The American Utopian Adventure

SERIES TWO

DAILY JOURNAL OF ONEIDA COMMUNITY
THE O.C. DAILY

DAILY JOURNAL

OF

ONEIDA COMMUNITY

VOLUMES 1-3

THE

O.C. DAILY

VOLUMES 4-5

WITH A NEW INTRODUCTION BY
ROBERT S. FOGARTY

PORCUPINE PRESS

Philadelphia 1975

First edition of *Daily Journal of Oneida Community,* Volumes 1-3,
Oneida, N.Y., 1866-1867.
First edition of *The O. C. Daily,* Volumes 4-5, Oneida, N.Y., 1867-
1868.

Reprinted in one volume 1975 by
PORCUPINE PRESS, INC.
Philadelphia, Pennsylvania 19107

LC No. 74-32359
ISBN 0-87991-032-1

Manufactured in the United States of America

ONEIDA *DAILY JOURNAL:* A BOOK OF COMMON PRAYER

Of all the nineteenth century utopias the Oneida Community (1848-1880) has had the greatest scrutiny and commentary. Historians, psychologists, philosophers, sexologists and community organizers have had a turn at understanding this varied and successful experiment in "Bible Communism," as they called it. Yet it continues to elude any simple analyses and provides new insights for successive commentators. Researchers have prized the *Daily Journal* (1866-1868)* since it gives an inside and unconscious view of community life unfiltered by our current preoccupations, later community scruples, or special pleading. It is a commonplace journal that records letters received, criticisms given, and the commings and goings of salesmen — all noted with the same fairness as a reference to yesterday's temperature. There are few conflicts and little heroism recorded in these pages; yet beneath the even statements one can detect major conflicts within Oneida and methods used to resolve them.

In general, there is an enduring sense of purpose, of humor and of collective spirit during what must have been the calmest period in community history. Some eighteen years had passed since the prosecuted Putney group, fresh from adultery charges against Noyes in Vermont, had moved to the burned-over district of New York. They were still a year away from the famed stirpiculture experiment in eugenics and the problems it created for the community. The years 1866-1868 are years before the storm which wrecked the society and caused it to dissolve into a joint stock operation in 1880. Oneida had been founded in 1848 by John H. Noyes and dedicated to his Perfectionist faith in Christian communism which he labelled "Bible Communism." The community was a logical product of Noyes' career as preacher, publicist and charismatic leader after his religious conversion to Perfectionism in 1834. But is was also a logical end product for the membership who came to Oneida in search of religious and economic security. These individuals sought and found at Oneida a social and sexual system that served their needs as no church or family had done before.

By 1866 the community consisted of 300 individuals, had a substantial economic base and comfortable surroundings, and had continued to sustain a religious life based on the primitive Christian model first introduced by Noyes in the eighteen forties. Oneida's most distinguishing characteristic, the practice of complex marriage, was still in force and gave to the colony a notoriety that attracted both visitors and national publicity. Some called it free love, but the members at Oneida practiced it within a tradition of religious sharing and, by 1866, were accustomed to the stares and comments of the "outside" world. Noyes inaugurated the complex marriage system at the Putney Community (1843-1848) in 1846. For Noyes the kingdom of heaven had arrived and he abandoned sexual exclusiveness in much the same way that property exclusiveness had been abandoned when the families organized on a communal basis in 1843. Noyes did away with the traditional marriage bond and took as his partner Mary Cragin, the wife of Charles Cragin, a Perfectionist believer. Noyes saw a new society in process "where the partition of the sexes is taken away and man ceases to make women a propagative drudge, when love takes the place of shame." As part of the complex marriage system Noyes instituted the practice of male continence, or coitus reservatus, in which partners enjoyed the early stages of sexual intercourse with men controlling themselves so as to avoid orgasm. Members were urged to place emphasis on the "amative" or "social" side of intercourse and to view it as a "joyful act of fellowship." In addition, there existed an ascending and descending fellowship in which individuals were instructed to associate with members who were spiritually on a higher plane. On a physical level young members were introduced into the practice of male continence by women past their menopause. As a result of these practices, the average yearly birth rate between 1848 and 1866 was two from an adult population over 175.

Oneida's prosperity came by the manufacture of traps and the leadership capacity to temper their ideals in a potentially hostile world. They elevated and spiritualized their work and believed that their success represented a triumph for Christ over Mammon. The key to success lay in their dedication and flexibility: dedication to the proposition that they were establishing a Perfectionist kingdom on earth and flexibility with reference to their varied business enterprises. After 1855 the community engaged primarily in the trap business; however, they maintained a lively trade in fruit preserves, travelling bags and silk goods. As the community industries grew they were forced to hire laborers — and repudiate an earlier idealistic theory about "hirelings" — in order to meet the commercial demand for their products.

Essentially Oneida was a unitary family which combined economic, religious and educational functions under one roof and under the guidance of their leader, Noyes. Noyes was at the center because the membership accepted his Perfectionist message of millenial salvation, his lineal authority from Christ and St. Paul, and his charismatic leadership. "Father" Noyes broods over these journal accounts though his appearances at Oneida between 1866 and 1868 were occasional; he preferred to live at Wallingford, Connecticut or at the New York Agency during this period. When the community reorganized itself in 1880 into a joint stock company it lacked leadership, religious unity and the will to continue. When these journals were recorded there was little to fear since Noyes, then 55, was in good health, the post-war boom held steady and a younger generation was schooling itself at Yale's Sheffield School and Columbia's School of Medicine.

The *Daily Journal* initially began in January, 1863 in manuscript form and was circulated within the community for a year before being suspended. A typescript copy of the earlier sections is at the Mansion House, Kenwood, New York and has the same flavor as these journals begun in January, 1866 for circulation within the community at Oneida and for the membership at Wallingford, and New York City. There are threee general areas which the *Daily Journal* covered: business affairs, internal social life, and communications with the outside world, particularly visitors.

BUSINESS AFFAIRS

Reports on production problems, canning quotas and sales projections fill these pages. For example, it is noted (December 16, 1867) that $40,000 in wages were paid out to workmen and that 230 workers were employed at a peak period (February 10, 1868) giving some data about the magnitude of their operation. Letters from salesmen to the community indicated how far west they ranged (St. Louis), what their concerns were while out in the "world," and how well they were received. It has been widely recorded that their salesmen underwent a spiritual "defumigation" when they returned home; there is little evidence in their letters that they felt threatened by what they saw. G.W. Hamilton reports from Columbus, Ohio (January 16, 1868) that while on his swing through the midwest he visited with cousin Rutherford B. Hayes, then Governor Hayes: "He [Hayes] spoke of visiting Wallingford some eight years since. Expressed himself as having no prejudice on account of our peculiar religious beliefs, and was well pleased at having a call from one of our people." Cousin Rutherford later accepted visits in the White House from members of the community who were always careful to minimize their illustrious family connections, so as to avoid embarrassing Hayes.

Insight into the "beeing sessions" at Oneida are valuable because they show how the community responded to business demands by a cooperative effort to meet larger orders. A "Queen Bee" account recorded on September 24, 1866 is a good example. The sudden arrival of 139 crates of peaches halted German and Theology classes for the day, brought the Willow Place workers to the preserve house and caused the hired help to volunteer their labor to get the job done. Some 171 persons made "the bee a complete success and yielded about 800 quarts of fruit to the preserves, which was all put up. We have never seen anything so brilliant. It was perfectly electric. The condensation of magnetic life produced a general sparkle and flash of mirth and humor throughout the bee."

The evening business meetings are detailed with managers reporting, work assignments given, and committees formed to investigate production problems or to purchase an implement. Oneida had an elaborately shifting bureaucracy with committees for every phase of community life from traps to clothing, to a once constructed manure committee that had to investigate a drainage problem. Community elders Woolworth, Hamilton and Hinds dominate such meetings and give flesh to the second line leadership that ran the community so effectively in Noyes' absence.

INTERNAL LIFE

The *Daily Journal* enlarges one area of understanding about Oneida that has been difficult to probe: its internal life. That religion was central to that life is no surprise, but the details, nuances and meanings from accounts of mutual criticisms, religious exhortations by Noyes and other elders, and a constant emphasis on spiritial renewal that fill these pages reaffirms the central role it played. It underscores that Oneida was first a religious, second a communal, and third, a sexual experiment.

Individuals offering themselves for mutual criticism did so as sinners approaching the anxious bench before witnessing. Those sessions were painful since a person's "faults" were told to him and he was instructed in the ways that he might improve. Manuscript reports were kept and the sessions were summarized in the *Daily Journal*. This November, 1866 letter from C. E. Underwood is typical of the attitude expressed by the membership after receiving community criticism: "I take the opportunity to express my thanks to the family for the sincere criticism of me in showing me my faults . . . I confess my love for Mr. Noyes, Mr. Hamilton and Mr. Woolworth as inspired men . . . I confess my love for the whole community family, and a spirit of   subordination to Christ at all times and under all circumstances."

Daily problems were the norm in the journal, but some significant ones consumed the community's interest. Victor Noyes' flight from Oneida is chronicled because his apostasy (or illness) had symbolic importance for the society. Victor (the son of John H. Noyes and Mary Cragin) left in August, 1866 in rebellion against his father. First, he fled to Gerritt Smith at Peterborough threatening to tell "all" about the community and failed to receive any encouragement from Smith, an old community supporter. Eventually Victor would up at the Utica Asylum having been placed there by his father. His "insanity" is discussed as a species of religious unbelief and Victor returns only when he has recanted of his sins. Whether insane or sinful Victor's case is a painful one for the community and tells us much about their attitudes toward disobedience, mental illness and the "Boston School of Literature' which Victor had been fond of reading prior to his flight and is cited as the cause of his unbelief.

Conflict about the social or sexual questions does appear though it is veiled in the community's language about such matters. It was their practice to refer to their sexual theory as a "social" theory: "In criticising individuals, sometimes, we talk about their being loose in social matters. I think in this connection we might profitabley inquire what constitutes true chastity or what in the kingdom of heaven, is the true standard of morality." The birth of a child was a rare occurence and when a boy, Eugene, was born to Myron H. Kinsley and Eliza Burt the event was announced "To the Community" in the *Daily Journal* (August 7, 1866): "We desire to keep free from all claim on him and offer him to the community as Christ's boy, to be governed and controlled as they see fit." There are a few accounts about "exclusive" love affairs, but they are minor and readers will have to rely on their imaginations or read between the lines for signs of conventional romance.

Published at Oneida, the *Daily Journal* kept members at Wallingford where the *Oneida Circular* was published, and at New York where a business agency operated, informed about vital community affairs. There are references to "Willow Place": it was a self-contained unit at Oneida where the trap production was carried on during the year. The journal appeared irregularly and the editor sometimes complained that there was little news to print though the internal life seems lively enough for a tri-weekly schedule.

VISITORS AND CORRESPONDENCE

One stereotype about communal organizations centers on their retreat from the world and their separation from the blandishments of a corrupt culture. Oneida may have fit that type in 1848 when they came in retreat from criminal proceedings at Putney, but by 1866 they were well connected with the world through commerce, publicity and most clearly through thousands of visitors who came each year. By their own count more than 16,000 visitors signed the register during a 5½ year period and they estimated that three times that number had actually come between 1862 and 1867. Some were famous like Susan B. Anthony, Tom Thumb and former Governor Seward; most were simply on a day's outing from Syracuse or Rochester to see the communists, sample their excellent cooking and stroll about the grounds. Many came on the Fourth of July and enjoyed the community's special strawberry shortcake prepared for the occasion. Visitors were instructed not to smoke, intrude into private rooms or drive their carriages off the roadway. The membership often tired of so many visitors and so many questions even if such contact was essential because the outside world had to be convinced that they were not free lovers, just a group of industrious and earnest Christians.

The roles reversed when others came to be looked over by the community and considered for membership. After the Civil War they received about 50 inquiries per month from individuals eager to join. How to sort the believers from the thrill seekers was a difficult task and prospective members were asked to study the community literature, read the Bible and, if their interest continued, come for a short visit. Richard Realf, the poet and planned secretary of state in John Brown's cabinet, was interested during this period; Charles Guiteau, Garfield's assassin, left the community in 1866 after a brief stay and later sued for back wages; and a contingent from another'"free love" community at Berlin Heights, Ohio were seeking admission. James Towner, a member of the Berlin Heights group, was granted admission and eventually became a major figure in the leadership struggles of the seventies. There were visitors and inquiries from other communists—most notably the Shakers—but also from old colony joiners who had been at Brook Farm or the North American Phalanx, or from new communards who were trying to start ventures on their own. For example, Charles Meeker visited in October, 1866 to do a story for the *New York Tribune* and may have come away with ideas for the 1868 Union Colony at what became Greeley, Colorado.

The journal ends abruptly during a March, 1868 economy drive and was continued in manuscript form according to the final editorial statement. Its brief but valuable history tells us more about Oneida than any other source. To be sure there are the periodicals, the books and, though still in private hands, the diaries; yet only in the *Daily Journal* is there a feeling that the audience was neither public nor private, just the "family." Self reflection and soul searching are absent from these pages as well as public posturing and messages: its message was to inform, encourage and instruct the workers in this heavenly community just where they stood—in practical and personal terms and on a daily basis—in relationship to the millenial kingdom they were working toward.

Robert S. Fogarty
Antioch College
Yellow Springs, Ohio

---

*The full title is *Daily Journal of Oneida Community;* the first issue, [Vol. 1], No. 1, was published January 14, 1866. Beginning with Vol. 3, No. 21, January 24, 1867, the title changed to *The O.C. Daily*.

PUBLISHER'S NOTE

This facsimile of the *Daily Journal of Oneida Community* is faithfully reproduced from a microfilm copy of the serial in the Oneida Community Collection of the George Arents Research Library at Syracuse University.

The printing quality and condition of the original issues vary considerably throughout the run of the serial; several original issues are illegible in part.

The original serial run contains more than 2,500 pages (measuring less than five by four inches). To facilitate the present one-volume reproduction, each issue, normally four pages in length, is reproduced on a single page in two columns of continuous text.

Errors in original issue numbering and dating are noted below.

ERRATA

Volume One

Issue No. 32. Incorrect day; February 21 was a Wednesday.
Issue No. 48. Incorrect date; should be March 12.
Issue No. 49. Incorrect date; should be March 13.
Issue No. 50. Incorrect date; should be March 14.
Issue dated March 31. Incorrectly numbered; should be 65.
Issue dated April 1. Incorrectly numbered; should be 66. Incorrect date; should be April 2.
Issue dated April 3. Incorrectly numbered; should be 67.
Issue dated June 14. Incorrectly numbered; should be 129.
Issue No. 131. Incorrect day; June 16 was a Saturday.

Volume Two

Issue No. 57. Incorrect day; September 6 was a Thursday.
Issue No. 137. Incorrect date; should be December 8.
Issue dated December 20. Incorrectly numbered; number 146 was used twice.

Volume Four

Issue No. 2. Incorrect day; July 2 was a Tuesday.
Issue No. 96. Incorrect day; October 20 was a Sunday.

Volume Five

Issue No. 1. Incorrect year; should be 1868.
Issue dated January 20. Incorrectly numbered; should be 17.
Issue No. 55. Apparently never printed.
Issue No. 73. Incorrect date; should be March 27.

DAILY JOURNAL
OF ONEIDA COMMUNITY.

A. D. 1866. JAN. 14. NO. 1.

SUNDAY.

OUR winter life is passing quietly. There is an earnestness in the family which seems deeper and more full of sustained power than ever before. The spirit Mr. Noyes breathes forth in all his talks and communications finds hearts here sympathetic and ready to receive it. Our unity with him, and with each other, is growing more vital. The faith that recogizes him as the chosen representative of Jesus Christ, and the ordained one who is to set up the kingdom of heaven in this world, becomes more clear-eyed and powerful every day. We recognize this faith as Christ's faith, as the bond of unity, and the condition and preliminary of success and victory on every. line. Our social life is taking a new and higher tone. It is rising through criticism into the purity and beauty of heaven. The passing away of special love, the judgment of the false, sensual, selfish, pleasure-seeking, slave-holding spirit, that has burst forth at Wallingford, are glorious signs that the Primitive Church is drawing near to us and baptizing us with its power and divine refinement. Perish from among us every obstruction to the social order and freedom of the resurrection!

The demand for traps and bags of late has been light, and much less is doing in the way of manafacturing than during last month.

The hired help at the trap-shop has been discharged. Only the following hired men are employed at Willow Place now: three blacksmiths, two machinists and one molder.

Machine-shop hands are busily engaged in making machinery and locks for the bag-factory.

The present force in the trap-shop is mainly engaged in making chains, a lot of 25,000 being under way.

J. C. Higgins, is devoting some attention to making Patent Bolt Shears. These shears are a very convenient and labor-saving contrivance for blacksmiths and waggon makers. There is some prospect that we may make a good profit by manufacturing them; at least it is thought worth while to try the market a little. Mr. Daniel Kelly owns the patent right for this State.

In the bag-factory only seven hired men and five hired women are now employed.

The ice-house has been repaired during the past week preparatory to getting in our next season's supply. Two courses of last season's supply are now on hand.

Some attention is given to quarrying stone at Willow Place.

The educational classes go on as usual and our people bid fair to reap a rich harvest of intellectual improvement this winter. The magnetism of study has passed outside the Community classes and affected our hired men and women, especially the latter. Sometime ago a wish was expressed by some of them that they might have classes like the Community family. This coming to the knowledge of their employers was of course sympathised with. Mrs. L. A Thayer volunteered to start an evening class with them. The class has been in operation a number of weeks. It meets for an hour in the evening three times a week. The present number of scholars is about eight; before many of the employees were discharged it numbered more than a dozen. Much enthusiasm has been manifested, and considerable improvement made.

Mr. John Kelly, father of our Wm. G., writes an interesting letter of sympathy with us. He seems to be getting hold of the truth in an earnest way; he has been studying the Berean and Bible Communism and indorses them. The spirit of his letter was very much liked. His conversion will be another blow to Oberlin.—Emily Otis also writes again. She seems to be strong in the faith, and growing. She mentions the fact that when Theodore Otis left Oberlin he gave his Berean to a young man who was living with Pres. Finney. T. used to read THE CIRCULAR to this young man and he was considerably interested. The Oberlin battlefield grows more and more interesting. New persons whom the truth is touching come into view every little while. Emily writes that her father and brothers are very much displeased and stirred up at her course in leaving Oberlin and embracing the truth. But she stands firm like a true soldier.—Mr. W. A. Knowles, who is absent at Champion, writes home in a good tone of faith and confidence in, and love for, the Community. Mrs. Knowles also writes to Mr. Seymour Nash. Her spirit of hardness and unbelief seems somewhat broken, and she apologises and asks forgivness for some of her past course, and asks for the fellowship and criticism of the Community. It remains to be seen however, whether she is really in earnest for salvation, or merely wants to find a personal home and sympathy.

There is good news from Bath by G. D. Allen. Mrs. Bushnell has another convert. A sister of Frances Hilliman, the girl who took Beulah's place in Mrs. B's family, has confessed Christ as a Savior from sin. She is fourteen years of age, and a bright and interesting girl.

We more and more realize the great relief brought about by the departure of Mr. Carr from among us. His presence, personally and spiritually has been a nightmare of unbelief and of obstructions to the free flow and organizing power of the Community spirit The atmosphere is clearer and more genially electric since he has been gone.

The weather for several days has been mild, threatning a regular "January thaw" and break up. To-day, however, it has resumed its winter tone, and at one o'clock P. M. the mercury is at two degrees above zero.

THE SALUTATIONS OF O. C. TO WALLINGFORD AND NEW-YORK.

DAILY JOURNAL
OF ONEIDA COMMUNITY.

A. D. 1866.   JAN. 15.   NO. 2.

MONDAY.

SOME indications of the working of a bad spirit among the boys, led to a meeting with them on Sunday, of those whom the boys had chosen for their fathers. The meeting was called, not so much for the purpose of special criticism, as for advising with them and inducing them to turn their hearts to their fathers. In the course of the meeting it became manifest that a very disobedient and disloyal spirit had been corrupting them. This spirit seemed to have its center in Orrin Wright. Since his return from the West, he has had little it any sympathy or fellowship with the Community. His face and heart have been turned toward the world. and he has been sowing discontent and disobedience among the boys. Homer Hazelton appears to have been the most affected by his influence, though all of his class have been disaffected toward the Community, and were plotting among themselves to leave, if they should be threatened with a whipping. Orrin and Homer were evidently ring-leaders. In regard to these two, Homer appears to have been the victim of Orrin, and Orrin is the victim of his father's unbelief, disobedience and infidelity. There was sincere criticism of the boys, and all but these two accepted it and endeavored to clear themselves. Mr. Wright's decision to leave and to take Orrin with him, appears to settle Orrin's case for the present. There have been indications in the past, that Orrin was good-hearted, and when obedient to good influences, loveable and disposed to seek improvement. But his father's influence and example have constantly tended to make him discontented, and insincere. His trip to the West was one of the worst things he could have done; and his father is responsible for it, and for his present state. Homer is still in a half-hearted state. Mr. Hamilton was very sincere with Mr. Hazelton in the meeting to-night for his attitude, his influence on Homer, and his past religious and spiritual character.

The state of the boys led to some sincere remarks in regard to the conduct of Mr. Wright in taking Orrin out West last fall, contrary to the advice and wishes of the Community, and allowing him to become filled with the spirit of the world, and then bringing him back and encouraging him in spirit to diffuse a corrupting influence among the Community boys. It was thought that no amount of service could atone for conduct so cruel and destructive.

Mr. Wright has decided to leave the Community. His letter announcing his intention was as follows:

Oneida Community, Jan. 15, '66.

Mr. E. H. Hamilton,

Sir:—I have made up my mind to leave the Community; please name some one to settle with me. Orrin goes with me.

Yours &c.,   A. D. Wright.

The letter was received with hearty cheers by the family. W. A. Hinds was selected by Mr. Hamilton to settle with Mr. Wright.

We are "comforted with apples" this winter, notwithstanding the prediction of scarcity that prevailed last summer. Besides all that are needed for kitchen and table use, Mr. Ackley every morning places three large baskets, filled with Greenings, Fall Pippins, Seek-no-furthers, Swaars, Henry Sweets, Northern Spys, &c., in convenient situations in the main passage ways of our buildings. From these baskets all are at liberty to help themselves.

Our friends from Wallingford seem to find no difficulty in organizing themselves into Oneida life. Mr. Seymour finds business every day at the Trap Shop. Mr. Perkins we notice is vigorously engaged at his favorite pastime of splitting wood.

Martin Kinsley reports $225,50 worth of pork sold since Jan. 1. The whole amount sold last year was $1529,30.

Dr. J. A. Roland, of the Attorney General's Office, Washington, who visited the Community last summer, has sent to Mr. Underwood, for the Community, several volumes of Public Documents. They include the Smithsonian Reports for 1862–3, Report of the Commissioner of Agriculture for 1863 and the two Vols. of Diplomatic Correspondence for 1864.

We have genuine winter to-day. Mercury at seven deg. below zero at 7 A. M. To-night the sky is cloudy and bids fair or foul, rather, for snow. We have had but little snow, and no sleighing thus far this winter. The ground is nearly bare, and the meadows, grainfields and strawberry plants all need their winter covering.

For the information of Messrs. Thacker and Barron we will mention, that during the cold weather last week the lowest figure marked by the mercury, was —20.

The maple grove at Willow Place, sometimes called our sugar bush, is being cut down and worked into firewood.

Mr. Cragin arrived at about midnight. We are all interested in the plans and prospects of the business of silk manufacturing, to which we understand Mr. C.'s mission here relates.

DAILY JOURNAL
OF ONEIDA COMMUNITY.

A. D. 1866.   JAN. 16.   NO. 3.

TUESDAY.

A SATISFACTORY settlement has been effected with Mr. Wright. The amount of his claim in money was $523,37. In addition to this he applied for a full suit of outside clothes, one muslin R. R. traveling bag, No. 9, 1 case (2 doz. cans) of fruit, and $30 worth of Fruit stock, mostly grape vines. For Orrin he claimed a suit of clothes and one hundred dollars. The Community agreed to pay him $400 and furnish him with the clothes, traveling bag and fruit asked for, and $40 worth of fruit stock. It was thought to be no more than fair to deduct from his claim the amount of his expenses out West last fall, as he assumed the responsibility of the trip and made it contrary to the advice and wishes of the Community. He agreed to this. He will leave next week, in the meantime visiting some relatives at Durhamville.

Orrin now wishes to remain in the Community. He has been much affected and apparently under conviction during the day, weeping much of the time. He talked with Mr. Hamilton and expressed his desire to stay in the Community. He said he had a sincere purpose in wishing to stay. 'Twas not because the Community was a good home, but because he believed in Mr. Noyes as we did, and that the Community was the kingdom of God. He had talked with his father and told him he wanted to remain here. Mr. Wright tried to persuade him out of it: told him that he (Orrin) did not believe in the Community principles, that he wanted to stay because he had been persuaded to, &c. He said that he (Wright) did not believe in some of the principles of the Community, never had and never should. Orrin fully sustained to his father his faith in the Community and his wish to stay. Mr. Hamilton and W. A. H. afterwards had some correspondence and conversation with Mr. Wright about the matter. He was at first indisposed to let Orrin stay; but he finally agreed to leave him free to stay on condition that Orrin should write to him once in six months, and let him know if he was discontented. He agreed that such correspondence should be carried on under the supervision of the Community, and that he would write nothing to Orrin to prejudice him toward the Community, or induce him to leave. He also agreed sign a contract relinquishing all claims for wages in case Orrin should hereafter leave the Community.

In the evening meeting the following communication from Orrin was read :

TO THE COMMUNITY.

I wish to separate myself from my father. I confess that I am not his son, but belong to the Community. I think I have had a bad, disobedient spirit ever since I went out west. I now wish to join myself forever to the cause of Christ and to become obedient and respectful to the Community. I confess my separation from my worldly relations. I believe Mr. Noyes is inspired and that this is the kingdom of heaven on earth. I would like the benefit of a criticism. I confess Christ a spirit of meekness.   ORRIN.

It was thought there was a spirit of earnestness in this note and sympathy was expressed for Orrin in his new position. Mr. Hamilton said he should be in favor of letting him stay until Mr. Noyes came, at least. The change in Orrin was the result of his own reflections and convictions, and took place without any interference from the Community. No one had talked with him since the meeting on Sunday, and he was then in a hard, disrespectful state. The case is an interesting one. It is a battle between the forces of faith and infidelity, and faith is proving itself the strongest.

It appears that Mr. Wright was intending to leave in the spring, and had been corresponding and making arrangements to that effect. We understand he had written to his wife inquiring if he and Orrin could make their home with her ; but she replied it would not be convenient. With his departure from among us we hope to bid a final adieu to the spirit of discontent, disunity, and infidelity.

The case of Mrs. Deborah Knowles was considered in the evening meeting. It was thought best before responding to her application for membership to administer a criticism as she requested. This was done, and notes were taken and will probably be sent to her.— It was thought in conclusion there would be no objection to her coming here on a visit.

A communication from Homer Hazleton confessing his purpose to take the Community for his home, was also read in meeting.

Lady Campbell's broken leg is doing well. She is very cheerful and full of thankfulness, making it pleasant to take care of her and to meet her at any time.

The health of the family is buoyant, and we notice that colds are less frequent than usual this winter. It is cheering to see the vigor and power of the resurrection so clearly at work, as it is in Mr. Cragin and others.

The office accommodations are to be enlarged by the removal of the bed, and the appropriation of the adjoining bedroom. A doorway into the bedroom has been cut through the partition.

The Green House, under the care of Mr. Kelly and Mrs. Sears, is prospering. With its green leaves, its opening rose and camellia buds, and its blooming primroses, heliotropes and fuschias, it presents a genial contrast to the whistling, gusty storm of wind and snow outside the doors. Small and unpretentious as it is, and requiring considerable care and labor to keep it in order and free from frost, it is a pleasant place to step into these wintry days, and refreshes one's memory of summer's green and bloom. Several of the magnificent Augusta roses are now in full blossom and fill the house with their rich perfume.

DAILY JOURNAL
OF ONEIDA COMMUNITY.

A. D. 1866. JAN. 17. NO. 4.

WEDNESDAY.

THE Bag-bees were brought to a close to-day, the first time in eight or ten years. The suspension will probably be brief, as it results only from the present light demand for bags. There is an interesting history of these bees which we hope will sometime be written. There has been romance in them as thrilling as anything in Scott's Novels. They have been a school of intellectual improvement as well as of industry. Hundreds of books have been read while thousands of bags have been making. A wide range of literature has been canvassed, from Scott and Cooper to Dickens and Thackeray and Charles Reade. The last popular new novel and the last Atlantic Monthly have been listened to while fingers were busily stitching. These bees played an important part in the solution of the problem of attractive labor. They have been means of fellowship between men and women, and between old and young. Who will ever forget them in the Old Parlor, under the Butternut tree on bright summer afternoons, in the New Hall, and in the Upper Sitting Room?

In the evening meeting Orrin was criticised. The stand he has taken in separating himself from his father and turning his heart to the Community, was commended, and a great deal of good feeling for him was expressed. But it was thought he would have to be very much in earnest, to carry out the purpose he had confessed, and become a truly spiritually-minded young man. He has much to repent of in the past, and must now prove by deeds his devotion to the Community and the truth. It was thought best to let him remain here a year on trial.

Startling apparition! "All at once a ghost appeared!" H. C. N. took care of her mother to-night. In the middle hours of the night she came out of Lady C.'s room with a dimly burning night-lamp in her hand, into the sitting-room, to look at the clock. Glancing across the room she beheld a white figure standing motionless in front of the entry door. With an emotion partaking slightly of the terrified, Helen cried out to the ghostly presence: "Who are you? Speak!" No answer. The figure lifts its arm and places it across its breast.—Helen's cry awakens Chloe, who was sleeping in an adjoining room. Chloe sprang out of bed and as she was coming out of her room found herself confronted with the mysterious figure. Though somewhat startled, she concluded it would be best to grapple with the mystery at once and so settle its ghostly pretensions. So rushing forward she seized the "Woman in White" by the arm; when, lo! the substantial form of Mrs. Kinsley appeared!! She answered not a word, but shook Chloe off with her arm and walked in dignified silence to a chair and seated herself. The terrified damsels retired to their rooms again, philosophizing on the materialistic character of ghosts. The object of their terror, we learn, soon after retired to her room and shook her sides a long while over the adventure.

At the machine-shop the handles are being fitted to several thousand mop-irons. This job closes up the mop business.

An ex-soldier called with pictures to sell. He was in the second battle of Bull Run, where he lost a portion of one of his hands. He afterwards lost his arm, by being run over by the cars.

To-day was clear and sunny until evening, when it assumed the usual stormy aspect. During the night a little snow fell, just enough to whiten the roofs and bare ridges.

The fruit-growers have been examining the buds of the plum and cherry trees, and find considerable injury done by the recent cold weather.

The ice-cutting machine, on trial, proves to be a success. It is properly named an ice-plow, and is drawn by a horse in the same manner as an ordinary plow.— A series of eight cutters are fastened on a line in an iron beam. Going back from the front end, each succeeding cutter is a little longer than the one in front of it, and consequently, when the plow is properly held, cuts a little deeper. The plow will cut a groove about half an inch wide and eight inches deep. It is provided with ordinary plow-handles. In cutting the ice a marking plow, with a gauge, is first used. The cutting plow follows the groove made by the marking plow. The ice is cut into square blocks.

Several typographical mistakes and omissions occurred in our previous numbers owing to the haste with which they had to be set up and printed in order to be in time for the mail. We hope to avoid errors of all kinds as much as possible in the future, and to make our little sheet an accurate transcript of the events and spirit of our daily life.

DAILY JOURNAL
OF ONEIDA COMMUNITY.

A. D. 1866. JAN. 18. NO. 5.

THURSDAY.

THE machine-shop barely escaped a serious injury this afternoon. Mr. Conant went into the shop while the machinery was stopped at noon, and wishing to grind an axe, asked Jacob, the colored man, to start the water-wheel. Jacob did not understand the business and raised the gate too high. The consequence was that soon the machinery was going at a very rapid and dangerous rate. The shop hands in the office discovering the trouble, rushed to the rescue, and the gate was shut down and the wheel stopped before much injury was done. Some of the bearings to the line shaft and other machinery were loosened and a belt was broken. It was a careless, thoughtless thing for Mr. Conant to have the machinery started without consulting the shop-hands, and contrary to the rules of the shop. The affair was referred to in the evening meeting, and the importance of having none but authorized persons meddle with the machinery was fully shown.

The spiritualist ambassador, A. Devine Wright, left for Durhamville this morning. He will return and get his clothes and other effects, before starting for the West. His mission to this government seems to have been a failure. His six years' residence here has not brought about any recognition on our part of the claims of hadean spiritualistic infidelity, or any wish to extend our acquaintance with the " principalities and powers" whom he serves. The prospect is that we shall continue to deny both his and their *divine right* to teach or lead us.

The sympathy and enthusiasm for the silk manufacturing business is steadily growing in the Community. The importance of the business is more thoroughly realized the more we study it. We feel sure that Mr. Noyes has a true inspiration in regard to it, and are glad to co-operate with him in carrying that inspiration out.

We note with much interest the business changes which have lately taken place at the N. Y. Agency, and would especially congratulate the brethren there, upon the addition to their number of so earnest a man as Mr. Easton, and of so loyal and true-hearted a woman as Mrs. Bloom. Her present effort at book-keeping is a beginning which will lead to glorious future results.

In the evening meeting Mr. Hamilton exhorted all to earnest devotion to business, and to not drop down in spirit in regard to it because of the lull in the trap and bag trade. Business is our religion now, and we should see to it that we are in rapport with Mr. Noyes and the heavens in our devotion to it. All our time, whether we work or study or pray, should be pervaded by a thorough business spirit.

The completion of a certain bed-quilt belonging to Mother Noyes, the beginning of which took place at Wallingford, was made the occasion of a pleasant supper-party in the Visitor's Dining Room. The supper was excellent, which is all that need be said on that point.— The quilt was hung up in the room, and the design was much admired. Considering the source from which a portion, at least, of the quilt was contributed, it is expected that Mother Noyes will take special " *delight*" in sleeping under it.

Mr. Cragin authorizes the Journalist to say that Wallingford may expect Charles Otis Kellogg to come there and assume the charge of the farm and out-door business.

The farmers have sold their barley to a dealer in Utica. They get 95 cents a bushel for it, delivered at that place. Some eight or nine hundred bushels are thus disposed of.

A trap order, amounting to $50, money inclosed, received.

The principal out-door business to-day, is cutting ice, preparatory to filling the icehouse. The ice-cutting machine is very much liked.

To-day has been warm, sunny and thawy, and the ground is nearly bare again in the valley. The hills south and west are still white.

ARRIVALS.—Preston Reeves Sherrard, formerly a refugee from Western Virginia, and recently a subscriber to THE CIRCULAR, at Wabash Water Cure, Indiana.— Mrs. Wm. Chesbro, from Fulton N. Y.

DEPARTURES.—Mr. Inslee, at three o'clock this morning, for New York, to obtain information about silk machinery.—G. D. Allen left yesterday morning for his silk-selling route west and south.

DAILY JOURNAL
OF ONEIDA COMMUNITY.

A. D. 1866. JAN. 19. NO. 6.

FRIDAY.

ONE of the leading events of to-day, was the receipt of the following letter by Mrs. Tobey.

Barnstable, Mass., Jan. 15, 1866.

Mrs. Tobey:—I enclose check for $150, and have the pleasure to inform you that at the Probate Court last week the guardianship over your estate was discharged. As soon as I get time, which will be in a few days, I will send you account of your affairs in my hands.

Yours Truly, &c., GEO. MARSTON.

This is a victory which will be felt along the whole line. Mrs. Tobey says she is now of age. She is seventy years old naturally, thirty-six spiritually and twenty-one financially. The event was celebrated by an attractive supper-party in Room No. 9, on the avenue. Mr. Hamilton remarked at the supper that it seemed to him that we were going to have a resurrection experience financially the present year.

Another leading event of the day, was the receipt of the following telegram, by Mr. Cragin:

New York. Jan. 18, 1866.

GEORGE CRAGIN, ONEIDA:—Come here Saturday.— Inportant business consultation on Sunday.

J. H. NOYES.

We should have mentioned yesterday, in connection with the account of the accident at Willow Place, that Mr. Conant displayed a very good spirit in confessing his fault in starting the machinery. His own criticism of himself showed that he fully appreciated the affair, and rendered further criticism unnecessary.

Roswell Hawley has gone into the machine-shop to work. He will undoubtedly make a first-class workman in that department, judging from his past career in the trap-shop.

The weather continues warm, the south wind blows and the snow is fast disappearing from the hills.

There is a continued and manifest growth of unity in the family, and more and more the hearts of the Community are becoming as the heart of one man. The expulsion of Carr and Wright from among us, has lifted a load of obstructing influences, and we breathe more in unison and see more nearly eye to eye every day. We begin to feel that henceforth we move in solid phalanx, every man's elbow touching his fellow's.

W. A. Hinds, Joseph, George Miller and the office girls, have formed a class for studying the science of detecting counterfeit money. They say it is an interesting study.

We have two classes in Rhetoric now, one of nine members under the teachership of Mr. Underwood, and the other numbering eighteen under that of Mr. Kelly.

The group engaged in getting ice, were obliged to discontinue their labor during the forenoon in consequence of the ice melting so much as to render it too wet to handle. Meantime the cutting machine will be arranged for cutting the ice into smaller blocks, as the width of the guage previously made them too heavy to handle.

The question of sending C. O. Kellogg to Wallingford was brought up in the evening meeting, and a unanimous vote in favor of the proposal was given. The general testimony was, that Otis is just the man for the place, though there was a little reluctance to part with him here. He is an invaluable man in his sphere. It is expected that his going to Wallingford will tend to unite and harmonize the farming interests of the two Communes. We wish him success and congratulate Wallingford on his accession to their ranks.

DEPARTURES.—Preston R. Sherrard. He is a young man of considerable natural ability and some culture. Has read THE CIRCULAR a year and is interested in it. Is out of health. Has been to the Dansville Water Cure where Dr. Jackson gave some treatment gratuitously. He seems to have swallowed Jackson whole. Jackso played the same game with him that he has played wit; thousands of others. He manages to get people unde obligation to him and to impress them with his impor tance and leadership, and so shuts their mouths so fa as sincere estimate and expression as to his character are concerned. It is to be hoped that his shameless egotisn and prostitution of himself and the truth to the love of money, will sometime find their fitting exposure and reward.

It may be understood hereafter that the DAILY JOURNALS will contain the latest news up to 12 o'clock the day they are printed. They have thus far only contained the news of the day previous.

DAILY JOURNAL
OF ONEIDA COMMUNITY.

A. D. 1866. JAN. 22. NO. 7.

SATURDAY.

AN order was received from Treadwell & Co., Boston, for the following traps:

12 doz. Otter; 12 doz. Beaver; 12 doz. Bear No. 5; and 2 Bear No. 6.

They want six months time on the order. The bear traps ordered amount to over $1000—the largest order for bear traps we have ever received. The whole order amounts to about 1500 dollars. Fearing there was some mistake in the ordering of so many bear traps, a letter of inquiry has been written to the parties.

Mr. Nash gathered from the field a large lot of greens to-day. This he esteemed to be a noteworthy event. Accordingly when he presented the editor of this JOURNAL, while at supper, with a plate of said greens nicely cooked, he avowed that it was for the purpose of getting them puffed. Though somewhat taken aback by so direct an attempt at bribery, we yielded and partook of the verdant dish. So here goes. They were as nice and tender as any we have eaten in June. Great is Mr. Nash and greens are his profit. May he always be green and growing, and never lack for greens while greens grow.

This morning the mercury stood at 52, with a warm wind blowing from the south. Only a few patches of snow were to be seen, even on the hills. At noon there was a sudden change. The wind veered round to the northwest, and by two o'clock the ground was white again and the mercury down to 25. Toward evening the sky became clear in the west, and the wind whistled a winter tune. At bed-time the mercury was at 13.

> There was a young lady named Ellen
>   ('Tis a very strange thing I am telling);
> The wind one cold night, blew her away in a fright,
>   That remarkable lady named Ellen.

P. S. There was no damage done.

In the evening meeting after the reading of the letters, including the criticism of Mrs. Bloom, there was a general expression of earnest sympathy with Mr. Noyes's remarks with regard to the control of the tongue.

SUNDAY.

An order received from E. H. Durfee, New York, through H. G. A., for the following traps:

49 doz. No. 1; 30 doz. No. 2; 20 doz. No. 4.

At 15 per cent off, the order amounts to $914.

In business meeting it was voted that Mr. Clark or Mr. Worden take a team, now while the roads are in good condition, and try what they can do in the way of selling plows.—Mr. Burt is to see that the ice-house at Willow Place is repaired.—The neighbors are inquiring if we have lumber for sale. It was thought best to select some of our best logs, and saw them up for that purpose. We can sell 20,000 feet of basswood lumber.— By proposal of Mr. Seymour it was voted that a set of clippers for cutting strawberry runners be made for Wallingford.

A general dance in the Hall, in the evening. In the meeting the character of C. S. J. as a writer, was analyzed, which will be reported by letter. We realize that these literary criticisms are having an important bearing on the effective power of THE CIRCULAR in the future, and are preparing the way for a more thorough baptism of inspiration and heaven's utterance.

We are stirred to the heart's core by the news from the agency. All of Mr. Noyes's utterances and movements are of thrilling interest. We shall watch for the report of to-day's events there, and believe they will be pregnant with important results, not only to the Community but to the nation itself.

The range of the thermometer, to-day, has been from 8 deg. in the morning to 13 at night. A very strong northwest wind has been steadily blowing all day, making it seem more intensely cold than the thermometer would indicate.

The people on Turkey Street are so highly pleased with the new school house the Community have built for this district, that they have applied to Mr. Hamilton for plans for a similar structure for their district. Mr. H. is accordingly draughting the plans.

ARRIVALS.—F. Norton, this morning, from Wallingford.

DEPARTURES.—A. D. Wright, for Wisconsin. Orrin was not present when his father left, and has avoided his society since separating himself from him.

DAILY JOURNAL
OF ONEIDA COMMUNITY.

A. D. 1866.   JAN. 23.   NO. 8.

MONDAY.

OLD Whitefoot again his own driver! He is reported to have started from Willow Place Factory this afternoon, with a load of lumber, which was distributed on the way home, together with seats, buffalo robes etc. The most serious result of the affair was the loss of one robe, and of the new teamster's *prestige* as a driver. *Mem.* Never leave a horse unhitched unless you have a definite understanding with him that he shall not start until you return, especially on such an uncomfortable day as yesterday, when any whitefoot might be excused for desiring to be in motion. This is the third time that old Whitefoot has lately dispensed with the services of a driver.

The reading of Dr. Kane's "Love-Life" was begun at seven o'clock. Nearly all the family turn out to hear it. It opens in an interesting way.

We were much interested in the report of the meeting at Wallingford on Friday evening, and the following remark of Mr. Noyes, especially, met with a hearty response:

"Why should it not be a regular excercise in any institution we set up, to give an hour or two every day to thinking, to simply minding your own thoughts and learning to reflect? I don't know why that should not be a regular study as much as algebra."

In the evening meeting Homer Hazelton was criticised. He has not been in a good state since the meeting with the boys, notwithstanding he has announced his purpose to stay in the Community. His spirit is hard and disobedient and full of unbelief. There is an indifference and dullness in him to spiritual truth, and if there is not a radical conversion of his heart to God and the truth, he will surely drift away from the Community. It was thought that his present state might properly be traced to the influence of his father's spirit; and there was sincere expression in regard to Mr. Hazelton. His course does not satisfy us. He does not take decided steps to identify himself with the truth. He hears criticism and is silent about it. While on the one hand he does not quarrel with it in an outward way, on the other hand, he does not yield his heart to it, and indorse and accept it clearly and positively. His position is a negative one, open to unbelief, and much out of the range of Community sympathy. While we would extend to him the utmost charity and kindly feeling and desire to help, that his case demands, we feel that he fails to realize the need he is in of help and salvation. His spirit affects Homer, and makes him spiritually dull and self-conceited. If Homer is to be improved and saved, criticism must go back of him and reach his father, and break up egotism and unbelief and the spirit of universalism there.

We hope for his own sake, and for Homer's, that he will come into sympathy in his inmost heart with the judgment of God against the false and corrupting spiritual influences he has been connected with in the past.

The following letter from Mrs. Kelly was read in the evening meeting:

Jan. 22, 1866.

To the Family:—From my childhood I have had an earnest desire to serve God and know the truth. I thank God that through Mr. Noyes the truth is being made plain to me. I confess my love for the truth, and a spirit that is receptive to it. I confess my love for criticism, and will gladly accept it at any time. "Spare not the rod."

I confess my entire confidence in Mr. Noyes and Mr. Hamilton as being inspired men. I confess my union with them and my subordination to them, as men of God.   L. Kelly.

The steady, piercing northwest wind which commenced Saturday forenoon, still continues. The thermometer ranges much the same as yesterday.

TUESDAY.

This morning the work of cutting and drawing ice was recommenced. The weather has moderated a little from yesterday, rendering this necessarily somewhat cold work, less tedious than it would otherwise be. The ice is over a foot thick, clear and good.

An order was received from Detroit for over a hundred dollars worth of preserved fruit.

There is a spirit of sincerity pervading the family. Criticisms both public and by committees are frequent. We realize that this is an indication that God is drawing near to us and preparing us for more unity and fellowship with himself, and with each other. This is always the effect of criticism truly given and received.

DAILY JOURNAL
OF ONEIDA COMMUNITY.

A. D. 1866. JAN. 24. NO. 9.

TUESDAY.

A BAG order received, through O. C. A., from Tracy and Bristol, St. Louis, amounting to about $650.

In the evening meeting the growing spirit of unity among us was spoken of. Mr. Hamilton in the course of the conversation remarked as follows:

"We have had considerable criticism going of late, and there are others in the family who have asked for criticism. I esteem criticism and like the love of the truth that is working. But I have had a feeling for a day or two that I did not want to let criticism take our whole attention, and turn our thoughts away from the goodness of God, and his work in and around us. With our criticisms there should be mingled an edifying spirit. I feel like opening my heart to general charity and good will. We are free from the bad elements that have been troubling us so long, and which have tended to annoy us and keep us in a chafe. But I feel that this occasion of offense is now gone from among us. I can now take in every body with a feeling of fellowship, love and charity.

*　　*　　*　　*　　*

"Persons come to me and talk with me, and want help. I have thought lately that the only good thing I can do for them, is to help their faith. We may as well set it down as an axiom, that we cannot have good experience without faith and trust in God. God is the giver of every good and perfect gift. If we are troubled about any desire, and feel cramped and our way hedged in, we should ask ourselves if that desire comes from a heart that believes and trusts in God. If it does that desire will be gratified.

*　　*　　*　　*

"I think there is at the present time a good state of unity with, and receptivity to, Mr. Noyes in the family. I think his ideas are magnetizing the life of the Community. I confess Christ a savior from all egotism. I will have no egotism stand in the way of the spirit and glory of the incoming kingdom."

WEDNESDAY.

It is a bright morning, cold, but spring-like in its beauty and absence of snow. There is a very general activity in business, and every one we meet appears happy.

An order from H. S. Gardner, Fulton, N. Y., for 25 doz. No. 1 traps with chains.

Also a letter inquiring our lowest net cash prices for traps, from The Russell & Erwin Manufacturing Co.

The ice group are having a successful time. Two accidents we hear reported. First, Old Grey, the horse used at the ice-cutting machine, slipped into the pond, and had to have some assistance in getting out. He apparently received no injury, though he did not seem to relish the experience much. Secondly, one of the workmen had a similar bath. He took it coolly, which considering the state of the thermometer was not surprising. We understand that Myron came near slipping in, and in saving himself, was the cause of Old Grey's ducking.

The committee on fruit preserving have decided to put up the following amounts respectively of fruit and vegetables the coming season: Sweet Corn, 40,000 cans; Peas, 10,000 cans; Tomatoes, 10,000 cans; Strawberries, 3000 bottles and 1000 cans; Raspberries, 2000 bottles and 2000 cans; Plums, 1000 bottles and 1500 cans; Peaches, 1000 bottles and 3000 cans; Pears, 500 bottles and 1000 cans; Pineapple, 1000 bottles and 1000 cans; Quince, 500 bottles and 500 cans; Blackberries, 500 bottles and 500 cans; Cherries, 2000 bottles and 2000 cans; Pie-fruit 2000 cans—amounting in all to 87,000 qts.; Jellies of various kinds, including strawberry, currant, blackberry, quince, crab-apple, plum, peach, raspberry, cherry, lemon, apple and pineapple, 3,650 pints and 2,450 half pints. It should be understood that of some kinds of fruit, particularly plums, we have a considerable quantity on hand. If this is all disposed of this winter and spring, some of the above figures will be increased.

DAILY JOURNAL
OF ONEIDA COMMUNITY.

A. D. 1866. JAN. 25. NO. 10.

WEDNESDAY.

OUR people have reduced the work of getting ice to a scientific basis, converting it from a heavy, dreary, tedious job, to a comparatively easy and pleasant one. The cutting machine does away with the old method of sawing, which was slow and difficult. Two men with a horse will now in a short time cut a quarter of an acre into blocks suitable for handling. The ice-plow does not cut to the full depth of the ice, but all that is necessary to separate the blocks is a blow or two with an ice-chisel. Then the loading, on to the sled or wagon, which used to be the heaviest and most back-breaking work of all, is now easily accomplished, without any direct lifting. From the point where the ice is cut out a canal is cut about three feet and a half wide and forty or fifty feet long, extending towards the point where the teams come to load. At the end of this canal next to the teams, an inclined plane, or ice-way, is constructed, of about the same width as the canal. This ice-way is made of five strips of scantling, twenty five or thirty feet long, fastened equi-distant from each other by cross pieces underneath. Upon the upper edge of each scantling an iron rod, three-eighths of an inch in diameter, is fastened, extending the whole length. At each side of the ice-way is a guard to prevent the ice blocks from sliding off. One end of the ice-way is placed in the canal and extends below the depth of the ice as it floats in the water. The other end is elevated to just the hight of the wagon-box or sled which is to receive the load, and is firmly secured there.

In loading, one man floats along sections of ice-blocks into the canal and splits them apart with his ice-chisel. Then two men, one on each side of the canal, seize each block, as it floats past them, with their iron pointed handspikes, and shove it before them up the ice-way nearly to the wagon. Then two other men, with a wooden cross bar, shove it forward into the wagon-box. In this way a load of ice is quickly transferred from the water to the wagon. The unloading is accomplished with similar ease and expedition. Thus the whole work, under the prevalence of a good spirit, really becomes sport.

To an observer at a little distance, the operations of persons using the ice-plow are somewhat novel, considering the time of year—they seem so much like ordinary plowing. The old nursery rhyme of Mother Goose, runs—

" There were three children a sliding went,
    All on a summer's day ;
The ice grew thin, they all fell in,
    And the rest they ran away."

Some one suggests that this now might be altered to

There were some men went plowing ice
    All on a winter's day ;
The ice grew thick, they plowed it quick,
    And drew it all away.

In the evening meeting E. P. I. was criticised by request. The principal fault criticised was, a tendency to be somewhat self-complacent over his own achievements and suggestions. His self-will and high opinion of his own talents and judgment make it somewhat difficult for him to coalesce with others and give up his opinion to theirs. He also has a rather rude way of speaking to his associates, particularly as leader of the Brass Band. He was thought to be steadily improving. He has a good spirit about music and is obedient to Mr. Noyes's suggestions in regard to the Band. He makes it very easy for persons to approach and ask a favor of him. What he most needs is to have his heart more thoroughly pervaded by the grace and spirit of Christ—to seek softness of spirit and depth of character.

At the machine-shop the temporary line-shaft has been removed, and the belting is being shifted to the permanent shaft, which extends the whole length of the shop.

A letter from Mrs. Deborah Knowles in answer to our letter of criticism was received to-day. It is as follows :

Rutland, N. Y., Jan. 21, 1866.

DEAR MR HAMILTON :—I heartily accept the criticism of the Community. I feel it a privilege to give myself up unreservedly to them, to be helped in any way they see fit. I am thankful for help from any one. I am in the dark, and I want to be led to Christ. I desire to clear myself of my old life in every way, and take Christ as a whole savior. I confess my entire separation from a disobedient spirit in any form, and from superficiality and insincerity. I confess brokeness of heart and faith in Christ. I confess resurrection life, and a spirit that will separate me from my worldly relatives, and from any spirit will separate me from Christ. I feel like giving up everything for Christ.

Yours in sincerity,   D. W. Knowles.

THURSDAY.

Treadwell & Co., Boston, in reply to our letter of inquiry, say they wish only 12 bear traps No 5, instead of 12 doz. This makes the amount of their order $543,92.

We are having the luxury of a north-east snow-storm, accompanied by a strong wind. It bids fair to give us good sleighing before nightfall. We do not remember a snow-storm that was more welcomely greeted than is this.

DAILY JOURNAL
OF ONEIDA COMMUNITY.

A. D. 1866.　JAN. 26.　NO. 11.

THURSDAY.

THE ice men were intending to finish filling the ice-house at Willow Place, this morning, and started out in force for that purpose; but the storm forced them to retire from the field.

In the evening meeting there was a criticism of Mr. Delatre, by request. There was but little said in the way of criticism. It was thought he did not organize quite easily enough with others, either in work or in study. He is slightly discordant in this respect. Has a somewhat legal and arbitrary tendency. In the past he has lacked a true appreciation of labor, but is improving, and growing in the public spirit. The general feeling of the family was expressed in the following remarks by Mr. Hamilton: Mr. D. wrote me sometime ago requesting criticism, and stating that he desired to begin the new year by putting himself in the best attitude for improvement. I will say for myself that my fellowship and good will have been growing for Mr. Delatre, especially during the past year. I thought he had improved in some of his habits. Formerly I was tried with his position in regard to business, but think he has gained some in that respect. I used to think he never slip," and include the financial statement, of January 1.

An order was received from Gunn and Tucker, Wellsboro, Pa., for 2 doz. traps with chains.

FRIDAY.

The snow-storm which began sometime on Wednesday night, continues. The snow falls moderately, and has not attained a great depth.

It is gratifying to note the working of the spirit of intellectual improvement among the elderly members of the Community, this winter. They engage in study with the same enthusiasm as the young, and seem to appreciate the privilege even more. It is one of the glories of Communism that it opens the doors of education to the old as well as the young, and makes personal improvement, in all directions, the imperative condition of fellowship in every one.

Dr. Fitch yesterday removed the bandages and other surgical arrangements from Lady Campbell's leg, thereby adding greatly to her comfort. She can now sit up, and by another week will be able to bear her weight up on her feet again.

The lamented " Q "'s unfinished volume, Maud, is being edited for the " press" sometime in the future. A page is daily revised and carefully corrected. Only the earliest written portions have as yet been examined.— The editor finds some tearful passages, but now and then a ray of sunshine lights up the page, and there are beauties in it that will linger long in the memory. We

entered into business on the basis of public spirit exactly, but his purpose was to work just enough to promote his individual interest so far as health was concerned. That was apparently the purpose which governed him. It seemed to me a selfish one. I thought he should rise up into a larger spirit of enterprise, and if need be sacrifice himself in order to secure some great end. I have the impression that he has risen out of that state into the spirit of service. It is possible for a person to pursue a similar policy to that which Mr. D. has pursued, and in a true way. Persons may seek employment and business responsibility, with a purpose of promoting spiritual health, and of putting themselves in a position where they are receptive to Christ. And that attitude is the spirit of service that says to the Lord, " Here I am, and I want you to make the most of me. I am entirely at your service." By putting yourself in that attitude you are in a sure way to secure the highest kind of health. I have spoken thus not because I think it especially applicable to Mr. Delatre now. But his attitude on this point was an occasion of disfellowship in the past. I think he is improving. I always liked him as a man. He has a pure taste, refinement and cultivation, which make his conversation attractive. I think, too, he has a rich and pure heart.

The Democratic Union, published at Oneida, has half a column of extracts from THE CIRCULAR, this week. They are taken from the column of " Community Gospredict that it will be more popular than Tennyson's " Maud," and more interesting than Whittier's " Maud Muller," when the time comes for its general circulation.

ARRIVALS.—Mr. Whitney, on a visit of a few days to get some clothes made, &c.

DEPARTURES.—Mrs Chesbro, of Fulton, N. Y., who has been visiting the Community for a week past.

DAILY JOURNAL
OF ONEIDA COMMUNITY.

A. D. 1866. JAN. 27. NO. 12.

FRIDAY.

YESTERDAY'S issue of the DAILY JOURNAL, was delayed beyond the usual hour of publication, by an accident to the printing-press. This will explain to our New York and Wallingford subscribers the failure to receive their papers by the usual mail.

The recent talk at Wallingford, on "Searching for the Cause," with its view of Hadean Spiritualism, and of certain spiritualists of the circulating, vampire order, is heartily sympathised with here at Oneida. The idea that these vampires are distributors of disease, is undoubtedly a true one. What is more probable than that the devil, as the Great Devourer and President of the court of death and hell, should have his special missionaries and itinerants, not only among the flies and invisible insects, but among his larger servants in human shape?

In a recent criticism Mr. Hamilton made the following remarks :

" I have some ideas which have come to my mind in relation to ——'s social character. I hope now that we are getting clear of unsympathetic, discordant material from among us, we shall be more free to discuss social matters here in our meetings, and that such discussions may enter into our ordinary criticisms ; because a man's social state and social practices have much to do with his character. My impression is that ——needs help in respect to his relations to women ; and I think there are others in the same position. I do not know as I can give a clear presentation to all the ideas that are working in my mind concerning this subject. But I see there is one way of loving a woman, which I would compare to making her your mistress. I do not mean this in a bad sense, exactly. I have been inclined to think that this was ——'s method of loving. In his social relations and combinations with a woman he has a tendency to make her his mistress. According to my idea of it, that kind of love elevates neither the man nor the woman. It cultivates self respect on neither side, and is not improving. There is a much higher standard than that.

" By studying Mr. Noyes's course you will see that he does not seek that relation with women. When a man marries a woman he elevates his love to a higher standard than that of treating her as a mistress. It is a love that cultivates more respect on both sides. The story of "Dr. Kane's Love-Life," that we are reading, shows one beautiful trait. The Dr. did not seek to make a mistress of his sweet-heart—he would not stoop to that, and soil his own honor and self-respect, but was determined to rise into a higher love, consecrated by the sacred bonds of marriage. His whole aim was to elevate her and make her a holy, pure-minded woman. He was a worldly man and we must take that into account, but his spirit in regard to this matter was refreshing, and something to admire and respect. She was much below him in her social position, and in her culture and development.

" This illustrates what we can seek in our love relations. We can seek to raise those we love, up into fellowship with God and Christ, and introduce the holy ordinances of the church between us as a medium. One very important method of securing that end is, in all our love affairs to secure some spiritual-minded third party, who shall be a medium between us and our sweet-hearts. I think persons fail in that respect. —— has failed to secure good spiritual cooperation.

" I throw these ideas out as something to think of, and perhaps we can talk of it again another time. I am well satisfied that no one can be very successful and improving as a lover until he adopts the higher kind of love."

SATURDAY.

An order is received from O. S. Hopkins for 200 No. 1 traps with chains and 10 No. 1¼ with chains.

It has been decided to increase the discount on our traps five per cent.

Half a dozen teams are employed drawing logs to the saw-mill.

Two orders for preserved fruit received by this mornings mail, amounting to about $100.

In consequence of the diminution of business in the shops, it has been thought best to sell a portion of the coal on hand. Accordingly sixty-five tons have been sold, amounting to about $775.

The Oneida *Dispatch* this week quotes several paragraphs from THE CIRCULAR, including the financial statement. It makes the erroneous statement that the bag-business has been suspended among us. It is not the bag-business but the family bag-bees that have been suspended. We learn, moreover, that the bees will be resumed again in a few days.

DAILY JOURNAL
OF ONEIDA COMMUNITY.

A. D. 1866. JAN. 29. NO. 13.

MONDAY.

THE following reply to Mrs. Knowles has been made by Mr. Hamilton :

O. C., Jan. 27, 1866.

DEAR MRS. KNOWLES :—Your letter has been received and read in our meeting, and I judge, found its way generally to the Community heart.

A proposal to invite you to come and live with us awhile " *on trial*," and so test the question of your ability or fitness to be vitally organized into the Community, was responded to by the family. Our Community was never more united than now. Bad, discordant spirits are cast out from among us, and the true hearts unite the more firmly. Our hearts are open to you, but allow me to be sincere and say, that while we are thankful for the words and earnest tone of your letter, yet we have learned from experience that by *faith-deeds* only, can confidence and unity become established. It seems to me that you will need desperate faith to get right with God and the Church after your long course of independence. But the Lord can save, and is stronger than the wicked one. Hoping that you may have grace to overcome

Yours truly,　　　E. H. HAMILTON.

The proposed covered passage way from the New House to the archway seems undesirable in several respects, and probably will not be built.

A consultation is to be held this afternoon, at Willow Place, relative to the manufacture and sale of the new small traps. Some of our agents think they could get orders for them, if we only had them on hand. About a thousand traps are ready for the springs.

The meetings for several evenings have been devoted to testimony and a general self-clearance from all sympathy with the malcontents who have left us, particularly the would-be financial autocrat. The real wickedness of this person's character and his effrontery and egotism were fully exposed to the gaze of all. Our contact with such persons, is revealing to us more and more clearly the practical truth of the doctrine that there are two seeds of men—that there is a class of men radically corrupt in their life, whom no amount of discipline, or culture, or friendship, or mercy, will change inwardly, whatever the outward semblance may be. They are coarse to the center, they have no chemical affinity with the truth, and they hate the judgment. Recognizing the essential corruptness of their hearts we are fully justified, when their character is clearly revealed, in utterly withdrawing all sympathy from them and cutting every cord that binds us to them.

Speaking of the doctrine of " principles not men" Mr. Hamilton remarked, last evening, that no man of deep spiritual views of organization and unity would hold to that doctrine, or to the idea of independence. " There is really no such thing as a man's holding to principles and not men, or of his really having an independent hold on principle and eternal truth for himself. W cannot do it. The spirit of the living God, is the foundation, origin and cause of all principle and of what th world ordinarily call truth. Men in the world say the hold to this truth or that principle. What are thos principles or truth ? They are nothing but the manifestation of the life that comes from God. There is only on true spirit, which we have all got to be organized into. I recognize that, and desire to be very modest in view the fact that I am nothing of myself, and that I canne be a good man unless I am organized into another spir and possessed by it, which is superior to myself. I rec ognize Mr. Noyes as my head, and the medium tha shall modify me and organize me into Christ's body.— The world may sneer at it and call it what they choose but that is the truth I accept."

On Saturday an accident occurred to James Vanvelze in the bath-room. While attempting the gymnastic fea of swinging to and fro, suspended head downward from the ceiling, he suddenly fell to the floor, a distanc of several feet. He was evidently considerably injured as for several moments (to use his own words) " every thing looked black" to him, while he turned sheet-pale Fortunately he struck on his hip in falling, otherwise he might have been much injured for life. We trus that all our boys and young men will learn a lesson from this accident.

We have an inquiry for four gross of mop-sticks, Myron reports the sale of $250 worth of Bags on Sat.

JUVENESCO.

My flowers, said the garden, are withered all ;
Not a poor, stray blossom is left me now ;
The star-shaped flakes through the still air fall
And the paleness of death is on my brow :
But my unborn roses lie safe below,
And when spring shall come with its warm, soft rain,
Then my darling flowers on my breast shall glow,
So I circle round to my youth again.

My light wanes fast, said the setting moon,
No longer my pearly radiance gleams—
With pale, pale face I look forth at noon,
Shorn of my fair and beautiful beams :
But beneath the nadir I quickly slide
And arise once more o'er the distant main,
Then with noiseless wings o'er the earth I glide
Thus I circle round to my youth again.

I am growing old, to myself I said,
There are sober lines adown my face
And here and there a silvery thread
Shines in my hair. But a quiet grace—
A sense of youth steals o'er my mind,
God's true elixir of life I gain—
The tender heart of a child I find,
So I circle round to my youth again.

W. H. H.

DAILY JOURNAL
OF ONEIDA COMMUNITY.

A. D. 1866.   JAN. 30.   NO. 14.

TUESDAY.

IN the evening meeting Mr. Higgins applied for criticism in the following letter:

To the Community.

DEAR BRETHREN :—I perceive the time has come for me to look to Christ, through his appointed means (which is criticism), to be delivered from an egotistical, superficial, idolatrous spirit. I see by looking back upon my past experience, that that spirit has harrassed me from time to time ever since my public confession of Christ as a savior from all sin. And previous to that time, a superficial spirit domineered over me to impede the spirit of inspiration in my heart.

I know that good is stronger than evil, as Christ is stronger than the devil among men. I wish to commit myself, body and soul to Christ, for his chastening and protecting care against every false and superficial spirit. I have considered myself in the judgment much of the time for the year past. As Mr. DeLatre said, I wish to begin this new year for God and his cause, with true and humble devotion to the Community spirit and interest. I know, as Mr. Noyes has said, that I have many habits to be purged out before the spirit of truth can have full sway over me.

I feel a compunction of conscience for not heeding Mr. N.'s advice before this. Sometimes I have felt a desire to improve by my own, and other's criticisms. And at this time I feel to trust God in committing myself to the brethren for criticism, at any time when Mr. Hamilton sees fit.   C. HIGGINS.

ONEIDA, JAN. 27, 1866.

He was thought to have improved in spirit a great deal during the past year. His old tendency to teach seems to have mostly passed away, and he is now docile and obedient in that respect. He is a Bible man, and fond of theological argument; but he dwells too much in the Old Testament. He needs to be pervaded more by the spirit of the New Testament. His will which has been a source of some trouble to him in the past, has grown more flexible and yielding to the Community spirit. He has less fear of criticism than formerly. Much love and respect was expressed for him. The following letter from Mr. Noyes to Mr. Higgins, written a year ago, was read by Mr. H.'s request; and suggested some interesting conversation in regard to old age, and the importance of elderly persons seeking criticism, and loving it as their deliverer:

Wallingford, Jan. 29, 1865.

DEAR BRO. HIGGINS:—I like the tone of your letter. God is waking you up to improvement. I doubt not that your inner heart is sound and loyal to the truth. But the same influence that has brought old age upon your body, has fastened some bad habits on your mind, and those habits are connected with your religious character and your love of the Bible, which makes it more difficult for criticism to get at them and overcome them. Old people ought above all to love criticism as an ordinance of salvation. By that God can make them young again. Yours truly,   J. H. Noyes.

A wish was expressed last evening that the evening readings might be continued. This will probably be done for a season, at least, if suitable and interesting books can be obtained.

Mr. Abbott reports the supply of water from the spring as short, and wishes all persons to practice economy in the use of it. It is lower than at any time last summer.

A small order for preserved fruit was received this morning.

Messrs, Burt, Woolworth, Hamilton and Cragin have been appointed a committee to select a man to take C. O. Kellogg's place in the farm management.

ARRIVALS.—Mr. Cragin, this morning, looking bright and happy. He walked up from the depot.—W. A. Knowles, from Champion, N. Y.

The boys now appear to be in an improving state. At a meeting held with them on Sunday, they all took a good position, and expressed their purpose to come into good relations with the Community.

The reading of "Dr. Kane's Love-Life" was finished last evening. The book has proved interesting and instructive, and has drawn a full house every evening.

The weather is again quite mild. The mercury stands at 37 deg. Sleighing is poor, but there are indications of more snow to come.

DAILY JOURNAL
OF ONEIDA COMMUNITY.

A. D. 1866. JAN. 31. NO. 15.

WEDNESDAY.

THE DAILY JOURNAL is now published about noon and is intended as a general thing to contain a report of the Community news from noon of the day previous. It is set up by Mrs. Dunn and Annie Hatch, corrected and printed by T. L. Pitt, and distributed after dinner by Abby Burnham and Sophronia Higgins. It is printed on Leonard Dunn's Press.

There seems to be considerable quilting going on among the in-door folks now-a-days. We heard of two quilts under way yesterday. According to our observation these quilting parties are generally ended with a supper, rather more select than the general course, to which a suitable number of the brethren are invited. The event is thus made memorable for a season, and the recipient of the quilt has the satisfaction of receiving with it a pleasant portion of the Community spirit.

Myron went to Boonville on Monday and sold about $700 worth of bags. We have the unusual good luck to have a full assortment of bags on hand to fill the whole order. Heretofore, in the case of nearly every order, large or small, a portion of the bags ordered would have to be manufactured before the order could be filled. This is the largest order we have ever had.

This week's CIRCULAR was highly commended in the meeting last evening. Much satisfaction was especially expressed with Mr. Noyes two articles, and the editorial on the "Highland Penny". Mr. Hamilton said he had wanted this last subject touched upon in the paper for some time. The whole paper is very interesting.

The bag-bees were resumed yesterday. The recent large orders are encouraging indications of increased activity in the bag trade.

Mr. Cragin gave a report of his journey, last evening, and of the proposal of Mr. Noyes to get the old horse barn ready to start the store by the 1st of April. This proposal was received with enthusiasm by the family, and we shall move forward at once to prepare the building for that purpose. The committee to decide on its location met this morning, and all present were in favor of letting the building remain where it now is.— It will be more convenient, in many respects, in its present location; some expense will be saved by not moving it; it will obstruct the view of some scenery from the portico, but less pleasant scenery than it would hide if moved further towards the present horse barn, and if finished up in good style, it will be an attractive feature in itself. Being so near it will probably be the means of relieving us of some of the freight that is now unloaded at our front door, and possibly it may eventually be found desirable to remove the present business-office to that building.

It is remarked that the health of the Community was never better than it is this winter. Colds, the common complaints of winter, are but little known. The children share in this general healthfulness, and present rosy-cheeked evidences, of their good condition.

This improvement and buoyancy of Community health is due we believe to the departure from among us of obstructing elements, and the growing state of unity that is prevailing.

We are conscious of a decided improvement in the spiritual atmosphere since the sincere clearing by the family, the other evening, of all sympathy with the unbelieving and disorganizing spirits that have left us.

The farmers dispatched their last load of barley to Utica to-day. The amount sold will measure about a thousand bushels. On Monday as the teams were returning home, some of the teamsters got into a strife of running by each other. One of them run his wagon off the side of the road, and got seriously hurt. He was taken up insensible, and remained so for eight or ten hours. He was cut and brusied considerably about the head and face. The doctor, however, says his skull is uninjured, and he will proabbly soon recover.

This winter is remarkable for its sudden and extreme changes, as well as for the small amount of snow that has fallen. Days of springlike mildness are succeeded by others with all the snap of winter in them, and these again by others sunny and pleasant. On the whole we enjoy the freaks of the season, with a considerable degree of satisfaction. The teamsters would like more snow, but on the other hand the skaters probably would not. The children find abundant enjoyment on the hillsides, and drink in some health and hardihood from their out-door sports every day.

DAILY JOURNAL
OF ONEIDA COMMUNITY.

A. D. 1866.   FEB. 1.   NO. 16.

THURSDAY.

THE following communications to the family were read last evening:

DEAR FRIENDS: I take this opportunity to express my thanks to God for his goodness to me through the past year, while I have been residing with you. I must say that it has been far the happiest year I ever experienced in all my life. I have not been without sorrows and severe trials. I find the last dying struggles of my old life are very severe, but I thank God through Jesus Christ our Lord, I believe he will bring me off conquerer over all the powers of darkness and opposition. I confess my love for Mr. Noyes and Mr. Hamilton as our leaders under the inspiration of God and I therefore place the utmost confidence in them under Christ our great leader and savior from all sin. I confess my love for and sympathy with the Community spirit, and endorse fully the doctrines of the Community as far as I understand them. I offer myself for criticism at all times whenever Mr. Hamilton thinks I need it. I think criticism very necessary as a means of improvement in spiritual life. I hope the family will not spare the rod, but use it as a scourge to whip all my old life and habits out of me, that hinder me from growing in grace and in the knowledge of our Lord and Savior Jesus Christ. I want all the wood hay and stubble burnt up that I may have about me. I may suffer loss, but I thank God I am ready to come to the judgment and have my work tried of what sort it is, that I might be saved yet so as by fire. I confess my loyalty to the Community spirit, and will endeavor to work at any post wherever the family place me, according to the best of my ability.

From your brother in Christ.   C. B. UNDERWOOD.

"I feel like acknowledging my dependence on Christ continually as my Savior from my old life. I confess a spirit of watchfulness, with a realizing sense of my own peculiar temptations. I find that my heart has grown into a more practical knowledge of Christ, since I have been here, than ever before, and that I can testify to the power of resurrection life within me. I am thankful for criticism, and feel like thanking particularly those who so faithfully criticise me. I confess a spirit that seeks to love most of all, those who are nearest God, and who are vitally organized into his Spirit. I feel thankful for all the blessings and happiness so freely given me, and confess a good spirit to actuate me at all times, that thus I may honor Christ.   PORTIA."

C. O. Kellogg offered himself for criticism last evening. Much love and commendation were expressed for him. The principal fault pointed out was his silence—he does not use his tongue enough. He should give more testimony for the truth, confess Christ more, and seek to edify and strengthen both himself and others by word of mouth. On this point Mr. Hamilton remarked: "I doubt if a man can build up a good spiritual character and be strong in the faith and the deep things of God, without using his tongue more in public. I have thought of this a great deal lately. Mr. Moyes has called attention to the use of the tongue and shown that effects are bad if it is used wrongly. But it is a great failure not to use the tongue at all. Our power of expression and discourse was given us to be used on the side of truth. I dont see how a person can build himself up in the faith without using his tongue for God and Christ and the truth. In that respect Otis might come under some criticism. He is too silent here in our meetings, and outside also. He might by confessing Christ, if it is only in a few words, create an atmosphere around him that would be a great benefit to him in all his operations. It would result in his own good and in the public good also."

The ice-harvest is now finished. Yesterday, while engaged on the pond, Mr. Thayer accidentally stepped off the solid ice and went down. Frederick Marks who stood near pulled him out nearly as quickly as he went in. No damage done except the wetting.

The proceeds of the barley sold amount to about $1000.

The committee on the location of the store reported their conclusions to the meeting last evening. The proposal to let the building remain where it now is, was unanimously approved by the family.

ARRIVALS.—A Mr. Lowell of Troy, N. Y., a visitor.— Mr. Inslee from N. Y.

DEPARTURES.—C. O. Kellogg, for Wallingford.

ANOTHER GHOST.

MR. EDITOR:—As I was wending my way through the last CIRCULAR, and quietly enjoying myself, on turning a corner—or page—I was suddenly startled by the ghost of lost "Q". Yes—on looking more closely I was convinced that it was the ghost of our dear old author of "Foot-Notes", who came to so sudden and mysterious an end in the neighborhood of Steer Creek. He appeared to be on to a new "spear". He had the same sharp eye—a little softened perhaps—the same curious twist of the mouth; and you could perceive traces of the old peculiar hitch in his gait that we always thought became him rather than otherwise. His step was more elastic, and he seemed so joyous in his new "spear" that he would occasionally give a hop, skip and a jump. Altogether he had an air of happiness, and seemed at peace with himself and all mankind, like one who had just got out of a *tight place*, or a good boy who has been *settling up* with kind but faithful parents. On the whole I was not scared, and hope to meet & often in the CIRCULAR.   H. E. H.

DAILY JOURNAL
OF ONEIDA COMMUNITY.

A. D. 1866.   FEB. 2.   NO. 17.

FRIDAY.

Mr. Cragin visited Mr. Leete, yesterday, and last evening reported the result of his interview. He found Mr. Leete ready to cooperate with us in the store enterprise, and to obey orders. Mr. Cragin proposed to him to sell his store-building and shop, in Verona, and build a cottage somewhere on our domain, where his family could be accommodated and provided for. This would obviate any objections that his outside friends might raise to his joining the Community. Mr. Leete was pleased with the plan; and it is sympathised with by the Community.

Mr. Inslee favored us with a report of his operations since he has been gone, which was very interesting. It seemed very evident that the providence of the heavens had been with him, opening men's hearts to give him the information he was seeking. After Mr. Inslee's report there was conversation about the proposal to send Charles Cragin to Willimantic, to learn the silk business. This was fully sympathised with, and it was thought best for Charles to go on to Wallingford this week. He will accordingly start to-night.

Much commendation was expressed of Mr. Inslee's efficiency and prompt business habits of late, particularly since engaging in the silk-business.

The number of persons in the Oneida family at the present time is 209. There are 79 adult males and 78 adult females; minors, under 21, males, 20, females, 32.

Our visitor, Mr. Amos M. Lowell, left yesterday afternoon. He is of New England birth. Some of his ancestors were the founders of the city of Lowell, Mass. He had learned of the existence of the Oneida Community through an article about us in the Troy *Whig*, two weeks ago. He will send the paper to us.

G. W. H. in visiting Watertown yesterday was, while at Rome, presented with a free pass over the R. & W. Railroad, by the chief foreman of Messrs. S. Adams & Sons, machine works. This gentleman visited the Community last season and was highly gratified with his reception here, and took this way of expressing his appreciation of G.'s hospitality.

A letter was received from a lady who visited us last fall, an acquaintance of Mr. Elmer, expressing considerable sympathy with the Community. The following paragraph indicates the tone and spirit of the letter :

"Almost daily I witness occurrences that make me desirous of the diffusion and prevalence of a Community spirit. The solicitations of the pinched and needy who only ask for "cold victuals," turn my mind at once to what is a sure and safe remedy for all the want, woe and wretchedness there is in the world ; i. e., the practical embracing of Christianity—the becoming one in Christ Jesus, *the* Great Family. It is without ceasing that I desire this end, and O that I may be able to make of my life *one great and unceasing prayer* for this glorious ultimate. In a condition of apparent isolation it is difficult to live in accordance with my highest convictions of right : instead of progressing myself and aiding others, my own growth is retarded, while others are in no wise benefitted by me. By a sad and painful experience, for which I devoutly thank God, I have obtained faint glimmerings of the truth which I trust naught shall ever make obscure. I should thankfully welcome any words of encouragement which you, or any of your family may see fit to address to me. Your prosperity as a family and Church I shall never cease to desire.

Yours respectfully,   M. S. CLARK.

A gusty snow-storm from the northwest, prevailed yesterday. To-day is mild, and a thin veil of falling snow hides all the hills. It is so finely sifted as to increase in depth very slowly.

An order was received this morning from the Russell and Erwin Manufacturing Co. for 44 doz. traps, Nos. 8 and 4, amounting to $609.

DEAR BROTHER PITT :—We of the children's department confess our union with Mr. Noyes's *great purpose* —A DAILY PAPER—and desire that our influence on the children may draw them into the same channel ; remembering that as the twig is bent the tree is inclined.

Oneida, Feb. 2, 1866.   R. L. H.

DAILY JOURNAL
OF ONEIDA COMMUNITY.

A. D. 1866.   FEB. 3.   NO. 18.

SATURDAY.

A MISSTATEMENT occurred in yesterday's JOURNAL. It was not the foreman of S. Adams and Sons' machine works who gave G. W. H. the free pass, but the master mechanic of the R. and W. Railroad.

A slight fire occurred in the engine-room, at the Tontine, last evening. A pan of ashes, with a few live coals in it, was placed in contact with a piece of plank at the back of the engine, and in the course of time set the plank on fire. No damage was done, except the destruction of the plank and the filling of the Tontine with smoke, as both the plank and ash-pan were isolated from all other combustible material. It was a hint however to watchfulness and certainty in the care of fire and ashes.

A company called in a sleigh last evening for the purpose of attending a concert, which they supposed was to come off in the Community Hall. As our programme for the evening did not include a concert, they were of course disappointed. They were, however, treated to a little singing.

In the evening meeting Charles Cragin was criticised. There was a very general expression of commendation of and love for him. He is very prompt and executive in his business habits, and has a great deal of force and resolute manhood in business. Has lacked a little in some details as a mechanic, is not quite thorough enough in his arrangements of machinery—is apt to toggle things up. He does not keep his business snug enough. The tendency of his spirit heretofore has been toward hardness. He has had a great deal of pride and intellectual ambition, and the vibration between pride and self-depreciation has tended to make him hard in spirit.— There has been a marked improvement in him the past season. He is loyal to the Community and Mr. Noyes, and his heart seems open to faith. We have confidence in him that he will honor the truth in the new position to which he is called, and our love goes with him. In the course of the criticism Mr Hamilton made the following remarks:

"Hardness and pride come from unbelief. It is the vibration of the mind between egotism and self-depreciation that hardens the character and produces lack of faith in God, and ennobling faith in one's self. In this connection I have thought with much interest of the following passage from John: "Behold what manner of love the Father hath bestowed upon us, that we should be called the sons of God; therefore the world knoweth us not because it knew him not. Beloved now are we the sons of God: and it doth not yet appear what we shall be; but we know that, when he shall appear, we shall be like him; for we shall see him as he is. And every man that hath this hope in him purifieth himself, even as he is pure." Here is indicated the only true foundation of improvement. No one can ever make real heart improvement who has not faith in God that introduces hope into his own life, and lets him see that there is noble blood in him through Christ. That is is what has lifted me up; and that is the gospel Mr. Noyes preaches. The blood of Christ is poured out into human nature, and gives hope and assurance that we may become good, noble and pure like Christ, and true sons of God. When a person gets in earnest and sufficiently sincere and refined to appreciate and receive such a gospel as this, he will find there is such a gospel. The experience that turns into this result is surely good for us."

TALK IN THE CHAIN-SHOP.

E.—I hope Mr. J. you will not feel *chained* down to your business.

J.—[Nonchallantly.] I hope not. [Arousing.] O ho! you are bent on punishing me with puns. I must have a *lynx* eye for you fellows.

E.—[Absently.] We must count these rings. How many rings are there to a pound?

J.—I thought from the abundant use we make of our hammers that there were a good many *pounds* to a ring.

Note.—It is unnecessary to give the name of the reporter of the above dialogue. We shall doubtless *see more* of his productions hereafter.   ED. JOUR.

DAILY JOURNAL
OF ONEIDA COMMUNITY.

A. D. 1866. FEB. 5. NO. 19.

MONDAY.

THE following correspondence needs no explanation :

Clyde, N. Y., Jan. 31, 1866.

MR. HAMILTON,

DEAR SIR :—I thought I would let you know my present feelings and wishes. In the first place I offer myself to the Community to serve in any place they think best. I am out of work, as Mr B. has let me off from the job which I had taken.

I should like very much to come back to the Community if thought best. If not can you give me work? I can get work here, but I would rather come to you if I could. But whether there or here I intend to work for the cause of Christ. I have to confess that I have not paid my way since I left the O. C.

Will you answer this as soon as convenient?

E. WHITNEY.

O. C. Feb. 2. 1866.

MR. WHITNEY :—You will probably remember a conversation you had with me when you were here the last time but one. It was the time Mr. C. was about leaving. Perhaps I cannot state just the words said, but the substance I remember well. You said that you had more or less of the same difficulty as Mr. C.—that was, lack of full confidence in Mr. Noyes's inspiration. I replied that it was very important for yourself to settle that point, and you should not seek to be received back until you had settled it. You made no reply of consequence, and your silence left me to conclude that you were still unsettled on that point.

The Community were never more united than now in their confidence in Mr. Noyes as an inspired leader, and in their purpose to have no fellowship with any who do not receive him as such. I do not think the Community would be willing to invite you to return without satisfactory testimony on this point.

Yours sincerely, E. H. HAMILTON.

A class for the study of draughting machine work has been started, under the teachership of Mr. Inslee and J. F. Sears.

C. A. Burt has been appointed pattern-maker for the machine-shop.

Edwin Burnham is to qualify himself to take C. A. Cragin's place as foreman of the trap-shop. In the meantime Joel is to have general oversight of the work.

The weather has continued stormy much of the time for the last four days. This morning was clear, with the mercury at —5 deg.

Considerable attention being turned, in the family, to criticism, it has been thought best to have some plan of organization, which would secure promptness in attending to cases of criticism, and relieve the general meeting from responsibility with regard to them. Accordingly, six committees or clubs of "Inquiry and Criticism," of ten members each, have been appointed. These clubs are to meet once a week or oftener.

The following note from Lady Campbell was read last evening :

DEAR FRIENDS :—Please to accept of this little note of thanks, which I, feel this morning constrained to write. I am truly grateful for all your kind words and deeds as well as for the spiritual strength which I have received : also for that baptism of hope and patience which has sustained me through so many wearisome days and restless nights. But thank that Goodness more abundantly not only for Mr. Noyes, but for all who have believed through him ; I confess my love for and union with them.

I have been thinking much about the good and bad use of the tongue since Mr. Noyes's remarks on the subject, earnestly desiring that my conversation may be in future in " simplicity and godly sincerity". I confess Christ in me a savior from old habits of thinking as well as talking. A. R. CAMPBELL.

A friendly and quite good letter has been received from Albert Ackley. He seems to be softened in spirit and evidently regrets his leaving the Community. He had heard reports from a late seceder, that there were a number of persons in the Community, particularly among the young, who were discontented and about ready to leave. He gives them his advice to remain where they are and not follow so foolish an example as his own. His letter has been responded to by Mr. Hamilton and several of the young men. He is at St, Johns, Mich., and contemplates going to Nebraska.

What is the difference between the states-prison method of punishing by the cold water bath, and the common one? One is by hydraulics, and the other is by rawhide-licks.

THE TRADER'S FUNCTION.

I.

Permit me, Mr. Editor, to express through the columns of your popular JOURNAL, my appreciation of the philosophy lately brought out by Mr. Noyes on the above subject : namely, that the producer and consumer stand related to each other as male and female ; that the trader is properly to be considered, not as an independent institution, but as the representative and agent of the producer ; that his true function is to seek the interests of both producer and consumer ; and that the present system of trade, which makes the agent, or errand-boy, more important than the one who makes the wares he sells, or than the one who uses those wares, is a great perversion of nature—a diseased condition—properly called priapism. W.

DAILY JOURNAL
OF ONEIDA COMMUNITY.

A. D. 1866.   FEB. 6.   NO. 20.

TUESDAY.

AN application from Albert N. Kneeland to be received into the Community, in company with his mother and sister, was read last evening. The Community thought we were not prepared to receive them all at present. A very favorable opinion was formed of Mr. Kneeland when here, a month ago, as a young man of good character and purposes. He seems to be very much attracted to the Community. It was thought, that for the present he had better remain where he is and devote himself to the interests of the Community in his present sphere. He can work for the cause as well there as here, and can help his mother and sister into a truer knowledge of and fellowship with the Community. The truth has suffered in that region heretofore in consequence of the misconduct of other members of his family, and he has a good chance to stand there now and honor the truth, and remove the stigma of the past.

Another fire occurred last night. Mr. Olds had filled the racks of the oven in the bakery with wood, for the purpose of drying it. During the night Harriet Howard who lodges in the children's house, was awakened and alarmed by an unusual quantity of smoke, which was filling all the lower part of the house. She aroused up some of the men, and the source of the smoke was soon found in Mr. Olds' oven. The wood had taken fire and was rapidly turning into charcoal, the doors of the oven being closed so that the wood could not blaze. Water was brought and the fire was soon extinguished. The only damage done, apparently, was the thorough blackening of the oven by the smoke and heat. It was providential that the doors of the oven were closed, otherwise the wood would have blazed, and possibly have set the neighboring woodwork on fire. The affair is another hint toward carefulness on part of all those who have to do with fire.

It being desirable to have some new small slide lathes for the machine-shop, G. W. H. and J. F. S. visited Rome yesterday, to examine lathes there and ascertain what improvements have been made in them recently, preparatory to manufacturing the lathes ourselves.

The statement in yesterday's JOURNAL to the effect that Edwin Burnham is to qualify himself to take the post of foreman of the trap-shop, was premature. Such a proposal was made in a trap-shop meeting and reported to the general meeting; but no definite action was taken on it, and it probably will not be carried out.

The latest item of news from the Janurary term of the court, is that a family of Thoroughfares are being tried for *sleighing* some of our most respectable inhabitants.

"Won': you *please* tell me who H. E. H., of No. 16 of your excellent JOURNAL, is?" How should *we* know, when the communication came by the secret conveyance of the Community Post-office? Did'nt we cudgel our brains over the same question? "H. E. H."—we never heard of him (or perhaps her) before. We feel an awe in attempting to solve the mystery. What if we too, should see a ghost!! Perhaps it is is a spirit communication. Ghosts are more likely to see ghosts than other people, we understand. What if, Mr. Inquirer, a whole troop of ghosts, with "Q" at their head, should come charging down upon us, screaming their battle cry, "*Procul, o, procul este, profani?*" Think of their "spears" ringing and clashing round our defenseless head!— Would'nt we have to make "foot-notes" with a vengeance? In view of such a possibility we must be silent, and fall back on the printer's rights, and only mentally *transpose* the first two letters of the mysterious signature. Perhaps this will furnish a clue. Who knows? We are dumb.

THE TRADER'S FUNCTION.

II.

If the producer and the consumer are related to each other as male and female, it is only necessary to ascertain what course of conduct, on the part of man toward woman, will insure the most permanent bliss in the social relation, in order to understand what course of conduct, on the part of the salesman (as the representative of the producer), towards the consumer, will produce the most perfect happiness in the commercial relation.

Now in the social relation the best interests of man requires that he should be considerate and gentle towards woman; that he should seek her interest and happiness; that his approaches to her should be governed by the laws of attraction; that while it is proper for him to call attention to his claims, any thing like forcing or extra urging produces repulsion on her part, and damages his own suit; that respect and confidence are the only sure foundations of love and happiness.

So, in the commercial relation, the salesman, as the representative of the producer, should treat the consumer as a maiden to be won and married; should pursue such a course of conduct towards her as will gain her respect, confidence and love; he should ever seek her best interests as well as his own; in presenting his goods he should avoid all forcing tendencies; and his interviews should always terminate with mutual satisfaction.   w.

DAILY JOURNAL
OF ONEIDA COMMUNITY.

A. D. 1866. FEB. 7. NO. 21.

WEDNESDAY.

DURING a late conversation in the evening meeting, on inspiration, Mr. Hamilton remarked substantially as follows:

"I was interested last night in thinking of Mr. Noyes' definition of inspiration—that it is a "stimulant or force." Inspiration works in many ways; I should not wish to say in how many or how few. I was however interested in noticing two ways in which it works. One way, and perhaps the one in which we are most accustomed to think of it as working, is in giving wisdom and instincts. We talk about an inspiration to do this or that thing, as something that has wakened up and stimulated the understanding, in a certain direction. This is a true and' very important part of the work of inspiration—to have our ideas directed rightly and our instincts inspired. But the idea is new that it also acts as a general stimulant to action, like the force of a great water-wheel—that it is a great force or power.

"Some of the most interesting ideas I have now-a-days, run in this direction. I feel my limits more in the direction of power than in any thing else; and this points me to the resurrection as the great center of our hopes. There is the mighty power of God that raised Christ from the dead, and overcame death itself. There we see the tremendous element of force or power at work. And in opening ourselves to this element of inspiration, we are opening ourselves to resurrection life. It does not matter what direction it takes, whether of business or something else, the inspiration of force is not the less important.

" I see that Mr. Noyes is the source not only of wisdom but of power to this Community. He has thrown this current of power into Mr. Cragin and made him a medium of power to us. This has interested me very much, and I wish to be wide awake, and quick in yielding myself to this inspired force. I see that God is going to give us prosperity in business not by wisdom and shrewdness alone, but by wisdom, shrewdness, energy and force combined. I confess my unity with Mr. Noyes in this respect. We must be prompt to catch hold of inspiration, and respond to it in acts."

The seven o,clock readings were resumed last evening. The book begun is " Across the Continent," by Samuel Bowles, of the Springfield Republican. Taking us over the line of the coming Pacific Railroad, and through the wondrous scenes of the Pacific slope of the Continent, it promises to give us much entertainment and instruction.

M. D. Flint of Cincinnati, orders five Lunch-bags.

The stone steps at the north end of the archway have been removed and a wooden stairway is being constructed in their place.

Another incipient fire was discovered yesterday, at Willow Place. Some rags and shavings had by some one been placed in the opening in the chimney near the floor, in the chain shop; and on building the fire by the stove some of the sparks fell down the chimney and set the combustible material on fire. The burning shavings rolled out on to the floor, but were discovered before any damage was done.

O. C., Feb. 7, 1866.

MR. EDITOR:—I was an eye-witness to the lamentable failure of "Simplice" to record her name in the annals of scientific discovery; but can hardly regret it, as it threw me into the most uncontrollable fit of laughter that I ever experienced.

There was a woman who said " See !
What a marvellous thing there may be :"
Then she furbished a dish till they all muttered " Pish !"
That ingenuous woman of O. C.

A friend suggests that if " Simplice" should be zealous for prosecuting further experiments in the line of " Tin Basins," it might be an economy of force if she were provided with such as had grown rusty by use. She could thus indulge her scientific tastes in a harmless way, and at the same time perform an actual service in burnishing a useful culinary utensil.   M. N. G.

THE TRADER'S FUNCTION.
III.

The common course of traders is far from the true one : they are prone to treat consumers (to follow up the illustration) as " common women," and are often ready to commit rapes when they cannot accomplish their ends by gentler methods ; for by what better terms can we characterize their urging, forcing practices ? It is not uncommon for them to assume that they know best what consumers need, and to insist that consumers shall purchase what they advise. They sometimes continue their solicitations after a positive denial has been given them. They resort to varied forms of deceit, such as representing their own wares as superior in material and workmanship, and the wares of other dealers as inferior in these respects, without strict reference to truth in either case. They are ready to take advantage of ignorance and innocence, in order to make what are called good bargains. All these things are entirely wrong and contrary to the true spirit and function of commerce.

W.

DAILY JOURNAL
OF ONEIDA COMMUNITY.

A. D. 1866.   FEB. 8.   NO. 22.

THURSDAY.

THE following response from Mr. Whitney to Mr. Hamilton's letter was received yesterday:

Clyde, N. Y., Feb. 5, 1866.

DEAR BRO. HAMILTON:—I heartily concur with the decision of the Community as stated in your letter. I can say that that point is settled with me. I wrote to Mr. Noyes soon after I was at Oneida, when Mr. C. left, confessing my sympathy with him in his judgment of that spirit; and also expressed a wish to return to the Community. When I returned from Oneida the last time I found a letter from Mr. Noyes approving of the spirit of my letter to him and also advising me, as you will see by the inclosed letter, which you will please return. I confess my faith in Mr. Noyes as an inspired man, sent of Christ to be the head of his kingdom on earth. However pleasant it would be for me to return to you, I am willing to wait till the Community are satisfied. I believe that Christ can and will make a Community man of me. Any criticism or advise which you or the Community have to give will be thankfully received, Yours in love and sincerity, E. WHITNEY.

The letter of Mr. Noyes referred to in the above was as follows:

Wallingford, Jan. 23, 1866.

DEAR BRO. WHITNEY:—Your letter to me came with such a spirit of earnestness and sincerity, that I feel bound to respond to it, and to say to you that I wish for your salvation, and no number or degree of past errors shall hinder me from helping you in any way I can to recover yourself from the snares of the devil. I don't know what the Community would say at present about your coming back; but I am sure that you can gain their confidence by patient continuance in well doing, and by corresponding with them in the spirit of your letter to me.

Yours truly,   J. H. Noyes.

Our teamsters are making the most of the present sleighing. Eight two-horse teams are sometimes seen moving in line, with heavy loads of logs or wood. They form an interesting cavalcade. At the present time they are hauling wood from Stockbridge hill, a distance of six miles. We notice that Mr. Kinsley, acting as teamster, occasionly leads the train and seems to engage in the business with all the zest of early days.

The meeting last evening was occupied with the criticism of J. P. H. The principal faults pointed out were 1, lack of personal neatness; 2, lack of faithful attention to details in positions of responsibility; 3, a kind of animal willfulness that does not respect the judgment and wishes of others, and sacrifices obedience and fellowship to having its own way; 4, some remains of his old tendency to love of ease and lack of enterprise; 5, some tendency to grumbling at his fare in the Community, particularly in social matters. It was thought that the manitestation of these faults was due to a great extent to the influence of his father's spirit; that he had dropped down somewhat in the tone of his character since his late intercourse with his father, and he was advised to make more thorough work than ever before in clearing himself from his father's spirit—to cut the spiritual connection entirely off. On the other hand much love was expressed for John and appreciation of his good qualities. He has a good purpose, and is loyal to the Community; is kind-hearted, and, aside from his faults, a very pleasant companion. He loves the truth and Mr. Noyes, and has a purpose to become a spiritual-minded man.

We have a letter of inquiry, to-day, about traps, from Greensboro, N. C.

Four gross of mopsticks have been sold the past week.

An order for 10 doz. cans of Corn was received this morning.

THE TRADER'S FUNCTION.
IIII.

Not less liable is the salesman, under the diseased condition described, to treat the producer without due respect. He often dictates the terms upon which he shall manufacture goods, the prices at which he shall dispose of them; and these terms are made primarily for his own advantage, and in the spirit which regards the producer as his inferior, and without reference to the true principle of bringing production and consumption together with the least delay and the least expense. Many manufacturers in the United States are bound by written obligations not to sell their goods to the consumer; others are bound not to sell their goods to consumer or retailer except at such prices as will cause the goods to pass into the hands of middle-men.

[At this point, dear Editor, let me make a confidential remark: I have concluded to bring this series of articles to an abrupt close. Why No. 1—Said articles appear to me a little inappropriate in a paper of the size and character of the JOURNAL; why No. 2—I wish to have the space which such articles might occupy filled with more sparkling matter. But in thus closing these articles let me say, I consider the subject treated as of great importance—that I believe the truth will yet effect a revolution in the whole system of trade; and that I am and will be in favor of the truth whether it "puts money in our purse" or not.   w.]

DAILY JOURNAL
OF ONEIDA COMMUNITY.

A. D. 1866.   FEB. 9.   NO. 23.

FRIDAY.

WE are having pleasant winter weather now.—
Sleighing is fair. The snow is not deep, but a little falls frequently. In the mildness and stillness of last
night, it came down lightly and rested on every evergreen leaf, every bare twig and post and roof and chimney, clothing the world with its wonderful purity and
beauty. The bending boughs of the hemlock and
spruce and cedar, seem touched with a grace of which
the artist of the winter alone knows the secret.

The machine-shop hands are rejoicing over a new
machine they have just bought. It is called a Shaping
Machine, and is similar in principle to the planing
machine. It is designed for planing and shaping small
work. Some of its operations can be made more thoroughly exact than those of the ordinary planing machine. Price $350. It was bought of the Remmington
Co., at Illion, and was taken in part payment of a note
we hold against them.

Mr. Leete came over yesterday to consult with the
Community about the store enterprise. He seems to
enter heartily into the project.

Mr. Brown, of Higginsville, continues very sick and it
is doubtful whether he will recover. His disease has
taken the form of consumption. Mr. Burt and Mr.
Hinds have gone to see him to-day.

Splitting wood is a job which any one who has opportunity can busy himself about now. The wood which
is being cut at Willow Place is sawed into suitable
lengths for firewood before being drawn home.

Myron returned this morning from a trip to Albany
and Troy, having sold over $700 worth of Bags, $300 of
Silk, $150 of Fruit, $100 of Hats and $100 of Collars and
Neckties.

We had several visitors yesterday. Mr. William B.
Powers, a friend of Mr. Horace Perry, called in company with his friend Dr. H. Spencer. They were from
Cortland. Were very courteous and made many inquiries. Mr. Powers spoke highly of the Lunch-bags; said
he saw them often on the cars, which he has opportunity to do as he is constantly traveling.—A Mr. Utley from
Bennington, Vt., also called.

A committee of eight was appointed last evening to
decide on a programme for the coming anniversary of
the 20th. The committee consists of E. H. Hamilton, W.
A. Hinds, O. L. Aiken, T. L. Pitt, H. C. Noyes, S. Van-
Velzer, C. A. Macknet and Elizabeth Hutchins.

Lady Noyes celebrated her 86th birthday, yesterday,
by a very pleasant party in the sitting room adjacent to
her room. L. A. T. and M. D. P. were her lieuten-
ants in getting up the party. There were about a dozen
guests. Mrs. N. seemed to enter into the spirit of the
occasion with much interest and vivacity, and opened
the entertainment by what she termed the " kiss of
charity," in which guests were to kiss each other all
round without reference to sex. We hope she will live a
thousand years and that every new birth day will find
her happier and younger than the one before.

Mr. Herrick writes that a firm in New York gave him
an order for fifty or a hundred deer-skins, and that if our
prices and judgment of the quality of skins should suit
them, their demand would be sufficient to keep a man
busy buying all the time. We have no skins on hand
at present, and do not see a way to profitably attend to
the purchase of them except in connection with the business of buying furs.

One of our wits, whose puns, like those of Ben Holla-
day's mail-agent, are sometimes " fearfully and wonderfully made," hands us the following original specimens
which were lately perpetrated at the chain-shop:

" Edwin, please take particular pains with those links
and not *burn 'em*. I should be sorry to *see more* of them
in that condition."

" One advantage they will have in starting the silk
business at Willow Place is, that the machine-shop will
be able to furnish all the *dies*."

A trap order was received from the Hudson's Bay
Company for 45 doz. Beaver, 10 doz. Otter, 9 doz. Fox,
and about 44 doz. Muskrat, 1 Bear, and a lot of springs,
amounting in all to about $1150 net. The traps are to
be sent during the Spring to several destinations.

DAILY JOURNAL
OF ONEIDA COMMUNITY.

A. D. 1866.   FEB. 10.   NO. 24.

SATURDAY.

THE proposal to send another woman to Willimantic was considered last evening and unanimously favored. The one selected to go is Elizabeth Hutchins. The order, " Women to the front !" is being carried out practically and rapidly. It is interesting to see how Providence is opening the way before us into the silk business. It shows that in following Mr. Noyes's inspiration we are on a sure path.

The new book we are reading—Bowles's " Across the Continent"—proves very interesting. It is well written and has a tone of candor and truthfulness about it that is quite refreshing. The author has a good knack of carrying the reader along with him, and keeping up a steady interest in all that he says. He sees and describes only as a New Englander can.

Mr. Burt and Mr. Hinds, yesterday, found Mr. Brown quite low. He has no expectation of recovery, and probably will soon depart. He was very glad to see them and was much rejoiced by their sympathy and conversation. His mind and heart seem to be very much attached to the Community, and the idea of meeting a community in Hades seemed to cheer him greatly. His disease was probably brought on in consequence of the persecutions he has had to meet. He testified that there was no truth in the charges which had been made against him.

A strong south wind with signs of rain prevails to-day.

The committee on the 20th met this morning and decided on the following general programme :

Breakfast at 7 o'clock.

Weighing and measuring, sleigh-ride for the children, and Brass Band music during the forenoon.

Dinner at 1 P. M., introduced by an anthem, and closed with a hymn by the family ; to be followed by toasts and speeches.

Games and Amusements from 3 to 7 P. M.

Evening gathering at 7½ o'clock, at which J. H. Noyes is expected to deliver an address from the stage.

President of the day, W. H. Woolworth.

Vice-President, H. A. Noyes.

Toast-master, W. A. Hinds.

Toast Committee, T. L. Pitt, G. Campbell, H. C. Noyes, H. J. Seymour, and H. M. Worden.

Committee on Music, Edward Inslee, H. C. Noyes and Homer Barron.

Committee on Amusements, E. L. Hatch, C. W Underwood, and Chloe Seymour.

Committee on Weighing and measuring, M. L. Worden and F. A. Burt.

Committee on Sleigh-rides, H. T. Clark, E. L. Hatch, A. L. Burt and Mrs. Whitfield.

Committee on Decorations, James Van Velzer, Manly Aiken, C. A. Burt, W. G. Kelly, O. A. Nash, L. E. Aiken, H. M. Hutchins and Beulah.

Committee on Table Arrangements, O. L. Aiken, F. Marks, D. Abbott, D. M. Kelly, B. Bristol, Joel Higgins, V. Hawley, W. R. Inslee, H. Burt, John Cragin, L. T Waters, Ellen Miller, Carrie, Jane Kinsley, Sophronia, S. K. Dunn, Alice Ackley, L. A. Thayer, E. Burt, Portia and C. A. Reid.

Table-Waiters, Abby Burnham, Edwin Nash, Edwin Burnham, Louisa Van Velzer, Ann Bailey, Ellen Nash, Martha, Alfred Hawley, Manly and George Miller.

Dish Washers, Mr. Perry, Mrs. Thomas, Miss Olds, Florence, Harriet Kinsley, Mary Jones, Meroa, M. D. Pomeroy, Mrs. Loomis, J. P. Hutchins and James Vail.

To wash Tumblers, Mrs. Burt, Martha, Louisa and Rosamond.

To wash Knives and Forks, Mrs. Underwood, Harriet Mallory, Alice Nash. Mrs. Kelly, S. W. Nash.

To wash Spoons, J. C. Bailey, Virtue, and D. P. Nash.

Arranging the Dining-Room Tables, Maria, AnnEliza, Annie, Mary Bolles, and Mary Baker.

Persons not named in the foregoing list are requested to assist in washing dishes, and arranging tables, and to make themselves generally useful.

DAILY JOURNAL
OF ONEIDA COMMUNITY.

A. D. 1866.   FEB. 12.   NO. 25.

MONDAY.

THE committees of inquiry and criticism began their sessions yesterday. There seems to be much interest centering in this movement. It is in harmony with the leading inspiration for unity which is pervading all hearts at Oneida this winter, and its effect will undoubtedly be to promote and intensify unity of thought and feeling and life. The number of persons in each committee is ten, and it is thought best not to increase this number by the addition of new members, but rather to form new committees if increased facilities for criticism are desirable.

A good letter from E. Otis was received on Saturday. She expresses much interest in Mr. Noyes proposed western visit, and wishes to meet him at O. Her school is closed and she is now out of employment, and uncertain what she shall do next. She has written home saying she will come there if they are willing.

E. Hutchins will start for Willimantic early Wednesday morning, accompanied by Mr. Cragin. Busy hands are preparing her outfit.

It has been decided to extend to Mr. Whitney the privilege of coming back to the Community. The spirit of his late letter was liked, and commended as the best thing we have had from him.

An order for $1000 or $1200 worth of bags has been received from a party in Rochester. Four months time is wanted on the order. It is not yet decided whether to accept the order or not.

The bag business opens more favorably this season than ever before, and the prospect of a large trade is good.

The furs and deer skins bought in Canada by the O. C. Fur Co., amounting to about $955, have been sold for about $1245, or at an advance of about $290, after paying the cost of selling and transportation.

All persons, either at Oneida, Wallingford, or the Agency, who wish to offer toasts, sentiments, or other communications at the coming celebration on the 20th., are requested to hand or forward them to the toast committee through the chairman W. A. Hinds.

In a letter from our large trap customer O. S. Hopkins, recently received, he inquires if we can sell him from two to five thousand muskrat skins.

A letter was received the other day from John Flawherty—a man who worked for us in 1864—dated in Ohio, stating that he owes us ten dollars, which he received by over-payment, and inquiring how he shall send it to us. It may interest Otis K. to mention that the letter was addressed to "Odious Kellige".

A note from Mr. Higgins was read last evening, expressing thankfulness for his late criticism, and stating that when he came to the conclusion to invite criticism, the dread of it was removed. He also says: "My experience in the year past has led me more and more into vital sympathy with Christ, with Mr. Noyes, and the leading members of this family. Also past experience has wrought in me more of that humble, meek and lowly spirit which Christ requires of his followers. I have great reason to thank our God for my present state of health and for the resurrection spirit that I perceive is working in my spirit and life."

In the business meeting, yesterday, Mr. Kinsley, Mr. Barron, and F. A. Marks, were appointed a committee to consider the matter of preparing a place to store sawdust where it will become dry and suitable for fruit-packing.—Messrs. Nash, Underwood, and De Latre were appointed a committee to investigate the expediency of burning kerosene in our night lamps.—The question of building a new dairy-house is to be considered, and Mr. Burt is to choose a committee, and report at the next meeting what seemeth best to be done.—Mr. Aiken, Mr. Campbell and S. K. Dunn were appointed a standing committee to provide clothing for persons when they are called to go away suddenly.

On Saturday and Sunday the weather was mild and rainy, the snow rapidly disappeared, and there were indications of a general break up and freshet. Last night, however, the wind changed, and this morning the snow is again falling.

It is suggested that we shall succeed in the silk business, from the fact that we have begun by going to the *Bottom* of it.

DAILY JOURNAL
OF ONEIDA COMMUNITY,

A. D. 1866.   FEB. 13.   NO. 26.

TUESDAY.

THE mail to-day brought orders for about $100 worth of silk, six barrels of apples, and letters of inquiry concerning traps and fruit. A hotel in Buffalo wishes to make arrangements with us to supply them with preserved fruit, if prices suit.

The article in the *Evening Post* of the 10th inst. attracted considerable interest and attention yesterday, and was read in the evening meeting.

A letter from Mr. Robinson states that Mrs. R. and Mrs. Wilcox wish to be present the 20th. Mr. R. writes in a tone of warm-hearted interest in the Community. He says:—" I find my heart full of love for you as God's little ones, and especially in your glorious mission, to cooperate with God in the establishment of his kingdom in this world, and to hasten the blessed time when His will shall be done in earth, as it is done in heaven.

" I have lately read with delight Mr. Noyes's discourse on Christian Faith, the same which charmed me 20 years ago as I found it in the New Haven Perfectionist, and opened to me at that time, the only way to God. It is still charming. Thanks be to God, for his love, in inspiring our true friend Mr. Noyes, to declare that soul-stirring portion of truth.

" The approaching aniversary must warm our hearts to increased appreciation of our inheritance; of our union with Christ and the Redeemed Church—the holy angels also, and all God's family in earth and hades

" With much love to all, I am happy to say,
" Your Brother in Christ, G. W. Robinson."

There is a girl with bright eyes,
Who all through the winter kills flies:
She expects in the spring, there'll be less flies on the
    wing;
That curious girl with bright eyes.

There's another woman, named Julia
    (She never lived in Apulia);
She makes bread and cakes, which an Old man bakes;
    That distinguished woman named Julia.

Our rhetorical scholars are progressing rapidly. We hear that one of them lately, on being asked by his teacher to give an illustration of sophistical reasoning, replied that he considered it a "sophistical argument, to maintain that a man did not need a lamp to go to bed by because he had eaten a *light* supper."

The editor of THE CIRCULAR seems to think that the atmosphere at Oneida is unfavorable to writing, arguing from the small amount of material furnished by this Community for his columns. We were not aware that getting up early in the morning had anything to do with the matter however. It is usually supposed that that occurrence has a tendency to make people wide awake.— Perhaps the Wallingford folks have discovered a different philosophy. We might question whether the fact of their living on a mountain had not something to do with their *superior* elevation of thought and clearness in the atmosphere of expression. A great deal of inspired utterance in past ages has come down from the mountains. Thoreau used to keep a mountain off east of him for literary and contemplative purposes. Perhaps we had better follow his example. David seems to have recognized the necessity of something of the kind also, for he says, " I will lift up mine eyes unto the hills, from whence cometh my help." However, if we do live in a valley, with a blanket of cloud over our heads, and don't write much for THE CIRCULAR, we are *trapping* and *bagging* an experience of life and feeling and interior blessedness, which will sometime bind the world with its *silken* cords of romance and beauty.

We take the liberty to be uneventful in our JOURNAL to-day. Dispatches from an army do not always tell of fields fought or battles won. Sometimes there are dynamic days which are comparatively unreportable, but which tell in their influence on the long campaign.

ARRIVALS.—Mr. Bradley, this morning.—Mrs. D. W. Knowles, yesterday.

TO MRS. P. NOYES.

ON HER 86TH BIRTHDAY.

What is a long life like your own,
To the forth-coming years that remain ?
How swiftly the moments have flown,
Strange mixture of pleasure and pain !
An age is as naught in His sight,
Who sees from beginning to end,
Who a thousand years counts as a day,
And holds the vast seas, in his hand.
Yet his heart is all tender and true
To the trustful and lowly in heart,
He has promised their youth to renew,
And bid e'en grim death to depart.
Thus the future is radiant and bright,
For the dark reign of error is o'er,
And Truth with her scepter of light,
Will sway the wide world evermore.

E. Y. S.

DAILY JOURNAL
OF ONEIDA COMMUNITY.

A. D. 1866.   FEB. 14.   NO. 27.

WEDNESDAY.

IN a conversation last evening about business organization, Mr. Hamilton remarked as follows:

"Mr. Noyes remarked in withdrawing Theodore from
his studies and sending him to New York, that he wanted to have his army in such a state that he could take a
soldier and precipitate him on a given point, whenever
such a measure was desirable. I have thought a great
deal about that, and see that it is very important that
we should all be ready at any moment to be pulled up
from our present quarters, and hurled upon any point
where the public interest may require us. Rapid work
is going on around us; and we should all be ambitious
to throw off every weight that will hinder us from being
used in any way that God sees fit. We should recognize wisdom in the appointing power and obey it, and
not judge it for ourselves. If the Lord sees fit to hurl
us upon any point, let us go ahead without stopping to
question. The old negro said if the Lord commanded
him to jump through a stone wall, he was going to
jump at it; that was his business, and getting through
the wall was the Lord's affair. When I feel that the
Lord sets me to jump at a thing, I expect to get through
it in some way.

"There is a certain principle involved here which it
may be well to lay to heart, as it is important to salvation, and as certain as fate. God will have long patience with us and dig about us and try to make us
fruitful, and then he requires of us that we shall be in a
state of readiness to obey his calls promptly and without a question: and those who cannot obey his inspiration promptly will find themselves huddled together in
the rear like the unorganized followers of an army.
God is going to have a thoroughly organized body, and
this fact should be laid to heart by every one. And
in holding back or shrinking from any appointments we
are cheating ourselves and failing of the grace of God.
The grace of God goes with his legitimate appointments. '

Mr Perry's sixtieth birth-day was celebrated by a party yesterday. The following communication was read
at the table:

Oneida, Feb. 13, 1866.

Through the good providence of God I am sixty years
old to-day. Spared beyond the years I expected to live,
I see many things to be thankful for, and from this point
raise my Ebenezer and say, hitherto hath the Lord
blessed me. Many hair-breadth escapes have I had
from my youth to the present time. A brother and
sister next older than myself, both by accident were taken away in their childhood, one by being scalded and
the other by laudanum administered by the nurse
through mistake. Twice in my childhood I barely escaped being drowned; once by falling into a well some

twelve or fifteen feet deep, from which I crept out alone
I have always thought that the angel of the Lord must
have helped me out. At another time I fell from a boat
on Cayuga Lake; when I was going down for the third
time an old man caught hold of me and barely saved
me. Three times I came very near being shipwrecked:
out of six vessels that left port the day we sailed ours
was one of two that came into harbor, the other four be
ing lost. I could mention other narrow escapes, but
these are enough to show the kind providence of the
Lord that has followed me all my days. I was early
subject to serious impressions, from ten until twenty two
years of age, when I was converted and joined the
church.

In the spring of 1834 I became a Perfectionist, after
reading the Perfectionist paper published by Mr. Noyes,
and, leaving the church I had belonged too, I became a
member with those who through faith and patience
have received the promise. My experience since my
joining the Community I need not recapitulate. In
looking over the past my heart is much softened and
my desires are being enkindled to run with patience
the race that is set before me. I am thankful for the
privilege of being a member of the O. C. with Mr.
Noyes for our leader; the prospect still brightens and
my heart says praise the Lord.

I can say farther that while others at the age of sixty
are growing old, I feel younger to-day than I did
ten years ago, and feel better prepared to live or die as
the Lord pleases. I no longer look at death as the great
purifier, but to Christ as my salvation. I am happy in
surrounding this table with loving hearts to sympathize
with. I confess my union with Christ and Mr. Noyes,
in the great work before us, and pray that from henceforth I may be more devoted to the cause of Truth.

W. H. PERRY.

An order for $74 worth of fruit was received to-day,
but we have only sorts enough to fill about half of it.

The attention of the family was, last evening, called
to the bag business. Our late large orders are taking off
most of the bags on hand of some styles, and all the labor
which the family can devote to this department, is desirable.

The spirit of organization is working in the machine-
shop. A free and sincere meeting of the hands and others was held last evening. The subject considered was
the relations of Mr. Inslee and G. W. Hamilton. Both
were free to state their feelings in regard to each other,
and the causes of a lack of fellowship and harmony, and
this was followed by frank criticism of each. It was
thought that Mr. Inslee should assume his position as
the head of the machine-shop; that he should be recognized as such by all; and that George's position should
be that of foreman of the trap shop in connection with
the general oversight or charge of the works.

ARRIVALS.—Mrs. Robinson and Mrs. Wilcox.

DEPARTURES.—G. Cragin and E. Hutchins for Willimantic.

DAILY JOURNAL
OF ONEIDA COMMUNITY.

A. D. 1866.   FEB. 15.   NO. 28.

THURSDAY.

A CONTRACT has been made with J. Neidling-en of New York for our annual supply of fruit bottles—one hundred gross—at $14,25 net per gross.

An accident almost of a serious character, occurred at Willow Place a few days ago. A belt having become out of order in some way, Douglass Hubbard in trying to regulate it got his hand caught and was drawn up against the pulley. The belt however broke, and released him before any serious injury was done.

Charles Cragin writes encouragingly about the silk manufacture. He says that with the assistance of one or two girls, the mechanical part of the business may be acquired in three or four months, without trouble. The greatest difficulty, or rather, task, is in learning to judge of the raw material. This is where manufacturers blunder oftenest. He says the foreman told him he saw no reason why we could not make better silk than any one else, as our hands would be trustworthy because all are alike interested. C. writes, "Every thing goes along well so far. Every one is kind and obliging, willing to give all the information in their power, and help me forward as much as possible. In talking with Mr. A. to-day, I described the situation of our building, and the room which we intend to devote to silk. The only objection that can be made to the room is on account of its dryness, as in the first "winding" if the silk becomes dry and brittle it breaks more easily. But this can be remedied without trouble by having a little water at hand and occasionally moistening it. We need be at no expense whatever, he said, to fix up the room unless we choose; and as for the dust and dirt, he remarked pointedly, "Oh! it don't make the least difference in the world how nasty your silk gets, you needn't be afraid that the dust or dirt will hurt it a particle, it is thoroughly boiled, in dyeing"—which was just the conclusion I had arrived at, after a few days observation.

"Mr. Swift gave me an account of the way most manufacturers make silk—using Canton stock, which is the poorest kind, but being coarse is worked more easily, and omitting the "cleaning," which though important is not absolutely essential, and otherwise slighting the work so as to secure a cheap article. But Bottom operates differently. He uses Shanghai and Japan stock, and has it worked in a careful, thorough manner—the result is, his silk is about the best in market. So you see it is providential that we got in here; for after we have learned to make a good quality, we can put up 2nd and 3rd if we wish."

A. F. Shapleigh and Co., of St. Louis, order 12 doz. Beaver traps.

Orders for 14 barrels of apples are also received.

A new bridge is building across the creek between our foundry and the saw-mill.

The new shaping machine has been set up, and on trial proves to be a very satisfactory addition to the shop.

The weather continues in its fitful mood—now a day or two of thawing and rain, and then a grand charge of all the forces of winter from the northwest. Yesterday and the day before were comparatively mild, with southerly winds and mist and rain; to-day the northwest breezes fairly scream over the roofs, and the snow that fell during the night is driven in clouds along the fields. The sunbeams burst through the turmoil of the elements occasionally and light up the conflict with their golden glory.

The teams finish drawing logs to-day, some five hundred having been secured.

Yesterday, Mr Harrison, from New Haven, the gentleman from whom the lumber was bought for the new printing office, called, in company with a gentleman from Albany. They were much pleased with all they saw.

One thousand bushels of Peas will be required the coming season by the preserving deparment. Our neighbors are anxious to raise them. Many have already petitioned for the privilege. One would like to raise four hundred bushels; another, two hundred; another, one hundred; another, all we want. Mr Barron will act as negotiator. The time may come when the Community will be able to supply all its near neighbors with such employment.

Our people recently purchased the cedar timber on three acres of land for one hundred dollars. They report that they have cut from it 830 hop poles, 1000 cedar posts and 16 loads of stakes for the vineyards and raspberry plantations. The value of the hop poles and posts is estimated at $200.

Mr. Olds is preparing to start on a western trip immediately after the 20th inst.

Mr. W. G. Kelly is to act as traveling agent in place of G. D. Allen who is to remain for a time at the New York Agency, after going over his route once with W. G. Kelly. G. D. Allen is expected here the present week.

A bed-quilt for the Agency is being prepared for practical uses, by some of the sisters to-day.

No letters from either Wallingford or New York, in to-day's mail.

DAILY JOURNAL
OF ONEIDA COMMUNITY.

A. D. 1866.　　FEB. 16.　　NO. 29.

FRIDAY.

MR. WHITNEY returned yesterday. He says he fully accepts the terms the Community offer him, and has faith that Christ will enable him to become a Community man. He also says that as soon as his heart turned toward God, it turned toward the Community with a desire to return. Mr. Noyes's talk to Mr. Carr also made a deep impression on him. He is sick of the world and says he don't wish to try it any more. We trust he will do well and become a thoroughly earnest and loyal man. There is certainly a spirit of charity and good will in the family towards him.

The weather excitement yesterday continued till late into the night, culminating about dark in a wild storm of wind and snow, sweeping over the fields with tremendous force, hiding every thing from view at a little distance. The result is the roads are filled with drifted snow and traveling is a difficult job, in some places.

Another class for learning how to detect counterfeit money commences to-day, of which C. Olds, Martin Kinsley, E. S. Burnham, L. E. Aiken. A. S. Bailey, O. H. Miller and W. A. Hinds, are members.

Orders for 10 doz. Beaver traps, and $50 worth of preserved fruit, were received this morning.

Letters were read last evening from a gentleman at Dansville Water Cure, and from a friend of Mr. Bolles, Mr. Claflin. The former expresses much interest in the Community and THE CIRCULAR. A paragraph of his letter reads as follows :

"I have been at 'Our Home' three years, during which time I have read THE CIRCULAR regularly ; and through its teachings, and the teachings of this Institution—the great cardinal principles of which it is believed here came to the originators of 'Our Home' through you—have been lifted out of the pit of darkness and infidelity in which, though a member of the Baptts church "in good standing", I had for years been sinking ; and now feel that my feet are firmly planted on the Rock of Ages forever. I want to come to you and speak my heart to you in words of such sincerity and fervor as could only be uttered by one who, like myself, has been raised from the dead into the fullness of life, by the love of Christ, coming to me through you his servants. I want to tell, also, of others who have been blessed through you, to tell you of the strong sympathy and love which men and women of intelligence and truth are coming to cherish toward you.

"I shall come to you under cover of a business errand. I have invented and perfected a combined Rule and Letter Scale, which is simple, convenient and accurate. It would require but little to introduce it, and I have the assurance of all my business friends, and from Munn and Co., T. P. How, and others, that it would pay handsomely. I cannot get time to attend to it myself, and have steadily refused to offer it for sale But I would be glad to have you take it, make a good thing out of it yourselves, and, by and by, pay me what you conscientiously think you can afford."

Mr. C. writes in a very friendly tone, and expresses a high appreciation of Mr. Bolles' character, and his faithfullness as a business man. He also expresses his intention of visiting Mr. B. in his Community home and endeavoring to learn the practical working of society here.

The following epistle, received lately by our bootmaker, afforded us considerable amusement last evening. We hope the writer will long enjoy his boots and be blessed with abundance of all kinds of happiness to boot.

Wallingford, Jan. 10th.

DEAR MR. VAN :—While sitting by the stove to-day, in a very comfortable mood, my thoughts involuntarily recurred to you. The immediate cause of my thought was my boots. Yes, *my boots.* Boots ! I love to speak the name. Boots ! what a charm there is now in that word, boots. For no man, before or since, ever possessed such a pair of boots ! So easy to my feet—fitting in every spot, and touching nowhere. O, my boots ! No man can know any thing about the luxury of wearing such boots without getting into mine ; which he will not be likely to do very soon, for I keep them on my feet all the while—yes morning, noon and night, my boots are on my feet. Slippers and every thing of the kind have gone out of date with me now, since I have discovered the real merits of these boots. Yes, I can hardly bear to pull them off long enough to warm my feet. So much have I become attached to my boots, I am even tempted to go to bed with them on, so easy and so comfortable are my boots. Not so very genteel and fashionable looking boots, to be sure, but so comfortable. Oh ! I look back with perfect horror and indignation on the past ; to think how I have been cramped, and squeezed, pinched and abused, by wearing the little, mean cramped up things called boots. But never again will I submit to such torture ; no, never, while *you* live, Mr. Van and are able to make boots. Oh ! I was a lucky man once, and that was when I got these boots. I shall always remember you, Mr. Van as long as these boots last ; and when they are gone, I shall never forget the comfort I enjoyed while wearing those truly wonderful boots.

With everlasting blessings on your head, I am truly yours,　　　　　　　　　　　　　　　H. T.

P. S. You had better not let anybody see this note ; for if it should get before the public, I fear you would never be able to supply the orders for boots.

DAILY JOURNAL
OF ONEIDA COMMUNITY.

A. D. 1866.   FEB. 17.   NO. 30.

SATURDAY.

MR. NOYES, in a letter from New York, received yesterday, relative to the business affairs there, writes as follows:

The result of my reflections about the relations between Oneida and New York is, that the Oneida Community must finally cease to consider itself as a local institution, doing business by agencies, and come to be an omnipresent body, doing business in *propria persona*, at many points at once. To carry out this principle here, we should simply put on our sign, "*Office of Oneida Community*," or even "*Oneida Community*"—no H. G. Allen, and no Agency—changing also our bill heads &c., correspondingly, and then give some one here, say Theodore, as he is book-keeper, power of attorney. On this plan the Oneida Community would be present here as really as it is at Oneida, with all its power and prestige and credit. We could then guarantee and enforce contracts, and borrow money, just as you can.— The only objection that I see to this, is, that it gives us too much power—more than you can trust us without of your sight. But this is not to be always a baby institution; nor are we to be always cramped for money, either here or at Oneida. We shall have to learn to trust one another, and trust God with our interests, outside and beyond the care and watch of the business board of any local Community. As long as I keep watch and ward here (which I mean to do till our interests here are safe and triumphant) there should be no special fear of indiscretions directed upon this point.— My impression is, that we are doing as safe a business here as anywhere, and that Oneida's great business battles for profit and power are yet to be fought here. We ought all to feel for a good while to come, certainly till we have accomplished our dream of a daily paper, that Oneida is present here, fronting and fighting the great world, not by a feeble Agency, but with her own right hand, and that here is the place where she is going to show her strength.

" The name of the Oneida Community has a prestige that ought not to be lost, as we progress in other places. It ought to go forth into omnipresence, *for the sake of unity*. Every new Community should be a *branch* of the one Oneida Community. The Community at Wallingford is not properly the *Wallingford* Community (though that term may be tolerated in common speech), but the Oneida Community *at Wallingford*, or the Wallingford *branch* of the Oneida Community, which might be expressed in initials by the letters O. C. W. B. Of course formalities are superficial and of small account in themselves; but *it is very important* that we should get above localisms in our spirits, and make the Oneida Community an omnipresent unit, ready to throw and even *hurl* the whole of its strength into any local point at the shortest notice."

The weather has cleared away its frowns, and to-day is cold, and brilliant with sunshine.

The members of the Oneida Community and its branches number, at the present time, 253. The average age of the members of the Oneida family, is 33 years and 29 days.

Mr. Hall and Myron returned yesterday from a trip in the sleigh to Hamilton and other places south, having sold four or five hundred dollars worth of silk collars and bags.

The Wallingford folks will probably be interested to hear that E. A. Miller has been selected to fill H. E. Allen's place in the Conspicuous family.

ARRIVALS —G. D. Allen, last evening.

There was considerable alarm in the Community for a little while last evening, at what appeared to be sign of a fire at Willow Place. Quite a large light was seen in that direction, and it appeared to be shining out of the front windows of the factory. As soon as it was discovered by Mr. Aiken and Myron, a man on horse-back was quietly dispatched to ascertain the cause; but continuing to increase, Mr. Hamilton came into the Hall where reading was going on and mentioned the matter and advised the men to start for Willow Place. Accordingly there was a grand rush in that direction. Before reaching the Hamilton bridge, however, Myron was met returning. He reported every thing *all right*. The light proceeded from the front windows of the boarding house, a number of which were quite brilliantly lighted up. The news relieved the solar plexus of the Community, and a long breath and a smile succeeded the intense sensations of a few minutes before. Mr. Hamilton remarked in the meeting that the devil would evidently like to frighten us with fire, and that we should refuse to be frightened under such circumstances, but be self-possessed and ready to meet any emergency.

Two small orders for preserved fruit were received to-day.

A letter was received yesterday from a man in Derby, Vermont, expressing interest in Communism, and a wish to visit us next month.

J. J. S. wishes to have some change of employment. In a letter to Mr. Hamilton, Mr. Noyes proposes that he go to Wallingford, to help on the paper and feel round for an educational career. He will probably go by way of New York, carrying with him a power of attorney for Theodore at the O. C. N. Y. B.

DAILY JOURNAL
OF ONEIDA COMMUNITY,

A. D. 1866.　　FEB. 19.　　NO. 31.

MONDAY.

IN a recent letter from New York G. W. N. says:

I will give you one or two ideas that Mr. Noyes has presented to-day. One is, that Christ in order to win his sweet-heart, the Jewish nation, is obliged to save the whole world. It is like the case of the man in the parable who found a treasure hid in a field, and who to get it went and sold all that he had and bought not the mere place where it was hid but the whole field. The Jews rejected Christ and would not look at him, and in order to get at their heart he must show his power and glory around them on such a scale as to gain the whole world.—The other point was, that the common idea of God that he is such an overpowering mighty being as to have every thing his own way must be corrected and we must rather conceive of him as the meekest being, one who knows patience and self-limitation and sweet acquiescence to what is inevitable in his circumstances.

Letters from Charles Cragin and Elizabeth Hutchins were received yesterday. They write in a good spirit. Charles seems to be more and more impressed with the providential aspect of the opening there, and thinks we have found the right place to learn the silk-business.

Another thaw is in successful progress to-day. A light rain having fallen during the night, accompanied by a south wind, a dispensation of slush prevails under foot. This is another of the sudden changes of the winter. A few days ago the mercury was below zero, 16 degrees below up the valley, at Hamilton.

We have frequent calls from visitors this winter, especially of late. They are mostly persons of intelligence and come in a spirit of inquiry. There is a feeling in the Community that we shall have a larger number of this class of visitors this year than ever before.

Mr. W. A. Brown of Higginsville, died on Wednesday last. Mr. Conant and Mr. Newhouse went to his house yesterday for the purpose of seeing him, but found him dead and buried.

The following communication to the family from Mrs. Knowles was read Saturday evening:

DEAR MR. HAMILTON:—I am thankful for your invitation to visit Oneida, and for the kind feelings manifest towards me since I came. I feel a strong desire to give myself up unreservedly to the Community to be guided by them in all things. I have been drifted here and there and suffered much by the enemy of all truth. I now feel like asking help of the Church and believe they can help me out of trouble. I want to be cleansed from my old life and be what God would have me, and come up in newness of life and be a faithful soldier of the Lord. I hope all will be free to criticise or advise me when they feel an inspiration to do so.

I confess Christ's resurrection life in my body and spirit.　　　　　　　　　　D. W. Knowles.

In the conversation last evening respecting the providential manner in which the way is opening for us into the silk business, Mr. Hamilton remarked, "I was thinking of the silk-business and of our business in general, how that it is taking a cleaner shape than ever before. Our business may be said to have commenced with the trap-business; but that and the silk-business were for a long while under a worldly spirit and administration. I trace the starting of our business on a new basis, and under the direction of faith in God's guiding providence, to the building of the factory at Willow Place. In buying that place and building the factory we followed Mr. Noyes's advice. He was the leader, and the measure was decided upon during the absence of the person most likely to oppose it, and who represented the spirit of the world in our business. It was by Mr. Noyes's advice that we were induced to put up the wing of the factory, now used for the mach-ineshop and destined to accommodate the silk-business.

"In this way things have been working until now we have our business more under the guidance of inspiration than ever before. I feel good heart that we can now go to work with the idea that it is the Lord's business we are called to—that we have got our job from him. We can all now have the consciosness that we are at work for the Lord. The Lord controls the seasons and the elements, and if we are about his business we need feel no anxiety as to the result. Let us all, from this day, say we are at work for the Lord. If we are at work for him our pay is certain, there is no failure about him—he is A. No. 1.

"I do not see through—do not yet see where we are going to get the capital to pay for all the machinery and meet all the expenses of starting and stocking the business we have entered upon, but I expect it is sure to come in some way, and I am not going to worry about it. I am going to live by the day and without anxiety.

"We have now five good businesses from the Lord, through Mr. Noyes. First, we have the trap-business, and then we have the bag-business, the silk-business, the fruit-business, and the store enterprise."

At the conclusion of the meeting Mr. Hamilton said: "Perhaps there are a good many who would like to say a word to show that they offer themselves to the Lord and dedicate themselves anew to his work. All who feel like making a new offering of themselves to the Lord, and saying to themselves, to each other, to the angels and the heavens above us, Henceforth we are the Lords servants, will please rise." The whole family rose to their feet.

We shall print no JOURNAL to-morrow.

DAILY JOURNAL
OF ONEIDA COMMUNITY.

A. D. 1866.   FEB. 21.   NO. 32.

TUESDAY.

THE 20th has come and gone—full of all its usual interest, happiness and prophecy of the future. We have only space in our little JOURNAL for the briefest mention, and must refer our friends to the forth-coming manuscripts of the reporters, for a sketch of what was said on the occasion, by the several speakers.

Mr. Noyes came in the morning, on a flying visit of business, and was gladly welcomed.

The general programme was followed. The day was moderately wintery without, closing at evening with a light fall of snow. Sleigh-rides and Brass Band music were the principal features during the forenoon. The dinner, as usual was served in the Hall. The bill of fare was bread and biscuit and butter, sliced cold beaf, frosted cakes, honey, preserved peaches, apples, oranges, nuts, coffee and wine. The repast was followed by regular and volunteer toasts and speeches. The following were the regular toasts:

The Event we celebrate.—Responded to by J. Burt.

J. H. Noyes.—Responded to by Mr. Noyes.

Inspiration—the bond and guaranty of salvation, the first rule of business, the source of genius, and the constitutional basis of the final government.—Responded to by E. H. Hamilton.

The latest order to the advancing column—" Women to the Front."—Responded to by H. C. Noyes.

THE CIRCULAR—its mission to present the truths of the Primitive Church to the world, and its destiny to become "a power in the land."—Responded to by W. H. Henderson.

The new principle of Trade—destined to effect a revolution in the commerce of the world.

Willow-Place the Second—the nursery of our business machinery as Willow-Place the First was of our spiritual machinery.—W. R. Inslee.

May the Community fire toast unbelief until it is burned to ashes.—Responded to by J. J. Skinner.

Our new members—good timber—may they enjoy the processes necessary to fit them for their places in the glorious temple of unity.—Responded to by L. Bolles.

W. C. the dual companion of O. C.—may their love and unity increase until they illustrate to the world the perfection and beauty of the divine order of society.—Responded to by H. J. S.

The Agency Brothers—Pioneers in the wilderness of selfishness—may they speedily make a broad 'clearing', and have such surroundings as are appropriate to the civilization which they represent.—Responded to by E. S. Burnham.

The growing happiness of the Community—the first fruit of the tree of life, destined to abound more and more.—Responded to by W. H. Woolworth.

S. L. Bloom—a refugee from marriage tyranny welcome to the home and hearts of the free.—E. Y. Joslyn.

THE JOURNAL—the commencement of a daily paper which shall yet electrify the world with its heavenly utterences.—A. M. Hatch.

From the volunteer toasts we select the following:

H. A. Noyes—The good angel of J. H. Noyes, and the *Mother* of his children—a free press, and the three Communes.

The Community Debt—A good *tonic* for faith and industry, and a good *cathartic* for unbelief, and parasites.

Mr. Seymour—*The Prince of Punsters*—May he be as fruitful as his vines, and may his writings shine brighter than DAY.

The old folks and the young folks—the two extremes of Community life,—in their meeting is the conquest of death—in the resurrection they rejoice together.

After the Hall was cleared, a variety of games were played, old and young mingling together in merriment and glee. The amusements were concluded by a masquerade dance, performed by eight couples. This was highly amusing. A curious medley of costumes was represented, from the Chinaman and the turbaned Turk, to Uncle Sam with his long tailed coat, strapped pants and bell crowned hat. One smooth faced young gentleman appeared as a fashionably dressed and becrinolined young lady, while a lady represented a plumed page. One young lady was a nun, another was dressed in the costume of sixty years ago. There was a sailor, a soldier, a Highlander and a fat man. There was a lady dressed in a costume like those worn by court ladies three hundred years ago, another as a ballet dancer, another in a somber dress bespangled with stars represented night, &c.

A meeting was held at 7½ o' clock; at the opening of which Mr. Noyes delivered an interesting address on the Purchasing Agency. He afterwards gave an account of his new edition of Salvation from Sin. After this some letters to the editor of THE CIRCULAR and to Warren Chase were read, and commented on by Mr. Noyes. Reports of these remarks will be sent in manuscript.

An order for 25 muskrat traps was received from Syracuse on Monday.

To-day, orders were received for 36 lunch bags, and 12 rail-road bags. The lunch bags were ordered from St. Louis.

An envelop was received this morning from G. Marston, Mrs. Tobey's whilom guardian, enclosing a statement of his operations as the superintendent of her property for the past five years. He says he now has in his hands certificates of bank stock valued at upwards of $3000, deed of house, &c., which are subject to her order. His charges for guardian services for the whole time are $170.

DAILY JOURNAL
OF ONEIDA COMMUNITY.

A. D. 1866. FEB. 22. NO. 33.

THURSDAY.

THE following letter from E. H. gives a glimpse o
life at the Willimantic Commune:

Willimantic, Feb. 15, 1866.

DEAR SARAH:—My first day at Willimantic is over
and now I feel just like writing you all about it. The
bell rings at half past six o'clock and we have just time
to eat our breakfast, make our bed, then off to the factory, which, providentially, is only a few rods from the
boarding-house. Harriet and I worked side by side to-
day at what they call cleaning the silk. The silk is
wound from one set of spools on to another, the thread
passing between two little knives placed so close together that no knots or coarse places can pass through.—
This you can see would cause a great deal of breaking.
After the bad place is broken out the thread must be
tied again with a peculiar knot. This work is not at all
difficult, one person can attend a good many spools,
when the silk is good. H. and I have worked ten and a
quarter hours at this business to-day, standing all the
time, only seating ourselves on an old box that stood
near, occasionally, for a little rest. This forenoon at
about eleven o'clock, I felt so tired I didn't know how I
should get through the day, but I felt good courage in
my heart, and knew where I could find strength and
life. My tired feelings gradually passed away and to-
night I feel fresh and strong.

"The machinery makes such a noise that we cannot
talk much, so we have good opportunity for reflection,
and I found it easy to-day to think good thoughts.

"Our boarding-house looks some like ours at Oneida
though it is not quite so roomy. The dining-room is
very small—has only one table that seats only twenty
girls, so Harriet and I eat in the sitting room with the
men, of whom there are only two at present, Charles and
Mr. Swift, our foreman. Our room is in the attic and is
poorer and smaller than any in the Oneida boarding-
house, and O how cold it is, but we lie close and so keep
warm. The bed is rather hard but clean. We have
enough to eat, and the cooking is pretty good. On the
whole I am happily disappointed and feel much more at
home than I expected to. The factory is warm and
clean, there is nothing dirty about the work."

A letter was received recently from Mrs. S. A. Clem-
ent, in which she expressed a wish to have the Community hire her husband, in order that he might come in
contact with our influence, and also in order that they
might thus be enabled to live near the Community.—
Her proposition was not thought admissable. Our experience in the past has not led us to think favorably of
such half-way connection with persons who are seeking
our sympathy. If persons wish to become one with us
in the gospel and life of Communism, it is better for
them to stand externally disconnected with us and in
the attitude of students of the truth, until they are prepared for a closer union, rather than to seek a mere
outside connection through the hiring system. Moreover, persons who are in bonds which prevent external
union with the Community, should remember that they
may become one with us in heart, and labor with us
in spirit just where they are, and furthermore, that
though they cannot come to us, the Community will
sometime come to them and loose their bonds and let
the oppressed go free. The mission of the Community
is to go forth into omnipresence, and fill the world with
its life, its power and its freedom.

The Plank-Road Company, who own the Turnpike
road from Oneida Castle to Utica, have lately proposed
to erect a toll-gate near Mr. Adams's house, about one
mile east of the Castle—which gate would impose a tar-
iff on nearly all the travel to and from the Community.
The project meets with much opposition from our neighbors, and those who will have occasion to pass through
the gate, or whose interests would be unfavorably affected by it. The Community would also seriously regret
the erection of a toll-gate at that point, and propose to
join with others in purchasing one mile of the west end
of the Turnpike now owned by the Plank Road Company, and at last advices the sum of $1000 had been agreed
upon as a compensation; for which amount the Plank
Road Co. will also guarantee that no toll-gate shall hereafter be erected, west of the Willow Place Trap Factory.
The Community expect to pay at least one fourth of the
above sum.

Mr. Hubbard came over yesterday for his annual
stipend towards the support of his father and mother.
He thought the Community should pay as Tryphena's
share $100, but the sum of $75, was finally agreed
upon. It should be understood that the Community,
several years ago gave Mr. Hubbard written promise to
pay him $50 a year for the above object, and he urges
that the increased cost of living entitles him to the advance asked.

Several accidents have occurred lately. Carrie Macknet sprained her ancle so that she has been unable to
walk on it for several days.—Mr. Higgins cut his foot
slightly yesterday while splitting wood.—S. K. Dunn,
yesterday slipped down and strained her arm somewhat.
None of these accidents are of serious character, and the
patients we believe are all doing well.

Yesterday's JOURNAL should have been dated Wednesday, instead of Tuesday as was the case by mistake.

DEPARTURES.—J. H. N. and C. O. for New York.—
G. D. A. and W. G. K. on their silk-selling rout—The
Baldwinsville delegation, consisting of Mrs. Robinson,
Mrs. Beach, and Mrs. Wilcox, for home.—Mr. Leete and
his daughter Mary for home.

What sheep is it that always loses a part of its fleece
whenever it *blows its nose* in winter? The we(a)ther.

DAILY JOURNAL
OF ONEIDA COMMUNITY.

A. D. 1866.   FEB. 23.   NO. 34.

FRIDAY.

THE following note from Mrs. Bolles was read last evening:

Oneida, *Feb.* 22, 1866.

DEAR FRIENDS:—I wish to make a public confession of God's goodness to me, in the year that has past.— It has been a time of great trial to me, and yet it has been the happiest year of my life. It is one year since I virtually received Communism. I am thankful to have a home in the true Church of Christ, and be permitted to bear some part in the great work of establishing Christ's kingdom on the earth. It is my purpose to be a sincere disciple of Christ, and a true Community woman. I confess my entire separation from my old life, and from legality in all its forms, particularly the marriage spirit. I desire to have every vestige of that spirit eradicated from my heart. I am thankful for Communism which delivers woman from the bondage of the marriage system. I thank God for Mr. Noyes, I regard him as the great deliverer of our sex. I confess my confidence in him, also in Mr. Hamilton, as our leaders, and confess my love for the family. I shall be glad of any criticism or discipline that will improve my character and make me more useful in the church.

Yours for the truth.   R. M. BOLLES.

We are in the midst of another thaw. A strong south wind prevailed all yesterday and last night. The snow is fast disappearing from the fields.

Miss A. M. Hatch has commenced taking lessons in book-keeping, in the office. She is to devote two hours a day to the business at present.

E. H. writes from Willimantic: "There are about twenty-six girls in the factory. They are a good and intelligent looking set of girls. They were quite anxious to see me in my short dress, so last evening I put it on much to their amusement. Some of them liked it very much. We are in hopes that we shall be able to wear them in the factory by and by."

H. E. A. says, "Last evening the girls said they wanted to hear about our home. We answered their questions and gave them the O. C. Pamphlet to read. None of them ever heard of the O. C. before C. came here. They all treat us well. We feel that the angels have us in charge."

In last evening's meeting, Mr. Hamilton referred to the large amount of attention that has lately been given to crochet-work and "tatting," especially among the younger portion of the family. He questioned whether it was not being carried to an unprofitable extent, and divert-

ing attention from more important and useful employments. It was not very enlarging to the mind. He thought the taste for ornamentation might find a better scope in the bag business, for instance, and so be brought into the public service.

A letter was received to-day from a man in Massachusetts, inquiring if he could find employment on our farm. He is somewhat out of health, and thinks if he could get out of the city and work on a farm for a couple of years, and "could get with a congenial society of people, where he could throw off all restraint and act natural, he could be perfectly happy." He is a spiritualist, has a family "who are all in a measure harmonious, when nothing happens to disturb their equanimity." Is a barber by trade, has worked at coloring photographs, and on farms both in this country and South America, and is twenty-three years of age, &c. We are hardly prepared to employ him.

A bag order was received yesterday but we have been unable to learn the amount. Several small trap orders have also been received within a few days.

There have been but few reportable events since yesterday. The family generally seem in good spirits.— All are busy as usual. There is much interest felt in Mr Noyes's project of a purchasing agency, and in the general aspect of things at New York.

ARRIVALS.—Mr. and Mrs. George Covill, of Higginsville, on a visit to the Community.

"What does make those men who work with the locomotioners, talk so much about switching injuns off the track? What good does it do to switch those insensibillious things?" said Mrs. Partington to Ike, as he was finishing his breakfast of biscuit and coffee. "Because they have a tender *behind*, I suppose," said he. The old lady seized the broomstick a moment too late to reach the young rascal as he rushed out the door with a broad grin on his face.

DAILY JOURNAL
OF ONEIDA COMMUNITY.

A. D. 1866.   FEB. 24.   NO. 35.

SATURDAY.

THE grand thaw of the winter is now in progress. The warm south wind has been blowing strongly and steadily for more than fifty hours. The snow in the valley, except where it is drifted, is gone, and it is fast disappearing from the hills. The creek is high, overflowing most of the Cragin meadow and chafing against the plank walk. The ice is breaking up, but has not yet (at eight 8 o'clock) begun to move. A rain storm appears to be now beginning. We shall hardly have so great a flood as last year, from the fact that the amount of snow to be melted has been far less than then.

Mrs. Thayer's school of employees, on the 20th presented her with an elegant silver cup, as a token of their appreciation of her labors, and of their interest in the school. We understand the school is well attended and popular among them.

The bag-business is in a prosperous condition at present. The sales during the present month have been thus far, three or four hundred dollars greater than during the whole of February last year, amounting to some $1400 or $1500. The number of hands in the shop is being increased. Eight hired men and five women are now employed. The opening of the trade this year is more promising than ever before.

Mr. Inslee reports a prosperous state of things in the machine-shop. The castings for the silk machinery have not yet reached us, but will probably soon do so. A full set of five machines is to be made to begin with; viz., a winder, a cleaner, a doubler, a spinner and a stretcher. Mr. Inslee thinks it will take about two months to get up the machines after the castings are ready.

Mr. S. W. Nash has been appointed assistant in the Green-house and flower department, to fill Mr. Kelly's place during his absence.

The bridge at the Foundry was finished on the 19th. It is built in the same style as the new bridge over the Oneida Creek, and is nearly fifty feet long. The attention of the carpenters will now be turned to fitting up the store.

Bowles's book, "Across the Continent," maintains its interest and draws quite a large audience every evening. Discribing the journeyings, adventures and observations of a party of eminent and interesting men, through the most wonderful scenery of our continent, giving us apparently a truthful glimpse of life and its great activities on the Pacific coast, it is a valuable book and should be read by every one who would understand the Far West—using the term in its newest and vastest significance—present and prospective, and who would comprehend the material greatness toward which this American empire is marching. Beginning at Plymouth Rock, and laying its dynamic foundations among the granite hills of New England, the Puritan civilization will yet, perhaps, reach its most conspicuous development amid the majestic scenery, and under the glorious climate of the Pacific coast. All who are interested in the Pacific Railroad should read this book. Its central thought and purpose is to stimulate interest in, and to show the importance of, this great enterprise. The point in the book which seems to us most narrow in statesmanship and social philosophy, is where the author treats of the Mormon question. Contrary as their social system is to the spirit of highest civilization, it may be doubted whether the attempt to destroy it by legal and governmental repression, is the wisest course. It is more important for the nation and its government to become representatives of that civilization and righteousness, which can judge the spiritual principality of Mormonism, than it is to merely destroy its exterior social order. Bring the spiritual root to judgment and all that is offensive in the outgrowth will pass away.

A letter of between twenty and thirty pages has been received from Mrs. Chesbro, giving an account of her proceedings since she left here for home. She is evidently full of fanaticism and the proselyting spirit, and her course has been such that the Community will refuse entirely to sympathise with it.

As we go to press the water is rapidly falling, though there is a rain-storm in progress. The ice in the creek has broken up and commenced moving downstream.

DAILY JOURNAL
OF ONEIDA COMMUNITY.

A. D. 1866.   FEB. 26.   NO. 36.

MONDAY.

MR. CAMPBELL expects to start next week for Canada, on a fur-buying tour.

E. H., writing of the silk-business, says:—" It is a very attractive business, and there is a real charm to me in learning it. There is a real charm too in feeling that I am at work for God and the Community. My heart is full of cheerfulness and courage, and I have found it easy to realize my union with Christ and you all, in a way that has fully satisfied my heart."

Myron reports sales during the last week, of hats, silk, bags, fruit, &c., to the amount of some $1200.

The weather after clearing the landscape pretty thoroughly of snow and the creek of ice, and made a vigorous attack on the frost in the ground, seems to have repented itself, and has gone vigorously to work repairing the damage done to the wintry aspect of things. The mercury this morning is down to 10, and the ground is all white again.

In the business-meeting yesterday, G. W. Hamilton was appointed to ascertain whether the engine boiler needs inspecting, and if so he is authorized to employ a suitable person to do it.—The subject of getting castings for a "stretcher", to be used in manufacturing silk, was considered, and it was proposed to have Mr. Cragin go to Willimantic and ascertain the best terms on which they can be obtained and order them. It appears that the machine is a newly patented invention and is owned by a company. The cost of the machine is only $350, but the right of using it to the amount of working up 100 lbs. of silk per week, costs $1000 more. Manufacturers pay $5,000 for its unlimited use. It appears to be necessary to have the machine if we would make first quality silk, and compete with other manufacturers.— Further effort is to be made to dispose of our stock of agricultural implements yet on hand: Messrs. Campbell, Worden, Clark and C. A. Burt were appointed a committee.—It was proposed that we adopt a cheaper mode of supplying our people with spectacles, by buying the bows and glasses in New York and fitting them up ourselves.—An arrangement is to be made with the Shakers, in respect to using the pea-shelling machine. as they hold a patent on it, upon which our unauthorized use infringes.—The Hat manufacturer at the Castle proposes to give us 8 per cent. on sales and let us sell all the hats he makes. No answer has yet been made to the proposal.

The Bangor *Daily Whig and Courier*, has republished the article on the Oneida Community in the *Evening Post*, and copied the *Post's* editorial remarks into its editorial columns, giving no credit in the latter instance.

The editors of the Springfield *Republican* appear to have observed the article in the *Evening Post*, for they begin an article this week on "Co-operation in Labor" with a reference to the Community and the facts as to our financial success. The paragraph ends in the following characteristic style:—"The moral condition of these Communities is vitiated by a false theory of marriage, the fruit of which in a few years must inevitably be the general degradation of the members and the breaking up of the communities themselves. All past experiments of the kind teach the same lesson. The divine law of marriage has never been defied without bringing social misery and ruin, and never can be."— It would be interesting if the advocates of the present social system would point out their exact authority for assuming that that system is founded on divine law.— The term, "divine law of marriage," has an imposing sound, but it stands much in need of a true definition: Under the Mosaic law, a man was permitted to have more than one wife, and in the Christian dispensation of the resurrection there is *no* marriage. But where between these two does the special divine enactment come in on which the present social order is so irrevocably based? Did the Primitive Church in passing out of the marriage system, either Jewish or otherwise, into the no-marriage of heaven, enter a state of "social misery and ruin"? And when the will of God, which tolerates no marriage in heaven, is done on earth, will it be attended with such disastrous results as the *Republican* predicts? Won't the editors and social philosophers look into the matter a little more closely?

Mr. John Flawherty has sent us the ten dollars, conscience money, which he wrote about some time ago.

A letter from Mr. Noyes, was received a few days ago, in which he criticised the intellectual and spiritual entertainment at the celebration of the 20th, as a rather heavy and sleepy affair. We are glad of the criticism and feel relieved by it. There seems to be a tendency to routine in the formal mode of toasts and responses which does not favor inspiration, and Mr. N. suggests that we shall have to invent a new style of social oratory. The profane way seems no better than the pulpit way.

ARRIVALS.—Mr. Olds, from New York.

DAILY JOURNAL
OF ONEIDA COMMUNITY.

A. D. 1866.   FEB. 27.   NO. 37.

TUESDAY.

THE meetings for several evenings have been occupied with conversations concerning our relations to Mr. Noyes, cultivating the business-spirit in all that we do—making it our religion, &c. A good spirit has prevailed and the meetings, though hardly of a reportable character, have been very edifying. The hints which Mr. Noyes has given us about the old spirit of New York Perfectionism, meet with an earnest response in our hearts, and we desire to be wide-awake in that direction.

The weather is again dark and stormy. A little more snow is needed to make our sleighing good.

Some rather ludicrous typographical mistakes have occurred in THE JOURNAL lately, such as "beaf" for *beef*, "wintery" for *wintry*, &c. In yesterday's JOURNAL there was a grammatical error. In the 2d line of the 4th paragraph the word "made" should have been *making*. There is really no excuse for such mistakes, for things should be done right, and the only thing to be said in palliation of them is, that the time allowed for correcting and printing the JOURNAL after it is set up, and the starting of the mail, is sometimes very short, and the work has to be done in a very hasty way. But we hope to overcome all difficulties, and if possible, as we know it is, avoid all such blunders or oversights.

The health of our elderly people is very good this winter. Lady Campbell has so far recovered from her accident as to spend much of her time in the sociabilities of the sitting-room. Lady Noyes is quite well, and seems cheerful and happy whenever we meet her.

Mrs. Abigail Kellogg's 75th birth day was celebrated by a party in the Lower Sitting Room, yesterday. All the occupants of the room were present, and we understand that it was a very pleasant affair. Among the congratulatory communications read, was the following from Mr. Seymour:

Away with talk of drear December,
Heralding the final slumber!
More of years canst thou remember,
Than is man's appointed number.

Thou wast born in such connection,
With the morn of resurrection,
Thou canst claim this sure protection,
Should grim death e'er bring an action.

THE CIRCULARS several times of late, have gone by to Syracuse, and consequently we have failed to receive them at the usual early hour on Tuesday, at which they are always so welcome.

An order for 12 doz. No. 4 traps was received from New York this morning.

DEPARTURES.—H. A. N. and E. A. M., for Wallingford.—C. Olds and J. N. Norton, for the West on a commercial tour.—W. A. H. for New York, on a business visit for a week.

(Communicated.)

The modesty of our editor will of course prevent him from referring in this newspaper to the lecture delivered Sunday evening in the Community Hall by T. L. Pitt, on "Canada and the Kanucks—Furs and Fur-buying and Life in the Woods." It was an interesting account of some experiences of our heroic brothers in their Canada campaign, not heretofore reported, together with a description of that portion of the country they traversed, and of the Kanucks with whom they came in contact, especially of noted trappers, and of others with whom our friends formed acquaintance, not omitting to mention Father McKillican and his genial companion, both nearly 70 years of age—their "splendid girls—bright and intelligent, obedient and industrious," and pointing out the general and special results of the excursion. We would like to make copious extracts from the lecturer's MS., but space forbids; yet we hope room will be found for the following closing paragraphs:

"Canada my Canada."

I vote for her—with her granite hills, her primeval **rocks; her evergreen forests; her blue-eyed lakes, pure** and beautiful, mirroring forever the skies of God in their liquid depths; her sturdy trappers, pioneers and lumbermen; her farmers; her Scotch hearts and hands; her beautiful, strong, magnetic daughters.

Land of health and hardihood,
Land of the northwest breezes,
Land of snow and the long, stern-faced winter,
Land of the moose and the caribou,
Land of the deer and the beaver, hunter's and trapper's land,
Land of the rude shanty by the margin of lake or river,
Land of the moccasin-shod, dark-eyed Indian,
Kanuck's land, my land forever and ever.

In conclusion I would express my thanks to the Community and to God, for that chapter in my life which I lived in the shadows of the Canada woods, among the rough hills, and by the firesides of her simple-hearted people. It abides in my memory with the charms of a romance—as an idyl of life, some of whose passages I would gladly repeat if an appropriate time should ever come.

DAILY JOURNAL
OF ONEIDA COMMUNITY,

A. D. 1866.   FEB. 28.   NO. 38.

WEDNESDAY.

THE first box of castings for the silk machinery, was received yesterday. Work will at once be commenced upon them.

A subscriber to THE CIRCULAR, in Wisconsin, expresses the hope that Mr. Cragin will not stay long at Oneida, if he cannot keep on with his "Story of a Life," while here. She says, "I find it very interesting.—Every thing connected with Mrs. Cragin always had a peculiar charm for me. I always loved her dearly though I never saw her."

A fine display of azaleas is seen at the green-house now-a-days. For much of the time during the winter a large Augusta rose—a climber—has hung its splendid clusters of flowers pendant from the roof, filling the air around them with their rich perfume and delighting the eye with their exquisite tints, their large size and beautiful shape. The camellias have also been a source of much enjoyment to beholders. The plants in the green-house all look remarkably healthy and repay care with their deep green, thrifty foliage, as well as with flowers.

There was certainly no "excuse" for *excuse* in the last JOURNAL.

A letter was received yesterday from Mr. McK., expressing a hope that the fur-buyers would come out to Canada again this spring, and asking us to buy some articles for him in case we should come. The letter was very friendly in its tone.

THE CIRCULARS came this morning, twenty-four hours after their usual time. A hint has been given to the Express Company, to the effect that if more regularity and promptness are not exercised, in the transportation and delivery of the papers, we shall possibly deem it advisable to give the job to Uncle Sam.

Our supply of seasoned fire-wood is nearly exhausted, and we have to turn to green wood as a substitute. Past experience has shown that seasoned wood is the most economical. A large supply is being split and piled for next winter's use.

The weather begins to give signs of approaching spring. The days grow longer, and the sun's rays daily become stronger in their genial, loving power. There is a subtle influence in the atmosphere that hints of the coming of magnetic days.

Mr. Campbell concludes to start for Canada to-morrow morning, in order to have more time there before the Reciprocity Treaty ends. After the 17th of March a duty of ten per cent. will be imposed on all furs coming from the British Provinces.

We notice among the minor events of to-day that some of the folks are busily engaged changing their quarters, which seems to be one of the periodical incidents of Community life. It is found desirable to delocalize persons on the small scale as well as on the large. And this change of rooms from time to time tends to quicken the circulation of the Community spirit and throw people into new personal surroundings.

Carrie Macknet called on the surgeon the other day, and found that the sprain in her ankle was rather more serious than she at first supposed. Thorough bandaging and rest will, however, probably soon restore it to its normal condition.

Buckwheat cakes were discussed, verbally, in the meeting last evening. Some people have scruples about eating them, deeming them unhealthy. The general feeling, however, seemed to be in favor of them. In some parts of the country buckwheat is a staple food of the inhabitants for six or eight months in the year, and we never heard that any deleterious results followed its use. It is sometimes said to be heating, and to produce humors in the blood, this however, we understand, is due to a small hull that adheres to the grain, and which may be removed before grinding, if proper care is exercised. It may be questioned whether the excessive use of butter and syrup with buckwheat cakes has not more tendency to produce the humors complained of, than the buckwheat itself. A newspaper article lately stated that some men, engaged in intellectual pursuits, testify that they can labor longer without nervous exhaustion, on a meal of buckwheat than on most other food. Buckwheat, we believe, is allowed by chemists, to be rich in phosphates, and hence is especially nutritive to the nervous and mental tissues, and stimulative of procreative power.

DAILY JOURNAL
OF ONEIDA COMMUNITY.

A. D. 1866.   MAR. 1.   NO. 39.

THURSDAY.

TWO young men called here on Tuesday. Both of them were born in England. One came from New-York, the other has been living with the Shakers at Mount Pleasant, Ky., for five months. They wished to become acquainted with the Community, and offered to work for their board. If we could not employ them they wished to find work in the neighborhood where they could have access to our publications. It was concluded to let them work a month. At the end of that time if we are satisfied with them, we may possibly hire them. Martin gives them employment on the farm.

C. C. H. was criticised last evening for a bad, disobedient, corrupting spirit in social matters. His case is a very serious one, and shows the power of false love in hardening the heart, and letting in darkness of spirit and disease of soul and body upon its victims. Mr. Hamilton used great plainness and severity in criticising C., and we trust that he will be able to fully recover himself from the snare of the devil into which he has fallen, and become a thoroughly earnest and God-fearing man. A report of the criticism will probably be forwarded to the Branches, in writing.

Mr. Campbell left last night about 12 o'clock, for Canada.

A letter was received from Mr. Mills, yesterday, through his Syracuse lawyers. It had no date, but appeared to have been written some time after receiving the money sent him some months ago, and before receiving the last payment. (It should have been mentioned that Mr. Hamilton went to Syracuse the day previous to the 20th, and paid Messrs. Sedgwick and Andrews the balance owing to Mr. Mills, and thus cancelled all our obligations to him.) He acknowledges the receipt of the former sum. Says he had no right to expect it before it was due, after what had occurred, and announces that he will not be out-done by Mr. Noyes in cultivating friendly business relations, but will do what he can to extend the sale of our traps, or buy furs for us, &c.

March comes in "like a lamb," to quote the old proverb. The south wind again prevails, and the snow is disappearing from the fields.

Small fruit and bag orders were received to-day. The sales of apples during the past month have amounted to $156.

A letter was received to-day from John Gage of Vineland, New Jersey, making inquiries with regard to the fruit-preserving business. He wishes facts as to the cost of buildings, apparatus, and general expenses of carrying the business on, &c. He also inquires if we know of a man who can be hired to take charge of such business and will invest stock in it. He speaks of their not being able to plow the morning he wrote on account of a hard frost.

There is not much news of an outward character to report to-day. There is much going on of an unreportable nature, criticism and heart-searching, whose results will sometime appear in improved character, and so be reported in living epistles, known and read of all men.

DAILY JOURNAL
OF ONEIDA COMMUNITY.

A. D. 1866.   MAR. 2.   NO. 40.

FRIDAY.

A PLAIN letter of criticism has been written to Mrs. Chesbro, condemning her course after leaving here, and warning her not to represent that the O. C. have any fellowship with her in her present spirit. After leaving here she spent several weeks on her way home, in visiting, preaching, proselyting, attending balls &c., all in a foolish, fanatical way. She was sincerely criticised while here, for her fanaticism and excessive tendency to talk and teach. But instead of taking the criticism she appears to have disregarded it entirely. It also appears from her letter that she is involved in social loosness with a physician. She seems to be a representative of New York Perfectionism, and manifests some of its most repulsive traits. She has been requested to visit the Community no more while in her present spirit. The Oneida Community has always set its face steadily against such works and such a spirit as Mrs. Chesbro has manifested, and always will.

A friend of Mr. Perkins, from the other side of Oneida Lake, is here on a visit. He has been in the army, where he lost an arm.

The conversation last evening turned on the present disturbed state of the national affairs. It was thought that God was humbling and criticising the nation and working to destroy the confidence of the people in mere human government that has no reference to the inspiration and leadership of God. The government seems to be crumbling and becoming disintegrated, preparatory to a new advance of the nation, and the turning of its heart to Christ. In this view of the matter it is to be regarded as a good thing that the people are in trouble, and made ashamed by Presidential foolishness, and the work of reconstruction goes on slowly. It is in vain to hope that the old system of government will be restored, with no higher guidance than President and Congress, and no higher principles of statesmanship than those contained in the Constitution of '87. Inspiration must be recognized by governmental authorities, and criticism and obedience to the truth must take their place in the halls of Congress and among the people, before peace and quietness will come to the national heart, and its affairs be settled in righteousness.

The birds begin to make their appearance. We have reports that robins, blue-birds and phebes have been seen and heard.

Mr. Hatch tells an interesting story about the way in which he has been supplied with spectacles. Some time ago he found that he needed some new spectacles, but hesitated to ask the financiers for the means to get a pair. He thought he would wait on the Lord about the matter, and expect to be supplied in some way.— He had been in this simple-hearted, faith attitude for some time, without any indications of the way in which his want would be met. The other day he was at work at the hen-barn, making some nests for the hens. On taking up some hay to place in one of the nests, his hand came in contact with a small roll of hay and paper, sticking out of which the end of a bent spectacles-bow was visible. On unrolling the paper and hay the other parts of the spectacles were revealed. They were blackened and rusty but a little scratch showed them to be silver. On bringing them home and cleaning them he found that they were good spectacles and *exactly what he wanted*. He regards the whole affair as an instance of providential care, and instructive and encouraging to faith.

The carpenters have begun work on the Store, and teams are busily engaged drawing stone for the foundation and basement.

The reign of mud has begun. To-day the mercury stands at 44 and signs of rain prevail.

Our hearts were electrified last evening by the report of Mr. Noyes's talk at Wallingford on business. Success to the new business principles which are being developed.

Mr. Jones is somewhat disabled and requires an assistant in the care of the furnaces. L. B. Jr. is at present officiating in that honorable capacity.

An order for preserved fruit was received this morning amounting to $100, only $40 of which can be filled, from the fact that our stock of tomatoes is exhausted.

DAILY JOURNAL
OF ONEIDA COMMUNITY.

A. D. 1866.   MAR. 3.   NO. 41.

SATURDAY.

THE conversation last evening related to the question of social morality. Mr. Hamilton introduced the subject by the following remarks:

"In criticising individuals, sometimes, we talk about their being loose in social matters. I think in this connection we might profitably inquire what constitutes true chastity, or what in the kingdom of heaven, is the true standard of morality, that should govern persons in their social relations. What is the opposite of this looseness we criticise? This is an important question There are principles of morality and chastity that govern in the kingdom of heaven, and in the Community as distinct and imperative as those which prevail in the world. What is considered in the world to be true chastity? It is marriage faithfulness and 'the bed undefiled.' Now I can see that the essence of all that, is in our system, and that the principles of morality and purity are more stringent in the Community than in the world. God is a jealous God, and the truth is jealous, and makes no compromises.

"In thinking of this matter, I can see that Spiritualism and New York Perfectionism, and all those false spiritual principalities that press upon us from without, are characterized by what we term looseness. The original, independent Perfectionism that Mr. Noyes had to come out against, was especially characterized by looseness in social matters, and insubordination. Mr. Noyes told us some time ago that we must beware of New York Perfectionism; and that it would be reaching out, and seeking to assimilate with us. I don't know but the temptation to looseness that we have been criticising in some of our young folks, has been caused by a baptism from these false spiritual principalities. Mr. Hamilton illustrated this spirit of looseness by referring to Mrs. Chesbro, whom he considered a type of New York Perfectionism.)

"I am certain that the Lord hates looseness. He has his standard of chastity and morality, and he is jealous in regard to obedience to it.

"We have our attention turned especially at the present time, towards being effective and faithful in business. Well, our social state and character has a direct bearing upon our business relations of all kinds, both outward and inward; and we cannot do a better thing for improving our business habits and efficiency, than to have a true standard of social chastity and faithfulness.

"The self-righteous world calls us a brothel. It don't believe it is possible to have a state of Communism in property and the affections, separate from looseness and 'icentiousness. But we are showing the world that we are models of economy and order in regard to the man-

agement of property; and I am sure that we shall be able to show also to all, that in regard to the affections and relations of the sexes, we are not licentious, but are improving characters—are governed by higher principles of morality, and are more faithful to the laws of chastity, than society under the marriage system. We have found a way to unite the freedom of Communism with the utmost purity of social relations.

"The glory and beauty of the marriage system of the world, does not consist in the mere play of the affections—in the strong action of passion or magnetism between male and female. There is beauty and power in all this. But it does not constitute the glory and righteousness of the system in God's eyes or in the eyes of worldly morality. That glory and righteousness, consists in the action of passion and magnetic attraction *in obedience and faithfulness* to certain established rules.—It is the subordination of the affections to obedience and faithfulness, that is glorified under the morality of the marriage system, and the thing which God values and approves. And in this thing it will be found, sooner or later, that we are far in advance of the marriage system, and those who uphold it. I believe the truth will be unfolded, in regard to us on this point, in a way that will shut the mouths of all objectors and satisfy all intelligent inquirers.

"The idea of the marriage system is that the body of the wife is for the husband, and the body of the husband for the wife. But do we necessarily come into a state of licentiousness where the principle of ownership ceases? Far from it. The social order of the kingdom of heaven makes the bodies of all belong to the Lord.—Not only the spirits but the bodies of both men and women belong to the Lord. And if we would come into fellowship and freedom with each other and the heavens we must be faithful and subordinate to that great principle. We must love without taking each other from the Lord. We must be the Lord's representatives and agents with each other. This is the opposite of all looseness, and the very highest obedience to principle.

"Under the marriage system we find men and women growing up side by side, full of magnetic power and beautiful attraction toward each other. But the Lord says to them, 'Hands off, till you are married.' And so he says to us, 'If you want freedom in love you must first become established in principle.' We cannot have freedom until we come into the spirit of the Lord. 'Where the spirit of the Lord is, there is liberty.' That sentiment is worthy to be engraved in letters of gold. In the light of this principle, it is prostitution for a man to draw a woman's heart away from the Lord, or for a woman to draw a man's attention to herself. The essence of prostitution consists in putting a thing to a use below what it was intended for. We should set the Lord always before our face, and any kind of influence or fascination which tends to subvert that principle, is prostituting us to lower and degrading purposes. I know if we go to the Lord he will teach us how to love without prostituting, either ourselves or the objects of our love, but on the contrary our love will become elevating and refining."

DAILY JOURNAL
OF ONEIDA COMMUNITY.

A. D. 1866.   MAR. 5.   NO. 42.

MONDAY.

IN the meeting Saturday evening, Mr. Hamilton referred to the fact that many of the leading members have been drawn off from Oneida, to serve in other places, and said, " What is the meaning of all this, and what are the consequences to follow ? I look upon it in this light : There is a general promotion taking place. Certain persons who have held leading positions here are called to other spheres; and their places must be made good by those who are left behind. We must all calculate to move right up, and have confidence in ourselves and extend confidence to others. We must put away all childishness and small-heartedness, and have no affection for sweet-heart or baby that shall cripple usefulness; but each one count it an honor to be considered a soldier ready to be handled as the Lord wishes.

" We should expect that the grace of God will abound in all directions among us. I feel like extending confidence to individuals, and expect that they will behave well, and do better than they have done in the past, and become good soldiers. The spirit of criticism and judgment is working, to be sure; but instead of crippling persons, that will set them free. I see that this is the result of the criticism that is working, and I am glad of it. I find it is good for me to enlarge my heart and stand up boldly, expecting the grace of God will be fruitful in me. That is the only way in which we can meet Christ and fulfill God's expectations. We must all be wide-awake and receptive to the inspiration God gives us. It is in that attitude that persons behave well, and rise out of temptations into harmony with the truth. The Lord will not have much to do with us unless we stand in that attitude. He cannot pour his Spirit into us if we are shrinking and standing back, full of small-heartedness and distrust. I feel like exhorting every one to stand up straight and be strong in the Lord, and take no counsel from fear and unbelief.

" We have got to press right forward and fill the places those persons have vacated who have gone to Wallingford and New York. Persons may find themselves called upon to fill places they had not even thought of. But let us not limit the grace of God. Instead of this, let us do justice to the labor that has been bestowed upon us. God has been at work a great while; and Mr. Noyes has labored with us faithfully and given us a great deal of truth. I should like to see a spirit of genuine ambition among us, that Mr. Noyes may see the result of his labors and be satisfied; and that the Oneida Community may be a splendid medium of power and inspiration, and a witness for the truth."

Mr. Hamilton then read the 12th chapter of Hebrews, and remarked that if the chapter had been written to us, it could not have been more appropriate in the general tenor and spirit of its exhortation.

In the business meeting yesterday, it was thought there was no necessity this year of going through with the usual formalities of business organization for the season. Persons are falling into their right places, and all seem willing to go where they are wanted. Mr Kinsley and Mr. Woolworth were appointed distributing committee.

Mr. Aiken, S. K. Dunn, H. M. Hutchins and Mrs. Conant, were appointed a committee to investigate the matter of getting a knitting machine. A new machine, apparently a very satisfactory one, is now offered to the public for $65,00.

Mr. Burt and W. A. Hinds were appointed a committee to take such steps as are deemed advisable, in respect to getting a patent on Mr. Burt's machine for cutting green corn from the cob.

Machinery for making bag frames and bag ornaments is nearly ready for use. It was voted that G. W. Hamilton employ several hands, by hiring, if necessary, and begin the business.

Mr. Burt was tendered a vote of thanks for his long and faithful service in the distribution of help. He is now turning his attention to the machine-shop.

W. A. Hinds reports that our use of rubber rollers for shelling peas, is no infringment on the Shaker Patent.

On Saturday we contemplated writing a paragraph about the fine weather we were having—how warm it was, how the snow was gone, how it had rained one night, how the grass was beginning to show its tender green amid the brown of the lawn, &c., &c. We have, however, concluded to defer the matter, at least until the present snow-storm is over, and the northwest breezes blow less vigorously. We don't intend to say any thing more about the weather until—there is a change.

A. H. Gardner and Co., Milwaukee, advertise our traps on their general list, as follows: " The Genuine Newhouse Animal Steel Traps. We would say to Trappers, purchase no other kind if you want a good and reliable article. We warrant all to be perfect and genuine."

Letters from Mr. Olds and John Norton, were received from Cleveland on Saturday. They report good luck, though sales were moderate, and business somewhat dull.

DAILY JOURNAL
OF ONEIDA COMMUNITY.

A. D. 1866.   MAR. 6.   NO. 43.

TUESDAY.

IN the meeting last evening Mr. Woolworth remarked as follows:

"This text has often been in my mind of late: 'Know ye not, that to whom ye yield yourselves servants to obey, his servants ye are to whom ye obey: whether of sin unto death, or of obedience unto righteousness?'— This seems to me to be the fundamental principle of the gospel of salvation. We do not seem to be called upon, and our salvation is not conditional upon, putting forth any great effort; but it is conditional upon the power of yielding ourselves to God and the spirit of truth. We are transformed by the truth as we yield to it. It seems to me that salvation is a continual yielding of our life to the spirit of truth. The truth takes possession of us as fast as we abandon ourselves to it.— That is the great secret of taking criticism well, to have a good, easy faculty of yielding to the truth. In that spirit there will be no quarreling, and no soreness that requires a long time to be overcome. That is the lesson I am studying. I am trying to learn how to yield myself simply and utterly to the spirit of obedience. I am certain that that will transform me and make me what God would have me."

Mr. Seymour leaves for Wallingford this afternoon, via New York. We have enjoyed his visit here at Oneida very much, and he carries with him the love of the whole family. We hope his shoulder will come back to its normal condition when he gets under the shadow of Mt. Tom again. We also trust that he will adjust his future relations to hickory-nut trees, on a more harmonious basis than happened to be the case last nut-time. It is a painful operation to fall out with them, or rather out of them, in such a vehement way as he did. However he seems as tough as hickory. May he live to be older than the big trees of California; may he climb hickory trees, and go to Roaring Brook in 2068, and may he *see more* nuts, and more strawberries, and more happiness, and write more soul-tickling articles for the Mount Tom Chronicle, every year that he lives.

Mr. Seymour last evening read an original poem from the stage, mostly composed while at Wallingford. It related to a visit to Roaring Brook, and a vision of millennial glory in 2068, or two hundred years hence.— We have not space to speak critically of the poem as an artistic composition, but much of it was pleasing and musical, full of the quaint fancy and originality for which Mr. S. is famous.

A new floor has been laid down in the back kitchen on the top of the old floor. People say they feel a little taller in consequence thereof, when going through the room.

THE CIRCULARS went by again to Syracuse last night. This express carelessness is getting to be an express bore, and if not expressly corrected will soon become expressly intolerable.

Our highest authority on birds, R. S. D., thinks the report was incorrect that the phebe had been seen and heard here this spring. His impression is that the bird referred to was a tom-tit. We have no doubt he is correct.

L. F. D. is improving in health and spirit quite markedly of late. Previous to the 20th he was in a hypo state and in much suffering of body. On the evening of the 20th, while Mr. Noyes was delivering his address on the Purchasing Agency, he seemed to get a new baptism of Mr. N.'s spirit, and his bad feelings of body and spirit passed away. Since then he has been steadily gaining he received a very encouraging letter from Mr. Noyes a few days ago. Since the 20th he has been staying at the New House.

The farmers have two men employed with a machine, threshing clover seed.

The trap orders to-day amount to $77.

On Friday afternoon a young man was seen triumphantly mounted on a large cake of ice, floating down the Oneida Creek, past the bridge and by the mill. He was in high glee, gesticulating, flourishing a pole, &c. A bend in the creek soon hid him from view as he continued his voyage toward the lake. A short time afterwards the same young man was seen about the Community buildings with a suit of clothes on entirely different, in texture, color &c., from those observed on him while on his voyage. This looked somewhat suspicious, and on diligent inquiry it was ascertained that his voyage had ended in shipwreck. His cake of ice suddenly parted in the middle and let him unceremoniously into the liquid element beneath. Finding himself in this uncomfortable position he made his way to the shore in the most expeditious manner possible, thence to the house and into a dry suit of clothes.

"The best laid schemes o' mice and men
   Gang aft agley."

The young man's name was Sidney.

DAILY JOURNAL
OF ONEIDA COMMUNITY.

A. D. 1866. MAR. 7. NO. 44.

WEDNESDAY.

LETTERS from Mr. Campbell came this morning, from Belleville. He reports good luck. Had received his money, and was ready to start up the road.— He finds prices of furs somewhat lower in Canada than he expected. He says:

" There is a strong reaction of feeling here in Canada at the failure of the negotiations for a new reciprocity arrangement. They lay it all to Uncle Sam's agents, and say they are going to wait now until the States want a treaty. They think the States will find they want one more than Canada does."

THE CIRCULARS were received last evening, after supper. They are highly entertaining this week.

The meeting last evening was mostly occupied with testimony, and confessions of Christ. An earnest desire pervades the family, to yield themselves to the truth and inspiration of the heavens.

Yesterday and to-day have given us genuine March weather, clear, cold and blustering.

One of the stockholders of a Connecticut Malcable Iron Company, located at New Britain, and which has been engaged in manufacturing the so-called Hudson's Bay Steel Traps, called at Willow Place yesterday. The company are sick of trap-making, and wish to sell us their stock, of which they have a great amount on hand. Their trap is the closest imitation of ours in shape of any that is made. It failed in quality. One of the samples the stockholder had with him broke while G. W. H. was examining it. They went into the manufacture under the lead of a Canadian, who appears to have had traps " on the brain" and was somewhat wild in his calculations. They started with plan, stock, &c. for 20,000 dozen. They made and sold about 2,000 dozen, when the demand seems to have ceased. About this time the dealers and trappers began probably to find out they were not quite equal to the Newhouse Trap. Mr. Newhouse courteously referred the stockholder to that chapter of the " Trapper's Guide," in which are given the testimonials in favor of the Newhouse Trap. He acknowledged that we had the inside track in the business. Our people did not give him any definite encouragement that they would purchase any of his stock.

There is much satisfaction and thankfulness expressed here, respecting the success of our brothers at the New York Branch in getting such a fine suit of rooms in the Moffat Building, for their business operations. The invisibles must have worked the wires for them. It is a grand step forward and looks like " moving immediately on the enemy's works."

The work on the store has fairly begun, and will now be vigorously prosecuted till completion. Mr. Hamilton last evening invited all to help at it who could, and make it a sort of pet job.

Mr. Mills in his recent letter inquired if he could obtain grape cuttings and cuttings of other small fruits, from us this spring. In a note to Mr. Hamilton, Mr. Noyes proposes we send him what cuttings he wants gratis, and if opportunity offers where he may be of use to us in selling traps, &c., encourage him in it.

ARRIVALS.—Mrs. Susan B. Munson, from Mass.

DEPARTURES.—Mr. Seymour, for Wallingford.

DAILY JOURNAL
OF ONEIDA COMMUNITY.

A. D. 1866. MAR. 8. NO. 45.

THURSDAY.

IN the meeting last evening, Mr. Hamilton remarked:

"I have thought I would allude to some of the matter and sentiments found in the papers at the present time. I don't feel quite ready, myself, to look at the South through Northern eyes—especially through the eyes of these extreme men. We read a great deal about the condition of the South, and the barbarism that prevails there. I have no doubt but that there is enough of that element working in the South, and yet I find myself restrained from letting my attention be taken possession of altogether by the Northern view. Possibly there is barbarism here at the North, almost as bad as that at the South. I want to face the truth. I hope there is better material to build upon in the South than some of these alarmists would lead us to think. I received the impression from Alfred after his visit to Western Virginia that there was something better about the people there than we would infer from the extreme Northern views. My own opinion is that we had better keep our minds clear from the strong prejudice shown in such papers as the *Tribune* and *Independent*.

"I cannot help respecting the high-toned morality and steady adherence to principle of such men as Sumner, Garrison and Wendell Philips. I cannot but think that the Lord is working through this class, and that he is introducing the great constitutional principles of heaven into the society where such persons labor; but still I have a feeling that there is a hard element of legality in these men that stirs up and provokes to wrath. They do not speak the truth in love. At any rate there is something about them that makes it desirable that we should not take them into too close fellowship. I confess a spirit that waits on the Lord and receives impressions from above, and will not suffer man to get possession of my attention."

The Librarian has been authorized to re-arrange the books in the library, and all persons in the family are requested to return books they have in their possession to the library for that purpose. The work will probably occupy several days.

W. A. H. arrived from New York last evening about ten o'clock.

In the meeting there was a general commendation of the spirit manifested by the silk-students.

E. H., in a letter from Willimantic, says:

"The days glide by quite swiftly—still when I look back it seems a long time since I left Oneida. *Dear Oneida* the mere mention of it makes my heart thrill, and I involuntarily say, thank God for such a home.

"We were very glad to see Mr. Cragin last night.— He came laden with good things—apples, cheese, cake and bottled fruit. We are thankful for the good things, but appreciate his presence more. How many things I think of these days to be thankful for. The one great thing that swells my heart with gratitude is, that God has given us an object worth living and laboring for.—

It seems to me that life would have but very little charm for me, if I had nothing more to look forward to than these girls around me have.

"Mr. Cragin brought fruit enough to give our whole family a meal, including Mr. Bottom's family also.— We shall have ours to-morrow, as many of the girls are away to-day. All who live near enough go home Saturday night. We hope to go home to Wallingford some time."

AN IDYL OF EVENING.

I sat in my chair at evening,
  And talked with a little girl,
And thought of the golden city,
  Its walls, and its gates of pearl.

And ever deeper and deeper,
  As we talked in accents low,
My thoughts and the mind's clear vision,
  Still back to my heart would go.

The walls of the golden city
  Within me I seemed to see,
And I longed that some blessed angel,
  Would open the gates for me.

Then o'er me a gentle stillness,
  As of heaven, there seemed to fall,
And I waited for some one to answer,
  For some one to hear my call.

Without still gathered the darkness,
  Round me and the little girl,
Within me a wonderful glory,
  Streamed down from the gate of pearl,

As open it swung on its hinges,
  Just touched by a radiant hand;
And there I saw, in the fullness
  Of beauty, a woman stand.

Around her there shone a nimbus,
  Of gorgeous splendor and light,
That all the bright heaven beyond her,
  Veiled from my ravished sight.

Then o'er me passed the thrilling
  Spirit of heavenly love,
That came like a gush from the fountain
  Under the throne above.

And there 'mid the golden glory,
  'Neath the pearly arch she stood,
Till deep in my heart I knew her—
  My guardian angel good.

As the gate swung again in music,
  Closing the beautiful scene,
My soul heard the name of the angel—
  'Twas Mary of Magdalene.

While within me the flame of heaven,
  Filled all my soul with power,
The little girl still sat beside me,
  And talked in the twilight hour.

DAILY JOURNAL
OF ONEIDA COMMUNITY.

A. D. 1866. MAR. 9. NO. 46.

FRIDAY.

IN the meeting last evening W. A. H. gave a report of his trip to New York, and his visit to the Shaker Community at Watervleit. We were very much edified by his account of the business school at New York, and the way in which Mr. Noyes's spirit is working among the brethren there.—Mr. Hinds found on consultation with the Shaker inventor of the Pea-shelling-machine, that our use of elastic rubber rollers, is an infringement on his patent, notwithstanding information to the contrary had been given us by Messrs. Munn & Co., of the *Scientific American.* The inventor refused to name any price for our right to use his invention, and said he would leave it entirely to the Community—they might pay him what they thought was right. We gathered from Mr. Hinds's report that his visit with the Shakers was a pleasant affair, and that he was treated in a very friendly and courteous way by them.

One of the lady Shakers observed to Mr. Hinds it was a pity that our Community being so near right should fail on *one* point. She thought if we were good *Shakers* it would be very pleasant to have visits between the Communes.

The project of buying one mile of the road, from the Castle eastward, and so avoiding the inconvenience of a toll-gate, seems likely to succeed. The sum asked for the road is $1000. $942 have already been subscribed, including $250 by the O. C. The subscription paper is still in circulation, and it is hoped that the balance of $58 will be raised without difficulty.

The fruit-growers, in using paper grape-boxes, last season, found them quite unsatisfactory in some respects. When transported long distances, the grapes sometimes get bruised a little, and the juice wetting the paper of the boxes often does much damage to the fruit. To obviate such difficulties our people have hit upon a plan for making wooden boxes, which are cheap and easily constructed, and are likely to be much more serviceable than paper ones. They are to be papered on the outside and will thus present a neat appearance.— About two thousand are to be made. The papering of them will be performed by some of the women.

ARRIVALS.—Mr. J. Barker and wife, and Mrs. J. Barker's daughter, Miss Robinson, from Castleton, Vermont.

J. J. S. left for Wallingford last night about 12 o'clock. He goes by way of New York. We wish him success and abundant happiness in his new sphere of labor.— He carries with him the love of Oneida hearts. The following is his valedictory to his boyhood home.

VALEDICO.

Farewell, a fond farewell, loved land of my boyhood How long will memory treasure up thy scenes and incidents, how often count over thy pearls and soothe m when weary, with sweet recollections of the days tha are past! Around all thy hills there circles the halo o remembrance. It dwells on all thy meadows, and lin gers in all thy woods and leafy dells. The "Island," whose glades the hermit-thrush thrills with its tremulous passion; whose trees I have climbed, to shake from their stems the butternuts for the waiting girls below; the brook that flows by, along whose banks I have wandered to the old elm tree that made the "Lover's Seat;" past the field of many a hard fought game of base-ball, to the larger elms at the high bank; to the bridge near which I waded in the rapids when a child; to the "swimming-hole" where, a merry crew of boys, we swam in summer and over which we felt a skater's joy in winter: on by grassy banks, the scenes of picnics and gala festivals unnumbered; onward, onward to the woods, where the muskrat dived, and the partridge whirred away a the sound of my foot-step: all these, and a hundred places more, are fadeless from my view, though I see them not with the outward eye.

And what can I say to the human friends from whom I part? Farewell, a thousand times farewell! And yet not sadly, for you go with me. Wherever I am I shall feel that your hearts are mine, the same as ever; that we are at work in the same cause, the same heaven smiles above us, the same God cares for us, and when He shall so order that we meet again, our joy shall more than equal the pain of the short separation. Once more Adieu, and may heaven bless the home and friends of my boyhood.
                                                          J. J. S.

DAILY JOURNAL
OF ONEIDA COMMUNITY.

A. D. 1866. MAR. 10. NO. 47.

SATURDAY.

IN the evening meeting Daniel Abbott was criticised. He is an efficient worker with his hands, and has attained to a good deal of skill and proficiency in his department. He is naturally amiable, friendly and obliging. His faults in the past have been a reserved state of life, that was not open to the Community spirit, and a tendency to insubordination, particularly in social matters. He never seems to have opened his heart thoroughly to the Community in a way to be vitally organized into it. His spiritual life has been more or less dormant and negative. His social insubordination was particularly dwelt upon. It was thought he needed to be in earnest to put himself in the attitude of obedience, and take some one as his head. The general feeling was that he is improving. It was also thought that some of his bad experience during the past year had resulted from his being associated and *identified* in business with an outside workman. Mr. Hamilton made the following remarks:

" I agree with the remark that Daniel, where his deepest interests are concerned, is not positive, as he is in outward things, but seems to be waiting for something to be done for him. He is waiting for God to do things for him that he should do for himself. Daniel is a very enterprising man in business; he has excellent judgment and is very observing. He may not be exactly what you call scientific, yet he is apt to examine closely into the causes of outward things pertaining to his business. Now he needs to have the same kind of enterprise in deeper, spiritual things. I think he has an insubordinate, reckless spirit in social matters. He has let the devil use him as a tool for working temptation in others, and has drifted along without manifesting much purpose to be edifying or conservative in his influence. He has caused me a good deal of anxiety in the past, but lately I have been feeling more hopeful and better towards him. I have been tempted to look forward to the approaching campaign in business with some dissatisfaction and unpleasantness when thinking of the department Daniel is connected with. In thinking of the spiritual state he was in, it seemed to me it would be quite unpleasant to be mixed up with him as much as I should have to be, if I gave as much attention to that department as I wished to do.

" I have been feeling that his spirit has been changing; and I have an impression that the new, practical organization that we are coming into, is going to help such persons as Daniel. He has never been organized, but has remained independent. There has been no individual whom he has been disposed to obey. Mr. Thacker was his nominal chief; but he did not respect him, and was irreverent at times. It is his special fault to lack respect for his superiors. He has inherited much of this tendency. Formerly that was Mr. Abbott's great fault—he was irreverent, discordant and unorganic. But on the other hand Daniel seems to have a genuine love of the truth, and this too he has inherited.

" I said I thought the new organization we are perfecting was going to help such persons as Daniel. For instance, I have felt that if Daniel would take hold and be subordinate to me and receptive to my spirit, that it would begin to work upon his spirit and moral character in a way to give him a new experience. His spirit has seemed softer and more receptive to me of late. And then I notice in him a disposition to fall in with Mr. Noyes's suggestions. He supports the administration.

" There is a profound depth of meaning in the old proverb. 'The fear of the Lord is the beginning of wisdom.' I realize its importance more and more. Irreverence, which is the root of disobedience, is the foundation of all evil; and reverence and fear of the Lord, is the foundation of all good. Fear of the Lord is the lowest form, but it is the *beginning* of wisdom; and there will not be any growth in wisdom that does not begin there—in the spirit that is careful to be obedient. In time this will carry a person on into the *love* of God, which casts out fear. I think Daniel needs to cultivate a nice taste, amounting to what is called fear of the Lord, which will make him careful to see to it that he is in harmony with a spirit more refined and better than his."

A very interesting report from Wallingford, on Empirical and Scientific knowledge as applied to the resurrection, was read last evening, also a letter from Mr. Cragin respecting the silk-business and the silk-students.

Mrs. Thayer closed her school last evening for the season. It has been in operation since the beginning of winter.

Letters from Mr. Campbell report his arrival at McKillican's on the 4th inst., after a somewhat tedious drive in a cutter from Madoc.

To-day is a cool, brilliant March day. There is just enough snow on the ground to whiten it.—Some of the farm teams are busy drawing manure.—For several days past a company has been sawing wood: and now splitting and piling are going on.

A number of bag orders have been received this week but we have been unable to learn their amount.

DAILY JOURNAL
OF ONEIDA COMMUNITY.

A. D. 1866.   MAR. 11.   NO. 48.

MONDAY.

LAST evening Mr. Hamilton called attention to the business-office, and the reasons there are for making it a more quiet place. He wished every one to feel at home there, but every one could see that it was not an appropriate place to frequent for mere conversation and gossip.

Work at the old barn or new store (which is it ?) goes on briskly, and that enterprise is gaining in Community favor. It is now proposed to broaden the wings, and thus make room for the shoe-shop, tailor-shop, business-office and silk-room, as well as the store proper.

G. W. Hamilton reports that he has consulted with Mr. Wood, the manufacturer of our steam engine, in respect to inspecting the boiler. He considers an inspection unnecessary at present. The law requiring a yearly inspection is limited in its operation to New York City.

The committee on the knitting machine has decided to postpone buying one till fall.

Mr. and Mrs. J. Barker, and Mrs. Barker's daughter, Miss Delia Robinson, left this morning. Mr. B. is somewhat interested in Communism, but knows little about us or our faith and doctrine. He had disposed of his property in Vermont, and was in hopes he could make some arrangement by which he could find a place near us to live, and get employment among us for himself and family, and thus have opportunity to attend our meetings and become acquainted with us, and our mode of life. The wife and her daughter manifested no interest whatever in Communism or the Community.— In our notice of their arrival we stated they were from Castleton. We learn that this was incorrect, they were from Derby Center. Mr. B. was originally from Maine.

In a recent letter, Mr. Robinson says:

" I can now and at all times reiterate an assurance of my love and fellowship. Particularly now also, when there are defections, here and there, I am happy to repeat my entire confidence in Mr. Noyes as God's chosen instrument to bear witness to the truth. He seems to have stepped into the shoes of the Apostle Paul."

Between 4,000 and 5,000 springs for No. 0 traps have been finished, at the factory. They are made from sheet steel. It is found that much less work is required to make them from sheet-steel than by the usual way from bar-steel. Mr. Newhouse and others wish to try the plan of making springs for No. 1 traps in the same way. The plan was sympathized with by the business board.

Mr. Hatch presented a bill to the business meeting, yesterday, for an investment in spectacles-stock amounting to about $50. The board favored his plan.

The new large lathe for the machine-shop is nearly completed. It will be a very valuable addition to the facilities of the shop. Its value at present prices is about $600.

Work on the castings for silk-machinery begins to-day at the foundry.

A company of visitors, came from Rome yesterday in the storm. The company included Mr. Dopp, the photographic artist, his wife and sister, Dr. E. Robellas and another lady, both of whom have been connected with the Blackwell's Island Lunatic Asylum. Dr. Robellas formerly had charge of an illegitimate son of Louis Napoleon, and succeeded in reclaiming him from a life of dissipation, in New York. For his services in this respect he was presented by the Emperor with a gold medal containing a lock of L. N.'s hair. He had the medal with him, and several of our people had an opportunity of inspecting the Imperial present.

Mrs. Jones and her son, of Baldwinsville, came on Saturday.

Mr. Burt is busily engaged in making a model of his corn-cutting machine, to forward to Washington with his application for a patent.

On Saturday Joseph Corney, the Englishman who worked for us two years ago, applied for the privilege of keeping one of our boarding-houses the present season, and to-day an Irishman at the Depot sends by his boy an application for the same honorable post.

O. H. Miller expects to start soon on an agent-excursion to Ohio.

M. H. Kinsley will probably start to-morrow on a trip to Springfield, Boston, Providence and other places, stoping two or three days at the N. Y. B., on his return.

Mr. Kelly arrived home on Saturday night.

Several conditional orders for agricultural implements, of respectable size, have lately been received through Messrs. Olds, Clark and others, some of which will be accepted. Mr Clark is now preparing to take a load of plows and castings to Cleveland, northwest of Oneida Lake.

DAILY JOURNAL
OF ONEIDA COMMUNITY.

A. D. 1866. MAR. 12. NO. 49.

TUESDAY.

IN the meeting last evening in conversation on the the conditions of Communism and salvation, Mr. Hamilton said:

"Communism and fellowship with one another can only come as we are saved from selfishness. Salvation from selfishness it appears to me comes in this way: before we can be saved from selfishness we must find some person, some society, government or power, that we have confidence enough in to yield our whole life to it or them and say, 'Here we are, take us and do with us what seemeth to you good. I don't see how persons are going to be saved from selfishness until they find some such power or person to which they can yield themselves. I don't believe the spirit of reform that has its roots in universal benevolence will save people from selfishness. And the reform that cannot save a man from selfishness will prove to be superficial. The great central assertion of selfishness is, 'I belong to myself. My business is to first seek my own good, and make all things, as far as I am able, work for my welfare and happiness.' The opposite of all that is what we must attain to; we must assert that we belong not to ourselves, but to God and Christ and the powers above us. Such is the only road I can see out of selfishness.

—"Now the question is, How can one get out of selfishness who does not believe practically in God and Jesus Christ, and in the work Christ has done for and in humanity? All these reforms that are based on any lower and less radical standard than the one Christ presented will, it seems to me, never amount to much.— Indeed I have no confidence in reforms that are based on universal benevolence. They are superficial in the ends they seek, and in the love and works they manifest. The spirit that believes in God is the only one sure to succeed.

"All folks require to make them happy is to get rid of selfishness. They must find a good power they can yield themselves to, and instead of working for themselves, go to work for some body else. But, manifestly, you cannot work for a power you have no confidence in.— And this leads to our definition of what it is to join the Community or the kingdom of heaven. Persons cannot join the Community until they see it in such a light that they can give themselves to it wholly, and say: 'Here I am person and property, and you can do just what you choose with me. If I can serve the interests of the truth better standing outside, I am content to do so. I have such entire confidence in the Community that I can put all my interests into its hands and go to work for it." That would be what I should call joining the Community. And by such a course a person would get out of selfishness.

—"Suppose a person were to come here and see all the happiness and comfortable surroundings that the Community has secured and given to us, and should be seized with a desire to share in them? That is not really seeking to join the Community. A true joining of the Community is the attaining of such confidence in it and its religion, government and central spirit, that you will boldly surrender your life to it.

—"I believe that under God Mr. Noyes will drill the Community till we shall all feel that we do not belong to ourselves; and we shall carry out that idea so thoroughly and perfectly that we shall gain the entire confidence of the world. We shall show them an organization that they can give themselves to, with perfect safety. This is one view of the calling of the Community, and one which kindles my ambition."

We are having a thorough spring thaw, and altogether a rainy, misty, muddy time. The snow has all disappeared except where it has been heavily drifted.— Every thing betokens the approach of spring. We feel it in the atmosphere, in the sun's rays, in the increasing mildness of the nights. We have almost daily reports of the coming of the robins. How interesting and full of vital power is the approach of spring—the season of springing grass, of bursting buds, and opening flowers! It awakens enthusiasm in every heart, it touches all things with a mystic influence, and fills all intelligent life with delight. From the morning of creation it has been the season of love and sexual reawakening. Tennyson says of it:

' In the Spring a fuller crimson comes upon the Robin's breast;
In the spring the wanton lapwing gets himself another crest;
' In the Spring a livelier iris changes on the burnished dove;
In the Spring a young man's fancy lightly turns to thoughts of love.'

But this increase of beautiful power, which as it were thrills through all creation, in this birth of spring, is given us not for the purpose of mere pleasure, but to equip us for the great business of the year. It is the bursting forth of the inner dynamic treasures which have been accumulated during the months of outward repose, and which if marshaled wisely and to great ends, will bring us into new sympathy with God, the creative, loving spirit of the universe.

Our visitor Mrs. M. left this morning. She was somewhat disappointed in not being able to find a home among us. Hitherto she does not appear to have had a very thorough knowledge of us or of our faith, and she has been associated more or less with the humanitarian class of reformers. Since she has been here, however, her attention seems to have been turned, by our sincerity toward her, to a deeper study of us, and of the Gospel. She confessed Christ as a savior from sin, last evening in the meeting, and accepted some very good advice from Mr. Hamilton. She bought a Berean.

DAILY JOURNAL
OF ONEIDA COMMUNITY.

A. D. 1866. MAR. 13. NO. 50.

WEDNESDAY.

WE have few business items to record in our JOUR-NAL to-day, so will give some paragraphs from correspondence.

Letters have been received from Mr. Olds and John Norton, from Detroit. Sales the first day in Detroit, amounted to $258. The following paragraphs are from Mr. Olds's letter:

" We find business in this city rather dull, and some people I should think have the '*blues.*' We called at a store to-day to sell silk, and on entering we saw six men standing round the stove waiting for customers.— They were a hungry looking set of fellows I assure you. Each I should think was trying to get ahead of the other to get a customer. But imagine what a disap-pointment when they found we came to sell and not to buy. Well, you ask, did you sell them any silk? No, we did not, for in such circumstances buying was not in their programme. We soon got them laughing over the matter, and I guess they felt better when we left.— At another store they thought they were out of pocket $10 a day for expenses.

" We found the clerks in another place having a mer-ry time over an incident that had just occurred in the store. The store was built with two rooms at right angles and fronting on two streets. A woman came in and called for some article, but the price did not suit, and after bantering awhile she went out without purchas-ing. On going out it seems she passed around she cor-ner on to the other street and went into the same store. The same clerk seeing her hastened to wait upon her, at the same time changing his countenance as much as possible. She called for the same article as before, and he named the same price. She made no objections but took it and went out, not discovering her mistake."

In a letter to his father, dated Madras, January 12th, Ernest Delatre writes as follows :

" You are very much mistaken, in supposing that the less religion you instil into your letters, the more ac-ceptable they are to us. I can say for myself (and I have reason to believe my remarks are equally applica-ble to Reg.) that I am not as I was. That I have had an awakening—and although it may be long before I find grace sufficient to turn my back on the world, yet religious matters interest me now habitually, in a way to which I was before a stranger. 'THE CIRCU-LAR', also, which you have so kindly persisted in sending, interests me in a way quite unwonted, and I appreciate more and more the harmony which exists between its sentiments and a true interpretation of the New Tes-tament.

" From the date of your receipt of this, I hope you will put my name down as a regular subscriber. I in-tend, as soon as I can spare it, to send you a remittance not only for THE CIRCULAR, but a copy of each of the Oneida publications. I want to send it now, but being engaged in starting my little business, I could not con-veniently spare it. I think the postage on THE CIRCU-LAR will amount to much more than the subscription.—Let me know."

A letter was received from a German inventor and philosopher, a few days ago, asking advice. He has in-vented two kinds of sewing-machines ; also a planctari-um, by which he claims to solve some of the motions of the heavenly bodies in a way not hitherto accomplished. He lacks means to bring these inventions before the public. To manufacture his sewing-machines he thinks requires a company with several hundred thousand dol-lars capital. His planetarium would only require some two hundred dollars to complete it. He inquires if we know of any rich men who are interested in scientific matters who would be likely to help introduce it to pub-lic attention.

The children's house folks have had quite a battle with colds and slight ailments among the children, of late ; but by meeting the troubles in a faith spirit they have been conquered, and Mr. Hatch reports the chil-dren as now doing well, and a bright, healthy spirit is prevailing.

THE CIRCULARS came yesterday at the usual morning hour, and were very welcome. We hear much commend-ation of the paper expressed of late. The new tract on " Salvation from Sin" has a very attractive look, and is well got up every way. The family voted last evening to have it read in the meeting.

We hear very favorable reports of Frederick Norton's skill and success as a dentist, now-a-days. He has made several sets of teeth, which we learn give good satisfaction.

The farmers have finished threshing clover-seed, and have 48 bushels as the result.

W. S. Knowles, brother of Atwood Knowles, came on Monday, and left to-day. He is engaged with an-other man in the manufacture of fishing tackle. He was somewhat interested to learn about the Purchasing Agency, and thinks they may patronize it with advan-tage.

DAILY JOURNAL
OF ONEIDA COMMUNITY.

A. D. 1866. MAR. 15. NO. 51.

THURSDAY.

JUDGING by the noise made, sawing wood is the most conspicuous business about home to-day. The wood-house is being rapidly filled.

Mr. Bradley has taken C. O. Kellogg's place on the farm, a fact which properly should have been historically stated some weeks ago.

One of the Rhetorical classes lately gave an entertainment to Messrs. Kelly and Underwood, the teachers; at which quite a number of rhetorical flourishes were skillfully executed.

Mr. Hamilton last evening called attention to the finances. He said we shall have to pay out quite a large amount of money during the next three weeks, and exhorted all to do what they could to limit the expenses of the family for the present. He thought a little continence in this respect at the present time, would lead to larger liberty hereafter.

The Home-Talk on Continence and Liberty was read last evening, and was received with expressions of hearty sympathy.

The "moving" operations of the family still go on. A large number of the members have changed their quarters within the last three weeks.

G. W. H. has been quite successful in getting up machinery for bending bag-frames.

The weather continues rainy and misty, and the frost is fast leaving the ground.

The boys are having very good success trapping muskrats. The skins bring a good price, being quoted in the circulars of the New York dealers at from 35 to 45 cts. apiece for common spring skins, and 50 cts. for black skins.

Mr. Hamilton has made architectural elevations of the front and north end of the store, and exhibited them on the bulletin. The building will present a very good appearance, especially in front, when finished. The two wings are to be enlarged to thirty-two feet in width, and their roofs carried up somewhat higher at the ridge than at present.

Mr. Burt has completed the model of his corn-cutting machine, and it will be sent to New York to-day. The model is very neatly got up, and was constructed by Mr. Burt himself. There appears to be little doubt of his obtaining a patent on it.

The fruit-growers propose this spring to plant a new cherry orchard of about one hundred trees, of the new hardy varieties. The object is a supply of fruit for preserving purposes. The kinds selected are the Shannon, Kirtland's Morello, Louis Philippe and Ohio. They have been ordered of Dr. J. P. Kirtland, of Cleveland, Ohio, well known among fruit-growers as a successful propagator of new varieties of the cherry. About thirty Damson Plum trees will also be set this spring.

Mr. Campbell writes that he has been up the Hastings Road as far as Doyle's, and picked up some fur.— Fowler had been up the road about a week ahead of him and got the most of the fur in the hands of the local dealers. Mr. C. has not yet seen Holland and Gunter but was about to do so, and after that he has some intention of going west to Peterboro, and up the Bobcaygeon Road. The principal furs to be picked up at this season are those caught by the Indians. The whit-trappers, as a general thing, do not begin spring trapping till sometime in April.

As we wish to be correct in all our statements, we will refer to one or two late mistakes. We stated that Mrs. Chesbro was several weeks on her way home from the Community. We learn that the time was between one and two weeks.—One man was hired with the clover threshing-machine, instead of two as was stated.

Portia has taken H. M. Worden's place as teacher of the children's school.

Mr. Leete is here—came yesterday. He is bright, and enters into the store project with much sympathy and enthusiasm. He says he shall be ready to take charge of the store when it is finished—he will come to the Community whether his family does or not. "If the door is kept open he will enter."

Hamilton Kneeland, brother of Meroa, and also of the young man who has lately visited the Community, in a letter lately received, expresses great interest in the Community, and says his wife sympathizes with him.— Their past conduct has, however, been such that judgment and repentance must precede their connection with the Community.

DEPARTURES:—Mrs. Jones and son, yesterday, for home.

DAILY JOURNAL
OF ONEIDA COMMUNITY.

A. D. 1866. MAR. 16. NO. 52.

FRIDAY.

MR. Wager requests that the amount due him on the Willow-Place property ($6,000), be paid him on the 1st day of April, in greenbacks.

Mr. Burt's model did not go to New York yesterday as was expected, the papers to accompany it not being in readiness.

The weather is still mild, cloudy and rainy, and the mud—well there will be less of it sometime, but at present it has the ground to itself.

Mr. Abbott reports the aggregate age of O. C. to be 7,749 years and about 10 months—average age 37 years and 29 days. The aggregate weight is 27,597½ lbs.—average 132 lbs. The aggregate hight is 1095 feet and 1¼ inches—average 5 feet 2 inches.

The reading of "Salvation from Sin," is continued in the meetings and is listened to with new interest. The following conversation took place last evening after the reading. Mr. Hamilton, refering to what had just been read said:

"I was particularly interested in the idea that we cannot be married to the law and to Christ at the same time. It may seem like going to destruction to swing off from the law. But we should reckon that we are married to a power greater than the law, as we come into conjunction with Christ. The world and the churches cannot see any righteousness that does not come from the law; and it seems to them that in abandoning the law they are abandoning all hopes of righteousness.

Mr. Woolworth.—I thought it was an interesting coincidence that this tract should be republished just at the time this revival movement is breaking out anew. I am sure we shall sometime have revivals that will go forward to salvation from sin as the only goal at which the converts will be satisfied to stop. [The papers report that revivals are numerous, and are extending throughout the country.]

Mr. Hamilton.—That is an interesting thought. It is well for us to be able to put a true value on the revival movement. We must feel right toward that and at the same time not drop down from our own position. The revival seems to me like the net Christ refers to in one of his parables. He likened the kingdom of heaven to a net that is cast into the sea, which when filled with fish is drawn to land by the fishermen, when they sit down to discriminate, and save some, while they cast others away. We might consider the revival as a net drawn in the sea of worldliness. After the haul is made, the test is to be applied. Mr. Noyes and Perfectionism came out of the former revival. And now there is another revival begun, and this doctrine of salvation from sin may be preached, and there may be another selection made from this ingathering. In this way we can sympathize with the revival as one of the Lord's measures.

Mr. Ellis.—Mr. Noyes prophesied there would be a revival after the close of the war, and it seems to be coming on.

Mr. Hamilton.—That is another interesting thought.—The war was a strife between the progressive spirit of liberty at the North and the barbarism of the South, in which the North conquered; but it was a gross kind of conflict such as we had to keep out of. The revival is perhaps a more refined method of carrying on the struggle. The work of the revival follows the war; and probably the work of Perfectionism is going to follow the revival. We are certain that all these great events are going to culminate in the kingdom of heaven."

The following note from S. B. C. was read last evening in the meeting:

I have had some thoughts of late on the subject of special love, or salvation from it which I would like to express. I have felt thankful for what has been done for me and for the Community in this respect, but have found myself hungering and thirsting for full salvation. We all know, doubtless what it is to be saved at times from this and that specialty, and to feel *free*, but the salvation we need and that is waitng for us, is that which **saves us from all *liability* to entanglements,** let the temptation be ever so strong. The earnest desire of my heart is, to be *saved* from uninspired attachments to man, woman or child, and *saved forever*, that I may be ready for every good word and work. "Be ye *clean*, ye that bear the vessels of the Lord."

I will add that I sympathize with Mr. Noyes and the Community in their present attitude towards business, and confess Christ my ability, whether I eat or drink, or *whatsoever* I do, to do it heartily as unto the Lord.

S. B. C.

DAILY JOURNAL
OF ONEIDA COMMUNITY.

A. D. 1866. MAR. 17. NO. 53.

SATURDAY.

CHLOE and Mr. Underwood have been very busy this week re-arranging and cleaning the library, and expect to nearly complete their labors to-day. It has been quite a laborious job.

The toll-gate between the Castle and Oneida will be thrown open on the 1st of April. Reason—the Charter of the company expires.

A letter was received yesterday from Dr. Rowland inquiring if some arrangement could be made by which his family could find a home somewhere "within our borders," for some weeks during the hottest weather of next summer. He also says; "My recollection is that there was something in THE CIRCULAR within a month or two about a school or university at Wallingford, but I cannot, in a hasty glance over the papers, find it, and I may be mistaken. Please tell me what the prospect is as to a school being started under the auspices or management of your people."

The clouds cleared away yesterday afternoon. During the night the ground froze, and there was a light fall of snow. This morning it is clear and cold, with a northwest wind blowing.

The amount of orders received for bags, for the week ending Friday, March 16, was $1195.

The first lot of castings for the silk-machinery was taken from the molds yesterday.

A lot of furs and deerskins was received from Mr. Campbell yesterday, amounting to $114,15.

Trap orders since March 6, amount to $594,32.

Fruit orders since March 10, amount to about $152.

There is great enthusiasm on the subject of greens, on the part of some of the family. Every time the ground is bare, the fields are scoured, and every little leaf of scurvy-grass that ventures to show its green face among the grass and withered leaves is forthwith made a victim and ends its life in the steam-boiler.

The manufacture of grape boxes is going on successfully, and a number of persons are engaged, when unemployed at other duties, in papering them.

Mr. Bristol, while engaged getting ice in the ice-house this morning, was suddenly made a prisoner. The northwest wind unceremoniously blew the door to, and it became fastened so that he could not open it. He remained there in a state of cool consternation, sometime, before he could succeed in alarming the neighboring population and secure a liberation from his wintry quarters. We judge from all accounts that the time of his imprisonment seemed rather long to him, though in reality it was quite brief.

Mary Whatley's brother arrived here this morning just from California.

Aleander Longley sends us a prospectus of another project of Community or Association, which he proposes to embark in, if he can find persons enough to co-operate with him.

G. B. Price of Watervliet writes that he accepts the offer of the Community, and forwards a paper guaranteeing to us in consideration of $40, the right of making and using pea-shellers involving the principles covered by his patent.

MY CONTRIBUTION.

It is said by some one that "no news, is good news," and we will apply it to our little daily. Though it may not have frightful accidents to record, or news from the wars to enliven its pages; still we will say, "it is good," and can we not supply their places with the effusion of a thankful, rejoicing spirit?

May we not hope, that every one that receives and reads the little JOURNAL, will feel it to be a privilege and a pleasure, to contribute to its usefulness. Though it may not always be "*credited*" it may be entertaining, and a receptacle for every bright thought, whether from old or young.　　　　　P. N.

DAILY JOURNAL
OF ONEIDA COMMUNITY.

A. D. 1866.　　MAR. 19.　　NO. 54.

MONDAY.

MR. OLDS writes from Detroit, about preserved fruit, as follows:

"Our fruit is getting a great reputation here. It is now pretty well introduced. The new firm who have been dealing in our fruit, have sold much more than they expected. One of them invited me to dine with him one day last week, saying 'they were going to have some of the O. C. corn, and would like to have my testimony as to its quality, &c.' I accepted the invitation, and found they understood preparing it for the table. It was indeed nice. This firm want 20 doz., more, and think they could sell more, even, but rather not get over stocked. They will want a large quantity this year, and will give an order on my return from the west.

Mr. Campbell, writing from Belleville, says:

"There is much excitement here about the Fenians. The streets are full of red-coated volunteers, who are under arms awaiting the Fenians' appearance. There is some talk about the Yankees allowing them to go on and organize and threaten to attack Canada, but if there is much ill feeling they don't manifest it to me."

The Springfield Republican came yesterday, with its second article on the Oneida Community and the "divine law of marriage." The Republican seems to be in a somewhat uneasy, nervous state with regard to the social question—and afraid that the present system will be overthrown, unless it keeps special watch and calls down the terrors of the law on all innovators. First the backward-looking polygamy of the Mormons must be put down, and then the "civil authorities" in the neighborhood of the advancing Oneida Community "have a duty to perform." It is doubtful, however, whether this knight-errant of the present marriage system will fare any better than Don Quixote in his contest with the wind-mills. The great mill of social progress and improvement will swing on before the breeze of heaven, and any daring champion who "pitches into" it will be likely to have the worst of the fight in the long run.

John F. Sears is to visit Willimantic for the purpose of getting information respecting some of the minute details of the silk-machinery. While in Connecticut he will call at the New Britain trap-manufactory, and examine their trap-stock.

Orders have been received and accepted, during the past week, for $734,31 worth of agricultural implements. Another order amounting to $350 is still under consideration. The prospect is good for closing up that branch of business the present season.

$123 worth of mops were ordered yesterday.

Steam-pipe and fixtures are to be introduced into the back kitchen for convenience in making paste &c.

It has been decided to finish off 800 beaver traps in addition to the 1800 now on hand.

Miss Sophia L. Nunns arrived yesterday morning, from New York.

The number of hired men in the bag-shop now is ten —eight more, we understand, than were employed last year at this season. The hired women number seven.

The reading of "Salvation from Sin," was finished last evening. It has been very edifying. The addition of the articles on "Christian Faith," and the "Spiritual Man," give a completeness to the argument which is very satisfactory. It was recommended to the young folks of the Community to study the pamphlet, and endeavor to get a thorough apprehension of the great truths it presents.

The weather continues cold, with occasional squalls of snow.

The project of buying a house in New York, for a Community home, excites very general interest, and all seem ready to follow Mr. Noyes's lead in respect to the matter.

Charles Reeves, the English farmer, who has worked for the Community several years, to-day starts for Iowa, taking his "pile of savings," with which he intends to purchase a small farm. He has relatives in that State.

Quite a thrifty little trade is going on in apples—Mr. Ackley and Mr. Worden acting as "middle-men" for our hill-neighbors, and obtaining fair compensation for their services. Apples are now sold by the farmers at the same prices asked last autumn.

DAILY JOURNAL
OF ONEIDA COMMUNITY.

A. D. 1866.　　MAR. 20.　　NO. 55.

TUESDAY.

IN the meeting last evening Mr. Hatch spoke of the experience he had had in dealing with the colds to which the children had been subject of late. He thought a spirit came in after the children were taken down that was very different from a quiet faith spirit.— He was led to study it, and was convinced that there were two spirits at work; one taking Mr. Noyes's view, that sickness begins primarily in the spirit and should be treated in that direction, and the other looking mainly to the body.

Mr. H. read some passages from the New Testament to illustrate his meaning and then said:

"I see that Christ in his dealings with persons who were sick looked altogether at the spirit, and hardly consented to say any thing about the body. In the case of the man who was sick with the palsy, it is quite noticable that Christ did not ask him a word about his body, but merely said, "Thy *sins* be forgiven thee." This made me desirous that we should be in earnest in our dealings with the children, and instead of looking at their bodies, learn to look to Christ. I have found that whenever we have done so, we have been successful. I hope we may as a Community turn our thoughts to Christ, when our children are ailing, and ask that they may have faith, and that we may have faith for them. The parents should stir themselves up to faith for their children. I am satisfied that if this could be done, it would be of great help to the children. I remember Mr. Noyes once remarked that if we would be successful we must strengthen the center. I thought this was the way to look, in order to help Mr. Noyes. We know he looks at the spirit, for the cause and for the cure of sickness. I wish to offer myself anew to Mr. Noyes's faith and hope.

Mr. Hamilton.—You will readily see by studying the New Testament, that Christ's object was not merely to heal diseases, but that this was merely secondary—a means to an end. Christ's miracles were means by which he sought to get at the spirit and internal life.— He frequently told persons not to mention what he had done for them, and forbade them to speak of it. Healing the body, in his view of it, was merely a superficial thing; and, as Mr. Hatch says, if we get our attention merely upon healing of the body, we are not sympathizing with the Lord. Frequently the Lord providentially makes use of suffering of the body, as a means of softening and chastening the spirit. If we wish to be in fellowship with Christ we should take that view of it, and try to keep the children in a good spirit.

Mr. Woolworth.—I have great confidence in the truth as a medicine for the body as well as for the soul.—

"The truth shall make you free"; free from disease from sin, and from bondage to bad spirits, from weakness, ignorance and foolishness. The truth is a good medicine for every thing that folks are afflicted with.— I find myself more and more in love with it, and have growing confidence in it as applicable to all conditions in all cases. It can be applied externally, internally, and *eternally*. I have great confidence in criticism, that is sincere and truthful, and given in love. I see when it is taken and given in love, its effects are almost instantaneous. Instead of creating soreness or despondency I observe in many cases the effect is right the opposite: it gives life, hope, strength and salvation. I have an ambition to be a good physician in administering the truth. I wish to be a physician of Christ, administer the truth so it will "go to the spot" as they say. I believe every one of us can get that art.

At this point the subject was changed, and Mr. Hamilton remarked: "I have been away to-day, on business; and I find the more I come in contact with the spirit of the world the more I appreciate my calling as a member of this Community. The life of the world seems very superficial and aimless. You do not seem to meet any love of the truth, or desire for righteousness, improvement and growth in goodness. The most that you see is love of money, and a great deal of bad principle. I notice that persons make a joke of goodness and truth. And then there is a great deal of trouble too, outside, as business is dull. Some persons do not know which way to turn, and their happiness seems to center entirely in the success of their business. I fully sympathize with the idea that love of the truth should claim our attention above all things else. I feel like taking home this saying of Christ's as applicable to business as well as every thing in life: "Seek first the kingdom of God and his righteousness." Seek first the constitutional spirit of the kingdom of heaven, and all these things shall be added.

Mr. Kelly.—While I was at the New York Branch, Mr. Noyes remarked that we should overcome the love of money by substituting the love of faithfulness and thoroughness in business.

Mr. Woolworth.—Persons are apt to think our business prosperity and success are geared into the affairs of the world, so if things are dull there it affects and damages our business. Possibly there may be a tendency to give too much attention to this view, and connect ourselves too much with the world's business system. I believe the Lord has the conditions of the world under his control, and the true way is to look to him, and trust him, instead of the world, to make our business good.

THE CIRCULARS were on time this morning, and were handed round to the family before eight o'clock.

O. H. M. starts to-day on his business trip to Ohio.

A letter from E. Otis, mentions the fact that the *Post's* article on Oneida Community, has been copied into the Lorain *News*, published at Oberlin we believe.

J. F. Sears left this morning for Willimantic.

An additional order for traps from the Hudson's Bay Company, amounting to $175, was received yesterday.

DAILY JOURNAL
OF ONEIDA COMMUNITY.

A. D. 1866. MAR. 21. NO. 56.

WEDNESDAY.

LADY Campbell has recovered so as to attend meetings. She is also able to walk without a cane.

Another of C. B. B.'s pupils writes, expressing a wish to join the Community. The letter uniquely says, " What I wanted to ask was, if the Community would let me come and see them ; and bring my trunk; and let me stay long enough to become well acquainted ; and, if they thought best, to let me stay *forever*. I do not think the Lord has wanted me to go before now, and now I think he does."

E. H. writes that the silk-students are improving in their business quite fast, and may possibly get through sooner than they expected at first. Their health is good and they enjoy their work very much. She says : " The silk we are winding is very poor indeed—they say we cannot possibly get a worse lot. So if we learn to work this up well we shall be ready for anything in that line."

A letter was received yesterday, inquiring if we could receive a colored woman, from the south, of good Christian character, into the Community. There was no evidence that either the writer of the letter or the woman herself understood any thing about the distinctive character and purpose of the Community, and of course a negative answer will be returned.

The weather now wears a quite unsettled aspect.— Yesterday was cold and cloudy, ending with storm of sleet. During the night the temperature moderated, and the storm turned to rain. This morning the fields are but slightly covered with snow, and begin to assume their brown appearance again.

The talk about financial principles, delivered at Wallingford, was read last evening, and was the topic of considerable conversation in the meeting. There was general sympathy expressed with the new views brought out by Mr. Noyes, and a desire to study and apply them to our business here as fast as we can. The system of prepayment is evidently the true one, and we must warp up to it, though it may require wisdom and some little time to adjust all our business arrangements to it.

Mr. Campbell arrived from Canada this morning. He had picked up what fur he could find, and as there was no prospect of getting more till April, he thought it was as well to come home, and see how furs were selling. He went as far west as Peterboro, where he purchased a lot of beaver.

Work on the Store progresses. The two wings of the old building have been taken down preparatory to building larger ones.

John Anderson, the young Englishman who came here from the Shaker Colony in Kentucky, left this morning. Martin paid him some money for his services. The other young man remains, and wishes the Community to continue to employ him.

Mr. Miller did not start yesterday for the west as we reported. He leaves to-day at 11 o'clock, and expects to be gone a month or more.

We do not know as any apology is needed for the brevity of our chronicle of to-day ; but after diligent inquiry and investigation we find but little to report.— Nevertheless a good spirit is working among us, and there is testimony from many of an increase of faith, and a deepening of their love for the principles of the Community, and the Gospel of Christ, and this is the best news that we can report.

DAILY JOURNAL
OF ONEIDA COMMUNITY.

A. D. 1866.　MAR. 22.　NO. 57.

THURSDAY.

THE following communication from L. F. D. was read last evening :

To the Family :—I was much interested in the talk last evening on the subject of finances. The plan of *prepayment* seems to me to be a sound business principle, and one that if fairly carried out would settle all the perplexing financial questions that now embarrass us, and the world. I do not understand enough about financiering to see how all the difficulties are to be overcome, in the way of putting such a great principle in practice, but I have confidence that it can be done.

Our present system of cash payment was not very popular with our customers when we first started it, but by representing to them that we adopted it from *principle* we soon gained their confidence, and secured to ourselves the very best class of customers in the country. I think that this experience should encourage us in trying to carry into practice the new principles that Mr. Noyes is bringing out.

I believe it is the destiny of the Community to revolutionize the worldly systems of trade, and introduce a system of its own, based on true, scientific principles.— The present movement seems to be in this direction, and I confess my hearty sympathy with it, and my desire to help carry it out.　L. F. Dunn.

A communication from Mrs. Loomis, expressing thankfulness for criticism and for God's goodness to her, was read last evening.

A communication was also read from Manly Aiken, expressing thankfulness for criticism and his purpose to seek the ascending fellowship, and to separate himself from the spirit of pleasure-seeking, which he confessed he had been under during the past winter.

The proposal to sell that portion of the Petric farm west of the road, is in a fair way to be consummated. Mr. Levi Petric, brother of the man from whom we bought the farm, came over yesterday and informed us that he wished to purchase the place. He offered to take it at our price, viz. $100 per acre. There are about thirty-three acres offered for sale. When the bargain is closed we will report the terms. It is regarded as a providential opening, and all feel glad to respond to it.

Mr. Campbell leaves this afternoon for Barnstable, Mass., to see what can be done in the way of hastening the settlement of Mrs. Tobey's affairs. He goes by the way of New York.

Martin reports the Ayrshire stock now on hand, to be as follows : full bloods, 1 cow, 1 bull, 1 yearling heifer, 1 three months old calf; half bloods, 12 heifers one year old.

Twenty-four cows are now milked, including fifteen new milch ones.

Thirty-three bushels of clover-seed have been sold for $6,50 per bushel. The farmers intend to sow about eleven bushels this season.

BRIBERY.

Dear Journal :—I wish to raise my voice against *Bribery*. My wrath is kindled against this great and growing evil. I cannot go abroad without meeting it. The hotel-waiter, the porter, the baggage-man and public functionaries generally, are becoming demoralized by it. There are doubtless many persons connected with every kind of employment who would sincerely shun any thing having the semblance of a bribe; but there are also others who seek it, expect it and labor to obtain it. Who has not learned that extra " quarters" judiciously distributed will insure him extra attention and accommodatio wherever he may go? The indifferent air assumed by hotel and railroad attaches often means : " If you have my good-will you must pay for it." I know of a city-bank where the clerks boldly ask for presents, and treat customers coldly until such favors are obtained. I know of a useful invention which was patented in consequence of a bribe thrown. to a clerk in the patent office. Not long since a somewhat noted Government official, in reference to an invitation to do only what was within the scope of his duty, intimated that his wife would like one of our fancy satchels! I felt insulted. Down with every form of bribery—let us accept only such favors as come by fair play and honest deal.　Derfla.

DAILY JOURNAL
OF ONEIDA COMMUNITY.

A. D. 1866. MAR. 23. NO. 58.

FRIDAY.

AS Mr. Underwood expects soon to leave for Wallingford, he requested criticism, which was administered last evening. But little was said except in the way of commendation. He was thought to be steadily improving, and growing in faith. He is gradually working out of many things which in the past have operated to cramp his faith and vital fellowship with the Community. His almost uninterrupted genial good nature was commended, though it was questioned whether it would not be more appreciated if it were sometimes tempered and balanced by a more decided and severe earnestness that would give him power to offend, even, where the truth demands it. And it is also true that while his outward life and deportment in the Community are very pleasant and agreeable, his spirit in regard to health has had to be resisted. But he seems to be working more into harmony with the Community in this respect. He has excellent ability as a teacher, and his services in this respect are greatly valued. He was also commended for his cheerful service in waiting on company during the past year. His course in this business has been very satisfactory. It is expected that his change of residence will bring him new and good experience, by bringing him into a new sphere of action and thought. He carries with him the love of the family.

The following note from Miss Nunns was read last evening:

To THE FAMILY—I thank you for the kind welcome you have given me, to your hearts and home. Many have said how well I look, so much better than they had expected to see me. It is true, I am better in health than I have been for many years. A spirit of obedience has been the good physician that has wrought the change. Mr. Noyes taught me to mind him, and since I have done so, I have steadily gained, both in spirit and body. There is a "charm about obedience" that lures one on, till an unspoken wish is perceived and obeyed as readily as if conveyed in words. I greatly desire that nice perception of the desires of others which will save them the trouble, and often pain of being obliged to speak to me. I confess Christ the keeper of my attention. SOPHIA.

In the evening meeting Mr. Hamilton made the following remarks:

"I have been led lately to think, in a very serious way, about our true attitude as a Community, toward those who come among us from time to time—new comers as we call them. I have my mind at the present time especially on the social influences brought to bear upon them. I see that we have men and women coming among us, and if we let things take a certain course, their attention is liable to become taken up with social matters. If women become taken up with the love of men and men with the love of women, and their hearts get enlisted in this way, it is *death* to spiritual growth. I see very much in earnest about this liability, and am disposed to be watchful and careful, and see that this result does not take place if it can be avoided.

We know all true prosperity is founded on loving God first and having the heart fastened permanently on spiritual things. But when persons come here into this free social atmosphere, there is a tendency for them to have their attention too much taken up with their social relations, and so get their hearts turned away from Christ and deep spiritual things. Those who stand as representatives of the Community spirit, must study this subject and see to it that their influence goes to turn the hearts of these individuals in the right direction. We are responsible for much of the influence that comes upon them.

I don't think it is a good plan to surround men or women, who come here and join the Community, with a great deal of attention and love, so as to make their hearts feel fat, as though they had come into a place where all they needed to do was to sail along and enjoy themselves; for that is not so: they have got to go into the judgment, and their hearts must be purified from pleasure-seeking and selfishness. I think at the present time, that some persons are suffering from the diversion of their attention from deep spiritual things, to their social experience. These persons are not sent here for their own pleasure, or for ours, but for the glory of God, and if we love them, we must in some way keep them in the fire of judgment for a good while. That is the universal rule. I don't believe persons can come here from the world without its being necessary for them to go through a good deal of self-examination, in order to become fit vessels for holding the new wine of the kingdom of heaven. Of course, there must be some venture, and persons must get into the water if they would learn to swim. But I think we can do a great deal toward helping these new members, and guiding them in the right direction. There should be a great deal of chastity and continence on the part of the Community toward this class.

"I am satisfied that this matter is worthy of the sincere, earnest consideration of the whole Community. I do not think there is any such thing possible as being born again into the kingdom of heaven, until in some way a person has got to that state where every thing is put out of sight and mind in comparison with receiving the soul's salvation. Persons in earnest to be saved must hate father and mother, sister and brother, sweetheart and lover, and every thing that stands in the way of having their relations to God established beyond all doubt. And this can never be done until continence of heart is reached in some way. No person will ever find Christ while the heart is taken up with lovers and sweethearts. God leads us along gently and with long patience; but I am satisfied we must all come eventually where we forsake all for the knowledge of Christ."

Mr. Noyes and Mr. Cragin arrived this morning from Wallingford.

DAILY JOURNAL
OF ONEIDA COMMUNITY.

A. D. 1866. MAR. 24. NO. 59.

SATURDAY.

SEVERAL teams are engaged to-day drawing sand for the store. The trench for the foundation is now being dug.

J. N. N. writes that notwithstanding business is very dull at the west, he and Mr. Olds are doing quite well.

The correspondence between E. A. Stillman and Mr. Noyes was read last evening. As the Branches at W. and N. Y. are already familiar with it, we will only remark that it was very interesting, and brought up historic scenes and facts in a very vivid way.

Mrs. Knowles is somewhat out of order, both in body and spirit. She is sick, and has been hard and full of unbelief, and indifference to criticism, for sometime.— Several things have transpired, which go to show that there has not as yet been much depth of sincerity in her separation from the spirit of the world. She has talked some about going away. To-day, however, we learn that there are indications that her spirit is softening somewhat.

Mr. Noyes and Mr. Cragin are warmly welcomed to Oneida. Mr. Noyes last evening gave an account of his objects in coming. His remarks will be reported to the Branches in manuscript, so we will not attempt to repeat them here.

The editor of the JOURNAL is informed by private dispatch, that the Willimantic students will spend the approaching "Sabbath" with the Wallingfordians, at Mount Tom. They will remain at that Commune till Tuesday afternoon, when they will return to their field of labor in Windham County. We are justified in whispering this secret in the public ear, by the fact that our paper will not reach the Mount-Tomites until after they have recovered from their surprise. Otherwise we should have preserved a profound and dignified silence.

The bag orders received during the week ending yesterday, amount to $711.

The gardeners are making preparations for their hotbeds.

The grove on the Willow Place farm has been all cut down, and the process of working it up into fire-wood is going on. Most of this work except the splitting is done by horse-power and machinery.

G. N. Miller is preparing to leave for New York next week, to assist in the business there.

The weather continues cold and raw. The landscape except on the hills is mostly free from snow. The sky, however, looks to-day as though there were more snow overhead.

A friend states his grievances as follows:

O. C., March 23.

MR. EDITOR:—Witness one of the ills of complexity. *Scene.* Office of O. C. Yourself busily writing. Enter well dressed stranger, who blandly inquires for C.

Off you post in search of that individual, confident of finding him in an adjoining room, but he is not there, and you go to the Library, and from thence through the Sitting Rooms, and (if near a meal time) through Kitchen and Dining Room, in a pursuit that becomes more eager as it is apparently more hopeless. Having exhausted the main series of probabilities, i. e. the public rooms, you bethink yourself of his private apartment. Where does C burrow? you ask of A, in despair. A tells you he is not certain but thinks it is somewhere in the old Mansion House; but while you are ransacking the dormitories of that building, you are assured by B that you are on a wrong scent, that C is his next neighbor in the Tontine. At the Tontine you find C's room, but C *non est,* and having no longer any clue to his probable whereabouts you wander about the halls and passages in a state of mind bordering on irritability.

Now Mr. Editor, as long as a man is not ubiquitous, and hence cannot be everywhere, and everywhere else, at the same time, we must expect to suffer some inconvenience of this kind, but I think we can and will sometime find a way to remedy it in a great measure.

MARCH.

We believe our correspondent's perplexities are already mitigated in a great measure by the use of signal strokes on the bell, which notify several of our official characters when they are wanted on special business. It is a question whether the Community has yet availed itself of all the advantages which this system of signals offers. Should there not be signals devised for *all* persons who are liable to be called upon to transact business with outsiders?

DAILY JOURNAL
OF ONEIDA COMMUNITY,

A. D. 1866.   MAR. 26.   NO. 60.

MONDAY.

MR. NOYES, this morning, announced the following new

PRINCIPLES OF BUSINESS.

1. Everything for sale except the soul.

2. Prompt clearing out of all dead property at any price that can be got.

The rule of prices—"SELL AS LOW AS YOU CAN," instead of—"Get all you can."

4. Pre-payment in buying and selling.

IN the business-meeting yesterday, it was voted to have the supper hour changed to 6 'oclock, and to have the schools, that will interfere with the business arrangements of the season, close this week.

A letter has been received from J. F. S., relative to the trap stock which the New Britain Company wish to sell to us. His report is favorable to investing in it. The Company do not ask for pay till the stock is worked up into traps and sold.

It has been decided to hire the boss molder at the foundry for six months longer.

Mr. Ackley has been appointed superintendent of the New House cellar, and is to see that it is kept in a neat and cleanly condition.

Mr. Clark has been appointed to superintend the measuring, selling and delivery of fire-wood to our hired people.

Mr. Newhouse and William A. Hinds have been appointed a committee to sell the guns in our possession that we do not need.

We learn that the proposed visit of the Willimantic students to Wallingford, did not take place yesterday, as our dispatch led us to expect, but has been deferred to a future period. Doubtless we might throw some light on the question as to when the visit will take place, but, as the war correspondents used to say, the success of the movement requires us to be silent on that point until the plan of the commanding officer is more fully developed. We predict, however, that the Mount Tomites will be taken completely by surprise, for at such an hour as they know not, the troop from Willimantic will come upon them.

Mr. Noyes has begun his protracted meeting with the Community, on the subject of Business. On Saturday evening he delivered a discourse of thrilling interest on the Pentecostal principle in regard to property. Last evening he discoursed on the subject of Prices, and Community-covetousness. At the conclusion of the discussion last evening, he nominated Mr. Cragin as Community-Agent, with full powers to sell, after due consultation with Mr. Noyes and the Community, all dead property, at such prices as he sees fit.

March is grim and wintry yesterday and to-day. One of our sweeping northwest snow-storms set in yesterday, and continues this forenoon. The wind roars over the roofs and through the trees, and drifts the snow at every available point. We hope it is the farewell storm of winter.

The sales of agricultural implements during the past week have amounted to over $400.

A son and a daughter of Mr. Jones are here on a visit to their father.

THE TRAPPERS.

Some mention of the organization, doings, and objects of the Community trappers may not be uninteresting to your readers. The organization is composed of the class of boys that attend Mr. Henderson's school, who have elected officers in regular military style; having a captain and secretary, the rest acting as privates. Their field of operations is quite extensive; commencing a little above the mouth of Bear creek on the Oneida creek and extending to what is called the picnic ground, together with a part of Mud and Sconondoa creeks. The boys are divided into three parties, and each party has a fair portion of the whole line to attend to. They have caught forty muskrats already, and say that they have but just begun. The adventures that attend trappers in more extended fields also attend these. They recount in glowing terms of no less than two overturns of the boat, thereby "ducking" its occupants—of many "narrow escapes" from the same fate—the building of one boat, and the wrecking of another &c., &c.

As to the objects of the organization, I am not very well posted, but this much I *do* know, that the boys have no private end in view; the proceeds from the sale of the fur going into the general treasury.

Up many times as early as half past four o'clock in the morning, they fulfil in a measure Paul's injunction, ' be instant in season and out of season."   E. S. B.

DAILY JOURNAL
OF ONEIDA COMMUNITY,

A. D. 1866. MAR. 27. NO. 61.

TUESDAY.

MR. NOYES has had the new business principles printed in the form of posters which have been put up in conspicuous places throughout the buildings.

Mr. Jones's relatives left for home yesterday.

The printing of yesterday's JOURNAL was delayed till afternoon, which will explain its non-arrival at the Branches by the usual mails.

Mr. Underwood and Charles Marks leave for Wallingford, by the way of Springfield, to-morrow.

Forty-two bushels of potatoes have been sold to Thorburn and Co., New York, for $2,75 per bushel.

Surveyors are here to-day for the purpose of surveying the Petric land, which is to be sold.

The weather is growing mild again to-day. The ground is covered with snow, not deeply however, except where it is drifted. The robins were merry this morning over the returning prospect of warmer days.

Mr. Noyes talked again on business last evening. The nomination of Mr. Cragin as Commissioner to sell property, was unanimously ratified, and Mr. Cragin made oath to be faithful to God and inspiration in the exercise of the duties of his office. The following were Mr. Noyes's remarks at the opening of the discussion:

"I find that the Pentecostal text I have been preaching on will carry us clear through; that it contains in it all the doctrines, really, that I have put on to that poster of "Business Principles." In the first place there is, "sell all." They sold their goods and lands, and of course all dead property. So far as the universality of the sales went, that point is evidently in the Pentecostal text; and it is implied and necessarily involved in it, that they put the prices down to the lowest figures, and on all dead property invited the buyers to fix their own price. So it is evident at once that low prices were included. Prepayment was also a part of the arrangement. It would never have done for them in selling goods and lands to have taken notes, or sold on credit. They wanted the cash to lay at the apostles' feet. When lively business is going on you must have cash. It is not said or hinted that they brought any notes or accounts to the apostles; they brought the money. Therefore the doctrine of prepayment is in that example.

"I don't think we can do better than plant ourselves firmly on that good old example and stick to it, considering ourselves a Pentecostal Church, and remain so forever. The business among the primitive believers was conducted in the most convenient manner; those who had property went and sold it themselves. Our circumstances are a little different. We have come into a state of Communism, where our business is the business of a single family, and we hold our property in common. Doing business in an organic way under such circumstances it will be necessary that we appoint some man as our commissioner. And in order to commit ourselves to the day of Pentecost principles, it is expedient that we should invite God to appoint a commissioner for himself, whose business shall be, to see what ought to be sold and then sell it.

"I may say that we individually deliver our property to God, and that in one sense it is important for us to do so. A man does but half own property unless he has the power of transferring it. Mere possession is not ownership, and God cannot be said to own our property here unless he can swing it where he wants it—unless it is in such a state that if he wants to transfer it for other purposes, he can sell it. Ownership is not complete until it gives transferrability—entails are not complete ownership. So far as our property gets into a shape where we cannot transfer it, or into land that we do not transfer, to that extent we lose the ownership of it. Property in that shape is but half as available as it might be if we held it where we could turn it. I want our property clear from all incumbrances and in the hands of inspiration, so that God can really own and use it as he pleases. I want to see it free from our covetousness and stickiness. I am not afraid that God will squander it, or leave it to go to waste. I have much **greater confidence in him than in landed titles. If he** gets it into his hands he will make it the most useful to us and to mankind.

"I feel a little anxious about giving such power as has been proposed to Mr. Cragin. He is a good man and I have great confidence in him. I don't know of anybody I would put into this office sooner than I would him; but it is a great and very important office. If he stands as the agent of God in the matter, he will be sure to do something, and likely as not he will do something that will make a panic in the Community. But I am prepared to risk it. What I want is, not that he should look out for the interests of the Community, but for the interests of God, and if he is going to be sworn in I am going to swear him to act for God in regard to the property of this Community."

Mrs. Knowles is improving, we learn, both in spirit and body. She accepts of criticism, and appears to be working out of the cloud of unbelief that has been over her.

Mr. Wildstrand, of Minnesota, writes to us that the Marist Community, of which he proposes to be the founder, will be set agoing in a few weeks. He says: "We would be glad to get all the advice you would give us, how to manage things, what to do, and what to make and every thing else."

DAILY JOURNAL
OF ONEIDA COMMUNITY.

A. D. 1866. MAR. 28. NO. 62.

WEDNESDAY.
TO THE FAMILY.

I HEREBY give notice to the members of the family, that I will be in the Reception Room, from quarter past six to half past seven P. M., for the purpose of receiving contributions of jewelry or other property that persons may wish to have sold or disposed of for paying off our national debt; also for the purpose of consulting with the members respecting the sale of Community property and other matters relating to the new Commission.

G. CRAGIN.

Mr. Cragin in his new capacity as Commissioner of Sale, yesterday issued the following notice, which was printed and distributed to the Community:

NOTICE.

Members of the Community who hold real estate, mortgages, notes, or property of any description, outside of the Community, are hereby requested to report the same to me or to those whom I may hereafter appoint as my assistants.

The members of the family are also notified that all dead property is to be sold or burnt up. Let nothing remain above ground that has not life in it. Either burn or bury whatever is not convertible into money or use for God and his cause.   G. CRAGIN.

The heavens appear to have ratified Mr. Cragin's appointment in a marked way. His first day in office was signalized by the sale of the steam-engine, for the sum of $1050. It was sold to a man in Clinton. He had met Mr. Clark and learned from him that we had an engine for sale and came over at once to examine it. He called at Willow Place yesterday afternoon, and Mr. Cragin happened to be in the office there at the time. Mr. C. jumped into the buggy with the man and they drove over to the engine. The man briefly examined it, and inquired the price. Mr. Cragin said $1200. The man said he could only give $1000. Mr. C. offered to split the difference. No. Mr. C. told him he could have it for 1000, if he would deliver it at Clinton himself. No, he had no teams. Mr. Cragin then offered it for $1050 and we would deliver it. The man agreed to this, and the engine was sold in five or ten minutes after they arrived from Willow Place.

The work of removing the engine to Clinton has already begun. It is desirable to have it all transported while the roads are in a good condition.

The Petrie land is sold; thirty-two and seventeen-hundredths acres. Price $100 per acre. $775 were paid down; the balance is to be paid between May and September 1. The Community contract to give a deed on the receipt of full payment.

The proposal is now under consideration to have an auction to sell cows, and other property suitable to be disposed of in such a way. It is thought that more can be realized by an auction, than by private sale.

Mr. Noyes resumed the business discussion with a criticism of the salesmen, particularly those of Oneida.— The criticism will be reported in full by D. J. B.

Mr. Leete is here on a short visit. He appears bright and in good spirits, ready for Community service.

METEOROLOGICAL.

March 27, 1866.

6 o'clock A. M. Mercury at N. side of old Butternut tree, 18deg. Wind N. W. Sun rises clear, but is soon hid by dark clouds across the S. E. horizon.

12 o'clock. Mercury at 28deg., nearly clear, wind slight and about N. W.

6 o'clock P. M. 26deg., clear atmosphere, gentle breeze from the west, beautiful but slightly hazy sunset.

DAILY JOURNAL
OF ONEIDA COMMUNITY.

A. D. 1866. MAR. 29. NO. 63.

THURSDAY.

IT is fully determined to have an auction—probably on the 7th of April. Some twenty cows and heifers are to be sold, besides a variety of other things, all of which we will announce in the JOURNAL when the advertisement is perfected.

A large amount of enthusiasm prevails in the family with respect to the proposed auction, and every one considers himself or herself a member of the committee of the whole, to hunt up dead property that can be sold. The women held a large and enthusiastic meeting on the subject yesterday, and appointed a committee to receive contributions.

The conversation last evening was on a variety of topics and somewhat fragmentary in its character. We will give some paragraphs:

Mr. Noyes.—While I was getting out the poster, "Antidote to the Cholera" &c., I seemed to come in contact with a diabolical spirit that brought a headache upon me, with which I suffered tremendously for three days. It was not a natural physiological affair, but a spirtual pressure producing headache, toothache, &c. I emerged from it and have been consciously more free in mind and strong in brain than ever before. But I was interested to-day to notice that when I turned my mind to fixing the poster for the proposed auction, I fell in with the same spirit, and was again struck in the head with the same sensations. I had the headache and toothache, and general nervous torment. The heart was at peace and all right, but the brain and nervous system seemed to be thrown into the fire. The thing happening so in both cases in connection with the attempt to get out a poster, makes it a rather curious and interesting fact.— It will bear some study.

My impression is that the devil, the evil one, the reprobate spirit that is keeping charge of this world, is jealous of my getting out before the public, or of my doing any thing that points in the direction of a push towards publicity. It is the effort of that spirit to keep all things quiet, as the sailors try to do when their ship gets on fire; they batten down the hatches and try to keep the smoke from coming out, and are very jealous of the blaze, and determined not to let it come out in sight.— Such seems to be the devil's theory about me. But sometime or other I shall be a public man.

Mr. Jos'yn.—The sooner that time comes the better.

Mr. Noyes.—I have got to break through the shell; but it seems as though there was somebody ready to strike me every time I tried to peck through.

Mr. Cragin.—I guess the devil only hits the shell, and perhaps he will make it all the easier for you to get out after all.

Mr. Cragin.—I feel that we are making good progress in breaking our way through the financial embarrassments that surround and beset us. But I don't want to be let up, and gravitate back into a state of unconcern I desire to keep wide-awake to do God's business, and not stop until we get out of debt, nor then either. want to learn to do business on a great scale, and handle and get possession of mankind, and be at home in all circumstances.

And here I will make a remark. Some have decided to give up little articles of fancy, such as finger-rings, and seem to feel a new spirit immediately after deciding upon such a step. Now I consider finger-rings dead property, utterly needless in every sense. Pins, that are useful for holding the ends of collars, may be serviceable to some extent. But I don't believe the time has come for us to wear finger-rings, which are mere ornaments and an inconvenience to the hands when at work. For myself, I had rather wait till Mr. and Mrs. Noyes set us the example. When we see Mrs. Noyes with rings on her fingers, I will vote to have all the women and girls provided with rings, black, white, or blue, to suit their fancy; but till she does set the fashion I think we had better part with all we have.

The engine was all loaded yesterday and part of it shipped to its destination. The two boilers, weighing about three tuns each, were drawn over to the turnpike. The whole is being sent forward to-day. I should have mentioned yesterday that the engine was sold according to the new principle of pre-payment.

The lot of beaver skins bought by Mr. Campbell at Peterboro, C. W., amounting to between eighty and ninety pounds, has been sold at considerable loss.

We learn that no potatoes have been sold to Thorburn and Co., of New York, as stated in the JOURNAL of Tuesday. An offer has been received through the Agency from R. L. Allen and Co., of $2,75 per bushel for Peach Blow Seedlings, and the Agency have been instructed to accept the offer.

Myron arrived home last night.

METEOROLOGICAL.

March 28.

6 A. M. white frost—cloudless sky, with almost an imperceptible haze in the East. Wind cold from the S. E. Mercury 18deg.

12 o'clock. Some wind from S. S. W. A general heavy haze over the whole canopy. Sun nearly obscure. Mercury 43deg. (At 11 there was a large circle surrounding the sun.)

6 o'clock P. M. Mercury 34deg. Wind nearly South, entirely cloudy with a trifling snow storm.

DAILY JOURNAL
OF ONEIDA COMMUNITY.

A. D. 1866. MAR. 30. NO. 64.

FRIDAY.

IN the meeting last evening we noted the following paragraphs of conversation :

Mr. Noyes.—I should advise the new commission to rely mainly on preaching the general principles of the Gospel of the day of Pentecost, and not much on personal demands. I don't like to have the impression of our general doctrine on this subject frittered away by too much talk about personal and individual matters, and small puttering with watches, rings, and such things. I should hope the truth finally would tear open the hearts of all, in such a way that whatever is right in these things, will come freely and not by dunning.—I think we have reason to be thankful for the movements that are being made. I see by adding up, that we have disposed of property within the week, that gives us extra funds to put into our business and meet demands to the amount of over $10,000. The figures I believe make out just about $11,000.

Mr. Cragin.—Mr. Noyes is in favor of our selling house-lots to our work people. If we do anything about it, we ought to have a good Committee for the purpose of examining the subject, and determining the locations where we would wish to sell such lots. I would suggest Mr. Hamilton appoint such a Committee to-morrow night.

Speaking of the auction, Mr. Hamilton said : " Mr. Noyes remarked that if we get free from covetousness ourselves, it will tend to remove covetousness in those with whom we deal. I have been interested in thinking of that to-day. I see that will be the way to handle masses of men. We must become in spirit what we would make other men. We must be a great reservoir of the spiritual fascination we wish to throw over them."

Mr. Noyes.—That is a very important idea. All kinds of spirits are catching, and the spirit of Pentecost among the rest. If we are fairly taken down by that spirit, we have every reason to expect there will be a great contagion of it that will spread all around us. We see what an outburst there was from the heavenly world 1800 years ago, of the spirit of true Communism. There is no reason for doubting that God will send forth that spirit again in the same power. This will be an antidote to the Cholera, a counter check, a counter movement. I want to have the Oneida Community take this for its ambition: to keep up within itself, and in all its branches and organs, at New York and Wallingford, and steadily press upon the world, the genuine spirit of the day of Pentecost—Communism with God. That is the fundamental principle of the Communism of the day of Pentecost—Communism with God; and from that growing out into Communism with one another. It was the assurance of faith that would resolve mankind into one family, as far as things admitted, and have faith take full possession of the hearts of all. It is the business and ambition of the Oneida Community to become the constant embodiment, reservoir, and medium of that spirit, flowing out and pressing upon the world around, and holding on patiently, and quietly, in faith, till the great barriers of covetousness give way, and the masses of mankind around us are swallowed up in the same spirit. Then all the capital that is now held in the service of selfishness will flow into the hands of God.

Now whatever you want other folks to do and be, do and be yourselves. Give place to God in your hearts and minds, and don't be afraid that he will make fools of you or lead you into fanaticism, or that he will waste your property. We have taken the principles of the day of Pentecost, and worked them out by a close analysis, and put them into ordinary language in those four principles of business, and one of the wisest business men in this vicinity—Mr. Henry Wilson—pronounces them sound. It is sure to be found that everything that Christ and the Primitive Church did, was sound. It is perfectly safe to risk all upon their principles.

Potatoes again ! " *New-York, March 29.* It was a bull about the potatoes. Mr. E., who saw Allen and Co., says they offered $2,75 per bbl., not per bushel, which I regret to report." The potatoes will not be sent.

The company who transported the engine yesterday, had very good luck. When they had got within about one hundred rods of their destination, the tire on one of the wagon-wheels broke. They immediately pried up the axle-tree, took off the wheel and carried it to a blacksmith and had it repaired. While this was being done the other teams went forward and unloaded. This was just accomplished when the wheel was fixed, and the other team was ready to unload. This was the only accident.

Myron's sales on his last trip were—bags, about $1800, silk $100, mops $100, hats $50, apples $30. Total $2100.

Nearly $11,000 worth of property has been sold during the past week, and thus made available for discharging the national debt. Mr. Campbell informs us that he has received about $1,200 of Mrs. Tobey's property, and sold her house and land for $1700 more. The Petrie land amounts to about $3200. The engine brought $1050. Cattle have been sold to the amount of $900. Total $10,950.

METEOROLOGICAL.
March 29.

6 A. M. Mercury 36 deg. Wind South. No sunrise. 12 o'clock. Mercury 31 deg. Wind nearly South. A trifling fall of rain and snow.

6 P. M. Mercury 32. Wind West. Cloudy.

DAILY JOURNAL
OF ONEIDA COMMUNITY.

A. D. 1866. MAR. 31. NO. 69.

SATURDAY.

IN the conversation Thursday evening, Mr. Noyes made the following remarks:

Mr. Noyes.—If any body will take the principle that I have been insisting upon, that we should be free and anxious to sell, and be very chaste about buying, I should be perfectly willing to risk the whole of our financial operations without keeping accounts, for our own benefit. I know we should get rich. I have no doubt but that if we should steadily pursue that principle and sell off all dead property and keep our productions or staple manufactures well sustained, we should clear ourselves from all mortgages and debts in a very short time.

I think it would be well in this connection to discuss what our policy should be about tenant houses. There are two courses we can take. One is to go on putting up tenant houses and renting them until we get a great village of tenants. The other way is to encourage our employees to buy lots and build their own houses, or get us to build them and pay us for them. We might encourage those tenants we have over across the creek to buy their houses and lots, and let us keep a part of their wages until they are gradually paid for. These are the two policies before us, and it is a fair question which it is best for us to follow.

Mr. Burt.—I think this is a fair question, and a great deal is involved in it. The present system throws a heavy expense of building upon us, and thus we are liable, from time to time to have our houses unrented, and so get no profit from them. On the other hand get men to build and own their houses and we are free from all liabilities and risks.

Mr. Noyes.—If we place a village off as far as the Hitchcock farm I should be as willing to have people own their houses as not. If we cannot control them by moral and spiritual influences I should not expect to control them by house rent. There are several disadvantages in going on with the present system and keeping possession of the houses we build. We should have to get such houses insured or else run the risk they are exposed to by men we cannot control and are not insured themselves in heaven. That is one objection to furnishing houses. Another is, that it is a notorious fact that it takes a very sharp, hard-hearted man to make money as a landlord, or to get what he ought to have, to make himself whole and cover all the repairs and liabilities from fire, &c. And then I may say it is not according to our policy or in keeping with our principles, to go on and cover the land with little tenant houses for single families. We expect to build great Communities. I had rather if we have got to make use

of the system for a time, leave it to somebody else to build and take care of such houses. This system of little families living in houses by themselves belongs to the old concern. We can spend our time, talents and means in something better than putting up isolated cottages for other folks. And at the same time it will be a good thing for those who live around us in this isolated way, and are likely to for some time to come, to be encouraged to buy, and live in their own houses. It will be an advance for them beyond living as tenants and paying rent. It would increase their civilization, independence and self respect, and really bring them nearer the state of actual communism.

So it would not only save us great trouble and responsibility, but it would benefit our tenants. And if our three water-powers are well employed we shall be able to give employment to a great many work-people in the trap, silk and bag businesses. I hope in time to see a village built up on the Hitchcock farm. Every thing seems to favor it. I think it would be good policy for us, in our minds at least, to lay that farm out into village lots, and perhaps invite persons who want to come and live near us to buy there. Such persons could labor for us in our factories, or could raise small fruits, and perhaps large fruits also, for us to use in our preserving department. I do not know why we may not offer folks as good advantages for making a settlement there as they do in Vineland. There are more chances of getting a living and of building up a village where there is a water power than in such a place as the Depot. Except for their railroads they have no special advantage in such a place as the Depot, while we have three good water-powers; and the Hitchcock farm lies midway between them and convenient to all. It is a good place for a village.

I would go on if I could and sell what we have already built. We must keep in mind that just as fast as we build up a village around us, we are making customers for our store, as well as laborers in our work-shops. I suppose the whole scheme depends upon our being willing to sell and on our being liberal enough to sell freely and wisely. I think you could easily get up an ambition among your tenants to buy and own their houses. I know it would be a real advantage to them.

Mr. Noyes left for New York yesterday at 5 P. M.

Mr. Campbell arrived home this morning.

Mr. Hamilton reported the following names for the committee on locating house-lots to be sold: Mr. Barron, Mr. Kellogg, Mr. Kinsley and Mr. Vanvelzer.

Bag orders for the week ending March 30, amount to $1450.

METEOROLOGICAL.

March 30.

6 A. M. Mercury 26deg. Wind west. Slight snow in the night.

12 M. Mercury 32deg. Westerly wind.

6 P. M. Mercury 30deg. Clear, no wind.

DAILY JOURNAL
OF ONEIDA COMMUNITY.

A. D. 1866.   APR. 1.   NO. 70.

MONDAY.

A PRINCIPAL topic of interest, and one sure to continue so during the present week, is the coming Auction. About one hundred and forty posters have been printed and are being distributed over the neighboring country. The poster reads as follows:

Annual Sales of Stock, Agricultural Implements, &c. The Oneida Community proposes hereafter to hold annually, on the grounds near the Community buildings, an Auction and Fair, for the sale of its productions and manufactures. The first annual sale will take place on Saturday, April 7th, beginning at 10 o'clock A. M. when the following articles will be offered to the highest bidder: 14 cows, 6 heifers, several half-blood Ayrshire calves, and 2 shoats. Also a variety of Implements of Agriculture from the Community Factory, consisting of about 60 Plows, including 40 Peekskills, Nos. 21 and 21H; 9 Harrows; a number of Corn and wheel cultivators; also clevises, coulters and wheels for plows; several Musical Instruments, including 4 Violins, 2 Flutes. 1 Fife, 1 Guitar, 1 Snare Drum &c., and various other articles too numerous to mention. A salesroom will at the same time be opened in the Community Mansion, where will be offered for sale at very low prices, Traveling Bags, Ladies' Satchels, Wool Hats, Green-house Plants, Pictures, &c., &c. Terms of sale: Cash on delivery of goods. Auctioneer, George Woodworth.

It has been decided to use the Ironing-room at the Tontine for a salesroom. The following Committees have been appointed:

General Superintendents and collectors of articles for sale: A. Kinsley, E. Kellogg, O. L. Aiken.

Committee of Women to receive and arrange articles in Salesroom: Mrs. Vanvelzar, Chloe Seymour, Helen M. Hutchins, Jane A. Kinsley.

Recorders of sales and money Receivers; W. A. Hinds, E. S. Burnham, Geo. Campbell, C. A. Burt.

Receivers at Salesroom: Mrs. Vanvelzar, Annie Hatch, Miss Nunns, Mrs. Sears, Myron Kinsley.

Committee on Stock: Mr. Kellogg, Martin Kinsley, A. Barron, L. H. Bradley.

Committee on Agricultural Tools: M. L. Worden, H. C. Clark, C. A. Burt.

Committee on Bags; W. H, Woolworth, E. S. Burnham, H. C. Noyes, A. S. Bailey.

Committee on Musical Instruments: E. L. Hatch, Charles Vanvelzar, E. P. Inslee.

Committee on Books: Chloe Seymour, T. L. Pitt, Geo. Campbell, L. A. Thayer.

Committee on Bee Hives: D. P. Nash.

Committee on regulation of Prices: E. H. Hamilton, W. H. Woolworth, H. C. Noyes, S. K. Dunn.

The amount of bags shipped during the month of March, was—to O. C. N. Y. B., $209; to other parties $5,000. Total $5,209. Total for the same month last year, $3,070. Balance in favor of this year $2,139.

There is some inquiry if our Foundry, and other property at that point, is for sale. In the business meeting yesterday there was a unanimous expression in favor of selling if opportunity offers. It was also thought it would be a good plan to advertise the property there as for sale, and W. A. Hinds was requested to make out a statement with regard to it.

It was also proposed in the business meeting to fit up the Red School house as a dwelling house, and put a cellar under it.

Mr Bennett the tin ware manufacturer at the Depot wishes us to make him a lot of hooks for holding cave-troughs.

Mr. Miller is to be instructed to examine into the merits of a new method of soldering tin fruit cans, that is in vogue at Cincinnati.

Messrs. Gillchrist of Verona last autumn mentioned to Martin Kinsley that they had a few thousand dollars which they would be glad to loan the Community. We did not then want to borrow, but after the demand for $6000 was made upon us by Mr. Wager, a couple of weeks since, Messrs. Gillchrist were notified that we were in want of money to meet said obligation; and they have taken considerable pains to obtain and loan us $3000, on note for six months, with the probability that the money will not be called for until the expiration of twelve months. It is proposed to use $2000 of the above money in releasing the Petric place from mortgage now held by Henry Wilson.

METEOROLOGICAL.
March 31.

6 A. M. Mercury 29. Wind South. Cloudy.
12 M. Mercury 43. Wind South. Rain.
6 P. M. Mercury 36. Rain. Snow on the hills during the afternoon.

April 1.

6 A. M. Mercury 37. Cloudy and dark, with but little wind.
12 M. Mercury 35. Wind South.
6 P. M. Mercury 35. Cloudy.

DAILY JOURNAL
OF ONEIDA COMMUNITY.

A. D. 1866. APR. 3. NO. 68.

TUESDAY.

THE trap sales during the month of March were $902, 83. Sales during the same month last year $975, 50.

The sales of Agricultural Implements during March were $858,61.

The principal and interest due on the mortgage held by Philip Wager ($6,420) were yesterday paid, and the mortgage assigned to Francis Whaley, Mr. Leet's friend, who has paid on the same $2,000, and is expected to pay $2,000 more to-morrow. Mr. Whaley assigned back to one of the Community members an interest of $2,000 in the mortgage, so that he owns only a $4,000 interest in it. Mr. Whaley agrees that this $4,000 may run three years at seven per cent, and that the Community may pay it in two years on giving him two months notice

The following remark was made by Mr. Cragin on Sunday evening:

Mr. Cragin.—I feel that we are starting on a new basis in regard to business, and I am anxious to walk in the spirit. I believe we can, and that God will give us grace. I know Mr. Noyes struck an effectual blow at covetousness and selfishness in the late move in regard to selling out whatever the Lord may wish sold.— I am anxious to co-operate with Mr. Noyes and carry out his policy effectually, and secure the results that his move anticipated. I believe God is more interested in this than in the minor point in regard to our securing a good income from the sales. He is looking for the destruction of the works of the devil, so as to make room for his coming kingdom. It is our work to destroy selfishness, so that God's kingdom can flow in. The work has commenced here in our midst. In a sense we have failed as a firm doing business on a worldly basis. And now we have made an assignment of all our property to God and Jesus Christ. When a man makes an assignment he has no control of the property after that, unless it is as an agent. It is in the hands of the assignee. We have made an assignment of our property; and hereafter we are attending to the business as agents of the Lord, to whom the property is made over. I believe he will give us his spirit to actuate us in doing business for him. He will help us fix the prices in a way to secure the end he has in view.

The annual dispensation of house-cleaning began yesterday. Mrs. Harriet Kinsley, Mrs. Kelly, and J. P. Hutchins appear to be the leading functionaries in the campaign. House-cleaning under the old order of isolated families was generally a simultaneous and vigorous attack on the whole house, the horrors of which to the masculine part of the family were once graphically portrayed by Dr. Franklin. In the Community, however, the field is so large that the attack has to be made by more gradual and strategic approaches which enable all sensitive bipeds to take warning and get things in order for a timely surrender to the artillery of mopsticks and bed-wrenches; and on the whole the warfare is conducted on more considerate and humane principles than in ordinary society.

Mr. Franks again urges the Community to become practically interested in his Virginia land. He has been informed that the Community have no desire of again entering into negotiations or even correspondence concerning it.

By a curious mistake our yesterday's JOURNAL was both dated and numbered wrong. The date should have been April 2, and the number 67, instead of 70.

Yesterday was a genuine Spring day. The sun shone clearly most of the day. The air was pleasantly warm. The snow had disappeared from the fields, except on the hills, and the drifts in hollows and under the creek's banks. Under foot the mud was abundant, which is one of the characteristic features of Spring at Oneida. Altogether the day was a pleasant contrast to most of our March days this season.

Mr. Kelly in a recent letter says:

" A little affair occurred to-day, which shows the benefit of account keeping. I left my two bags of silk in the wholesale room of Rosenblatt & Co., over night. This morning I went there to get a part of my silk, and in changing my silk from one bag to the other I laid a roll of stick twist on the counter, and started away without putting it into the bag. Had just got across the street when it occurred to me that I had left the twist out. I went back and found the man who takes care of their silk mixing my twist up with their silk. He supposed it was some they had bought—thought they had bought a "heap of it." He did not know anything how much he had taken of mine. So I had to take account of my stick twist and find out how much belonged to me.— Found he had taken four or five hundred. My account comes out right every night."

METEOROLOGICAL.

April 2.

6 A. M. Mercury 32deg. Cloudy—no wind.
12 M. Mercury 46deg. Clear and pleasant.
6 P. M. Mercury 40deg. Clear and fine.

DAILY JOURNAL
OF ONEIDA COMMUNITY.

A. D. 1866. APR. 4. NO. 68.

WEDNESDAY.

A TRAP order was received this morning for 6 doz. muskrat, 6 doz. otter, and 12 doz. beaver, amounting in all to $292,50.

To-day is the third pleasant and beautiful day, with which April has already favored us. The robins, the sparrows, the blue-birds and the crows have been jubilant in the warmth and sunshine, and this morning a veritable phebe arrived, and added its notes to the chorus of song. Wild ducks are seen occasionally following the course of the creek. Somebody's boys were seen fishing in the creek yesterday. Whether they found any thing larger than minnows is doubtful.

Several letters have been written to Mr. Strong, by the Northern Vermonters, rejecting his pretensions of spiritual paternity, and fully indorsing Mr. Noyes.

The Green-house presents the finest display of flowers now that we have ever seen in it. The Azaleas, of which there are a number of varieties, have been in full bloom during the past week. Several varieties of roses are also in bloom, including the Lamark, a most delicate and highly perfumed white rose, and the splendid Augusta, which has been flowering for several months, and bids fair to continue for a good while to come.— The Cactuses are putting forth their great flower buds. Orange blossoms fill the air around them with their rich perfume. Pelargoniums and numerous other flowers add their beauty to the scene. There are forty-three different kinds of plants in blossom, besides many varieties of some kinds. There are nineteen varieties of Azaleas in full bloom.

Ransom Reid was one year old on Monday. He walks alone, and is a bright, lusty boy. Little Maud grows finely.

Lady Campbell is now able to go to her meals in the dining-room, without assistance, and seems cheerful and bright withal. Mrs. S. B. Nash is also quite smart these days, and yesterday went to the dining-room to dinner, the first time for many months.

Not quite right yet. We notice on examining a file of the JOURNAL that the numbering has been wrong since Saturday last. Saturday's paper was numbered 69 instead of 65. Hence, Monday's paper became 70, instead of 66. Hence, moreover yesterday's paper should have been 67 instead of 68. It is not necessary to explain how the mistake originally started, or how it was perpetuated yesterday. We are right again now, and intend to keep so.

The conversation last evening was mostly on the subject of the principle of Pre-payment. There was a feeling of hearty sympathy with it and a desire expressed to carry it out in all our business operations as fast as possible.

Pruning trees and preparing hot-beds are going on.

The work on the foundation of the Store has begun and the carpenters are busy with their part of the job. It will probably take till some time in May to finish the job. The building has been raised about fourteen inches.

METEOROLOGICAL.

April 3.

6 A. M. Mercury 30 deg. White frost. Clear.
12 M. Mercury 54 deg. Clear and pleasant.
6 P. M. Mercury 52 deg. Clear.

DAILY JOURNAL
OF ONEIDA COMMUNITY.

A. D. 1866.   APR. 5.   NO. 69.

THURSDAY.

A LARGE flock of pigeons was noticed flying eastward this morning.

L. F. Dunn appeared at the dinner table yesterday. There has been a marked improvement in his spirit and health of late.

In the course of the meeting last evening Mr. Cragin made the following remarks:

"I have an impression that there is now a good deal of harmony between Mr. Inslee and George Hamilton, and that there has been a great victory gained in their case. When I was here six or eight weeks ago, there was more or less trial and lack of harmony and unity between them in their business.

"Surely there is no limit to the grace of God. I confess my hatred of unbelief in every form. We should love to receive orders, no matter if we are apparently on the invalid list. I confess I am not on that list, and do not intend to be. I don't care how weak I am, or how much suffering I may have, I keep up the confession to myself that I am a well man, and that the resurrection life of Christ is in me, contending against disease and death. I believe that is consistent with the doctrines and philosophy of Christ's gospel. We all certainly believe, or at least I do, that Christ is in us; and hen if he is in us it is a fact that his resurrection is in us—there is immortal life in us. It is working: it is mighty in overcoming unbelief and evil in every form. I desire that this whole Community may give place to that life in us, and not give place to any thing that denies these facts. There is the point of conflict between unbelief and faith—between the power of the devil and the power of Christ. I am sure we shall be victorious just in proportion as we side with Christ against symptoms, appearances and feeling.

"We need this same resurrection-outlook of faith in our business, as much as in personal victories. I think God is interested in us mainly as a unit composed of many members. He is deeply interested in the organic, vital work that is knitting us to Mr. Noyes as our true head. I believe that as we honor Mr. Noyes in the spirit of loyalty to the truth, we honor Christ."

Mr. Delatre's favorite bird, the Purple Finch, has made its appearance again, and is full of song and activity these sunny days.

Four stone-masons are at work on the foundation of the store to-day. There was some talk last evening as to when the building would be ready for occupation.— Mr. Hamilton thought it would take about five weeks, after the stone work was completed. Mr. Cragin said he should be satisfied if the building was all ready by the 1st of June. The unfavorable weather for the past two or three weeks, has delayed the work on the foundation.

A trap order for 3 doz. otter, was received this morning from Walsh, Coulter & Co., New York.

Martin Kinsley and one of the hired men have been engaged for several days in breaking a colt. She appears to be a very bad tempered animal, and is disposed to kick a great deal. When first harnessed she would allow nothing to touch her hind legs, without a grand kicking demonstration. Several days steady driving with another horse appears to have given her some new ideas as to her proper function in this world, and there is some prospect of making a decently behaved beast of her.

Every one is hoping that our fine weather will continue till after the Auction is over.

To-day is beautiful—warm and full of sunshine. The atmosphere is smoky, and the hills and sky remind one of Indian Summer.

METEOROLOGICAL.

April 4.

6 A. M. Mercury 50 deg.
12 M. Mercury 68 deg.
6 P. M. Mercury 66 deg.
The day was clear and beautiful throughout.

DAILY JOURNAL
OF ONEIDA COMMUNITY.

A. D. 1866.   APR. 6.   NO. 70.

FRIDAY.

THE frogs began their concerts last night.

Letters from Mr. Olds were received yesterday. They were criticised some for their continued iteration about business being dull. No matter if it is dull, it is a poor plan for our agents to be talking in that strain all the time.

Preparations for the Auction are going on vigorously. The women by extra exertion finished their ironing yesterday, so that the room could be used to-day for arranging the articles for sale. The grounds around the house are being cleared of their winter accumulation of rubbish. The agricultural implements will be sold at the horse-barn. Other articles will be sold at the Tontine. The auctioneer engaged is said to be one of the best in the country.

NOTES OF LAST EVENING'S CONVERSATION.

Mr. Woolworth.—I was thinking to-day of our new business principles, and of the proposition that we should adopt pre-payment, as soon as possible. I thought I should like to get into Mr. Noyes's spirit, and have true faith about this matter, and not look at it through unbelief and the spirit of the world. I wou' look at it in the true light. I am satisfied there is an important revolution involved in this movement. But I don't want to see any bug-bears that are not there—not any that unbelief suggests, at any rate. Every such important principle as this, before being adopted, has to encounter a certain amount of opposition from unbelief. The devil is always ready to throw cold water upon it and make it look very formidable.

Mr. Hamilton.—W. A. H. and I had a consultation to-day and made a little beginning in the direction of pre-payment. We concluded to put on all bills going away, after this time, an offer of one and a half per cent. discount on all remittances made immediately on the receipt of the invoice or bill. I believe that is, substantially, what they are doing at the Agency. Probably we shall print something on the bills when we are fully determined what to say. I am inclined to think it would be a good resolution to begin with, to take all the funds we receive in pre-payment and use them in pre-payment again.

Mr. Cragin.—Are you now buying on the thirty days system for any department?

Mr. Hamilton.—We have not made any decided change in policy. We have not bought much lately, and are not fairly up with the old thirty days accounts.

Mr. Hinds.—Do you think, Mr. Cragin, we had better adopt the policy of pre-payment, immediately?

Mr. Cragin.—My feelings run in that direction. The more I think about what Mr. Noyes said to the family and to me, the more anxious I am to have a beginning made. I should like to have the family go into a committee of the whole, and have all our business men and women make this a matter of prayer, and seek to know the best way of pleasing the powers over us.

I am anxious to push the sale of landed property as fast as we can. I would like to have bills got out very soon, offering the Wilson place, saw-mill, foundry, etc., and also the stone quarry across the creek on the Wager farm, for sale. I have a strong inclination to advertise. I have got by any sensitiveness in reference to having it known that we are pretty heavily saddled with debt, and are anxious to sell off all unprofitable property in order to pay our debts. I don't know but we are going to be called upon to sacrifice our reputation for being wealthy, and so lose our credit. We have had the credit of being so wealthy that it would be safe for any one to trust us even to the amount of $50,000. It is just as safe now as it ever was, for we should meet all obligations some way. But perhaps we have had too much pride and worldly feeling about our reputation and the trust people reposed in us, and may have looked to man too much, and not enough to God, to sustain our character as a business Community. I think it has been the fact that we have rather dropped down upon our landed property as the basis of our credit, in stead of regarding it as resting in God and Christ. I am now prepared to be stripped of everything and have no credit with the business world, and be obliged to pay cash down for everything we buy. We are a great deal better prepared for this now than we were eighteen years ago. This is of course looking at the case in an extreme light. But at any rate I want the inspiration of God to control us hereafter in both buying and selling.

I had some reflections to-day, in reference to our past experience, that were profitable to me. When we have been prospered in business our wants have multiplied in proportion. Our expenses have increased without inspiration. Perhaps God is now putting us through a discipline calculated to prepare us for handling any amount of money without being contaminated and having our personal wants multiplied, or becoming puffed up in any way; learning us to handle his property as faithful agents and servants. We must attain to that state where we can have any amount of property around us and not be tempted to any thing that is not dictated by inspiration. That is the state for us as a Community to attain. It is the purpose of God and of Mr. Noyes that we should have a great business in New York, and make a great deal of money without being in the least contaminated by the handling of it.

METEOROLOGICAL.

April 5.

6 A. M. Mercury 56. Hazy sunrise.
12 M. Mercury 76. Clear and fine.
6 P. M. Mercury 72. Hazy sunset.
During the afternoon the mercury rose to 84 deg.

DAILY JOURNAL
OF ONEIDA COMMUNITY.

A. D. 1866. APR. 7. NO. 71.

SATURDAY.

THE bag orders for the week ending April 6th, were $685.

NOTES OF LAST EVENING'S CONVERSATION.

Mr. Cragin.—In reading the chapter Mr. Noyes quotes from, saying "Owe no man anything", I was interested in the verses connected with that passage. "Owe no man anything, but love one another". And then love is spoken of again in the verse following. That led me to reflect somewhat on the vital principle of the gospel. We understand from Christ that the vital element is love. And Paul teaches that though a man may have faith that will move mountains, if he is destitute of love, it amounts to nothing. I am interested in the great fact that "God is love", and the gospel is love. That love which proceeds from God, should underlie our whole organization—should pervade every part of our life. In adjusting principles of business that bring us into contact with the world, this principle should not be overlooked. Evil is to be overcome with good. We find selfishness rampant everywhere; but in many instances those under the influence of selfishness have been affected by a good spirit, so that they would act generously and very differently from their ordinary course.

I am convinced that our future prosperity as a business Community will depend upon our being bathed in the love of God. All of us, and especially our agents should learn to depend more upon the influence of a good spirit than mere shrewdness in the way of trade. We have learned that some of our agents in the past were not popular with business men. But it will be so, and it is now to some extent, that people will trade with us when they do not want our goods, just for the sake of bathing themselves in the good spirit our agents bring with them.

We can see that Mr. Noyes, in solving the business problems that present themselves goes to Christ and Paul and the church above us for instruction. I felt, on reading his letter, a prayer in my heart that I might come into the state of receptivity to that church that Mr. Noyes has attained, so that I might expect their assistance in helping me out of difficulties.— I regard Paul as the great financier. He certainly was the model in this respect in the Primitive Church, and was at the head of their financial department. He has had 1800 years of spiritual practice in financiering, and of course must have made great progress. I move therefore that we as a Community give place to Paul's spirit in our finances, and expect he will give us wisdom and assistance in carrying on the work before us.

I say with Mr. Noyes, "Hurrah for Paul!" [Applause.]

Saturday, 11 A. M. The day is favorable, cool and cloudy, but not stormy. The Auction has not began yet, though some private sales have been made. People come somewhat slowly. Probably they are holding off for dinner.

O. H. Miller is succeeding very well in obtaining bag orders.

ONLY A FORMALITY.

C. S. J., as a necessary preliminary to being "admitted to the bar," desired certificates from the legal fraternity at Oneida of his good moral character, general intelligence, etc. So I called yesterday on Esquire Loomis, who seemed pleased with the opportunity to do his friend Joslyn a favor—he had formed a high opinion of Mr. J.'s ability and modesty, and thought he would be likely to achieve eminence in his new calling. Justice and attorney Ferry did not at first remember our candidate for legal honors, but afterwards concluded he had seen him a few times; but the attorney signified that it was not of the slightest importance whether he was personally acquainted with Mr. J.: "it is all a mere formality." Next I called on attorney Jenkins, who did not at first have any recollection of C. S. J.; but on recalling to mind that he *had played base-ball with Charles four or five years ago*, said he would cheerfully make out the desired certificate! w.

METEOROLOGICAL.

April 6.

6 A. M. Mercury 48.
12 M. Mercury 46. Cloudy.
6 P. M. Mercury 42. Some indications of rain.

ional
DAILY JOURNAL
OF ONEIDA COMMUNITY.

A. D. 1866.   APR. 9.   NO. 72.

MONDAY.

MYRON went to Oswego last week, and sold on the trip—three days—bags, silk and collars to the amount of $530.

Sales at auction on Saturday $1234,89. Sales at the Tontine Salesroom $56,57. Two cows, two half-blood calves, and some other property were disposed of at private sale after the auction, making the total sales on Saturday about $1500. The agricultural implements sold generally at fair prices, and the cows brought nearly their value with two or three exceptions. The musical instruments, bee-hives, and some other articles went at very low prices; but, on the whole, we have reason to be satisfied with this commencement of the annual sales. The audience was neither so large nor respectable as we could have desired, which may be accounted for partly by the fact that there were at least three auctions in operation at the same time within the distance of a few miles, and partly by the fact that it seemed to the public hardly possible that the Community should have an auction excepting for the purpose of selling useless articles, and their poorest cattle. All think another year will witness a much larger crowd.

The auctioneer repeatedly informed his audience that the Community intended to have sales of this kind annually, and no doubt the idea will be circulated for scores of miles around before another Auction and Fair takes place here. The goods in the Salesroom were well arranged, and excited no little admiration.— Many of the men wished they had brought their women, and many of the women wished they had "only known and told their neighbors." One table was covered with a fine display of green-house plants; another with preserved fruits and jellies; another with all the varieties of satchels and traveling bags we make; another table had a show-case which contained sewing-silk, &c.; two other tables were covered with contributions—offerings to the pentecostal spirit. The walls were hung with pictures and specimens of artistic effort, including three beautiful shell-covered what-nots, two flower-wreaths, &c., &c. On the shelves were seen wool hats, steel traps, and "books going at 5 cts."— Some of us think a room thus filled and ornamented should be one of the institutions of the Community.

From the evening conversation which followed it appeared that the spirit and manners of the auctioneer employed on the occasion were not entirely satisfactory to the Community, and the purpose was evolved of educating our own auctioneers, who shall represent at such sales the true spirit, and avoid the deceptions and corruptions which are now connected with auctioneering.

Our neighbors, Messrs. Davis, Adams and Hubbard wish to have us supply them with strawberry-boxes, this season. In the business meeting yesterday it was decided that, if they will pay $2 per hundred, Mr. Thayer be authorized to furnish the boxes.

W. A. Hinds reported statistics to the business meeting respecting the Wilson property, from which it appears that at the present time this property is paying a better profit than most of our other property. Our mistake seems to have been that after buying the property we were drawn into buying the agricultural stock, upon which we shall loose more than a thousand dollars.

Mr. Davis offers us $150 for the horse we bought of him last season. The Committee on horses are to consider the matter.

Mr. Cragin leaves for New York to-day.

METEOROLOGICAL.

April 7.

6 A. M. Mercury 32 deg.
15 M. 36 deg.
6 P. M. 34 deg.
No sun visible to-day.

April 8.

6 A. M. 35 deg. Leaden sky.
12 M. 46 deg. Sun shines.
6 P. M. 40 deg. Nearly clear.

DAILY JOURNAL
OF ONEIDA COMMUNITY.

A. D. 1866.   APR. 10.   NO. 73.

TUESDAY.

TO THE COMMUNITY AGENTS.

Uniformity of prices among our agents cannot be maintained unless there is frequent communication between them and the home department.

Pre-payment at home requires that agents abroad should make quick returns of sales and collections.

For these and other reasons, all persons traveling to obtain orders for O. C., are requested to write to Oneida *as often as once a week*, reporting their operations, and the general prospects of trade and such observations as they may deem of importance to the home department, and naming the places where and the times when letters will reach them on their intended route.

All agents selling goods and soliciting orders for the O. C. N. Y. B. are requested to generally communicate *twice a week* with New York (always *once*), stating amount of collections, amount of sales, prospects of trade, remitting at the same time all the money they can spare (unless they have a very small amount on hand, or are to reach home in a few days), giving an idea of their intended route, and specifying the places where and times when letters will reach them—together with such observations as they consider will be of benefit to the O. C. N. Y. B.

All orders for goods to be filled at either Oneida or New York should generally be transmitted the same day they are received, and should contain all necessary information in respect to prices, discounts, style of goods and shipping directions.

Important collections should be reported and the money forwarded as soon as possible.

As a general rule, all monies, including collections for Oneida, may be forwarded to New York, with a statement of what amount is for collections and what for sales. If the collections are for New York, state explicitly the names of firms and the sum paid by each firm, together with amount of discounts, and the reasons therefor. When money is sent to New York on collections for O. C., send with the money simply a record of how much was collected for O. C., and send the particulars to the book-keeper at Oneida.

Communications containing information for the book-keepers should always be addressed to the book-keepers.
w.

O. C. N. Y. B. PRICE-LIST.

REPORTED APRIL 9, 1866.

Mach. Twist,	"O. C".	Bl'k and Drab.		$14,50 lb.
"	"	"	White.	16,00 "
"	"	"	and Corticelli, (100 yds.)	2,25 doz.
"	"		Union	2,10 "
B. H.	"		Black.	11,50 lb.
"	"		Drab	13,00 "

Embroidery silk		(weighted.)	$2,25 C.
"	"	(pure.)	2,50 "
Col'd sewing	"		2,20 "
10 oz. Box	"		1,10 oz
10 " "	"		1,15 "
8 " Package "			1,00 "
7 " "		(Drab)	11,50 lb
Stick Twist			2,00 C
Wide Straight Ladies' Collars			6,25 M.
Narrow " "			4,25 "
Circular "	"		8,00 "

NOTES OF LATE EVENING'S CONVERSATION.

Mr. Hamilton.—I feel a great deal of interest in the subject of the resurrection. I wish we could turn our attention toward it this evening, and concentrate that attention by conversation. There are some encroachments of disease just at the present time, nothing very serious, but just enough to show the pressing down and rushing in of a spirit that would do mischief if it could. It seems to me that the two worlds, hades and the resurrection, are rushing and pushing for the possession of this world. I believe the resurrection world is near to us, and that it is good for us to reach our hearts and spirits out toward it. The love of God is back of it all and will have its way sooner or later.

Mr. Cragin.—It will be remembered that Christ's inability to work miracles in his native place was on account of unbelief in those around him. That spirit of unbelief is the only real obstruction to the influx of the **resurrection church among us. It is not distance but a** state or condition that hinders their approach. Then what are the specific obstructions to the influx of the resurrection life? Fear of death is one and quite a large obstruction. The fear of disease is another. If we look at the outward world with our attention upon our bodies rather than our souls, we are looking away from the resurrection, away from the point where that world will enter our life; and it is evident that in order for the Primitive Church to fully embody itself in this church there must be a spirit of faith and receptivity—a belief that they can come into us. We must remove the fear of death and disease, and stand where Christ stood in the power of his Father. Paul made little account of death. He was willing to die if necessary. His attention was drawn away from his body, and outward visible life to the interior life of Christ. If we do that we commit the physical life to God. I find in my own case that Christ told me to go to work when it was apparently impossible; and when I obeyed he made me a well man right in the face of disease. He cured me by getting my attention on the interior world and truth. I desire very much that we may make it easy for God and the Primitive Church to dwell with us and give us their presence, as I know they are anxious to do. Their presence will secure to us happiness and prosperity in every direction.

The bag-bees were resumed yesterday, after an interval of two weeks.

METEOROLOGICAL.

April 9.

6. A. M. Mercury 26 deg.   Clear.   White frost.
12 M. 45 deg.
6 P. M. 42 deg.

DAILY JOURNAL
OF ONEIDA COMMUNITY.

A. D. 1866. APR. 11. NO. 74.

WEDNESDAY.

THE following letter was received yesterday:

Draft Rendezvous, Jackson. Mich.
April 4, 1866.

DEAR FRIENDS:—I wish to visit you for the purpose of observing the workings of Communism as illustrated by you. I believe in Christ, and in Communism as the legitimate fruit of faith in him, but am not decided, whether in endeavoring to "work out our own salvation" and to spread the Gospel, it is best now to join in organized efforts such as yours, or to work as we can in our *present* relations to each other and the world. I wish to determine that question, and believe a visit to you would aid me. Furthermore, I wish to come within the sphere of your personal influence for a time, that whatever may be the result so far as the above question is concerned, I may through that influence be brought near to Christ; learn of him through you, and be helped in my endeavors after salvation.

I will give you a few particulars of myself and family. I am 42 years of age; my wife is 37; and we have three children, two boys and one girl, aged 15, 10, and 6, respectively. Myself and wife were reared under the influence of Methodism. At 20 I professed faith in Universalism; at 27 became a preacher of that doctrine, preached five years, then stopped because not satisfied with practical results. At 35 commenced the practice of the law and at 37, in 1861, went into the army and am still in the military service. I was wounded in battle, losing the left eye. My health is fair; that of my wife is rather poor, from chronic affection of the liver; that of my children is good.

I wish to leave the military service, and having now no permanent or fixed home, I wish, before choosing one, to visit and live with you for a while, at least, if it be consistent with your views and interests. I believe that myself and wife are measurably free from the bondage of the marriage spirit; she has worn the short dress most of the time since our marriage; and I would come with my family and live with you *as nearly as may be*, as though we were members of *your* family, expecting, in all things to submit to your direction and guidance. If this be not practicable, I would come myself. I have some money and other property; in all, about $2400,00, and should bring with me some $1700,00 to be used, or not, as might be considered best.

I am used to most kinds of manual labor, have a good knowledge of law and of business generally, and my oldest boy has a decided aptitude for mechanic arts. Should you wish further particulars before answering me decisively, they will be freely given.

I inclose our photographs. The left eye of mine is artificial. I should add that my wife's wishes are the same.

Truly and faithfully yours, J. W. T.

To the Oneida Community.

O. C. April 10, 1866.

MY DEAR FRIENDS:—I confess my entire separation from my old life, and from every spirit that would interfere with the full operation of the truth in me.

I confess Christ in me a soft and humble spirit—a perfect Savior from all evil; and I now consecrate myself anew to his service.

I am grateful to you all for the tenderness and sincerity with which my case has been handled. The expressions of kindness and encouragement which many of you have shown me during the past week have touched me deeply, making me feel that it is the judgment of God that has encompassed me, and not the judgment of the world.

I confess my union with Mr. Noyes and Mr. Hamilton.

I am, sincerely yours, W. H. Henderson.

Myron has gone to Rome to-day with samples of our traveling-bags, satchels &c., for the purpose of getting them photographed. The photographs are to be used in selling instead of samples.

A number of persons in the family are suffering from colds and hoarseness at the present time.

Lady Noyes has been quite feeble for a number of days. She is very quiet and peaceful, and apparently has but little suffering.

Some difficulty is experienced in getting masons enough to carry on the stone work of the store as rapidly as is desirable. Several of our men and some of the hired carpenters are now engaged in laying stone.

The grounds and fences around the cottage occupied by Mr. Radford, our Shoe-maker, are being put in order.

(Extract from a letter by H. G. Allen.)

" Mr Noyes says we have given our property unto the Lord, and that now we must go a step further, and give our *services* unto the Lord. We must see to it that we work in earnest for him, and have the true spirit of *faithfulness*. If we have Paul's spirit of earnestness in regard to business we shall accomplish much more than we now do,—our workmen will feel it and be influenced by it."

Sales from farm in March $1237,20; in April $1341, 53—total $2578,73.

There was a free criticism of Mrs. Knowles, Monday evening in the meeting. She has not commended herself to us since she has been here, and has shown no true repentance of her old faults and unbelief. No one feels confidence in, or sympathy with her. She has been under the power of disease, and an inlet of that spirit to us. It was thought that there should be an entire separation of our spirits from her, and that she had better withdraw from amongst us.

METEOROLOGICAL.

April 10.

6 A. M. Mercury 28 deg.
12 M. Mercury 34 deg.
6 P. M. Mercury 52 deg.

DAILY JOURNAL
OF ONEIDA COMMUNITY.

A. D. 1866.   APR. 12.   NO. 75.

THURSDAY.

LADY NOYES died last night at about 10½ o'clock. Her departure was very quiet—a peaceful falling a-sleep of the body, without a struggle, a word or a movement. She said but little, and took little notice of things around her all day yesterday. We doubt not that for her to " die is gain," and though she is resting for a little while in hades, she is still journeying to the resurrection, and will ere long attain the fullness of victory.

The funeral will take place to-morrow.

Spring operations among the gardeners and fruit growers have begun. One acre has been planted with potatoes. The early peas have been sown. Yesterday the teams were plowing and sub-soiling ground for grapes. Some 8,000 raspberry plants are being taken up and healed in. They are all to be set in our own grounds. About 2,000 plants are required to the acre.

The journalist would offer THE JOURNAL to the Wallingford and New York Branches for criticism. As it is written and printed mainly for their benefit it is desirable that we should know how it pleases them, and wherein they think it can be improved.

There are indications that we are gradually getting the attention and patronage of the trappers. Yesterday another letter was received from Samuel Shannon, otherwise " Riley Hunter," of Sandusky, Ohio. He is one of the large trappers of the West. He has been a trapper 35 years; was born on the Indian Reserve, in Ohio, and afterwards lived among the Chippewas; trapped and bought furs for the American Fur Company for ten years; left the service of the Company in 1848, and since that time has trapped on his own hook. For 34 years he says, " I have been most of my time either in the bush, prairie, marsh, or on some water in the pursuit of wild game." He also says, " I wrote once to the editor of THE CIRCULAR, published at Wallingford. My motives for writing were to compliment you trap-makers, but I thought from the heading that he gave the article, that he thought I wanted to become the hero of some great story, of which I am very clear, for I never cherished flattery." Of his last trip to Canada he says : " I caught on the Bradford Marshes 937 muskrats, and 34 minks, and then I left Bradford for the country near Lake Nippising, where I caught, great and small, 56 beaver, 17 otter, some few fisher, 3 linx, killed two moose, caught 3 bears and could have taken many more if I could have used them, they were plenty, killed a a great many spruce partridges. Could catch any amount of brook and salmon trout, the finest I ever found. Caught a few pine martens, and killed deer enough to make a hide cover for camp, and we left the skins exactly where we used them. Brought my birch bark canoe

back to Lewiston, N. Y., and sold it to the proprietors of the American Hotel of that place. I bought the canoe at Big Winds Islands, up at Nonogotogamog or Lake of Four Bays. I came down the Northern rivers to Collingwood, and then across to Toronto by the Northern Railway, and took my canoe across the lake on steamer. Was gone 121 days." He has trapped with 40 doz. traps, new and old, of our make and has only had 22 broken springs.

Another trapper named Mc Cluer writes from Austin, Nevada, inquiring about traps. He says " I have trapped for fourteen years in California and Oregon, and last fall I accidentally got hold of a trap in San Francisco, bearing the address of this letter, which far excelled any thing for power and mechanism that I ever saw in the trap line. The trap that I have reference to was a small double spring and would when set probably spread four or five inches."

The father and mother of Mr. Bolles were here yesterday, on their way home. Their visit here was brief and friendly. They seemed to cheerfully acquiesce in Mary's decision to give herself to the Community.

A Mrs. Sheldon from Utica is here.

To-day is clear, warm and beautiful. Only a few small snow-drifts on the hills are now visible. Some wild anemone blossoms were brought from the woods a few days ago.

S. A. B., E. M., and Temple and Leonora, arrived last night about 1 o'clock. We understand that they were delayed on their way from the Depot, by the breaking down of the wagon. No one was injured however. Particulars will undoubtedly be supplied by private correspondence.

METEOROLOGICAL.

April 11.

6 A. M. Mercury 40 deg.
12 M.   "   56 deg.
6 P. M.   "   54 deg.

There was a slight shower in the morning, after which the clouds passed off, and the afternoon was clear and pleasant.

DAILY JOURNAL
OF ONEIDA COMMUNITY.

A. D. 1866.   APR. 13.   NO. 76.

FRIDAY.
TO THE COMMUNITY AGENTS.

With this you will receive revised price list of Bags.

On comparing it with the old list you will note important changes. Muslin common (lined and unlined) have been reduced from $1,50 to $2,50 per doz.; Muslin Pelissier $4,00 doz.; Gent's. B Sacks an average of $5,00 doz.; C ditto $3,00 doz.; Solferino $6,00; Magenta $10,00; Fancy and Leather Pelissier $6,00; Ladies Satchels from $6,00 to $9,00; and Lunch Bags from $12,00 to $16,00 per doz.

These reductions are made partly on account of reductions in cost of stock, but mainly with a view to making a price list which shall be generally acceptable, and which shall represent the new policy of " selling as low as we can, instead of getting all we can."

Our prices may not now be in all respects as low as those of some other parties, but we trust they will be found nearly so considering the quality of work; and we promise further reductions as rapidly as the cost of stock and manufacturing can be reduced.

Last year the net profits of the Bag department were 10 per cent. on sales: we shall be contented this year with 5 per cent.

The rates of discount have also been changed, and it will be understood, in selling at the new price-list, that the best retail dealers are to receive only 5 per cent. discount; country jobbers seven and one half per cent., and wholesale dealers and jobbers in New York, Boston and perhaps a very few other large cities ten per cent. The smallest retailers should be sold to at list-prices or two and a half per cent. discount.

For pre-payment or remittance on receipt of invoice, in New York par funds, one and a half per cent. from the net amount of invoice, will hereafter be allowed.

W.

NOTES OF LAST EVENING'S CONVERSATION.

Mr. Hamilton.—There is one interesting fact about Lady Noyes's death. It is rather singular that with all her large circle of relatives, children and grandchildren, not one was present at this time. I think this will be found an edifying fact if we consider a little. Her attention was not turned toward her relatives, and she did not want to see them. I believe she did not call for any of them. She pleasantly spoke Mr. Noyes's name, "John," once or twice, but I infer that in this case it was not so much for personal presence as for spiritual support and sympathy.

She was not alone, but was well cared for. And best of all, she was in good relations with God and the heavens, so that her attention was in that direction. I think it a great commendation to the school and church organization that is formed here, that such a state of things could be; that here is a spiritual organization that will carry persons through such an experience and meet all their wants, not only physical, but even spiritual wants, and really overcome the fear of death and give support and strength. You may surround persons with all the sympathies of the flesh, and if they lack spiritual support it is all worse than nothing.

Mr. Woolworth.—I think it a very interesting fact that she did not trouble herself about the arrangement of her circumstances; it was proof to me that she had got well out of her own little family into the great family of Christ.

We had a thunder-shower early this morning, which has given a refreshing tone to the atmosphere, and caused an obvious start of the grass. A visible greenness begins to overspread the fields and lawn, and the brown shade of the elm blossoms appears on the face of the woods.

Mr. Jones is in poor health now and sits up but very little.

Mr. Worden has begun his campaign on the roads.— He reports them to be in such good condition that but little more is required this spring than to level them off with a scraper.

METEOROLOGICAL.
April 12.

6 A. M. Mercury 44 deg.
12 M. Mercury 70 deg.
6 P. M. Mercury 55 deg.

THE ROBINS.

One happy morn of an April day,
    So warm that it almost seemed like June,
Three robins came to our lawn to play,
    Each one singing his own sweet tune.

In musical language each seemed to tell
    Some happy tale of his own dear love,
While his voice in gladsome song would swell—
    But they knew not who sat in the boughs above.

Two lady robins—two darling birds
    Were sitting quite near on a hemlock spray,
Listening in glee to the songs without words
    So sweetly sung by those lovers gay.

Down from the bough they lightly dropped,
    Fluttering coyly toward the others—
First a sweet, clear note, then on they hopped—
    Why not? The three were only their brothers.

Quickly the three heard the joyful sound,
    And I saw them coming to meet the two;
Quickly the two arose from the ground,
    And back to the hemlock bough they flew.

Then a gush of merry notes and long
    Came from the two as they watched the three,
Who followed them still with amorous song,
    Flitting about from tree to tree.

Soon they all flew off and left me there—
    In their playful flight I saw them pass,
Then the place was still; but the fragrant air
    Stirred softly over the tender grass.

W. H. H.

DAILY JOURNAL
OF ONEIDA COMMUNITY.

A. D. 1866. APR. 14. NO. 77.

SATURDAY.

A VISITOR, Mr. Shelley, of Indiana, is now here.

The funeral of Lady Noyes took place yesterday at 1½ o,clock, in the usual quiet way of the Community.—We hardly realize that there has been any death in the family, so little of the hadean shadow has been present.

Miss—not Mrs.—Sheldon, left for home this morning. She is a seamstress, hires a room and lives alone, somewhat after the style described in "Seeking a Shelter," we judge. She has read THE CIRCULAR for a year or more, is somewhat interested in Communism, and came here to see for herself. She appeared to be honest and intelligent.

The Bag Department has lately turned out a new style of Satchel, which is designated by the letter O.

Edwin Burnham is making some experiments as salesman, and may soon be numbered among the regular Community agents.

Mr. Kelly arrived home last evening, and to the query, Are you ready to go out again? promptly replied, "Yes;" and at 8 o'clock this morning was again on his way.—He is expected to return this evening.

NOTES OF LAST EVENING'S CONVERSATION.

Mr. Hamilton.—Mr. Pitt says he has no newspaper report, and no letters to read this evening. We have received no mail to-day from either New York or Wallingford. I believe it is good for us to be shut off once in a while from reliance on these outward sources for edification. All these things are good in their place; but I am led to think the Lord would have us rely less on these outward things and more upon him. I am led to see that it is a state of poverty, for instance, to be relying so much upon the daily newspapers for the food that goes to make up the sum of our daily happiness.—There is no mistake but that this is a poverty-stricken state to be in. It is a good thing for us to turn away from these outward sources of happiness and entertainment. There surely are higher sources of happiness. I have felt, for myself, when I had my whole attention turned to the Lord that new channels of inspiration and enthusiasm were opened.

I was thinking it would be well for us to watch daily for the heavenly influx of news. There may be a mail train that passes here every day from the upper world that would throw out something to us if we were wide awake to receive it. Let us study the subject in this direction. It always does me good to do so.

W. A. Hinds.—I have been led to appreciate Mr. Noyes's last visit here. I think he did a great work and that his spirit is still with us calling us in the same direction. I desire to yield myself to it entirely.

Mr. Burt.—It seems to be a time when we are called more emphatically than ever before to wait upon God and to introduce inspiration into all our business.—This idea of the Pentecostal spirit has interested me great deal. I see it is all-important that we as a Community should get where we can continually recognize that spirit, and carry it into all our business.

Mr. Hamilton.—I join with others in reference to Mr. Noyes's work when here last. I know he did a great work in the Community, and I confess he helped me a great deal. I am very thankful for the individual benefit I received.

Mr. Hamilton then read the first chapter of 2 Peter, and commented particularly on the passage—"We have also a more sure word of prophecy; whereunto ye do well to take heed, as unto a light that shineth in a dark place, until the day dawn, and the day-star arise in your hearts."

A member of the house-cleaning company thus unburthens himself:

MR. EDITOR:—House-cleaning is absorbing a good deal of attention these days, but principally from those of us engaged therein. We have been at work about two weeks, and it seems as though we had only commenced, when we look over the whole field and see what is yet to come.

To-day, Homer Barron (honor be to him and his posterity after him), presented us with a beautiful and handy little machine for nailing down carpets; and I assure you it does all it promises. Why, Mr. Editor it revolutionizes our profession at once. It would do your heart good to see it work, particularly if you had just emerged from a fortnight's siege of finger-pounding, leg-cramping, back-breaking carpet-nailing, as we have. We were about to set up such a wail through your JOURNAL, Mr. Editor, against house-cleaning in general and carpeting in particular, as would have melted the heart of a stone, much more these tender Community hearts, but this charming little invention combined with our natural good nature has tranquilized us into a state of acquiescence, and we say with Petroleum Nasby, "we see light."

Success to new inventions. Yours truly, J. P. H.

METEOROLOGICAL.

April 13.

6 A. M. Mercury 51deg. 12 M. 49deg. 6 P. M. 45deg.

DAILY JOURNAL
OF ONEIDA COMMUNITY.

A. D. 1866. APR. 16. NO. 78.

MONDAY.
SELLING BY SAMPLE

Is one of the highest branches of trade—quite superior in many respects to selling goods that are at hand. It involves more skill on the part of the salesman, and more sagacity and confidence on the part of the buyer. The largest mercantile transactions are now carried on in this manner. Larger commission houses sell goods by samples; cargoes of flour, grain, sugar, etc. etc., are bought and sold by samples. At the great exchanges in New York immense values daily exchange hands, and both buyers and sellers base their judgment on sample-goods. This indeed becomes indispensible in proportion to the magnitude of business operations.— It was easy enough, for instance, at one time to carry around the country in satchels all the silk we had capital or courage to purchase; and at an earlier period Mr. Daniel Nash trundled through New York city in a hand-cart all the Traveling Bags manufactured by the Community! All this has become quite impossible; our agents can now carry with them only a fair assortment of samples; and it is quite likely that our manufactures will ere long become so extensive that agents will not be able even to carry samples, and will have to rely on pictorial representations.

But the point I wish to urge is that in extending trade, very much will depend upon our faithfulness in obtaining and executing orders. The sample system being based in a large degree on confidence, that firm which shall prove itself best entitled to confidence must in the long run be most successful. And it is not enough that we are *honest:* we must also be accurate, careful, and vigilant to see that orders are filled exactly as they are given. Practically there is often no great difference between a careless honest man and a rogue.

To show that exhortation on this point is not superfluous I will, in another number, recapitulate a variety of blunders which have been made the present season in transmitting and executing orders.   w.

BUSINESS MEETING ITEMS.

Mr. Hatch was instructed to either shut up the hens or sell them, so that Mr. Radford and the occupants of the Burt house may proceed to make their gardens.

Mr. Hamilton has engaged parties to construct a patent gravel walk in front of the New House.

Mr. Burt and Mr. Conant were appointed a committee to attend to the placing of brush-wood at proper places in the creek to protect the banks.

Mr. Clark was appointed to superintend the repair of wagons the present year. Mr. D. M. Kelly was added to the wagon committee.

It is proposed to have a peddling wagon going most of the time this season, and the wagon committee was requested to take into consideration the matter of furnishing a wagon for that purpose.

An exhortation was given in favor of more promptness in filling orders for goods.

The Hermit Thrush has made its advent for the season in the woods at the head of Parsons's Gulf or Ravine. Last evening it was making the woods vocal with its clear, mellow notes.

Mr. Shelley, our Indiana visitor, left this morning.— He appears to be somewhat posted with respect to the Community—has read the Berean, Mr. Noyes's Religious Experience, and THE CIRCULAR.

Mr. Potter, an acquaintance of Mr. Bolles, came Saturday evening and left this morning. He appeared to be favorably impressed with the Community.

METEOROLOGICAL.
April 14.

6 A. M.	Mercury 32 deg.	Heavy frost.
15 M.	"	62 deg.	Pleasant.
6 P. M.	"	54 deg.	Wind and slight rain.

April. 15.

6 A. M.	Mercury 40 deg.
12 M.	"	50 deg.
6 P. M.	"	47 deg.

Clear and pleasant throughout the day.

DAILY JOURNAL
OF ONEIDA COMMUNITY.

A. D. 1866. APR. 17. NO. 79.

TUESDAY.

NOTES OF LAST EVENING'S CONVERSATION.

Last evening there was conversation in regard to our treatment of visitors. We glean the following paragraphs from the report:

Mr. Hamilton.—I have been thinking about visitors, and that it would be a good thing for us to spend an evening in discussing the subject and trying to get at the true way to meet them. We have lately appointed Mr. Bolles to serve the Community in receiving and attending to visitors. This is a very important office, and it is very important that the Community should be rightly represented. It is essential that the person who stands in such a position should have wisdom and strength given him to meet persons in the right spirit, and not become involved and weakened by communication with them. I think it will be a good thing to talk about it, and if we have any advice to give Mr. Bolles, we will do so and fortify him as well as we can. We might include Mrs. Joslyn and Chloe Seymour, as they also stand in this capacity toward visitors.

I think Mr. Bolles is well adapted by experience of a certain kind to fill this office. It is true, as he says, that he has not been long in the Community. That is something of a draw-back, with me, I confess, but in looking around, I could not see any one else who was so available for the place as he

Christ said to some of his disciples who were fishermen, "Follow me and I will make you fishers of men." I think that remark gives us a good hint of the way we should deal with visitors. In one sense, we are called to be fishermen. Through the good providence of God, we have come ashore, and all the world about us are floundering around in an indefinite sea. Our hearts are established in practical subordination to God.— "Seek first the kingdom of heaven and its righteousness, and all other things shall be added." The Lord has established the Community on this ground, and that is the source of all the good things that we possess, and the satisfaction and strength of heart that we feel. It is a fact that we please folks who come here, very much, but it is because we have sought the kingdom of God and its righteousness. We must see to it that the folks who call here and are so taken with us, *swallow our bait*—and not we theirs—that we do not go down into too much sympathy with them. If we can get them to swallow the bait of Salvation from Sin that Mr. Noyes has brought forth, well and good—let them swallow it and run. But it will not do for a man like Mr. Bolles to have them in tow, and swallow a good deal of their talk and spirit. We must look out and not let him get into the slush and be swallowed by their spirit.

I think we as children of God are called upon to manifest a general good nature and good will toward all. Then on the other hand there are things in which we must be chaste and economical. God does not waste his life and we must learn not to waste our life by too much talk with visitors. It will not do to drop down to them and suffer them to drain our life out of us by talk. We can be good-natured and still hold folks off, and not be deceived by them. Christ, while the magnetism of his life and the truths of his gospel were drawing crowds around him, was yet continually shaking them off and rebuking self-seeking. He was searching them—sifting the true seed from the self-seekers.

I confess I feel sharper than usual in regard to our business with visitors. I feel on the one hand free and glad to have persons come and see the good there is here, but if they don't come to trade—to sell their old life, I don't want much to do with them. We should be sure and make something on them, and not let them speculate on us. I don't feel satisfied to have men and women come here and spend several days, and go off feeling nice and let that be the end of it. I want to harpoon them with the truth—so that they will feel troubled and be in the judgment. At least I don't think it is safe to let them have much of our sympathy. We are squandering our life if we do.

Mr. Bolles was criticised somewhat for a tendency to drop down to visitors and talk too much with them, and **was advised to study reserve of life and spiritual reticence.**

100 cherry trees have been received from Cleveland.

Ellen Hutchins has put her boy into the Children's House, and has gone into the kitchen to work.

A brother-in-law of Mrs. Knowles is here, having come by her request. We understand she intends to leave with him.

THE CIRCULAR was received promptly this morning.

Mr. Kelly and Mr. Seymour Nash are engaged in laying out a new flower-garden on the plot of ground north-west of the large reservoir.

On Sunday evening Myron was criticised; a report of will be forwarded in manuscript.

ADVANTAGE OF A LUNCH-BAG.

Edwin Burnham and I concluded to take a lunch-bag with us yesterday, on our trip to Utica. So friends filled one with bread and butter, boiled eggs, pie, nut-cakes, &c., which afforded us a "good square dinner" and a good square supper." The first cost of the food we took from home could not have been over 50 cts., and it saved us a hotel bill of at least $3,00, and considerable time; and we had the additional satisfaction of eating food of home-preparation, preferable for us to any hotel-are. **w.**

METEOROLOGICAL.

April 16.

6 A. M. Mercury 35 deg. Cloudy.
12 M. Mercury 57 deg. Clear.
6 P. M. Mercury 55 deg. Clear.

DAILY JOURNAL
OF ONEIDA COMMUNITY.

A. D. 1866. APR. 18. NO. 80.

WEDNESDAY.
BLUNDERS ABOUT ORDERS.

A lot of Traveling Bags were ordered to be sent to Cleveland as *freight ;* they were sent by *express*, and the firm who ordered them refused to pay the extra charges. The same firm assert that they ordered bags with *painted fronts*—plain bags were sent them, because nothing was said in the order received from our agent about painted fronts. It is not certain whether the agent or the firm is responsible for this mistake.

A firm in Mass. ordered a lot of satchels through one of our agents, expressly stipulating that they should all be furnished with *flat* handles. The agent neglected to write particularly about the handles until after the satchels had been sent off with *round* handles. The firm was of course disappointed and displeased.

A firm in Michigan ordered *plain* Pelissier Leather Bags : *Pocket* Bags were sent ; and the firm refused to pay the extra expense, and a considerable reduction had to be made to compromise the matter.

A man in Utica ordered some Delaware Grape vines through one of our agents some time since. The agent neglected to inform the horticulturists, and when he was ready to set out the vines and again spoke to us about them, we had none to spare.

A quantity of groceries was received last Saturday from New York ; the Purchasing Agency will take note that of the tea, coffee and molasses sent, no invoice has yet been received. Mr. Aiken has sold some of the goods without being able to fix upon a definite price.

Quite a number of Bag orders have lately been received from our agents, nothing being said about rates of discount. All such omissions are occasions of perplexity to the home department.

Orders have been received lately from agents which did not state how the goods ordered were to be sent—whether as freight or by express.

The above items are recorded here for the purpose of impressing upon the Community agents the great importance of first fully understanding the orders they receive, and then in transmitting them—of stating explicitly all particulars, in respect to style of goods, rates of discount, shipping directions. The home department must also be equally careful in filling orders. I believe we can and shall convince the business-world that the Community is not only strictly honest but also perfectly reliable and free from stupid blunders.   w.

NOTES OF LAST EVENING'S CONVERSATION.

Mr. Hatch.—We who live at the children's house and have charge of the children feel as though God was calling upon us to take a higher stand in regard to faith. Our experience is of that kind that leads us to hope, yet we find we need more faith. We realize that we are dealing with principalities and powers. The old principality that we have always had to contend with more or less—that is the family-spirit, or what is called the motherly-spirit—still affects the children to some extent. We feel that this is Community business, and we want the sympathy of the fathers and mothers, and of the Community generally.

I thought it best to present our views here, as we have been considerably oppressed of late. When we find the children sick or a little out of sorts, so that we have to pay attention to them, then the mothers are interested and come to give special care and sympathy to their own children. I found formerly the children's house women had a great deal more respect for the mothers of the children than for Mr. Noyes's instincts. I suppose it was owing to their sympathy, which worked in the wrong direction. I have no particular fault to find with the past, however; but I think we have learned better now. I think we have had experience enough so that we, as a department, should stand first; before the motherly spirit; and we should have the sympathy and support of every father and mother.

We can see that the important thing is to have the children possessed of a good spirit. I don't and can't think so much of the bodies as I do of the spirits. At the same time that I fully sympathize with the trials of the mothers, I think we should be reckoned first. We want to stand first, as a department that Mr. Noyes has taken a great deal of pains with, and let his spirit enter and direct our course.

I have no criticism of individuals, but feel that parents should hold their children loosely, and feel that they are God's children and that they do not belong to the mothers. We should feel that every child that is given to the Community belongs to the Community and not to the mother. We consider our department open to criticism at any time.

Mr. Hamilton.—I am surprised from time to time to see the great change that takes place in the children when their parents cease to give them so much attention, and are careful not to get between them and the Community spirit. The children have really suffered from the effects of the parents standing between them and the Community. The parents may think it kindness to their children to act in this manner, but it is *cruel* blindness. Disease and trouble follow in the train of the family spirit. It is a spiritual law which you may be sure will prove true in every instance, that where you let the family spirit come between the children and the Community spirit, there you will find trouble, disease and a bad spirit working. I could point out several marked cases where this is the state of things at the present time.

Mrs. Knowles left yesterday.

Mr. Chesbro, of Fulton, N. Y., came here yesterday to see if he could find employment, and a place near us where his family could reside. His plan was not favored, and he left this morning.

Preston Reeves Sherrard, the young Southerner who visited us last winter, is now employed in the Bag Shop.

METEOROLOGICAL.
April 17.

6 A. M. Mercury 42 deg. Clear.
12 M.   "   61 "   Wind S. E.
6 P. M. "   60 "

DAILY JOURNAL
OF ONEIDA COMMUNITY.

A. D. 1866.   APR. 19.   NO. 81.

THURSDAY.

AN old man—a German—came from Utica yesterday, for the purpose of joining the Community.— He was accompanied by his son, who had heard of the Community through Homer Smith when he lived in Utica. Of course the application was respectfully declined.

Mr. Edgett, of Camden, N. Y.—the man who is engaged in the fruit-preserving business at that place—is now here.

A Mr. Ingersoll, formerly a member of Congress, from New Haven, called here yesterday.

Daniel Abbott started for Cincinnati on Monday, to investigate concerning the machine for making tin fruit-cans. If the machine is satisfactory it is proposed to buy one. The price, we believe, is about $175.— According to the accounts we have received of the machine, it effects a great saving of labor.

The stone-wall of the store is gradually approaching completion. The south wing is finished; the main part nearly so; and the north wing is under way. The carpenters have begun work on the south wing.

The horticulturists are planting grape-vines.

The remainder of the Virgalieu pear trees in the orchard are to be grafted over with other varieties. The Virgalieu has proved an almost total failure, from its tendency to crack. Mr. Bristol is engaged in grafting the trees when not working in the bakery.

Greens are a great institution here now, and nearly every day witnesses the disappearance of large piles of them into the steam-boiler.

Another letter was received from Samuel Shannon, the trapper, yesterday. He incloses two photographs of drawings made by his son who once went with him on a trapping expedition. Of the pictures he says:

"No. 4 represents myself and Wm. Softiron, my companion, as we were hunting for a beaver-trap that was carried away the night previous by a beaver. The animal cut the tally-pole and carried the trap into the dam, and I think that that beaver dam will ever retain a specimen of the labor of the Oneida Community.— That dam is on a small stream that empties into Cobbamojeckamog Lake.

"No. 5 represents Big Winds Island, a station where the Indians congregate after their hunt is over, preparatory to starting homewards. That is a point at which some one of the agents of the so-called Hon. Hudson's Bay Company generally calculates to meet the Indians and swindle them of their furs. The Island in question lies about the middle of Nonongotogamog or Lake of Four Bays. It appears to be about the center of the hunting grounds of the Ramas, Snakes, Muskokas, and Chippewas and the Little Currents. It is, as near as I can calculate, about four hundred miles from the Sault St. Marie River."

"I commenced to ascend the Muskoka river last year on the 8th day of April, and I found the snow six feet on the level in the heavy wood, but the margins of all the streams were clear of snow, and for several rods back the grass commenced to start. The streams very seldom freeze over, owing to the great quantity of snow. It appears that so much snow keeps the earth warm, and as the streams are generally rapid, the melting snow furnishes water to keep quite a current running, consequently there is very little if any ice, and of course the beaver and otter have things all their own way, especially during the absence of Yankee trappers."

Scene R. R. Ticket Office—Night Baggage-man reclining on wood-box. Enter Community Agent.

"Halloo there, Community! How do you do?"

"Very well sir; but do you know all the Community people?"

"Yes."

"How?"

"I don't know how, but *I can tell them every time.*"

METEOROLOGICAL.

April 18.

6 A. M. Mercury 48 deg.   12 M. 69.   6 P. M. 67.— Wind south, blowing quite hard in the afternoon.

DAILY JOURNAL
OF ONEIDA COMMUNITY.

A. D. 1866. APR. 20. NO. 82.

FRIDAY.

NOTES OF LAST EVENING'S CONVERSATION.

Mr. Hamilton.—I like very much indeed what Mr. Noyes said at New York about working with the heart and communing with God, I will read it again.

"I have been threatening to criticise the Community for not having enough activity and industry, but now I feel more like criticising them for not having the true kind of activity—activity of the heart. I don't know but there is fully enough of outward activity—employment of the hands, at present.

"We insist upon it that our agents shall make returns to us regularly of their sales and business prospects, and we all ought to make returns to God in the same way, and learn to be receptive to his orders. Every man who wants to grow, ought to have a time of meditation and talking with God every day. Activity in that direction is more important than activity of the hands in business. That was the activity Christ had."

Mr. Woolworth.—I feel that this is something all of us will consider indispensable, sooner or later, as much so as going to the table. We shall not have to force ourselves to it, either, any more than we do to the table. We shall feel hungry and unsatisfied without such a season of communion every day.

Mr. Hamilton.—I cannot help feeling that there is a great lack in the Community on this point. All bad experience can be traced to this want of reflection and talking with the Lord. We think we must go to the dining-room three times a day, and then when we get up in the morning we must wash our hands and face and comb our hair, and look in the glass to see that we are tidy and presentable. But these are unimportant things compared with washing our spiritual faces. We must find out the way to daily wash ourselves from the spirit of the world. A neglect to do so may be as offensive to the Lord as it would be to us to have people go along months without combing their hair or washing their faces.

There is one Lord and one spirit; and the more we get into this habit of meditation and falling back on God, and communing with Him, the more harmony we shall have. We shall see more beauty and happiness in everything, and find ourselves thinking and acting in unison.

Mr. Pitt.—I believe that talking with God in the way Mr. Noyes recommends, is the true foundation of success in business, and in all that we do.

Mr. Woolworth.—I think it is the only way we can be successful in this great warfare with evil and the plagues of the world.

O. H. M. is having good success in his Ohio trip—sends home many bag orders, and makes no complaint about the dullness of business. The following letter was received from him on Wednesday:

DEAR FRIENDS:—James says, "Ye adulterers and adulteresses, know ye not that the friendship of the world is enmity to God." James must have had deep spiritual experience, or he could not have seen the broad line between the world and the truth. The world is adultery—the lust of the flesh is the ruling dynasty.— Men are haunted day and night. They commit adultery in the streets. How far must such be from God. They are classed with liars, unbelievers and murderers, who shall have no part in the kingdom of God. I have been particularly impressed in meeting the world, this time, with the adulterous spirit which prevails. Men stare at women as they pass in the streets. Look at the advertisements in all the city papers—doctors advertising to cure private diseases. This is the world. In contrast with this picture, I have thought much of the doctrine of male continence. It seems like a resurrection thought, one which causes thankfulness and gives hope. Waiting on the Lord is a blessed privilege. *Gloria in Excelsis* for male continence, civilization, patience and victory!

Yours in Christ, O. H. M.

There is a good deal of activity in the bag-business now, and a demand for work in the afternoon bees. Last evening Mr. Hamilton and Mr. Woolworth called the attention of the family to the importance of helping as much as possible in the bees, at the present time. It is a good ordinance for every one who can attend the bees to do so, for it pays not merely in dollars and cents, but in personal experience.

RELIABLE AGENTS.

Extract from a letter of Mr. Noyes to W. A. H:

I see clearly that all our great projects of a world-wide Purchasing Agency, sustaining a world-wide Daily and a world-wide radiation of missionary work, depend absolutely on our raising up an army of *conscientious, reliable, faithful Agents.* This is the great want of all commercial business enterprises. Hobart Herrick says that if he could get *reliable men* to work for him as agents, he could control the whole flour trade of the country. He cannot get them; but we can, and will. Our moral and social machinery was invented on purpose to manufacture *good men,* and we will have them and plenty of them too, to manage the biggest complication of business for body and soul that the world ever saw.

Who can read the above without saying in his heart, "AMEN—IT CAN AND SHALL BE DONE?" w.

G. D. A. arrived yesterday to take W. G. K.'s place on his silk-selling route, Mr. K. being somewhat disabled by his former trip. G. and Edwin Burnham go to Oswego to-day.

D. Abbott arrived home this morning. He was successful in his business. He found the tin can machine quite satisfactory, and engaged one for $225. He was very lucky in meeting Mr. Miller at Cincinnati Mr. M. had been looking into the merits of the machine and had made arrangements to have the machine at work, so that he could observe its operations, just in season for Daniel's arrival.

Mr. Knowles is quite sick—was taken down immediately after Mrs. Knowles's departure. He has suffered very severely with pain in his head and side.

METEOROLOGICAL.

April 19.

6 A. M. Mercury 60 deg. 12 M. 66. 6 P. M. 68.
Pleasant. Southerly wind, and signs of rain during the day.

DAILY JOURNAL
OF ONEIDA COMMUNITY.

A. D. 1866. APR. 21. NO. 83.

SATURDAY.

MRS. H. A. Hall submitted to a surgical operation yesterday. For many years—ever since she was at Putney—she has had several excrescences growing on her head, somewhat similar in their structure to the swelling on Mrs. Abbott's neck. Yesterday they were removed by Dr. Fitch. Mrs. Hall bore the operation, which was quite painful, with fortitude.

Edith Waters also had a swelling on her neck, which has been troubling her for some time, lanced by the doctor.

The conversation last evening turned on the subject of the cultivation of fortitude and strength of heart, in meeting disease, by fellowship with Christ, and laying hold of his faith and resurrection power.

The following note from Mrs. Kelly was read last evening :

April 20, 1866.

DEAR BROTHERS AND SISTERS:—It is one year to-day since we came to the Community. It is a year long to be remembered. I cannot but look back and see what a wreck I was then in body and spirit. I can hardly realize that I am the same person. Now I think I can do as hard work as any woman in the Community, and am well and happy. I thank you all for the great kindness and patience shown us as a family. My prayer is that each one of us may prove a true soldier in " the army of the Lord."

Your sister in love of the truth. L. E. KELLY.

Another letter from "Riley Hunter" :

GENTLEMEN:—I received the trap springs yesterday, also one copy of the Trapper's Guide, which as yet I have not had time to read. I think the Guide is a good thing for young trappers, or new beginners, and it will meet with the approbation of many of my large circle of acquaintances.

Inclosed you will please find five dollars. Send me that amount in copies of the Guide. You will please send one of the copies and THE CIRCULAR, to the address of P. F. Cavaliere, Fremont, Ohio, as he has a desire to see THE CIRCULAR.

I consider myself under many obligations to you for those springs, and will endeavor to exert my influence for the benefit of the honorable Community for the furtherance of their already wide sale of traps.

I notice in the Trapper's Guide two new kinds of traps lately introduced. Those two traps have never been in this region to my knowledge. The mink trap I think will be quite sure to find ready sale here when once introduced. The small traps I would prefer by all odds, if they should prove of sufficient strength to hold the marten, on account of their lightness, as a man could carry a greater number of them. In this letter you will find an extra dollar, for which you will please send me one of each as a sample, and I will show them to the trappers here. Yours Respectfully,

SAMUEL SHANNON.

Mr. Jones is improving, and is well enough to go about considerably. His suffering of body appears to have been the occasion of much improvement in his spiritual experience, and we understand that he enjoys a clearer sense of justification and union with Christ than ever before.

METEOROLOGICAL.

April 20.

A. M. Mercury 60 deg. 12 M. 86 6 P. M. 85.
The day was very pleasant. In the afternoon the mercury rose to 90 deg. and there were thunder-clouds and signs of showers. During the night there was some rain.

SONG.

How happy the birds are ! I heard one this morning singing in a strain that seemed expressive of such intense delight that one could easily suppose the well-spring of gladness in its breast so strong, that it *mus.* break forth thus in song, or the bird would die.

There is a kind of joyfulness inherent in some of God's creatures, that demands musical expression as its own peculiar outlet, and which feels itself restrained, hampered and pent up if it find not this its chosen utterance. This is true of birds, and frequently also of mankind. I know not if it is strictly true of any other creatures.

I have heard Signora Piccolomini and other noted female singers who, in their higher flights, tossing aside all the conventional restraints of formal, measured music, seemed to pour forth their whole souls in glorious outbursts of delicious song, as if a fountain of unmixed joy arose from their bosoms, flooding the atmosphere and filling the hearts of the audience with unspeakable delight.

Warbling so ecstatic as this, cannot be called "singing"; the word is too tame. I know no word that can describe it. The influence that such a performance has on a susceptible listener, it is difficult to imagine. The eloquence of a great orator may accomplish more, and has a wider scope, but it cannot produce such intense, unmixed happiness—happiness reflected from the singer, and which, for the time, seems like that of the lark, knowing nothing, remembering nothing, anticipating nothing, but completely absorbed in the glad sensations of the moment.

Yet perhaps it is not to be regretted that pleasure of this kind comes not often and comes not to all. What it gains in intensity it loses in breadth. We may safely assume that mere melody-happiness is at least nearly akin to bird-happiness. But the happiness of God is broad, deep and " endureth forever." The poet was very nearly right when he said

"There is no joy but calm."

W. H. H.

DAILY JOURNAL
OF ONEIDA COMMUNITY.

A. D. 1866. APR. 23. NO. 84.

MONDAY.

A BORE.

A person called at this Community a day or two since with a model of a new patent hay-fork, which he desired to exhibit to us. We politely informed him that it would be of no object to do so as we already had a hay-fork which was satisfactory, and we could not possibly be induced to engage in the manufacture of hay-forks for sale : besides we were quite busy, and had no time to examine his model. But nothing we said appeared in the least to discourage him. He would not take "No" for answer, and was evidently determined that the Community should in some way become practically interested in his patent invention ; and we were forced to appear rude to him, and turn to other matters, even in his presence. Finally, he went away, and we congratulated ourselves that we were delivered of his presence and conversation ; but, no—he soon returned with model in hand, and was about to expatiate thereon, when he received a rebuke so positive as to induce him to beat a speedy retreat. It is not sufficient to say that this person was a bore. He was a bad case of mercantile priapism, and really intended to commit a rape upon us. Such an example may serve a good purpose as a contrast to the true spirit of a tradesman, which is modest and courteous, and never forgets the golden rule.   w.

BUSINESS MEETING ITEMS.

The subject of repairing the roads was before the Board. It was thought that the work necessary to be done now, could be accomplished without hiring help. Mr. Clark was appointed to furnish teams, and Mr. Kinsley to furnish help.

The question of straightening the road near the Red School-house was left to a committee.

Mr. Burt was appointed to attend to such repairs as are necessary on the Willow Place dyke.

Mr. Wilson has inquired if we would sell him a plot of land in the rear of his garden, so that he could extend it down to our pond. The project was not favored. Mr. Thomas also wishes to buy a lot of land.

Mr. Noyes's inspiration, and the spirit of harmony and brotherly love in our business, was confessed.

Several parties went riding yesterday, and others to ramble in the Park.

The pleasant spring weather attracts people out to the fields, and makes excursions popular. Mr. Hamilton referred to the matter last evening, and thought the family should guard against the tendency to scatteration and pleasure-seeking that is apt to come in at this season. The meeting was taken up with testimony and confessions of Christ.

Mr. Knowles's sickness has been quite serious, but it is believed that he is slowly rallying, although he is not able to leave his bed ; he has been removed to the back parlor where he receives every kindly attention.

G. D. A. left to-day on his trip to Buffalo.

Mr. Thayer cut the first asparagus of the season yesterday—about 10 lbs.

Our term of warm weather closed yesterday apparently. This morning it is cool and cloudy, with prospect of rain.

E. H. writes from the silk-factory as follows:

"The time of our sojourn here grows shorter every day, and it will be but a little while before we shall see our Oneida home once more. You may calculate on seeing us in five or six weeks at the farthest, I think.—H. and I think we have thoroughly mastered the art of winding, and next week one of us will begin spooling and the other something else. There are several things to be learned yet, but nothing that will require near the time that the winding has taken. Our work goes on first-rate and we enjoy it much, especially now as we begin to see our way through so soon.

"Our surroundings here are very wild and romantic and we enjoy strolling off among the hills and valleys, where the charming little brooks are making their way under the tall trees and bushes. It seems to me that I never enjoyed a spring as I do this one—perhaps it is because we have so few other outward things here to attract our attention."

METEOROLOGICAL.

April 21.

6 A. M. Mercury 63 deg. Some rain early in the morning.

12 M. Mercury 75 deg. Cloudy.

6 P. M. Mercury 67 deg.

April 22.

6 A. M. Mercury 53 deg. Cloudy sunrise.

12 M. Mercury 66 deg. Clear.

6 P. M, Mercury 60 deg.

DAILY JOURNAL
OF ONEIDA COMMUNITY.

A. D. 1866.　APR. 24.　NO. 85.

TUESDAY.

NOTES OF LAST EVENING'S CONVERSATION.

Mr. Hamilton.—If we watch for the resurrection, how shall we look for it ? and where shall we expect it to appear and take effect ? These are questions we might study. I desire to be receptive to the truth in this direction. I want to know how to watch and wait for the resurrection in the true way. It has seemed to me sometimes that there might be a selfish desire and eagerness for the resurrection to come in the body. It may be looked for in a selfish way that God cannot sympathize with. I am interested at the present time in looking for the effects of the resurrection in my spirit. I feel that the power of God will work first in the spirit and then in the body.

Christ frequently said when he healed persons, "Go and sin no more, lest a worse thing come upon thee." He recognized an intimate connection between the health of the spirit and the health of the body. The more I look in this direction and the more I desire to be in the resurrection, the more I am led to pray for purity of life. It seems to me there are certain principles we can lay hold of and apply in a way to help our sincerity and direct our prayers. The power of God working in our spirits will transform our bodies. We know that the character of a person's spirit expresses itself—a person's moral character is stamped upon the face, and is conspicuous to any acute observer. If a person yields himself to debauchery, crime, or evil passions in any form, the effect is marked upon the face, so that every body can see it. And then if a person is moral, studious, and upright, this also is manifest in the face. We can reason right back in this way, and strengthen our faith with the assurance and hope that the work of the Gospel and the discipline that God is putting us through, is breaking up selfishness, self-will and pleasure-seeking; and that becoming acquainted with God and giving place to his life and energy, is going to make its mark on our bodies.

It takes a clear eye to see the truth; and it takes a pure heart to see God. And so it takes a pure heart to see and appreciate the resurrection. We see that the Lord has been purifying us, and that there has been a great advance in the general character of the Community within the past two years. Take for instance, the time Mr. Noyes started the project of transferring THE CIRCULAR to Wallingford, and I think you will find a great change has taken place since then. The general life of the Community is now much purer than it was then. Much bad material has been cast out. There is a great deal more compactness and unity of life and freedom of spirit now than there was then. I believe that in all this we are so much nearer the resurrection, and so much more available to God and receptive to his spirit. And yet probably there is still a great deal to do in purifying the life of the Community. I dare not hope for the resurrection till we attain purity of life.

In the world they are guarding themselves against the Cholera in a negative way by removing uncleanliness and corruption. We may hasten the resurrection and draw near to it by helping God remove obstructions in the spirit. We are not doing in this respect like the world. They are trying to keep out evil by removing the occasion of it. We are trying to invite a good power to come and take possession of us by creating a receptive atmosphere and by removing all obstructions. If God is stronger than the devil, or the resurrection life stronger than the Cholera, then our case is the most hopeful. I feel like having a strong heart, and expecting good to work in my life. I would exhort others to awake from sleep to the consciousness that good is strong in all, and not lie down under evil, and think that evil habits have got hold of them that cannot be broken. The resurrection is working back of all these things, and I believe it is going to be easy for us to be good.

A gentleman in Cleveland, Ohio, writes to Mr, Newhouse as follows:

"Some time since I bought of one of the hardware dealers in this city, Mr. G. Worthington, one of your Bear Traps. I purchased it for the purpose of protection against burglary and chicken thieves. Three nights since I had the satisfaction to catch one of these light-fingered gentry. I am recommending these traps as a protection against burglars; and the idea of their use seems to be received favorably by our citizens. I wish. to know what you would charge for fifty of these traps"

W. A. Hinds left for New York yesterday on a business visit.

Mr. Knowles appears to be gradually improving.

METEOROLOGICAL.

April 23.

5 A. M. Mercury 41 deg.　12 M. 47.　6 P. M. 48.

A cold rain-storm has been in progress since yesterday forenoon, accompanied by a strong wind. This morning we notice occasional small flakes of snow mixed with the fine rain.

OUT RIDING.

The other day a party of excursionists who were going out riding, invited me to join them. We had a a pleasant drive; the fresh, delicate verdure that enameled the earth, and the light green buds that were bursting from the trees, filled the atmosphere with the spirit of youth, and our hearts with suggestions of resurrection life.

Much of the land we saw appeared good, and would probably yield a fair return for its cultivation; but when we passed some of the more rugged parts, where the farmer seemed to have a hard battle with nature to win daily bread, we thought how much better it would be, were such misapplied labor directed rather to the building of railroads and other means of locomotion, to connect the comparatively sterile portions with those richer regions, where one hundredth part of the agricultural force expended in less favored latitudes, would raise food enough for the entire human race. Why should not the Tropics along with such lands as those of the great West where corn is often used as fuel, be the farms and orchards of the whole world? The main things we lack, are the facilities for rapid and cheap transportation.

These less productive sections that are now the scenes of so much toil, might then be fields for the exercise of artistic improvement—pasture lands, lawns, groves and parks, with pathways winding through copse and garden, thus literally realizing the ancient prediction that 'the desert should blossom as the rose." 　　w. h. h.

DAILY JOURNAL
OF ONEIDA COMMUNITY.

A. D. 1866.   APR. 25.   NO. 86.

WEDNESDAY.

Mr. Knowles still improves, though unable to sit up much yet. He occasionally gets off a joke. Last night, he remarked, while feeling somewhat uncomfortable in consequence of a large blister on his side : "Paul says it is better to marry than to burn. I got married once, and got terribly scorched, and now I'm burning."

The Express Company performs its duty now with respect to THE CIRCULAR with commendable regularity and promptness. Several delays, however, have occurred in the delivery of the papers at the Community, in consequence of the Community mail agents failing to call for them on their Tuesday morning trips.

House-cleaning still goes on vigorously. We heard yesterday that the company had cleaned about sixty rooms, large and small. There are some thirty or more rooms yet to clean. The work appears to go off cheerfully and in a good spirit. J. P. H. is enthusiastic over his new machine for fastening carpets.

D. P. N. and a company of women and girls, went off this morning scouring the country for greens. They propose to secure enough for supper for the whole family this evening.

Messrs. S. Nash and W. G. Kelly have of late been occupied in laying out the ground on the west side of the lawn—between it and the privet hedge. Their present plan is to have it chiefly in grass, with a few flower plots. Some gracefully winding walks have already been constructed, with rose bushes set along the borders. This "new garden," considered as the complement of the lawn, will have a fine effect.

In a letter from the N. Y. B., Mr. Hinds says :

"We had an interesting conversation this morning about ownership of property in persons and things.

"Mr. N. says a man does not fully own anything until he gets it into such a state that he can freely *swing* it. The Lord has been at work with us some time on this point. He showed us last winter that we had not a *sure hold*. Now we are to seek a *swinging* hold. God thinks more of perfecting the ownership of the property we have, than of our getting more. We have only half-ownership of property so long as we cannot do what we have a mind to with it.

"Something similar is going on with reference to persons in the Community. God has only half-ownership of persons until he can swing them where he pleases. So long as a man is attached to persons and things he is not convertible property—the Lord cannot have full control of him. The Lord's way is first to get a *sure hold* of persons, and afterwards a *swinging hold*. That is

what we are trying to do with our agents. It will not answer to swing our agents very much until the Lord and the Community get a sure hold of them. The trouble in A. W. C.'s case was, that the Community never got a sure hold of him.

"This philosophy explains the social experience of the past year or two, more especially. God wants the ownership of our hearts and affections, so that he can *swing* them where he pleases. A man whose heart is fixed in certain special directions is like a mortgaged estate—not convertible property."

The work on the store goes steadily forward. The south wing is being raised—the rafters will be put up to-day. The wall of the north wing is about two-thirds laid.

Mr. Leete is here. He came over to glaze the sash for the Store; but finding that job already done, has turned his attention to laying the floor.

Last evening Mr. Hamilton spoke as follows :

"Sunday evening while George Allen was here, he called at my room and wanted to talk some with me, and cultivate good relations by opening his heart. He said he had some temptations to feel babyish on coming here, about going out again. He began to feel homesick and as though he wanted to stay at home. He said that Mr. Kelly had spoken of having the same feeling. I have thought of this a good deal since ; and I am not going to be satisfied with having our peddlars come home here and have such an experience as that. There are some reasons why they should feel tempted, and why it is more comfortable to stay here than to go out. But for all that, I feel for myself that I want to have such a spirit as will make every one seek service. I hope there will be such a spirit of devotion to God's will and service here, that it will electrify and strengthen our agents, instead of making them feel weak. I want to have such a spirit prevail, that when they come here, they will see that everybody is about the Lord's business—that there is no fellowship or interchange that is not founded upon that spirit ; and that there is not any loose, easy state of circumstances, that persons can drop into ; but that all are wide awake and enterprising for service. These thoughts arose in my mind while thinking of my conversation with George.

"The only heaven is in having the spirit of service. I confess my union with Christ's spirit where he said it was his meat and drink to do his Father's will. There is no mistake but that this is the truth, and we are miserably deceived if we are looking for happiness in any other way. I pray to be possessed by that spirit. I am thankful for the enlightenment in my mind, that sees the beauty and profit of that attitude. I confess, sincerely and modestly, that the spirit of service and seeking to do God's will, is eating up the love of ease in my heart. I believe that this thing is going on in the whole church—that the love of ease, comfort and happiness, in any other way than in God's service, is being displaced."

METEOROLOGICAL.

April 24.

6 A. M. Mercury 35.   15 M. 34.   6 P. M. 34.

There was a light rain all day, sometimes inclining to snow. During the afternoon the wind veered round to the West, and in the night the curtain of dripping clouds blew off. This morning it is clear and cool, but without frost.

DAILY JOURNAL
OF ONEIDA COMMUNITY.

A. D. 1866.   APR. 26.   NO. 87.

THURSDAY.

Martin and his agricultural corps are now busily engaged in repairing the fences.

Since the old horse barn has been consigned to the hands of the carpenters, it is found necessary to have a place for farm tools and implements. Excavations are in progress a few rods west of the Tontine, with the view of building a shed for that purpose. The wings of the old horse barn will supply the material necessary.

A writer in THE CIRCULAR is quite eloquent in his— or her—praises of mathematics. Apropos of that, we observe that although the regular classes have been closed some time since, there are several enthusiastic students who keep up the study with undiminished interest. The other day we observed a group poring over an intricate equation of the second degree. At Oneida
The " New Tonic,"
Has become chronic.

A COMMUNICATION.

MR. EDITOR.—I should like to correct a statement in yesterday's JOURNAL. It reports me to have said that I felt babyish about starting out peddling. I think the report came from some conversation I had with G. D. A. to this effect: that on returning home, the first influence I met, was of the more superficial kind, and was not satisfactory—that it sometimes took two or three days to get through this superficial influence into the peaceful, quiet influence of the central spirit ; and I thought in his circumstances the effect of this kind of influence would be either to make him wish he had not come at all, or would make him dislike to go out again.
Yours truly, W. G. KELLY.

Mr. Reynolds has lately been subject to some of his old temptations to irritability and evil-thinking. Last evening he offered himself to the family for criticism. The truth was spoken to him in a kind and thoroughly sincere way, and we trust he will be greatly benefited thereby.

Mrs. S. B. Campbell is suffering from quite a severe attack of erysipelas.

This morning we are having a practical illustration of the old adage about " Winter lingering in the lap of Spring." The mercury in the thermometer is slightly below 33 deg., a series of snow-squalls is creating a turmoil in the atmosphere, and the ground is white.

Mr. Henderson is now engaged in learning job-printing, and promises to become a successful master of the art.

The sale of the Red School-house, together with 1½ acres of land adjoining, to Mr. Radford, has been effected. He pays $275 for the property.

Mr. Nash and his verdant company made a successful raid on the scurvy-grass in Mr. Hubbard's strawberry field, yesterday, and the result was an abundant supply for supper. Our troops that march under the "Green Flag," this spring, have thus far been more successful than the Fenians. We expect they will eat scurvy-grass a good while yet, before O'Mahoney takes Ireland.

Speaking of the Fenians, we noticed on a bit of pine board the other day, the following effusion by some ambitious Community " pote." Whether he intended to slander the patriotic members of the " Irish Republic," or no, we are unable to say:

" B. Doran Killian
Was a great Fenian,
Who with O'Mahoney
Got a great deal of money
From the sons of Kilarney
By their Fenian blarney."—
Here the afflatus seems to have " kinder gin eout."

METEOROLOGICAL.
April 25.

6 A. M. Mercury 33 deg. Clear. Wind west.
12 M. Mercury 35 deg. 6 P. M. 34 deg. The afternoon was cloudy, with a tendency to snow. We were incorrect in stating that there was no frost yesterday morning. The ground was slightly frozen in some localities.

DAILY JOURNAL
OF ONEIDA COMMUNITY.

A. D. 1866.　APR. 27.　NO. 88.

FRIDAY.

The following note from Mrs. Abbott was read last evening :

O. C. *April 26*, 1866.

I should like to thank the family for their kindness to me the past year. I feel it is due to the faith and sympathy I have received, that my life has been spared. I believe that had I been in the world, I should have died ; it seems as though I came as near the other world as I could, and stay in this. I can say the Lord is good. I can thank Him for the past, and trust Him for the future. I have learned many valuable lessons in faith and patience. My prayer is, that I may have the inspiration of God in all I do, and be a help to Mr. Noyes, in carrying out whatever he may suggest. I confess Christ a humble receptive spirit.　LAURA ABBOTT.

Mr. Jones wishes to express his thankfulness to God for His dealings with him and to confess his faith in Christ as a perfect Savior of body and soul.

Mr. Hamilton leaves to-night for Wallingford, accompanied by Arabella Woolworth. Mr. H. expects to return, by the way of New-York, about the middle of next week.

The prospect of a good crop of apples and plums is very fine. Many of the plum trees are heavily loaded with blossom buds. This is particularly the case with the Lombards and McLaughlins. The Catherines promise a fine crop. Several seedling trees will do well. The seedling tree on the bank west of the little fish-pond, has proved to be a very hardy variety. It bears a good plum, especially for preserving. The tree is loaded with blossom buds.

After application at seven different nurseries, we have been unable to find any Damson Plum trees, this Spring.

The Oneida *Democratic Union* copies the article " A Village in Futuro," from THE CIRCULAR.

Mr. Radford, our shoe-maker, has, for the last week or two, been at work on the store, laying stone-wall &c.

Among the visitors yesterday was a Swede. He is at present attending the Madison University, and came down to the Community with a fellow-student, the son of Mr. Crane, one of our hired carpenters. His name is Theodore Truve, of Gothenberg, Sweden. He was a missionary for several years in his native country, preaching the Baptist faith. For doing this, he was much persecuted. The national and state religion of Sweden is the Lutheran, and he represents the people as quite bigoted, and intolerant toward any innovations on the popular religion. He was among the first who received Baptist views. Since then, he states, some thousands have adopted them. After he gets through with his course at the University, he proposes to return to Sweden. He is about 35 years of age. He was considerably interested in what he heard and saw of the Community, and thought he should come here again in the Summer.

S. B. C. is somewhat more comfortable to-day.

Mr. Knowles is steadily improving.

METEOROLOGICAL.

April 26.

6 A. M. 33 deg.　Snow.　12 M. 37 deg.　Strong west wind.　6 P. M. 39 deg.　Cloudy.

Our little snow-storm yesterday soon passed away. The day was cool, gradually moderating toward night. The culmination of the cold term seems to be past, and we judge there has been no serious injury to vegetation.

THE PRESENT TENSE.

The Imperfectionists lay a good deal of stress upon Paul's use of the present tense in the 7th. of Romans— " I am carnal" &c.—arguing from the tense of the language, that the apostle was a " carnal" sinner at the time he wrote.

We would politely request such persons to try the application of the same rule of interpretation, to Carlyle's " History of Frederick the Great," where the author— himself writing only a few years since—informs us that " It is now May, 1728," that " Frederick is twenty-one," that Maurice, son of the King of Poland, " resembles his father," &c., from which statements, if interpreted according to the above rule, it would be inferred that Frederick was twenty-one, and that Maurice resembled his father, at the time Carlyle wrote, and that Carlyle wrote in the year 1728.

Indeed, throughout all the years of his History, Carlyle makes himself present wherever it suits him, and writes accordingly.

Now if Carlyle uses this privilege, much more may Paul, especially when it is remembered that his Epistle is something more than a mere chronicle, the narrative element in it being clearly subservient to the argumentative.　W. H. H.

DAILY JOURNAL
OF ONEIDA COMMUNITY.

A. D. 1866.   APR. 28.   NO. 89.

SATURDAY.
THE LICENSE QUESTION.

Some of the Community agents have had the impression that it is necessary for them to have both a Commercial Brokers' License and a Peddlers' License. I have recently consulted an Assistant Assessor in New York, and also M. Barnet, the Assistant Assessor at Oneida Depot, on this point; and received assurances from both, that only a Commercial Brokers' License is required for the Community agents who travel, soliciting orders and delivering goods. Accordingly, only Commercial Brokers' Licenses will be procured for our agents; and if any person claims that another license is also required, the claimant should be referred to the Assistant Assessor to whom application was made for the Commercial Brokers' License.   w.

Bag orders were received during the week ending April 27, to the amount of $292.42.

A new boat, capable of holding several persons, has been built for use on the pond at Willow Place. Being constructed with bass-wood boards, it is quite light and easily handled.

Good progress is being steadily made in fitting up the silk-machinery. Mr. Inslee expects to have a portion of it ready for running by the 1st of June.

The manufacture of bag-frames, is fairly inaugurated with us, and has been in progress for some time, under the supervision of George Hamilton. A very good article is turned out. The locks for the frames are also made at the machine-shop. Mr. Noyes was much interested, when here last, on learning that this branch of manufacture was begun. He remarked that it was the beginning of our Newark.

A new martin-box has been made and fixed on the horse-barn; another on the cupola of the Mansion House; a third, of more decorated style, will be placed on the Tower. See Psalm 84.

Mr. Abbot has been clearing out the rubbish from the old shed at the mill. Yesterday, he sent off about a ton of old iron which has been picked up there and at the boarding-house.

Mr. A. Smith, of Verona, was here yesterday. He repaired the pump on the road opposite the Mansion House; and has been engaged to make a tool for fitting pump-logs. It will cost $5.

Some time since, Mr. Noyes, in a letter to Mr. Hamilton, suggested that in locating building-lots to be sold on the Hitchcock farm, we should consider the feasibility of altering the course of the road to Willow Place. The road at present is somewhat crooked, bending to the west so far as to form quite an angle at the Hamilton bridge. Mr. Noyes proposes to run the road straight from the Mill Bridge to Willow Place, forming a "Broadway" from one factory to the other. By this plan, the road would run several rods further east than it now does in front of the Community Mansions—east of the barns, and would cut the high creek-bank, and enter the Hitchcock farm a considerable distance east of the boarding-house. The plan contemplates the eventual possibility of a horse railway from one factory to the other, and the extension of both road and railway from Willow Place to Oneida, by way of Sconondoa. The whole plan is received with much sympathy by the Community.

Mr. Knowles and S. B. Campbell continue to improve. Jane Seymour has been very feeble of late, but to-day is quite comfortable, and manifests a very cheerful, happy spirit.

Note to the family from Tryphena Seymour :

April, 27.

I wish to renew my confession of Christ in me a Savior from sin, and to express my sympathy with, and desire to more fully appreciate, the Resurrection truth lately presented to us. I wish to give myself, my child, and every person and thing in which I have life, to God, that all my interest in them which is of the flesh, may be made the most of for the service of the church.

I confess Christ a Savior from a spirit of care and anxiety about my child, and an inordinate affection for her.

Since my late criticism, the Spirit of truth and of judgment has been searching my heart, showing me many faults and shortcomings, and I pray earnestly that everything may be removed that hinders the free course of the Community spirit in me.   T. S.

METEOROLOGICAL.

Thermometer, April 27.

6 A. M. 36 deg. 12 M. 45. 6 P. M. 47. Clear all day, with chilly westerly winds.

DAILY JOURNAL
OF ONEIDA COMMUNITY.

A. D. 1866.   APR. 30.   NO. 90.

MONDAY.
BUSINESS MEETING ITEMS.

We are still in want of a blacksmith who will do horse-shoeing, and machine-forging. It was thought best to advertise for one, and G. W. Hamilton was authorized to advertise in the local papers, and also to prepare a proper notice to be inserted in THE CIRCULAR.

The committee on trap prices, and the trap committee, are to take immediate steps to ascertain the cost of the two new sizes of traps, and perfect their price list in time to issue a revised list by the 1st of June. The trap committee meets this morning at Willow Place to consider the matter.

It was suggested that measures be taken to remove the compost heap at the west end of the wood-shed, and that a more suitable place for garbage be provided.

It was also thought that there was a lack of vigilance on the part of the sanitary committee. In view of its being a cholera season we should be vigilant to keep every thing clean. S. W. Nash, Mr. Henderson, Mr. Ackley, Harriet Mathews and Sophronia Higgins, were appointed as a thorough-going, executive sanitary committee.

Yesterday may be remembered as the Day of Winds. For nearly twenty-four hours, from Saturday evening to sunset of yesterday, a northwest gale blew with an almost continuous blast. We remember nothing like it during the last twelve years, for duration and extreme violence. On the exposed hills, it was difficult for a person to keep his position in face of it. One could lean back against it at quite an angle and be supported. Not a bird could trust itself before it. On our grounds the robins might be seen in a silent half-terrified mood seeking shelter on the ground under the hedges and low evergreens. A great cloud of dust kept continually rising from the sand hills west of us, and sweeping across the valley, far up on to the East Hill beyond Olmsted's woods. Back of Petrie's there is a deep ravine running down from Johnson's hill. This ravine and the land on each side of it, had been plowed and sown with oats. Here the wind and the sand held revelry. The wind would gather in the sand from either side, and forming a cloud at the bottom, would send it whirling furiously out at the mouth of the ravine. Much of the time the cloud would be so dense that for rods nothing could be seen through it. We heard of no accidents or injuries. Several square feet of the cement-roofing on the Tontine were blown off.

Mr. Hall returned Saturday afternoon from a peddling excursion of four days, having made the following sales: Bags, $27,00; hats, $37,50; silk, $366,13; total, $330,63.

The Saturday evening conversation turned on the care of the sick. It was thought there should be chastity and reserve in regard to turning our attention toward those that are sick. They should have good care, and all necessary nursing and sympathy, but the Community should go about its business and not suffer its attention to be distracted from its work and purpose, and turned to the wounded and sick. This is the best way to help the sick. They need to give their attention to Christ and the Church, and not to their own bodily ailments and symptoms. The Community is an army in a warfare and on a march, and it will not do to stop the march or turn from the fight for the sake of the wounded. They must be cared for by the proper ones, but the fight must go on until the victory is won. The devil would like to divert our attention, and have us all thinking about, and taking care of the wounded, giving him a chance to prey upon us where he likes. Even if those who are sick or wounded die, the most that can be said of them is, that they are taken prisoners, and will have to be delivered up before the war closes.

In Saturday's JOURNAL an omission of a line in Mrs Seymour's note occurred. On the 545d page, 2d line from the bottom, after the word "may," the sentence should read as follows: "be destroyed, so that my whole being may be made the most of for the service of the church."

METEOROLOGICAL.

Thermometer, April 28.

6 A. M. 40 deg. Clear. Wind S. S. E. 12 M. 68.—Slightly hazy. 6 P. M. 71.

April 29.

6 A. M. 41. 12 M. 50. 6 P. M. 49. Clear. Wind N. W., blowing a heavy gale all day.

WHAT FEAR YE?

All day the sky had been of azure hue
But in the evening, the celestial blue
   Had changed to gold;
And when the sun set in the glowing west,
A flood of glory on the lake's calm breast
   Benignly rolled.

It was Gennesaret's lake; the light streamed o'er
The placid stretch of sea from shore to shore.
   The dazzling mass
Scarce stirred; and in its stillness seemed to be
Not living brine, but some enchanted sea
   Of carven glass.

Cleaving the slumb'rous water with strong oar,
There glided from the Galilean shore
   An antique ship;
But as the middle of the lake was gained,
Each sun-browned rower toiled, with sinews strained
   And compressed lip.

For, as the night went on, had risen at length,
First, faint and low, but growing in its strength,
   So fierce a blast,
That each, though strong of heart and firm of hand,
In anxious hope to reach the distant land,
   Looked round aghast.

No longer now in beauty shone the sea,
But shook its foamy mane as if in glee,
   And rose, and fell;
The pale moon looked from out the troubled sky
Upon the haughty wave-crests tossing high
   Above the swell.

As thus, through drifts of cloud, those slanting beams
Fell on the surf in fitful, broken gleams,
   Strange fear and awe
Came o'er the toilers; and one cried "O, look!"
Then blanched was every lip, each strong limb shook
   At what they saw.

For, with firm footstep, gliding through the storm,
The straggling shafts of light revealed a form
   That still drew nigh;
Borne, as a spirit, o'er the reeling deep,
With steady grace its course it seemed to keep;
   Then rose a cry

Of terror from the rowers—a wild shriek—
When, lo! they, wondering, heard the phantom speak
   In accents clear;
And, calming their tumultuous thoughts, it said:
"Tis I, your Master; Why are ye afraid?
   Be of good cheer."

*   *   *   *   *   *

And even thus, when fiery trials roll
Across the path of life, and wring the soul,
   Is heard Christ's voice—
Christ's kindly words like light through darkness breaking,
Giving the troubled mind sweet peace, and making
   The heart rejoice.   **W. H. H.**

DAILY JOURNAL
OF ONEIDA COMMUNITY.

A. D. 1866. MAY 1.   NO. 91.

TUESDAY.

Yesterday the man who was engaged to lay the new walk in front of the house, came and commenced operations. The composition of which the walk is constructed consists of coarse gravel, coal-ashes, fine gravel and coal-tar. It is laid down about four inches thick, and is said to make an excellent walk, or pavement.

The fruit-growers have got nearly all their raspberry vines tied up, and are now at work on the grape vines. Two hired women are employed at this work, and do well. The tieing of the raspberries was nearly all done by them.

Last evening Mr. Inslee gave some account of what they are doing at the machine-shop in the way of fitting up the silk machinery. He thinks they are making very good progress, and the work goes on very satisfactorily. The testimony of the hands is, that it is a great pleasure to work on this job. Fourteen machines are to be constructed, viz., four winders, three cleaners, four spinners, one doubler, one stretcher and one soft-silk winder. In addition to these, some spooling-frames will be required. Mr. Inslee thinks that a portion of the machines will be ready for use by the 1st of June.

Mrs. Sherrard, the mother of Preston Sherrard is here. She wishes to obtain employment for some weeks, until she can make arrangements with reference to returning to Virginia. The family formerly resided in Fredrerick County in that State, and was broken up by the war. Preston made his escape through the Rebel lines with great difficulty to avoid being forced into the Rebel ranks. Mrs. Sherrard, we understand, is a lady of cultivated taste and fine education. She is an artist by profession.

The sanitary Committee have gone thoroughly to work. They yesterday made arrangements to have the compost heap, which has always occupied some point near the house, and which of late has been located near the wood-shed, discontinued altogether, and to have all rubbish, dirt and garbage deposited at the barn-yard where it will be speedily converted into manure. All our noses rejoice at the final abatement of this nuis_ance. To-day the committee are investigating the condition of the cellars.

Note to the family from Ellen Hutchins, read last evening :

"I thank God for his goodness to me in giving me a place in his church. I also thank Him for the privilege of giving my child to the Lord, and I confess Christ my helper to enable me to do it cheerfully and heartily. I confess an earnest spirit in separating myself from all horizontal and descending fellowships, and in seeking only the fellowship of those who can help me to for-get the past and press forward. I pray God to enable me to make speedy work in clearing away all obstructions in my spirit to the free flow of His Spirit in my heart, so that I can always walk by the clear light of inspiration. Yours for the freedom of the angels. in the service of the Lord, E. F. HUTCHINS."

The subject of conversation last evening was the idea of progressive perfection, advanced by Mr. Noyes in his conversation with the people at the Phalanx. A general sympathy was expressed with Mr. Noyes's doc-trine on that subject.

THE CIRCULARS failed to make their appearance at the Depot this morning. Our mails have been quite meager for several days, bringing us but little from either of the Branches.

House-cleaning still goes on vigorously. The Parlor. Business-office and Library are now undergoing the scouring and renovating operation. Abby says that the work has gone off this Spring easily and cheerfully.

The trap sales for the month of April amount to $752, 79.

W. A. Hinds has gone to Rome to get a lunch-bag photographed. The bag was furnished with bread and butter, cake and raisins, arranged in an attractive style.

The letter of Mr. Towner, published in THE JOURNAL some time since, was replied to. The Community did not deem it advisable for him to bring his family here, as he proposed, without further acquaintance. His other proposal to visit the Community himself, was favored. A letter was received from him to-day, expressing satisfaction with our view of the case, and saying that he should avail himself of our permission to visit the Community at his earliest opportunity.

METEOROLOGICAL.

Thermometer, April 30.

6 A. M. 34 deg. Clear. Wind West.
12 M. 46. deg. Clear. Chilly West Wind.
6 P. M. 44 deg.

DAILY JOURNAL
OF ONEIDA COMMUNITY.

A. D. 1866.   MAY 2.   NO. 92.

WEDNESDAY.
THE LICENSE QUESTION, AGAIN.

The following reported decision of the Commissioner of Internal Revenue, from Saturday's *Tribune*, puts an entirely new phase on the license question as applied to the Community agents:

"Persons traveling about the country as the agents of manufacturers, or dealers seeking orders for goods as agents of one person, or firms only, such as salaried clerks, or men hired by the month, should not be required to take licenses as Commercial Brokers—all parts of decision No. 150 inconsistent herewith, are hereby revoked."

Immediate measures will be taken to find out just what licenses, if any, will be required for our agents, in view of this recent decision.   w.

The patent walk in front of the New House was laid yesterday. It extends from the north east corner of the tower to the south end of the curbing in front of the portico, and thence along the south end of the portico. The process of laying the walk was as follows: A lot of sand and gravel from the creek was sifted. The coarse gravel and stones were thrown into one pile and the fine gravel and sand into another, coal ashes being mixed with each. Then into each pile a sufficient quantity of coal-tar is mixed to thoroughly saturate the whole mass, so that each individual grain or pebble is completely coated with it. The foundation of the walk being prepared by excavating to the depth of three inches, the coarse part of the prepared material is laid down and carefully leveled with a rake. Then the fine material is laid on and leveled in a similar way. A sprinkling of the dry sand and ashes is then thrown on, and the whole surface leveled by being heavily stamped with a plank and pounder. Another sprinkling of dry sand is now thrown on, and evened with a broom, and the walk is then rolled with a stone roller about two feet long, fourteen inches in diameter and weighing six hundred pounds. This rolling process is continued for some time, until the material is thoroughly compacted, and the surface well shaped and evenly graded. Another sprinkling of fine sand is added, and the walk is finished. The result is a very satisfactory walk, smooth, impervious to water, and durable. The inventor and patentee is Mr. D. French, of Syracuse. Associated with him is Mr. W. E. Lansing, formerly member of Congress from this district. Messrs. French and Lansing were both here. Mr. French is an old pavior, superintends the business and takes hold of the hardest of the work personally.

A man at the Phalanx House, Red Bank, N. J. having seen the paragraph about the "Village in Futuro", writes to know if he can find employment in our manufactories. His name is Charles M. Nye.

The cellar wall of the store is nearly completed. The carpenters are shingling the south wing.

We had a fine rain last night. To-day is warm and the fresh green grass of the lawn is beautiful, beneath the sunshine.

Mr. Hamilton was expected home to-day. The following letter explains his delay :

New York, May 1st, 1866.

"I am busy helping move, and Mr. Noyes wants I should stay over till to-morrow. I shall try and be at Oneida Thursday noon.

"It is a splendid room, but awfully dirty. I wish we had Abby, John P. Hutchins and Co. here a day or two. I believe I am getting filled with a good spirit.

      "Yours,   E. H. Hamilton."

The comic scene described in the Wallingford Journal, of Mr. Noyes's beginning to talk on a delicate subject, unconscious of the presence of a stranger, was repeated here on a larger scale last evening. The Hon. Mr. Lansing and Mrs. Sherrard, were present in our meeting. As the reader of the journal came to the description of the scene, persons began to whisper to each other, wondering if the reader knew of the presence of the strangers. Miss N. grows nervous, and tries to get Edwin Burnham to check the reader. Failing in making Edwin understand, she gets Mrs. W. to whisper to him. Just as the reader approaches the climax of the story—G.'s "hoarse whisper"—Edwin jumps up, frantically seizes the reader's arm, and whispers "There are strangers present !" The reader, who fully understood the case, smiled, and replied by reading G's whisper and the remainder of the description. A long breath of relief came from the audience, as it became apparent that no report of the "delicate matter" was coming.

Would it interest our readers to learn that the old saying " Welcome as flowers in May" was gracefully illustrated yesterday, by one of our children finding a wild strawberry blossom in the woods?

Some of our orthoepists think that the mistake of spelling the word " rhythm" with only one h, as " rythm," in THE CIRCULAR, should be corrected. The mistake has occurred several times lately.

Mr. Seighman has written to Mr. Hamilton inquiring about the land we propose to sell. He asks for a description of the land, price, terms, distance from the Community buildings &c. He says : " Being a sympathizer, I would like to settle near the Community. I am engaged in merchandizing in this town, at present, but would prefer giving up matters here, and living near the Community, if I could see my way clear. One of my brothers and my mother, are in favor of the move."

METEOROLOGICAL.
Thermometer, May 1.

6 A. M. 33. Cloudy and white frost. 12 M. 50.—
P. M. 44. Begins to rain.

DAILY JOURNAL
OF ONEIDA COMMUNITY.

A. D. 1866.　　MAY 3.　　NO. 93.

THURSDAY.

Mr. Hamilton arrived this morning about 7 o'clock.—We are all glad to hear that the N. Y. Branch have been successful in their moving operations, and that they have got so good business quarters. *Vive les Shakers!*

The late cool weather has checked the progress of vegetation somewhat, and slight injury by the frost is noticed in some places.

Martin Kinsley, while harnessing a colt yesterday, had his foot stepped upon, and in attempting to extricate it, wrenched it badly. Alice Ackley also, has sprained her ankle, and experiences some inconvenience therefrom.

A number of bag-photographs have been received from the Rome artists, and are very satisfactory. They bid fair to be a great convenience to our salesmen.

We were mistaken yesterday in announcing that the Mr. Lansing associated with Mr. French, was the Hon. W. E. Lansing. His name is Jacob S. Lansing, and he is *not* an ex-member of Congress. In making our report we followed a statement which, at the time, we supposed to be correct; but the "reliable gentleman" who made the statement, was misinformed.

The house-cleaning company have attacked the Upper Sitting-room to-day, and are making thorough work.

Mr. Knowles has had a return of his bad symptoms during the last few days; but to-day he is better, and we trust will continue to improve.—Mrs. S. B. Campbell is getting quite well again.

From last evening's conversation, we take the following paragraphs:

Mr. Pitt.—I had some thoughts to-day about this battle with disease, that we are engaged in. I remember that some time ago, after the Community had cast off Warren Chase and his hadean influence, Mr. Noyes remarked that probably the next principality we should have to meet would be New-York Perfectionism. I have questioned whether in this battle we were not fighting that principality. I trace the beginning of this dispensation of disease, to the time Mrs. K. came here. Before she came, the Community were remarkably free from ailments of all kinds, and had been so for a long time. There was a buoyant state of health among us. Mrs. K. was a thorough representative of New-York Perfectionism, and was formerly known as such in the region where she came from. She came here full of the evil-thinking devil, and full of disease. While she was here, every one who sympathized with her, was more or less affected by disease. And when she went away, she sent a diabolical shaft of disease into Mr. K., from which he has been suffering ever since.

Now I have no doubt that the head-quarters of New-York Perfectionism, are in Hades. The leading spirits of that dispensation, have passed into that world. The old reprobate leaders who tried to crush New-Haven Perfectionism, are there. But they have their mediums in this world, and I have no doubt we have been in contact with one of them in this case. Mr. Noyes told us to beware of New-York Perfectionism. I felt to-day that I wanted every vestige of sympathy with that principality, cleared out. Another indication that we are in a battle with that spirit, is the fact that Mr. Cragin has been exposing the corruptions of New-York Perfectionism in the recent chapters of his history.

[Several spoke of having similar impressions in regard to this matter.]

Mr. Woolworth.—If this experience serves to stir us up to put on the whole armor of God, it will be good. I believe that is the lesson God would have us learn.

Shortly since, a gentleman who shall be nameless, spent two days here on business. On both evenings, he was courteously invited to be present at meeting, but he respectfully declined. He was sitting in the Library when THE CIRCULARS arrived, and one of them was offered to him but not accepted. We learn that his *better half* had prudently warned him against our influence; hence his shyness. Here was a reversing of the dynamic and conspicuous!

Jane Seymour died this morning about 10 o'clock.

METEOROLOGICAL.

Thermometer, May 2.

6 A. M. 39. Cloudy. 12. M. 44. Wind west. 6 P. M. 40. Very chilly day. Mr. Hall reports having seen snow on the northern hills.

DAILY JOURNAL
OF ONEIDA COMMUNITY.

A. D. 1866.　　MAY 4.　　NO. 94.

FRIDAY.

John S. Freeman of Schenectady writes to us as follows:

The Lord seems now to have opened the way for me to come to Oneida, if it is the wish of the family. As you know, I am a babe in righteousness, and need the milk of the word and criticism; but I wish to grow in grace and the knowledge of Christ; and I know of no place so favorable to growth as with you.

If the Community accept me and think it best that I should come this spring, or wait longer, please let me know when convenient.

I am now engaged in the nurseries near us. The next College term begins Monday, April 30, which father is very anxious I should attend, but I leave it all to your direction, and "await orders."

We are glad to see the "Story of a Life" appear again, and are very much interested in it.

　　　　　　　　　Yours sincerely, J. S. Freeman.

Emily Otis's letter and the report of the talk at Wallingford in relation to it, were read last evening. There was a general expression of sympathy with the talk.

The pale green tints of early leafage begin to come upon the woods; but spring delays to clothe herself, under the influence of our cool nor'westers.

The general spring work seems to be going on well, and all are cheerful. We hear of no jars now in any of the departments.

Mary D. Pomeroy is gaining ground apparently every day, attends bag-bees, and is around the house more or less with her cheerful, smiling face.

Mr. Campbell has gone into the machine-shop to work.

Mrs. Campbell addressed the following note to the family last evening:

I wish to express my thanks in the congregation of the saints, for my late experience—for my sickness, and for my restoration, and especially for the spirit of victory that has been given me. I have proved that the Lord can control the attention in the midst of great distractions. I confess my confidence in him as the greatest charmer in the universe.

I also wish to express thanks for the kind care and attention that I have received, and above all for the strengthening of my faith. I believe I have, by the grace of God, begun anew, and I confess Christ my ability to walk in the Spirit.　　　　　S. B. C."

The funeral of Jane Seymour takes place to-day, at 11 o'clock.

The stone-masons having got through with the store wall, are now engaged laying the foundation for the tool-house. This building is situated on the west bank of the ravine, back of the Tontine, and nearly opposite the North end of that building.

The store progresses visibly now each day. The south wing is shingled, and work has been begun on the front of the main part.

An occasional plum blossom begins to open, notwithstanding the cool weather.

The florists keep steadily at work, remodeling the flower beds and forming new ones.

Mr. Thayer displays his customary activity in the vegetable line this spring, and his hotbed plants are in a promising condition.

The green-house keeps up its attractive show of flowers. We are having a fine display of cactus blossoms, now.

MOVEMENTS OF AGENTS.

W. G. Kelly expects to start for New-York to-morrow, and will soon *agent* his way back.

E. S. Burnham expects to go to Rome and Utica to-morrow. Mr. Hall has returned from a successful trip of two days.

Mr. Olds and John Norton have separated for return trips. The latter writes from Freeport:

"My intended route is as follows—from here to Rock-Island and Davenport—Muscatine and Burlington—Keokuk and Quincy, thence to Chicago, via Chicago, Burlington and Quincy R. R. From Chicago to Detroit via "Michigan Central," stopping at Kalamazoo—Battle Creek—Jackson—Ann Arbor and Ypsilanti. From Detroit to Cleveland, via Adrian, Toledo, and Sandusky City.　　　Yours as ever,　　　J. Norton."

Mr. Olds, we suppose, is now at Millwaukee, but he intends to go to Chicago, thence to St. Louis, and return again to Chicago before coming home. The following suggestion in his last letter is important:

"I find some of the samples of Bags we have are not lettered, and I am sometimes at a loss to tell which is which. It seems to me that all our Fancy Bags in particular should be numbered and lettered, as we have no other way to distinguish the different kinds."

The Bag department has lately ordered new stamps, and it is not likely that any one will long be troubled in the manner described above.

Mr. Miller is expected home soon.

METEOROLOGICAL.
　　　　　　　　Thermometer, May 3.
6 A. M. 38.　12 M. 40.　6 P. M. 42.　The day was cloudy with cold westerly winds.

DAILY JOURNAL
OF ONEIDA COMMUNITY.

A. D. 1866.   MAY 5.   NO. 95.

SATURDAY.

The creeks and ponds are becoming quite attractive to the disciples of Izaak Walton. White fish, suckers, chubs and bass are brought home almost daily, and may be seen, served up in dainty fashion at the breakfast table. The frogs also, who we presume are second cousins to the fish, sometimes share a similar fate. We saw a delicious mess of them lately, kicking in the frying-pan.

Speaking of Izaak Walton and frogs, we are reminded that the dear old angler had quite a love for these amphibians. When he baited his hook with one, he used always to put it on in such a manner as to "keep it alive as long as possible." What a tender-hearted old dear he was!

Our trapper correspondent Shannon, sends us a copy of the *Fremont Journal*, containing the following notice:

TO HUNTERS AND TRAPPERS.

S. Shannon, the trapper of Riley, has received an enormous Bear Trap of the celebrated Newhouse pattern. It was presented to him by the Oneida Community, of Oneida, New York. He has also ordered samples of two different grades of this noted trap for mink and rats, which have been recently introduced. He invites all trappers to call and examine them. He has also the Trappers' Guide Book. It contains many very essential instructions to trappers and hunters, as it gives the experience of several trappers who have spent half a century in trapping. It also gives a description of the different grades of the Newhouse trap, and the habits of animals they are adapted to catching. It is a very interesting book. Call at my residence, on Fox Island, and get a copy, or address, box No. 1, Fremont, Ohio, and I will send you a copy on receipt of the Publishers' price, 75 cts.

SAM'L SHANNON.

The bag orders for the week ending May 3, amounted to $414,63.

Yesterday the first trap-order of the opening trade, was received from Merrill Ryder of St. Paul, for the Red River region, amounting to $271,88.

To-day, an order for preserved fruits and vegetables was received from Milwaukee, amounting to about a thousand dollars. The order is to be filled in the fall.

Mr. Thayer reports the new strawberry plantation as all set. It occupies a little over three acres. The leading varieties, as usual, are Wilsons and Triomphes. In addition to these, beds of French's Seedling, Oscar, Agriculturist, Russell, and Oneida Seedling, have been set.

The fruit-growers have secured the services of a young Englishman, who has had considerable experience in an English fruit garden at St. Albans. He appears to be intelligent and trustworthy in the business, and will probably prove a valuable assistant in that department.

Nearly five acres of raspberry plants have been set this Spring. They comprise the following varieties: Brinckle's Orange, Fastolf, Hudson River Antwerp, Hornet, Philadelphia, and Doolittle's Black Cap.

Last evening Mr. Hamilton gave an interesting account of his visit to New-York, and of affairs at that Branch. It stirred up our hearts to new interest in the operations at that post, and brought Mr. Noyes very near to us all. We feel more than ever, that New-York is the central point of interest now, and shall gird up our hearts and minds, and bend all our energies to sustain the brethren there.

The Tontine roof is being repaired to-day. A section about four feet square had been blown off.

Lawyer Foote of Morrisville, was here yesterday with a lady, and took dinner with us.

The house cleaners are at work in the entries and vestibule of the New House. The Show-room at the head of the vestibule stairs is to be dispensed with, and the room will again be used as a dormitory.

The plateau north of the cow-barn has been plowed and planted with potatoes.

The gravel that was washed out of its place by the overflow of the creek in spring, has become available for a useful purpose. Several teams are busily at work to-day conveying it to different points on the road, where, under the management of Messrs. Worden and Co., needful repairs are being made.

METEOROLOGICAL.
Thermometer, May 4.

6 A. M. 40.   12 M. 50.   6 P. M. 48.   Clear, pleasant day, with westerly wind.

DAILY JOURNAL
OF ONEIDA COMMUNITY.

A. D. 1866.   MAY 7.   NO. 96.

MONDAY.

On Saturday, just as the "bag-bee" had met, we observed quite a company of gaily dressed ladies and gentlemen, over west, who seemed to be wending their way towards our grounds quite rapidly. We were sure of this soon after, as Mr. Bolles and Mrs. Burt escorted them around the domain. We afterward learned that they were teachers belonging to the Academy at Oneida—Professor Swett, and the Preceptress, Mrs. Leonard (who formerly resided at Meriden), besides other teachers and several pupils. They took supper, and left just before six o'clock. While Mr. Swett was in the Hall, he asked Mrs. Burt if each member had a chair of his own, inferring as much, we conjecture, from the great variety in size and shape of the Hall chairs.   H.

The following Receipt will explain itself:

May 5, 1866.

$150,00.

Received of Oneida Community one hundred and fifty dollars, in full payment for my services and those of my son Homer, and of all other demands whatsoever.

S. K. HAZELTON.

Mr. Hazelton and his son leave the Community to-morrow.

A trap order amounting to $1175 net, was received from the Hudson's Bay Company on Saturday evening. They order mostly large traps, including 500 beaver and 50 bear.

The prospect of a lively trap trade is very good.— Letters of inquiry come in almost every day. The demand also increases for large traps. Immediate steps are to be taken to put up 5000 beaver and 200 bear traps. G. W. Hamilton, Mr. Newhouse and J. C. Higgins are appointed a committee to attend to the business.

A plan has been proposed and is to be carried out, to move the clothes-yard to the ground back of the Tontine. At present all the clothes have to be carried up the hight of one story, before they can be taken to the yard. The new plan will obviate this.

Yesterday an order was received through Mr. Olds, from W. B. Burbank of Chicago, for about $1500 worth of preserved fruits and jellies.

Mr. Winter, a German gentleman from Syracuse, came here on Saturday evening and left this morning.— He is an architect and designer by profession—has been studying community organization and has been connected with some unsuccessful attempts at combination in Iowa. He came here to see a practical illustration of communism on a religious basis, and is much pleased with what he saw.

He showed a spirit of modesty and good sense, and has some good ideas of religion, which he has taken means to improve by purchasing the tracts "Salvation from Sin" and "The Oneida Community."

He had with him a great many very beautifully executed architectural drawings done by himself, and is evidently a man of superior talent and cultivation.

Last evening, Mr. Hamilton reported some of Mr. Noyes's remarks, at the N. Y. B., on the subject of faith, which were very interesting and edifying, and formed the topic for conversation and testimony during the meeting hour.

We have occasional singing from Plymouth Collection in the evening meeting. The appetite for family singing seems to be reviving somewhat.

A man in Ohio writes to the Oneida Trap Co., as follows:

GENTS:—Please send me a Circular and Price List of your Quaker traps, as I wish to buy some.

Messrs. Burt and Dunn yesterday received from Munn and Co. the specification papers relating to their corn-cutting invention, and to-day the papers have been duly signed before a Notary Public, and returned to Munn and Co., who will immediately transmit them to Washington with an application for a patent.

There was quite a frost this morning, but it is thought that no injury was done to the fruit. A portion of the plum blossoms are out, but though the mercury was two degrees below freezing, they do not show any signs of being hurt. Since early morning the weather has grown steadily warmer. The day is clear and very pleasant.

It is remarked that we are having more clear weather here than usual this spring. Mr. Messenger, who called this morning, and had returned the other day from the western part of the State, said that things were much more forward here than there. Some of our crops begin to suffer for want of rain.

Abram and D. Kelly spent a portion of yesterday at the carpenter's shop, making a set of croquet balls and mallets for the principal of the Oneida Academy. For the eight balls and eight mallets they get $7,00.

METEOROLOGICAL.

Thermometer, May 5.

9 A. M. 42. Cloudy.

12 M. 50. Clear.

6 P. M. 50. Clear. Beautiful sunset. Westerly winds throughout the day.

May 6.

6 A. M. 41. Wind west. Clear, pleasant morning.

12 M. 54. Somewhat cloudy.

6 P. M. 50. Clear.

DAILY JOURNAL
OF ONEIDA COMMUNITY.

A. D. 1866.   MAY 8.   NO. 97.

TUESDAY.
A MACHINE FOR CUTTING GREEN CORN FROM THE COB.

A machine for this purpose has been invented by J. Burt and L. F. Dunn, members of the Oneida Community; and for which, measures have already been taken to secure a patent. This machine will be found well adapted to the use of large boarding-houses where corn in considerable quantity has to be prepared for the table. The particular design, however, in getting it up has been to facilitate the business of preserving corn in cans. For this purpose it was thoroughly tested last summer at the Oneida Community and was found to perform the work of six persons with knives. The Oneida Community are now prepared to manufacture these machines to order on short notice. They will be furnished to boarding-houses for a small advance on the cost of manufacturing. To other parties, the price will be proportioned to the amount of business to be done. [The Circular is invited to copy the above.]

Mr. Hazelton and Homer left this morning. He goes to Strafford, Vermont, where he expects to find a place for Homer. Beyond this, he has no settled plans. He seems to be the victim of false spiritualism and false social theories which have prevented him from coming into organization with the family, and until his eyes are opened to his condition and need of salvation, it is better for both sides that he withdraw. We wish him well—thorough emancipation from the bondage he is now in.

Mrs. L. A. Thayer received by this morning's mail a letter from Mrs. Mead, relative to Lady Noyes's death and expressing her appreciation of the kindness and care with which her mother was attended by the Community, and by Mrs. Thayer in particular.

Last night, the fruit-growers being a little apprehensive of another frost, F. Marks and Orrin spent great part of the night in warding off the enemy by burning brush-heaps in the neighborhood of the plum orchard. Let us think of this in Summer when we eat the fruit.

Arrived last night, Mr. Easton with his two children, Emily and George. When Temple met Emily, who, he thought, required a little encouragement, he raised his forefinger in quite a dignified manner, and said, " If you stay here, you will get *acquainted* with us."

Every one is charmed with the beautiful weather we are having to-day. Spring, beaten back in her early advance by her wintry competitor, is returning to the charge with new vigor, and bids fair now to conquer and permanently occupy the field. We wish her complete and unchecked success.

Two pairs of robins, lately married, we suppose, have commenced building among the evergreens close to the window of the children's house. They very likely expect to have a family themselves, and have no doubt chosen their site, with the view of having *their children* brought up as near to ours as possible. As their nests appear somewhat feathery, we may perhaps consider them as " wings" to the children's house.

The family were pleased on first stirring about, this morning, to find The Circulars already distributed through the rooms, they having arrived by the same train that brought Brother Ambrose.

Several of the hermit-thrushes have been heard in the woods about here this spring. One was heard the other evening in the cedar swamp across the creek, on the Petrie farm.

The purple finches also are quite numerous in this section, and are very musical. The Report of the Commissioner of Agriculture states that this bird is on the increase in some of the Northern States.

The annual campaign against the apple-tree worms has begun. We notice that Mr Perkins has been trying the effect of kerosene oil on some of the nests. It is an extinguisher of the worms. Two years ago, the writer of this, while at Wallingford, thoroughly tested oil— common machine or lamp oil—as a remedy for these worms. A few drops spurted from an oil-can into the center of one of their nests, would in a few minutes effectually kill all that came in contact with it.

The north wing of the Store is now going up.

The first corn of the season was planted yesterday.

The conversation last evening related mostly to the ideas advanced by Mr. Noyes in the criticism of G. E. C. in regard to the body being the temple of God. There was a general confession of sympathy with the doctrine, and a desire to more thoroughly study and understand it. At the close of conversation, Mr. Hamilton remarked as follows:

" If we are going to make the most of our circumstances, and of ourselves as men and women, we must have a great deal of spiritual boldness and faith. We must draw nigh to God with a great deal of assurance. The kingdom of heaven, in one sense, suffereth violence, and the violent take it by force. Persons should first be honest of heart, and then bold. I am satisfied God likes that quality of spiritual boldness, enterprise and faith."

METEOROLOGICAL.
Thermometer, May 7.
6 A. M. 32. Bright frosty morning with no wind.
12 M. 56. Clear.
6 P. M. 53.

DAILY JOURNAL
OF ONEIDA COMMUNITY.

A. D. 1866.   MAY 9.   NO. 98.

WEDNESDAY.

A LETTER FROM H. G. ALLEN—IMPORTANT TO AGENTS.

New York, *May* 8. 1866.

DEAR W.,—Our revised price list for silk &c. is sent you to-day, and our agents are at liberty to deduct 5 per cent. from same, when large orders are received.— We are desirous of starting a thorough system of recording the names and address of all our customers in the various branches of trade we are engaged in. With this end in view we should like to have all of our agents commence at once keeping a memorandum of their customers, giving the standing kinds of goods they purchase &c., &c. As the agents return we should like complete lists of our customers made out, over the routes they have traveled—having the lists properly classified and forwarded here.

One object we have in view, is to be prepared to send circulars and price currents to all of our customers as often as we may wish.

Mr. Noyes says that we must study and see how much we can make the press serve our business.   H. G. A.

O. C. N. Y. B. PRICE-LIST.

REPORTED MAY 9, 1866.

Mach. Twist, " O. C.",	Black		$14,00	lb.
" " "	Drab		14,50	"
" " "	White		16,00	"
" " "	(100 yds.)		2,15	doz.
B. H. " "	Bl'k ($1,40 per. spool)		11,00	lb.
" " "	Drab ($1,60 " ")		12,00	"
Embroidery Silk	White (pure)		2,40	C.
Col'd Sewing "			2,10	"
10 oz. Box "			1,05	oz.
16 " " "			1,10	"
7 " Package "	Drab		10,50	lb.
Stick Twist			2,00	C.
Goldsmith's Collars	P. P.	Byron	22,00	M.
" "	" " (Less than M.)		24,00	"
" "	" Shakspeare		40,00	"
" "	" Garrote		20,00	"
"	Cuffs		4,50, C pairs.	

Mr. Easton leaves for New York this afternoon. His visit has been a very pleasant affair, and we are glad of the opportunity to become acquainted with him. His children have got so well "inquainted" with the other little people that they will hardly miss him.

Mr. and Mrs. H. R. Perry and their two children arrived this morning.

Two visitors of another kind delighted our hearts with their notes at an early hour to-day—one, the Baltimore oriole or golden robin, the other, the bobolink. Good morning, Oriole! Good morning, Bobolink! Make yourselves at home, both of you.

A letter from Mr. McKillican was received this morning, stating that he had sold about $20 worth of our traps. His letter was very friendly. Annie and Christie also write, expressing their thanks for the Berean and THE CIRCULAR.

The conversation last evening was mostly in relation to Mr. Hazelton's departure. There is a general feeling of relief. It becomes more and more evident that there was no union or sympathy of spirit on his part with the Community. He is in bondage to Hadean Spiritualism, and willfully adheres to its teachings and philosophy In spite of all criticism.

Messrs. R. S. D. and C. E. have been improving Spring Grove by clearing away dead branches &c. They have set out the wild azaleas and other shrubs that were sent from Wallingford last fall, and contemplate extending the walks. We like to see progress of this kind,

METEOROLOGICAL.

Thermometer, May 8.

6 A. M. 41.   Clear.   Some frost.
12 M. 66.   Clear and pleasant.
6 P. M. 62.   Cloudy, with indications of rain.

Vegetation has come forward the two past warm days very fast. The apple trees will soon be bursting into bloom. The birds grow merry again and new ones make their appearance. We hear the swallows this morning.

DAILY JOURNAL
OF ONEIDA COMMUNITY.

A. D. 1866. MAY 10. NO. 99.

THURSDAY.
FINCHIANA.

MR. EDITOR:—There is often much ado in the world when a prince is born, or some heir to a large fortune &c., but really I never cared as much for such things as I now do to announce the prospect of another purple finch family on our lawn. You may remember how tame they were last summer, receiving crumbs from the hand while on the nest. Well, the same bird, apparently, is at it again, only a few rods from the spot selected last year. Our birds are all getting more and more fearless. Shall we not soon be able to " put salt on their tails"? ORNITHOPHILOS.

There was a lengthy and quite interesting conversation last evening on the question of the permanency of the Community movement, suggested by a report from W. A. Hinds, of a conversation he had lately with a Shaker elder.

There seems to be a bright, joyous spirit prevailing in the family. Since the departure of our last Hadean ambassador, the spiritual atmosphere is a great deal clearer. We trust the last of the copperheads is gone, and that now the power of resurrection life will have free scope among us.

Yesterday, there called at the office of the DAILY JOURNAL, a visitor who is an old acquaintance of our P. D. Assuming the privilege of familiar friendship, he proceeded to chaff the P. D. on his new profession.

" Well, can you print any yet?"

" Yes, some."

" Can you set type ?"

"A little."

" Well now, tell us, don't you sometimes set the type upside down ?"

Such ignorance of the Caxtonian art, was too much for the P. D., who promptly replied with a grin of satisfaction, " Yes, we *always* do."

Can our readers guess who this visitor was? Could he have been a monk ?

Extract from a letter of Charles Olds, dated, Milwaukee, May 6th :

" I am out here in obedience to the Community, and in accordance with my own wishes, and I expect to ' face the music,' and not retreat till I have finished my business. If, in any particular, I have been turned aside from doing faithfully the business of the Community,' seeking first the kingdom of God and his righteousness,' it will only operate by leading me to find the sure path; and in all things I shall ' learn obedience by the things I suffer.' So I am not discouraged. No,

not by any means. And in fact, it is a small matter where we are, or what we suffer as individuals, provided we are in the service, and in harmony with the great purpose of God. I wish to learn to endure hardness as a good soldier and fear no evil. James says, ' Blessed is the man that endureth temptation, for when he is tried, he shall receive the crown of life, which the Lord hath promised to them that love him.' I confess my union with Christ and Mr. Noyes and their inspiration.

TRAP TRADE PROSPECTS.

" There are very encouraging signs of a great trap trade next season. Gardner and Co. are confident of a great sale. They say, if furs continue as high as they are now, when the spring trade closes, there will be a greater sale of traps another season than we ever had. They are selling traps now. They like the new No. 1½ trap (single spring), and think they will order 20 or 25 doz. of this kind for the fall and winter trade, and hope we will have them ready. They don't think much of the new trap No. 0, although they may want a few of that kind. What does Mr. Newhouse think of it ?
C. O."

Mr. Miller arrived this morning from his Ohio trip, having been absent about six weeks.

A son of Mrs. Chesbro, called here last evening, with letters from his mother, for the purpose of finding employment. Of course he was disappointed in his expectations, if he sincerely entertained any. He left, this morning.

One of the Oneida Indians (Christjohn, by name), now residing near Rome, desires the Community to receive and educate his "very smart boy." Said boy is nine years of age, and "reads in the Fifth Reader—very smart boy indeed." This request indicates the respect which our Indian neighbors have for the Community; it is not probable, however, that it will be complied with, as we are averse to receiving into the Community, children whose parents are not in full sympathy with us.

The appearance of advertisements of THE CIRCULAR, in *The Nation, The Tribune* &c., is viewed with satisfaction. In the Tuesday's *Nation* the first three letters in the word Oneida and the letter o in " or", are missing. Mr. H. R. Perry suggests that H. G. A. had better call at the office of the paper and direct the attention of the publisher to the omission; otherwise the error may run through the month.

METEOROLOGICAL.
Thermometer, **May 9.**

6 A. M. 48. Cloudy, with southerly wind.

12 M. 55. Cloudy.

6 P. M. 53. Clear.

During the early part of the day, there were indications of rain, and a few slight sprinkles; but the clouds passed off, leaving the thirsty fields unsatisfied.

DAILY JOURNAL
OF ONEIDA COMMUNITY.

A. D. 1866.　　MAY 11.　　NO. 100.

FRIDAY.

In the evening meeting the same subject of conversation as on the previous evening was continued.

The reports relative to the Purchasing Agency from N. Y. B. interest us very much, and the steady growth of that business is very encouraging.

Our colored hostler, Timothy Thomas, died suddenly in a fit, this morning, before he had risen from his bed. He was a very faithful hand and much liked by our people. He leaves a wife, who is *enciente*.

The north wing of the Store building is up and nearly ready for shingling. Every day shows a visible advance toward the completion of this job.

Seated at the harmonium last evening, (it was the chord of the dominant seventh, I believe, which my fingers were resting on) I had just attained that delightful state of nerve when harmony is full of richest thrill, when C. came into the Hall in search of recruits for some kitchen work. I caught his inspiration in a twinkling, and shutting the instrument, soon found myself within the magic circle of a fish-cleaning bee. The court was full of busy, cheerful men, women and girls, the laughter of whose happy voices kept pace with their active hands. The glitter of the scales that flew in every direction and stuck in everybody's hair, the prattle of children in the corridor above, and, above all, the good spirit that prevailed, ennobled the humble work into Divine service, so that I was sorry when it was over; for I had found in it a delightful ordinance of fellowship with the church.　　P. D.

The call for extra help in the bag-bee, yesterday, in consequence of the receipt of a large order from Milwaukee, was heartily responded to. There are many indications of a growing love of work in the Community.

The gardeners were planting melons yesterday.

The dwarf apple-trees and also the pear-trees are fast coming into bloom. There is a splendid promise of a large crop of both apples and pears.

We notice that Mrs. Burt is improving very much in health and vivacity lately. She and Lady Burnham appear in a high degree to enjoy stirring each other up. The other day we witnessed quite an exhilarating scene between them. We will not attempt to describe it; but those who know the capacity of each to make fun, will no doubt enjoy the simple mention of the matter.

Babydom appears to be in a flourishing condition just now. The several new members form an interesting accession, and all are in a growing condition. Little Maud makes vigorous exertions in the line of "foot-notes" every day. We expect that ere long her understanding will be so well established that she will give running commentaries on pine boards.

R. J. Hollingworth, the inventor and patentee of the Can-making machine lately purchased in Cincinnati by the Community, arrived this morning, and will remain until to-morrow; and if the can-machine comes in the meantime, Mr H. will see that it works successfully before leaving. Mr. H. is on his return from Baltimore, where he expects to introduce his can-making improvements, although he met with much opposition there from the members of the Can-makers Union.

The Bag orders obtained by Mr. Miller on his late trip amount to $1538,26.

W. J. Slingerland, agent of Bradstreet and Son of New York, publishers of "Bradstreet's Commercial Reports," was among yesterday's visitors. He appeared to have a tripple object in visiting the Community: 1st to become somewhat acquainted with the institution; 2nd, to obtain a subscription to the "Reports" ($125, per year); 3d, to obtain statistics for a Manufacturers' Book soon to be published by Bradstreet and Son. He thought the Community the only firm in the town of Lenox whose productions were sufficiently extensive or in sufficient general demand to deserve a notice in the proposed work. The "Reports" which purport to give the business character and standing of nearly all firms in the United States and Canada make no mention of the Oneida Community.

Mrs. Tobey yesterday received the balance of her Barnstable estate; and to-day congratulates herself and her friends on the fact that at her seventieth birth-day, she is free from the world and has made full consecration of herself and property to the glorious cause.

EXACTLY SQUARE EVERY NIGHT.

I was pleased to notice, in looking over Mr. Miller's Memorandum book, that he kept a strict cash account during his absence, and that he had been able to make an exact balance every night, with the single exception that at one time it was out one cent! and equally pleased to hear Mr. Miller say that he has had a good experience in keeping an exact record of every thing, and on the whole had rather enjoyed it.　　w.

METEOROLOGICAL.
Thermometer, May 10.

6 A. M. 45.
12 M. 64.
6 P. M. 63.
Clear and beautiful day.　Westerly winds.

DAILY JOURNAL
OF ONEIDA COMMUNITY.

A. D. 1866. MAY 12. NO. 101.

SATURDAY.

Mr. Olds writes that the prospects are good for preserved fruit this season. "I believe," he says, "there will be a *great* demand for it. Many are giving large orders for it now."

T. Jones Jr., Editor of the *Insurance Monitor and Wall St. Review*, called yesterday. He formed the acquaintance of some of our members a few years since up in the North woods, and expresses much interest in our movement. We regret to state that there were unmistakeable indications in his appearance that he had lately had "a brick in his hat."

The bag orders for last week amount to $1111,89.

Mr. Underhill, formerly of the Unitary Home, N. Y., who is now giving public entertainments partly musical partly phrenological, called yesterday with two other gentlemen who are associated with him. One of them, Mr. Lavender, played the violin in a style that showed a good deal of natural talent. Mr. U. sang and played a piano accompaniment. Among other pieces, he gave "The Monks of Old."—Mr. Lavender has studied the Berean and THE CIRCULAR, and professes a keen interest in the cause.

We have quite a large congregation of little folks now. Harley is the oldest of fifteen who live at the children's house. In addition to these there are two, yet under maternal care.

To-day the house-cleaning company have attacked the children's house in their usual thorough way.

In respect to licenses for our agents, H. G. A. writes; "The assessor of this district advises that we take out a ten dollar license, as fourth class peddlers, for all of our agents who travel and take goods with them to deliver. As *he* understands the law we are not obliged to do this, but as others understand it differently he thought our our agents would be troubled without these licenses: and we take out four of them to-day."

Mr. Hollingworth, our visitor from Cincinnati, has ordered a Corn-cutting machine of the Community. He thinks it a fine invention, and says if it was generally known and appreciated our machine-shop would have all the business it could do in filling the orders we should receive.

Mr. Olds found it necessary to pay $20, for a city license in Milwaukee—rendered so by recent action of the Common Council of that City. The license can be used by any of our men, and is good for one year.

A long and interesting letter was received to-day, from Samuel Shannon. He is very much pleased with the No. 0, and No. 1½ traps. He thinks the No. 1½ is preferable to No. 1 for trapping muskrats, and that it will supersede No. 1 in that part of the country. His reason for liking it better is that it has greater weight, and spread of jaws, which for trapping on marshes where there is but little depth of water, he thinks is very important, as the rat is liable to be caught higher up, and thus prevented from legging himself, and, receiving more injury is liable to die or be drowned sooner. Of the No. 0, he says:

"No. 0 is the very trap that I am in for. Were it not for one thing, I would prefer it for my northern and northeastern tramps before any other trap that ever came to my notice, on account of its smallness and lightness; as I think it is sufficiently strong to hold the marten, and northern mink which are not much more than half as large as our mink here.

"The greatest advantage of the Newhouse traps is that any trapper can at any time change his springs, chains, jaws or groundworks by means of the nut on the jawpost. This cannot be done without bending the jaws or groundwork of the No. 0, and the rivet will become loose in the course of time, and the trapper is not at all times and places provided with implements to tighten up the rivets.

"One more reason why I should prefer the screw and nut, is I could make a No. 1. spring answer on the No. 0, if I should need it, and only for the absence of the screw on the jawpost I should order a few of them for marten and northern mink.

"The No. 1½ is a capital mink trap, and better for rats than the No. 1, but I have caught several hundred mink, 47 this last winter, in the No. 1 and never yet had one pull out."

TO AGENTS.

We are instructed from N. Y. B. to quote Goldsmith's Shakspeare Collars at $35 per M.

METEOROLOGICAL.
Thermometer, May 11.

6 A. M. 47.
12 M. 74.
6 P. M. 70.
The day was clear and very beautiful. At 2 o'clock the mercury stood at 80 deg. in the shade.

DAILY JOURNAL
OF ONEIDA COMMUNITY.

A. D. 1866. MAY 14. NO. 102.

MONDAY.
BUSINESS MEETING ITEMS.

Mr. Hatch asked the mind of the board about appropriating the ground in front of the Tontine for a play yard for the children, as the present yard is too small for the number of children. The board thought the proposed ground was too public a place—the children would be exposed to the unprofitable attention of visitors.

It was proposed to build a neat board-fence on the east side of the road from the new store building to the site of the old one.

Mr. S. W. Nash suggested the plan of attaching fixtures to the present steam-engine for throwing water in cases of fire. The board thought that a small hand fire-engine could be procured cheaper.

Mr. Burt asked for the mind of the board about making an additional number of corn-cutting machines as there is a probability that they will be wanted the coming season. The plan was favored. Messrs. Burt, Hinds and G. W. Hamilton were appointed a committee to determine the price of the machines &c., and are to act in consultation with Mr. Thacker.

Mr. Miller proposed that we buy our oil for burning from first hands in Pennsylvania, as he found when he was there, that there was a kind which was already fit for use directly from the well, needs no refining, and is much cheaper than that we are at present using. The board were in favor of trying a barrel of it.

Martin Kinsley proposed that some one be appointed to have the oversight of the grounds around the boarding-houses, and see that things are kept neat and orderly. It is also necessary for some one to supply the boarding-houses with wood. Mr. Kellogg was appointed to this office.

NEW PRICE LIST OF TRAPS.

In accordance with Mr. Noyes's suggestion a committee was some time since appointed to revise the Price List of Traps. The committee after considerable deliberation, and some consultation with the Agency, have decided upon the following:

Price List.

No. 0 Rat	Traps.	Without Chains.	With Chains.
" 1 Muskrat	"	$3.00 doz.	$4.25 doz
" 1 1-2 Mink	"	3.50 "	5.00 "
" 2 Fox	"	6.00 "	7.50 "
" 3 Otter	"	9.00 "	10.50 "
" 4 Beaver	"	12.00 "	13.75 "
		14.50 "	16.50 "

Bear Traps. No. 5, $9; No. 6, $16, each trap net.

On comparing the above with the old list it will be seen that very great reductions have been made.

It is expected that traps will be sold to trappers at list;

to retail dealers at five per cent. discount from list; to jobbers at ten per cent. discount; and to the largest dealers in New York and elsewhere fifteen per cent. discount; but that in no instance a greater discount will be given.

With the new list and new discounts the profits of the Community in the manufacture of traps will be reduced about one half.

But it is hoped that the reductions made will put an end to competition, and enable us to "sweep the deck."

The profits on chains have heretofore been quite limited, and the list price of them has not been correspondingly reduced.

New cards containing the revised list will soon be printed, and also a Circular notice to be sent to our customers.   w.

TO AGENTS.

Permit me to call your attention to the suggestion in H. G. A.'s letter (printed in the JOURNAL of the 9th inst.), that our Agents should keep a memorandum of their customers, and on their return make out complete lists of the same, properly classified, and send them to N. Y. B., together with observations respecting their business standing and the character of their trade. It is very important at the present time, and will be indispensable as we grow into a large Commercial Company. Such a system of reporting will prove our best insurance against losses by trade with irresponsible firms—far better than the Commercial Reports of Bradstreet and Son, or those of any other Mercantile Agency. I hope the Agents will commence at once to carry out this suggestion. We have now here at O. C. a pretty full list of all of our Trap Customers and Bag Customers, and measures will be taken to make out a classified list of our Fruit Customers. If the N. Y. B. would like a copy of these lists we will accommodate them. Concerning old and proved customers, already classified and listed, it will be unnecessary, I judge, for our Agents to take note, except of changes in their trade or business prospects; but of every new customer a careful record should be made and forwarded to N. Y. B. or O. C.—perhaps in many cases to both places. About Silk Customers it will only be necessary to report to N. Y. B. Let the Agents themselves study this matter, and offer such thoughts thereupon as may occur to them.   w.

☞ Two orders were lately received from one of our Agents for Lunch-Bags which did not state whether the Bags were to be furnished or not. An order for Ladies Satchels was received at the same time from the same Agent, which did not state whether the Satchels were to have steel or gilt trimmings. Bad blunders!

On Saturday it was found that the aqueduct had burst. Thanks to Mr. Abbot's skill, the leak was soon found and a new log inserted instead of the broken one. The stoppage at the kitchen faucets did not occur till after supper time and caused but little inconvenience.

Mr. Hall returned last Saturday from a week's trip, having sold—Silk, $526,56; Bags, $28,01; Hats, $47,83.

METEOROLOGICAL.
Thermometer, May 12.

6 A. M. 69. 12 M. 75. 6 P. M. 74.
Bright, beautiful weather all day.

May 13.

6 A. M. 67. 12 M. 66. 6 P. M. 44.
Considerable rain during the day.

DAILY JOURNAL
OF ONEIDA COMMUNITY.

A. D. 1866.   MAY 15.   NO. 103.

TUESDAY.

Messrs. Underhill and Post, called again last evening and remained over night. They are brothers-in-law, and Dr. Post is a son of the Dr. Post mentioned in Mr. Cragin's history, and was at one time, we believe, an office-boy for Mr. Cragin when the latter was publishing agent for the Moral Reform Society. The Dr. got hold of the vol. of THE CIRCULAR containing the earliest chapters of Mr. Cragin's Story, and soon became very much interested in it. He intends to call at the N. Y. B. and purchase the vols. of THE CIRCULAR containing Mr. C.'s history. Mr. Underhill professes much interest in our movement, and also expresssed his purpose to call at the Moffat Abbey and become acquainted with Mr. Noyes. After the proposal of Mr. Underhill and his party, on Friday, to call here again and perhaps repeat part of their programme of entertainment, there was some repugnance in part of the family to having them come with such a purpose in view, as we were not pleasantly impressed with their style of performance. On arriving last evening, however, they expressed themselves as not wishing to bore us with their performances, as they came to observe and learn of us, though they would be willing to sing a few songs or tell a story if we wished it. Nothing more was said about the matter and the evening passed off without their being called on for this purpose. They expressed themselves as being very much pleased with their visit, and left this morning. Dr. Post said that his mother would be much interested to see Mr. Cragin again.

Mr. George S. Phillips ("January Searle"), of Chicago, in a recent letter says:

"Oh! how I wish I had known about that farm of yours only two months ago. I have just bought a place an hour's ride from this city, or I would certainly have bought yours, for the society if for nothing else."

On Sunday, Mr. Burt and others went over to Cook's Corners to see the butter and cheese factory that has been started there. The cheese is made of the milk which has just been skimmed, the new morning's milk and the butter-milk from which the butter has just been taken. This seems to be an economical arrangement, and the result is quite a good cheese. The enterprise has been started by a Mr. Pardee to whom we wish all success.

DISCOUNTS.

As the prices of our manufactured goods are reduced, it becomes more and more important that our Agents act wisely in respect to the matter of discounts, and that their course be in harmony with instructions from the home department.

Our Price List of Bags, for instance, is graded so as to hit the New York jobbing trade; and it will be readily seen that if Agents give the highest discount to country dealers it will at once defeat this object, or compel us to increase our discount to the New York jobbers, which we cannot afford to do.

So with our new Price List of Traps, the highest rate of discount should be limited to the very largest dealers, such as New York houses, Gardner & Co., Hudson's Bay Co., the Dailys and others. If fifteen per cent. discount is given to smaller dealers it will soon make trouble in the family, and tempt such firms as Gardner & Co. to think they should have more than fifteen per cent. which cannot be afforded.

Several small orders for Bags, at seven and one half and even ten per cent. discount, have lately been received from Agents, without any explanation. Perhaps in most of these instances, the Agents had good reasons for taking the course they did; but it would be better in case of any departure from general rule, to send home some word of explanation.

We appreciate the difficulties our Agents have to meet in obtaining orders, and will gladly help them all we can, especially in the way of acceptable Price Lists, we trust they will see the importance, on the other hand, of wisely managing this matter of discounts.

Several steps have been taken this spring in the direction of low prices, and others will probably come. We are confident that the new Trap List will prove satisfactory, and a further reduction in the price of Bags (especially of Muslin) will soon be made.

As agents stand where they can best judge of the prices of our goods as compared with others, let them feel free to indicate from time to time what changes they would like to have made in prices, quality and style of goods, &c.   w.

SALUTATIONS.

"Salute no man by the way," said Christ when he sent his disciples forth. "Why? What was the harm?" I used to ask; but the churches never gave me any satisfactory answer.

I had not been long in the Community when I was enjoined to beware of entering into fellowship with outsiders and to be reserved and reticent even in forming friendships among the family. "Why? What's the harm?" I again wondered.

But I have now no difficulty in comprehending both Christ's injunction and that of the Community. He who would give his life to God, cannot afford to let it out much in fellowship toward any but those who are above him and can help him. The spirit of true chastity requires reticency even in the matter of salutations. P. D.

By a new arrangement of the Post-office Department, our morning's mail from New York hereafter does not reach Oneida until 9 A. M. The afternoon mail for New York leaves at 2½ P. M.

METEOROLOGICAL.

Thermometer, May 14.
6 A. M. 80.   12 M. 45.   6 P. M. 46.   Cold westerly winds prevailed during the day.

DAILY JOURNAL
OF ONEIDA COMMUNITY.

A. D. 1866. MAY 16. NO. 104.

WEDNESDAY.

Mr. Noyes arrived this morning about 10 o'clock. It is unnecessary to say that we are very glad to have him with us.

Dr. Gleason, a water-cure physician from Elmyra, was here yesterday—came with the Verona Springs folks. He was very courteous, made many inquiries, and said he was watching our movement with much interest. He thought we were working out valuable physiological results, and said that we showed a remarkably high degree of health.

Abram left for the Moffat Abbey on Monday afternoon, for the purpose of fitting up the salesroom with suitable shelving arrangements.

Mr. Leete has been detained at Verona longer than he expected, by sickness in his family. Mrs. Leete and Mary have both had the prevalent lung fever. They are now recovering, and Mr. Leete hopes to be soon released.

Mr. Knowles is gradually gaining strength, and seems in a fair way of recovery.

The funeral of our late hostler, Timothy, took place yesterday. He was buried near our new burying ground.

The house-cleaning group end the labors of the spring campaign to-day. Their *last* point of attack is the bootroom at the old Mansion house. It is expected that this being their sole job now, they will turn up jack, and end off with a scrub race to boot. They have been engaged about seven weeks, and report a jubilant, victorious time throughout. No hired help has been employed in our house-cleaning this year, which has been quite a saving, financially, as we used to pay one dollar per day for help in this business.

Mrs. Sherrard—we should have mentioned the fact some time ago—is now stopping with Mrs. Hubbard, who, not being very well and hearing of Mrs. Sherrard's visit here and her wish to find employment for a season, offered her a home till June.—Preston still works in the bag-shop and spends most of his leisure time studying Mr. Noyes's writings. He does this, Bible in hand, examining every passage that is quoted. He remarked to Chloe, the other day, that he apprehended salvation from sin—that some six years ago he realized the justification of Christ, but that now, he believed he was saved from sin. Chloe asked him if he confessed Christ in him a Savior from sin, and he said he did. He seems to be a well disposed, ingenuous young man; and if he can work out of his water-cure theories and early education and habits, into practical faith in Christ and a practical estimate of life, he will make an interesting character. We should judge that much of his past life has been in the world of books.

AN ELOPEMENT.

Yesterday afternoon, a youthful scion of the O. C. was sent off with the old Grey and wagon to Willow Place. On arriving there, the young charioteer finding he had plenty of time, hitched the Grey to another equine quadruped that happened to be standing there, in the shape of a saw-horse, and strolled into the machine-shop.— But Grey did not fully relish being mated with so contemptible a caricature of horse-flesh—it certainly was a degradation to him—so shortly after, G. W. H. was surprised to see the noble creature galloping off full speed, wagon and all, dragging his humble companion along with him.

Chase was soon given and property recovered, yet not until Grey had disengaged himself from his pseudo brother of the saw, disclaiming all relationship and leaving him far behind. Grey is slightly lamed, we believe—got a kick probably, from his rival.

A SECRET.

Yesterday, it was told me as a great secret that J. H. N. was expected to come this morning. I was warned not to tell any one, so that the family might have a pleasant surprise when the journal was read.

Well, believing that I had got a veritable cat in the bag, I resolved to keep its mouth shut—I mean the bag's mouth, not the cat's—and said not a word to any one. An hour or two afterward, however, H. told me the same secret; still later, P. repeated the mystery, then C., till it became evident that the cat had got out, and when the official announcement came at meeting, however welcome it might be, it certainly produced no surprise.

P. D.

METEOROLOGICAL.

Thermometer, May 15.

6 A. M. 39. Cloudy.
12 M. 64. Clear and pleasant.
6 P. M. 64.

DAILY JOURNAL
OF ONEIDA COMMUNITY.

A. D. 1866. MAY 17. NO. 105.

THURSDAY.
LETTER FROM MR. OLDS.

Milwaukee, May 13.

DEAR BROTHER:—Yours of the 3d and 10th were received yesterday on my arrival here from Chigago.—Also the two packages containing Photographs of bags, traps and fruit. I think most of them are splendid pictures. I am much pleased with them. Getting up these photographs is going to be a good thing not only for our Agents, but for our whole business. I find it gives a good impression. I like too, the suggestion made by Mr. Noyes of "studying to see how much we can make the press serve our business." I am persuaded we can help our business very much in this way. I find the Price List of silk published in the "Daily Journal" is helping us in the silk trade. Parties see we are a regular business institution in New York City, having printed lists of prices &c., which gives them confidence "we are somebody." This tends, you see, to make it easier for us Agents to do business. Get the press to work, and we shall have the O. C. and its several branches of manufacture before the business world in a way to have all the business we can do. We have a high reputation, well established, so far as we are known, for manufacturing the best goods. This being understood, there is no danger but that it will spread if we take measures, guided as we are by inspiration, to get it before the public. I apprehend if there is any danger, that it will ultimately be in having more orders than we can fill.

In regard to deviation from the regular prices on silk, would say, I have found it necessary in a few instances. I find I must do so in some cases in order to sell to my old customers where the Beldings are selling. I think, it will be unnecessary to deviate long, after we get our system to work. And I shall seek inspiration in this matter as in every thing else.

I shall arrange my business if possible so as to return home, as you request, by the 16th of June.

I don't know as I have any thing to say about Fruit Price List. Only I have expected we should make considerable deduction from last year's prices. In fact I have encouraged parties to expect this. How much we shall make is a question for calculation in cost of material, &c. We are starting off this season in the bag department by being satisfied with lower profits.

I hope this policy will extend to all the other departments, and that we shall get out price lists, as we have begun—at reduced rates.

I wrote you that I was much pleased with the new Price-List of Bags. I think now we can sell if we can find parties that want bags. C. O.

BUSINESS CIRCULARS.

The sending of a Circular to our business patrons, as Mr. Noyes suggested in his speech on the 20th of Feb., will be a great auxiliary to the business agents, and will also induce buyers to call on us, and send orders, for goods. We know the benefit of line upon line, and precept upon precept. The circulars will appear over the wide field of our customers at about the same time. It was a help to me to have the prices printed in the JOURNAL. I found success in showing it to those who disputed our prices. One man in particular, said he would give $13 for silk. He was shown the printed list, in which the price was $14,50, and he thereupon readily paid it. O. H. M.

A fine young walnut tree that grew in the pasture beyond the creek, east of the barns, has lately been wantonly cut down without the permission of the Community. In meeting the other evening, there was some conversation about it, in which it was suggested that it may have been taken in misapplication of an old law which grants to the aborigines the right of cutting down forest trees for purposes of manufacture. But it is understood that if such a law really exists, it does not apply to trees growing on cleared lands. Nothing is known, however, as to who the depredators are, and we can only resolve to keep wide awake in future.

We continue to receive letters in reference to the prospective village. Some of the correspondents inquire whether the children of settlers can have the privileges of the Community schools. There was considerable discussion of this point last evening. The conclusion was that it would not be possible for us to open our schools to outside children. Perhaps, however, as the village grows up, and there is a demand for a higher order of schools and teaching than prevails under the public school system, the Community will be able to furnish teachers. A report of the conversation will be sent in MS.

The fruit-growers have begun their campaign against the curculio. Ninety-one were found this morning.

A letter was received yesterday from Mrs. L. B. Smith, saying that she wishes to build her a house, and asking the Community to lend her four hundred dollars on eight per cent. interest, and take a mortgage on her property.

METEOROLOGICAL.

Thermometer, May 16.

6 A. M. 53. 12 M. 54. 6 P. M. 46.
Gentle rain throughout the day.

ONEIDA.

Sing of the name we hold so dear,
Sing it with voices strong and clear,
Sing it aloud with hearty cheer;
  Oneida!

This name that binds, like silken band,
Sisters and brothers hand in hand,
Shall one day ring throughout the land,
  Oneida!

O, happy birds of sheeny wing,
Whene'er your thrilling voices ring,
Take up this note and loudly sing
  Oneida!

O, winged winds, to Westward go,
Breathe out your music full and low;
And chant this name where'er you blow;
  Oneida!

Proclaim it where the loaded wain
Comes from the fields of yellow grain,
And cry in accents clear and plain,
  Oneida!

Over the wave-crests wreathed and curled,
Bear it, ye ships, with sails unfurled;
Say, when ye reach the Eastern world,
  Oneida!

Speak thus to all oppressed with fears:
The dawn of hope shines through your tears,
Aglow with light and truth appears
  Oneida!

Echo it wide o'er every land,
To aching heart and toiling hand—
Echo this word in chorus grand,
  Oneida!   W. H. S.

DAILY JOURNAL
OF ONEIDA COMMUNITY.

A. D. 1866.   MAY 18.   NO. 106.

FRIDAY.

In the meeting last evening, Mr. Noyes gave an account of the life of Socrates, and of his influence in preparing the Greek mind for the reception of Christianity. After this a portion of the address of Socrates to his judges; and the description of his death, as given by Plato, were read. 'Twas all deeply interesting and affecting, causing many of the family to shed tears.

The bag-bees are quite well attended now-a-days and there is considerable demand for work. Ten dozen muslin bags were made in four days last week. Victor Hugo's "Toilers of the Sea" is now being read in the bees.

The north wing of the store is shingled and rough boarded. The front of the main part is now receiving the attention of the carpenters. The building will present an attractive appearance when finished. Since the wings were raised the view of neighbor Parson's establishment from our Portico is completely intercepted.—This, however, is not considered a mournful loss.

Mr. Ellis, to-day is sawing off all the dead stumps of branches from the old Butternut Tree. The old tree appears to be putting forth with all its usual vigor.

The work of reducing the Price List of bags is again going on. Our bagmakers and financiers seem determined to command the market, as well by the lowness of their prices as by the superior quality of goods. Seventy-six sizes of Traveling Bags, Gent's and Ladies' Satchels and Lunch Bags, are now manufactured. The various names of the bags are as follows: Enameled Muslin, lined, unlined, Gothic and Pelissier; Brussels Carpet, Common and Pelissier; Gent's Leather Sacks; Gent's Leather Solferino Sacks; Gent's Leather Magenta Sacks; Fancy Pelissier, Half Morocco and Full Morocco, lined; Leather Pelissier, Plain, With Pocket; Ladies' Leather Satchels, Gilt Mounted, and Steel Mounted, A. D. E. H. and O; Ladies' Quadrille Satchels, Plain Lock and Eagle Lock; Ladies' Muslin Satchels; Leather Lunch Bags, Drill Cloth Lunch Bags, Leather Cloth Lunch Bags and Ladies' Lunch Bags.

Twelve hired men and five hired women are employed in the shop now.

Letters of inquiry about the village lots have been received from Mr. and Mrs. Jeffrey of Canada West, and Mr. Warren Ball, of Goshen, Mass. Mrs. Jeffrey is the daughter of Mrs. Cockril.

Victor Hawley is slightly disabled by a sprain of his left hand, caused by a fall in the machine-shop.

The lawn presents a very attractive appearance now.

Messrs. De Latre and Nash are busy most of the time, attending to the walks, flower-beds, &c.

A Price-List of Preserved Fruits and Vegetables is in course of preparation. The list for this year comprises, Strawberries, Raspberries, Huckleberries, Plums, Peaches, Quinces, Pears, Pine-Apples; Pie-Fruits such as Pie-Plant, Apple and Huckleberries; String Beans, Sweet Corn, Tomatoes and Tomato Catsup. A variety of Jellies in pint and half-pint tumblers will also be put up. These comprise Strawberry, Blackberry, Peach, Currant, Quince, Crab-Apple, Plum; Black, Orange and Red Raspberry, Lemon, Grape and Pine-Apple.

There has been some correspondence with a Mr. Nye of the Millennial Fraternity at Phalanx, N. J. On seeing the announcement of the proposed village in THE CIRCULAR and the opportunity for employment offered in the Community Manufactories, he wrote, expressing a wish to find employment here, with the object in view of becoming acquainted with the Community. As he mentioned that he had been at work making tin files we thought that perhaps he might be a useful hand to employ in the tin can shop, and wrote to him that we could probably give him employment in that department. In reply he accepted of our proposal, but objected to work at soldering, as being unhealthy. As soldering was the business we wished to employ a hand to do, Mr. Hamilton immediately wrote to him that we should decline to employ him.

METEOROLOGICAL.

Thermometer, May 17.

6 A. M. 38.   12 M. 66.   6 P. M. 65.
Fair day throughout.

There was some frost in the morning, but we do not learn that any damage was done to the fruit-trees.

DAILY JOURNAL
OF ONEIDA COMMUNITY.

A. D. 1866.   MAY 19.   NO. 107.

SATURDAY.

Yesterday Mr. Worden was away hunting for potatoes for kitchen and boarding-houses. But few can be found, and they are held at not less than 88 cts. per bushel. They were but 50 cts. recently, but all at once it was discovered that potatoes were very scarce in this section; and Mr. W. says that "now it seems as if they would go beyond reach and sight."

The following note was read one evening last week, and should properly have appeared in THE JOURNAL several days ago:

To THE COMMUNITY:—I wish to make a full and un-reserved surrender of myself and whatever I may possess to Christ and the Community. I recognize Mr. Noyes as a true and inspired leader, and gladly acknowledge my subordination to him and the Community.   H. R. PERRY.

Mr. Leete is here again, but returns to Verona to-day.

Mr. Knowles begins to ride out in the wheel-chair on pleasant days. He has evidently passed the crisis of his disease and is steadily gaining.

Mr. Noyes suffers considerably with his teeth yet.

Most of the meeting last evening was occupied with an interesting conversation about Socrates and Greek civilization, which will be reported elsewhere.

One hundred and twenty-five Norway Spruces, four feet high, have been bought. Forty-two of them have been set in a circle round the new burying ground; the most of the remainder have been set in the hedge south of the house, in place of those of last year's planting which died.

W. A. Hinds left for New York, yesterday noon, on business.

A quite serious accident happened at the bag-shop this morning, involving a surgical operation. The favorite cat of that establishment—a very remarkable cat—a cat whose equal has never been known in this part of the country—a cat whose history is sometime to be written, we understand, by a learned and competent individual, who has collected a variety of *memorabilia* concerning him—well, this cat—this Thomas cat—met his friends this morning with a fishhook painfully fastened in his cheek, from which he was anxiously desirous of being relieved. A council was held on his case, the result of which was that Surgeon Dewey cut the hook out. The superior intelligence of Thomas, it is hoped, will hereafter lead him to avoid meddling with fishhooks, however temptingly they may be baited. Would it be correct to consider Thomas a catfish in future?

We are pleased to observe that the CIRCULAR is advertised in the "State Journal" of Springfield Ill.; also in the "Daily Journal" and "Daily Gazette," both of Indianapolis, Ind. This looks like dropping "seed corn" in the fertile West, said to be a good corn country. Watch this seed, won't you? and see if it don't grow and bear a luxuriant harvest. Both of the Indiana papers give editorial notices as well as the advertisements; one of them refers to the "Communionism" advocated by THE CIRCULAR. To this we say; Good for Indiana or any other Anna. Long may she wave!

Two regiments of infantry, each consisting of six men including officers, marched against the common enemy the Curculio at half past four this morning. General Marks's division killed 172, Gen. Abbott's 241, total 413. We may add, in confidential whisper that it is contemplated to make similar raids every morning till the enemy is exterminated. But we hope no one will be so indiscreet as to mention this to the Curculios; none of them subscribe for THE JOURNAL; if they ever did, their names have been struck off the list. Enough said.

The regular weekly ablution of the infantile population took place in the Tontine wash-room yesterday. It was the first of these at which the two little Es have been present. When they saw the whole swarm casting off the "fetters of the falser life," they seemed to be in some hesitancy, till, amusing to relate, George drew Emily aside and held a private consultation with her, after which, both submitted at once, cheerfully, to be stripped and washed. The precise terms of the *tete a tete* have not been divulged, but the result was good.

Much satisfaction is expressed here with the poem entitled "The Choice" in last Circular. It is considered to be one of the least exceptionable poems of home production that have appeared in our paper. The Circular as a whole, is certainly in the ascendant and reflects much credit on its conductors.

METEOROLOGICAL.

Thermometer, May 18.

6 A. M. 50. Somewhat cloudy.
12 M. — Fair.
6 P. M. 60.
A fine day of alternate clouds and sun shine.

DAILY JOURNAL
OF ONEIDA COMMUNITY.

A. D. 1866.   MAY 21.   NO. 108.

MONDAY.

BUSINESS MEETING ITEMS.

Mr. DeLatre inquired what provision there was for mowing the lawn. It was proposed to try the mowing machine on the open space, and that the Appropriating Committee furnish help to cut around the trees. The Lawn Committee were instructed to inquire into the merits of the hand-mowing machine used in the Central Park.

The Road Commissioner has called on us to do some road-making out of our usual province. It was moved that we signify our wish to the Commissioner to be relieved from such liabilities in the future, as we now do more work on the road than our tax amounts to.

A note was read from Alfred Barron asking the services of Mr. Worden during the strawberry harvest at Wallingford. The plan was sympathised with and it was voted that Mr. Worden be free to answer the call.

A letter from Mr. Cragin was also read expressing a wish for a little help in the carpentry line. It was proposed that Mr. Woolworth go on there for a couple of weeks.

It was proposed to put more help in the trap-shop at once, and not confine ourselves to the making of large traps. The prospects of the trade are such as to warrant us in making provision for a large demand.

Voted that Roswell have liberty to introduce improvements in the forge-shop.

Yesterday forenoon, a jolly party of Community brethren carrying hoes, spades and shovels, started for the Park, where they spent a few pleasant hours in extending the walks. These now reach far beyond the grove, into the pond hollow, and after many windings, pass by a well-known tree inscribed with familiar initials, such as C. A. M., W. A. H., E. H. H. &c., then push pioneer like, toward some other Ultima Thule where space may be found for a revised edition of arborigraphs. Such is human progress. The ancients were continually setting up boundary lines—Chinese walls—saying, " Thus far and no farther;" but whoever is on the right track, may safely assume that there is no boundary to improvement, because there is no boundary to truth; and truth has no limit, because its source is in God who is illimitable.

We had a very little rain last night, and to-day the clouds look showery. A steady pouring rain for a day or a night would be gladly welcomed.

There is a wonderful profusion of apple blossoms in the orchard, and if the crop of apples proves to be correspondingly abundant, it will astonish the oldest inhabitant of these regions.

The Grand Turk hunters destroyed 560 yesterday.— To-day the numbers were 413, including prisoners. Capturing the insects alive, forms a novel feature in this branch of horticultural labor, which originated in a wish expressed by some of the family to see "the varmints.' A few fat specimens were brought home in a phial and handed about on exhibition, after which they were given over to the executioner for capital punishment.

Last evening Mr. Noyes gave a talk on Dentistry as illustrative of our System of Criticism, suggested by his late experience. It was very interesting and will be fully reported in MS.

The new arrangement of the mails is somewhat unpleasant, and it is hoped that some modification of it will ere long be effected. We do not now receive our New York mail until after 10 A. M. and have no N. Y. mail on Sundays.

Mr. Towner, and his sister Mrs. Lasley, wife of J. P. Lasley of Berlin Hights, came on a visit to the Community, on Saturday.

Mr. Woolworth left for Wallingford this morning.

The following communication from Mr. H. R. Perry, to the family, was read last evening:

"I wish to say to the family that all my early training was a warfare against cant. All was negative with nothing positive. It was a constant criticism of God and religion as represented by the popular churches, a continual tearing down without building up. As I was under such teachings for the first twenty years of my life, they made a very deep impression. Until I read Mr. Noyes's writings, I never found anything that was positive and at the same time satisfactory to my heart and mind in relation to God and eternal life. I find it difficult, even yet, to shake off the impressions of my youth, which I now see were just in accordance with the devil's plan and wishes in my case, to keep me from the true knowledge of God. I wish to separate myself from all sympathy with unbelief, and commit myself to God and his truth for eternity. I want the devil to understand that I am henceforth and forever on the Lord's side.

H. R. PERRY.

METEOROLOGICAL.

Thermometer, May 19.

6 A. M. Clear and pleasant 55. deg.

The day was warm and beautiful, but I was away.— The whole spring has been remarkably fine and favorable for business—farmers have plowed their land and put in the crops without interruption; but it has been too dry—wheat looks thin and rather poor, and grass is not very promising up to this time.

May 20.

7 A. M. 70. Fine and clear.
12 M. 81.
6 P. M. 80.

The mercury rose to about 86 during the afternoon and in the sun at 4 o'clock stood at 112.   M. L. W.

DAILY JOURNAL
OF ONEIDA COMMUNITY.

A. D. 1866. MAY 22. NO. 109.

TUESDAY.

Mr. Towner made the following communication to the family last evening;

O. C., May 21.

DEAR FRIENDS:—I wish to express my gratitude to God for your kindness in receiving myself and sister, and affording us an opportunity for so pleasant and profitable a season as we have enjoyed since we came here. The object I proposed to myself, in my letter to you of April 4th, is already accomplished. I said then, that though having faith in the ultimate triumph of Communism, I was somewhat in doubt whether it was best now to organize or not. I am fully satisfied with your example; for the servant of Christ to see it, is to believe in it. I feel a strong desire and determination to unite myself with the body of Christ, outwardly, as well as inwardly, and wherever, whenever, and with whomsoever God shall appoint. I am determined to do his will; to hold myself in readiness to obey His voice, and do the work He appoints me to do. When I left Detroit to visit you, I proposed to myself a visit of ten or twelve days. I thought it necessary, to enable me to learn of you what I wished to learn. But I find it is not. I am satisfied with what I have already seen and felt, without a longer stay. Hence, I feel that I can do the Master's will better by returning, than by a prolonged stay in the nature of a visit. I would be at work.

If it be the good pleasure of the Community, I desire to continue my correspondence with you, hoping and desiring to preserve and secure as vital a connection with you as possible. If you shall find a work for me, you can command me. I have found Christ here exceedingly precious, and I thank God that through Mr. Noyes and the Community, I have been led to him, and found him a complete Savior.   J. W. TOWNER.

A number of evergreens are in course of being set out towards the south-west corner of the square, back of the New House, in place of the trees that had been killed or injured, and at various points where good taste required some such pleasing object to meet the eye.

A cold rain-storm is in progress to-day. This morning was so cool that it was thought unnecessary to hunt the Grand Turk.

Last evening Mr. Noyes gave a long and thrilling talk on the Calling of the Community, Worship in the Future, &c.

THE MOUNT TOM CHRONICLE arrived this morning, and looks interesting as usual. The new mail arrangement luckily does not affect the arrival of THE CHRONICLE.

The nest of young robins reared in the children's yard, have taken wing, and are occasionally seen about the grounds, still attentively attended by their parents. Each year the birds on our grounds seem to be growing tamer, as well as becoming more numerous. In this case the nest was built in an evergreen, only a few feet from the house, about six feet from the ground. Under and about the tree the children were playing every day. After the young were hatched the old bird would fearlessly feed them while a person was standing close to the nest watching the operation.

W. G. K. has gone to Utica on a business trip.

ABOUT ROADS.

The Road Commissioner of Verona has decided to give the Community, for the tax on the Hitchcock farm the road from Hubbard's towards Parsons's as far as our land goes, for our portion, and to give it into our charge.

The path-master intends to call out his help on Turkey Street this week and make repairs on the Willow Place Road, as he will probably accept the invitation of Wallingford to go there and assist them during the Strawberry season.

I want to enter protest against the practice of throwing any vegetable matter such as grass, bits of turf or any sort of yard or garden rubbish into the roads, as it it is both wasteful and injurious. I sometimes see old chips, leaves of trees and such—the best of fertilizers—thus thrown away and made a nuisance and a pest to travel over.   Yours respectfully, M. L. W.

METEOROLOGICAL.

Thermometer, May 21.

6 A. M. 53. Sunshine.
12 M. 55. West winds, floating clouds.
6 P. M. 50. Strong wind, cloudy and cold. We hear of a great hail storm in the vicinity of Rochester yesterday causing much destruction of fruit, such as peaches &c.

PRAYER.

Far as our upward-stretching thoughts can reach
In feeble word,
To give the flower and blossom of our speech
To Christ our Lord—

To yield our bodies in devotion free,
Our purpose this;
That, in the end, the ripest fruit may be
Our perfect bliss:

Not setting forth our prayers in formal ways,
On bended knee,
Nor mouthing them in antiquated phrase
Of "thou" and "thee,"

But using still the unaffected "you"
As to a friend
Quite near to us and, in his goodness, who
Will apprehend

The purpose of the heart however dressed—
Who still holds dear
The prayers of all his own, and makes them blessed
Because sincere.   W. H. H.

DAILY JOURNAL
OF ONEIDA COMMUNITY.

A. D. 1866. MAY 23. NO. 110.

WEDNESDAY.

It is the Road Commissioner of Vernon, not of Verona, as we printed yesterday, who proposes to give us charge of the section of road from Hubbard's Corners easterly through the Hitchcock farm. Mr. Worden reports that we shall accept the proposal.

Butter is now 35 cts. a pound wholesale and 40 cts. retail.

Mr. Towner and Mrs. Lasley left for home last night, after meeting. Mrs. Lasley before leaving handed in the following note to be read in the family:

To the Oneida Community,

Dear Friends:—I wish to express my gratitude for your kindness to me, since my stay with you, and I sincerely wish to join, and further identify myself with you.

I confess Christ in my heart and my union with him. I desire to do his will.   Maria Lasley.

Marriage seems to be popular among our hired people. Three couples have been married during the past six or eight months. In the last case the marriage of Charles Primo and Fanny Adkins was kept secret for several months, for what special reason we are unable to say. From all we hear, the matches appear to have turned out agreeably to all parties.

A Mr. Adams from Bridgeport, Conn., came yesterday to inquire about the Community. He is a mechanic and is employed in Howe's Sewing Machine manufactory. He is still here.

Last night was quite cool, but we believe there was no frost sufficient to injure the fruit.

A mason is now at work on the chimney of the store.

Our hired colored man, Jacob Thomas, has returned from a visit to New Jersey, accompanied by his parents. The latter propose to live on a small place which Jacob has bought of Mr. Andrew Smith of Verona. Jacob has been absent for several weeks and had the misfortune, while he was gone, to be robbed of a considerable sum of money.

Notwithstanding the coldness of the morning, the raiders started at the usual early hour, and had the satisfaction of killing one curculio. We presume they must have felt somewhat as Percy did when, after having " killed some six or seven dozen Scots at a breakfast," he " washed his hands and said to his wife: Fie upon this quiet life! I want work."

A young man from Herkimer, walked into the Reception Room this forenoon, and helped himself to a chair, and without taking off his hat, or introducing himself, inquired for " The Foreman," and intimated that he would like to hire out to the Community as a teamster.

He was sent to the barn to talk with Martin Kinsley and Mr. Bradley. He soon returned, however, to the Reception Room, seated himself as before, and inquired

" Do you receive members into your society ?"

" Occasionally. We have many applications, but only receive such as fully appreciate our purposes and objects. Those who apply for the sake of a comfortable home are generally refused."

" What are your rules of admission ?"

" We have none. Those who desire to join are advised to study our publications, and become acquainted with our principles."

" Have you any pamphlets, containing some sketch of your principles ?"

" Yes, here is one, " Conversation with a Visitor," which will give you some idea of our Community."

" I have seen that."

" Here is another, which will give you an idea of our fundamental doctrine of salvation from sin or selfishness; and then we have some larger works."

After examining the last tract about ten minutes, with hat on head, he threw it down, rose and left the room without saying a word.

Mr. Noyes leaves for Wallingford this afternoon, accompanied by Ormond.

Mrs. Perry is having a new experience since coming here. The Lord seems to have shown her the truth and drawn her heart to himself. She confesses Christ as a Savior from sin, and is desirous of coming into sympathy with the Community. Mr. Perry is greatly rejoiced at the change in her feelings.

A letter was received yesterday, from E. J. Robinson, of New York City, in relation to the locality &c. of the building lots of the new village. The writer, who appears to be a lady, thinks she shall wish to purchase if she can exchange with us some property she owns in Illinois,—which is quite doubtful.

In meeting last evening, Mr. Noyes mentioned that he had taken a walk over to the Park last Sunday, and observed a number of outsiders strolling about. He thought that as the improvements we have been making there serve to make the place attractive to pleasure-seeking parties that are not in sympathy with us, there. by defeating our purpose of keeping a pleasant place for parties of our own family, we had better discontinue our improvements in that direction and turn our tastes to the beautifying of the grounds immediately around the barns and other home buildings where privacy is more likely to be secured. A full report of the talk will be sent in MS.

METEOROLOGICAL.
Thermometer, May 22.

6 A. M. 40. Clouds and wind.
12 M. 44. Strong Northwest wind.
6 P. M. 44.

DAILY JOURNAL
OF ONEIDA COMMUNITY.

A. D. 1866.　　MAY 24.　　NO. 111.

THURSDAY.

W. G. K. started to-day on his regular business trip —expects to be gone several weeks.

E. S. B. also started for Syracuse and Oswego this morning—expects to return on Saturday evening.

A beginning has been made at the sweet-corn planting.

Mr. Burt has four new corn-cutting machines finished and ten more in embryo. Those finished look finely and appear competent to do their appointed work. They are worth $100 each.

Mr. Burt has also greatly improved the Pea Sheller.

Frederick Norton was criticised last evening. There was a good deal of commendation of him for his skill and pleasant deportment as a dentist. It was thought there was some tendency to answer people abruptly when they spoke to him about their teeth when away from his shop. It was also thought that he needed to cultivate a thankful spirit and open himself more to the Community. He is too isolated and independent in his habits, and at the same time he drops down too much to the boys and those below him, for fellowship. The true spirit is not stiff and independent toward those around us, but child-like and simple and at the same time gravitates toward those who are superior to us.— Frederick is becoming very successful as a dentist, and his work is much liked. He should look to it that he becomes equally successful as a spiritual man and a student of heavenly things. It was remarked that he was loyal to Mr. Noyes, and seems to have a very high appreciation of him. Mr. Hamilton's concluding remarks were as follows:

" I have had occasion to talk with Frederick, from time to time, in a frank sincere way, and have always found him ready to listen, and accept what I said to a certain extent. There is a truthfulness and manliness of spirit about him that makes me feel near to him when I talk with him. The main fault I find with him is that which has been mentioned, that he is too isolated. That is an external fault with him, but I don't know that I should dislike it more than a certain kind of familiarity and superficiality. In the light of Mr. Noyes's recent talks, the strongest criticism I should give Frederick would be that he does not worship God enough. He does not let himself be known sufficiently as a worshiper. We do not hear his voice here in the public assembly in the way of doing justice to God, as much as we should. He is too silent. I feel now more than ever before, that we should all be known as thankful persons. God deserves so much worship from every one of us; and our thankfulness should be expressed publicly, so that we may be known as persons who do justice to God. I seems to me, that what Frederick needs, in order to do justice to God, is, to have his heart all broken to pieces under the sense of God's goodness. It is the love of God in our hearts that makes us one. The spirit of the world is the spirit of pride, independence and hardness. The spirit of the world, tends to shut the heart up and prevent us from dropping down into what might be called the foolishness of love. But the school we are in has the opposite effect. The teachings of God and the Holy Spirit tend to make us soft and loving and gentle, and break up all this hardness of the old man. The mere study of the science of dentistry, as Frederick has been studying it, especially if he were successful and skillful in practice, as I think he is, would tend to make him professional and independent. He needs to to be modified by the social spirit of the family."

Wood is being hauled from the former wood-lot at Willow Place. There is a great quantity there still of both long and short wood, and being mainly maple, it is of the best quality; but as there is not room to store it under cover, it follows that it must suffer some depreciation during the season.

There is considerable wood also in and about the swamp, cut and gathered up by Mr. Higgins and others, which is good for summer burning.

Twenty-three bushels of potatoes were delivered here yesterday at 75 cts.—Mr. Worden having engaged them on Saturday near Munnsville.

Mr. Noyes made considerable sport yesterday on the prospect of Ormond's trip to Wallingford. He remarked that " it was customary when ships were about to put to sea to ask several important questions. These were, first, Has she taken in provisions? secondly, Has she discharged her old cargo? thirdly, Has she pumped out all her bilge water? If these things are attended to, start the engine." We presume these were important questions in this case. We hope however, that Capt. N. had a successful voyage with his craft, and that he came into port with sails in good order from jib to mizzen.— We shall await a copy of his log-book with interest.

METEOROLOGICAL.

Thermometer, May 23.

6 A. M. 40. Sunshine, and west wind.

12 M. 46. Cloudy with occasional drops of rain.

6 P. M. 47. Cloudy.

A few small flakes of snow were observed during the day.

DAILY JOURNAL
OF ONEIDA COMMUNITY.

A. D. 1866. MAY 25. NO. 112.

FRIDAY.
TALKING WITH GOD.

What Mr. Noyes said the other evening about our talking with God, and always considering him present, let us be doing or saying what we may, seemed to bring heaven into my heart, and I felt very near to God and Mr. Noyes and the Community. I desire to get my tongue free in His service. I think it a very beautiful idea that the gift of speech is to be devoted chiefly to the worship of God. The idea of talking with our dear Father, kindles my heart with enthusiasm, and makes me long to get rid of all the rubbish that would hinder the free course of God's spirit in me. One might think that if we always realized the presence of God, we should be awe-struck, as it were, and should never be playful and jovial, nor act ourselves out in a free and easy manner. But I believe our God to be a cheerful, loving Father, full of charity for his children, and that he delights to see us joyous and happy in the sunshine of his love. And if we walk about, and stumble in his presence sometimes, he invites us to try again and again, and gives us courage to think that we shall overcome all our faults in time. C. A. REID.

Two twin, half-blood Ayrshire calves, a bull and a heifer, made their appearance the other day.

Work on the new section of the road was begun yesterday, with hired help.

Two "fatted calves" have been killed, and partaken of by the family during the present week. Yesterday some nice home brewed beer was an accompaniment of our dinner.

Albert Ackley arrived here from Michigan. We do not know yet what his purpose is, but we understand he intends to remain east for several months. He is quite well.

There are some signs of rain again, which we hope will be fulfilled. Some of our people think that we are having the severest general drought they ever saw at this time of year.

Mrs. S. B. Nash is quite smart. Yesterday she rode over to Willow Place, and walked about the shop some.

A letter was received the other day from Mrs. Munson. She seems very desirous of joining the Community.

The mowing of the lawn has begun. The trial of the mowing-machine upon it did not result very satisfactorily. We greatly need a lawn-mower.

The conversation last evening related mostly to the subject of talking with God.

ICE–HOUSES FOR PRESERVING FRUIT.

Some of your readers may be interested to know about the Patent Ice-House for the preserving of fruits, which has come into existence within the last decade. There is one in Rochester, one in Cleveland, and others in other cities. The one in Cleveland is a house 80 feet long by 44 feet wide, nearly two stories high. Its sides consist of two sheet-iron walls three feet apart, the space between which is tightly compacted with shavings. On the first floor are the sales- ante- and fruit-rooms; on the second, is the ice-room. The fruit- and ice-rooms are separated by sheet-iron. The entrance is into the sales-room and thence to the ante- and fruit-rooms. The fruit-room is divided into two apartments; each apartment is bisected by an aisle, and on each side of the aisles the fruit is placed.

Apples are kept largely, also grapes, oranges and lemons. Apples keep good the year round. A bunch of grapes which I ate on the first of May were truly wonderful in goodness and flavor. These are sold at twenty-five cents a bunch. Such houses must be profitable in cities. O. H. M.

METEOROLOGICAL.

Thermometer, May 24.

6 A. M. 43. Clear. A little frost was seen at the barns.
12. M. 63. Clear with westerly winds.
6 P. M. 58. Cloudy and calm.

TO THE BIRDS.

Come, Bobolink, prepare to sing;
 We saw you flutter past us now:
Come, Blackbird with the glossy wing:
 Sit near, upon this maple bough.

And build within our hemlock hedge,
 Or in the shrubs about our lawn;
Your young are safe to grow and fledge
 At evening dusk or early dawn.

These nests, embowered by tender leaves,
 Recall the song of Hebrew king :—
"On God's own house, beneath the eaves
 The swallows forth their young ones bring."

And though that cedarn house, of which
 The poet-king sang, is no more,
Build freely in each sheltered niche
 You find by lattice, porch or door.

This house is God's, as much as that
 Which stood in fair Jerusalem :
If *there* the sparrows safely sat,
 The charm guards you that sheltered them.

Come, Oriole and Hermit Thrush—
 Come Purple Finch, your dear mate bring;
By well-kept lawn or tangled brush
 We love to hear you warbling.

W. H. H.

DAILY JOURNAL
OF ONEIDA COMMUNITY.

A. D. 1866. MAY 26. NO. 113.

SATURDAY.
THE LICENSE QUESTION SETTLED.

It has been decided, by Assistant Assessor Barnett, and by other authorities, including the highest tax functionary at Washington, that the following recent decision of the Internal Revenue Commissioner, applies to the Community Agents:

"Persons traveling about the country as the agents of manufacturers or dealers, seeking orders for goods, as agents of one person or firm only, such as salaried clerks, or men hired by the month, should not be required to take licenses as Commercial Brokers. All parts of decision No. 159 inconsistent herewith are hereby revoked." E. A. Rollins Com. Int. Rev.

According to this decision, our agents, in seeking orders, will require no license; but if they carry goods to deliver, they become thereby peddlers of the 4th class, and will require a ten dollar license.

As some Tax Officers are not so well posted as they should be in respect to the decisions of the Commissioner, and might through ignorance call on our agents for a Broker's license, it would be a good plan for each of them to carry a copy of the above decision; and all who deliver goods should be provided with a peddler's license or some paper showing that they have made application for such a license.   w.

There is evidently a good deal of active thought and feeling going on in the Community in reference to the truth lately brought out on the subject of worship and the constant recognition of the presence of God.

A mistake occurred in Mr. Miller's article yesterday. The price of the grapes which he mentions having eaten of at the preserving house, was twenty-five cents per *pound*, instead of per *bunch*.

This morning is chilly and there was some frost.— Yesterday's signs of rain failed. The sky is clear of clouds again. The atmosphere is smoky, like Indian Summer.

The meeting last evening was mostly occupied in giving expression to the spirit of thankfulness by the whole family.

Mr. Hatch has constructed a wheeled chair for Rose, which is very light and handy, and having large wheels, it can be easily drawn up and down stairs.

The birds—we will add another item about them—continue to astonish us with their tameness. We hear of their coming into the kitchen, and yesterday two of the little chipping sparrows came into the bakery, where they gave Mrs. Ackley an opportunity of illustrating a certain proverb about "a bird in the hand." Whether they had read the verses in yesterday's JOURNAL, is at least doubtful, but we are certain they appreciate the Community spirit.

We were gratified to receive the intelligence of the safe arrival of Mr. Noyes and Ormond, in New York. The "log" of their voyage was piquant and interesting.

A slight error occurred in the paging of THE JOURNAL yesterday. Instead of 436, 7, 8, it should have been 434, 5, 6.

A young man named Draper, called at Willow Place yesterday, and asked for employment. Some encouragement was given him that we could furnish him with a job. He afterwards came over here, and became considerably interested in inquiring and reading about the Community. He formerly lived in Steuben County, in this State. He has been married, but his wife had proved unfaithful to him and they had dissolved partnership. In the settlement of the case he seems to have lost considerable property. He left this morning, thinking that he should perhaps return next week and work for us.

An impertinent letter was received to-day, addressed to THE CIRCULAR, asking for a list of our subscribers in Syracuse, Cazenovia, Liverpool, and Auburn. The writer represents that he is a traveling agent, and wishes to do all the good he can by exhortation and conversation. He concludes his letter as follows: "Do not fail to include the names of the ladies, because they are the most useful members that we have." He signs himself, "H. H. Hines." We suspect that this agent is well described in 2 Timothy. 3: 6.

The bag orders last week amounted to $1231,72. The present week the principal order received is for ten lunch bags.

MENTAL HYGIENE.

Amid the bustle of manufacturing business that distinguishes the mother Community from her literary and commercial daughters, we are glad to observe a good deal of literary study going on. One class is reading the Bible in French with E. H. H.; two young ladies may daily be seen bending over some ponderous Latin tomes; while another group are busily acquiring German under Professor H. R. P. We looked in upon this last class the other day and heard some reading from Goethe's unique poem beginning:

"Wer reitet so spat durch nacht und wind?"

The homogeneity of this language and its susceptibility of regular musical rhythm, give it, in our opinion, an immense superiority to French. Where is the line of French poetry that could be compared with that we have just quoted? Besides, owing to the abundance of Germans among us, we can have more frequent opportunities of talking German than of talking French.   w. H. H.

METEOROLOGICAL.

Thermometer, May 24.

6 A. M. 54. Cloudy. Southwest wind.
12 M. 57. Wind Northwest.
6 P. M. 58. Clear and pleasant.

DAILY JOURNAL
OF ONEIDA COMMUNITY.

A. D. 1866.   MAY 28.   NO. 114.

MONDAY.
BUSINESS MEETING ITEMS.

S. W. Nash was appointed to attend to the erecting of another lamp post. It is to be placed in a position where it will light the walks in the rear of the buildings.

It was proposed to proceed at once with the cementing of the Store cellar, as it may be needed for dairy purposes.

More vigilance is needed in keeping account of the time and payment of the hired men, and measures are to be taken accordingly.

A water-wheel is needed at the Foundry. A man at Rome wishes to put in one of his iron wheels, in order that we may test its work by the side of the other kind. It will cost some two or three hundred dollars. Referred to Mr. Burt, G. W. Hamilton and Mr. Kinsley.

John Norton returned from his western trip on Saturday. He had been absent just three months. He reports himself as glad to get home, and as having met with nothing that had any attraction for him in society outside. Mr. Olds is expected home in the course of two weeks.

1076 curculios were found in yesterday morning's hunt, and 456 in this morning's.

Messrs. Bristol and Bradley went to Black Creek, yesterday, and caught some fine pickerel. A number were brought home alive and placed in the fishpond at the Park.

Our drought seems to have fairly come to an end.— Yesterday and last night it rained finely, and to-day is cloudy and showery. These droppings from the clouds have been thankfully received.

Mr. Worden expects to leave some time this week for Wallingford.

On Saturday, Mr. Worden and his company were employed on the Parsons Road, which was found much worse and needing more repairs than was anticipated. Mr. W. reports his three miles of road, except the newly added portion, as good as the best in the town.

The following conditional order was received a few days since, through the N. Y. B., from Stanton & Co., of Chicago. It is possible that satisfactory terms may not be arranged, but those interested in the fruit department may find some pleasure in looking over the figures:

ORDER.

Dozens in glass: 5 Damson Plums, 5 Green Gage, 5 Lombards; 20 Strawberries; 20 Orange Raspberries, 25 Red do.; 10 White Cherries, 10 Red do: 10 Pears.

Dozens in Tins: 600 Tomatoes; 450 Corn; 75 Peas. Jellies in Cups, Dozens: 4 Grape, 8 Raspberry, 60 Red Currant, 6 Strawberry, 4 Black Currant, 15 Blackberry, 4 Quince.

In addition to the above he wants Hodge's order, from Chicago, for 1865, amounting to $319, duplicated.

Speaking of Stanton, H. G. A. says: "I called his attention to the Lunch-Bags, and found he was much pleased with them. He sells lots of Lunch-Baskets and had down on his order book to purchase 6 doz. He gave us an order for 1 doz. to be sent on as samples, and says if his folks at Chicago think as well of them as he does, they will give a larger order. I think he is just the one to take hold of the Lunch-Bag at Chicago. He ordered one for his own use at once. I think if we deal with Stanton as proposed, on the prepayment system, we shall get over the trouble we have had in the past."

It may be explained to the W. B., that their failure to receive the Monday's JOURNAL was due to the fact, that, after being put in the envelop for W., it either dropped out or was taken out by some one, and remained unnoticed in the bottom of the letter-box for several days. Two other JOURNALS have not been printed in time for the mail and had to lie over one day. The mail is always carried down in season to go by the 2.35 train for New York. We intend always to have THE JOURNAL ready in time, and think we shall hereafter succeed.

METEOROLOGICAL.

Thermometer, May 26.

6 A. M. 42.   Clear and pleasant.
12 M. 68.   Clear.
6 P. M. 65.   Cloudy.

May 27.

6 A. M. 58.   Cloudy,
12 M. 62.   Rain, with Southwest wind.
6 P. M. 62.   Cloudy, with southerly wind.

There was a slight rain during the night, and several fine showers during the day.

DAILY JOURNAL
OF ONEIDA COMMUNITY.

A. D. 1866.   MAY 29.   NO. 115.

TUESDAY.
BAG PRICES.

A New Price List of Bags was printed yesterday afternoon, and copies will be sent to-day to the Community Agents and to a number of our customers. On comparing the new list with its predecessor a number of changes will be noted. The price of Enameled Muslin has declined six or eight cents a yard since the previous list was made out, which enables us to make important reductions in the prices of Muslin Work of all kinds.— The distinction about painted fronts to Pelissier Bags has been struck out.

New and thorough estimates have recently been made of the material and labor in a great variety of Bags ; the labor of manufacturing has in several cases been materially diminished ; and pebble leather is now purchased two or three cents a foot lower than in early spring, and the prices of other materials have somewhat declined.— All these things have been taken advantage of in making out the new list, and such reductions have been made as seemed feasible. Leather Pelissiers are reduced six dollars per dozen. Ladies' Leather Satchels are reduced from four to ten dollars per dozen, and the Eagle Lock clause abolished. Persons can have the Quadrille Satchel with choice of lock at list price.— Lunch Bags are reduced from two to six dollars per dozen. The price of C. Sacks is reduced, but a difference of eight dollars instead of six is made between the different sizes to correspond better with the difference in cost. A new C. Sack of 16 inch frame has been added, at the suggestion of Mr. Burnham ; also a smaller size of the Ladies' H. Satchel, which looks well ; also a larger size of the Quadrille.

The same rates of discount will be continued, as stated in the 76th JOURNAL, viz., the best retail dealers are to receive only five per cent discount ; country jobbers seven and one half per cent ; and wholesale dealers and jobbers in New York, Boston and perhaps a few other large cities, ten per cent. The smallest dealers should be sold to at list, or at two and a half per cent discount.

Send on the orders—the more the merrier.   w.

———

Mr. Thayer reports that the strawberries are looking quite well notwithstanding the drought and the hard winter. He thinks we shall have a fair crop, if the rest of the season is favorable.

The rain of yesterday and the cool night were unfavorable to active operations by the Turks, so that only 89 were captured this morning.

An error having occurred in omitting to change the day of the week, at the head of yesterday's Journal, in those printed to send to W. and N. Y.; corrected duplicates will be sent by to-day's mail.

In accordance with Mr. Cragin's proposal, an invitation will be extended to John Freeman to come to the Community.

Several old apple-trees which were either beginning to decay or did not give very important returns in fruit, are being cut down.

The Store is now all clapboarded and shingled. The window-sashes are in, the chimneys finished, and the floors mostly laid. The stairs are being put up, partitions set, and every thing got in readiness for the plasterers.

The conversation last evening turned on the cultivation of quietness and faith in meeting disease, and thorough separation of our hearts from the spirit of unbelief.

Our meetings now are usually closed with singing, for which there seems to be a growing appetite in the family.

———

A SQUIB—NO FIB.

Mr. Hatch in looking around, down in the hen-barn yesterday, found a clandestine nest with seven times three excellent eggs which immediately he, seeing them right before his eyes, carried away as a lawful prize.— For whatever view may be held by the hen ; eggs may be lawfully taken by men : and of these twenty one, we may safely say, they were certainly *hatched*, though not in the way meant by the bird that did them lay.

This item was handed me, Mr. Pitt, by Anna Kelly, who wished that it might appear in THE JOURNAL, I suppose, just as she wrote it, in simple prose. But in turning it over with inky claw, a chance for rhyming I very soon saw, so I've changed the prose into verse, you see. Very respectfully yours, P. D.

P. S. It may interest some to know, the hens were all killed a month ago.

———

METEOROLOGICAL.
Thermometer, May 28.

6 A. M. 52.   12 M. 54.   6 P. M. 48.

Cool westerly wind throughout the day, accompanied with intervals of rain.

DAILY JOURNAL
OF ONEIDA COMMUNITY.

A. D. 1866.   MAY 30.   NO. 116.

WEDNESDAY.

A letter was recently received from a man in Iowa, containing an extract from the Boston Investigator. The extract was in the form of comments on the passage from Dr. Trall's book which was published in THE CIRCULAR sometime ago. The writer is full of Infidel horror of the social innovations of the Community, but seems to feel very much relieved in view of the fact that the Community is not an Infidel institution.

In the meeting last evening the fifth chapter of Matthew was read, accompanied by comments by Mr. Hamilton. Albert Ackley's visit here was also referred to by Mr. Hamilton and others. On the one hand he is outwardly friendly, on the other he is full of unbelief, and in such a condition in this respect, that we cannot afford to extend him any fellowship.

Mr. Powell, formerly of Newark, now of Nauvoo, Ill., is here on a visit to Mr. Inslee. He wishes to interest the Community in a knitting machine on which he has made some improvements. He talks some of joining us; but his ideas on that subject are rather vague and indefinite.

Mrs. Munson's letter has been answered to the effect that we see no opening to invite her to come here at present. She professes to regard this as her home, but she does not give evidence that she apprehends or appreciates our central doctrines and faith.

If the visitors, register can be relied on, we are having more visitors this season than last. During the month of May last year, there were 41 names registered; this year there are about 111.

Mr. Conant yesterday received a letter from Mr. Quimby of Oregon requesting that two copies of the Berean be sent him and inclosing five dollars for the same.—He expressed considerable interest in the Community and desires to be remembered to Mr. Burnham, whom, it seems, he knew in Vermont, and with whom he would be glad to correspond.

Yesterday, there came to hand part of one thousand dollars worth of tin lately sent for. The can-making corps has been joined by John N. Norton. Such changes of occupation put us in mind of "Hard to find." Old Nick is possibly looking for John somewhere out west just now.

J. N. Sherrard, a brother of Preston's came here this morning; he is in quest of employment.

We must give another bird item. A robin is now building her nest in the evergreen at the southeast corner of the old Children's House, right by the path which is constantly traveled from one house to the other.—The nest is within arm's length of the path. One reason of the tameness of the birds is undoubtedly to be found in the fact that there are no cats about the buildings this season. The only cat we have is the remarkable Thomas at the bag-factory.

The fruit-room is being cleared of its winter accumulation of boxes, boards and other material, preparatory to the fruit business of the season.

Mrs. Sherrard called here yesterday from Mr. Hubbard's. When she went there some weeks ago, Mrs. Joslyn, loaned her Mr. Noyes's "Religious Experience," as she expresses a desire to read it. Mrs. J. took particular pains to find a copy which was not bound in connection with the Bible Argument. She read it with much interest, and she seems to feel a good deal of respect for and confidence in Mr. N. While she was conversing about it yesterday, she remarked that she had read the Bible Argument. And on Mrs. Joslyn's inquiring where she obtained it, she said that old Mrs. Hubbard had a copy which she kept hid, and she gave it to her (Mrs. S.) to read! Mrs. S. as far as she understood it seemed greatly pleased with it.

Mr. Hall started on a business trip yesterday.—Charles Vanvelzer accompanies him with the view of getting initiated into the peddling business.

Our cloudy weather continues, and this morning we are having a series of refreshing showers.

10½ A. M., THE CIRCULARS have just arrived.

Mr. Worden left for Wallingford yesterday afternoon, going by the way of the N. Y. B.

METEOROLOGICAL.

Thermometer, May 29.

6 A. M. 55.   Clear.
12 M. 56.   Cloudy.
6 P. M. 56.   A fine shower in progress.

DAILY JOURNAL
OF ONEIDA COMMUNITY,

A. D. 1866.   MAY 31.   NO. 117.

THURSDAY.

Last evening the following confession from Mrs.
Perry was read :

DEAR FRIENDS OF THE COMMUNITY :—I came to you
having no sympathy with you or your views, but
merely to please Mr. Perry.

Although I have been with you but a short time, I
feel that the Lord has shown me by his Holy Spirit that
this is truly a godly people, and I feel willing, if it is
his will, to walk with them. I confess Christ my Savior from sin, and ask the prayers of all, that his Spirit
may guide me and lead me into all truth.

AMANDA E. PERRY.

The other night, one of our boys was suddenly awakened out of his sleep by a strange thumping noise.—
What was it? Surely some one had fallen out of bed.
Who could it be? Thus he wondered for a few moments,
till at last the truth flashed upon him. Some one *had*
fallen out of bed; it was *himself*. The hero of the adventure related it to us in good e(a)rnest.

In the absence of Mr. Worden, Charlotte Maria and
Anna Kelly attend to the meteorological record. We
presume it is already generally known that they are the
regular type-distributors of THE DAILY JOURNAL.

A letter was received from Mr. Seighman, indicating a
purpose to shape his business affairs so that he can come
and settle near the Community.

A letter was also received from a young lady, who
writes confidentially, over an assumed name, and whose
residence shall be nameless, expressing a wish to join
the Community, if it is such an institution as she has
heard it represented to be. She wishes to join us without the knowledge of her parents, under the guise of
working for us. She apparently knows but little about
the Community. Of course her application will be respectfully declined.

Buttermilk seems to have great attractions for some of
our people now-a-days, and a morning draught of it is
one of the institutions. We noticed this morning a red
flag displayed in front of the dairy-house, and on inquiry as to its meaning, learned that it indicated that
the supply of fresh buttermilk was ready for its
votaries.

A good letter was received, yesterday, from E. Otis.

We are gratified to learn from H. G. A. that he has
seen the mail agent, and that, if possible, a more satisfactory arrangement of the New York mails will be
brought about.

The " Talk for the benefit of Oneida," was read last
evening, and we all felt very thankful to receive such
a commendation, from such a source. Afterwards the
goodness and providence of God in sustaining Oneida
and giving her such great financial prosperity, formed
the topic of conversation during the meeting. Oneida
feels it to be a privilege to be an agent in helping forward the great cause which Mr. Noyes represents. At
the close of the meeting the hymn, " On the mountain-
tops appearing," was sung.

For the convenience of watering the flower-garden
near the green-house, Mr. Nash has inserted a lead pipe
with faucet in the pump-logs leading to the large reservoir.

A fine Ayrshire bull, nine months old, was bought
yesterday of Messrs. Walcott and Campbell, of New
York Mills. Price $150.

A wagon shed 124 feet long is in course of construction, in the yard east of the horse barn.

The benefit to vegetation that has already resulted
from our rainy weather is incalculable. The foliage of
the trees which a week ago seemed slowly struggling to
develop itself, has come forward very rapidly, and begins to assume the customary luxuriance of spring.

Mr. Powell, who is still here, appears to be more interested in our cause than he at first seemed to be. He is
quite desirous either to join us or to settle in our immediate vicinity so as to be as much within our influence
as possible.

The tulip beds on the lawn are making a fine display. Their brilliant colors, seen against the background of green form a beautiful contrast, and a delight
to the eye. Nor is color their only attraction. Many
of them, especially the double ones, exhale a rich,
fruity perfume.

METEOROLOGICAL.

Thermometer, May 30.

6 A. M. 46. Rain.
6 M. 62. Cloudy, but pleasant.
6 P. M. 50. Rainy.
Cool westerly wind throughout the day.

DAILY JOURNAL
OF ONEIDA COMMUNITY.

A. D. 1866. JUNE 1. NO. 118.

FRIDAY.
LETTER FROM MR. TOWNER.

Berlin Hights, Ohio, May 29, 1866.

DEAR FRIENDS OF THE O. C.:—Having opportunity on Sunday, the 27th, I publicly confessed Christ, avowed my faith in Him, and delivered my testimony in favor of Oneida Communism before a goodly number of the Berlin socialists in their Hall at this place. Two reasons moved me to thus improve the opportunity afforded me; the first was my former connection with them, and the second a desire to state publicly and unqualifiedly my renunciation of, and separation from the radical error of Berlin socialism, viz., individual sovereignty, and my surrender to the sovereignty of God and Christ. There was a free meeting. The occasion was quite interesting, and yet to the seeker of the kingdom of God, to the earnest worker for God and humanity, it was mortifying. It was sad and mortifying in the extreme, to see so large a number of intelligent, and as a general thing, superiorly endowed men and women together, apparently inquirers after the good and true, and yet so discordant and antagonistic, a moral and spiritual Babel, having no recognized unifying sentiment or power.

I think there is little hope in this quarter for Christian Communism, at present. There is now in existence here a small Community, the seventh attempt, I am told, at organization here, within as many years; and this is based upon articles of faith, professedly religious, yet, in one of which, it is stated, that "we see God in death as well as in life, in evil as well as in good."—This being the case, it seems strange that any one should seek to escape or ward off either death or evil. On such a basis all moral efforts are absurd and stultifying. One thing may as well be as another, and all we have to do is to fold our hands and float along. Moral distinctions are out of place; conscience is an interloper.

A few persons here have faith in Christ and look to Oneida Communism as the only practical form of social re-organization. Some others give their adhesion conditionally. Many of the latter class are wedded to Berlin Hights as *the* place for work and cannot think of separation. They would like to see Oneida come to Berlin, but cannot think of Berlin going to Oneida. The *animus* of Berlin socialism(?) is for disintegration rather than for co-operation. Any attempt to establish Christian Communism here would doubtless encounter more actual opposition from socialists than any other class of people. Here are those who rely upon science alone to save the world; those who say it is to be done through the harmonial philosophy, to whom every thing *now* is right and nothing is wrong; those of religious pretensions, who would lean upon the popular churches if they could; those who are indifferent, who have seen only failure thus far and prophesy against future success, pronouncing the world itself a failure; those who believe Oneida Communism good as far as it goes, but think its light pales before the transcendant illumination which they are expecting but have not received; and, finally, there are the "roughs," profane in speech, boorish in manners, mere distractives; most of whom would contest the field with Christian Communism and resist in one or another form, its establishment.

Faithful testimony from those who confess Christ may work a change here, even, before long. The number of these is increasing, and their utterances are becoming more clear and positive. Several have come out within a few days. I hope the O. C. will find itself able to encourage them, to extend to them the hand of sympathy, and help them to be steadfast and immovable in the position they have taken.

Truly and faithfully, J. W. TOWNER.

The bag-orders since May 19th amount to $1053,86. Sales for the month of May, $3262,31.

The trap sales for the month of May amount to $2441,47.

Mr. Leete is at work to-day painting the store.

Abram arrived this morning. He has brought with him three beautiful gold fish which will be quite an addition to the aquarium. They have stood the journey well and are quite vivacious.

Mr. Kelly says in a letter received yesterday, that the prolonged rain has had such an effect on his customers that they have bought up his entire stock of blue silk.—We are glad he has "given them the blues" in so wholesome a manner and hope they will catch the scarlet fever next and buy up all his reds.

May, after coquetting with us for a whole month, sometimes in the laughter of warm sunshine, sometimes in tears of rain, left us last night, to make way for her sister June. In leaving she was saucy enough to give a parting snap of frost by way of farewell. This recalls the Eastern story of the merchant who offered to sell his goods to a beautiful lady for a kiss, and who, on taking his price, bit her cheek. We believe, however, that Jack Frost did not bite so hard as the merchant.—It was hardly more than a spicy kiss after all.

Quilting for the N. Y. B. has been going on for several days.

Mr. Thayer reports 1511 tomato plants set out. The varieties and proportions are as follows: Early 359, Fegee Island 720, Cook 432. About 500 more plants will be set.

June begins to-day with all her banners unfurled in the glorious sunshine. Though the morning was cool and slightly frosty—the mercury sinking one degree below 40—a warmth begins to pervade the atmosphere this forenoon more genuinely summer-like than anything we remember in May, though the mercury does not record so high perhaps.

The old, rotten fence on the east side of the road in front of the house is being removed to the wood-pile, and will soon be used to manufacture steam for our washing and cooking.

METEOROLOGICAL.

Thermometer, May 31.

6 A. M. 50. Cloudy.
12 M. 57. Pleasant.
6 P. M. 52. Clear.
West wind throughout the day.

DAILY JOURNAL
OF ONEIDA COMMUNITY.

A. D. 1866. JUNE 2. NO. 119.

SATURDAY.

June 1, 1866.

To THE FAMILY:—It is one year since I confessed Christ, and it has been the happiest year of my life. I thank God for showing me the truth. I confess my entire separation from my old life, and wish to become a true soldier of Christ. I confess my sympathy with Mr. Noyes's late talk on worship; it has drawn me near to Christ. I confess my union with Mr. Noyes and Mr. Hamilton, also a soft and receptive spirit and one that is open to criticism. H. M. SIBLEY.

In Mr. Knowles's room is a cot mounted on rockers—a kind of cradle—for the use of any one who attends him during night. Last night the attendant was Mr. P. D.; and when some others came in to relieve him in the morning, the following colloquy took place:

P. D. (*stretched on the cot*) "Well, I havn't been in a cradle before, since I was a baby."

Mr. K. "Yes, I've been sitting up with him last night; he slept pretty well."

P. D. "No wonder; Mr. K. put me to sleep with his snoring."

Mr. K. "I'm glad I didn't wake you up with it."

This is but a single example of Mr. K's. usual facetious humor.

Mr. Hall returned yesterday, having left C. V. at Boonville. He has given Charles a fair start in the business, and left him now to his own resources.

Little E., the other day, was called over to his mother K's. room to try on a new suit. Finding a number of women present he felt rather embarrassed and declined the honor. A. suggested, however, that she would place a chair before him, and this would obviate the difficulty. As he was proceeding with the operation, he caught sight of A's. face peeping over the chair, and all at once energetically cried out: "*There are not chairs enough!*" We did not learn whether any further aids to his modesty were furnished.

The committee on prices of entertainment, the present season, recommend that last year's prices be continued with one or two exceptions.

A teacher at Solsville, Madison County, inquires if the Community will entertain her school of twenty scholars, about the last of June.

The dairy department began carrying milk to the cheese-factory, for the season, last evening. Butter-making will now be discontinued for the season. With the last churning to-morrow, they will have made since the first of January, about 1435 lbs. During the month of May 779 lbs. were made.

As soon as the store is finished we believe it is the intention to remove the dairy-house, and fit up the main part of it as a dwelling for our hostler. Since the store has been fitting up, the desirableness of having the dairy-house removed has become more and more evident. The South wing has become considerably dilapidated and unsightly. And the whole institution is too conspicuously near our front doors.

Neighbor Parsons is in some difficulty with the cheese-factory authorities about the quality of milk he sends to the factory. It is claimed that on certain occasions there were unmistakable evidences that said milk had been diluted. Mr. P., at latest advices, had acknowledged the fact, and stated how it happened—which statement exonerates him from personal blame. The rule is, that if a patron of the factory is proved to have sent diluted milk he shall withdraw from the company, and forfeit all interest in the milk previously sent to the factory.—We understand that the offence is also punishable by a fine of one hundred dollars and imprisonment for six months.

Our neighbors have been engaged by Mr. Barron to raise several acres of Sweet Corn; and two or three of them have set out raspberry plantations the present spring as tributaries to our preserving establishment.

The Cheese and Butter Factory at Cook's Corners, mentioned in a late JOURNAL, has concluded to confine its operations to cheese-making.

In meeting, Mr. Hamilton made a call for volunteers for the erection of a new fence to extend from the store southwards as far as the corner. We are glad to observe this morning that the call is vigorously responded to. The work seems to be engineered by Abram, whom we are glad to see among us again.

This morning while trying vigorously to obtain some news for our daily sheet we were informed by an intelligent and observing lady that she had heard of nothing, and that THE JOURNAL got ahead of even the *women* in the line of news, and that she frequently found information in it which she had not heard of before. Was not this complimentary? We shall not despair of the TONTINE LUMINARY maintaining its character as an entertaining publication, if it continues to keep ahead of the conspicuous part of the Community.

There are about fifteen acres of strawberries to be harvested in our neighborhood the present season; and strawberries are likely to sell at low prices unless some of them can be shipped to New York, and the large cities. To effect this object some efforts will be made to have the 9 P. M. evening express stop at Oneida Depot. Fruit shipped on this train would go right through and arrive in New York early the next morning.

It is estimated that the Community will not have many strawberries to market—our expected 200 bushels will be mainly sold, eaten and bottled at home.

William Inslee called here last evening and spent the night with us. He is looking well and hearty; and had been to Syracuse on business for Messrs. Hewes and Phillips.

The silk-spinner is finished and Mr. Inslee only waits the arrival Charles Cragin before setting it up.

The machinists have successfully introduced the casting of brass at the Foundry; and thereby will save considerable outlay, as they have some ninety pounds to cast for parts of the silk machinery.

METEOROLOGICAL.

Thermometer, June 1.

6 A. M. 58. Pleasant. South wind.
12 M. 68. Clear. 7 P. M. 65.

DAILY JOURNAL
OF ONEIDA COMMUNITY.

A. D. 1866. JUNE 4. NO. 120.

MONDAY.

On Saturday 666 curculios were captured. Yesterday they were hunted both morning and evening and the result was that 1744 more ceased their depradations and came to an ignominious end.

Yesterday a Mr. Leverett Appleton, called here. He is a great pedestrian and had just come from Boston on foot. He has traveled over a great part of Europe on foot and is now pedestrianizing in this country. He was acquainted with Thoreau, and knows many of the literati of this country. We did not learn what definite object he has in his travels.

G. C. Cone, of McGregor, Iowa, orders twenty dozen of the new trap No. 0, and says, "I wish you had got out this size before, then I would not have bought any of Blake's traps."

Our dry weather during May was not without its compensation. The work on the store progressed much more rapidly than it would have done had the weather been stormy. Now the building is all inclosed, and the inside work goes on without interruption.

Our friend, R. Sparrow Ornithophilos, is very enthusiastic about the birds this season. Now that he has equipped himself with a pocket telescope, we hear reports of sundry discoveries he has made. Yesterday he was off to the hills, and brought home glowing accounts of having found the Hermit Thrush, the Wood Thrush and the Scarlet Tanager. We notice that he is getting more severely scientific in his notions. We even heard him say yesterday that if he had had a gun with him he would have shot one strange bird that he saw, in order that he might have closely observed it, and determined its order and name! Think of the hardihood of such a suggestion. We shall not be surprised, hereafter, to see him negotiating with Mr. Newhouse for the loan of a cane rifle or shot-gun.

G. W. Hamilton reports that in making 80 dozen Railroad bag frames 36 per cent. profit was realized after paying for the labor; and it is thought 50 per cent. will be attained. On the common bag frames the profit is not so much.

Last night and to-day we have been having a splendid series of showers. Great good therefrom will be realized in the strawberry and grass crops.

A company went to Black Creek yesterday, and caught a fine lot of pickerel. The neighboring trout brooks are also frequently visited this spring. We saw several dozens of little fellows on their way to the frying pan yesterday.

In order to have uniformity in the hours of labor all round, and prevent some confusion that now exists between the hours of labor of the various departments, and between the time of our own people quitting work and that of the hired help, it was thought best, in the business meeting, to have a new system of ringing the bells all round. They will accordingly be rung hereafter at 7, 12, 1, and 6 o'clock. To suit this arrangement our dinner hour is put forward to 12½ o'clock.

Messrs. Burt and Dunn received the following letter from the Patent Office, Washington, this morning:

Washington, D. C., May 14, 1866.

Sir :—Your application for a patent for an improvement in Cutting Green Corn from the Cob has been examined and allowed. The patent will be engrossed for issue on the receipt of 20 dollars, the balance of the fee payable thereon, if received within six months.

Respectfully,   T. C. THEAKER.
                       Commissioner.

METEOROLOGICAL.

Thermometer, June 2.

6 A. M. 59.   12 M. 74.   6 P. M. 72.

The day was clear and beautiful, and during the afternoon the mercury rose to 87.

June 3.

6 A. M. 64.   12 M. 72.   6 P. M. 67.

OUR AQUARIUM.

In the green-house, stands our aquarium. It is about three feet long, eighteen inches wide and one foot deep. It contains, in addition to fragments of rock, pebbles and aquatic plants, 4 bullheads, 3 gold fish, 2 bass, 2 roach or sunfish, 5 Crabs, 2 tadpoles just on the eve of metamorphosis, 2 clams who exhibit their powers of locomotion by taking continual journeys from one end of the aquarium to the other and of whom or of some other shell fish the poet asks:

"Did he stand at the diamond door
Of his house in a rainbow frill ?
Did he push, when he was uncurled,
A golden foot or a fairy horn
Thro' his dim water-world?"

Then there are 3 Renatae fuscae, 8 minnows and lastly, 4 water newts in defense of whom, allow us one word. We quite frequently hear expressions of disgust for these harmless and really pretty little creatures; but to those who indulge in such prejudices, we would recommend the reading of "The Ancient Mariner" whose bad luck came by shooting the Albatross, and who learned by a terrible experience to love even

"The slimy things that crawled with legs
Upon the slimy sea."

There was once a frog among this happy family, but it was silly enough to leap out and try the world again.

W. H. H.

DAILY JOURNAL
OF ONEIDA COMMUNITY.

A. D. 1866. JUNE 5. NO. 121.

TUESDAY.

In allusion to the subject of governing children, the other evening, Mr. Hamilton made the following remarks:

"It is an important truth, which we must lay to heart, that in governing children, or in trying to convert and reform other folks, we cannot make them what we are not ourselves. We cannot teach what we do not know; neither can we impart a quality of spirit we do not ourselves possess. We cannot raise good fruit from bad seed. This is a simple truth but a sweeping one. If we are not good children ourselves to God we cannot expect to make our children good to us, but devils will possess them. And if we want to cast devils out of our children and secure their obedience, the first thing we must do is to become all right with God, and let him cast all the devils out of us."

We are receiving some responses now-a-days to letters lately addressed to our fruit customers. Here is a specimen:

Cincinnati, May 31, 1866.

ONEIDA COMMUNITY:—In reply to your favor May 28, we take pleasure in giving our opinion as to the quality of your fruits, which each one of our firm has used in his family for the past two years.

We consider them by far the finest we have ever used, and for the quality of fruit, much cheaper than we can put them up ourselves, even counting our labor at home as worth nothing.

Of the hundreds of cans of fruit and vegetables of your brand which we have examined and used, we have never yet found the contents of any one, when opened, otherwise than in perfect order and evidently as fresh as when first preserved.

What first attracted our attention to your fruits was their fine flavor which we think is nearer the fruit just from the tree than any in the market.

Respectfully Yours, R. W. BOOTH & Co.

William Inslee left for Newark on Sunday evening.—From what we hear he enjoyed his visit here very much, and was agreeably surprised at his reception. He confessed as he was going to the Depot with Edward, that he had some misgivings about coming and almost decided at one time not to come. He was very much surprised at the state of things here, and at seeing such a fine machine-shop. He thought our shop was the finest he had ever seen outside of the city. He has some thoughts of getting married though we believe there is no definite arrangement in regard to the matter: and he admitted to his father that there was a better way.—He expressed much thankfulness for his Community education, and said it had been a great means of saving him from the temptations of the world.

Mr. A. Barnes, subscriber to THE CIRCULAR, from Massachusetts, is here. He came to look into the matter of buying some land of the Community and making himself a home near us. He is a carpenter, and has been a reader of our publications for twenty years. He says he does not feel quite ready to join the Community but he would like to live near us.

THE CIRCULARS were on hand at an early hour this morning, for which we were all thankful.

SINGULAR, BUT TRUE.

It is not uncommon for persons to take advantage of the stupidity of an old yellow hen, and make her mother a flock of goslings, or a flock of young ducks, or turkeys. I once invited her to hatch and rear a dozen partridges. She hatched them, and reared them about three days, when they reared themselves out of her sight and mine too. A white bantam rooster at Wallingford, several years ago, was instructed in the useful art of brooding, and learned to spread his wings in good fatherly style for a number of little chicks, and seemed to take much satisfaction in his new calling. Yellow hens and white bantams are, however, not supposed to be very gifted in sense and judgement, and are liable (especially the yellow hens) to be blinded and fooled by the undue action of philoprogenitiveness; but think of a sage cat nursing a grey squirrel, and treating it in all respects as though it were her veritable kit! A few weeks since an Oneida paper contained this statement:

QUEER FREAK.—C. Y. Chapman has a curiosity at his store in this village, viz: A cat performing the part of mother to a kitten and a *squirrel*, both receiving nourishment from the cat. The kitten and squirrel are both young, having had their eyes open but a few days.

It seemed probable that there was some humbug about this story; and I thought no more of it until my attention was arrested yesterday, as I passed by Mr. Chapman's store, by the kitten and squirrel themselves. They were playing together in a small glass-globe house, made expressly for them I judged. The old grimalkin was not present, and had probably weaned them, as the kitten was full half grown, and the squirrel seemed nearly full size, and a handsome fellow. It was singular enough to see them rolling and tumbling, and jumping and biting, like two kittens or two squirrels—both enjoying themselves finely. A little selfishness was apparent in the squirrel, as he undertook to conceal from his companion some bits of cracker, which had been given them.

After witnessing this curious combination the old story that Romulus, the founder of Rome, and Remus his brother, were suckled by a wolf, does not appear so incredible.   w.

METEOROLOGICAL.

Thermometer, June 4.

6 A. M. 52. Fine warm rain.
12 M. 66. Cloudy.
6 P. M. 72.
A fine shower at 7 o'clock in the evening.

DAILY JOURNAL
OF ONEIDA COMMUNITY.

A. D. 1866. JUNE 6. NO. 122.

WEDNESDAY.

A Mr. Ira Porter, of Chicago, is now here. He claims to be a social reformer, and has issued the prospectus of a new order of society which he wishes to inaugurate. He proposes to reform the world by a system of "Self-sustaining Industrial Colleges." We have read his prospectus, but—"don't see it."

A letter was received yesterday from Mr. G. F. Lewis of Detroit. The writer says:

"Mrs. L. has long desired to live in a Community of spiritual and noble people" and "has long thought a higher social state was to come on this earth, but as yet has not seen her desire gratified." "She has thought much of visiting you. She is an earnest, sincere, religious woman, whose whole soul yearns for a higher life. Be pleased to advise upon what terms she can be admitted to your Community upon trial or as a learner."

G. B. Price, a Watervliet Shaker and inventor of a Patent Pea-Sheller, called at the Community yesterday to talk about our making his Pea-Shellers for such as may apply to us for them—to examine the corn-cutting machine and to see the folks. He expressed himself as agreeably disappointed in the appearance of the buildings and grounds, and indeed of all he saw, including the children, women and short dress. He said at once that the corn-cutter is a fine thing, altogether superior to the one a Shaker brother had been working at ten years. He said that on his return, he should advise the Trustees of his society to obtain one of our corn-cutters, and if it worked satisfactorily, he had no doubt, it might lead to the sale of a dozen among the Shaker families at Watervleit, Lebanon and other places.

Mr. Price said he had seen our Community and Mr. Noyes, in a vision, before the Community was started, and took great interest in looking at Mr. N's. photograph. He is one of the few live men (comparatively speaking) of the Shaker brotherhood, and it was evident that he is unsatisfied with the spirit and genius of Shakerism.— Speaking of the cultivation of music, he acknowledged that there was no valid objection against it, and that the Shakers were now governed in this respect by the prejudices of their old people, who had been taught to look upon it as evil. He said the principal thing now taught among the Shakers is obedience, and reverence for those who had preceded them as having been inspired and taught the whole truth. To the question, "Does that satisfy such a mind as yours?" he replied, "It has to satisfy it." "That is a singular answer." "It is the best I can give."

Mr. Price requested that no mention whatever should be made in THE CIRCULAR of his visit to us, which request I hope will be respected; and said confidentially, "If you wish to keep on good terms with the Shakers you must stop reviewing," which remark I hope will not be heeded. It was a cowardly utterance, and indicates that " the swamp angel" is doing effective service in Shakerdom.   w.

We have come to the last of our apples, Four barrels were sold yesterday, for $6 a barrel. Mr. Ackley says that the last for family use will appear to-morrow.

The lawn has been mown, and under the genial influence of the warm weather and frequent showers, daily adds to its attractions.

The indications of a revival in the trap business continue. A large order was received a few days ago from Montreal. Mr. Olds also writes encouragingly.

The farmers finished planting their 30 acres of sweet-corn, to-day.

Our supply of news seems to be quite limited to-day. Our rainy weather continues, the birds are wonderfully musical—all the morning as we have been at work on THE JOURNAL, the mellow, curiously swinging song of the Veery has come into the window from the swamp across the creek, while a general chorus of Bobolinks, Robins, Sparrows and Orioles and Catbirds, has been going on about the lawn. Every body seems busy, good-natured and happy. Those that were sick are getting well. Mr. Knowles is getting quite smart— rides out every day or two, sits up a good deal and occasionally tries his hand at a game of checkers. The sprained ankles appear to be doing well. We notice Alice goes without her crutches much of the time.—L. F. D. seems to be steadily gaining. He busies himself considerably at the bag-business now-a-days.—Mr. Jones also is quite efficient at bag-work.

The new road-fence south of the store is finished or nearly so, and is a great improvement. We believe it is the intention, to put up a new fence on the same side of the road, from the store to the barns.

The store has received its first coat of paint. It is to be a light drab, we understand, with dark brown or maroon cornice, window and door frames.

METEOROLOGICAL.
Thermometer, June 5.

6 A. M. 66. 12 M. 74. 6 P. M. 77.
There were several fine showers during the day.

DAILY JOURNAL
OF ONEIDA COMMUNITY.

A. D. 1866.　　JUNE 7.　　NO. 123.

THURSDAY.

The Trappers' mare, brought from Canada last winter, foaled a fine colt last night—a grey stallion. Both mare and colt are in excellent condition this morning, and we hear that the latter is already valued at $100 by some of the lookers on.

A man in Chicago, wishes to interest the Community in a patented invention of his. It consists of a Trunk or Door Brace, for holding open trunks and doors. It may be a useful invention, but we have business enough in manufacturing our own inventions, and shall not be likely to give much attention to this one.

Mr. Porter left yesterday morning.

The following letter has been received from John S. Freeman :

Schenectady, N. Y., June 4, 1866.

My Dear Brother :—I received yours of Wednesday 30th May, in good time, and to-day yours of June 4th.

I thank God for the invitation which you have given me, for I feel that the privilege of coming to Oneida is a great blessing.

Perhaps it may be best for me to finish this term in College (which closes the last of next month), and assist father in making his wine, before I come to make trial of Community school.

Mother thinks of coming to make you a visit in strawberry time.

Yours Affectionately, John S. Freeman.

A Mr. Truesdell, a Hydropathic physician, arrived here this morning from the west. He is acquainted with the Dansville people, and was intimate with Giles.

Mrs. Kelly was criticised last evening with much sincerity. It was thought there was a good deal of self-complacency, and wholeness about her that makes her hard and egotistical. There is a tendency to superficiality and to seek outward popularity. It was also thought that her influence on Mr. K. was injurious. He has been somewhat discontented of late and has talked some about leaving. His trial seems to be with the marriage spirit. It was thought that her influence tended to hold him to her, while outwardly she preached separation. Her views of the separation of husbands and wives in the Community are not exactly correct, are too legal and sweeping. She needs to take a more humble position and attend to her own salvation, and not try to superintend Mr. Kelly so much. On the other hand, she has manifested a good deal of faith and love of the truth, and there is much love for her in the Community. We hope that both she and Mr. Kelly will turn their hearts to Christ, and become so thoroughly grounded in his purpose and love that nothing can move them.

In the bag-bees, the reading of "The Toilers of the Sea" has been finished, and the book now in hand is another of Hugo's—"The Hunch-back of Notre-Dame."

On Sunday, Sidney went fishing in the trout-brooks, over cast, and brought home 91, including some quite fine ones. The same day Homer and J. P. H. caught sixty or seventy in the Clockville brooks. In view of such results we can condole with our Wallingford friends, whose experiences were so graphically described in a late Circular.

Frank Hillerman arrived this morning from Bath.

Orders for 524 dozen traps were received yesterday.

Our lovers of buttermilk have come to grief. The milk is now taken to the Cheese-factory; consequently there is no more churning, Uncle Heman's red flag is no longer unfurled in the early morning, and we hear various utterances of lamentation from the numerous followers of the buttermilk banner. Mingled with the lamentations are praises of the health-giving properties of the beverage that is gone. We have no doubt of its excellence in this respect and hope an occasional churning will still be found both economical and desirable.

METEOROLOGICAL.

Thermometer, June 6.

6 A. M. 69.　Sunshine and south wind.

12 M. 75.

6 P. M. 62.

About 2 o'clock there was a heavy shower accompanied by a strong west wind.

DAILY JOURNAL
OF ONEIDA COMMUNITY.

A. D. 1866. JUNE 8. NO. 124.

FRIDAY.

Our June thus far is in marked contrast with our May. The clear, dry weather of May has been succeeded by an almost continuous dispensation of clouds and showers. It rains wonderfully easily, and under the genial drippings of the clouds, the meadows which a few weeks ago threatened a great failure of their crop of hay, are now rapidly improving, and promise a goodly yield.

Only 3 two-wheeled cultivators are now left at the agricultural works—Plows, Harrows, Rollers, and all else having been sold; and it is probable these three cultivators will soon be called for. Hurrah!

A of root-beer has been brewed by Mrs. Langstaff and has furnished a supply for the table several times of late.

Yesterday's New York Journal was very interesting. Every thing we hear of Mr. Noyes's sayings and doings finds a response in our hearts.

Mr. Burt received a letter from Mr. Noyes making the proposal that one of Mr. B's. Corn-cutting machines be sent to the Agency for exhibition and that measures be taken to call the attention of the public to the invention.

The fruit growers and preservers are making preparations for the season's campaign. The fruit-room in the basement of the Tontine is being re-arranged. The partition has been removed, and the whole space made into one room. The rooms on the floor above have been thoroughly cleaned, and the large one has been whitewashed.—A new

for carrying fruit from the fields has been fitted up.

Miss Hillerman states that her parents were at first opposed to her coming to the Community, but when they found that she had made up her mind to come, consented to it, and her father assisted her in starting on her journey.

In meeting last evening, Mr. Hamilton made some interesting remarks about cultivating simplicity in our relations to Christ, and avoiding all cant in our thoughts as well as in conversation and confessions.

Mr. Knowles has moved out of the back Parlor, and the room is being cleaned and put in order for visitors.

The spooling machine which Mr. Inslee and Co. have been making for Mr. Bottom, is finished, and was on exhibition in the upper sitting room the other evening.

Mr. Daniel Nash has been constructing a frame for a lamp which it is proposed to have placed in the rear of our buildings.

PEAT.

In Scotland, peat is much used by the peasantry of certain districts, as fuel. It is not found in swamps but in sections which, however they may at one time have been covered with water, are now high and dry, and are known as peat-mosses. The peat is cut out in pieces rather larger than an ordinary brick and of much the same proportions. When cut out, they are set upright—some half dozen together—to dry, after which they are ready for use. There are two kinds of peat; one very dark brown, nearly black, and pretty hard, the other of a lighter brown, somewhat soft and spongy, and can easily be broken to pieces with the hands. Either kind consists of a mass of fibres varying in thickness from one eighth of an inch to the merest thread, reticulated into a confused mass, the interstices between, being filled up by a blackish, vegetable substance which appears to have been formed by sedimentary deposit. It is the greater preponderance of this, that makes the difference between the two kinds mentioned, the lighter sort being almost destitute of it.

Peat is a poor conductor of heat, so much so that a small piece of it may be held in the hand while one side of it is on fire. It gives no flame, but merely smoulders; and when once ignited, it is quite difficult to quench the fire. I have frequently seen a burning piece plunged in water, and on being taken out and the water shaken off, it was found to be burning on as if nothing had happened. W. H. H.

METEOROLOGICAL.

Thermometer, June 7.

6 A. M. 60. 12 M. 64. 6 P. M. 62.

A cool westerly wind throughout the day, accompanied much of the time by a light drizzling rain.

DAILY JOURNAL
OF ONEIDA COMMUNITY.

A. D. 1866.   JUNE 9.   NO. 125.

SATURDAY.

Willow Place is one of the great attractions of the Community. The steady progress of the silk machinery, the increasing activity in the

business, and the genial, enthusiastic spirit of the brethren there, combined with the splendid building and conveniences, and prospective development, make a visit there a very interesting event. It is like taking a bath in the inspired atmosphere of mechanism and power.

The following letter, received last evening, is another indication that the articles in THE CIRCULAR on "Shaker Communism" are producing some commotion among the followers of Mother Ann. H. A. N. will please see that the request for discontinuance is complied with:

Shaker Village, Albany, May 4, 1866.

FRIEND HAMILTON :—I thank you for the pamphlets you sent me, and for THE CIRCULAR thus far; please discontinue and oblige.   Yours truly, E. B. PRENTIS.

A letter of warning and threatening was received a few days since from " Frederick Hyren, Prophet of the Most High," addressed to Theo. R. Noyes. As Theodore had promised him that his letters should in future be committed to the flames, this communication was speedily burned.

Mr. Hatch's sister has been here since Thursday, and will stay till Monday.—Last evening, Daniel Bailey was criticised by request. The criticism was very full, sincere and kind, and will doubtless be sent to the other Communes in MS.

The ornithologists tell us that the cow-birds are at their tricks again. At Spring Grove, a simple-hearted veery is incubating on two eggs, one of her own and one of the cow-bird's. We hear also of a silly little sparrow who is raising one of these insidious parasites along with her own brood.

Mr. Kinsley with a company of the hired men, is laying a cement floor in the cellar of the store.

To-day we are having a little sunshine filtrated through the clouds, and a cool southerly wind is blowing.

Testimonials in favor of our preserved fruits continue to come in, some of which are very interesting and commendatory.

Dr. Truesdell is still here. He was present at meeting last evening where he heard a good deal of sincere talk in the form of criticism. He expressed himself very much interested in it, and said that it gave him a truer idea of the spirit and character of the Community than any

thing he had met with. He seems to be honestly seeking the truth and is a man of considerable discrimination and spiritual discernment, and quite a thinker.

An arrangement has been made to sell Mr. Hubbard's strawberries the present season for a Commission of fifteen per cent., he to furnish boxes and crates, and defray all expenses of freight, cartage and expressage.

The construction of a board fence in front of the

barn, and the yard of the large barn has been begun.— We hope soon to chronicle the fact that the grounds in that section are in a more attractive condition than when Mr. Noyes was here last.

FULL DRESS.

In the world, it is customary for fashionable people never to shew themselves in public, nor even to their visitors, except in full dress, and perhaps the rule is not a bad one—at least for them. But we have known persons who appear to follow a similar rule in regard to spiritual things—who never shew themselves but in a kind of spiritual full-dress. They seem " finished to the finger nail" and to hail us with a full, round "All's well, God bless you !"

Now we protest against this. If such people have any true experience, they cannot always feel so airy. Figuratively speaking, they are not always really in full dress, but are sometimes in soiled—even ragged, or at best, working garments ; and there is no need for them to doff these and put on silk and broadcloth in order to receive us. We would rather meet them just as they are.   W. H. H.

METEOROLOGICAL.

Thermometer, June 8.

6 A. M. 56. West wind.
12 M. 66. Cloudy.
6 P. M. 63. Cloudy.
Beautiful sunset.

DAILY JOURNAL
OF ONEIDA COMMUNITY.

A. D. 1866. JUNE 11. NO. 126.

MONDAY.
GIFTS.

The O. C. may be considered as an organization for the giving and receiving of gifts. From the "unspeakable gift" downwards through wide gradation of spiritual, intellectual and material gifts till we reach the apple or flower sent from one branch to another as a token of remembrance, the whole is redolent of gifts. There is quite a nack in the graceful giving of a gift; for instance when the giver is unknown, and the gift seems to drop down from the heavens, whence indeed all good gifts do come from. The writer received one in just such a way, yesterday. There it lay with its fresh, pure, clean look—without speck or flaw or imperfection of any kind —oval, shining, with all that appearance of lightness and coolness which delights the eye in Summer—a comfortable, easy-fitting straw hat braided by some kindly hands that know the happiness of giving.   W. H. H.

BUSINESS MEETING ITEMS.

The committee on selling land at Willow Place are to meet and decide on prices, &c.

Messrs. Burt, Kinsley, Hatch and Myron were appointed a committee to see that the high chimney at the Children's House is put in a safe condition.

Mr. Burt wished to know if it was best to make more than ten Corn-Cutting Machines at present. It was thought that if orders should come in for more than that number we could soon make more by having some of the parts on hand.

Mr. Delatre presented the subject of mowing the lawn. No one has the responsibility of cutting and disposing of the grass. The system of depending on volunteer help is somewhat uncertain, taking a long time to get over the lawn. Mr. S. W. Nash was added to the Lawn Committee and will take the responsibility of cutting the grass. The board were in favor of purchasing a Lawn Mower, if one can be got at a reasonable price.

Mr. D. P. Nash wanted to know the mind of the board about purchasing a machine for making eaves-gutters. The probable cost of the machine is $5,00.— Left to Mr. Nash and Mr. Hinds.

O. C. June 10, 1866.

To THE COMMUNITY:—I should like to thank God for all the mercies and judgments I have received. I knew that God had dealt with me in great wisdom and loving kindness, but it seemed as if I could not say until the past year, I am thankful for all his dealings with me. For a long time after the death of my children, I was tempted with regrets for the past, unreconciliation with the present, and fear for the future. My prayer was, "Lord lift upon me the light of thy countenance." Reading the Home Talk on the discipline of the affections seemed to settle me, particularly this passage, "That the past should be just as it has been, that the present should be just as it is, and that the future should be just as it will be." I now realize the peace of God dwelling in my heart, and it is worth experiencing the loss of all things to receive. The consciousness of abandoning of one's self to Christ, with all that we hold dear, is of far more worth than thousands of this world's possessions laid at our feet. I desire to realize the presence of God at all times, and that my purpose in all I do may be to please him. My heart is filled with gratitude for a home with those who are serving God, where we can be saved from our old life, and find that rest which the world knows not how to give. When passing through those trying scenes, the Community home was to me, as a beacon light to the mariner on the stormy sea. Temptations and darkness gathered thick around, but within was a light that beat back the tempter and I knew that good was stronger than evil.
S. J. Clark.

W. G. K. and C. A. Cragin arrived on Saturday night from New York,

A change seems to be working in Mr. Daniel Kelly's spirit. Yesterday after some conversation with W. G. K., and a letter from Mr. Hamilton, he wrote Mr. H. the following letter:

Oneida, June 10, 1866.

DEAR MR. HAMILTON:—After reading your note I came to the conclusion that for me to stand out against the will of God and the Community would be utter folly.— I do believe that the devil had got full possession of my will, and was taking me away from the Community.— There has a wicked devilish spirit got hold of me. I confess my entire separation from such a spirit and every kind of spirit that tends to draw me away from Christ and the Community. My prayer is that God will subdue my stubborn will, that I may have a soft and receptive heart ready and willing to do any thing that Christ or the Community finds for me to do. I confess my entire separation from the marriage spirit. I give up all claims to wife, children and every thing else and ask the prayers of the church to help me. I thank God that he has put me into the judgement. My prayer is that I may be cleansed from every thing that is false. I confess my union with Mr. Noyes, Mr. Hamilton and the family, and ask for criticism whenever they see I need it.

Ever your brother in love of the truth, D. M. KELLY.

METEOROLOGICAL.
Thermometer, June 9.

6 A. M. 66.   12 M. 70.   6 P. M. 66.

June 10.

6 A. M. 64.   12 M. 78.   6 P. M. 79.

DAILY JOURNAL
OF ONEIDA COMMUNITY.

A. D. 1866. JUNE 12. NO. 127.

TUESDAY.
LETTER FROM MR. TOWNER.

Detroit, Mich., June 8, 1866.

DEAR FRIENDS OF THE O. C.:—I send you words of greeting on my return to my present home and duties. My visit to you will be remembered as one of the most profitable experiences of my life. I trust that the new inspiration I have received thereby will be as permanent as it is refreshing and vitalizing. I feel strengthened and established; I have come to realize as I have never before known, Jesus, a Savior from sin. And I should keep back a part of the truth did I not acknowledge my allegiance to Mr. Noyes as a man approved of God by the work he has done, and is doing, a medium of Christ in the establishment of his kingdom on earth.

I gladly confess Christ in me a Savior from egotism and vanity; in me, a spirit of humility and docility.— Since I wrote you on the 28th of May, I had the pleasure of meeting some friends at Berlin Hights, who, confessing Christ, have resolved to engage together in the work of studying the Bible and the Berean for the purpose of learning of and coming more fully into union with him. There were nine persons beside myself and Mrs. Towner, They desire to connect themselves with the O. C. as the "Head Center" of light, and to separate themselves from the spirit of infidel free-love Berlin, and I am confident they will do it. We had a free conversation and the utterances and confessions were clear and searching. A good work is begun there, which will, I doubt not, have your sympathy.

For myself, I can not refrain from now saying that I yearn for membership with your family, if I might be worthy, and it be found for your good as well as mine. On this point, I may write more fully ere long, if you will allow me.

Faithfully yours,   J. W. TOWNER.

DEPARTURES.—Mrs. Wells, sister of Mr. Hatch left yesterday.—Mr. A. P. Truesdell also left yesterday.— The residence of this gentleman at present is in Minnesota. He professes much interest in our movement, and took with him the Berean and Bible Argument. While here he read the articles on the Second Coming, The First Resurrection and the Origin of Evil, and said he accepted the views therein presented as the most satisfactory and rational of any thing he had ever met with. He, however impressed us as being somewhat superficial and intellectual in his tendencies, and as rather too much absorbed in his own individual leadings and experience.

Mr. D. Kelly was criticised last evening, a report of which will be sent in MS.

The weather since Sunday has been very fine. Days of sunshine are highly appreciated after a week or two of clouds and rain. Every thing is in a fine growing condition. The strawberries will be late this season.— A few ripe wild ones have been brought in, but from the plantation few will probably be harvested under eight or ten days.—The raspberries are now in blossom and promise a goodly crop.

Mrs. Sherrard who has been stopping at Mr. Hubbard's for some weeks, leaves to-day for the home of her sister in Western Virginia, in company with her youngest son. She was quite anxious to be employed by the Community, and to find a home with us or near us; but as she has no vital faith in the Community or in the Lord, we could not receive her or assume responsibility in regard to her, simply on account of her unfortunate circumstances. We, however, presented her with twenty dollars towards defraying her traveling expenses. She left her husband, Col. Sherrard of the Rebel army, on account of his conjugal infidelity, but intends returning to him, as he claims to have reformed and promises better behavior. She proposes to have her husband send a box of tobacco to the O. C. Agency to be sold to remunerate us for money advanced to her and to supply her oldest son, Preston, with funds to return to Virginia.— Preston will work for the Community only a few days longer.

The trap orders received since Saturday from New York, and from the West through Mr. Olds, amount to 1052 dozen, mostly of the smaller sized traps. 125 doz. No. 0, and 105 doz. No. 1½ are ordered. We understand the orders will take off the greater part of the Muskrat traps that are on hand.

The mare and colt are doing well. We believe the latter is considered by good judges as a very fine specimen of juvenile horse-flesh.

The second coat of paint is being put on the store.— The building will be a fine addition to our surroundings, and we judge that all are satisfied with its present location.

EDITOR OF JOURNAL:—Our ancient Thomas of the Mill, a well known personage to many of your readers, was to day the hero of an exploit which has had a tendency to relieve him of the odium resting upon him in consequence of his Quixotic attempt at fishing with a hook a few days since. He discarded all artificial contrivances, like hooks and lines, and evidently "*went in* on his muscle." His appearance indicated this when he presented himself to his friends of the Bag Department, dripping wet from his *waist* downward, and bearing in his ponderous jaws a huge sucker which measured from the tip of its probosis to the extremity of its caudle appendage fully eight inches. He walked in with his accustomed dignity and a very knowing look, as much as to say "*Don't you wish you had it*," and having received the congratulations of his friends, immediately commenced an operation which while it was evidently fine for Thomas, was death on the sucker. Sucker as he was he was *catfished* in short order.   X. Y. Z.

METEOROLOGICAL.

Thermometer, June 11.
6 A. M. 59.   12 M. 72.   6 P. M. 64.
A clear and beautiful day, closing with a fine sunset.

DAILY JOURNAL
OF ONEIDA COMMUNITY.

A. D. 1866. JUNE 13. NO. 128.

WEDNESDAY.
QUICK RETURNS.

The practice of drawing on parties, when their accounts are overdue, is becoming more and more common here and at the Agency. Hence the importance of our Agents making immediate reports of all collections.— Otherwise there will be great liability of persons being drawn upon who have already paid their accounts, which accident is to be avoided if possible. A case of this kind happened lately. The Agent who made the collection for Oneida, reported the same to the Agency, but the O. C. book-keeper did not hear of it until after the party had been drawn on; now this might have been avoided if the Agent had reported the collection at once to Miss Macknet. Money collected for Oneida may be sent to the Agency whenever convenient, but a report of the same should always be sent here soon after the collections are made. And please remember to write about all such matters directly to the book-keeper, and not to some other person, as that is liable to occasion delay and negligence.   w.

Last evening the subject of meeting and treating visitors was up for discussion, and there was some criticism of Mr. Bolles for dropping down too much in spirit to them, and indulging too much in the preaching spirit. It was thought this was quite apparent in his intercourse with some of the recent visitors.

Our fair weather is over for the present, and this forenoon we are having a southeast rain storm.

We should have mentioned before that Charles Vanvelzar returned from his peddling trip on Saturday night. He had quite good luck we believe. He went north into Lewis and Jefferson Counties.

The tall chimney at the children's house has been taken down. A new chimney for the use of the children's department will be put up near the center of the building.

THE CIRCULARS came yesterday morning at an early hour, and were eagerly sought for, as usual.

A small bill of type has been ordered from New York, for use on THE JOURNAL and for job work.

The dairy house is to be dispensed with and removed as soon as other business will permit. The main part will be fitted up for the hostler. The location selected for it, is east of the vineyard which extends south from the horse-barn.

Mr. Hatch says we may report that they "have got a dozen cocoa-nuts to make *mince pies* with for the children."

The fence between the Weed lot and the Hamilton meadow has been removed. With the exception of the swamp, all the land west of the main road and north of the road leading to the Red School-house, is in one field. Communism makes broad fields.

The curculio hunting still continues. This week two of the women volunteered to take part in the morning hunts. The "Varmints" appear to be diminishing in number, though some of them are increasing in size. A huge one was caught this morning, which Mr. Bristol talks of sending to the Editor of the Horticulturist.

Mr. Miller has gone to New York, and E. S. Burnham to Oswego, on business.

For the benefit of G. W. N. we would state that his hemlock hedge is very beautiful this season. It is now just in the glory of its new growth, and the light green of the young shoots amid the dark green of older leaves forms a charming contrast. We wish the Editor of THE CIRCULAR could see it. Several Norway Spruces have been planted at the western end of the hedge for the purpose of making a more artistic termination in that direction.

We received a letter to-day from a gentleman and lady who stand in conjugal relations to each other, expressing a wish to visit us. The letter was signed "Sylvanus Ward and wife (according to law)."

METEOROLOGICAL.

Thermometer, June 12.

6 A. M. 58.   12 M. 68.   6 P. M. 66.

Cloudy during the latter part of the day with signs of rain.

DAILY JOURNAL
OF ONEIDA COMMUNITY.

A. D. 1866. JUNE 14. NO. 125.

THURSDAY.

L. F. D. is now engaged in assisting Frederick in the dentistry business. We hear that he pulled five teeth for Mrs. Harriet Kinsley this morning.

Mr. Newhouse went over to the Siloam trout brooks on Saturday afternoon and came back on Sunday, bringing with him about 140 of the speckled beauties. Mr. N. thinks the reason why the Mount Tomites have no better luck, is that they "dont understand how to do it." In reporting his opinion we do not wish to be understood as fully indorsing it.—Abram, Homer and Mr. Bristol, also visited the brooks over east on Sunday and met with very good luck.

Mr. Thayer reports $58 worth of plants sold from the hot-beds.

The digging of the cellar for the hostler's house was begun this morning.

The larger part of the store is lathed, and the plastering is going on.

The fence northward from the store is now in course of construction. A fence will also be built in the rear of the store, at such a distance from it as will allow of a driveway round the building.

The fruit preservers are beginning to make arrangements for the season's supply of fruit. Martin will go out west next week to investigate about cherries and raspberries. The country about here has been canvassed for cherries by Mr. Ackley. We find that the crop will be quite small.

In noticing in yesterday's JOURNAL the removal of the fence on the south side of the Hamilton meadow, we spoke of the fence as separating the Weed lot from that meadow. We should have said Calkins lot. We presume however the matter was understood by most of our readers.

In the meeting last evening the subject of dealing with visitors was continued by Mr. Hamilton.

We were all glad to hear the report of C. S. J's. interview with A. C. S. Mr. Smith's attitude shows the power of the truth to subdue and control character.

We are having very warm weather to-day. The sky is almost cloudless, a warm south wind is blowing, and the sun pours down its rays with great power.

The second mowing of the lawn is in progress. Mr. Underwood is quite efficient with the scythe now-a-days.

The fruit testimonials received lately in response to a circular addressed to some of our customers are very encouraging. A Chicago firm in a letter received yesterday says: "I take the earliest opportunity to let you know that I wish you to consider me as a customer of yours for the coming season, and at all times hereafter as long as I continue in this business." A St. Paul customer writes: "We take pleasure in assuring you that all who have used your fruits here concur in our opinion that they are decidedly the best fruits ever offered in this market." A number of these testimonials will soon be printed in a circular with price-list for the present season

As we go to press the rain is pouring down.

Orders for 134 dozen traps were received to-day.— One trapper writes as follows: "You inquire whether I had read your Trapper's Guide. I answer, Yes, five times, and find it a very pleasing book. Some valuable hints, and yet I do not trap otter and fox in the way described by Mr. Newhouse, as I could not catch one in ten. They are scarce here and hard to catch. I would send you my way of catching the two animals if it would be worth any thing to you. But I suppose where they are plentiful they can be caught any way."

PRICE OF PATENT-CORN-CUTTER.

For the information of all whom it may concern, be it known that it hath been decided to charge preserving establishments for a Patent Corn-Cutter one hundred dollars, and hotels, boarding-houses and other parties sixty dollars.

METEOROLOGICAL.

Thermometer, June 13.

6 A. M. 60.   12 M. 60.   6 P. M. 70.

In the afternoon the clouds and rain ended with a very heavy thunder shower from the northwest.

DAILY JOURNAL
OF ONEIDA COMMUNITY.

A. D. 1866. JUNE 15. NO. 130.

FRIDAY.

Mr. Woolworth arrived yesterday afternoon.

Last evening Mr. Woolworth gave an interesting report of Wallingford and New York affairs, Mr. Noyes's talk, &c. Afterwards Mr. Hamilton read the 1st chapter of the 1st Epistle of John, and talked some about the importance of walking in the light.

The reports from Wallingford on "Old Age, Dress, and C. H. Weld's Influence" are very instructive and edifying. The view taken of a certain former member of the O. C. by Mr. Noyes and others at New York, meets a hearty response here.

We received the following letter the other day, and as the writer wanted it printed, we correct the spelling and grammar somewhat and print it here:

North Bay, Oneida Co., N. Y., June 4.

J. H. NOYES, DEAR BROTHER:—I take my pen to drop a few lines to your Community, which you are at liberty to use as you please. If I could spell my words right I would like to have this letter printed; but don't like to make myself appear ridiculous in the eye of the public. But I wish to express my feelings to the Community; not that I wish to become a member of your Community, but I wish to become one of your warm-hearted outside friends, and be permitted to call you brethren, and sisters. May I have that privilege?

I have received THE CIRCULAR for nearly two years past, for which I am very thankful. I read it with great pleasure. I sent to THE CIRCULAR office for a pamphlet; I see it was sent and marked on my paper, but it did not reach me.

I know nothing about you only by THE CIRCULAR.— The reports I hear about you are unfavorable. The sects say there is no religion in your paper. My answer is, If there is no religion in their paper I don't know where to find it. I never saw any of your people, except the Band here on our Fair grounds. I calculate to come and see you this season. There are some things in your theory I cannot agree with, but I am no sectarian. My creed is, no creed but the Bible, no test of fellowship but Christian character. I love God's people every where. I can repeat the Lord's prayer, not only by heart, but from my heart. Union, O how sweet it sounds! Love, What word so dear? In heaven all is love and union. Is my action in harmony with my prayer? If not I am a hypocrite. Call no man on earth father, for one is your father in heaven, said Christ. What I not say father Wesley, or father Calvin, or Luther. No, nor father Noyes; none but our Father in heaven. Then I must call you all brethren and sisters. But you say

you are Perfectionists. I am glad you are, I wish I were one. I wish to be holy in heart.

My wife sends her best respects to your family. She says she feels an interest in your prosperity, and would be glad to come and see you all. We live in harmony together; never had a jarring word between us. We have our morning and evening prayers.

I am a poor man in health and property, so good bye; God bless you all. J. B. JOHNSON.

It is hardly safe, at least we thought so yesterday, to say much about the weather—it changes so often. But to-day—that is just now—10 o'clock A. M.—is very beautiful. The sun shines gloriously, and only a few fleecy clouds are seen in the sky. The west wind plays gently among the leaves, and every thing looks as if washed clean by yesterday's shower.

We have a specimen of parasitism on our lawn just now, in the shape of the cow bunting, which is being waited on by two song sparrows. One of the disgusting things about it is that while the sparrows are laboriously attentive to its wants, the cow bunting keeps up a continual teasing cry, reminding one of the daughters of the horse-leech which cry "Give, give."

Mr. Leete came last evening.

Letters were received to-day from G. W. Reeve and wife of Berlin Hights, expressing sympathy with the Community and its faith in Christ.

METEOROLOGICAL.

Thermometer, June 14.

6 A. M. 60. 12 M. 78. 6 P. M. 78.

DAILY JOURNAL
OF ONEIDA COMMUNITY.

A. D. 1866. JUNE 16. NO. 131.

FRIDAY.
OUR LITTLE WORLD

MR. EDITOR:—To give you some idea of the risk incurred by the feathered race in the rearing of their young, I will just state that out of four attempts by our favorite finch this season, on the lawn, only one has succeeded. I am thinking of contriving some means of guarding them from the attacks of their foes—made evidently at night, by cats, or as some say, by skunks.—Perhaps you will say, "cui bono?"—but it is hard to look on and do nothing at such times. We feel tender toward our little proteges whose welfare (though but temporal) we have so much at heart. Perhaps we will report to you from time to time, how it goes with this little parish of ours, extending as it does, some way into the valley in which we live. To begin with, we can announce to you the approaching exodus of a promising young family of finches from the same Norway spruces selected last year, who will probably not forget the home of their infancy, when another spring calls them northward.   Your friend, ORNITHOPHILOS.

Yesterday afternoon the children who attend Portia's school had a grand foot excursion to the swamp beyond the cheese factory, to gather wintergreens. Including their attendants, there were twenty-three in the company, from Marian up to George Henry. The afternoon was just suitable for such an excursion and all appeared to enjoy it very much. Some of the little ones, and we believe some of the children of a larger growth, got somewhat tired. Going and returning, the walk was about three miles.

The new chimney for the children's house is being put up to-day. It starts in the back kitchen, near the sink.

Miss Betsey Jane, the colt which Martin broke lately, played Ernest an ugly trick yesterday. He was mounted on the sorrel, which he was bringing home from pasture, when Betsey came along-side and made a maneuver which resulted in a painful though not serious bruise on Earnest's leg, just under the knee. An application of arnica, and a quiet rest in bed will soon set our equestrian all right again. A little hurt like this, has sometimes quite a good effect in composing the mind and inducing reflection.

Last evening Mr. Henderson was criticised by request.

Two men were here from the Depot yesterday to get Edward Inslee and Charles Vanvelzer, to play for a Festival of the Baptist Church Sunday School. The proposal was respectfully declined. Our musicians do not wish to respond to individual invitations of this kind, preferring to go abroad only when the whole band goes and when there is some general public interest to serve.

Preston Sherrard's connection with us was brought to a close yesterday—at least we thought so when, having augmented his wardrobe and purse, we saw him take his departure. But like some of the newly-fledged robins on our lawn, he made his appearance again in the evening, requesting permission to stay in the nest one other night. He had been as far as Gerrit Smith's, seeking employment. We hope he will be more successful to-day.

We have a few visitors every day, and frequent calls for meals or refreshments.

The construction of the silk machinery at Willow Place is progressing very rapidly and forms an attractive feature in the machine-shop. A party consisting of some half dozen, paid a visit there yesterday; among them were one or two of our sisters who had not been at Willow Place since the fall of '64. The very idea of any thing silken in a place which has always been associated in most of our minds with iron-filings and grease, seems like the placing of Eve beside Adam.

Several days ago the agent of Oliver Ditson and Co., music publishers in Boston, was here. He was quite a sociable, hearty sort of a man and evidently an enthusiast in musical matters. He sang several pieces with excellent voice and quite good expression. He was very enthusiastic over New England and Massachusetts, and Boston in particular. He spoke of the Greatorex Collection of Music as the best collection that has ever been published in this country. It is published by Ditson and is used, we believe, by the Protestant Episcopal Church.

METEOROLOGICAL.
Thermometer, June 15.

6 A. M. 73.   12 M. 73.   6 P. M. 79.
Clear and pleasant throughout the day.

DAILY JOURNAL
OF ONEIDA COMMUNITY.

A. D. 1866. JUNE 18. NO. 132.

MONDAY
BUSINESS MEETING ITEMS.

Mr. Burt brought up the subject of buying a mile of the turnpike, so as to prevent the putting up of a toll-gate between Willow Place and the Castle. We have in our hands considerable of the money that was subscribed for that purpose, and Mr. Wilson wants us to pay it to the company who own the road on rather insufficient security. Some persons have paid with the understanding that there is to be no gate put up west of the present one, and it was the opinion of the board that we could do nothing with the money that was not implied in the contract.

The Business Talk given by Mr. Noyes at New York, recommending self-possession and flexibility was read.

The desire was expressed that we might be able to keep self-possessed and not get excited if we have a great many orders.

The house occupied by Mr. Kelly, the Willow Place founder, needs a cistern. Mr. Kinsley was appointed to look into the matter and report.

Martin thought there was rather too much demand for teams for fishing parties, and it was suggested that a little continence in this respect was needed.

The plan of getting up dies and other tools, for the purpose of punching out springs was spoken of, and a desire to experiment upon it expressed. No objection was made to trying it, but the board thought nothing should be done to hinder our efficiency in making traps. G. W. Hamilton thought Mr. Newhouse should give his attention to getting up patterns, thereby carrying out the suggestions of the Talk that had been read.

The Vineland Fruit Preserving Company of Vineland, New Jersey, sent an agent to the Community last Saturday, who ordered for them one Pea Sheller and one Corn-Cutter—the former at $65, the latter at $100. We have to pay Mr. Price of Watervliet $25 for each Pea Sheller sold by us, on account of his patent interest. Mr. Edgett of Camden has been hired by the above Company to superintend their establishment the present season.

Mr. "S. Ward and wife (according to law)", have been here—came Saturday and left this morning. Mr. Ward is a spiritualist and interpreter of prophecy on his own hook, and evidently thinks he is "some" in that line. He has had his divers dreams, visions, impressions, leadings, revealings, &c., &c. He understands all about the beast whose number and mystery has puzzled Biblical students for more than six hundred three score and six years. He predicts that the number of the beast ends with the present year. He has had his brain opened and seen remarkable things, after which it was shut again. Since then he has been able to see more than most folks would care to brag of. He thinks the O. C. is nearer his ideal than any other association he has met with, but thinks it would take six months to find out all about us. He understands so much, has seen so much, and can predict so much, and evidently thinks he is so muchly himself, that it is somewhat singular we never should have heard of him before.—We did not ask him if he were going into the "show business", like his relative "A. Ward of Baldwinsville." He subscribed for THE CIRCULAR and paid $1.00, which was the best thing we heard about him. His wife according to law seemed modest and unassuming, but evidently had considerable faith in her legal other half.

MR. EDITOR:—I wish to make known to the readers of your JOURNAL that, whereas I have not been able for the last six years to read a word except large print like the headings to newspapers, I can now by the means of a magnifying glass read the print of THE CIRCULAR. I read a chapter in the Testament yesterday, also one to-day, without injury. I am more than realizing my dreams. I have a good many times dreamed of reading and the letters always looked large and plain. It was a great pleasure to me to have such dreams and the effect would last for days.

I am thankful to God for all of his dealings with me in the past and the present, and I can with the fullest assurance trust him for the future.   J. C. ACKLEY.

In making up our Saturday's paper we omitted to change the day of the week, consequently it read Friday.

Last evening Charles Cragin offered himself for criticism. Little was said except in the way of commendation. His course and public spirit in the silk business were liked, and it was thought he had done well while absent.

Mr. Knowles has so far recovered that he can walk across the room.

To-day Mrs. Hatch, Fidelia and Abby have gone to Willow Place, to clean the Office.

Edward Insler starts this afternoon for Newark to visit his mother's family. He will carry with him an invitation to his mother and sister to visit the Community.

Mr. Daniel Kelly has finally decided to withdraw from the Community, and will leave as soon as his things can be got ready. His family refuse to go with him.

Mr. Olds arrived home on Saturday after an absence of between three and four months. We were all glad to see him.

METEOROLOGICAL.

Thermometer, June 16.

6 A. M. 70. Clear. 12 M. 73. Clear. 6 P. M. 55.
During the afternoon there was a thunder shower accompanied with considerable hail.

June 17.

6 A. M. 57. 12 M. 60. 6 P. M. 63.
A drizzling rain throughout the day.

DAILY JOURNAL
OF ONEIDA COMMUNITY.

A. D. 1866. JUNE 19. NO. 133

TUESDAY.

Mr. Burt has begun making ten more Corn-Cutters. He had made four before, one of which is sold and the other three are wanted for our own use. Mr. Burt anticipates we may have considerable many orders for them during the season.

We noticed yesterday a new improvement in heating springs at the forge-shop. Heretofore it has been necessary to have a man at every furnace to attend especially to the heating of the springs. This necessity is now dispensed with at the furnace connected with the drop presses that punch and shape the bows. Two endless chains, running on pulleys and worked by the action of the press, are arranged on the front edge of the furnace, forming what may be called a chain-way. On this chain-way the springs are placed, with one end reaching over to the hottest surface of the fire. The springs are first placed on the end of the chain-way farthest from the presses and by the time they have reached the other end, by a gradual motion, they are hot enough to be transferred immediately to the presses. A small boy is employed to keep the chain-way full of springs, while one of the pressmen can have an oversight of the fire and the movement of the springs. The whole arrangement is ingenious and economical.

Mr. Daniel Kelly left this morning for some western destination. Mrs. Kelly manifests a good spirit and is loyal to the Community.

Mr. H. R. Perry was criticised by request last evening. Very general satisfaction with his course since coming here, was expressed. He was thought to be a loyal hearted, upright, genial and harmonious man. He was recommended to thoroughly study Mr. Noyes's writings, to cultivate faith and to avoid personal entanglements.

New York, June 13, 1866.

Dear Bro. Pitt:—I have sometimes queried whether the "Tontine Luminary" was put to legitimate use as a medium of individual disquisitions and yet "Gifts," in the 126th No. provokes me to add something quite similar to that of "W. H. H." Day before yesterday I too, was made the recipient of a gift, in the shape of a pair of Congress gaiters, from O. C. They were acceptable and I was thankful; but on removing the wrapper I discovered some writing on the bottom of one of them signed "From, Guess Who." On the bottom of the other gaiter was written a similar note in phonography. I am unable to transcribe the words for contact of the gaiters with city pavements has utterly erased the writing, but in both notes there were hints of the apparent necessity that my "soul" needed replenishing or something to this effect. This was serious. But more; on testing the *fitness* of the gaiters neither of them could I get my foot into. Had our good purveyor, Mr. V., failed in his function. I would not judge too hastily.— So inserting my hand instead of my feet, what should I find but a lump of candy in each shoe. Enough said; only that "Guess Who" has my thanks without being *guessed ;* and yet the *gift* is none the less savory on that account. H. W. B.

Jenkins and Doolittle of Oswego say that they shipped for Wallingford Community, on the 16th inst., 5 barrels of Double Extra Flour, at $15 a bbl.

LETTER FROM CARLTON RICE.

Hamilton, June 16, 1866.

Mr. Hamilton:—In June last I received very pleasingly a friendly invitation from you to visit your domain with my family, and enjoy the hospitality of your folks. At that time I could not accept the invitation. I should be pleased to visit you with a portion of my family, during the strawberry season now approaching. Will you be so kind as to let me hear from you and know when your strawberries are in perfection?

With great respect to you and to your people at the Community, I am your friend, CARLTON RICE.

AMONG THE GROVES.

About a mile due west of us may be seen a piece of woods forming a very charming resort. Try it every one of you who like to be tickled. There too, you may hear the carolling of the stately Hermit Thrush—perhaps two of them together, as it was my luck to do last evening. A fine spot for reflection among those tall overarching trees, if one could only gag the chattering squirrels—a sight of them, to be sure, there is about there— good enough when the *tarush* is not at it. Well—at last we got a sight of one of those notable songsters! He is of the usual thrush dimensions—of rather a slender make—his color lightish ; but having sallied forth this time *minus* a glass (which be assured, shall not happen again) we can say but little on that score. But do go and try that grove, thrush or no thrush. O.

METEOROLOGICAL.

Thermometer, June 18.

6 A. M. 66. 12 M. 71. 6 P. M. 72.
Southerly wind throughout the day.

DAILY JOURNAL
OF ONEIDA COMMUNITY.

A. D. 1866. JUNE 20. NO. 134.

WEDNESDAY.

One hundred and twenty quarts of strawberries were sent to Utica this morning at 33 cts., to supply a festival. They were raised by our neighbors, Adams, Davis, Hubbard and Smith. Our own strawberries are unusually late—two quarts were, however, picked by Mr. Thayer day before yesterday.

Two Roman Catholic Priests were here yesterday.— One of them was the parish priest of Durhamville and Rome and the other of Utica. They came ostensibly to see the Community and to buy strawberries and garden plants. They were courteous, and intelligent. One was an Italian unable to speak much English. They bought the two pamphlets and made some inquiries as to our organization—were surprised that we had no written rules or constitution. Mr. Bolles told them that in some points we thought their Church nearer right than the Protestant, which remark seemed to please them.— They were probably on a visit of inspection and it will not be strange if their visit is reported to the Holy Father at the "Eternal City."

An old trapper was here yesterday—came to see about getting traps for a fall campaign. He had lived in Canada and had traveled through the region where the Community trappers were last fall. He seemed to be quite an enthusiast in the trapping line. We took him through the house and up on to the tower. After surveying all, he said, "Well, you have every thing very nice and I don't see why you cannot take a great deal of comfort; but after all *I had rather be in the woods.*" He intends to come again when the strawberry season is further advanced and bring his wife with him.

THE CIRCULARS were received promptly yesterday morning.

A letter was received a few days ago from a lady in Galveston, expressing a wish to visit the Community, and also if possible to effect a junction with us. She appears to have been an acquaintance of Mr. North's but evidently knows but little about the Community.

Our horticulturists think their experience this season will impress upon them one good lesson—viz., to cultivate the Wilson strawberry in hills, and not let the vines exhaust themselves by making runners. They are confident that larger berries, and a greater quantity, with less labor, can be obtained by cultivating plants in hills than in beds.

A charming little nosegay—chiefly roses—with a pink or two, and just the slightest dash of soft green, was handed to the writer last evening in meeting. It came so unexpectedly, and the odorous breath was so agreeable that for a moment, a spirit of selfish appropriation seemed to say "This is for me." But the feeling was only momentary; the bouquet was a public one, and quickly passed from hand to hand, shedding perfume as it went, till it was lost sight of in some distant corner of the Hall.

A FIGHT WITH A ROBIN.

I had a fight with my namesake to-day—I was just going to take a peep into a Robin's nest in which were two young ones. No such easy thing, Sir. Down came the male bird as large as life, feathers all stretched out to the utmost, screeching and snapping his beak at me furiously. I had never seen such a show of fight. Well, I thought I would just see how far he would dare to go, so I made as though I would *Rob* the nest, but he flew at my hand repeatedly—striking sharply. As often as he paused (he was so close to me) I struck out, expecting to grab him most surely—but no, he was too quick for me. Again and again he returned to the charge, snapping viciously, nay venomously. It was fine to see the figure he cut—wings, tail and crest all spread out. The fellow must have taken me for a panther. But what a fuss! and yet they build almost any where, the careless chaps. I am going to know something more about that character before he gets through, I can assure you. o.

METEOROLOGICAL.

Thermometer, June 19.

6 A. M. 56. 12 M. 66. 6 P. M. 60.
Somewhat cloudy but pleasant day.

DAILY JOURNAL
OF ONEIDA COMMUNITY.

A. D. 1866. JUNE 21. NO. 135.

THURSDAY.
FROZEN FRUIT.

Our comrade, Daniel Abbott, is given to close observation and useful speculations. Among his fruit experiments he placed on the 23d of December, a box of fruits and vegetables where they would be exposed to the lowest temperature—the fruit in bottles, the vegetables in cans—with the purpose of ascertaining two things—whether the bottles would burst, or the fruit and vegetables be injured in consequence of the frost. Yesterday said box was brought forward and it was found that not a bottle had cracked; and those who tested the fruit were agreed in saying that it could not have been damaged in the least. The vegetables, corn, tomatoes and peas, were heated and seasoned and put to the test by several judges, and the general verdict was 'Not guilty.' Some thought the corn had been slightly improved, and on the other hand, one thought the tomatoes had been slightly damaged by the frost, but the general mind was that the vegetables, which had been thus frozen, were as good as any we have had on the table.

The result of this experiment is very satisfactory.—We have generally been very careful about shipping our fruit in cold weather, fearing that we should lose both fruit and bottles; but hereafter we shall not be afraid to send it at any time excepting the very coldest weather, and even then there might not be any danger. Our customers too, cannot ask for any better evidence that our fruit is put up in heavy syrup.

The following extract from Lampman and Robinson of Cleveland, Ohio, indicates that another and unwished for experiment had the same fortunate result:

"With reference to the Fruits sent to us last winter which got miscarried and became frozen, we can only say, when they reached us, we took them out of cases and placed them on our shelves which gave them a moderate temperature; though they were badly frozen they gradually yielded to the temperature and so far as we could judge, they suffered no material change from having been frozen except to be somewhat softened. We sold them all, and never heard a complaint."

Mr. Abbott also states, as the result of his observation, that our preserved fruit improves by age in the same way that wine does. Fruit which has been kept two or three years has a smooth, rich taste wanting in fruit recently sealed.   W.

Mr. and Mrs. Blood, with their smallest child, arrived last night.

C. A. C. informs us that a box of assorted fruit has been sent to Mr. Swift, foreman of Mr. Bottom's silk-factory.

A letter was received from John S. Freeman the other day, saying that he was meeting with considerable opposition from his father and friends, since his decision to join the Community. His father had called on Dr. Hickok, President of the College, and got him to talk with John, advising him to go through with the College course. Under these circumstances John is somewhat disposed to give up his plan of going through with the present term, which ends the latter part of next month. Dr. Hickok was careful apparently to say nothing against the Community, but remarked that disregarding the family relation "was contrary to his principles."—John says, "Now, I have laid the matter before the Lord, wishing to do what is best, and it seems to me to be his will that I should 'seek first the kingdom of God and his righteousness,' the other things (education included) being sure to follow. I have written as though I were talking with you, freely, and I would like to know what you think about my remaining till the end of the term (last of July), under these influences."

A letter was received from Robert J. Hollingsworth of Cincinnati—the man of whom we obtained the new can-making machine—ordering one Corn-Cutter, one Pea-Sheller and 100 doz. cans of strawberries. The whole order amounts to $660. He also wants the privilege of ordering 100 or 200 doz. more strawberries within a week or two at the same rates—$4,95 per doz.

A letter has been received from Bottom, Swift & Co., expressing satisfaction with the Spooling Machine which Messrs. Inslee & Co. made them. It is thought at Willimantic that if all our machinery is got up in as good style as the Spooler, we shall have an excellent lot of machinery. They wish to have our machinists overhaul and repair one of their present Spoolers, which we are disposed to do.

The sister of Mrs. VanVelzer, Mrs. Smith, with her daughter are here to-day—came yesterday afternoon.

Yesterday fifteen quarts of strawberries were picked from our beds! One year ago yesterday, over 1600 qts. were picked.

Last evening Mr. Olds made a report of his and John Norton's late trip. The amount of their sales of silk, fruit, traps &c., with the orders they obtained, was over $19,000.

Mr. Noyes's talks on Brotherly Love, and Spiritual Microscopy, were read last evening, and elicited a hearty response.

METEOROLOGICAL.
Thermometer, June 20.

6 A. M. 55. 12 M. 74. 6 P. M. 90 in the sun.
Very beautiful day.

DAILY JOURNAL
OF ONEIDA COMMUNITY.

A. D. 1866. JUNE 22. NO. 136.

FRIDAY.

The following communication to the meeting from Mrs. Kelly, was read last evening :

I have been under Universalist influences all my life up to the time of my coming here, and never was taught to hate evil or to think there was any devil. And I have been under Spiritualist influence somewhat. I deeply and earnestly desire to separate myself both from Universalism and Spiritualism, and confess my hatred of them as very dangerous things. I desire to separate myself from a smooth, outside, deceitful, goody spirit, that I have always been a slave to, and which is a great hindrance to my entering the kingdom of heaven. I have learned to hate it so much that I feel like swearing to rid myself of it.

I heartily indorse what Mr. Hamilton and others say about Mr. Kelly. I think he has a wicked, diabolical spirit. I desire to separate myself wholly and forever from his spirit. L. E. KELLY.

It was stated in yesterday's Journal that Mr. Hollingsworth had ordered canned strawberries at $4.95 per doz. It should be understood that our price is $6.00 per doz., and that a discount of 10 per cent. is given on such large orders as that of Mr. H. We, however, offered some three weeks since to deduct 50 cts. per doz. on an order of 100 doz., if he would order at once and send on the money, as we had that quantity of strawberries left over. Negotiations are now pending concerning this order.

C. VanVelzer returned yesterday from another peddling trip, and reports that he had good luck.

The curculio campaign is about closing up. The number slaughtered, according to Major-Gen. Marks's report, is 9,175.

Yesterday, Messrs. Burt and Dunn received the Letters Patent for their Corn-Cutting Machine, through Messrs. Munn & Co., of New York.

Martin returned yesterday from his trip among the fruit growers of Western New York. He finds the cherry crop not so abundant as was expected—some varieties are suffering from a species of blight. He thinks, however that we shall be able to secure as many as we want for preserving, if we are wide awake. The peach and plum crops promise well.

An interesting letter was received yesterday from Mr. Towner, from which we make the following extract :

"I am informed that Mr. Warren Chase, as he travels about, represents himself as having been unhandsomely treated by the O. C. and especially by J. H. N.; representing among other things, that from the correspondence published in THE CIRCULAR, material portions of his letters were suppressed, so as to convey a partial and unfair view of his attitude toward the Community. I know nothing of this, but from what I do know of Mr. Chase, I consider him essentially dishonest. When one goes up and down the country denouncing "free love" and glorifying dual marriage, and at the same time practices what he denounces, and leaves the fruits of his practice to the loneliness and destitution which is the lot of children thus begotten and born, one cannot well help regarding him with distrust and suspicion. 'Modern Times,' unless I am greatly misinformed, could unfold a tale. I think the refusal of the O. C. to have further communication with him was eminently proper and prudent."

G. W. Hamilton having business at Hampton, invited a sister to accompany him. They called by invitation at the house of Mr. Shattuck, the gentlemanly overseer, and also one of the proprietors of the Iron Works at that place. A famous wedding was absorbing the attention of the quiet little village, and Mrs. S. in enumerating the bridal presents "rich and rare," mentioned a fine leather, Ladies' Lunch Bag, purchased at Utica. This seems to be introducing the Lunch Bag under favorable circumstances, and it is pleasant to hope that a little of the Community spirit may be left lurking in the bag as a good savor for the young couple. Mrs. S., who is a lady of much taste, expressed her admiration of this present to her friend.

METEOROLOGICAL.

Thermometer, June 21.

6 A. M. 68. 12 M. 86. 7 P. M. 84.

Clear and beautiful, and the most thoroughly summerlike day of the season.

DAILY JOURNAL
OF ONEIDA COMMUNITY.

A. D. 1866. JUNE 23. NO. 137.

SATURDAY.
IMPORTANT TO AGENTS.

N. Y. B., June 21.

DEAR MR. PITT:—Having some difficulty in filling orders for Silk and other goods sent in by our Agents, I concluded to write out a list of the mistakes that are made by some of the Agents in sending orders; and if you think proper to it insert in THE JOURNAL, please do so.   Yours truly, G. D. ALLEN.

The importance of our Agents being accurate in giving orders for goods is shown by a few examples like the following:

Order No. 1, for 1 lb. *Red* 6 spools O. C,. OO, oz. spools.

The supposition of course was that *Red* Machine Twist was the article wanted. Being unable to find it—notified the Agent. His reply was—"I wanted Bottom's Black Machine Twist."

The *Red* being an abreviation for *Bottom's ounce Machine Twist, black*, O. C., *Red* Label. We did'nt understand it !

Order No. 2, for ¼ lb. assorted drab B.

Difficult to decide whether to send Machine Twist ounce or ¼ ounce, or to send drab Sewing Silk. Had to write to Agent.

Order No. 3, for one spool each B. and O *Red.* The same mistake as order No. 1—*Red* meaning O. C., Red Label.

Order No. 4, for ¼ lb. 16 oz. Box Silk.

No letter being given, four orders were kept waiting three days in consequence—had to wait and hear from Agent.

No. 5, 1 box assorted C yds.

Did he want Black, Drab or bright Colors assorted ? We did not know.

Order No. 6, for 25 No. 2 Sin. needles.

Is the order from a shoe manufacturer or a tailor?—If for a tailor he wants the Round Pointed Needles, if for a shoemaker he may want either Round, Flat, Chisel, or Twisted Point. Not knowing which are needed, must write to Agent for more definite orders before the needles can be sent.   Respectfully, G. D. ALLEN.

P. S. Would suggest that the *price* of all goods ordered be written out in full and *not* refer to Printed List for terms, as we occasionally change our prices—hence the liability of quoting from wrong Price List. G. D. A.

WILLOW PLACE ITEMS.

The Silk Factory *in futuro* has been partially cleared out, and the silk-machinery taken up stairs, and placed in position, preparatory to receiving the final touches.

The second swarm of bees was hived day before yesterday at the W. P. apiary.

One of the noticeable features of the boarding-house front yard is a woodchuck, so tame that he will eat from the hand ; a little doubt, however, still being felt as to whether or no he is thoroughly " reconstructed," some slight strictures on his personal freedom yet remain.

C.

It is proposed to move the dairy-house during the coming week. Mr. Aiken is busily engaged preparing to move his establishment to the store building.— The cellar under the company dining-room is being cleaned and fitted up as a place for keeping milk and cream during the summer.

44 meals, were furnished to visitors yesterday ; also nine boquets, four of which were made mostly of rose-buds and were sold for $1 each. Among the visitors yesterday was a bridal party. A gentleman and lady from New York accompanied by their daughter, bought $18.00 worth of bags.

By way of correcting mistakes we would mention, that our announcement some days ago, of E. S. B's. departure for Oswego was incorrect. His destination was Syracuse, only.

Mr. Delos Dunton, of Pekin, New York, was here yesterday accompanied by three ladies and a little girl.— The ladies wore short dresses, and had been attending the Dress Reform Convention at Syracuse. Two of them were M. Ds., who had studied at Dr. Trall's Hygienic School. They stayed till after meeting, and seemed to be well pleased with all they saw here. One or two of the ladies were acquainted with Dr. Mary E. Walker.

The strawberries are gradually ripening. 76 quarts were picked yesterday. Several of the new varieties promise to be acquisitions. French's seedling is early, large, handsome, good-flavored and of fair productiveness. Mr. Thayer regards it as a desirable berry. We tasted the Agriculturist this morning and were very much pleased with it. It is a noble looking berry, of fine flavor. We shall be unable to fully judge of its productiveness the present season, from the fact that our bearing plants, exhausted most of their strength in making runners last season ; but it promises well.

THE SUMMER YELLOW-BIRD.
THE COW-BIRD OUTFLANKED !

In one corner of the lower flower-garden, a small bush is tenanted by one of these little creatures, a model of patience, perseverance and good humor—a tiny little thing, with a very black, sharp looking eye. She has a nest in that bush, but it was speedily discovered, first by the cow-bird and then by the girls. The former dropt her egg there of course, then the girls saw it and made a fuss, and then by some means one or two of the eggs were missing, then again the finger of curiosity found its way there almost hourly, until we had given up all idea of its coming to anything.

But dear me, there they are at this moment, the two young aspirants, thriving as if nothing whatever had happened. You approach her domain, and she meekly slips out, not a word of reproach, and when your back is turned she as meekly slips back again. A bird will often forsake its nest on the very first intrusion. The steady and quiet persistence of this little thing is touching.

We have it, on the authority of the Cyclopædia that this little mite has wit enough to outflank the lubberly cow-bird. She cannot cast out her egg, but she *perforates* it, and builds again on the top of it, sometimes even sacrificing her own eggs to effect this. Then she lays again, and if interfered with a second time, will repeat the process—thus making a three story house of it ! In this case, however, the obnoxious article had been abstracted by human aid.   O.

METEOROLOGICAL.

Thermometer, June 22.

6 A. M. 66   12 M. 77.   6 P. M.   No observation.

DAILY JOURNAL
OF ONEIDA COMMUNITY.

A. D. 1866. JUNE 25. NO. 138.

MONDAY.
BUSINESS MEETING ITEMS.

Homer Barron called attention to the matter of having our goods that are sent to us, so marked that it may be known to which department they belong. He will make out a list of the proper directions for the several departments and put it in shape so that all can understand it.

A bell is wanted for the Willow Place factory. A trial is to be made this week of depending on the Mansion House bell for notifying the help at the Bag Shop as to the hours of beginning and quitting work. If found satisfactory the Bag Shop bell will be removed to Willow Place.

Messrs. Burt, Kinsley and Conant were appointed to examine the bank at the boarding-house, which is beginning to cave in a threatening way, and report what ought to be done.

It was proposed that the former custom of each department fastening their doors and windows when they quit work be revived, instead of leaving it to devolve on the watchman.

Mr. Cragin and others will be interested to know that the wood-pile is at length completed. The greater part of it consists of new wood cut down during the bygone winter; but a considerable proportion is also made up of old wood from the late horse-barn and fences, and stumps taken out of the Calkins lot which was plowed in the spring. Mr. Higgins, who has had the management of this job reports that the pile is about twice as large as our wood-piles generally are.

The latest catastrophe:—a catbird caught in a trap set for a rat.

The work of moving the dairy-house began this morning. It will be carried forward as expeditiously as possible.

265 qts. of strawberries were picked yesterday.

69 meals were furnished to visitors on Saturday, and 60 yesterday. Besides these many persons had strawberries and bread and butter.

Mr. and Mrs. Blood, and boy, left for home last night. They received an invitation to make their home with us, and with that end in view go to settle up their affairs, as soon as practicable.

Twelve strangers were lodged on Saturday night; viz., the three Bloods, and seven of Mr. Underwood's relatives, including Helen and Florence and Delia Stetson—the three latter remained till this morning—Mrs. Freeman and her little daughter, who came on Saturday, and are still here.

A great funeral took place at the Depot yesterday.—

Mr. C. Y. Chapman died a few days since very suddenly. Being a Free Mason of high grade, the fraternity assembled from Albany to Buffalo, we understand to bury him with high honors. Dolphus Skinner preached the funeral oration.

Martin went to Troy last night with three crates of strawberries, to try the market. We are selling at Utica and Rome &c., for 25 cents.

Mr. Hall started on a peddling trip to-day.

In the meeting on Saturday evening the interesting and suggestive article in the last Atlantic Monthly, entitled "The Case of George Dedlow," was read.—Last evening there was interesting conversation in relation to the suggestions of the above article, and also on the subject of worship. The latter subject is one of abiding and growing interest with us.

DEAR JOURNAL:—Yesterday, I saw walking familiarly around the house a young man with a heavy mustache and smooth cheeks. Not knowing him, I wondered who he could be, and asked J., who told me that it was —— a young man of the Community. Of course J. was joking, as the stranger did not resemble —— except in slight degree. In the course of the day several other young men of equally strange appearance have been moving around among us, mingling familiarly with the family at meals and in private rooms. They came to meeting without invitation and stayed with us over night. Who they really are, may not transpire till they have spent some time at Jericho, but they seem like very agreeable young men, though a little bare-faced.

Yours,   BARBARIAN.

METEOROLOGICAL.

Thermometer, June 23.

6 A. M. 60. 12 M. 82. 6 P. M. 84.
A clear and beautiful day, closing with a splendid sunset.

June. 24.

6 A. M. 64. 12 M. 84. 7 P. M. 82.
Clear, still, hot.

DAILY JOURNAL
OF ONEIDA COMMUNITY.

A. D. 1866. JUNE 26. NO. 139.

TUESDAY.

We have at length entered on the season of strawberry bees. The first one took place on Sunday evening.— Last evening the bee was interfered with by a shower, so that a call was made for one this morning at 5 o'clock.

We reported yesterday that 265 quarts of berries were picked on Sunday. When we came in from the bee we expected to have a larger number to report, and were somewhat surprised that it was otherwise. The mystery however, was explained yesterday afternoon, when a chest of 60 boxes of berries was found in the Fruit House, which had been overlooked. As it was thought they would hardly keep in good condition long enough to send to market, they were hulled and furnished the family with a rich treat at supper. We heard some remarks to the effect that the oversight was Providential. They were certainly partaken of with thankfulness.

A letter was received yesterday from Mr. Hollingsworth countermanding his order for a Pea-Shelling Machine.

Mr. Parker, with his machinery, is here to-day moving the White-house. The additions have been taken down, and the south wing will also be taken to pieces, leaving only the main part to be moved.

Mrs. Barron has been relieved in the dairy department by Miss Mathews.

H. M. W. was criticised in the evening meeting, a report will be forwarded in manuscript.

Monday brought its usual relief from the crowd of visitors during the several previous days.

Fruit preserving was begun to-day, Strawberries being the first fruit preserved.

A letter was received from Mr. Towner and his wife a few days ago, making an application for membership. They profess to be in full fellowship with our faith and principles. Mr. Towner is about to leave the Army, and his property is now in hand, in a controllable state, and he dislikes to make any investment of it outside of the Community. When he was here we were very favorably impressed with his character and spirit, and his letters have been excellent since he returned home.

THE CIRCULARS came to hand at the Community about 10 o'clock this forenoon.

There is a growing demand for the Trapper's Guide, and orders or inquiries for it are frequent.

A letter from E. Otis was received the other day, saying that she had been called home on account of the sickness of her mother. Her relatives say that her mother is deranged, but Mrs. Bushnell who visited Mrs. O. lately, writes that she saw no evidence of insanity. On the other hand, Mrs. O., though prostrated in body, was in her right mind and rejoicing in the truth as never before. She said she saw the truth about the social theory and fully received it.

Letters have been received from the men of whom Martin engaged cherries, saying that they are ripening, and requesting persons to come and attend to the picking. Mr. Van Velzer and Mr. H. R. Perry will go on at once.

A WAGON LOAD.

On the hind seat of a wagon (I've a story to tell),
   Two Hs were sitting by the side of an L;
On the next seat to that were two Bs and a J;
   While forward of them sat two Ns and a K;
To the Community trap-shop all on the way,
   And all on one side sat L, J and K
And the rhymer's initials are W. J.

METEOROLOGICAL.
Thermometer, June 26.

6 A. M. 78. Clear.
12 M. 90. Somewhat cloudy.
6 P. M. 88. Cloudy.

A hot day ending with heavy showers passing to the north and south of us. Just as the sun was setting it broke through the clouds and formed a vast rainbow in the southeast.

DAILY JOURNAL
OF ONEIDA COMMUNITY.

A. D. 1866. JUNE 27. NO. 140.

WEDNESDAY.
TO AGENTS *ET AL*:

The price of the leather used in our fancy satchels, and leather Pelissiers and Lunch Bags has advanced to 24 cts. per foot. This advance on the part of the leather dealers necessitates an advance in the price of our goods; but as we are not prepared to get out a price-list a reduction of discounts is recommended. For the present, let 5 per cent. be the highest discount on leather work given to largest wholesale dealers and jobbers in New York, Boston and other cities, and all other dealers be sold to at list. On muslin and carpet work previous discounts may be given, viz., ten per cent. to retail dealers. **w.**

---

476 quarts of strawberries were picked yesterday.

H. R. Perry left yesterday afternoon for the western part of the state, to attend to the picking and forwarding of cherries.

A few bushels of cherries were received yestyrday by the preserving department, and were promptly put up.

The White-house was removed as far as the horse-barn yesterday. The course taken with it was down the road through the lawn. The frame of the south wing was found in such good condition that it has been decided to move it without taking it to pieces, as we mentioned yesterday. The plan now is to move it to some suitable place and make a cottage of it.

1019 qts. of strawberries were shipped this morning—over 600 of which were raised by our neighbors Hubbard and Davis. The demand for this fruit is greater than we have ever known it, and good prices are realized, though much lower than those received for the Wallingford fruit. Our neighbors are jubilant over their good success the present season; and we are inclined to rejoice with them. We are pleased to have the producer receive a full reward for his labors. The fruit gathered yesterday by Mr. Davis from one acre will net him nearly $150. All of the strawberry growers in this vicinity are harvesting more fruit, and receiving much better prices for it, than they expected a few weeks since.

A yard is being enclosed on the edge of the pond at Willow Place for the accommodation of bathers. It is to be furnished with steps descending into the water, and a spring plank.

Another machinist has been hired, there being quite a rush of business in the shop—Silk-machinery, Pea-Shellers, Corn-Cutters and Trap-shop tools are the leading items.

Mr. Aiken has moved his goods and groceries into the north wing of the store building, the large salesroom being yet in an unfinished state. The tailor's shop is also in the north wing second story.

James Vaill was criticised last evening. There was considerable commendation of him for his general respectful disposition and spirit. He is well liked. On the other hand it was thought that he was pleasure-seeking in regard to his work, and when in any occupation that he does not fancy, is given to teasing to be relieved—asking to be placed in some department that he thinks he should like. He is small-hearted in this, and should study to wait on the Lord for the arrangement of his circumstances, and in whatever place he is called to work, learn to be content. His relations to the other boys are somewhat unpleasant, and it was thought that the boys were as much to blame as he for that state of things. Considerable criticism was given Ernest for being lazy and shiftless, and Erastus Van has been considerably affected by fellowship with him. On the other hand, Orrin Wright was much commended by Mr. Hamilton and others for his manly, public spirit and devotion to the Community.

Mr. John H. Tobitt of New York is here—came yesterday.

NOTE.

DEAR DAUGHTER WALLINGFORD:—As the weather here is very hot and sultry I should feel greatly obliged if you would send me a loan of—of—of the Quinnipiac.
Your affectionate Mamma, ONEIDA.

METEOROLOGICAL.

Thermometer, June 26.

6 A. M. 73. 12 M. 89. 6 P. M. Very warm, but no observation made. The day was clear till afternoon, when showers rose in the west and passed north and south of us. After meeting there was a fine shower, accompanied by a great display of electricity.

DAILY JOURNAL
OF ONEIDA COMMUNITY.

A. D. 1866. JUNE 28. NO. 141.

THURSDAY.

TO AGENTS—A CORRECTION

In yesterday's JOURNAL by the omission of a clause in the article "To Agents," the concluding sentence was made to read differently from what was intended. The sentence should read:

"On muslin and carpet work previous discounts may be given; viz., 10 per cent. to largest wholesale dealers and jobbers, and from 2½ to 5 per cent. to retail dealers."

The mistake occurred from a failure to read the article by copy before going to press.

The Community have bought Mr. Davis's strawberries—about two acres, which are expected to yield 200 bushels—for $775. Mr. Davis picks the berries in the bargain. He thinks there will be a 1000 quarts to-day.

We had considerable company yesterday. Among others was a company of about thirty-two from Canastota, Wampsville and a number of other places. They had a general understanding and appointment to meet here. Some of them came about thirty miles. Being shut into the house during most of the afternoon by the rain, and also being at the highest key of hilarity and good humor, they overflowed the house generally. They seemed, however, to manifest no intentional disrespect, and when checked in some of their tendencies to rudeness took it in good part and helped to keep each other within appropriate bounds. There were a number of fine singers and musicians among them, and they seemed to enjoy gathering in the Hall and playing and singing in various ways—solos duetts, full chorus &c. They called for $1 dinners, and left about six o'clock.

Another five o'clock bee this morning. Result 237 quarts. Picking will probably go on all day if the weather permits. About a dozen hired pickers are employed at 2 cts. a quart.

320 quarts were picked yesterday.

A letter was received a few days ago from Mrs. Munson, showing more earnestness than any of her previous ones. She is still at Ridgeway in this State, and wishes to know, if she should go east this season, whether she can stop here for a visit of a few days.

The work of moving buildings goes on. The rain interfered with the operations somewhat yesterday. To-day the White-house is being placed on its foundations, and the carpenters are busy getting the wing ready for moving. Meanwhile the stone wall of the old cellar is being carted away.

52 dinners were furnished to visitors yesterday.

To-day is cool, cloudy and pleasant—a fine day for berry-harvesting. The berries picked this morning were very fine, and the beds yielded quite abundantly.

Three crates and two baskets of cherries were received this morning in good condition. They cost 7 cts. a lb.—40 lbs. to the bushel.

The night-blooming cereus at the green-house, opened one of its magnificent white flowers last night, and was the center of attraction for some time after meeting.

Martin came home about 8½ o'clock last evening, and started again for Troy at about 11½ P. M. He had succeeded in making more favorable arrangements with the Express Company for the transportation of berries, and all the berries he could get to Troy to-day he expected to sell for 25 cts. a quart.

Mr. VanVelzer finds it difficult to leave the shop to go west to attend to cherry picking, and consequently some other man will probably be selected for that purpose.

METEOROLOGICAL.
Thermometer, June 27.

6 A. M. 69. Cloudy. 12 M. 80. Cloudy. 6 P. M. 67. A heavy shower came on just after noon, and most of the afternoon was rainy.

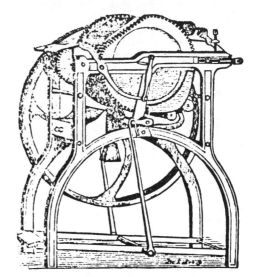

DUNN'S ROTARY PRESS,

On which the ONEIDA JOURNAL is printed.

DAILY JOURNAL
OF ONEIDA COMMUNITY.

A. D. 1866. JUNE 29. NO. 142.

FRIDAY.

1144 quarts of berries were picked yesterday from our own beds. 810 qts. were received from Davis. 990 qts. were sent to Martin at Troy. We have already received 1170 qts. from Davis since purchasing his berries, and the prospect is that we shall make a good thing of the investment.

We are all rejoiced to hear by Edward Inslee that we may expect Mr. Noyes next Monday night, in company with little Ormond.

Mr. Woolworth and Mr. VanVelzer went west yesterday afternoon, to attend to the forwarding of cherries. Mr. V., we understand, intends to be absent only a few days.

Mr. Nash and Mrs. Sears are engaged taking up the tulip bulbs from the beds on the lawn.

Mr. Delatre has received a letter from Reginald, dated "Dinapore Station, East India Railway, Bengal Division, May 1, 1866." Speaking of the Community he says:— "You say you hope you do not tresspass on our patience by mentioning little Community matters. Why, that is just what we like to hear about! I wish you would tell us every thing about the Community that you think of. I should like more particulars now and then: names of persons or places or any thing that would remind me directly of the days we spent there, would be very interesting, also the doings of individuals that I knew &c., &c. How do you manage the children's department now?— What has become of our old "ogre," Mrs. B.? We have to thank her for our leaving the Community. Why don't you go hunting too? Have you lost your fondness for the sport? Do any of the people there ever ask about us or seem to remember us? You never mention any one sending remembrances as of old; that is because we are of the "world;" or perhaps long years of abscence have caused them to forget our existence. There are many I should like to name but I have not room now. Perhaps you will give my kind remembrance and regards to them all."

50 dinners were furnished to visitors yesterday. It has been decided to charge from 75 cts. to $1 for meals according to quality. A good dinner will be furnished for 75 cts., while for a first rate meal $1 will be charged.

This morning was so cool that fires were called for in the furnaces.

Mr. Tobitt left yesterday. He expressed great satisfaction with his visit, and appears much interested in the Community. He proposes to come again some time this season and bring his wife with him.

535 bottles of fruit were preserved yesterday, 189 of which were strawberries, and the remainder cherries.

Last evening, Mr. Guiteau was criticised by request. A report will probably be sent in manuscript, so we say no more about it here.

Men and teams are busy to-day clearing away the stone and rubbish from the site of the White-house, and we hope by to-morrow night to have the grounds there in an orderly condition.

Nine crates—two bushels each—of cherries were received this forenoon.

Mr. Leete is here, busily engaged painting the store.

Our friends will be interested to hear that Sir Christopher *Wren* and family occupy "Squash Hall" as a residence for the season. Unable, however, to fill the whole space with their usual effects, and being somewhat crotchety on this point, they have succeeded with no little *architectural* skill, in reducing its dimensions by the introduction of a mass of incongruous material, and will no longer feel lost in its immensity! "Squash Hall" may be visited at any hour of the day, by the aid of a short ladder, the foundations having been laid high. It is situated in "Pear Orchard."   o.

METEOROLOGICAL.
Thermometer, June 28.

6 A. M. 61. 12 M. 63. 6 P. M. 63.

SOUNDS OF JUNE.

All day the Veery's song is heard
  From out the hemlock grove,
All day the Hermit's far refrain
  Deep thrills his woodland love.

The Robin's home-like song at morn,
  Awakes the Sparrow's lays,
The Catbird's merry notes call forth
  The Thrasher's hymn of praise.

The Red-winged Blackbird's liquid tones
  Beside the river's brink,
Are echoed from the meadow-weed
  In mirth of Boboliak.

The Wood-Thrush in the forest glen,
  Most sweet of all the throng,
Awaits the cadence of its mate,
  Then lifts its mellow song.

Thus, underneath the myriad leaves,
  In sunshine and in cloud,
The anthem of the summer hours
  The Birds pour forth aloud.

DAILY JOURNAL
OF ONEIDA COMMUNITY.

A. D. 1866. JUNE 30. NO. 143.

SATURDAY.

LETTER FROM W. A. H. TO H. G. A.

Oneida, June 29, 1866.

Bro. H.:—Small fruits are so high, and likely to continue so high, that we think the prices already proposed for our new price-list of Preserved Fruits not sufficiently high. We shall certainly have to add 50 cts. (perhaps a dollar) per doz. on strawberries. We calculated in our estimates that strawberries would not cost us more than one shilling per quart for canning and bottling. They have not been less than 20 cts. per quart here, and are likely to be worth 25 cts. or more all next week. Thus you will at once see that we shall be unable to put them up as cheaply as was expected. I write this thinking you might have opportunities for receiving orders before the new price-list is printed. Even if we should make the prices for strawberries in cans $7,00 per doz., and in bottles $8,50, it does not appear to us that they would be high when compared with the prices at which fresh fruits are now selling. At Wallingford they are selling strawberries at from 50 to 75 cts. per quart; and at the prices for our preserved fruits last named we should not average quite as much for our strawberries after they are canned and bottled, to say nothing about the cans, bottles, sugar, and other expenses incidental to preserving. On account of the high price of strawberries, we shall put up only a limited quantity. Fruit orders are now coming in occasionally, and the prospect is that we shall have little difficulty in disposing of what will be preserved. We are now receiving very fine cherries from Messrs. Perry, Woolworth and Vanvelzer. Truly, w.

Among the visitors yesterday afternoon were the temperance lecturer Mr. Hewlet and his daughter. Both being excellent singers they entertained us with several songs. The young lady is a daughter by a former wife and is a lineal descendant of Pocahontas the Indian maiden of historic celebrity. She has a very superior and well cultivated voice, and is simple and unaffected in her manner. We thought we saw in her finely moulded and beautiful features a suggestive resemblance to her beautiful ancestor. A fine bouquet was presented to her on leaving.

414 bottles and 157 cans of cherries and 45 bottles of strawberries were put up yesterday.

435 qts. of berries were picked from our own beds yesterday, and 330 received from Davis.

128 meals were served to visitors yesterday, besides a very large number of ice cream and fruit luncheons.—

The day was very pleasant for riding, and people seemed disposed to improve it by visiting the Community.

Mrs. Freeman left for home this morning, having been here about a week. She was well liked and seems to be an earnest Christ-seeker.

Mr. Harrison, the machinist recently hired at Willow Place, proves to be the brother of David Harrison, friend and follower of J. H. N. during the early days of Perfectionism. Mr. Harrison was living in Meriden at the time when his brother and J. H. N. were there, and remembers the latter well; remarking that "they were together a great deal."

Mr. Miller arrived last night about 10 o'clock, having left New York on Monday, via Hudson River route. He saw Martin yesterday in Troy and found him active in the strawberry business—selling at 25 cts. a quart.

A letter was received to-day from Isabel Welchman, of Boston, a lady who visited Wallingford some time since, saying that she should leave Boston on the 2d of July on a trip to the west, and would like to make a short visit at the Community.

To-day is cool and pleasant, and the visitors are numerous.

METEOROLOGICAL.

Thermometer, June 29.

6 A. M. 59. 12 M. 69. 6 P. M. 67.

A cool, clear day.

END OF VOLUME FIRST.

DAILY JOURNAL
OF ONEIDA COMMUNITY.

VOL. 2.   JULY 2, 1866.   NO. 1.

MONDAY.

The proprietors of St. James Hotel, New York, send us the following testimonial to the merits of our fruit:

New York, June 28, 1866.

To THE ONEIDA COMMUNITY, GENT.s:—You will please allow us to express unto you our most entire satisfaction with all the canned fruits and vegetables purchased of you last season; a very few of which we still have on hand, but they are in as *good order* and *fresh* as when put up. While fruits purchased of other parties we were compelled to return to them, on account of poor quality, yours proved to be all we could ask of them as to quality &c.   Yours truly, LACHMYER & HOTCHKISS.

The patterns for two Hop stoves, different sizes, have just been finished, the casting of which will afford quite a large job for the foundry.

Mr. Goakes, the night watchman at Willow Place, employs the time when he is not occupied in going his rounds, in making strawberry boxes, for which he receives 30 cts per hundred.   He makes from 200 to 500 a night.

There are at present twelve hired hands employed in Trap making.   A lot of 40,000 No. 1 are under way in the Finishing Dep.   In the Forge Shop 11,000 No. 4 springs are about to be tempered.

We are now sending berries to Boston, to Hilland and Smith.   They telegraphed on Saturday that the berries were received in good order, and sold for 35 cts.

1177 qts of strawberries were picked yesterday.

On Saturday 141 meals were furnished to visitors; yesterday 93 meals. $40,50 worth of bags were also sold yesterday.

H. R. P. writing about several of the persons with whom he deals for cherries, says:

DEAR BRO. HINDS:—Mr. M. delivers his cherries and quietly starts for home without saying a word about money no more than if he were a member of the O. C., but the man who is acting Lieutenant in Mrs. L.'s Empire of Cherrydom and who is known here as *Joe* Parsoll is quite another individual.   On delivering his fruit last evening he suggested that it would be well enough to settle for each lot as they were delivered.   His cherries amounted to between fifteeen and sixteen dollars, and so, as he is to deliver another lot this evening, I surprised him by handing him twenty dollars and telling him to give the O. C. credit for that amount which would be less trouble than to figure the matter to a cent.   He seemed agreeably surprised on seeing the money forthcoming, and I hope to keep him good natured and in working order so that he will let us have all of his cherries.   In order to do this, it will be best to lubricate each delivery with greenbacks or their equivalent, and you

had therefore better send me fifty or seventy-five dollars. He does not seem to be fully posted in relation to all affairs in the Community, as his first question was, as to whether we continued to have trouble with our leader, Mr. Mills.   On being assured in the negative and informed that Mr. Mills never was the "*representative man*" of the O. C., a little light seemed to dawn upon his mind. He evidently does not take THE CIRCULAR and is no no great historian—at least never read the "History of the Mills War."

As there is a prospect that we shall have a great crowd of visitors on the 4th, all our forces have been thoroughly organized for the occasion.   General business will be suspended and a combined effort made to meet all the requirements of the occasion.

The work of filling up the White-house cellar and grading the ground is being completed.   The improvement of the general effect of our front grounds will be much appreciated.

1545 quarts of strawberries were shipped this morning, of which 675 qts. went to Martin at Troy, 180 to Saratoga, and the balance were distributed at various places between Oneida and Albany.

METEOROLOGICAL.

Thermometer, June 30.

6 A. M. 57.   6 P. M. 79.

July 1.

6 A. M. 61.   12 M. 71.   6 P. M. 74.
Clear, beautiful days.

WEST HILL AND ITS INHABITANTS.

Who knows how much we owe to that "West Hill," each time we look at it from our windows?   Just imagine the whole of that generous slope, lowered to a plain! Ah! it would indeed be a comparative blank! And where would be the Wood Thrush?   He too, would flee away to mourn its loss, for he loves to look off from the topmost hights.   There, perhaps, he feels nearest to the source of his inspiration.   May it not be owing to that, that he gives you the feeling that you may expect almost anything from him in his improvisations.   His pauses seem to promise something new at every time.— He appears to be selecting.   There is an air of confidence about him, as though his resources were endless.   We could not resist this impression.   It is a peculiar charm attending the efforts of this artist.   The Hermit Thrush soothes and elevates, but this bird of the uplands fascinates you—creates a home-feeling too, because he is ever greeting some fellow-companion, singing, as he usually does, in concert, with some other bird of his kind, always listening, it would seem with the utmost deference for the response of the other, before uttering his rejoinder. The effect is bewitching.

You will find him on "West Hill," friends.   Now, don't spare your muscles.   o

DAILY JOURNAL
OF ONEIDA COMMUNITY.

VOL. 2. JULY 3, 1866. NO. 2.

TUESDAY.

Mr. Noyes and company arrived last night in good spirits.

Miss Susan B. Anthony was here on Sunday, and spent a large portion of the day.

Yesterday the editor of the Syracuse *Courier* was here. He remarked that he intended to give the Community a notice in his paper.

Mr. Newhouse has discovered that the upper part of Oneida creek is quite rich in speckled trout, and has had good luck several times in that region. We merely whisper this to H. T. and G. W. N.—not to the public generally.

32 meals were furnished to visitors yesterday.

James Prindle arrived yesterday noon, and leaves to-day we believe.

Mrs. Lynde's daughter and child came last evening.

Mr. Bolles received a letter from his sister expressing a wish to visit Mr. B. and the Community, if she could be allowed the privilege. She sent for the Community pamphlets and Bible Communism. She professes to be interested in Communism. She says:

"Mother thinks that she never saw children so well trained as they are at the Community, and says it is a splendid place. I think from all accounts that it must be a desirable place to live. I do not understand all your doctrines but am open to conviction. If there is a class of people devoid of selfishness, it must be Communists. I believe selfishness is the besetting sin, the root of all evil."

Our purchase of Mr. Davis's strawberries may be regarded as in some sense an act of mercy. The Davises (father and mother and son) found themselves with their two acres of strawberries somewhat like the man who drew the prize of an elephant. Having only two or three regular customers, and being quite uneducated in the business of selling fruit, and unknown to dealers, they would have had their hands full if they had gone on a few days longer. As it was they were greatly hurried in body and mind. Mrs. Davis told me last evening that one night neither she nor her husband had a moment of sleep. At one o'clock Mr. Davis took his son Frederick and some strawberries to the Depot, and he had to meet the next train at half past four with more fruit; and the balance of the night was occupied in leveling and packing. The crates were new and not made in the best manner—the boxes did not go in right in all instances—one crate refused to receive its quota on account of being too small; whereupon, after much vexatious trying, Mr. Davis threw it in his wrath against the wall. Mr. Davis prides himself on regular habits—says he nearly always goes to bed at about half past nine, and "sleeps like a rock until morning." But all such commendable habits had to be entirely abandoned.—For several days, he declares, he did not sleep at all; but this statement may be questioned, since his wife declares that on one occasion, after returning from the depot, he undertook to milk his cows, and fell asleep twice before finishing! All this vexatious experience they now avoid and receive a reward for their culture which should satisfy any fruit grower. The Community find no difficulty in disposing of all their own strawberries, all of Mr. Hubbards, all of Mr. Davis's; and what we can buy of two or three other neighbors. **w.**

"St. Patrick's is a great deal better man than ever the Fourth of July was," said one of our work-women a while since.

The south wing of the late White House now stands on the site of the old store of former years. The old cellar, which had been so long in disuse will thus come into play again when the little cottage is put into habitable shape.

1101 qts. of Strawberries were shipped this morning; 720 qts. to Martin at Troy, and the balance to ten customers.

A letter was received from a trapper yesterday, giving his method of catching otter, which is somewhat different from the method described in the Trapper's Guide.

We should have mentioned yesterday, that two of Mrs. Tobey's half sisters called here on Saturday.

Extract from a letter from D. Macoy:

Cambridge Borough, Vt., June 25, 1866.

DEAR COMMUNITY:—Having just partly recovered from a bed of sickness, I feel my heart overflowed with gratitude to God for his preserving care; and regarding you as his faithful servants and representatives here on earth—the only sect who live to serve Him in the exact way prescribed by his only begotten Son, our Lord and Master—and in endeavoring to partly compensate you for the good teachings and sound principles which the good old CIRCULAR communicates to me and to my fellow men, I would beg leave to ask you to regard a barrel of maple sugar consisting of one tub and several cakes which I have this day forwarded to your address by Express, as a token of my sympathy in your labors and creed. I would gladly have visited you this spring were it not that almost constant illness has prevented me from traveling; although I hope to be able to bear the pains and fatigues of journeying in a month or six weeks hence, and I shall rejoice in the privilege offered to me to see in person that class of people and their great and fruitful works which deserve the praise and acknowledgement of all mankind.

In order to be enabled to live near your Community, I would gladly buy a small place consisting of a dwelling-house and a garden spot, where I could raise sufficient vegetables to entertain me; you would therefore show me a great favor by letting me know if I could possibly get such a place within a half mile or a mile from your Community, and what price it would command.

Mr. Macoy is at present in the mercantile business, and thinks if he continues in it that he would like to communicate with the Purchasing Agency, and have them procure his goods for him. He also wishes to know the price current of maple sugar. Can the P. A. inform him.

METEOROLOGICAL.

Thermometer, July 3.

6 A. M. 62. 13 M. 75. 6 P. M. 77.

Clear, until evening, when it became cloudy, threatening rain.

DAILY JOURNAL
OF ONEIDA COMMUNITY.

VOL. 2.   JULY 5, 1866.   NO. 3.

THURSDAY.

The 4th passed off quite pleasantly. The day was somewhat showery, which probably lessened the crowd. but, on the other hand, kept them within doors more.— Several hundreds were here during the day. No formal programme of entertainment was made out. We endeavored to furnish people with all they wished to eat and drink in the form of good dinners, fruit, ice-cream, lemonade &c. There was music in the Hall at various times during the day, by the brass band, violinists, pianist and singers. People seemed to enjoy themselves well, and we heard of nothing especially unpleasant or disturbing. $292,68 were taken at the office. Of this amount $52,97 were for horse keeping, $6 for bouquets, $2,30 for pamphlets. The remainder was for meals. At the store the sales amounted to $76,35; at Tontine $30,83; at Fruit Room $72,84. Besides attending to visitors considerable business was done at fruit preserving. 452 cans of strawberries were put up and 315 cans of cherries. 342 qts. of strawberries were picked by hired help. Over $600 worth of fruit was shipped during the day.

A letter was received yesterday from Justin Carter, son of Henry Carter of Waterbury, Vermont, asking for employment with a view to becoming acquainted with the Community and ultimate membership. The letter was accompanied by another from his father, stating that he had advised his son to write to us; and also saying that if his son should join the Community he should furnish him with his share of money to invest with us.

A letter was also received yesterday from Thomas Rutter of Winooski Falls, Vt., expressing considerable sympathy with us, and a desire to find a location for his family near us. He also wishes to be instructed in the doctrine of male continence.

Emily Otis came yesterday morning. She was on her way home, with Theodore, and wished to come on here before going to her father's. On mentioning the matter to Theodore he favored her coming. Her mother is much better, and there seems to be no pressing call for her to return home immediately.

Mrs. Welchman left yesterday. She made many inquires while here, and seemed disposed to make the most of her time in this respect. She is connected with the Kindergarten and Training School, corner of Chaales and Chestnut Streets, Boston, having charge of the Kindergarten department.

One of our Indian visitors yesterday said he came " to get some Independence."

Mr. Kelly returned home on Tuesday night, having had very good success in business.

Mr. Noyes talked on Tuesday evening on the subject of Woman's Position. Last evening the principles that should govern in receiving new members were discussed. Full reports of the talks will be sent in MS.

The large dwarf apple-tree north of the Tontine, which has had various accidents and removings in the past— being at one time nearly killed by the mice, and at another split open by the snow—last night blew over. On examining it this morning it was found broken off just below the surface of the ground, the center of the trunk being in a decayed state.

Cherries come thick and fast. The fruit preservers began operations this morning with 50 bushels, and more are expected during the day. A bee for picking them over commenced at 5 o'clock.

The farmers have begun haying, and the meadow below the pear orchard was mowed yesterday.

The store salesroom is nearly finished except the painting. The goods were placed on the shelves for yesterday's operations, but were moved out again this morning, to make room for the painters. Mr. Leete is here, busily engaged in his department.

Visitors are numerous again to-day, the pleasant and partially cloudy weather after the rain making it attractive riding though somewhat warm.

METEOROLOGICAL.

Thermometer, July 3.

6 A. M. 68.   12 M. 85.   6 P. M. 79.
Clear, pleasant, hot.

July 4.

6 A. M. 68.   12 M. 75.   6 P. M. 76.
Cloudy, and showery.

DAILY JOURNAL
OF ONEIDA COMMUNITY.

VOL. 2. JULY 6, 1866. NO. 4.

FRIDAY.

835 cans and 570 bottles of cherries were put up yesterday. 50 bushels were on hand in the morning, and 40 bushels more came during the day. 75 bushels of these were sorted over ready for bottling before night, entirely by our own folks. A large day's work.

Mr. Noyes talked last evening on the effects of habit in narrowing and falsifying affection, and the progressive character of true affection. He also gave some account of the social history of Mr. Finney and his family, as learned from E. Otis. The facts were not very creditable to the influence of Oberlin legality.

1178 qts. of strawberries were picked yesterday, by hired help.

Mr. Noyes and Ida Kelly leave for Wallingford this afternoon.

Mrs. N. A. Morse of Lafayette, Onondaga Co., an old subscriber to THE CIRCULAR and an acquaintance of Lady Hamilton, arrived yesterday.

E. O. brought with her the copy of the Berean which Prof. Finney has read and annotated. His notes, which are neither copious nor profound, are attached to the articles. "Infidelty among Reformers," "Spiritual Nature of Man," "Origin of Evil," "Paul's views of law," "Christian Faith," "The Sabbath," "Baptism," and "Fiery Darts Quenched." They show considerable bitterness and are characterized principally by a tone of denunciation.

Mrs. Lynde's daughter, Mrs. Gaines, left last night. She seemed much pleased with her mother's Community home and appeared to be a candid and agreeable woman. She said she should visit us again.

The editor and office hands of the Tontine Luminary, would express a due amount of gratitude to the compositors of the Mount Tom Chronicle for their recent contribution, and hope to be able sometime to make a suitable return.

It is thought here that the journals from New York are rather infrequent. We have had none since last Thursday and only one for the five previous days. We should like to hear daily even if there is but little to report.

Mr. Ellis cut his foot somewhat severely the other day while bathing in the creek with the boys.

The perils of crinoline were illustrated on the 4th., in our green-house, by a gentleman's getting his foot entangled in a lady's hoops and falling at full length on the floor. We did not learn that he was seriously injured, though we understand that considerable effort was required to extricate him from his embarrassing bondage.

As Abby was stepping up to her type case in the printing office this morning, she suddenly started and gave a slight scream on seeing her stool occupied by a huge black cat. Mr. Hatch came opportunely to her rescue and carried off the monster to the children's house to be thoroughly trained and subdued.

One of our hired strawberry-pickers remarked on coming in from the field in the evening that she had eaten nothing since about 3 o'clock in the morning. The remark fled on the wings of rumor, exciting a good deal of sympathetic comment: "What a pity!" "She ought to have had some dinner offered to her," &c., &c. It turns out, however, that the sympathy was entirely wasted, as it often is; she had her dinner with her, but wishing to earn as much as possible, did not eat it. She and her little boy seven years old earned $3,75. It is hoped he took time to eat his dinner.

Be it known for the relief of those who regret the shooting of robins, that the progeny of a single pair (incurring no loss) would amount, in the space of ten years, to the respectable figure of 60,466,176 pairs! that is, allowing twelve birds to be the annual produce of each pair, for they rear *three* broods every year, always laying *four* eggs each time. And, as it would not be too much to say that these birds may live at least 10 years (since even smaller ones have been known to live longer) the original pair would in that time have started *nine more* lines of progeny, embracing in all, 12,093,234 pairs which, added to the sum given above, would make an aggregate of 72,559,410 pairs!! We may imagine the loss they sustain.   o.

METEOROLOGICAL.
Thermometer, July 5.

6 A. M. 68. 12 M. 81. 6 P. M. 78.

About 6 P. M. a fine shower accompanied by a strong wind.

DAILY JOURNAL
OF ONEIDA COMMUNITY.

VOL. 2.   JULY 7, 1866.   NO. 5.

SATURDAY.

Nearly 1400 cans and bottles of cherries and over 300 of strawberries were put up yesterday.

Yesterday was the most sultry day we have had this season. The mercury at 2 P. M. stood at 89 deg. in the shade.

The largest picking of strawberries this year was on Tuesday, when 1880 qts. were gathered.

The peas are beginning to ripen and during the coming week will require the attention of the preservers.

Charlotte Maria on going into the water yesterday where Mr. Ellis injured himself, cut her foot on the same sharp substance, not very seriously, however.— The creek is to be examined, and the dangerous thing removed.

Rose has improved lately and is now able to walk considerable. She walked down to the store and back the other day.

73 meals were furnished to visitors yesterday and 66 the day before.

Several Methodist ministers from the villages south of us were here yesterday. One of them has read our paper for several years, including the time of the Mills war.

The buying of Davis's strawberries proves to be a good speculation. We have already realized several hundred dollars more than was paid.

Hiland and Smith of Boston send us word that some Triomph de Gands which were sent them the other day brought 40 cts. a qt. Wilsons brought foom 30 to 35 cts.

WILLOW PLACE ITEMS.

Of the first lot of silk-machinery begun, the Winder, Cleaner, Doubler and Spinner are completed. The Stretcher, which is not needed till the silk is well started, is being put together. The pulleys and countershafting for the machinery will be finished by the first of next week. As yet nothing has been done to the room: this however, will be but a short job when once begun.

The copper pipe used to cool the water for hardening trap-springs is undergoing thorough repairs: when first put down the joints were soldered, but many of them have proved defective, causing the loss of much time, brine and patience, so they are now to be brazed.

The Hop-stove speculation seems likely to prove a success: Mr. Clark has already obtained orders for four, and has partially engaged two more.   c.

After diligent observation and inquiry we come to the conclusion that there is not much to report to-day. Every body is busy in the several departments, though the pressure of business in the fruit-rooms is less than it was yesterday. The sky is clear but not cloudless. The temperature is on its way up toward the nineties. The hills look beautiful in the hot clear atmosphere. The woods seem to invite one to their shadows and cool retreats. We hear the music of the mowing machines in the Elm meadow and know that the farmers are haying. We see lines of carriages on the road and know that visitors are numerous. Below our window the steam engine keeps up steady motion and works tirelessly for the cooks, the bathers, and the fruit-preservers. The Depot team comes a little after ten o'clock with the mail, and the semi-diurnal load of cherries. The fruit men tell us they have put up more than their quota of cherries, and the season will soon close. The quality of the cherries received this year is the best of any we have ever had, and they have arrived here in the best condition. So with cherries in our mouth we bid you good bye till next week.

METEOROLOGICAL.
Thermometer, July 6.

6 A. M. 68.   12 M. 88.   6 P. M.   No observation, but over 80.

DAILY JOURNAL
OF ONEIDA COMMUNITY.

VOL. 2.   JULY 9, 1866.   NO. 6.

MONDAY.

Mr. Perry arrived home from cherrydom on Saturday evening bringing with him some 25 bushels. In all he has sent home about 140 bushels. He was located at Cayuga. Mr. P. remarked that although he had had a good time in his business while absent, yet he was glad to get home. He realized that there was quite a difference in coming to a home where one or two hundred were glad to see him instead of one person, as formerly. He said he accepted it as the first instalment of the hundred-fold promise of Christ.

Henry G. Allen came on Saturday night, on a business visit.

Martin also come home on Saturday night, having finished his berry-selling campaign at Troy.

A woman from Ohio, named Goodwin, came on Saturday and is still here. She claims to have been sent here by the Lord, but we don't exactly see it in that light. She seems to be a cross between Second Adventism and New York Perfectionism and is abundantly charged with fanaticism. She came without any previous correspondence. Some criticism has been administered to her.

A young man named Flint came here on Friday evening and staid till Saturday evening. He was from Indiana, was born in this town, had but recently heard of the O. C., and came to learn what he could about us.

Last September when the bees were destroyed, two hives were reserved and taken to Willow Place. Mr. Newhouse who has had the charge of them reports that from the two hives he has had four large swarms.— The first, we believe came out the latter part of May.— On Saturday a fifth swarm came out from this oldest o the four swarms. Things look promising now for a successful apiary at Willow Place.

Note from Portia to the family:

God has shown me that I have been very unbelieving in regard to myself—that I have not surrendered my whole life to Christ in faith, expecting victory, but have reserved it where I was most weak—most needed a Savior. I see that Christ's strength made perfect in weakness can manifest itself in me, and I now surrender myself unreservedly to Him, believing His life is my life. It has seemed to me very difficult for my social character to be organized into and subordinate to Christ, and I have rather expected defeat even when confessing strength. I now confess my separation from all my past experience, forgetting the things that are behind and claiming Christ's promises fulfilled to me. I confess Mr. Noyes's victorious spirit in me and my love for him and all who lead me to God. I believe Christ is in me an element of strength, and confess my hatred of the unbelief that has kept me from apprehending it. I resign myself forever to Him and His faithfulness.

943 cans of cherries and 211 bottles of strawberries were put up on Saturday. 165 cans and 98 bottles of cherries, and 124 of raspberries were put up yesterday.

The first raspberry picking took place yesterday. 14t qts. of black caps were gathered from about two thirds of the ground.

The dangerous thing in the Creek which had wounded two of our bathers, was found on thorough search to be a broken bottle. The wounded are doing well.

Last evening there was some conversation about the children, and particularly Ormond. He has manifested a very mischievous spirit since coming back, and it was thought there was too much attention given him and that his mischievousness was rather smiled at than criticised as it should be. Mr. Hamilton and others also criticised the article about Ormond which appeared in the paper some time ago. It was thought that it did not present the true philosophy about his mischievous spirit, and rather palliated it than otherwise. The truth is that a mischievous spirit is a devilish spirit and ought to be dealt with accordingly. It was also thought that our children were getting a too prominent idea of the distinction between their natural mothers and the family generally, and that there was a spirit at work among them that fostered this idea.

S. W. N. is this morning engaged cutting a direct path from the main entry of the New House to the office door of the Store, intersecting the oval green in front of the portico. A kind of contest has been going on in the minds of a good many between the taste that preferred to keep the oval intact and the necessity that demanded the path; but it may be assumed as a safe principle that beauty and utility are never really antagonistic. At some future time the paths and grass plots may be entirely re-arranged in conformity with new requirements and new ideas.

BUSINESS MEETING ITEMS.

Messrs. Kinsley, Burt, Kellogg and Barron were appointed to appraise our land lying north of Scanandoah Creek.

It was thought best to remove the bag-shop bell to the Mansion House, and to remove the Mansion House bell to Willow Place. A. L. Burt is to see that the job is attended to.

Messrs. Kinsley, Conant and Clark were appointed to see what is best to be done in the way of repairs at our coal-yard at the canal.

Our folks are requested to discontinue the practice of digging fish worms under the fruit-trees.

Mr. Campbell is authorized to take down the old sign at the Foundry, as we no longer make plows, and put up another sign, such as he may think suitable.

Mr. Clark was authorized to furnish pipe for the hop-stoves, that may be ordered.

A. L. B. is to attend to the disposal of the coal in the yard at the wood shop.

Messrs. Hamilton, Abbott, G. W. Hamilton and Aiken were appointed to attend to providing the store with running water.

METEOROLOGICAL.

Thermometer, July 8.

6 A. M. 72. 12 M. 80. 6 P. M. 74.
A short, but heavy shower in the afternoon.

DAILY JOURNAL
OF ONEIDA COMMUNITY.

VOL. 2.   JULY 10, 1866.   NO. 7.

TUESDAY.

Mrs. Goodwin left yesterday afternoon. She had recently parted from her husband and had spent most of her money in coming here. We gave her $6 to assist her to some other place.

Mrs. Robinson and a daughter of Mr. Jones arrived yesday.

The raspberry crop promises to be very fine and abundant this year.

The strawberry harvest will close in a few days.— Some portions of the beds will now hardly pay for further picking. We shall report results as soon as we can.

The success of our neighbors the present season in fruit-growing is likely to stimulate them to further enterprise in that direction. On the other hand our own experience in buying and disposing of our neighbor's fruit, has been very encouraging.

Among the visitors yesterday was a Welch company from Utica. One of them, a Mr. Jones, is the editor of the Welch paper called the "Drych," published at Utica. This is the only Welch paper published in the United States and has a circulation of some 60,000. The company remained till after 9 o'clock and attended meeting. They seemed to be pleasant people. The Editor promised to send us a copy of his paper—and said he should be pleased to exchange with us—which will be a curiosity to those who are unacquainted with Welch orthography. Here are a few specimens:

Gwir yn erbyn y Byd
" Truth against the world,"

Duw a phob daioni,
" God and all that is good,"

Gair Duw yn uchaf,
" The word of God above all."

Enw Duw yn uchaf,
" The name of God above all."

O gweddw ddawn! ei gwaedd a ddwg
Mawr gwynion Bro Morganwg,

" O widowed Genius! thy wails convey
The deep lamentations of the region of
Glamorgan."

The weather is pleasantly cool and breezy to-day, and the sky bright and almost cloudless. P. S. We record this fact for S. S. II's. benefit.

We got from Mr. Davis,s strawberry field yesterday, 325 boxes of berries, being more than we expected from him. After emptying a few of the boxes the reason of the large quantity became apparent. A great many of the boxes appeared to be shallower than usual, and, on examination, it was found that the pickers employed by Mr. D.—mostly boys from the Depot, we believe—despairing of making good wages picking berries at 2 cts. a quart had put bottoms belonging to other boxes into the ones they filled. Ninety extra bottoms were found, there being from one to five extra in each box. One box was nearly filled with leaves, there being barely berries enough to hide them.

What added to the "fun" of the thing was, that young Davis happened to be over here with a party of friends just as the trick was discovered. He joined heartily in the laugh against himself, saying he thought in the morning when he got them to pick for two cents a quart, that he had made a good bargain, but concluded now that *they* had got *him* instead. He had observed a large quantity of hoops with no bottoms lying around and had thought that some of the boxes were lighter than usual but had no idea that he was the victim of such a hoax. It was evidently a concerted plan as Davis says that every time he took the tally of boxes picked he observed them to laugh among themselves. One of Davis's friends observed that this showed the natural dishonesty of human beings. Some one standing near rather objected to this wholesale statement, but thought it might show the natural dishonesty of certain small boys and girls from Oneida Depot. This was in all probability the last picking which accounts for their temerity.   E.

The carpenters are now engaged in putting up the Gardener's Tool House west of the Tontine.

Two hired women are almost constantly employed in the vineyards now, assisting at the pinching and tying.

THE CIRCULARS were received about half past ten this morning.

Only about two bushels of cherries were received yesterday.

The fruit committee in connection with H. G. A. are deliberating on the preserved fruit price list.

METEOROLOGICAL.

Thermometer, July 9.

6 A. M. 69.   12 M. 78.   6 P. M. 77.

DAILY JOURNAL
OF ONEIDA COMMUNITY.

VOL. 2. JULY 11, 1866. NO. 8.

WEDNESDAY.

We understand we were in error in stating that the Welch paper at Utica has 60,000 subscribers. It has about that number of readers.

Emily Otis left for her father's on the 11,20 train last night. Her visit here has been refreshing and strengthning to her faith and has doubtless prepared her to be a help to her mother.

Mr. Woolworth arrived home yesterday, from his cherry campaign at Fairport. He had very good luck, and his services have been much appreciated. He had the market pretty much all to himself, the crop was abundant and fine, and to dispose of the avalanche of cherries that poured in upon him some days required great activity. He however found two good assistants in a son and brother of Mr. Howard, one of whom had been engaged in the forwarding business. He boarded with Mr. Howard, and found him in quite a good state, expressing much sympathy with Mr. Noyes and interest in Paul's gospel. Mr. Woolworth was much commended for the spirit he has shown in the business.

It is proper to state that Mrs. Goodwin on leaving here proposed to return to her friends in Ohio. She professed to be anxious to know the truth. We told her if this was so, the first thing for her to do was to find a way to bring about a reconciliation with her family.— The money that was furnished her she accepted as a loan, saying she should take measures to repay it as soon as she arrived at Cleveland.

H. G. Allen. leaves to-day for New York.

Mr. Peter B. Mead, late editor of the Horticulturist, sends us the following testimonial to the quality of our preserved fruit.

New York, July 9, 1866.

GENTLEMEN :—During the past year or so I have used your "preserved fruits," and I owe it to you to say how much I have been pleased with them. Nothing, in my opinion, can be better, except the fresh fruit itself, the natural flavor being preserved to a nicely. It is amazing to me that people will eat "sweetmeats" when they can get such fresh fruits as are put up by the Oneida Community.

Yours very truly, PETER B. MEAD.

Mr. Hatch is fitting up a place at the creek where the children—the girls more particulary—can bathe, and learn to swim.

The pea-preserving has fairly begun. Mr. Burt has two shellers in good working order.

Anna Main, a singer of considerable culture and fine voice was here yesterday afternoon and favored us with several songs. Some thought that in some respects she excelled Miss Pocahontas Hewlett.

Morning bees for picking raspberries are the order.— Most of the strawberries have been picked by hired help, the demand on the family for work in the fruit rooms being such that it was thought not expedient not to over-tax ourselves with strawberry bees. But since the strawberries and cherries have been disposed of, and there is less call for help in the preserving department, the family cheerfully yield to the call for raspberry bees.

The following letter was received from Mr. Towner to-day. His application for membership we believe has not yet been answered:

Detroit, Mich., July 7, 1866.

DEAR FRIENDS :—I wish to say to the Community that my faith grows stronger and clearer every day. I have no hope of salvation but in the name and through the power of Jesus Christ. And I wish further to say that my faith in Christ does not depend in any sense upon my expectation of realizing through it, a high ideal of life, as in Community, for example. No; I would not be found seeking the Kingdom of God *for* the things that shall be added to me. Come what may, I will cling to Christ. Wherever I may be, whatever my relations may be, however much I may at present fail of my aspirations for want of means or propitious circumstances, I will trust in him, the loving and Holy One, as the way, the truth and the life. To this end, I ask your prayers and sympathy. Faithfully yours, J. W. TOWNER.

METEOROLOGICAL.

Thermometer, July 10.

6 A. M. 69. 12 M. 81. 6 P. M. 75.
Clear with westerly wind throughout the day.

DAILY JOURNAL
OF ONEIDA COMMUNITY.

VOL. 2. JULY 12, 1866. NO. 9.

THURSDAY.

Mrs. Burt and Ann Eliza, accompained by Charles Cragin, leave for Wallingford by the five o'clock train to-morrow morning. Charles goes on silk-business—buying stock, visiting the Paterson factories &c., and will bring H. E. A. and E. H. home with him to start manufactoring.

Neighbor H. is in some trouble with the cheese-factory folks, suspicions having arisen that the milk furnished by him was not of the proper richness of quality. On applying the usual tests this was found to be the fact.— He however stoutly denies all charges of its being tampered with in any way. The factory authorities to ascertain the truth of the matter appointed a committee to milk his cows and test the quality of the milk. Martin is on the committee, and they began their labors last evening. It is quite an important case, as the party involved is one of the leading members of the association, having charge of the selling of the cheese. The committee we understand hope for favorable results for Mr. H., though circumstances have compelled the factory authorities to make a thorough examination of the case. It seems like the working of practical criticism in the affairs of the association, and is watched with much interest by the adjacent public.

Rose walked as far as the Bag-factory the other day. She had the promise sometime last season, from A. S. Bailey, that when she could walk as far as the factory she should have a bag. So she went down and claimed the gift. Mrs. H. C. Noyes brought her back in her arms.

A. B. will please understand that W. A. H. has assumed the responsibility of reporting the results of our strawberry crop.

A grand bee was summoned to the raspberry field at an early hour this morning by the brass band. 78 persons were counted in the field, and 266 qts. were picked. The family voted last evening to pick the raspberries themselves, without the assistance of hired help. The bees are a good ordinance, stimulative of unity of heart and resurrection influx.

The haying is going forward successfully, and some of the farmers say that it will be accomplished with comparative ease. The yield is quite good, notwithstanding the unfavorableness of the early part of the season for the growth of grass.

A company from Hampton were here yesterday.— Among them were Mr. and Mrs. Shattuck and their little girl. Mr. S. is the foreman of the Maleable Iron works at that place. The little girl it was observed by many seemed like a second edition of T. C. M., in her early days.

Our stream of visitors continues. On Monday, Tuesday, and Wednesday, respectivley, 9, 32, and 37 meals were furnished.

An illustration of the excessive modesty that is sometimes manifested by certain individuals, occurred in the green-house the other day. A lady visitor on observing a certain flower remarked to Mrs. S., "That is what you call *rooster's* comb, is it not?" "That," replied Mrs. S., "is a *cock's*-comb." The lady thereupon looked as though she had been convicted of something rather silly. She must have been related to that other lady who once called here and who on going to the barn with Mrs. B., asked if a certain quadruped was a *male* cow.

The Home-Talk in the last CIRCULAR on the Perennium is regarded with great interest here, as a wonderfully lucid statement of the Community faith, and the gospel which God has revealed through Mr. Noyes.

The fashion is growing into favor among the mothers and women here of loving and specially caring for other children than their own. The plan works well, and is enlarging and communizing to the hearts of those who enter into it. The children seem to like it, and some of them behave much better when with their adopted mothers than with their natural mothers. Temple remarked the other day that "Miss Fidelia was his mother some, and that Mrs. Ackley was his mother."

We learn that a man of whose existence we were unaware till many years after the O. C. was founded, announced recently in a neighboring city that he was the original discoverer of the social principles upon which we are based, and that he imparted them to us. Verily, the vagaries of egotism are remarkable.

A floral curiosity in the shape of a double dahlia has been on exhibition in the library for several days—two perfect flowers exactly opposite each other on a double stalk. One of the flowers is a little further advanced than the other, otherwise they would present the appearance of a floral globe.

METEOROLOGICAL.

Thermometer, July 11.

6 A. M. 72. 12 M. 81. 6 P. M., no observation. The day was clear.

DAILY JOURNAL
OF ONEIDA COMMUNITY.

VOL. 2. JULY 13, 1866. NO. 10.

FRIDAY.

YESTERDAY'S ITEMS.

423 qts. of raspberries were picked. General bees are now held morning and evening.

Mr. Mills's legal adviser, J. Cooper Esq., was here with a party of friends and took dinner.

The health of the family here appears to be buoyant and improving.

36 dinners were furnished.

It was recommended in the meeting that the family avoid as much as possible attention to or discussion of the cheese-factory troubles, and regret was expressed that Martin should have had anything to do with the matter. We should not have mentioned the subject yesterday but for the fact that he had become in some way connected with the Committee. We understand nothing but circumstantial evidence has been elicited.

Another night-blooming cereus opened its petals last night at the green-house.

TO-DAY.

Mrs. Morse left on the early morning train. Her visit here has been quite pleasant to all parties we believe. She joined freely in the family work and made herself quite useful.

The pea business progresses; the new machines shell a bushel in from five to eight minutes, according to the state and quality of the peas. Some of the best peas obtained from our neighbors, are raised by the Indians.

A different method of preserving peas is in progress this year. They are first placed in a large tin cullender and set in a boiler, where they are quite thoroughly boiled. They are then put into the cans and sealed and the cans are boiled one hour and then drawn. The result is that the peas when the process is completed have a much finer flavor than by the old method. This method was recommended by Mr. Edgett, and we understand it is also followed by the New York preservers. Mrs. Vanvelzer's experiments with it have thus far proved successful.

The family were called up at sunrise to the raspberry bee by drum and fife. Uncle Heman, Mr. Underwood, and S. W. Nash, performers.

A platform is building at the north end of the Tontine to facilitate loading and unloading wagons at the door.

We have concluded to authorize the Agency to purchase 182 tons of Lehigh coal. Mr. Geo. Coville, of Vienna, wishes to do the boating of the coal for us, intimating that in this way he would like to contribute fifty dollars to the printing-office fund. We are disposed to accommodate him.

A letter was received by this morning's mail from Richard Realf, dated at French's Hotel, New York, asking information about the Community, conditions of membership &c. If we recollect aright he was one of the original "John Brown men," and escaped from Harper's Ferry when Brown's raid failed. He writes to the "President of the Perfectionist Association" and says that he recently heard of the existence of our society for the first time, at Vicksburg, from a former comrade in arms. He states in regard to himself:

"That I am 34 years of age, pretty well educated, that in the various grades of private, non-commissioned officer, and officer, I served four years in the volunteer army of the Union; that I have in my possession the official proofs of this, beside the proofs of the recommendation on the part of seven general officers, of being appointed to a First Lieutenancy in the regular army of the United States (from which my refusing to endorse the policy of President Johnson barred me); that I am an occasional contributor to the Atlantic Monthly, Harper's Monthly and Weekly; that since my muster-out of service, three months ago, I have resided near Vicksburg, Miss.; that I came north, partly, on account of pecuniary losses, sustained in consequence of the proscription to which loyal men are subjected, and partly for the purpose, if it were possible, of associating myself with your own or some other Communistic society,

"Far off from the clamor of liars belied in the hubbub of lies
Where each man walks with his head in a cloud of poisonous flies."

"I arrived in this city this morning; and I hasten to address you this brief note trusting to elicit from your courtesy a reply to the request I have expressed, as well as a statement whether and under what circumstances, I should be eligible for membership.

"I am quite poor, and unaccustomed to manual labor. I am willing, however, to overcome my ignorance; and I should not at all object to pay my board until I had learned to make myself useful.

"If you give me the information sought for, and accord me permission to hold a personal interview, I will bring with me letters and papers corroborative of the statements I have made."

METEOROLOGICAL.

Thermometer, July 12.

6 A. M. 75. 12 M. 82. 6 P. M. 77. Clear throughout the the day.

DAILY JOURNAL
OF ONEIDA COMMUNITY.

VOL. 2. JULY 14, 1866. NO. 11.

SATURDAY.

YESTERDAY'S ITEMS.

377 qts. raspberries were picked.

A letter was received from Susan Dunn of Bakersfield, Vermont, aunt of Leonard and Fidelia, giving an account of the death of her mother, Mrs. Margaret Dunn, and also expressing a wish to join the Community.—She says :

"Can I have a home at the Community? My heart has been there for years, and I feel that my term of trial here is about ended. My trust is in God, I know he will never forsake me—he who has sustained me in the adverse scenes that I have passed through for a few years. I feel an attraction for the home of homes, that is the Community."

The farmers in their haying during the past three days have averaged twenty-four loads a day.

A Mrs. Tupper of Lakeport, came in the afternoon, on a visit to the Community. Her husband had previously visited us and was so much interested in the Community as to wish his wife to come and see it for herself. Mr. Nye, brother of Mrs. Tupper, came with her.

Mrs. Robinson and Miss Jones returned. Mrs. R. was criticised by a committee. She came we understand for this purpose principally.

TO-DAY.

80 persons were out to the 5 o'clock bee. They were roused from their slumbers by the brass band, it having been suggested in meeting that possibly it would be a good plan for the band to do their practicing at that early hour instead of during the evening bees.

The robins had become so numerous and destructive among the raspberries that quite severe slaughter has been going on among them during the past week. Tho' somewhat unpleasant to the feelings of some it has been found on the whole that the criticism of the birds was necessary.

A hot term has again begun. Yesterday was of very fervid temperature and to-day is not less so. On the whole we enjoy it; and feel sympathetic toward the "monks," who are favored with still warmer conditions. If they will send us a sea-bath occasionally, we will endeavor to forward them a mountain-breeze in return.

The fruit preservers have considerable trouble with their bottles. The breakage, owing to the poor quality of the glass, is quite serious. They have abandoned corking before boiling in consequence of this difficulty.

A letter was received from Mrs. Goodwin, from Cleveland, inclosing six dollars in payment of the amount loaned her.

We do not find any thing more in the line of news, to-day, so we will conclude by inserting the following dissertation concerning

SLEEP.

Our friend X complains of sleeplessness.

We reccommend him to adopt our theory that sleep is a far less necessary institution than is popularly believed, and seek a higher method of recuperation.

He rather laughs at the idea, and thinks he would prefer having a good night's rest to our theory.

We think, on the other hand, that if he sticks to his present position he will soon be in the rear of human progress. Experience is teaching us that six, eight, or ten hours sleep out of each twenty-four is by no means a necessity, and that there are other means of bodily and mental recuperation far more effective and life-giving.—We believe others will find this true if they study the matter in a scientific way.

A man may be dependant on sleep, and feel exhausted and weakened from loss of it, or he may rise above this dependence, into fellowship with the unsleeping energy, and life of God. He can turn his wakeful hours into seasons of communion with the inner world, and talk with God and the angels. He may open himself, to influx from this ascending direction, and be refreshed by its reception, in body, mind and spirit, far more than by the deepest and most restful slumber. "There is no night there," and the abounding vital energy, love, and intellectual illumination of that bright world may be ours, if we find the true way of yielding our souls to their fellowship.

David who was a profound student of the higher human relations, says "My reins instruct me in the night season." The dependant on undisturbed and regular sleep may learn what that instruction means, if he will study his bodily relations to the omnipotent source of uncreated Life and Love.

We believe it is the destiny of the resurrection to lift us out of the sleep-slavery, and in so doing it will have done much toward lifting us out of the death-slavery that binds with the chains of hades. The whole institution of sleep needs to be brought into the light, to be judged and purified, and placed on the basis of Resurrection-Repose. As it now reigns it belongs to the "fashion of the world which will pass away."

METEOROLOGICAL.

Thermometer, July 13.

6 A. M. 76.   12 M. 84.   6 P. M. 82.

DAILY JOURNAL
OF ONEIDA COMMUNITY.

VOL. 2. JULY 16, 1866. NO. 12.

MONDAY.
YESTERDAY'S ITEMS.
BUSINESS MEETING.

Mr. Burt was appointed to make arrangements to have some one take Mr. Kellogg's place in driving the Willow Place team.

A Mr. Thomas wishes to get maleable iron of us for 400 traps. There is no objection if he will take what iron he wants all at once.

Mr. Hamilton, Mr. Burt and J. D. Conant were appointed to look into the matter of modifying the heat in the ironing room and have what can be done to effect that object accomplished.

Mr. Hamilton was appointed to make arrangements for buying the right to lay down all the patent walk we wish to on our domain.

The question of renting a portion of the Burt house to Mrs. Goaks, mother of Mr. Goaks, was referred to the rent committee.

The bell question was reconsidered. The Mansion House bell is to remain where it is, and the bag-factory bell is to be removed to Willow Place.

The following communication was presented to the meeting last evening:

DEAR FRIENDS:—Since coming to the Community I have been feeling under a good deal of condemnation on account of my old life, but God finally gave gave me courage to reveal it to Mr. Hamilton, and since doing so I have felt a very great relief from the devil's condemnation.

As I look back on the snares into which I have been led by the devil I feel thankful that God has at length enabled me to escape. My prayer is that I may not be led into temptation and that God will give me strength to resist evil in all its forms.

I confess my separation from my old life and my hatred of it, and my desire to be clothed upon with the life of Christ. I wish to disown all sympathy with the spirit of the Mr. Royce who bored Mr. Noyes with his talk a few days since. H. R. PERRY.

Mrs. Perry, who has been in some trial and judgment lately, and manifested some tendencies to fanaticism, was very sincerely criticised in the meeting. A report will be sent in MS.

This was the hottest day of the season, thus far, the mercury in the thermometer at one time in the afternoon standing at 95. deg.

On Saturday 149 qts. of black caps were picked and 46 qts. of other varieties. Yesterday 271 qts. of black caps were picked. Notwithstanding we have had but little rain for the past two weeks the raspberries have been finely developed. They begin now to show the need of rain, and the hot weather will probably bring us a shower ere many days.

An immense bee was held before breakfast to gather strawberry leaves. It was more numerously attended than any bee this season, and more leaves were secured than were gathered last season. Mr. Aiken, general-in-chief, proposes to hold one more bee.

A corn-cutter was ordered on Friday, by Mr. E. F. Edgett of Newark in this state. If it works well he says he shall want one or two more.

The Tontine printing-office was moved from the garret to the second story room formerly occupied by silk; the silk and hat business having been moved to the second story of the south wing of the store. This is a very pleasant and desirable change. The low ceiling of the room in the garret made it a very warm place to work in summer, besides the light was rather insufficent. We now have a light and airy room, with high ceiling and three large front windows. We are also one flight of stairs lower down, which is by no means an unimportant item. We rather think our office compares favorably now with the far famed one at Mount Tom. At least we hope to merit more fully hereafter in the quality of our JOURNAL the commendation of our Circularian brothers and sisters.

Oneida, July. 16, 1866.

BEAUTIFUL SURROUNDINGS.

Some persons are satisfied with a front-yard containing a few trees and rose bushes; others are not content unless they have also a small and well cultivated garden; others still desire to have two or three acres of ornamental grounds and gardens; while another class aspires to have a large farm well cultivated, and ornamented with thrifty orchards. Communities are somewhat noted for having rich and well cultivated lands, and some of them aspire to ornamented grounds on a large scale. The O. C. might perhaps be reckoned of this number. But if this object is attained, should it satisfy us? No. That would indicate, it seems to me, a sort of Community selfishness, and would not be in harmony with the real spirit of our institution. Let our interest in beautiful surroundings by no means be confined to our own domain; but, on the contrary, wherever we go in this wide world let us do all we can to stimulate the love of improvement and beauty in our neighbors. I confess that I feel a growing purpose about this Oneida valley. I am not content that this Community should have pleasant grounds, fine gardens and fruitful orchards. I want to see this whole valley of several thousand acres all under the highest cultivation—one great garden, devoted to the greatest variety of fruits, vegetables and cereals. A beginning is already made in this direction. Many neighbors stimulated by the example of the O. C., are raising strawberries and other fruits extensively.— Let us encourage this movement and help it onward.— Let this valley in a few years roll out the strawberries and other fruits by the thousand bushels per day. Even this season, over one hundred bushels of strawberries have been harvested in a day within an area of a couple of miles. Ten years ago we should have thought it impossible to dispose of that quantity, and the idea of raising so many at least Quixotic. Let us not be content until we can ride or walk for miles in any direction from our home, and be ever surrounded with thrift, improvement and beauty. w.

METEOROLOGICAL.

Thermometer, July 14.
6 A. M. Somewhat cloudy. 12 M. 81. 6 P. M. 81.
July 15.
6 A. M. 80. 12 M. 92. 6 P. M. 85.
The day was perfectly clear and ended with an unclouded sunset.

DAILY JOURNAL
OF ONEIDA COMMUNITY.

VOL. 2. JULY 17, 1866. NO. 13.

TUESDAY.

YESTERDAY'S ITEMS.

During the mowing season our men have volunteered to do the milking at night.

Our thirty or forty acres of wheat looks well, and promises a good yield. We believe it has not suffered from the depredations of the weevil to any serious extent and as yet shows no signs of rust.

A curiosity is seen at the ice-house now-a-days—wheat growing in ice. Some of the wheat grains from the straw covering of the ice have germinated and pushed their slender roots into the solid blocks of ice. We suppose the evolution of vegetable life in the seed generates heat, and as the rootlets push forth they melt a space in the ice in front of them.

The farmers last week cut seventy acres of grass for ourselves and sixty acres for our neighbors. They charge $1.12½ per acre for mowing for outsiders.

Chauncey Hamilton and wife, and a sister of Lady Hamilton with her husband, came here yesterday. The two former went home last night, the others staid over.

A call was made in meeting for two volunteers to start the pea-shelling machines this morning at half past four. One hundred bushels were on hand to begin with. Three machines are now in working order and are kept in vigorous service.

In the meeting there was some conversation on the subject of sleep, suggested by the article on the subject in a recent JOURNAL. Mr. Hamilton and others indorsed the doctrine which had been advanced, and regarded it as important that we should have true ideas about sleep, and not get into bondage to a mere animal form of it.

FRUITS, VEGETABLES AND JELLIES,
PUT UP BY
THE ONEIDA COMMUNITY.
Price-List, 1866.

VEGETABLES IN CANS.
Per dozen qts.

Tomatoes,	$2,75.
Sweet Corn,	3,50.
Green Peas,	4,25.
String Beans,	4,00.

FRUITS IN CANS AND BOTTLES,
Per dozen qts.

	Cans.	Glass.
Pears (Louise Bonne de Jersey),	$6,00,	7,50.
Peaches, assorted,		
Cherries : Mazzard,	6,00,	8,00.
" May Duke	6,50,	8,00.
" Black Eagle,	6,50,	8,00.

" Black Tartarian,	6,50,	8,00.
" Yellow Spanish,	7,00,	8,50.
Plums : Damson,	6,50,	8,00.
" Lombard,	6,50,	8,00.
" Yellow Gage,	6,50,	8,00.
Quinces,	6,00,	7,50.
Pineapples,		
Raspberries : Doolittle's Black,	7,00,	8,50.
" Brinckle's Orange,	7,50,	9,00.
" Fastolf (Red),	7,50,	9,00.
" Antwerp (Red),	7,50,	9,00.
Strawberries	7,50,	9,00.
Huckleberries	6,00,	7,50.
Blackberries	6,00,	7,50.

PICKLED FRUITS IN GLASS JARS.
Per dozen qts.

Pears	$6,00,	7,50.
Crab Apples	6,00,	7,50.
Peaches		

JELLIES IN CUPS AND TUMBLERS.
Per Dozen.

	6 oz. tumblers.	12 oz. cups.
Strawberry	$ 3,00,	5,50.
Blackberry,	3,00,	5,00.
Currant,	3,50,	6,50.
Quince,	3,00,	5,50.
Crab-apple,	3,00,	5,50.
Plum,	3,00,	5,50.
Pineapple,	3,00,	6,50.
Grape,	3,00,	5,50.
Peach,	3,25,	6,00.
Black Raspberry,	3,00,	5,50.
Red "	3,50,	6,50.
Orange "	3,50,	6,50.
Lemon,	3,25,	6,00.

☞ The Vegetables put up by the O. C. are all raised in the immediate vicinity of the Preserving Factory, and great care is taken to have them harvested at the best moment, and canned while they are fresh.

The Fruits are preserved in heavy syrup made of best white sugar and will be found right for table use without further preparation. The aim has been to put them up in the best manner.

Our packing cases hold two dozen cans and one dozen bottles; and parties are requested to order full cases. Jellies are packed in cases of one and two dozen, as desired.

Shipping directions will be strictly followed, and goods will be delivered at the nearest Railroad station in good order without extra charge; but the Community will not be held responsible for any breakage which may take place after the goods are shipped, or for any loss which may occur in consequence of misdirection, (when they have been marked according to order,) or for any negligence on the part of freight agents or others in handling the goods after they have left our charge.

Orders will be received at the Community, or at their office, 335 Broadway, (Room 9), New York

METEOROLOGICAL.

Thermometer, July 16.
6 A. M. 80. 12 M. 94. 6 P. M. 88. There was a slight shower just after dinner, scarcely laying the dust however.

DAILY JOURNAL
OF ONEIDA COMMUNITY.

VOL. 2. JULY 18, 1866. NO. 14.

WEDNESDAY.

YESTERDAY'S ITEMS.

About 141 bushels of peas were shelled and canned. A bushel makes about eight cans and a half.

The season thus far has been rather unfavorable for the pea crop, the hot, dry weather ripening and drying them very rapidly.

The new method of preserving peas does not work so well as it first promised, and has been abandoned.

In meeting Meron Kneeland was criticised. Much dissatisfaction was expressed with her present unimproving and disobedient state, and it was thought that if there was not a thorough change in her spirit she would have to be invited to leave the Community. She is inefficient in business, is gross in her alimentiveness, and spends a great deal of time in reading novels and newspaper stories. A committee was appointed to talk with her and find out what her real character and purpose are and determine what course shall be taken with her.

A letter was received from Mr. Blood saying that he and his family would start for Oneida on the 15th of next month, unless advised to the contrary by the Community. It appears that not receiving any reply to their letter in April, they did not expect, when they came here on a visit, to receive an invitation to join so soon, and had made arrangements to remain where they were till another season. It was thought at the time that they received the invitation somewhat coolly, and Mr. Hamilton wrote to them to that effect and suggesting some criticism. We judge from a letter received from them a day or two ago, written before they received Mr. Hamilton's letter, that they had felt some compunction on this point. They profess however, to be hearty in the move and determined to go forward. They think that they shall settle up square with the world so far as money matters are concerned. The letter was considered very satisfactory. There seems to be a modest, good spirit in both Mr. and Mrs. Blood that leads us to hope they will work into the family well.

The saddler's shop is this morning being removed to its new quarters in the store. The room appropriated to this department is in the upper story of the south wing. One branch after another thus finding its way into the new building makes it a kind of multum in parvo—an epitome of Community labor and industry.

On Monday a young man by the name of Gunn called and inquired for work. He has worked for two or three years at Dr. Jackson's cure, but having lost his situation there on account of temporary illness, he was advised by one Dr. Parker of that institution to come here. Said he was very anxious to get a good permanent home, where he could live on true vegetarian principles. He was furnished with a few numbers of THE CIRCULAR, two pamphlets and a modicum of advice.

Mr. Bradley had quite an entertaining hunt for a calf a few days ago. The old cow had hid her baby in the grass, and pretended not to know anything about it while Mr. B. and others were looking for it. She would occasionally give a note of warning, as much as to say, "Lie low!" Finally the old cow was put in the barn and kept some time—then again turned into the lot. She went towards the calf, but noticing the hunters she gave her word of warning, and passed on to another part of the lot. The calf was finally found lying very flat upon the ground.

The right for laying down French's patent walk has been purchased of a man at Oneida who owns the right for this County. The price paid was $100. This walk proves to be very satisfactory, and is rapidly coming into use at Syracuse and other places. Chauncey Hamilton said when here the other day that the first that was put down in Syracuse five years ago, is now in as good condition, apparently as when newly put down.

TO-DAY.

The pea-preservers began operations this morning with one hundred bushels.

METEOROLOGICAL.

Thermometer, July 17.

6 A. M. 82.   12 M. 92.   7 P. M. 72.
In the evening we had several fine showers.

DAILY JOURNAL
OF ONEIDA COMMUNITY.

VOL. 2. JULY 19, 1866. NO. 15.

THURSDAY.

YESTERDAY'S ITEMS.

In the afternoon we had a number of splendid showers, which have given the ground quite a soaking. The fruit-men rejoice, for the berries were beginning to dry up, and we hear no complaints from the hay-makers.

The wheat is now ready to harvest, and will be attended to as soon as the weather will permit.

A very large bee was called out this morning by the band to pick raspberries. The family seemed to have lost none of their enthusiasm after a respite of a few days. There has been a real inspiration attending these bees, and every one has enjoyed them and felt better for attending them.

H. E. A., E. H. and Mabel arrived in the afternoon. Charles arrived in the evening having been detained at Albany and Troy. They came up on the Troy boat, and on arriving at Albany, in having their baggage removed from the boat the Express bag from the Agency was overlooked and went on to Troy. Charles went after it, leaving the girls to come on alone.

The enrolling officer of the State militia has called for the names of our men between the ages of 18 and 45.—The law requires an enrollment once every two years.

A young man named Griswold, formerly of Westmoreland, and an acquaintance of the Seymours, was here. He is now connected with the *Cincinnati Times*, and is the author of the articles which have been somewhat extensively copied "By Our Fat Contributor." He is an acquaintance of "A. Ward."

A large company of Germans were also here from Rome. Some of them could not speak English and it was amusing to see them gather in groups and hear them talk in what to us was an unknown tongue. Perhaps they were equally amused with our demonstrations.

About 500 cans of the peas which were put up according to Edgett's method of boiling but one hour after sealing, have spoiled. Luckily we had not many more to spoil.

Mr. Hall returned on Tuesday evening from a two day's peddling trip, having sold $186 worth of goods.

1178 qts. of peas were preserved. The method now pursued is to boil them from thirty to forty minutes before putting them into cans, and then boil them three hours after sealing. Nothing but pure water is used in the cans with the peas.

The talk by Mr. Noyes on "Life compared to a Tube" was received, and read in meeting, and followed by expressions of sympathy.

We have not had so many visitors this week as last.—Yesterday, however, we furnished 28 dinners.

TO-DAY.

Gravel is being drawn for the patent walk from the house to the store.

The lawn in front of the house is being mown for the fourth time this season.

The fixtures at the store salesroom are finished and painted, and Mr. Aiken has moved in his goods. The room is a fine one for the purpose, large and light.—The shoe department is to be moved into the lower story of the north wing.

We are having a cool, breezy day. This morning the thermometer stood at 58. We notice that subtle feeling in the atmosphere, that peculiar aspect of the landscape, that fullness and depth of color in the forest foliage which mark the culmination of the season. We note that this turning point of the season takes place in this latitude somewhere between the 15th and 25th of July. Generally there comes a shower or heavy rain, after long hot days; we go to bed with all the summer magnetism thrilling us. We wake in the morning apparently in a different season. Summer has begun to recede, and the year begins to pass toward the more sober and fruitful days of Autumn. We may have hot days afterward, far on into September, yet to him who studies the finer phases of the season, such days will be quite different from those of equal temperature that came before this culminating point.

METEOROLOGICAL.

Thermometer, July 18.

6 A. M. 76.   12 M. 74.   P. M. 72.

DAILY JOURNAL
OF ONEIDA COMMUNITY.

VOL. 2. JULY 20, 1866. NO. 16.

FRIDAY.
YESTERDAY'S ITEMS.

A company of Roman aristocracy was here. Unpleasant people, very. Brought their brandy bottle with them, had evidently patronized it before coming, did so while here, probably did so after leaving here. After leaving, one of our goblets, which they had been using, was missing. When last seen it was in the hand of one of the men.

The committee on Meron Kneeland's case reported to the meeting the result of their investigation and consultation. They sought simply to be governed by the mind of the Lord and the best interest of the cause and not by mere human sympathy or benevolence. In so doing the best light they could get led them to conclude that it was best for her to withdraw from the Community.— While, so far as she alone is concerned, it might possibly have seemed well to have let her remain some time longer on trial, yet considering the case in connection with her child, Emily, it was deemed best for her to go. The child shows few if any evidences of improvement, on the contrary, she has of late apparently been retrograding. Her influence is bad and stupifying on the other children, and we feel that the interests of the cause and of the children's department demand that she should be removed from here, and that those to whom the care of her naturally and properly belongs should assume the responsibility, and not allow it to be imposed upon us. We have kind feelings toward both and wish to do our whole duty in the case, but the Community is not a charitable institution and cannot be governed by questions of that character. Moreover, so far as the question of charity is concerned, we feel that we have done all that is required of us, and even more. The case of the child is one which neither we nor our principles are responsible for. Yet while this is true and well known to us, it is not known, or not recognized by the public who gaze upon us and judge us merely by the results which they see. The children's department is one which attracts a good deal of attention from the public, and is one in which the fruits of our system should be fairly shown. But we feel that this is not the case, while Emily in her present condition is there and is a prominent object of observation and a medium of obstructing influences. Furthermore we think it will be a good thing to test Meron's earnestness and real love of the truth to have her go away and be placed in circumstances where faith and a thorough, loyal purpose will be demanded.

THE STRAWBERRY HARVEST.

Mr. Thacker, in THE CIRCULAR of July 9th, while speaking of the general failure of the strawberry crop, remarks that " in some favored spots the crop was fair." These words apply to the Community neighborhood. There certainly has been here a fair, though not large yield ; and the prices realized have been unusually high : so that, on the whole, it has been a good season for strawberry cultivators in this section. The net proceeds of their strawberry ventures were never greater.

The Community, it must be admitted, have not taken the lead in successful culture this season. Others have raised more fruit on the same space of ground, and have gathered, with the exception of a few bushels of Triomphes, as well developed fruit. The winter was an unusually cold one, while the depth of snow was less than usual, and consequently all the strawberry fields suffered from slight protection, but ours probably most of all. To this cause is partly attributed the light crop.

Another cause is found in the course of cultivation pursued. When the vines were set out last season, from which the present crop has been harvested, the idea prevailed, with those having charge of horticultural matters, that some important advantages would result in cultivating the vines in beds instead of rows, even though the fruit should be smaller. The present season's experience has dispelled this illusion, and convinced all that the best manner of raising the Wilson, Triomphe, and perhaps other varieties, is to cultivate the vines in single rows with hills from eight to ten inches apart. The vines, not exhausted by throwing out runners, become large and strong, bear larger fruit, and more of it, and the labor of harvesting is diminished.

Still with these drawbacks we have occasion for gratitude in view of the harvest just completed. From the old bed of seven-eights of an acre 1110 qts., or nearly 85 bushels were picked—enough to pay well for keeping it over, considering the high prices realized. Yet the gardeners are not generally in favor of harvesting more than a single crop from the same vines, especially of the Wilson variety. They so thoroughly exhaust themselves by the first year's bearing that only a meager crop can reasonably be expected the second season.

From the new bed of three acres 8498 qts., or over 265 bushels, were gathered, or about 88 bushels per acre.

The picking from our vines commenced June 18th, and ended July 13th—our neighbor Mr. Adams commenced picking nearly a week earlier. The greatest picking took place July 3d, when 1887 qts. were secured, or over 58 bushels.

It is impossible to ascertain exactly how much has been realized from our strawberries, as several hundred quarts have been used at the family table—more have been served in various ways to visitors, and 2868 qts. have disappeared in the preserving factory.

For those sold at home and abroad the price has ranged from 20 to 25 cts. per qt.—a few have been sold for less than 20 cts., and a few of the earliest at a higher figure, and a few hundred qts. sent to Boston brought from 25 to 30 cts.—one crate of Triomphes were sold in Boston at 35 cts. The net value of the Community strawberry crop the present season, allowing over one hundred quarts as lost and wasted, and reckoning the balance at 18 cts. per qt. here, must be $1700. Allowing $200 for picking, and $100 for use of crates and boxes, and $1400 is left for the four acres under cultivation.

More to-morrow.

METEOROLOGICAL.

Thermometer, July 19.

6 A. M. 58. 12 M. 70. 6 P. M. 76. The day closed with a most beautiful sunset.

DAILY JOURNAL
OF ONEIDA COMMUNITY.

VOL. 2. JULY 21, 1866. NO. 17.

SATURDAY.
THE STRAWBERRY HARVEST.
(Concluded.)

Of new varieties of strawberries the *Agriculturist* promises well, though we have not yet given it a full trial; Buffalo seedling and Russel's Prolific rather poor bearers, not good for shipping, but fair in size and flavor; French's seedling is a beautiful berry, of fine flavor, nearly equal to Burr's New Pine, good bearer, but too soft for marketing—does best cultivated in hills.

Some of our neighbors must have realized better figures than the Community for the use of their land. Mr. Hubbard will receive from some less than two acres, after paying expenses of selling, picking, use of crates and boxes, nearly or quite one thousand dollars.

Mr. Davis, from about the same amount of land will receive as his reward, after paying for picking, &c., not less than $850—probably over $900. The Community purchased the balance of his crop, after he had gathered several hundred quarts, at $775, but of this sum about $100 must have been paid to pickers. Mr. Adams probably received more for his berries than any other one, but he is not very communicative on this point.

The amount of berries received from Mr. Davis was 5552 qts. During the very hot weather which followed the 4th of July we lost of this lot perhaps 100 qts.— The balance were mostly sold in Troy, and the price realized could not have been less than 22 cts. above express charges, making total receipts $1199.44. Deduct from this amount $24.44, for Martin Kinsley's expenses to Troy, and $25 for use of crates and boxes, and the amount left for our labor and profit is $375. Mr. Davis himself acknowledges that he probably has realized more for his fruit than he would if he had himself marketed it, as he was not acquainted with the business, and had not the facilities for handling fruit that the Community have.

For selling Mr. Hubbard's berries we received a commission of 15 per cent. The total amount of commission received from him will be over $160.

We purchased also some strawberries from our other neighbors Parsons, Adams, and Smith, on which there were small profits. It is safe to say that $550 were received for selling the fruit of our neighbors; and our having the control of so large a proportion of the strawberries raised in this section enabled us to obtain better prices for our own fruit than we otherwise should.

In conclusion, let me express gratitude for the good luck which attended all the operations connected with the strawberry harvest. There were no accidents, and but few unpleasant experiences. Let me also express my appreciation of the zeal and good nature displayed by Messrs. Thayer, Marks, Barron, Burnham, Joslyn, Wright and others. They were ever ready for cheerful exertion.   **w.**

In the spring of '65, Mr. Kelly set a cutting of oleander in a flower pot and as it seemed to have "struck" and to be doing well, he sold it; but the purchaser did not come for it, so it continued in the greenhouse where it still remains. Shortly since, Mrs. Sears, seeing no signs of growth in it pulled it up and found that it had never struck at all; not a fibre of root was to be seen. No apparent growth or decay had taken place for upwards of a year. But as its half dozen leaves were still green, it was placed in water, where it has thrown out a thick cluster of white roots.

We are having many more visitors this season than last. Already the number of meals sold exceeds by 300 the number up to the same day last season.

T. R. Noyes arrived last evening.

A new pea-sheller with rollers two feet long is now in operation. It shells a bushel in three minutes. We have been unable to shell the Champion peas with the small machines, on account of the pods being filled so compactly with the peas that the rollers would not grip them. This new machine, however, shells them without difficulty.

Our Indian neighbors are making good use of the opportunities which our fruit preserving business afford them. Some of them are raising peas successfully.— The best peas we have received have been raised by the Indians. The Indian women and children are also bringing us many wild raspberries. Yesterday they brought over one hundred quarts. The wild berries are very abundant and fine this season, and make excellent jelly.

Charles Underhill, of Bath, brother of Portia, was here yesterday with his wife. His wife has been visiting at Oneida for several weeks and has called here twice before. He met Portia in a very friendly way and seemed to be quite favorably impressed with the Community and its surroundings. On leaving he took with him "Salvation from Sin" and the "Familiar Exposition."

Mr. Hamilton talked in a very interesting and edifying way last evening, on ideas suggested by Meroa's case.

Willow Place will by and by need a new wing to hold its menagerie. In addition to the woodchuck a young hawk is in course of reconstruction at the factory. But although it seems to know its keepers and condescends to accept the frogs with which they occasionally supply it, yet we doubt if it will ever become "as gentle as a sucking dove." Another feature in this menagerie is to be found in a small drawer where lamp-wick is kept. Open it carefully and you will see among the soft cotton, a litter of young mice. Their mother is never seen; she probably slips out by the back of the drawer when any one opens it. But the young—what sweet little dears they are (!) sprawling over each other with shut eyes! They are almost as pretty as young pigs.— We never look at them without thinking of the exquisite, sentimental song of "Three blind mice."

METEOROLOGICAL.
Thermometer, July 20.

6 A. M. 62.   12 M. 76.   6 P. M. 72.

DAILY JOURNAL
OF ONEIDA COMMUNITY.

VOL. 2. JULY 23, 1866. NO. 18.

MONDAY.
CHANGE OF DISCOUNTS.

Oneida, July 21, 1866.

Bro. Burnham:—In view of the facts communicated in your letter of the 19th inst., that notwithstanding the advance in price of leather, Bag Manufacturers are not making a corresponding advance in the price of their goods, and that leather is not likely to go higher at present, it is concluded to return, as advised by you, to old rates, viz., ten per cent. discount to wholesale dealers and jobbers, in large cities; seven and one-half per cent. to country jobbers; five per cent. to the best retail dealers—the smallest dealers to be sold to at list or two and a half per cent. discount.

The advance was made in view of the rise in gold and of the probable advance of pebble leather to 25 cts. per foot. If it does not go above 23 cts. we can give the rates named above, and make a reasonable profit except on Leather Pelissiers, and we shall not lose on them. I trust you and other agents will communicate freely with the home department, and make such suggestions as may occur to you from time to time.

Hoping that you will be prospered in your journeyings, and send many orders for Bags, Traps, Fruits, Jellies, Vegetables, Bag-Frames, Corn-Cutters, Sewing-Silks, Photographs, Publications &c.

Truly yours,   w.

$219,13 were handed in a few days ago, proceeds of milk sent to the Factory for about fourteen days.

In the strawberry article of Friday, read "one crate of Triomphes were sold in Boston at 40 cts.," instead of "35 cents."

The farmers cut their wheat on Friday and Saturday; all except one field which is later than the rest. It is said to be good and well filled.

Some mowing is yet to be done at Willow Place.

From June 12th to July 12th over 1600 meals were furnished to visitors.

Portia resumes her school to-day after a vacation of a number of weeks.

A letter was received on Friday last from Dr. O. H. Wellington asking for admission for himself and family into the Community. Of course the proposition cannot be entertained.

BUSINESS MEETING.

Mrs. Conant expressed a wish to have some straw saved to fill beds for the boarding-house. Martin was appointed to save a quantity sufficient for the purpose.

Mr. Burt reported that Mr. Ratnor wants to hire the small cottage near Willow Place, to dry hops in. After some conversation on the subject, it was thought best to leave the matter over for future consideration.

Mr. Campbell reported that the old sign-board at the plow-works is claimed by Henry Wilson as his property. No counter claim will be made by us, but Mr. W. will be requested to take the article away.

Mr. Hamilton spoke of the necessity of re-roofing the Mansion House and adjoining buildings. He spoke of plastic slate as a new kind of roofing that is coming into general use. It consists of pulverized slate mixed with pitch. The main objection to it is the smell of the latter; but the odor of pitch is said to be a good disinfectant. It was suggested by some, on the other hand, to have the roofs shingled and coated with Mr. Kelly's fire-proof preparation. Messrs. Burt and W. G. Kelly were appointed to correspond with Mr. Kelly with the view of having him roof one of the smaller buildings by way of experiment.

G. W. Hamilton reports the Foundry roof as in want of repair and Mr. Hatch that the roof of the Children's House is out of order. Both roofs are to be attended to with as little delay as possible.

G. W. Hamilton suggested that more stock be ordered for making the O Traps. After considerable conversation on the trap business generally, it was decided to order malleable iron sufficient for two thousand more.

Last evening the talk on "Life Compared to a Tube" was read again and talked about. The view of life there presented is very interesting and suggestive. It shows us where to look for God and how to draw nigh to him and recognize his presence.

An invitation has been extended to Justin Carter of Waterbury, Vt., son of Henry Carter, to visit us. He writes that he shall probably be here sometime this month.

The Augusta rose, in the greenhouse proves to be a remarkable as well as magnificent bloomer. Since the 1st of January it has been in almost continuous blossom.— The other day we counted a cluster of thirteen buds more than half which were in full bloom. A number of other clusters and single flowers were in bloom at the same time. We know of no flowering plant that pays better for care and culture than this rose.

METEOROLOGICAL.

Thermometer, July 21, & 22.

6 A. M. 62.   12 M. 74.   6 P. M. 72.
6 A. M. 64.   12 M. 76.   6 P. M. 73.
The afternoon was quite hot.

DAILY JOURNAL
OF ONEIDA COMMUNITY.

VOL. 2. JULY 24, 1866. NO. 19.

TUESDAY.

A second letter was received yesterday from Mr. A. P. Truesdell. After his first letter was received about four weeks ago, two letters of criticism were written to him by Messrs. Bolles and Pitt, as the Community were not satisfied with his assumption of fellowship with us, and as he had invited us to criticise him freely. From some misunderstanding these letters were not sent. His second letter shows that he is engaged in preaching his version of our doctrines as he has superficially gathered them from the Berean and Bible Communism, at a water cure at Clifton Springs, and is also engaged in what he terms healing the sick by laying on of hands or animal magnetism. We do not know how far he puts himself forward as a representative of the Community and its principles. But we have no confidence in him, and feel that as far as he attempts to represent us in his present state he will only bring the truth into reproach. The two former letters which were written to him, supplemented with brief additional letters from Messrs. Bolles, Pitt and Burt, the persons with whom he conversed principally while here, will be sent to him at once.

Mr. Burt is contemplating some improvements in his corn-cutter, whereby the feeding and working of the machine will be greatly facilitated. He proposes to have it so arranged as to feed by a hopper, and to be run by machinery, instead of by hand, as at present.

The silk company are busily engaged getting ready for operations. The room is being whitewashed on the sides and ceiled over head, and the windows are being thoroughly cleaned.

The Circular came promptly this morning and looks very interesting. It would do the hearts of the editorial and printing corps at Mt. Tom good to see the interest and avidity with which their paper is seized and read as soon as it comes. This week's number is entertaining, though we have only had time to glance at it. Oneida thanks and blesses you all for your labors of love.

An excellent letter was received from Emily O. this morning. She seems to be full of faith and victory, and with her mother stands up bravely for the truth.

We are having delightful weather to-day after the late rain. The trees, the grass, fences and buildings are all washed clean, and every growing thing seems revivified with the droppings of the clouds. How exquisite are the showers of summer, in their comings and their effects! No wonder David says of Christ and his government and influence, " He shall come down like rain upon the mown grass: as showers that water the earth." This is one of the finest comparisons in all literature.

Oneida, July 23, 1866.

To the Family:—I feel like responding to Mr. Hamilton's suggestion for persons to testify of what they have to be thankful for. We all have unbounded cause for thankfulness for the gift of salvation, and for the gospel which has brought life and immortality to light: and for the clear manner in which Mr. Noyes has brought out the truth of this gospel before the world. But what I am specially thankful for is that I have had *grace* and *faith* given me to *venture* my all on the promises of the gospel. I fully believe I have given all for Christ—that I hold nothing so dear but that I could freely give it up when the cause of God or his church require it. I am thankful that my confidence in Mr. Noyes and the church is fully established. For the last two years I have had hardly a temptation to doubt the truthfulness of their position. I am thankful for a home in a Community of brothers and sisters who believe in the immediate government of God, and are devoted to his service. I am thankful too for the social experience I have had. This has been a school in which I have been through some severe discipline; but I can truly say it has yielded me far more of happiness than suffering; and I am encouraged to believe that I have learned some valuable lessons. I am also thankful for all the trials and discipline I have been through in the Community, and for the humility and softness that have been wrought in my spirit. I believe it has taught me obedience and receptivity towards my superiors, which I know to be the foundation of all good both in time and eternity.

JOHN ABBOTT.

METEOROLOGICAL.
Thermometer, July 23.

6 A. M. 60. 12 M. 69. 6 P. M. 76

DAILY JOURNAL
OF ONEIDA COMMUNITY.

VOL. 2. JULY 25, 1866. NO. 20.

WEDNESDAY.

Cornelius Hatch was criticsed in meeting. The general feeling was that he was in an improving state. Mr. Hamilton talked in an interesting way to the young men generally, exhorting them to cultivate the revival spirit. and become thoroughly devoted to God.

A letter has been written to Dr. Wellington declining his proposal to join the Community.

Ominous sounds proceeding from the big pyramid of Pea-cans, which had been erected in the lower room of the Preserving factory, indicated that all was not right.—A council of war was held, which resulted in the determination to give the pea-cans an additional steam bath of three hours ; so at it the preservers went on Monday afternoon about 4 o'clock, and continued at it until last evening. The number of cans thus re-heated is some over five thousand. The great majority of the cans stood the test and will probably give no further trouble, but several hundred "swelled heads" are now thrown aside.

Of course there are many inquiries for the cause of this luck. The first failure, previously reported, is generally ascribed to the short time of cooking the peas ; and this happened from following too closely what was supposed to be Mr. Edgett's advice of first cooking the peas in an open vessel half an hour, and afterwards cooking them one hour in cans. But in a letter recently received, Mr. E. says he never has cooked them less than two and one half hours in the cans. This last lot were cooked half an hour in an open kettle, and then three hours in cans. This, it was supposed by all, equivalent to the cooking the peas received last year, and which generally kept well. Peas which are hereafter put up the present season will be cooked from four and a half to five hours.

All realize in the preserving business that they are dealing with powerful and mysterious forces, and that they need the help of science and inspiration.

It may be mentioned that at the time most of the peas were canned the weather was very hot and that the peas were not themselves properly matured—some were too green, while others had been wilted and became hardened before getting their growth. It may also be mentioned that the Community is not alone in their experience. H. G. A. writes that the peas put up at the North American Phalanx this season are "blowing" and Mr. E. writes from Vineland : "Peas are acting very bad here, we have lost some that I cooked three hours then opened and cooked five hours longer making eight hours in all. They act a great deal as the corn did last year."

The carpenters are inclosing and fitting up the tool-house.

Half the wheat was brought in yesterday: the other half will be got in to-day. There is about sixty loads of it altogether.

Another of our sisters fell heir to the crutches the other day by slipping her foot. We give no names, as she has enjoined us " not to put her in the JOURNAL." These crutches have been used by so many of late that one lady has been practising with the view of being prepared when her turn comes. The spirit of lameness has been so much laughed at of late that he ought to be ashamed of himself and hobble off, crutches and all.

Here and there in quiet corners may be seen one or two of our elder sisters picking over a nice heap of strawberry leaves. There is something so provident and motherly about such work, done in this quiet way, that one feels like sitting down to join in it. say for two or three minutes, just for the sake of the fellowship.

No, Mr. ED. CRit., there is no mistake about it, wheat is growing in our ice-house *in contact* with the ice. The seeds germinate while lying directly on the surface of the ice; the white shoots, just touched sometimes with a tint of green, are found growing along the surface of the blocks and melting little channels in which they coolly lie ; the roots penetrate into the clearest and apparently most solid ice—we have just pulled one out of such ice, which had penetrated more than an inch. In the porous snow ice the roots have in some instances penetrated several inches. Are you satisfied? P. S.—Mr. Bristol has just brought a piece of our best ice into the office into which the roots have grown at least two inches.

"Every thing for sale except the soul" says one of our business principles. One of our neighbors, who is quite a business man, inquires what we will take for Willow **Place with its water privilege, machinery and whole** stock. Should H. W. & Co. ask the question in sober earnest, we might perhaps be willing to make a bargain ; only we should name a good round figure.

O. C., July 24, 1866.

To THE FAMILY :—I am glad to respond to Mr. Hamilton's invitation to give expression to thankfulness.—There has been a great change wrought in my heart since I first came here. I am thankful for all the suffering I have had, and accept my freedom as the gift of God. To be able to say that I am rejoicing in the love of God, is worth the price that has been paid for it.

Since Mr. Noyes's talk about the "Presence of God," it has been my prayer that I might realize it more fully, and really feel that confiding love in him which would make it easy for me to talk with him and be guided by his inspiration. He has answered my prayer, and I do realize his presence as fully as I do the gifts he has so liberally bestowed upon me. I fully believe that we can be led by inspiration, and find it a better and surer guide, if we are thoroughly obedient to it, than any other.

It is six months since I left Hoboken, and it has been without exception the happiest period of my life. I have learned to love and appreciate women more than ever before, and I acknowledge my indebtedness to my sisters for much that a worldly education did not teach me.

I confess my love for Mr. Noyes, Mr. Hamilton and Mrs. Dunn, and a spirit of obedience to them. I am happy when I feel that I am in fellowship with them.—My cup is full and running over. I thank God for his goodness and I love him with all my heart. SOPHIA.

METEOROLOGICAL.
Thermometer, July 24.

6 A. M. 62, 12 M. 78. 6 P. M. 74.

DAILY JOURNAL
OF ONEIDA COMMUNITY.

VOL. 2. JULY 26, 1866. NO. 21.

THURSDAY.

A letter was received yesterday from a German who wishes either to join the Community or find employment in one of our factories. He objects to our religious theories and says he has "no much faith in Jesus Christ."— To which we might answer, that we have no much faith that he would suit us, either as a member or as an employe.

A letter was received also from Mrs. Munson, addressed to Mr. Noyes, expressing a great desire to join us.

A letter was also received from a young man in Canada asking for information. He has heard the Community commended by a friend, is a moral and temperate man, and if our regulations suit him thinks he will send an application for admittance.

G. B. Price, inventor of the pea-sheller, writes: "Some three or four of our men are building corn-cutting machines of different varieties, so that I may not be able to sell your machine this year. I now think of going to New York to see about some pea-shellers sent to Stephen Provost, and which do not work well. If I cannot give him satisfaction, I will advise him to order machines of you, if you have no objections, as I am about sick of the world and pea-shellers in general, and think I will try my hand or head at something else—preaching I guess."

Mrs. V. had a lot of bottles boiled yesterday in soap and water, and afterwards filled with fruit, and only three broke of more than one hundred. This experiment will be continued while it brings such good luck.

Meron and Emily Kneeland started yesterday noon for Ohio. R. R. tickets for a part of their journey were purchased for them, and they were well furnished with clothing, and given twenty-five dollars, with the privilege of asking for twenty-five dollars more when they most need the money. We heard several say that they had liked Meron better since her late criticism than for some time previous, and that they had considerable hope that she would commend herself in her new circumstances. Meron was herself disposed to take the right attitude of spirit in leaving, saying she only wanted to please the Community. She however, dreaded a return to her worldly relatives. A sincere letter was written to Mrs. Kneeland, criticising her and her son for their course and treatment of Meron and her child in the past, and recommending them to assume and faithfully discharge the responsibility in regard to her and Emily which naturally devolves upon them, and not allow the truth to be wrongfully reproached through negligence or insincerity.

The conversation last evening was on using anæsthetics in dentistry, some recent experiments having been made with them. It was thought that the introduction of such agents should be made a Community matter. T. R. N. was requested to consult with Mr. Noyes and get his mind in regard to their use.

BIRTHDAY TESTIMONY.

Oneida, July 25, 1866.

To THE FAMILY :—As this is the anniversary of my birthday I thought it a fitting time to give expression to thankfulness. As the causes for thankfulness are too multiplied for me to enumerate, I will mention a few of those which have a special claim on my gratitude. I am thankful to God for his watchful care during the long period of sixty eight years, all of which except the last two, have been spent in a wicked and gainsaying world, in which my experience therewith had filled me with disgust and turned my attention to a higher life.— And most fervently do I thank God for a home in this Community, among genial and loving hearts, who are looking for my best good. But more and above all do I thank him for faith in a risen Savior, bringing in the hope of the resurrection, and man's immortality and destiny, sweeping away the last vestige of skepticism and placing my feet on the rock of ages. I am thankful for all the experience I have had since coming here, though I have passed through suffering and trial; yet those very trials have been lessons of wisdom in which my spirit has been softened and made more receptive to good influences. I am also thankful for the ardent desire to make progress in spirituality which I feel working within me, leading me to high resolves and sacrifices for the cause of Christ.

The other day as I came from the dining room and stood for a moment gazing at the passers by, a much loved friend and sister stepped before me and said, "You look very solemn, what are you thinking about?" when I promptly told her what was then passing in my mind; that I envied none their new clothes or fine things, but if I envied any, it was that they had made greater attainments in spiritual growth and the graces which adorn the Christian character than I; and as this is the one great desire of my heart, I should be especially thankful for your sympathy and criticism to aid me in my efforts.

I feel that I already owe much to Community life for the vigor and youthfulness of feeling which has animated my spirit, and notwithstanding the years that are numbered to me, I feel younger to-day than I did ten years ago and am better able to perform my daily labor. For this too I have great cause of thankfulness. And so long as I live will call on the name of my God and confess Christ my helper and preserver.

SUSAN UNDERWOOD.

METEOROLOGICAL.

Thermometer, July 25.

6 A. M. 61. 12 M. 80. 6 P. M. 80 in the sun.

DAILY JOURNAL
OF ONEIDA COMMUNITY.

VOL. 2. JULY 27, 1866. NO. 22.

FRIDAY.
YESTERDAY'S ITEMS.

George E. Cragin and Milford J. Newhouse arrived in the afternoon.

Mary and Sarah Leete and two children came during the day and remained over night. Mr. Leete has been here for several days, but is now absent.

W. G. K. is absent on his peddling route.

Raspberry bees continue after supper and are likely to for three weeks to come.

The other day while the farmers were getting in their wheat a shower came on causing them to suspend their job. But instead of quitting work they proceeded to Willow Place and began getting in hay, the shower not extending so far north as that. Martin remarked that there was some advantage in having a farm large enough so that when it rained on one side of it, they could go to the other and continue work.

A letter was received from Mr. Realf, stating that he purposed to leave New York for Oneida yesterday.

Mr. Justin Carter arrived this morning.

Mr. Hamilton has written to the carpenter in Canada Mr. Isaac Carey, of Brighton, that if he will visit us we will furnish him with employment for a month or so.

The value of using ether in some cases of dentistry was shown yesterday in an operation on Edwin Nash.— He had two front teeth removed, and probably without the use of the anæsthetic would have been unable to have endured the operation without great nervous prostration and without being held by others, the roots were so firmly fixed, having grown to the process of the gum so that the latter had to be broken or cut in order to extract them. By using ether, the operation was painless, and effected with comparative rapidity and ease, and without any injurious or unpleasant results.

TO-DAY.

We have had several good trap orders lately, including one from J. M. Warren and Co. of Troy, for 95 doz.; one from Walker and McIlvaine of Peoria Ill., for 50 doz.; one from Sidney Shepard and Co., for 25 doz.; one from George R. Barton of Syracuse, for 80 doz.; and a 50 doz. order from Botsford and Co., of Chicago. Besides these a number of smaller orders have been received.

We have fine weather—days of golden splendor, and clear, bright nights. The mercury ranges between 64 and 90, but the heat has not of late been oppressive. Our Oneida summer, this season, has had, we think, more than the usual proportion of clear days.

We have nothing more to report to-day. The family seems to be in good spirits, and there being so little news of an outward kind is no sign we are not happy and busy. "Blessed is the nation whose annals are silent," says some one.

> Brother-love is growing.
> Hearts are interflowing.
> Work to sport is turning.
> Souls are heavenward yearning.
> Each day seemeth better
> Than our yesterday.
> Each day breaks some fetter
> Of death and old decay.

METEOROLOGICAL.

Thermometer, July 26.

6 A. M. 68. 12 M. 80. 6 P. M. 81. in the sun.

A SUPPER-PARTY.

All the little folks, yesterday
    Took supper together out of doors;
They made it a time of pleasant play,
    Thinking it better than carpeted floors.

There were ever so many children fair
With three good mothers taking care—
Jessie and Edith and Marion,
    Lucy, Harley, and Willie Sears,
Full of the gladness of childhood's spring,
    The joy that belongs to infant years—
Sunshine of life without its tears.

George and Emily Easton,
    Rose and little Cosette were there;
Happy Mabel and sober May,
    And Virgie dear with her sunny hair.

Carrie and Lillie and Rosamond,
    Two Harrys, Ormond and Leonora—
I wonder whether I've counted all—
    Temple and Anna and Theodora.

With bread and butter and cups of milk
    And cookies set out on a pretty tray;
Crackers and cheese and good things else—
    A merry company were they;

Grasshoppers leaping high in the grass
    And music up in the trees above,
And a good spirit in every child;
    'Tis a dainty feast that is eaten in love.

DAILY JOURNAL
OF ONEIDA COMMUNITY.

VOL. 2. JULY 28, 1866. NO. 23.

SATURDAY.

YESTERDAY'S ITEMS.

T. R. N., by request, lectured last evening on the diseases of licentiousness.

The following letter was received:

Buffalo, N. Y., July 26, 1866.

To the Oneida and Wallingford Communities,

Gentlemen:—Another young gentleman and I are anxious to become two of your family. We have examined your religious and social theories, and find nothing in them but what we can fully indorse. We have watched your operations and mode of conducting business, and read your publications for some time, and find every thing satisfactory.

We shall be glad to answer any questions, and to furnish references.

Our ages are respectively 25 and 29 years; of sober business habits.

A line by return of post will oblige

Yours respectfully, WHITAKER & SMITH.

The Leetes left for home in the afternoon.

TO-DAY.

T. R. N. left for New York this morning.

The fruit-preservers have been obliged to abandon the attempt to shell the Champion peas with the machine.— When they began using the large machine and while the apron was dry it promised to do the work, but as soon as the apron became wet it did not work well. There was a great deal of waste. The Champion pods seem to be thinner and more compactly filled with peas than the other kinds, and at the same time they do not open so readily. The pea campaign is drawing to a close. This week from 12 to 50 bushels a day have been put up.

We would inform Mr. Leonard that the bundle of printing paper has arrived.

The fruit-growers are becoming deeply impressed with the importance of applying more manure to the raspberry plantations than in previous years. The finer varieties, more especially, show the need of it this year.

The old bridges about here seem to be giving way generally. Not long since the bridge over Mud Creek broke down while one of our teams was passing over it. The other day the bridge at the south end of the Mill gave way under similar circumstances.

The various hedges have been undergoing their annual clipping the past week—two of the hired men officiating at the business.

Mr. Towner writes that he has been mustered out of the U. S. service, and is now at Berlin Hights, where he awaits our answer to his application for membership, before entering into permanent business outside.

The cans which contained the spoiled peas are undergoing a process of purification; they are first taken to the creek and rinsed, and are then thoroughly boiled for an hour or more.

The apple crop does not promise to be so abundant as we were led to expect in the spring. The fruit-growers say it is "very light." Probably there will be some compensation in the extra size and fairness of the fruit. The plum crop on many of the trees will be good, the branches of some of the trees having already to be propped up to prevent breaking. The pear crop will not be very abundant, but the fruit is large and fair.— Grapes promise well, the Delawares are the finest we have ever had at this season.

WILLOW PLACE ITEMS.

Part of the new Silk Factory has been ceiled over head, the walls whitewashed and the posts and ceiling painted; to-day the floor is being scrubbed. Actual operations in the manufacture of silk are expected to commence on Monday next.

About 2500 No. 0 Traps have lately been finished off and inspected. 20,000 No. 1 are now being put up and 200 Bear traps are also under way.

METEOROLOGICAL.

Thermometer, July 27.

6 A. M. 72. 12 M. 85. 6 P. M. 80 in the sun.

DAILY JOURNAL
OF ONEIDA COMMUNITY.

VOL. 2. JULY 30, 1866. NO. 24.

MONDAY.

Yesterday again brought us some unpleasant company from Rome. One young man was so disrespectful and disgustingly rude that he had to be sharply rebuked.— The company who were with him were apparently no better than he, but were not so conspicuous in their demonstrations.

On Saturday evening G. E. C. made his report of the analysis of pie-plant, which was interesting and instructive but not finally conclusive as to whether the free use of the plant is injurious—that question must finally be settled by future experiments. So far as himself was concerned he thought he should continue to use it until its injurious character was more fully demonstrated. He found about *one grain* of oxalic acid to the ounce of juice. The analysis of pie-plant wine is not yet concluded. The fruit-preservers seem disposed to accept Mr. C's. view of the matter, as we notice that they have begun putting up pie-plant to-day.

Mr. Knowles left this morning for Jefferson County, in company with S. W. Nash. He goes to effect some satisfactory settlement of his affairs with his wife, and secure her a comfortable home. He is not very strong yet, but it was thought that it would do him good to assume the activity and responsibility of this work. We believe he also thinks, as soon as he is well enough, of engaging in selling silk on the northern route. Last evening the following communication from him was read:

To the Family.

As I am expecting to leave in the morning, I thought I would like to express my thanks to the family for their kindness to me since I first came here, particularly during my sickness. I could not have had better care, both spiritually and temporally, than I have received since I have been sick. I am very thankful for the sincerity that has been extended to me and hope it may prove a lasting benefit to me. I am also thankful for the unity I feel with Mr. Noyes and the family generally, and for the privilege I have had of living in the Community so long as I have. The year I have spent here I think has been the most profitable year of my life. And in going away, I can address myself to the work before me with good courage, because it seems to be the course that God in his providence has marked out for me. Were I to consult my natural feelings of course I should rather not go. I would prefer to remain in the Community. I desire to look away from my bodily weaknesses and give my attention to the spirit of the resurrection that is working in the family at the present time, that I may be a good medium of that spirit and be wholly possessed by it. My heart and sympathies are all with the Community, and I am thankful to be a co-laborer with them in the great

work in which they are engaged. I ask for your prayers, that I may go forth in the strength of God, and be a good soldier for the cause. With much love,

Yours truly, W. A. Knowles.

The back parlor is being cleaned and fitted up for Lady Hamilton's use.

Last evening the talk on intuition was re-read and made the basis of conversation.

BUSINESS MEETING.

Frederick Marks reported that he has been setting out a lot of raspberry and other vines on land naturally poor, while much of the manure formerly at the disposal of the horticulturists is now used for other purposes. It was the unanimous feeling of the meeting that manure for this purpose must be had. Mr. Hamilton remarked that it seemed to be the mind of God and is certainly the mind of Mr. Noyes, that fruit-growing should take the precedence of farming, and that we may expect good luck if fruit-growing be made of primary consideration in the disposal of manure as well as in the general thought and attention of the Community. Some further conversation was held on the desirableness of saving soap-suds from the wash-room, after which it was moved and seconded that the horticulturists be appointed a committee to see about obtaining manure.

S. W. Nash reported that the can-soldering furnace, as it now stands, is in rather unsafe proximity to the wood-work. John N. Norton was appointed to see that it be built around with brick on the sides next to the wood-work.

G. W. Hamilton reported that the boat and bathing facilities at the Willow Place pond are attracting outside boys to the orchard to an extent that is becoming a nuisance. A feeling was expressed that, if possible, the public should not be disallowed from bathing in the pond at certain times; and it was decided that the boat should always be locked up when not in use, that the springing-board should be taken away, and that suitable posters be got up and placed on the fence to regulate the behavior of outside boys who come there to bathe.

Myron stated the need of having greater facilities for carrying the hands to and from Willow Place, the necessity being augmented by the circumstance that two of our sisters will now have to be taken to the Factory and back every day. Messrs. Kellogg and Clark were appointed to make such arrangements as they thought best.

METEOROLOGICAL.

Thermometer, July 28.

6 A. M. 72. 12 M. 80. 6 P. M. no observation.

29.

6 A. M. 70. 12 M. 80. 6 P. M. 80 in the sun.

HURRAH FOR THE CABLE AND CYRUS FIELD!

DAILY JOURNAL
OF ONEIDA COMMUNITY.

VOL. 2. JULY 31, 1866. NO. 25.

TUESDAY.

The three principal items of news which electrified the Community yesterday were—

1. Cyrus Field's report of the successful laying of the Atlantic Cable,

2. The Atlantic Cable telegram announcing peace between Austria and Prussia.

3. The beginning of Silk Manufacturing at Willow Place.

In the meeting C. A. Burt was criticised. Notes were taken and a report will be forwarded to the other Communes.

John S. Freeman arrived yesterday.

Mr. Justin Carter left for home this morning. He says he goes to settle up his affairs, preparatory to coming back. He thinks he shall be able to work for us if he cannot live with us, though he hopes to be able to do the latter.

Mr. Ackley reports that the fruit-preservers finished putting up peas this morning. 833 bushels have been shelled, 121 of which were raised by ourselves. The remaining 712 bushels were bought of our neighbors at 75 cts. a bushel—$534. From 8½ to 9 quarts of shelled peas have been obtained to the bushel.

It is probable that John and Andrew Heyl will be hired for another year to work in the Satchel Factory. John intimates that he may want to live with us always.

The Sterling Gazette, published at Sterling, Ill., of July 28th, contains a very enthusiastic and rose-colored account of the O. C., written by a correspondent at Utica.

The Community have purchased their annual supply of coal, consisting of 2 boat loads of Lehigh from New York, and 80 tons of Scranton from Syracuse.

Mr. Geo. W. Covell has drawn one load of coal from New York, and deducted from his charges $50, as his contribution to the Printing-office fund. W. C. will please take note.

Capt. Covell was delayed at Little Falls three days by the breakage of the Canal. He says there was a string of boats extending about twenty-five miles, or about twelve miles on each side of the break.

Capt. Covell says canal boats do not generally move three miles an hour, but "there is no night there"; and some idea of what they accomplish even at this slow motion may be gained from the fact, that since the 20th of June his boat has taken a load of salt from Syracuse to Buffalo—a load of grain from Buffalo to Albany—a load from Albany to New York, and brought back 103 tons of coal to Durhamville, arriving there July 29th.

The Silk manufacturing is likely, for a time at least, to make Willow Place a popular place with visitors.— We were there a few hours yesterday afternoon, and during that time, three parties of visitors, of three or four persons each, mostly women, called in to see the works. We also understand that many of the young ladies of the region round about are anxious to obtain employment at the factory, when the business is far enough advanced to demand hired hands.

A party of young men visited the cascades near Perryville, eight or ten miles distant, on Sunday. They report very fine scenery. The fall of water is said to be 130 feet—90 feet of which is an unbroken leap. There is undoubtedly much picturesque scenery within a half-day's walk of our home which we have never known or appreciated. The East Hill, for instance, contains many wild and romantic ravines, down which trout-brooks find their way to the creek, and where great rocks and old woods meet the eye. The scenery of this section has had the reputation of being rather tame, compared with Wallingford and its environs. But study and investigation will reveal new beauties at many a turn where we least expected them, and will show much more to admire than the superficial observer would suppose.

WILLOW PLACE ITEMS.

SILKEN.—The opening year brought a change in the Community programme. The order came—"Prepare for silk making—Forward, march!" On the 20th of Jan. Mr. Inslee went east to make investigations in regard to the construction of the requisite machinery. By the 15th of February, three students had been established in the factory of C. L. Bottom, whose Machine Twist stands highest in market. E'er the 10th of June the last of the three had graduated. July 17th Mr. Hadden & Co. sold to the Oneida Community one bale of raw silk, weighing 103 lbs., valued at $12,25 per lb., 3 per ct. off. Saturday the 28th inst. found the first lot of machinery in running order, and a part of the fine room devoted to silk making fitted up. Monday the 30th of July came, and with it the beginning of silk manufacturing by O. C. The acorn has sprouted. A vigorous young sucker from the Communistic oak, watered by the rain of special Providence, and warmed by the sunshine of loving hearts. All day a changing group of admiring spectators hovered around the Winder, watching the slender threads as they were slowly reeled off.

"Is it horse hair?" soberly questioned a six year old urchin.

"Not much," we replied.   C.

METEOROLOGICAL.

Thermometer, July 30.

6 A. M. 66.   12 M. 66.   7 P. M. 66.

DAILY JOURNAL
OF ONEIDA COMMUNITY.

VOL. 2.   AUG. 1, 1866.   NO. 26.

WEDNESDAY.

Mr. Nash returned last night. He convoyed Mr. Knowles as far as Watertown where he resigned his charge to E. Knowles, who had come there by appointment to meet his father. Mr. N. had calculated to spend a day or two in the north, and make some investments in fruit, but did not do so, as the markets were unfavorable.

Our excellent brother, and paragon of honesty, " Elias which was for to come," contrary to all precedent, as well as all expectation, got into a scrape on Monday. Only think of it in a man of his unimpeachable character, a man who wherever he goes in all the region round about is regarded as a man of the uttermost veracity and reliability, who won't sell any silk except that which is made in the dominions of King Victor Emanuel as Italian Silk—such a man to be pounced upon by an officer of the law and caught selling goods without a license! Even so.— He went down, or up, or over to Cazenovia, and worked away diligently among the merchants until he had canvassed the whole town, and was just starting for the next village west, when a venerable official personage stepped up to him and invited him to step into an office just at hand. Always willing to oblige, he favored the hospitable man with his personal presence at the place designated. On entering the precincts of the august representative of Uncle Sam, Uncle Elias was subjected to the following impertinent question :

" Have you a license for selling goods ?"

To which with his usual imperturbable courtesy he replied :

" Yes, I have a license, but have not got it with me."

Public functionary returned to the charge with—

"That will not do; I must request you to present your license, or take out one here."

Uncle E. replied :

" But I can bring you ten men, merchants of your village, who will testify to my word."

" Won't do. Would not take the testimony of all Cazenovia. In business between you and me, I would take your word ; but my *official* capacity requires me to demand that you show your license, or if you have none to show, to require you to take out one."

So rather than leave his team there on expense and foot it home to get his license, our veteran salesman paid $15 and took out another license; Mr. Official Capacity agreeing that if Mr. Hall would forward to him the statement of Assessor Barnett, of Oneida, to the effect that he had already taken out a license, or applied for one, he (Mr. Official Capacity) would refund the money. Mr. Barnett has accordingly forwarded a statement to that effect, and Mr. H. awaits the answer. Our Agent hereafter will probably go "armed and equipped as the law directs."

The following letter was sent to the Shaker Society at Lebanon :

F. W. EVANS,

FRIEND :—Learning that you have, in a recent letter to our sister Commune at Wallingford, made some inquiries concerning our new patent machine for cutting green corn from the cob, we take the liberty of making the following offer to the society with which you are connected : We will send you a machine and a man to superintend its first operations and give all necessary instructions ; and if the machine gives good satisfaction we shall expect only our usual price, and if it does not give satisfaction we will withdraw the machine, defray all expenses and make no charge. We are confident that you will not choose to part with a machine after you have once seen it work. Please advise us soon whether the above proposition is received favorably by your society, and oblige,

Yours Respectfully,   ONEIDA COMMUNITY,
by W. A. HINDS.

Another member was added to the Community yesterday, a little after noon. He is yet quite young and inexperienced, but his mother, Eliza Burt, having long been a valued member of the family, there was no hesitation in receiving him into our home and hearts.— Both he and his mother are doing well.

Mr. Noyes's letter on " Male Continence," was received yesterday, and was read in the meeting. It is regarded here as a masterly presentation of the subject. Mr. Hamilton remarked that putting that subject before the world in this way, was a greater event than the Atlantic Cable.

METEOROLOGICAL.

Thermometer, July 31.

6 A. M. 62.   12 M. 78.   7 P. M. 68.

DAILY JOURNAL
OF ONEIDA COMMUNITY.

VOL. 2.   AUG. 2, 1866.   NO. 27.

THURSDAY.
YESTERDAY'S ITEMS.

Ormond received a lesson yesterday which will likely be of some service to him in the future. While no one else was present he climbed upon the table at the children's house and tipped over a large kerosene lamp.—The oil came down on his head, saturating his hair and running into his eyes, causing him to give loud outcries for help. The result was that he had to be put into a tub of soap-suds and subjected to a thorough scrubbing. He will doubtless remember, hereafter, that it is not altogether a light matter to meddle with kerosene lamps even if they are not burning.

In the meeting there was some talk about Victor's case and the connection between the spirit of insanity and disobedience. After this, followed confessions and the meeting closed as usual with a hymn.

A letter was received from a harness-maker in New Haven, named Geo. B. Kirtland, inquiring upon what terms he could become a member of the Community.

A letter was also received by Mr. Hamilton from H. W. B., written at Pittsburg, warmly expressive of brotherly love, and also giving some account of his business operations.

Maj. Priest of the Central Railroad was here with a company. He bought a $10 lunch-bag. Among others with him was Mr. Boardman of the firm of Boardman and Co., piano manufacturers.

TO-DAY.

G. E. C. in connection with the fruit preservers is prosecuting investigations into the causes of the pea failures. One point is established and there are indications that the main cause of the difficulty is found. It is this: Water boils at this altitude from the sea at 210 deg. But 212 degrees of heat are required to kill the yeast plant which causes fermentation. Hence, though the vegetables in the cans are heated to the boiling point, and even boiled many hours, if the heat does not rise above 210 deg. there is no certainty that they will not ferment. Last year in boiling peas, D. A. Abbott says that the covers of the boiling vats were fastened down, and hence a pressure of steam was secured which probably carried the heat up to 212 deg. or over, and there was but little loss by fermentation. This year the lids have not been fastened down. Experiments and improvements are being instituted which we confidently hope will result in making the whole business a sure and successful operation. Fruit preserving generally, we judge, has hitherto been mainly an empirical business.

We hail the application of more exact science to it with much satisfaction.

A letter was received the other day from E. A. Stillman to T. R. N., partially in answer to inquiries about huckleberries. He also states that the pressure of his business is such that he is forced to give up the idea of visiting the Community at present. He thinks he may wish hereafter to avail himself of the services of the Purchasing Agency in ascertaining the prices of some kinds of lumber which he manufactures.

Martin left early this morning for Troy, Saratoga, Whitehall and Plattsburg, to make collections at first-named places, and join a huckleberry party at the last place. We obtained our supply of huckleberries last season at Plattsburg, and if prices are satisfactory, Martin will purchase about thirty bushels.

Yesterday afternoon, Miss Mathews went over to Verona and hired two girls to work in the Silk Factory. Miss M. took as her *compagnes de voyage* three little maidens who had made themselves useful to the bag bees, by threading needles, and who had long looked forward to some little excursion by way of reward.—They had refreshments with them which they ate in picnic fashion under a tree by the wayside.

Mr. Dunning and family have left the boarding-house across the creek, and the care of that establishment now devolves on Mr. Aiken and Mrs. Conant.

We thankfully report that the preserving department are having better luck with the bottles, in consequence of their being boiled for a time in soap and water—a device of Mrs. Vanvelzer's.

☞ Persons who go to Syracuse, Utica and other villages near us, are requested to give previous notice to the office folks, when practicable.

METEOROLOGICAL.

Thermometer, Aug. 1.

6 A. M. 64.   12 M. 76.   6 P. M. 76.
The day was cloudy, with occasional drops of rain.

DAILY JOURNAL
OF ONEIDA COMMUNITY.

VOL. 2.   AUG. 3, 1866.   NO. 28.

FRIDAY.

YESTERDAY'S ITEMS.

W. G. K. and M. L. W. returned home last night.

A Baptist minister accompanied by three ladies and two children, from Oswego, called here yesterday. They had been attending the Commencement at Hamilton and were on their way home. They wished to stay all night, but the proposal was declined. The father of the minister, whose name was Hughes, was born in a religious Community which was founded in Wales some time in the last century, by Howell Harris, a revivalist and contemporary with Wesley and Whitfield. The party were acquainted with Mr. Franks, and Mr. Hughes expressed much interest in the Community.

Mr. and Mrs. Perry went to Durhamville to visit Mrs. P's. sister. Mrs. P. will remain several days. Mr. P. returned in the afternoon. Mrs. P. appears to be doing well at present.

We were edified yesterday by the receipt of numerous reports of talks by Mr. Noyes at Wallingford and New York.

Several bushels of peas have been bought for the purpose of continuing experiments in heating &c.

We have had quite a large increase of company this week—16 dinners were served on Monday, 36 on Tuesday, and 14 yesterday.

Yesterday, a very select entertainment was given in the old parlor. Only a limited number of invitations had been issued so that the affair appeared to be almost private. The curtain, which was extemporized for the occasion, was withdrawn about 4 o'clock and there was the sole performer, Master Eugene, lying in dramatic attitude on a pillow, with shut eyes and sprawling fingers, the very image of his grandmother—at least in regard to one of his facial organs; for we heard a voice from behind the scenes, which we recognized as Eliza's, saying: "He has mother's nose exactly."

TO-DAY.

An order for 1¼ doz Bear traps, No. 5. was received this morning from Haywood, Cartledge and Co., Chicago.

The class of girls who formerly studied French with Mr. Hamilton now have Mrs. Easton for their teacher.

Letters and orders in response to the fruit circulars which have been sent out begin to come in in encouraging quantities. It begins to be evident that we are getting the inside track on fruit. We have already got the short track on traps, and shall undoubtedly get it on silk as soon as we get fairly started in manufacturing.

This is a very quiet day, and we cannot find much family matter to report.

DAILY JOURNAL
OF ONEIDA COMMUNITY.

VOL. 2.   AUG. 4, 1866.   NO. 29.

SATURDAY.
YESTERDAY'S ITEMS.

Among the guests here yesterday, was a Methodist minister from Lowell, Oneida Co. His name was Shepard. His wife was with him. He has read THE CIRCULAR for some time, and seems to be considerably interested in the Community.

Another visitor was a Miss Wheeler, an accomplished singer, who favored us with several songs.

A party, consisting of Mr. Hatch, Harriet Mallory and Charlotte Maria, visited the Cascades yesterday.

The trap sales for the month of July were $4,309.21.

G. W. H. and G. E. C. were at Utica investigating the cost and practicability of getting some kind of metallic boilers for the fruit-preservers. We have not yet learned the definite results of their journey, though we understand they were satisfactory.

In the afternoon Mr. Freeman commenced working at the machine-shop. We understand he has heretofore worked in a boiler shop in Schenectady.

Mr. Noyes and Victor arrived about 12 o'clock last night.

TO-DAY.

The weather this morning is cool, cloudy and somewhat rainy.

The fruit-growers are now employing women to hoe strawberries. One half of our three-acre plantation has been hoed out by them. Hired men will hoe from 12 to 14 rows a day. The women hoe from 10 to 13 rows, and do their work better than the men.

The old canes have all been removed from the black raspberries. The new ones are making a fine growth.

Our grape crop generally is in very fine condition, and we note a few facts concerning it:

Delaware, crop large, free from disease, clusters well and evenly filled.

Hartford Prolific, crop large, clusters well filled, berries finely devloped.

Concord, crop moderate, slightly affected with rot, but promises well.

Diana, crop light, rotting considerably.

Creveling, crop good, berries a little uneven, free from disease.

Ontario or Union Village, promises well.

Rogers's No. 19. Heavy crop, splendid.

The Iona will fruit for the first time with us.

Several of the teams are now busily employed in drawing coal from the Canal.

Mr. Realf, who did not visit Oneida last week as he had purposed to do, now writes to us that since his former letter he has been very sick with the typhoid fever. He is now slowly recovering. He says that as soon as he gets strong enough he shall go to a friend's in the country, after which he shall carry out his intention of visiting the Community.

The other day, after Martin had gone, a man called here from Plattsburg, and from him we learned that there is a large crop of huckleberries this season in that section. He recommended that we go to the region north of Plattsburg, near to the Canada line.

WILLOW PLACE ITEMS.

Yesterday, while the men were at work at the Drop in the Forge Shop, the upper part or lifter broke, and a ten pound bit of iron came down and narrowly missing the head of one of the men, scratched his hand. A difference of ten or twelve inches in position alone saved his life.

Five hired girls are at work in the Silk Factory. The work goes on well, though of course somewhat slowly

Yesterday the Winder and Cleaner were both in operation. The machinists are going on with the additional machines all of which they expect to have ready by the 1st of December.

☞ Agents sending orders for Preserved Fruits, will please bear in mind that we already have orders for double the quantity of Orange raspberries we shall be able to put up the present season.

METEOROLOGICAL.

Thermometer, Aug. 2.

6 A. M. 64.   12 M. 70.   7 P. M. 68.

August 3.

6 A. M. 62.   12 M. 78.   7 P. M. 70.

DAILY JOURNAL
OF ONEIDA COMMUNITY.

VOL. 2. AUG. 6, 1866. NO. 30.

MONDAY.

Last evening Mr. Noyes gave a deeply interesting discourse on some hitherto unexplained events in the history of the Community.

Mr. Hall has received back the $15 he paid to Mr. Official Capacity at Cazenovia, the latter being satisfied with the statement of facts furnished him by Assessor Barnett.

Our cool weather continues. Yesterday was cold, cloudy, and occasionally rainy. This morning is the same only a little more so.

Pine-apples are the order of the day in the fruit-preserving rooms—some 2,000 having arrived from New York on Saturday.

Our mowing was finished last week, though the hay is not quite all in the barn yet. The crop has been fair, and has been secured in good condition.

C. Vanvelzer left this morning on a peddling trip round Oneida Lake.

A curiosity is to be seen in the New House cellar. In the spring Mr. Nash, left some Canna and other roots covered with dirt at the foot of one of the stone piers.—Forgetting to remove them as he intended, he found them growing quite vigorously the other day. Some of the Canna stalks are about four feet high, and standing where the light from a window strikes them are quite green.

BUSINESS MEETING.

Charles Vanvelzer made application to have a wagon assigned to the use of Mr. Hall and himself, better than the one they now have. It was urged that the wagon now in use for this purpose, gives no shelter to goods or persons. W. A. Hinds thought that if the peddling business alone were concerned, it might hardly be necessary to get such a wagon, as we do not know how much longer we may continue this branch of business; but he thought that a wagon might be got which would be useful for general purposes and which might be available for peddling when wanted for that purpose. It was voted that the wagon committee be appointed to obtain such a wagon as will be best.

Mr. Hatch presented the inconvenience felt by the women in carrying water to the rooms on the corridor. A wish was expressed to have a tank fixed to hold rain water from the roof for the convenience of the upper stories. Voted that Mr. Hatch, G. W. Hamilton and A. L. Burt be appointed a committee to consult with Mr. Hamilton as to the cost of such a tank.

A letter from H. G. Allen was read stating that Mr. Farwell of Boston, "writes that he wishes another Silk Spinner and would like to know how soon we could get one out for him." Mr. Inslee stated that the only difficulty in the way of filling such an order is the fact that the machine-shop is at present pretty fully occupied with work for our own silk factory. G. W. Hamilton expressed a wish to accept the order should we get it. Mr. Hamilton concurred in this wish, considering it as important to encourage the influx of work to the machine-shop. Moved and seconded that Mr. Inslee and J. F. S. be appointed to decide on a fair price for the job, and that we hold ourselves open to accept this or any similar orders received.

G. W. Hamilton reported that an application has been made to purchase one of the presses used in the Trap works. Voted that the matter be referred to G. W. Hamilton, J. C. Higgins, Mr. Inslee and Roswell Hawley.

With reference to the above orders, powers were given to the managers of the machine-shop to engage another good machinist if such can be had.

The committee on the Laundry furnace, report that it is unnecessary to lay out any expense on that department at present.

W. H. Woolworth expressed a wish to have a case fitted up for bags, as some of them are getting injured.—It was thought that as the carpenters are at present fully occupied, nothing should be done in this matter further than can be done with the facilities we already have.

O. C., Aug. 6, 1866.

DEAR LUMINARY:—I have some good friends to whom I wish you would quote the old rule of politeness—"Never look over a person's shoulder when he is writing." These friends I know have no wrong intentions in the matter. They appear entirely at ease, and unconscious of doing aught amiss, and what is most strange, do not appear to have the slightest thought that I am unpleasantly affected by their operations. Perhaps they say to themselves, 'He is only adding up figures,' or 'He is only writing a business letter,' or 'He is only writing in the account book, certainly there is no harm in my looking over his shoulder.' Could they feel for a moment as I sometimes do I am confident they would correct their habits in this respect; and yet I am not otherwise easily disturbed while writing.

I can get along very well when there is considerable noise and communication going on in the room ; but to have one walk up deliberately behind me and stand there till he has read a whole page is altogether too much. I am perfectly willing persons should read all the letters I write, if they will wait till I have finished them, and (if not too much trouble) ask permission ; and common politeness would seem to require as much as this in nearly all cases. SCRIBO.

METEOROLOGICAL.

Thermometer, Aug. 4.

6 A. M. 60. 13 M. 74. 6 P. M. 56.

August 5.

6 A. M. 60. 13 M. 60. 6 P. M. 60.

DAILY JOURNAL
OF ONEIDA COMMUNITY

VOL. 2.   AUG. 7, 1866.   NO. 31.

TUESDAY.

YESTERDAY'S ITEMS.

Mr. Robinson arrived in the afternoon.

Mr. Burnham has sent us an order from J. B. Glen and Co. of Cleveland, for Preserved Fruit, amounting to over $1100 net.

Mr. Noyes discoursed last evening on the Organic administration and development of Salvation from Sin.

Mrs. Perry arrived home yesterday, and seemed glad to get back.

TO-DAY.

Mr. Lampman of the firm of Lampman and Robinson, of Cleveland, is here this morning. This firm have dealt considerably in our preserved fruit.

The fruit preservers are having some cast-iron heating vats made at Willow Place.

We find it quite difficult to obtain good butter at present in this region, as most of the milk is sent to the cheese-factories. We hear that in Smithfield there is a factory at which both butter and cheese are made, and a trial will be made to get good butter there.

Mrs. Robinson has written to us a letter expressing thankfulness for her criticism while here, and saying she had derived a great benefit from it.

The clouds have cleared away and we are having a clear, cool day, so cool that it seems like fall.

The Tontine printing-office corps were treated to-day by Mr. Nash, with portions of an orange which has ripened in the greenhouse. The appearance and perfume were much like what we have been accustomed to in oranges, but the flavor bore but little resemblance to that of those ripened under southern skies.

The following notes were presented to the family on Saturday evening;

To THE FAMILY.

By some things that I have heard, I judge that some may think that I do not like to take the responsibility of being the father of Eliza's child. I would say to all that I do accept it; and have felt like doing so in the past.

I wish also to take a humble attitude towards the truth and be receptive to it, and let it and criticism work in my heart. I confess the true spirit of obedience in all things.

M. H. KINSLEY.

To THE COMMUNITY.

We thank God that he has given us a little boy, and if the Community like the name, we should be pleased to call him Eugene.

We desire to keep free from all claim on him and offer him to the Community as Christ's boy, to be governed and controlled as they see fit. We desire always to be receptive and open to criticism or advice about our relations to the child or each other. We confess Christ in us strength and wisdom.

MYRON H. KINSLEY.
ELIZA E. BURT.

ABOUT PRESERVED FRUITS.

We are likely to have many more orders than we shall be able to fill. Shall we call it good or bad luck? We have not yet heard from many of our old customers, and yet of the finer varieties our orders already run far ahead of the probable supply. Agents will keep this fact in mind, and not solicit orders for Red and Oranges Raspberries in bottles or cans, for Yellow Spanish and May Duke Cheries in bottles, for Mazzard Cherries in bottles or cans, and for strawberries in bottles. Pine-apples cost so much more than usual that only a limited supply wil' be put up. They can not be afforded at less than $11.00 per dozen bottles, and $9.50 per dozen cans. We have a good supply on hand, and not ordered, of Black and Yellow Spanish Cherries in cans, and of Strawberries in cans, and expect to be able to fill orders received for Pears, Peaches, Plums, Quinces, Huckleberries, Blackberries and all the different kinds of Jellies and Pickled Fruits named in the Fruit Circular. If the Peas stop spoiling now, we shall have about 5000 cans, and the probability is we shall have from thirty to forty thousand cans of Corn. Several hundreds of cans of String Beans will be put up, more than are at present ordered, and a large quantity of Tomatoes will also be preserved.

From this statement Agents and others will be able to judge what is the best course for them to take in soliciting orders. They should be cautious about taking orders for those kinds for which we are already better supplied with orders than fruit. But such orders as we can fill will be gratefully received, especially those for Vegetables and Jellies.

The unprecedented demand for fruit the present season will no doubt induce much greater enterprise in this department of business another year.   w.

METEOROLOGICAL.

Thermometer, Aug. 6.

6 A. M. 60. Cloudy.
12 M. 65. Cloudy.
6 P. M. 65. Cloudy.
The day ended with a beautiful sunset.

DAILY JOURNAL
OF ONEIDA COMMUNITY.

VOL. 2. AUG. 8, 1866. NO. 32.

WEDNESDAY.

YESTERDAY'S ITEMS.

Mr. Kelly's father arrived last night in response to an invitation to experiment with his new roofing material on the wing of the Mansion House.

On the cars he was made a victim of the confidence game. As we heard the story, a man asked permission to sit on the seat with him, and immediately entered into conversation, inquiring where he was going, &c., stating at the same time that he was himself a merchant, and had just started a store about eight miles from Oneida. Soon another man stepped up to Mr. Kelly's companion, and inquired whether he could pay the a- mount due him. He replied that the conductor had promised him the money, but he could not attend to the matter until he had been through all the cars. The creditor urged that he could not wait; so the debtor solicited Mr. K. to lend him fifty-four dollars for a few minutes, until he could obtain it of the conductor.— Mr. K., unsuspecting, complied with the request—his "friend" disappeared at the next station: and after an unsuccessful search through the cars, Mr. K. was forced to conclude that a rascal had taken advantage of his simplicity and generosity. A lesson may be learned from the affair in regard to fellowships, worth more than fifty dollars.

Among the visitors was Orson S. Murray, formerly of Vermont and now of Ohio, and well known as an apostate Baptist minister, infidel and Anti-Slavery lec- turer and writer. He came, ostensibly, to examine Mr. Burt's Corn-Cutter, and remained over night. He was a disgusting looking object, wearing long hair and beard, both of which looked, and doubtless were, dirty. He made one or two attempts to vent infidel poison but was promptly rebuffed by Mr. Bolles. His presence here in- duced Mr. Noyes to have read the old article in the Per- fectionist, entitled, "Come out from Among Them." After this Mr. N. gave a very interesting talk on Anti- Slavery, and the apostasy of Garrison and other leaders into infidelity.

Mrs. Munson persistently endeavors to have us receive her as a member, notwithstanding we have repeatedly informed her that we do not think she is fitted for such a relation. From the two last letters which have been sent her she has appealed to Mr. Noyes, in the last instance forwarding to him Mrs. Joslyn's letter, complain- ing of it as cold and stern. How little cause she has for such a charge may be seen by reading the letter, which, as Mr. Noyes remarks, "is excellent, and ought to be pub- lished for the benefit of those who will appreciate it more than Mrs. Munson does."

Oneida, July 26, 1866.

DEAR MRS. MUNSON:—Your letter of the 20th inst.. written to Mr. Noyes, was sent here yesterday, and read last evening in our meeting. On the back of the envel- ope was penciled the following: "I don't know anything about the writer of this and therefore send it to Oneida J. H. N." To-day Mr. Pitt handed it to me to reply to. I asked Mr. Hamilton if he had any thing to say to you —any word to send. He said he had no word for you only to refer you for a reply, to Mr. Noyes's Home-Talk in the last CIRCULAR, on the "Admission of new mem bers." Had you seen that article before you wrote him. you probably would not have written him as you did There is a general rush toward us at the present time and petitions for membership multiply, so that, unless we steadily persist in waiting until we know the mind of the Lord, "our life-boat" will certainly get swamp- ed.

We are expecting a family of five from New Hamp shire next month. They have long stood knocking for admission.

We certainly feel for you, and sympathize with you in your homeless condition, and benevolence, and a kind of fellow feeling, would prompt us to open our doors. and offer you an asylum. But it is plain to us, that for some cause the way is hedged up. God knows for what. *I*, for one, cannot think you are so well fitted for mem- bership as you think you are yourself—yet I have hope in your case. I don't think it probable that you will be called to join us at present, therefore would it not be better for you to seek a home and some regular employ- ment, and not be drifting here and there without any purpose other than connecting yourself with us? I think you told me that you were not concerned about a liveli- hood, and I should think, judging from your natural activity and energy of character, that you would make your way in the world without much trouble; and you can, at the same time improve your relations to us, by seeking to know more of Christ and his gospel of salva- tion from sin. If you prove to us that you are an ear- nest Christ-seeker, instead of a Community-seeker, the veil between you and us will be rent. *My* greatest de- sire every day I live, is that I may please the Lord, and if I please him I shall be acceptable to the Community spirit. If we draw nigh to him he will draw nigh to us. If you lay your life open to the judgment and are sin- cere with yourself, you can be a helper to the cause right where you are, and act in harmony with us.

I have written thus plainly because I felt that you were indulging in hopes in reference to joining us, that could not at present be realized. What future years may bring forth in respect to your case, I cannot foresee, but of one thing I am certain if you are one of Christ's flock, you will sooner or later be gathered into his fold. Com- fort your heart with this thought, and quietly and patient- ly wait on the Lord.

Yours in truth and sincerity, E. Y. JOSLYN.

METEOROLOGICAL.

Thermometer, Aug. 7.

6 A. M. 61. 12 M. 72. 6 P. M. 71.

DAILY JOURNAL
OF ONEIDA COMMUNITY.

VOL. 2.   AUG. 9, 1866.   NO. 33.

THURSDAY.

O. H. M. started on a peddling trip on Monday.

D. F. Knowles arrived last night.

In the meeting the talk at Wallingford on the good points in Victor's character, was read, after which Mr, Noyes delivered a discourse on the young folks and the prospective growth and permanence of the Community.

Martin arrived home on Tuesday evening. He found the huckleberries scarce, and secured only twelve bushels. Yesterday afternoon the berries were received, having been delayed sometime on the way. They were in a somewhat crushed condition, but had not spoiled. They were received about five o'clock and were sorted over and ready for canning before dark.

In the afternoon the children's department, by invitation of Mrs. Dunning, visited Willow Place, and took supper at the boarding-house. The old omnibus was brought out and the party, dressed in their best, were seated—25 inside and 4 on the top—and driven over between three and four o'clock. After their arrival they enjoyed themselves in play and sight-seeing for a while, and then gathered into the house, where three tables were set for them, and Mrs. Dunning and her assistants served them with an excellent supper. The children behaved well, and all parties enjoyed themselves exceedingly.

Mr. Robinson returned home yesterday.

The pine-apple bees ended yesterday. Some of the people were apparently glad of it, for we noticed the skin was nearly taken off their fingers by the acid juice.

Mr. Burnham writes from Cleaveland under date of Monday as follows: "A. W. C. was here last Friday and stole the march on me in selling silk. But the point is that he was taken, as of old, to be the agent of the O. C., and he not only did not deny it but actually offered to take orders for P. F. and send them on to us."—Comment is unnecessary.

The first order for "Male Continence" which has come to Oneida, was received the other day from Dr. **Pusey** Heald of Dansville Water Cure.

Twenty-two bushels of string beans are being disposed of this morning by the preserving department.

We are having a cool, misty, rainy day.

Note to the family from Mrs. Hutchins:

I feel greatly indebted to Christ and Mr. Noyes for what I am, and for all I expect to be. I thank the family for their kindness and long forbearance with me. I love to read my Bible and the Spiritual Magazine. They are always new. I know I love Christ because I love his children. A verse in Psalms has seemed to me very beautiful: "One thing have I desired of the Lord, that will I seek after: that I may dwell in the house of the Lord all the days of my life, to behold the beauty of the Lord and to inquire in his temple." Truly the one thing I have sought for many years I have found to the joy of my heart—a people who love God with all the heart and their neighbor as themselves. My faith and confidence in Mr. Noyes as the true medium of Christ remains firm and unshaken. I confess my obedience to Christ, Mr Noyes and Mr. Hamilton. I confess a spirit that will neither give nor take offence.   FANNY P. HUTCHINS.

METEOROLOGICAL.
Thermometer, Aug. 8.

6 A. M. 60.   12 M. 78.   7 P. M. 66.

DAILY JOURNAL
OF ONEIDA COMMUNITY.

VOL. 2.   AUG. 10, 1866.   NO. 34.

FRIDAY.

Mrs. N. A. Morse writes to us of her return home, and expresses much thankfulness for her visit here.

In the meeting the conversation was mainly in reference to a tract for visitors which Mr. Noyes proposes to write, to take the place of the late pamphlet "Familiar Exposition."

The fiery charger which flies to and fro over the W. P. route, despite his undoubted willingness, is scarcely equal to transporting twenty-four passengers at once; so Mr. Conant has come to his assistance with a double team: he makes a morning and evening trip. The passage is usually made inside of 12 minutes.

F. W. Evans, the Shaker elder at New Lebanon, writes that our offer relative to the Corn-Cutting Machine is accepted by his society, and that he will notify us as soon as they are ready to have one sent.

Mr. Burnham writes from Cleveland, giving an account of a visit he has made to Prof. Nyce, the inventor of the Patent Fruit House. He says:

Very soon after my arrival, a lady brought in several clusters of Catawba grapes and a plate of apples—among which were specimens of apples grown in the summer of 1865. Both grapes and apples were of fine flavor—and the apples were as hard and plump as you could desire. Mr. Nyce was very free in conversation—and although I have a clear impression of much valuable truth, both of a scientific and practical nature, which he uttered, I can give you but the merest epitome of it.

He is just now engaged in certain experiments in the line of canning corn and vegetables which bid fair to result in greatly shortening the process of boiling or steaming, as practised by us. I had with me a copy of THE CIRCULAR containing W's article on Fruit Preserving, and at his request, read that paragraph in which it speaks of corn boiling 5 hours—making a vent for the escape of steam &c.

His theory about the matter is this: that these fixed gases in the grain must be set loose and expelled from the can, but that 5 hours boiling more or less does not necessarily do this while the can is perfectly tight. His method is to make a small puncture in the can, at the outset of heating, not so large as to let air *in*, but sufficiently large to allow the air inside to escape. He then drives a sharp fire—watching, meanwhile, the operations at the vent. So long as the current is outward, the boiling must be continued but soon it begins to diminish in force; and then to determine whether the gas is all out he makes a thin paste, or perhaps uses thick soap suds and with his fingers puts it over the hole. If the paste, or whatever is used bubbles up, then the heating must be continued, but if not, he considers the process ended, the little opening is soldered over and the can placed away in the cellar.

He is not through with his experiments, but so far as he has gone, everything is in favor of his theory. The boiling process does not occupy over 30 minutes.

He says that these gases cannot be eliminated *if confined*, they must have room for the atoms to move freely about, and hence the mistake in boiling with the cans air tight. He thinks he will be through with his experiments in a week—and, as I gave him your address, he will write you on the subject.

A letter was received from Prof. Nyce this morning making many inquiries about preserving vegetables.

A man named Tichenor, of Schenectady, ordered a dozen tracts on Male Continence, the other day.

A company of eight—Mr. Conant, John Conant, Manly Aiken, John Kinsley, Mrs. Abbott, Mrs. Lynde, Jane Abbott and Frank Hillerman—have gone to the Oneida Cascades this morning.

Several very large orders for preserved fruit were received this morning. One from E. C. Hazzard & Co. of New York, for a general assortment, including 200 dozen Peas. Another from Christiansen and Bush, Detroit, for over 460 dozen fruits, vegetables and jellies. Several smaller orders were received. In all, the orders amount to between $2000 and $3000.

Our rain is over and gone, and to-day is very pleasant the sun shining clearly except when occasionally obscured by the great cumulus clouds that float slowly eastward.

METEOROLOGICAL.
Thermometer, Aug. 9.

6 A. M. 59.   12 M. 59.   7 P. M. 58.

DAILY JOURNAL
OF ONEIDA COMMUNITY.

VOL. 2.   AUG. 11, 1866.   NO. 35.

SATURDAY.

YESTERDAY'S ITEMS.

Among a gay party of visitors yesterday, was a Miss Rice, a professional singer from New York, who sang a number of songs and other pieces in very good style.— She has a clear, full, contralto voice—rich and mellow and of unusual power, especially in the lower notes. Her singing was just the counterpart of Miss Hewlett's, heard by us lately, the excellence of which lay rather in the nicety and precision with which she rendered the lighter, rapid, soprano passages. We should like to hear the two in a duett. Miss Rice has sung at the recently destroyed Academy of Music in New York and is now, we understand, connected with the choir of one of the Brooklyn churches. We heard some one say that her family were formerly residents of this county.

42 meals were furnished to visitors.

Dr. Strong, Frederick Norton's dentist-teacher, arrived in the afternoon from New Haven.

For some time, preparations have been going on for inaugurating Croquet among us. Yesterday afternoon the croquetorie and ground being in readiness, an arena was marked out on the lawn in front of the rustic summer house, and the stakes and bridges arranged for playing. Several experimental games were afterwards played. The game bids fair to prove very entertaining, and to afford a pleasant and graceful excercise. We have not yet sufficiently mastered it to enable us to speak intelligently of all its beauties, or its scientific points, but it seems to combine in a rare degree many interesting qualities. Here is what the author of "Croquet; as played by the Newport Croquet Club"—a little manual which we would commend to all beginners as a very clear exposition of the rules and manner of playing—says of the game:

"The origin of this game is unknown. No man invented whist or chess, and croquet like them seems to have been evolved by some process of nature, as a crystal forms or a flower grows—perfect, in accordance with eternal laws. There is in all these games a certain theory which furnishes interpretations for all cases that arise in actual play. The rules are grouped about a central principle. The mimic battles have a unity, and are homogeneous in all their parts. If the rules are indefinite or contradictory the game loses its distinctive character. If the rules are accurate and rigidly enforced, croquet is a game of the highest interest. I am informed by a scientific billiard player that though croquet is inferior to billiards in affording opportunities for delicate manipulation and manual dexterity, that it far excels that elegant game in the field it opens for the exercise of the higher qualities of combination and foresight. Whist exercises the memory and the power of calculating probabilities; chess the imagination and the faculty of abstract reasoning; but croquet, though it taxes these mental qualities less, combines them with the delights of out-door exercise and social enjoyment, fresh air and friendship—two things which are of all others most effective in promoting happiness. Those who have been in the habit of regarding croquet as a game for children may, perhaps, smile at my enthusiasm; but let them procure a perfect ground, balls and mallets, play half a dozen four-ball games in strict accordance with the rules, and when they can claim to have mastered the game, they will acknowledge themselves converts."

In meeting Mr. Noyes delivered a very interesting discourse, criticising the doctrine of Illusion as presented in the poem in the last CIRCULAR.

The husband of a certain lady who is in full sympathy with the Community, living in a certain inland town of this State, has written the following note to W. G. K.

B—— August 8, 1866.

W. G. Kelly:—You are hereby requested to keep away from my house entirely, and if any of my family come to the Community send them away.   H. B.

TO-DAY.

Mr. Noyes says the fact that Boyle has begun his warfare against the Community is evidence that we are coming near to the "end."

The carpenters are engaged in re-roofing the wing of the Mansion House. It is to be shingled, and then coated with Mr. Kelly's composition, which it is claimed will render it proof against all ordinary liabilities of fire from sparks or even brands.

This is one of old George Herbert's perfect days—

"So cool, so calm, so bright,
The bridal of the earth and sky."

METEOROLOGICAL.

Thermometer, Aug. 10.

6 A. M. 60. 12 M. 70. 6 P. M. 69.

DAILY JOURNAL
OF ONEIDA COMMUNITY.

VOL. 2. AUG. 13, 1866. NO. 36.

MONDAY.
BUSINESS MEETING.

S. W. Nash reported that the turkeys and other fowls kept by our hostler are quite a nuisance. We had *our* poultry killed on account of our own and our neighbor's gardens, and Mr. N. thought it needless that we extend a privilege to our employees, which we do not reserve to ourselves. Frederick Marks said that he had mentioned the matter to the hostler, telling him that as he found it necessary for the preservation of the fruit, to shoot the robins occasionally, it was quite possible that he might mistake the turkeys for robins and shoot some of them. Messrs. Burt and Kinsley were appointed to look into the matter and speak to the hostler that he have his poultry removed.

Martin mentioned that our Hay-cutter is in very bad order; it has been repaired a number of times and is getting worn out. It was decided to have it put in thorough order for the present; and that we have it in view to purchase a better one when we hear of such in the market.

F. A. Marks inquired how far our hired people should be allowed to help themselves to fruit. It seems they have been doing so very freely although our own family do not. Martin said that he should take care that none of the farm hands should take any such liberty—if they did, he should discharge them at once. The heads of other departments will be expected to take equally firm measures with those under them.

Martin called the attention of the board to the necessity of having a Dairy House, as the cellar presently used for keeping the milk will shortly be wanted for other purposes. Several solutions of this question were proposed, after which Messrs. Hamilton and Darron, Mrs. Harriet Kinsley and Mrs. Barron were appointed a committee to consider the matter.

Mr. Clark reported that the girls employed at the Silk Factory would like to be carried to the Depot and back once a week. As it is probable that we shall by and by have quite a large number of operatives in this department, it was thought well to have a distinct understanding on this subject at the outstart. Voted that the managers of the Silk Factory, when they hire hands, make it clearly understood by them that we come under no obligations to afford them any regular means of conveyance.

Mr. Burt proposed that an excavation be made west of the Tontine to receive the waste soap-suds by a drain from the wash-room, and to receive muck or compost as absorbents. The proposal was referred to the committee on Manure.

WILLOW PLACE ITEMS.

The Doubler has been running several days, and on Saturday the Spinner was started. Both machines work well. The long expected Reel arrived from Atwood's the other day and has been set up. This is a new invention of Mr. Atwood's—ours being one of the first ever built. The Reel and Stretcher complete the number of different machines necessary to "throw" silk, i. e. get it ready for the dyer.

E. P. J. has invented an ingenious machine to be used on the Iron Planer for planing angles.

R. Hawley is at work on an endless-grate for furnaces, designed to keep the fire always in order. c.

On Saturday evening Mr. Noyes talked about his own position in the Community in regard to criticism. Last evening after talk about the sore-eye devil that is trying to find entrance to the Community again, he made some further remarks on the subject of Illusion.

To-day is cool and somewhat rainy.

We learn with pleasure that Mr. Thacker intends to soon visit the O. C., and spend a week or two, with his eye on the interests of the horticultural department.

48 meals were furnished to visitors on Saturday, and 14 yesterday.

The probability is that L. F. D. will go to Wallingford in F. Norton's place.

Dr. Strong left last night: he appeared to be very much pleased with his visit. He spoke very highly of the short-dress, and wished it might be introduced into New Haven.

Shutters to the Store are being hung.

METEOROLOGICAL.

Thermometer, Aug. 11.

6 A. M. 60. 12 M. 72. 7 P. M. 69.

August 12.

6 A. M. 66. 12 M. 80. 7 P. M. 76.

DAILY JOURNAL
OF ONEIDA COMMUNITY.

VOL. 2. AUG. 14, 1866. NO. 37.

TUESDAY.

Mrs. Leete has been very sick of late, and Mr. Leete has thus been prevented being of much help at the Store. Mr. Leete writes that she has been improving for the last few days, though she has had to be kept under the influence of stimulants most of the time.

Messrs. Marshall, Wilson and Case, of Vernon were here yesterday, for the purpose of inviting the Community to participate in their coming town fair, in October. Mr. Hamilton gave them encouragement that we would do something in that way. At the conclusion of the conference they hinted in a delicate way that if the brass band should favor the fair with their presence, it would be very pleasant and acceptable.

It appears that the inquiries as to whether we would sell the Willow Place property, were the result of some ideas that are entertained by certain citizens of Vernon relative to starting a woolen or cotton factory. It is not likely that we shall seriously consider any proposition to sell.

Mr. H. R. Perry recently learned that an aunt of his, in Fulton, N. Y., had some money that she would like to loan the Community. Accordingly by the advice of the financiers, he visited her, to look into the matter. He returned yesterday with about $1100.

All signs go to show that we shall have a good trade in traps this fall. Orders or inquiries for them, and orders or inquiries for fruit are received almost daily.

Mr. Noyes talked last evening on some new plans for education which he has recently received—involving the starting of a Community family at New Haven &c. The talk was electrifying to the whole family.

To-day is dull and cloudy.

The lawn is undergoing the mowing process for about the fifth time this summer.

Mr. Bradley goes to Syracuse and Cylde to-day on matters connected with the fruit department.

Mr. Kellogg's brother and his wife arrived here this forenoon. They reside in Ohio, and have been on a visit to friends in Connecticut.

Tryphena's mother is also here to-day.

The circle around the new burying-ground has been set with strawberry plants, by Messrs. Bradley, Bristol and others. The evergreens that were set in the spring are doing finely.

The shingling of the wing of the Mansion house, which has been interrupted by the rain, is resumed to-day.

Mr. Spencer, the optician, of Canastota, called here yesterday afternoon. He brought with him a magnifying glass, which had been ordered by Mrs. Hawley when she had charge of the greenhouse. The price of it was $15, five dollars less than would have been charged to other people. The glass is a very good one, and is very acceptable to Mrs. Sears. Mr. S. also made Mr. S. W. Nash a present of another magnifying glass, of less power and value.

The fruit-preservers are putting up string-beans again to-day in large quantities.

Mr. Bradley has been relieved from the farming department, and will turn his attention to other business.

METEOROLOGICAL.

Thermometer, Aug. 13.

6 A. M. 60. 12 M. 6 P. M. 64.

DAILY JOURNAL
OF ONEIDA COMMUNITY.

VOL. 2.   AUG. 15, 1866.   NO. 38.

WEDNESDAY.
PRESERVED FRUITS.

The way the fruit orders are coming in is very gratifying. Most of them are in reply to the Circular sent out a short time since.

It is important that our customers have no good cause for complaint, even that we have disappointed them in respect to filling their orders; and with this in view I will endeavor to keep agents and others posted through the *Journal* of the actual condition of the fruit business—the supply and the demand. And persons will be written to who give orders which we lack fruit to fill.

Look over the fruit circular, as you read the following, and you can tell how matters now stand :

It is intended to put up from ten to fifteen thousand cans of Tomatoes; 3012 are ordered. About 5000 cans of Peas have stopped swelling; 3744 are ordered. 5094 cans of Corn are ordered of the 40,000 we hope to have for market. 1793 cans of String Beans are on hand; only 824 have been ordered. Shall probably be able to fill orders received for Pears. It is too early to speak definitely about Peaches, but prospects are now favorable for getting a good supply of this fruit. Get no orders for Mazzard Cherries either in bottles or cans, for Mayduke Cherries in bottles, and for Yellow Spanish in bottles.— Of Cherries unordered there are on hand Maydukes in cans 524 ; Black in bottles 435, Black in cans 1576 ; Yellow Spanish in cans 2305. Prospects are good for Plums and Quinces. Pine-apples are nearly all ordered, but the present intention is to put up another thousand or two. Of Red and Orange Raspberries more than twice as many are ordered as we have on hand, but of Black Raspberries there are still on hand 516 bottles, 1585 cans. Of Strawberries there are only 431 bottles and 1275 cans uncalled for. There are about one hundred cans of Huckleberries on hand. There is no immediate danger of our receiving too many orders for Blackberries : the indications are favorable for an unusually good crop of this fruit. All the Currant jelly likely to be made is already ordered, but send on the orders for the other varieties.

☞ Orders for vegetables especially desired.   w.

The meeting was mostly occupied with conversation on a communication from John Leonard, in which he revealed some of his spiritual troubles. He appears to have been suffering for several years from torment in his solar plexus, which appears to have been the legitimate result of the spirit of grumbling which he has formerly tolerated and cultivated. This spirit several years ago seems to have come to a head and led him to speak some hard words against his Community home. After this a reaction came on, attended with this sense of torment or suffering in his solar plexus. His statement of his difficulties was very clear, and was thought to be the best thing we have ever heard from him. There was no grumbling in it as there has been in nearly all his former communications. He seems to have come to a point where he can look clearly at his own faults and imperfections and judge them, without grumbling with people and things around him. We may now expect that soon he will work into a permanent state of rejoicing and contentment.

Croquet, for the past few days has been quite popular with those who have had a spare hour to learn its movements. Old and young appear to enjoy it with equal zest. It seems well adapted to the promotion of friendship and good feeling. There is as much sport in being croqueted by your "enemy" as in croqueting him. Then victory depends on such delicate conditions that when you are almost sure of it, the next blow of a mallet may be the signal of your defeat. The game is thoroughly scientific, and affords a fine opportunity for the cultivation of skill and grace, and is pleasantly exciting to mind and body.

Mr. Olds left this forenoon on a trip to the west, expecting to be gone about two months.

Milford leaves to-day for Wallingford.

OUR BUTTERNUT TREE.

Dear to our hearts is our Butternut Tree,
Waving its branches so graceful and free,
Standing erect, in its glory and pride,
Robed like a queen, or some beautiful bride.
Storms beat against it, and tempests assail,
Blasts of mid-winter to cripple it fail,
Deep-rooted and reaching its arms towards the skies,
Alike all their fury, and wrath it defies.
Once it seemed pining and drooping with age,
And its speedy decay some did sadly presage,
But ere long a new life, and new vigor were seen,
And the tree once more shone in its beautiful green.
Oh ! if it could speak, what a tale it might tell,
How it dwelt in a forest, with those it loved well,
How the woodman's sharp axe, with its severing blow,
Cut down its companions and laid them all low.
Blest tree, how we love thee ! We rest in thy shade
Till autumn's chill frosts all thy leaflets shall fade,
And thy fruit ripe and pendant, is garnered with care,
That each of its richness and sweetness may share.
Like the tree, Truth Immortal unyielding shall stand
While the broad streams of error that deluge the land,
All lashed into fury, dash 'gainst her in vain,
She stands, all resplendent, without spot or stain.

DAILY JOURNAL
OF ONEIDA COMMUNITY.

VOL. 2. AUG. 16, 1866. NO. 39.

THURSDAY.

Mr. Wm. Hepworth Dixon, editor of the London *Athenæum*, arrived here yesterday, bringing a letter of introduction to Mr. Noyes from Horace Greeley. He is accompanied by two friends, Mr. and Mrs. Haywood, of London. Mr. Greeley's letter was as follows:

New York, Aug. 10, 1866.

Dear Sir:—The bearer, Mr. Hepworth Dixon, Editor of *The Athenæum*, has come from London expressly to study our people. He wishes especially to know *your* people, having long been familiar with your writings. I commend him to your confidence and hospitality.

Yours, Horace Greeley.

John H. Noyes, or his successor, Oneida Community.

Mr. Dixon had gained some knowledge of the Community from fragments of our publications in the British Museum. He appears to be considerably interested in socialistic questions. He is on a tour of observation, and intends to visit Brigham Young's dominions before returning to Europe.

Prof. Bancroft of Utica, was here yesterday afternoon, accompanied by his wife and daughter and several friends, including his daughter's husband, Mr. Johnson. Prof. B. and Mrs. Johnson favored us with several songs, in their usual superior style.

In meeting Sidney Joslyn was criticised, a report of which will be sent in Manuscript. In the course of the conversation the new game of croquet was alluded to, and the tendency to let in the spirit of competition, as there seems some liability of doing, was criticised. It was thought that it there were not other things in the game besides competition sufficient to make it interesting and attractive, it would be short-lived among us.

About two weeks ago the following letter was received from Messrs. Fowler and Wells:

389 *Broadway, N. Y., 4th. Aug,* 1866.

Friends and Gentlemen:—We desire answers to the following questions:

Who were the ancestors, of J. H. Noyes? and where —what country or nation—were they from?

When and where was J. H. N. born? Where did he spend his youth and where was he educated? and for what calling? We wish for a Biographical Sketch, such as may be authentic. We wish to publish the same, with some account of his life and labors, in the *Phrenological Journal,* for the information of our readers and the public.

It would be proper to state in connection therewith, the principles on which your Communities are conducted.

We propose to give a brief description of Mr. Noyes—

that those interested may form a general idea of his personal appearance.

Hoping you may be able and willing to grant our request, or to put us in the way of obtaining what we wish, We are truly your friends,

Fowler and Wells.
per S. R. W.

A favorable answer to the above was returned by W. A. Hinds. A few days after a second letter was received, which was as follows:

389 *Broadway, N. Y., 9th. Aug.,* 1866.

Mr. Hinds, for O. C.,

Sir:—Yours of yesterday, is received with thanks.— The sketch would be most acceptable, if received within a month. It may occupy two or more pages of the A. P. J. It *should* embrace the *origin* of the O. C., with some account of its progress and *prospective* condition. Its industrial, educational, social and religious condition.

When in Europe, we took occasion, in our lectures, to mention your organization, and we wish now, to fulfil a promise then made, to tell our patrons more about you. We should like to give at least an epitome of the whole matter.

Our readers are of a class, to look at your movement appreciatively and without prejudice. Of course there are many crooked sticks among them. Some are radical —liberal—ultra. But many are of the better class. We have some 2,000 Clergy on our list—many Teachers, Lawyers, Physicians etc. We print,—stereotype,—from 25,000 to 30,000 each No.

In a paragraph, please give the personal appearance of Mr. N. size—height—complexion, color of eyes— hair, etc., so that one at a distance, may see him as he is.

Give principles on which the O. C. are governed.

Let it not be too general; but *practical,* sharp and descriptive. If it shall serve your purpose by way of "sending grists to your mill," in a business way, all right—but it must be something more than an advertisement.

Hoping all may be made to work together for good,

We are truly yours, Fowler and Wells.
per S. R. W.

In response to the above invitation, W. A. H., at the request of Mr. Noyes, has prepared a sketch for publication, which will be forwarded to Messrs. F. and W. The publishers of the P. J. intend to accompany the sketch with an engraved portrait of Mr. Noyes.

DAILY JOURNAL
OF ONEIDA COMMUNITY.

VOL. 2.   AUG. 17, 1866.   NO. 40.

FRIDAY.

The following communications to the family were read last evening:

TO THE COMMUNITY.

I take this occasion to express my thanks for the criticism and advice I received last evening, and for the sincerity that was manifested.

I wish to thank Mr. Noyes for his sincerity, especially in regard to times long past. I well remember when I felt very near him and used to converse freely with him; and I consider those my happiest days. I have always regretted my leaving him as I did. I *loved* him, and I am sure that had I continued with him, I should have been a better man and a greater help to him and the Community. I am certain that my love for him *then* has helped me a great deal *since*, and has been steadily growing ever since, in spite of adverse circumstances, and in my darkest hours his spirit shone forth and strengthened me and helped to dispel evil spirits. I wish to confess my love for Mr. Hamilton and my confidence in him as a leader. I thank him sincerely for his long-continued patience with me and his untiring efforts to bring me near to Christ and the Community.

I confess Christ the controller of my tongue and a spirit of humility,   SIDNEY.

Oneida, Aug. 16, 1866.

DEAR FRIENDS:—I wish to testify to the grace of God, in saving me from the spirit of evil-thinking and grumbling, and filling my heart with thankfulness and rejoicing. I thank God for a home in the Community, and desire to devote myself to his service. I believe what Mr. Noyes said about salvation from sin, and I confess my union with him and my love for him, and should like to become better acquainted with him.   E. WHITNEY.

Our English visitor, Mr. Dixon, left this forenoon to take the noon train west. Mr. Haywood and his wife left yesterday noon for Niagara. Mr. Dixon last evening talked for an hour or more to the family, giving interesting reminiscences of his late tour in the Holy Land. He is very entertaining as a conversationalist.— Daniel took notes and we presume a report will be sent to the other Communes. Mr. Dixon is intimately acquainted with Carlyle.

Mr. Noyes remarked this morning, after playing a fine game of croquet, that he had got a new view of the subject of competition. He says that, accepting our doctrine about the war, that God is on both sides in every fight, as true, we may apply it to all games, and in so doing find that there is a legitimate place for competition and that it is a good thing. By loyally recognizing God in the game, and that he controls the result and gives the victory to whom he pleases, we may enter into it heartily and exercise our utmost skill and power to win. In this way it becomes a field for the development and manifestation of character and individual power and destiny, and competition instead of being a mere exhibition of antagonism, becomes a harmonic co-operation with God. Mr. N. intends to talk on the subject in meeting to-night.

The late cool, wet weather appears to have caused the mildew to attack some of the grapes. It shows itself mostly on the leaves, and affects the Delaware vines rather more than any of the other leading sorts.

H. G. A. sends an order for 125 doz Tomatoes in quart cans, and 25 doz in two quart cans; and adds: "It looks now as though fine fruits would command almost any price here among the fruit men, after a while." Again, "I think we can afford to stiffen on the price of our fine fruits as things now look." Several other fruit orders were received to-day.

WILLOW PLACE ITEMS.

A room 11 by 16 ft. has been partitioned off on the first long floor of the wheel-house, wherein S. Newhouse (who is about to remove from that sunny corner of the Silk Room), will continue his varied mechanical pursuits.

About 25 lbs of silk have been wound off and the greater part of it cleaned and doubled. A small quantity was twisted the second time to-day and stood an even test with C. L. Bottum's of the same letter, though as yet unstretched.

An order has been taken from Bennett, of Oneida, for 17 cast-iron window caps at $7,50 apiece. A good pattern has been bought and it is thought that more jobs of the same kind may be procured.

21 Hop stoves have been sold this season mostly of the 300 lb. size.

Mr. Burt has just finished an additional contrivance for his Corn Cutter. It consists of a series of longitudinal knives which will slit the kernels before they are cut off. This was got up originally to satisfy the Shakers, who wished their corn cut finer than the machine usually leaves it, but as the corn is thought to be improved by this process, it is likely we shall adopt it for ourselves.

The machinists are just finishing a large cast-iron steam-box for fruit preserving: it will be capable of sustaining quite a high pressure—as the sides are half an inch thick and strongly braced.   C.

METEOROLOGICAL.
Thermometer, Aug. 16.

6 A. M. 50.   12 M. 60.   7 P. M. 60.

DAILY JOURNAL
OF ONEIDA COMMUNITY.

VOL. 2. AUG. 18, 1866. NO. 41.

SATURDAY.

A letter from Mr. Abbott to Mr. Noyes:

DEAR BROTHER NOYES:—I would like to confess my love for you, and to thank you from the bottom of my heart, for the benefit that I and my family have received through you and your friends. It seems to me that, under God, I am indebted to you for all the blessings I enjoy, worth living for or that would render existence a blessing. For the last two years or more, I have been thankful and contented with my circumstances, and have felt it to be an invaluable blessing to be a member of this body, and am sincerely thankful for all the *faithfulness, forbearance* and *longsuffering* that have been bestowed on me. I pray for grace and wisdom to do justice to my benefactors.

For more than two years past my social experience has been very satisfactory—far better than I could reasonably ask or expect—for which I am truly thankful, as my greatest trial before leaving the Community was I think on this subject.

I think my case may be encouraging to others who find it difficult to harmonize with the Community, as I think no one had more pride of independent thought and judgment and individualism, than I had; but truth and love are almighty, and have gained the victory.

Truly yours forever, JOHN ABBOTT.

P. S. I am thankful for the brotherly love that is given me for Messrs. Hamilton, Burt, Cragin, Ackley &c.

J. A.

The preservers are putting up their last lot of string-beans—about 20 bushels—this morning.

Sidney and Frederick started last evening for Vienna, after a load of blackberries, and expect to return early to-morrow morning.

The carpenters still continue the work of re-roofing.— The L of the Mansion House has been shingled, and the wood-house roof is now undergoing the same process.

Mr. Bradley returned yesterday having had good success in making arrangements for a supply of peaches and plums.

Mr. Bradley has been at A. Mallory's establishment, Rochester, in quest of grape-boxes. He brought home some really beautiful samples with grotesque oriental patterns on the lids. We could almost expect the fruit to taste better for being packed in such boxes. We are negotiating for a supply of them.

Mr. Ackley is selling apples—Red Astracans—for $3 a bushel. He would like to know if it is true, as was stated in the W. Journal, that Mr. Thacker sells apples at New Haven for $5 a *bushel*. It is thought that possibly the writer meant to say *barrel*. How is it, T. C. M.?

We regret to say that several of our tenant-houses favorably noticed in THE JOURNAL last spring, have remained unoccupied all summer. The dwellings we refer to are small, it is true, are placed at rather high altitudes and have no stairs, having been intended for winged tenants. Perhaps C. E. will succeed better in suiting the martens next year.

Last evening W. A. H's article concerning Mr. Noyes and the Community, written for the Phrenological Journal, was read to the family. It is an interesting and satisfactory document and has been prepared under the supervision of Mr. Noyes. If accepted it will fill two or three pages, or more, of the P. J.

Several fine orders to-day for fruit, including one for 200 doz. corn, and one for 30 doz. plums—both from Agency.

Our visitor, Mr. Dixon, expressed himself as highly gratified with his visit here. He goes on direct from here to Atchison, Kansas, and expects to leave that place for Salt Lake on Thursday next. On his return he will pass through some of the Southern States, and will visit Lee at Lexington. Returning to New York, he will visit Wallingford: thence to Boston and home.

METEOROLOGICAL.
Thermometer, Aug. 17.

6 A. M. 59.   12 M. 70.   7 P. M. 61.

DAILY JOURNAL
OF ONEIDA COMMUNITY.

VOL. 2. AUG. 20, 1866. NO. 42.

MONDAY.

The present "father" of the Kitchen, J. P. H., has invented an ingenious automatic faucet stop for the boiler that stands on the Kitchen stove. It has been a thing of frequent occurrence for persons when filling the boiler to open the cover, set the faucet running and go off to attend to other duties, neglecting to come back till warned by the hissing sound of the water running over on the hot stove. The new automatic stop consists of a sealed fruit-can filled with air, which floats on the water in the boiler: this connects with the hook which holds the cover open, in such a way that when the boiler is filled up, the floating can disengages the cover and lets it fall, while the cover, being connected with the faucet by a chain turns off the latter in falling. We can give the invention this praise: that it works well.

On Saturday evening Mr. Noyes delivered a discourse on the study of Theology, and the importance of having a school started for the training of some of our young men as orators and religious teachers, who will be able to present the truth to the world in an effective and acceptable way. He anticipates that there will be a call ere long for us to send out lecturers and preachers. He nominated Mr. Bolles to start a school of Theology and Elocution here. Last evening Mr. B. commenced his labors by giving a lecture on the subject at 7 o'clock, in the Hall.

Orders for 158 doz. traps were received this morning. The largest order was for 100 doz., from Love and Hamilton of Rochester.

Victor for some time past has been in an independent, disobedient state. On Saturday the spirit in him seemed to come to a head, in his taking an attitude of disrespect and insubordination to his father and the whole Community. A committee was called together in Mr. Hamilton's room, and after some very severe criticism of him by Mr. Noyes, Mr. Hamilton and others, the spirit seemed to give way, and he retracted what he had said and confessed his sin. Since that he has been gradually coming into a better state, and seems to be disposed to do the right thing and take the right attitude. The following notes are the result of his late experience:

TO THE FAMILY.

I wish to confess my indignation and separation from a spirit of insubordination and disobedience which has been upon me for the last week or two. I recognize this Church as the Church of God, and as God's only Church upon earth. I confess my subordination to Mr. John H. Noyes as God's appointed leader, to Mr. Hamilton as the head of the family, and to the Community generally, as the Lord's people. VICTOR NOYES.

TO THE FAMILY.

I wish to confess my recognition of Theodore as my spiritual head, and one to whom I owe obedience and subordination. I confess Christ's humility and spirit of organization. VICTOR NOYES.

BUSINESS MEETING.

G. E. Cragin, on the part of the women who work at the Bag-shop, called the attention of the Board to the offensive accumulation of flood-wood and dead animals at the rack close to the Mill. It was thought that in a sanitary point of view, something ought to be done about it. Edwin S. Nash and A. L. Burt were appointed to have such objects removed and to see that nothing else of an unwholesome kind be allowed to collect.

S. W. Nash expressed a wish that all litter of a combustible nature should be cleared away from the yard at the Mill, and that the piles of waste lumber should not be allowed to stand so near the buildings. Recommended that A. L. Burt, who it is understood has some plan with reference to this matter, attend to it as soon as convenient.

G. W. H. reported that a heavy demand for traps is coming on, and the question was raised whether the hands now working in the trap-shop who were formerly employed in the bag-shop, should be transferred to the latter department, where there is also an increasing demand for goods. Mr. Hamilton thought it would be well not to transfer any hands from the trap-works to any other department at present.

G. W. H. called attention to the necessity of obtaining additional help on traps, and wished also to know how far he can depend on our own folks for help at Willow Place. Mr. Hamilton thought it would be good to exercise faith in God in respect to help.

Mr. Burt called attention to the disposal of the old flume at the Wilson place. Left to the disposal of Messrs. Burt and Kinsley.

D. P. Nash reported that, in view of manufacturing silk-machinery for the trade, he and J. F. Sears have been trying to construct a perfect cylinder and have not succeeded. Mr. Nash thought that J. F. Sears might go on to Willimantic and learn the art. The cylinder-maker there had offered to explain the secret for twenty dollars. G. W. Hamilton and John F. Sears were appointed a committee to find out how this art can be most easily learned, and to act upon such information as they obtain.

METEOROLOGICAL.
Thermometer, Aug. 19.

6 A. M. 13 M. 66. 6 P. M. 66.

DAILY JOURNAL
OF ONEIDA COMMUNITY.

VOL. 2. AUG. 21, 1866. NO. 43.

TUESDAY.

The following notes were read to the family last evening:

Aug. 20, 1866.

DEAR MR. NOYES—I have been under a dark cloud lately, which has made it hard for me to have faith and trust in God. At times I would almost say, What profit is it to serve God? and be tempted to murmur that he did not help me to feel in more unity and fellowship with you and others. The talk last evening has helped me to see the truth more clearly. I know the difficulty has all been in myself, and I wish to give myself up to the *truth* and *judgment,* to be cleansed from all obstructions.

I have been criticised *justly,* for independence, and complacency, and now I say that I do not think I have ever had a true spirit of subordination to my superiors. Underneath a pleasant exterior, I have been too free to think my own thoughts. When other young women have been put forward into leading positions, I have been tempted to grumble because I was not chosen. There is naturally a strong spirit in me that desires place, and the good opinion of those around me. But I thank God that nothing short of deep sincerity and devotion to Christ will make us popular. I now separate myself from every spirit that hinders heart fellowship with you, Mr. Hamilton, and the leaders of the church—praying for humility that will make me receptive to the truth whenever it is presented. I thank God for the blessings of this school—for all the criticism I have had, and hope in future to prove myself a good scholar, that will devote all my energies to *true organization.*

Your sister, FIDELIA A. BURT.

Letter from Mr. Higgins to Mr. Noyes.

Oneida, Aug. 19, 1866.

DEAR BROTHER NOYES:—Since my interview with you a few days ago, it has been a time of serious reflection and meditation with me. Your remarks and advice to me sank deep into my heart and spirit. I consider it just for me to acknowledge the many blessings of divine providence bestowed through your agency upon the Community enterprise. I feel a desire to take a humble, obedient position in heart and spirit among the brethren.

I am conscious that the old deceiver, the accuser of the brethren, has deceived me, which has caused my offense to you, and others in the family. And now I have no where else to go but to God and those brethren for forgiveness and help to victory over the world, the flesh, the devil, and all bad habits.

There are numerous things to be thankful for, such as a Community home among brethren, and that God has raised up leaders to criticise and instruct &c.

I confess Christ my health, and my victory over the seducer. Yours for improvment, C. HIGGINS.

I thank God for this brotherly and sensible letter, and hope brother Higgins will not remember unpleasantly the sharp words that I used toward him, but will think of me in the spirit of peace. J. H. N.

Oneida August, 19.

TO THE FAMILY:—I wish to acknowledge to the family—for it is just—that I never have had the first cause to complain, or to think evil in the least thing, from my first acquaintance with the Community to the present time; but have always been treated kindly, respectfully and with all long-suffering, forbearance and forgiveness.

The cause and source of all of my suffering and adverse experience, has been in the perverseness of my own spiri and insubordinate will.

I wish now to ask the forgiveness of Mr. Noyes and the family, for past offenses; and do now give myself unreservedly to Christ and the Community to do their will and pleasure—knowing no will, purpose, er pleasure of my own—in entire submission to criticism and to the judgment of my superiors. I am thankful to God for a home and place in the family, and for the kindness I have received.

I confess Christ in me a soft heart, new life and experience, and my ability to honor, and glorify Him forever.

J. R. THOMAS.

Oneida Aug. 20. 1866.

TO THE FAMILY:—I have been through a good deal of trial and temptation this summer from low spirits, and have felt lately that it was a judgment on the spirit of competition and individuality, which I can see has affected me more or less up to the present time. I am encouraged to hope that the truth is working to effect a thorough cure, and wish to do what I can to help the matter by confessing the truth about it. I find that as I get meek and humble I get nearer to God and am thankful for any experience that produces that result. I confess my hearty sympathy with the truth and principles lately brought out on the subject of unity and organization, and consider it a privilege to submit my life to them. I join heartily in Mr. Abbott's testimony, that I am indebted for what I have and am, that is of any value, to my connection with Mr. Noyes; and confess the spirit of subordination and loyalty to him, to Mr. Hamilton, Mr. Cragin and all others who are my spiritual superiors. GEO. CAMPBELL.

Mr. Noyes leaves this afternoon for New York. The family here realize that his visit has been a great blessing, and we all thank God for it.

Mr. Noyes talked last evening on several topics—first about Messrs. Easton, Herrick and Henderson; secondly, about some revelations which Miss Hawley had made of having in the past been in communication with a familiar spirit; and thirdly, he made some remarks on the Organic Duality which is manifesting itself in the Communiy, and its relation to the final victory.

Mr. Hatch and Rose left early this morning for Wallingford.

A late Agency Journal says: "A Shaker from Watervliet called to see the Corn-Cutter. On learning that Mr. Burt is going to Watervliet with a machine he concluded to postpone any thorough examination until he reaches home." The Oneidians were supprised at this announcement, supposing that Mr. Burt was intending to take a machine to a Shaker Society at Canaan 4 Corners.

☞ Persons are hereby requested not to take the copybook of "Talks" from the counting-room, without at least notifying Mrs. S. B. Campbell, or such other person or persons as may have charge of copying the "Talks."

☞ Mr. Herrick writes: "The fruit men here do not expect any more Pines this season." As the Pine-Apples now on hand are nearly all ordered, the fruit department have to request that no further orders will be solicited for this kind of fruit.

METEOROLOGICAL.

Thermometer, Aug. 20.
6 A. M. 59. 12 M. 69. 6 P. M. 59. Mean 62½.
Clear and pleasant.

DAILY JOURNAL
OF ONEIDA COMMUNITY.

VOL. 2.   AUG. 22, 1866.   NO. 44.

WEDNESDAY.
ABOUT THE GRAPES.

Now is a good time to look at the grapes. The enjoyment is not alloyed with any alimentive temptation, as may be the case a few weeks later. If you are fortunate enough to secure the company of Sidney or Frederick in your walk your pleasure will be greatly enhanced.— Either will convey to you much information you might not otherwise obtain; and Sidney at least will show you how all the finer varieties have been layered and double-layered, and tell you that he has counted 2854 layers, 733 cuttings, and 400 two-year olds; for which at least six hundred dollars will be realized, as they are all ordered at good prices. He thinks the greatest profit can be obtained by giving special attention to the propagative department of grape-culture.

The grape vines look well at the present time, with the exception that the Delaware and some other kinds are slightly affected with some sort of blight resembling mildew, and promise a fair yield. It is estimated that there will be at least a score of

loads, or from six to ten tons, provided, of course, that Mr. Murphy's old

and his scraglio are kept away. Is it not a little surprising that these bipeds have been seen on our lawn within a few days, notwithstanding all the resolutions which have been passed? They are nearly as voracious as

which never seem satisfied, and as lawless as a flock of

I fear if they should get a taste of ripe grapes they would do more damage than a yoke of

rushing through the vineyard.

It may interest some persons to learn that the Community vineyards contain the following varieties of grape vines: Deleware, Concord, Hartford Prolific, Isabella, Creveling, Rogers's Nos. 15, & 19, Diana, Israella, Iona, To Kalon, Adirondac, Rebecca, Union Village, Perkins, North America, Louisa, Logan, Northern Muscadine, Clinton; but the greater proportion of the vines are included in the six or eight varieties first mentioned.

I judge that grape-culture is one of the most profitable businesses we have, as well as one of the most pleasant; but I hope an accurate record of the labor and other expenses attending the crop, and of the proceeds will be kept for a few years, that we may have more reliable data on the subject. Fancy paper boxes or "pockets" have been ordered, and efforts will be made to introduce grapes the present season into more distant markets than heretofore. They will be sent, at least for experiment, to Boston, Saratoga, Troy, and perhaps to Montreal and other Canadian cities. Mr. Olds has been advised to ascertain whether grapes can profitably be sent to some large cities of the West.

It is hoped that the Community table will be well favored with the presence of this fruit. What more beautiful or more delicious! Let epicures continue to praise that curious mixture known as

salad, and that combination of potatoes, onions, bread or crackers and

known under the term "chowder," and descant at length on the delights of

soup, we will not envy them, while our table is ornamented with a plentiful supply of grapes and other fruits.   IONA.

---

8 A. M. We will begin our record by the commonplace remark that it rains—rains hard, and there is a fair prospect of a rainy day. The weather however is so changeable that we will not venture to prophesy.— 9½ A. M. Our continence of prediction was pertinent to the occasion. The sky is now clear, except where a few fleecy clouds are floating eastward, and the sun shines with genial warmth.

Last evening Mr. Hamilton gave some account of Mr. Justin Carter, who visited here some time since. He has been a roaming, ungoverned boy and apparently has never had much discipline of will. He has been to Australia, among other places. Though seemingly a good hearted young man, Mr. Hamilton doubted whether he would be a proper person to hire, and he is certainly not prepared to join the Community.

We omitted to mention yesterday that John H. Cragin accompanied Mr. Noyes to New York.

W. G. K. left yesterday on his silk-route.

Frederick Norton left for Wallingford this morning.

Mr. H. R. Perry leaves to-day on a business tour in the Western States.

J. P. H's automatic faucet-stop does so well and is found so convenient that he has had an air-tight float made on purpose for it instead of the fruit-can which had been used at first by way of experiment.

METEOROLOGICAL.
Thermometer, Aug. 21.

6 A. M. 53.   13 M. 70.   6 P. M. 63.   Mean 62.
The day was cloudy with some rain.

DAILY JOURNAL
OF ONEIDA COMMUNITY.

VOL. 2. AUG. 23, 1866. NO. 45.

THURSDAY.
FRUIT AT THE WEST.

Mr. Olds writes from Detroit, Aug. 19, as follows:

"From what I can learn since I came here, I am pretty well persuaded that the Peach crop is very small in many parts of the country, and that we had better calculate to put up all we can. I find that fruit is and has been very high here all through the season. It has been so high and scarce that families who have heretofore put up their own preserved fruit, did not do it this season. The obvious reasons for this are, in the first place, parties found fruit was so high and scarce that it was difficult to get it, and in the second place made up their minds it would be cheaper to buy it already put up. People know that fruit will be high, but we may be sure that these parties who have money and did not put up fruit, intend to have it and will buy it if they can get it. No doubt this is pretty generally the case everywhere. Would it not be well for us, under the circumstances to put up all the Peaches we can, provided we can get them within reasonable bounds? This is rather my mind in regard to the matter. I find Christensen and Bush have the same opinion. I should not be surprised if they should want to double their orders for some kinds of fruit. I think they will want more Peaches. They are making calculation to advertise and solicit orders from their customers. I told them we might not be able to fill their orders.— Well, we will trust God and do the best we can."

We presume some, if not all of our readers yesterday laughed at our "ducks," and perhaps thought we were making "game" of them. We have to acknowledge that there was a little *quackery* in the matter. It must be admitted that we know "snipe," if we are not up to "ducks" yet in our artistic accomplishments.

The sight of the delicate, filmy threads at the S. F. tends to stimulate our young people to the study of natural history. Yesterday, J. V. brought into the *Journal* office a specimen of silk which he had drawn from one of those large yellow and black spiders that are to be seen at this season in roadside nooks. The "silk" was of gossamer thinness, and measured from fifty to sixty yards. James held the insect between his thumb and finger and drew out the thread, winding it on a reel as it came. It appeared so strong that we don't know why it should not be spun. James has about a dozen captives which he intends to experiment on at his leisure.

Three Catholic priests were here yesterday—one from Baltimore, one from Boston, and the third from Utica. There was no special interest attached to their visit, except in so far as it indicated that the Roman hierarchy is taking observations of the new apostolic church.

Mr. Crandall of Baldwinsville came yesterday and remained over night. He is an acquaintance of Mr. Robinson's.

The Journal was premature in its announcement of Mr. H. R. Perry's departure. He did not leave till about 7 o'clock this morning. His business will be quite complicated, as he proposes to act as general Community agent, in obtaining orders for Bags, Traps and Fruit, and procure advertisements for the Lafayette Journal, a western paper with which he was connected before joining the Community. He intends to stop at several of the principal places in Ohio, such as Mansfield, Newark, Columbus, Springfield, Dayton, Cincinnati; from which last place he will probably go to Louisville, Ky.— He will go to Terre Haute, Lafayette, Indianapolis, and perhaps as far West as St. Louis.

A game of croquet is reported to have been played last evening after nine o'clock. There was beautifully clear moonlight, and the game would have been completed had all the players remained a few moments longer. As it was, two became "rovers" and the other two advanced far beyond the "turning stake."

The World's Fair! J. C. Higgins will prepare the samples of traps to be forwarded; H. C. Noyes the the bags; and Mrs. Vanvelzer the fruits.

218 doz. traps ordered to-day. The largest order was from Lloyd and Supplee, La Crosse.

FRUIT ORDERS.

We still have on hand unordered, one hundred and fifty dozen cans String Beans, 12 doz. cans Pie-plant, 25 doz. cans May Duke cherries, 25 doz. bottles and 75 doz. cans Black Cherries, 110 doz. cans Yellow Cherries, 30 doz. bottles and 118 doz. cans Black Raspberries, 20 doz. bottles and 28 doz. cans Strawberries, of the fruit and vegetables already put up; and that is all. The other varieties of cherries and of Raspberries, the Huckleberries, Pine-Apples and Peas are all ordered. At the rate orders are coming in, the above named supply will soon be all called for. In view of this fact I suggest that persons receiving orders be very careful about promising that they shall be filled; and further, that they do not take great pains to get orders for fruits of any kind. Efforts will be made to secure a large supply of Blackberries, Plums, Pears, and Peaches; but there is every indication that we shall be able without much effort to dispose of all we can put up of these fruits. Orders are still desired for all kinds of Jellies on the list, excepting Currant; and orders for Corn and String Beans received with special favor.   w.

METEOROLOGICAL.
Thermometer, Aug. 22.

7 A. M. 63.   12 M. 68.   6 P. M. 59.   Mean 63.

DAILY JOURNAL
OF ONEIDA COMMUNITY.

VOL. 2. AUG. 24, 1866. NO. 46.

FRIDAY.

A trapper writes from Larrabee's Point, Vt.:

"Please to send me six dozen more of your No. 1 or muskrat trap. The trappers here are giving away their old traps and ordering the Newhouse."

Mr. Blood writes that he and his family will start for O. C. to-morrow. He says:

We are very glad we have got so near through here. We shall have some queer things to tell you when we get to Oneida. I think we 'have advertised the Community pretty well here during the last two weeks. I rather believe that it would not have made more talk if we had been taken up bodily into the air out of sight, instead of the move that we are making.

However that may be, that the cause of truth, and God's Kingdom may be advanced, is our hope. We are not troubled by the excitement, we are trusting in God, and are determined to follow what seems to be the direction of his spirit, always regardless of what those that have no regard for the things of the spirit, may say or do.

My pecuniary matters are coming out much better than I had dared to expect, and I have got nearly settled up, and have only to pack up what things we have left and rest perhaps one day, then we will start as I have said.

Hoping soon to be with you, I am yours in the love of Christ,   D. E. BLOOD.

A Boston Spiritualist called yesterday. He was just from the oil region in Pennsylvania, where he has been trying his skill in discovering oil by some kind of spiritual or clairvoyant process with a big name. He did not "strike ile" however, and complained considerably of the unbelief of the people down there. We don't blame them for being unbelieving in quackery.

Wm. Wallace, a machinist who has worked for us for the last eight months, quit last Saturday on account of some disagreement with the boarding-house keeper. He was a man of very industrious habits—a fact appreciated by no one more than himself. He left with the firm conviction that we never should be able to find another such man. On the whole however, the machinists don't particularly care if they do not. Another machinist, a Mr. Glydon, has been hired.

Mrs. Rondthaler writes from New York City that she and Bertha are in quite straitened circumstances, and asks for a return of the three dollars which she sent some time since for pamphlets, or its equivalent in preserved fruit. She also wishes that Bertha might have the privilege of visiting the Community for several weeks.

Our Summer has been quite vibratory—first a warm term and then a cold one. April and early May warm; later May and most of June cold; July very warm; August cold. August thus far has been more like fall in its temperature than like a summer month.

Nineteen meals were served to visitors on Wednesday and thirteen yesterday.

Two men were here yesterday experimenting on a new kind of well. They bored down some 29 feet near the Burt House but failed to get water, and gave up the job. No charges were made, as they volunteered to come and only receive pay if they succeeded. The failure seemed to have been caused by a deep bed of compact clay, apparently almost impervious to water, and of which they did not succeed in reaching the bottom.— At the Depot it is said there is a number of these wells in successful operation. The process is to bore down till they find indications of water and then insert a tube, which terminates at the lower end in a point and is full of little holes. The upper end is attached to a pump.— In favorable situations a constant supply of water is thus obtained.

Mr. Burnham sends us the following testimony to the quality of our preserved peas, from a dealer in New York who does a large business in supplying "upper-ten-dom" in that city:

"DEAR WILLIAM:—Hazzard has tried the Peas sent down to him yesterday and says they are very nice. He would like another 100 cases but I declined the order."

LETTER FROM MR. NOYES.

New York Aug. 23. 1866.

DEAR WILLIAM:—All has gone very prosperously with us in the negotiation with Wells & Co. He has read the manuscript and says he shall put it all in as it is. We have also engaged a first rate picture of large size— 1 lock 5 by 3¾ inches—price 30 dollars. Wells will only use the block for stereotyping, and then it will be ours—he paying us for the use of it what he pleases in copies of the Phrenological Journal. He also has dictated to his reporter a full examination of my head, which is to accompany the picture. So I am likely to get fairly to the front before long. This matter is to come out in the October number, which I suppose is published some time in advance of its date. We are to have opportunity to correct the proof.

Yours heartily.   J. H. N.

METEOROLOGICAL.

Thermometer, Aug. 23.

6 A. M. 59. 12 M. 60. 7 P. M. 59. Mean 59¼.

DAILY JOURNAL
OF ONEIDA COMMUNITY.

VOL. 2.　AUG. 25, 1866.　NO. 47.

SATURDAY.
THE BUSINESS SITUATION

Is now very interesting. The indications of sprightly music in all departments of Community industry were perhaps never more favorable. The demand for fruit is unprecedented; the trap orders come in so freely that the trap-makers have resolved to make the best use of their present facilities, and increase their force as rapidly as they can advantageously; the cry of "more help —twenty orders behind!" comes up from the satchel factory; the horticulturists are likely to be efficiently busy in harvesting their varied fruits, and the farmers, with all their teamsters, are busy in many ways. It is indeed a grand harvest time; and as Mr. Hamilton remarked yesterday, let us make the most of it, with our attention on the great educational projects which have lately been placed before us.

Let us thank God for the present opportunity to make money—not for its own sake—but for the results which may be accomplished by it.　　　　　w

We are having good luck in getting blackberries. 13 bushels were received yesterday and 12 bushels this morning. They are obtained in Vienna, Oneida County.

A Mr. Pierce of St. Charles, Illinois, a subscriber to The Circular was here last night. He had been to Rutland, Vt. He was a pleasant, well-informed man, and came to see the Community at the earnest recommendation of a friend. He expressed himself as highly pleased. For a wonder, he made no inquiries about the Social Theory.

Orders for 200 doz. traps, besides 7 bear traps, were received yesterday. By this morning's mail orders for 182½ doz. were received.

We are having a very fine display of dahlias—finer we think than ever before. Mrs. Sears's garden grows daily more brilliant with its many-hued annuals.

Last night was quite clear and cold, and some thoughts of impending frost crossed our minds as we went to bed. But before morning a gentle breeze sprang up and the danger passed off. We trust the cold term has reached its culmination, and that now we shall have a return of summer weather.

Mr. H. R. Perry's German class have now finished Bokum's "Introduction" and are about to commence Goethe's Faust, using Hayward's translation as an aid.— Their teacher has gone out West for the present and will probably be gone some time; but they have got a sufficiently good start to enable them to continue the study in his absence, which they are diligently doing. So it is not always true that

When the cat's away
The mice will play.
The members of the class are W. H. H., D. J. B., J. Freeman and J. V.

WILLOW PLACE ITEMS.

Mr. Farwell of Boston called on Thursday and left an order for a Spinner, two Spoolers and a Spooling-table, amounting in all to about $675. He wished some alterations made in the journals of the spindles on the Spinner, which were agreed to, after a short discussion. He is a practical silk manufacturer and knew precisely what he wanted, having thereby the best side of the argument.

A letter was received from H. G. A. stating that Rose and Belding would like us to make Stretchers for them for $250, apiece, delivered at Albany—the matter is yet under discussion.

Considerable activity prevails in the Trap-Shop Finishing Dep., and heavy shipments are made almost daily.— Something is doing in the Forging Dep., though it is not fairly under way yet.　　　　　c.

METEOROLOGICAL.
Thermometer, Aug. 24.

6 A. M. 52.　12 M. 63,　7 P. M. 53.　Mean 55½.

DAILY JOURNAL
OF ONEIDA COMMUNITY.

VOL. 2. AUG. 27, 1866. NO. 48.

MONDAY.

Oneida, Aug. 24, 1866.

I wish to thank God for Mr. Noyes's late visit here, and the truths he brought out. I desire to let them sink deep and work in my heart. I have thought with growing interest of the idea that Salvation was not an individual but an organic thing, and it has made me more desirous than ever of seeking unity with my superiors, and to be thoroughly organized into the church. It opens to me a new field of truth and hope, and gives me a greater assurance of salvation.

I thank God for all his dealings with me, and confess a humble loving heart.   C. A. MACKNET.

Frederick reports the results of the raspberry harvest as follows:

Brinckle's Orange, 974 qts. or about 30¼ bushels.
Red,   480 qts. or 15   "
Philadelphia,   450 qts. or 14¼   "
Black Cap (Doolittle's Improved), 114   "

The first crop of Black Caps from one acre was a fraction over 60 bushels. It is expected that another year the crop from the same ground will be at least double that amount. The labor of caring for an acre of this kind of fruit Frederick estimates to be but little more than that required by an acre of corn.

Mr. Burt starts to-day for Portland, Maine, to exhibit the Corn-Cutting machine to the "Packers" in that vicinity. H. G. A. writes that several firms near Portland are desirous of seeing the machine in operation; and if it please them, he thinks they will order quite a number. Mr. Burt will stop on his way at the Agency to put a machine there in working order; and will also call on the Shakers at Canaan 4 Corners, and instruct them in regard to the working of the machine already sent them.

Orders for about 53 doz. traps were received yesterday and to-day.

Mr. Blood and his family arrived on Saturday night.

55 bushels of blackberries were received from Vienna last week. Mr. Bradley and Mr. Worden superintended the buying of them and Mr. Conant attended to the transportation. Mr. Worden is still there and expects to obtain more berries this week.

H. G. A. writes from Portland, Me., that one man in that vicinity intends putting up the present season 500 acres of corn.

Mr. Bradley leaves to-day for the Western part of the State, to attend to the Peach harvest.

BUSINESS MEETING.

Mr. Hamilton on behalf of the Dairy Committee reported that he had consulted with Mr. Noyes as to the best location for any new building that might be erected for dairy purposes—that various sites had been proposed and that the plan now considered the best, was to appropriate the present fruit-room to dairy use as soon as it can be had and to build an addition to the north-west corner of the Tontine so as to have increased accommodations for the growing necessities of the preserving business. The Committee did not intend this plan as a final decision, but merely as a proposal to be thought over by those interested.

George E. Cragin, on behalf of the women expressed a wish that some reform should be made in the women's and children's compartments of the privy building. He thought that the wooden receptacles for slops should be replaced by iron ones and partitioned off from the children's place,—further that the building in question is too near the dormitories in the west end of the Avenue, which, he suggested might be used for some other purpose than that of sleeping apartments. Voted that A. L. Burt and F. A. Marks be appointed a committee to make the necessary improvements without delay.

Mr. Hamilton reported that a quantity of chips and shavings has been accumulating in the cellar at Willow Place. Recommended that G. W. H. see that they are removed.

W. A. Hinds reported that he had had some conversation with Mr. Noyes lately about Mr. Aiken and the tailoring business. It was thought Mr. Aiken's growing usefulness in buying and selling is such, that it would be well to release him from tailoring altogether, as soon as possible, and have some of our young men learn the business and be ready to take his place. Mr. Hamilton did not think we could spare any of our young men for this purpose at present, and that a better plan would be to advertize again in THE CIRCULAR for a tailor who would sympathize with the views and purposes of the Community.

G. W. H. consulted the board on the expediency of having some one put into the inspecting department at the Trap Factory. He also expressed a wish that those of the family who occasionally help at riveting, should come on to-morrow and aid that department.—Some conversation was held on appropriating C. A. Burt to the Trap-works, provided he could be relieved from it when wanted on Corn-cutters. Mr. Hamilton thought all should be flexible and willing to communize labor by each leaving his own particular business and help in another at a push. Recommended that those who are engaged at Willow Place consult together and each department aid the other in a spirit of Communism and flexibility.

METEOROLOGICAL.

Thermometer, Aug. 25 & 26.

7 A. M. 59.   12 M. 63.   7 P. M. 59.   Mean 60¼
7 A. M. 59.   12 M. 70.   7 P. M. 62;   Mean 63¼

DAILY JOURNAL
OF ONEIDA COMMUNITY.

VOL. 2.   AUG. 28, 1866.   NO. 49.

TUESDAY.

Alfred Barron and Augusta Hamilton arrived last night.

On Sunday evening the first meeting of the Theological and Elocutionary class, met at the call of Mr. Bolles, in the School room, and had an hour's conversation on the objects and purposes of their proposed organization. About twenty-five persons were present, and an earnest spirit of unity prevailed. It was concluded best to meet twice a week at present—on Sunday and Thursday evenings. The following subject was adopted for consideration at the next meeting: What are the best methods of promoting the objects of the class?

Our cold term seems now to be fairly over. Yesterday the temperature began gradually to rise, and to-day is clear and warm.

Miss H. M. Hutchins has commenced taking lessons in dentistry, with a view to qualifying herself for service in that department.

Those who would appreciate the labors of brother Higgins and others should take an occasional trip around the wood-house. There they may see large quantities of old boards, rails and other flood-wood piled and stuck up in orderly manner, to season and be ready for kindling our fires during the cold winter days to come.— May Mr. Higgins dwell long on the earth, and his days be blessed.

Mr. Nash and Mrs. Sears are busy this forenoon cleaning the green-house. Bugs and spiders, mildew and parasites of all kinds, are subjected to a thorough bombardment with the syringe.

Preparations are going on for re-roofing the Mansion House, and applying Mr. Kelly's fire-proof preparation to it. Mr. Kelly returned home some time since, after having given Abram and others sufficient instruction as to the mode of mixing and putting on the paint.

A letter was received yesterday from two ladies in Chittenango, asking the privilege of spending two weeks here next month. They say: " We do not wish to come to gratify curiosity but simply to get away from care, and because we can wear a suitable and convenient dress. Last year we spent a month at Dansville Water Cure, pleasantly and profitably. And if you do not take strangers for more than a day or so, we will be disappointed to be sure—but think just as kindly as ever of you, feeling assured you know your own business best. We only care for a sleeping room, wishing to spend most of the time out of doors. Please answer immediately and oblige, stating price of board per week &c."

Of course this proposal was respectfully declined.

On Sunday evening Mr. Hamilton gave a very interesting talk on seeking the spiritual qualifications and power to cast out evil spirits, and the importance of cultivating meekness and humility.

It has been noticed lately that visitors are quite free to go through the vineyards and fruit orchards, and some have been seen helping themselves to fruit. It is thought best to have some notices placed in conspicuous points on the paths leading to the fruit grounds, reminding visitors that they are expected not to enter such grounds without special permission or an attendant.

Heavy orders for traps this morning. Gardner and Co., Milwaukee, order 400 doz. No. 1, 50 doz. No. 1¼, 25 doz. No. 0, 20 doz. No. 2, 10 doz. No. 3, 5 doz. No. 4, and 6 bear traps No. 5. Hibbard and Spencer, Chicago, order 58 doz., Foster & Co., of the same place, successors to Geo. T. Abby, order 67 doz. A letter of inquiry was received from Baltimore.

Mr. Conant arrived home from Vienna this forenoon with over 27 bushels of blackberries, and called immediately for another load of crates to take back with him.

METEOROLOGICAL.

Thermometer, Aug. 27.

7 A. M. 60.   12 M. 79.   7 P. M. 60.   Mean 66⅓.

DAILY JOURNAL
OF ONEIDA COMMUNITY.

VOL. 2. AUG. 29, 1866. NO. 50.

WEDNESDAY.

Victor left the Community Sunday afternoon and has not been heard from since. It was first thought he had probably gone down to Vienna where the blackberries are being picked, but Mr. Conant when he returned yesterday said he had not been there. The family feel quiet about the matter, and believe it will turn out for the best in some way.

Charles Vanvelzer writes from his peddling route as follows:

Champion, Jeff. Co., Aug. 25, 1866.

DEAR WILLIAM:—I am stopping with Mr. Knowles over Sunday. He makes it very pleasant for me. I feel thankful to God for his watchful care over me so far on my journey. I often think of those splendid talks that Mr. Noyes gave, especially the one he gave to the young men the night before I left. The more I get acquainted with the world, the more thankful I am for my Community home. I think I shall get around home this week. Business is somewhat better than it was. I have sold out most of my load except silk; I have quite a quantity of that, but mostly of colors unsaleable at this time of year. I have sold nearly $400 worth up to this time.   Yours, C. VANVELZER.

Mr. Leete is here—came yesterday morning, and we understand will return this evening.

Orders for 24 doz. traps were received this morning.

Work in the Trap Shop now commences at 5.30 A. M. and continues till 7 P. M., half an hour being allowed for each meal.

Orrin Wright has left the Horticultural Department to assist C. C. Hatch in inspecting Traps.

The first load of plums was received yesterday afternoon, part of them from Syracuse and part from Mr. Bradley, farther west.

Fires are becoming quite numerous in this part of the country. Last night Peckham's store at the Castle was burnt, and a few nights ago there was a large fire at Oneida. On the night of the latter, the conductor of one of the railroad trains said that it was the sixth fire he had passed since leaving Rochester that night.

G. E. Cragin is busily engaged fitting up the new iron steam-vat, which bids fair to be a great improvement on the old wooden vats. It is made strongly of cast-iron, and will stand a heavy pressure.

A corn-cutter was shipped yesterday by express, to Mr. Burt at Portland.

A ditch is being dug on the eastern side of the road near the Hamilton bridge, for the purpose of straightening the Creek, which threatens to seriously undermine the high bank near the boarding-house.

The talk on the Cragin Family was read last evening and heartily sympathized with. Much love was also expressed for Mr. Cragin. George and Charles fully endorsed Mr. Noyes's view of their relation to each other and to their father.

The upper story of the main part of the Store is being plastered and finished off.

The new tool-house is being painted brown.

To-day is warm cloudy and misty.

From F. M. Bradley, the great grape grower of East Bloomfield in this State:

"I receive your CIRCULAR regularly, and peruse it with great interest. May God speed you in your good work."

METEOROLOGICAL.

Thermometer, Aug. 28.

7 A. M. 66.   M. 70.   7 P. M. 58.   Mean 67.

DAILY JOURNAL
OF ONEIDA COMMUNITY.

VOL. 2. AUG. 30, 1866. NO. 51.

THURSDAY.

WILLOW PLACE ITEMS.

G. W. H. gives the following information in regard to the ability of the Trap-shop to meet orders. Of No. 0, about 5,000 are now being finished off. Of No. 1, 4,000, or 5,000 on hand—a lot of 30,000 under way. No. 2, none on hand—4,000 or 5,000 can be put up next week if necessary. Nos. 3 and 4, nearly out. 2000 No. 3, and 4,000 No. 4 will be put up in two or three weeks. Twenty-two hired hands are employed in the Trap-Shop together with ten of our own folks.

A juvenile whose ideas concerning *meum et tuum* were doubtless a little foggy, was disagreeably interrupted in his labors in one of our apple trees by Orrin Wright, who surprised and captured him before he had got his basket nearly filled. When arraigned before Mr. New-house and mildly questioned, he made, amid many tears, numerous confused and contradictory statements. It was finally discovered that his grandfather lives near by; whereupon the young man was requested to leave his basket, and go home and ask his grandparent to give us a call.   C.

Orders for about 175 doz. traps were received this morning.

11 orders for preserved fruit, mostly for small amounts, were also received by to-day's mail.

Our first meal of tomatoes this season was served yesterday for dinner.

Our trapper friends, Messrs. Holland and Gunter, of Canada, in a recent letter, give the following results of their trapping during the last three years:

"We give the amount of Furs we have caught for three years, for the trapping class to judge of for themselves, and to encourage those in new countries who, besides farming during the Summer, may have opportunity for trapping in Winter. For the years 1863 and '64 we will give the No. of skins we caught, as we kept a memorandum of them. In 1863 we caught 98 mink, 52 marten 14 fisher, 10 otter, 53 beaver, 5 wolves, 13 coon, 7 foxes and 280 rats. In 1864 we caught 89 mink, 47 marten, 9 fisher, 9 otter, 10 foxes, 6 coon, 240 rats, 5 wolves and 63 beaver. In 1865 we kept no account of the No. of skins, as we sold in so many parcels, but we will give the sales. First in the Spring $138, in the Fall $222,50 at one time, $77,50 at another, and $67 for fur sold in March caught in 1865, in all $505. In these three years we caught 137 deer.

"The most of our furs of last year's trapping we sold to the Oneida Community, to whom we recommend all trappers to sell, as we found them to be honest in all respects; and we think they are entitled to the first offer of furs, as they make the best traps now in use in America.   PETER M. GUNTER.
                                          ROBERT HOLLAND.

" *Millbridge, Hastings County, C. W., Aug. 1866.*"

TO THE COMMUNITY.

O. C., Aug. 28, 1866.

DEAR FRIENDS:—I thank God, and you, for the kindness and care which I have been and am receiving of him at your hands. I don't feel that I have any right or claim to it, but my heart swells with gratitude to both Him and you for it, as I conceive of its pure and disinterested character. And I confess through Christ who is the mediator of it all, a thankful, loving heart in return for it. I also take this opportunity of confessing my love for Mr. Noyes, and my acceptance, as the truth, of his ideas lately brought out relating to Salvation from sin, being alone within the Community or church.

Yours for improvement,   WILLIAM JONES.

CAUTION.

We would call the attention of the family to the importance of using great care in disposing of salt water, from the ice cream works or any other source. It should never be thrown upon the lawn or grass plots, or near any shrubbery. Several fine shrubs have been either injured or killed, and one large Norway Spruce has been injured, this summer, by the want of caution in this respect. We hope every one will remember hereafter the dangerous character of brine to vegetation.

METEOROLOGICAL.

Thermometer, Aug. 29.

6 A. M. 69.   12 M. 69.   7 P. M. 60.   Mean 66.

DAILY JOURNAL
OF ONEIDA COMMUNITY.

VOL. 2.   AUG. 31, 1866.   NO. 52.

FRIDAY.
VALEDICTORY.

The undersigned having secured a suitable successor in E. Y. J., to occupy the editorial chair of the TONTINE LUMINARY, respectfully makes his bow and retires. He has no doubt that the same kindly sympathy and help which it has been his good fortune to experience, will be extended to the new editor, and that under her care and management the paper will steadily improve in interest and vivacity as a record of our daily Community life.

Affectionately to all his readers,   T. L. P.

P. S.—The immediate occasion of the writer's retirement, is a contemplated trip to Canada, a month hence, to buy furs. There are indications that we secured a good opening into the fur trade in that section, last season, and Mr. Noyes thinks it will be well to follow it up further and see what we can make of it.   T. L. P.

Quite a quantity of bags have been sold at the Store during the last month, including three or four lunch bags. They were bought mostly by visitors, and but few of them would have been sold if they had not been in the Store. Over $40. worth of goods was sold yesterday. Our trade is evidently increasing.   S.

The Theological class met again last evening, and it was decided to use the Berean in connection with the Bible for our Text Books, and any other theological literature which was suitable. There was a free discussion upon the best method to be pursued and all minds fell into unity upon the plan of using the Berean &c. It is contemplated to vary the exercises as inspiration may lead, perhaps by short speeches by the members, upon the subject of study. There was some talk about a name for the class and several suggested "Bereans"; but it was agreed to refer this point to Mr. Noyes.

A large wagon load of our people enjoyed a pleasant moonlight ride last night after meeting,—the objective point being a fire somewhere on Turkey St. The exact whereabouts of it however was for some time uncertain, though two or three veracious young gentlemen successively, announced in the most positive manner that it was the Foundry, the Iron Store House, John Thomas's Cider-Mill, Mr. Filley's Cider Mill, the Tile Factory, and most any thing that was situated on the north side of the Street. A brush heap was finally settled upon, and the party turned homeward before reaching it. Mr. Dunning was presently overtaken who informed us that the conflagration was a barn belonging to Mr. Myers with 20 or 30 tons of hay—no cattle. As no lantern had been used there, it was supposed to have been set on fire.
     C.

Mr. Thacker arrived last night, from Wallingford.

The following orders were received by last evening's mail, from H. G. A. from Canada. 146¼ doz. traps, and over $800 worth of fruit and vegetables.

Ten trap orders were received by this morning's mail, in all 570¼ doz. Willis Cornell and Carey of New York, order 105 doz., Quackenbush Townsend and Co. of New York, 108 doz., and Enoch Woods of Chicago, 128 doz.

TRAP DISCOUNTS.

The letters of our agents indicate that they are occasionally tempted to give the highest of discount, 15 per cent., to the second or third class firms, who may offer to order one or two hundred dozen traps; and the home department is sometimes subject to the same temptation.

As remarked in a previous JOURNAL, (about the time the new trap-list was issued,) the highest rates of discount should be limited to the very largest dealers, such as New York houses, Gardner and Co. of Milwaukee, the Daileys of St. Paul and the Hudson Bay Co. If 15 per cent. discount is given to smaller dealers it will soon make trouble in the family, and tempt such firms as Gardner and Co. to think they should have more than 15 per cent., which cannot be afforded.

Our agents should of course have some discretionary power. They may meet with cases where the interests of the trap trade will require them to deviate from the above rule, but such cases will evidently be rare. The indications are that the Community is getting nearly the whole trap trade, "sweeping the board,"—the prices are now so reduced that fur dealers will not buy other traps if they can obtain the Newhouse traps; so that it cannot be often necessary to deviate from the general rule, by the doz. at list; to common retailers at 5 per cent. discount; to jobbers at ten per cent.; to the very largest houses at 15 per cent. It is hoped that our agents will study to act wisely, and not use too much bait while fish bite so readily. Gardner and Co. recently sent an order for over 500 dozen of large and small traps. Firms giving such orders can complain with apparent reason if the same discount allowed them is given firms who only purchase one third as much, and to whom they have perhaps, themselves formerly sold.   W

ON TO NEW HAVEN—LATEST DISPATCH.

New York, Aug. 30, 1866, 8 P. M.

DEAR DANIEL:—Mr. Cragin has bought a house in New Haven, for two thousand eight hundred and fifty dollars ($2850)—possession Sept. 15. This will give us a home for the students.

In fearful haste,   F. WAYLAND SMITH.

METEOROLOGICAL.

Thermometer, Aug. 30.

7 A. M. 60.   12 M. 70.   6 P. M. 69.   Mean 66⅓.

DAILY JOURNAL
OF ONEIDA COMMUNITY.

VOL. 2.   SEP. 1, 1866.   NO. 53.

SATURDAY.
A DAY'S RIDE.

A party of eight visited the Cascades, near the lime kilns yesterday. The day was everything that could be desired, and the enjoyment of the party seemed to have as little alloy as could be anticipated by the most sanguine. Though this delightful scenery had been visited before by several of the company, yet its many charming features had lost none of their attractiveness. One recalled the time of a visit there in company with the ex-editor of the CIRCULAR, and of his transports over the rocks and scenery, almost hugging the bowlders in the fervor of his enthusiasm.

What with wading and spattering in the pools, and showering under the cascade, the water was not the least attractive feature of the place.

Mr. B. threw a hook and line into the water under the falls thinking that perchance a trout might be induced to add grace and variety to our well filled basket of edibles, but only some of the plebeian tribes could be induced to take the bait. An old dry saw-mill on the border of the cascade, and near its head—in the last stages of decay and dissolution, offered an interesting object for those of speculative tendencies and for antiquarian curiosity.

The ride home through the valley of Siloam, and over West hill, if in some respects a little tedious, gave Geo. E. the pleasure of reviewing some of the scenes of his *first Silk peddling* trip, and of recounting his trials, and fortunes. He had not forgotten the house where he made his first sale, after repeated trials, and the encouragement he derived from it though the amount of the sale was but one cent. And then the grand view from the summit of west hill, of the lake, and the expansive and variegated valley, contributed to put all in good humor for the remainder of the ride.   n.

We have had lively times in the Bag-Shop lately—have been considerbly behind our orders, but are gaining a little now. The oldest order on the book, yet unfilled, was received Aug. 18th. Two women are now employed to work in what has been considered the men's department. They do well.

Bags sent off the last week amount to $669,26. Bags sent off in the entire month of August $2779,31.

Mr. Bradley writes that he has secured two hundred bushels of peaches—the best at $3.

Arrangements have been made by Mr. Bradley and others for a large supply of plums.

Three times as many blackberries have been preserved as was at first intended.

10½ A. M.—Our last load of blackberries has just arrived, and with it our brother M. L. W. who has been absent nearly two weeks, to oversee the collecting and forwarding of the fruit.

Phœbe is about house again, and shares with the other women, in the labors of the family. Her eyes are steadily improving.

Victor has not yet reported himself.

The greatest activity in business prevails at the present time, and every one seems enthusiastic and desirous to do their best to secure this harvest of our industry.—An earnest spirit too, is felt in our evening meetings and a desire is manifest for closer and more vital unity with Christ and the heavens. Mr. Hamilton's talk last night on Victor's case, and the tests by which to distinguish between true and false spirits, was very interesting and instructive.

WILLOW PLACE ITEM.

Yesterday forenoon a young woman with sharp black eyes, came into the Office to settle about those "hooked" apples. The captured boy was her nephew. "Her sister" she said, "told the boy to gather some of those apples, but did not direct him to club the tree." She added scornfully that "she didn't suppose that we cared for *them* apples; the tree was so far off, she didn't imagine we ever thought of gathering them." (The tree stands on the northern edge of the Pond.) She was informed that it is our purpose to gather all our fruit, though our neighbors occasionally save us the trouble. Mr. Newhouse labored with her, till some faint glimmerings of the right in the matter seemed to dawn upon her, when he returned the basket of fruit to her, and dismissed the case.   c.

THE NEW STAMP TAX

Which takes the place of the five per cent. ad valorem tax after October 1st, in respect to all canned fruits and vegetables, will affect the Community interest fovorably, excepting in respect to vegetables. On these the stamp tax will exceed the *ad valorem :* on Tomatoes the tax will be increased about one shilling per doz.; on Corn about eight cents, &c. As the margin of profits is now small on these goods, I would suggest that in taking orders hereafter our agents keep in mind the increased tax and give lower rates of discount than formerly.   w.

WANTED!

A watch for Roswell Hawley. If any person can spare a time-piece, he will do well to hand it to Roswell, whose present responsibilities require him to carry one.

METEOROLOGICAL.

Thermometer, Aug. 31.

6 A. M. 69.   12 M. 75.   7 P. M. 70.   Mean 71½.

DAILY JOURNAL
OF ONEIDA COMMUNITY,

VOL. 2.　SEP. 3, 1866.　NO. 54.

MONDAY.

YESTERDAY'S ITEMS.

Among the visitors was a party from Utica, including Mr. Grove, Editor of the Observer. His daughter Miss Nettie Grove, played a number of pieces on the piano with excellent execution: she also sang Tennyson's "Break, break, break," and other songs.

There was also in course of the afternoon some music by some of the family including several instrumental quintettes by C. A. M., E. P. I., G. E. C., J. F. S. and C. L. V.

Mr. Henry Smith from Canada came here on Saturday evening with a note of introduction from H. W. B. and staid till yesterday afternoon. He had called at the N. Y. B. with a note from Mr. Ames an old friend of H. W. B.'s. A neighbor of his, an Englishman who has taken the Circular several years, desired Mr. S. if he came here, to learn all he could about us.

Henry G. Allen arrived on Saturday afternoon.

Chas. Vanvelzer returned yesterday, having had a successful trip.

Mr. Perry is succeeding well in obtaining orders for Community productions.

Mr. Thacker and Mr. Worden go west this morning to join Mr. Bradley in buying peaches.

The shoemaking establishment has at length been removed to the store building. It occupies the lower story of the north wing. The front room is fitted up as salesroom, and the room to the rear as workshop. We understand it is Mr. Vanvelzer's wish that all orders should be given to himself personally *in the salesroom*. Of course the shoe cupboard in the Mansion House will no longer be used as formerly.

130 bush. of Blackberries have been received, 4,200 qts. put up in bottles, and 1000 in cans. The remainder were consumed in the family. They were mostly collected by L. H. B., M. L. W. and Mr. Conant in the wilds of Vienna, about 22 miles from here. The job was not a very attractive one in itself considered, as it was attended with a good deal of labor and difficulty; but nevertheless, it was done cheerfully and heartily.

☞ Orders have already been received for 9024 cans tomatoes; and though it is expected that the preserving department will put up several thousand more, it is thought best not to receive unconditional orders for any until we are certain of being able to fill them. Agents will keep this in mind, and only receive *conditional* orders for tomatoes.

BUSINESS MEETING.

O. H. Miller mentioned that Mr. Ackley has been somewhat disturbed by the Red Squirrels making nests in the peach-boxes. It was thought that such animals cannot really be considered as ornamental if they are mischievous. The several departments that find the squirrels troublesome were directed to use means for destroying them.

D. F. Knowles reported that there has been some private conversation about the placing of the new wheel at the Foundry water-power. It was considered important that it should be so fixed that the power might be available for various different purposes. Messrs. Hamilton, Kinsley, Inslee and Knowles were appointed a committee to consider the best way of doing it.

S. W. Nash reported that the trees and shrubbery along the front bank are getting badly injured by the cows as they pass daily to and from pasture. The matter was referred to the Lawn Committee to be considered and reported on.

G. W. Hamilton stated that he has had some difficulty in getting goods conveyed from the Depot to Willow Place, jobs having sometimes been delayed for want of material which was lying at the Depot waiting for transportation. The fruit business has of late produced a good deal of extra pressure on the teaming facilities, and it was thought that Homer has as much work on hand as he can well attend to. It was thought however, that while all the responsibilities must rest with Homer, he should be considered free to call on Mr. Clark for help at a push, rather than let any Willow Place goods lie over till he has opportunity of bringing them himself.

Martin reported that Mr. Hubbard has, for a year past, been urging the necessity of straightening the Creek so as to prevent it washing away the land. Messrs. Kinsley, Conant, W. A. Hinds and Martin were appointed a committee to attend to the matter.

G. W. Hamilton mentioned the necessity there is of having a ditch cut at Willow Place to carry the rainwater right down the road instead of allowing it to wear a channel for itself by the side of the building. It was voted that Messrs. Hamilton, Kinsley and Roswell be appointed a Committee to examine the location and report.

Horace Burt inquired whether J. P. Hutchins cannot be relieved from the kitchen to work on trap-springs.— Mr. Kinsley replied that the Appropriating Committee has had that case under consideration, but that there has, of late, been so much difficulty in supplying hands for the different departments that the Committee felt almost as if they were required to make bricks without straw.

METEOROLOGICAL.

Thermometer, Sep. 1. & 2.

7 A. M. 69.　12 M. 84.　7 P. M. 79. Mean 77¼.
7 A. M. 79.　12 M. 82.　7 P. M. 70. Mean 77.

Yesterday was a hot, sultry day. A sudden, short and heavy shower fell about six o'clock P. M.

Brilliant rainbows were observed on both evenings at the same hour, 6 o'clock.

DAILY JOURNAL
OF ONEIDA COMMUNITY.

VOL. 2.   SEP. 4, 1866.   NO. 55.

TUESDAY.

Every part of the Store is at last finished; the plastering of the upper rooms was completed some time last week. The most of our Artisans are now engaged at Willow Place, finishing and ceiling the silk-room.— Some, however, have to be briskly employed in making boxes for packing fruit.

In the store-room adjoining the fruit-room, a set of shelves has been put up to hold the large stock of jellies, jams and pickles which the preserving department has been putting up. The shelves reach from end to end of the store-room, and rise, tier above tier from floor to ceiling. The goodly array of sweetmeats is quite a tempting sight. Were the renowned Vathek, the eater of "three hundred dishes" to get a peep, it would make his mouth water.

The hop crop in this vicinity promises an abundant yield; but the warm weather of the last few days, together with the frequent rains, has caused the hop growers to hasten the harvesting, lest lice should attack the vines. Many loads of hop-pickers passed by yesterday. A man came here this morning to see if he could engage some of our folks to assist him in picking. He did not of course succeed. We are unable at the present time to obtain all the hired help we need at the bag shop.

63 letters were received by this morning's mail, mostly on business.

Thirteen bushels of peaches were received this morning.

We commence putting up corn to-day. It is on a small scale however, and commenced thus early, that George E. may have a chance to experiment upon it before leaving.

Sidney reports that 18 bushels of plums have been gathered from our own trees; they are very nice.

Mr. Hall started this morning on a short peddling trip, of two or three days.

Mrs. Loomis who has had charge of the beds and bedding, making quilts &c. the last year, has handed us the following: Quilts made during the year, 52. Comfortables, 27. Bed Ticks, 24. Mattresses, 22. Pillows, 16 pairs.

157 doz. traps ordered this morning, mostly small orders.

Yesterday's departures: Alfred Barron, and Agusta Hamilton for Wallingford and H. G. A. for New York.

Yesterday's blackberry report was not quite correct.— Besides the 130 bushels collected by Worden and Co. and a few berries brought in by the Indians, several crates were received from other sources—exact quantity unknown. Of these, we have preserved 4,200 qts., 1000 qts. of which were put up in bottles, and the remainder in tin cans. We hope to be more careful in future.

As we are very desirous to improve, and to make the JOURNAL, as much as possible, a faithful, daily record of home life, we invite criticism or any suggestions of improvement at any time, from the family We enter upon our new work with much fear and trembling, and with a keen sense of our incompetency. We look to the family for sympathy and strength.

The following anonymous article was handed us for insertion in the Journal. We think with the writer that if persons would avoid the mortification of seeing their published articles appear in a mutilated state, they should be particularly careful to write them in a fair legible hand.

Willard of the Utica Herald, who is now writing from England to that Journal, complains of the mistakes made by the printer in his letters. It does not seem probable that such mistakes should occur in such a Journal as he mentions, if his manuscripts were legibly written.

It may be no more than just that the complaints of writers to the printers, should fall upon themselves.

The manuscripts of our own Journalists, it has been thought by some, might be improved. They are found difficult to read by those who are not very familiar with the writing. Would it not be well to aim at the best standard of chirography and not make peculiar letters of our own?

METEOROLOGICAL.

Thermometer, Sep. 3.

6 A. M. 68.   12 M. 79.   7 P. M. 60.   Mean 69.

The cold and wet of August have given place to a delightfully warm September. The air is clear and transparent, and all conditions are favorable to the perfecting of both flowers and fruit.

DAILY JOURNAL
OF ONEIDA COMMUNITY.

VOL. 2.　SEP. 5, 1866.　NO. 56.

WEDNESDAY.

YESTERDAY'S ITEMS.

Two men from N. Vt., acquaintances of the Kinsleys, called here in the afternoon and staid till half past ten, P. M. One was Orrin Bentley, a nephew of Harry Montague, and the other Mr. Leach, the husband of young Bentely's sister. We understand they were quite gratified with their call, and would have been pleased to have stopped longer.

An acquaintance also of Mr. Abbott's, Dr. A. N. Henderson from Buffalo, was here to supper. He pretends that he can cure all diseases of whatever name or nature by his Electropathic treatment. Mr. Abbott thinks him a quack, miserly and avaricious, and not very honest.

An infidel named Hyatt called here and made himself very disagreeable to Mr. Bolles by putting forth his offensive doctrines after being requested to desist. He took supper with us, but thought himself ill used because Mr. B. declined to extend fellowship to him. He was treated with more courtesy than he deserved.

The Hamilton stage, crowded with passengers, wishing either to see, or to be seen, or both, drew up toward the house, as if to leave some one of its number, but it passed on steadily and slowly, and in close proximity to our front door.

TO-DAY.

37 Crates of peaches and plums just arrived. Ten crates were sold at the Depot. Now, 11, A. M., the quick stroke of the bell is summoning all hands to the bee.

WILLOW PLACE ITEMS.

Seated at the Inspector's bench, armed with hammer, file and pan-twister the quondam editor of the Luminary may be seen, for the present at any time from 7 A. M. to 6 P. M., noon hour excepted. "P—takes hold well," the Oracle was heard to observe.

6000 or 7000 traps behind orders, is the latest from the Trap-Factory. _Opus fervit._

New faces are seen at the machinery up stairs, and the crowd of small boys perceptibly increases. M. Scheer and J. Solman have each a "caip" in the Chain Room, chattering alternately in German and English.

A new Winder has been started in the Silk Factory, and the Stretcher will be in operation to-day.　c.

LETTER FROM MR. BURT.

On board the cars from Lebanon to Boston, Sep. 1, 1866.

DEAR BROTHER WM.—I arrived at the Shakers on Friday evening, put up the machine in order on Saturday and cut a few ears of corn—enough to try it. They are not ready for general business, and will not be so till the latter part of the week. My plan is to stop there on my return and spend a day in running the machine. There is one feature about their corn-cutting which is new, i. e. they boil the corn before cutting. The effect is to soften the cob so that in some cases the driving-rod will penetrate the cob instead of driving the ear through. This however is not the case except with immature ears. I think I shall be able to suit them. My trust is in God for good success.

I went to Lebanon on Saturday evening and spent Sunday there—was treated quite respectfully by the leading men among the Shakers—attended their meeting, in short had a good look at Shakerdom generally. I was drawn into some considerably interesting conversation in the way of comparing notes on our relative principles. They had read "Male Continence." They commenced upon me by conceding that we are right in the main but wrong in our views about sexual intercourse; they assumed that our true course is to back out of our position and accept theirs—that theirs is the only gospel ground. I sat quietly and heard them through, then boldly but calmly took my position and assumed that they did not, as they supposed, understand us—that we in reality stand on a higher plane than they do—that we have got the key to salvation for the sexual organs—that instead of giving them up to destruction, we consider them the highest instruments of praise and worship in the Heavenly world. I told them that whilst we claim liberty for the the free use of our sexual organs as a means of social enjoyment, improvement and refinement, we at the same time claim them as instruments of discipline—that in reality our liberty is a far more potent engine of crucifixion and destruction to the old, carnal nature than their abstinence is. I told them that instead of their being able to absorb and swallow us up, we expect in the end to absorb them and that ours is a higher calling than theirs.

Well, in the foregoing I have given you but an outline instead of a detailed account of what was said. I had several different talks, they beginning each time and at the same time treating me with respect and courtesy.—

I was by the grace of God enabled to keep cool and aboveboard in my spirit. I felt that the Lord was with me.

What I have written has been whilst the cars were in motion or at the stations. If you can read this I shall be glad. I shall give fuller particulars when I get home.

With much love to yourself and to the whole Community, I am yours &c.　　J. BURT.

METEOROLOGICAL.

Thermometer, &c.

7 A. M. 64.　12 M. 80.　7 P. M. 79.　Mean 74⅓

DAILY JOURNAL
OF ONEIDA COMMUNITY.

VOL. 2.   SEP. 6, 1866.   NO. 57.

WEDNESDAY.

Stirring indications of business meet the eye almost every where throughout the entire Cosmos of the O. C.; but there are points of special interest from which the extent of the Community commerce and manufactures may be comprehended at a glance. One of these is the Store Cellar, 70 feet long, and 40 feet deep at the widest part, appropriated with a trifling exception, as storage for Preserved Fruit and Vegetables. Not only around the walls piled up in orderly rows, but in longitudinal lines of cases built up above each other, extending throughout the wide area, with only narrow passages between, the luscious *fruits* of our industry await the Midas-touch of Commerce to change them into gold—or greenbacks.

Charles Burt returned yesterday from Newark, whither he has been to put a Corn-cutter in working order. He was successful in his mission, proving to Mr. Edgett, the man who ordered the machine, that even an inexperienced workman can cut with it on an average eighteen ears per minute. Charles appears to have had a pleasant time generally. On his return from the preserving factory to the cars he was taken by the old Fox house where the rapping manifestations first commenced in this state. It is now uninhabited, dilapidated and a fit abode for murky spirits.

After the usual news and letter reading, our prospective M. D., G. E. Cragin, occupied the meeting hour, at Mr. Hamilton's request, with a lecture on quackery in medicine and surgery. G. took his stand on the stage, and in a cool, matter-of-fact manner, interspersed with occasional jokes and sarcasms, sketched the history of medical quackery and surgery. The presentation was edifying to all, and instructive to many who had not given the subject any special investigation before.

Mr. Wilson of the firm of Tracy, Irwin and Co. N. Y. called yesterday. He did not seem to know much about us, but made many inquiries and expressed warm sympathy with the movement. On leaving, he contributed $2 to the Cause.

From our window, almost every day, we see Mrs Hamilton slowly walking in the yard. It is a real pleasure to call in her room and witness the cheerfulness and faith with which she bears her severe trials. Surely, God gives her grace equal to her day.

The O. C. sympathizes heartily with the N. Haven project, and wishes Wallingford all success, in her educational pursuits. Mr. Noyes was driven from N. H. 32 years ago in disgrace. But in the long run God suffers no defeat. Mr. N. returns now, armed with 30 years experience, and with the good will at least, if not with the consent, of some of the best men in town, and quietly takes possession of the place. Is it not grand?

The Helianthus or Sunflower, is not usually considered a *fine* flower; but the display made by a group of them at the back of the green house, is really magnificent. There is one double corrolla which measures fully nine inches across.

Mrs. Sears has just brought into the Printing Office, a beautiful little bouquet, composed wholly of white flowers. It is to be added to a splendid one, that one of our workmen procured last night, and is we understand to grace a bridal party.

The carpenters are now busy, finishing the White House. It will soon present a cosey dwelling for an hostler when we find one whom we can like.

A cement floor has been laid in the root-cellar at the cow-barn. Nothing but improvements!

Mr. Joslyn's brother from N. Vt. arrived here to-day with his Wife.

The following letter was received last week from Mrs. Freeman:—

"Schenectady, Aug. 28, 1866.

DEAR JOHN:—Your father has been at work ever since you went away, picking up every thing he could find that he thought was against the Community, and he has almost canvassed the city to publish all to the people of Schenectady, Albany and Troy. He has been to Troy and Albany three or four times. Now, he has gone to New York to see what he can do. He says, that last tract that Mr. Noyes published is enough to condemn him, I heard from several that he was going to break up the O. C. I did not pay any attention to it. This morning he told Kate he was going to New York; I asked him if it was true that he was going to try and break up the O. C.; he said he was. He got a package of those tracts several days before I received that one you sent.— I asked if he sent for them, he said No, he got some one else to send for them.   *   *   *   T. F."

GOOD VERSUS EVIL.

Good is stronger than its opposite, Evil:
The one is of God, and the other, the devil.
Whatever is beautiful, lovely or bright,
Has God for its Author, blest Spirit of Light;
But sickness and sorrow, all discord and strife
That darken this earth, and poison our life,
Proceed from the devil, the father of lies,
Who roams through creation with covetous eyes.
But good, like its Author, must surely prevail,
And all the delusions of satan, must fail,
Christ's Banner is waving, "Salvation from Sin,"
And His Glorious Kingdom, is ushering in.
                                        E. Y. J.

METEOROLOGICAL.
Thermometer, Sep. 5.

7 A. M. 72.   13 M. 80.   7 P. M. 64. Mean 72.

DAILY JOURNAL
OF ONEIDA COMMUNITY.

VOL. 2. SEPT. 7, 1866. NO. 58.

FRIDAY.

Letter from G. E. Cragin to the family, read last night:

Oneida, Sept. 6, 1866.

As I leave for New York to-morrow to resume my medical studies, I wish to express my thanks for my six weeks visit at Oneida. It has been a rich treat to me and I feel like thanking God for it, and for the privilege of being a member of the family, which to me appears a wonderful embodiment of the grace of God.

My heart has been full of love towards all and every one since I have been here, and my desire is that I may become a perfect medium of the Spirit of Truth and love which I feel all around me.

I confess my love for Mr. Hamilton, and entire confidence in him as an inspired man—one whose obedience and receptivity to Mr. Noyes's spirit renders him worthy the love and confidence of all. GEO. E. CRAGIN.

Mother Oneida heartily appreciates her son J's affectionate Good bye. His visit here has been a useful one. The reforms he has instituted, his scientific labors in the preserving department, his lectures and his genial fellowship, will not soon be forgotten by the family. We look forward to a career of wide usefulness for him. The education he has already had has been put to so good use that all feel encouraged by the prospect of what he will yet gain by his further studies.

PEACHES.

Mr. Olds writes from Milwaukee: "Have you succeeded in getting Peaches? Will you be able to get all we want? Great demand for fruit, and will be, no doubt through the season. Put up all you can."

For the information of Mr. Olds and others interested it may be stated that the list price of preserved peaches will be $7 per. doz. in cans—$8,50 in bottles.

Mr. Perry writes from Cincinnati:

Bro. HINDS:—Enclosed I send Mr. D. Flynt's order for bags.

I find two Jobbers have just received invoices for Traps ordered of you direct, viz. Dickson, Clark & Co., and Heron, Rogers & Co. Another firm, Hiram, Hobart & Co. I have induced to write to their buyer who is now in New York, to be sure and call at the Agency and purchase from 800 to a $100 worth. They would have given me the order but did not know what he might have bought. They very much want the Newhouse trap in preference to any other. I think I will go down the the river this afternoon to New Albany and Louisville.

Peaches are selling here by the box at from 5½ to $7 per bushel. Mr. Hollingsworth wanted to come and take charge of Fruit-canning &c. at $1500 per year. I told him I would tell you.

His department here is not as great as Mrs. Van's, and is perfumed with about forty different and distinct smells. I have received the price lists &c., also the letter, inclosing that of Mr. Olds.

Bags and traps were a little dull yesterday, and I took a turn at advertising, and made more money than I have spent yet. I suppose you will now direct to me at La Fayette. Yours, H. R. PERRY.

WILLOW PLACE ITEMS.

Ten hired girls now find work in the Silk Room. Not far from 60 lbs. of silk have thus far been wound off, cleaned & most of it doubled; the spinning has begun in earnest. The Stretcher and Reel both work well so far as they have been tried. The carpenters have finished ceiling the room, and the walls have been thoroughly whitewashed. It begins to look like a real Silk Factory.

A letter was received from Farwell yesterday ordering a Cleaner, with a hint of several more machines he should wish us to make for him ere many months, if we suit him as to workmanship, terms etc. c.

Another Catholic Priest called here yesterday; we understand he is from the West Indies. The existence of the O. C. is really a more serious occasion of alarm to the Roman Hierarchy than the preaching of Martin Luther was.

Mr. Thacker writes that he has met a man who "saw Victor at Smyrna:" the man "thought he was half crazy." Mr. Hall thinks he may be mistaken in the person, as he has himself seen a man there, that he thought was crazy.

Last evening, G. E. C. addressed a few words of caution to the family on the use of ether.

There was a grand family bee this morning at 5 o'clock. 25 crates of plums and 2¼ bushels of peaches were got ready for the preservers.

The carpenters have got their scaffolding erected in front of the Mansion House and will commence shingling it immediately.

Carrie walks around now, without the aid even of a cane, and goes down and takes her meals with the family. Alice N. too, has walked without crutches more than a week.

Two ladies from Vineland, one the wife of M. L. W's nephew, staid here last night. Mrs. Worden was quite disappointed in not finding her Uncle at home.

Mr. Joslyn's brother and his wife left this morning, well pleased we should think, with their short visit.

W. G. K. arrived home this morning.

METEOROLOGICAL.

Thermometer, Sept. 6.

6 A. M. 70. 12 M. 72. 7 P. M. 70. Mean 70⅔

DAILY JOURNAL
OF ONEIDA COMMUNITY.

VOL. 2. SEPT. 8, 1866. NO. 59.

SATURDAY.

Mr. Burt writes an interesting letter from Boston.—Speaking of his visit to Mr. Rumery's establishment he says: " I put my machine in order and cut my first basket-full of about 150 ears at the rate of about 30 per minute with a crowd of spectators around me. I put the whole basket-full through without stopping. Countenances brightened up considerably one after another, and the remark was made, 'I guess you will succeed after all.'"

Mr. B. adds " I have got pay for coming here in what I have learned of their plan of filling cans."

This being the season of bees we might mention that the winged sort have been somewhat troublesome of late. The hives that were kept in the meadow south of the horse barn have been sending their agents into the preserving room to help themselves and annoy their neighbors. So the other evening, Mr. Conant, D. P. N. and Myron started off with the hives in the direction of the W. P. apiary; but although the doorways of the hives were pretty well secured, the jolting of the wagon at once wakened up the captives and set them at liberty. And then—what a time there was! Old Grey had to be unhitched leaving the wagon and hives by the roadside, but by no means leaving the bees. Alas, no!—All were stung but Myron who was saved by forswearing the use of his razor. *He combed seven out of his beard!* Hence the propriety of beards.

Bags sent away during the week ending Sept. 7, amount to $472,74. There are 20 unfilled orders on the books of this department, and the scarcity of help makes it almost impossible to keep up with the demand.

210 doz. trap orders received yesterday, including 60 doz. from Mr. Olds, Milwaukee, 75 do., from Geo. R. Barton, Syracuse, and 53 doz. from G. C. Cone, Mc Gregor, Iowa.

Some of the first-fruits of our vineyard were gathered yesterday, and 24 Pockets of the Luscious Delawares were sent to Highland and Smith, Boston.

An interesting letter from Mr. Towner was read last evening and will be forwarded to the other Communes. The invitation contained in it, we rank with such other events as Mr. Dixon's visit, the recent notice in the Evening Post, the forth coming, article in the Ph. Journal, the New Haven project &c., all of which shows how the tide is moving.

H. M. H. called at the printing office this morning with a pair of new forceps in her hand. With their fierce jaws and scaly-like handles, we could only compare them to a young alligator, but Helen seemed to gloat over them with the eye of a savant in dentistry.

Little Ransom has been teething, and has not been very well of late. He has manifested a wilful spirit at times, and Sunday, it seemed to culminate in a fit of obstinacy. Mr. Woolworth was obliged to correct him and it was 2½ hours before he yielded, which he did at last heartily. He has been more docile, and better in health ever since.

To give the Printing Office staff of our Mount Tom exchange some idea of the contrast between the leisurely and oft-repeated proof-readings of their weekly, and the hurried push and drive of our daily, we might say that most of the letters we print reach us about 11 A. M. and have frequently to be transcribed before passing to the compositors. The proof-reading is necessarily confined to the merest glance, and the papers have to be driven through the press with a rush in order to catch the mail at 1 P. M.

We trust our brothers and sisters will take these things into consideration, and not be too severe upon us, if, under these circumstances, mistakes do some times go uncorrected.

In the great pressure of business, our Croquet ground seems comparatively deserted. A few persevering ones however, catch half an hour's leisure occasionally, to spend in this interesting amusement.

O. C., *Sept. 6, 1866.*

DEAR LUMINARY:—Will you let your light shine upon a little fault some of the more thoughtless are addicted to, that they may see and reform? Certain ones, who may here be nameless, have a practice of winking insinuatingly when desirous of pleasing, cajoling, or simply to give force to what is being said; others of pouting out the lips very invitingly when piqued. Both practices become habits with those who indulge themselves in them. Though innocent enough in themselves, these acts are liable to be misconstrued, and to produce different effects from those intended. Should it not be borne in mind that we are almost constantly under public inspection? Besides, should pretty mouths make themselves unnecessarily tempting to those who with difficulty refrain from tasting of forbidden fruits?

Very respectfully and earnestly, OCULUS.

METEOROLOGICAL.

Thermometer, Sept. 7.

7 A. M. 70. 12 M. 72. 7 P. M. 60. Mean 67½.
Cool and showery.

DAILY JOURNAL
OF ONEIDA COMMUNITY.

VOL. 2. SEPT. 10, 1866. NO. 60.

MONDAY.

BUSINESS MEETING.

G. W. Hamilton presented the necessity there is of having some improvements made on the Willow Place boarding-house. It seems that the sitting-room is in a very unattractive condition, its furniture deficient and its wall-paper dirty. The want of improvement is felt all the more on account of our having a number of women boarding there now. Voted that the Boarding-house Committee be instructed to have the room fitted up comfortably.

W. A. Hinds spoke of the worn-out condition of the pump over the engine room. Voted that Mr Inslee and G. W. H. be appointed to examine the pump and have a new one if necessary.

W. A. H. reported that a letter has been received from a Tailor at Port Byron in reply to the advertisement in the Circular. Action on the matter was postponed until details should be learned regarding a similar application that has been made at Wallingford.

Myron stated that all ice used in the home boarding-house has heretofore been carried thither by hand daily. It was suggested that the best remedy for this inconvenience be thought over so as to have better arrangements next year.

W. H. Woolworth suggested that, owing to the press of business in the Bag-department and the want of help, it might be necessary to notify our agents that they exercise caution in accepting orders for these goods. W. A. Hinds thought that all orders should be generally accepted, but that agents should notify our customers that it may not be possible to fill their orders immediately.—He thought it quite important that we do all we can to fill the bag orders received and so retain our present customers. If they find that we cannot supply them, they will be induced to order from other manufacturers, and thus we may lose, not only their present, but also future trade.

It seems that the chief difficulty in regard to help, is the want of lodging accommodations. After some general conversation on the subject, Mr. Hamilton suggested that by the family's economizing our own sleeping accommodations, we might be able to give up the bed-rooms in the Tool-house and perhaps of the Tontine for the use of help during the next six weeks, and so make room for as much additional help as would carry us through our present press. Some remarks were made about appropriating the Dunn cottage to the use of our hired help. Mr. Hamilton thought it would conform better with Mr. Noyes's ideas, to reserve that cottage as a sanctum for the Theological class—perhaps for Mr. Bolles. It was a good place for prayer and meditation. There was some conversation on the full tide of business that seems to be coming in upon us. W. A. H. remarked that God seems to be granting this success in business as the complement of the inspiration which has thrown out the New-Haven project, and other educational schemes. G. W. Hamilton thought that a spirit of humility should be cultivated in connection with our success. Mr. Hamilton considered that God is now educating our faith: we have, of late, made some heavy investments and have had some considerable expenses, some of which were unlooked for at the time and God had the other day supplied $3000 most opportunely. Mr. H. thought that we are under the influence of Heavenly Financiers, who would have us look to them —that we should cultivate a spirit that does not fret, but acts under faith and inspiration.

PRICE OF PEACHES.

In accordance with the suggestion of H. G. A. and other agents, it is thought best to hold the Peaches at $7 50 per doz. in cans and $9.00 in bottles, instead of $7. in cans and $8,50 in bottles, as stated in Friday's Journal.   w.

☞ Agents are hereby informed that the stock of D, Ladies' Satchels is exhausted, and that no more of this style will be manufactured.   w.

"I've brought home the first skein of silk." These were C's words when he returned from W. P. yesterday where he had spent the greater part of the day; and we forthwith expected him to take from his vest pocket a shining little five-cent skein of sewing silk. But we were completely mistaken. What he showed us was more like a skein of white woolen yarn, only that the threads were quite fine, and instead of their being glossy they were quite dull, owing, we believe to the soap-suds that had been applied during manufacture. In fact this skein of silk was ready for the dyer, but by no means ready for use.—If there is any such thing as luck in days, we take it as a good omen that these first fruits of the S. F. were gathered on the first day of the week.

The preservers have begun putting up tomatoes. The demand for them is great. One man in N. Y. city would like to engage 1000 doz. Some of the enthusiastic talk about raising 25 acres of tomatoes next season.

L. H. Bradley, "the flying artillery," as Mr. Thacker calls him, returned home Saturday night, or rather Sunday morning, about 2 o'clock, and started back again last night. He has had good success thus far, ably seconded by Messrs Thacker and Worden. He is instructed to furnish us with three hundred bushels of peaches and one hundred bushels of plums the present week. He expects to pay over one thousand dollars for fruit within the next six days.

Mr. Hatch returned on Saturday night. The children were overjoyed to see him, expressing their delight in a thousand little innocent ways, as children best can.— Mr. Woolworth is to remain in the children's department for the present, and Mr. Hatch will engage in other business.

Our company yesterday, was composed chiefly, of Hop-pickers; several loads called, during the day.

Several mistakes occurred in the last No. of the Journal, the most ludicrous of which, was relative to Trap orders—instead of 210 doz. trap orders, &c. it should have read 210 doz. traps ordered—Mr. Burt's letter also was written from Portland instead of Boston as reported.

METEOROLOGICAL.
Thermometer, Sept. 8 & 9.

7 A. M. 64. 12 M. 70. 7 P. M. 69.   Mean 67¼
7 A. M. 64. 12 M. 72. 7 P. M. 64.   Mean 66⅓

DAILY JOURNAL
OF ONEIDA COMMUNITY.

VOL. 2. SEPT. 11, 1866. NO. 61.

TUESDAY.
PRESERVED FRUITS, &c.

I promised to keep Agents and others informed through the Journal, of the condition and prospects of the fruit business.

10,802 cans Tomatoes ordered—can't accept any more unconditional orders at present—would not advise giving more than five per cent discount on orders received conditionally on our being able to fill them—better if sold at list.

16,040 cans Sweet Corn ordered. We hope to put up 40,000 Send on the orders.

More Peas ordered than didn't "swell up."

About 130 doz. cans String Beans are unordered.

Would rather not receive unconditional orders for Pears in either cans or bottles at present.

Nearly all the Peaches that will be put up in bottles, are ordered. 4,963 cans are ordered; it is expected that several thousand more cans of Peaches will be put up. The price of peaches, it is finally concluded, will be $7,50 per doz. in cans, and $9,00 in bottles, as stated in yesterday's Journal.

We can fill orders for Black and Yellow Cherries in cans, and for no other cherries either in cans or bottles.

Unless we have special good luck in procuring Lombard and Damson Plums, we shall be unable to fill any more orders for these fruits. We have on hand a good supply of Yellow and Green Gages in both cans and bottles.

The present prospect is that we shall be able to fill all orders for Quinces we shall be likely to receive, but only a limited quantity will be put up in glass, and Agents are requested to receive orders only for Quinces in cans.

No Pine-Apples unordered.

Of Raspberries there are still unordered about 200 bottles and 1,250 cans of Doolittle Black.

Strawberries and Huckleberries are all ordered.

We are better prepared to fill orders for blackberries than any thing else.

Of pie-fruits (i. e. fruit put up without syrup) we have only Blackberries at $5 per doz.

We shall probably have what pickled fruits will be ordered, though not anxious at present for large orders.

Orders are acceptable for all kinds of jelly excepting Currant.

DEAR EDITRESS:—The above statistics may appear dry and uninteresting to some of your readers; but their publication will serve a good purpose in conveying useful information to the several agents, and will save the trouble of writing to each one of them.　　　　w.

"Croquet may be a very fine affair; but commend me to a turn at the good old-fashioned game of nine-pins." By some such expression as this we can imagine our New York brethren handling the well-turned pins which Abram has been making for their use. We wish our monastic brethren much good fellowship in their play.

Victor came home this morning at about 4 o'clock.—Myron went to Sherburne after him, and though he at first objected to coming, he at last consented.

Our Community now presents itself to strangers as a hive of industry; who can doubt it? And yet we are not like the world devoted to mammon.

Christ says to his disciples: "This is the work of God, that ye believe on him whom he hath sent." This work of faith is the principal thing with us at least, and no amount of outward activity will atone for the neglect of cultivating it.

Mrs. Chesbro came just at dusk last night. Not finding our folks at the Depot, she came up on foot. The first words she said were: "Am I welcome?" She wrote to Mr. Hamilton some time ago, expressing regret at her course and asking forgiveness. We should think she had suffered a good deal in consequence of being cut off from us, and was desirous to do anything, or take any position that would bring her into sympathy with the family.

A letter was received a few days since, from a young lady in Woonsocket R. I. She has heard of us, and is desirous to join; says she can bring good recommendations.

Traps, ordered, Saturday and Monday, 150 doz.

The Circulars arrived in good season and seem peculiarly sparkling.

METEOROLOGICAL.
Thermometer, Sept. 10.

7 A. M. 59.　12 M. 68.　7 P. M. 64.　Mean 61¼

DAILY JOURNAL
OF ONEIDA COMMUNITY.

VOL. 2. SEPT. 12, 1866. NO. 62.

WEDNESDAY.

HINTS TO CROQUET-PLAYERS.

One secret of the popularity of this game, evidently is its adaptation to both sexes. Then the question arises, how can the men best preserve this social and civilizing feature—the partnership of the women? First, I should answer, let the gentleness and moderation of the women, modify the tendency to excess and competition in the men. The violent way in which many of the men croquet their opponent's balls, seems very directly calculated to spoil the attractiveness of the game, especially for the women, and more or less for all parties. Very hard striking of the balls is clearly at variance with the character and intent of the game, and is repugnant to the more refined and delicate feelings of those who engage in it. Again, violent striking is destructive to the implements, the balls and mallets. No one who has observed, can have failed to notice with regret, the way balls and mallets have been broken and used up, since the game was introduced here. Lack of implements, and disinclination of any body to make more, will soon deprive us of the game unless reform and a higher civilization are introduced.

The toning down of the eagerness and excess of the masculine element, would, in the humble opinion of one at least, add very much to the attractiveness of the game, and serve very much to perpetuate it, as a pleasant and improving pastime.   H.

We were not a little amused the other day, while out on the Croquet ground. Several of the younger boys were playing with a good deal of zest, we thought, when one of the urchins received report that supper was nearly ready, and was to consist of fried potatoes. "Here, who'll take my place!" he exclaimed suddenly, at the same time dropping his mallet, "Fried 'taters for supper—I can't play any more now—I must go in this minute," and away he ran, evidently very much excited.   L. M.

We sat in the mellow sunlight admiring the splendor of the ripening foliage and all the inexplicable charms of a fresh morning in early Autumn. Presently the rain began to fall and blend with the glittering rays very beautifully. This suggested a rainbow; and on turning to the west, lo! a gorgeous iris spanned the heavens, made all the more striking by a background of dark-frowning clouds. The effect was inexpressibly charming. Rain soon fell quite copiously; yet the sun shone calmly down till at length the fast-rushing clouds obscured his rays. But in a few minutes, thanks to a westerly breeze, the shower had passed.   X.

"Now, don't be putting that in the Journal"—"There now, they're sure to have it in the Journal." These and like expressions salute our ears from time to time when we are in quest of items. Sometimes the very children, when anything befalls them, warn each other—"Take care: you'll be put in the Journal." One day we were quietly sitting at dinner with calmest feelings when somebody came and said a great many dreadful things to us, all because they had got into the Journal. Has the Wallingford Journalist any such experience as this?

We have, as yet, shingled only the east side of the Mansion House, and that was done almost wholly in the rain. Abram thinks he shall not attempt to do any thing to the other side till the Barometer indicates fair weather.

The drain and vat for economizing soap-suds have been completed and will serve an excellent purpose.— It seems to us one of the phials of Nature's laboratory— She is the true alchemist who transmutes objects least pleasing to the senses, into waving fields of grain and clusters of aromatic fruit.

71 crates of Peaches came last night, in a condition that required immediate attention, so a bee was called for this morning at 5 o'clock.

There is something quite charming about these family bees. The various little knots of workers, grouped unceremoniously around the end of a table, elbow to elbow, knee to knee—the rippling laugh or vivacious chatter—the ever active fingers—all combine to make such gatherings like the very cream of Community life.

Our Plum crop is harvested. The amount gathered is 61 bushels: mostly Lombards.

Our farmers are ploughing the middle pasture of the Hitchcock farm, and sub-soiling it to the depth of six inches. They are mowing rowen on that place, but experience great inconvenience, from the repeated rains.

The scientific corps of the Luminary now includes Rosamond, who makes the regular meteorological observations.

Miss Rice the noted songstress, accompanied by a young gentleman was here again day before yesterday and took dinner—she did not sing, however, this time.

A niece of Mr. Higgins's from Ohio, with another lady came last night.

METEOROLOGICAL.

Thermometer, Sept. 10.

6 A. M. 69.   12 M. 60.   7 P. M. 69.   Mean 69.

DAILY JOURNAL
OF ONEIDA COMMUNITY.

VOL. 2. SEPT. 13. 1866. NO. 63.

THURSDAY.

We make short extracts from Emily Otis's letters received yesterday :

"Father tells me that I ought to be doing something to earn my living; I told him I would like to be a typesetter but I did not expect to go out in the world and do it, as the world is now. I do not think he would oppose my going to Oneida, and would feel relieved, but Tilton tells him he must not say I may go, as that would be countenancing the Community. I expect to have a talk with him this week and have it settled. Would the Community be willing I should come if he did not oppose? When I first came home, mother said she wanted me to stay as long as she did, for there would be such an opposition, and she dreaded to meet it, but yesterday she told me she was getting where she could face the shame, and rejoiced that she had a daughter that was counted worthy. They expect if she is away from Mrs. Bushnell's and my influence, she will give it up, but I feel that she will gain her own freedom."

"If I come this fall, and it seems best for mother to visit you I shall be glad. I have picked more blackberries this summer than ever before. I have sold about six dollars worth to Uncle Francis and Sophie, besides having all we wanted in the family for present use and for winter; we put up more than usual as other fruit is scarce excepting grapes at Hammondsforte. It was the first of my picking berries to sell, but I enjoyed picking them. Theodore said he was afraid I would use it for the Community. I told him I did not know where it would go—it might be there and it might not—I should do with it just what I thought God wanted me to."

We are so far removed from the world, and our worldly relatives, that a visit from them, necessarily causes a faint ripple on the surface of our life. Such was the case a few days ago, when Mr. Joslyn's brother whom he had not seen for fourteen years came unexpectedly to see him.

He came from the Depot, with a horse and carriage, that Homer procured for him, because his own wagon was so heavily loaded. On arriving here, and assisting his wife to alight, and not seeing a place at the New House to hitch his horse, he drove directly over to the Mansion House and commenced fastening his horse to the chain post, at the corner of the house, leaving his carriage standing directly across the road.

Mr. J. was just emerging from the house and seeing him (a stranger as he supposed) hitching his horse right in the passage way he said to him in rather a rough way

"You will find entertainment, sir, at the other house and some one to take care of your horse; that is no place to hitch him." "I found no place over there to hitch him" said he, "and I came to see *you*."

"Well I am to be seen" said Mr. J. "but I dont know you;" he kept walking slowly along all the time, and scarcely deigned him a look, and it was not till his brother said the second time, "I came to see you, and Hannah came with me," that he recognized him as his brother, and replied "Is it possible that it is you, Israel."

YESTERDAY'S ITEMS.

Yesterday, the family were taxed to the utmost, and the call for "more help," from the preserving room, was oft repeated. In the afternoon the girls from the Bag-Shop were called in to assist, and not far from 80 bushels of peaches were put up during the day.

360 lbs. of Delaware grapes and Hartford Prolific, picked yesterday. 600 in all, have been picked this season.

G. W. H. went to Seneca Falls, yesterday, and purchased a new pump, for the Steam Engine.

Traps ordered yesterday 391 doz. Among others,
75 doz. from Pratt & Co., Buffalo,
48 " " R. D. Cone, Winona, Minn.,
50 " " Terrill & Johnson, Auburn, N. Y.,
42 " " Pruyn & Son, Albany. N. Y.,
50 " " A. H. Gardner & Co., Milwaukee.

TO-DAY.

To-day we received from Mr. Perry one bag order and six trap orders. He writes from Springfield, Ohio :—"The Indianapolis Journal gave me a 'Pass', so I thought I would take a little shoot out this way."

The fruit agents are having excellent luck in securing peaches.

Four women are now employed to pack grapes, and it is thought it will require at least a dozen, as soon as the fruit is all ripe.

Mr. W. H. Graves, from Hoosick, in the eastern part of this state, a nephew of Miss Thomas's, called on his way west, and staid over night.

METEOROLOGICAL.

Thermometer, Sept. 12.

7 A. M. 70. 12 M. 72. 7 P. M. 70. Mean 70½

DAILY JOURNAL
OF ONEIDA COMMUNITY.

VOL. 2. SEPT. 14, 1866. NO. 64.

FRIDAY.
A QUEEN BEE !!!

There arrived at the Depot yesterday, one hundred and thirty-nine crates of peaches, of which about twenty were sold at Oneida and the rest brought home. To meet the necessities of such a supply, the Theology and German classes were suspended, a bee was started immediately after supper, and the fruit-room was soon well filled. The Willow Place hands soon joined the party, and then the room was crowded to overflowing. A further addition consisting of hired help who had volunteered their aid, (about thirty we believe,) soon made their appearance and were accomodated in the laundry, while a few of our own people, forming a cozy group of their own, met in the parlor of the old childred's-house. Altogether, the numbers, including the preservers down stairs, amounted, we understand, to 171 persons.

The bee was a complete success, and yielded about 800 quarts of fruit to the preservers, which was all put up. We have never seen anything so brilliant. It was perfectly electric. The condensation of magnetic life produced a general sparkle and flash of mirth and humor throughout the bee. The arrival of Uncle Horace was hailed by a chorus of sopranos calling " Come and sit by me," " Come over here," or " This way, Uncle." So cordial a welcome would have mellowed Uncle H's heart if it hadn't been mellow before, and he contributed several songs, of which, in the wealth of our recollection, we can only remember something about a " little dog, sixteen feet high," and a " large horse about four inches high." These songs brought our good Uncle the most unprecedented applause. Several rondos and songs with choruses, were sung and participated in by the mass.

Among other songs, " Dearest May" was given by Mr. Inslee, " John Brown" by Abram, and " There was a man in our town" by a company of jovials. It was at first intended to drop the bee at half past eight and have the ordinary meeting; but the affair was too good to be broken up so early, and so was kept up till nine o'clock, about which time a musical deputation went into the ironing-room and serenaded the volunteers who were mostly in that room enjoying themselves immensly.— We are not sure but that the hilarity of the occasion was owing in some degree to the expectation of Mrs. Skinner's arrival. Certain it is that long after the bee was over, the excitement seemed to prolong itself in the various sitting-rooms.

There is one point further, worthy of peculiar note.— While most merry-makings which we have seen in the world were succeded by miserable lassitude in the morning, with this, as with most Community merry-makings, it was quite different. We felt the flashes shooting athwart the breakfast table this morning like the last tossings of a storm sparkling into sunshine.

WILLOW PLACE ITEM.

ACCIDENT.—One of our juvenile Teutons had an experience not altogether felicitous with a belt, yesterday. While at work in the Tom Room he amused himself by putting a peice of leather between a belt and pulley.— Unfortunately, he did'nt let go of it soon enough; his hand was caught and carried around the pulley, jerking his body against the shaft and his head against a post.— He was picked up half senseless, but recovered so as to be able to go on working. It is thought that he will exercise more care in future.   c.

Old Whitefoot ran away again this morning. One of the hired men was unloading some boxes, and leaving him alone for a moment, old Whitefoot started. He ran thirty or forty rods, and only stopped after he had broken off one thill completely, splintered the other and barked his own shins and heels.

Mrs. Chesbro left yesterday afternoon. She seemed quiet and receptive, not so talkative as formerly, and we all liked her very well. She was thankful for the criticism sent her last winter, and has improved by it we think.

Mr. Perkins while gathering apples yesterday, fell a distance of 8 or 10 feet and hurt his back quite seriously. The ladder on which he was standing slipped, and as it did so, he caught hold of a branch of the tree, which broke, and let him down. He has suffered a good deal all night, has not slept any, and can move himself with difficulty.

Mr. Thacker came home in the afternoon, Mr. Burt in the evening. Mrs. Skinner came also on the 11 P. M. train. It is unnecessary to add that she was thrice welcome.

A Mrs. Morgan from Oswego Co. a sister of Mrs. Vanvelzer's, with her daughter, are here on a visit; we understand she is very friendly to us.

it will not be a strange thing if the Journal these days, smells strongly of peaches, for we live and move and have our being in the midst of this delicious fruit. It meets our eye, and its aroma greets our olfactories, almost, at every step. This week, however, will close up peach preserving, or nearly so, for the season, and the less attractive, though not less palatable tomato will take its place.

123 doz. Traps ordered yesterday. Mostly small orders, Workman and Griffin, Ottawa, C. W. order 42 doz. including 18 doz. No. 4.

☞ In consequence of the bee, Mr. Bolles's class did not meet last evening, but will be held this evening instead.

METEOROLOGICAL.
Thermometer, Sept. 13.

7 A. M. 72.   12 M. 60.   7 P. M. 60.   Mean 67

DAILY JOURNAL
OF ONEIDA COMMUNITY.

VOL. 2. SEPT. 15, 1866. NO. 65.

SATURDAY.

The following letter from Mr. Burt indicates some of the results of his Portland excursion. It should be remarked that Mr. B. is entirely confident he can readily adapt his machine to the cutting of ears of corn of any size.

Gorham, Sept. 9, 1866.

Dear Brother William:—I am at present stopping at this place about 9 miles from Portland.

The company here are packing about 8,000 cans of corn per day. I came here Friday evening with my machine, and set it in operation yesterday, on the whole with good results. Mr. Baxter one of the principal proprietors of this firm, is a very fine man and is disposed to give me all the chance I wish, to exhibit my machine, and is quite favorably inclined towards it.

He is the man Mr. Webb sold to. Mr. Webb is the man who saw the machine at New York. He officiates here still as an overseer and is quite active in helping me. Since coming here, I have made an important discovery about the machine, i. e. that it cannot cut their largest sized corn. When I started on their medium size, such as we raise at Oneida, (which, by the way embraces two thirds of all they raise here), the machine ran beautifully, and I put through several bushels, in a way that charmed all with its work. Well, next, I tried some large ears, but I soon discovered that the cobs did not come through in good condition. I went back to smaller ears, but still there was the same result.

On examination I found the knives were bent and disarranged. I put them in order, and again went to cutting small corn; all went well again as at first, but on making another trial on large ears, the same result followed as before. I straightened up and repeated my effort but to no purpose. On close examination I found that in opening the knives too far, it gave the cut an outward incline, so that the tendency was for the knives to run out towards the surface of the ear and thus spring the rods and, after a while the knives would get bent. Well upon discovery of these facts, I frankly reported the deficiency of the machine to the parties interested I explained to them the difficulty, and showed them where I could remedy it hereafter. I made my proposition to them viz.: that under the circumstances, I would not seek to sell the machine, but if they would furnish a good man, I would stay long enough to instruct him how to run it, and then leave it with them for the season, to be run with corn adapted to it. They appeared glad to take it on these terms. I offered it to them, because it seemed to me the best I could do.—Other shops were unwilling I should give any exhibition whatever. Mr. Jones, the largest packer here, said he should like to see it run if I would get it going in some other shop, but he had very little confidence in its answering his turn—said he had 300 hands at work in his establishment, and he did not like to have their attention diverted from work by such a kind of novel exhibition.

You may guess I have had some blue times here, but am feeling well and happy now, and have been learning some good lessons—shall have considerable to tell when I get home.

Mr. Webb appears to be a fine man and is responsible as far as I can learn. He evidently is a good deal interested to have me succeed, and will, I think, do what he can, in that direction, with the hope of hereafter, in some shape, acting as an agent in this region. I have as yet however, made him no special promise to that effect. I now intend, if nothing happens to hinder, to leave here for home Wednesday, shall stop at the Shakers, but shall not attempt to work the machine there, as theirs is the largest kind of Stowel corn.—Good bye, with ever so much love to all.   J. Burt.

Mr. Bradley writes: "Mr. Morse's children (at Cayuga) saw me coming, and all ran and met me at the gate, taking hold of me, and shaking my hand, as though I had been ' Pa'—sitting down by me, wanting to know where I had been, how long I would stay, &c."

From Lockport he writes: "Fifty-nine tons of Peaches were shipped from this place day before yesterday, and I think there must have been more to-day. You should have seen the teams waiting to unload. There was a string from the car back one-fourth of a mile, from four to half past six; as fast as one team unloaded at one end of the string another arrived at the other, each having from 16 to 50 crates. The peach crop has not been so large for years in Niagara Co. Buyers from some new point arrive every day; they are shipped every where, in all directions, to Boston, New York, Montreal, Philadelphia, Baltimore, Washington, Cleaveland, Chicago, Cincinnati, and all intermediate places. The growers are just finding out that they are worth more to them to ship than they are getting here, and they begin to stiffen on prices."—"We think, however, that to-morrow, Peaches will be plenty and cheap, as it has rained and prevented picking for nearly two days, but it has been fun to see the buyers snap them up. Crawfords go quick to-day at $12. You can see the buyers standing along the road and when a load comes along, run at it: the one who first says ' Are they sold?' has the right of way and can proceed at his leisure; and if he does not strike a bargain, there is another strife to see who shall be first. This afternoon 2 loads came along at once; while I was talking with the first another fellow went at the second; after telling the first that I wanted his peaches, I turned to the other and said 'How many crates did you say you have on?' 'Sixteen' said he. On hearing that the buyer left, and walked on a little way leaving me to make my bargain at leisure.   Your Bro. L. H. Bradley.

Another bee, last night, for cutting peaches, at the Tontine—not quite so brilliant as the night before, but in which good service was done. It held till half past eight, when we repaired to the Hall, to hear letters and reports.

Mr. Perkins still suffers a good deal with his back.—Under the influence of morphine, however, he slept a little last night.

Edwin Burnham returned from New York in the night. He went there Tuesday, and as it was his first visit to the city, he was much pleased with the trip.

Received only one order for traps yesterday, and that was from Sidney Shepard & Co., Buffalo, for 50 doz.

METEOROLOGICAL.
Thermometer, Sept. 14.

7 A. M. 50.   12 M. 63.   7 P. M. 59.   Mean 60.

DAILY JOURNAL
OF ONEIDA COMMUNITY.
VOL. 2. SEPT. 17, 1866. NO. 66.

MONDAY.

NOTE TO THE FAMILY.

Our hearts overflow with thankfulness that we are in this school—also for Ransom's improvement; and our prayer is that we may do nothing to mar the work of God that is going on in and around him.

F. P. and E. F. HUTCHINS.

P. S. I sometimes wish folks would not talk to me so much about Ransom. E. F. H.

C. O. writes to Mr. Bolles from St. Paul, Minn.: "I see by the Daily Journals that you are organizing a class to train public speakers to preach the gospel. I sympathize with you very much: the time is near at hand when there will be a demand for lectures. I never had so much preaching to do as on this trip. There seems to be a wish to hear what our religious views are. People are astonished, as of old, at our doctrines and our success. They don't know what to make of us. The reputation of the O. C. stands so high that all who know or have heard anything about us, want to hear more. I think people generally have a greater respect for us after they know we are believers in Christ and the Bible, are more radical in our views of Christian faith and are deeper and more thorough than the different sects. I find this to be the case more and more. There is a large class who will always respect God-fearing people, though they may not see exactly as they do."

It will interest the family to know that our friend W. A. Knowles is still improving in health. He writes to S. W. N.: "I have slowly gained strength and am able to walk 40 or 50 rods at a time. My heart is strong in the Lord and I rejoice in the God of my salvation. I confess the resurrection life of Christ in me."

A letter was received from Mr. Towner a few days since, requesting that his wife and two children might be permitted to make us a visit: we understand an invitation has been extended to her to come.

As we gathered in the Hall Saturday evening, we felt, as one expressed himself, as if we had been from home. The interruption of two nights, gave all, we should think a higher appreciation of our evening gatherings. The magnetic current of love seemed to circulate freely, and Mr. Hamilton said that he felt a good spirit with us.— Last night we had some interesting talk about faith, and "every man's being rewarded according to his works." It was remarked that faith-work, was the kind of work that would ensure the greatest reward—that it required intense activity of the heart to believe, and that a lazy, shiftless person, would not be likely to exercise saving faith.

WILLOW PLACE ITEMS.

Mr. Henry Ratnor the next neighbor on our side of the road west, sold his farm the other day for $10,500.— This includes cattle, horses, farming utensils, buildings etc.,—possession to be given March next. Mr. R. bought the place a year and a half ago, paying $6,000 for it.

We have now three hired machinists at work, all first' class workmen. c.

"C." left last night for Willimantic, taking with him about 50 lbs. of silk to be dyed. A handsome basket of fruit was sent by him to Mr. Botum's family, and a box of grapes to Mr. Swift. C. will return by the way of New York, where another bale of raw silk will be purchased.

Messrs. Worden and Bradley closed up their peach campaign, and returned home Saturday night, bringing with them 140 crates, and yesterday, the family turned out en masse, to perform the manipulations necessary for canning them. Work commenced at 6 o,clock A. M. and, with only a short recess for dinner continued till 3 o'clock P. M. 1639. qts. of peaches were put up during the day, and 381 qts. of plums—the largest day's work of the season. The remainder of the 140 crates is to be sold, or otherwise disposed of, we are told.

Mrs. Sears has been calling our attention to the beauty of our cock's-combs. Their size and general splendor give them a very prominent place among the beauties of the garden. In depth and brilliancy of hue, they surpass all our conceptions of Tyrian purple, while in richness of texture they are beyond anything that ever came from the once-famed looms of Damascus.

Mr. Macoy, from N. Vt. and Mr. John Smith from Saratoga, came Saturday night. Mr. M. is delighted with our surroundings and wishes himself connected with us. He has never read the Berean, but wants to obtain it now—says he appreciates the Circular more and more.

Yesterday, the public interest was so completely absorbed by the peach bee that the usual board meeting was adjourned without transacting any business.

204 doz. traps ordered Saturday. Harwood and Ryder, St. Paul, ordered 100 doz.; Stratton, Orton and Corey, Boston, 40 doz.

Mr. Perkins is decidedly better, though he is slow to admit it—says he slept hard last night.

Mrs. Vanvelzer's sister and her daughter leave for home to-day.

ERRATUM.

In Saturday's Journal, on the last page, the fifth line from the top, for $13 read $2.

METEOROLOGICAL.

Thermometer, Sept. 15 & 16.

7 A. M. 46. 12 M. 51. 7 P. M. 49. Mean 48½
7 A. M. 43. 12 M. 57. 7 P M. 54. Mean 51½

DAILY JOURNAL
OF ONEIDA COMMUNITY.

VOL. 2. SEPT. 18, 1866. NO. 67.

TUESDAY.

NOTE TO THE FAMILY.

I wish to thank God publicly for his goodness to me, and his care over me. I also wish to return thanks to the family for their many tokens of love and sympathy for me. At the same time I desire to return it all back to God, the fountain of all goodness.

The talk last evening, stirred up my heart to do justice to God and the truth, by renewing my confession of faith and cofidence in Mr. Noyes as an inspired man and successor of Paul.

I confess my faith in the Primitive Church, and their care over us, and am thankful for any place in the Kingdom of God; and above all things, I pray for a meek and quiet spirit that is receptive to the truth.

S. H. HAMILTON.

It is amusing to observe the cool manner in which our joking friends manifest their sympathy. For instance we were riding home from W. P. in the rain the other day. Our friend S. had provided himself with an india-rubber blanket and an umbrella and sat in serene contentment under their protecting expansion, while we and a dozen others were becoming thoroughly saturated in the descending shower. When nearly half way home S. looked complacently from under the rim of his umbrella, and remarked to our dripping self, "My old overcoat was at W. P.; you might have had it, and welcome."— Wasn't that a comforting assurance in the circumstances? You may be sure we were thankful for it.   *

Some Indians were in the shoe-shop yesterday, and, among other subjects of conversation, expressed their appreciation of Mrs. Joslyn. It seems they miss her somewhat, when they come to the kitchen to make their small transactions, and have not yet got acquainted with her successor Mrs. Abbott. It was rather curious to observe that the main point in Mrs. J's character that struck their admiration was that she was *honest.* They are not quite sure yet, how much confidence they can place in Mrs. A., but no doubt she will gain their esteem by and by.   F.

We have had singular weather this month—thus far very few pleasant days. We are sure we shall appreciate the sun's rays should he deign to smile on us once more, and gladden our hearts with his genial warmth. We are not disposed, however, to complain of his withdrawal, for could we soar high enough to penetrate the dark clouds that hang over us we should find him faithfully performing his appointed work, and should discover that it was not his fault that his rays were hidden from our sight. So, in the midst of spiritual darkness we will not forget that the Sun of Righteousness still shines with unabated effulgence, though dark spirits have come between and shut out from our hearts, the consciousness of the warmth and love that his presence inspires. Faith lifts the veil and we are comforted with the thought that,

"The darkest day— Live till to-morrow, will have passed away."

Messrs. Macoy and Smith, left this morning for home. Mr. M. hopes to sell out his property in Cambridge, and persuade his wife to come and live near us. We understand he bought $40 worth of goods from the store to take home with him, including a few traps.

The Phrenological Journanl, brought by Mr. Noyes, has been on exhibition in the reception room throughout the morning. The portrait of J. H. N., is considered, on the whole, a good likeness—better than the average of wood-engravings that appear in illustrated papers. The sketch of Mr. N's phrenological development appears to be just and satisfactory.

Traps ordered yesterday, 261 doz., the largest orders are from Russel and Erwin, Mfg. Co., 143 doz., and Sidney Shepard, and, Co., 86 doz.

Mr. Noyes arrived this morning in the rain, a little before 6 o'clock.

HYMN.

Jesus dweller in my heart,
All thou hast, yes, mine thou art;
I am just as fully thine;
All is thine and thine is mine.
Thou dids't give thyself to me,
From myself to make me free:
I do give myself to thee,
Thine forever more to be.

This, then, makes our spirits one,
Thus is Heaven on earth begun,
And this union ne'er shall cease,
But eternaly increase.
So the magic life is shed
Through the body from the head:
All the members feel the fire,
All made one by one desire.

All the burden and the strife
Of a false and selfish life,
Cease to mar and vex the soul,
While we make a glorious whole.
Earth has no such bliss as this;
Jesus makes his chosen his.
Love so pure and life so strong
Shall forever be our song.   B.

METEOROLOGICAL.

Thermometer, Sept. 17.

7 A. M. 60.   12 M. 64.   7 P. M. 60.   Mean 63¼

DAILY JOURNAL
OF ONEIDA COMMUNITY.

VOL. 2. SEPT. 19, 1866. NO. 68.

WEDNESDAY.

A Mr. Lovell, who had called here last Sunday, has written to Mr. Bolles, and as the letter was quite unexpected, and is somewhat interesting, we quote a sentence or two: "On our return, a lady asked me what we had seen, I told her ' we had seen more of heaven than we could see anywhere else, this side of the Delectable Mountains.'—I trust we shall meet again, with another favorable opportunity of investigating the workings of this inner life within your inner world. I say 'your world,' for in my opinion, you are nearer the great source of all goodness—of a purer happiness than we can find in our system."

A letter was also received yesterday, from Lucinda S. Wilcox, M. D. of Detroit, addressed to Mrs. H. A. Noyes. She says: "For twelve years I have been trying to patch up broken down women. This has led me to think more seriously than before, upon the causes of so much suffering in society. I have been reading the Circular for the last few months with intense interest. I get more inspiration from it than from all other reading. Every number makes me more and more anxious to visit you. It is not curiosity, but an earnest desire for truth (if I know myself) that actuates me.—O, I want to grasp the hand and look into the face of an *earnest* woman. Pardon me if I am too presuming."

We shall give the writer of the above, an invitation to make us a visit.

Messrs. Noyes and Hamilton, with Mrs. Skinner and E. S. B., went to Utica yesterday, and took Victor to the Hospital. From there, Mr. Noyes went directly to New York without returning to Oneida. Mr. H. and company came home a little before 10 o'clock, P. M.

As to Mr. Kelly, it is next to impossible for the Journal to keep track of him.' He reminds us of the boomerang used by the Indians of Australia, which they throw with a twitch so skillful that it will kill bird or beast or foe, and curve round again to its owner's feet. Mr. K. is constantly appearing and disappearing. We suppose him at Rome, when, lo! we find him eating his breakfast at our left elbow. We inform some one that he can be found at the office; when, straightway, it turns out that he has gone to Utica. All success to him. In Rome, yesterday, he secured, among other business, a silk-order amounting to about $500.

Just as the Journal was going to the press yesterday, the sun shone out, for a moment, and Mr. H. said "Report it, quick, do," but it was too late; and it was well, for very soon, the clouds closed up again, and a dark rainy afternoon and night succeeded. This morning, the watery element continues to pour itself upon the already saturated earth, with unprecedented liberality, and fair weather seems quite in the future.

Mr. Brooks, husband of Roswell Hawley's cousin, is here just now, from Brooksville Vt. He has lately sold out his axe-manufacturing business, and has driven all the way in his own conveyance, being on a business tour partly to wind up his own affairs, partly to obtain orders for the firm he has sold to. We have not heard what he is going to engage in next.

Through G. W. N's hemlock hedge, a pretty wild vine with delicate, whitish blossoms, has been twining itself. Some called it Wild Clematis.—The other day, we noticed it all shriveled up, and we suspect Jack Frost has been around, nibbling with his destructive tooth.— The other beautiful vine which adorns the Fruit-house is fast robing itself in vermilion. Indeed, everything around warns us that summer

"advances toward
Its mild decline."

Our children are all, without exception, well, at the present time—full of life and activity. One cannot help pausing, in passing through their room, to hear their chatter, and to inhale the freshness of their young life.

Parson Brownlow passed Oneida in the cars last evening, and, we believe, made a short speech at the Depot.

Mr. Bradley left last night for Lockport, to buy peaches.

A Mr. Morrell from Albany is here. He wishes to sell us a few thousand acres of land in Kentucky. Very like a whale.

Mr. Inslee and Lady, from Brooklyn, arrived to-day, on a visit to *our* Mr. Inslee. Mrs. I. has, we believe, been giving some music in the Hall.

264 doz. traps ordered yesterday, including 128 doz. by Harwood & Ryder, St. Paul; and 42 doz. by Proebsting & Voigt, Peoria, Ill.

171 bushels of tomatoes have been put up during the last two days.

We commenced shipping our new fruit yesterday, by sending off 150 cases. A good beginning!

METEOROLOGICAL.

Thermometer, Sept. 19.

7 A. M. 49. 12 M. 60. 7 P. M. 59. Mean 56⅔.

Delightful Scotch mist. M. L. W. rubs his hands together and says "Fine growing season—suits me exactly."

DAILY JOURNAL
OF ONEIDA COMMUNITY.

VOL. 2. SEPT. 20, 1866. NO. 69.

THURSDAY.

A letter has been received from a Mr. M'Laughlin, M. D., of Cumberland giving a short, sketch of his life, and expressing a wish to know more of our system and beliefs. He writes that it is about eighteen years since he first got hold of some of our writings, but was not attracted to them till lately. He says he has lost his wife and child, and is alone in the world, starving, not only religiously, but socially, though he has abundance of the material things of life. He once went to the Shakers at New-Lebanon with a view of joining them, but their doctrine of celibacy seemed so unnatural, that he could not feel in much harmony with them.

"For some time past" he writes, "I have desired to visit your Community for the purpose of learning more about the practical workings of the society, and if possible to unite with you in membership."

He remarks, that he was always religiously inclined, and joined, the M. E. Church when young. At the advent of modern spiritualism, he turned his attention to that, and was cast out of the church, and had been living at a starving, dying rate ever since.

He says he has been from the first, unreasonably prejudiced against our order, and looked upon us as a company of profligate, licentious characters, who had put on the cloak of religion to screen ourselves from the eyes of the world—that he was always in favor of exclusive love or dual mateship, but, from a very remarkable experience he has had on this subject, and from re-reading our writings, "Bible Communism" in particular, he is convinced that we have the truth in part, if not the whole, on the subject. He says in conclusion, "If you have instituted the great school for the race, I want to know it, and labor in the cause. Will it be asking too much of you, to write me a line informing me of the best course, to become fully acquainted with your order? Enclosed I send 50 cts. for which please send me a few Nos. of the Circular."

A letter was also received from a woman of Toledo, Ohio, of spiritualistic pretensions—a medium—requesting help in correcting and publishing her writings, when she was in an entranced state. She says she is very ignorant, and her letter plainly indicates it.

A large portion of the family met in the Hall last evening at 7 o'clock to hear some music. The Brass Band played some favorite pieces, and Abram and Alice sung several duetts, after which Mrs. Inslee played several pieces on the piano in quite a pleasing style. We may add that Mrs. L expressed, in a quiet way, a good deal

of interest in us and seemed somewhat open to spiritual sympathy with us. She took with her several copies of the Circular and one of Salvation from Sin. When the party visited the Journal Office, she requested a Journal, in a way which it would have been difficult to refuse. The one she got, was that for Sept. 12, containing "Hints to Croquet Players."—Mr. I. seemed well pleased with us, but his sympathy was merely of an intellectual kind.—They left, early this morning.

Mrs. Whitfield has left the children's house, where she has acted as mother, for two and a half years, and Miss Jane A. Kinsley takes her place.—Mrs. W. has endeared herself to the children and to all, by her long and faithful services in that department. May her mantle fall upon her successor.—Mr. Hatch is with the children again, as Mr. Woolworth's services are needed elsewhere.

Our present scarcity of water, caused chiefly by the immense demands of the Preserving Department, makes us wide-awake for anything like a leak. One has been discovered in the wooden pipe between the reservoir and the company kitchen; and workmen are busy, replacing the wooden by an iron one. It is contemplated, at some future time to continue it down to the Store.

We beg to call the special attention of our readers to the medical advertisement on our last page.

A Mrs. Pomeroy, a sister-in-law of Mary's, with her grandson, a young Mr. Willis, both of New Haven, Conn. stopped over night with us. They are on their way to the western part of the state, we understand, to visit some relatives.

Four workmen are now employed in constructing a new water-wheel at the Foundry.

Traps ordered yesterday,		426 doz.
The principal orders were—		
J. and C. M. Daily,	St. Paul,	85 "
C. L. Grant,	" "	120 "
Cheritree and Farwell,	" "	37 "
Enoch Woods,	Chicago,	100 "

METEOROLOGICAL.

Thermometer, Sept. 19.

7 A. M. 59. 12 M. 62. 7 P. M. 58. Mean 59¾.
Steady rain.

DAILY JOURNAL
OF ONEIDA COMMUNITY.

VOL. 2. SEPT. 21, 1866. NO. 70.

FRIDAY.
DEALERS AND CONSUMERS.

O. C., Sept. 21.

Bro. Olds:—Your customers, Rice Brothers of Milwaukee, write:

"We do not like the idea of your taking small orders from consumers here at such low figures, as it cuts into our trade. Our object in making large orders was to have control of that trade."

Miss Nunns has replied, that the Community will in future endeavor to take such a course as will not interfere with their trade. Still the question arises, What is our true policy? While it appears to be for our immediate interest not to sell many goods to consumers in places where we have received large orders, I cannot forget what has been said by Mr. Noyes and others about our favoring the consumers. There is a large and growing class who prefer to secure their supplies directly of the Community; and I confess that while anxious not to offend the dealers, I take special satisfaction in sending our fruits and vegetables directly to the consumers; and am inclined to think we should retain this privilege.—Is it not a fair and sufficient compromise with the dealers, to assure them that we will not sell to consumers at less than list, while we give them five or ten per cent. discount, according to the amount they purchase? I would like to hear from you and others on this subject. In the meantime, caution should be exercised in taking orders where we sell largely to dealers; and I have noticed with pleasure that you have in nearly every case, on your present trip, sold our fruit at list prices.

Truly, w.

☞ Now is the time, for such as croaked at the building of the Willow-Place Factory, to pay a visit to that establishment.—I think a walk through the different rooms would induce the most obstinate of evil foreboders, to prophesy good results, and to acknowledge that the expense involved in the new building was neither unwise nor ill-timed.

☞ It is only fair that those who doubted the expediency of Mr. Noyes's policy in urging that the prices of our manufactured goods, especially traps, should be reduced, and that we should "sell as low as we can," —should acknowledge that his policy has been crowned with grand success. The demand for traps is unprecedented; and the low prices of the Community traps prevent competition instead of stimulating it. Mr. N. said, at the time the new price-list was made out—"I hope we shall sweep the board this fall," and it is being swept quite thoroughly. w

Mr. Perry, writing from La Fayette to Mrs. Perry and speaking of a visit he made his married sister, says—"I thought it was an awfully selfish and lonesome way of living, in comparison with our beautiful home, and I felt to thank God for enabling us to live in the Community. I think more and more of Mr. Noyes and Mr. Hamilton, and their faithfulness to Christ and God, even though foolish and selfish worldly-minded men may pretend to despise them.

My greatest pleasure and ambition is to be true to the Lord, and I know he will be true to me; and the world is going to find out, by and by, that it is greater wisdom to seek after God, and to know and do his will, than it is to stumble along in their own selfishness and corruption. I never can be too thankful that the Lord has finally enabled you and me to see the truth alike, so that we can work together, instead of drawing apart, as we used to. The devil kept us both, just enough blinded to the truth, to make us both unhappy, when we knew that we loved each other dearly and truly."

Last evening, Mr. Bolles called the attention of the Theological class to the subject of singing, making special reference to Mr. Noyes's lately expressed ideas on the subject. Mr. B. recommended that each one should accustom himself to sing alone before the class; and a call was made for volunteers who would be willing to do so. More than twenty volunteers, male and female, responded, by giving in their names. Mr. B., setting a good example, closed the meeting by singing the hymn published in last Tuesday's Journal. The class were pleasantly surprised to hear so pure and sweet a voice in one whose musical talent seems hitherto to have been "under a bushel"—at least since he came to the Community.

Miss Pomeroy's friends left last night at 10 o'clock.—Mrs. P. was quite well pleased with her visit, and the young man particularly so. He has been a member of the Methodist Church since he was ten years old and quite devoted, taking an active part in their religious meetings. He was charmed with the spirit he felt here, and said the meeting was a "real treat" to him—that the day he spent here, would be long remembered. He expressed his pleasure, that our people were going to New Haven. Miss P. says his father lives only a quarter of a mile from our new place there.

It has been decided to extend the iron pipe mentioned in yesterday's Journal, right down to the store at once; so the workmen, under Mr. Abbott's superintendence, are busy at it with spade and shovel.

John Freeman was criticised in the meeting last night, by his request. But little fault was found with him, and he was commended for the earnest spirit he manifested in joining us, for his general good deportment, since, and for his industry and quietness.

A fine breeze, this morning tempted the boys out with their new kite; they were quite successful in raising it, but a dark cloud was pending, and the rain soon poured in torrents, scattering our juveniles, and breaking up the sport.

Traps ordered yesterday,   57 doz.

ERRATUM.

At the commencement of yesterday's Journal, on the first and second lines from the top—

for   "M'Laughlin M. D., of Cumberland,"
read   G. B. McLaughlin, Cumberland, Md.

METEOROLOGICAL.

Thermometer, Sept. 20.

7 A. M. 54.   12 M. 53.   7 P. M. 54.   Mean 53½.

DAILY JOURNAL
OF ONEIDA COMMUNITY.

VOL. 2. SEPT. 22, 1866. NO. 71.

SATURDAY.

Vernon Centre, Sept. 20 1866.

Mr. T. L. Pitt:—I have the honor to inform you that you have been selected as one of the Judges on Apples at the Fair of the Vernon Agricultural Society to be held at Vernon on the 4th. day of October next.— We trust you will not fail to be with us, and let me say to you that we are not only hoping, but expecting that your folks will rally with us in making the effort to make the exhibition one that will be a credit to all concerned. Mr. Hamilton gave us encouragement that you would join with us, and if you fail to do so, we shall be greatly disappointed in making it a success. You have all the material to make a good exhibition of yourselves; but let us join our efforts with yours, and success will be certain if the weather is favorable. We will endeavor to make ample preparations for space and convenience for you in the tent. And lest but not least, we want your band to volunteer on the occasion. Tell them to drive to Reid's Hotel and put up their team, and get their dinners and the society will save them harmless from paying any thing for entertainment.— We want exhibited the firstlings of your flocks and herds, and specimens of your industry generally, together with samples of fruit and vegetables, and the handsomest of all, don't let the *Ladies* forget the *Flowers* and to be well represented themselves.

Now we are induced to make this draft on you, not only because you have the material, but it is because a large part of your well cultivated domain is part and parcel, of the old town of Vernon, and you must consider self protection the first law of nature. And hence if the people of Vernon fail in this effort, we want you to share with us, but there can be no such thing as fail, if we but make a reasonable effort.   *   *   *

We shall be pleased to receive from you a favorable response giving us assurance that your intentions are to be with us and lend a helping hand in whatever you may deem essential in promoting the object of the industrial Holiday.   With much respect &c.,

Levi T. Marshall.
Secy. Vernon Agl. Soc.

It has been decided to respond to the above invitation; and T. L. P. and W. A. H. have been appointed a committee (with power to add to their number,) to select and forward such articles as will best represent our industry.

It was quite a relief last evening to have a meeting at which no one was present but our own family. We have been pretty well "cousined" of late, as a certain lady remarked. Mr. Hamilton took advantage of the privacy of the occasion to give an account of the late visit to

Utica. The description was very gratifying to all, and gave rise to some general conversation. C. A. Cragin, on passing through Utica yesterday, called at the Hospital, and although he did not see Victor, he learned that he is quiet and contented.

Notwithstanding the rainy weather, our indefatigable purveyor, M. L. W., has been scouring the country in quest of butter lately. He has had, on the whole, good success. This morning, five tubs at 40 cts. came in. It is a good article.

The preservers are now busy putting up Pears and Corn.

Traps ordered yesterday,   66 doz.

RHYMES OF PROGRESS.

Dare you give the Truth a hearing,
   Be its message what it may;
Stand not idly, doubting, fearing;
   Boldly enter on the way,
Striving in true emulation,
Free from boastful ostentation,
   For the coming of the day
When the bonds of sin are riven,
And the earth is one with Heaven.

Men, we hold, were made for action,
   Not like cabbages to grow:
Brother-like, above all faction,
   Onward ever, we will go,
To whatever task invited,
Resolute to see wrong righted;
   Quick to deal the telling blow
In the great, important contest,
Ending death by lawful conquest.

We, at war with foolish fashions,
   Fearless face the world's disdain—
Seek to educate the passions
   For God's service, not in vain.
Surely, what he has created,
Howsoever now perverted—
   Made to serve in Evil's train—
Was for noble ends provided
When by inspiration guided.

Yield we not to vain illusion;
   Truth is grander, brighter far:
Blessings flow in best profusion
   When we take things as they are:
And who truly loves existence,
Pierces through the mists of distance,
   Which his just conceptions mar:
Faith and Science, then uniting,
Make a prospect most inviting.

O. C. Sept. 21, 1866.   T.

METEOROLOGICAL.

Thermometer, Sept. 20.

7 A. M. 69.   12 M, 70.   7 P. M. 64.   Mean 67⅓.

We are most happy to say that the sun shines once more, and our Equinoctial storm seems to be at an end. We are certainly thankful.

ERRATUM.

In yesterday's Journal, in the last clause of W's letter to Mr. Olds,
   for,   "sold our fruit at list prices,"
   read,   sold our fruit *to consumers* at l'st prices.

DAILY JOURNAL
OF ONEIDA COMMUNITY.

VOL. 2. SEPT. 24, 1866. NO. 72.

MONDAY.
BUSINESS MEETING.

O. C., Sept. 23, 1866.

Mr. Kinsley suggested the necessity of purchasing half a dozen arm chairs for use in the Hall. It was decided to make such a purchase, and Mr. Hatch, W. A. Hinds and J. H. Barron were appointed a committee to act in the matter.

Mr. Abbott introduced the subject of the insufficiency of our present supply of water. There was some general conversation as to the best way of getting an increased supply. Suggestions were made with reference to various adjacent springs and also to the rain water shed from the different roofs. Messrs. Burt, Clark, Abbott, Woolworth and G. W. Hamilton were appointed a committee to consider the subject and report.

Mr. Woolworth suggested that as our corn is, for the most part, too large for the corn-cutting machines as they are at present constructed, some patent knives, like those described by Mr. Burt as in use at Portland, should be bought for the Preserving Department.

F. A. Marks stated that there is a muck swamp for sale near the cheese-factory. It seems that our own swamp muck is not of first rate quality, is fast giving out, and the excavation of it, is making unsightly holes in our farm. Mr. Conant, who has seen the swamp now for sale, considers the muck of good quality.— Messrs. Kinsley, Barron, Hinds and Martin Kinsley were appointed a committee to learn the price at which the swamp can be bought, and the best means of access to it from our farm and orchards.

W. A. Hinds introduced the subject of Fruit Labels. It has been thought desirable to have a new style of these in which each different kind of fruit put up by us, should be represented on its own label. If they are to be got up in time for next year, it will be necessary to take early action in the matter. Mrs. Miller is ready to commence work at once on the new designs; and Mr. Leonard considers that a new printing press will be required for printing them. A committee was appointed consisting of Mrs. Vanvelzer, Messrs. Hamilton, Pitt, Thacker and Hinds.

G. W. Hamilton spoke on the subject of apparatus to raise water at Willow Place. He had seen, in use at Seneca Falls, a pump, suitable for such a purpose, which cost $110. It was thought very desirable to have some such facilities, considering the amount of valuable property we have at Willow Place. Voted that Messrs. Inslee and G. W. Hamilton be appointed a committee to learn the entire cost of such an apparatus, and report.

G. W. Hamilton stated that for $300 or upwards, a movable six-hand fire-engine could be had, suitable to be kept near our home buildings. No action was taken on this subject.

The following Committees have been selected to attend to the exhibition of articles at the Vernon Town Fair:

Fruits:—F. A. Marks and S. Y. Joslyn.

Preserved Fruits:—S. Vanvelzer and E. Whitney.

Agricultural Stock:—Martin Kinsley and J. A. Conant.

Bags:—H. C. Noyes and E. S. Nash.

Traps, Corn Cutters &c.:—J. C. Higgins and J. Burt.

Flowers:—A. C. Sears and S. W. Nash.

Silk;—Elizabeth Hutchins and C. A. Cragin.

Fancy and Needle Work:—H. M. Hutchins and S. S Higgins.

General Superintendents:—W. H. Woolworth, M. L. Worden and Chloe Seymour.

The general superintendents will take charge of all articles selected and see that they are placed on exhibition. They will also decide what articles shall be exhibited of those offered.

Abram gives good accounts of our young carpenter E.—says he will make a good workman. E. is fond of gunning too, and makes a good shot. The other day he brought down a squirrel which he picked up and slipped into his pocket, then passed leisurely on in quest of other game. Suddenly, a suspicion crossed his mind that all was not right, and he felt his pocket, at the same time glancing hurriedly around, when, lo! there is Mr. Squirrel darting up a tree " like a streak."

Some sweet corn has been bought from neighbor Darling, and a husking bee was called yesterday morning. Many hands made light work and soon it was ready for the preservers. This same neighbor D., it seems, is quite a conscientious man. The ground on which the corn grew was recently purchased by him and had on it at the time, a fine young plantation of hop-vines. But Mr. D. did not think that the Lord wanted him to raise an article that was liable to be put to a bad use, so he dug up the whole and raised this corn instead.

On Saturday night, the florists, feeling the chill of the atmosphere, were seen covering up their favorite flower-beds with sheets, so that the garden had almost the appearance of a bleaching ground. The forethought was timely but availed little. On Sunday morning it was found that the hoar frost had committed fearful havoc.

"Swift summer into the autumn flowed,
And frost in the mist of the morning rode,
Though the noonday sun looked clear and bright,
Mocking the spoil of the secret night."

We learned this morning, that Mr. Newhouse has been to Wallingford on a business trip, and returned Saturday night. H. W. B. came also, Saturday afternoon. He is going further west, peddling, we believe; and is to remain here only two or three days.

We leave the Journal for a day or two, in charge of our co-laborer W. H. H., and go to Utica for the purpose of visiting our sisters, at their urgent and oft-repeated solicitations. ED.

Traps ordered by mail on Saturday and Sunday, 222 doz.

DAILY JOURNAL
OF ONEIDA COMMUNITY.

VOL. 2. SEPT. 25, 1866. NO. 73.

TUESDAY.

The result of brother Bradley's raid of last week, was one crate of peaches for which he paid the sum of $4. He had been as far Niagara County, had attended a Millerite meeting where he was very much tempted to call out "He's come"—had heard speeches by Barnum and General Banks, and had gone in a hired conveyance into the peach country, but all in vain, and the single crate had to be bought at Rochester on his way home. When he jumped out of the cars at Oneida, he saw the said crate jolting along on somebody's wagon, and called out to Homer—"Have you sold my peaches already—what did you get for them? "Four Dollars" was the reply.

The identical basket, half full of apples, which Mr. Perkins left on the tree twelve days ago, has been found hanging there just as he left it, and will probably remain till he is able to come for it. This seems like a homely counterpart to the Arab tale of the Sleeping Palace where all life and motion stood arrested for a hundred years, waiting for the fairy prince. Mr. P., who got as far as the breakfast table this morning, like the newly wakened King in the story, can say—

"My joints are something stiff or so."

The trimming of labels for the fruits and vegetables is becoming a regular branch of Community industry.—Labels for bottles require to be cut to an outline of points and curves well calculated to try the patience of one not skilled in the use of the scissors. Those for the cans, though of simpler outline, require considerable cutting also. In addition to what is done in meeting by volunteers, and by the children—who seem to like the work, and do a good deal of it, a regular bee is now held every afternoon to prepare them for use as fast as required.—We understand S. K. D. superintends this bee with characteristic efficiency.

We had the painful satisfaction a few days since, of placing ourselves in the hands of the Dentist, for the purpose of having a decaying tooth built up after the latest modern style. The operation was not a very pleasant one, in itself considered, but it was nevertheless very nicely and substantially Dunn (done.) What with scraping and boring, and wedging and malleting, and to cap all, withdrawing the wedge at last, we thought, our mouth and jaw, should have been made of something more substantial than flesh and bone, to go through the operation unharmed. The result is, a fine solid tooth, and we would advise all who are troubled with defective teeth, to go and do likewise. E. Y. J.

What strange speeches children sometimes make! The other day a little one was heard saying "I wish God wouldn't make flies; I don't like to have Him do it.

WILLOW PLACE ITEMS.

A letter was received the other day from Hanks, a silk manufacturer, enquiring how soon and at what price we could furnish two spoolers. "In six weeks and at $60." was substantially the answer we gave. It is found that we cannot make spoolers for $50, the Patterson price unless we copy the Patterson shiftlessness, which it would be hardly advisable to do.

The silk hands are at work on the new bale. The reason why this bale cost less than the first is quite apparent. It is sluggy and rather brown.—Two new girls have lately been hired. C.

Mr Porter, tailor, from Port Byron, came here yesterday. He leaves to-day at noon, but will return in a few days and work for us a couple of weeks on trial.

During the late rain, we heard Brother Leete threatening to break the barometer; but we are glad to say that, under Brother D.'s care it is doing pretty well now, the weather being clear and windy.

The Mount Tom Luminary has arrived this morning. The baby paper of the Tontine, observing the double column of extracts, thanks his amiable Ma, the Circular, for such ample appreciation, and will do his best to merit her continued notice.

At the close of the meeting last evening, there was some singing in addition to the usual hymn. One of the pieces was an old fashioned hymn by H. W. B. We were all glad to hear his voice again.

The arrival of another lot of corn necessitated another husking bee. Sixteen volunteers gave in their names last night, and W. called them, lantern in hand, a little before five o'clock this morning: the work went on well.

Eight Indians and squaws came this morning to husk corn. They have been hired and set to work.

Yesterday, the Preservers put up 1896 cans of tomatoes and 53 cans of pears. This looks like work.

Mr. Aiken arrived last night.

Traps ordered yesterday, 114 doz.

HYMN.

From God, through Christ, comes every good
　　Which to mankind is given—
Salvation, life, and health and food—
　　Inheritance in Heaven.

All science, of whatever age,
　　Improvements of the past,
And all that shines on history's page
　　We'll own as Christ's at last.

And all the comforts men possess—
　　From where, else, do they flow
But from the Source of blessedness,
　　Through Christ whose love we know?

By Him consisteth everything:
　　The worlds were made by Him:
For all, to God, we'll tribute bring
　　And praise in grateful hymn.

W. J.

METEOROLOGICAL.
Thermometer, Sept. 24.

7 A. M. 50.　13 M. 62.　7 P. M. 59.　Mean 57.

DAILY JOURNAL
OF ONEIDA COMMUNITY.

VOL. 2. SEPT. 26, 1866. NO. 74.

WEDNESDAY.
LETTER FROM H. R. PERRY.

Chicago Sept. 23, 1866,

Brother Hinds :—During the summer I have heard something said about getting a knitting-machine this fall. Please hold on about it until I get home, as I am getting one of Lamb's, in the advertising line.

I have not seen anything of Mr. Olds here, but I shook hands with a lot of our traps which I saw hanging out at a store door on Lake Street a day or two since. As soon as they saw me, they sprung and commenced wagging their jaws, and made many enquiries about Mr. Newhouse and several others of their old acquaintances.

When I was at La Fayette a few days since, I drew on the Agency for $75 on traveling expenses; I suppose they have informed you. The La Fayette Journal folks wanted very much that I should come up here for them, so I have been in the advertising line for the last three days. I have made some money for them, and for the Springfield, Ill. Journal, and in the meantime it has fully paid me for my time and expenses.

I have let the Bag and Trap business lie quiet here, as I did not wish to interfere with Mr. Olds's programme.

I return this evening to La Fayette and then go immediately to Springfield, Ill. and St. Louis. I see by taking a second look at Mr. Olds's route that he visits Keokuk and Quincy. I shall not go to these places therefore, as I had before intended—guess I will get home in about two weeks. Love to all.

Yours T. uly, H. R. P.

A gentleman from Rochester, agent for the principal nurseries there, called here this morning. The horticulturists showed him our Delawares, which had been thought by some to be scarcely equal to what we had had last year. But this agent says they are " the best he has seen anywhere." He returns here on Monday to purchase grapes from us as samples to take vine-orders by.

George Vaill came here yesterday; he made application to be admitted into the family, or at least to be allowed to work for us. Permission was given him to remain for one or two days, but it is not thought advisable to receive him into any kind of connection with us.— His old bias already shows itself in the contradictory accounts of himself he has given to different members of the family.

We passed through the upper sitting-room this morning in quest of items and found a delightful bag-bee, including Maud among the number, grouped around the stove. During our brief stay, we heard some such eloquence as might well commend itself to the emulation of the Theological class.—This bee may be considered as very suggestive not only of the flushness of work in the bag-department, but of the atmosphere of work and industry that pervades the Community generally. It is impossible to touch the O. C. at any point, without feeling the nimbus of a healthy activity.

We think it speaks well for Master E. Kinsley, that he *escorts* his mother to meeting almost every evening. It is true that he does not come in, but waits in an adjoining room where he can hear equally well. The fact is, that he has not yet been invited to come in, as he might want to "speak" in meeting, and it is not considered that his talk would be very edifying.

A letter was received a few days since from Meroa.— She is near where her mother lives, and works out, doing house-work. She gets $2 per week. She writes that Emily cries a good deal to go back to Oneida—wants to see Father Hatch and the children.

Gunning parties are quite common in these days.— We know of three young men who took a stroll through the woods the other day and brought home twenty grey squirrels and twelve red. Squirrels may appear small game for a hunting party of Nimrods but they are sweet eating.

In justice to Mr. B., it ought to be mentioned in connection with yesterday's peach story, that in course of his trip, he transacted some other important business rather more profitable than the crate of peaches was.

In addition to our music on the Harmonium, John F. Sears has of late, played the violoncello as an accompaniment to our congregational singing, the effect of which is very pleasing.

Mr. Gillson and his wife from Boonville arrived yesterday and are still here. They were in meeting last evening, and were pleased. Mr. G. has been a subscriber for the Circular for the last eight years, and expresses a good deal of sympathy for us in a quiet way.

A brother of Miss Matthews, with his wife and three children came here yesterday afternoon. They are not much interested in us, though not opposed.

The peach stones which have been saved during the season, amounted to nearly twenty bushels and have been sold for $20.

The horticulturists picked 640 lbs. of grapes yesterday; 3,500 lbs. have already been harvested this season.

Traps ordered yesterday, 50 doz.

METEOROLOGICAL.

Thermometer, Sept. 25.

7 A. M. 40. 12 M. 54. 7 P. M. 40. Mean 50⅓.
Rain, rain, rain !

DAILY JOURNAL
OF ONEIDA COMMUNITY.

VOL. 2. SEPT. 27, 1866. NO. 75.

THURSDAY.
FRUIT UNORDERED, SEPT. 26.

	Cans.	Bottles.
Black Raspberries,	1,059	170
Damson Plums,	800	
Lombard "	1,660	
Y. Gage "	1,493	648
Peaches,	2,136	1,319
Black Cherries,	883	
Yellow "	1,121	
Blackberries,	2,591	477
Pickled Crab-Apples,		144
String Beans	1,462	

We have not yet finished putting up Pears or Quinces, and of course cannot say how many we shall have more than are now ordered. It is probably safe to receive small orders for these fruits.

We shall put up a few dozen more of Pickled Peaches and Pickled Pears than are now ordered.

It is safe to receive small orders for all Jellies excepting Currant, Pine-apple, Grape and Strawberry.

Peas and Tomatoes; all ordered long ago.

Would prefer not to have large orders taken for Sweet Corn until we are able to ascertain more definitely what amount will be put up.

Miss Nunns estimates the amount of fruit and vegetables already ordered, at over $30,000; but some of the orders can only be partly filled. w

---

We are glad to resume our post, once more, after an absence of two days. Our peep into an isolated household although it was blessed with many external comforts, and above ordinary society, in intelligence and refinement, will suffice us for the present. The contrast it presents to our own loved home and its higher, nobler objects of pursuit, has made us doubly thankful, and more than ever desirous that the truth of Communism may rapidly prevail, and swallow up these petty family interests, that so cut the world up into discordant factions. Ed.

Looking round for items of news for the Journal this morning, we encountered Mrs. Ackley who was complaining of her lame shoulder. She said she could work only with one arm and Mr. B. her associate in the bakery, was disabled in one hand, and so that made them one, as there was only two hands that could be used between them. A new way that, thought we, to solve the great problem of unity; but not more absurd than to expect that unity of heart can be generated, in a church composed of 40 families, each one having separate interests, and whose bond of unity is creeds and forms instead of Christ.

H. G. A. writes from the Agency that a letter has been received from Seth Kinman the celebrated California hunter, inquiring about our traps and inclosing photographs of himself and of the unique chairs presented by him to Presidents Lincoln and Johnson.— The pictures are in Chloe's possession and will, along with one of Mr. Dixon, be taken to Wallingford by Mrs. Skinner when she goes.

Our stock of "ile" gave out a few days since—all but what was in the lamps, and that also has failed in a number of instances. But although some of our young ladies had "no oil in their lamps," last evening, no one could justly consider them "foolish" as they had supplied themselves with tallow candles instead. We confess there was something quite pleasing about the mild light of these candles—all the more primitive like, from being stuck in cucumbers for candlesticks.

The Theological Class, which has hitherto been held in the schoolroom in the Tontine, had grown too large to be accommodated there, and met in the Hall last evening; it will hold its regular sessions there in future.

George Vail left yesterday afternoon. It seems that while at the Depot on his way here, he picked up the acquaintance of a Madison County farmer who offered to hire him; so he has gone to accept the job.

The new spooler at the S. F. commenced operations yesterday, and Olive Ann is learning to run it.

Some of our young girls are making themselves quite efficient as mothers in different departments. Harriet Olds is connected with Jane Abbott as mother in the kitchen, and we are told is quite responsible, and does finely.

S. W. Nash is building a new chimney to the greenhouse.

There was some singing last evening by eight of the family, including H. W. B.

We suspect we did *violence* to J. F. S's double bass viol yesterday by calling it a violoncello. But, no matter: "a rose by any other name &c."

The Gillsons left this morning, well pleased with their visit. Mrs. G. said if she "could live here altogether," she would be "extremely happy."

H. W. B. left this morning. He goes in the direction of New York, doing some peddling on the way.

2590 qts. of corn put up yesterday, all done without the aid of machinery.

Traps ordered yesterday, 116 doz.

ERRATUM.

Add to the list of Fair Committees published in Monday's Journal,

Vegetables:—H. W. Thayer.

METEOROLOGICAL.
Thermometer, Sept. 26.

7 A. M. 50. 12 M. 54. 7. P. M. 51. Mean 51½.

DAILY JOURNAL
OF ONEIDA COMMUNITY.

VOL. 2. SEPT. 28, 1866. NO. 76.

FRIDAY.

Fairport, Sept. 27. 1866

DEAR BRO.:—Your kind letter of the 23 inst. came duly to hand, informing us of the shipment to us of preserved fruits by the Oneida Community, all of which was received last evening in perfect order.

Now brother, need I tell you how much we appreciate so valuable a gift, especially the expression of so many kind hearts? It is above price.

You will please accept our hearty thanks for the same, and through you I wish to express my heart-felt gratitude for this token of remembrance and kindly feeling of the Community family. Was pleased to hear that you were so successful in obtaining a supply of peaches, which was (as I learn from the CIRCULAR) a cause of bringing in requisition "*A queen bee.*"

Yours affectionately, J. E. HOWARD.

When the store goods were first moved from the old White-house to the new building they presented a rather small appearance. One felt, on going into the large new Store, and seeing the apparently slim supply of goods, as if one could stuff the whole stock into a moderately capacious pocket. But the shelves have been gradually filling up, and Mr. Aiken's last trip to New York has resulted in a large accession to the stock; somewhere between two and three thousand dollars worth has been bought, chiefly dry goods.—Such an emporium presents a decided attraction to the ladies; we met quite a bevy of them the other day, holding a very animated confabulation over the respective merits of different favorite patterns.

Our tin can making has come to a close for the present, a sufficient quantity having been made. For several months past we have had, working in this department a hired man who had "taken his wife into partnership with him;" she slipped on the tops and bottoms and he soldered them. The arrangement was a good one and worked well.

In these days when we are doing so much to cancel our own national debt, Uncle Sam claims a levy to defray his, in the shape of an internal revenue stamp on every can or bottle of fruit we sell. Over $600 has already been expended this season on these miniatures of George Washington: the putting of them on is almost a business by itself, besides their being cancelled in the Dana press.

As it was important that our corn should be picked Wednesday and it was a very rainy day, we hired men to do it, and gave them each 50 cts. per day extra wages.

The scaffolding is erected on the west side of the Man-sion House, preparatory to shingling it. The long delay has, in part, been caused by the continued rain. The weather promises fair this morning.

There are twenty five or more hired people, including some Indians engaged in cutting corn, besides eight Indians who husk. The corn-cutting bees are very efficiently superintended by Mrs. F. A. Burt.

We have just been down into the preserving room and passed around, to witness the lively operations going on there. One squaw, we observed, had her hair tied up in a style very much resembling a waterfall with a net drawn over it nearly as coarse as a fish net; another one had her long hair quite prettily beaded in two neat braids. There were Irish and Dutch and one or two of the dark sons of Ham—quite a motley set.

Our people are collecting apples for making cider.—We have of late been obliged to buy all our vinegar, at the high price of twenty five cents per gallon, by the barrel. We hope to make cider enough, this fall, to furnish us all the vinegar we shall need the coming year.

The autumnal tints begin to add new beauty to the prospect from our window, and though they point to the coming winter, and nature's long sleep, yet we enjoy the sight, nevertheless.

Last evening, W. made a call for men to husk at five o'clock this morning and women to cut corn at a quarter before six. W's call was immediately succeeded by another from the kitchen folks for a bee to open clams. At this point, Mr. Hamilton, asked "Any more bees wanted?" when a somewhat *thin* voice responded "Would like a bag-bee to-morrow forenoon." We understand that all three bees have been well attended.

According to the theory of the Saturday Review as given in last Circular, sitting up late at night is a mark of advanced civilization. Well, the O. C. is certainly not behind even in this feature of progress. D. P. N. and Mr. Blood continued their yesterday's work in the Preserving room till one o'clock this morning.

We are realizing good prices for our Grapes. Some are sent as far as to Boston, others to New York, others to Syracuse and Utica. Hiland Smith and Co., of Boston write, "Your fruit comes in good order, and the style is very neat."

Our men are at present relieved from the unpleasant task of milking, as it is done wholly by our hired help. We milk now, sixty cows.

Mrs. Bushnell, Mrs. Otis and Emily arrived last night. Miss Mathews' brother and family left this morning.

Traps ordered yesterday, 53 doz.
Including the following:
Walsh, Coulter and Co., New York, 57 doz.

METEOROLOGICAL.

Thermometer, Sept. 27.
7 A. M. 46. 12 M. 60. 7 P. M. 59. Mean 55.

DAILY JOURNAL
OF ONEIDA COMMUNITY.

VOL. 2. SEPT. 29, 1866. NO. 77.

SATURDAY.

Mrs. Towner with her two children arrived last evening, bringing with her, the following note:

Berlin Hights, O., Sept. 27. 1866.

DEAR BRO. PITT:—I feel thankful to God that I can commend Mrs. Towner (who will bear this note to you) and Freddy and Lillie, our children, to the sympathy and love of the Oneida Community. I hope their visit may be to their and your mutual good. I desire to have them remain as long as is conducive to that end, and while they do stay, I wish the children, if practicable, to share your children's discipline and life.

Whatever expense is incurred on their account will cheerfully be met to your satisfaction. Patiently and cheerfully waiting, I am faithfully and fraternally yours,

J. W. TOWNER.

W. G. K. received a letter from his brother Daniel yesterday, in which he speaks of a report having been circulated, that he has been speaking against the Community and trying to draw his family away from it. He disclaims all authorship of such rumors and expresses the best feelings towards us.

Mrs. Atwell from Naples, whom Mr. Cragin will recollect as his correspondent, and to whom he returned the $50 with a criticism, came here last night, and left for home this morning. She has been to Philadelphia to visit her brother, for the express purpose, she says, of calling on us, unknown to her husband, as he was unwilling she should visit us. We liked her appearance very well, and Mrs. Bushnell who is acquainted with her says, there is a favorable change in her spirit since her criticism. Mrs. A. says she has always believed we held the truth, and she said on leaving, "When you get ready to let me join you, will you let me know?"

A young man by the name of Camp, from N. Haven, Conn., came last night. He has studied, he says, to the injury of his health, and partly on that account, and partly to become acquainted with us and our principles, he wants to get employment here. He has visited Wallingford and has read the Circular some—has been a "flaming methodist," but is quite dissatisfied with his religious experience, and believes there is a better way.

The weather is at present remarkably clear and bright. The rustling of brown leaves under our feet, reminds us that   "Leaves have their time to fall

And flowers to wither at the North wind's blast."
Speaking of flowers, we are led to wonder where our floral contribution to the coming fair is to come from. The late frost desolated our garden for the present season irremediably. We shall have to trust to the greenhouse.

Mr. Porter the tailor, his wife and two children came yesterday: we understand they are to occupy Mr. Aiken's room at the Store, for the present, and board in the family. Mrs. P. seems a good deal interested in the Community. Mr. P. is busy at work.

We have now four hired women in the washing department, and one more is expected next week. They iron all the women's clothes, with very few exceptions, dresses included. Mrs. Mallory says there were over fifty dresses washed last week.

Our first lot of silk came back from the dyer yesterday, and has a very fine appearance. The spooling of it, will commence next Monday.

There were 3,420 cans of corn put up yesterday. The husking is usually started by our own folks in the morning and carried on throughout the day by hired help.

We are now supplying the Boston market with pears for which we receive from $16 to $20 a barrel. The costliest kinds are the Flemish Beauties and Louise De Bonne.

The sales at the store yesterday, to outsiders, amounted to $72,15, besides what was sold to members of our own family.

The dispensation of tallow candles has come to an end. Oil has been "struck."

G. W. N. arrived last night, having walked up from the depot. He is warmly welcomed at Oneida.

Mr. Morse was here again and staid over night.

Traps ordered yesterday,	113	doz.
The principal orders were—		
A. H. Gardner, Milwaukee,	87	"
also 6 No. 5 Bear.		
Scudder, Rogers & Co., Boston.	17	"
Morland, Watson & Co., Montreal,	25	"

RHYMES FOR THE TIMES.

It is a vain tradition
That the family position,
    An isolated one,
Is the only state that's free,
Where the parties both agree,
And that love and unity
    Are found in that alone.

Oft the yokes that men have made
And on our necks have laid
    Are hard enough to bear,
But Christ's yoke is free and light
To the humble and contrite,
And to wear it, all delight
    Who his love may share.

METEOROLOGICAL.
Thermometer, Sept. 28.

7 A. M. 59. 12 M. 70. 7 P. M. 59. Mean 62⅓.

DAILY JOURNAL
OF ONEIDA COMMUNITY.

VOL. 2.   OCT. 1, 1866.   NO. 78.

MONDAY.
HURRAH FOR J. BURT AND THE CORN-CUTTER!!!

If, when it was found some weeks ago that the corn-cutters could not be used on thick ears of corn, many of us felt as we had done when the first cable snapped. truly the complete success that now crowns good Father Burt's efforts, scuds a thrill through every heart. His genius has at length, through patient thought and faith, made such changes in the machine, that it now not only adapts itself readily to ears of whatever thickness or taper, but works much more easily than before.—In our limited space, it is impossible to give a discription of the improvement, but this much we may say, that the changes are so radical, that we might almost call the machine a new one altogether. To see the grain so rapidly and perfectly stripped from the cob, is quite wonderful.

BUSNESS MEETING.

S. W. Nash spoke on the liability of accident from the careless use of matches. He mentioned a new safety match to which Mr. Aiken has lately been calling atten tion. This new kind cannot be lighted by mere friction, but only when brought in contact with a kind of chemically prepared emery paper, a piece of which accompanies each box. Messrs. Nash, Campbell and Aiken were appointed to take measures for introducing these matches into partial use in the family, by way of trial.

The following facetious note was received this morning in reply to a letter notifying the writer that we shall not be able to fill his entire order:

ONEIDA FRUIT(LESS) DEPARTMET;—Aint you getting a little too kussed popular in your phicksuns? Its thundering hard that a fellow can't get a few tomatoes even, before they are all ripe at home.—Send all I ordered that you have, and where glass is skaice, send tin of course. Pack them ready to ship, and on receipt of invoice, I will send funds, and you can forward them. Dont trust any body 5½ minutes by Frodsham's Chronometer. If you can, by them ere "intuitions," tell what you are gwine to raise next season, send a price list, and I'll fill an order and for once in my life be in season!

Yours (always in the drag),   J. M. Beckett,
Boston, Mass.

We were rather amused yesterday with an interesting group of visitors, consisting of three or four women and a corpulant old gentlemen who was acting as their guide. He seemed to be explaining everything to them with the air of an oracle. On passing up the main stair-way, where some specimens of feather-like pampas grass have been standing ever since last fall, we saw him ele vate his cane in portly style and point to the grass with the air of a naturalist. "The cotton plant." said he to his fair companions. Doubtless, they felt as if they had learned something.—Another youth asked one of us if he might "see that ocean"—meaning the aquarium.

G. W. N. gave a lecture last evening on "The Lesson of History." The unity of plan maintained throughout the lecture, together with its comprehensiveness, made it deeply interesting. We should think that such a lec ture is just what is needed, to show the world the place which Communism is destined to occupy in the develop ment of God's plans.

Our neighbors, the Indians, have turned out en masse this morning to husk corn. They occupy the shed north of the Tontine. There are old men and old women, young folks, children and pappooses.—one old squaw, entirely blind and another one on crutches, some smok ing, some chewing, and all seemingly quite contented with their lot, and willing to work. They are not all to be trusted, however, in their count, and Mr. Barron, who keeps tally, says he has to keep a sharp look-out.

It seemed necessary, yesterday, that our work in the preserving line should go right along, as there were to matoes that were spoiling, and pears that would not keep long, and the putting up of corn could be delayed only one day, so a bee was commenced in the morning and continued till half past 4 o'clock P. M. 1,408 quarts of tomatoes were canned and 283 quarts of pears. Many strangers looked in upon us, some of whom doubt less thought, as neighbor Davis expressed himself, that we were growing worldly minded, getting rich &c,. He said it however, apparently in sport, and with the best intentions.

Sidney went on Friday last to East Bloomfield to vis it Mr. Bradley's vineyard which consists of eight acres of Isabella vines. He also went to Rochester, where he visited the nursery of Elwanger & Barry for the purpose of engaging some plum trees. He did not succeed in finding any, but the observations he made amply repaid him for his trip. He returned on Saturday.

The fine weather brings its crowd of visitors—quite a rush yesterday—of quite a good class, on the whole—nineteen dinners served.

G. D. Allen came Saturday night and spent Sunday with us. He leaves again sometime to-day.

Traps ordered Saturday,	150 doz.
The principal orders were—	
C. Shepard, Milwaukee,	80 "
Sidney Shepard & Co., Buffalo,	73 "
Dickson, Clark & Co., Cincinnati,	27 "

Thermometer, Sept. 29 & 30.

7 A. M. 59. 13 M. 70. 7 P. M. 60. Mean 63.
7 A. M. 59. 13 M. 69. 7 P. M. 60. Mean 62½.

DAILY JOURNAL
OF ONEIDA COMMUNITY.

VOL. 2.　OCT. 2, 1866.　NO. 79.

TUESDAY.

We subjoin a few extracts from a letter received this morning from Mrs. Atwell who was here a few days since:

"I am very thankful for the delightful hours spent at the Community, night before last, Your principles (and I think I understand them some), are prized, if circumstances do prevent their being fully practiced. I have found the philosopher's stone &c.—On my way home I called at the O. C. N. Y. B. which seems to be composed of very reliable and trustworthy young men I am hungering and thirsting after righteousness, and am striving to accept Christ as my magnetizer."

Your friend,　　E. M. ATWELL.

In meeting last evening Mr. Burt related some of his experience in reference to the improvement of the corn cutter. He said, the new idea came to him at Portland while he was under the pressure consequent upon the failure of the machine to work, and that his mind was occupied with it constantly, till the object was accomplished. He said he wished to give God all the credit of his success.

Mr. Perkins has so far recovered as to be able to walk round, with the help of a cane. Yesterday he went down and measured the distance of his fall, and found it twenty feet, instead of ten, as reported. He says it would have killed a common person, and the reason of his surviving it is because he was so tough. We tell him that it has improved him, that he is straighter, and walks lighter than before his fall.

Mr. Cocks of Brooklyn arrived last evening and left this morning. He has hitherto read the CIRCULAR at the house of a friend, but is so much pleased with what he has seen, that he wishes to have it for himself and handed Mr. Bolles $5 as his subscription.

Mr. Camp, whom we mentioned in Saturday's Journal, de-Camped on Monday morning. He professed to "hear the word with gladness," made some spasmodic attempts to make himself useful at our bee, and was quite enthusiastic to have us hire him. Having gone over to an Indian Methodist meeting (which his presence, we suppose, made into a Camp meeting), we found his views so far modified that he took his departure on Monday morning, ostensibly because he "felt as if he were going to be sick."

A beggar called one morning, wanting some breakfast, and enquired if he could be hired. Mr. Woolworth told him he guessed we did not want to hire him, but he might work enough to pay for his breakfast. After he had eaten he was seen walking off, but James Vaill followed him and reminded him of the conditions upon which his breakfast was furnished him. He attempted some faint excuse and said he was in a hurry—wanted to meet some one &c, so James let him off.

Where do our thoughts come from? and why do they flow so freely at one time, while at another we feel as barren and dry as the wintry heath? If there is an inexhaustible fountain within, why is it, that at times the treasure seems sealed up, and no amount of labor can unlock it? We are convinced that evil spirits have something to do in producing this uncomfortable state of things, and that were there no devil, there would be no hindrance to the free flow of inspiration in our hearts.

As there was no stove in the room occupied by the Porters, they have removed to the old Tool-House, and occupy John Norton's room. Mrs. P. seems desirous to get acquainted with the family.

Mr Ackley thinks that persons might get a wrong impression, from what was said in Friday's Journal about our vinegar. He says we have bought only two barrels and we use fully thirty, in the course of the year.

One of our children, a little four-year-old, was whining around with his arm up over his eyes in great trouble because the children plagued him—so to comfort himself he said, "I'll go up in the tower and tell God about it." Quite an orthodox idea.

One of our employees came into the Journal Office the other day to have a Circular put up in a wrapper for the mail, and having heard that a paper of some kind was issued here, was quite surprised that this was not the office of the Circular. Baby must surely be very like Mamma, to be mistaken for her in this way.

On getting up this morning we were all agreeably surprised to find the CIRCULARS already distributed.— The hasty reading we have given them, was quite refreshing.

Mrs. Ackley is superseded by Jane Abbott in the Bakery and takes her place as mother at the children's house for the present.

35 crates of peaches came to the depot, to-day, eleven of which were sold there and the rest brought home. Mr. Bradley is away purchasing this fruit.

G. W. N., Mrs. Skinner and J. A. Kinsley, left early this morning for Wallingford.

Arrived in the night, Mr. Hawley, Emma, Rose and Mr. Easton's little girl, Fanny. Also a hired man, who is to work in the Trap-Shop.

Over 3,100 quarts of corn put up yesterday.

Value of bags shipped in September, $2,500. This department is three weeks behind orders.

Traps ordered yesterday,　　　　　　　171 doz
Including—
Orders sent by Mr. Olds from Davenport, Ohio, 101 "

Thermometer, Oct. 1.

7 A. M. 50.　12 M. 61.　7 P. M. 59.　Mean 59⅓.

DAILY JOURNAL
OF ONEIDA COMMUNITY.

VOL. 2.   OCT. 3, 1866.   NO. 80.

WEDNESDAY.

We overheard a conversation between two young persons in the tent-room a few days since, which disturbed our equilibrium somewhat, though it was spoken we presume without much reflection.

A. "How different this room looks from what it used to, when I roomed here. The curtains were new, with blue trimmings, the beds were made up sleek, and the room nicely carpeted."

N. "I suppose that persons who room here now, are pretty much those of the last generation."

Indeed!—thought we to ourselves as we listened—and that is the cause—is it?—of the general dilapidation and unattractiveness of the place! Better extend your sympathies to those, who consent to room there, notwithstanding its time-worn condition, and who have waited patiently, long years, for the magic wand of the carpenter, to transform it into comfortable dormitories.

Notwithstanding the late abundant rains, our scarcity of water led Mr. Abbott to suspect there was a leakage in the pipes somewhere.—They had not much trouble in finding the leak, and stopping it yesterday, but this morning another, and more serious one is being searched out, and men are digging in front of the Tontine, to see if they can find it. Although the water ran into the large reservoir as much as usual during the night, there was little in it this morning, which indicates that the trouble in the pipes, is not far off.

Mrs. Bushnell has in her possession, and brought with her as an antique curiosity, the veritable bib that the traitor Arnold wore in his infancy. It is made of fine linen, with a strip of ornamental needle-work in the centre, about one and a half inches in width and extending from top to bottom. It was presented to Mrs. B. by one of the descendants of that distinguished personage, and may serve as a relic to perpetuate the memory of his perfidy.

After the usual readings, last evening, there was some conversation about the approaching Fair. Presently Mr. Hamilton called for a story, and Mr. Burt responded with a humerous account of his fruitless efforts to resist sea-sickness during his late trip.

We had some visitors, yesterday who made themselves quite disagreeable in various ways. They went into the room where our people were packing grapes, and helped themselves unsparingly to grapes and pears.

Mrs. Leete is here on a visit.

Mr. Gonkes, who was the regular night-watch at W. P., is now occupied in running the corn-cutter, his place as watchman being filled by volunteers from the family.

The first samples of O. C. sewing silk have been on exhibition for a day or two in the upper sitting-room.—It is black and of very beautiful quality—was spooled by Olive.

A company, yesterday, were looking at the curiosities of the show-case, when on examining the big tooth and jaw of the Mastodon, a gentleman remarked, "That's *ossified.*"

Mr. Burt is now turning his attention to the invention of a new corn-husker. An experiment was made this morning, but the machine is only in an incipient stage.

The weather this morning is cloudy and cold, and a storm seems pending.

Our corn is all picked, and the work of canning it, closes up to-day. 3,733 quarts were put up yesterday.

Value of Traps shipped in September,		$19,666 03.
Traps ordered yesterday,		248 doz.
Including the following orders—		
Geo. S. Saxton,	St. Louis,	60 "
G. Bremerman & Co.,	"	17 "
Jno. G. Alexander & Co.,	"	53 "
Hibbard & Spencer,	Chicago,	50 "

MORNING NOTES.

Mechanics off at early morn, prompt at the hour if foul or fair;

Maidens plying the dreaded broom over the carpet and down the stair;

A group of natives husking corn, with faces dark and raven hair;

The sons of Erin drawing cans, and Mr. Barron's watchful care;

The Tontine, too, a swarming hive, where many hast'ning steps repair;

And here the florist, working hard for coming winter to prepare;

The Journalist is seeking news, much perplexed, but not in despair;

Yonder seen in Sanctum's nook, the Editress with thoughtful air;

Mr. Bolles escorting the guests, who but seldom forget to stare;

Such are scenes of our outward life—but from comment we now forbear.   T.

Thermometer, Oct. 2.
7 A. M. 59.   12 M. 78.   7 P. M. 60.   Mean 65½.

DAILY JOURNAL
OF ONEIDA COMMUNITY.

VOL. 2.   OCT. 4, 1866.   NO. 81.

THURSDAY.

Some months ago, when volunteers were called for to sleep at the Mill, names were handed in, to the number of from thirty to forty, and it was arranged that they should take turns, each accepting a dormitory at the Mill for one week. But what was at first accepted as a duty has now become something of a privilege, and it is hard to persuade people to be content with one week in this delightful retreat. Not to speak of its quietness, and the beautiful view had from the north windows in the morning, of the creek rippling along under the bending

branches of yellow and green, there is a domestic animal at the Mill, which rejoices in the expressive name of Skipper. Skipper is a kitten of collossal size, much larger than the grown cats found around here. What he *will* grow to, time alone can show. He is of spotless white—every hair of him; and his disposition corresponds to the spotlessness of his coat. His abilities as a hunter, cannot be disputed, and if rats and mice do not shortly vanish from our premises, it will only be because this noble cat disdains such paltry game. He looks more like a match for a panther.—Like all great personages, he is magnanimous, and shows high respect for his superiors, being much attached to Man. "Man is the dog's God," says the proverb—and the cat's too—we should say.

To give some idea of the manner in which the O. C. is represented at Vernon Town Fair, we subjoin a synopsis of our principal contributions:—

Fourteen Satchels, eight Traps, thirty-four sorts of Vegetables, twenty-four head of Horses and Cattle, twenty-one sorts of Grapes, thirty-nine sorts of Apples, and twenty-one sorts of Pears: besides samples of Sewing-silk, Benedict Arnold's bib, crayon Drawings by C. A. M., Work-boxes and Baskets coated over with sea shells and nuts or acorns, Needle-work, a tiny Chair made of goose-quills, &c.—One team of horses will be entered at the plowing match. The brass band went to di course sweet music, and a party of the family, including several ladies have gone, by way expressing our good will, as well as to "see the Fair."

The last machine necessary for the production of machine twist, was started yesterday. It is the soft silk winder, used for winding silk from the skein in which it is dyed, on bobbins ready for spooling.—A young lady called at the Factory yesterday to buy some sewing-silk to use in making a new dress. She purchased a small spool for thirty-five cents. She will probably be the first to put the O. C. silk to the test of actual use.

One really handsome bouquet was sent to the Fair, and we might have sent more than one, had it not been for the impoliteness of our Tuesday's visitors. They had the legality about them that would not allow them to eat their dinner till they had said grace, yet they helped themselves to flowers enough for two bouquets after being told that we wished to send what we had to the Fair and could spare none for other purposes.

We know of a lady who, the other day, went to look in the dictionary for a word. Presently, she was heard affirming that it wasn't there. "It must be there," said some one; "it's a perfectly common word." "Can't find it," was the rejoinder, after further search; "it isn't here at all." And, sure enough, it wasn't; for she was looking in the *concordance.*

It was quite a sight to see our band start off for the fair this morning. The wagon in which they rode was a hired one, with six or eight seats, and drawn by three span of horses. They drove around the house several times, and attracted the attention of all the hired folks, who turned out to see them, including the hands at the Bag Shop.

We are amused at the ease with which one of our hired men carries a well filled two bushel basket on his head, though we confess to some trembling, lest we should see it precipitated to the earth, scattering the contents at his feet.

Mr. Hatch has taken the largest class of boys that live at the children's house to the Fair, together with the girls of Charlotte Maria's age.

We are happy to say that the shingling of the Mansion house is completed, and the rubbish around is removed.

There was a severe frost last night, and it felt quite wintry this morning, but the day, though cold, is very pleasant.

Traps ordered yesterday,	135 doz.
including the following orders—	
Wells and Hale, Milwaukee,	50 "
Pratt & Co., Buffalo,	50 "
James N. Stephenson, St. Louis,	20 " Fox.

Thermometer, Oct. 3.

7 A. M. 49   12 M. 60.   7 P. M. 59.   Mean 55¾.

DAILY JOURNAL
OF ONEIDA COMMUNITY.

VOL. 2.   OCT. 5, 1866.   NO. 82.

FRIDAY.

VERNON TOWN FAIR.

We have not been able to obtain full particulars regarding the Fair; but such details as were within our reach, although fragmentary and imperfect, may be interesting to readers at the Branch Communities.

No one entering the large oblong tent at Vernon, yesterday, and glancing around the really brilliant display of goods useful and ornate, could fail to observe the large proportion of articles marked "From the Oneida Community." Indeed the very decided preponderance of our stock, manufactures and productions over those of any private competitors, led the judges to adopt the unquestionably wise course of not really placing our goods &c. in competition with those of other exhibitors at all. So that the report of the judges, spoken at the close of the Fair, distinctly stated, with reference to our Ayrshires, Traps, Preserves, Sewing-silk, Pears &c., that they "swept the board and took all the premiums;" while the premiums were very properly given to the productions of individual effort, with the saving proviso. "excepting professionals."—In a few things, however, we were placed on a level with other competitors, and to rank as follows:—

Yearling Steers,	1st. & 2nd.	Premiums
Fall Apples—best six varieties,	1st.	"
Winter "	2nd.	"
Hand Bouquet,	1st.	"
Hearth-rug (Mrs. Bushnell's),	1st.	"
Show-case of Fancy Articles,	1st	"

Vegetables, "beyond all comparison and worthy of all the premiums." The Corn-cutter, operated on by Mr. Bart, was described as "a marvel of ingenuity."—As no teams were entered for plowing but our own, no "match" was held.—In passing to and from the Fair, our teams were allowed to pass the toll-gate free of charge.—The brass band were very hospitably entertained at Reid's Hotel. At first, they were in the general crowd at the dining-room door, waiting to take their chance of obtaining seats; but the host, on seeing this, signaled them to follow him round by another way and gave them comfortable seats before the other guests were admitted.—On thinking over the position awarded to the O. C. on this occasion, we were led to wonder whether the public cannot read a lesson from it. Do they not see that it is really Christ that "swept the boards", was "worthy of all the premiums" and was "beyond all comparison?"

Another letter from Meroa was received yesterday. She complains of being homesick, but on the whole gets along very well. She professes much love for the Community and desires to keep in fellowship with them.—Also a letter from a Mr. Crawford, of Millville, N. J., a tailor, making inquiries, about his chance of getting into business here, what wages we give, and whether we could give his wife and two daughters employment. He has read the CIRCULAR, some, and professes to feel interested in our principles. He says his wife has worn the short dress, the last seven years.

———◆◆◆◆———

We are informed that Mr. Clark has brought home a kid, and the children are quite jubilant over it. One person we hear, is making great calculations about milk for the children when the cows fail, and one of the girls is anticipating the time when she can have a pair of kid gloves made from its skin.

———◆◆◆◆———

There are indications of trouble among the cans of preserved corn. Some seem rather restless in their confined condition and are indeavoring to break their bonds. Measures are being taken to quell, if possible, their inquietude, by an extra cooking.

———◆◆◆◆———

This morning at six o'clock the thermometer stood at 13 deg. below freezing; a piece of ice half an inch thick was brought into the house, and the hoar frost had to be swept off like snow from the balconies. The days, however, are remarkably brilliant.

———◆◆◆◆———

Those who were unable to visit the Fair, have an opportunity of seeing the principal part of our contribution, to-day. The fruits and vegtables have been arranged on tables at the back of the New House and make a very fine display.

———◆◆◆◆———

Last evening, Mr. Hamilton called attention to the very large influx of business we are having in the Trap department. He spoke of this prosperity as "a gift from the Lord," which we ought justly to appreciate as such. We trust our readers do not overlook the daily reports of Trap-orders given in our columns.

———◆◆◆◆———

Traps ordered yesterday,	293 doz.
also five Bear.	
The principal orders were—	
Standart Brothers, Detroit,	125 "
James H. Foster, Chicago,	52 "
C. E. Mavo, St. Paul,	51 "
A. F. Shapleigh & Co., St. Louis,	80 " No. 2.

———◆◆◆◆———

Thermometer, Oct. 4.
7 A. M. 40.   12 M. 41.   7 P. M. 39.   Mean 40.

———◆◆◆◆———

DAILY JOURNAL
OF ONEIDA COMMUNITY.

VOL. 2.   SATURDAY, OCT. 6, 1866.   NO. 8

SWEET CORN.

From present indications, we conclude that only a limited portion of the 25,000 cans of Sweet Corn put up the present season, will answer for shipment. As 18,000 cans are already ordered, it is not advisable to receive further orders.

The present is perhaps not the best place to discuss the cause of the failure. It may, however, be stated that the method pursued was substantially the same as that followed last season.   w.

Another letter was received a few days ago, from Mrs. L. S. Wilcox M. D. She is disappointed in not making us a visit as early as she hoped, but thinks she may come in the course of a week or ten days. She says—

—"My thoughts turn involuntarily and almost constantly, to your Community as the brightest light of this blind distracted world.—I am not able yet to see the truth of all its teachings, but the unfaltering endeavor to make practical all the truth received, commands my admiration—my worship. O! we have long enough been tantalized by theories of christianity—by talk of fraternal love—by essays on self-abnegation. The practical is what is needed.—The world must have examples. I am tired—heart-sick of dealing with effects: I want to grapple with causes.—How I have longed, these many years to be in a condition where the whole nature would be developed harmoniously! How sadly I have felt the need of criticisms made in the spirit of love. Mr. Noyes says, 'God means we shall become wise enough to trim ourselves;' but who is able to do it?—especially under unfavorable conditions. Can a plant grow to its greatest perfection with no sunshine—no cultivation, and surrounded with weeds and thistles? No more can a human spirit grow into all it is susceptible of becoming in society as it is.—Pardon this liberty.

Yours for a true life,   LUCINDA S. WILCOX."

Speaking of the Vernon Fair, the Utica Herald says: —" The competition on fruit, and on almost everything else, between the Oneida Community and the rest of the town of Vernon, was close, but preponderating in favor of the former, as was acknowledged by the Committee on Premiums. This was pre-eminently to be noticed in the articles of manufacture and in vegetables. In this connection we would notice the neatness and durable appearance of ladies' and gentlemen's traveling satchels exhibited by the Community. Also, a very complicated and ingeniously contrived, yet very effectual machine for cutting green corn from the cob. The machine was invented by Mr. JONATHAN BURT, and entered at the fair by the Community."

Miss Mathew's brother who was here last week, and spent three or four days, writes to his sister, that he found on a scrap of wrapping paper she gave him, some allusion to the discovery of Male Continence. He says, "I claim to be an earnest seeker after good, and this has the appearance of being something good, as well as new and I wish to know more about it, it it is consistent." Miss M. will send the tract, "Male Continence."

The boys who have hitherto assisted in keeping the cutlery in order, are quite pleased to find their labor considerably lightened by an invention which Mr. Dunn has set in operation for scouring forks. It consists, simply, of a circular brush which revolves on a spindle connected by a gearing with the steam engine. The fork is dipped in a mixture of water and pounded brick, then drawn lightly over the surface of the revolving brush so that the bristles pass lengthwise between the prongs, when in less than half a minute all rust-specks and spots are removed.

Mr. Brooks, a gentleman over eighty years of age from Elmira, and a Miss Gates with an adopted daughter of hers, from Yellow Springs, Ohio, staid with us over night. Mr. Brooks is the father-in-law of Dr. Gleason of the Water-Cure in Elmira, who, with his wife made us a visit last summer. Miss Gates is an intimate friend of the Gleasons, and is on her way to Boston, to visit the child's father, and put her charge to school in the City. The father of the child is an Irish Lord, and holds large estates in his native country. Miss Gates is a woman of a good deal of strength of character, we should judge—has read the writings of Swedenborg a good deal, but they do not satisfy the longings of her heart for truth. She expressed herself a good deal interested in our doctrines.

Our tomato patch consists of 148 rods. From this, 70 bushels were picked on Thursday, which closed the harvest for this season. The entire crop has amounted to 608 bushels, of which $100,05 worth has been sold, and the rest canned and used in the family and boarding-houses.

Mrs. Otis left for home last night. She has mixed up with the family in their work, and made herself generally useful. We trust she will return home much comforted by her visit.

Traps ordered yesterday.	155 doz.
The principal orders were—	
A. H. Gardner & Co.,	315 "
W. D. Foster, Grand Rapids,	100 "

Yesterday's temperature—
7 A. M. 22.   12 M. 49.   7 P. M. 40.   Mean 37.

DAILY JOURNAL
OF ONEIDA COMMUNITY.

VOL. 2.   MONDAY, OCT. 8, 1866.   NO. 84.

BUSINESS MEETING.

C. A. Cragin mentioned that he had lately visited a silk-factory, at Northampton whose silk is noted for the regularity of its twist. It seems that while in most factories, the twisting is regulated by mere guess work, this Northampton factory manages this matter with the accuracy of science. The foreman has offered to communicate to Charles the secret of doing it, for one hundred dollars, and it was for the board to decide whether the offer should be accepted. Voted that with Mr. Hamilton's approval, Charles should make arrangements to meet with this foreman and accept his offer.

Some conversation was held on the subject of husks for beds. Mr. Bradley and E. F. Hutchins were appointed to take measures for obtaining some, either from the Indians or otherwise.

Mr. Burt spoke of the improvement he had made on the corn-cutter. He wished to know whether it is necessary to have a new patent, as the first one does not cover this improvement. It was thought that *practically*, the patent already obtained is a sufficient protection to the new improvement, although it does not cover it specifically, seeing the improvement could not well be used except on the basis of the original machine.

S. W. Nash and M. L. Worden were appointed to see to the laying of the cement walk, weather permitting, as soon as the tar arrives.

Voted that we consider the season as closed for getting dinners for company; but that substantial luncheons almost as good as dinners, should be provided in the family dining-room to such guests as call for them.—The company dining-room will be fitted up as a dairy and milk-house.

Sunday Oct 7.

We wish to acknowledge our appreciation of the public expressions of love and welcome, from Mr. Hamilton and the family to us, since we came here, and confess our union with them through Christ. We hope that Mr. Hamilton's expectation that we shall prove to be good soldiers for Christ, may be realized, and that we may always be found united in heart and purpose with those that are fighting evil, and laboring for the building up of God's Kingdom on earth.

DAVID E. BLOOD.
MARY L. BLOOD.

Seth Otis, a distant relative of Emily's, called yesterday and staid an hour or two. He was U. S. Consul in Switzerland during Filmore's administration, and is at present agent of Claflin and Co., New York. He had been at Vernon on business, and knowing that Emily was here, came over to see her. He expressed himself as rather surprised at the "elegance" of things here—especially the Hall. He thought it a "strange move" in E. to come here, and does not sympathize much with us, but was, on the whole, very gentlemanly, and intends to learn more about us.

Our florists were rather amused the other day with the remarks of two women who visited the Greenhouse. "What's the name o' that flower?" asked one. "Earrings;" replied the other, with the air of one who knew something. "That's the century plant that blows every fifty years—ain't it;" added the other, turning to Mrs. S. "That is the century plant," was the reply. "I've heard," rejoined the visitor, "that when it blows, it can be heard a mile off."

We have stopped sending our milk to the Cheese Factory for the season, and commence setting it for butter, to-day. The company dining-room has been fitted up as a dairy and milk-house, and Mrs. Harriet Kinsley resumes charge of it for the present.

We shall not realize as much profit from our grape harvest as was anticipated in the summer. The failure is to be attributed in part to the cold rains of August, and partly to our early frosts, both of which have been a great hindrance to the ripening of the fruit.—We have sold, however, over $1,200 worth.

The weather has been delightful for the last two or three days—mild, bright and suggestive of that mellow ripeness which satisfies the mind.—Mr. Dunn's health has so far improved that he walked over to the Park yesterday.

On Friday evening, over eighty of our employees met in the home boarding-house where they had a dance.—They were very well dressed, and behaved themselve with propriety. The meeting broke up a little after ten o'clock.

The Porters left us on Saturday. We learn that an offer has been made them, and they are to let us know by Tuesday, whether they will accept it. Our people are going to fit up the Burt house, for the accommodation of a tailor.

Mr. Bradley returned Saturday. He bought while out 100 bushels of quinces, and paid for them $211.

Mary Leete has been here several days on a visit.—She went home this morning.

Our tax in the month of Sept. on traps alone, was $1000.

Traps ordered Saturday,   132 doz.

Temperature, Saturday and Sunday—
7 A. M. 40. 12 M. 59. 7 P. M. 49. Mean 49½.
7 A. M. 51. 12 M. 72. 7 P. M. 69. Mean 63.

DAILY JOURNAL
OF ONEIDA COMMUNITY.

VOL. 2.   TUESDAY, OCT. 9, 1866.   NO. 65.

The article in the Phrenological Journal has drawn some communications to Oneida as well as to the Branch Communes. One young man writes from North Hampton, L. I., in a tone so self complacent and at the same time so importunate that we are tempted to print an extract from it for the amusement of our readers, retaining the original spelling. He says:

" I am Thirty Two years of age single. I think that I have Devoted myself to the same Objects the Communities have in view I love the Principals of such society. I have carefully read the General Principals of your society. I am not selfish I like to do good for the good of the Community. Therefore I think it is Just the Place for me. Will you Please admit me into your Family I can be of some service to you as I am a lone in the world or that is I have not many of my stamp to associate with in this Vicinity I will make Application to you Please accept me and my good wishes for your success.—I have Been Studing and practicing those habits Which you Believe and Practice for a number of years And I think that I have perfect controll of myself So that I can fully comply with your Principals and rules as laid down in the Journal which I have read and Studeyeed for a number of years. Please write me if you will not accept me now Please write me if there is any chance in the Future.

Yours Respectfully,   STEPHEN W. BISHOP.

P. S. I have seen what your rules and terms are I know that I can comply to them. Please Admit."

Victor Hawley was criticised last night by request: but little fault was found with him, and much commendation of his course was expressed. He is quite a naturalist, and carries his investigations right along with his work. He was exhorted to become more in earnest for spiritual attainments, and to use his tongue more freely in testimony of experience and confessions of Christ, in our evening gatherings, and elsewhere.

A Mr. Crandall from Baldwinsville, came last evening bearing a letter of recommendation from Mr. Robinson. He wishes to work for us. It is uncertain, as yet, whether we can employ him.

SONNETS.
i.

Well I remember, in my childhood's years
My young life bounding with exultant beat,
My hopes all flushed with visions fair and sweet,
Soul-music ever sounding in mine ears—
Those happy strains of joy that childhood hears—
How I then dreamed in life's path I should meet
Great men, or at some noble Teacher's feet
Should one day sit. But ah! I woke to tears;

And chilling mists curled round my manhood's prime :
The visions paled, the pulse began to miss
Its early flash, faint grew the music's chime—
When lo! the Truth has changed the whole to this :
Joined with the best and foremost of my time
In purpose good, my life is crowned with bliss.

ii.

And now, once more, the early music swells
With richer harmony, with fuller tone ;
Far higher hopes around my path are strewn ;
On earnest truth—not dreams—my spirit dwells.
Up from my heart a living current wells ;
No longer stand I in the world alone ;
A leader and a brotherhood I own,
Living the grand, though quiet life that tells
Upon the world. Thus has my course been brought
To find the good that once seemed far away :
The living Truth exceeds my dreamiest thought ;
Around my path the happy sunbeams play ;
With golden threads my web of life is wrought ;
I see the morning of a perfect day.

W. H. H.

We called on Eugene this morning, and presented him with a Luminary. He took it and held it in his hand a moment, laughing and making sounds that might pass for reading. This is certainly a clear proof that he is of a literary turn of mind. The famous Samuel Johnson wrote verse at the age of four years; but Eugene beats that : he studies the Luminary at an age of less than as many months.

Four Stone masons are at work laying the wall to the cellar of the wing of the old dairy house, which, it will be remembered, stands on the site of the store that was burned. It is to be fitted up as a cottage for some of our tenants. The Burt House is to be moved forward so as to be in line with the new building near it. The cellar is now being dug.

As the work of riveting at the Trap-Shop is behind hand Mr. Burt is round among the men this morning, calling for volunteers, and has succeeded, we believe, in getting three or four hands.

It is proposed to have our Black employees, the Thomases, removed to the old packing shop, back of the Mill, as their *peculiar* habits are quite annoying to their near neighbors.

We had quite a lively bee at the Tontine, last night, at half past six o'clock, for pairing and cutting apples to dry.

Rosamond has resigned her post of recording the temperature. She is succeeded by Arthur H. Bloom.

A light shower fell last night.

Traps ordered since Saturday   80 doz.

Yesterday's temperature—

7 A. M. 52.   12 M. 70.   6 P. M. 60.   Mean 60⅓.

DAILY JOURNAL
OF ONEIDA COMMUNITY.

VOL. 2.   WEDNESDAY, OCT. 10, 1866.   NO. 240.

WORK.

A peep at the Trap Factory, is worth something in these days. We spent half an hour, yesterday, in going through this department, and lo, what a racket there was! And no wonder. Just think that with the material which, of course, was got ready beforehand, the number of traps put together and completed during last month, presents the neat little figure of 42,000. To turn out goods at such a rate as this, many hands are required. Consequently, we have forty nine hired workmen and twenty members of our own family, all busily engaged in this single department. These sixty nine persons are distributed through many different branches of the work, from the original designer, down through a long grade of processes too numerous for particular mention. There are blacksmiths and machinists who keep the tools in order; those who roll out the bars of steel, who cut out springs and who temper them; those who tom the different pieces, who put them together, who nail and rivet them; those who cut out the dogs, who bend them, who put them in; those who weld chains, who put them on, who test them; and many others whose specific craft we must pass over till we reach the group who inspect the finished article and hand it over to the packer to be got ready for shipment.

It is something of a "steep comparison" to pass from all this clang and clatter into an adjacent room where we hear the incessant murmur of the Silk machinery.— Here fifteen hired girls and five members of the family guide the almost invisible attenuations that magically vanish from one bobbin to another, till it reaches the final spool. But these spider-web-like filaments, when many thousands of yards have been doubled and spun and twisted and colored and spooled, present another important contribution to the market. Our first regular lot, consisting of eighteen or twenty pounds, goes to the Agency to-day. Success to it.

In connection with the Trap business, we give the following extract from a letter received a few days ago:

"I have just received the traps you sent 11th S. p'. and 1 case is almost "whipped." You may expect a full sale of traps this season, because wheat is all very poor, say 52 lbs. to the bushel, and corn is not half a crop. Water froze here ½ of an inch, which rather "hurt" corn—consequently the pork season will be early and and light. Farmers will not realize good returns for their crops, and will naturally take up something else to make up their losses, and fur is on everybody's thought.
Respectfully Yours,   G. C. CONE."

The fruit-preserving department is this morning at work putting up quinces. Mr. Bradley pares them on a machine, and we noticed eleven hired women with one of our own, cutting and putting them in cans.—A Mr. Rowley from Philadelphia, was here to supper last night. He came for the purpose of selling our people a lot of tin cans.

In continuation of the poem published in yesterday's Journal, we now add the following:

SONNET.
iii.

My home-surroundings when I contemplate,
   How, with a grace more perfect than a King's,
   The truth is told me of my shortcomings,
By gentle friends, of heart too good and great
To do a thing ignoble; and who wait
   With Christ-like patience for the blossomings
   Of slow but true improvement;—all these things
Fall on my heart with touch so delicate,
They seem more grateful to my inward sense
   Than, to my outward, breath of violets is.
When thus, the Spirit of Good, tender, intense,
   Like atmosphere of gardens, fills with bliss,
And round me floats in very affluence
Of grace, I say: "Even this to me! and this!"
O. C. Oct. 1866.   W. H. H.

Much sympathy was expressed last night with Mr. Noyes's talk about the character of the Circular, and a desire was manifested by some, to contribute more to its columns, than heretofore. Reference was had to the time when writing for the Circular was a matter of the first importance which was discussed from time to time in our meetings, and all exhorted to do what they could to sustain it. It is the unanimous sentiment here, that we ought certainly, now when the world is beginning to appreciate its truths, to feel doubly interested in its prosperity. We love the CIRCULAR and appreciate highly the labors of Wallingford in that department.

Yesterday we sat with our windows wide open, enjoying the soft and balmy breath, of a delightful autumnal day. But like human experience, a few hours has changed the the whole aspect of things. The weather to-day is cold and windy, with indications of rain, and we instinctively draw around the fire for warmth and comfort.

H. R. Perry arrived to-day.—Also, Albert Ackley.

Traps ordered yesterday,	123 doz.	
The principal orders were—		
Walsh, Coulter & Co., New York,	50 "	
R. & E. Mfg. Co., "	11 "	No. 4.

Yesterday's temperature—
7 A. M. 59.   12 M. 63.   6 P. M. 60.   Mean 61¼.

DAILY JOURNAL
OF ONEIDA COMMUNITY.

VOL. 2.   THURSDAY, OCT. 11, 1866.   NO. 87.

THE WHEEL MOVES.

Mr. Meeker, agricultural reporter of the New York Tribune, arrived here yesterday. He intends to stay long enough to "do us up" thoroughly. He is a middle aged man, simple and unassuming in his manners and wholly free from "airs." Messrs. Hamilton, Pitt and Bolles have had more or less conversation with him and find him quite a pleasant man and a careful observer. He has made a good many inquiries about our religious principles as well as our general organization, setting down everything in his note-book, apparently with much care. He expects to make very extended notes, and afterwards to digest and concentrate them into an article that shall occupy about two columns of the Tribune. He had an opportunity of seeing a large and animated apple bee last evening in the Tontine. He attended meeting last evening, and at the close, observed that "It had just dawned upon his mind that this is a Christian Community." We are glad he has found out so much already.

TO THE FAMILY.

I have for some time past been at the mercy of egotism—excessive individuality. I have identified myself with all evil in my spirit and character, and felt that all blows against that, were aimed at me. I now begin to see my way out, thank God. I confess entire separation from my old life. It is no longer I, but my enemy. All that is worthy of being called 'me' is a part of Christ and the church. I therefore wish to turn right about, and stand with the truth, facing all evil in my character and spirit, reckoning myself, by virtue of union with Mr. Noyes, dead indeed unto my old life, and alive to all that is good and true. I confess the humility of Christ, that will maintain this position.

SARAH B. CAMPBELL.

A letter was duly received from Mr. Porter, the tailor, stating that, on mature reflection, he and his family had decided not to accept our offer; Mr. Crawford, the other tailor, was then written to, after which, to our surprise, Mr. Porter arrived here yesterday to re-file his application. He says that from the time he wrote this last letter, declining our offer, he and his wife had felt as if they had not taken the wisest course; and now he has come to see if we cannot accept them on the same terms as before. It is doubtful if we can treat with him on the subject, until our negotiations with Crawford are closed.

Mr. Perry's trip has some interesting features. While it has been a decided success as regards the obtaining of orders for O. C. manufactures, Mr. P's extensive business connections in the west, enabled him to obtain passes on many of the railroad lines and thus save considerable expense. He has been doing more or less in the advertising line and has brought home one German copy and an English one of "Headly's History of the Rebellion" which he had received as pay for advertising; also a copy of "Camp, Battlefield and Hospital," got for writing a notice of the same. Mr. P. did not forget, among his many responsibilities, the educational wants of the Community, and has brought a general cargo of interlinear translations of "William Tell" &c., in German and one interlinear "Cæsar." He brought also, an interesting contribution of fossils, mostly trilobites, with some fragments of cephalopoda, picked up by him from the bed of a creek in Warren County, Ohio. The orders obtained by him, on this trip, for Bags, Traps and Fruit. amount to $4,260, while by Advertising, he earned $231 besides part of his Hotel and Railroad expenses.

A note was read in meeting, night before last, from Homer Barron, expressing some of his temptations, the past year, and inviting criticism. As there was not time that evening, the criticism was deferred till last night, when it was administered faithfully, and in a spirit of love. A manuscript report of it will be forwarded to the other Communes.

S. W. Nash has cleared out all the old-fashioned matches from the Mill buildings and replaced them by the new safety matches. Similar changes are being made in the Tontine, and are contemplated at Willow Place. Very shortly, the new article will probably entirely supercede the old, which will be a considerable saving of anxiety to many who used, with good cause, to look nervously at every stray match that lay where it ought not.

Charles A. Cragin left last night for Springfield. He will be absent only a few days and will return by way of New York. We ought to observe that the foreman whom he is to meet, offers to give his secret on the liberal conditions, that Charles is to judge for himself of the value of the information *after receiving it*, and only pay the $100, if he considers the instruction really worth it.

Mrs. Norton and Mrs. Smith from Prospect, arrived in the night. They came on a visit, and propose to stay a week or more.

ERRATA.—By substituting "glass jars" for "tin cans" on the third page of yesterday's Journal, our readers will perhaps be able to *see through* the article a little better.—On the second page, fifth line from the top—for "five," read "four."

Traps ordered yesterday,	193 doz.
The principal orders were—	
Wm. Read & Son, Boston,	74 "
Sidney Shepard & Co. Buffalo,	50 "

Yesterday's temperature—
7 A. M. 49.   12 M. 54.   6 P. M. 58.   Mean 53½.

DAILY JOURNAL
OF ONEIDA COMMUNITY.

VOL. 2. FRIDAY, OCT. 12, 1866. NO. 88.

O. C. COMMERCE.

There is, at present, among the dealers, a great demand for our productions: letters are daily received from city jobbers and firms doing a large wholesale business, inquiring the prices of our traps, fruits, etc., and frequently enclosing orders which would have startled us a few years since by their magnitude. This is all well; but still let us keep in mind the fact, that our nearest and best relations are with the consumers, and that our true policy is to seek the interests of the consumers, and not "give them the cold shoulder," for the sake of favoring the "middle-men." We must not forget that we are mainly indebted to the consumers for the increased demand for our productions, and not primarily to the efforts of the dealers in circulating them. The demand has grown in this way: the consumers first find out that the Community can be relied upon for good, honest articles; and they trouble the retail merchants until they conclude to order a limited supply; then the retail dealers and country merchants trouble the city jobbers and wholesale dealers until they find it for their interests to take hold of our wares; and then they claim "especial privileges," "exclusive right of sale," and assume that they ought to be allowed to control and monopolize the entire trade. The "middle-men" have a proper and useful function to perform; but they should not be allowed to interfere unnecessarily with the relations of the consumers and producers.

W.

Inter alia, the INDEPENDENT's article by Joel Benton, about the Wallingford Community, was read in meeting last evening. Although it contained an erroneous statement regarding Mr. Realf, yet we thought the article, so far as it went, gave as fair a representation of us as could be expected: it certainly stands in marked contrast to the public notices we have had in former years.—G. E. C's description of some of the doings at Bellevue, read a few evenings ago, had much scientific interest; we hope shortly to read something of the same kind in the CIRCULAR.

Our group of little children are at the present time not the least interesting feature of the Community. By the increase of new members, the past season, we have now eighteen, under seven years of age.—Our home boarding-house is crowded to its fullest extent: there are over forty boarders, and Mrs. Conant still oversees the work.—They have, at present, a hired man to assist in the kitchen, which is a great help.

Our colored neighbors, the Thomases, have bought a house in Verona, of Andrew Smith, and started for

yesterday, bag and baggage.—Michael Scherr's child, boy about seven years of age, had the ambition, yesterday, to attempt climbing an apple-tree; but his skill and muscle, not proving equal to his aspirations, he fell and broke his arm, a little above the wrist. It was bandaged by Dr. Carpenter, and is doing well.

Messrs. Wells and Lowry, from De Ruyter, are experimenting with the view of obtaining water for us at the Burt House. They sunk their tubes to the depth of thirty-five feet yesterday, and certainly struck water, but failed to draw up any with their pump. On withdrawing the tubes this morning, they found about twenty feet of quick-sand in them. They are now operating on the east side of the road, where it is hoped they will meet with better success.

Favorable indications are reported concerning the corn.—The remainder of our grape crop is being turned into wine.—Mr. Bradley started yesterday for the vicinity of Lockport, "to see the folks, and get some peaches."

Mr. Meeker visited the Bag-Factory yesterday, in company with Mr. Woolworth, and Willow Place with Mr. Hamilton.

Between ten and eleven thousand dollars worth of fruit has already been shipped the present month.— Agreeable odors proceeding from the Preserving Room, greet our olfactories this morning, assuring us, in a silent way, that the aromatic quince is undergoing the necessary preparations for canning. The parings and cores of this fruit are boiled, and the juice manufactured into jelly.

Albert Ackley leaves to-day. He seems rather softened by his late sickness, but fails to have that stability and earnestness of purpose, which will lead him to seek Christ for his portion, instead of the world.

Mr. Olds writes that he will be here to-morrow afternoon from his long trip to the West. Welcome Brother!

Traps ordered yesterday,	403 doz.
The principal orders were—	
Enoch Woods, Chicago,	105 "
A. R. & G. H. Miller, Chicago,	50 "
Treadwell & Co., Boston,	96 "

Yesterday's temperature—
7 A. M. 44. 12 M. 63. 6 P. M. 56. Mean 54¼.

The DAILY JOURNAL is printed by the ONEIDA COMMUNITY, for the use of the families at Oneida and the Branch Communes.

DAILY JOURNAL
OF ONEIDA COMMUNITY.

VOL. 2.   SATURDAY, OCT. 13, 1866.   NO. 69.

OUR LATE VISITOR.

" A chiel's lmang ye takin' notes,
An' feth, he'll prent 't.

Mr. Meeker is a very plain, unpretending man, about fifty years of age evidently a keen observer, quite original and full of a quaint, dry wit. He was interested in the Association movement of twenty years ago, and with his family, lived for four years in the Trumbull Phalanx in Ohio. This old experience, he said, made it easy for him to become interested in new social experiments. He also said that he thought it would be quite easy for him to become a communist and to live here with us. The longer he staid the more interested he seemed to become, and he left very much impressed with the importance of our movement. He said he should tell Mr. Young the editor of the Tribune, that in sending him here to "do up" the Community, he had given him the biggest job he had ever had.

He expressed great admiration of our grounds, thought they were the finest he had ever seen. He said the whole arrangement of things here showed great tact and ability. He took with him the Berean, Bible Communism, the 'Familiar Exposition,' 'Salvation from Sin,' 'Male Continence,' the Phrenological Journal and several numbers of the Circular. He read 'Male Continence,' and took several of the tracts, saying he should give one to "Horace." He said Young would also want one.— He thought he ought to stay here a month in order to do justice to the subject.

He said he should go out to his boarding-place in New Jersey, and study the whole subject, before he attempted to write anything. He asked a great many questions about our religious and social views and life.

He did not manifest any special opposition to any thing, though, in theology, we thought there were indications that he tended rather to Universalism or Restorationism. He again and again, with great heartiness expressed himself as glad that he came here, and his increasing sense of the greatness of the work that was going on here.

On some points in regard to our religious views he expressed considerable sympathy. The doctrine of the duality of God, and our idea of perfection— that it is consistent with eternal progress and improvement seemed to meet much favor with him. He expressed himself as having a great respect for genuine religion, though he was not in any special sense a religious man himself.

We heard our visitor Mr. Meeker tell some interesting things about Mr. Greeley and the Tribune. He said Mr. G. read the Tribune through every day—every word of it, including advertisments, and that he never slept more than half the night. He said he came into the office a few days ago with paper in hand and walking straight up to one of the editors who sat at his desk writing, raised his spectacles from his eyes, and said to him, "This brother's article has more than a hundred errors in it which I can point out;" he then asked who wrote a certain article on a horse race, remarking: "It is the best description of a horse race I have ever seen." Mr. M. said it was astonishing to see how much time it required to select from the mass of material that was furnished, articles suitable for publication. A great deal of copy was laid over, and a good deal of what was in type, was pushed out, by more important matter, that came in at a later hour.

He mentioned a rather interesting fact about the Bible in the Tribune office. They have one copy in the editorial rooms and he said it was in use most of the time, one or another of the twenty men at work there, inquiring for it very frequently. He said there were wagon-loads of the Tribune carried to the P. O. and it took fifty men to mail them.

Mr. Meeker said he had seen the most astonishing things since coming here, that he had ever seen in his life, and yet he had seen a good many strange things; but the strangest of all, was to see strong men submit themselves, the one to the other. Persons in the world who were unqualified to rule, were generally, the first to take upon themselves responsibilities, and the last to yield to others. He said his salary was small, but he thought he should be the gainer in coming here, and **was surprised that he had not heard of the O. C. before.**

The Journal breathes freely again. The plenipotentiary of the Tribune had visited the sanctum on Thursday when we were bending over the galley containing the article entitled "The Wheel Moves;" while yesterday we set up the form with very much the same feeling we used to have when we improvised a hasty "sum" on one side of the slate to meet the coming teacher's eye, knowing that on the obverse, there was a life-like, picture of him. But he is gone now—went yesterday at 1 P. M. having received a Luminary to read by the way. Just fancy him perusing our little Tom Thumb in the cars, while others have their great "Posts" &c· Well, there is this comfort, that *taking notes* is a game that can be played by two. His idea of his visit may be inferred from this : Mr. Hamilton asked him just as he was leaving—"Well, have you got through?" "No" was the reply, "I've scarcely begun yet."

We do not claim any credit, that our Journal is of a (Meeker) character to-day than usual.

Traps ordered yesterday,		217 doz.
The principal orders were—		
Chas. Busch,	Detroit,	24 "
Ducharme & Prentiss "		41 "
Buhl & Ducharme, "		96 "

Yesterday's temperature—
7 A. M. 43.   12 M. 58.   6 P. M. 52.   Mean 51.

DAILY JOURNAL
OF ONEIDA COMMUNITY.

VOL. 2.　　MONDAY, OCT. 15, 1866.　　NO. 90.

SQUIRRELS & CONSCIENCE.

The other day I went to a tree where a few butternuts had been found. After a diligent search, a dozen or so graced the bottom of my basket. Coming near the roots of the tree, a tempting pile presented itself packed away under the protecting bank. I wanted them, they seemed so precious this year; but is it not too bad to take them? for Mr. and Mrs. Squirrel had evidently been

Up in the early morning, just at the peep of day
Searching the hillocks, and storing the choicest nuts away.

What must be done? thought I. If a man is much better than a sheep that gives coats to our backs and hose to our feet and mutton "while we move in the flesh," surely a sheep is much better than a squirrel, that scampers away with our choicest tit-bits. Then they want something to do to keep them out of mischief—so storing these conclusions away under my hat, I soon began to store the yellow coats away in the basket, but as my hand groped in the dark hollow, certain misgivings crept in like these: what if Mr. and Mrs. S. have hired a sentinel, and he should pounce upon my unprotected fingers? But then "nothing venture, nothing have," so on I groped, until what appeared the last nut would just alow me to tickle its sides with the tips of my fingers in a very tantalizing way. I did not now like to leave one nut, but necessity compelled this venture, so onward I went, rejoicing and thankful for this way that providence chose to give me that peck of good nuts.

C. E.

"Our best span of horses are missing," were the words that startled many of the family last Saturday morning. "They've been stolen," suggested one, "Or have run away," chimed in another. So Mr. Clark and Martin went to try if they could get upon the track. But all this excitement might have been saved, if it had only been remembered that ours are educated, accomplished horses. The chain halter, fastened with a T inserted through one, or even two links, is no gordian knot to the analytical powers of our equines, who, by a little *dentipulation* (pardon this coinage), can unloose 'most anything. In short the "best span" were found quietly grazing in the pasture, their chain halters dangling at their necks.

A letter has been received from Batavia, Illinois, requesting the Community to receive "a boy of thirteen years of age, strong and healthy and of as good habits as boys generally have" and can "read and write. The The boy when an infant, was left on Mr. Todd's doorstep, and has been brought up by him. He has sold his farm, and "cannot now do for the boy" as when he was

farming—His "business calls him from home" and it is "impossible" for him to "give the boy the instruction he ought to receive." He says: "Mrs. Mills will recollect me." We may add that the Community decline to accept the boy.

BUSINESS MEETING.

The committee on the devising of water-works for W. P. reported that a pump and hose suitable for the purpose could be had for $480, or $500 at most. Voted that the report lie over till next meeting, when a larger attendance may be expected.—In connection with this subject, Mr. Burt led some conversation on the possible construction of water-works for our home buildings, in connection with the water power at the Mill.

F. A. Marks spoke on the subject of the vineyard of Diana grapes. He said that after our experience of several years with that variety, it had from various causes which he mentioned, been found unprofitable, and he suggested that the vines be taken up, and the ground set with some kinds of small fruits and Louise de Bonne pear trees, a quantity of which are now ready to be transplanted and could not be well moved at all if not moved soon. As this was a move of some importance Frederick requested that some persons be nominated to advise with the department on the subject and share their responsibilities. T. L. Pitt, W. A. Hinds and Daniel Abbott were appointed for this purpose.

Mr. Olds gives an interesting report of a visit he made to Berlin Hights by request of Mr. Noyes. He took dinner with that small party who have been seeking our fellowship and had some conversation with them. While he considers them as less spiritual and less earnest than we had hoped, yet, on the other hand, they have separated themselves from the fellowship of the other socialists there, have confessed Christ, and acknowledged Mr. Noyes's leadership; and these steps, we would not undervalue. Though little or no allusion was made to social matters, Mr. O. received the impression that the importunity of the party to be recognized by us, proceeded too much—at least on the part of some of them—from the desire to have social freedom. Mr. O. considered that for us to drop down to them, would neither be good for them nor us, and he exhorted them to study our writings and keep their attention turned toward the Community. He did not forbid them to hope, that at some future time, we may send some one among them to help and strengthen them.

Dr. Pike, oculist and optician, from Utica, called last week. He had a large lens with which he examined the eyes of those who wished to consult him. Mr. Hatch considered him trustworthy and skillful, as well as very gentlemanly in his way of doing business. Several pairs of spectacles were bought from him, and he is to call again in December.

The Horticulturalists report that during the month of August and September, 137 barrels of apples were picked; and from October 1st. to October 11th, when the harvest closed, 291 barrels; the entire crop was thus 428 barrels.—H. W. B. and W. G. K. have succeeded in selling off old fashiond satchels to the amount of $460 worth. They have been a long time on hand, and were considered as dead stock.—Twelve Fruit-orders were received on Saturday.

<hr>

To the Community.

DEAR FRIENDS:—I desire to express my thankfulness for your sincerity and kindness towards me. I never before so fully appreciated the warm loving heart of the Community, as during my late criticism. I have some times been on the point of giving up my own case as nearly hopeless, but am resolved to accept my case as it is, and take Christ's estimate of me. I desire to honor the Community spirit in all that I do, and confess my love and respect for all.   J. H. BARRON.

<hr>

25 crates of peaches came from Mr. Bradley Saturday night, so W. A. H. spoke of it in meeting, and requested the family's aid yesterday, in putting them up. The call was well responded to, and the job completed, by 3 o' clock. The peaches we get now, are quite small, but come much cheaper than in the summer, and it was thought good policy to put up, at least 100 bushels more.

Mrs. Wilcox came on Saturday to make her long contemplated visit. She impresses us quite favorably, has none of the masculine element, that we should expect to find in an M. D., though she is evidently a woman of a strong mind and cultivated intellect.

<hr>

Mrs. Loomis's son, daughter, and niece, and a young man from Philadelphia a relative, of theirs we believe, came here Saturday night and returned home yesterday. Mrs. L. says her children read the CIRCULAR with a good deal of interest, particularly the daughter and are much attracted toward the Community.

<hr>

Mr. Hamilton left in the night for Wallingford in compliance with a request, by telegraph, from G. W. N.

<hr>

Lists are being made out of our different class-books, and these are to be kept in future in the small cup-board in the lobby, where boxes of fruit are usually kept in the company season. We will probably be prepared to open classes for study rather earlier this season than usual.

<hr>

A letter has been received from Isaiah Morris, Blainstown, Iowa, announcing that "Mrs. Lidia V. Peet, a widow, and Mrs. Phebe Allman, a married lady," propose to start for Oneida to pay us a visit if agreeable to us. The writer says: "I assure you that we would not spend the necessary amount of money and time, merely to gratify an idle curiosity; but we are earnestly and honestly desirous to learn something from you for our benefit."

We are enjoying magnificent weather.

> "The leaf—turning yellow
> Falls, and floats adown the air.
> Lo! sweetened with the summer light,
> The full-juiced apple, waxing over-mellow,
> Drops in a silent autumn night.
> All its allotted length of days,
> The flower ripens in its place,
> Ripens and fades, and falls, and hath no toil,
> Fast-rooted in the fruitful soil."

One party went to Oneida Lake yesterday, while another company gave enthusiastic descriptions of the romantic falls at Perryville which they had visited.— They say it even surpasses Roaring Brook.

<hr>

Abel Carter, John Conant's uncle, called on Thursday and stayed over night. He had been out West, and was on his way back to his home in Vermont.

<hr>

We are happy to give our readers a "double portion" to-day, as the Meeker topics of Saturday, had crowded out much interesting matter that appears worthy of publication.

<hr>

Saturday night we had to furnish lodging for eleven visitors.

Traps ordered Saturday and Sunday,	291	doz
The principal orders were—		
Westphal & Hinds, Dubuque, Iowa,	25	"
Geo. Worthington & Co., Cleveland, O.	28	"
Enoch Woods, Chicago, Ill.	110	"

Temperature, Saturday and Sunday—

7 A. M. 40.   12 M. 61.   6 P. M. 52.   Mean 51.
7 A. M. 40.   12 M. 70.   6 P. M. 64.   Mean 58.

DAILY JOURNAL
OF ONEIDA COMMUNITY.

VOL. 2.　　TUESDAY, OCT. 16, 1866.　　NO. 91.

THE NEXT CABLE.

Some of our enthusiasts propose to gently agitate the project of having the O. C. connected by telegraph with the other Communities and "with all the world besides." The resulting advantages will readily occur to all. A few think the necessary outlay would eventually prove a good financial investment. Certain it is, that it would save, in the course of a twelve-month, a great number of journeys to the depot, and if the Willow Place Factory were included in the circuit, much pedal labor of horse and man might be avoided. Then, how convenient for the N. Y. Agency to be in telegraphic communication with the silk-factory and other departments here! And who shall describe the greater spiritual and social advantages which might result from instantaneous communication between all the Communities? The project may appear distant and Quixotic to some of our readers of the JOURNAL, but I am inclined to think, a few years will see it realized. The expense will not be so great as I had supposed, but on this point I will communicate again when able to give more definite figures.　　w.

The talk last evening was upon labor, and the effect the motives we have in engaging in it, have upon our spirits in overcoming laziness and making work attractive. The subject drew out some testimony calculated to show us plainly how far we are removed from the motive power that acts upon the world in respect to labor, and to give us a greater sense of what God has done for the Community, in saving them from care and anxiety about gaining a livelihood. Whatever may have been our experience in the past, it is the universal testimony now, that we have not one lazy person among us.

BY MR. OLDS.

The following is a statement of the business done on my last trip:

Trap Orders obtained,		9,326 54.
Fruit	" "	4,310 74.
Silk	" "	2,253 65.
Bag	" "	1,301 67.
Total	" "	17,192 60.
Cash sales for Silk		513 00.
Collections		4,068 75.
Aggegate amount,		$22,374 35.
Distance traveled by Rail		3,148 miles.
" " water		80. "
" " Total		3,228.

c. o.

Yesterday, a carriage, containing some fashionably dressed ladies, drove around the buildings and passed in front of the children's house. Conspicuous among a group of children at play, was Temple, perched on an inverted wheelbarrow. The carriage stopped.

"Where are are your parents, little boy?"

"My papa Noyes and mamma Miller are at Wallingford."

Now, the ladies evidently felt themselves on the right track. Another charge as successful as this, might result in storming the fortification.

"Miller! that's a nice name; and what's your own name besides Miller?"

The reply had such amplitude, such rolling fullness, such *naivete* and simplicity, so much of that frankness which fears nothing, that we love to record it.

"My name is Temple Noyes Dunn Burt Ackley."

We need scarcely add that the enemy was astounded, repulsed, utterly discomfited, and "sped away."

We make a few extracts from a letter Portia received a few days since from her brother Charles:

"I should love dearly to write you and that often were you where I could do so without remorse when the public know where you are. I deeply regret the course you have taken, and the choice you have made, being led into that which you must know is contrary to all your former teachings.—But if you wish to leave there and be a good girl and sister, I will do all I can for you as long as I live and nothing prevents. I am very sorry you are where you are, and what is worse I suppose you call it right. Read your *Bible carefully and you cannot fail to change your mind* and see the error of your choice. *I* think you were honest in your motives when you went there and thought it was right. You certainly cannot feel so now.—Until I know you are totally ruined and lost, I am your true and affectionate brother,

CHARLES.

We started on our eight-pager, yesterday, partly in fun. Part of the matter had been set up on Saturday, and lay temptingly on the galley, inviting us to use it in getting up an extra. Indeed, the idea of doing something of the kind, some day, had been bandied about in a playful way, for several weeks past. So it was done yesterday, and we can assure our readers that however simple a thing it may appear to them, our "joke" turned out to be something of a serious "job" by the time it was nearly completed. We feel that we need a good deal of charity from readers, not only with reference to the JOURNAL in question but to our general performances.

Mr. Ellsworth, a nephew of Mrs. Maria Kinsley's, with his wife, came here last night. They live in Cambridge Vt., and are on their way home, having been farther west, to visit some friends.

Mr. Elias Hall returned, Saturday, from a week's peddling trip. He sold while absent, $430 worth of silk and bags, mostly silk.—Peach- and quince-preserving are the order of the day now, and work is quite lively in that department.

Traps ordered yesterday,　　46 doz.

Yesterday's temperature—

7 A. M., 42. 12 M., 63　6 P. M., 54. Mean, 52½.

DAILY JOURNAL
OF ONEIDA COMMUNITY.

VOL. 2.   WEDNESDAY, OCT. 17, 1866.   NO. 92.

AT SEA.

Mrs. Wilcox's short visit did not admit of our becoming very intimately acquainted with her. She is a woman forty-six years old, was married three years ago, and buried her husband after less than six months.—She received her medical education at the Hydropathic College, at Cleveland, Ohio, but her present mode of practice is the use of the Electro-Thermal bath, in which she seems to have great confidence. In early life she joined the Baptist church, 'from persuasion,' she says, 'more than from any honest conviction of the truth of its doctrines.' She afterwards drifted into infidelity, and has been for many years in an unsettled state of mind, expecting that the good there is in human nature (which she did not admit was Christ), would in the end assert itself, and revolutionize the world. She has taken the CIRCULAR since last spring, and has read it with increasing interest, and appears anxious now, to investigate our doctrines, but is slow to believe, or take other people's testimony; said she was not sure that credit was due to Christ for the improvements she saw here, and she expressed herself as not believing in a personal devil. She is very frank and acknowledges that the worst side of her character was always the most conspicuous. We felt that there was a dark spirit of unbelief over her, but from her increasing earnestness, we could not but feel hopeful, that she would at length emerge into the light of truth.

Mrs. W. is a decidedly intellectual woman says little and seems to ponder much, over both what she hears and says. Yet although her present struggles seem to be chiefly of the nature of intellectual apprehension, she says much about heart improvement. On being asked what was the standard by which she seeks heart improvement, she replied, after a few moments, "The ideal." It was suggested to her that if she would take Christ as the embodiment of the highest "ideal," she would, thus find something less vague and more definite on which to base her "heart improvement."

C. A. Cragin arrived home yesterday. He has been at Springfield and bought the secret of silk-twisting, as contemplated, paying $100, for it. We hope the investment will yield a hundred fold.—Charles returned by way of New York, where he bought two bales of raw silk, one of Hadden & Co., the other of Goodridge & Co.

"We are nearly swamped with orders," says one connected with the bag-business; and this expression gives but a fair idea of the pressure. As a further illustration, we quote from a letter received, the other day, from J. R. L.: "Will you inform me if those orders from New Haven have been filled. You cannot imagine what a blowing-up I got, when last there, for being so slow in filling them." There are fourteen hired men and women at work and eleven of our own family, twenty-five in all, trying to gain upon the orders, but the faster they work, the more numerous are the demands. Another hired hand is expected next Monday. On the whole, it is a good thing to have plenty of work a-head—to be under just a *little* pressure, and to accept it as from the LORD.

DEAR LUMINARY:— There is a kind of delicacy which might be more generally cultivated than it is: I mean that thoughtful courtesy that does not too frequently nor too abruptly remind people of their deficiencies, but chooses the proper time and place for giving hints and conveys them in the spirit of inspiration and prayer and with a distinct view to improvement. There are several of my friends, who have a *habit* of saying in a thoughtless way, things that, by their constant repetition, have become quite unpleasant.

Yours for improvement,   C.—N.

Mrs. Towner and her children, together with Mrs. Wilcox left in the night, for their homes. They are to travel in company as far as Buffalo. Mrs. Towner has been here two and a half weeks. She had quite a sincere criticism while here, which she received in a good spirit and seemed thankful for it. She lacks in the government of her children, especially her little girl—seems quite amiable, passive and receptive, but lacks energy. We thought she seemed a good deal more in earnest after her criticism than before. We trust her stay here, will be a benefit to her in every respect.

Mr. Perry's German class have, for the present, laid aside "Faust," and taken up "William Tell," using the interlinears which their teacher brought with him when he returned from his last trip. It is quite a delightful change to pass from the metaphysical speculations of Goethe to the ringing music of Schiller.

Our churning is done at the Tontine, every two or three days, by steam power. We have thus far churned about thirty-five pounds at a time, which all lovers of good butter, enjoy highly. Buttermilk too, fresh and new, is quite a treat to many.—3,170 lbs. of broken glass was sold yesterday, at one cent per pound.

D. P. Nash started early this morning for Wallingford, and Philena B. Hamilton, for Putney.

Traps ordered yesterday,	418 doz.
The principal orders were—	
Hibbard & Spencer, Chicago,	150 "
Wm. Blair & Co., "	50 "
Enoch Woods, "	100 "
Rice Lewis & Son, Toronto, C. W.	80 "

Yesterday's temperature—
7 A. M., 54. 12 M., 65. 6 P. M., 51. Mean, 56½.

DAILY JOURNAL
OF ONEIDA COMMUNITY.

VOL. 2.   THURSDAY, OCT. 18, 1866.   NO. 93

THE PRESERVING DEPARTMENT.

The labors of the Preserving department, if it keeps fewer hands at regular work than some other branches of our industry, yet, dealing as it does in material that is more or less perishable, requires, in addition to occasional bees, a steady course of incessant labor from its regular corps. We cannot but admire the unwearied and methodical activity that has presented itself to our observation every time our business has led us into the basement where the principal operations are performed. Within the last three days, 851 quarts of peaches have been put up, and 1131 quarts of quinces, besides 210 quarts of peaches for family use, making in all 2,492 qts This gives an average of over 830 quarts per day.

It may give a further idea of this department to say that fourteen different kinds of jelly have been made this season: and although the jellies are not nearly all made yet, there have, up to the present time, been put up 2,803 pints, and 3,080 half-pints. In addition to all this, a quantity of jams has been made, of which we cannot now give particulars.

The hands, including those in the fruit-room, comprise six of our own family and thirteen hired people.

One of the great curiosities of the greenhouse at the present time, is the Augusta rose. It has grown and spread itself so rapidly, that it has already overshadowed the other flowering shrubs, of more modest pretensions, and has reached the extremities of the roof, where its climbing propensities, and higher aspirations receive a sudden check. One solitary rose, "the last rose of summer" it would seem, remains upon its branches; since its first blossoming, in January last, there has been no time, when it has not had buds or blossoms upon its stem. The scarlet Salvia, and two varieties of the Veronica are in bloom now, and are very beautiful.

After the late frost, our gardens presented a miserably blackened appearance; but the milder weather we have had since, has wooed back a few beautiful bright tints from the stocks and verbenas.—For two weeks, we have had no rain, and the weather has been the finest of the season and the sky cloudless. The traveling is the very best, though somewhat dusty. We begin to feel the need of rain, and there are indications this morning, that our wishes in this respect, will ere long be gratified.

The fine weather brings us a good many visitors, and calls for fifty-cent meals, or luncheons as we term them, are frequent. Saturday last, we furnished meals of the above description to nineteen.

A small order for traps was received yesterday from a firm in Bath. For testimonials of their reliability, they say, "we refer you to Mrs. Bushnell of your institution."

Wells and Lowry gave up their attempt to find water at the Burt house, but we shall likely have them at work in another quarter, soon. Our supply of water at the home buildings, being insufficient, negotiations have been under way with neighbor Johnson, for the purchase of a plentiful spring on his grounds, near our own springs in the Grove. He offers to let us have it, if we will dig a well for him close to his house; so Wells and Lowry have been engaged to sink tubes at the required spot, and should they fail, we shall likely dig a well for neighbor J., as the spring he offers would be very valuable to us. It is said to yield six gallons per minute.

Since the above was "set up," a note has been received from Mr. Johnson, stating that his family are opposed to the arrangement, and requesting us not to proceed with the well-sinking at his house; but we are not without hope that so valuable a spring can be had on terms, perhaps equally favorable to us.

Stepping to the front door this morning, we saw a man in patches, sitting on the piazza, whose face looked quite familiar, yet whom we failed to recognize. He looked at us, with a familiar "how d'ye do?" when we recollected him, as one of our most important customers in the past: a beggar of the worst description. We turned quick, and went the other way, not caring in our haste, to listen to his pitiful story, or to be annoyed by his importunity.

Whitefoot has been trying his speed again, and asserting his freedom, by running away. He was standing at the door at W. P., and Mr. Kellogg was waiting a moment for some one to get ready to go home with him, when he suddenly gave Mr. K. the slip, and came home without much ceremony, depositing himself as a rational horse should, safely in the barn. We hear that little damage was done.

Mr. Hatch has commenced a class with the little girls, to teach them to sing by note—quite an undertaking.—Crawford, the tailor, has written to us, declining our offer; and we have opened the way again to the Porters to come on if they wish.

Mr. Smith from Prospect, came here yesterday, on a visit.—The Ellsworths left, yesterday.

Mr. Bolles was criticised last evening by his request. A MS report will be forwarded.

Traps ordered yesterday,	215 doz.
The principal orders were—	
Sargent & Co., New York,	50 "
J. M. Warren & Co., "	25 "
Howell, Gano & Co., Cincinnati,	34 "
Pratt & Co., Buffalo,	50 "
Kennedy & Spaulding,	80 "

Yesterday's temperature—

7 P. M. 51.   12 M. 64.   6 P. M. 50.   Mean 55.

DAILY JOURNAL
OF ONEIDA COMMUNITY.

VOL. 2. FRIDAY, OCT. 19, 1866. NO. 94.

LETTERS.

From Capt. Joseph M. Chase, Shobonier, Illinois.

"MR. NOYES, Dear Sir:—As I am desirous of learning somewhat more of the Community Society than the
account contained in the PHRENOLOGICAL JOURNAL,
please forward to me the CIRCULAR published at the
Wallingford Branch, also BIBLE COMMUNISM and the
tract MALE CONTINENCE—should be glad to have the
BEREAN and CONFESSIONS, if in book form and for sale.
Myself and wife are believers in a free salvation, liberal
Christianity—used to belong to the Methodists, but have
not now for some time—manage to keep up family worship. Our ages are 30 and 29 years—very anxious to
investigate the theory of government in your Society."

From Mrs. M. E. Austin, Morenci, Mich.

"MR. NOYES:—I have just been reading the interesting
description of the Oneida Community in the PHRENO-
LOGICAL JOURNAL, and I cannot find words to express
my gratitude that there are a few who dare to live out
correct principles in direct opposition to morbid fashionable opinion. I too, though struggling along alone,
have tried to reach a higher life and live out true principles, but I have found it a trying business. It may be
interesting to you to know that I have worn the reform
dress exclusively, everywhere and on all occasions for
12 years, and, in various innovations, have made my
mark upon the false conditions of society. I would like
to know more about you and your society, and feel that
I should receive strength to do right, by being in correspondence with you or some of your Community. I
would like to better understand the principle of ascending fellowship and I would like your tract on Male
Continence for which I enclose $1,00. Please send me
any such papers or books as you think would instruct
or interest me, and oblige your friend and co-worker in
every progressive movement."

The Theological class has lately developed a new feature: a short address is given each evening from the
stage. This seems like a parallel to the inspiration that
is turning the attention of the "Monks" to elocution.—
The efforts of this kind, hitherto, have been very fairly
successful; and there can be no doubt that should any
of our people be called on to lecture outside of the Community they would find it *much easier* to speak the Truth
to an audience who were unacquainted with our gospel,
than to members of the O. C.—The ordinance of
singing is still kept up with enthusiasm.

Part of the meeting hour, last evening, was occupied
in reciprocal exhortation from the groups that occupy
different parts of the Hall, to speak out when they said
anything, so as to be heard by all. It was observed that
several persons who spoke in very indistinct tones the
first part of the Meeting, improved considerably toward
the end. Some instances of this kind, gave rise to some
good-natured pleasantry.

A letter was read from Dr. Wellington, requesting us
to transact some business for him at Syracuse. He contemplates buying a mill there for a friend and wishes us
to make inquiries about it and assist him in negotiating
the matter. The Community think favorably of the re
quest.

In order to hasten the work at the Trap Factory, elev-
en of our hired workmen, besides one or two of our
own family, are engaged there now till half past nine
every evening. Two men worked all last night at the
presses.—A lot of silk—about thirty-five pounds—is sent
off to-day to be dyed white. This is the last part of the
first bale bought by us.

Dr. H. Bascom of Philadelphia, an elderly gentleman,
called yesterday, who had spent the greater part of his
life in South America. He had served three years as surgeon in the army of Bolivar, and spoke of the wars in
Venezuela, as very barbarous. He returned to this country about three years ago.

Mrs. Mary L. French of Winooski Falls, Vermont,
has written to us, expressing a wish that we would give
her some kind of employment here. She made us a
visit two years ago, and has since manifested some sympathy with the views held by us.

We spoke yesterday, of indications of rain, but they
soon disappeared, and the sky resumed its wonted clearness. To-day is warm and summer-like, and instead of
seeking the comfort of a fire, we instinctively throw our
windows wide open.

We notice, this morning that a man is engaged in sifting gravel in front of the New House, preparatory to
laying the anticipated cement walk.—About two bushels
of barberries have been used in making jelly besides
what has been picked for private use. The crop is not
yet exhausted.

Mrs. Dilts from Fulton, a cousin of Horace Perry's, and
a Miss Butler from the same place, came here on a visit
yesterday.—Mr. Dunn went to Syracuse yesterday on
business and returned this morning.

Traps ordered yesterday,	125 doz.
The principal orders were—	
Ferris & Co., Montreal,	38 "
Morland, Watson & Co.,	26 "
Henry Phillips, Toledo, O.,	31 "

Yesterday's temperature—

7 A. M. 48. 12 M. 64. 6 P. M. 57. Mean 56¼.

DAILY JOURNAL
OF ONEIDA COMMUNITY.

VOL. 2.   SATURDAY, OCT. 20, 1866.   NO. 96.

ON DIT.

When I am out in the world, I sometimes hear persons from various parts of the country tell interesting stories of the productions of the O. C. For instance, when I was at Lockport, I chanced to make the acquaintance of a Boston fruit-dealer, whose stand is next to that of Hiland Smith and Co., to whom we send our grapes. Speaking of that firm, he said to me:

"There is not another such set of men in the whole United States to sell produce, and especially fruit. Why, sir, I was in their place the other morning, and seeing some of your grapes (Delaware), in those neat, fancy pockets which you ship them in, I said,

"'Smith, let me have one of those pockets for my little girl,' and I took out my porte-monnaie to pay; but Smith said,

"'Take it sir, take it sir; keep your money; I will give the grapes to your little girl; now sir, look this way and see how we sell these Community grapes.'

"So I went with him into the sales-room where there were half a dozen customers ordering goods in this way:—

"'Put me up a box of those grapes,' said one.

"'And me one'—'and me'—'and me,' added several, calling for various other articles equally costly; then one would say—'What is my bill?'

"Smith figured it up," continued my acquaintance, going through the appropriate gesture, "and these gentlemen took out their purses and paid fifty cents each for our smallest pockets of grapes, and bought other things in proportion, without ever questioning their charge; and that sir," he concluded "is their style of customers."

L. H. B.

Some of the commercial letters received in these days, are very interesting. Sidney Shepard & Co. write, "We are suffering for No. 1 Rat Traps with chains. Please let us have all you can at once, and the balance, as soon as possible."—Another merchant, writes for a price-list, and closes thus: "I remain, your obedient servant and a friend to the Newhouse trap."

The hostler has, for some time occupied the cottage which now stands by the barn, thus vacating the Dunn cottage, which will be duly renovated whenever the press of business will allow. The other little cottage, formed of the wing of the White House, is now boarded in and is fast assuming the appearance of a habitable dwelling.

We are tempted, every day, to speak of the weather, it is so splendid. We wonder if Wallingford has such unclouded skies, and an atmosphere as mild and soothing? The children are wonderfully happy, even the smallest of the group is out doors, on the run from morning till night, and they are scarcely willing to remain in the house long enough to take their meals.

We understand that there is to be a wedding to-day of two of our employees, Billy Smith, as they call him, and Libby Coakes, and our people are making a wedding cake. Myron promised Billy several years ago, to furnish him with a wedding cake, should he ever get married—and a few days ago he notified M. that the cake in question would soon be needed.

The kitchen group, with Miss Thomas and Beulah for mothers (though we think that honorary title expires with them to-day), are seen at their post, Mr. Hawley and James Vaill co-operating, together with a corps of willing workers, who take pleasure in serving the family in this department.

The masons are busy, constructing a cistern at the northeast corner of the store.—Our crop of beets is now safely housed in the barn cellar. They amount to 1,500 bushels.

Four days ago, Maud took a sudden start, and walked clear across the room alone. It is even thus that new powers and faculties manifest themselves, which had long been lying hid, while the strength that was to make the final development, had been silently accumulating.

Mrs. Dills, and Miss Butler left for home this morning. —Three of Mrs Loomis' friends staid here last night.— We are buying husks for beds, of the Indians, and pay eight cents per pound for them.

The laying of the cement walk is proceeding so rapidly that if it is not finished by the time the JOURNAL is printed, it will be shortly after.

Traps ordered yesterday,	228 doz.
Also two bear.	
The principal orders were—	
Crathern and Caverhill, Montreal,	46 "
Haywood and Ryder, St. Paul,	133 "

Yesterday's temperature—
7 A. M., 54. 12 M., 76. 6 P. M., 63. Mean, 64.

Erratum :—In the list of Trap-orders published yesterday, for 'Ferris,' read 'Ferrier.'

DAILY JOURNAL
OF ONEIDA COMMUNITY.

VOL. 2. MONDAY, OCT. 22, 1866. NO. 96.

BUSINESS MEETING.

Mr. Abbott reported that our large reservoir leaks, and needs repairing; he thought the best time to attend to it, would be immediately after the washing, as then the least quantity of water would run to waste. Mr. Abbott and Mr. Clark were appointed to attend to it.

G. W. Hamilton inquired if there could not be an arrangement made by which Mr. Kellogg might attend to the coopering at the Trap-shop, for the present. It was proposed that Mr. Underwood, if willing, should take the W. P. team for a time.

G. W. H. reported that the chain-making does not proceed fast enough—it was desirable to run the chain welding, day and night, for a while. The hands we have are fully occupied with day-work, some of them working till half past nine, and our boarding-houses being quite full, we do not see our way clear to engaging another set of men. It was mentioned that Mrs. Town is willing to lodge eight or ten men for us and it was thought that by a greater number of our own family eating at the second table, we might board them. G. W. H. thought we might get up a company of our own family to work at night, as our liability to run short of stock, made it a questionable policy to engage more help—the low figure at which we are selling traps, will not allow of the manufacture being conducted on any other than the most economical plan. Mr. Burt spoke of using the Tin-shop press, and getting up another welding furnace, so as to drive a double business during the day and save the necessity of working in the night. The supply of help was referred to Messrs. Burt and Woolworth.

F. A. Marks called for a report from the Committee on the buying of the muck-swamp. It was found that this Committee had not met; and it was remarked that if the business board think any matter important enough to have a committee appointed for its management, such committee should act promptly.

Mr. Burt reported the action of the committee about securing more water for the house. It met last Sunday—went over the grounds where the springs are, looking at the different springs—pretty much made up their minds in favor of negotiating for Mr. Johnson's spring and laying down iron pipes. Mr. Abbott had made some measurements and found that Mr. Johnson's spring discharges six gallons per minute, and the fish-pond two gallons per minute, while the waste water running in the ditch amounts to four or five gallons per minute; half of this last might be secured. Reported that while Mr. Johnson would be dissatisfied with a tube well, he would be willing, if we will dig him a good well, to deed his spring to us, reserving only this privilege: that he shall always be free to draw water from it at any time when the well should fail from drought of the weather or from any other cause. The committee are in favor of taking measures to secure the water, and get ready to bring it here in iron pipes next spring. There was considerable conversation about the thickness of pipes necessary for such a purpose; and it was calculated that the entire cost of digging the well and laying the pipes would be about $3,000. As it was thought desirable to act deliberately about this matter, it was voted that it be reconsidered at some special meeting of the board or at the regular evening meeting of the family.

TO THE COMMUNITY.

For a long time I have been under a proud, unbelieving spirit, and one that is independent and insubordinate.

I believe these spirits are the enemies of improvement, and as such, I hate them and wish to separate myself from them.

I confess my union with, and obedience to Mr. Hamilton and the Community. CHARLES BURT.

The boxing department prospers. The boxers are again giving lessons to new aspirants. Blows are given thick and fast, yet no bloody noses, nor bruised heads appear although our *nails* are freely used. But all is taken in good nature, and pleasant jokes pass around. Are there not worse amusements than boxing? I think it pays. Though the charming weather invites to walk or ride or row the boat as much as in lovely May.

> We deal our blows yet know no foes,
> From early morn till daylight's close.

C. E.

We copy the concluding paragraph of a letter received a few days since from Albert Ackley:—"Give my love to Alice, and tell her I never think of her as separate from the Community, and never have any desire to do so. I am glad she has got such a good home and am glad she can never be taken from it."

Mrs. Wright, a sister of Mrs. Joslyn's, with her son, both from Utica, came here on Saturday afternoon, and set for home this morning.—Also Mr. and Mrs. Ellsworth spent Sunday with us—left at the same time.

Traps ordered since Saturday	410 doz.
The principal orders were—	
Sidney Shepard, & Co.,	172 "
A. Fisher, Clyde. N. Y.	50 "
Wm. Blair & Co. Chicago,	50 "
Wm. Read & Sons, Boston,	56 "

Temperature—Saturday and Sunday,
7 A. M., 56. 12 M., 7. 6 P. M., 61. Mean, 67¼.
" 57, " 75. " 60. " 67.

DAILY JOURNAL
OF ONEIDA COMMUNITY.

VOL. 2.   TUESDAY, OCT. 23, 1866.   NO. 97.

TRUE PROGRESS.

The worldly idea of perseverance is narrow and superficial. The world sticks to one course with a mulish obstinacy as long as it can, and gives it up only when obliged to do so. Outward prosperity is all that is thought of, and so long as that continues, it is considered the merest folly to "back out" of any operation. But God's perseverance has an infinite width of scope, yet is marked by repeated stops: God is continually breaking off and starting anew again, and that is perhaps one way in which he maintains his eternal youth. A superficial observer might think his course was only a succession of failures, while really he is rounding off the most perfect successes. Geology is constantly revealing ideas of organized existence which the genius of God had developed to a certain point, and then dropped; and we can easily imagine how Satan looked at these; his short-sightedness would reckon them up as failures. But God knew better.

We believe it is the true attitude for us, to be of God's mind in this respect. We expect to make the greatest progress in the end, by being willing to drop the most apparently prosperous of our minor schemes, in order to attain quiescence with the mind of God—to say with Paul, "What things were gain to me, these I counted loss for Christ."

A VOICE FROM THE JOURNAL OFFICE.

Our JOURNAL's not a small affair,
Requiring little thought or care,
As many think; and though we love
The work, all other work above,
Yet time it takes, and patient thought
To pen and publish as we ought;
To gather facts, and write them out,
And tell what the O. C. 's about.
We run to gain a bit of news,
For our small DAILY to diffuse;
We grasp it, write, and send to press,
In half a "jiff" and often less.
Then, when at last the mail arrives,
Oh, how, sometimes, our business drives
To read, transcribe, and copy set,
And for the mail our JOURNAL get !
To write with speed, and do it well
And in few words our story tell;
This is our loved, our daily task,
For which all sympathy we ask.

E. Y. J.

Last evening, expressions of welcome were given by the family to our visitors Mr. and Mrs. Smith, and it was remarked that they have lately admitted two new members to their Community, Mrs. Norton and her mother. It is a good idea to have a new Community in Prospect.

Early this morning, the ex-editor of the Journal, left here en route for Canada. We know not what privations he may encounter on his journey, but we know of a certain luncheon which he came very near missing. "Hold there," cried some one in the kitchen last night, "dont eat that; that luncheon's for Mr. Pitt to take with him."

"What a Pit(t)y !"—was the remorseless answer.

Our house-cleaning commenced yesterday, under the supervision of S. B. C. and E. F. Hutchins. We are expecting a hired woman to assist.—Mr. Hall started this morning on a peddling trip, of three or four days.

The new turbine wheel at the Foundry has been in operation for some days. It is forty inches in diameter and is said to be of sixteen horse power. It has scarcely had a fair trial yet, but seems to work well.

Helen and Florence Underwood and their sister-in-law from the west, together with Mr. Howard, the father of the latter staid here last night. The sister-in-law is on her return west, to Fond Du Lac, Wis., and Florence goes with her. Helen is to be married to a Mr. Brown, one of the attendants, at the Insane Hospital at Utica. He is to meet Helen at the depot this morning, and the nuptial ceremonies are to be celebrated to-day at Syracuse. Mr. Underwood has gone with them to attend the wedding.

Among our visitors of last Saturday, was a Miss Grant of Boston, niece of the great General. She played some pieces on the piano and appeared to be a very agreeable young lady.

The moon was about full last night and the air perfectly transparent: the mildness of the day was succeeded by a very slight chill, scarcely felt, perhaps, by the croquet players, who, we observed, kept up the game till pretty near eleven o'clock.

Our women had quite a lively bee in the upper sitting room, yesterday, to assist with their needles the sisters who are preparing to leave for Wallingford on Thursday.

There was a lively apple-cut last evening: eighteen bushels were pared and cut; they are to be put up in stone jars for family use.

Traps ordered yesterday,   55 doz.

Yesterday's temperature—
7 A. M., 54.   12 M., 75.   6 P. M., 62.   Mean, 63⅓.

ural
DAILY JOURNAL
OF ONEIDA COMMUNITY.

VOL. 2.   WEDNESDAY, OCT. 24, 1866.   NO. 98.

AT THE PHALANX.

New York, Oct. 20, 1866.

DEAR MRS. VANVELZER:—I have just returned from the North American Phalanx, and as I had some talk with Mr. Bucklin the Fruit Preserver, I thought I would give some of the results to you.

Mr. Bucklin's fort is in preserving Tomatoes. His method is to turn off the liquid portion, filling the can with the solid tomato as far as can be readily done, and *scaling the can before the fruit is cooked.* He leaves no orifice for the escape of fixed gasses, but cooks the Tomato, thus hermetically closed, about 30 minutes. The result is (as he claims), that the original flavor is preserved and he does not lose one can in a thousand. His Corn, Peas, Beans and fruit of various kinds, are, like the Tomatoes, steamed after the cans are soldered. This is different from Professor Nyce's method as reported by me several weeks ago, and, as I suppose, different also from your method. Am I correct? Five minutes' boiling is all the time given to Peaches, also most other fruits.— Corn, this year, he cooked thoroughly, ten hours, and even then, like us, he lost quite a percentage. The reason for this, he is unable to decide on satisfactorily, although this much he has observed: that corn planted late, is more likely to pack well.

Corn cooked in a copper kettle becomes discolored at the kernel. An enameled kettle is better, or a copper kettle, tinned.

Tomato Catsup is made from the skins of the fruit and not from the fruit itself. The first cost is about $1,00 per barrel—his wholesale price for the same is $12,00.

Mr. Bucklin is a very practical man, and I could not but feel (and I told him as much), that he and some of our practical Fruit Preservers ought to confer together and compare notes as often as once in two years at least.

He reaps much benefit from having his vats out of doors so that by the perfect light he can detect any defect in the soldering before it is packed away in the store-room.   H. W. B.

THE SUN.

I.

Burning star within the sky,
Looking down with dazzling eye,
Quick'ning all things with your beams—
Far and wide your radiance gleams.

II.

See you everything that grows,
Every stream of life that flows:
All is nourished, day by day,
By your universal ray.

iii.

Look you down on human life,
On the peace and on the strife,
On the love and on the hate,
Peopled lands and desolate.

iv.

On the hamlet, on the town,
Streams your living glory down;
Look you daily, none the less,
On the sandy wilderness.

v.

Whence your power? Who is it gives
The secret strength which in you lives?
Whose glory shines your splendor through?
Who is He, looks down on you?

vi.

Know you Him whose finger bright
Kindled first your flaming light?
Know you Him whose mighty power
Sustains your being every hour?

W. H. H.

DEAR LUMINARY;—I once had some experience which showed me the nature of persistent and persevering effort, in the right direction. For a long time I had it in my mind to write an article for the CIRCULAR, and the subject on which I wished to write, was ever present to my thoughts. Once and again I made a feeble attempt, but failed to satisfy myself, or do justice to the subject. I was tempted to give it up and doubtless should have done so, had not an invisible power urged me on. At length I grew tired of my half-hearted efforts; my will was thoroughly roused; I said to myself, "I *can* do it and I *will*." I had little trouble after that, and the result was quite satisfactory.   s.

Mr. Porter arrived here yesterday and has commenced work. His family will not come until a house is got ready for them.—The German class has been dropped for the present.—F. Norton returned from Wallingford yesterday. We give him a hearty welcome, as his services in the Dentist's Office are very much needed.

Mrs. Perry has had a niece from Durhamville here on a visit of a day or two. She returned home yesterday—Mr. Perry left on Monday last for New York, on business; he expects to be absent about a week.

Mr. Higgins is cutting up pumpkin to dry. He places it, on poles in the Dry-house, where it is dried quickly and easily.

Traps ordered yesterday,	124	doz.
The principal orders were—		
Pratt & Co., Buffalo,	29	"
Mulford & Sprague, New York,	85	"

Yesterday's temperature—
7 A. M., 46. 12 M., 73. 6 P. M., 60. Mean, 58⅓.

DAILY JOURNAL
OF ONEIDA COMMUNITY.

VOL. 2.   THURSDAY, OCT. 25, 1866.   NO. 99.

SILK.

To give a somewhat intelligent idea of our success hitherto in silk manufacture, we present some facts about the first bale. Seventy-nine pounds have already been spooled from it, and we expect to put up sixty-five pounds more that are being dyed, besides a small remainder not yet worked. (It should be understood that in spooled silk, ten ounces make one pound). A rough estimate of the proximate cost and proceeds of working this first bale, has been made, and is as follows:

Silk Dr.	
To Raw material,	$1,232.
" Wages and board of hired hands	250.
" Dyeing, Spools &c.,	100.
" Probable profit,	268.
	$1,850.

Contra Cr.	
By 144 lbs. silk at $12 60,	$1,800.
" Small Remainder,	50.
	$1,850.

This calculation shows a profit [$268], sufficient to cover our own wages very well. An accurate statement will be made when the bale has been spooled.

It is a common saying among experienced silk manufacturers, that every one who goes into the business loses money the first year or two. But it seems that Communism presents a favorable exception to that rule.

The cheaper of the two bales of silk lately purchased, is being worked, and is found to be a very good article—better than was expected.   c.

BERLIN HIGHTS.

We make the following extract from a letter received from Mrs. Towner yesterday :

"Tongue cannot express my gratitude, for the good I received from my brief stay with you. Through the awakening power and vitalizing influence of the Community, I have been aroused to new life—have thrown off passivity and unbelief, and have been able to put myself in a positive condition towards evil. I feel that Christ is within me, permeating my whole being, and that through Mr. Noyes and the Community he has saved me from unbelief and doubt. I feel to repent in regard to the things in my past life which have been contrary to his gospel and to confess him in me a broken contrite spirit.

"I am very thankful for the criticism I received and hope I may ever be so mindful, as to profit by it. I shall ever hold in grateful remembrance, those of you who treated me with such kindly consideration during my visit.

"Mr. Towner reports progress in his class here, and thinks they have improved much, since I left. Mr. Olds's visit here has been very beneficial indeed; it has given them a new impetus. Last Sunday, Minnie Waite expressed herself as being free from unbelief, and confessed Christ in a broken spirit—said that she had been vacillating till then, and had even doubted whether the Community life was the true way.

Yours truly,   c. s. t."

Mr. Towner writes: "If we are united to Christ, if we recognize and acknowledge the existing fact that Christ is in us, then we can be united to the O. C., but in no other way. This I feel more and more sensibly day by day, and if thus united, the union will be lasting, eternal. 'He that believeth hath everlasting life.' If we have faith we shall have all else, as certain as God is.

j. w. t."

Our beautiful weather of four weeks' continuance, with scarcely a drop of rain to moisten the atmosphere, has given place to clouded skies and threatening storms. But little rain has fallen however, as yet, though we much need, and hope for, abundant showers.

Last night we had a sincere criticism of Charles Vanvelzer by his request. It was thought there was first-rate material in Charles, on which to build up a good business character, and if he had a sufficient spiritual basis, he might make himself very useful in peddling. As it is, though he attends steadily to his business; and does well in that respect, yet he gets off the track, and is more or less affected by the spirit of the world.

Mr. and Mrs. Smith started at 4 o'clock this morning, for Prospect; also Tryphena Seymour and Lucy, and Emily Otis, for Wallingford.

Owing to the demand for springs, C. O. H. and J. N. N. run the rollers day and night, working five hours each alternately.

The silk machinery for Farwell advances rapidly towards completion; but it is doubtful whether it will be finished by Nov. 1st, as desired.

Traps ordered yesterday,	203 doz.
The principal orders were—	
Gale, Perrin & Co., Kalamazoo, Mich.,	46 "
Love & Hamilton, Rochester,	50 "
Lloyd & Supplee, La Crosse,	50 "

Yesterday's temperature—
7 A. M., 44.   12 M., 42.   6 P. M., 35.   Mean, 40¼.

DAILY JOURNAL
OF ONEIDA COMMUNITY.

VOL. 2.   FRIDAY, OCT. 26, 1866.   NO. 100.

A HUSKY ODE.

Now is the season of Husks.
The noise of wagon wheels is heard,
And an Indian Queen
(We ought to say squaw),
Is straightway seen
To gracefully draw
Up in front of the house and ask for Mr. Bradley,
Who is harrassed badly,
(If he is n't, at times,
Still, excuse us for the sake of the rhymes),
But he comes with quick tread,
And buys the Husks; for he thinks of the bed
Whereon we may
The weary head
And tired limbs lay
At the quiet close of some busy day.

Once, these Husks wrapped the ears of corn
With kind embrace,
But from the cereals they've been torn,
And now they've a higher place,
Serving, in honor, the human race.
Now is the season of Husks.
We pass up stairs
In a thoughtful mood,
When, quite unawares,
We're obliged to stood
Close up to some door,
And make ourselves astonishingly thin
In order to let some Husk bed in.

We are intent with pen or book
When lo! our sister with smiling look,
Beckons or calls for our humble aid
In making a tre-men-dous raid
On Husks;
And still we count the task as light,
For in husk-beds we delight.

Give me no bed of feathers;
In all sorts of weathers,
Give me Husks.   W. H. H.

V. Calvin of Albany writes to Mr. Newhouse that he is preparing a criticism of the TRAPPER'S GUIDE, which he will forward soon. He makes some inquiries on the subject of winter fishing and other subjects, and closes thus:—"Please answer immediately (if at all), and remember, you may save a human being from being hard pinched by hunger at times—if not worse.

I am &c., V. C."

NOTE TO THE FLIES.

Offspring of Beelzebub, depart; take yourselves off: quit our borders; come not near our faces any more.—Touch not with your maculating proboscos, anything that belongs to the O. C. Alight not on our walls, pictures, books nor windows—and above all things, keep far off from our food. You belong not to our principality—avaunt! Amen.   ONEIDA COMMUNITY.

We hate the toothache. Who does not? It must be one of satan's devices to torment us. If ever we are tempted to feel cross or grumble it is when suffering from a long, tedious and unmitigated attack of tooth ache. They are surely temptation-proof who can bear it in a cheerful, hopeful and buoyant spirit. We doubt not, that it is one of the "all things" that work for good, but it is a mysterious providence that can extract good from an evil so annoying, thus foiling the enemy of the harm he intended us.   .Y.

Our expected guests, Mrs. Peet and Mrs. Allman, from Blainsville, Iowa, arrived last evening.—Also a Mr. Loring, his wife and niece, from Courtland Co., stai l her over night, and left this morning. Mr. Loring is an old acquaintance and friend of Mr. Hamilton's: they were school-boys together, and it sounded strange to us to hear Mr. Loring accost Mr. H. with the familiar name of "Erastus." Mr L. takes the CIRCULAR, and seemed pleased with his short visit.

Our neighbors who raise Grapes are sometimes urgent, soliciting the services of our men in trimming their vineyards. Mr. Morris yesterday offered Messrs. Marks and Joslyn $12. to trim his vineyard of one acre; but it is doubtful whether they can find time to do services away from home.

The charge of conducting our evening meetings, devolves now upon Mr. Woolworth, instead of Mr. Hamilton, as heretofore.—A faithful criticism of Mr. Aiken was given last evening, at his request.

Seventy-eight persons took dinner at the Willow Place boarding-house yesterday: the number is not likely to be any less, so long as the rush of business continues.—Half a dozen new arm-chairs have been got for the Hall.

$23,000 worth of Fruits, Vegetables and Jellies have already been shipped.

Our new Tailor, Mr. Porter, after some perturbation of experience, has concluded to remain.

We notice a man engaged in painting over the roof of the New House.

Erratum. In the silk account given yesterday, for "$13 60," read "$12 50."

Traps ordered yesterday,   87 doz.

Yesterday's temperature—
7 A. M., 33.   12 M., 39.   6 P. M., 32.   Mean, 34⅓.

DAILY JOURNAL
OF ONEIDA COMMUNITY.

VOL. 2.   SATURDAY, OCT. 27, 1866.   NO. 101.

A PROJECT.

The Theological class has been occupied for the last two or three of its sessions in studying the list of bible texts at the close of the article on the Second Coming, in the Berean. There has been some talk about having the texts printed in full, in pamphlet form, JOURNAL size and several have volunteered to assist at the work on successive Sundays until all the passages are in print. This is a good proposal; and we hope it will be carried out. Such a vade mecum of authoritative statements might some day do good service in the cause of the Truth and would certainly be very serviceable in the present class.

We have already paid over $160 for husks, and we are still buying them. Some of the more thoughtful and prudent in the family, are beginning to feel, that we are paying a good round sum for husk beds, quite too much, though the price at present is a little reduced. Some of the men shake their heads ominously with, a "dont know about it, guess we shall have to plant a field of corn next year." One reason for the extra call for husks is, that we are making a good many new beds this fall, and our old ones are much reduced.

The Burt House now stands secure on its new foundation. When the cellar was being dug, the moistness of the ground, showing itself as it did, in little pools in every cavity, led to the hope that a well might be found. We do not wish to incite premature hopes on the subject; but we may say that, from the well-hole about five feet deep which has already been dug, about a dozen pailfuls of water have been baled daily for two or three days past. Time will tell.

Maud has been given up to the children's department. We called there yesterday, and found her enjoying herself happily. She did the honors of the house to us in a handsome way by rubbing a quantity of moistened cracker on the shoulder of our coat.

The work in the Bag department goes on efficiently. Some time ago, they were somewhere about forty orders behindhand, now they are about twenty. Orders are still coming in.

Our visitors from Iowa appear quiet and reserved, though quite interested in all they see and hear. They have read the CIRCULAR seven or eight years, are quite intimate friends, though they live thirty miles apart.

They say Mr. Morris's wife does not sympathize with her husband much, in his religious views though she is quite a reformer and wears the short dress.

We have an old man working in the Bag-shop now, who has been a clock-maker in his day, and who makes himself very useful to us by doing such odd jobs as we used to send to the Depot. He has put several of our clocks in order successfully; and is busy with some others to-day. His name is Walden; he is the father of Mrs. Smith who works in the bag-shop.

A portable clothes-rack has been made and is now in use in the children's house. There are nearly twenty pegs in it, each one labeled with the name of the juvenile to whom it is appropriated—Ormond, Emily, Ransom and so on.

By day, this rack may be seen ornamented with a row of night gowns; at bed-time it is brought forth to have these exchanged for a row of dresses, stockings &c. It is a delightful sight.

A board floor has been laid on that part of the Greenhouse that was not paved. It forms a decided improvement to the slippery clay we used to step on whenever we went to admire the flowers.

Apple bees are much in fashion at present. There were several last evening—or rather there was one, consisting of several groups—in the Bakery, the Kitchen, and the Cellar. This was after the similitude of the O. C. which is one, yet has a foot at Oneida, another at Wallingford, a hand in New York and one in New Haven——Head ubiquitous.

Since Mr. Pitt's departure, the office of Reader has devolved on E. S. B.—We observe Mr. Woolworth at work among the house-cleaning corps.

H. W. B. arrived last evening, on his usual peddling route.—Mr. Hall came home last night.

Now that the weather is showery, we know the good of our cement walk to the Store.

Traps ordered yesterday,	279 doz
The principal orders were—	
Sidney Shepard & Co.,	25 "
Russell Erwin Mfg. Co.,	104 "
Darling & Co., Montreal,	48 "

Yesterday's temperature—
7 A. M., 31. 12 M., 44. 6 P. M., 32. Mean, 35.

DAILY JOURNAL
OF ONEIDA COMMUNITY.

VOL. 2.   MONDAY, OCT. 29, 1866.   NO. 102.

BUSINESS MEETING.

It is desirable to have a covered carriage to convey the workmen to and from W. P. Several plans were proposed, but it was finally left to the wagon committee to investigate, and report at the next meeting.

Mr. Burt introduced the subject of getting a greater supply of water. If we succeed in getting Mr. Johnson's spring, it will give us six gallons per minute more than at present. The board were in favor of making preparations to lay a cast-iron pipe between here and the springs, early next season. Messrs. Burt and Abbott were appointed a committee to make experiments near Mr. Johnson's house, to see if water could be obtained by digging a well. Voted to lay a four inch cast-iron pipe to convey the water from the springs here.

George Hamilton stated that there was a lot of 25,000 traps to be put up, and he would like to have an extra effort made to get them through this week. It is desirable to do *all* we *possibly* can for the next two weeks, as our customers are calling loudly for traps. They write that if they cannot have them now they shall not want them at all.

It was thought that the walk in front of the house had better be deferred until warm weather, and have Mr. Worden's help for a while in the shop. It was proposed to have Messrs. Whitney, Nash and Bradley help what they can now.

D. Edson Smith from Onondaga Co., came here last Saturday, and left this morning. We were quite favorably impressed with his appearance and spirit. Since he was here a year ago last September, he and his wife have been South and spent a year. They were sent out as teachers, by the New York Freedman's Relief Association, and were stationed at City Point, Virginia, where they suffered many privations.

Mr. S. said he always had great reverence for the Bible—was formerly a member of the Baptist church, but latterly drifted into Millerism. He was rescued from that snare by reading Mr. Noyes' views of the Second Coming. When he was here before, he bought the Berean, and he said that he and his wife made it their indefatigable study all last winter. At first he was disposed to criticise it some, but finally, we should judge, from what he said, they had received its doctrines fully and heartily. Mr. S. is a young man 29 years old, fine looking and quite gentlemanly in his deportment.

S. W. N. spoke in the meeting last night, of the new matches. They have been in use in the family two weeks, and he wished to know how they were liked, and whether we could not dispense with our old ones. All seemed to like them much, now they had learned to light them. The family were exhorted to be cautious in throwing them down on the floor, or elsewhere, as there was more wood in them, than in the old ones, and they were not as soon extinguished. Mr. N. said that while we use the utmost precaution to avoid accidents by fire, it was ever present to his thoughts, that Christ was our true protector.

It has been decided to print the Bible Texts on the Second Coming of Christ, as referred to in Saturday's JOURNAL. It is intended that the first Number shall be printed next Sunday, and the rest on consecutive Sundays, until the little book is completed. It is believed that about two hundred copies will be sufficient to supply Oneida and the Branch Communes.

In the meeting Saturday evening, we had a faithful and sincere criticism of the JOURNAL, which we hope may result in its improvement. We are thankful, that there is a spirit here, that can detect any deviation from the true standard of Journalism, and can set us on the right track when we are disposed to wander from it. We confess Christ our helper, in the work, our wisdom and our guide.

In connection with the trap business, G. W. H. reports that we are 42,000 traps behind orders. There are 25,000 springs all ready and many of the other parts belonging to these, and as it is very desirable to finish off this lot during the present week, all possible help from the family is called for, even to the temporary inconvenience of other departments. Among others, Mr. Reynolds, who is a "tower of strength" in himself, has gone into the trap-making, while a wagon-load of young recruits of Arthur's size, were seen taking their departure for Willow Place this morning.

G. W. H. spoke in the meeting of Mrs. Dunning of the Willow Place Boarding-house, as worthy of much commendation, for her untiring efforts, in our great press of business, to accommodate all the boarders she possibly could, and putting up, with much good nature, a good deal of inconvenience on that account.

We were particularly edified and strengthened by the good spirit that prevailed in our meeting last night; Mr. Hamilton said he was thankful for the work of Christ that he saw in the men and women around him.

In the four days Mr. Hall was out peddling, last week, his sales amounted to $460,60.

Traps ordered since Saturday,   78 doz.

Saturday's and Sunday's temperature,
7 A. M., 43. 12 M., 49. 6 P. M., 35. Mean, 42½.
7 A. M., 38. 12 M., 46. 6 P. M., 40. Mean, 41⅓.

DAILY JOURNAL
OF ONEIDA COMMUNITY.

VOL. 2.   TUESDAY, OCT. 30, 1866.   NO. 108.

OUR VISITORS.

Our visitors from the west, leave for their homes to-day. Mrs. Peet bought a small Lunch Bag, to take home with her, and Mrs. Allman subscribed five dollars for the CIRCULAR. Neither of them had ever seen a member of the Community before, and both seemed highly gratified with their visit, and thought it would be a great benefit to them in the future.

Mrs. Peet is a widow lady, lives at Blairstown, and is a near neighbor to Mr. Morris, in whom she has great confidence. To show the faith she has in the O. C., she stated that, before leaving home, she made her will, in which, in case of her death while absent, she willed her children (two sons and three daughters, the oldest fourteen years old) to the O. C. if they would accept them, together with her property, amounting to about $8,000, and she appointed Mr. Morris, her executor.

Mrs. Allman lives about thirty miles west of Blairstown, at Iuka, a place recently settled. She says her husband is a believer, and would like to make us a visit, but on account of his work could not leave home now. They both seemed simple-hearted and receptive to truth, though in Mrs. A. we thought we discovered a tinge of self-righteousness. Both of their parents were Quakers, and they seemed to have quite a respect for the religion of their fathers.

Lady Hamilton suffers the crucifixion of the flesh with Christian fortitude and heroism. Her flesh fails, but her inward life rises in cheerful faith and victory over the destroyer, who can only kill the body. She seems to have accepted the truth that her body is dead property, and turned unreservedly to the renewing of Christ's resurrection, with abiding hope and confidence.

She is at present so helpless as to require to be moved from one bed to another on sheets.

We had a good many visitors here last Sunday though the weather was not the fairest: thirteen luncheons were furnished. Among the number was Mr. and Mrs. Hunt and their adopted daughter, from Verona Springs. The young lady played with much skill, and with first-rate execution, three very difficult pieces on the piano, which did her much credit as a performer and artist.

We are at last happy to report rain—yes, rain in good earnest—not a slow drizzle, but the actual outpouring of the overcharged clouds above us. We all say: Thrice welcome!

To give our absent friends some idea of what the O. C. has to do by way of entertaining company these days, we would inform them, that last week, the meals cooked for our home visitors amounted to ninety-nine. We are glad to be instrumental, in any way, to the spread of the truth, and do not grudge any amount of labor and expense that tends to that end.

A good deal of work was accomplished at the Trap-Shop yesterday, and great enthusiasm prevailed.—It is desirable that the boys should be exempt from their usual chores about the house, while they are engaged at the Trap-Shop, and the women will see that they are relieved.

We clip a paragraph from a letter received last night from Utica:

"Myself and neighbors are overrun with rats and one neighbor has one of your steel rat-traps and is making great slaughter amongst the varmint: I have got a notion that you had better send me one dozen traps and I will try them myself. Please send bill with them."

    Very Respectfully,   J. B. LOAK.

The grape-vines were all laid down and covered over, some days since.

Abram Burt was criticised in last evening's meeting, a report of which, will be sent in manuscript.

Mrs. Norton started for home at 4 o'clock this morning.

Traps ordered yesterday,	12½ doz.
The principal order was—	
Wallingford Community,	12 "

Yesterday's temperature—
7 A. M., 49. 12 M., 52. 6 P. M., 55. Mean, 52.

DAILY JOURNAL
OF ONEIDA COMMUNITY.

VOL. 2.   WEDNESDAY, OCT. 31, 1866.   NO. 104.

FROM BERLIN HIGHTS.

DEAR FRIENDS:—I wrote once to you and called you Brothers and Sisters, I feel now that it may have been presuming in me to do so, but I feel that you are my friends and teachers and I will wait until you feel to acknowledge me as a sister in Christ before I claim that relation.

When Mr. Olds was here he told us to write, and keep writing, not stop because every letter did not get a personal answer: I feel that I would be ungrateful indeed should I in spirit ask any thing of the kind when the CIRCULAR comes every week freighted with rich blessings. On opening the last CIRCULAR my eye caught. 'WHY THEY DON'T SHIRK.' I want to say, that labor has become a matter of worship with me. "Whatever I do is done heartily as unto the Lord." I feel a "motive power strong enough to make all kinds of work attractive." God bless you for expressing it for me, I could not have done it so well of myself.

I have learned in my life that two or more persons can say the same words and mean quite differently, but I feel very confident that when Christ, or the spirit of Christ, speaks in those persons, the same words will mean the same thing. I wish I could be with you just long enough to receive just the criticism I need most, perhaps I shall be sometime; I think God will make the way plain when the time comes, and I do not want to come to see with my external vision merely, or to let you know that I understand your position and principles but that you may answer me this question "What lack I yet?" Perhaps experience will teach me that I do not know what I am talking about, but I am hungry for criticism.   MARTHA S. REEVE.
                                 G. W. REEVE.

About two thirds of our raspberry vines have been laid down and covered. The young vines of the Red and Orange varieties have been "heeled in" for the Winter. They propose setting out new raspberry plants, this Fall, wherever old ones have failed and to set out about three fourths of an acre besides.—F. A. M., who has charge of this department, had occasion, the other day, to administer a little wholesome criticism to the hired hands, who it seems were indulging in idle conversation to the hindering of their work. A good effect has been produced, and the work goes on rapidly again.

Mr. Perry returned yesterday from New York, via Buffalo and brought with him, a knitting machine, that he bought when out on his last trip. He paid sixty-eight dollars for it, and he has learned to run it. He brought home a little stocking knit by himself, which showed the capabilities of the machine for family service. The stocking was all finished with the exception of binding off the heel and top of the stocking, and fastening the sides of the heel to the foot, and it took Mr. P. only fifteen minutes to knit it. The machine is Lamb's Knitting Machine No. 1, and was obtained at Rochester.

If our women are disposed to give a nod of approbation, as of course they will, to this new acquisition to our labor-saving machinery, some of us may perhaps nod in a more uncomfortable way, in our evening meetings, should knitting by hand come to be entirely out of vogue with us.

The attention of the committee on obtaining muck, has been directed to our own wood-swamp, in the south and south-east portions of which, a bed of excellent muck is found, of sufficient quantity to last us at least several years. The excavation of it, it is thought, will not disfigure our domain.

We were much interested in the account of Bellevue matters, read last evening—also in the information contained in the New York Journal, although the Reader was much embarrassed by the illegibility of the copy.

In meeting last night Mr. Hawley related some interesting experience he had had, since he came from Wallingford, and in connection with his work in the kitchen. He has felt the baptism of a youthful spirit—testified that work was not drudgery, but a pleasure to him, and that he could accomplish much more than formerly, without fatigue. The subject of humility was also introduced as a topic of conversation, and elicitated some very instructive ideas on that subject. We shall all learn sooner or later, from our own experience, that "before honor, is humility."

The foundation is laid, and the doors and window frames already made for a small addition of 17½ feet by 12 to our Willow Place boarding-house. This will enlarge the kitchen, and make it much more comfortable for cooking purposes.

Our potatoes have all been harvested and safely housed. There were about five acres of them. The crop is rather a poor one, a good many having rotted.

Traps ordered yesterday,	103 doz.
The principal orders were—	
Edward Wilson & Co., Albany,	23 "
Westphal & Hinds, Dubuque,	50 "

Yesterday's temperature—
7 A. M., 50.   12 M., 45.   6 P. M., 39.   Mean, 44½.

DAILY JOURNAL
OF ONEIDA COMMUNITY.

VOL. 2.   THURSDAY, NOV. 1, 1866.   NO. 105.

LETTERS.

Thanet, C. W. Thursday Evening Oct. 25, 1866.

DEAR BROS. HINDS AND CAMPBELL:—I arrived here this evening at 5½ o'clock, having had very good luck all the way. I got into Kingston about 4 P. M. the day I started. The passage was quite rough, there being a strong west-wind on the lake all the way. Like Mr. Burt I was called upon to pay a slight tax to the rolling "powers that be"—nothing very serious, but just enough to appreciate the matter, and to know what folks mean when they talk of being "sea-sick."

Everything was pleasant at the custom-house at Kingston. I got through without having my baggage examined, paid $3 30 duties on guns, traps and preserved fruits—15 per cent. Should not have had to pay anything on the guns if I had simply said, I did not intend to sell them, but I preferred to pay and retain that privilege. I arranged the whole matter with the Collector personally. He was very gentlemanly and pleasant—remembered our company that went out last year. I told him frankly what I had, where I was from, and what was my business. He seemed to be desirous to give me as little trouble as possible—thought I had rather a large number of cartridges with my rifle, but passed them without duty. After he had got through with his questions, he mentioned such articles as would have to be entered, asked me to mention them to the clerk, and without my asking it, gave directions that my baggage should be passed without examination—which was a very pleasant favor. Mr. Meagher, with whom I was slightly acquainted, was very kind and helpful in assisting me through. I thought my mentioning to the Collector that I was from Oneida Community was not without some service and influence in making the whole affair pleasant, and successful,—I felt that in doing it, I was confessing the Community.

From what I have been able to gather about prices I think good mink will be difficult to get for less than $3 to $3 50. I hear that Fowler offers $3, though he has not been up further than Madoc. I have not yet come in contact with any trappers, though I hear of a good deal of trapping going on. The idea seems to have got into the heads of some on the Hastings road that there has been some decline in the price of furs since last fall.

I shall be as quiet as possible in my operations, and only to do a safe business, watching for the leadings of inspiration.

The following are the Montreal prices as quoted in the TRADE REVIEW of Oct. 19.

Mink, $3	to $1 50.	Otter, $4	to $5.
Fox, $1	" $1 25.	Beaver, $1 23 "	$1 50.
Rat, 12c. "	18c.	Fisher, $4	" $5.

I hope Mr. Campbell will watch and investigate the market and report to me often and promptly.

I find the people I meet, who recognize me, are pleased, apparently, to see me. I tell them I came in, to hunt a little and to look after our traps, saying as little as possible as yet about buying furs.   With love to you and all, Your brother in the service.   T. L. PITT.

TO THE COMMUNITY.

For some days past, I have been under temptation about my late criticism in connection with the Daily Paper. I have tried to accept the criticism by conforming in a legal way with the hints and recommendations given me, at the same time keeping my heart whole.—But God has shown me that such external conformity is the very least of the things He requires of me, and that the chief thing is brokenness of spirit.

I confess Christ in me, a soft, contrite heart.

I thank the Lord that He keeps His covenant with me and will not let me go unsaved.   W. H. H.

A letter was received yesterday from a Mr. F. H Meeker, Cincinnati, Ohio. Too lengthy for insertion in the JOURNAL, we can only quote from it some of the juiciest passages, in which the munificent generosity of the writer appears to best advantage. Mr. M., while reading the sketch in the PHRENOLOGICAL JOURNAL, was "strongly impressed with the idea" that Mr. Noyes' "sphere of usefulness might be enlarged" and our "numbers considerably increased" &c. &c. &c., by a certain "proposition," which he "submits" "upon the strength of his impression."

Indeed the opening paragraph assumes such a tone of disinterested concern for *our* good, that even the least amount of sagacity would naturally suspect such professions in one who is an entire stranger. So that no one need be surprised that the body of the letter is occupied with a glowing account of a piece of property he wishes to sell us.

He gives a minute description of the property which according to his account, is a very fine affair. The keen, worldly shrewdness which is manifested as the "proposition" unwinds to its full length, is in marked contrast to the preamble. Nothing is forgotten to secure self.—He wishes a loan of $10,500, and an annuity of $3,000 per annum, the whole to be "secured" in a very satisfactory manner.

Mr. Perkins has not been able to work, since his fall, till last week. He now assists in out-door labor some, and goes to the Trap-shop to help there, every rainy day.

The sky is unclouded to-day and our rain storm seems to be over. We had a trifle of hail and snow yesterday, and the air this morning is cool and bracing.

Yesterday's temperature—
7 A. M., 36.   12 M., 41.   6 P. M., 30.   Mean 35⅔.

ered
DAILY JOURNAL
OF ONEIDA COMMUNITY.

VOL. 2.   FRIDAY, NOV. 2, 1866.   NO. 106.

AN EXIT.

One of the trap-packers shipped himself last night, and left the following among the freight receipts be made out yesterday:

DEAR MR. HAMILTON:—I thank the Community for their kindness to me and wish them prosperity and happiness; but after much prayer and mature reflection I have to confess that I don't want to spend all my days *tied* to a Community, and seeing no good reason why I may not as well quit, first as last, I have decided to return to New York now.

My object in leaving clandestinely is twofold; First, to obviate the necessity of a personal interview, and secondly, to go as *quietly* as possible, thereby sparing the feelings of all parties concerned. I therefore hope that you will look charitably upon the peculiar manner of my exit. In this connection I wish also to state that I sincerely think a great deal of the Community, especially of Mr. Noyes, and of others, but as I said before, so say I now again, I don't want to spend all my days *tied* to a Community.

In regard to a financial settlement I have to request that you send me *immediately* a sight draft for seven hundred dollars, on the Tradesmen's Bank, in New York City; the same to be made payable to my order. Should there be any doubt in your mind as to the propriety of refunding the money that I put into the Community, as I have suggested, I beg leave to present the following facts. 1. That the Community have already had the *use* of it since February 1864, (nearly three years), *without interest.* 2. That they have also had the use of it for 15 months longer than they expected to; as I have been creditably informed that they were about to refund it in July 1865, before I thought of returning to the Community. 3 It should also be noted that they have had the use of it at a time when finances have been very tight, and now that money is coming in freely it seems no more than *fair* that they should refund it as I have suggested; and I ask them as *Christian* men to do it.

Again, thanking the Community for their kindness to me and again wishing them prosperity, and happiness, I bid you all a hearty farewell.   Yours &c., c. j. g.

P. S. I intend to qualify myself for a position in some Bank until I can do better. My Post-Office address, for the present will be,

      CHARLES J. GUITEAU.
      Care of Sweeny's Hotel, New York City."

2. P. S. It may be proper to state that through the kindness of an outside friend I have been able to procure fifty dollars, thus making my exit easier than it otherwise might have been.

In connection with the above, an extract from a letter just received from C. J. G.'s father will be read with interest.

The CIRCULAR has been full of good things to me lately. I should hardly know how to get along without it. Sometimes in my imagination I compare it to the leaves of the "Tree"(spoken of in the book of Revelations) as being in the Holy City, whose *leaves* are for the healing of the nations. It seems to me a sure thing that those who are faithfully co-operating together in scattering the leaves of the CIRCULAR, will in time feel that they are abundantly rewarded for any temporary trials or discomforts they may be called upon to endure in their work and labor of love.

Many people are gradually being enlightened by it, who will one day rise up to bless those who are faithful and true in their efforts to spread the light of the Gospel of Communism. With much love and sympathy for you all, I remain, Yours truly,   L. W. GUITEAU.

It was reported last night, that 5,600 traps were inspected, yesterday, 5,000 put up, and about the same number shipped. G. W. H. said it was the largest day's work ever done in the shop.—A call was made last night, for extra help in the Trap-Shop to-day, to supply the place of some of our hired men, who would be absent attending to their political registry.

We received yesterday, $22 premium, on articles exhibited by us, at the Vernon Town Fair, held a few weeks since.

Mr. Henderson has left his work in the Printing Office, for the present, and takes the place so abruptly vacated by C. J. Guiteau, at the Trap-Shop, packing traps. M. E. Kellogg will take his place in the Office.

It is interesting to see the zeal with which some of the younger class of our young men (those of 16 or 17 years of age), engage in business, at the present time. They volunteer, and take their turn in working nights at the Trap-Shop. One of that class, said to-day, "It is astonishing how my eyes have stood it, if I had been at work for myself, they would have been put out, long ago."—Good testimony that in favor of Communism.

Among the enthusiasts at the Trap-Shop yesterday, might be seen little Harley H. and Eddy Blood, both rigged in overalls.

Traps ordered Wednesday and Thursday,   90 doz.

Yesterday's temperature—
7 A., M., 30. 12 M., 45. 6 P., M., 40. Mean 38¼.

DAILY JOUR.
OF ONEIDA COMMUNITY.

VOL. 2.   SATURDAY, NOV. 3, 1866.   NO. 107.

A GENEROUS DEED.

The horticulturists have sent a party of men to Wampsville to cut cedar stakes for use in the Raspberry plantations, &c. The owner of the cedar allows us to cut what we want "without money and without price." This is considered a rare opportunity, and it is estimated that every man's time who works there will be worth at least 75 cts. per hour. As might be anticipated, the Horticulturists manifest very much the enthusiasm, that we imagine adventurers do when they strike oil, or a rich vein of the precious metals. Two or three hired men have been sent to cut the stakes, who will board near the scene of their labors. Mr. Barron and Thayer also engage in the enterprise, coming home every night. The two quart bottle of new cider, they smuggled into their wagon this morning as they started off, testified that these men are lovers of good cheer, and have found out a chemical affinity between cedar and cider.

House-cleaning goes on very efficiently and quietly.—. Mrs. Goakes the elder, comes here early every morning, and works at cleaning till dark; she is over sixty years old, but looks much older. She seems to have great power of endurance, and probably has seen some hard times.—There is a lively company at work cleaning the dinning-room to-day.

Mrs. Vanvelzer and Mrs. Reid finish to-day, their long and arduous campaign of Fruit-Preserving which has lasted over five months. The last, of their hired women will be dismissed to-day.

A bee was called for, and well attended yesterday, in the upper sitting-room at the New House, to assist the Bag-Shop hands in finishing off a lot of bags, that were needed to fill their orders—another bee is expected to-day. One of the sisters remarked, that the bee reminded her of H. A. N , and her labors of love, and gave her a renewed desire to see her.

Our cherry trees west of the Concord vineyard, 70 in number, are being taken up, as they have for many years proved themselves unfruitful, and the merciful cry to 'spare them yet another year" has given place to the sterner accents of justice which says cut them down, " why cumber they the ground."

We bake and send over to the Boarding-house at Willow-Place, every day, ten loaves of bread, and shall do so, till the addition to their kitchen is completed and they have better accommodations for baking.—Twenty dinners are also furnished from our kitchen, and sent there daily.

The Burt-House progresses to completion, slowly, as only two hands are employed in the work. Mr. Porter says his family will be obliged to come on soon, as the house they now occupy is rented.

Our Horticulturists are preparing three and one half acres of land, principally for raspberry bushes—have sub-soiled it to the depth of eighteen inches, and are now engaged in ditching it.

A large order for over $400 worth of Bags, was received from a firm in Boston yesterday.

SALES IN OCTOBER.

Pres. Fruit,	$27,005.21
Trap,	17,097.80
Bag	3,045.50

Traps ordered yesterday,	188 doz.
The principal orders were—	
Pratt & Co.,	53 "
Geo. R. Barton,	50 "
C. E. Allen, Quincy, Ill.	30 "

The latter has formerly dealt in Peck, Smith & Co.,'s Traps.

Yesterday's temperature—
7 A. M., 45. 12 M., 46. 6 P. M., 34. Mean 41½.,

DAILY JOURNAL
OF ONEIDA COMMUNITY.

VOL 2.   MONDAY, NOV. 5, 1866.   NO. 105

BUSINESS MEETING.

The committee on procuring a covered wagon for carrying passengers between here and Willow Place, report it as their opinion that they cannot provide one in season to be of much service this fall. After some discussion the same committee were authorized to fit a cover we have on hand, to Mr. Kellogg's single wagon, and to take measures to procure one during the winter, suitable to hold twenty persons, at least, so that we can have the benefit of it next spring.

A communication from M. L. Worden, reporting the condition of the roads in our district, the amount expended during the past summer, in repairs, on the same and calling attention to the bad condition of the bridge across our dyke-race, and asks for the appointment of a committee to examine the same.

Messrs. Worden, Kinsley, and Clark were appointed as such a committee.

He also reports several days labor yet due on the road from our neighbors, which together with contributions from the Community, he recommends to be laid out on the roads in fall repairs.—The Board accepted Mr. W.'s report, and authorized him in connection with Mr. Clark, to cause the same to be done.

D. F. Knowles suggested the propriety of putting a pipe and pump to the well at Willow Place Boarding-house, for bringing the water into the kitchen instead of going out doors for it, as at present. Messrs. Abbott, Kinsley and Burt were appointed a committee to investigate the matter, and report at the next business meeting.

Mr. Kinsley reported the action of the committee on purchasing the muck-swamp belonging to Dr. Cherry & Co., but as negociations in relation to said purchase, are still in progress, it was thought best to let the matter lie over, till our next business meeting.

Mr. Pitt writes:

"Every thing appears to be working quite well thus far. I have seen Holland and Gunter. They will have a fine lot of fur—especially mink—better I think than last year, of which I shall have the *first* offer. They have already as many mink as they had last year three weeks later. They wish to sell about the 20th of November. I have also seen John Ray, and secured the first offer of his fur. He called at McKillican's the morning after I got in to see the bear trap, which he seems rather inclined to take. He had seen me on my way up the road. He said he had made up his mind not to sell till we had seen his fur, if we came in. He said that Holland and Gunter had told him that they preferred dealing with us to any fur buyers that had ever been on the road. I shall go up the road this week and see Long and Robinson, and if possible secure the refusal of their fur. These will be the *three* principal lots on the road, and would doubtless amount to $600 or $700 gold. They will probably all be for sale between the 12th and 20th of November.

Haw, (Mr. Campbell knows the man), will have quite a large lot of mink to sell three weeks hence. He and his son, and another man in company with him have already over 25 mink, from middling to fair quality, and what they catch after this will probably all be good.

I feel very good so far about the work before me, and find it easy to keep my mind and heart on my business and on Christ. I seemed to have special good luck in meeting Ray, Holland and Gunter."   T. L. P.

We propose to facilitate the working of organization by carrying it into the childrens department in a more thorough way. We have found in our past experience that children become tired of play-things in a few days, however nice and costly they may be, while ordinary things frequently changed give entire satisfaction. Our plan is to have a set of play-things for every day, each day to close by putting them all away, with the expectation of new ones to-morrow.   E. L. H.

Over 22,000 traps were finished off last week, and if the springs had not failed, G. W. H. said they would easily, with the help they had, have put up 80,000. Mr. Hamilton enquired if any one felt that they had worked too hard, or were tired? Some testified that they felt fresh and vigorous, and the past week had to them been a very happy one. It was remarked that the hired men seemed to catch the spirit of enthusiasm that prevailed in the shop, and that they worked better and more effectively than ever before.

In addition to what was reported in Saturday's JOURNAL about the cedar timber our people are cutting, we would say that the owner of the land is a Mr. Cobb, and that our people have engaged to cut all the timber on his lot. He gives us freely all the sticks, less than three inches in diameter, (which are of sufficient size for our use), and pays our people for cutting the remainder.

Traps ordered Saturday,	82 doz.
Traps packed and shipped last week—	$7325,12.

Temperature Saturday and Sunday—
7 A. M., 29.   12 M., 40.   6 P. M., 31.   Mean 33⅓.
7 A. M., 33.   12 M., 40.   6 P. M., 26.   Mean 36.

Erratum:—On the last page of Wednesday's JOURNAL, for 17½ feet by 12 read 17½ feet by 16.

DAILY JOURNAL
OF ONEIDA COMMUNITY.

VOL. 2.　　TUESDAY, NOV. 6, 1866.　　NO. 109.

OUR VISITORS

Two gentlemen staid here last night, and will leave this forenoon. One was William A. Bryan, Chief of Bureau Inspector U. S. P. O. Department, Washington and Private Secretary to the Post Master General, Judg. M. Blair. The other man's name is Smith, both are from Lewis Co., and came with their own horse and carriage.

Mr. Bryan is a man about 40 years old, we should think, of middle stature, and quite gentlemanly in his appearance. He has traveled quite extensively in Europe and at one time spent two years at Vienna. He has a fund of knowledge and renders himself quite interesting in conversation, and talks in an easy familiar way. He married his wife in Lewis Co., and is now on his way to Binghampton, where he is building him a house, and Mr. Smith is to oversee the building of it. He had with him an English hunter and coach dog, white all over, and dotted with small black spots, which he seemed to think almost as much of as though it was a child. Last night, he spoke of his dog—said it was in his carriage in the barn, and had had no supper, and asked us, if we would not please to send one of our *subordinates* to the barn and give the dog something to eat. We had some music in the Hall before meeting, with which he expressed himself much pleased, also with the privilege of attending our meeting. He had heard of us through a friend of his, who visited here, and he has seen occasionally a No. of the CIRCULAR, but further than that, had little knowledge of us, though he expressed himself interested in our movement. He expects to visit Southern Europe, another year, and will be happy he said, to send us some token of remembrance from there. He spoke of the Shakers, at New Lebanon, whom he had recently visited, and thought their system similar to ours. [Not quite, thought we to ourselves, as you will probably learn at some future day.] He seemed desirous to collect all the information he could, about the Communistic movements in our country, before making his contemplated tour.—Mr. Bryan spoke last night of the coming Election, and said the politics of the country had become so corrupt that he had not voted for a number of years.

Election day interrupts our business some, as quite a number of our hired men are voters. Only one or two however are absent from the bag-shop, as most of them were disqualified by change of residence for voting.

Mr. Hubbard has interested himself in getting all our hired men who vote the Republican ticket to register their names, and be promptly at the polls.

Outsiders in our vicinity seem to understand our position in respect to politics pretty generally, and we do not get lectured as formerly, or reproached for dereliction of duty.　　　　　　　　　　　　　　E.

The gravel, tar &c., that have so long lain in front of the New House, and which was designed for our cemetery walks, we are happy to say has been removed. One load of the gravel was deposited in the children's yard for the especial benefit of the little three-year-olds. A half dozen of them can be seen these fine days, (for the weather is again splendid,) perched on top of the mound of gravel, each with his little wheel-barrow and a broken shingle, or whatever else can answer the purpose of a spade, loading, and wheeling the gravel into the little shed that stands back of it. They enjoy it "mightily," we should judge, and from the assiduity with which they load and unload, they might be taken for a company of "paddies" working for day wages. The heap of gravel is however, from the constant treading of their little feet, becoming quite hard, and sport for them in this direction must soon cease.

It is known to many, but perhaps not to all, that the scattering of apple bits and pearings on the walks, or stairs, exposes people to serious accidents. It is not uncommon to read in the papers of broken limbs from such, and similar causes. Now there is not a day passes but some of the cautious ones stop and pick up apple pearings from the stairs leading to the archway. Will not every one commence a reform on this point at once? By so doing, they will satisfy themselves and the Community in this matter.　　　　　　　S. B. C.

Yesterday Willey's Father gave him a nice little house with two chimnies, one near each end of the roof. After turning it in all directions, and examining it carefully, he suddenly came to the conclusion that all boys do, and with a string around one of the chimneys, it was soon seen swinging around the circle, with Georgy and Harry and Temple, who were already playing horse.

Twenty four Britannia pitchers have been purchased for the use of the family, which it is earnestly hoped, may be used carefully, and kept exclusively for the table. -Twenty two comfortables for our beds, have been made since the 4th of October.

Traps ordered yesterday,	133 doz.
The principal orders were—	
Homer Bishop & Co., Boston,	34 "
F. H. Luse, Iowa City,	50 "

Yesterday's temperature—
7 A. M., 25.　12 M., 32.　7 P. M., 26.　Mean 27⅓.

DAILY JOURNAL
OF ONEIDA COMMUNITY.

VOL. 2. WEDNESDAY, NOV. 7, 1866. NO. 110.

LETTERS.

We extract the following from a letter received a day or two since:

Bates Ill., Oct. 30, 1866.

VERY DEAR FRIENDS:—I think that when I wrote to you some months ago, I asked you a very important question, important to me, viz., Can you, or will you s nd a person to help me start a Community here? Which question *was never answered.* I write now again in hopes of an answer. Since I wrote and became a subscriber of the CIRCULAR I have studied your principles attentively, and like them well. I have sent and got the PHRENOLOGICAL JOURNAL for Oct., and am studying it attentively. They give a very good report of you and it is very interesting to me. Why? I am an old reformer and glory in the name. I have hopes that spiritualism will do good, but as yet it is too much theory and not practical like your reform. O, how I rejoice that you have succeeded so far. The way seems already open and the kingdom of heaven near at hand. I have read and thought much upon the social principles for the last twenty years, and when I see a state of happiness so near, that we can all reach it, if we will, it seems that nothing will satisfy or suit me but a practical experiment.

Well, what say you, brothers and sisters? Is it not time to think of a Community in this region? Ira Porter, I suppose will go to New Jersey. Wildstrand is away in Minnesota too far north. This is a beautiful prairie country, fruit grows large, luxurious and luscious. O, if I could only help in such a noble enterprise as founding a Community, would I not be happy? The hope of it is a happiness to me now.

Dear Friends, I beg pardon for so frequent use of the pronoun *I*, but a spirit urges me on and I can't help it. Do, please answer this and much oblige and gratify an ardent reformer fifty-six years old.

May the God of all grace bless, comfort and guide every one of you, into the kingdom of heaven.

W. GOULD.

Last evening W. G. Kelly offered himself for criticism, and the spirit of carelessness that has troubled him of late in his business transactions was severely criticised. This fault of Mr. Kelly's gave rise to a good deal of talk about the bad effects of a careless spirit, both upon the person who indulges it, and upon the Community, with which he is connected. Some testified that they had thought a good deal of late, about the disastrous effects that sometimes follow in the train of an act of carelessness, and Mr. Noyes' recent Home-Talk on that subject had stirred them up, to rid themselves entirely of that pernicious habit. Some confessed their faults and thought it was a good way to help ourselves, in overcoming the spirit of carelessness, to let in the light.

While at Elmira recently, I got into conversation with two young men, about the Community, our manner of conducting the meetings &c., when they replied, why, that is very similar to the daily prayer meetings we attend at Thomas K. Beecher's church. Said they did not have any formality about them, but they took the form of familiar conversation about spiritual things, and if any one had a desire in his heart for any thing, they would express it in a simple way without rising up or kneeling down. They became quite interested in learning about the Community, and I left them the tract "SALVATION FROM SIN" which they said they would read. W. G. K.

The CIRCULARS did not reach us, till last evening. We have of late received them so early in the morning, that we were some disappointed in waiting all day, though we confess to an increased appetite, and high relish for reading them when they came.

Mrs. Ellis' eighty fourth birth-day was celebrated yesterday, by a small party assembled in her room.—Mary Leete came here again, yesterday.

Mrs. Sears is learning to run the Knitting Machine, and is making some progress, though it will take time, to master it completely.

If we pare our pears, and put them up in pairs, who has a right to find fault with us?

This is the third week of the children's school vacation which they seem to enjoy much.

The O. C. shipped yesterday to I. Farwell Jr., Agent, Boston, Mass., the following machinery, manufactured at Willow-Place.

1 Silk Spinner,	$550.00
1 " Cleaner,	$297.00
2 " Spoolers,	$100.00
Spooler, Table and fixtures,	$40.00
Boxing and Packing,	$20.27
Total,	$1007 27

John F. Sears started for Willimantic last night, for the purpose of getting the cylinders to the above machines made at that place.

Traps ordered yesterday, 101 doz.

Yesterday's temperature—
7 A. M., 25. 12 M., 41. 7 P. M., 26. Mean 30½.

DAILY JOURNAL
OF ONEIDA COMMUNITY.

VOL. 2.   THURSDAY, NOV. 8, 1866.   NO. 111.

OUR VISITORS.

Dr. Wellington came last night, and a lady friend of his, a Mrs. Curtis from New York City. The Dr. is on his way home from the far west, and Mrs. C. is on her return from Cleveland Ohio, where she has been spendding some time, with a sister living in that City. Dr. W. has given up teaching, and has been engaged several years in curing insanity by what he calls "Obsession"; and he states that he has been very successful, often dis-possessing a person of evil spirits, in ten minutes time. He could not tell *how* it was done, he only felt as his experience had proved, that he had the power to do it, and he called it faith in Christ. Though his business is lucrative, yet he longs to quit it, and has been waiting long for an opening to connect himself with us. He says he has been a Communist 25 years.—They were not invited to attened meeting on account of F. Norton's criticism.

Mrs. Curtis is the widow of a physician, and after the breaking out of the rebellion she was employed two or three years as nurse, in the Hospitals both at Washington and Nashville. She made a good many enquiries about us, said she had wanted to visit us before, but she seemed almost entirely ignorant of our religious faith.

I am always interested to read anything in the JOURNAL that comes from the children's department, and as I am one of the assistants at the present time, I would like to add my mite, however small it may be. In their meeting this morning, Mr. Hatch gave his impressions about different ones, and then showed them the importance of having a good spirit. He read a chapter in the Bible, where it speaks of prayer and said it was just as easy and simple for the children to ask God to help them, as it was for the older people. He also spoke of the Golden rule—said they should "do to others as they would have others do to them", illustrating it in such a way that it was very easy for them to understand. I observed one of the older boys in tears, which impressed me that such meetings soften their hearts, as well as ours, and bring us nearer Mr. Noyes and the family.

P. A. S.

As we are about closing our out-door plays, for the season, will our friends give us the benefit of their thoughts and suggestions, in regard to in-door amusements for the winter; what will be improving, edifying and amusing, for our small circle of fifteen children under seven years of age?   E. L. H.

"Give us this day our daily bread" springs up sponta-neously from our hearts, every morning, as we enter the Office. We will do the best we can, in collecting items for the JOURNAL and then rest satisfied with what we can obtain, whether it be little or much, trusting that if the Lord has set us about our work, as we believe he has, all will be well. He has already done more for us and far better than our fears, thus rebuking our unbelief.

Mary Leete returned home, this morning. When she was here last, she was criticised by a committee, which we should judge, had been quite a help to her, as her spirit seemed more soft and genial than heretofore.

If it was a little later in the season, we should call the delightful weather we a e having, Indian Summer.—November seems trying her best, to out-vie her departed sister, in clemency and sunshine.

Our carrots are all harvested, 800 bushels.—We commence threshing our wheat to-day.

We think an apology is due to the readers of the Journal, for the frequency with which we have mis-spelled the words, pare, and parings, or rather our oversight in correcting them in proof-reading. No two words have bothered us like those—even after they are in print (p-e-a-r), &c., we are slow to detect the error. We think this blindness must be the effect of carelessness, which we certainly are desirious to put far from us, and to reform, wherever reformation is needed.

Traps ordered yesterday,   86 doz.

Yesterday's temperature—
7 A. M., 34.   13 M., 50.   7 P. M., 31.   Mean 35.

DAILY JOURNAL
OF ONEIDA COMMUNITY.

VOL. 2.   FRIDAY, NOV. 9, 1866.   NO. 112.

LETTERS.

Stowe, Vermont Nov. 5, 1866.

MR. S. NEWHOUSE: DEAR SIR:—I have received a pamphlet from Fowler and Wells, called the "Trapper's Guide." I have read it with interest as I am a lover of hunting. I have just returned from a trip to the Saranac Lakes, and had a good time generally. I learned on my return that Black Bears are quite troublesome here this fall, and some attempts have been made to capture them, but the bears have proved too much for them as yet. I see you advertise bear traps for sale with swivels and chain. I want to get one and try it.— The track made by one of the bears is eleven inches long, and five wide. It will need to be a pretty large trap for such a foot. I think the seventeen pound trap will be about what I shall want. I don't know what your prices are or I would send you the money in advance. You may send me one marked C. O. D. (collect on delivery). Please send by Express as soon as you receive this and oblige,

Yours Respectfully,   H. W. WILLIAMS.

Three accidents occured at Willow Place yesterday afternoon, none of them serious though. Providence said very pointedly, "Take care!" Mr. Kellogg's hatchet glanced, whilst coopering and made what he calls a slight scratch on his leg, which Mr. Henderson sewed up. Mr. K. says he had a decided instinct not to use his hatchet in the way he did, but persisted till the tool itself stopped him. He is at work as usual this morning.

H. E. Allen climbed up a ladder to put on a small belt. This being accomplished, (a feat she can do as well as a man,) she was preparing to descend, when the ladder, slipped back and fell to the floor, striking the Reel on its descent. H., who was bound never to give up the ship, hung to it till it had fairly reached terrafirma. The shock was divided up, among both thumbs, right wrist, left elbow, head and leg, so none of the wounds were very serious. Her thumbs were strained some, so that she will stop work for a day or two.

A lighted kerosene lamp was knocked on to the floor, in the Finishing room, and broken. The oil took fire and began to spread. A croud of boys rushed upon it at once and began to stamp about. A. Hawley pulled off his coat and threw upon it which was followed by one or two other garments. The flames were soon subdued, no damage being done except to the coats, and Alfred's face which got slighthly scorched.

On the other side, the company of welders who worked from 6,30 P. M., till 12, had a very enjoyable evening. All felt the presence of a spirit of worship in labor.

c.

Out-door work is being closed, and the Business campaign for the season is about ended, but interior activity now commences. Our hearts are drawing together into unity with each other and the heavens.

The less conspicuous but more dynamic work of the mind and heart will go on, to result, we trust, in forthcoming flower and fruit of good works.

We notice the arrival of a fresh supply of Robinson's New University Algebra.

We are frequently asked, how does Rose get along these days? Our answer is, Well. Her bodily health continues to improve, and since her return from Wallingford, she takes her place with her class of girls—eats at the family table, takes her part in the appointed work, attends school, plays croquet, sings in the class, is interested in sports, and plays generally. This is not all; Rose, we think is a girl of faith. Her sickness of three years, has not been lost; it has softened her spirit, and improved her character generally.   E. L. H.

Mrs. Whitfield has taken Miss. Pomeroy's place, in taking care of Lady Hamilton, as Miss. P. was getting some tired and needed a change. Her faithful services, performed so cheerfully and heartily, are much appreciated by the family, as are also, those of Mrs. Jane Kinsley who has been associated with her. Their labors of love will be rewarded. "Inasmuch as ye have done it unto one of the least of these my brethren, ye have done it unto me."

Dr. O. H. Wellington and Mrs. Curtis, left here yesterday afternoon. Mrs. C. was desirous of purchasing the Berean, but as we had none here, Miss Chloe told her she could probably obtain one at the New York Agency. She said she would do so, and she should make it her study the coming winter, to acquaint herself with our theological views and principles.

Mrs. Bushnell is one of the daily distributors of the clothes, at the ironing-room. She carries her Berean with her, and when she has a half hour's leisure, she reads aloud. The ironing girls try to be as still as they can, and Mrs. Mallory thinks that some of them, are getting quite interested in the reading.

Mr. Worden has taken Mr. Aiken's place, in the supervision of our Boarding-houses. He enters upon the duties connected with them to-day.

Traps ordered yesterday,   52 doz.

Yesterday's temperature—
7 A. M., 39. 12 M., 56. 7 P. M., 38. Mean 41.

DAILY JOURNAL
OF ONEIDA COMMUNITY.

VOL. 2.   SATURDAY, NOV. 10, 1866.   NO. 113.

Trap-Shop.

A visit to the trap-shop at the present time, will afford animated pleasure to any one who has a taste for business enterprise and execution. The forging department especially, with its glowing furnaces, and the clash and chorus of its presses and rollers, and its motly groups of workers, presents a very interesting spectacle of industrial operation. Foreman R. Hawley, estimates that with their present force and facilities, they will be able to turn out two thousand springs per day. The finishing department will easily supply all parts requisite to make finished traps.   n.

House-cleaning is nearly finished for the season. The Reception-room, however, remained to be done, and as there was no company here, Mrs. B. and T. decided yesterday to clean the room to-day. Mr. Whitney was seen at an early hour, taking up the carpet, having moved the furniture, by the help of the Willow-Place men. Presently, Mrs. B. came down stairs to say that they would defer the work, as she was disabled; but it was too late. Miss Thomas would surely be on hand.— No, she was reported sick, and needed care herself.— What should be done? We had gone so far, that the room must be cleaned, to-day. In a short time, the state of things was known among the women and girls, and one after another volunteered to help as soon as their morning's work should be done; and now, the work is going forward rapidly, and to all appearance it will be completed sooner and with greater ease, than it would have been, had the usual company been at their post.

It seems sometimes as though circumstances were thus providentially arranged, for the purpose of drawing out the talent and public spirit of different members of the family.   S. B. C.

Our band of little ones enjoy wonderfully the privilege of getting out-doors, such beautiful October-like weather, as we are having at the present time, and if they do appear a little like young colts, just turned out to pasture, and require considerable attention, we feel well paid for our trouble, when we note their enjoyment and see their happy little faces and sparkling eyes. To-day we took them out on the Croquet ground, and they enjoyed watching the players, and the older ones like Fanny, Temple, Harry, &c., seemed to have quite an idea of playing a game themselves, judging from the way they used the mallets, and knocked the extra balls about. From there, we took them down to the Great Barn, to watch a company of men, who were threshing wheat with four span of horses, going round and round in a circle. They were delighted to see them and stood peeping through the fence very quietly, and with intense interest, for nearly an hour. Maud and Ransom were of the party in their little carriages, and seemed to enjoy it all, as well as the older ones who could run all about.   E.

Mr. Bradley has, for a little time past, taken the place that Mr. Kellogg has so long and faithfully filled, in going to and from Willow Place, carrying passengers, luggage, &c. He thinks he has contrived a method by which our horse, White-foot, will be effectually cured of his runaway proclivities. He fastens his halter to a heavy iron and lays it down on the ground. The horse tied his skill at fleetness, a few days since by running from Willow-Place as usual, but was arrested in his course by Martin, who stopped him near Mr. Hubbard's.

Mr. Ackley has put up 205 barrels of apples for winter use, 156 of which, are of our own raising. The barrels are all marked with the name of the apples that the barrel contains, and then put in the Fruit-house. We have besides these, quite a quantity of fall fruit, that we do not put in barrels, as it will be used right along as we need it.

The "bites" on the edges of the JOURNAL are occasioned by having our form too large for the capacity of the press. Our only feasible remedy is to cut down the width of the JOURNAL one fourth of an inch on each page. Shall we do it?

Four little girls of Edith's class went to the Trap-shop yesterday, to help on the chains. They were quite efficient and have gone again to-day.

Traps ordered yesterday,	34 doz.
The principal order was—	
A. F. Shapleigh & Co., St. Louis,	20 " No. 2.

Yesterday's temperature—

7 A., M., 50.   12 M., 60.   6 P., 38.   Mean 49¼.

DAILY JOURNAL
OF ONEIDA COMMUNITY.

VOL. 2.   MONDAY, NOV. 12, 1866.   NO. 114.

BUSINESS MEETING.

S. W. N. motioned that a committee be appointed to cause the removal of the accumulated rubbish around the Willow-Place buildings. Messrs. Campbell, John Leonard and the Willow-Place teamsters were appointed a committee to attend to the matter.—Mr. Abbott reported the result of the investigations relating to bringing water into the boarding-house at Willow-Place. The water would have to be raised twenty-five feet at an expense of $20. Mr. and Mrs. Dunning would prefer to have another cistern instead. Messrs. Abbott, Kinsley and Burt were appointed a committee to favor them with another cistern instead of a pump.

After some discussion concerning the importance of crowding the business of trap-making for the next few weeks, Messrs. E. H. and G. W. Hamilton, Hatch and Burt, were appointed a committee to decide upon the best method of furnishing the necessary help. To this committee was referred the matter of employing hired women in chain-making.

As the 300 cords of stone quarried since last fall have all been readily sold, and the prospects are that the demand will be equally good for stone another season, W. A. H. proposed that measures be taken to prosecute this branch of business the ensuing winter; Messrs. Kinsley and Burt were instructed to have at least as many quarried as have been disposed of the past season.

There was some conversation respecting the true policy to be pursued by the Community towards the two great mail express companies—the American and Merchant's Union. There are some features in the organization and management of the latter which, it was thought, entitle it to, at least, a share of our patronage.

———————

A Miss Lowell, from Portland, Maine, came here last Saturday. When her father was here some months ago, he requested that his daughter might be permitted to make us a visit—consent was given, with the proviso, that he should write and let us know before she came. It seems that her father became some acquainted with C. W. Underwood when he was here, and though the lady did not write that she was coming, she enquired for Mr. Underwood at the depot, expecting, it appears, that he would meet her there. For some cause she refused to come with Homer, and hired a man at the Depot to bring her up. She says she is only twenty-eight years of age, but she looks much older. She has been married, and after living with her husband five years, she left him, because he was dissipated. She expressed a wish to join the Community, thought she understood us pretty well as she has read one of our papers and the tract "Oneida Community." We do not think much of her honesty and shall not regret her leaving, as she expects to, to-day. Miss L.s' father lives in Troy, and she goes from here to visit her parents in that City.

———————

Our efforts to obtain water at the Burt House, are at last crowned with success. There were indications while digging the new cellar, that water might be found there, and on digging down to the depth of five feet below the bottom of the cellar, they found it in great abundance. They have stoned up the well, and the water has risen to the surface of the ground. It remains to be seen whether there is a living spring there.

———————

Mrs Allman and Peet met with many tedious delays on their return home. They started from here Tuesday noon, and did not reach Blairstown Iowa, till 9 o'clock P. M. Friday. Mrs. A. writes: "Though we feel ourselves almost worn out, yet we are gratified in the belief that we have visited a God loving, and truth seeking people."

———————

In consequence of the pressure of business at the Trap-Shop, the commencement of the school, is deferred a week or two longer. Two of our women have volunteered to take turns in going over to the shop, to work with the little girls and take charge of them.

The men who were employed last week in hanging out clothes from the wash, have handed us the following statement. Whole No. of articles in the wash during the week, including stockings, handkerchiefs, collars &c., was 3,589, and the estimated No. of square yards of cloth contained in the garments and articles was 5,681, excluding stockings and collars from the calculation. If these clothes were all spread out to dry, they would cover a surface of one and one eighth of an acre.

The principal articles were—

Women's and children's aprons, dresses and other calico garments,	460.
Pieces of women's and children's apparrel,	578.
Table-cloths, Bed-spreads, flannels and overalls,	68.
Linen Pocket Handkerchiefs,	290.
Men's and boy's shirts and drawers,	294.
Towels great and small,	620.
Pillow-cases,	816.

The above statement includes the boarding-house washing.

———————

Traps ordered Saturday	72 doz.
The principal order was—	
Pratt & Co. Buffalo,	50 "

———————

Temperature Saturday and Sunday—
7 A. M., 40.   12 M., 54.   6 P. M., 34.   Mean 43½.
7 A. M., 45.   12 M., 53.   6 P. M., 44.   Mean 47.

DAILY JOURNAL
OF ONEIDA COMMUNITY.

VOL. 2.   TUESDAY, NOV. 13, 1866.   NO. 115.

SWEET-CORN.

Wallingford, Oct. 8, 1866.

BRO. WILLIAM:—In accordance with your suggestion, I tried the sweet-corn, and found it first-rate. You need have no fears of our suffering in reputation, if the rest of the corn is as good as the five cans I have opened. But one thing I noticed which was unfavorable—the cans were not evenly filled. Two of the five were full weight; the rest varied from one to two ounces, which difference can easily be made in careless weighing. I have never heard how serious the loss in corn was, or whether you have found out any satisfactory cause of some failing to keep. Were the farmers who raised corn for us, faithful in bringing it freshly picked? I have also questioned the policy of stacking the cans together in large bodies, perhaps before they were thoroughly cool, &c. However, these suggestions may not be to the point. It seems to be a precarious business, judging from the many failures, but I hate to give up *beat*. If we decide to do anything at the business another year, I would suggest the propriety of making it a separate thing from the fruit preserving. At the time of putting up corn, the business is liable to be more or less interfered with by tomatoes, late peaches, pears &c., which come along about the same time, and perhaps not giving time to do as much at either as would be desirable; under a pressure of business, things are liable to be done in a hurry or left too long undone. But perhaps we can do all the business we want to in this line, in preserving fruit alone, without doing anything at putting up peas and corn.

Yours for truth and science,   H. T.

O. C. Nov. 12.

BRO. THACKER:—Thanks for your letter and the suggestions it contains.

There has been talk of having a sweet-corn thanksgiving. The final results of corn-packing this season are likely to be much better than any here expected.—We have shipped twenty thousand cans, and have now on hand about eight hundred. The number of "swelled heads," which have been seen around home, is estimated as not far from three thousand. Only one customer has yet made serious complaint, and to him the corn was shipped early in the season. Some others may claim deductions for poor corn; but still there is occasion for gratitude that it has turned out so well.

I judge that the general impression now is, that the failure of a part of the corn was on account of its being heated before it went into the preserving-room. At different times there was corn enough picked in the afternoon to last the huskers and cutters till ten o'clock or later the next forenoon. Considerable pains was taken in spreading the corn, but we learn that at least one load was badly heated when brought by our neighbor Davis. I understand that successful corn-packers are very particular, and will not receive any corn picked after twelve o'clock, and that they sometimes induce those who raise the corn to commence picking at three o'clock in the morning.

The fact that our corn spoiled "in streaks" favors this view. Of some lots nearly every can puffed itself into uncomfortable shape, while it was difficult to find a "swelled head" in other lots.

It should also be mentioned that it was not possible to boil the corn under so much pressure as was desired, on account of the distance of the bath-room from the engine, and the great amount of other work it had to perform.

Perhaps other important reasons might be given.—Mrs. Vanvelzer thinks as you do, that the cans ought not to be stacked together in large quantities until entirely cold.

The preservers here do not yet consider themselves "masters" of corn and pea preserving, and any hints you or others may have for their benefit I know will be thankfully received.   W.

We have realized from our field of wheat, about 400 bushels.

The recent criticisms of O. H. Miller and Frederick Norton, particularly the latter, have had the effect to stir up the community, especially the young men, to clear themselves of bad influences, that have been at work among them for a long time past. Night before last, several communications were read from the class of young men of Ernest's age, exposing the workings of a dark, secretive spirit among them, and expressing a desire to come to the light, and be purged from false influences.

Some of the family sat up last night to witness the anticipated periodical display of meteors. As Mr. Hawley was to rise at 4 o'clock however, to get breakfast, he volunteered to get up an hour earlier, and call the family, should any uncommon phenomenon make its appearance in the heavens. So the majority of the family slept soundly, and nothing unusual transpired. We shall watch with interest again to-night.

Traps ordered yesterday,	107 doz.
The principal orders were—	
May & Co., Boston,	39 "
and three Bear Traps.	
W. H. McConnell, Grand Rapids,	24 "
Murfy & Clark, Cleveland,	15 "
Worthington & Co., "	15 "

Yesterday's temperature—
7 A., M., 37. 12 M., 44. 6 P., M., 33. Mean 38.

DAILY JOURNAL
COMMUNITY.

VOL. 2. WEDNESDAY, NOV. 14, 1866.　　NO. 116.

THE WAY TO DO IT.

The teams had been hauling fruit and vegetables to Mr. Bennett's storehouse at Durhamville for nearly three weeks, and in the meantime none had been shipped east.

At least thirteen tons were there awaiting shipment, besides 5000 lbs. of scrap steel. We began to grow anxious on the subject, and wrote to Mr. Bennett to ship it at least by Tuesday of this week if he possibly could, without waiting for an expected boat of the Ithica line. He replied that he thought it better to wait for the boat from Ithica, which was probably on the way.— We then telegraphed to the agent of the Ithica line, and got word that he could not move our goods immediately. Letters were daily received from customers urging us to "hurry forward their fruit." Something must be done—we could not sleep first-rate nights, with that fruit lying still at Durhamville. Homer and I concluded Monday evening it must move by canal yesterday, or by railroad to-day, and he volunteered to go down and hail every boat that passed, till he found boats to take it. Towards evening he sent up this dispatch:

"All off but L. G. & Co. 74 cases, and O. C. A. 50, and old scraps. Guess I shall come it by sunrise."

But he did not have to wait till "sunrise." At 7½ o'clock last evening he arrived with the pleasing announcement, "The goods are all off!"—If they had not been taken away yesterday they would probably have had to remain at Durhamville two weeks longer, or been drawn back to the Depot, and sent by Railroad, as the papers inform us that there is a serious break in the canal near Palmyra, which may stop boating operations twelve days. We feel thankful for good instincts and good luck.　　　　　　　　　　　　　W.

We have several times lately been reminded of what Mr. Noyes has said in some of his Home-Talks, that "Words are seeds sown", by some one's saying to our little ones without taking thought for its effect, you are a rogue, or you are a naughty boy. One little fellow who had been visiting his parents, came to us, with his mind disturbed, and trying to solve the problem, "my papa say my mamma naughty girl. Is she naughty girl?" How shall we answer? He evidently expects us to give him a satisfactory answer and set his mind at rest. Children believe all that is told them, and why should they not? Shall it not be one of our early improvements to overcome the habit of idle talk?　　　　E. L. H.

Those who sat up last night to witness the expected meteoric shower, were again disappointed. At 11 o'clock the sky was cloudless and the air transparent, and a few quite brilliant meteors shot onward from the north-east, But. We noticed two, in their appearance of rockets, and they might have been rockets, sent up from Rome, or from some place in that direction—others were of a paler hue; but as the night advanced the atmosphere became hazy, and although there were small phosphorescent lights, darting here and there, from time to time in all directions, yet nothing of any magnitude was to be seen.

Daniel Kelly writes to his brother, Nov. 4th: "I feel that my whole heart is with Christ and the Community, and I feel ready and willing to do anything that the Lord has for me to do. I am studying the Berean now, and I think it is doing me a great deal of good. I would like to return to the Community, if they feel (considering the circumstances in which I left), that they could receive me back, and try me again. I am perfectly willing to leave my case with God and the Community, and feel that I shall be dealt with justly."

A new exercise has sprung up almost involuntarily in our evening meetings. It is this: some one is called on to read the hymn before singing. This practice was started by Mr. Hamilton, (at Mr. Bolles's suggestion, we believe), by his proposing to read the hymn himself, and the next evening, he asked Mr. Woolworth to read it.— The following night, and the night after, some of the women were called on to read, and so the fashion is fairly started, and there is no knowing where it will end.

A man by the name of Burdick, from Guilford Vt., a nephew of Mrs. Lynde, staid here last night. He has been in the army four years and is on his way to Michigan.

Bad Spelling.—A letter was received yesterday for Elisabeth Quance, directed thus:

"Libthabuss Quanch
　　　　oneida kamunity N Y"

A business letter recently handed in to the office for mailing, contained the following abbreviation of two common words: "havto."

Traps ordered yesterday,	133 doz.
The principal orders were—	
Markley, Alling & Co., Chicago,	50 "
A. R. and G. H. Miller, "	50 "

Yesterday's temperature—
7 A., M., 25.　12 M., 42.　6 P., M., 28.　Mean 31¼.

DAILY JOURNAL
OF ONEIDA COMMUNITY.

VOL. 2.   THURSDAY, NOV. 15, 1866.   NO. 117

FRUIT.

The following interesting statistics have been collected by Miss Nunus and her assistant:

Bottle Cases sent away,		1200.
Can, " " "		2607.
Jelly, " " "		469.
Total No., " " "		4276.
Total value of Fruits, &c., sent away,		$34,769.20.
Shipped, 6 oz. Jellies,		326½ doz.
" 12 oz. "		305½ "
Value of Jellies,		$2894.31.
Value of goods shipped to Chicago,		$6798.18.
Value of Fruit &c., sent to Dealers,		$23656.35.
" " " Consumers,		$11112.85.

Fruits &c. have been sent to 9 Western States, 4 Eastern, 3 Middle, States, 43 Western Cities, 43 Eastern.

It may be added that if the cases required to ship the Fruits and Jellies now on hand be added to the above, the aggregate would be about 4500.

There are still on hand over $4000 worth of fruits and vegetables, besides what have been reserved for family use. The following table will indicate to agents and others what they can safely receive orders for:

Tomatoes, Corn, *String Beans; Quinces in cans and bottles: Damson Plums in cans and bottles;

*Lombard,	"	"
Blackberries,	"	"

Yellow Spanish Cherries in cans:

*Black Raspberries,	"
Huckleberries,	"
Pie-plant,	"

Peaches *cut, whole and pared and whole unpared, in cans.

Blackberries in *bottles, and in *cans with and without sugar.

Brandy Peaches	in bottles,
Strawberries,	"
Crab-apple Pickles,	"
Black Raspberry Jam,	"
Strawberry Jelly, 6 oz. and 12 oz.	
Blackberry, "	"
Currant, "	"
Grape, " "	
Peach, " "	"
Black Raspberry,	"
Lemon,	"
Barberry,	" "
Cranberry,	" "

Of those kinds designated with a * we have extra quantities on hand.

There are but few Jellies on hand of any variety.

Of the general financial results of the Fruit Department the present season we cannot speak definitely, but the profits will probably exceed those of last year. w.

New-York, Nov. 11, 1866.

DEAR MRS. J:—I see by Friday's JOURNAL that Miss Chloe told a visitor at O. C. that she could probably purchase a Berean at the New-York Agency, as they had none for sale at O. C. Now the fact about the matter is that we have no Bereans here to spare—we have scarcely enough for our own use. We have just commenced our Theological class in earnest and every available copy of the Berean is in active demand. The truth is we have no Bereans to sell. It seems to me that the best we can do for our outside friends who wish to read the Berean is to *lend* it to them. The conclusion several weeks ago at W. C. was, that the edition was exhausted, and its advertisement was accordingly withdrawn from the CIRCULAR. Notice was also given to O. C. in the regular New-York Journal, to the same effect, but as there still appears to be some misapprehension about the matter, will you please to mention it in your JOURNAL.

For myself, I never appreciated the Berean as now and is this not the case generally throughout our Communities? It is coming to be our *text book*, something like the Bible itself, and I imagine the time is not far away when it will in some form be reprinted.

Truly Yours, H. W. B.

Mr. Brown from Brentwood L. I., who visited here more than a year ago, and who called at New-York Agency in June last, and was criticised while there, came here this morning.—Mr. Burdick will leave to-day.

Traps ordered yesterday,	133 doz.
and Bear Traps,	six and one twelfth "

The Bear Traps were in a California order, the whole of which amounted to $865.

Yesterday's temperature—
7 A. M., 26.   12 M., 52.   6 P. M., 39.   Mean 39.

DAILY JOURNAL
OF ONEIDA COMMUNITY.

VOL. 2. FRIDAY, NOV. 16, 1866. NO. 118.

LETTERS.

Extract from Mr. Pitt's letter of Nov. 9th.

" Please have the CIRCULAR sent to Mr. John Lewis of Belleville, C. W. He said he neglected to write for it when the notice was published to subscribers. I judge from the way he spoke, that he rather wants it, and he remarked that it circulated among quite a number of respectable citizens, when it formerly came to him. As he is obliging to us in a business way, I should be in favor of sending it to him as long as he cares to have it, without any regard to pecuniary return.

I have concluded to start up the road this afternoon The present prospect is, that mink will range from $3½ to $4, and possibly for extra skins $4½. I shall do all I can to buy below $4. I judge that Haymes here in Belleville will be our principal competitor. He is quite well established in business I should judge, and evidently manages to, or is managing to manipulate the local fur buyers back on the road so as to get their trade as much as possible. He talks on the "full" side to them, and Cleak follows suit.

I have concluded also to draw on you to-day, Nov. 9, for $400 at .our days after sight. This will enable me to buy what fur I have in prospect, if it is possible to get it. If I fail to get the fur at safe rates I shall be able to return the money in a few weeks. Possibly I could get along with $350, but if I get what fur i shall try for, it would have me rather a small margin I fear.

I confess the successful principality and faith of Christ in me as my controller and guide, and am resolved to fully trust him for good luck.

I confess my union with you all and my love for the whole church in heaven and on earth. I am happy and contented in my work, but shall be glad to return home as soon as I have got through. I feel that I am taking hold anew on Christ, and becoming emancipated from much that has been a hindrance to my usefulness and clearness as a medium of Christ and Mr. Noyes.

Yours in the service, T. L. PITT.

The study of Algebra is likely to become even more popular with us than it was last winter. We hear of one class that has already commenced, and many in the family are quite enthusiastic to improve every leisure moment in studying it in private. Some are commencing the study for the first time, and others are hesitating, and the question is heard to drop from their lips, " do you think I could learn Algebra? Am I not too old and too obtuse to try?"

It appears to us that if anything will arouse persons from their apathy, and awaken their dormant faculties, it is Algebra. In this respect it seems well adapted to elderly persons, many of whom are averse to close thought and investigation. If the study seems hard at first sight, a little patience and perseverance will soon overcome the difficulty and it will become a real pleasure.

Mr. Brown leaves to-day. He claims to be in sympathy with us and asks for advice. He has buried his children, four in number, and has separated from his wife. At the present time, he is living in a sort of Community way, with a man and woman at Brentwood, L. I. We understand he would like to connect himself with our Community if we would receive him.

We are having rainy weather now, and the farmers are improving their time, by doing their semi-annual task of oiling their harnesses, thirty in number. We have, at the present time twenty-two horses and three colts and yet our people employ only one man in the horse-barn.

Our little cottage across the way, is plastered, and very nearly finished. It is to be occupied by Billy Smith and his newly wedded wife.—The Burt-House is finished on the outside and vigorous measures will be taken to complete the inside work.

Martin says he shall employ two hired hands all winter to work in the cow-barn. The farmers have at the present time, three teamsters at work doing up their fall jobs. Mr. Clark thinks he shall need four hands all winter to do team-work.

The horticulturalists report that the ditching (150 rods) on the Raspberry plantation is finished. The greater part of the ditches were dug 2½ feet deep ; about 40 rods however were 3 feet in depth.

Mr. Bradley reports success in obtaining husks for the New-York Agency, and he says he will send them on, as soon as they are sufficiently dry.

Two evenings have been principally occupied with the criticism of D. J. Bailey.

Traps ordered yesterday, 143 doz.
The principal order was—
Hibbard & Spencer, Chicago, 100 "

Yesterday's temperature—

7 A., M., 43. 12 M., 54. 6 P., M., 52. Mean 49½.

DAILY JOURNAL
OF ONEIDA COMMUNITY.

VOL. 2.　　SATURDAY, NOV. 17, 1866.　　NO. 119

LETTERS.

Prospect, Nov. 11, 1866.

DEAR JOHN:—Since my return from Oneida, my thoughts often, yes, very often, fly back to that dear home, where so many loved ones dwell, and in imagination I can see the family moving about in their different occupations or assembled in the Hall in their evening gatherings, where in union they testify to the goodness of God, and express thankfulness for favors received.

I feel renewed thankfulness to God from day to day for his care and protection over me. How often the words of the Psalmist come to my mind; "The Lord is my shepherd I shall not want. He maketh me to lie down in green pastures; he leadeth me beside the still waters. He restoreth my soul; he leadeth me in the paths of righteousness for his name's sake; yea, though I walk through the valley of the shadow of death I will fear no evil, for thou art with me; thy rod and thy staff they comfort me." The rod spoken of in the above quotation represents I suppose afiction or criticism admin istered by a loving hand whenever we stray away from the right paths—as soon as we humble ourselves before the Lord, and return to his allegiance, his staff which means his supporting grace comforts us. The rod and the staff are both necessary for our spiritual welfare, al though the application of the rod, is not always agreea ble to the natural man, it should be borne patiently, and received thankfully for the benefit which the staff con ers. I confess my faith in Christ and the Community and my allegiance to both, and I desire to so live as to make myself acceptable to God and the Primitive Church.

Dear John, I want to just say a word to tell you that I appreciate your labors of love, and feel grateful to you for your untiring devotion and thoughtfulness to supply my every want while at Oneida—and I feel thankful for every act of kindness extended to me by you and others while I was there. I look upon you now, as not belong ing to me, but as one with the family, belonging to Christ and the Church; and I thank God that you are where you are; I feel no anxiety about you, believing as I do, that all your wants will be supplied, both spiritual and temporal. I thank God for his goodness, and pray that before long the way may be opened for my return to Oneida.　　Your affectionate Mother,　　P. H. N.

The Theological class take up for their next topic of discussion "The Origin of Evil." In the last meet ing when a volunteer was called for, to speak on the stage at the next meeting, two persons, Messrs. H. R. Perry and J. S. Freeman, happened to speak at the same time, and so it was proposed that both should ad dress the class when we meet again, one at the com mencement of its session, and the other at its close.— The class increases steadily, both in number and enthu siasm.

We saw on exhibition in the Hall last night, a very pretty picture of quite a remarkable family, Mr. and Mrs. Quance of Camden, with their fourteen children. The children are all living, the eldest being twenty-six year of age and the youngest four. The parents are placed in the center of the picture, and the children form a circle around them, the two youngest standing inside the group, one at the top, and the other at the bottom of the picture There are one pair of twins among them, two girls.— The second son is a Tin man by trade, and has been in our employ some months past. At the present time, he is at work in the Trap-Shop, and his wife finds employ ment at the Bag Shop. One of the girls also assist at the home Boarding-house.

Mr. Edgett of Vineland, came last evening on a visit He wishes to make some arrangement with the O. C. N. Y. B. by which he can engage them to sell the products of a fruit preserving Co. at Vineland, of which he is the Superintendent.—H. W. Burnham came again last night

---

There is no abatement of activity at the Trap Shop— 3,000 traps were inspected, boxed and shipped, yester day. We gain on our orders so rapidly now, that an other week will give us more leisure, to turn our atten tion to study. The large room in the Tontine that has been used through the summer for preparing fruit and vegetables for preserving, is being partitioned off, and a part of it is to be used for a school-room.

Those who have been engaged in Fruit-preserving through the summer, invited the criticism of the family, last night. No fault was found with them, but their general course, and the spirit that has prevailed among them was much commended.

H. G. A. writes: "Our Silk business is much better than we expected it would be. Saunder's man, on calling yesterday, said we were doing more than any one else among their customers."

Traps ordered yesterday,　　　　　81 doz.

Yesterday's temperature—

7 A. M., 45. 12 M., 46. 6 P. M., 37. Mean 42½.

DAILY JOURNAL
OF ONEIDA COMMUNITY.

VOL. 2. MONDAY, NOV. 19, 1866. NO. 120.

BUSINESS MEETING.

.The subject of the use of coal and its waste, sifting ashes &c., was introduced and elicited much discussion As our coal in many cases has to be carried quite a distance, it was thought that men should take the responsibility of doing it, and leave less of the burden of carrying the coal to women and boys. Messrs. A. Kinsley, S. W. Nash, J. Abbott and W. H. Woolworth were appointed a standing committee, to have the oversight of the use of coal, and to make any improvements they may see fit.

W. A. Hinds said it was of some importance to have some consultation about the fruit business for the next season. If we double the business, a great deal of lumber will have to be purchased and some one will have to do it. There has been a question whether we should put up corn and peas, and also whether we shall alter the size of our cans, and bottles? By having the sizes smaller, we can save one half the tax, probably $1000. We want to give our orders for bottles in the course of two months. W. A. Hinds was empowered to convene a committee to consult and to decide upon the matter.

Mr. Inslee enquired if we had not better get castings for more lathes, and have them made up, as they are always a salable article. As we have to pay hands who work on the lathes $3,00 per day, and a proposal has been made by the proprietors of the silk stretcher, to make stretchers for them, it was thought, that if we accept their proposal it would be more profitable for us to work on silk machinery, as there seems to be quite a demand for it and we do not have to give the workmen employed, as high wages.

Mr. Woolworth is to see that the earth is removed that has slid against the brick shop, and Mr. Kinsley will put up a stone wall for its future protection.

Lumber is growing scarce and high, and at the same time we shall want more and more boxes. Messrs. A. Burt, J. Burt, E. H. Hamilton and D. F. Knowles, were appointed to see if we can adopt a more economical way of making our boxes.

We had quite an exhibition on the stage just before the close of meeting, last night. Mr. Burnham had exhibited to some few of the men at the barn, in the course of the day, the manner in which Mr. Frobisher commenced with them his lessons on elocution, so it was proposed that Mr. B. should give the whole family a similar specimen. About a dozen men volunteered, and took their stations on the stage with Mr. B., as his pupils. The exercise of inflating the lungs, and giving the vowels the lowest sound possible, was quite amusing, and gave us all a hearty laugh.

Among our company of employees at the Trap-Shop are several little Irish boys, who from time to time make us considerable sport by their shrewdness. A little fellow last Friday morning after having eaten hash for his breakfast was reproved by one of the other boys for having eaten meat. In reply he said there was no meat in the hash, it was cod-fish, and to decide the question he asked one of our men what hash was made of; meat and potato of course, was the reply. Another boy coming in just at that moment said to the conscientious questioner No. 2, " What made you eat meat for dinner it's Friday." " I forgot that it was Friday," said the little urchin, rather nonplussed at being detected on the spot in meat-eating, " till I got my meat on my plate, and then the Holy Virgin herself, could not stop me." On being asked what punishment their parents would inflict on them should they discover that they had transgressed in this respect, they said, " they would give us a sound whipping, and shut us up in dark rooms for three days."

In our meeting last night two short notes to Mr. Hamilton from O. H. Miller were read, which were anything but satisfactory. Then considerable criticism of Mr. M followed. After that a letter was read from C. A. Burt, which showed that sincerity and criticism in his case, was softening his spirit, and lifting him out of his past difficulties, by giving him a broken and contrite heart.

Charles Vanvelzer writes from Watertown: " I have really got out in a snow-storm this time. It looks now as though I should get snowed in. If it is so I can get along to-morrow I shall take a *B* line for home, and thankful I shall be when I get there. Business has been quite fair."

Mr. Porter and his family came Saturday afternoon. Mr P. had been absent from here a week, making arrangements, and preparing to move. They are to occupy the quilting-room and an adjoining bed-room, until the Burt-House is completed.

Mr. Underwood was sincerely criticised, in Saturday evening's meeting. He is to start for Wallingford, early to-morrow morning.

Mr. Hamilton having gone to Utica to-day, and the trap-orders for the last two days not having been booked, we defer the report till to-morrow.

Temperature Saturday and Sunday—

7 A. M., 37. 12 M., 40. 6 P. M., 33. Mean 36¼.
7 A. M., 39. 12 M., 49. 6 P. M., 36. Mean 41¼.

DAILY JOURNAL
OF ONEIDA COMMUNITY.

VOL. 2. TUESDAY, NOV. 20, 1866. NO. 121.

NOTES TO THE FAMILY.

I was not in meeting the evening of Mr. Miller's criticism, and so did not know about it at first. I have thought as Mr. Vanvelzer said last night, that Mr. M was eccentric, and have always felt inclined towards sympathy and friendship for him; but as I am more or less involved in the same spirit of pride and independence, which leads to murmuring and discontent, I wish to accept the criticism for him and myself, and take this occasion to separate myself from him in that spirit, and from evil in all its forms, by confessing my union with Christ and the Community spirit.

I confess a spirit of humility and docility, and the power of Christ's grace to overcome all my faults and save me from all evil. M. L. WORDEN.

—

I take this opportunity to express my thanks to the family for their sincere criticism of me in showing me my faults at this present time, as I am on the eve of going to Wallingford. I confess it to be one of the greatest parting blessings that could have been conferred upon me, and therefore I accept it as the truth about myself. I have been sensible that I have had a strong family-spirit, and when it was proposed that I should go to Wallingford I felt very glad on that account. Christ will accept no relatives in his kingdom on earth, but such as do the will of his Father in heaven, and I pray that I may have the mind of Christ in all things. I have suffered a great deal from egotism. I believe it is the greatest hindrance to my spiritual growth of anything I have to contend with. I confess Christ in me a Savior from all sin and unbelief. I confess my love for Mr. Noyes, Mr. Hamilton and Mr. Woolworth, as inspired men, and I truly desire to follow the lead of their inspiration. I confess my love for the whole Community family, and a spirit of subordination to Christ at all times and under all circumstances. I desire your prayers that I may "stand fast, in the liberty wherewith Christ hath made me free, and be not again entangled in the yoke of bondage."

Yours for the love of the truth,
C. B. UNDERWOOD.

—

For sometime past I have had a desire in my heart to confess publicly my love for, and union with the Community. I feel, as Mr. Hamilton said last night, that the time has now come for us to testify which side we are on. I thank God that by his grace I can say that my desire is to be on the side of truth. My great stumbling-block has been an idolatrous love for my husband. I wish to separate myself from that spirit, and pray God to remove all idols from my heart. I confess a humble [...] [...] of [...] Christ that in his strength I should be able to overcome all evil.

I confess my love and union with Mr. Noyes and Mr. Hamilton, and desire to be receptive to their spirits. I wish also to take this opportunity of expressing my sincere thanks to the family for their loving kindness to me and my children, and receiving us into their hearts. I feel now as I have not felt before that I can thank God for a Community home. LOUISA EASTON.

—

I have been under a hard, wicked spirit lately. The devil has been setting schemes before me, to draw me out of the Community, and has been tempting me to think evil of my best friends. And I have been tempted all the while to think that God approved of my course, so that I hugged the sentimentality of my own nature and tried to make believe that it was the spirit of Christ.

I feel indeed, as if the devil had been dragging me through the dirt and making a fool of me; and I am thoroughly ashamed that I have yielded to him so long; I hate his deceitful and seducing course with me, and pray Christ to take entire possession of me and give me a broken penitent heart. I want to be thoroughly washed and cleansed, and to have my old life completely rooted out of me.

I confess Christ in me a spirit of subordination to Mr. Noyes and Mr. Hamilton, and I ask the aid of the family to make a new man of me. W. H. H.

———

Mr. Hamilton gave an interesting account in last evening's meeting, of his call at the Insane Hospital at Utica, and his visit with Victor. We should judge from what Mr. H. said that he thought Victor had improved some, and that the discipline of the Hospital, was having a good effect upon him.

———

The devil tries hard, our young men to seduce,
But he'll soon give it up, and confess, " It's no use,
They may start on my train, but as sure as the day,
At the very first station, they'll all run away.
So the most that I gain for my labor and pain,
Is chagrin, that I cannot my captives retain."

———

Traps ordered since last report— 55 doz.

———

Yesterday's temperature—
7 A. M., 40. 12 M., 50. 6 P. M., 45. Mean 45.

DAILY JOURNAL
OF ONEIDA COMMUNITY.

VOL. 2.   WEDNESDAY, NOV. 21, 1866.   NO. 122

LETTERS.

THE INDEPENDENT, Editorial Rooms,
No. 5 Beekman Street, New York, Oct. 25, 1866.

MR. JOHN H. NOYES: MY DEAR SIR:—The bearer of this, Mrs. Georgiana B. Kirby, of Santa Cruz, California, is an earnest seeker for truth on every subject that concerns the welfare of mankind. She was for a time a resident at "Brook Farm," near Boston, and has never lost her interest in the great social problems which the movers in that, and in so many other enterprises of a similar character, hoped to solve. She has a strong desire to see the Oneida Community, and to inquire carefully into the principles upon which it is founded. She is a woman of noble character, beloved of all who know her, and I am sure you will take pleasure in seeing her and answering her inquiries.

Yours respectfully,   OLIVER JOHNSON.

—

Syracuse, Nov. 17, 1866.

MR. J. H. NOYES: DEAR SIR:—Seventeen years ago just as I was starting for California, I saw at the house of Dr. Joel Shaw, a gentleman from your Community who wished me to visit Oneida. I told him I expected to be gone three years, and should certainly avail myself of his invitation on my return. My interest in your movement, as in all efforts to improve the condition of human society, has increased rather than diminished, and I am therefore very desirous of passing a day in your midst. Will you be so kind as to write me if I could be accommodated in case I had to stay all night. I am staying here with a friend for ten days—at the latest two weeks.

Mr. Johnson intimated that he wished I had a note of introduction from some one who stood better in your estimation than himself.—Please direct to me, care of Chas. B. Sedgwick.   Very truly yours,

GEORGIANA B. KIRBY.

The above letters were received yesterday, and an invitation has been sent to Mrs. Kirby, to make us a visit.

DEAR FRIENDS: I feel very thankful to you for your kindness to me since I have been in the Community. I confess my faith in Christ and my belief that this is indeed the Kingdom of God begun on the earth. I desire to be obedient and receptive to the truth, and to do my duty in all things, as unto the Lord. I ask the prayers of the family to strengthen me in my good resolutions. I have rather dreaded criticism, but am thankful for that which I lately received from a committee, and trust the Lord will help me to profit by it.

AMANDA E. PERRY.

We called in to see a sister, M. D. P., last night, who for several days had been suffering from an attack of disease. She remarked to us that she did not know but the dread lest her case should be noticed in the *Journal* had kept her from giving up entirely. She is almost well again.

Mr. Noyes's Home-Talk that was read in meeting last night, contrasting the faults of the old and the young, and striking the balance in favor of young life and activity, was heartily responded to by the family. Some spoke of the last CIRCULAR—thought there was a good tone to it, &c.

A bed has been put up in the silk-room at Willow Place, and C. A. Cragin has volunteered to sleep there. He thinks there is too much property at stake there; to be left without special care.

Mrs. Freeman came yesterday, on a visit of a few days.—W. A. Hinds started yesterday afternoon for New York.

The weather is colder, and some snow is falling this morning—the first of the season.

Traps ordered yesterday,	145 doz
The principal order was—	
A. H. Gardner, Milwaukee,	100 "

Yesterday's temperature—
7 A. M., 50.   12 M., 50.   6 P. M., 42.   Mean 47½.

DAILY JOURNAL
OF ONEIDA COMMUNITY.

VOL. 2. THURSDAY, NOV. 22, 1866. NO. 123

LETTERS.

Extract from a letter received from D. M. Kelly. Dated Nov. 15:

"I received brother William's letter criticising me for the course I had taken in leaving the Community, and I feel like thanking him for it. I think that God's spirit has been working in my heart about ever since I left the Community, but I resisted its warning voice, and would not yield to it. There was something within telling me that I had done wrong. I finally came to the conclusion, that I would not hold out against Christ's spirit any longer, but yield, and give myself up entirely and without reserve to him. I can, and am willing to see the wickedness of my ways, and do heartily and sincerely repent of them, and ask the prayers of the family that I may become as a little child. I confess, at times I was tempted to doubt Mr. Noyes's inspiration.—I now see, that it was the temptation of the devil, which has long since passed away. I believe him to be a man chosen by God to lead his people, and teach them the way of life and salvation. William asked me what assurance I had that under the same circumstances I should not again yield to temptation? I can say that I believe Christ is able to deliver me from the temptations of the evil one, if I only put my full confidence and trust in him. That is the only assurance I have.—I confess my entire obedience to Christ and the Community, fully believing that they are able to, and will deal justly with me if I will give myself up entirely to them. With much love I remain truly yours."

D. M. K.

—

Mrs. Towner writes Nov. 15, that they have moved their family to Cleveland, and that they are very glad to get away from Berlin. Mr. Towner has bought a house and lot, a little out of the City, and they are well pleased with their locality. Mrs. T. says "Freddie and Lillie have not forgotten what Mr. Hatch taught them. They confess Christ, and I find I have less difficulty in controlling them, since we were with you. Their hearts are with the Community still. Although I am absent from your family in form, yet I feel that I am ever present with you in spirit. I am thankful that I have been raised from doubt and unbelief, through the grace of God."

To the Community.

DEAR BROTHERS AND SISTERS:—I think for nearly a year past, I have been made a partaker of the spirit of Christ, he being the resurrection life which flows to us through Mr. Noyes and the Community family.

I confess an earnest thankful spirit that is receptive to the truth. I have received much strength by attending the theological class.—I hope the family will feel free to criticise me, when I need it. Yours forever in the bond of love, L. B. LYNDE.

———

Cyrus Field's long speech, made at a banquet given him in New-York, and published in the TRIBUNE, was read in meeting last night. The graphic description he gives of his experience in projecting and laying the Atlantic cable is of thrilling interest, and shows plainly the guidance of good spirits and inspiration, in this great enterprise. His untiring perseverence in overcoming almost insurmountable difficulties, that stood in his way, and in rising above temptations to discouragement, is well worthy of imitation.

———

Business at the Trap-Shop is driving as usual this week, the children working there the same as last week. School however will commence again in a few days, and their sport in work will be over.

———

We have for a quilting room now, the south garret of the Mansion House, but in the present demand for quilts and comfortables, they are using also, the lower sitting-room of the New House, for that purpose.

———

George Kellogg and Mrs. Bristol arrived here safely yesterday, by *daylight*.

We hear that one of our neighbors set a small trap to catch rats, when on going to examine it, he found a raccoon securely caught in it.

———

Traps ordered yesterday,	220 doz.
The principal order was—	
Hibbard & Spencer Chicago,	165 "

———

Yesterday's temperature—
7 A. M., 34. 12 M., 35. 6 P. M., 28. Mean 32¼.

DAILY JOURNAL
OF ONEIDA COMMUNITY.

VOL. 2.   FRIDAY, NOV. 23, 1866.   NO. 124.

NOTES TO THE FAMILY.
Thursday, Nov. 22.

MR. HAMILTON, *Dear Sir:*—I confess that I was wrong yesterday morning in being so quick to determine in the way I did, to go away immediately, (but I felt that you would rather not have us in the family unless we were in full spiritual sympathy with you), and I submit myself to the criticism of the family for that, and also for my life generally since I came to the Community; so that all the past may be settled up, and so that if I have not been in the relation to the Community most proper for me, I may begin a new one if thought best. Now I wish to ask you if you are willing to hire us to work for you, Mrs. Blood, Henry and myself, in the departments in which we can be of most service to you, and set apart a place for us at your table the same as you did for your hired help in the summer, giving us sleeping rooms as much apart from the family as is convenient for you to do, and have our other children do what they can to help you the same as heretofore, and controlling them entirely as to their character and religious instruction, and as to what they are to do?

I make the above suggestion with the idea, that it is possible that by a longer acquaintance with the Community now that I understand more fully than I did when I came, their *real* purpose and idea of organization, that I may in time come, into *full* sympathy with them. I believe that in my present state that would be the best relation for the Community and us to stand in towards each other.

I wish to express my appreciation of the kindness of the family to us yesterday, and also to ask their forgiveness for taking the course to cause them so much trouble. I wish to express my love for them as christian men and women. It seems to me I should enjoy working for the Community in some such way as I have suggested, and *I think* you can rely upon our being discreet in such a relation. As to compensation I would leave that entirely to the proper persons in the Community, so that if it was considered that they could give us only our board for the present, we would be satisfied.

Yours Respectfully,   D. E. BLOOD.

Mr. Blood who has of late been tempted with evil thinking, and doubts about Mr. Noyes's inspiration and position in the Community, decided Wednesday morning to leave and take his family with him. As it was desirable that they should go as soon as possible, the day was spent by the family in getting them ready. The help of tailors, seamstresses &c. &c., was called in requisition to furnish them with suitable apparel. Three women were dispatched to look up sheets, pillow-cases, table-cloths, &c., that the Bloods brought when they came here, which were scattered if not to the "four winds," at least to as many buildings, including both boarding-houses. Before dark, every article with one exception, was found, washed, ironed, and ready for packing. In the evening there was some change in Mr. B's spirit, and the next morning he seemed a good deal broken. His letter published to-day, will speak for itself. Last evening, a faithful criticism was given him, and his case at the present time remains unsettled.

—

I take this opportunity to express my unshaken confidence in the administration of this church, and Mr. Noyes as a leader appointed of God to lead us into all truth. I abandon myself to the truth, that will separate me from all false affections, and especially that which centers in my family. I know it is a selfish, hateful, secretive spirit. I now give myself unreservedly to this family for criticism, and to be saved from my old life and habits. I believe this is the Kingdom of God and that we are surely in the judgment.

A. W. BURNHAM.

Yesterday there was a bee proposed by the women for the purpose of assisting Mrs. Conant in her sewing. Accordingly after dinner about a dozen of the "Sisters of Charity" who had volunteered, could be seen hastening to the boarding-house, where a cozy little room was prepared to receive them. In a few minutes all hands were busily engaged in this work of love. While sitting there my thoughts turned to the bees I used to attend a few years ago, where there was all splendor and outward show, but in heart a lack of unity and sisterly love. I could not but contrast the two. After supper we used to have long prayers asking for God's blessing, while here, after partaking of a nice repast, we all returned home feeling that if we have a good spirit, we already have God's blessing.   L. E.

Mrs. Dascomb, a widow lady, with her son, a lad of ten or twelve years of age, came here last night. She is an acquaintance of Mrs. Bushnell, and formerly lived in Cameron a few miles from Bath. She came here from Marathon where she has been engaged for some time, teaching. She has read our writings some, and expresses herself interested in our enterprise.

The ground is covered with snow this morning, to the depth of about two inches, and it is still falling. Every tree shrub and fence is clothed in white, and presents a fine appearance.

Yesterday's temperature—
7 A. M., 28.   12 M., 32.   6 P. M., 28.   Mean 29⅓.

DAILY JOURNAL
OF ONEIDA COMMUNITY.

VOL. 2.　　SATURDAY, NOV. 24, 1866.　　NO. 125.

Bill Thomas, a resident of Turkey Street, and a genial hearty forger in the trap-department before its removal to Willow Place, was unexpectedly found yesterday at his old occupation in the new shop. In answer to the surprise expressed at finding him there, he said he was only there for a few days, that he accepted our invitation to help straighten a lot of springs they had just finished rolling; and in further conversation about the shifts he made to get a living he said, " I eke out a miserable existence any way," at the same time referring to the " death blow" he got while working in the dark, damp basement of the forge-shop of Wilson's Plow-factory.

His countenance lighted up when he spoke of the time when he worked for the Community; these he said were my happiest days; and he said it evidently not for effect, but as something that had a real existence in his memory—a bright spot that he did not forget amidst all the trials and vicissitudes of his life.　　　H.

We were interested last night, in hearing Augusta Hamilton's letter to her father, read, as also Mr. Hamilton's letter to Mrs. Fisher, Augusta's grandmother in reply to one she wrote Augusta. Considerable conversation followed about the bitter spirit Mrs. Fisher and the Wilders had always manifested towards the Association, and Mrs. F's claims on Susan and the children, trying to draw them away from Mr. H. and the Community. The family spirit in her case shows its cloven foot, and we shrink from contact with it, but in other cases it assumes a more plausible seductive form, and is on that account the more dangerous.

We desire to attach ourselves so firmly to Mr. Noyes, and to the one family of Christ, of which Mr. N. is the visible head, that these outside influences can have no power over us.

Mr. Blood's spirit seems to have been favorably changed by the faithful, sincere criticism of the Community, and the new light that is breaking in upon his understanding, leads him to retract his hasty decision to leave the Community and to ask for further trial. He with his family, will probably remain on probation for the present.

The committee that was appointed sometime ago to decide upon what articles of our manufactures should be sent to the World's Fair, are busy in collecting and preparing such articles for shipment. We understand they are to be sent the first of next month.

It continues to snow a little, and the weather seems quite wintry. The boys have fine sport with their sleds sliding down hill.

We hear that Mr. Worden has engaged turkies enough for thanksgiving, to furnish both boarding-houses, as well as our own family, with a good supply.

W. A. Hinds returned from New-York yesterday, also W. G. Kelly.

Charles Vanvelzer returned from his peddling trip yesterday. We understand he had fair success in the business.

We shall be under the necessity of sending out a short JOURNAL to-day, for the simple reason, that there is little to report.

Traps ordered yesterday and the day before, 87 doz
The principal order was—
Sidney Shepard, & Co.,　　　　　　　50 "

Yesterday's temperature—
7 A. M., 30.　12 M., 32.　6 P. M., 25.　Mean 29.

DAILY JOURNAL
OF ONEIDA COMMUNITY.

VOL. 2.   MONDAY, NOV. 26, 1866.   NO. 128

BUSINESS MEETING.

Charles Cragin, asks for some arrangement to carry the silk factory girls down to the depot. They now sometimes hire a cab. Two of our hired men wish to know also if we can bring them up Monday morning, they are willing to pay their passage. Mr. Clark has difficulty in accommodating the girls who go to the depot to trade, they all have the idea, that they are entitled to a free ride once a week. This is a practice that does not obtain at other manufactories, and as we increase our help, it will become more and more a business. It is a question whether we ought to carry them free of charge?

G. W. H. spoke of the present status of the trap business. We wish to fill all our orders, at the same time as we are generally out of stock, have not enough to keep all our hands employed, have just discharged several, some of the orders will have to wait: George would like advice. He would like to keep some few hands right through: shall we try to shape our business to do so? We are out of most kinds of traps: shall we buy any more steel? The impression is, we shall have a moderate but steady demand for traps all winter, that there will be a steady demand for No. 0. Messrs. Hinds, Olds and Campbell were appointed to look into the market, and the statistics of sales.

The dumb-waiter at the Mill is considered in an unsafe condition. The other day passenger and load descended suddenly to the bottom. Abram is to confer with Mr. Woolworth, and if there be no decided objection the waiter will be thrown out of use.

Mr. Clark said we need some new horse-blankets. The cheaper way will be to buy the material in New-York, and have Mr. Reynolds make them up, not only enough for ourselves, but also a few for sale; Mr. Clark, Martin, Mr. Reynolds and the store hands were appointed to find out what they wanted, and order the cloth.

Mrs. Dunning has spoken to us about a woman who would like to take our nearest boarding-house. Such an arrangement would relieve Mrs. Conant. Left to the boarding-house committee.

It is not thought best to raise water to the corridor till we carry out the plan of bringing our water in iron pipes, it can then be done easily.

The prospect is that we shall have to pay more for saw-logs this winter than formerly. We need not hesitate however to keep on buying the best we can, as we shall want a great many more boxes the coming year, than last.

We had considerable talk Saturday evening about our schools and education in general. Mr. Hamilton thought that the Community should now turn their attention to study, with the same spirit of enthusiasm that they have shown in labor—said he thought that the work of judgment and criticism that we had had, was a good preparatory step to study. Messrs. Hinds, Campbell, Kelly, and E. S. Burnham, L. A. Thayer, H. E. Allen, and Chloe Seymour, were appointed a Committee to organize classes, and look after the educational wants of the family. It was thought best to have the school for the small children re-opened to-day, and the class of boys of Erastus's age should have a school all day through the winter, and be thoroughly drilled in the elementary branches of study. E. S. Burnham is to be their teacher.

Mrs. Dascomb and her son, also Mrs. Freeman, left this morning. A little over a year ago Mrs. D. became interested in reading our publications, but being a conspicuous member of the methodist church, and a contributer to the "Guide to Holiness," a methodist paper she evidently came here with the idea of impressing us with the magnitude of her own righteousness. She had also met, a brother of Mr. Carr who though in sympathy with many of our doctrines, yet was grieved that Mr. N should claim to be inspired, and refuse that gift to others, (A. W. C. we suppose). He represented his brother as being a very godly man, and he warned Mrs. D. of falling into the Community current, and in worshiping Mr. Noyes.—Mrs. D. admitted this morning, that she had been benefitted by her visit, that much of her experience that she thought was the leadings of the spirit, she now saw was the devil's leadings, and she confessed Christ in her, to deliver her from all prejudice against the inspiration of Mr. Noyes.

We learn by Mr. Worden that the turkeys for thanksgiving, are soundly engaged, but the credit of the purchase is not due to him, but to Mr. Aiken and Martin.—A grand B. is invited to-morrow P. M., to pluck their feathers, and otherwise prepare them for cooking.

About one ton of scrap tin from the can-shop was sent to New-York this morning, for which we expect to receive $60.

Traps ordered since Friday,   95 doz.
The principal orders were—
Russell & Erwin, Mfg. Co.,   27 "
Love and Hamilton,   40 "
Edward Wilson,   25 "

Temperature Saturday and Sunday,
7 A. M., 24. 12 M., 30. 6 P. M., 23. Mean 25⅔.
7 A. M., 18. 12 M., 30. 6 P., M., 20. Mean 22⅔.

DAILY JOURNAL
OF ONEIDA COMMUNITY.

VOL. 2.   TUESDAY, NOV. 27, 1866.   NO. 127

EDUCATIONAL PROGRAMME.

Class No. 1, 5 Young Men; E. S. Burnham Teacher 6 hour's study.

Class No. 2, 10 Young Men; W. A. Hinds Teacher half-day.

Class No. 3, 6 Girls; Chloe Seymour Teacher: half day.

Class No. 4, 8 Young Women; C. B. Bushnell Teacher 2 hours.

Class No. 5, *Grammar*; 27 Pupils—George Campbel Teacher.

Class No. 6, *Geometry*; 8 Pupils—E. H. Hamilto Teacher.

Class No. 7, *Geography*; 11 Pupils—M. L. Worde Teacher.

Class No. 8, *Phonography*; 7 Pupils—S. B. Campbe Teacher.

Class No. 9, *Colburn's Arithmetic*; 10 Pupils—A. C Sears Teacher.

Class No. 10, *Thomson's Higher Arithmetic*; 21 Pupils— John Freeman Teacher.

Class No. 11, *Elementary Algebra*; 29 Pupils—L. A. Thayer Teacher.

Class No. 12, *ditto*; 22 Pupils—A. S. Bailey Teacher.

Class No. 13, *ditto*; 20 Pupils—John F. Sears Teacher.

Class No. 14, *Robinson's New University Algebra*; 14 Pupils—H. E. Allen Teacher.

Class No. 15, *ditto*; 13 Pupils—William G. Kelly Teacher.

A few of the above classes will be divided if found to contain too large a number of students for the best progress.

There are a few small classes in French and other studies not included in the above list.

We get one or more letters every day directed to J. H. N. from persons who have heard about the Community in the PHRENOLOGICAL JOURNAL. To-day, (Sunday), four such letters came. These letters all have a very friendly tone and many of them express much joy that such a state of society as Communism is realized in this world. Many of them say that our life, judging from what they have read, embodies their long cherished ideas of society. Most of these writers ask for more information, for publications, or letters that will give them a clear insight into the internal machinery of the institution. Others want to come and make a visit of a longer or shorter time. Others again want to know if they cannot come and work for us for a few weeks or months paying their board in that way, perhaps earning something besides, and thus have time and opportunity to study the Community and get acquainted with its members. And then again quite a proportion of the write are anxious to join as soon as possible; they have become convinced that the religion and socialism of the Community are in accordance with their views of justice and right, and they are sick of the world and long to escape from its antagonism and corruption. Now and then one pleads with us to receive them for their children's sake, who are exposed to the evils and temptations of a wicked and perverse generation. We write to some and send papers and pamphlets to others. Short visits are encouraged where people desire it. "Male Continence" is in request more or less.   H.

I wish to thank the Community for my criticism, and take sides with the truth, which I most thankfully accept. I desire to be entirely free from a wicked diabolical spirit which has oppressed me for a long time. In the fore part of the summer I thought I never saw my way more bright through it. But when I have been out on business, this spirit would come upon me and almost paralyze my faculties and make me feel as though was not fit to be among folks. This spirit has had the most power over me through my social nature. I confess the power of Christ's resurrection of soul and body I am desirous of taking any place to prove my obedience.   Hoping this will prove satisfactory,

O. H. MILLER.

We clip the following paragraphs from a letter received from Chicago, a few days since:

"Have you any fruit to sell? If so what kinds and at what prices, in glass and tin? We would also like to talk about a supply for next year, and begin in time. Will you let us have all the fruit you put up for sale, except what you may sell east of Buffalo? If we can make a satisfactory arrangement we should be glad to do so.

Can you not talk this matter over fully, so that when Mr. Olds comes out again, he can be prepared to make an arrangement with us?"

Yours truly,   STANTON & CO.

Mr. Abbott, who is our glazier, and might in truth be called "a repairer of the breach," at least in respect to windows, has given us the following statistics:

Whole No. of panes of glass, in all our buildings including boarding-houses, green-house, hot-beds, &c. &c., is about 15,500.

Yesterday's temperature—

7 A. M., 23, 12 M., 32, 6 P., M., 21, Mean 25¼.

DAILY JOURNAL
OF ONEIDA COMMUNITY.

VOL. 2. WEDNESDAY, NOV. 28, 1866. NO. 128.

OUR VISITORS.

Mrs. Kirby from Syracuse, also two gentlemen, one from Fulton, and the other a Mr. Wright from Monroe Co., came last night. Also Mr. Macoy and his step daughter from Vermont. Mr. M. has sold out his property in Cambridge, Vt., and has come here for the purpose of buying a place and locating himself near the Community. He brought us a nice tub of maple-sugar. Mrs. Kirby goes back to Syracuse to-day. She is a woman of English birth, and we should judge from slight acquaintance, of strong mind and intellect. She reasons philosophically, but has few ideas in common with us. She repudiates the belief in a personal devil and denies the divinity of Christ. She represents her stay at "Brook Farm" as a bright spot in her life; says she formed attachments while there, that will be as lasting as life. She says there was an inner circle of about twenty in that Community whose experience ought to have been written out, to show to the world what persons could do in trying to serve one another.—She represented them as entirely free from self-seeking and governed by the law of love, in their deal with each other. Mrs. K. returns to her home in California, sometime the coming winter.

A VOICE FROM THE KITCHEN.

We had a pretty good illustration, Saturday last, of the old adage, "*Misfortunes never come singly.*" The kitchen company had calculated upon a heavy day's work, as short-cakes were to be got for dinner, and preparations made for the coming Thanksgiving. The work commenced with unusual vigor. One of the "Mothers," was suffering from the toothache, which was the beginning of sorrows. The other "Mother," flew around with the greatest activity imaginable. She startled us once, with a sharp outcry, occasioned by a slight scald, as she attempted conducting water in a tin pipe from the small reservoir, to the steamer. This, however, proved to be very slight, and we still worked on with great energy. Just at dinner time when the pressure was greatest—when short-cakes were to be buttered and spread for dinner, and other things to be placed on the table, another accident occured which might have proved serious. Some tremulous hands, in moving the dripper containing hot gravy, to the back of the range, spilled over a small quantity on to the stove, which blazed up instantaneously; this was followed by the sudden dropping of one end of the dripper, which caused a great commotion, pouring half the gravy on to the stove, which was immediately enveloped in flames, reaching even to the ceiling, and our floor, completely deluged with the greasy fluid. No one was burned—*not a scream was heard!* All was silence, and for an instant we stood in blank amazement. But not long. In 2 minutes the floor was mopped, and the dinner on the table in good style. Two or three little accidents followed upon this, but of two small moment to be noted. After dinner we quietly retired into the bakery, and were busily at work, when we were summoned into the back-room to see "*how somebody had spilled the bluing.*" And sure enough there it was, slowly dripping over shelves, platters, plates, etc. We were sure that all the plates would require re-washing, and the shelves a good scouring. This occasioned a good laugh. Some one suggested, "*There's nae luck about the house,*" but we told them on the contrary a good Providence had been over us, and that we had enjoyed the day highly.

DEAR MR. HAMILTON:—For some time past I have been under the influence of a bad and wicked spirit and I have not had the courage to resist it and do right. But what you said last night softened my heart, and led me to think that Christ would help me if I would trust him, and I think I have trusted him. I want to go on with the Community and learn all I can of Christ, and be as much like him as I can be. I confess a spirit that is subordinate to you and the Community, and I wish to gain the love of all around me.

Yours in the love of the truth, H. P. BLOOD.

Mr. Pitt writes that he has purchased furs to the amount of $250, and sent them on by Express, but we have not yet received them. We give the following short extract from his last letter:

"I feel my heart growing more soft, and impressible to the spirit of faith, and I am thankful for it. I long for the time when my old, individual, natural life shall be wholly crucified, and Christ have entire control of every thought and deed, and I welcome every judgment and criticism and mortification of the flesh, which will tend to bring it about. I see that that is the true preparation for all usefulness in the church of Christ, for all preaching of the gospel, whether by word of mouth, by pen, by spirit, or by example. Yours truly, T. L. P."

Our Silk-Factory girls are all fast adopting the short dress. We have been pleased every Monday morning for a month or two past, to see some new one appear in short dress and pants, who left the Saturday before in long skirts and hoops. This morning we noticed but three long dresses among our group of 16 girls—and we doubt not these will soon give place to the more convenient, and I can truly say more *becoming* short dress. E

Traps ordered since last report— 96 doz.

Yesterday's temperature—
7 A., M., 33. 12 M., 41. 6 P., M., 27. Mean 33¼.

DAILY JOURNAL
OF ONEIDA COMMUNITY.

VOL. 2.   THURSDAY, NOV. 29, 1866.   NO. 129

LETTERS.

Extracts from a letter of Mr. Guiteau's to Mr. Hamil ton :

"Perhaps it is useless for me to say that I was much grieved at the intelligence of Charles's desertion—and my heart almost sinks within me at the thought of th terrible consequences that may ensue unless the good ness and long suffering of God, shall lead him to retur with genuine humility and true self abasement. It i evident to my mind, that he does not realize the fearfu consequences of "putting his hand to the plow and then looking back." There is evidently a species of insanity hanging about him, and it seems to me that this ha been the case for a long time. May God have merc upon him, and give him humility and repentance unt life.

With reference to paying Charles (*his* money as h seems to call it) I hold that he or any other person wh understandingly and voluntarily put their money int the Community are guilty of doing great injustice, t set up any claim for a reimbursement, or withdrawal o it or any portion of it; and it seems to me as I now view it, I could not have the face to ask it; and if i should be driven to the conclusion after a fair trial that I could not remain in the Community, the most I could say would be, do with me in the premises as you see fit.

As to the question what is expedient and best for you to do about refunding any or all of what Charles claims, I hardly know what to say, I am quite sure of one thing that it probably would not be long before he would run through with the whole of whatever you might place at his disposal—and he might possibly after spending all his living, and feeding for a while upon husks among swine, come to his senses and return penitent and humbled like the prodigal son of old. Though the thought is distressing to me yet I don't know but it would be best to give him a chance to run his race and the sooner the better. I however have every confidence my dear brother, in the judgement and instincts of the Community, and shall be quite satisfied with whatever course you may see proper to take in the premises.

With love and thankfulness,   L. W. GUITEAU.

BAG-SHOP EXPERIENCE.

Our contribution of a Lunch-Bag to the World's Fair at Paris, was called for much sooner than was expected. Three days only were left us for getting out patterns, design &c., and part of the materials at least, in Utica and New-York. Our courage was at a low ebb, very, when we thought of the short time, and of those skillful Frenchmen the other side of the water ready to laugh at our Yankee attempts. We remembered also that the Lunch-Bag sprung from an inspired idea of Mr. Noyes's. so setting aside the thought of competition, and re solving to let it stand on its originality for merit, w determined that it should be done. With this, good luc started. No time was lost waiting for articles, thanks t the Agency brother who so fully entered into the exige cy of the occasion. At the required time the Bag wa finished, being quite appropriately surmounted by th American Eagle and stars for a lock. We could not bu notice that a good Providence was over us, and that the invisibles were helping us. We were also struck wit a certian admiration for the working of the Expres lines, the Railroads and other conveniences, so near annihilating space in this wonder working age.

The Bag was made of Turkey morocco, nearly blue (the skin of the goat or chamois, with the most minut seeds pressed upon its surface), with a raised figure a trimming. A silver fork, with silver plated knife an lunch-box completed the out-fit.   N.

Mr. Felix Foucou, a gentleman from Paris, France called here last night and took supper, and staid two o three hours. He is a mining engineer, and has spen four months in visiting the mines, on the upper Missi sippi. He had heard of us in the south of France whe some were a good deal interested in our experiment.— He seemed anxious to get our publications, and sub scribed for the CIRCULAR, taking with him some of the back numbers. He bought also four dollars worth of our pictures to take home with him. He said he would be happy to do us any service in his country, that lay in his power. He has a wife and one child in Paris, and expects to return there, the last of next month. He will pass from Boston to New York about the 22d of Dec., and intends calling at Wallingford. He thought he might call here again in about a week, and perhaps stop over night. He expects to come to America again next year, and will bring his wife and child, in which case he said he hoped to make us a longer visit. He is very gentlemanly, bright and intelligent, and speaks our language quite fluently.

We are now only about 5000 traps behind our orders, yet as they are wanted at once, it is desirable to get all the help we can to put them through. Now that we are so near the end of the race, it is hoped that no one will grow slack until the work is completed.

One of the leading Shakers at Watervleit has written to have us send him several of our tracts, "Male Continence."

Traps ordered yesterday,   42 doz.
Yesterday's temperature—
7 A. M., 37.   12 M., 47.   6 P. M., 42.   Mean 42.

DAILY JOURNAL
OF ONEIDA COMMUNITY.

VOL. 2.   FRIDAY, NOV. 30, 1866.   NO. 130

To the Community.

Nov. 28, 1866.

I wish to judge and separate myself from the spi: of Mr Carr. The suggestion about him in the talk o "The Evil Eye" read some evenings since, has set r upon studying his character and my experience in conne tion with him. I had a good deal to do with him in on way and another from the first, and though I had n sympathy with his self-will and insubordination I ca not but think I took on more of his spirit than I wa aware of. I have had a good deal of unsatisfacto experience for the past two or three years that I cou not understand—have many times been under seve pressure from the spirit of unthankfulness, evil thinkin and unbelief, when I felt I had no fellowship with it i my heart, and could not account for it. It used to be ac companied sometimes with a singular apprehension of evi and of something wrong in my spirit. I am constrained to think that much of this trouble, was occasioned by the poison of his spirit, though doubtless I had a weak ness of character that exposed me to it, and more o less tinder in me to take fire.

I am satisfied he was not only full of independen. and self-exaltation but also of jealousy and unthankful ness, and perhaps I ought to say bitterness of spirit towards those who stood in his way. I have a sense of the hatefulness of his peculiar way of seeing the faults of others and the evil in things around him—of watch ing for evil, that makes me desirous to thoroughly clear myself from even the taint of it.

I thank God for a new appreciation of his goodness that fills my heart with love and thankfulness, and for the influx of a spirit that watches for good and for heavenly things.   Geo. Campbell.

II. G. A. writes: "The 5th Avenue Hotel has con cluded not to keep our corn, and release us from all obli gations.—I have called at the St. Nicholas Hotel—it has not found any bad corn, and paid for the same.—The Fifth Avenue Hotel folks were much pleased with some string beans I presented them, but did not like so well the pie blackberries.—Have just filled an order received from the German Consul at St. Louis, for eight dozen peaches to go to Germany."

Thanksgiving day passed off, very quietly and pleas antly all round. The family went on with their usual work. The Trap-Shop hands came home to dinner, (which consisted of turkey and its usual accompani ments), and returned again to their work at the shop.— The day was very warm for the season, and rainy.

There were two or three hard showers in the afternoon and it has rained nearly all night. The Creek overflow its banks this morning, and the mud is very deep.

The new Bibles our people are having were referred t in meeting last night. They are very nice and hav cost already, $52. Mr. Hamilton said that although h was gratified to have our young people and all other turn to the study of the bible, yet he did not quite sym pathize with the purchase of such costly ones. Tl Financial board also, should have been consulted befo buying them.

Mrs. Gibbs and her little girl, and Mary Leete, we here to dinner yesterday, and spent the night.—A son-i law, also, of Mr. Cockerell, a Mr. Jeffreys from Canad came just before dark, and staid with us all night. H takes the Circular.

II. M. Hutchins has just finished a set of artificia teeth for Mrs. Lynde. It is II.'s first attempt. She ha only the assistance of L. F. D., who had never made : set on rubber base. The work gives excellent satisfactio

---

We finished yesterday our web of fifty-seven yards o rag-carpet. Mrs. Hutchins has sewed all the rags wit the exception of five or six yards. Mrs. Conant wo about twenty yards, and E. F. Hutchins the remainde

Lady Hamilton fails slowly. A man sleeps in the adjoining bed-room to lift her in the night, if occasion requires it, and a woman sits up to watch, or lies down in the room, if Mrs. H. sleeps comfortably.

We hear that there has been recently an addition to our Ayreshire stock, of a fine heifer calf.

56,700 Traps have been shipped since Oct. 30th.

Traps ordered yesterday,   71 doz.

Yesterday's temperature—
7 A. M., 00.   12 M., 63.   6 P. M., 40.   Mean 55.

DAILY JOURNAL
OF ONEIDA COMMUNITY.

VOL. 2.   SATURDAY, DEC. 1, 1866.   NO. 13

LETTERS.

Cleveland, O., Nov. 26, 1866.

DEAR O. C.:—I feel that I have neglected myself having so long failed to communicate with you. I desire to preserve and strengthen the ties of sympath which have connected me with you. Myself and fami have lately moved from Berlin Hights to this plac where we are now settled to remain until God shall c us elsewhere in our search after his kingdom. I hav heretofore regretted the necessity of having again buy property and locate in isolation, but it is evident the Lord's will, and I rejoice that he has given me grac enough to be content to work in whatever field I called, and to pass through cheerfully whatever prepar tory discipline may be necessary to fit me for his kin dom.

The labor of finding a place to live, and moving an getting settled being now done I turn my attention re-opening correspondence with you. I wish to sa that the business which I shall follow here, next to stud and spiritual improvement, is the question that claim my attention. I am inclined to shrink from undertaking **to resume the practice of my profession, the law.** I d not fear but that I can practice law, and be honest and upright, scorning trickery and injustice, but successful practice presents so many hindrances to spiritual growth, so many temptations to tempt one away from the doctrine of Christ, that I prefer not to engage in the profession as a business. I have been in the apple trade, this fall, rather like it, and think perhaps I shall continue in it here another season. But I wish further to do something that will bring me into more direct and tangible relations with you. Hence I propose this: to become an agent here for the sale of your productions, especially your fruit, traveling bags and silk, either one or more of them as may be practicable. I think I might, both to your advantage and my own, undertake something of this sort.   *   *   *   *

I confess Christ a spirit willing to work for God and his glory, and wish to feel that what I am doing is for him.   Very truly yours,   J. W. TOWNER.

BRO. HAMILTON:—I am thankful for the sincerity manifested in my late criticism, and accept it heartily as from the Lord. Having embraced Perfectionism in 1834 I embraced some of the views of N. Y. Perfectionism; was, that we no longer need the teaching of man.— I became established in individualism and concluded that I had light enough to take care of myself, not considering the truth that the gifts of God belong to the church. I became egotistical, and instead of entering in,

I have stood outside of the body of Christ, fighting ev on my own basis. I have found it hard, uphill work and shall hereafter consider it none too good for me, (i the Lord shall count me worthy), to be saved with the church. I wish to renounce my own will in this an every thing else and become identified with Mr. Noyes and the family spirit in all things. I am aware that I have been proud and self-willed, which has made it hard for me to yield to the Community spirit. I wish to la all upon the altar without reserve, and accept of Chri to save me upon any terms. I confess my abandonme of my old life and offer myself to Christ and the Chur to be made the most of for his service, and pray for mility that will make me content with any position how ever low, in the service of Christ.

Yours for union with Christ and submission to th perfect will of God.   W. H. PERRY

We were agreeably suprised this morning to hear the arrival, in the night of H. A. Noyes, Oneida b i her a cordial welcome.

We hear that one of our elderly women got so absor ed in mathematics yesterday, that the premonitory stro of the dinner bell failed to reach her ear, and on s plodded, till some time past one o'clock. She roused length, on seeing some man putting on his overcoat, p paratory to going away, and said, "what, you are r going till after dinner are you?" This caused a general laugh in the room, which recalled our mathematician from her abstraction, to this mundane sphere, and to the physical wants of the body.

We received yesterday from E. G. H. a pretty bouquet accompanied with the following note.—"I have the good fortune to be able to present you with a beautiful bouquet of flowers from the garden, fresh and fragrant as those of summer. It is composed of Pansies, Primulas, Anterrhinums, German Stock, Iberis, (umbelata), Iberis, (hardy perennial), Ribbon grass, Trumpet Honeysuckle, commonly called woodbine, Lonicera sempervirens. A wreath of Myrtle encircles it with its pretty blue flowers."

Autumn in retiring from the field and giving place to her sterner sister, winter, has spread a slight mantle of white over the earth thus making the appearance of nature more attractive.

Yesterday's temperature—
7 A. M., 42.   12 M., 40.   6 P. M., 36.   Mean 39¼.

DAILY JOURNAL
OF ONEIDA COMMUNITY.

VOL. 2.   MONDAY, DEC. 3, 1866.   NO. 13.

BUSINESS MEETING.

The Board are in favor of getting a machine to do the printing on the wrappers of the CIRCULAR, to take the place of hand-inscribing. Machines are in vogue at all large offices, in which one man can print 10,000 in two hours. Several kinds are in use; one kind can be purchased for $10,00 charging $50 more for a perpetual right to use it. Another kind, supposed to be better costs $300. William will write to the Wallingford folks to suit themselves.

Geo. W. Hamilton, wished to know if there was any objection to having the willow trees cut down, that grow on the bank of the Dyke. His theory is, that when the wind blows the trees, the roots and earth are so disturbed as to cause the Dyke to leak. It is thought, before they are cut down, it had better be found out whether they really do any mischief. The trees are ornamental and it is not so easy to grow them as to cut them down. Left to Mr. Burt and G. W. Hamilton to investigate.

Mr. Clark is to get a covered wagon body made, for the Willow Place line, that will seat easily sixteen persons, and of suitable stength for the purpose. It is thought that in about a year or two we shall want to take hold of the railroad enterprise, and also to establish Telegraphic communication between here and Willow Place.

It is desirable to enrich the lawn. The application of ashes on some portions, and guano on others, was proposed. S. W. Nash is to ascertain the price of guano.

Mr. Inslee received a letter a few days since, from his brother at Brooklyn, (who with his wife visited here last summer), from which we extract the following:

"You seem to regret that things were not propitious for our enjoying our visit. You need not, for I assure you, we did enjoy it in the highest degree. The storm made it uncomfortable, but this we must necessarily have borne, anywhere. Both Julia and I, really enjoyed our visit with you, so entirely beyond anything we had anticipated, and beyond anything I can tell you of, that it is really a delightful spot in our memory.

Whatever may be your peculiar views of life and revelation, spiritually or temporally—whatever may be your peculiar precepts or practice, no one who has a true and active perception of love reigning in the heart and life, can help feeling that its very atmosphere is there. And it was this that impressed us, I think, and has carried its power with us, so that we cannot forget it. When any friends speak to us about you, we say to them, you must go and see and feel for yourself, and you will come away with new thoughts, such as you could not conceive of before. I called at your rooms in New-York after my return, and spent an hour happily there, and now get your paper regularly, and find much pleasure and instruction in reading it."

Mr. Asa Patten from Hammonton, N. J., came here last Saturday, and staid over Sunday. He is on his way to Wisconsin, and called here at the earnest solicitation of several individuals in that place, who, he states, are a good deal interested in our movement. One of them Dr. Lawrence, who has visited us sometime in the past told him that if he came here, he would find himself little nearer heaven, than he had ever been before. Mr. P. did not say whether he felt that to be the case. He lived with the Shakers, near Pittsfield, Mass., till he was thirty years of age, and one of his brothers was an elder there. Mr. P. is said to be quite rich.

A charming sight was seen in the upper sitting-room Sunday afternoon, which was Mr. Dunn and Rose waltzing. Rose with some of the other little girls had just finished a lively dance, when some one reminded Mr Dunn of his promise, (given to Rose when they both appeared to be hopeless invalids), to dance with her, some time. "O yes said Mr. D., I can dance as well as ever I could," and the dance was performed gracefully, and with ease, by both the parties—a striking contrast to their appearance a year ago.   H. M.

Mr. Macoy and his step-daughter, Mrs. Story, started for home this morning. Mr. M. succeeded in buying him a place on Turkey Street, the second lot east from the corner near Willow Place, on the south side of the road. He paid $1,600 for it and will move his family here in the spring, if not sooner.

Mr. Jeffreys left for home Saturday noon. He wanted to buy and settle somewhere near the Community, if we would engage to give him steady employment. We did not give him any encouragement to come with that expectation.

They are making preparations at the Foundry, to cast the iron pipes, for bringing water from our springs to the house, instead of the wooden ones that have proved so leaky.

SALES FOR NOVEMBER.

Traps,	$20,722.11.
Preserved Fruit,	$9,127.78.
Bag,	$2,541.26.

Temperature Saturday and Sunday,

7 A. M., 24.   12 M., 30.   6 P. M., 28.   Mean 25½.
7 A. M., 42.   12 M., 40.   6 P. M., 36.   Mean 39½.

DAILY JOURNAL
OF ONEIDA COMMUNITY.

VOL. 2.   TUESDAY, DEC. 4, 1866.   NO. 13

NOTES TO THE FAMILY.

DEAR MR. HAMILTON:—A few years since I becan a believer in Mr. Noyes's doctrines and on coming to the Community, with his consent, I placed myself in the school of Christ, for further instruction in righteousnes. and though I am quite sensible of being a dull schola I am nevertheless resolved, through Christ's strength to learn my lesson, though my progress may be marke occasionally with a stunning blow.

I am truly thankful for your patience and forbearance with me, and am thankful for criticism; I look upon like holding a mirror before me that I may discover the devil's lurking places in my spirit, enabling me by the light of truth to resist his wily devices. I have beer brought to see very clearly of late my worldly-minded ness and idolatrous love of my family. I confess te that pride and self righteousness have been a great hin dranco to my spiritual growth. I wish now to separate myself from the family spirit, in a way I never have before, and forsake all for Christ's sake and the gospel'.

It seems to be God's purpose that I should have not. to lean upon save his own right arm, and he means shall learn the lesson through experience, hard though it seem. I desire to separate myself from my old life, though it clings to me with persistent tenacity. I still feel the assurance that Gods grace will be sufficient for me.

I confess a spirit of obedience to my superiors in all things, and desire to become a helper in the great work before us, and with true humility of heart to be willing to become anything, or be counted as nothing, "if so be hat I may win Christ" and be gathered into his fold, to go no more astray.

Yours in the love of the truth,   S. UNDERWOOD.

I wish to take sides with the family in judging the wicked spirit that F. Norton has been under. I have been more or less intimately mixed up and influenced by is spirit. I wish to subject myself to any judgment or criticism that will purge that spirit out of me. I have felt for a long time past that there was a barrier between me and the Community, and it was hard for me to get into as good relations with the central members as I wanted to. I have had seasons of very unsatisfactory experience from time to time, and instead of going to the right source for help to conquer it, I have poured forth my thoughts to F. in a way that was not good for me. More than a year ago I was aware of the wicked spirit that was over him, and said as much to some persons at that time. I feel very thankful that he has been brought to judgment and I sympathize with every thing that has been said. I think it will be easier for me to serve Go than ever before.   C. VAN VELZER.

Our educational campaign is fairly opened, and en thusinsm for study runs to the highest pitch. One can not look in any direction, and scarcely at any hour o the day, but they will see persons hastening with book: slates &c., to find their place in some class; and in almo: every corner or private room, little clusters are sec gathered for study. Yesterday, as Mr. Hamilton, Mr: Noyes and Mrs. Dunn were returning on foot from Wil low Place, Mr. Perkins hastened past them, and bein asked why he hurried so, he said "I am afraid I shall t late to school." Some one called to see Mr. Vanvel: at his shop, but he was not to be found, he too was : school, and so it is all round.—We called in yesterday, : see Mrs. Porter the tailor's wife, and she said she neve saw anything like our mania for study. Had Solomo. lived in our day, I don't know but he would be oblige. to retract his wise saying, that, "there is nothing nev under the sun," for though the spirit that prompts t action is as old as God himself, yet its manifestation i this world, acting upon the old, as well as the young, is as all must admit, something new,—Our hired folks have caught the infection and have solicted our people to fur nish them with a teacher, as we did last winter. The question whether we shall do so remains to be decided

The dentists extracted a singular specimen of a tooth for Delight Bristol, a few days since. About ten years ago, her mouth was prepared for a full upper set of artificial teeth. After waiting nearly a year for her mouth to get settled, the dentist discovered a tooth just making its ap pearance through the gum near the place occupied by the second molar. As the tooth resisted all reasonable efforts to remove it, it was left in the mouth, and the ar tificial plate fitted around it. The tooth had given her much trouble for a few years past and she applied to the dentist to have it extracted. On removing it, the crown of the tooth was found to be enlarged to nearly double its natural size. It is the intention to send it to the Medical students for examination.

The CIRCULARS came early this morning and were distributed in good season. Passing through the upper sitting-room, we were struck with its stillness, and on looking round to discover the cause, we saw every one with paper in hand, reading, and the same state of things prevailed in all the lower rooms—all work is dropped for the time, and the Circular has the entire attention.

Yesterday's temperature—

7 A., M., 28.   12 M., 42.   6 P., M., 38.   Mean 36.

DAILY JOURNAL
OF ONEIDA COMMUNITY.

VOL. 2. WEDNESDAY, DEC. 5, 1866. NO. 134

We make some extracts from Mr. Pitt's last two letters, of Nov. 23d and 26th.

DEAR BRO. CAMPBELL:—I have been resting and thinking some to-day, and this afternoon took a hammer and went out and hammered the rocks some. I found plenty of quartz, but did not see any gold. Quartz however is one of the "indications;" and as the gold seldom appears on the surface of the quartz veins, there may have been plenty of it several feet below my hammer for aught I can say to the contrary. I bantered Mr. McE. as to what he would take for his lot up by Mynzies where his "extraor'nary" quartz "mind" comes to the surface, but he thinks he will hold on and see what may turn up. By the way, I do not know but it might be a good plan to look after our Salmon Lake "clearing," as I hear Frazer, at Gulf Lake has found gold on his place. If there is gold any where here, I should think it would as likely be found among the rocks on the north shore of Salmon Lake as in any place. If I remember rightly I saw a good deal of quartz rock there.

Speaking of Salmon Lake reminds me that when was at Canniff's, I saw Mr. Baubell. He was very friendly and enquired particularly about you. Mr. Canniff said that he read the CIRCULAR with much interest. I got better acquainted with him than ever before and rather liked him. He seems to be a very kind-hearted gentlemanly Englishman. He told me if I would come over, sometime, he would take his boat and go up to Salmon Lake with me.

The gold fever rages more intensely every day. Gold quarters may be seen every day between Jordan and Madoc. A stage runs once or twice a day, I believe, from Madoc to the Richardson mine. Cameron generally brings a load up twice a week. Parties are actively scouring the country, having mineral rights, hunting up and "concessions," and prospecting with pick and shovel, hammer and pan, or some sort of tool. I have not seen or heard of many north of the "Hole in the Wall" yet, but when Spring opens, the tide of miners and speculators will probably reach York river. The California miner estimates that if the Richardson mine turns out a paying concern, that there will be 25,000 old Californians in Madoc next season.

Enough about gold. I have not felt much of the excitement, though I occasionally look at the rocks as I am traveling about. If I had a chance however, and the season was not so late, I should like to explore a little on Salmon lake.

I have been thinking for the last few days considerably about the fur business, and trying to get at a true view of it. For one thing I see that fortunes are not made by merely buying furs *from* the trappers and selling them *to* dealers and manufacturers, although oftentimes fine profit *may* be made in that way. It is however a precarious and uncertain business. For instance, Fowler who had the run of this region last year, made money at the beginning of the season and lost at the close. To make the business most profitable, it must be organized on the basis of manufacturing. That is where the most money is made in these days in the business.

As we were coming to the office this morning, Mrs. Ackley related to us some of her experience with the children. Some of our folks had occasion to call on Dr. Carpenter, at the depot day before yesterday, who after remarking that it was very sickly among children, at the present time, enquired who we employed to doctor our children? On being told that we had no occasion for a doctor, and that our children were all, without one exception well, he said, that they must have excellent care bestowed upon them, to keep them in such a state of health, while so many children around us were suffering and dying from disease. What the Dr. said was told to Mrs. Ackley who is the mother at the children's house, and she said that with it, there seemed to come in a spirit that sensibly affected the children. Yesterday three or four of the little ones were attacked with cold and indications of croup, and last night two of them were quite sick, and required the closest attention all night. But the battle was fought and the victory won, and this morning they were seated at the table as usual and as though nothing (un)usual had happened.

Mr. Nye, a young man who came here from Lakeport last summer in company with his sister, staid with us again last night. We understand that he came to buy a few traps for his own use. He is enamored with the Community and wishes he was good enough to join. He seems to be a person of a very sensitive nature, who has suffered a good deal from the deceit and treachery of men; this has had the effect to sour him toward all the race, and make him misanthropic.

Mrs. L. A. Thayer was criticised last night. But little fault was found with her at the present time, but she was much commended for her faithfulness in the public service and for her general course in the family.

Mr. Hamilton stated last evening that all our trap-orders were filled, which report caused a hearty cheer from the family. Mr. Woolworth said that the bag orders were also nearly filled.

Yesterday's temperature—
7 A. M., 38. 12 M., 46. 6 P. M., 43. Mean 42½.

DAILY JOURNAL
OF ONEIDA COMMUNITY.

VOL. 2.   THURSDAY, DEC. 6, 1866.   NO. 135.

We make the following extract from a letter Mrs. S. I. Nash received yesterday, from Mrs. Wealthy Knowles of Champion:

"I have just received the CIRCULAR and have been reading it. It don't seem as though folks living in the Community could enjoy reading the paper as I do. I am sure I never can feel anything but thankfulness so long as I can have the CIRCULAR to read. It is a real feast, and I don't know what part I like best. I like the 'Notes of the Evening' and what is said in the last paper about the 'Second Coming of Christ.' It has always been the great truth of truths with me. I alway's like to read Mr. Noyes's Home-Talks. His picture in the last paper is beautiful—he is a noble looking man.

I don't know but I should feel disheartened some, if should allow myself to think of myself and my surroundings, all the time. If we are God's children, he will place us in circumstances, best adapted to our spiritual growth, if it costs us a life of suffering. He wants w should be strong-minded men and women and be able to 'endure hardness.' Self is of little consequence—but a little speck when compared with the great whole I shall always rejoice in the prosperity of Christ's kingdom, and I feel one with the Community and take an terest in all your doings, as much as though I was here personally."

The Community has in use a large number of watches, and the expense of keeping them in repair is quite an item every year. It is thought that a little attention and care on the part of persons who carry watches would save us some expense for repairs, and that the watches would last much longer than they now do. Perhaps he following suggestions may be of service:

Never, habitually carry your watch key in your pocket: If you dislike to have it on your watch-guard, hang up in your room. Then if you are likely to be called away from home keep an extra key in your pocket to be used only in case of emergency.

Turn your watch pocket inside out and brush off the dust and dirt, once in two or three weeks, or oftener.

Do not allow your watch to run when it is out of repair: by doing so it may take more damage in a week han it would to run for years in good order.

Send your watch to a *good*, *honest* workman to be repaired. It may cost more, but it will pay in the long 'un. Watches are often spoiled by being "tinkered."

Always have a regular hour to wind your watch if you would have it keep good time.   D.

Mr. W. A. Knowles came here, yesterday, for the purpose he says, of resting. He is much better than when he left in the summer. We understand he has had some rough experience in getting settled since he went away, but has at last succeeded in buying back his old place. His son will assist him in carrying on the farm. Mr. Knowles stands firm with us, and he regrets that his circumstances are such that outwardly he must be separated from those he loves.

Mrs. Sears is making good progress in learning the use of our new machine; and though it is not designed for knitting very fine yarn, yet common sized yarn, such as is commonly used for men's socks and women's every day stockings, Mrs. S. knits without much trouble, and the work looks very well.

For several days the weather has been warm for the season, and very pleasant, with frosty nights. It is cloudy this morning, however, and there are indications of a storm.

Mr. Ely, an old Perfectionist and an acquaintance of Mrs. Tobey, came here this morning.

Mr. Morse from Cayuga, staid here last night.

Yesterday's temperature—
7 A. M., 41.   12 M., 49.   6 P. M., 40.   Mean 43.

DAILY JOURNAL
OF ONEIDA COMMUNITY.

VOL. 2. FRIDAY, DEC. 7, 1866. NO. 123

Short extract from a lettter received from Mrs. M. E Austin, of Morenci, Michigan.

" I had not thought much about your society from a r ligious point of view, but I feel that there is a ligh beaming up from your Community, which will shed it radiating influence far and wide, enabling woman to cast from her the shackles which the false conditions o society have put upon her, that she may stand up in he purity, thus elevating humanity in a social and domes tic point of view.—I feel anxious to learn more of you society, and will say, that my heart is with you in th great and good work you are trying to do, in remedyin the evils of present social life of which there is grea need."

In looking for the passage, "The fear of the Lord i the beginning of wisdom," my eye fell upon this, "Th fear of the Lord is the beginning of knowledge." I wa impressed by it, and also comforted. Several time since, when studying, or trying to understand som problem, and when my head would seem confused an my mind dark, I would think of the same passage, an also, "In Christ are hid all the treasures of wisdom an nowledge." Let us all fall back upon this during our ntellectual revival, and never for a moment give place o discouragement. Let us on the one hand be earnest or improvement, and on the other, be patient with urselves, and depend more on Christ within, than on y mere human effort or capability. S. B. C.

It may interest Mr. Thacker to learn that his recent rticle, on winter covering for plants and vines, has been opied into the *Utica Herald;* some other one (Mr. Cra n I guess) to learn that his article on Husk-Beds, writ nnd published a year or two since in the CIRCULAR, s just made its appearance in the *Democratic Union;* nd the purveyors of the CIRCULAR in general, to learn at the Oneida papers copy nearly every week, one or ore items from the Journal column.

Quite a scene occurred in the Trap-Shop, in the pack g-room, the other day, when it was announced that e last trap was packed, and our orders were all filled. 7e heard at first that there was such an uproarious shout at it reached the ears, even of Mr. Jones and Kinsley n an adjoining room; but we afterwards learned that ar coming in just at the time when the noise was the eatest, was entirely accidental. This rather takes vay the cream of our story, but we give it nevertheless.

We have decided to furnish the applicants at our near

boarding-house, with teachers, and Mr. Inslee and L. A Thayer are appointed to fill that office. They will hav their school session three evenings in a week, at from 6 o'clock to 7½.

CHRIST WITHIN.

Our God is so near,
That to us it seems clear,
We have nothing to fear
From the world's scoff or sneer,
Or for friends we hold dear,
From within or without;
For he gives us his grace,
All our faults to erase,
Every evil to face,
Nor to turn in disgrace,—
And abandon our place
But the enemy rout.
We are strong for the right,
And will act with our might,
And be girt for the fight,
(Though in peace we delight,)
For the good and the true;
And the sword of the spirit,
Which in Christ we inherit,
(And hence have no merit,)
We'll furbish anew.

Miss Thomas was criticised last night by her request. he was commended a good deal for the improvement she .ad made in overcoming her past difficulties, and for her aithfulness, and public spirit.

A third grammer class is being organized, with L. F. Junn for teacher.

Yesterday's temperature—
7 A. M., 34. 12 M., 48. 6 P. M., 42. Mean 41½.

DAILY JOURNAL
OF ONEIDA COMMUNITY.

VOL. 2.   SATURDAY, DEC. 8, 1866.   NO. 137

LETTERS.

Cleveland, O., Nov. 29, 1866.

DEAR FRIENDS OF THE O. C:—I most respectfully
and humbly present myself to you for such criticism as
you may see fit to give me, and as you may be able to
give at this distance. I confess my besetting sins to have
been willfulness, individual sovereignty, and of course
infidelity. I hope I have repented of them all, but presume I have not fully escaped their malign influences.—
To save you time and labor, I will say that your criticisms may be reported in Phonography and sent me thus
as I am familiar with the art. Hoping I am not asking
too much,   I am truly yours,   J. W. TOWNER.

Mr. Towner's letter was read in meeting, but it was
thought that we were not sufficiently acquainted with
him to criticise him.

—

The bag of furs, that Mr. Pitt sent some time ago,
has not yet reached us.—Mr. Pitt writes, Dec. 4th:

" I send you to-day via. A. F. Woods & Co., two bags
of furs, of which you will find an invoice inclosed. I
trust they will reach you, promptly and safely. I have
forwarded a similar invoice to Woods & Co. to be sent
with the furs. I fear the other bag has been delayed by
my failure to forward a detailed invoice, as Wood's &
Co. have been called upon by telegram for such invoice,
and I have forwarded one to them. I feel criticised for
his blunder. Had I followed my first instinct, all
would have been right ; but I could not recollect at the
time, whether you used to send anything more than a
general statement. I shall learn something by the affair,
at the worst.

I find it is pretty slow business getting furs, and sending them off, *alone*. I have worked *hard* for a week, to
get this lot, and get it started to you. It has been a
week of mud and rain and snow, and I am thankful I
have succeeded in getting them started."

—

We received yesterday the following scrap, from P. R.
Sherrard, the eccentric young man who worked for us
for a time last spring, in the Bag-shop. It was written
on the blank side of a bit of wall-paper.

Grafenberg, Dec. 5, 1866.

DEAR MR. W.:—I have twenty-two inventions on
which I want patents; but as I have no money to get
them through, I must assign them to some party who
will bear the expense and share the profit. Could not
your Community take them up? Please let me know
early. I am burned out of house and home, the Hygieotherapeutic Institute in which I was employed being
destroyed by an incendiary. In bonds of affectionate regard and christian fraternity,   P. R. SHERRARD.

The present weather with its soft south winds, and
genial skies is more suggestive of April than December,
and what tends to heighten the illusion is the singing
and chirping of birds, and the green grass by the way-
sides interspersed with the dandelion as yellow and
bright as in spring-time. How soon northern blasts
with driving snows may dissipate the illusion, remains
to be seen : but there seems to be no pining for the reign
of the Frost-king unless we except some of the juveniles
who manifest a little impatience to vary the routine of
life, with the use of sleds and skates, and snow-balls
understood, if not expressed.   H.

—

We heard one of our elderly men, who has just commenced the study of Algebra, say, that he was so
charmed with it, that he could think of nothing else all
day, and he dreamed about it all night. This is only
one specimen, of the general interest that is felt in the
study.

—

A bed has been put up in the chamber of the Store
building, in the room that Mr. Reynolds occupies for a
work-room, where Mr. R. will be snugly and pleasantly
domiciled for the winter.

—

This fine balmy weather invites the flowers to peep
out, as though they thought spring had come. Friend
Thacker, might find a number of his favorite dandelions
between the house and the mill. But the flower-garden
can boast of the pansy and polyanthus, quite gay and
flourishing. Mr. Nash has put the climbing roses to bed
for a long winter night, and tucked them up, with the
hope that they may come forth in the spring, rested and
prepared to bud and blossom again with renewed beauty.

C. E.

Traps ordered the last week,	232 doz.
The principal order was—	
H. W. Corbet, New York,	40 "
mostly large traps for the Pacific coast—	Amount $500.

Yesterday's temperature:—

7½ A. M., 41.   13 M., 49.   6 P. M., 38.   Mean 43½.

DAILY JOURNAL
OF ONEIDA COMMUNITY.

VOL. 2.   MONDAY, DEC. 10, 1866.   NO. 138

BUSINESS MEETING.

Mr. Noyes has expressed a wish that the yearly inventory might be got out promptly, and it is desirable that it should be. It does not effect the value of our property but it is of interest historically. Mr. Hamilton said had had some thoughts of putting the job on William school. It would be a good exercise for the school. would be of practical application and a good discipline for them to take it up and go through with it. They might get together and distribute the business, to the heads of the different departments, and get up the thing in good shape. Those who furnish statistics should prepare them so well that they would not have to be written over. William, Mr. Campbell and Edwin were appointed a committee on the subject.

The board are in favor of disposing of all our hired help, except enough to enable us to carry through successfully our educational project.

The committee appointed to see about getting much report the practicability of getting it from our ced swamp. Upon discussion, it was thought that o swamp had not better be cut away, or large holes dug it. The timber is growing, and will always be more ess valuable to us for poles and stakes; besides it is a pleasant jungle to stroll into, so near home. We have gone too much of it.—The ten acre muck swamp in market, can probably be got for 15 or 16 hundred dollars. This swamp can be drained, and would furnish us muck and peat for years to come; after it is cleared it will make the best of meadow. It will not be a bad bargain to get it at that price. It was unanimously voted that the committee be authorized to purchase the land. They can feel their way, and if the Lord wants we should have it, the way will be open.

Mr. Burt inquired what we should do about the corn-machines? He thought it was time to give them some attention in the way of getting up the style, if we mean to do any thing about it. It is thought that though the machine seems to be a success now, in its details it might possibly be improved.—We ought to learn from last year's experience not to offer the public, what we have not proved ourselves, and finished in its details. Mr. Burt had better advise with John Sears, or Mr. Inslee, and get up what we want, for ourselves, and two or three extra ones to exhibit abroad, next season. If you get a machine right, you cannot test it till the corn season, and then there is not time to introduce it. You have got to overcome the prejudice existing against it, caused by exhibiting it prematurely last year. If we prove the machine, and are satisfied with it ourselves, and they see for themselves, (for instance at such a place as Port-

land), that they are *the thing*, there will be no difficulty in introducing, them, next season.

Mr. Worden petitioned that an ice-house be put up our near boarding-house. The subject was referred the building Committee.

There was quite a discussion about the new match that are in use. They are not very convenient, and a not much safer, it is thought, than the old ones, as the boxes have in two or three instances taken fire. It seer that this prepared surface is very combustible and therefore liable under certain circumstances to ignite. It was voted that we use up what matches we have on han and then return to the old ones.

Mr. Woolworth enquired whether the elevator at the mill, could not be made as safe as the one at Willow Place. It is much needed to raise heavy boxes, coal, &c from the basement to the garret. Referred to G. W Hamilton and Mr. Inslee.

An interesting report of the state of our finances was read last night, and statistics given, which forms a striking contrast to last year's report. Our present prosperi is attributable to the expulsion of Mr. Carr's spirit from our midst, and in following Mr. Noyes's inspiration, in placing a man of faith at the head of our business operations. A good deal of talk followed, recalling past times, and acknowledging the hand of God in guiding our ship safely to port, in the midst of such a terrific financial storm as we encountered a year ago.

TWO SIDES.

Some of the letters received from persons to whom fruit has been sent are not very pleasant reading, on account of occasional allusions to poor corn, "swelled heads," cracked bottles, broken tumblers, &c. But *per contra*, we are encouraged with such words as the following:

South Hadley Falls, Oct. 12, 1866.

Please send to my address the enclosed order for your *very* excellent canned Fruit.

Respectfully,   Mrs. Joseph Carew.

Milwaukee, Nov. 1, 1866.

All the Preserved Fruit in glass seems to be very nice, and so far we have no complaint to make.

Yours truly,   Ledyard & Co.

Chicago, Ill., Nov. 5, 1866.

The goods are received and give entire satisfaction.

L. H. Lawrence Agt.'

Situsville, Pa., Nov. 29, 1866.

I have tried the Tomatoes, Plums and Beans and have found them to be very nice, and in perfect order. Place me on your list for an annual Circular of fruit &c.

Yours truly,   L. H. Severance.

Temperature Saturday and Sunday,

7½ A. M., 48.   12 M., 54.   6 P. M., 50.   Mean 50½.

7½ A. M., 34.   12 M., 40.   6 P. M., 33.   Mean 35½.

DAILY JOURNAL
OF ONEIDA COMMUNITY.

VOL. 2.   TUESDAY, DEC. 11, 1866.   NO. 139.

NOTES TO THE FAMILY.

I feel dictated by the spirit of Truth, to confess my entire dependence on Christ, and to confess him my Saviour from doubt and unbelief. In months and years past I have asked God to put me through such discipline and trials, as would fit me for a subject of his kingdom. I have had trials in consequence of my egotism and old habits, and I want to expose my temptations, and free myself by the help of the brethren and the spirit of truth, from the evils that beset me in this respect. I had confidence in Mr. Noyes's inspiration long ago, and believed him inspired, and I now believe that he is trying his best to free me as well as others, in the Community, from the spirit of egotism and idolatry, that we may worship God in spirit and in truth, and do his will in all things. I thank God for a home in the Community and I wish to take a position that shall gain the affection and confidence of all.

Yours for victory over the temptations of the evil one,   C. HIGGINS.

—

DEAR FRIENDS:—Allow me to express my thankfulness for all your faithfulness in the past, and for your kind sympathy in helping me to overcome my many failings and imperfections. My prayer is, that I may prove worthy of your love and good wishes. I was not prepared for so much commendation as was given me the other evening, but will try and return all to the right source, and magnify the grace of God, by yielding myself to him, that he may make the most of me for his service. It warms my heart, when I think of the privilege I enjoy, of helping push on the great car of progress, with so many brave brothers, and heroic sisters, while so many around us, had rather step on and ride, than to help in the good work.   C. K.

Community people in times past have been considered lacking in concentrativeness, but had an observer passed through the lower sitting-room the other day, he would have received quite an opposite impression. The idea of a "school-house on a battle-field," or the man watching the clock with a "Here she goes, there she goes," in spite of all interruption, no longer seems impracticable. At the table sit three of the brothers, deeply engaged in the study of Algebra. One is reading the example, another performs the operation, while a third demonstrates. These gentlemen perhaps, fancy themselves in class, and consequently their voices are raised considerably above a whisper to say the least. At the other side of the table sits a lady absorbed in Arithmetic, apparently undisturbed. Two more are studying their lessons aloud, (grammer and phonography), while the sewing machine in the adjoining bed-room keeps lively time. A rather facetious old lady, (one of the occupants of the room), perceives the state of things, and proposes to herself to read aloud an article from the CIRCULAR. This she does in a clear loud tone, without in the least diverting the attention of any one. All, with one exception, confess that they were ignorant of what was going on around them, and the reader from the CIRCULAR affirms, that she never had so good an understanding of what she read before.   AN OBSERVER.

WILLOW PLACE ITEMS.

A Miss Barber, niece of neighbor Cole, has been hired in the Silk-Factory, to learn to spool. She gets along with this somewhat particular branch, much better than could be expected, of an entirely green hand.—The number of hired men has been diminished to twelve in the Finishing department, and about the same number in the Forging-shop.

We witnessed an interesting operation to-day, conducted by Mr. Pritchard, our prince of blacksmiths.—He had been rejuvenating an old anvil, and wished to harden the face of it. After being heated to cherry redness in the forge, it was lifted from thence, by means of long iron bars, and placed upon a wheel-barrow.—Prussate of Potash was then sprinkled over the glowing surface, whereby a greater hardness with a lower degree of heat is obtained. Striker Ashleigh then wheeled the barrow around into the wheel-house, directly over the end of the flume. It was then let down through a hole in the floor, and placed in position before the waste gate, "all ready;" tip goes the gate, and a jet of water two feet wide and fifteen inches deep, strikes squarely on the heated mass. In five minutes the anvil, though still warm, is pronounced cool enough, and pulled up.— "First-rate temper," says Pritchard, after a brief examination, "hard as glass," and Ashleigh trundles it away.   C.

In working on the Burt-House our people discovered in the little "cuddy" over the wing, a number of letters, the principal part of which, proved to be the correspondence between Mr. Burt's father and mother, previous to their marriage. We noticed one dated 1790. They breathe a serious tone, very, and show plainly the religious character of Mr. Burt's ancestors.

One thing that struck us, as peculiar about the letters, was the respectful, but cold and distant manner of their address. Every letter commenced with only the title, "Sir, or Madam"—not even the qualifying term "Dear," attached to it. Quite a contrast we thought, to the fervent manner of address, of modern lovers.

Frederic Marks starts to-day noon for Wallingford via New-York.

Yesterday's temperature—
7½ A. M., 20.   12 M., 24.   6 P. M., 20.   Mean 21½.

DAILY JOURNAL
OF ONEIDA COMMUNITY.

VOL. 2. WEDNESDAY, DEC. 12, 1866. NO. 140.

TO THE COMMUNITY.

I wish to thank the family for my criticism. The fear of it, is all gone, and I am sure that it is an experience to be enjoyed rather than dreaded. If I had no other evidence that this is the kingdom of God than the good effects of criticism on character, I could truly say it is enough. I confess Christ my ability to improve by such means, and to learn to walk in the spirit. I never had so high an appreciation of our system of criticism as now.

I confess my union with the family, my love for and confidence in Mr. Hamilton and Mr. Woolworth as inspired men.   J. R. THOMAS.

Mr. Pitt in his letter of Dec. 8th, speaking of the many perplexities he has had in getting his furs started, says:—" I have got some insight into the cooking of tariffs and customs, which I did not have before, and think I shall be able to lecture on the ' Perplexities of a Fur Buyer' hereafter. However I know the Lord's hand is in the whole matter, and I had rather learn by severe experience to trust him and walk by his inspiration, even if I blunder some, than be guided by worldly foresight and wisdom. I am very thankful that he has watched over me and let things go no worse than they have."

A brother remarked to us last night, that the little article in the JOURNAL yesterday, from "An Observer" reminded him of olden times when several of the musicians were wont to resort to the old school-room, (for the want of a better place), for drilling. He said there were flutes, horns and violins, and every one played on his own hook, without any reference to his neighbor.—In speaking of that experience, he said he wondered how they could have done it.

We noticed yesterday, the small boys putting on their skates, and on enquiring if they were going to try the pond, they said, no, they were only going on to the ice where the water was about a foot deep.—A committee has been appointed consisting of G. W. Hamilton, Mr. Newhouse and Myron, to decide upon, and report when the ice on the pond at Willow Place is considered safe for skating.

Alfred Hawley was criticised last night, and Mr. Hamilton took occasion to say in the course of the criticism, that he never had such pleasant relations with the young people as now.

Some visitors called the other day, and after they were gone, a poor little puny kitten was found in the Reception-room. What their object was in leaving the little creature on our hands, we cannot tell, but it seemed to us rather a mean trick. They must have been affected with cat-a-(left)-sy, we think.

AN ODE.

i.

While the worlding fights for fame,
Which but proves an empty name,
For the goal of truth we aim :
  This we hold most dear !

ii.

God our efforts will inspire,
Light our hearts with heav'nly fire,
Fill our minds with high desire :
  He is with us here !

iii.

Hero come, the cause is grand !
Who with us would fear to stand ?
Who will serve with voice and hand,
  Let it now appear !

iv.

Give your life, in Jesus's name,
To the cross : despise the shame :
Thus you'll win immortal fame,
  Hailed by prophet's peer !

v.

Who would yield to sin, a slave,
Led in fetters to the grave ?
Rather let us Satan brave :
  Ring defiance clear !

vi.

Boldly front the lurking foe,
Christ and angels aid the blow
That will lay the demon low :
  Never yield to fear !

                                 MIDAS.

We had quite a serious criticism last night from one of the family, for forgetting to insert Mrs. Noyes's departure on Thursday night last, in the JOURNAL. They did not know that she had left, till yesterday, because as they said, the fact was not publicly announced as it should have been. We ask pardon for the negligence.

The reign of winter has fairly commenced, though in its mildest form. The ground is frozen and a slight sprinkle of snow covers its surface. Every thing indicates that the weather is settling down into its accustomed routine of storms and calms, for the season.

Yesterday's temperature—
7½ A. M., 15. 12 M., 24. 6 P. M., 20. Mean 19⅞.

DAILY JOURNAL
OF ONEIDA COMMUNITY.

VOL. 2.   THURSDAY, DEC. 13, 1866.   NO. 141.

Edenton, N. C., Dec. 4, 1866.

DEAR FRIENDS OF THE O. C.:—I have just finished reading No. 37, (present Vol.) of the CIRCULAR, and I wish I could make you understand how my heart thrills with sympathy toward its writers. But language is too tame. God only can understand my feelings. I used to think that no paper was like a certain Advent paper; but since my eyes have been opened to see the truth on the great question of Christ's Second Coming, those papers have lost their interest, and become insipid. In some things the stream that flowed from those papers was nearer the fountain head of truth than where I had formerly drank; but the CIRCULAR is so much nearer than they, that I have no cravings for a drink lower down stream, but rather higher up. O that I could have the privilege of sitting at Mr. Noyes's feet as did those in the "Putney Corporation," and there learn the way of truth more perfectly. I used to think differently.—I was struck with the forcibleness and truth of an article on "Independence," in No. 36 of the CIRCULAR. I too used to be a victim to the false theory of independence; but I have been some humbled, and now wish to be controlled by the spirit of organization. I feel dependent on Christ for power to shun evil, and I desire to learn of all who are better than myself. In fact I want egotism entirely removed from me, and myself entirely subjected to Christ's spirit. The world knows nothing of this spirit, and are astonished at its manifestation. Even members of churches cannot appreciate the idea of one individual working for all; they know nothing about giving up *all* for Christ's Kingdom.

I wish I could occasionally drop into your meetings, and thereby become more fully charged with Christ's spirit; for evil spirits cannot force the solid spirit of unity and truth that surrounds you, as when one is in the world. Still I believe God knows best and will enable me yet to become a perfect man in Christ Jesus.

Is there not some way in which I can come under the influence of faithful criticism?

Yours in much love.   D. EDSON SMITH.

D. M. Kelly, in writing to his brother from Toulon, Ill., Dec. 7th, sends a draft on New-York for $800, the money that was due his wife, we believe.

He writes:—" I confess my obedience to the Community, in whatever they think best for me to do. I feel like turning my attention to Christ entirely. I have faith to believe that he will direct my steps in the right way. I shall stay here as long as I can find work enough to pay my way.—I wish you would send me the back numbers of the CIRCULAR from about the 14th of Nov."

We were very much interested in Mr. Noyes's talk last evening, on the "inspired use of natural means" as agents sufficient to overcome all difficulties, old age included. This view of the "situation," takes from us all excuse for imbecility of body or mind, and should nerve us to greater activity of heart and faith, to avail ourselves of the resources that lie within the reach of all.

Night before last, as one of the hired men was taking the milk from the barn to the house, the can that was left unfastened, fell to the ground, spilling nearly all the milk, and injuring the can. About fourteen pans of milk were lost. We send at the present time about one third of all the milk we have in the morning to Willow Place boarding-house.

Mr. Noyes arrived about 4 o'clock P. M. yesterday. In the evening he gave a particular account of his call at the Hospital at Utica, on his way here, and his talk with Victor. He thinks V. has improved a good deal, but said in conversation with him, he saw indications that there were still some remains of his old difficulties.

The folks at the children's house, have had quite a serious fight with colds, influenza, &c., among the children. They are all well again now, and as full of life and sport as ever.

Our ironing-girls, have caught the enthusiasm for study that runs so high in the family, and bring their grammars and keep them open on the table before them, as they iron.

As the pond at Willow Place was pronounced safe, yesterday, the ice being fully two inches thick, some of the young-men enjoyed an hour or two skating, in the afternoon.

Mr. Knowles left for home in the night. As his health is, it was not thought best for him to go alone, and S. W. Nash accompanied him.

Three bags of fur from Mr. Pitt, have just arrived.

Yesterday's temperature—
7½ A. M., 20.   12 M., 28.   6 P. M., 20.   Mean 23¼.

DAILY JOURNAL
OF ONEIDA COMMUNITY.

VOL. 2.   FRIDAY, DEC. 14, 1866.   NO. 142.

Mr. Noyes's talk last night on spiritual wife-dom, or "split beans," as he termed it, recalled to our recollection the excitement that prevailed in Northern Vermont on that subject, twenty-five years ago. There was a class in that region that followed in the train of the Second Adventists, and who believed as they did, more or less, but did not fully endorse their doctrines. S. K. Hazelton was one of that class. They were called spiritualists, because they professed to have made greater attainments in spirituality and to have reached a far more satisfactory stage of experience than the churches. They were distinguished for their fervency and zeal in prayer and their fanatical tendencies. There were some women among the number who took quite a leading position, and who accompanied the brethren from place to place attending protracted meetings held by the Second Adventists, and laboring with them to save souls. It was finally whispered round, that some of them believed in having spiritual wives and discarding their old ones, or treating them coldly. It produced quite an excitement, and gossip with her hundred tongues, was busy enough.

We are not able to trace the history of the affair further, though we remember that one of the women, a young lady of fine appearance, had an illegitimate child as a consequence, we suppose, of finding her affinity, or the other half of the "split bean."

Mr. Nash returned at one o'clock this morning, from Watertown, where he had been to accompany Mr. Knowles, on his return home. When he reached Richland, he encountered a heavy snow-storm, and the snow was so deep (three feet), that when he arrived at Watertown, the train was more than five hours behind time. Egbert met his father at the depot, but Mr. Nash thought from his appearance, that he was far from welcoming him home. Mr. N. said it was evidently a concerted plan, between him and his mother, to get Mr. K. off *their* hands and on to the Community for the winter. It is hard for Mr. K., in his present weak state, to look on the side of faith, and his tendency is, to sink into discouragement and hypo.

We hope the grace of God will sustain and comfort him, in the exceedingly trying circumstances in which he is placed.

Mr. Perry in obtaining an order for Bags from a firm in LaFayette, Ind., on his late trip, gave a greater discount than he intended. The following was received in response to a letter apprising them that a less discount would be allowed them:

"Having been very well satisfied with your goods, the five per cent discount shall not keep us from ordering hereafter. Please add to our former order, &c."

Letters were received yesterday from two firms, asking for more sweet-corn, "like that last sent."

A firm in Kingston, Canada, writes, "Your fruits give good satisfaction."—[We omit some *per contras*.]

The mercury was down this morning, to within six degrees of zero, and the day is cold but sunny.

Yesterday's temperature—
7½ A. M., 18.   12 M., 28.   6 P. M., 24.   Mean 23½.

DAILY JOURNAL
OF ONEIDA COMMUNITY.

VOL. 2. SATURDAY, DEC. 15, 1866. NO. 143.

Fort Howard, Wis., Dec. 8, 1866.

MR. NOYES, DEAR SIR:—I saw in a paper a short time since, a notice of your Community. Upon what terms can one join. And if a man and woman whom the world will not let live in peace should join you, can they enjoy each other's society exclusively if they wish? Any work or paper on the subject will be attentively perused and willingly paid for. I remain yours &c.,

L. H. NELSON.

Mr. Noyes's talk last night on idolatrous attachments and special relationships, interested us very much. In the view of the subject as he presented it, the sin of idolatry is the great sin of the age; and what renders it still worse is the fact, that both clergy and laity, those who profess to stand in nearest proximity to God and truth, are in total ignorance of its existence, and glorify special attachments, as beautiful and lovely.

Stepping into a room the other night, occupied by one of our elderly men, one who has signalized himself, for his zeal in our business campaign the past season, we found him poring over his algebra with the same spirit of enthusiasm that has characterized him in his work. We asked him if he had any items of news for the JOURNAL? He answered promptly, no, and immediately said, "I'm all engaged in algebra,, and I like it, too." Thinking there was not much chance to gather up items there, disconnected with algebra, we withdrew.

We heard of another person, who having occasion to get up in the morning, at an unusually early hour, found herself trying hard before rising to work out the unpleasant problem by algebra, instead.

Mr. R. M. Quinby from New-York City, came here last night. He was here a little more than two years ago, and bought some of our books. He is a bachelor thirty-five or forty years of age, and heir to large estates, if he can succeed in wresting them from other claimants, and can establish his own title. He is a quiet sort of a man, and does not seem much interested in us or our enterprise. He has gone over to Willow Place this morning.

The family took a unanimous vote night before last, in favor of the proposition Mr. Noyes presented, which was to have Mr. Frobisher invited to pass the **Christmas** holidays at Oneida. He is to give the family, as many of them as choose it, lessons in elocution during his stay, and we are to pay his traveling expenses from **New-York here and back.**

The Augusta rose bush has again commenced her blossoming career. We noticed to-day, one delicate rose upon its stem, surrounded with eight promising buds just ready to open.

A company of eight girls, or young ladies rather, went over to Willow Place yesterday, and had a fine time skating.

Traps ordered the last week,   116 doz.

Yesterday's temperature—
7½ A. M., 7. 12 M., 11. 6 P. M., 17. Mean 11½.

DAILY JOURNAL
OF ONEIDA COMMUNITY.

VOL. 2.   MONDAY, DEC. 17, 1866.   NO. 144.

BUSINESS MEETING.

The teamsters wished to know who they could depend upon, to do the wagon and sled repairing this winter? It was thought that Daniel Knowles would be a good hand, and that it would be the most convenient in many respects, to have it done at Willow Place, where it is handy to the blacksmith. Left to Abram, Daniel, and Mr. Burt to arrange the matter.

The tin can business needs to be prosecuted. One of the small presses at Willow Place, can be removed to the tin shop, and our machinists will endeavor to furnish another within a few weeks.

It would be economy to have one more pair of sleds, than we have teams for. In good sleighing as much can be done in one day, as in five days of such going as the present. The wagon committee are authorized to supply themselves with what they need.

Voted that we have a light strong wagon built this winter, to ply between here and the depot.

The means for providing water in case of fire at Willow Place was referred to, and it was moved that something be done. E. H. Hamilton, G. W. Hamilton, Mr. Inslee and W. A. Hinds, were appointed to take such measures as they thought proper.—It is thought that there is more liability of fire originating in the wood-shop than elsewhere; consequently, that a separate building for a wood-shop would be safer and better than our present arrangement.

The committee appointed to decide the question relating to the elevator at the mill, report that they found the greatest difficulty in the matter to be, lack of care. They recommended that so good a piece of machinery had better be fitted up with the proper safety guards, and that its management then, be put into the hands of one or two responsible persons. To do this, it will cost about $40. Referred to G. W. H., Mr. Inslee and Mr Woolworth.

Mr. Abbott reported the leaky state of the aqueduct. Unless we use the water sparingly, there will not be enough for the washing. It was recommended to follow it up and find the place of the leak.

Our youngest children to the number of twelve were favored with a rich treat last night, in the form of a supper party, got up for them by the folks that live with them, to which Mr. Noyes and Mr. Hamilton were invited guests. The cause was this; Ormond with one or two more of the little ones had called over to see Mr. Noyes, and their talk about their visit, had excited a desire amongst the rest of them, to see Mr. Noyes, one after another saying, "I want to see papa Noyes",

which being reported to Mr. N. he said he should like to take supper with them before he left.—The table was spread in the parlor at the children's house and at the appointed time the little ones, on the tiptoe of expectation were seated around it. When Mr. N. made his appearance, every countenance brightened up and the murmur passed around "papa Noyes, papa Noyes," little Ransom calling out in a loud voice, from the further end of the table "Noite." On the whole it was a pleasant affair, and enjoyed by all.

It commenced snowing yesterday forenoon quite moderately at first, but increasing more and more, till all the afternoon and evening, we had what we should call a driving snow-storm, the wind blowing strong from the southeast. We have now good prospect of sleighing, as the snow this morning is about a foot deep.

There was a concerted plan among the young men yesterday, to take their place at the dinner table by the side of Mr. Noyes, and crowd out the young women and girls who had been in the habit of sitting by him when taking his meals. They thought the girls had monopolized Mr. N.'s attention, quite too much, both in his room and at the table, leaving *them* altogether in the back ground; so at an early hour they came into the dining-room, filling nearly the whole table, and leaving only a seat for Mr. Noyes. The girls on entering, stared some, to see their accustomed places occupied, but soon comprehended the joke and retreated with a good grace to another table. Mr. Noyes too, on seeing the change, hesitated about taking his accustomed seat, till one of the sisters who understood the matter told him all was right. After being seated he made the remark, that "when the women get out the way, the men will learn to love one another."

Mr. Burnham, who passed Sunday with us, gave us on the stage after meeting last night, as a specimen of elocution, a burlesque of the speech of a back-woods Lawyer, made in defence of his client who was accused of stealing. It was quite amusing.

Mrs. Jones from Baldwinsville is here on a visit.

Temperature Saturday and Sunday,
7¼ A. M., 11.   12 M., 23.   6 P. M., 19.   Mean 17¼.
7¼ A. M., 18.   12 M., 20.   6 P. M., 24.   Mean 20¾.

DAILY JOURNAL
OF ONEIDA COMMUNITY.

VOL. 2.   TUESDAY, DEC. 18, 1866.   NO. 145.

DEAR BRO. HAMILTON :—I feel to join heartily with Mr. Noyes in his raid against special love. Ever since I have been in the Community, I have been striving to have my own way in love matters, independent of all the counsel that has been given me, and this has been one of the reasons of my standing outside of the family. I have been determined that if I could not have love in my own way that I would not have it at all. I am ashamed of my obstinacy, and ask forgiveness of God and the family. I am determined to surrender, and from henceforth give up my will and be governed by the church and accept of her truly as my mother.

I heartily endorse the kind expressions made to you and Mrs. Dunn last evening, and confess that I have had a growing appreciation of your labors of love in the family. Confessing Christ my ability in all things, I am your brother,   **W. H. PERRY.**

The Theological students have finished their study of the "Origin of Evil" and at their next session will take up for investigation "The Divine Nature," a short article in the Berean. Mr. Noyes was present at the meeting of the class Sunday evening, and recommended them to look up and investigate the articles in the old "Perfectionist," on Swedenborgianism. He said those articles cost him a good deal of study, and they would have been published in the Berean as he designed to have them, had there been space, but they were crowded out by other matter. His talk on this subject, in his discourse on "The Divine Nature" in the Berean, he thought, might be a good introduction to further thought and investigation.

The plan adopted in the Theological class for persons to sing and to speak on the stage, has had a good effect we should judge, in breaking up bashfulness and mortifying egotism, if not curing it wholly. It requires a good deal of strength of purpose for a young woman, especially, to place herself in such a position before the public; yet why should we feel timid when the fact is, we are brothers and sisters of the same family, and all scholars in the same school.

Meroa Kneeland writes, that she and Emily have both been sick, and that she needs the money she left, $25.— She says she has not read a novel or looked into one, since she left Oneida. She says Emily improves, goes to school, and is a better reader than children of her age in that place.

Mr. Blood is again talking of going away. He is not

established on the point of Mr. Noyes's leadership and inspiration, and of course in that state he will not find much peace with us. His wife feels badly, is in sympathy with our views, and would choose to remain.

Mr. Noyes went to Utica again yesterday, and saw Victor, and had a visit of an hour with him, which was quite pleasant. He saw also Dr. Gray and had a pleasant chat with him; on the whole he said his call was quite satisfactory, much more so than the first.

The CIRCULARS came in good season to-day. They look very interesting, but we have not yet perused them much. We are glad to see a continuation of Mr. Cragin's article on "The Putney Corporation," as that seems to be the natural sequel to his "Story of a Life."

The weather is quite mild, and to-day the sleighing is very good. The boys enjoy the snow, though it spoils their fun of skating.

Yesterday's temperature—
7¼ A. M., 26.   12 M., 24.   6 P. M., 24.   Mean 24¾.

DAILY JOURNAL
OF ONEIDA COMMUNITY.

VOL. 2.   WEDNESDAY, DEC. 19, 1866.   NO. 146.

Blairstown, Iowa, Dec. 12, 1866.

DEAR BROTHERS AND SISTERS:—Enclosed, find Tax Receipt. I have not found a chance to sell your land yet, but have at last got a man to look after it specially. I hope I can report favorably soon.

I learn by our lady friends, that J. W. Towner has applied to become a member of the Community. I think he would be able to tell the value of said land. I feel under great obligation for the kind and hospitable manner, in which you entertained our friends, Mrs. Peet and Allman. I was sorry they did not stay longer, but they stayed long enough to become very much in love with you, and your mode of life. Were you a little less Orthodox, or they a little more so, I think they would both have been knocking at the door ere this. As it is, they are both praying over it. I do not know whether they have written to you. They felt a little delicate before they went, about letting people know where they were going; but since they have come home, they make no secret of it, but declare openly in your favor. I do not know whether they manifested themselves to you, but we are, nearly all of us, rather inclined to be Spiritualists, or Harmonial Philosophers. If I had been there, or any where else, it would have been known as far as I was concerned. Nevertheless we are bound to give in, that your practical life is right, and we have to admit, that that is a very strong argument in favor of the correctness of your theory. I have never met with an Orthodox people, who would tolerate you at all, while among Spiritulists, or Freethinkers, I always find a willingness to read and hear of you, and your doctrines. Individually I feel that I am in position to learn, rather than teach; so I will carefully read the CIRCULAR, and await the result. You will consider me as ever, a

Devoted Brother,   ISAIAH MORRIS.

NOTE.

Artemas Ward's " N. B. This is sarkasum," should be understood, after most of the remarks concerning the Willimantic Boarding-House, in Monday's CIRCULAR. Two or three sentences, intended to convey such an idea, (rather too pointedly perhaps,) were ommitted by Ed. Cir. The description, as it now stands, is much nearer rose color than accords with truth. The Willimantic Trio have no desire to complain of the discomforts that fell to their lot, while at school; but they do feel, that the article in question, should not reflect on the veracity of the statement they have made at various times, about their experience while there.   C. A. CRAGIN.

Alfred Hawley in coming down the stairs at the Tontine, last night, with a lighted lamp in his hand, slipped and fell, and for a short time he was insensible. The hard blows bestowed upon his back, however, soon restored his lost breath, and this morning he feels pretty well, with the exception of a little lameness in his back. What was wonderful about the fall, was the fact, that the lamp was not broken or extinguished. It was found standing right side up, on the floor at the bottom of the stairs. The attempt to save his lamp, which was a large one, was doubtless the cause of his heavy fall.

Mrs. Jones left for home, yesterday, and Mrs. Langstaff went with her as far as Syracuse. Mrs. L. has been suffering for a long time, with sore eyes, and some time ago, she went to Syracuse, and consulted Dr. Slocum, the man who was so successful in curing Mr. Hatch's sore eyes. The Dr. gave her a wash for her eyes, that she has been using ever since, with good results, she thinks. But it seemed necessary that she should go and see the Dr. again, as he wrote to her to come. She may stay several days. Dr. Slocum has recently moved to Camillus, a station a few miles west of Syracuse.

Our people are to have a dinner of fresh codfish to-day. On opening one of the fish, yesterday, a large bearded hook, four inches in length, was found in him. We think it must have lain hard upon his stomach some time, as it was quite rusty.

John Smith arrived yesterday afternoon. We should not have recognized him at all, as the John Smith that left us when quite a small boy. He looks robust and healthy.

All our hired carpenters are discharged, with the exception of two hands.

Yesterday's temperature—
7½ A. M., 24.   12 M., 34.   6 P. M., 30.   Mean 29½.

DAILY JOURNAL
OF ONEIDA COMMUNITY.

VOL. 2.   THURSDAY, DEC. 20, 1866.   NO. 146.

NEW FARM.

The committee, appointed recently by the Business Board, with instructions to negotiate for the purchase of a certain ten-acre Muck Swamp, yesterday made a verbal contract for the same. Terms: $1475.00—about one-half of this sum to be paid April 1st, 1867, and the balance to remain on interest after April 1st. Possession is to be given as soon as the necessary papers can be drawn and executed. The new farm is bounded, on the North by Mr. Wells's lot; on the South and East by B. Stiles's land, on the South-east by the Cheese Factory; and on the West by more Swamp. This purchase will afford all the Muck, that the Farmers and Horticulturalists will require for many years.   w.

Vernon Center, Dec. 19, 1866.

ONEIDA COMMUNITY:—As I am about to write a *Report* for the year, of the "Vernon Agricultural Society" to send to Albany, for publication in the Transactions of the State Agricultural Society, it has occurred to my mind, that a detailed history of the Manufacturing and Agricultural productions of the Community, appended to our Report, would be read with interest, and be creditable to all concerned.

Your *Report* should embrace every thing deemed of interest, the number of acres of farm, and its several divisions of productions, with theory, and practice pursued in Agriculture, Horticulture, Fruit and Flowers, together with Manufacturing products, and details of buildings, grounds &c., which may suggest to the reader the history of Oneida Community.

Please accept this as an invitation to do as I propose, and if you will consent to comply with my request, please inform me by letter at your earliest convenience, and oblige,   Your friend and obt. servant,

LEVI T. MARSHALL.

Secy. Vernon Agl. Soc.

P. S. The *Report* should go to Albany in the month of January or as soon as practicable.

AN APPEAL.

DEAR EDITRESS:—Are you aware of the mischief that is going on among the groves on West Hill? Winter after winter bears witness to the laying low of many a stately tree, and of course this would ere long complete the ruin of every single grove on that beautiful slope. But where would be found the charming Wood Thrush? where the hours of delicious revery, while imbibing those bewitching strains?

It may not be known to many that this species of Thrush not only confines itself to the high lands, but appears to select such groves as are furnished with underbrush. We failed altogether to find them in open woods, while in every instance where there was underbrush, there we found this bird, and they are far superior, in our opinion, to the Hermit Thrush in point of song.

Now there are but a very few such groves within a circuit of ten or twelve miles from our homestead; and two of them lie on the slope of the hill opposite to us, and that is where they are doing the mischief. Wouldn't I though, were I a rich man, and had a chance, buy up those groves? Yes, they should be an everlasting home for those sweet songsters, as long as they chose to favor us with their summer visits. Other groves there are of the kind, but they are farther off in an opposite direction. Could we not do *something* toward rescuing, at least, *one* of those wood-lots from utter ruin? But it is not only the Thrush that we should lose, but also the jubilant Gross-beak, and the gorgeous Tanager—both of them famous for vocal powers. Who will sympathize?

Your old friend,   ORNITHOPHILOS.

We had a call yesterday, of an hour, from Parker Pillsbury, known as a big gun of the Garrisonian Abolition and Woman's right's school. He had quite a fine looking lady with him, Miss Bisbee, with whom he is traveling, attending conventions and lecturing from place to place on "Equal Suffrage," which with them, includes woman as well as the negro. He expressed his dissatisfaction with the world as it is, and also with the measures and prospects of reforms, as superficial; and said, "Perhaps we may be drifting toward you, I don't know; I want to learn more about you. If you are as you appear, you must be very happy." He was introduced to Mr. Noyes, and they had a pleasant chat about old times, Garrison, Boyle, &c. The lady was quite interesting and intelligent. She went in to see the children, and on leaving, there was a general out-call, "come again," which pleased her much.

We had two splendid Sun-dogs this morning, one on each side of the sun, about 15 deg.'s each way and about 10 deg.'s in hight. They looked like pillars of fire, though with rainbow colors. It is said they are ominous of cold weather. It is clear and cold this morning, and splendid sleighing.

The mercury sunk during the night, 23 deg. and stood early this morning, 5 deg. below zero.

Yesterday's temperature—

7½ A. M., 30.   12 M., 36.   6 P. M., 33.   Mean 33.

DAILY JOURNAL
OF ONEIDA COMMUNITY.

VOL. 2.   FRIDAY, DEC. 21, 1866.   NO. 147.

I wish to thank the family for the kindness and christian charity which they have manifested toward me since I have been here. I confess my union with this family as the church of God; and with Mr. Noyes as a man chosen and inspired of God, to lead and instruct the church in the things pertaining to the kingdom of heaven; and I confess my entire separation from every spirit contrary to this idea.

I ask your prayers for me, that I may seek more earnestly to know the will of God, and submit myself to him in all things.   MARY L. BLOOD.

A NIGHT'S EXPERIENCE IN THE GREEN-HOUSE.

Last night was so very cold, that I had much difficulty in keeping up the usual temperature of the Greenhouse. I labored hard with my fires until past midnight, but without success. The stove in the east part of the house, seemed to have lost all the draft it ever had, and baffled all my efforts. The mercury, at a distance of ten feet from the stove, steadily maintained a downward tendency until it reached 40 deg. above zero. Not liking to be beaten, nor to see the plants frozen, I resolved on desperate measures. So I dumped the fire in the large stove, and built a wood fire. This changed the condition of things at once, and brought the temperature up to the desirable point. I then applied a fresh supply of coal, and at 15 minutes of 2 A. M., having fairly "carried the day," and got things in a shape that I could leave them safely, I gladly retired for the remainder of the morning.   S. W. N.

Mr. Noyes announced to the family this morning, that he should leave us this afternoon. He said two or three days ago, that he did not like to be questioned so much, about *when* he was going, but when he made up his mind to start, he would inform us. We are thankful for his good visit.

Rev. C. A. Hammond from Peterborough, of the Mill's war notoriety, called here yesterday, and staid an hour. He came for the purpose of leaving a book, the 2nd Vol. of Mr. Greeley's "Conflict," for which our people had subscribed. He enquired if we offered the hospitalities of a tavern, to persons who wished to stay with us over night, and intimated that he should like to stay and attend our meeting, and see Mr. Noyes; but Mr. Bolles was pretty cold, and would not understand him.

At W. A. Hinds request, Mr. B. introduced him to Mr. Hammond. W. A. H. wished to probe him a little, about his shameful treatment of us two years ago. Mr. H. said, that what he did for Mills, he did for money,

and finding the atmosphere becoming more and more uncomfortable, and free respiration difficult, he buttoned up his coat and said he must go.

We observed the other morning, some time after daylight, that the lamp, that is placed in the rear of the Mansion House, was still burning, the watchman having failed, as we supposed, to do his duty in extinguishing it, the night before. What made it still more ludicrous was the fact, that the moon shone brightly all night, and not a cloud was visible in the horizon.

Now a lamp is a good thing in its place, but it cannot compete with the light of the sun or of the moon even. Are not the Orthodox churches in something of the same condition with the poor lamp? They try to shine us in the past darkness, but their light is the merest flicker, the brighter rays of the true Gospel, having eclipsed it almost wholly.

We have learned since the above was in type, that the lamp did not burn all night, as we supposed, but was lighted for a particular purpose, toward morning.

When Mr. Noyes commenced his talk on "Spiritual witchood," he requested the family to aid him in his investigations, by writing out what they knew about the loose proceedings of the New York Perfectionists, in the early stage of their experience. Accordingly quite a bundle of such documents were handed in, and, as many of the family wished to hear them read, Mr. Woolworth read a part of them, in the Hall after meeting, last night.

John Smith left this morning. Mr. Noyes spent considerable time with him. He was much interested and threw out, occasionally, obscure hints about connection with us; thinks it would be easy for him to work in, &c.

Quite a stylish company from Munsville, called yesterday, to warm. They were on their way to the depot.

The Thermometer from which we make our daily observations, for sake of convenience hangs on the north side of the Mansion House, which it is said modifies it, in some degree. We have another one, that hangs on the north side of the reservoir, from which the following observations were taken this morning:

5 o'clock 25 deg. below 0.
5¼   "   26   "   "   "
6   "   27   "   "   "
6¼   "   28   "   "   "
7¼   "   30   "   "   " at the fish-pond.
8   "   26   "   "   "

Yesterday's temperature—
7¼ A. M., 3 deg. below 0.
12 M., 0.
6 P. M., 5 deg. below 0.   Mean 2¼.

DAILY JOURNAL
OF ONEIDA COMMUNITY.

VOL. 2.   SATURDAY, DEC. 22, 1866.   NO. 148.

EVENING MEETING.

Mr. Hamilton : In his room before leaving, Mr. Noyes made some remarks about John Smith. He thought it might be profitable to consider his career, and future prospects, as it might be instructive to our young men. What is the result of the course he has taken? He went away from the Community and has had his own way, I suppose, ever since. Mr. Noyes said he was rather smart naturally, and that he had made money and then lost it again, till he is now poor and likely to be. He has been mixed up with things and taken on habits, Mr. Noyes said, that would probably prevent his ever becoming a member of the Community, although he is dropping hints that he thinks he could work in again. Mr. Noyes thought he had lost all religious conscience. He seems to abandon himself to float along on the surface of events, and enjoy himself as he goes, without any effort to be a good man or any hope of becoming one.—Surely the future of our young men is much brighter than his. He tries to treat everything lightly, and in the way of a joke, and pass on through all sorts of experience in an easy manner. He may treat all these things thus lightly and pass them by, but he will find by and by that they won't pass *him* by, for, "Whatsoever a man soweth that shall he reap."

Mr. Woolworth : He is now poor and comes to the Community to improve his means of getting a living by seeking a business connection with us.

W. A. Hinds : What is said of him ought equally well, to apply to the other young men who have left us. His prospects are full as bright, I should think, as those of Leonard Burt, George Hatch and others.

Mr. Woolworth : He made a remark about the children, showing the way he should manage them, or not manage them, and Mr. Noyes thought it a pretty good indication of his practice and life. His remark was that, if he had fifty boys he would try and give them a good education, and then let them take their course. If they wanted to run away, they might, and he should never hinder them. Mr. Noyes thought that was the principle that governed his life, and that it would keep him out of fellowship with us.

It was mentioned that this clique of young men, including John Smith, Leonard Burt, &c., had never become reconciled to the discipline they received while in the Community. This was thought to indicate a small view of life. The wisest man is thankful for all discipline received from his superiors.

*Mr. Burt :—*I wish to express thankfulness for the criticism received last evening. I feel as though what Mr. Noyes said about me was all true. It has been a great relief to me, and I regard it as an answer to prayer. I did not know the nature of my own disease, but I feel that he has clearly pointed it out. I accept every thing he said and wish to take it into my heart.

Thankfulness for Mr. Noyes's visit was expressed, and Mr. Woolworth and others were very hearty in confessing a purpose to help him do the work of God that he is engaged in.

"PROBING."

I fear the remark in yesterday's JOURNAL about my probing Mr. Hammond may convey an incorrect impression. I endeavored to treat him courteously, and, on learning his name, expressed the hope that he was *not* a certain Hammond, who two years since used his pen in behalf of one Mills and against the Community!— That was all the probing I did. He replied that he was the man, but added, by way of apology, that it was simply a business transaction between himself and Mr. Mills— as though the fact that he was paid for the job justified him! As Mr. Bolles afterwards remarked, Judas could have excused himself in the same way; he too, was paid. But never a word was said in reply.   w.

We were quite surprised this morning, to hear that Mr. Noyes came back in the night. The cars being detained at Verona, for some repairs, they were behind time, and finding that they would not connect so that Mr. N. could reach New-York in season to go up to Wallingford to spend Sunday, he got off at Rome, and came back, as he said, "to connect with us." He had concluded to walk up from the depot, when he met James Vaill, who had fortunately gone down after Frederick Marks, and who took Mr. Noyes instead, as Frederick did not come.

It was noticed this morning that the thermometer had risen 60 deg. in the previous twenty-four hours, which "the weatherwise" say, is an unprecedented change in that length of time.

We are expecting Mr. Pitt now every day. He says in his last letter, "I shall be very glad to bid *good bye* to Canada, I assure you."

An order for fruits and vegetables has just been filled, which are to go to England—18 cases.—value $214.00.

Traps ordered the last week,   72 doz.

Yesterday's temperature—
7½ A. M., —2½. 12 M., 4. 6 P. M., 5. Mean —4½.

DAILY JOURNAL
OF ONEIDA COMMUNITY.

VOL. 2.   MONDAY, DEC. 24, 1866.   NO. 149.

NOTES OF BUSINESS MEETING.

R. Hawley, J. C. Higgins, and J. P. Hutchins were appointed a Committee, to investigate the condition of the salt-water vats at the Trap-Shop, and to report what changes, according to their judgment, should be made, in order to stop present leaks, and prevent further waste.

L. F. Dunn, E. L. Hatch and the Financiers, were appointed a Committee to consider the matter of supplying the family with spectacles, and to report their mind as to the best method.   Some of the Board were of the opinion, that considerable deception is practiced by spectacle-peddlers, and that probably the Community interests, in this respect, will never be satisfactorily attended to, until we have a Community Optician, who makes it his special business to attend to the spectacle wants of the Community.

It was voted, as the mind of the Board, that persons who have occasion to drive teams to the barn should never leave them unhitched, and should make sure that they will be properly cared for, even if this involves their going to the hostler's house; and, still further, the Board recommend that the smaller class of boys should not be invited to drive teams to the barn.

To H. T. Clark, Geo. W. Hamilton and W. R. Inslee, was referred the subject of making patterns for casting three kinds of stoves, most commonly used in the Community. We have now over one hundred stoves, and much expense would be saved if we could cast such parts of stoves as often need replacing; and if we could cast the entire stoves we might supply ourselves and dealers in the neighboring villages.

We at the Printing Office, are sometimes placed in rather an embarrassing position, by our folks inviting strangers into the Office. If visitors call, they must be told that we print a Daily, and the next thing is, they want to see it, or if they see them lying on the table or shelf, they are free to take them up and read them.— Sometimes, to be sure, we should have no objection to their doing it, but it is not always so. Would it not be better, if it is considered necessary to invite persons who are unacquainted with us, into the Office, to let us know beforehand, that the JOURNALS may be put out of the way.

It was reported to us, yesterday, that Mr. John Kinsley, who is sixty-nine years old, has, since last spring, with the exception of two days and a half, been over to Willow Place every day, Sundays excepted, and worked as many hours in the shop as the other hands. This he has done cheerfully and heartily, and he enjoys his work very much. His labors are highly appreciated, as is also his society and humorous companionship in the shop.—We heard it suggested, that he be invited to spend the Holidays at home, to study and recreate.

The Students in Theology, have, by a unanimous vote of the class, changed their Programme, somewhat.— Volunteers for singing can, if they choose, invite some one to sing with them, and, instead of questions and answers from the Berean, as has been the practice, one individual is to read and explain a part of the lesson, then another; each one occupying a limited space of time; the whole performance subject to the criticism of the class. A large number volunteered their services, to sing and also to read and expound.

There was quite a scene occurred in the kitchen Saturday. Some one observed Mrs. Bristol fingering round one of the posts and trying to hold on in a singular way. At length her efforts failed her, and she fell backward, Mrs. A. S. Burnham catching her in her arms: she had fainted. She was carried into the open air, where she soon recovered. She had not been very well, for a day or two, but she is about the house as usual, to-day.

Mr. Porter's oldest son spent Sunday with us. He is a young man about seventeen or eighteen years old, we should judge. He is engaged in some Printing Office in Canastota, and his mother says, he is a young man of excellent habits.

We have a sudden change in the weather. The warm south wind and rain of yesterday, has melted off the snow, and the ground is again bare.

Mr. Hall was out on a peddling trip last week, and brought home about $300—the avails of his sales.

W. G. Kelly and F. A. Marks came home yesterday morning.

Temperature Saturday and Sunday,
7½ A. M., 28.   12 M., 36.   6 P. M., 35.   Mean 33.
7½ A. M., 39.   12 M., 43.   6 P. M., 42.   Mean 41½.

DAILY JOURNAL
OF ONEIDA COMMUNITY.

VOL. 2.   TUESDAY, DEC. 25, 1866.   NO. 150.

To the Community.

I want to give thanks to God publicly for restoring me to health again. I was seized with a violent attack of cold and fever, which threatened to become serious. I was determined not to give way to it, nor be deprived of the privilege of work, class or meetings, while Mr. Noyes was here, and I kept the resolution until I fainted. But now I want to begin with new energy and purpose, to be a helper to Mr. Noyes, in a small way if I cannot in a larger one; although I should very much prefer to become qualified, to be a helper in every good word and work.   DELIGHT BRISTOL.

Mr. Clark saw Mr. Carr at the depot one day last week, and had some talk with him. Mr. Clark asked him if he was on his way West to peddle silk? Carr said no, he was going to his brothers; that the game of silk-peddling at the West was played out with him, as our people sell lower than he could afford to. Mr. C. said to him, it is natural for *you* to make money, anywhere; " But I didn't though," said he, in reply, " sixteen years, not for myself." He asked a good many questions about the Community, the Agency, &c., how business was with us, and if " Noyes" was here? Mr. Clark said he was so disgusted with the disrespectful way in which he spoke of Mr. Noyes, that he quit talking with him, and came away.

Myron Kinsley and Homer Barron, while making out their inventory, last night, in Mrs. Jane Kinsley's room, upset the swing table on which they were writing, and precipitated ink, paper and lamp to the carpet. The lamp was not broken, but the oil and ink intermixed ran over the carpet. Quick as thought, some milk was procured, and the unpleasant mixture washed from the carpet. The oil spot was removed by passing a hot iron over it, and when Mrs. Kinsley, who was absent during the catastrophe, returned, scarcely any trace of the accident remained.

Christmas dawns upon the world bright and mild.—The little children hung up their stockings, as they usually do, and though Santaclaus was rather sparing of his gifts, yet the little that he did contribute, afforded immense satisfaction to the little ones, quite as much so, we thought, as more elaborate gifts.

Our people have bought over three hundred saw-logs on West Hill, and during the few days of good sleighing we had last week, seventy-one of them were drawn to the saw-mill. One or two teams are engaged now, in drawing, on wheels, our cedar stakes from Wampsville.

Our new tailor gives good satisfaction, both in making and fitting. His wife and little girl have been absent two weeks, at Port Byron. We have been told that their house is nearly ready for them.

Committee of arrangement for Mr. Frobisher's visit, Mr. Woolworth, R. S. Delatre, S. K. Dunn and H. C. Noyes. Mr. F. and J. R. Lord have just arrived.

Some of our hired help are keeping Christmas. All the girls at the Silk Factory are absent, and three of the girls in the ironing room, we observe, are missing.

871 tons of coarse coal were consumed by the Community last year, and thirty tons of a different kind, at the blacksmith's shop.

Mrs. Vaavelzer is mother in the kitchen, which the hands that work there, consider quite a treat.

Yesterday's temperature—
7½ A. M., 43. 12 M., 44. 6 P. M., 36. Mean 41.

DAILY JOURNAL
OF ONEIDA COMMUNITY.

VOL. 2. WEDNESDAY, DEC. 26, 1866. NO. 151.

EVENING MEETING.

Mr. Noyes: It appears from an item in the CIRCULAR arrived to-day, that Mr. Dixon won't have the benefit of our investigations in this book he is about to publish, for that is to come out the 1st of January. He wrote to me for information that I supposed was going to be put into that book; and I have been at work partly to get the necessary information, and expected to write to him soon. I suppose it will be of no service to him now, unless he is going to publish another book. But I acknowledge it has been a great benefit to me, to study old fashioned Perfectionism and the various sects that have been concerned in what we might call the great revolution of the past thirty years.

I hope the spirit of historical investigation will get working among us finally, in a thorough and effectual way, and that each one will get in the practice of studying his own history. I don't know but it would be good for every one to be preparing to write his own history, for the benefit of himself at least. It would be very beneficial to us to study our own lives and understand them; and besides the benefit to ourselves, there is nothing so interesting as autobiography. If we want to provide matter for an interesting paper there is no better way than to study our own lives and get ready to tell the story. Nobody can tell a person's story so well as he can do it himself, if he is honest and simple-hearted: for he knows his own story better than anybody else.—There is no life so barren, that a respectable novel could not be made of it.

Mr. Woolworth:—I can readily believe there is an immense amount of material of this kind that might be made very interesting. I have an idea that Mr. Kinsley here, will have an interesting story to tell sometime, and I don't know how many others there are.

W. A. H:—It is quite a laudable ambition for us all, to be able to write interesting stories of our lives. Mr. Noyes has remarked that a thing was not done, till reported. I don't know why that principle should not apply to one's life. It seems to me the daily papers of the world, might be made much more interesting, if partly filled with good stories of men's lives, than when filled with accounts of wickedness and political squabbles as at present.

Mr. Noyes:—Don't you believe the time will come when true stories will be told, that will be far more interesting than the novels that are being written that the papers are so full of?

Mr. Woolworth:—The most interesting novels are those which approximate nearest to autobiography, of which "Jane Eyre" is one of the best specimens.

Mr. Noyes:—It seems to me like labor thrown away, to invent stories, when far more interesting stories might be found in real life. Where would you find anything in a novel, half so interesting as Mr. Cragin's "Story of a life?" The fact that you know those things actually took place, nearly doubles the interest, while the story itself would compare well with anything you would find in the novels. I should hope the actual rehearsal of the lives of men and women would become a substitute for novels. When men and women become honest enough to tell the whole truth, and have good taste and rhetoric enough to sieze the true points of interest and tell the story in good style, it seems to me novel writing and reading will go out of use.

Mr. Noyes:—I am glad to express my pleasure at the entertainment we have had here this evening. I think the whole family will be benefited by merely seeing graceful action and hearing correct speaking. Those that do not take part in the daily drills may be benefited by looking on.—Others expressed much satisfaction with Prof. Frobisher's performance.

Prof. Frobisher met a class yesterday in the Hall, composed mostly of young women, and drilled them an hour, in the elementary exercises of Elocution; but, as we were not present, we cannot describe the *modus operandi.* At 7 o'clock in the evening, all the family assembled in the Hall, to listen to the reading and recitations of the Professor, some of which were comic and caused a good deal of laughter. The exhibition he gave us of ventriloquism, shows to what the human voice can be trained, and his elucidation of "the way he did it," was quite satisfactory. On the whole, his stay with us opens rich. To-day, a class of men meet at 9 o'clock A. M., and a class of women at 10½ o'clock for drilling, and both are to take lessons again in the afternoon. The exercises for the evening will be the same as those of last night.

Mrs. Loomis took the stage yesterday afternoon, for Hamilton, to visit a sick brother.—Mrs. Langstaff returned home day before yesterday.

Yesterday's temperature—
7½ A. M., 31. 13 M., 32. 6 P. M., 30. Mean 31.

DAILY JOURNAL
OF ONEIDA COMMUNITY.

VOL. 2.   THURSDAY, DEC. 27, 1866.   NO. 152.

We were all very much surprised and highly entertained with a song, sung at the close of the meeting
last night. The solo was performed by Abram, and the
chorus by G. W. H., E. S. B., E. P. I., and C. A.
Burt, with piano accompaniment by Miss. Annie M.
Hatch. Where the song came from was at first quite a
a mystery; but it was at length whispered round, that it
was not designed for Oneida, but was purloined or taken
stealthily from the brothers at Moffat Abbey, by a
certain gentleman who has mixed freely in their circle.
However that may be, the music was Oneida's own,
improvised for the occasion; and although we are not
sure, but we shall be the losers, nevertheless Oneida
generously proposes to exchange "notes" [musical] with
the New-York brethren, at their earliest convenience.
The following are the verses in question:

I.

In a city old, where the white winged ships
   Came sailing from over the seas,
'Mid the rustling crowd far away from the sound
   Of birds and flowers and trees,
Stood an Abbey gray, where a race of monks
   Lived a holy life of rest.
They ate their bread and sang their hymns
   And harbored the distressed.

> Alas! where have the good monks gone!
>   Their Abbey is dreary and still;
> One winter's night they sped away
>   When the wind was blowing chill

II.

They bought and sold for their Church's weal,
   And stored their minds with lore;
They loved with more than woman's love:
   Each other's burdens bore.
They said, who saw their cheerful mien,
   "These, drink from hidden wells;
Their joys, are joys we know not of,
   This love, God's heaven foretells."

> Alas! where, &c.

III.

In a sunny vale where the flowers in spring
   Came earliest in the wood,
On a green hillside was a cloister old,
   The home of a sisterhood.
As purely their lowly life flowed on,
   From care and sorrow free
As the river, which under the willows ran
   Its winding way to the sea.

> Alas! where; &c.

IV.

One night a sound of mirth was heard
   From the cloister's olden walls;
The manly voice and the silvery laugh
   Resounded through it's halls.
With the swelling hymn and earnest prayer
   For the strength and will to do
Their Father's work, and to be for aye,
   Brothers and sisters true.

> O! there is where the monks have gone,
>   Their Abbey is dreary and still;
> But with life and love they're coming back,
>   Its tower once more to fill.

The men's Elocution class, went out on the lawn,
last night, for their vocal exercise, so as to have plenty
of fresh air. Mr. Henderson, who was just starting for
home from Willow-Place, at the time, heard a singular
noise, and on listening, he came to the conclusion that
it was a pack of dogs. But what could they find to
bark at? As he walked on and the noise became more
distinct, he found it was not the barking of dogs: what
was it? Before reaching home however, he divined
from whence the noise proceeded—that it was neither
more nor less, than the explosive power of forty or fifty
healthy lungs, well inflated.

We have tried to get some one who was better gifted
in the art of reporting, than ourselves, to draw a life-like
picture of our 7 o'clock entertainment last night, but as
we have failed to get help, we shall be obliged to refer
Wallingford to the band of brethren, who have so long
sat under Prof. Frobisher's instruction. The most of
our employees were present to enjoy the treat.

For some time past we have had three carnation pinks
in bloom, that have been quite a source of pleasure to
those of the family, who call at the Green-house. Sometime between yesterday noon and this morning, one of
them disappeared. Now, though, I do not feel like criticising any one for picking it, yet I would suggest to
them whether it would not after all, really afford them
more satisfaction to have it where *all* the family could
enjoy it, than to appropriate it to their own private gratification. We think it would.   S. W. N.

It snows finely this morning and the prospect of good
sleighing brightens.

Mr. Noyes's letter to Mr. Dixon was read last night.

Yesterday's temperature—
7½ A. M., 23.   12 M., 30.   6 P. M., 31.   Mean 28.

DAILY JOURNAL

OF ONEIDA COMMUNITY.

VOL. 2.　　FRIDAY, DEC. 28, 1866.　　NO. 153.

The classes for study have for a few days past, occupied the back ground in the picture of Oneida life, and
conspicuous in their place, stands physical science, particularly the cultivation and improvement of the vocal
organs. On account of both the teacher and a part of the
pupils, being engaged in taking our annual inventory
W. A. Hind's school is having a week's vacation.—
Other classes too, have only met at irregular intervals;
but we expect after this week, that things will settle
back into their accustomed channel, and the appetite
for study will be only the keener, for this temporary
check.

We have had a very blustering night, and the snow
that we thought yesterday, was going to afford us such
fine sleighing, is to-day all in drifts.—Our people started
for Willow-Place this morning and went as far as Mr.
Hubbard's, and were then obliged to turn back, as they
could get no further.—Prof. Frobisher expected to leave
us to-day, but it seems now, doubtful whether he will be
able to do so on account of the blustering storm and drifts.

When Mrs. Langstaff went to Camillus she lost her
shawl, having left it on the cars when she got off at
Syracuse. Homer was requested to try to find it, but
he did not know to what place to send a telegram.—
At length Homer talked with the man who has charge
of the baggage on that line, and engaged him to try to
look up the shawl; last Monday morning, to his surprise
it was handed him, the baggage man having been
faithful to his promise. Homer said he was so thankful to
find, in this benighted world, one honest man, that he
gave him $1.50 for his trouble.

Mrs. Sears and I have put up new curtains in the
Green-house, lately. The old one had become so completely rotten, worn and torn, as to be nearly useless.—
It covered nearly the whole of the south roof of the
wing and was all in one piece, so that if we used any
part of it we must use the whole. For convenience
sake, the new ones are put up in three sections, so that
if we wish to shade one portion of the house, or protect
it from cold, we can do so without darkening the whole.
We think we shall like this arrangement much better
than the old one.　　　　　　　　　　　　　s. w. n.

The class of women that Prof. Frobisher has drilled
in the use and intonation of the voice, is not far from
twenty-five, and the men's class numbers about thirty.—
Pro. F. gave us last night, readings from Shakspeare,
intermixed with humorous, and comic recitations. The

family proffered him a vote of thanks for his untiring
labors while here. His stay with us has been very
pleasant, and we trust profitable to us all.

J. H. Barron went to the depot last Tuesday, and
sending his team back, he staid there all day and settled
up accounts with fourteen men. He reports that he received orders at the depot in one week, for $86 worth of
bags, and $32 worth of silk. Besides this, he sold to a
grocer who has recently moved in there, $41 worth of
Preserved Fruit.

The two last notes that we owed the Bank were paid
yesterday, though they were not either of them due.
At one time during the press of the Fruit-Preserving
business in the fall, our liabilities at the Bank amounted
to $9600.

Mr. Noyes's talk about Gerritt Smith, last night, will
be read with much interest.

Just as we are going to press, 12 M., who should
make his appearance, but our long absent brother T. L.
Pitt. He must surely have been borne to us on the
wings of the wind.

Yesterday's temperature—
7½ A. M., 29.　12 M., 30.　6 P. M., 28.　Mean 29.

DAILY JOURNAL
OF ONEIDA COMMUNITY.

VOL. 2.　　SATURDAY, DEO. 29, 1866.　　NO. 154

Mr. Frobisher left yesterday afternoon, notwithstanding the snow and drifts. We were informed, that in meeting with his classes, by his suggestion, two or three from each class, whom they thought the most competent, were selected to take the lead. He advised them to continue their exercises—to go on and perfect themselves in the art of Elocution.

Mr. F. manifested some surprise at seeing such unmistakable evidence of our prosperity, and expressed a wish to J. R. L., to read some of our publications, that he might become better informed about us. J. R. L. handed him the Oct. No. of the Phrenological Journal, and pointed out the article relating to Mr. Noyes and the Community, for him to read. He also read "Conversation with a visitor," and asked for "Male Continence," which J. R. L. gave him. He seemed quite pleased with the "Daily Journal," and wanted a copy to send home to his wife. He came into the Printing Office and made himself quite at home. He thought it would be nice if he could have a Printing-press in his own house, and do his own printing—said he should like to learn to set type &c. J. R. L. said he thought his visit here would set him to thinking, and perhaps lead to a thorough investigation of our doctrines.

The truth brought out by Mr. Noyes last evening, met with a hearty response in my heart. While on the one hand I felt criticised, and seriously so, on the other, it seemed like a star of hope. Can any sacrifice be too great for us women to make, that will bring us into true relation to *man?* I think not.

In reflecting on the subject, I had an earnest desire to give my attention to it; and I believe it can be done in the same way that we concentrate our minds upon any difficult problem in Algebra or Geometry, thereby "seeing through it." By so doing, the truth will work in us like leaven and purge us from all obstructions to being true help-meets to the men. I confess Christ my sufficiency in this matter.　　　　S. B. C.

It still snows, though the wind has subsided. Some of the men made their way over to Willow-Place through the lots in the afternoon, yesterday, on foot, but the principal part of the hands enjoyed a nice holiday at home. The great business of to-day is shoveling snow and breaking roads. Three or four teams with ten or a dozen men are breaking roads to Willow-Place. The drift between Mr. Hamilton's door and the Piazza was so high, that Mr. H. dug a hole through, forming an arch of snow above. They say Mr. H. has been through

it, but we opine that he had to stoop *considerably low* to do it.

Mr. Noyes talk to, and criticism of, the women in the Community, made a deep impression upon us, which we sincerely hope may not be lost. We certainly desire above every thing else, to become thoroughly organized into Mr. Noyes's spirit, that his life may circulate freely through us, making us more efficient helpers, and co-laborers with him than we have been in the past.

DEAR FRIENDS:—I thank God for the victory he has given me through Christ, over a certain characteristic of the old life, which I have had to contend with in the past. The sight or knowledge of this victory, brought with it hope or assurance of overcoming what I have to contend with now, for which also, through Christ, I thank him.

W. JONES.

Traps ordered the past week,　　　　　94 doz
The principal order was—
Patrick & Co., New-York,　　　　　48 "
mainly of the large sizes, for the California trade.

Yesterday's temperature—
7½ A. M., 16.　12 M., 20.　6 P. M., 15.　Mean 20½.

DAILY JOURNAL
OF ONEIDA COMMUNITY.

VOL. 2.   MONDAY, DEC. 31, 1866.   NO. 155.

EVENING MEETING.

Mr. V. testified that a thorough self-examination had revealed the fact that he had been badly affected by the "old granny" spirit. A sort of impotence and stupidity overshadowed him, making him go to sleep in meeting, in the midst of interesting discussions. It seemed like a night-mare to him. He was troubled too with forgetfulness, and the feeling that he was getting old, though in spirit he felt as young as he did thirty years ago. He wanted to expose this spirit and offer himself to the family to be cured of all tendencies in this direction.

Mr. V.'s remarks raised a regular insurrection against the principality of sleepiness that has troubled so many in the meeting. Persons confessed a purpose to be separated from weakness of every form. J. P. H. wished to publicly announce his resolution, made some time ago, to become a good business man and a good student. He had felt blessed since forming such a purpose. Joining in the general testimony Mr. Hamilton said : I have found in my experience in writing in the Office that I could work a great deal easier after getting warmed up with a purpose to do all I could in a given time. I found to sit down and work in a moderate way would tire me ; but when I would get warmed up with some resolution I could do a great deal more, and not get into this dull sleepy state. That is also true of my experience about a great many things. In order to work easily and keep out from under this sleepy, stupid spirit, I have to get warmed up, and have my whole soul awake and enlisted. I thought that was one trouble persons have in their religious experience : they are not more than half awake, and do not work easily. It is easier to be real manly, whole-souled and energetic, than it is to try to get along in a half-awake, sleepy, shadowy state. I noticed Professor Frobisher is very earnest to get persons warmed up, and have them speak not only with their lips, but with their whole body and spirit. He wants them to speak so that every fiber of the body will take part. Take the old comparison Mr. Noyes has used about the ships, and we find every thing works best when we are under headway. It is hard work to do things when there is no headway. I liked John Hutchin's testimony. I think an inspired purpose of that kind, which puts your own spirit in union with God, will help you to dodge a great many evils and temptations. A mere resolution of the will would not be worth much ; but a real inspired purpose would strike right against this sleepy spirit. Perhaps the difficulty with these persons who are so sleepy is, that they have not got warmed up with some good purpose. I have noticed in my experience that I have most trouble with this sleepy spirit in the afternoon after eating dinner, generally along about two or three o'clock. If I get really enlisted in some enterprise, and well warmed up, I can get over that bar and not be disturbed ; but if I am rather listless, and not under the influence of some purpose, I am apt to have trouble with this spirit about that time of day.

Mr. Noyes:—Probably we are not aware how much of that influence comes from the world and the general mass of men that we are in one way or another connected with. We do not entirely clear ourselves from the influence of the world so but that it works upon us. Now I notice the sleepy spirit comes on, as Mr. Hamilton says, after eating dinner. It comes just the same whether I have eaten much or little. It does not seem to depend on the amount eaten. If you fast it will come. Why is it ? That is the time when the whole population of the nation around us and the world have stuffed themselves, and the great overshadowing spirit of sensuality and stupidity is taking a soak. It settles down upon and works in us. What leads me to think so is, that while it is true that this spirit comes on generally after eating our dinner, it is also true that it comes very especially on Sunday. Sunday is the sleepiest day in the week. There is no reason why it should be so with me, for my habits are the same on Sunday as any other day. There in Connecticut I used to feel that Sunday was a stupid, sleepy, sensual day as regular as it came. I am getting out of it some now. I reckon it is an indisputable fact that the listlessness, laziness and sensuality of the Sunday experience of the mass of people around affects us. We must get our eyes to see this clearly, and then not be discouraged and condemn ourselves for it, but turn our faces toward Christ, and expect he will help us to overcome this great principality, and that he will expel this disease—for it really is a disease—out from among us, and from the people around us, through us ; just as he is expelling the cholera and diphtheria.

I don't suppose that Mr. V., for instance, is personally responsible for the feelings he has. The probability is that the great spirit of old age, working in every body and all around every where, is at work on him, trying to chew him up and digest him ; and it will chew him up and digest him if he does not find a way to get into partnership with Christ and set going a counter power that is stronger than the devil himself.

The schools and classes resume their studies to-day.

Mr. Noyes and Burt left for Wallingford in the night.

Temperature Saturday and Sunday,
7½ A. M., 12.   12 M., 21.   6 P. M., 18.
7½ A. M., 20.   12 M., 30.   6 P. M., 20.

END OF VOLUME SECOND.

DAILY JOURNAL

OF ONEIDA COMMUNITY.

VOL. 3. TUESDAY, JAN. 1, 1867. NO. 1.

In addition to what was reported of Mr. Hamilton's talk the other evening, the following remarks, which we consider very interesting, were omitted:

"I like to think of Christ's expression, where he says, 'I have come that they may have life and that they may have it more abundantly.' I believe Christ's influence begets manliness and resolution to attempt things. It gives control over ourselves, and awakens a desire for righteousness." * * * * *

"I was thinking the Lord had given us a pretty good holiday present this year. So far as outward things are concerned we have had a treat in Prof. Frobisher. We gave him a vote of thanks; and now I don't know but we had better move a vote of thanks to Mr. Noyes for bringing him here. [Approved.] We have had a better treat here for three evenings running than the entertainments they get up at the depot could furnish, I dare say. Then it has been instructive withal, and will give us a good lift on the very point where we need help. If we are chaste and do not look outward toward the world, I believe we shall find that the Lord will give us entertainments, as in this instance, and do better by us than we can ask or think." [We might add, that we consider it a greater treat, after all, to have had Mr. Noyes here, and to listen to the rich talks he has given us.]

———◆———

H. G. Allen writes:

"Have just called on Whital, Tatum & Co. They have agreed to accept our order for 75 gross of quart fruit bottles at $11.50 net per gross, to be delivered at Ithica Line Canal Boats about May 1st. Terms cash, payable thirty days from date of shipment. We are free to duplicate the order within two or three months, if they do not stop their blast before that time."

"Am pleased to note the *marked* improvement in the appearance of notes and orders received of late from C. Vanvelzer and also his father. Charles has *greatly* improved."

"The silk Inventory received from O. C. yesterday, will add about $500 to the earnings of our silk business for 1836. It will make the profits of the business over and above the expenses of Agents over $9000. All things considered, our showing is as well as could be expected, and we feel that the Lord has blessed us in temporal as well as spiritual things."

A party from Munnsville called here last evening during the meeting hour. They said they were out on a New-Year's ride. On being told that we did not like to entertain company at that hour, they expressed their regret that they had intruded.

———◆———

I.

The Community "Life Boat," one twelve month ago,
Was locked in fierce fight, with a desperate foe;
And a Financial storm, with its threatning wave,
Essayed to engulf her, in one common grave.

II.

But brave men stood manfully firm in that hour,
And with faith in their hearts, they defied all the
    power
Of the devil, the vessel to sink or to shatter,
The crew to unman, or their forces to scatter.

III.

The *cause* of this terrible gale was then sought,
And the "Jonah," who on them this tempest had
    brought,
Was into the turbulent element cast,
When, lo! every vestige of danger is past;
And the vessel, relieved from the weight that op-
    pressed,
Is speedily moored in a Haven of rest.

IV.

So the year sixty-six, with its victories bright,
We will gratefully cheer, as it fades from our sight,
And the new one we greet, as its dawnings appear,
And heartily wish all, "A Happy New-Year."

Capt. W. Bridgman who is commander of the Steam Ship, City of Cork, and Thomas Rice, M. D., Surgeon of the ship, in company with P. J. M. McQuade, and several others from Utica and New-York, made us a call yesterday. The Capt. remarked that being longer in port than usual, they were improving the opportunity to enjoy the Holidays. He is a relative of Ex Mayor McQuade (whose son was of the party), and was making a visit at Utica. He says he has seen our fruit in England. He and the surgeon reside at Liverpool. They went through the house and to the Store to look at the Fruit, Traps and Bags, and expressed much gratification. They said they hoped to come again in the Summer.

———◆———

We enter upon the New-Year with thankful hearts and with a renewed purpose to surrender our whole being to God and to Mr. Noyes, to serve cheerfully to the best of our ability, in any place to which we may be called.

———◆———

Not much work is being done at Willow-Place yesterday and to-day, as our hired hands are, the most of them, keeping New-Years. The ironing-girls too, are all of them absent to-day.

———◆———

The day is very mild and pleasant and the sleighing very good.

———◆———

Temperature Saturday and Sunday,
7½ A. M., 7. 12 M., 21. 6 P. M., 20. Mean 17.

DAILY JOURNAL
OF ONEIDA COMMUNITY.

VOL. 3.   WEDNESDAY, JAN. 2, 1867.   NO. 2.

We give below, some extracts from a letter Mrs. Bushnell received from a young man by the name of Warne, of Fort Madison, Iowa. Mr. W. was studying to become a Baptist preacher, and during his vacation last summer, he went to Bath and taught school, and boarded at Mr. Bushnell's. He became so much interested in our doctrines, that he relinquished all thought of the ministry, and gave his ecclesiastical friends to understand the *cause* of the change in his life-programme.

"I have not forgotten your many kindnesses, nor the many pleasant readings of the Berean, and our long conversations upon vital themes connected with the christian hope. No! such an experience as that of mine in Bath is not one that could be faintly remembered. It was an epoch in my life, and its influence will be engraven upon my nature forever.

"I doubt if you ever saw so much of the inner life of a young man before; for I was frank and open with you, as I have been with few. I had the feeling that God had brought me to your house, and I desired to have the temper and teachableness of a child, in the way of truth. Such a disposition of mind I certainly had sometimes, though many of my spiritual exercises were not those of a child.

"It will interest you to know, that when I was in New York I hunted up Moffat Abbey. It gave me pleasure to see some originals of photographs in your album and several besides. They seemed pleasant, quiet, undemonstrative sort of men, attending to their business like other folks;—nothing monkish, certainly. I obtained the CIRCULAR three or four different times, calling for it every week. Of course with my unfortunately reserved manners I made no progress in acquaintance, though I had brief conversations with several. Once I saw Mr. Noyes; would have liked to converse with him, but didn't. I sent on for the CIRCULAR as soon as I came to this place and thus have kept up the connection of interest unbroken.

"I have taken up the Berean again and have read it with new interest. How often you are brought to mind in reading it. I continue in the confession of Christ, but can give you no idea of the spiritual conflict I have passed through in the last two months; darkness and tempest have enveloped and swept around me, and it seemed as though the evil one had taken complete possession of me as of Job, and my mouth has been smitten dumb in my trouble.—It may be I need to pass through all this, to shake to their foundations, the huge structures of lifeless beliefs, built by wrong teaching and thinking, upon my heart. I am constitutionally greatly averse to change, and my conscientiousness, I mistrust, is in league with an evil spirit often, barring any advance on my part to true freedom.—For some days past, however, a calmer state has come over me, and I feel more quiet trust in the work of God within me. I wish to be rid of all disposition to cling to dead formulas, and to hold to nothing but the living truth, to be able to say I *know* in whom, and in what, I have believed."

———————

Mr. Hatch presented last night, the older class of boys under his charge, for criticism. He thought they needed the help of others besides himself. He could see many things in which they had improved during the past year. They were very studious. On the other hand they were not very faithful in doing their chores, and frequently got into little difficulties among themselves and with other persons. He looks to George Henry for help and sympathy, more than to any other one, but for some reason he does not get it. He liked Arthur and Lorenzo better. It was thought the young men should search themselves and see that their influence on the boys was good. It was believed that some of them had helped to foster this hard state George Henry is in.—Considerable talk and criticism followed which we have not room to report.

———————

We had a visit yesterday from an old man with "a mission," an infidel preacher of the genus, vagabond. He gave his name as "Walter of Greenburg." He goes about the country hauling a hand cart—preaching that there is no personal God—that he was born into the truth eight years ago and knows all truth, and that truth is God—that it is wrong to use money, buy, sell or pay taxes &c. After ventilating his views, as he showed no signs of moving on, he was told that we could not keep him; but he insisted upon staying, as he did not know *where* to stay. He was offered fifty cents to pay for his lodging, but this he refused, as conscience would not allow him to handle money. Upon this, as all other means to get rid of him had failed, and as his odor and filthy looks disqualified him for any bed we had, he was told flatly to take his things and "budge," which he did. Mr. Skinner will perhaps remember his calling here some years ago, under the name, Vandusen.

———————

The classes for Elocution are fairly organized. The men and women have two classes each; the latter meet only once a week, Sunday—while the men hold their sessions every other night, for the present. We are told that a good deal of enthusiasm prevails, in all the classes to become good readers and speakers.

———————

Mrs. Ellis is in her eighty-fifth year, and she told us yesterday, that she had not been absent once, from the evening meetings for more than a year.

———————

Yesterday's temperature—
7½ A. M., 27. 12 M., 32. 6 P. M., 28. Mean 29

DAILY JOURNAL
OF ONEIDA COMMUNITY.

VOL. 3.   THURSDAY, JAN. 3, 1867.   NO. 3.

ANNUAL INVENTORY.

Net Profit at O. C. in 1866,	$17396.86.
" " " Agency Branch in 1866,	1222.95.
	18619.81.
Expense more than Income at W. C. " "	5421.07.
Net Profits of United Communes, " "	$13198.74.

The increase of Capital has exceeded the profits, as more capital has been received from new members than has been abstracted by seceders, and there has also been added $3300, not included in previous inventories on account of unavailability; so that the Capital now stands:

Capital Inventoried at O. C.,	$247319.92.
" " " Agency Branch,	8313.72.
" " " W. C.,	30184.56.
	$285848.20.
Total Inventoried Jan. 1, 1866.,	267681.71.
Increase of Capital,	$18166.49.

It should be mentioned, in this connection, that the Agency books indicate a gain for the past year of $2378.88, and record the present capital as $9499.65. The discrepancy between their books and our Inventory is accounted for by the fact, that we have preferred not to include in our estimate an account of $1155.03, which stands on the Agency books.—It should also be understood that in estimating the gain at the Agency the manifold services of the Agency brethren for the other Communes have not been considered. If only moderate charges had been made for these, their annual exhibit would have been greatly improved.

The capital inventoried at Oneida includes the New Haven property; but the expenses of that station are included in the expenses of the Wallingford Community.

The expenses of O. C. the past year for clothing, food, and many other things, have been greater than they were last season, partly on account of high prices, and partly on account of improved fare.

The incomes of the principal business at O. C. for the past year have been:

Horticultural, including Strawberries,	$3501.24.
Farm, Dairy and Teaming,	7332.97.
Bag-Making,	2033.89.
Fruit-Preserving,	13442.32.
Trap-Making,	10792.78.
Foundry and Saw-Mill,	2190.20.

In estimating the profits of different businesses the labor of our own people is not considered.

The profits of the Bag Department in 1865 were $9835.20, nearly five times what they have been the past year, and the profits of Trap Business in 1865 were $18266.43, nearly as much as they have been the past year, although the Trap sales in 1866 greatly exceeded those of 1865. These results are accounted for, in some measures, by the new policy, inaugurated last spring of low prices and small profits; it will, however, doubtless prove our best policy in the end.

It will be noticed that, the income of the Wilson Property, (Foundry and Saw-Mill), has been more than one-third of its original cost.

The profits of the Fruit-Preserving Department in 1866 tell a good story, when the losses on Corn and Pea are taken into account.   W.

EVENING MEETING.

The Inventory being read, W. A. Hinds observed: "I think we have reason to be thankful for this showing.—Perhaps it is not all some might wish, but taking everything into account, our expenses here, with those at Wallingford and New Haven, of the educational and publishing departments, the Communities, it appears to me, have much occasion for gratitude.

Mr. Hamilton joined in this and then said: "In reflecting on this subject of our business, I compare it to the human body. Money, in one sense, is like the blood in the body. I am not very much of a physiologist; but I believe the blood is mainly manufactured by the stomach. I don't think it is God's purpose to make us immensely rich, in the sense that a great many men and companies in the world are. I cannot think God cares much about having a great deal of unemployed capital. I believe his purpose is to make us strong and rich in the sense that we shall have a great deal of property invested. We have now got over a quarter of a million.—Our ambition should be to have capital enough to enable us to carry on our business to good advantage. God wants we should have money enough in the treasury to supply all demands—to serve as blood. It seems to me that individuals and corporations, when they begin to amass property that does not play an important part in their business, and in their moral influence in society, are like persons who are getting a big, overgrown belly. Now a man does not want to carry round a larger belly than is necessary to help furnish all the blood he wants. I should think from all I hear that the Shakers are potbellied. They are immensely rich, but this wealth does but little good in society. I like to be in good condition and see others so, and I am ambitious to see the Community grow strong and acquire a great deal of power, but I don't believe God purposes to have us become potbellied.

"It is a comfort to me to think that we have a man like Mr. Noyes, who is governed by God, and who has led us on in this way, printing the paper and giving Christ a medium, and sending the young men to school. Our business has answered the purpose of healthy circulation and education. It has not hurt us, but been just what we wanted the past summer.—I feel faith growing in my heart that the capital accumulated in the world is going to be available in the kingdom of heaven. In one sense, we need not feel that we have got to earn our living. My faith is growing, that we shall have all the money we want for education and the development of our organization. If we devote ourselves to God we shall live like the birds. We do not love fat but good muscle and healthy development. I believe we shall have that. We shall have capital enough, to become a useful and powerful business organization in the world."

Yesterday's temperature—
7½ A. M., 17.   12 M., 32.   6 P. M., 11.   Mean 20.

DAILY JOURNAL
OF ONEIDA COMMUNITY.

VOL. 3. **FRIDAY, JAN. 4, 1867.** NO. 4

A WINTER LANDSCAPE.

Our " West hill" presented this morning a scene of enchantment. The sun was welcomed by a cloudless sky, and an atmosphere crisp and transparent; and as he threw his first oblique rays upon the western hill with its varied and snow-enameled surface, the effect was magical and bewitching. All the prominences of the hill-side caught the roseate hues from the beams of old, faithful, genial King Sol, and reveled for a brief space in all the beauty and witchery that art and imagination have given to the land of the fairies. The shadows that were thrown into the dimples and depressions of the hill-side, brightened as ever the effect and beauty of the scene.

The forest trees that range along the hill-top, and form groups in the slope, reflected a richer and warmer light, and contrasted charmingly with the more delicately rose-tinted features of the picture. It seemed as though every dormant bud of the forest stirred with a premonition of returning Spring.—One section with its broken billowy surface, lying in alternate light and shade, became, with very little aid of fancy, a miniature ocean swelling and rolling from the effects of a recent storm. Who would not hesitate thought I, in view of such a scene, before exchanging our northern latitude for tropical climes.　　　　H.

" A soft answer turneth away wrath." The following correspondence will illustrate this truth :

Columbus, Ohio, Dec. 14, 1866.

MESSRS. OF ONEIDA COMMUNITY, ONEIDA, N. Y.
GENTLEMEN :—On the 24th September you sent us a small bill of goods. We were led to suppose from the representations made by the gentleman offering the traps, that you had but one price, and that we were buying at the best figures you gave. Such being the case, and the fact coming to our knowledge that the same gentleman selling to us, offered to sell to one of our neighbors, and unless we are misinformed *did* sell to another, (Gill and Sons,) at better rates, we feel justified in asking, that you either correct the price, or give no further trouble to yourselves in calling on us. We are aware that the business loss is nothing to you, if we buy nothing of you —if all Columbus or half Ohio ceases to patronize you. But there is a certain line of business rectitude, you nor none of us can deviate from, without loss *to the man.*

Respectfully, ST. CLAIR & SCOTT.

Oneida, Dec. 20.

MESSRS. ST. CLAIR & SCOTT,
GENTLEMEN :—Your rather sharp letter of the 14th inst. was duly received. We accept your rule of judgment, that it *is* more important for us to do right, that to have the trade of all Columbus or Ohio—and though we think we do not deserve your censure in this instance, still we are pleased to find a business house setting up such a standard.

Our agent affirms that he offered you the same rates he offered others, (we have no hired agents), and they are under no inducement to have two prices. [Here follows an explanation of our classification of trade and rates]. These rates we adhere to, as consistently as possible, and for this, we certainly do not deserve your blame.

Hoping to retain both your esteem and your trade, we remain yours respectfully,

ONEIDA COMMUNITY, by E. H. H.

Columbus, Ohio, Dec. 28, 1866.

MESSRS. OF ONEIDA COMMUNITY :—Yours of 20. Dec has been to hand several days. The writer hereof has been necessarily absent, and correspondence devolves on him.

Where we think we are not treated as others are, we do write sharply, sometimes—the writer is an old printer, and has not forgotten how to say a thing smoothly and make the edge incisive. A young man in one of our neighboring houses advised us, that he saw your Agent on the cars—probably between here and Cleveland, and that he was offered the traps at the lower rates. As he may have misunderstood the 10 pr. ct. off offer, and applied it to any quantity; or even misrepresented the case, (though from the character of his dealings with us we doubt if he would do such a thing), it affords us a sense of relief to say that we were wrong and not you. It is not easy to feel a loss of confidence in those we have trusted, and we would much rather feel assured of being mistaken ourselves, than be compelled to cease trusting those we have trusted.

Hoping you will accept our apology for what we may have said in error, you will permit us to say that the goods ordered have been satisfactory—although we have to work against cheaper imitations. We think that in a few years we could sell a fair amount of them, even in the face of cheaper goods.

Respectfully, ST. CLAIR & SCOTT.

A few days ago we borrowed for trial, an apparatus for producing local anæsthesia by narcotic spray. The apparatus is very simple, consisting of a small rubber hand bellows, with an arrangement of rubber and small metalic tubes by which ether, or other volatile fluid, is blown upon the part to be operated on in the form of narcotic spray. The rapid evaporation of the fluid produces intense cold and consequently insensibility. From the trial we have made, we like the method very well.— The instrument seems to have the power, when rightly managed, of producing complete insensibility over a small surface, sufficiently so to make the extraction of teeth a painless operation, and we think the use of it will in a short time nearly or quite supersede the use of all other anæsthetics in dental Surgery. DENTISTS.

Yesterday's temperature—
7½ A. M., 3. 12 M., 20. 6 P. M., 14. Mean 12.

DAILY JOURNAL
OF ONEIDA COMMUNITY.

VOL. 3.   SATURDAY, JAN. 5, 1867.   **NO. 5.**

LETTERS.

New-York, Jan. 2, 1867.

MY DEAR FRIENDS:—To-night, [Wednesday] I give my first drill to the class at the Abbey since their return and I now send the paper's relating to Cooper Union &c., and also return the overshoes for which I am *much* obliged to Mr. Lord.

I arrived one o'clock Saturday the next day—it was rather tedious but still I got home in safety.—I slept in Albany and took the first A. M. train as we missed connection and no train behind on time.

Give regards to all,   J. E. FROBISHER.

In the letter from Mr. Warne from which we made extracts Wednesday, he speaks of his correspondence with a friend and prominent Baptist clergyman at the West. Mr. W. sent him " Salvation from Sin" and a CIRCULAR, and was copying for him from the "Berean," "Two classes of Believers." Mr. G. writes to him:

Tell me the rules of the O. C., I am ignorant. The paper you sent me did not specify. It only spoke of some of their principles. Do you own that Theological **work you recoomended me to buy?** I am full of desire to understand the belief and practices of this peculiar, and I am disposed to think, much abused people. If they have anything of a spiritual nature that I have not I want it. And as God is no respecter of persons, I believe he will give it to me if I seek him aright, I do want to be spiritual. I do hunger and thirst after the deep things of God. Be a helper to me if you can."

Mrs. Goodwin of Akron, Ohio, who made us a short visit last summer, writes to Mr. Hamilton, that she has heard through a friend in Cleveland, that an article was published in the CIRCULAR relative to her visit here, and she wishes us to send her the paper containing such article, that she may reply to it, if necessary. She says:

" I am sorry (as an honorable Community, whose order and ladyship I so very much admired) that you did not better understand me. My main object in visiting your Community was suggestive, in view of the approaching storm, the most terrific, since the creation of the world—being now in the calm which preceeds it—between the first and second woes—as you undoubtedly know. The world's next great events come under the 6th. angel—the pouring out of the 6th. vial—the opening of the 6th. seal."

Night before last in meeting, Mr. Aiken brought up the subject of making candy. He did not know at the present high price of sugar, how far the practice of making it, would be sanctioned by the Community.— It was proposed that a committee be appointed to look into the matter and decide upon it.—This talk led to some criticism of the practice some of the young men have, of congregating in the kitchen and cellar after meeting. It was thought that the bad experience of some originated in their unprofitable gossip while there, and the temptation they have to go to the cupboard and help themselves to eatables.

Mrs. Chesbro, of Fulton, writes, requesting permission to come and make a visit and bring her two small children. We have replied, that the whole Community are too much engaged in study, to give her much attention, and on that account, her visit might not be very pleasant for her; but, if, under the circumstances she chooses to come, she is free to do so.

The horticulturalists are improving the sleighing to transport thirteen thousand cedar stakes from Wampsville, where they were cut in the fall for use in the Raspberry plantation. The work of sharpening one end of them proceeds as they are delivered.

It was voted in meeting night before last, to dispense with our dinners on Sundays, during the winter, and to have breakfast from eight to nine, and supper at 5 o'clock P. M.

Mr. Hamilton is very low, and it is with difficulty that he speaks so as to be understood. Miss Pomeroy and Mrs. Whitfield have the care of her.

The weather is mild, and the sleighing passably good.

Henry Allen arrived yesterday afternoon.

ERRATA.—In Mr. Woolworth's article in yesterday's JOURNAL under the signature of H., on the last line of the first paragraph for " brightened" read hightened; and on the second line in the next paragraph for " in" read on.—Also on the last page, last article, a little above the middle, for " narcotic spray" read minute spray. There are also some slight grammatical errors in the first letter, that escaped our notice.

Traps ordered the last week,   24 doz.

Yesterday's temperature—

7½ A. M., 12.   12 M., 30.   6 P. M., 29.   Mean 23⅓.

DAILY JOURNAL
OF ONEIDA COMMUNITY.

VOL. 3. MONDAY, JAN. 7, 1867. **NO. 6.**

NOTES OF BUSINESS MEETING.

Mr. Clark was selected to dispose of sleigh shoes, plow-points, and other castings, in the neighboring villages, for old cast iron, of which we shall require from ten to fifteen tons to make the new water-pipes.

Messrs. Hatch, M. Kinsley, G. W. and E. H. Hamilton were appointed a Committee on the subject of introducing a steam pipe and pump at the children's house, with power to act.

H. Barron and the Muck-swamp purchasers were appointed a Committee on the matter of selling the muck.

It is supposed that some person or persons purloin wood from the open shed near the Foundry. A. Kinsley appointed committee on the subject.

The Rent Committee were instructed to hand a monthly rent-statement to the book-keepers.

Messrs. Thayer, M. Kinsley, Clark and Marks, were authorized to make arrangements for securing our annual supply of Ice.

NOTES TO THE COMMUNITY.

I desire to thank God publicly for the victory he has given me over the coughing principality. Three years ago when I was sick with fever and very weak, I coughed almost constantly. It was made plain to me that it was an imposition of the evil one, and I was led to look to Christ for help, and confessed him in my throat and lungs, and said down deep in my heart that I was not going to cough, and by holding something tight over my mouth, and looking steadily to Christ for strength, I gained the victory over it. I have been tempted in the same way many times since, and have not felt at liberty to be indifferent about it, but have been strengthened to resist it. I have had some experience of late in this line that has been a source of thankfulness to me.

I look back to the sickness spoken of as a bright spot in my experience, and thank God for it, and for any suffering that will soften my heart and make me receptive to faith and trust in Christ. I thank the family for their kindness to me since my lameness; it has touched my heart many times and made me love you all. Yours for overcoming egotism and unbelief in all its forms.

E. HIGGINS.

—

I have felt a desire since the beginning of the year to dedicate myself anew to Christ, and to the spirit of improvement; but find obstructions to overcome.—I confess Christ to help me and give victory over all evil. I wish to take sides against the spirit of discontent and unbelief, and separate my life from their influences, that I may walk in the Spirit, and serve the truth acceptably.—I thank God for his goodness, and confess union with Mr. Noyes and the Community Spirit.

M. L. WORDEN.

Mrs. Hamilton's sufferings ceased yesterday morning about six o'clock, and her spirit peacefully withdrew within the veil. None but those who were her immediate attendants, can have any idea of the sufferings she has passed through for months, and more particularly the last few weeks. Rest to her must be unspeakably welcome, and the separation of her spirit from its mortal clog, an unutterable relief. We cannot follow her to her new abode, but we are sure that the same faith in God, that has sustained her, during her long, and severe trial, will not fail her now, and that she will meet with a cordial welcome, from many whom she will recognize as fellow-soldiers, who like her have fallen in battle.— Her burial will take place at eleven o'clock to-day.

Mr. Henderson left us quite suddenly Saturday afternoon for New-York, from whence he purposes to take passage immediately in some steamer for Glasgow, Scotland.

The cause of his abrupt departure, was a letter he received from his brother, informing him of his wife's sickness. Mr. H. has for some months past, been rather uneasy about the condition of his wife and child, and at one time, not long ago, proposed to go to Scotland, and see if he could not persuade his wife to come back with him, or if she would not consent to come, to let him have the child. This the Community did not sympathize with fully, so the project was given up. He wrote his wife a letter, however, making provision to pay her passage to America should she consent to come.—On the receipt of the letter she was too low to have it read to her, and Mr. Henderson's brother wrote a reply.

Mr. Henderson left, hoping if his wife lived, to make some arrangement by which he could return to us soon. He left his trunk and books.

An accident occurred in the Can-shop this morning. Mr. Abbot in cutting some tin with the gauge-shears, cut off the ends of the two smallest fingers on his right hand. The piece cut from the little finger was small, but from the finger next it, about a half inch was taken off, including a small piece of the bone.

It has snowed some, yesterday and to-day, which has improved the sleighing considerably.

H. M. Worden takes Portia Underhill's place in teaching the small school.

Temperature Saturday and Sunday,
7½ A. M., 28. 12 M., 38. 6 P. M., 34. Mean 30.
7½ A. M., 28. 12 M., 31. 6 P. M., 30. Mean 29½.

DAILY JOURNAL
OF ONEIDA COMMUNITY.

VOL. 3. TUESDAY, JAN. 8, 1867. NO. 7.

EVENING MEETING.

Mr. Hamilton:—I feel like giving public thanks for the goodness of God, and his providence manifested in various ways during mother's sickness and last hours. I feel thankful for the way she was sustained by the grace of God, and for the work that was wrought in her spirit; also for the kindness, inspiration and strength, members of the Community had in taking care of her. Then, too, I am thankful for the strength that has been given my heart to not be depressed and come under the anxiety persons in the world feel on similar occasions. I feel that I have come nearer the resurrection, and obtained a clearer idea of the resurrection world than ever before. I don't think the devil or hades have gained anything, but the kingdom of Christ and the resurrection have gained.

Mr. Woolworth:—I am thankful God makes all things work together for good to us. We can say death is ours as well as life.

By request Mr. Noyes's last talk at Oneida was read. Mr. Woolworth then observed: " Unity itself is a miracle, one of the greatest of miracles. There are many things that the devil can counterfeit, and does, with a view to deceive; but I don't believe he has the power to counterfeit unity. It is God's exclusive right to give unity and love: This carries more weight and power in proof of God's work than any other one thing. The Spiritualists are destitute of this miracle. However many other wonders they may be able to work they do not know the miracle of unity. They are independent and scattered. They may be very good mediums of hades."

Mr. Hamilton:—" I hate the spirit of unbelief. I hate the spirit of weakness. I love faith and strength."

The following extracts are from a letter Mrs. Bushnell received from Mrs. Dascomb, who visited the Community not long since.

" I fear that it was indeed a false inspiration that led me to be afraid of Mr. Noyes' writings, and I praise the Lord for the faith and strength he gave me to visit you and the people of your choice. I saw there an inspiration I have failed to find elsewhere—a unity of purpose and feeling—*a oneness of spirit*, that I have never seen manifested in the world or in any branch of the visible church. The last meeting I attended was with you, and it seemed a very happy place to me, notwithstanding the tender criticism that was given me and which I now desire to thank you and the Community for, with all my heart. The writings of John came to me with a new and precious fullness when read by Mr. Hamilton that evening.

" I have thought much of the general characteristics of your Community, since my visit there. The perfect harmony, order and neatness, together with the spirit of love and improvement, seemed to prevail everywhere. There seemed to be a spirit of inspiration in work in every department of business, which elevates labor to worship, robbing it of all connection or association with the curse pronounced upon Adam, for nowhere did I see anything which seemed like drudgery in work.

" The exceeding '*straightness* of the gate,' I never apprehended so fully as I now do—*so straight* that it takes all our friends—father, mother, brothers and sisters, children, aye, even our own life—for flesh and blood cannot enter through."

Having been with Mrs. H. most of the time for several months, I feel like testifying to the goodness of God, which was very manifest in her case. Although she suffered a good deal, the grace of God was still more abundant, and she felt that her experience was a necessary discipline to separate her from her old life and fit her for the resurrection state. She suffered but little the last few days, which she attributed to the victory she had obtained over the flesh. She spoke of her past life as being very hateful to her; says, "O Mary! I have had a great deal of evil thinking, but it is all gone—I have nothing but love in my heart." She was very heroic and courageous to the last.

I am thankful for my experience; the effect has been to bring my own spirit more in rapport with the resurrection world, and instead of losing anything by her departure, I think we have made an advance—an onward march toward victory over death. M. D. P.

I feel like thanking God publicly for my late experience in helping to take care of Mrs. Hamilton, for her faith and trust in God, and her loyalty to Mr. Noyes as his chosen one, shone brightly in her heart. The victory of the spirit, over the flesh, was very manifest. I realized many times that the resurrection was here, and that we were one with the Primitive church. I had many tokens of the fact,—one is this. At times when not attending to her wants directly, I would take my algebra, and I had as clear a medium as though I had been at school for the purpose, and I can testify to the grace of God, in her case, as being a helper to my faith. It does my heart good to think of my fellowship with such a soldier of Christ; and I cannot help thinking of it as a green spot in my experience, because that victory over death appears clearer, brighter, than ever before. E. W.

A beginning was made yesterday, of cutting ice for the Ice-house, and to-day all hands are called out to assist in getting and packing it. W. A. H.'s and E. S. B.'s schools are consequently both suspended.

They are having quite lively times in the upper sitting-room making mittens for the men who are at work on the ice.

Yesterday's temperature—
7½ A. M., 22. 12 M., 24. 6 P. M., 30. Mean 25½.

DAILY JOURNAL
OF ONEIDA COMMUNITY.

VOL. 3.   WEDNESDAY, JAN. 9, 1867.   NO. 3.

EVENING MEETING.

Mr. Hamilton :—I don't know but this is a good time to make some remarks about the spirit and experience connected with mother's case. I had some talk with Mrs. Whitfield and Mary Pomeroy to-day on the subject. I didn't like that little notice about mother in the DAILY JOURNAL of yesterday. I thought it exaggerated her sufferings some; and the tendency of it was to promote a doleful, foreboding spirit, I should think, and to make people fearful about death and suffering. I have no doubt mother suffered a great deal; but the impression left on me, (and I found it was so with those who had most to do with her), was, that although she suffered, her sufferings were swallowed up in victory. That was the general feeling, that death and disease in one sense were swallowed up in her improvement, and cheerful, victorious spirit over the flesh and the will of the flesh. The idea came out in my talk with Mrs. Whitfield that there was a more victorious faith spirit there in the sick-room than there was in the family, where persons were apt to exaggerate the evil of the case. The spirit of the resurrection was in the sick-room. Mrs. Whitfield said she

d not feel that she needed pity or as though it had been a terribly hard task. It was true the task was a disagreeable one; but where such a victory has been gained, you do not think so much about the sufferings in the case. I think myself that the experience in this case of mother's, if the spirit of it could be known, as it was known by those dealing with this attack of disease and death of the worst form, as you may say, would encourage everybody to trust in God and not to fear death. That is the victorious feeling in my heart, and I have found it true of all those who have had most to do with mother.

When I first saw what the result had got to be I felt a good deal of shrinking and dread. Though I was not with her much, the spirit of the thing of course weighed upon me more or less. But all that was completely swallowed up in victory, and I could say with Paul, "O death where is thy sting! O grave where is thy victory." I never felt more victorious over the fear of death than in this experience.

G. W. Hamilton :—I never felt so little of the worldly spirit of death as I did in this case of mother's.

Many made similar confessions, when Mr. Hamilton said : "I attribute all this experience to the victorious spirit of Christ's resurrection."

———

I have often felt thankful for the experience I had while taking care of Mrs. Hamilton for a short time during her sickness. I was thankful to overcome an effeminate spirit that dreads the sick-room, and I considered it a privilege to become better acquainted with her and to witness the grace and faith given to sustain her in such a trying situation. I never heard a murmur or scarcely a groan escape her, and most of the time she was cheerful and victorious. Her confession of Christ was always at hand and was expressed in simplicity and meekness. She would sometimes talk with spirit and power, of the goodness of God, and of her confidence in him. She valued criticism and profited by it.

She manifested great interest in my studies, especially in that of geometry, and would inquire about the lesson, and the progress of the class. She related her experience in studying geometry several years ago, when Mr. Noyes advised the Community to give attention to it; said she was thankful for it, as it helped her now to sympathize with others. She really enjoyed having some of the theorems demonstrated to her.

I can say sincerely that I thank God for such a sister, and for the hope and assurance that she is joyfully wending her way to the resurrection.   B. B. C.

———

O. H. Miller in his present state of hardness, has been requested not to obtrude his presence upon the family in their Sitting rooms or Library. Accordingly he has been furnished with a room in the Tontine garret with a stove in it, that he may not be under the necessity of going to other rooms to warm. A note from him was read last night, professing to accept the criticism Mr Noyes gave him years ago, and with which he has so long quarreled, insisting that the record of it should be erased from the books. Whether he is sincere in this, remains to be seen.

———

Seven teams are engaged in drawing ice to-day. They will finish filling our ice-house this forenoon, and will commence this afternoon, the work of filling the one at Willow-Place. The ice is ten inches thick and very nice.—The neighbors are improving the opportunity to get *their* ice, and from twenty to twenty-five teams are out to-day, our people helping them load.

———

Mrs. Bailey was criticised last evening by her request, and the conversation reported in to-day's JOURNAL, was drawn out by some remarks made in the course of her criticism, of the spirit she had, in connection with her care of Mrs. Hamilton. It was thought Mrs. B. sympathized quite too much with disease, which effected her own spirit unfavorably.

———

We had a company of eleven here from Hamilton yesterday, who took lunch. The family entertained them with music, both instrumental and vocal, with which they seemed much delighted.

———

The Burt-House is completed at last, and the Porters moved in last Saturday.

———

We have not yet received Monday's CIRCULARS.

Yesterday's temperature—
7½ A. M., 13.   12 M., 18.   6 P. M., 19.   Mean 16⅓.

DAILY JOURNAL
OF ONEIDA COMMUNITY.

VOL. 3. THURSDAY, JAN. 10, 1867. NO. 9.

EVENING MEETING.

Mr. Hamilton:—It has occurred to me it would be well to make some remarks about the finances, and especially concerning the showing of the Bag-department. The earnings of this department were not very large the last year, and some of the members connected with it were tempted to feel discouraged. I have not seen anything very serious, but I thought it was a rather small view to take. Others, perhaps, think it would hardly pay to carry on a business that doesn't give better returns. I thought it would be well to show how that department was situated.

Last winter when we made our inventory, the Bag-department had a large supply of stock and finished work on hand. All this was charged to the department when purchased, and then what was on hand at the end of the year, was credited in the inventory to the amount of about $20,000. At this year's inventory their stock on hand was only about $7000. While they have not earned only some two or three thousand dollars, they have turned a good deal of property into cash, and have helped us pay our debt in that way. That has been our business this last year. We had a heavy stock on hand in both the Trap-department and Bag-department which we have greatly reduced. It would have been good policy to turn this into cash, rather than to carry it along another year, even if we hadn't made anything on it above the first cost.

The Bag-business had a good deal of competition to contend with and was pretty hardly run, as so many went into it the season before. Then business was very dull for a good part of the year. But we have kept our foot-hold, and stand now where we can go ahead and probably advance our prices some the coming season.— So as I understand it the Bag department has furnished us some $14,000 or $15,000 toward paying this debt the past season. That is pretty good. They earned more last season, but it didn't help our finances because it was all put into stock.

Mr. Woolworth:—I am glad to have this statement made for I think it is just, and necessary to the correction of some erroneous impressions.

Arcata, Humbolt Co. Cal., Dec. 5, 1866.

S. NEWHOUSE ESQ: DEAR SIR:—I have come in possession of one of your traps. I have in former years been something of a trapper and hunter, and the sight of a good and perfect trap, has induced me to try my hand with them again.—I have sent to San Francisco for an outfit of traps, but could find none of your traps in the City. * * * * * * *

If you will have the goodness to write me immedi-ately, telling me the price of the different sizes and the weight of each, I can manage to fix the matter so they will come safe.

There is a good amount of game here, such as bear, (three varieties), California lion, panther, wolves, (lots), otter, fisher, wild-cats, martin, mink coon, skunk, fox &c.—We have seals also, the sea-lion, which weighs from 500 to 2,000 pounds. I think they can be taken with a No. 5 trap, with a heavy weight to the trap to drown them, and can be found by a long line and buoy or float.

Do you make traps with *spread* enough to take in the foot of a grizzly bear? I have measured some tracks in the dust, which measured eleven by thirteen inches. Takes a big trap to take in that foot—I last season helped to kill one, the foot of which weighed twenty-two pounds! Is there no way one man can set one of those big traps? Some of the bear traps I have seen here, will take all the settlers in the neighborhood to set them. * * * * * * * * *

I should be pleased to hear from you *very* soon—if there is anything an old trapper like yourself would like to learn of the game and sport here, I should take much pleasure in furnishing any information you desire.

Please address, JAS. A. BOUTELLE.

With others, I should like to add my testimony to the goodness and grace of God that helped to sustain Mrs. Hamilton during her late illness. It was strengthening to my faith to be with her, and I felt that her sufferings were not for her alone but for the benefit of the church. It was a growing time for all that took care of her. Her mind was always clear, she did not seem like a sick person in that respect. She was much interested in the different classes for education that were forming about the time I took care of her. She liked to have her curtain drawn, so that she could see the Grammar class go to their place of recitation. I should think this was her favorite study. Mr. Noyes's last talk with her, gave her the crowning victory over death and the grave. C. A. B.

Among the improvements of to-day, what is particularly gratifying to the Office hands is, that our Printing-press has been connected with the Steam power, so that foot-power is no longer called into requisition for printing.

A snug little room about eleven feet square, has been partitioned off from the Store-chamber on the front side, and nicely finished. A new carpet has been put down and a stove put up. Mr. Leete is to occupy it this winter.

We conclude that the CIRCULARS are snow-bound, as they do not yet make their appearance.

A $2000 order for traps, was received yesterday from the Hudson Bay Company.

$54 worth of ice was sold to the neighbors yesterday.

Yesterday's temperature—
7½ A. M., 15. 12 M., 30. 6 P. M., 24. Mean 23.

DAILY JOURNAL
OF ONEIDA COMMUNITY.

VOL. 3.　　FRIDAY, JAN. 11, 1867.　　NO. 10.

The meeting hour last night, was spent mostly in reading Mr. Noyes's recent talks. The one on the "Beard" caused a good deal of laughter, and was particularly gratifying to those who dislike long beards. His talk on the Pacific Railroad and the Indians, had quite a thrilling effect, and was heartily cheered. It seems clear as Mr. Noyes said, that every thing that stands in the way of progress, will in some way or other be removed.

Mr. Woolworth observed :—" I guess we have all had a secret feeling that the Pacific Railroad was going to have an important bearing upon our destiny and future."

J. R. Lord :—What Mr. Noyes said about that region as a good market for our Preserved Fruit, puts me in mind that I had some talk with a gentleman in Danbury, who had been to Pike's Peak and California. He asked me why we did not transport our Preserved Fruits into those regions, and said any amount of it could be sold there, and that it brought very high prices. I believe we shall find great market in that direction for our fruits as well as our traps.

After the reading of Mr. Noyes's criticism of the CIR-CULAR, and his suggestion that it would be well to confess our faults in the paper, the failure in Corn, Peas, &c., Mr. Woolworth said : " I trust we shall be open to the truth about this Fruit-business, and not try to cover up anything or seek to evade the criticism. I believe God has some good lessons for us ; and we want to learn them, and get all the profit we can out of our disasters.

Massillon, Ohio, Jan. 9, 1867.

GENTLEMEN :—Pardon me, if I should make an improper request, for I ask in good faith. Having read your CIRCULAR of December 31st, I read " Malthusian Colloquy," and I am in the same situation Mr. Eber is in, in the above.

I was married at twenty-five, and am now thirty-eight years old, and we have seven children, (no twins), more than we can support, and feel easy and comfortable ; the mother as a natural consequence broken down in health and spirit. Our habits are moderate, don't believe in quacks.

Will you please send me a copy of a tract you call 'Male Continence," I will adhere to its instructions, for the sake of prohibiting superfluous propagation.

Yours truly,　　GEORGE YOST.

We shall send Mr. Y. the tract, of course.

Lansing, Mich., Jan. 2, 1867.

J. H. NOYES: DEAR SIR :—Being desirous and somewhat anxious to hear and know more of your Communi-ty, I take this opportunity of writing to you for more information.

I have read your publications and have been a reader of the CIRCULAR for the past year more or less, and like its teachings well. It seems to me that you are engaged in a good cause, and I would like to join you and work for the cause.

When I look around me and see the selfishness and wickedness, that is abroad in the land, it is enough to make one blush for shame and cry for reformation, of some kind.

There seems to be an influence that directs me to you. I would like to come and make the Community a visit, and stay the winter with you, if I could work and pay my way.

Please write and oblige one that is seeking after light and truth.　　A. C. KENT.

We continue to have contradictory reports of our Preserved Fruits and Vegetables. One firm at Detroit, Mich., writes that nearly all the Corn it has sold has been returned. A firm in Utica reports that sixteen cans out of twenty-four were bad. On the other hand, a firm in Chicago, who had received forty doz. cans of Corn, has just sent an order for fifty doz. more ; and yesterday a duplicated order for Corn was received from Freeport, Ill. But, on the whole, the Corn of last season must be regarded as a bad failure. And the same is substantially true of the Peas.

The other canned goods, so far as we are at present able to judge, have given better satisfaction. We occasionally receive such expressions as the following :

" I ate some of your fruit in Janesville, Wisconsin, and think it the best I ever tasted."

Again, from the Hudson Bay Company, " The three cases of Preserved Fruit, sent to my address, have arrived. I find them excellent. EDWARD M. HOPKINS."

C. A. Mackuet had a telegram from her brother, yesterday, informing her that her father had had another paralytic attack, and requesting her to come immediately. She had a letter three weeks ago, stating that he was suffering from a previous attack, though a good deal better. Carrie started for Newark in the night, accompanied by S. K. Dunn and Henry Allen, the former for Wallingford and the latter for New-York.

Our statistician, J. Abbott, gives us the following :

Whole number of persons in all the Communes at the present time,	271.
At Oneida Community,	209.
At Wallingford,	50,
Including New Haven Branch, and Victor at Utica.	
At New-York Branch,	12.

H. R. Perry is added to our list of traveling agents.

Yesterday's temperature—
7½ A. M., 22.　12 M., 36.　6 P. M., 26.　Mean 28.

DAILY JOURNAL
OF ONEIDA COMMUNITY.

VOL. 3. SATURDAY, JAN. 12, 1867. NO. 11.

EVENING MEETING.

Mr. Noyes's talk concerning Graham bread was applauded. After some discussion, it was unanimously voted to abolish it entirely. Among other things said on the subject Mr. Pitt remarked as follows:

" I used to think considerable of Graham bread, but since I went to Canada I have not wanted it, and even rather not have it come in my sight as a general thing.—I have been persuaded for the last year or two that there was a spirit connected with it that I could feel old . . . every time I undertook to eat it.

Mr. Hamilton:—Do you think it would be a good thing to have Mr. Cragin go to Canada?

Mr. Inslee:—I like the sentiment of that talk just read. I have no fellowship with Graham, nor am I in any bondage to his bread. I have used Graham bread in preference to the other kind because I liked it better, and I have used brown bread, in preference to Graham bread because I have liked that the best. But I am generally satisfied with whatever I happen to get.

Mr. Hamilton:—I used to rather like it, but of late it has seemed so **unattractive and repulsive** that I never touch it.

Mr. Kelley:—Giving up Graham bread will be cutting the last link of sympathy between us and the Water-Cure people. They make a great hobby of Grahamism.

Mr. Bolles said he tried living on the Graham system for nearly nine months, and he had no doubt that it would have killed him if he had continued till the end of the year. He took to eating roast beef and soon got better, and had hated the sight of Graham bread ever since.

Mr. Reynolds said he lived upon it for about a year, more as an experiment than anything else. That satisfied him in regard to Grahamism, he believed it to be injurious to the body and spirit when one gets wedded to it. Mr. Hamilton suggested that might be the cause of Mr. Reynold's difficulty with his stomach now.

Mr. Woolworth:—I once boarded with Dr. Graham a few days. One day he came to the table in a very doleful state, and said this disagreeable duty of eating, had to be attended to once in about so often. That shows what kind of an ordinance he made of eating.

Mr. Bolles:—Mr. Noyes seems to make more account of the spirit than anything else. I think that is the correct view. There is terrible bondage to the flesh in these hygienic and dietetic systems. The idea is that our life consists of what we eat and drink.

Mr. Pitt:—It is a gospel that tries to save men body end foremost.

Mr. Woolworth:—It is very important that we should discern the Lord's body in our eating and drinking. I guess in eating Graham bread, people do not discern the Lord's body; but perhaps if they were sharp, they could detect Graham's spirit.

Mr. Hamilton:—I don't believe Graham bread makes very good backbone. I heard Dr. Graham lecture once, and he had one foot up in a chair and leaned upon his knee like a man that hadn't backbone enough to stand up straight.

Mr. Woolworth:—Mr. Pitt's experience is interesting. He says going to Canada cured him of Grahamism. I have an impression it did work a great revolution in him. It seems to have given new tone to his whole life.

W. A. Hinds:—George Miller writes that Mr. Meeker has called at the Agency and notified them that his article about the Community will not appear in the *Tribune.* He left a copy with them which will probably be sent here. This did not disappoint me, as I thought if it was going to appear at all, it would have come out before this. It seems to indicate a lack of backbone in the *Tribune* somewhere.

Mr. Pitt:—Probably Greely has not given up Graham bread.

W. A. Hinds:—Do you think if he had been to Canada he would have published it?

It was thought rather weak in the *Tribune,* to send a man here to investigate—have him spend a week or two in writing an article—put it in type, and then distribute without printing it. It was thought Mr. Ripley might be at the bottom of the back-out. He was absent when Mr. Meeker was sent here, and but recently returned to the *Tribune* Office.

Mr. Carr was recently at Utica selling silk. One merchant told me of some conversation he had with him. Mr. Carr said he had spent 16 of the best years of his life at the Community, and he was no better off now, than he was when he first went there. He said he had nothing against the Community—thought it was a good Institution. The merchant asked him why he left it then? He replied, on account of a difference between him and the leaders; they were getting too selfish for him. **W. G. K.**

It was proposed last evening that we have a dance, to-night, in celebration of the victory we have gained over the principality of Grahamism. We have not had a dance for nearly a year, and the young people in particular, are anticipating it with a good deal of pleasure.

Among the frequent changes we have these days, we notice that Fidelia Burt has taken H. C. Noyes's place at the Bag-shop, and Miss Nuns, Ann S. Bailey's place.

The teams are engaged at the present time in drawing saw-logs from West hill. A little more snow fell last night which will improve the sleighing considerable.

Traps ordered the past week,   227¼ doz.
mostly large traps.

Yesterday's temperature—
7½ A. M., 23.   12 M., 28.   6 P. M., 21.   Mean 24.

DAILY JOURNAL
OF ONEIDA COMMUNITY.

VOL. 3.   MONDAY, JAN. 14, 1867.   NO. 12.

EVENING MEETING.

Mr. Hamilton:—The spirit of delocalization that Mr. Noyes has said so much about has interested me a good deal, and is doing so more and more. I think I understand the way Mr. Noyes is advancing in that direction. I see there has been quite a change in some respects, or at least a development of that idea, since Mr. Noyes made the movement of having the paper printed at Wallingford, and of making his home there a part of the time and here a part, to begin with; and finally he began to spend part of his time at New-York, and so on round to New Haven, until you see at the present time he has no special home anywhere. You don't know whether he will be at Wallingford, New York, New Haven, or Oneida. I love the end he is seeking, which is, it seems to me, to have his home wherever he goes, and not get attached to places and surroundings or persons. If we can get delocalized so that we do not care where we are, and so that we are at home with God and the redeemed of the New Jerusalem, and all who are one in the body of Christ, wherever we may be, it seems to me we shall have passed beyond death.

I was thinking about it the other night in connection with our agents. I should think their service tended towards delocalization, perhaps more than any other branch. I thought they were not settling down here and there into routine. Mr. Noyes is determined to get them delocalized, and where they won't be hampered by personal or local attractions. It seemed to me this was a kind of service that was favorable to the resurrection. I felt in my heart that I wanted to join that service, and reckon myself as one with our agents in commencing the coming campaign. If I stand here all the time I want to reckon myself as in that service, ready to go anywhere and do anything without fear or thought of hardships or inconvenience, but leave all that in God's hands.

In this view of the subject the service of our agents is a high and great calling, and God will be with them more and more. What I recommend is, that the agents should all seek to come together and unite their hearts so that they would be one wherever called. This would be a continual safeguard from the spirit of the world, and would form a stronger bond of unity between them and the Church. That is really the way to go home—to get into that spirit and keep there. I see that for me to settle down into the spirit that loves ease, and try to make myself a nice, comfortable nest, would be just the way to get farthest from the heart of the Church and the inspiration of the resurrection. All of us who stay at home can study this and get into the spirit of it.

Great battles are yet to be fought. Death is not overcome. We have got to be soldiers and agents for God; to fight and go on service. We must drive the devil out of the world before we can have any permanent peace, and before heaven can come upon the earth.

Mr. Olds:—I am thankful for Mr. Hamilton's remarks in regard to the agents. I am thankful for the privilege of remaining at home so long, and for the chance I have had of attending the Theological class. I now feel better prepared to go into the world than ever before. It is my ambition to become all I can be for God and be a thorough helper to Mr. Noyes in fighting this battle.

J. R. Lord:—I should like to express thankfulness for the victory I have gained in my own spirit about going out. About a year ago I had quite an experience. The feeling came over me that I was called away from home so much that I might about as well be outside. About that time I had a pretty severe criticism. I feel now there has been an entire change in that respect. I can say I am thankful to be in any situation I am called to, whether it is traveling, or at home. I do not prefer to stay at home when I am called away. I am thankful for the privilege of serving in the cause.

Mr. Olds and Kelley were both faithfully criticised last night. But little fault was found with Mr. Olds, and his business course was a good deal commended, and his spirit generally. Mr. K's business habits were thought to be in rather a loose unsatisfactory state, and required great improvement.

A party of eight went to the Lake, yesterday, for fishing some said, but after their return having caught but one fish, some that went affirmed, that their object in going was not particularly to catch fish, but to have a good ride.

Mr. Olds starts to-day for his Western tour. He hopes to get through in a month; certainly before the 20th of February.

Mr. Kelley also goes out to-day on his business trip of a week or more. They both have our hearty sympathy.

The dance Saturday evening was very satisfactory we believe. A good spirit prevailed, and all seemed quiet and pleasant.

7¼ A. M., 12.   12 M., 16.   6 P. M., 14.   Mean 14.
7¼ A. M., 10.   12 M., 15.   6 P. M., 16.   Mean 13¾.

DAILY JOURNAL
OF ONEIDA COMMUNITY.

VOL. 3.   TUESDAY, JAN. 15, 1867.   NO. 10.

A letter (of which the following is a copy,) has been addressed to the Chairman of the Ways and Means Committee of the House of Representatives at Washington, and also to the Commissioner of Internal Revenue.

We are not very confident that either of the requests preferred will be granted; but as a prominent Revenue Law official of New York City gave it as his opinion that they were reasonable, and further said that the Oneida Community is entitled to a 'voice' at Washington, it has been thought best to forward the following letter to the officials first named:

Oneida, N. Y., Jan. 14, 1867.

"Permit the undersigned, (a firm of two hundred persons extensively engaged in preserving fruits and vegetables), to call your attention to the fact, that the Internal Revenue Law, as at present amended, imposes excessive taxation upon fruits preserved in glass bottles, as compared with those preserved in tin cans.

"By Schedule C., section 170, the stamp tax for 'every can, bottle, or other single package, containing meats, fruits, vegetables,' &c., is rated according to the weight of said can or bottle 'with its contents.'

"**By a subsequent provision**, 'Tin cans used for preserved meats, fruits, vegetables,' &c., are exempted from the manufacturers' *advalorem* tax. But glass bottles when used for precisely the same purposes are still subjected to this *advalorem* tax.

"As the Law now stands, and is construed, the same quantity and value of fruit which in a tin can requires only a one-cent stamp (because with the can not exceeding two lbs.) requires, if preserved in a heavy glass bottle, a three-cent stamp, (because exceeding with the bottle three lbs.,) in addition to the five per cent. *advalorem* tax previously paid on the bottle by the manufacturer.

"We beg permission to urge, that this unequal taxation bears heavily upon those who are engaged in preserving fruits in glass, and to pray that such changes may be made in the Internal Revenue Law that the tax required on fruits preserved in bottles, shall be the same as that required on the same fruits in cans. This would result from having the stamp tax imposed upon the *contents* of can or bottle, instead of upon the can or bottle *with its contents*, as at present; and by making the can as well as the bottle subject to the manufacturers' *advalorem* tax.

"If this request cannot be granted, then we would further urge that the present exemption of tin cans from the manufacturers' tax, when used for preserving purposes, may be extended to glass bottles when used for the same purpose for which cans are exempted."

Very Respectfully,
Oneida Community,
By WM. A. HINDS.

DEAR FRIENDS:—Dr. Carpenter called here yesterday, and the favorable state of my case caused him to hope that I am cured. If so, I accept it as the work of the Lord, and take this method to thank him publicly for it. In the early part of my affliction I confessed Christ alone my physician, and when the Community proposed having me go to the doctor about it, it gave me trouble, lest in submitting my case to the doctor, I should not be trusting it with the Lord. I felt that I would rather die than not to trust him, and told Mr. Burt so. He represented to me that I had a Christ of my own, independent of the Community, and I think that was so. I looked at the matter, and came to the conclusion to take the Community as Christ to me, and I told him I would do so. I have ever since, through his grace, been obedient to their advice as unto the Lord, and have been blest by his presence and support in so doing.

In one instance, dreading a surgical operation which was about to be performed, I committed myself to Christ in the matter, and all dread of it passed away, and quite a strong desire to have it done took its place. It was soon over, and my heart became thankful. Then followed a manifestation of the presence of the Lord in the faith, joy and loving heart he gave me. He manifestly alleviated my pain, and made it easy to bear; and when I think of the cure done on me, I can give the glory of it and the praise to none but the Lord. The doctor is but his instrument. WM. JONES.

Our home boarding-house has furnished the past year to our employees, exclusive of the persons engaged in preparing them,

Meals,	22,315.
Cost according to the Books,	$4,271.20.
At Willow Place—Meals furnished,	22,818.
Aggregate cost,	$4,315.54.
Meals for hired men,	13,421.
Women,	2,354.
Community folks,	5,946.
The fewest in any month was in February,	678.
The most in November,	4,729.
Cost per week at Willow Place,	$3.97.
At the home boarding-house,	$4.04.

A man by the name of Mallory, from Rochester, staid here last night. He is the gentleman who manufactured the paper boxes, that we had last fall for packing grapes. He came we understand, to engage us to buy of him again, another year.

It is clear and cold this morning. The mercury stood at 5 o'clock, 14 deg. below zero.

Yesterday's temperature—
7½ A. M., 10.   12 M., 14.   6 P. M., 8.   Mean 10½.

DAILY JOURNAL
OF ONEIDA COMMUNITY.

VOL. 3. WEDNESDAY, JAN. 16, 1867. NO. 14.

EVENING MEETING.

In reference to the return of Grace Mills to the Community several expressed themselves as sympathizing with Mr. Noyes's view of the subject. Mr. Hamilton observed: " I am not afraid of her corrupting our girls. If she comes here on probation and doesn't do well then she can be returned."

Mr. Woolworth :—One thing looks hopeful in the case. She seems to have had a deliberate purpose. We heard through Ellen six months ago that Grace would be glad to come back ; so it does not seem to have been a mere impulse of the moment.

Mr. Bolles :—I think it would be quite a victory over the Mills principality if one of his children could be snatched from him and saved. Visitors from this part of the country ask a good many questions about Mr. Mills. I am in hopes before Mills goes into hades, the Lord will force him to take back what he has said about us.

Mr. Hawley :—I don't think he will ever go to hades until he does do it.

Mr. Bolles :—I owe Mills a special grudge. There was a particular devil's providence through Mills, calculated to break off my connection with the Oneida Community. * * But considering the result I don't know that I ought to owe Mills any particular spite.

Mr. Kinsley :—I was thinking you should be thankful for that experience.

Mr. Bolles :—I am thankful to God but not to Mills.

Mr. Hamilton :—In a good many respects I think Mills was made a means of grace to us. He may see this himself sometime, and turn around and go the other way out of spite. I have read about a very good man who had a terible vixen for a wife. He was a Methodist, and once some of the brethren of the church were condoling with him on his hard fate, in having been matched with such a woman, when he replied, that it had been the greatest blessing of his life, as she was a means of grace to him, in keeping him in the right attitude. She happened to hear about it and said, she wasn't going to have him go to Heaven over her back, and turned around and made a very good woman.

The remainder of Mr. Meeker's article was read, which caused great laughter in the Hall. Considerable conversation about Mr. M. and the article followed.— Mr. Hamilton said, " In regard to Meeker's article and what he says about my talk with him, I didn't take notes and don't know as any one else did ; but he has'nt given a very good representation of what I undertook to tell him. I attempted to say that the social theory was not the great object we were aiming at, but that we were seeking to do God's will and promote the best interest of society, and that we could live as Shakers or as married people as a matter of expediency. But I guess he must have been a little sleepy."

Mr. Hatch :—I don't know but everybody else likes his piece, but it seems to me he doesn't represent things at all truly. He represents Homer's criticism, so that persons wouldn't be apt to take it at all as it was given.

Mr. Pitt :—He admitted when he went down to the reception-room, that he was asleep during most of the criticism.

Mr. Hamilton :—If he has much to do with us we will invite him to submit to criticism, and see how he likes the performance.

Mr. Bolles :—I have a great objection to his sacrilegious way of turning everything into a joke, as though we were put up here to be laughed at.

J. R. Lord :—I think it would be well to have his article pretty well criticised if it is going to be printed.

Mr. Hamilton :—I see in this, one of those Providences where everything is overruled for the best.

* * *

In looking into my past experience I can see that I have sometimes deviated from full sympathy with Mr. Noyes and others. For instance, when we were building the Factory at Willow-Place, I had some doubts as to the propriety of making so large a debt, particularly in going to Utica for brick to finish building. Whether I was under the influence of Mr. Carr's spirit in that thing or not, I will protest against every spirit among us, that is not in sympathy with Mr. Noyes as an inspired man in financial matters.—In the debate with Mr. Carr before he left, Mr. Hamilton said that our preparation at Willow-Place, was a stepping stone, to other facilities in business. I see that I have been short-sighted, and it becomes me to take a humble position among my brethren, and look to God for wisdom and inspiration to direct in future. CORNELIUS HIGGINS.

* * *

Mr. Goakes has a cow which has produced the last year besides what they have used in the family,

230 lbs. of butter, sold at forty cents per. lb.,	$92.00.
42 lbs. at thirty-three cents per. lb.,	$13.86.
323 qts. of milk, sold at six cents per. quart,	$19.38.
Whole amount,	$125.24.

CORRECTION.—In the statistics given yesterday, instead of $4.04 as the cost per week, of board at the home-boarding-house, it should have been $4.02.

* * *

Yesterday's temperature—
7¼ A. M.,—9. 12 M., 10. 6 P. M., 2. Mean 1.

DAILY JOURNAL
OF ONEIDA COMMUNITY.

VOL. 3.   THURSDAY, JAN. 17, 1867.   NO. 15.

WILLOW PLACE ITEM.

A kerosene lamp exploded about 10 P. M. night before last at the boarding-house. It was standing on a bureau in Mrs. Dunning's bed-room. Mrs. D. had just been in there, and examined the lamp, and saw that it was well filled, and in a safe position, and had gone out again, leaving the room vacant. Presently she heard a slight tinkling of glass—feeling uneasy, she made her way again into the bedroom. The room was filled with flame and smoke. She rushed out—gave the alarm and fainted away. Mr. D. hearing the alarm, grasped a pail of water and started for the room—saw his fainting wife, and stopped to catch her. A shop-hand who was near by, took the water and succeeded in extinguishing the flames. The bureau, carpet, and a basket of towels, were the principal articles damaged. Mrs. D. estimates her loss at $10, aside from the bureau, which is entirely ruined.   c.

Another scene occurred at home, in the Reception room, yesterday, in which a kerosene lamp acted a conspicuous part. Mr. Bradley got up on a high stool, to fix a window curtain, and whether his sudden elevation caused him to become giddy-headed, as is the case with some, certain it is, that in descending, he forgot his high position, and stepped backward, imagining that he stood on a lower plane. The consequence was, that he fell his whole length on to the floor; upsetting in his fall, the table with its contents, including a globe lamp, breaking the globe and spilling the oil on the carpet. We believe Mr. Bradley was not seriously injured, judging from the way he ran to the Tontine for hot irons, to extract the oil from the carpet.

Mrs. Brown, of Brattleboro, Vt., writes to her sister, Mrs. Lynde, "It always does me good to hear from you and the dear Community family, for they are always on the bright side of resurrection truth. My heart is gladdened and cheered with the prospect of victory over the last enemy.

. I am learning to be humble and patient, and at times hopeful and joyful. I believe J. H. N. to be an inspired leader,—a chosen disciple of Christ, to lead his people out of darkness into this marvelous light."

It has been asserted by some, that fish could be frozen solid, and afterwards restored to life. I have always doubted the assertion; it sounded too "fishy" for me to credit. Finally I thought I would try the experiment myself. I therefore obtained a perch from the Oneida Lake, of about one-half pound weight. One cold night, I cut a hole in a large block of ice, and filled it with water, and put the perch into it, and left it in it all night and the next forenoon; in all; about seventeen hours. In the meantime, the mercury sank to twenty degrees below zero: so there could be no possibility of doubt, that the fish was frozen solid. I then put the block of ice into a tub of water, and left it to thaw out, which it did in the course of the afternoon: and upon examining the fish it was found to be dead.

I still hold to the opinion, that if a fish is thoroughly frozen, it cannot be restored to life again.

GEORGE R. KELLOGG.

Mr. HAMILTON:—I liked what W. A. H. said, that it would be necessary for me to humble myself more, before God and the Community. I desire a humble and repentant spirit, that there may be an entire separation between me and my old life. Nothing too bad can be said of it. It has no place in the Community. I endorse what you said of it in your criticism; egotistical, shiftless, lazy and wicked. I am thankful for the judgment that has been brought upon it. I wish to have no will of my own, or desire any thing not in accordance with the will of God and the Community. By the strength of Christ, I will serve God and the Community. I pray for a meek and lowly spirit, and a spirit of unity.

O. H. MILLER.

In meeting last night, Mr. Woolworth brought up the subject of the Bag-business, for discussion. He thought that department needed strengthening, and it was proposed that more hands from the family, be put into the work, and the Bag-bees resumed. The proposal was heartily sympathized with.

Mr. Pitt is reading in the Theological class, the unpublished correspondence between Mr. Noyes and Prof. Bush, written in 1845, on Swedenborgianism. It is very interesting.

Our employees, boarding at Willow-Place, clubbed together and bought oysters, and night before last had a nice supper, which they seemed to enjoy wonderfully.

A member enquired of one of the little boys, whose child he was; he replied, "he was all the Community's child."

Charles Cragin started for New-York yesterday afternoon, to buy stock.

It snows this morning, and the weather is quite moderate again.

Dr. Slocum, from Camillus staid here last night.

Yesterday's temperature—
7½ A. M.,—13. 12 M., 18. 6 P. M., 13. Mean 6.

DAILY JOURNAL
OF ONEIDA COMMUNITY.

VOL. 3.   FRIDAY, JAN. 18, 1867.   NO. 16.

EVENING MEETING.

Night before last, a meeting was called for, to be composed of those who were connected with the fruit preserving business, and others who might feel interested, to consider the question of building a new house for that department, the coming season. Accordingly, such a meeting was held yesterday, and a report given last evening, by W. A. H. as follows:

"All know it had been the plan to erect a large brick building near the Tontine, for the use of the fruit-department. Mr. Hamilton said he had given considerable thought to the subject, and several times had resolved to make drawings and estimates of cost; but for some reason he hadn't commenced the work; and in talking with Daniel he found some difference of opinion about the building required. Altogether, he was led to inquire whether it was best to put up the building the coming season. He seemed to feel that it was not; and in course of the conversation it appeared that others had had the same query; and before we got through I think the feeling was unanimous, that the erection of a building had better be postponed, at least one year.

"The reasons urged in favor of this course were, first, that we do not know exactly how large a building we need; secondly, we are undecided where to place it; and thirdly, the subject has not been sufficiently studied, so that we are certain what would be the best arrangements that could be made for such a building—what are the best labor-saving contrivances that might be put into such a structure. Then another important consideration was, that by putting up the building the present season, we should tie up, so to speak, quite an amount of capital which we need in our business.

"As we do not design to can a large amount of vegetables, corn, peas, &c., it was thought we could get along the coming season very well, with our present accommodations, with some changes. For one thing, it is proposed to erect a large wooden building near the Tontine, probably west of it, which shall be used as a store-house, and perhaps have a jelly-room connected with it. With that addition, it was thought the department would get along very well the coming season ; and after the summer's campaign, we shall be better able to decide with reference to the future.

"A remark, made by Mr. Noyes, had some weight with Mr. Hamilton and the committee. He said we might want to build on a very large scale for the fruit-department, and perhaps it would be better to put up a wooden building in the mean time. It is evident it would be perfectly wise and safe to erect this wooden building, for it will always be in demand in that place for storage and other purposes.

"In the course of the conversation there was a view taken of the future development of the fruit business that may have an important bearing on our building operations. The fruit business has gradually increased in dimensions, and it is difficult to say why it should not continue to do so, and become at least a dozen times as large as it is now—why it should not double every year if we choose to have it. If that is the true view, then the question arises, whether there is not a limit to the amount of business we can do here profitably, and whether we shall not eventually contrive some way to preserve different kinds of fruits in the localities where they grow most abundantly; peaches, for instance, in New Jersey, plums near Rochester, quinces somewhere else; and blackberries and huckleberries in still another locality. Or, better, a Community may yet be started in the midst of the best fruit region. Some one remarked that Rochester and its vicinity was one of the best localities in the State, and perhaps in the whole country, for growing a great variety of fruits We now get all our peaches, nearly all our cherries, and a large proportion of our plums and quinces from that region. It is about one hundred miles from here, and would fall in with Mr. Noyes's plan, of having a line of Communities from Wallingford to the Pacific. I don't know how soon something of that kind may take place; but certainly, it is worthy of consideration. I confess the more I think of it the more enthusiastic I get over the idea. The trap-business and the bag-business, in a financial point of view, might be said to have made the Oneida Community. Why is not the fruit-business capable of making another association as large as this Community or larger? You see at once, there would be a great many advantages in having the preserving factory right where fruit is most plenty.—This would save a large amount of expressage. We must have paid several hundred dollars for expressage last year. And then there is always considerable loss by decay, where fruits are transported any distance, and more or less is purloined while on the way. Then we might have our factory so near the railroad, that it would save a great amount of carting, which is expensive.

"The main object the committee had in making this report, was to find out if the Community would sympathize with this plan of postponing building, till we are better prepared." [The report was approved.]

The changeable, freaky state of the weather, is almost unprecedented. Yesterday morning, it was comparatively mild, and snow was falling gently; but in the afternoon and evening it grew cold—the wind changed and blew almost a gale, piling the snow into drifts. This morning the weather is cold and windy.

Yesterday's temperature—
7½ A. M., 13.   12 M., 24.   6 P. M., 10.   Mean 15½.

DAILY JOURNAL
OF ONEIDA COMMUNITY.

VOL. 3. SATURDAY, JAN. 19, 1867. NO. 17.

Blairstown, Iowa, Jan. 11, 1767.

BROTHERS AND SISTERS:—I am going home to Ohio to visit father and friends, and if I felt that I was good enough I would ask you to allow me to visit you, but I must wait. Please send the CIRCULARS to me at Mt. Gilead, Monroe Co., Ohio, until I order otherwise. I send my likeness; won't you send me the likeness of some of the men and women there, who are the most harmonious communists. I want to see them. The picture I send you is very correct. I love you, and only wish I was sufficiently in possession of the true spirit of religion, to come and aid you in the good work but I fear that I should be a garden as yet; but I earnestly hope for better days. There is quite a revival of religion in our town at present, and the more I am with them, the more I think of you, and think I see you living religion every day, about your business, as much as though you were in meeting. I send our paper; you will see by it, that I am closing up every thing here. I don't know where I shall go. Don't publish any of this. but if any brother or sister should feel like writing to me, I should be glad. I am tired of the competition of business, and of the wickedness it generates, and I could no longer refrain from writing to you. Mrs. Allman, Mrs. Peet and I were together night before last; they talked of nothing but you.

The Allmans have sold out and are unsettled. Mrs. Peet has sold the most of her property. We feel we are not fit to come to you, and are not qualified to start a Community ourselves, and are not satisfied to stay as we are. Won't you please present us to the throne of grace sometime when it is well with you? I send $5,00 to pay for pictures if you have them, if not, apply it to the paper. I feel so blue to-day that I can't write to my own satisfaction, and still I want to write. Is J. W. Towner with you? have you got room for any more, or are looking towards establishing any other branches of the Community? Please address me at Mt. Gilead, Monroe Co., Ohio, as I expect to be there in a few days. If you have any other information that I have not asked for, that you may think proper to give me, do so. Mrs. Morris is in Ohio. She wrote me to send her the CIRCULAR at once, as she felt lost without it. She is Orthodox and quite devotional. I have a son eighteen years old, a good tinman by trade; he is attending Commercial College in Delaware, Ohio. If he should wish to visit you in the spring, could you make him useful at his trade for a while?   As ever your Brother,
ISAIAH MORRIS.

Two evenings have been principally occupied with the criticism of the boys that attend E. S. B.'s school.—

They were not thought to be in as good a state in reference to their studies, as they were at the commencement of the winter. Distracting influences had come in, and diverted their attention from study. Besides, they were too much absorbed with each other, and did not enough seek association with persons older and better than themselves. A good deal of interest was manifested for them, and a desire expressed, that they should take a new start—seek the ascending fellowship, and become helpers to Mr. Hamilton and the Community. Mr. H spoke of Orrin Wright as having had satisfactory experience in the past, and he still hoped, that though he had dropped down into fellowship with those below him, he would recover himself, and become truly a Christ-seeker. Much love was expressed for them.

There is considerable complaint this winter, of our neighborhood school. It is a branch of the Union free school at Oneida Castle, and governed by the same Trustees, of whom Barnes Davis is one. Well, his daughter a young girl of sixteen is made the teacher of this branch, but she is not liked by some, and the school of about thirty children, has dwindled to seven or eight For some reason our tenant, Michael Scheare, does no send, although he has a large family that ought to be schooled, and lives close by the school-house.

Others complain; Mr. Radford and Heyl have with drawn their children.—Perhaps the Community ough to enquire into the matter, as we have a large tax to pay for the support of schools, and also an interest in the education and improvement of all, especially the families of our tenants and employees.   M. L. W.

Our classes for elocution are still quite enthusiastic over their ba, be, bi's, &c., and though we have not had the pleasure of a drill in that school, yet we hear them vocalizing, above, below, and on all sides of us.

S. L. Hun takes this opportunity to inform the family, that her name is neither Nans, Nunn or Nunus, but simply Hun, and none other.

Our teamsters are now drawing logs from East hill, where they have engaged about one hundred.

We have to report to-day, cold weather, a cutting north wind and drifted roads.

C. A. Cragin arrived last night at about 10 o'clock.

Traps ordered the past week,   19 doz.

Yesterday's temperature—
7½ A. M., 0. 12 M., 8. 6 P. M., 5. Mean 4⅓.

DAILY JOURNAL
OF ONEIDA COMMUNITY.

VOL. 3.   MONDAY, JAN. 21, 1867.   NO. 13.

NOTES OF BUSINESS MEETING.

Is it not time that the Willow-Place Factory was furnished with a trip-hammer? The probable cost of such an one as is wanted is estimated at $900. All were agreed in thinking that the Factory should some time have a good trip hammer; but in consideration of the outlay involved, the matter was referred to E. H. Hamilton, W. A. Hinds, Geo. W. Hamilton, J. C. Higgins, and W. R. Inslee.

G. Campbell was appointed to take charge of selling the quarry-stone at Willow-Place.

The Financial Committee, in connection with Mr. Vanvelzer are to decide upon the expediency of procuring a Sewing-machine for the Shoe-shop.

G. W. Hamilton, W. R. Inslee and J. H. Barron, were appointed a Committee, to consider and report upon the subject of lighting the Community buildings with gas.

The Fuel Committee reported the recommendation that coal stoves be used wherever practicable, in places where fire is kept up most of the day, and that no more new wood stoves be purchased, as coal is now considerably cheaper than wood.

G. W. N. writes to us, that much of the "Oneida Gossip" furnished by the JOURNAL is not transferable to the columns of the CIRCULAR, on account of its being in the form of propositions; "It was decided to do so and so &c.," and, that though Wallingford likes to have things reported in this prospective shape, for their own private reading, yet the ripe form of accomplishment, is all they ought to use in the CIRCULAR; and he suggests to us, a little more copious mention of things after execution. In a P. S. he adds: "The above ideas suggest the question, whether it would not be well for each department to make a systematic (however brief) report of its labors and transaction, to your bureau from time to time." [We heartily say amen to the above postscript. ED.]

———◆◆◆———

Mr. Ackley and Worden have exchanged rooms for the time being. The former has been troubled with lameness for some time past—his left leg below the knee having become swollen, sore and painful. Of late his difficulty has increased so that he has been nearly confined to his room, and needing some care and attention, a warmer and more commodious room was desirable for him.

———◆◆◆———

C. A. Cragin purchased when in New-York, two bales of raw silk, quite good, for $12.75, per pound, three per cent off.

JUVENILE.
SOLILOQUY OF THE EVENING WATCHMAN.

I.
Twenty little shoes, all set in a row,
Side by side on the old bureau;
The little owners have gone to bed;
A pillow holds each sleepy head.

II.
Twenty little dresses hung in a row,
With little red stockings swinging below.
The little wearers are wrapped in sleep;
And I am here their watch to keep.

III.
Twenty little throats, O! tell me how?
All warbling at once, just now; just now;
But all is hushed. Methinks I seem
While listening here, to hear them dream.

IV.
Twenty little dreamers; what do *they* care?
What the future in store, has for them to share;
They dream of naught but their gambols, I ween;
So let's not awake them, but let them dream.

———◆◆◆———

We clip from the report of the meeting of the Farmers Club, in the New-York Semi Weekly of Jan. 18th, the following: "Mowing by Moonlight;"—D. H. Gould of Salem Franklin Co., Maine, says, "It is a moonlight fact, that a man can mow more grass on smooth land by moonlight, than by sunlight, when the mercury stands at 99 degrees." Another one adds, "This may be true, but there is something wrong when a man works nights. Recently we heard of a man ploughing corn, night after night, because some of his female relations had joined the Oneida Community."

MONDAY MORNING:—Our teamsters say that they have finished hauling logs from the West Hills, but are now engaged at wood in the same vicinity.—Notwithstanding the wind and storm, last night, and the snow this morning, some half dozen wood teams were seen at 7 o'clock on their way, as we have one hundred cords of dry wood to draw a distance of five or six miles.—On Saturday teaming was suspended, on account of snow drifts and the cold.

The Bag-bees commenced to-day. They are held in the upper Sitting-room at ¼ to 10 o'clock A. M., and continue one hour.

———◆◆◆———

Temperature Saturday and Sunday,
7¼ A. M., 5.   12 M., 12.   6 P. M., 18.   Mean 11¼.
7¼ A. M., 10.   12 M., 20.   6 P. M., 18.   Mean 16.

DAILY JOURNAL
OF ONEIDA COMMUNITY.

VOL. 3.   TUESDAY, JAN. 22, 1867.   NO. 19.

EVENING MEETING.

Mr. Hamilton:—I have promised myself that I would sometime criticise the habit of making excuses and apologies, when we attempt to do anything: it seems to have grown considerably upon the Community of late. I have met it recently in many ways, when persons have attempted to work out a problem on the blackboard, demonstrate a theorem in geometry, or come on to the stage before the elocution classes to speak, until my indignation has been aroused against it. I query if that is not one of the worst influences working among us at the present time, and one that belittles folks and hinders faith more than most anything else. Almost all will remember, that Mr. Noyes criticised this habit long ago. If persons had anything to say, he disliked to hear them begin with an apology.

I have noticed in the elocution class that I attend, that in several instances when persons come forward to speak their pieces, they do it in an apologetic way, and then if they don't succeed very well, they apologize for the failure. I believe we should do better all round if we did just as well as we could, and then took credit for what we are able to accomplish. If you fail don't try to plaster it over with excuses. I don't believe that practice is pleasing to God. I consider it a very vicious habit of spirit, as it destroys all manliness and assurance of heart We need to cultivate the opposite, as Christians and **strong-hearted believers, and go forward, not with false** assurance and pomposity, but with simple-hearted child-like confidence.

The spirit of Christ working in our hearts and lives, instead of making us do less than we expect will enable us to do far better. As near as I can find out there is a great deal of this apologizing spirit in the classes, and perhaps it is one of the most disagreeable things the teachers have to meet. It has its source in egotism and unbelief, and I for one dislike it very much. [Approved.]

Mr. Woolworth:—We hear a great deal said nowadays about breaking up egotism, and in a good many ways we are breaking it up and getting freed from it. And yet this spirit that makes excuses and apologies is egotism trying to save itself. I have no fellowship with it.

W. A. Hinds:—And as usual it defeats its own object.

Mr. Henton:—Yes, as William says, it defeats its own object in more ways than one. If a person is going to do anything he wants all the assurance of heart that he can have. If he assumes the attitude that he is not prepared to do this or that, and cannot do it very well, he puts himself into rapport with the spirit that is not able to do it. If a person wants to be overcome by fear, the most sure way is to assume the attitude of fear.

Mr. Inslee:—It is a common saying that those who excel in making apologies are good for nothing else.

Mr. Hamilton:—It is a very good saying. It is best not to go into the battle unless you have made up your mind to fight; but having once entered you should throw away the scabbard. And so of anything: make up your mind to go into it whole-heartedly and run the risk, or else not try at all.—I feel a great deal of interest in this effort to break up egotism in various ways and get our freedom. I believe I have got my share of the work to do. I mean to keep clear of apologies, and if I do not, I hope I shall be criticised.

Mr. H. R. Perry gave us a very interesting and instructive lecture during the meeting hour last night, on the origin of the popular belief so prevalent in Christendom, that the devil is a fallen angel. He thought the idea originated in heathen mythology, and was incorporated into the creeds of religionists, during the dark ages.

SONG OF THE PACIFIC RAILROAD.

Over the rivers, over the plains,
    Over the Rocky Mountains,
On through the valleys, up to the hights,
    Up by Sierra's fountains:
Thus we go marching, steady and sure,
    Swinging the pickaxe and shovel,
Marching on o'er the buffalo fields,
    On by the Indian's hovel.
        Down with the ties, down with the rails,
        Up with culvert and trestle!
        On with the engine, coaches and mails,
        Ho! there, the Westward whistle!

Laborers! haste ye over the seas,
    Workers, from all the nations;
Many we want on ev'ry mile,
    Builders at all the stations:
Chinamen! from the Yang-tse-Kiang,
    Irish! from banks of Shannon,
Soldiers! who fought the war to the end,
    Facing the Rebel cannon!
        Down with the ties, down with the rails,
        Up with culvert and trestle!
        On with the engine, coaches and mails,
        Ho! there, the Westward whistle!

Glorious labor!—song of to-day—
    Better than war and plunder;
Banner of empire, leading the way!
    Chariots rolling in thunder!
This is the dream the prophets beheld—
    This is the ancient vision:
Banding the earth with progress and truth—
    This is the final mission.
        Down with the ties, down with the rails,
        Up with culvert and trestle!
        On with the engine, coaches and mails,
        Ho! there, the Westward whistle!

Builders are we for ages to come—
    Ages of brightest story,
Blending the nations' hearts into one
    Unity, love and glory.
Hail! then, the peaceful march of to-day!
    Hail! to the workers in motion!
Hail! to the hearts that lead in the way,
    On to the Western Ocean!
        Down with the ties, down with the rails,
        Up with culvert and trestle!
        On with the engine, coaches and mails,
        Ho! there, the Westward whistle!

ERRATUM.—An omission occurred in yesterday's JOURNAL, near the bottom of the third page. For "Semi Weekly," read Semi-Weekly Tribune.

Yesterday's temperature—
7½ A. M., 18. 12 M., 33. 6 P. M., 26. Mean 25½.

DAILY JOURNAL
OF ONEIDA COMMUNITY.

VOL. 3. WEDNESDAY, JAN. 23, 1867. NO. 20.

EVENING MEETING.

Mr. Hamilton:—I have been over to the boarding-house this evening, as they sent to have me come to an oyster supper, the boarders had been getting up. When Mrs. Conant first told me they wished to have me present, I didn't know what to think about it; but I finally concluded if they had sent and invited me to come, I would go as a representative of the Community and the Community spirit, and look in upon them. So I went over and took supper with them, and staid to see them commence dancing and then came home.

But the thought that worked in my mind about the matter was, that the time would come, as we increased our business and the number of our employees, that we should exert our influence over them more and more. I thought our employees were a very smart wholesome looking set of folks. I hope sometime, we shall have a large boarding-house with better conveniences for such parties. It does not appear to me to be an impossible thing, to elevate all those around us out of the ways of the world, into the ways of the Kingdom of Heaven more or less.

Mr. Hawley:—I believe the Community spirit is having an effect on all our employees, and whoever surrounds us, and that this influence is constantly growing stronger. I like Mr. Hamilton's idea very much of lifting them out of their present position into one that is higher and better.

Mr. Hamilton:—I felt free to meet them with all the sympathies common between us. I felt I could do it and have the balance of influence on our side.

Mr. Hatch:—I liked the idea of having our folks furnish music, and keep the control of it, better than to have them go and get outside players. I thought the effect upon them would be much better.

Mr. Woolworth:—I should suppose such a party would seem quite like a Community.

Mr. Hamilton:—Yes, there was something quite pleasing about it. I thought it was an advance in civilization, as far as it went.

Mr. Vanvelzer:—A good many persons appreciate working for us.

By request Mr. Woolworth read from the CIRCULAR the article "Life Compared to a Tube," and then remarked as follows:—"I think this is a good subject to recur to often, that we may as fast as possible realize the conditions presented in this article. I believe it reveals the great secret of happiness and salvation. The sure condition of peace is here revealed. In the world we shall have tribulation, abundance of it. We know that is true."

One who has had considerable to do with the culinary department gives the following recipe for making cake:

"The three principal ingredients of Cake are *beat*, *stir* and *mix*. First use beat, beat, beat, on eggs until they become froth. Next compound: beat with butter until the butter becomes cream. (Making butter of cream is a common thing, but to make cream of butter will be found quite a different thing by those who try to do it. Then take the froth and cream, and add several parts of stir, stir, stir. Then throw in some flour, a little grated nutmeg, a few currants and a few raisins. Now add the last ingredient, viz., mix, mix, mix, mix, mix, mix, until your hands are tired and elbows ache, and still continue to add this important part, until some one mercifully cries out, "That will do."

It is mild and still, this morning, and the snow is falling gently. The roads are so badly drifted between here and Willow-Place, that free passage is difficult—the sleigh at any moment, being liable to become upset.

The Hamilton stage, which is a covered conveyance turned over into a snow-drift opposite our home boarding house, a few days ago. We believe there were no women aboard, though there were several men.

The hands at our home boarding-house, in imitation of the example set by their Willow-Place associates formed themselves into a club, bought oysters and had a supper and dance last night. Several of our people were invited, Mr. Hamilton among the rest. Our musicians furnished them with music for the occasion, and all went off pleasantly.

Mr. Andrew Smith, of Verona, the man who laid down our pump logs several years ago, and who with his wife has frequently called here, was buried yesterday. We understand he died of cancer in the stomach.

We have now, employed in the silk-factory, nineteen hired women and girls, and one man.

THE CIRCULARS for some cause are delayed again, and have not yet reached us.

Yesterday's temperature—
7½ A. M., 20. 12 M., 28. 6 P. M., 20. Mean 22⅓.

THE O. C. DAILY.

VOL. 3. THURSDAY, JAN. 24, 1867. NO. 21

EVENING MEETING.

Mr. Woolworth :—I was interested in what Mr. Noyes said about improving our meetings and rising out of routine. I think we are liable to fall into some stereo typed formulas, especially in our criticisms, that are unedifying.

A. L. Burt :—I remember Mr. Tinsley used to say a good deal about our use of " I do;" and many times he would get up quite a labored speech just for the sake of avoiding that form, and showing what he could do, and then afterwards say something about it. I much preferred to hear our folks say " I do", than to hear *him* tall fifteen minutes.

Mr. Campbell :—I have an impression that bashfulness has more or less to do with these set phrases. It is said " Out of the abundance of the heart the mouth speaketh." When we get freedom to talk out of the heart, perhaps we shall have more variety of expression.

Mr. Hamilton :—It is a good time now to take a new departure, and get room in the first place, to enlarge our hearts towards God. We must trust him to inspire us, and he will enable us to rise out of routine. It is a good time to look to God to give us new inspiration about many things. Mr. Woolworth and others will be called on to take charge of the meetings. The inspiration of God if we look for it, will start new things and awaken new interests. There is a great deal of material and a great deal of life and power here in the Community, if it could be waked up, brought out and made the most of. One good thing about this elocutionary drill that we are having is, that it is breaking up egotism and getting persons free to do just what they can. I appreciate it very much in that respect.

Mr. G. W. Reeve from Berlin Hights, came here yesterday forenoon, and left after meeting last night. He had business at Buffalo, and finding that he should be obliged to stay there over night, he chose to come on here, though he could stay only a short time. He went over to Willow-Place, and looked round as much as he could, in the little time he spent here. He seemed quite pleased, and claimed to be one with us, though he confessed that he was not fully settled on all the doctrines we hold, but he hoped to be.

John Heyl started yesterday for New York, sent by the Bag-department for the purpose of getting some ideas in reference to the new styles of bags, frames &c., that may help him in getting up new, and as much as possible, original styles for our trade. We pay his expenses, and he is to spend a week in looking round among the Bag manufacturers, wherever he can gain admittance.

Our meetings close now, precisely at 9 o'clock, unless something very important prevents. We had gradually departed from our original practice of holding them one hour only. Mr. Hamilton called attention to the subject a few evenings since, and it was decided that we should in future, be particular to break up at 9 o'clock.

Passing through the children's room this morning as they were taking their breakfast, we asked the mother *pro tempore*, what we should say about her children?—Nothing, she replied, except that they are every one well; perfectly so.

They have commenced reading, in the Bag-bees, " Felix Holt," a new novel by the author of " Adam Bede." Mrs. H. C. Noyes is the reader.

It rained some yesterday and last night, and this morning every tree, twig and shrub are covered with ice.— It is also very slippery.

The CIRCULARS came last night, and glad were we to get them.

Yesterday's temperature—
7½ A. M., 23. 12 M., 29. 6 P. M., 26. Mean 26.

THE O. C. DAILY.

VOL. 3.   **FRIDAY, JAN. 25, 1867.**   NO. 22.

EVENING MEETING.

In the criticism of C. A. Bart last night, but little fault was found with him—it was thought he had improved since his last criticism, though he still lacked resurrection life and energy. Mr. Hamilton remarked as follows: " It is the real soldier spirit that is wanted. You have got to go into it rough and tumble if you are going to beat the devil. You must have real masculine vigor and tone to your spirit. I am well assured that is what God gives—that is the fruit of his spirit in our life. That old, subdued, noncombative, noodemonstrative kind of religion that is so much lauded in the churches is not the kind that belongs to God's army and his power. The spirit of God working in a person's heart makes him strong and sure. I feel like saying to Charles, 'awake out and put on strength and majesty.' I want to see him become a fighting man—if you choose to use the term—for Christ and his cause.

God is very patient and good-natured. He tries to get possession of mankind; but frequently he fails to do so till men and women are on their death-beds, as it were, and stripped of their glory. He is working differently with us. He wants to get hold of men and women right in the prime and pride of their strength and glory. If we can find out the way to give ourselves to God entirely, while we are in full possession of our vigor of life, we shall be so much more worthy of him. It is a splendid sight to see strong men and women, young men and women, right in the pride of life, wholly subdued to God, and that work wrought in their spirits which is frequently only wrought in a person when on his death-bed. I believe it can be done; that we can give ourselves to Christ, and that he is strong enough to take possession of us with all our powers, and make everything draw us toward God. "The joy of the Lord is our strength." I am ambitious and pray that there may be no weak and feeble ones among us. I want to see all stand up strong in the joy of the Lord.

Charles has a good deal of trouble and temptation, or has had, about love &c. The question is, what is the cure for that experience? It is freedom from idolatry, and the attitude that takes the joy of the Lord instead. There is nothing else that can make people truly happy. You may swing around the whole circle of creation, and revel in the beauty and glory of the outward world, but you never will be happy till you get where the joy of the Lord works in your life. Until this is done you cannot love in the true way—in the way to worship God and do good. To me there is a great deal of meaning in that expression, "The joy of the Lord is your strength." Get the joy of the Lord in your heart and you will trample on temptation, and digest and cast it out.

Mr. Woolworth :—We see there is a heaven of fellowship that is open to every one that will walk in the light. We need not feel poor or starved, for we have fellowship with this church and with the church of the first-born in the New Jerusalem, every day and hour. I believe that is what we are invited to.

Mr. Hamilton :—Charles was in my room the other day and I had some conversation with him. I told him I thought he needed more vigor of faith and life. He seems to be tempted some yet. Sometimes it seems as though his life was pitched on the minor key. There is a certain child-like simplicity I have seen about Charles lately, that I have liked very much.

Mr. Woolworth :—Charles has impressed me as being in a somewhat negative state. I should think he had faced around in the right direction, but he does not seem to have got in motion yet. There does not seem to be very much enthusiasm for the cause. I don't know but it is working in his heart. I judge it is. I wish however he would give it more way, and think in that way he would kindle and get into a more positive state, and have more of the missionary spirit. I think there is a good deal of native power and ability in him.

<hr>

At the request of Mr. Marshall, Secretary of the Vernon Agricultural Society, a report has been made on " The Oneida Community: Its Buildings, Manufactures Agriculture &c.," to be submitted for publication in forthcoming Annual Volume of Transactions of State Agricultural Society.—Mr. Pitt, who made out the report, yesterday delivered it to Mr. Marshall. Mr. M. was much pleased with it, and stated, he should either forward it at once by mail, or deliver it when he attended the annual meeting of the Society in a few weeks. It may also be mentioned, that Mr. Marshall in one of his previous reports made a brief but favorable mention of the Community, which was published in the Annual Volume for 1862.

<hr>

GOVERNMENT OF THE TONGUE.

I have thought a great deal about this subject lately, and have often wondered why we could not testify on the right side as well as the wrong. I know that I use my tongue very recklessly, and it is with a great deal of difficulty, that I am able to control it; but I know if we stop and confess Christ, that he will help us to overcome this great evil. I desire to let Christ's spirit come into me, when I am talking, and keep him constantly in mind; if we do this, we cannot have anything but good thoughts, and we shall not be likely to talk in a light frivolous way. I have worked myself into a very bad state, just by gossiping with folks that I knew would not do me any good. I felt very much discouraged this evening, when one of my companions came along and spoke to me, and I answered back in a sharp disrespectful way. I was very sorry; I did not have any right to use my tongue so, it does not belong to me, but God, and I ought to use it to please him. I remember when I was a little girl, that the folks told me when I got provoked, to fill my mouth full of water, so that I could not say anything, but I think confessing Christ is a great deal better, and I mean to do it. I pray that sometime I may be able to testify boldly for the truth, and let my tongue go in that direction.   FLORENCE.

<hr>

Yesterday's temperature—
7¼ A. M., 28.   12 M., 32.   6 P. M., 26.   Mean 28⅔.

THE O. C. DAILY.

VOL. 3.   SATURDAY, JAN. 26, 1867.   NO. 23.

EVENING MEETING.

Mr. Hamilton :—I like all Mr. Noyes says very much, both about Mr. Thacker and the principle of unity. I thought of Christ's saying right in this connection : "All power in heaven and earth is given unto me." It came home to me forcibly that this power was given to him because he had discovered the secret of unity. He knew that he was one with God, and that God was one with him. Probably he had this in mind when he said, "Where two or three are gathered together in my name there am I in the midst." This principle of unity is a great spiritual power. There is no unity where there is selfishness and egotism. I have thought a good deal lately about the passage, "Blessed are the pure in heart for they shall see God."

I have been feeling for some time, that before we went into another campaign of fruit-preservering, the Fruit-department should receive a more thorough criticism than it has yet had. I think Mr. Noyes has given a suggestion that we can now apply to that department in the way of criticism. Perhaps we shall have more light and inspiration to find out what has been the trouble there, than we have had heretofore. This department was criticised sometime ago but there wasn't much said. I would suggest that all connected with that business offer themselves for criticism to-morrow night.

Our good sleighing brings us considerable company these days. Among the parties yesterday was one, of six young men from North Brookfield, a hotel-keeper and his predecessor in the same function, with four others, three of whom had never been here before. All expressed serious and lively interest in our movement. Although they chewed tobacco and were evidently somewhat rough, they evinced a hearty honesty, quite refreshing.

One of their objects in coming, was to get the use of the Hall, music and entertainment generally, for a dancing party from their place. Mr. Hamilton said that we might sometime be prepared to respond to such applications but could not do so now.—Mr. Hall who has on his peddling trips, occasionally put up at their Hotel, says that they were in the crowd who cleaned out the Loomises. They enquired for Mr. Underwood, and five of them subscribed for the CIRCULAR.

Mr. and Mrs. Dunning from Willow-Place, came here by invitation yesterday, took supper, and staid to the evening meeting. They seemed to enjoy themselves very much, and our people took considerable pains to make it pleasant for them by way of entertainment.— Mr. Hamilton inquired of Mrs. D. if she had not got to be almost a Community woman ? She replied that she thought so, as she kept the Willow-Place Branch. She said to some one after meeting, "Wouldn't I hate to be criticised in that great Hall."

We had a long letter of nine pages, from a Mrs. Chapman of Summit Co., Ohio, giving a history of her life, family &c., and wishing to connect herself with us, or to come with her little girl ten years old, and board with us a few months, if agreeable to us.

The Horticulturalists have commenced making boxes for grapes. They design to make 500, which, added to 500 which was left over last season, will, they think, be all they shall need the coming season.

Several sleigh-loads of our people went to ride, yesterday afternoon. The sleighing, where the roads are not drifted is very fine, which together with the mildness of the weather, makes sleigh-riding an agreeable pastime.

Two or three inches of snow fell last night and this morning, which has more than repaired the loss, by the rain and warm weather we have had a day or two past.

We had two songs last night, after meeting, one by Alice and the other by Abram. The one sung by A., "Who'll save the Left" was very inspiring.

Traps ordered the past week,   12 doz.

Yesterday's temperature—
7¼ A. M., 26. 12 M., 34. 6 P. M., 31.   Mean 30¼.

THE O. C. DAILY.

VOL. 3.   MONDAY, JAN. 28, 1867.   NO. 24

EVENING MEETING.

Mr. Woolworth:—I have had some thoughts lately about fellowship. It seemed to me it we could enter into that, it would solve the problem of social life, and re move all the difficulties, embarrassments and torments people are now subject to, more or less. "If we walk in the light as he is in the light we have fellowship one with another," or communism as it is properly rendered. In that relation there is permanence; and that is what the human heart wants and seeks after—something that is not subject to decay or to be lost, but is permanent.— I know we get that in Communism or heart fellowship. It is something that will go on eternally, independent of time or place and is in no way dependent on the presence of any object. There will be fellowship if indi duals are ten thousand miles apart, for they will be with each other in spirit. If they go to hades, or the New Jerusalem the chain will hold good.

That is the kind of fellowship I want, and nothing less than that will satisfy my heart. For instance, want fellowship with Mr. Hamilton, whether he is here or in China, or in any other place where he may be called; and I desire the same fellowship with Mr. Noyes, and with all true believers on earth, or in heaven, or hades.

I am certain if we can enter into true communism it will solve all the difficulties and perplexites of social life and experience. If persons undertake to appropriate individuals to themselves and make heaven in that way they will find no security. There is constant insecurity and fear in that state of things, and to the happiness built upon it. "Fear hath torment." There is no fear in love and true communism, or fellowship. "Neither height nor depth nor any other creature can separate us from the love of God." That is the very essence, it seems to me, of delocalization. Communism of heart is not broken by distance or space.

NOTES TO THE COMMUNITY.

I wish to thank God publicly for restoring me to health again. I was attacked quite violently with pain in my head and stomach last Wednesday afternoon. At first it seemed as though I lost all control of my own faith, or heroism in helping myself to throw off disease; but Mrs. Noyes and Whitfield's quiet faith and trust in God turn- ed the current, and I soon found myself looking for help in the same direction they did. I am thankful for the experience, and also for the kind care bestowed upon me by Mrs. N. and W, also others, who occasionally came to my room. I offer myself anew to Christ and the Community to be made the most of. I want to be a true soldier in the cause, and a helper to Mr. Noyes and Mr. Hamilton. I confess my separation from all my worldly friends, and my union with, and love for the family.

—

I wish to separate myself from a spirit of weakness, that has tempted me some or late. I am aware it is the result of a lack of faith and trust in God, and "Whatso- ever is not of faith is sin." I desire not only to be loyal to Mr. Noyes, but I want a strong and vigorous heart, that is not moved by circumstances. The Lord seems to be calling on us to lay off any remains of weakness and narrow-mindedness of spirit, and rise up into sym- pathy with Mr. Noyes's unity of heart and purpose.— There, seems to be our only hope of success in overcom ing evil.—Mr. Noyes's late talks on unity, have been very instructive and edifying. I desire very much to partake of their spirit, in a way that will make me bear fruit unto God.   M. D. P.

A Mr. Aldred, his wife and two little children, came here Saturday forenoon, staid over Sunday and are still with us. They are from Wisconsin, and are *en route* for Texas, where Mr. A. hopes to be able to make a pur- chase of land, and form a sort of colony there. He knows nothing respecting the Community, except what he has gleaned from a few CIRCULARS that he has read. He did not impress us very favorably, either as an earn est seeker for truth, or as having "an ear to hear." He seemed full of his own ideas of things, and put them forth quite immodestly, we thought. He is an English- man, a printer by trade, and a Universalist in sentiment.

Birds are quite numerous this winter, I think their number is unprecedented. There are two varieties of the snow-bird, also one or more of the wood pecker, be- sides the familiar chick-a-dee. This morning the wind blows and the snow flies; the birds nothing daunted go back and forth with their merry chic-a-dee- ee. A day or two since, a flock of birds were observed on a tree in front of the Tontine, chirruping quite socially, although the weather was bitter cold. We are informed that Mr. Delatre takes pleasure in feeding them, and this may account for their frequent proximity to the win- dows.   E. G. HAWLEY.

We have to report snow and drifts again to-day, and we are quite blocked in. Some of our people attempted to go to the depot yesterday, went nearly to Hubbard's and turned back. Then they started on the other road, and succeeded in getting over to Johnson's, but no further; so they gave it up. This morning all hands and teams were called out to break roads to Willow- Place. On account of the state of the roads, Mr. Ham- ilton did not start in the night for Wallingford as he expected. The snow is still falling.

Mr. Kelley returned Saturday, between 9 and 10 o'clock P. M., in company with Mr. Clark, who had been to Albany on business.

Temperature Saturday and Sunday,
7¼ A. M., 30.   12 M., 40.   6 P. M., 32.   Mean 34.
7¼ A. M., 30.   12 M., 27.   6 P. M., 22.   Mean 23.

THE O. C. DAILY.

VOL. 3.   TUESDAY, JAN. 29, 1867.   NO. 25.

EVENING MEETING.

C. A. Cragin was criticised last night by his request, and the following are some of the remarks made on his case.—*Mr. Woolworth :*—I have had a great deal of admiration for Charles's business capacity and energy. I think he has marked abilities as a manager, or superintendent of business. I have similar impressions, however, to those expressed by others, that he relies on himself too much, and not enough on inspired action and organization. He should seek to organize his business as perfectly as possible into the Community spirit and the general business. If he should do that, he would work with more ease to himself, and give better satisfaction in the long run. I have an impression he finds a good deal of friction. I know he has great enthusiasm, and a strong purpose to carry it through and make it successful at all hazards; and yet I have the feeling that he doesn't work with the ease, pleasure and satisfaction that he might, if his own spirit was more perfectly organized and in rapport with the Community spirit. It would be less wearing on him, as he would feel strengthened and supported more than he does now. I think any amount of sympathy and support are ready to be extended to him, whenever he puts himself in the attitude to receive them.

C. A. Cragin :—I have felt the business wearing on my life some of late, and I think Mr. Woolworth has hit upon the reason.

Mr. Woolworth :—I guess you have got it too much on your own individual shoulders. I am afraid you will not be able to carry it in that way. It would be likely to break you down before you had fulfilled your mission or destiny.

Mr. Inslee :—I have thought there was danger of that, as I have noticed his care-worn appearance.

H. E. Allen :—I have sometimes thought him too open toward outsiders. He is not sufficiently reticent toward the help. It is too easy for him to confide his plans and schemes to outsiders. He is rather isolated, and spends most of his time at the factory. He doesn't seem to mix up much with the family in a social way. He is too impetuous, and frequently makes up his mind without sufficient thought or deliberation. I think he has good purposes and means to have a good spirit.

Libbie Hutchins :—I have thought since my acquaintance with Charles, that he did not appreciate sympathy and union with those around him. There is an individuality about him that makes him independent of others. I think he has improved in that lately, and begins to appreciate sympathy. I was very much impressed with this trait when we were in Willimantic. He didn't seem to appreciate fellowship with Harriet and me, but felt perfectly competent and rather preferred to stand alone. I think he needs to be pretty earnest in regard to his fellowship with outsiders, as he is very apt to be open and free with them.

I would like to endorse the criticism given the other evening, of Daniel Abbott; also what was said of the Abbott spirit. I know it is a prominent trait of the Abbott character to be very self-reliant and independent, to stick to their own views and judgment in a very obstinate, egotistical manner, in a way to exclude the judgment of others or the Community spirit from coming in to lubricate and modify their judgment in the premises. I wish to confess Christ a saviour from an isolated independent judgment, and I confess him in me a spirit that is modest, and esteems others better than myself, and is conducive of unity, brotherly love and true organization. I believe what Daniel and I both need, is to die to egotism and our old life, that the meek, humble, childlike spirit of Christ may have full possession of our hearts.   JOHN ABBOTT.

Mr. Aldred and family left yesterday afternoon. He offered to pay for his board while here, said he expected to do it; but Mr. Bolles told him we did not charge him anything, and on his insisting to pay, Mr. B. told him if he wanted to give any thing for the cause, he might do so. He left five dollars.—Mr. Hamilton also left for Wallingford, on the afternoon train.

REQUIEM.

Old Tom is dead, that good old cat,
  We ne'er shall see him more.
He used to watch for rats and mice,
  Beside our old shop door.

When Tom was young, a little kit,
  A neighboring man one day,
Quite kindly left him for our use,
  And then went on his way.

We fed him well, he grew apace,
  A goodly cat was he,
Who once was seen to catch at once
  Of mice, no less than three.

He lived to see the Trap-shop moved,
  The Bag-shop in its place ;
Yet he remained a faithful cat,
  The cutest of his race.

The years sped on ; as Tom grew old,
  He grew so *very* cross,
That of his former pleasant ways
  We deeply felt the loss.

Peace to his bones ; we'll let him rest :
  His mousing toils are o'er ;
He's gone to join the race of cats
  Like him, who've died before.   B. B. H.

The sun shines beautifully this morning, the first time for many days, but the wind blows, and the snow flies, and withal, it is pretty cold.

Yesterday's temperature—
7½ A. M., 18. 12 M., 28. 6 P. M., 30. Mean 25½.

THE O. C. DAILY.

VOL. 3. WEDNESDAY, JAN. 30, 1867. NO. 26.

EVENING MEETING.

Mr. Woolworth :—We see that Mr. Noyes does no forget the old fields, notwithstanding he is looking t new scenes of enterprise and expansion. He doesn' forget where the seed has been sown in years past.— The Putney field looks rather dreary and desolate now but there must be a good deal of seed buried there, tha will spring up and bear fruit, sometime.

Mr. Pitt :—I like the large view Mr. Noyes takes, ir cluding hades as well as this world.

Mr. Inslee :—I feel deeply interested in this talk. I brings clearly to my mind some remarks Mr. Noye made two years ago, when I was at Wallingford. H spoke of the fact that the people in that vicinity wer very much interested in his preaching during the reviva season, while he preached on the new-measure principle but after he turned Perfectionist they felt that he ha gone astray, into a wild-fire they could not approve o follow him into. He said he was ambitious to sti prove to them that he did not go astray, but had gon steadily on from that time to this, in the course of thing they had so much admired at first. He had been doing what would save both himself and them still, if they would but give him a fair hearing.

"Winter has come in all his hoary majesty, and locked the earth in a cold embrace. The cold, white blanket that he has spread over nature, is thicker than usual; the highways are already blocked up; but still he continues to sift his feathery flakes over the earth, as though he would smother from nature the last remains of her vitality.—The north wind sweeps across the glistening plains, and howls in the ears of shivering hedges and shrubs, its dismal tales of polar bergs.

"The pines on the lawn are huddled together as though they had discovered that unity is warmth as well as strength; and are bitterly complaining that Boreas is making them his sport; they are singing the same mournful cadence as they sang of old, when the wind first descended to earth and sought among them, a voice. Those Norway spruces too; I will warrant, they have at last found a clime parallel, at least; with that of their ancestors; as they stand half buried in snow, writhing in the northern blast. The aspen shakes as it never did before; while a few remaining winter-seared leaves, are fluttering and clinging, as it were, for life, to the young maples by the road-side; lest by some mishap they should lose their hold and be at the mercy of the storm. Nothing seems to escape the fury of this storm, but the fishes in the pond. I wonder if they feel it, as they lie nestled among the rocks under the cold ice. While I write I hear the wind whistling through the registers and flues; screaming around the corners of the building; frolicing with the window-sashes and the clinging vines about them ; and all this mingled with the mellov tones of the distant organ, as they swell and die on my ear amid the stormy din. My soul is thus inspired with a reverential awe for the God of the elements."

We take the following extract from one of the girl's compositions.—" If persons possess the earnestness anc humility of Christ, they find it easy to overcome bac habits, thus enabling them to become graceful and re fined. I have lately observed some of the habits anc the appearance of a class of the young women. A care less or love-of-ease spirit will often prompt them to very unlady-like postures—such as sitting on one foot wit the other twisted around the chair, or seated with th feet elevated considerably, while leaning back, &c.—ther In standing to converse with a person, it does not seen necessary to be writhing and twisting—leaning first or one foot, then on the other; these attitudes are said by some to be very easy—but it is well known that a true lady does not require such habits to be at ease. When I describe the habits and appearance of others, I find i necessary to judge myself. I will here mention that has been observed that the custom of retiring at a lat hour is not in good taste ; one will in time, find it d mental to the health, and the company that is fo near the hour of midnight, is not always improving associate with. Slang words and phrases should also avoided and we should learn to thoroughly bridle ou tongues." E. M. M.

We received a letter yesterday, from Mrs. Sherrard of Winchester Virginia, the lady to whom we loaned money to enable her to return to her home in Virginia, last summer, and the mother of the eccentric young man who was for a time employed in the Bag-shop.

She says :—" The object of this communication is to assure you that I have not forgotten the obligation I am under to your Community, and though I have been *once more* duped by the man who had so often deceived me before, I do not despair of being able *some time*, to cancel the amount I am owing you.

My husband detained the proffered " Box of Tobacco," for which he offered various pretexts, until he found I had finally concluded not to return to bondage—not to resume again the yoke made so grievous by his obliquities, and then he refused to send it except upon the condition that I should meet him at a place designated by him, and accompany him home. This of course was not to be thought of, after my mind had been made up as to the course I should pursue.

He writes to my brother-in-law of this place, 'She is *mine* and ought to be made to know it, by all reflecting men and women.'"

Mr. Bliss of the firm of Buck and Bliss, Toledo, Ohio, called last Saturday, and left an order for bags, amounting to $215. They are old customers and buy only our best work. Mr. B. inquired for Mr. Olds, and commended him as a genial business man and Agent.

Yesterday's temperature—
7½ A. M., 12. 12 M., 22. 6 P. M., 15. Mean 16½.

THE O. C. DAILY.

VOL. 3.   THURSDAY, JAN. 31, 1867.   NO. 27.

Buffalo, N. Y., Jan. 28, 1867.

To the Oneida Community :—Within the past two days, arrived from Wallingford Ct., a letter of the 24 inst., and three Nos. of the Circular, and the Oct. No. of 1866, of the American Phrenological Journal. In the middle column of page 101 of which Journal, is " referred" to, 1st, " Confessions," 2nd, " Berean," 3d, " Bible Communism" and " Male Continence ; which if in pamphlet form, please mail to my address.

In the " Circular," last column, is announced " Price list" of " steel traps," " traveling bags," &c., &c., a price list of each, please mail to me.

Within, is a one dollar bill, to pay, so far as it goes, for what is so requested. Please also to mail, " Pictures of your Community buildings and grounds, price 75 cents." The above is suggested from my reading the above, though perhaps not fully appreciated.

It may not be inopportune here to suggest, that New York Statutes as to marriage and divorce, are illy adapted to man's true progress and improvement, still, Monogamy (one mate; one husband, one wife,) seems to accord with the equal numbers of the sexes and with the sympathies of pure kindliness or affection : and further, that the now soon expected new constitutional amendment, and statutes in our Nation and States, may have radical changes.

Hence, 1st ; may not New York State and other state and national Statutes, be modified ? and 2nd ; may not the entire people, be practically educated to a higher standard of morals, founded on self-control and wise abnegation, so as to unite conformity with our Maker's organic (inevitable) laws, and improve man ?

Do you guess this writer has some bitter experiences, (dear tuition)? If leisure permit one to read an " Expose," (which will be mailed to you with this), that one may guess from facts in that Expose, 144 pages.—With kindly greeting to all studying the right,

Respectfully Your friend,   Le Grand Marvin.

The course of travel to Willow-Place is now a tortuous affair, Mr. Worden's highway being in nearly complete possession of the snow drifts. The drifts between the barn and Hamilton bridge are in some places about seven feet deep, and from Hubbards to mud creek they are higher than the fences. Up to the last storm, teaming had been kept up on top of the drifts; but we are at last driven fairly off into the field. The passage now is made through the orchard west of the road to Hamilton bridge, thence by the boarding-house door to the Hitchcock barn, thence via Hubbards barn to the west side of the road, thence to Mud creek bridge, thence to the top of the hill, thence through the field to Mr.

Town's cow-yard, thence round the southwest corner of his barn and the [illegible] to the [illegible] turnpike, thence west to the factory. Mr. Newhouse suggests that Town's property will increase in value, now that he lives on a *corner* lot.

In calling at the different stores in Utica yesterday, the most of the merchants had something to say about our financial showing. They all seemed to think we had made fine profits the past year. Some of them would repeat the different items, indicating that they had read our report with a good deal of interest.   w. g. k.

The weather grew suddenly mild, last night. At eight o'clock the mercury stood at zero, and at nine o'clock it had risen to twelve degrees above.

L. F. Dunn was sincerely criticised last night, a report of which will be forwarded in manuscript.

T. R. Noyes and C. A. Macknet came in the night We give them a cordial welcome.

Yesterday's temperature—
7½ A. M.,—2. 12 M., 10. 6 P. M., 0.   Mean 2⅓.

THE O. C. DAILY.

VOL. 3.   FRIDAY, FEB. 1, 1867.   NO. 28.

REPORT FROM THE WEST.

Chicago, Jan. 27, 186.

DEAR BROTHER:—I have called on Williams, Ye and Kaas, of this city, and found them well pleased the corn, and pleased to hear that you had shippe balance of their order.

They speak in high terms of its quality. It occurred to me, on my way here, that they were the parties I called on last fall, by request from one of our trap custom ers. This proved to be so, and I took a small ord that time.

They are greatly delighted with our fruits and veg bles, and give me an order for 100 doz. corn, and 20 fruit of different varieties, for the coming season. So you see the orders begin to come earlier than usual. The prospect in this section is, that we shall have an increas ed demand this year. Parties seem more ready to give their orders early than ever before. Yesterday I called on E. J. Bowen, 492 State street, of this city, and found him apparently a very fine man, and much pleased with our goods. He would like to give us an order now for the next season.

I expect Burbank will give his order. I have not yet seen Stanton and Co., but it is reported that they are not going to deal in our goods another year. If this is true, it is *good* news. I shall see him before I leave.

I found Markley Alling and Co., complained some of the corn. Smith, one of the firm, said out of the case he had, there were only four cans good. I told him we would send him another case (two doz.) free of charge, if he would pay the express charges, &c., which he very readily accepted. So you will please send him a case by *either* Express company, marked W. B. Smith, Chicago, 51 Lake Street. Burbank has a little spoilt fruit in bottles, but has not heard much about bad corn. Other parties do not complain much. So on the whole, since leaving Detroit, the good *odor* of the corn has prevailed. The sweet odor is getting to be the general rule, and the bad the exception. We may, however, hear of some more bad corn before next June. But "the Lord reigns," you *know*, so it will all work for good in the end. As we expect to put up a limited amount of corn this year, perhaps it is not best to take many orders. What do you think? I don't really like to have parties get the idea that we are not going on to put up corn and peas. At the same time we must be sure we are right, before we can go ahead. I suppose we shall have to experiment more this year, in order to be able to succeed every time. "*Success,*" you know " is the test." and it is not going to do for us to back out, and say " we can't do it." No, we must go on till we succeed. This is my faith, and I presume it is

yours. Mr. Noyes seems to think so, and by inspiration we shall find the way to do it. Truly yours,
CHARLES OLDS.

We have had a partition put up in the packing ro of the Bag Department dividing it into a Store-room bags, and an Office. We hope by this means to have bags always in good order, free from damage done dust and exposure. Our Office we expect will be, vaded by a good Community spirit, and be a more at tractive lodging place for our night watchman. We say; " success to the Bag business," and we expect it.

John Heyl returned Wednesday, bringing with him several patterns, a sample bag, and a new style of fe for common pelissiers recently patented.

Bag sales for Jan., 1867, $973.19.

We had some talk in meeting last night, about kitchen, and the extravagant use of butter and gar particular. There has been so much butter used in cooking—in making doughnuts, pastry &c., and in cook ing potatoe, that the food had become quite unpalatable to many, and a reform in these respects, was loudly call ed for; also in putting too much sweetening into cakes and pies. It was thought too, that a spirit of rivalry had crept in among the mothers, which was not good, each one trying to outdo her predecessor, in point of cookery. It was remarked, that we did not wish to live any poorer, but better; hence the criticism.

It rained considerably last night and is warm to-day; consequently we have soft treading, and the prospect that our snow-drifts will diminish, though we hope not too suddenly, lest we be swallowed up in the flood.

Mr. Ellis has been engaged for some time past, in re pairing furniture; bureaus, tables, chairs &c. Some of the bureaus that were old and dilapidated, under his magic touch, look almost as well as new ones.

Yesterday's temperature—
7½ A. M., 18. 12 M., 23. 6 P. M., 28 Mean 24½.

THE O. C. DAILY.

VOL. 3.   SATURDAY, FEB. 2, 1867.   NO. 29.

EVENING MEETING.

Last evening Mr. Hamilton gave a particular account of his visit to Wallingford, and his call on Victor on his return home. There is good evidence that Victor is almost wholly recovered, and will be able to return to his friends soon. Theodore remarked :

" Victor wrote to his father a while ago to the effect that the doctors did not wish the CIRCULARS to be sent to him any longer on account of the bad moral influence the paper exerted. Dr. Gray said he looked that letter over, and said to Victor he did not think he told the truth strictly, in ascribing his stopping it to that cause. Victor was free to draw his own inferences, but he had said nothing about the moral character of the paper either way, and didn't care about giving him his reasons for stopping it. It was enough that he wanted it stopped. He then told us he stopped it solely on medical grounds, in his treatment of the case. He explained it in this way : When in the stage of acute mania, patients are easily excited and stimulated to a high pitch. Their brains are very active. That runs its course, and then comes a reaction, in which the patient passes into what is called dementia. In the stage of acute mania, they run down in flesh and suffer from lack of nutrition. When they pass on into the state of dementia they gain in flesh, as pretty much all they do is to eat and sleep. Some land in that state and never come out of it. When they gradually come out of it there is danger that excitement may bring on another attack of acute mania.

" Dr. Gray said when Victor first came there he was very mischievous, and very insubordinate, and disposed to get away. He was very abusive in his references to his father, and was always playing some pranks, like pulling handkerchiefs out of peoples pockets, opening the windows, or whatever he could think of to annoy people. During this period he run down in flesh, and became quite thin. After that he went into the state of dementia, grew dull and was disposed to sleep most of the time. He then passed into a state where he did'nt want to see any one, and was very sensitive about his position. In that state he liked to have him read the CIRCULAR, because it stimulated his intellectual powers, and helped him to get rid of torpor. Now he had passed out of that state and begun to hold discussions with the other patients, and if his mind was over-stimulated, he would be in danger of another attack of acute mania. He is in a ward with a number of persons who have a great deal of religious ardor, and they are very opinionated, as such persons are apt to be. If left to hold their discussions, there

would be no end to them. The Doctor said he would not allow discussions on politics, any more than on religion. He has a number of persons there, who were engaged on the side of the South, in the late war, and if he should allow discussions on political subjects, they would have a strange time of it. He said he told the Southerners they must stop their discussions, as he would not allow them to go on. There was one in particular, very fond of recounting his exploits, and he told him, ' I have no sympathy whatever with what you have done ; but as a sick person and my patient, I do sympathize with you, and for that reason I want you to stop these discussions.' He stopped the CIRCULAR because it was getting to create quite an excitement every week, as Victor would bound out into pretty fierce discussions, and it was having a bad influence in a medical point of view.

" I thought the doctor was quite careful to disclaim passing any opinion on the moral aspect of the CIRCULAR. He said in the course of six or eight weeks Victor would be so far recovered that he could be taken out, and it would do him good to study some, in a steady way, if he did not do too much, in order to get his mind in a state where he could reason systematically without excitement.

" I was quite interested in talking with Dr. Gray.— He strikes me as a person who is in some sense a genius and well adapted to his position. He seems to have a good deal of decision of character, and insight into the ways of the insane. He said to me that when young persons were taken with acute mania they run risk of having the development of their brains and intellectual powers arrested. If attacked by acute mania before the brain is fully developed and the intellectual powers matured, the development is stopped, and there is danger that it will never be completed. In fact it was quite rare he said for young persons to fully recover from such an attack.— They generally showed some evidence of arrested mental development through life. But he said from present symptoms, he should think Victor was going to entirely recover, if he keeps on as well as he is doing, and that would be rather an exception to the rule."

I wish to express my thankfulness to the family for their sincerity in criticising me. I have realized as I never did before, that the truth, however mortifying it may be, is the only thing that can save me from my old life. I do not think that I have ever truly appreciated criticism, but have stood in fear and dread of it. I hope by the grace of Christ, that hereafter I shall always give it a warm loving place in my heart.

L. F. DUNN.

Yesterday's temperature—
7½ A. M., 43. 12 M., 44. 6 P. M., 34. Mean 42.

THE O. C. DAILY.

VOL. 3.   MONDAY, FEB. 4, 1867.   NO. 30.

We give below an extract from a letter received from Mr. Reeve, of Berlin Hights, the man who made us a short visit week before last.—" My heart wants to say something to you, but my head, or mouth does not know what to say; (I guess it's egotism; can't say it quite satisfactory—don't you think so ?) I must acknowledge, that I was troubled with egotism the day I spent with you. Although I said to you (Mr. Bolles especially), that I wished you not to leave your work to care for me, yet there was a complaining spirit with me, when I was left alone. What an ugly, lying spirit it was: I am ashamed to speak of it, only to be truthful, I must confess.

" I do feel that your prayers have followed me, and I have felt constantly blessed by you, since there; and if you had been a little better acquainted with my case, and had given me a good criticism, *that* would have been a good shower-bath for my egotism; I had been *more* blessed I suspect.

" A Mr. Leonard, from Oberlin, is with us, expresses himself interested in the O. C. &c. He is the gentleman that wrote to Mr. Noyes sometime since, upon the subject of 'Usury;' feels considerably nettled about the remarks of G. in the CIRCULAR of Dec. 10. A diagnosis of his case seems to reveal the usual complaint ' egotism,' somewhat aggravated at that: yet he permits us to tell him that is his complaint, with quite a good grace, though of course he does not think this to be true. He feels that we are too much inclined to make Mr. Noyes our God. He would like to help build up a Community somewhere west; would not like to go east, thinks we might take the O. C. for a model, &c.

" I desire your prayers for a speedy sale of my entire stock of egotism.   Yours unworthily,
        G. W. REEVE."

My heart and my whole life belong to God, and I wish anew to abandon myself to his love and service; to consecrate all I am, or can be, to meekness, unity, and ... organization. I confess Christ an Almighty Saviour ... and confess a receptive ... I have had a view of the family spirit lately, which leads me to hate it, and to desire exceedingly to be saved from it. I confess my hatred of, and separation from, the spirit which longs for idols, or wishes to be an object of idolatry myself; also from the family spirit to which my old life belongs; a spirit that is careless about the will of God, loves its own life, and hates criticism. I confess my love, union, and identification with Mr. Noyes, the Community, and the new life of Christ, that thoroughly loves truth and righteousness, and hates iniquity.

I desire courageously to offer myself to criticism, and judgment, that I may be purged from my old life, abide in the vine, and bear fruit to God. My relatives are those who do the will of God. I confess my love for all such, and my separation from all others.   H. M.

Mrs. Freeman writes to John, that his father's bitterness toward the Community is by no means abated; that Mr. F. is writing a long document which he carefully conceals from her, though she has seen enough to know that it is the outpouring of his wrath, and intended for publication. Some one ought really to notify the gentleman, that he is behind time—that it is too late in the day to harm us—that he is spending his strength and ammunition, for nought.

In meeting last night Mr. Hamilton alluded to the letter and the position Mr. F. assumes towards the Community. He thought that John and his mother ought really to take the responsibility of his case—thought that they had it in their power, effectually to silence his barking at us.

In a letter from Mr. Olds, dated Chicago, Jan. 25th, he says :—" I think the trap-market here is not overstocked unless it is in some of the large sizes. On the contrary, some parties could have sold several hundred dozen more, if they could have got them on here in season. All seem to think we did very well in filling orders. It looks now as though we should have a good trade in the spring.—I may get some ... and had only a part of a case, &c."

Eighteen or twenty men with three spans of horses, were engaged all the forenoon Saturday, in shoveling and breaking out the road between here and Willow-Place. In the afternoon sleighs went over there, all the way in the road, instead of through the fields, as they have done more or less, for many weeks. Saturday evening there was rain accompanied with lightning; but this morning it is colder, and the present prospect is, that our thaw is at an end.

In accordance with an arrangement just completed, Mr. Jarvis Quance and wife, assume charge to-day of the home boarding-house. Mr. Q. will continue to work in the can factory as heretofore. So long as the above arrangement continues in force Mr. and Mrs. Q. will receive for their services fifty-five dollars per month.

Grace Mills arrived Saturday afternoon.

Temperature Saturday and Sunday—
7½ A. M., 23.   12 M., 28.   6 P. M., 30.   Mean 27.
7½ A. M., 40.   12 M., 43.   6 P. M., 39.   Mean 40½.

THE O. C. DAILY.

VOL. 3.   TUESDAY, FEB. 5, 1867.   NO. 31.

EVENING MEETING.

The discourse by Mr. Noyes, " Form and Substance," was re-read and called out the following remaks:

Mr. Hamilton :—Mr. Noyes said considerable on this subject there at New Haven, and seemed to be very much interested in it, and held it as important. It took great hold of my attention and has been a new key-note to me ever since. I appreciate the form of Communism, but I think more of the substance.— I see here in the Community, that we must be sure and get our hearts on the substance. Where the spirit of God rules, there is the kingdom of heaven.

Mr. Woolworth :—There is great advantage every way in being free from bondage to forms. The Primitive Church were comparatively free from forms : they held them all loosely. After the second coming the apostate church built up forms and surrounded itself with them, until it became a dead, lifeless form of godliness without the power. The Primitive Church had the power that wrought miracles, and saved men from sin and selfishness. There was substance there. They were in fellowship with the Holy Ghost, and could afford to be pretty careless about forms. At the same time they looked forward for the country where all hostile surroundings and restrictions would be removed.

T. R. Noyes :—This talk furnishes me with a good deal of profitable thought. It seems as if it pointed out, in a way to come home to every body, that mere living in the Community is not salvation. Being content to live in the Community, and loyalty of that kind is only useful as it enables a person to take hold of interior life and join Christ in that way. Communism is only a means to that end ; and those who live in Communism and do not realize *that*, will make just as bad a failure as those who live in the world and make the same mistake.

Mr. Hamilton :—That is true. I see that we need to pray for a revival, not in the world alone but in the Community also. We need a revival in the Community that shall melt all hearts and make them receptive to the Spirit of God. I desire to give myself to this work as important above everything else.

Mr. Woolworth :—Folks can have the substance any where and ask no odds of society or circumstances.— They can have unity with Christ, salvation from sin, the spirit of victory and rejoicing, and all that anywhere. They can have unity of hearts and fellowship with all saints, and Communism of the interior kind under any conditions of outward life.

Mr. Hamilton :—I had some talk with Theodore right in this line, and he expressed a wish to do what he could to promote the spirit of heaven, and conversion to the heart and substance, among the young folks. I have had some queries as to the best way to get at it. I would suggest, as a begining or experiment, that all the young men, for instance, who are interested in the subject, meet with Theodore and myself, and perhaps one or two others, to-morrow night, at a quarter to 7 o'clock, in the Reception-room. No matter if it interfers with the classes a little, I think it would pay. The young folks have a good deal to do with the tone of the family. Let all pray in a simple, childlike manner, that God will give us his spirit.

I wish to thank the family for their faithfulness in my criticism last evening. I can now see that I needed just such a chastisement to give me that humility and brokenness of heart, which may qualify me for what is to come, and separate me from superficial connections. I hate weakness and a superficial life and that egotism which prevents the influx of the life of Christ and the Community.

I thirst for that water which Christ promises " shall be a well of water springing up into everlasting life." Will you pray for me?   L. BOLLES JR.

A Roman Catholic Priest, from Utica, called here yesterday, accompanied by a lady. The gentleman called once last summer, and was so much pleased, that he was induced to come again. He could not speak English, but the lady, who was a fine appearing woman, was his mouth-piece. Mr. Bolles gave them two or three numbers of the CIRCULAR, for which they seemed thankful.

Our anticipations yesterday morning, that the thaw was over, were dissipated before noon, and the snow continues to melt, the weather being warm and spring-like.

F. Norton resumes his practice of Dentistry to-day. There is at the present time a great deal of work to be done in the Office, and his services are much needed.

Mr. Greeley is to deliver a lecture at the depot next Saturday evening, on " Self-made Men."

Yesterday's temperature—
7½ A. M., 30.   12 M., 44.   6 P. M., 33.   Mean 35⅓.

THE O. C. DAILY.

VOL. 3.   WEDNESDAY, FEB. 6, 1867.   NO. 32.

THE GREEN-HOUSE.

Because we are Communists, it does not necessarily follow that each individual attends to every body's business, or that he has not enough business of his own to keep him from troubling himself very much about that of his neighbor's. On the other hand, every man has his round of duties to perform; he has an important place to fill in the working of the great machine, and is expected to be more faithful at his post, than he who is laboring for himself alone.

But I have to own, that I got a little out of my usual beat, this morning, and found myself, the first time for many weeks, in the Green-house, inhaling the fragrance of its flowers, and my eye charmed with their beauty. I was greeted with a full blast of summer if I may so express myself. Mr. N. and Mrs. S. were watching and watering their plants something I imagine, as Adam and Eve did in the garden of Eden. Some of the little bright-eyed mountain daises seemed to reproach me for staying out in the cold all this dreary winter, when a tropical clime was so near me. There I found besides many of our summer flowers in their full fragrance and bloom, lemon trees, with ripe and green fruit, and also blossoms, all on the same tree.

I was surrounded with flowers of many varieties, both great and small; from the mass of overhanging vines, that trailed about the glass over my head, and the thorny Cactus, with its club-like shoots, down to the sweet-scented Mignonette and minute flowering Mosses, that crept along the earth. The Calla (*Water Arum*), supported on its stately stem one large white blossom as pure as snow, and in fragrance somewhat resembling the Water-lily. Mrs. S. said that its fragrance alone, sometimes filled the whole apartment where it was situated. There too, was the Flowering Maple with its variegated and bell-shaped flowers, dangling over head. On entering another apartment, I was greeted by a long row of Chinese Primroses; their pink and purple faces looking as bright and cheery, as though no storms had blustered, or north winds howed within a few feet of them, all this long winter. The little Sedica vine, and the *Lobelia Gracilis*, were running down over the sides of their earthern pots, like over-flowing fountains, and I wanted to lie down on a bed of moss that was near by, and listen to their tinkle; but I did not feel quite clear about broaching the matter to Mrs. S. She told me the names of many flowers and shrubs, among which was the Acacia; its long green branches touching the glass over head, the Euphorbia also, a tall plant, divided into two prongs, at the top of which are situated two tufts of scarlet leaves, which present a charming appearance.—Mrs. S. said that most people, on entering the Green house, gave their attention to the large and showy flowers, but it was the sweet Elisia Jassamine, and little Mosses that most reminded her of summer.

After I had counted five hundred flower pots, great and small, I began to be a little frightened at the labyrinth of pots into which I was getting, and estimated what I had counted to be about one third of of the whole. I went away with a determination to make the Green-house another visit at an early day, and a strong desire to become a botanist.   J. P. H.

We had a call yesterday from Mr. John Iverson, of North Bloomfield, Ontario Co. He is an old friend of E. A. Stillman and was engaged with him in the Fourierist Association at North Bloomfield, twenty years ago. He is an Englishman and was a disciple and personal acquaintance of Robert Owen. He has also been acquainted with Mrs. Bushnell and Beulah for a number of years. He is still interested in Social reform. Is now a subscriber to the CIRCULAR, through the advice of Mr. Stillman. Is quite a modest, genial, thinking man; seemed much interested in what he saw here. Lacks faith in Christ as a personal, spiritual leader, but claimed to have great faith in what he termed the *principles* of Christ. Said he had nothing to offer in opposition to our belief; that we were more advanced than he, and might be entirely right, though he did not yet see as we did.— He thought it was our duty to go forth and hold meetings and tell the people what we had attained, and how we had attained it. Said the people were ready to hear us, and that the field was fast ripening for new truth. He staid over night with us, and his call was a pleasant affair all round. He expressed considerable regret that Mr. Noyes was not here, as he had wished to meet him.

Mr. Hamilton and Bolles started on their contemplated mission to Deruyter, this morning, at a quarter past seven o'clock. They contemplate going via. Peterboro, and calling on Gerrit Smith. The Community heartily sympathize with the move, and bid them God speed.

We have received, through Mr. Olds, an order from J. M. Alcott & Co. of Milwaukee Wis., for $201.44 worth of Bags.

Mr. Olds says; "I find parties want *new styles*. I hope we shall be able to get up something *new* that will take in the market. I think we are behind the times in this respect."   N.

A RIDDLE.

A blind beggar had a brother, and he (i. e. the brother) died. Deceased had no brother. What relation was blind beggar to deceased?   GERRIT.

Yesterday's temperature—
7½ A. M., 37.   12 M., 38.   6 P. M., 30.   Mean 35.

THE O. C. DAILY.

VOL. 3.   THURSDAY, FEB. 7, 1867.   NO. 33.

Cleveland, O., Feb., 3, 1867.

DEAR FRIENDS:—I want to say to you that my interest in Christ is unflagging, and that my desire to be conformed to his will, and to be organized into his body, increases day by day. I find myself in great need of his spirit and his life, to enable me to overcome the world, with its passions and lusts, and to withstand the temptations and onsets of the devil with any degree of success. "There is salvation in none other." Of this truth I am becoming more and more deeply impressed.

Whatever I may do, I wish to do for Christ. If I remain here, I think now, notwithstanding I have some aversion to it, that I shall practice law. I would do it, if possible, as for God. As Moses commanded the Hebrews; " Ye shall hear the small as well as the great, ye shall not be afraid of the face of man, ye shall not respect persons in judgment for the judgment is God's;" so I would do. The will of God, the justice and righteousness of God—to seek this, as the sole object, I would aim. Pray for me.

Thine truly,   J. W. TOWNER.

I desire to give myself anew to Christ, Mr. Noyes and the family. For some time past I have had a growing desire that I might be possessed by the spirit of unity and brotherly love, and also that I might become localized, and detached from all persons and things, that prevent my becoming Christ's freeman, and useful in his body.—I confess hatred and separation from all spirits that would divert me from Christ and Mr. Noyes. I confess separation from a spirit that draws persons or things to myself, from pleasure seeking, false love and egotism. I desire that the revival spirit may have full place in my heart, and that I may be soft and receptive toward it.

I wish to express my thanks to the family for all their faithfulness and love to me. My prayer is that I may be a help in some way to the church. I confess my union with Mr. Noyes, Mr. Hamilton and with the family.   JOSEPH C. ACKLEY.

WILLOW-PLACE ITEMS.

Two new Winding-frames have just been set up in the Silk-Factory, and but one more is needed to complete the number desired. Three more Spinners and two Cleaners are in process of construction.

By Monday next, the number of hired girls will be twenty-four.

The amount of silk made, varies from twenty to thirty pounds per week, according to the fineness of it. O. S. Chafee, Mansfield, Conn., lately ordered through the Agency, two Spoolers, to be paid for in silk.

The Bag-frame business is again started in the east side of the Machine and Finishing shop.

Our Florists were somewhat disturbed by the incorrectness of some of the statements, made in J. P. H's article publised in yesterday's DAILY. They do not think that any unfairness of representation was intended, and they attribute the use of wrong names, and mis-statements, to their true cause ; viz, ignorance of botany.—We confess to the same ignorance, and will in future avail ourselves of the help of the Florists whenever articles of that kind are placed in our hands for publication.

We have not yet completed our sets of playthings for the little children, so that we can distribute a new set every day ; but we find that children with a good and thankful spirit, will be happy and contented with a few things. The last play introduced, was whittling. What ! you will say, give knives to children two or three years old? Certainly, why not ? We find from experience that it works well. After going the rounds of other plays, they divert themselves with splitting small blocks prepared for them, and in this way pass many a pleasant hour.

Last evening, the O. C. DAILY was offered to the family for criticism. The principal faults pointed out were, 1st, a too lengthy report of the evening meetings; 2d, the insertion of ordinary compositions; and 3d, not giving a more detailed account of the business transactions of the Community and other items of interest.

Mr. A. C. Smith is here on a visit. He came yesterday ; also a Mr. Gray, who has called at the Agency, and with whom T. R. N. was some acquainted. We understand that Mr. Gray came to the depot and remained there, till he had written and sent us a letter and obtained a reply with an invitation to visit us.

Mr. Blood is engaged in making up a lot of tin ware, for the use of the family, the coming season. He has recently finished eighty-seven boxes for the Lunch-Bag, which it is thought, will be a sufficient number for the season.

It froze hard last night, and this morning the boys are having fine sport with their sleds, drawing the little children on the crust.

Yesterday's temperature—
7½ A. M., 31.   12 M., 40.   6 P. M., 33.   Mean 34⅔.

THE O. C. DAILY.

VOL. 3.   FRIDAY, FEB. 8, 1867.   NO. 34.

MEDICINAL—A PURGATIVE.

Our noble water-wheel lagged wearily yesterday afternoon. Water had leaked and spattered into the inside of it, till it was thickly coated, and a mass of mingled ice, snow and water, "slosh," in school-boy vernacular, kept sliding, slopping and tumbling about in it. By 4. 30 P. M. the crisis came. The gate was shut down—the wheel blocked—and blacksmiths, trap-men and machinists, armed with shovels and hammers, went into it and cleaned it out. At 5. P. M. water-wheel was again on its way with a lighter (stomach.)   C.

SHOE–SHOP ITEM.

I went to Syracuse a few days since, taking with me my man Hillis, for the purpose of purchasing a Sewing-machine for the Shop.—We had the good luck to buy a $75.00 one, No. 2, Singers, for $60.00. The man that sold the Machine remarked : "your folks all have a remarkable faculty to buy cheap, and sell for a good price."

We have long been in need of a Machine, and we are thankful to get a good one—it works to a charm, and will be a great help to the Shoe-shop, and quite a relief to Mrs. Higgins, our binder.   L. V. V.

Philadelphia, Pa., Feb. 5, 1867.

I am 34 years of age and unmarried. I think I would like to join your Community. I would like to hear from you and have the necessary information, and know whether you would receive me. I have had a good College education, and have been engaged in teaching as you will see by my card. My family is well known here. I should of course work in common with others. Will you please let me hear from you at your earliest convenience. I am familiar with the general principles of your Society. Hoping to hear from you soon, I am,   Yours very respectfully,
MELVILLE MALCOM.

DEAR FRIENDS:—I wish to ask your forgiveness for my past conduct. I feel that I have done you a great wrong, but still you receive me back, and give me another chance to become a true Community woman. I will improve that chance by a thorough conversion of my heart. My object in coming back, was to give my heart to God, and I knew I never could become a true christian in the wild, giddy world. I confess Christ my helper. My case is open for public criticism.   GRACE.

Mr. Hall and Clark have been out together two days, with their own horse and sleigh, the latter selling plow-castings, and Mr. Hall as usual selling silk.

Mr. C. sold about $100 worth of the castings, and Mr. H. not far from $100 worth of silk, besides receiving one small order of sixteen dollars, for Bags.

Music has been composed by E. P. Inslee and set to Mr. Pitt's song, "The Pacific Railroad." It was sung in the Hall, a few evenings since ; Solo by Abram, chorus by three young men with piano accompaniment. The effect was quite thrilling.

Our people have bought 100 hemlock logs in Verona swamp, two miles below Oneida depot, and the teamsters are at the present time, engaged in drawing them.

Both Mr. Porter's children attend our school.— They commenced when they were boarding with us, and our people consented after they moved, to let them remain.

Received yesterday two trap orders, one from Failing and Hatt, Portland, Oregon, amounting to $460, the other from Netherland & Co., Louisville, Ky., amounting to $87, all large traps.

The weather still continues warm, though we have cold nights, and the snow on that account does not melt so rapidly, as it otherwise would.

Yesterday's temperature—
., A. M., 31.   12 M., 34.   6 P. M., 34.   Mean 29½.

THE O. C. DAILY.

VOL. 3. SATURDAY, FEB. 9, 1867. NO. 35.

We received a letter yesterday, from Miss Susan B. Munson, the first we have heard from her for six months. It is dated at Dansville, where she is at present stopping. She writes:

"I made up my mind, that I never would write to you again, until I had found some steady employment; but I do not know as that time will ever come, and I want to hear from you all so much; and then, I do not feel as if I can live much longer without the CIRCULAR. I tried to borrow some to read of the Dr. and of others who take them here, but have not succeeded as yet. I came to Dansville the 4th of Oct. I at once fell in love with the place, and made up my mind, if possible to make this my home for the present, as I could dress and live here more to my mind than any where else, except ————. I had encouragement given me, of having the care of the Dr's. Cottage in the spring, but there has been great changes since then, and the Dr. and family take their meals now at the Cure. I shall stay here in Mr. Johnson's employ until May, I think. I can lay my plans no further, but I feel there is one who can plan for me better than I can for myself, and I am ready to give myself into *his* hands, who doeth all things well.'

"So you see it is not my fault, that I do not find ... ... as you advised me to. So ... ... not send me any more. That letter of yours grieved me very much, it would not hurt me now, I was sick then.

"I have often thought that you must have a very persevering family at Oneida, if they have all struggled as hard as I have to gain admittance. About fifteen years ago a still small voice whispered to me of a true spiritual and social life on this earth. About two years after, I heard of Oneida, and my heart yearned to know more of you—I improved every means to know and understand you. I wrote to you—my letter was miscarried. I wrote again and received a reply; also a third and a fourth I think. I afterwards obtained permission to visit you. After leaving, I wrote, and received a reply; I wrote again, received no reply. I then wrote to Mr. Cragin, received no reply. I then wrote to the Editor, received no reply. I began to feel as if I was entirely cut off from you, but thought I would try once more. I then wrote to you and said considerable about the Community. In reply you told me you did not think I was as well prepared to join you as I thought; but you did not tell me what other preparation I could make. I am just as much in the dark to-day, with regard to it, as I was then.

"I have given up all, even my children, and I desire to be guided wholly by Christ, and love him with my whole heart. I try to live up to my highest ideal of a true life, every day of my life. In Bible times, if any one asked, they were told; and if there is anything more, I am anxious to know what it is. I also asked permission to call on you, on my return to Boston, as I visited you the most unfavorable season in the year to see the external beauties of your home—you did not answer my question. I afterwards wrote to Mr. Noyes, but received no reply. Now, I write to you once more, hoping to hear from you soon."

In the Theological class one evening last week, Mr. Pitt was called on to close the exercises, by singing, as he had previously volunteered to do. He complied, and sung a song of his own composing, which we have tried in vain to obtain for insertion in the DAILY. It was so characteristic of its author, and sung with so much self-possession and earnestness, (if not with perfect correctness of intonation), that it "brought down the house," by repeated and prolonged cheering. Mr. Inslee has succeeded Mr. Bolles, in conducting the class.

Mrs. Aiken was criticised last night, by her request. It was thought she had improved considerably, the last six months, and had overcome some of the faults for which she had formerly been criticised—was more spiritually-minded. She still lacks faith in respect to her bodily difficulties, and needs to look ... ... with more earnestness, for help in that direction. She has done good service in her connection with business at the store, and her labors in that department are much appreciated.

Not far from 150 distinct "pitch-holes" so called, and a corresponding number of hummocks to match, now diversify the Willow-Place road. A ride over and back in the antiquated pung now plying on that route, is productive of a series of sensations more marked than agreeable. Imaginative persons compare it to boat-riding—if the waves were *frozen* the similitude would be more apparent. ONE WHO HAS TRIED IT.

FOUND.—In the Hall this morning, some money. The loser will please prove property, pay charges to Mr. Clark, the finder, and it will be restored.

It rained considerably last night, is foggy and misty this morning, with plenty of "slush."

Traps ordered the last two weeks. 79 doz. mostly large sizes.

Yesterday's temperature—
7½ A. M., 34. 12 M., 46. 6 P. M., 34. Mean 38.

THE O. C. DAILY.

VOL. 3.   MONDAY, FEB. 11, 1867.   NO. 36.

Mr. Woolworth, Dear Sir:—I feel that I cannot leave your happy society without expressing my
thanks for the kind and courteous reception I have
received from the members of the Community, and I
shall always pray that you may prosper in your endeavors to show to the world, a life of real christianity.
        Truly yours,   George Gray.

P. S. Please accept the enclosed [fifty dollars] for
the publication of the Circular.

After Mr. G.'s note was read, Mr. Woolworth said:
"I trust he did not feel that this money was necessary
to establish our good will toward him, or to gain our
friendship. I confess my interest in, and respect for
him. [Approved by many.] If he gives this money
heartily for the Circular, we shall appropriate it
conscientiously for that purpose."

Quite a desire was manifested to hear some of Mr.
Gray's adventures. After several hints Mr. Gray said:
"At some future time I will try and write some things
that may be interesting."

———————

Mr. Smith said last night, "I am thankful for the
invitation Mr. Noyes gave me to visit Oneida, and for
the kind attention I have received since I have been
here, especially from Mr. Pitt. I confess my union
with the Primitive Church, and with Mr. Noyes and
the Community. I feel that the Lord is truly around
and about you. The glorious work that has been
wrought here since I left, is very apparent to me, I
contemplate leaving in the morning. I feel that I
have got a good package to take home with me and
look over after I get there, and that I am richly paid
for my visit."—Mr. Woolworth said, "I am much interested in Mr. Smith's visit, and am glad to hear this
testimony from him.

———————

Our thaw of a week's continuance is fairly over,
and cold blustering storms have resumed their wonted
sway. We think we can say with safety, that yesterday was the most tedious day of the season, and that
is saying a good deal, considering the many tricks that
Boreas has played us all through the winter, piling
the snow into high drifts, thus rendering our roads
and paths impassable, and making plenty of work for
man and beast. This time however, he has found
comparatively little snow to revel in, but what little he
could command, he sprinkled in our faces through
tiny cracks in the windows, or dashed unmercifully
upon us if we dared venture outdoors. This morning however, the wind has subsided and the sun has
risen clear and bright. We thought of our mission-
ating brethren yesterday, and wondered where their
lot was cast, and whether they were shielded from
the storm.

11 o'clock.—Since the above was in type, the wind
has commenced blowing again strongly from the
southeast, and it is quite cold and tedious being outdoors; so that in respect to the weather we can say
truly, "we know not what an" hour "may bring
forth."

———————

Poor old white horse! There you stand in front
of the New House, with your eyes half shut, looking
meek and tired, waiting we suppose, for your load,
and for the sound of your master's voice to break your
revery, with the well known, "get up." Can you tell
us (for we do not know), how many times in a day,
you wend your way over to Willow-Place and back
—down to the Bag-shop and back, to the Foundry
and other places? Are you conscious of the importance of your calling, and how much more highly
honored you are, than is your race generally? The
Community discipline has effectually cured you, we
think, of your runaway proclivities, and you can now
be trusted to any extent, without clog or halter.

———————

T. R. N. leaves us to day. His visit has been
every way pleasant, and will, we trust, prove to be a
great help to the young men in particular. He has
met with them three evenings, which has had a tendency to unite and strengthen them to take hold with
. . . . he met yesterday
with the young women, which will be a help to them
we trust.

———————

Mr. Pitt went to Geneva last Thursday, and came
home Saturday. He went on business connected with
his getting out a new Edition of "The Trapper's
Guide." He will report himself to-morrow.

———————

Theodore gave us in the Hall last night, a specimen
of his elocutionary reading, which was quite entertaining, and pronounced first-rate.

———————

Temperature Saturday and Sunday—
7½ A. M., 42.   12 M., 48.   6 P. M., 33.   Mean 42⅓.
7½ A. M., 15.   12 M., 16.   6 P. M., 10.   Mean 13⅔.

THE O. C. DAILY.

VOL. 3.   TUESDAY, FEB. 12, 1867.   NO. 37.

Mr. George Gray our visitor left here yesterday.— He gave me a brief sketch night before last, of his life, occupying some two and a half hours. He has followed the sea from his youth, his first voyage being to Europe in 1844, the 14th year of his age. Since then he has taken four voyages to the Pacific, via. Cape Horn, visiting the Sandwich Islands and numerous other Islands in the Pacific and Atlantic; spent ten years coasting between California and British Columbia, visited the Gold mines twice, without realizing any financial prosperity. He has taken two trips to the Mediterranean, visiting several of her most important cities, including Naples, also the Ruins of Pompeii, of which he had with him a number of fine photographs, which he purchased in Naples. On leaving he generously gave us the pictures. On two of his voyages he had very cruel commanders, though he was always treated kindly himself, yet the harsh treatment the other sailors received, grieved him quite as much as it would to have received the same cruelty himself.

He went aboard a Merchant vessel at San Francisco, bound for London, and before they had been out **twenty days the first mate knocked down a young** sailor and stamped on him for some trifling offence, and when he turned his back, the young man sprang up and stabbed the mate in the back, with his knife, (which sailors always carry in their belt)—the mate sprang to his state-room for his pistol, saying he would shoot the d————d rascal—but fell as he reached his room, and in fifteen minutes was dead. The Captain was very sick at that time, and not expecting to live, and there was no one aboard but Mr. Gray, that could take the ship's reckoning, therefore that duty fell upon him and he took her safely into port at London; a four months voyage. He stood at the wheel one time and saw every thing washed overboard that was on deck, masts and sails blown away, &c., &c. He told about his visit to Frazer river, the account of which was very interesting as were his adventures generally.   J. R. L.

WILLOW-PLACE ITEMS.

Notice is hereby given that any one wishing to gain admittance into the Willow-Place Factory between the hours of nine P. M. and six A. M. will probably be obliged to give their names to Mr. Millbury, the night watchman, before he will allow them to enter. If they are unacquainted with him, they may have to state their business, or in some manner convince him of their citizenship.

The immediate cause of the adoption of the countersign is this: about four o'clock Sunday morning Mr. M. saw a man loitering about the corner of the building; he did not recognize him but presumed it might be a Community man. Presently the individual knocked. "Who's there?" sung out Mr. M. "Let me in!" was the curt reply. "I thought he was a Community man," the Teutonic sentinel afterwards remarked, "he spoke so short,"—so the door was rather cautiously opened. An "awful big fellow" presented himself, and made vigorous attempts to enter. A smart scuffle followed, at the close of which the big man found himself locked out again, and vented his surcharged feelings, by "curses long and loud." Mr. M. wishes to run no risks in future.

One of the blacksmiths, a Mr. Greene, has just finished a model of a machine he has invented for filing saws. All that is necessary to do, is to put the saw-blade between the clamps, and turn the crank a sufficient number of times, and the saw is filed. He is about to patent it through the Sci. Am. Agency.

D. F. Knowles was sincerely criticised last night. He has up to this time, used tobacco more or less, and in a note addressed to the family, he asked them for help, and criticism. It was thought he would have to be a good deal more in earnest to separate himself from the world, than he has been in the past. He fraternizes with the hired help at the shop and seems to choose to stay with them, in preference to staying in the Office with our folks. His living in a worldly atmosphere was thought to be the cause of his prolonged appetite for tobacco.

We went down yesterday, and called on the Porters. Mrs. P. is well contented and pleased with her situation, particularly in having her children attend our school. The boy, who is eleven or twelve years old, goes regularly to the children's meeting, and his mother says, is much interested, and would not on any account stay away.

The well in the cellar furnishes an abundance of water, not only for them, but for their nearest neighbor, though the water is pretty hard.

Mr. Smith did not leave for home yesterday, as he expected, but staid till this morning. He seemed very much gratified with his visit.

Yesterday's temperature—
7½ A. M., 9. 12 M., 27. 6 P. M., 29. Mean 21⅔.

THE O. C. DAILY.

VOL. 3. WEDNESDAY, FEB. 13, 1867. NO. 38.

Mr. Hamilton and Bolles came home yesterday afternoon. In the evening meeting they gave an account of their proceedings and experience while absent, which was listened to with intense interest by the family. It is very evident that their going out was an inspired move, and we may expect corresponding fruits. It was a bold step, and we are thankful that they had courageous and strong hearts, to break their way into the enemy's camp, and silence, at least, the tongue of slander. Mr. Hamilton had some bitter experience in doing it, but he was rewarded with success, and a consciousness of internal growth and expansion, that must be a sufficient reward. Mr. Bolles being a stranger in the place, was saved from the disagreeableness of meeting opposing spirits in old acquaintances, and was in his element we should judge, and a great help to Mr. Hamilton. Skeptics in the little village of Deruyter may say as did the unbelieving Jews of Thessalonica in reference to Paul and Silas's labors among them : " These that have turned the world upside down have come hither also." The following notice of their intended lecture, was posted, and read in the churches in the village :

" A free lecture on the Religious faith of the Oneida Community, will be given by two of its members, E. H. Hamilton and L. Bolles Jr., on Monday Evening, Feb. 10th, in the Town Hall, at 7 o'clock."

Our children enter into studies and business, with as much enthusiasm as the adults. The boys spend an hour before breakfast in study and braiding. One of them has braided enough for six hats in three weeks, mostly before breakfast. Their chores have been done in a much more satisfactory manner than formerly. The girls are enthusiastic in learning to read music, preparatory to taking lessons on the Piano, or other instruments.

Mr. Hallenbeck from Wallingford, with whom some of our people were acquainted, spent last night with us. He married a cousin of H. E. Allen, and is here we believe on business connected with the strawberry culture.

We ship to-day for Wallingford, a machine we have been constructing for sawing wood. It is valued at about $50.

Mrs. Editor :—As your allusion to the following song, seemed to imply that you wished to have it appear in the Daily, I have revised it and hand it to you. It is an imitation or parody of " The Battle-Cry of Freedom," so popular in the war, and several of the lines of that piece, with some alterations of word and sentiment, are made use of.　Yours,　T. L. P.

THE BATTLE CRY OF HEAVEN.

Yes, we'll rally round the truth, boys, we'll rally once again,
　Shouting the battle-cry of heaven,
We'll rally from the hillside, we'll rally from the plain,
　Shouting the battle-cry of heaven.
Chorus.—King Jesus forever, Hurrah ! boys, Hurrah !
　Down with the devil, up with the cross !
While we rally round the truth, boys, rally once again,
　Shouting the battle-cry of heaven.

On our banner is the cross, boys—for love of it we'll die,
　Shouting the battle-cry of heaven,
And beneath its gleaming rays, boys, we'll march to victory,
　Shouting the battle cry of heaven.
　King Jesus forever, &c.

All our brothers down in hades shall hear the sound we make,
　Shouting the battle-cry of heaven,
And from out the sleep of death they shall suddenly awake,
　Shouting the battle-cry of heaven.
　King Jesus forever, &c.

Up from out the spirit realms they will gather to our ranks,
　Shouting the battle-cry of heaven,
And with resurrection life we will turn the dragon's flanks,
　Shouting the battle-cry of heaven.
　King Jesus forever, &c.

Thus we're springing to the call of our leader gone before,
　Shouting the battle-cry of heaven,
And we'll fill his glorious ranks with many millions more,
　Shouting the battle-cry of heaven.
　King Jesus forever, &c.

We'll welcome to our number the loyal true and brave,
　Shouting the battle-cry of heaven.
And although they may be poor, none to sin shall be a slave,
　Shouting the battle-cry of heaven.
　King Jesus forever, &c.

So we're springing to the call from the east and from the west,
　Shouting the battle-cry of heaven.
And we'll hurl the devil's crew from the land we love the best,
　Shouting the battle-cry of heaven.
　King Jesus forever, &c.

Death and hell shall flee before us, when marching for our king,
　Shouting the battle-cry of heaven.
And the New Jerusalem, boys, with victory shall ring,
　Shouting the battle-cry of heaven.
Chorus.—King Jesus forever, Hurrah ! boys, Hurrah !
　Down with the Devil, up with the cross,
While we rally round the truth, boys, rally once again,
　Shouting the battle-cry of heaven.

Yesterday's temperature—
7½ A. M., 30. 12 M., 40. 6 P. M., 38. Mean 36.

THE O. C. DAILY.

VOL. 3.   TUESDAY, FEB. 14, 1867.   NO. 39.

We had a long letter a few days since, of six or seven pages from a young man by the name of Tupper, of Nashua, N. H. He writes that after mature thought, he would like to join us. He says: "I first became acquainted with it, [our society] by finding some stray papers published by your Community. At first I took no particular notice of the institution excepting there were some features which tempted me to investigate more fully its objects and purposes, and wherever I found information I carefully studied the sources, and weighed and balanced with reasonable forethought the arguments in favor, and objections brought against it, and at every stage conviction triumphed over prejudice, and at this present stage I am fully convinced of the uprightness and justness of the Community.

"Taking as you do the Bible for your foundation, and the sublime tenets of the Christian philosophy for your frame-work, how can you be otherwise than successful. * * After giving you my ideas and motives calculated to let you understand that it is after proper forethought and investigation that I make this proposal, I will try and give you some idea of my circumstances. I am twenty-six years of age, single, of a strong constitution and sound body, and I think a clear head and willing heart.—My early years were spent in an orthodox family, in the bosom of the _____ church, eschewing all light, or romantic _____. I always possessed a great desire to read everything of a historical, biographical and scientific character, which came within my reach. At sixteen, I was nearly prepared to enter college.

[He did not go to College as he expected, but studied Law, until the breaking out of the war, when he enlisted and served in the army four years. Then he finished his studies, and was admitted to the Vermont Bar a few months since.]

He says: "I ask for admission from neither selfish, ambitious, or degraded motives, but from a pure, devoted respect of the principles of your Community, such as have been known to the world through your publications.

" _____ _____ _____ the common stock, about _____ _____ _____ _____ solid, substantial, sound reading, besides other things which I think would be of value to the Community and add to the interest of the concern. You must not think I am taking a step impelled by the nervous action of the enthusiast, for such is not the case. I have carefully examined the premises, and find them consonant with my ideas of right and wrong."

The hour for meeting last night, was pretty much taken up, with reading letters and reports. T. L. Pitt and H. C. Noyes, were selected to appoint a committee to make arrangements for the 20th. Mr. Hamilton remarked, " Mr. Bolles leaves for Wallingford to-night, and I will take this occasion to express my love for him. He said he became more acquainted with me during this trip we have had together than ever before. I can say the same of him; and the more I see of Mr. Bolles the more I love him. I think him a very pure-hearted man—simple-hearted and truthful. I am thankful for such a brother in the cause. I admire the simplicity of his spirit. [Others joined in this.]

DEAR MR. NOYES:—It was a year ago that father went away, and at that time I chose to remain in the Community. Mr. Hamilton said I might remain a year on probation. The year is now up, and Mr. H. thought I had better write to you, with regard to joining. I think you being the spiritual head of the Community, are the door through which I must enter.

I wish to make a full surrender of myself to you and the Community, and take any place you may wish to have me. I confess Christ in me a humble, obedient spirit. Your son in the cause,   ORRIN.

The above note was read in meeting last night, after which it was unanimously voted, that Orrin Wright be hereafter considered a member of the Community.

I wish to express my thanks to the Community, for their kindness to me since I came here. When I first came, I was glad, because I thought there would be more pleasure here, than in the world. Now, I feel very different. I want to commence now and become one of Mr. Noyes' true children, and a boy that Mr. Hatch can have perfect confidence in. The criticism that the boys had, encouraged me more than any other thing, and I have felt ever since, a desire to have a good spirit in my heart. I confess Christ a soft broken heart.   L. BOLLES 3d.

The number of bushels of wheat we raised the last year was 452 bushels, 420 of which, have been sold for $3.00 per bushel, amounting to $1260. The remaining 32 bushels are white wheat, and valued at $3.25 cents per bushel, which will be kept for home consumption.

The warm weather we are having again, together with frequent rains, have taken pretty much all our snow, and we are obliged to go to and from the depot on wheels. The creek overflows its banks and runs across the road this side the bridge, though it is said to be slowly falling this morning.

Mrs. Perry has a sister visiting her, from Durhamville.

Mr. Bolles started in the night for Wallingford.

Yesterday's temperature—
7½ A. M., 44. 12 M., 55. 6 P. M., 50. Mean 49½.

THE O. C. DAILY.

VOL. 3.   FRIDAY, FEB. 15, 1867.   NO. 40.

CONCERNING MR. A. C. SMITH.

Mr. Pitt:—I might make some report of Mr. Smith's visit here, as I had considerable communication with him. Soon after he came, Mr. Worden mentioned that he was here, and asked me to go in and see him. He met me very pleasantly. I might say, when I first joined the Community at Brooklyn, and became acquainted with Mr. Smith, there was a good deal of fellowship between us. I have always felt an interest in him since that time. He seemed very glad to get here, and thankful that Mr. Noyes had invited him to come. That evening or the next morning, he related some circumstances in regard to his early connection with Mr. Noyes. Some of them appeared to come up quite fresh in his memory, though he said he had not thought of them before in a good many years. They related to his submission to Mr. Noyes there at Kingston, while Mr. N. was stopping with him. One day, Mr. Noyes came out and claimed the position of a spiritual father to him, and demanded that he should submit to him and accept the relation. This position at first seemed strange to him, and he did not understand it; but Mr. Noyes insisted upon it, and made it the condition of his fellowship and sojourn with him. Matters soon came to a crisis when they had sat together as much as an hour, neither of them speaking a word, but thinking and praying, or at least he was, for light to do the right thing. All at once it seemed to be revealed to him that that was their true relation to each other, and he burst out laughing, it seemed so clear and simple to him. He said to Mr. Noyes that he accepted the position. Mr. Noyes then proposed they get their skates, and have a skate upon the river. They did so, and skated up some ten or twelve miles and took dinner, and then returned home.

The next morning Mr. Noyes told him he wanted him to go to Putney as he had business for him to do. They looked over their purses and found they had about eighty cents. I won't be certain as to the exact amount. Mr. Noyes advised him to put on his skates, go up the river as far as he could. He skated to Troy and then walked over the mountains. When he came to the foot of a mountain he stopped over night. The next morning he started early. There was snow on the ground, and it happened that he took a wood road, instead of the right one, and this led him to the top of the mountain, and there it stopped entirely. He concluded he would not go back; and as the sun was just rising, he laid his course with the expectation of striking the road on the other side. It was a terribly rough place to get through, down one mountain and up another, but he traveled on for about eight hours, right through the woods without a compass or guide of any sort, as the sun soon after noon became obscured. There was no road whatever. Finally he grew tired and lay down upon the snow. He soon fell into a light slumber, but suddenly awoke with this question running through his mind: "Does the Lord want me to lay my bones on this deserted mountain?" He got up and pushed on, and in a short time came out to the road.

Soon after this, a man came along in a sleigh who took him in, and carried him within six miles of Putney, without charging him anything. He went on and in a short time collected and sent Mr. Noyes considerable money, I think he said some over a hundred dollars. At the same time he had good success in preaching.   [Conclusion to-morrow.]

WILLOW-PLACE ITEMS.

A new line shaft is being put up on the east side of the machine-shop, at present more particularly for the use of the Bag-Frame business.

A revolving coal-sifter has just been completed for the use of the Shop. It consists of a cylinder of wire-netting, about four feet long, with a shaft running through its centre. One end of the shaft projects about two feet and has a crank attached. The cylinder is placed in a frame, one end being about ten inches higher than the other. A hopper at the upper end—a spout at the lower. Pour the coal into the hopper, set the scuttle under the spout, and turn the crank. In a half minute the grist is ground out.

It is the invention of Mr. R. Hawley.   c.

The class in Theology are now reading and investigating the articles in the Berean, on "The Resurrection." We have adopted the practice of having the pieces read through publicly, by volunteers, and discussed afterwards, or at the next meeting of the class. The present method has thus far proved very interesting, as the subject under discussion have been presented in a clear, concise manner.

We have a letter before us from Mrs. Mary S. Arnold, of Galveston, Texas. She intended to have visited us last summer, but was disappointed. She sent a dollar bill, and says, "Please send us something to read." The tract "Salvation from Sin" was mailed to her. She exhorts us to burn her letters and not make them public.

It is cold again this morning and the ground is frozen quite hard. We understand that one cause of the sudden rise of the Creek yesterday, was the blocking up of the ice above. It moved down stream at length, and the water settled back into its accustomed channel. The Creek is now as far as we can see, clear of ice.

Yesterday's temperature—
7¼ A. M., 49. 12 M., 48. 6 P. M., 32. Mean 43.

THE O. C. DAILY.

VOL. 2.   SATURDAY, FEB. 16, 1867.   NO. 41.

TALK CONCERNING MR. SMITH CONCLUDED.

All the time Mr. Smith was here, his mind appeared to be turned back to that old experience connected with his submission to Mr. Noyes. He told me that the night Mr. Woolworth first called upon him to speak in meeting, it came so suddenly that he did not know what to say, and so did not say much. That night he did not sleep any, and this old experience kept coming up over and over again in his mind. On Sunday he wished to have some talk with me, and I found he was laboring some on his relations to the Community. I might say from the moment of my first meeting him he seemed in a soft state, more so than I ever saw him before.

He seemed ready to take criticism if need be.— During my conversation I had a pretty strong feeling to be sincere with him in regard to his relations to Mr. Noyes, and to ascertain whether he had indeed really apprehended Mr. Noyes's position in the Church. The more I talked with him the more I saw that he never had fully apprehended it. I felt quite an inspiration to present that subject to him and sincerely press it home. I had a good deal of freedom in presenting the subject of Community organization. The day before I went out to Geneva I read him the talk, "Salvation From Sin, Community Property." He said it presented the subject in rather a new light to him, but the more he thought of it the more he was disposed to accept it, and I felt his spirit yield. He had purposed to start for home on Monday morning, but concluded that night to remain another day and study the subject farther. Next day I read him several Home-Talks on the subject of organization, and had a good deal of freedom in talking with him. I felt his spirit yield more and more to the truth, and he still grew more earnest in regard to his relations to Mr. Noyes. He seemed to see that his only hope of salvation was in getting back to the old point of submission to Mr. Noyes, taking him as his head.

I was a good deal interested in my experience with him. It was a profitable season to me whether it helps him or not. I felt that age had done a good work in him, in breaking down self-righteousness and egotism. He said he felt that he was poor spiritually, and these doctrines of " Salvation From Sin Community Property" and spiritual organization that we had developed here, showed him that he had never really been saved from sin, in the full sense of the word, and that there was a great work yet to be done in him. He said he should go home and study it all, and then write to us. He purposes to go down to New York some time this spring, when he would try and meet Mr. Noyes, as he had long wished to have a season of reflection and conversation with him.

I could not help thinking of his trip to Putney as typical, somewhat, of his whole course. He has wandered off into the wilderness and come very near laying his bones on the barren mountains of isolation. I felt a strong prayer in my heart that he might work through and come out safely. He said he loved Mr. Noyes very much, that he always had and always should. He also said that for a long time he had dreamed about the Community nearly every night, and seemed to be here with us.

He joined the Methodist church some years ago, but does not seem to have a great deal of sympathy with it. They make him free to talk in their meetings if he chooses, but he feels that he has been growing out of fellowship with them for some time. They appointed him trustee lately, but he told them he should not act, as there were points of difference between him and them that he could not give up. For this reason he did not wish to take any responsible position among them. I judge they have fished for him, and tried to get him into their organization, as much as, or more, than he has sought it.

WILLOW-PLACE ITEMS.—The skating is quite good on the Willow-Place pond; but the attention of our people seems to be pretty much absorbed in other things.

C. Primo succeeded in "dumping" a load of folks out of his sleigh, yesterday afternoon. They were just opposite a pile of wood that stood on the road-side, near Mr. Hubbards—horses on a lively trot, when— Presto, over! and folks, wood-pile, sleigh, buffalo robes, and Mr. Austin, our painter, with a pail of paint, were in a chowder. For a minute or two things were stirred up like a bumble-bee's nest with a boy over it. When they got straightened, their losses were found to be, J. F. Sears, one piece of skin, and E. Austin a little paint; otherwise all right.

A WORD FROM THE BUSINESS OFFICE.

We are occasionally asked if we have an item for the DAILY? But as our work is such that we do not vary much from day to day, we seldom answer in the affirmative. It is not a very busy time of the year, and we have some leisure for studying and sewing. As there are four of us we take turns in relieving each other from staying there all the time. Our mail comes generally between 10 and 11 A. M., then we have letters to answer—pamphlets, papers and pictures, that are ordered, to do up and mail. The two former are called for a great deal, and the many calls we get for CIRCULARS and Pamphlets, give us an idea that people are becoming more and more interested in us, and desirous to know more of us.

We girls find it good once in a while, to turn away from work, and give our attention to interior, spiritual things. We have proposed to have a meeting among ourselves, and read Mr. Noyes Home-Talks, or something of the sort. It tends to promote unity, and that we find we must have in order to promote happiness.

A.

A letter was received yesterday from Mr. Henderson, dated Liverpool Jan. 29th. On account of head-winds, he was fifteen days making the voyage, which is usually performed in ten or twelve days. He is stopping with a brother-in-law in Liverpool, where he says, he was kindly received. He writes that his wife is nearly recovered from her late illness, and he expects her to join him shortly at L. He says:

" I cannot of course say definitely when I shall be in America, but I hope Agnes' health will allow of our sailing about the month of May."

A man by the name of Budine from Tioga Co. Penn., came here last night. He has formerly been connected seventeen years, with the Shakers.

Yesterday's temperature—
7½ A. M., 27. 12 M., 35. 6 P. M., 32. Mean 31⅓.

THE O. C. DAILY.

VOL. 3.   MONDAY, FEB. 18, 1867.   NO. 42.

St. Paul, Minnesota, Feb. 9, 1867.

DEAR SISTER:—I have an incident to report, that may interest your readers. While in the city of Jackson, Mich., a few weeks ago, I called in at a shoe-store and walked toward the counting-room, and saw before me posted up near the desk, a small sign with gold-leaf letters which read as follows: "J. H. Noyes, U. S. Assistant Assessor, Jackson, Mich."

I stopped to look at it, (for I could not help it), wondering who it could be, and what kind of a man he was. I had a curiosity to see him. So I made some inquiry of the proprietor of the house, who said he was book-keeper for him, in connection with his official duties as assistant assessor. Said he was not in just then, but would be soon, &c. I did not wait to see him, but called again soon after, and found him in. I introduced myself by inquiring if his name was Noyes; he replied it was. I said in return, I know a man by the same name as yours, and took out of my pocket the CIRCULAR containing Mr. Noyes's engraved portrait, with a discription of his character as given by Mr. Wells, and handed it to him saying, *there is the man.* He took it, looked at the picture a moment, and said pleasantly, "he is a good looking man for a Noyes." He thanked me for the paper and said "he would like to read it." Shall be interested to know how he likes it.

He is a young man of medium size, good looking, intelligent, rather light complexion, but black hair, with an open pleasant countenance. Says his ancestors were from *Vermont.*

We are having severe cold weather here in St. Paul, the thermometer over twenty degrees below zero. The snow is much less here than at O. C., not over one foot deep.

I shall not get back by the 20th as I intended. Extending my Journey to this point, and being subject to more or less detention, by reason of storms and cold weather, it will be impossible to return before the first of March.   Truly yours,   C. OLDS.

It was mentioned in business meeting yesterday, that Mr. Carr and other men, stop at the depot to sell silk, and it was thought that our folks were not as wide awake as they should be to supply the depot with silk. We ought to be able to supply the market around here, a little better than any body else. J. R. Lord thought if we would institute a plan for supplying them regularly every week, they would be pleased, and would not buy of others. J. H. Barron, E. Hall, and W. G. Kelley, were appointed to supply the depot regularly with silk, every two weeks.

TO THE COMMUNITY.

The care of the boarding-houses, has devolved on me, mainly, this winter, and now the Spring arrangements are in progress I feel new responsibilities for their good order and economical management: and I desire the sympathy and co-operation of the Community.—If there are words of advice on this subject, or criticism of management, or otherwise, I shall be glad of its expression.—I confess the spirit of humility, and desire patience and faith, and God's blessing on all I undertake to do.   M. L. WORDEN.

PROGRAMME OF THE 20th.

Breakfast—at 7 o'clock.
Meeting—from 10 " to 11.
Dinner—at 2 o'clock.
Presents distributed at 4 o'clock, in the Hall.
Amusements of various kinds at ½ past 5 o'clock, and the exercises to close with an evening meeting as usual.

As the two meal per day system, for Sunday, did not work very well in our large family, we have returned to the old plan of three meals, the same as on other days.

ERRATA.

DEAR ED.:—After the notice of the tip-over came out in Saturday's issue, I became aware that my informants "good jog" was not synonymous with "lively .... but meant merely an easy walk. Moreover, it was .. .. J. F. Sears that was lost as that comma made me say, but only a portion of the cuticle from one of his wrists.   C.

[Excuse the over-sight; we confess we are not very sharp in punctuation. ED.]

A young man from Skeneateles came here Saturday evening, and staid over Sunday. He came to get work, but as we could not employ him he left this morning.

DEPARTURES.—W. G. Kelly Saturday morning for Lockport on a short peddling trip. Mr. Hamilton starts this afternoon for New-York, and Alice Ackley for W ... ... Division; also Mr. Ballac leaves to ....

ARRIVALS.—H. W. Burnham Friday—C. W. Underwood Saturday.

Temperature Saturday and Sunday—
7½ A. M., 34.   12 M., 34.   9 P. M., 34.   Mean 34.
7½ A. M., 36.   12 M., 38.   6 P. M., 36.   Mean 36⅔.

THE O. C. DAILY.

VOL. 3.   TUESDAY, FEB. 19, 1867.   NO. 43.

TO THE COMMUNITY.

I have for some weeks thought of making some expression to the family, but the feeling that I could not say anything that I knew would be satisfactory to them, has kept me from doing so till now. But as it has been suggested to me that they would like to hear from me, even if I were not going to stay, and could not say that which would be perfectly satisfactory, I will try to give some idea of how I feel in some respects.—[Mr. B. goes on to relate his experience before coming here—the effect of his reading the BEREAN and CIRCULAR—his confidence in Mr. Noyes as an inspired man, and his love for him &c., which we have not room to print.] Since coming here, [he continues,] I have been in such a state from various causes, that I have not perhaps seen and appreciated Mr. Noyes's work in the Community, as it is; perhaps have not appreciated the good there is here, as I ought to have done, but I believe that Mr. Noyes was inspired of God to do a certain work, and that he is the true head of this Community. I confess my faith in Christ as a whole saviour, and my love for all that are his, and my willingness to receive and accept *all* truth that he gives me to apprehend. Whether I continue with the Community or not, I am *determined* to do his will, just as fast as by the aid of his spirit, I can find it out, even if I loose all things, and my own life also.   D. E. BLOOD.

I have been for a few days past in deep tribulation. There have been two spirits striving in me to see which was the strongest, and I think good will prevail, because I have been led to see more clearly than ever before, the hatefulness of a hard unbelieving heart. In examining myself, my thoughts run back to my domestic life and I can see clearly many happy and profitable seasons I might have had at my own fireside, had it not been for that robber of social life, a hard heart. When I think of the many wounds I have inflicted without cause, I feel like humbling myself before God and asking his forgiveness. I feel that I have outraged God and the Community, by suffering myself to be held captive by this spirit so long, and I humbly ask forgiveness of all.—I am thankful for any circumstances that will stir me up to earnestness, and I pray that the judgement fire will continue to burn until the old life is consumed, if it takes body and all. I confess my union with, and subordination to Mr. Noyes, Mr. Hamilton and the Community spirit.   L. VAN VELZER.

P. S. I feel as though I could not close this without saying God be praised for opening my eyes.

We have on exhibition just now, a relic of exquisite penmanship about two hundred years old. It has come down to our day as an heir-loom, we suppose, in the family of Mr. Crane (one of our hired carpenters). It is a sample of the celebrated Edward Cocker's books of writing exercises.—The amateur could not fail of a treat, should he happen to cast his eye upon its pages. Verily such execution must have taken a lifetime of practice. His style was thought to rival the Italian.—Many will recall the name of Edward Cocker as an authority in Arithmetic.—We shall make no attempt at description, but apparently, there's nothing under the sun that he could not have represented with a flourish of his pen, had he only *chosen* to do so.

R. S. D.

We have examined the book of penmanship Mr. D. speaks of, with a good deal of pleasure. There are fourteen capital letters, whose superficial contents, could they be accurately measured, would average over eight inches each. The outline of each letter is formed with bold strokes of the pen, which are filled up with numberless graceful curves, flourishes, and devices, executed with great taste and with entire precision. Within the compass of some of the letters, and forming a part of them, are accurately drawn pictures of faces, fowls and animals. In one there is a tiny little squirrel sitting upright, cunningly nibbling a nut.

We were sitting in our room last Saturday evening, absorbed in study, when there burst in upon us three little girls, with the exclamation, "O Mrs. J.! we have got something for the DAILY; will you put it in? O! will you? do, do, it's so funny." They were so eager to get a promise from us, that it was some time before we could get the particulars of what had happened. It seems that one of the small girls in taking down a bowl of molasses from the cupboard, had tipped it over, spilling the contents on the top of her head, which had run down all over her face, neck shoulders, and to the skirts of her garments. The showering with molasses was not a great treat to the poor lass, and the washing and scrubbing she had to be put through, to relieve her of her extra sweetness, will long be remembered by her, as one of the bitterest sweets of her girlhood.

Among the changes of to-day, (which are not a few), we would report that L. F. Dunn has commenced working in the machine-shop; besides, there is a general stirring up and changing rooms of a dozen or more.

Mr. W. H. Perry has been gone two or three days to Herkimer, to attend the funeral of a neice. His object in going, he says, was to see his relatives together, and have some talk with them on subjects connected with our religious faith.

We shall omit publishing the DAILY to-morrow.

Yesterday's temperature—
7½ A. M., 29.   12 M., 40.   6 P. M., 38.   Mean 35⅓.

THE O. C. DAILY.

VOL. 3. THURSDAY, FEB. 21, 1867. NO. 44.

Freeport, Ill., Feb. 16, 1867.

I left here on Thursday last for Dubuque, Iowa, reaching Dunleith on this side of the Mississippi River about 10 P. M. On arriving there I learned there was to be no crossing over the river that night with teams, as it was considered dangerous on account of the ice breaking up. Being anxious to get into Dubuque that night, I in company with a woman passenger, and a young girl (about 10 years old) started on foot to cross the river, a distance of half or three quarters of a mile. At first we were under the necessity of taking a small skiff, for a few rods in order to reach the sound ice. Then we directed our steps for the other shore without pilot not knowing what we should find there. After we had got two thirds of the way or more, we noticed other passengers coming behind us. This gave us courage, thinking we were not alone on that great river at such an hour of the night, (between 10 and 11 o'clock). Although it was not dark, yet it was somewhat difficult to see where the river was open. But as a good Providence would have it we found our way to the other side in just the right place, as it proved, although at first we began to think we might have to stay on the ice for some time. We found the river open several rods from shore as it was on the other side, and no one to take us across, and so we began to walk up and down on the ice, looking for some safe place to cross, being at the same time careful not to get too near where it was open, lest we break through. In this situation, I thought of the woman and girl, thinking they must be tired from the long walk, but No; they did not complain, nor did they seem to be frightened. About this time several men, passengers on the same train came up, and just then we saw a man near the place on the shore where we first reached, who in answer to our calls, said he would take us over. I guess our hearts were *glad* and *thankful*, at least mine was. I could *see* that God had delivered us, in directing us to the right spot, as we might not have found another place at that late hour.

We were soon safe on shore, though not without some difficulty. The next day I returned, but it being in the day-time, got back safe again. Yours, c. o.

The 20th passed off pleasantly though with less formality, show or parade, than has been our custom in years past. Business was suspended in most of the different departments of labor, and the family were all at home. We met in the Hall at 10 o'clock A. M., and immediately after assembling, it was announced that Messrs. Cragin and Thacker had arrived. They were invited into the Hall, and were received with lively demonstrations of welcome. Dinner was served up at 2 o'clock P. M. Tables were set in the dining-room, kitchen, and cellar, sufficient to seat all the family including the children. Our bill of fare consisted of coffee, biscuit and butter, cheese, apple-sauce, (the nicest kind) fruit-pie, baked potatoes, oysters, wine, nuts and raisins. Two large tables were spread in the Hall, on which were placed the presents that had previously been prepared for the children. At 3 o'clock, we had music by the Brass band, and at four, the presents were distributed, which made lively times for the children. At half past four, there was an impromptu concert, consisting of music by the small Orchestra, songs and recitations, and at a quarter past six, a dance. We had our meeting at the usual hour, in which many expressed themselves as feeling increasing desires for newness of life, and softness of heart.

WILLOW–PLACE ITEM.

For a month or more J. F. Sears has been at work constructing a machine for measuring silk as it is put on the spool. A few days since it was finished, and is now on trial. Though the machine lacks perfection in detail, it does its work well. The greatest objection discovered thus far is, that it takes a good deal more time and care to spool with it than in the usual way. But we can afford the extra expense for the sake of putting up silk " on the square." The machine is not a new invention, but only an amplification of a hand measuring machine used by the trade to test the length of a spool of silk.

" BETTER LATE THAN NEVER."

This is a common expression. When people are behind time and are half an hour late, I often hear them say " Better late than never." Supposing a person walked to the depot some dark stormy night, and got there just after the cars left. Would they say " better late than never?" Perhaps not. What if Engineers were governed by this rule and not have any special rule for passing trains; would that do? Does God like such a spirit? I believe he likes promptness, and for my own part I want to be prompt in all the affairs of life. 7,

The event of secret at O. C. is often sorely pressed of the journals and Not unfrequently say, " How I do wish, the one who writes the items would write a little clearer! It is almost impossible to decipher this"! Will not the friend who writes them think of our reader, and be a little more precise in the formation of the letters, or strive for a bolder, plainer hand? s.

The Willow-Place Works were closed for the 20th, Mr. Dunning taking charge of the shop.

Temperature Tuesday and Wednesday—
7, A. M., 25. 12 M., 30. 9 P. M., 23. Mean 27½.
7, A. M., 18. 12 M., 33. 6 P. M., 38. Mean 36.

THE O. C. DAILY.

VOL. 3. FRIDAY, FEB. 22, 1867. NO. 45.

TO THE FAMILY.

As I am to leave to-morrow for New-York, I will take this opportunity to express my thanks for the pleasant and profitable visit I have had with you. I feel that my heart is softer than it was when I came, and I hope and pray that the work may go on until I become one with Christ in thought and deed.—If you have any advice or criticism for me it will be thankfully received.

Yours for brokenness of heart, J. R. LORD.

Much love and fellowship was expressed for J. R. L. and thankfulness that he had been permitted to stay here so long.

VISITOR.—Dr. G. M. Weeks, from Broom St., N. Y., on his way to Minnesota. A scientific not a religious man. Had heard enough of us to become thoroughly interested. Wished to see results; our woman, children &c.—was army surgeon during the war—married five years ago—practiced "Male continence"—had no children. Lungs weak—thinks the fogs of New-York bad for them, and therefore goes to Minnesota to inhale the pure dry air of that region, for a month or two this spring.—He leaves this afternoon.

COMPOSITION.

It's not easy to tell of the terrors that dwell
  In the mind of young ambition,
Of that wondrous rule they have made in school,
  About writing composition.

He must write, they say, one every day,
  No matter about his condition;
He must torture his brain, if the goal he would gain,
  So wonderful is composition.

At length, with a sigh, he says I will try;
  And he puts himself into position;
And subjects his brain to a terrible strain,
  But pshaw! what a vile composition.

He flings the thing by, with a tear in his eye;
  How vain is worldly ambition;
He is heard to say, that he rues the day
  When he embarked in composition.

But after a while he is seen to smile
  The grim smile of desperation.
His white teeth grind—and now he's blind
  To all, but his composition.

He knits his brow, he is desperate now.
  (Such tells on the fate of nations),
He will obey the rule, and present to the school,
  To-morrow, a composition.

But no! that poor soul was destined to fail,
  How wretched is his condition;

He ought to have known that he was not born
  To succeed in composition.

Alas! luckless youth; we are bound to say truth,
  When we say of his sad condition,
It was ten and more, times worse than before
  He dabbled in composition. J. P. H.

In meeting last night Mr. Cragin presented the subject of building a new house for the children, for the consideration of the family, and gave his own views in reference to the site, size, and construction of said building. The discussion of the subject was deferred till Sunday evening, when there is to be a general expression of the family in regard to it. All, particularly the women, are invited to think over the matter and present their views relative to it.

The class in Theology have adjourned *sine die.*—Many expressed themselves as having received much benefit from the exercises of the class, and the study of the Berean, and the hope was expressed that at some future time, we might be reorganized and enter upon another course of Theological study.

A letter was received from Mrs. Chesbro a day or two since, enclosing $6 which she says was a gift to her from a sister, and she wishes to put it into the Lord's treasury. She says, "I am so thankful that ... into my heart to do so."

Mrs. Robinson is here on a visit. She came Wednesday morning, for the purpose of passing the 20th ... She came to the depot the day before, but ... the Oneida conveyance, she staid all night with an acquaintance.

G. E. Cragin arrived yesterday, quite unexpectedly to many. In the meeting he gave us a brief history of New Haven affairs, which was very interesting indeed.

The snow has fallen some two or three inches the last twenty-four hours, and it is still snowing—so we have ... prospect of sleighing once more.

Yesterday's temperature—
7½ A. M., 23. 12 M., 31. 9 P. M., 28. Mean 27.

THE O. C. DAILY.

VOL. 3.   SATURDAY, FEB. 23, 1857.   NO. 46.

From Mrs. Dascomb of Cameron New York.

" My thoughts have turned toward you as a people involuntarily and almost constantly since my visit to Oneida, and my heart has often been drawn out in love to all my dear brothers and sisters at Oneida who have come up through great tribulation and have washed your robes in the blood of the Lamb, and yet I have not studied you as a people so much as I have a spiritual body—as the professed members of Christ's body, and the embodiment of his Kingdom in the earth; and the more I read your writings and reflect upon the oneness of spirit which I saw manifested in you with many other evidences of inspiration, the more am I constrained to believe that God is with you in deed and in truth.   *   *   *   I am reading the Berean and can no more doubt the inspiration of God in its author, than I am able to doubt that of Paul or any other leader that has been raised up to establish and build up the kingdom of heaven on the earth. The leaven is working—will work in spite of all opposition from man or the author of all evil.   *   *   I doubt if there is any thing more perfect and beautiful connected with your present organization than the self-abandonment which characterized its leaders and founders in laying down their lives and reputations if need be, in an untried experiment to establish truth in the face of a blind and persecuting world. That God is honoring your faith and abnegation of all selfishness must be evident even to the most skeptical that have watched your progress.

" One of the strongest evidences in my own heart that the God of the Bible is with you, is the spirit of Judgment that has rested upon me in turning from you and seeking an independent inspiration."

Just before night, yesterday, a Mrs. Francis, from Bridgewater, Vermont, was brought up here from the depot, and she requested to stay over night. She looked the very picture of sadness, and so out of compassion we concluded to let her remain. She says she started from home and came to Rutland, twenty miles, to see a Dr. whom she wished to consult about her health. Not finding him at home she concluded to come on here, though she knew not a word about us, only what little she could gather from the article published in the Tribune, some time ago. She has the same piteous story to tell, so oft reiterated in our ears of late, of separation from her husband, and a houseless, homeless condition—a little child two years old to provide for, with the prospect of another before many months. She refused to give us the reasons for her separation from her husband; said she chose to say nothing about it. She was urgent to join, said she thought she might be happy here, as she could have her child with her, which she could not have in her present circumstances. She said her mother was a Methodist professor, and she was brought up to respect that body of religionists more than any other; but as for herself, she never professed religion, and was not religiously inclined. As she cannot reach home if she starts to-day, I suppose we shall be obliged to keep her over Sunday.

Mrs. Loomis has at last left the Community, to the great relief of those who had the most to do with her. Mr. Clark started with her this morning, for Hamilton, with every thing she brought here and *some things she didn't*. She professes to go away through respect for Mr. Hamilton's advice, given her before she went to visit her friends, but she evidently is in a quarrel with his criticism given her some time ago.

She says in going away, she is not going to forsake the truth, but she shall seek to find out what the trouble is between her and the Community, and prepare herself to return to us, some future day. She tried hard to make every thing on her side appear fair and smooth.

E. S. Nash was criticised in meeting last night, by his request. But little fault was found with him, but a good deal of commendation of his general course, his public spirit, business habits &c. It was thought he lacked spirituality, and he should cultivate that side of his character, which was so essential to his success as a foreman.

Our people are improving the little sleighing we have, to draw wood. They had for several days previously, been sawing it by horse-power.

Mr. Kelley spent the 20th at Bath. He reports that our silk is pronounced first-rate by his customers, all on the route he takes in his peddling trip.

One of Mr. Van's workmen, Thomas Hillis, left yesterday. This leaves Mr. V. with only two hands except himself in the shop.

Our people have bought a yoke of oxen recently and paid $250 for them.

Mr. Pitt and John Lord left yesterday afternoon for New-York.

Yesterday's temperature—
7½ A. M., 29.   12 M., 33.   9 P. M., 22.   Mean 28.

THE O. C. DAILY.

VOL. 3.   MONDAY, FEB. 25, 1867.   NO. 47

The discussion last night, about building a new house for the children, resulted in appointing a committee to locate the same, draw a plan &c. The feeling was unanimous that such a building should be put up the coming season, if brick could be procured.

A committee, which met during Friday and Saturday afternoons of last week, to consider the amount of fruit and vegetables to be preserved the coming season, decided on the following

PROGRAMME FOR 1867.

VEGETABLES IN CANS.

Tomatoes,	15,000.	Green Peas,	5,000.
Corn,	5,000.	String Beans,	5,000.
	Pie Plant,	600.	

FRUITS.

	CANS.	BOTTLES.
Pears,	3,300.	1,700.
Plums,	6,700.	3,300.
Peaches,	6,700.	3,300.
Raspberries,	4,000.	4,000.
Quinces,	2,500.	1,000.
Cherries,	6,700.	3,300.
Strawberries,	3,500.	3,500.
Huckleberries,	800.	400.
Pine-apples,	12,00.	1,200.

PICKLED FRUITS, IN GLASS JARS.

Pears, 600.   Peaches, 600.   Crab-apples, 300.

JAMS, IN GLASS JARS.

| Blackberry, | 150. | Black Raspberry, | 150. |
| Currant, | 150. | Red   " | 150. |

750 doz. Tumblers of Jellies.

Making a total of	65,000	Cans,
	20,700	Bottles,
	2,100	Jars,
	9,000	Tumblers.
	96,800.	

Saturday Mr. Charles Parry came up from Troy to join us. He was a healthy robust well formed man ; but he was broken hearted, and he had such dark, sad, earnest, truthful, trustful eyes, that mine would moisten sympathetically whenever I looked into them.

He had been a soldier for a number of years—had fought for the republic, also for a higher life—had lived with the Shakers a year and a half. He spoke evil of no one in the sketch he gave me of his trials. He wanted to *rise*, he said, and his yearnings and aspirations for spiritual improvement were so strong that they almost overpowered him.—He could get neither sympathy nor appreciation in the world.— **His wife did not sympathize with him, although** she was a noble hearted woman—church members did not respect him, and in consequence, much against his inclinations, he was a solitary, in the midst of a crowded city. It was evident that his mind and heart were so absorbed in interior things, that he did not give a wholesome regard to outward things—the amenities of social life, personal tidiness and cleanliness &c., and accordingly failed to make himself acceptable. We gave him some of our publications, and a few words of advice, and he took the return train for Troy.   U.

San Francisco, Jan. 29, 1867.

MR. J. BURT OR L. F. DUNN : DEAR SIR :—Please send us description circular, price and all particulars concerning your green corn-cutter patented last year.

Yours truly,   CUTTING & CO.

REPLY.

Oneida, N. Y., Feb. 25, 1867.

MESSRS. CUTTING & CO.: GENTS :—We have yours of Jan. 29th and reply : The machine for cutting green corn from the cob, patented by Mr. Burt and myself, has not yet been perfected so as to work in an entirely satisfactory manner, and we are not now offering the machine for sale. Should the machine be perfected so as to work to our satisfaction we will give you the information you desire at the earliest moment.

Yours respectfully,   LEONARD F. DUNN.

AN ECHO FROM THE SHOE-SHOP.

DEAR EDITRESS :—Perhaps it may be interesting to some of your readers to learn that nearly all the waste scraps at the Bag-shop are turned to good account at the Shoe-shop. From a lot of scraps that were carried to the Shoe-shop at the time of their last inventory, there has been cut out between 50 and 75 pairs of women's and children's shoes ; and the pile is not half exhausted. Besides this, the lightest of the pebble scraps are found to work well and be very suitable for piecing out boot legs. Also the best part of them compare nicely with oil dressed goat-skin, and works in well, for quarters ; and when the shoe is made up, none but the best judges of stock could tell it from oil dressed goat-morocco, and as the shoes are cheaper, and do not require to be blacked to keep them bright, it is proposed to substitute them for calf skin, for our women's every day wear, which I think will be much more satisfactory to them. Who sympathizes with this kind of economy ?   S. S.

Mrs. Ackley has resigned her post as mother at the children's house, and Mrs. Hatch takes her place.

Temperature Saturday and Sunday—
7½ A. M., 29.   12 M., 38.   6 P. M., 28.   Mean 31⅓.
7½ A. M., 40.   12 M., 40.   9 P. M., 30.   Mean 36⅓.

THE O. C. DAILY.

VOL. 3.   TUESDAY, FEB. 26, 1867.   NO. 48.

Wilson County, N. C., Feb. 19, 1867.

Mr. J. H. Noyes, Dear Sir:—In reading the American Phrenological Journal a short time since, I saw a sketch of your life and the Community organized by you, and I fully agree with you as to your opinion of marriage; and the manner of working suits me in every particular, for what can be more pleasant to a person than to labor for the general welfare of the people among whom he lives, "Doing unto others as he would that they should do unto him."

I am a young man nineteen years of age, have no trade but that of a farmer, have seventy acres of land which however I am not in possession of yet. I would like very much to become a member of your Community. Trusting to hear from you soon, I am respectfully yours &c.,   H. D. Lucas.

TO THE FAMILY.

I would like to thank the family for my late criticism; I believe it was just, and given in a good spirit; I hope to profit by it.—I have been sensible the past winter of being oppressed by a hard, worldly, unbelieving spirit, that has greatly obstructed my fellowship and union with the heart of the Community. My purpose has been not to yield to its temptations, or influence; yet I have had to be in unceasing warfare with it, in which I have been sensible of a good deal of weakness of spirit, and I think it has quite seriously affected my health. For the last few weeks I have been somewhat tempted with a discouraged spirit; my old life appeared perfectly hateful; and the way to full and permanent union with the power of life seemed very difficult. * * I confess my willingness to serve, to the best of my ability in this war against the powers of darkness and unbelief, however much of suffering it may involve, until all sin and selfishness and death are destroyed, and Christ's kingdom is fully established on the earth. I wish to abandon myself unreservedly to Christ and Mr. Noyes, to help forward the cause they are engaged in.   John Abbott.

Our visitor, Mrs. Francis, left yesterday morning, seemingly in much better spirits than when she came. She spent her time principally while here, in reading our publications, in which she seemed to take a good deal of interest. She is only twenty-five years old, but has suffered a good deal for a person so young. She married her husband in Michigan, a young Dr., and he, having enlisted, left soon after for the army, and she returned to her friends. Two years after, he returned to her a drunken sot, and she refused, after learning what his habits were, to have anything to do with him. We thought she was honest, but quite secretive, as she had not informed her mother with whom she is now staying, of her present condition. On leaving, we gave her the tract, "Salvation from Sin" and a few Nos. of the Circular for which she seemed very thankful.

We came across quite accidentally, the following lines written by M. E. Cragin in 1851, which we do not recollect ever having seen in print:

"Lines suggested by hearing Mr. Noyes remark that, 'the resurrection power created a bright spot in the heart, that no clouds could dim.'"

"In a dark gloomy vale rose a beautiful star,
Its radiance was steady, its light from afar
Dispelling the darkness and clouds all around,
Bade the valley rejoice in the friend it had found.

For now said the star I will pierce through the gloom;
I will brighten thy evenings, and gladden thy noon.
No clouds can o'erwhelm me, no darkness dismay,
I will bring to this valley, the light of the day.

And true to its promise, the beautiful gem
Was the star of the valley, its bright diadem.
It would vapors and storms, yes, e'en tempests defy,
It had power to shine—but no power to die.

Fit emblem methought of the star in the soul,
Shining on through all tempests, which over it roll;
Unbelief may envelop, and doubts may rise high,
And the tremulous heart seems to heave its last sigh.

But the star in the centre with life giving ray,
Turns the gloom into sunshine, the darkness to day.
Oh repose in its beauty and trust in its power,
'Tis our link to Jehovah, our fortress, our tower."—

The subject that is exciting the most interest at the present time in the family, is our new project of building. There are various opinions, as to the best thing to be done, but, we trust, all will at length as heretofore, fall into harmony with whatever plan the most advanced minds among us shall see fit to make. For our own part we rest quietly, assured that,

"Ever the right will come uppermost,
And the very best thing be done."

The weather for a few days past, has been pleasant and spring-like, every thing indicating that that interesting season is close upon us. Our schools are to close this week, and also the classes that interfere with business. The hope was expressed in meeting last night, that the same spirit of enthusiasm that had characterized study, the past winter, would be transferred to our business operations, which would be equally improving, if performed in a right spirit.

G. E. Cragin started for New-Haven yesterday afternoon.

Yesterday's temperature—
7½ A. M., 20.   12 M., 32.   9 P. M., 26.   Mean 26.

THE O. C. DAILY.

VOL. 3. WEDNESDAY, FEB. 27, 1867.   NO. 49.

Miss Munson writes to Mrs. Thayer, Feb. 22d:

"I received your kind letter last Wednesday, also six papers, and a photograph, for which many thanks.

"I am sorry my letter affected you so unpleasantly. I did not mean to grumble, or find fault, but only to let you know how many difficulties I had passed through, so far. But I see things very different now, from what I did when I wrote that letter. I have always felt since I first heard of you, that if I could live with you at the Community, you could rouse me out of the condition I was in. A short time previous to receiving your letter, I went to bed one night, but not to sleep. I was thinking how fast I might grow if I was only with you—it seemed like a dream, but I know I was awake—when a voice seemed to say to me, ' not there, not there my child, but come to me.' I seemed to see a more beautiful picture of Christ than I have ever seen painted. I went to him and nestled in his bosom, as a little child would go to a loving father, feeling he was its best friend. I have been very happy since, he seems to be in all my thoughts and acts. My prayer is that I may always feel thus. I think I can be happy any where now, everything looks more beautiful to me, and when I look into the face of Mr. Noyes, he seems to look at me approvingly. Now when I read the papers, and re-read the letters you have sent me from time to time, I wonder I could have been so blind, when you have pointed out the way so clear. I am sorry I have been such a trouble to you. But with the help of God, I hope to be able to see more clearly in future.—I find there is a great interest in you here. I have agreed to lend the CIRCULAR to five different persons. I have also lent the BEREAN, &c.

"It seems very pleasant to me to see the CIRCULARS once more, it is almost as good as a letter from you every week.

"From one who is with you in spirit. Love to all,
SUSAN B. MUNSON."

Mr. Cragin suggested in meeting last night that it would be profitable, as there are to be some changes, for the different departments to offer themselves for criticism. He said, "I confess a good spirit in the investigation of our affairs, and the spirit of brotherly love in our criticisms of one another. I believe we can tell the truth in love and softness of heart, and that it will result in drawing us nearer together. I have a good deal of fellowship with the men of the Community. The experience that our men have had at the Agency, and their visit at Wallingford during the Christmas-week was to me quite miraculous and very interesting. This growing attachment between the men and the freedom they have to open their hearts to each other, and pray for one another, is pleasing to heaven, for it came from heaven."

TO THE FAMILY.

I feel like publicly acknowledging what Christ has done for me of late. I have been deeply interested in Mr. Noyes' late talks about the soft heart. I have had an earnest prayer that Christ would break my heart and fill me with his spirit. I think my prayer has been answered, and that I have had a new conversion. I feel as I used to when I was a young convert, joyful and happy; my faith in the Community and Mr. Noyes is growing. I feel a flow of love and unity with Christ, that I never felt before; every interest of my life is identified with the Community. You can use me as you see fit. I thank God for the revival spirit.   Yours for a soft heart,   R. M. BOLLES.

As the present prospect is, that apples will not be very plentiful with us this spring, Mr. Worden went out yesterday, to see if he could buy some. He procured a few, for which he paid $1.50 per bushel. He has also bought recently, fifty bushels of potatoes for the boarding-houses, and paid seventy-five cents per bushel for them.

We commence reading in the Hall to-night, at 7 o'clock, Mr. Dixon's new Book. We hope to derive some pleasure from the same, though we confess we shall be compelled, judging from the many wrong assertions he has made about the Community, to take his words at considerable discount.

Mr. Kinsley went last Monday to see Mr. Hall, the Brick-maker, to see if brick could be procured for the new building in season to put it up the coming summer. He reports that the brick can be had by the last of July, and it was decided last night, to engage them immediately.

Mary Leete is spending a few days here. She is having her teeth repaired.

Yesterday's temperature—
7½ A. M., 20.   12 M., 34.   9 P. M., 33.   Mean 25½.

THE O. C. DAILY.

VOL. 3. THURSDAY, FEB. 28, 1867. NO. 50.

We have received recently, several Nos. of the "Optimist" a paper published at Berlin Hights, Thomas Cook Editor, from which we copy the following:

HOPING FOR THE KINGDOM.

THOMAS COOK, MY FRIEND:—Enclosed please find fifty cents; for which you will send to me the *Optimist and Kingdom of Heaven* one year.

I am glad to find even "Tom Cook" in the "Kingdom of Heaven," and working for its enlargement.— As that Kingdom is yet very small on earth, there is ample room for it to grow larger.

But there are so many institutions in this world, each claiming to be "the Kingdom," that I prefer, as yet to be satisfied with the Heaven in my own individual heart At the same time rather rejoicing that Thomas Cook, and the Oneida Perfectionists, with many others are prospecting for that "Kingdom" on a larger scale; fully believing that out of all of these revelations will come a glorious hereafter.

JOHN CORWIN.

Five Corners, Cayuga Co., N. Y.

We believe with Solomon, "Train up a child in the way he should go and when he is old, he will not depart from it." Christ endorsed the wisdom of Solomon by saying, "Suffer little children to come unto me and forbid them not for of such is the kingdom of heaven." There is our labor and our study to know how to impress on the minds of little children this saying of Christ. We remember strong religious impresions before we were six years old. We are sure that children are impressible very much younger here and really capable of receiving Christ; but as a fountain can raise water no higher than its source, so we can raise them no higher or nearer Christ than we stand ourselves. x.

"BE STRONG."

[From the Cooper Union Journal.]

Ye knights of toil whose sweat decides
The meed ye drain from stores of life,
Whose iron arm and will provides
The food for little ones and wife,

Be strong.

Ye slaves of grief, whom fortune shuns,
Ye sons of sires now cold and still;
Ye tracks o'er which in orbit runs
The force of Fate's remorseless will,

Be strong.

Ye men who lead the thoughts of time,
Ye toilers o'er the cliffs, that bar

From vulgar gaze the hopes sublime,
That cluster round advancement's star,

Be strong.

O God! but 'tis a fearsome sight
To view the great and good go down
Unknown, uncared—amid the light
That gilds the worthless with renown!
Oh, break, ye surfs of venal waves!
Oh, roar, ye gales of human scorn;
A ray of hope my bosom craves;
A whisper to my soul is born—

Be strong.

D. T. GARDNER.

"O. C.:—Would you please send a copy of your 'Male Continence,' and oblige a poor young man, with a rather large small family. Find enclosed ten cents. Address A. Armour,

Tamarack, Ill."

The chicken-pox has broken out among the little children, eight or nine of them being down with it, though none of them what we should call *very* sick, but still requiring considerable attention. At first we could not conceive how they could have taken it or in what way been exposed, but on reflection we remembered that Mr. Aldred and his wife who were here the last of Jan. and staid over Sunday, had a little girl that was sick, though we did not know what ailed the child, and as Willie and Theodora were the first that had it, and as they are over to the New House more than the other children, we came to the conclusion that the disease must have been communicated to them, through this child. Mr. Bolles will remember the peculiar, and unpleasant odor Mr. A. and family brought into the house, but we did not then suspect that it proceeded from the disease that was upon the child.

We cannot help feeling a little anxious sometimes, at night and after meeting, about matter for the coming DAILY, when nothing has transpired worthy of record, nothing reportable in the evening meeting, and no letters. Such was the case last night. We lingered in the Hall a while, talked with this and that one, but could get nothing except one short item. We obtained one or two promises however, which encouraged us some. Then we canvassed the upper Sitting-room, with some of the adjoining bed-rooms, and all we got was a promise from one of our leading business men, of an item to-morrow. So we went to our room, not disheartened, but, as we said before, a little anxious for the fate of to-morrow's DAILY, yet trusting in God, who has hitherto given us our "daily bread," sometimes in almost a miraculous way.

Yesterday's temperature—
7½ A. M., 31. 12 M., 34. 9 P. M., 29. Mean 31½.

THE O. C. DAILY.

VOL. 3.   FRIDAY, MARCH 1, 1867.   NO. 51.

WILLOW-PLACE ITEMS.

The quarries at Willow-Place are quite an institution, or would be considered such if worked by a private individual. Five men have been employed at them all winter with a net result of about 300 cords of stone quarried, at the time of this writing. Of these, 100 cords are at the quarry by the foundry, and 200 at the one by the new dam. 85 cords have been sold and mostly drawn away. Quarrying stone on a bleak creek bank might seem to be rather severe employment for winter, but they have kept it up through snow and blow, with the exception of occasionally a day or two in the severest weather. The stone are in horizontal strata, or nearly so, the dip being scarcely perceptible. They vary in thickness from mere slate to about a foot or eighteen inches of impervious rock. The quarry is about six feet in depth and underlaid with a bed of slate. Much of the stone loosens up readily with a bar and pick skillfully applied, but the more solid strata have to be started with powder and fuse. The stone are of varying quality, but sell at an average of about $3,00 per cord, the limits being $2,50 and $3,50. This would give us $900 as the result of the winter's work, but we pay $1,50 per cord for quarrying, besides some other incidental expenses for tools, powder, &c., amounting to perhaps twenty-five or fifty dollars more.   G.

Our sawyer, Mr. Tipple, has left the Sawmill recently, and rented a farm on the Street. Another sawyer, a Durhamville man, has been hired, but as he did not come when he agreed to, Mr. Kinsley and D. F. Knowles are running the mill.

A man called at the shop the other day, who used to work in the old Morrisville Silk-factory, but for eight years has been employed in a Woollen mill. He expressed considerable surprise at the various improvements in the machinery, and also the new inventions. I asked him about the failure of the Morrisville Company. He said that they were successful at first, but after Mr. Gurley became sole proprietor, things were managed very shiftlessly. Mr. G. spent but little time in the mill—leaving two or three boys to look after the business as well as they could. Such management led in time to the inevitable conclusion—failure   C.

About three weeks since, Mr. Clark, in coming from the depot, lost off from his sleigh, a machine about the size of a small Straw-cutter, for cutting enameled cloth, that was purchased in Newark, and cost $35. Homer Barron looked for it soon after it was missed from the sleigh, but it could not be found. Much inquiry was made for the lost machine to no purpose, and finally it was advertised, and a reward offered for its recovery.—Last night, after we had almost despaired of ever seeing the machine again, three Indians came and delivered it to us. In answer to the question why they kept it so long? they said they could not read the name on it. Oneida Community was written on the card attached to it in a bold hand. We paid the finder $2.00 and his black eyes glistened with pleasure, as he took the money.   H.

We have calls in the Office from all manner of folks, rich and poor, the vagrant who asks for money or bread, the rich man who wishes to order refreshments, persons seeking their fortunes and wishing to join, the well to-do farmer, who comes to sell us his butter, the poor Indian who cannot write, but makes his mark, and occasionally some one who wishes to have us invest, in some Patent Right.

We had a call from one of the latter class a short time since, who wished us to make a patent fixture for adjusting ladies skirts. It was so arranged that by pulling a string at the pocket-hole, the skirts could be raised *before* on going up stairs, and *behind* on going down ; or with an extra pull and fastening, the whole could be raised at once on going through the mud. He prefaced his remarks by saying that he would take off his coat so that he could "blow." The women were in the Office, and one of them told him that we had as much as we could do to attend to our regular business, and did not think we should want to turn aside for anything of that kind.— But said he, " You can make a dollar and thirteen cents on every one of these you make, and you can't make that on every rat-trap." We told him that traps would very likely be wanted for some time to come, but this was something that probably would not be used a great while—certainly would not be if all went to wearing short dresses. What ! said he, " Do you expect every one is going to throw away the fashions and wear these short dresses ?" We told him mildly, we did not know but they would.— He replied, " These short dresses may be very nice to wear in the mud, but for my part I do not like them."

But to appease the man, we went in search of Mr. W. But he met with no better success in talking with him, and on leaving said, if it had not been for the women, he thought he should have been more successful, in selling us territory.   A.

Birmingham, Pa., Feb. 25., 1867.

To THE O. C.—I have been reading your publications for some time. I wish to join your Community. What must I do? Pass not by this note, but please answer it, either by letter, or through THE CIRCULAR.
                                    JOHN DAVIS.

Two evenings have been spent in criticising the farming department. Great changes are anticipated in that line of things, as soon as practicable.

Miss Susan Dunn, of Bakersfield, Vt., an Aunt of Fidelia's, came here yesterday to make a visit.

Yesterday's temperature—
7½ A. M., 28.   12 M., 50.   9 P. M., 40.   Mean 39¼.

THE O. C. DAILY.

VOL. 3. SATURDAY, MARCH 2, 1867. NO. 52.

WILLOW-PLACE ITEMS.

FORGE-SHOP.—A lot of 30,000 muskrat springs are now being tempered; 6,000 Fox, and 3,000 Beaver springs are under way. Of the five hands employed there, three work the most of the time repairing the springs which have been damaged in making. These have been accumulating for several years, but this season they are going to clean them all up.

FINISHING-SHOP.—Between two and three thousand beaver traps are now in process of construction, and over two thousand otter traps are ready to be put together, and a lot of forty thousand muskrat traps have been started. Seven hired men, and seven communists constitute the regular force.—We have a double team on the Willow-Place route, now-a-days, and it is needed. A portion of the road is quite muddy, while the remainder consists of very dirty looking snow-drifts, the track through which, is corrugated in a manner approaching the marvelous.

BAG-SHOP.—The month of February has been a busy month with us, and Spring opens with our arrangements for a business campaign, pretty well completed. We have had more shelves put up in our store-room. Our leather work is thoroughly protected from dust and light by paper curtains, dropping from each shelf. Printed names on each curtain will designate what style of bags is to be found underneath.

Our Office is a pleasant place. A tent-curtain at one end, partitions off a bedroom for our night-watchman. We think he must have pleasant dreams here; our own experience during the day makes us feel sure that angels always come where an earnest and happy spirit invites them.—John Heyl has been getting up four new style bags, two of them quite handsome.— We expect to have them out soon.　　　　N.

We have made the past month, 51¼ dozen Bags valued at　　　　　　　　　　$2,086.72.
Ordered the past month,　　　　　　　36 doz.
Sales the past month,
Bag Department,　　　　　　　　$1,837.44.
Trap　　"　　　　　　　　　$1,113.91.
Silk-Factory sent to N. Y. B., and sold,　$1,714.75.
The first shipment of Traps of the Hudson Bay Co.'s order, was consigned yesterday to W. Macnaughton, 52 Cedar St. New-York, amounting to,　$306.85.

We receive some letters from our Trap-customers, enquiring for our lowest cash prices.

Grand De Tour, Feb. 24, 1867.

DEAR FRIENDS:—It has been over two years since I left the Community, and a long two years it has been to me. Many times has the folly and wickedness of my leaving the Community arisen in my mind, and as many times have I cast it aside, but it will return.

I have not found what I was looking for, but I have found that it is an utter impossibility to attain perfection without the help of Christ and his church, and the more I think upon this subject the more I become convinced that the Community is the best place for me. My friends have nothing to do in influencing me to write this letter; on the contrary they would prefer that I should not return, (for such is my object in writing this) neither has my folks at the Community any thing to do with it, but the world itself has made me come to this conclusion.

I read the CIRCULAR and derive great benefit from its columns, especially from J. H. N's Home-Talks. I also see that Grace Mills has returned and has been admitted as a member—hope that I may one day be permitted to follow in her trail.　I remain yours in Christ,　　　　　　　ISRAEL S. BAILEY.

Last evening I closed my class at the Boarding-house. It has passed along pleasantly and quietly all winter, and I have been interested in seeing the general spirit manifested by those who attended. They have been, not only desirious of improvement in their studies, but kind and respectful to one another, free from competition, and always ready to assist each other if necessary. They have made it pleasant for me all winter and seem to appreciate the interest the Community take in them, and have improved and gained my respect. I am satisfied that whatever we do toward the improvement of our employees, has a healthy and communizing influence on the character, and on society.　　　　　　　　　　L. A. T.

New steps have been put down, recently, on the stairs leading to the second floor of the Mansion House, the old ones having been pretty thoroughly worn out. We are told that this is the first time the stairs have been repaired since the building of the house, which, considering the almost constant treading to which they have been subjected, seems quite remarkable.

As several of the classes close to-day, and many school-books are likely to remain idle for a time, it is requested that students should hand to Mrs. L. A. Thayer such books as they have in their possession which they do not wish to retain; and she will carefully preserve them for another campaign of study.　　w.

We received an order yesterday, from N. B. Harwood of St. Paul, for 100 doz. traps No. 1, and one case of otter; also from one to two hundred dollars worth of silk. The letter was addressed to Mr. Olds, and written in a very confidential tone. He closes by saying, "My wife joins me in an invitation to you to make our house your home, whenever you come to St. Paul."

Yesterday's temperature—
7½ A. M., 38. 12 M., 45. 6 P. M., 44. Mean 42¼.

THE O. C. DAILY.

VOL. 3.　MONDAY, MARCH 4, 1867.　NO. 53.

WILLOW-PLACE ITEMS.

The Bag-Department has ordered over 200 dozen frames from the Willow-Place Works, which are now in process of construction.

Eight young men and boys at the Willow-Place Boarding-House, have formed an anti-tobacco league. The period of abstinence is to be one month to begin with, "because" as one of them remarked, "if we can leave it off a month, we can for the rest of our lives." Two or three pale faces around the shop to-day, indicate that the struggle is no slight one.

Mrs. Dunning at Willow-Place had expressed a wish to see our baking operations and visit the kitchen in its every-day suit.—So one day last week by Mr. Worden's invitation, she, in company with her friend and lady boarder, Mrs. Glidden, came over and staid to dinner.—They seemed to take great pleasure in inspecting the bakery and kitchen preparations for an hour before dinner, after which they returned, expressing much satisfaction for the privilege.

Mrs. D. remarked that she wondered why it was, that she had never before looked in to our ways of doing things, and thought it instructive and gratifying to do so. She had frequently called, and with friends had visited the Green-house, garden and grounds, but had not seen so much to instruct and please her.

OUR WILLOW-PLACE ROAD.

The Willow-Place road is an exceeding rough way,
　So *very* rutty indeed, that my comrades say \
That such riding, ought, and they are sure it can
　Shake volumns of poetry out of a man.

Now all of this is exceedingly plain,
The truth of which I would stoutly maintain;
　But would that man write poetry again?
Here is a matter that's not quite so plain.

Now our road lies over a drift of snow—
And the wheels go down to the ground below;
　When one side comes up, down the other will go,
The effect of which every one *must* know.

"Hurry up there!" we call, "driver, let us get on."
　But see, we are bounding like popping corn.
And O, the wry faces, and looks forlorn!
　For each man is treading on his neighbor's corn.

"Stop! Stop! now, driver!" we vigorously call—
　We are tumbling about here, like a foot-ball.
We look at each other and smile; that's all,
　As we out from among the buffaloes crawl.

But enough of this, let's have no more—
　Spring has come, it will soon be o'er;
Over our way the lark shall soar;

And the swallow skim the meadows o'er.
The bobolink too, shall wax jocose,
　And the bluebird fly from post to post;
While from where he was wont to sit the most,
　The kingfisher will watch the scaly host.

J. P. H.

The criticism of the Horticultural and Fruit-preserving Departments, has occupied the last two evenings. The criticism last night turned principally on W. A. H.'s case, and was very searching and pungent. We were quite surprised to hear him, after so many years experience in the Community, make the attempt to justify his past course. We thought how easy it would be for him to emerge from all his difficulties in the twinkling of an eye, could he find a way to obtain a soft heart. We felt like praying that the Lord would touch and melt his heart and show him the truth.

Mr. Cragin has proposed to the young men to commence a series of Sunday meetings. The first one accordingly, came off yesterday, and Mr. C. attended. Almost every one present, spoke of the benefit he had received from the meetings held while Theodore was here, and they all wished them continued. It was thought that some such ordinance would serve to unite the young men, and bring them all into line in God's army. The most noticeable feature of the meeting however, was the reconcili ation of the young men as a class, with Mr. Cragin, "something" as S. Y. J. remarked, "that he never expected would happen in his case."　Q.

We received a letter a few day since, from Mrs. Reeve of Berlin Hights, in which she expresses her thankfulness that liberty has been given her to make us a visit, which she shall gladly avail herself of, as soon as the way opens. She seems to be struggling against surrounding influences, and anxious to know the truth, and come into good relations with the Community.

Now that the classes are closed, the women are going into the study of elocution in earnest. They have engaged Mr. Underwood as teacher, and are to meet for practice four times in a week, in the Hall, between four and five P. M.

We have wintry weather again, the snow having fallen during the night about two inches and the atmosphere being cold and chill.

The supper hour is changed from half past five o'clock to six.

Temperature Saturday and Sunday—
7½ A. M., 52.　12 M., 38.　6 P. M., 23.　Mean 37½.
7½ A. M., 9.　12 M., 34.　9 P. M., 28.　Mean 30½.

THE O. C. DAILY.

VOL. 3.　　TUESDAY, MARCH 5, 1867.　　NO. 54.

Hart Lot, Onon. Co., N. Y., Feb. 28, 1867.

To the President of the Oneida Community :

Please send me a Circular containing the principles of the constitution of your order. I have heard much concerning you and the order which you represent, and I am solicitous to become a member of your society, if I find the principles which are established in keeping with my views.

I have been laboring for some time to establish a system similar to yours in many respects, though perhaps more radical, and if I can be so fortunate as to find one already existing, I shall not be backward in availing myself of the fraternal inducements held out by a brotherhood so commendable as yours.

I am fraternally yours,　　　　B. T. Munn.

Mr. Woolworth said last night that he thought we might profitably have a little discussion about business, now that we are starting for a new campaign. This winter we have had a very good time for study and improvement. We have had a very liberal allowance of time and means of all kinds, and our studies have been prosecuted with zeal and enthusiasm. Now the same spirit should lead us to turn this zeal into business, and make us single-eyed in our devotion to it.— We have a great enterprise before us, and I am sure our business is going to enlist all our energies. The bag-business is quite prosperous; and we have every reason to think there are great quantities of traps to be ordered before long, and that the market will demand them. So too there is a prospect of a good demand for our other productions. I don't know that there is any special occasion for this exhortation ; but it seemed desirable that we should make the transition from study to industry as quick as possible. I believe God's blessing will attend us.

G. W. Hamilton remarked that he had had some thoughts in the same direction. They were started by something his brother said to him before he went away. He said he wanted to see our Trap-shop well stocked', so far as business over there was concerned. He expressed the same ideas Mr. Woolworth has done, that we have had a good time for study, and should now turn our enthusiasm right into business enterprise.

We received letters a few days since, from Isaiah Morris and wife, dated Mount Gilead, Ohio, where they have been stopping the past winter. Mrs. Morris wishes to make us a visit, says she is convinced that our system is the true one, and she is anxious to witness its practical working. Judging from what Mrs. Alman and Peet, (who knew her well) said of Mrs. M.

when they were here, we should think there had been a great change in her spirit. Mr. Morris evidently would be glad to join us, but has hitherto been opposed by his wife.

LARGE RESULTS FROM SMALL BEGINNINGS.

When the fond Hebrew mother hid her boy,
(Too beautiful for Pharioh to destroy)
Three months, with sad affection, pure, and deep,
Till she no longer could the secret keep,
Then mournfully, a wicker casket made,
And hid him in the rivers rushy shade.
Turning with hasty steps and tearful eye,
From his lone wail—she could not see him die—
She little dreamed that slave-born child should be
A conqueror; and set his Nation free,
Give laws to Kingdoms, rule in distant climes,
And be the great Historian of his times !　A. B.

One of the young women circulated a paper yesterday afternoon, to get the names of those in the family who would prefer to have the children's new house placed north of the Tontine, and also those who would choose to have it built on the site now occupied by the wood-house. The result was ninety-one in favor of the former location, and nine of the latter.

We have two new hands in the washing and ironing, two having left. Mary Garlock goes into the tailor's shop to learn the trade. She receives no wages the three first months, but only her board. She has commended herself as a good worker, and has improved in her general deportment and spirit since she has been in our employ.

We get the Circulars now regularly, Tuesday mornings. Dixon's articles, together with J. H. N's comments, are sought after with nearly the same eagerness that we felt during the Mills campaign.

W. A. Hinds left last night for Wallingford.

Yesterday's temperature—
7 A. M., 22.　12 M., 38.　9 P. M., 28.　Mean 29⅓.

THE O. C. DAILY.

VOL. 3. WEDNESDAY, MARCH 6, 1867. NO. 55

Mr. Cragin remarked last evening, in reference to what Mr. Hamilton said in his letter on Homer Barron's case :

"I hope, pray and expect that we are going to have conversions every day. I believe God will answer our prayer for conversions, if we can receive the blessing in a way not to make a bad use of it. Freedom from the hard heart is a great thing. God knows how to make us free from hardness and keep us soft, but he must have some security that it won't be wasted upon egotism and the devil. I hope that subject will be studied, and when persons have had a new experience, and found themselves in a new state, that it will work humility instead of high-mindedness or exciting too much rejoicing about it.

Then I know if Homer feels as I think he does, he must feel humble to think he had a hard heart for so long a time, and that God was so merciful to suffer him to go on in such a state. I confess I feel humbled myself to think I had a spirit in reference to Grahamism that tormented me more or less, and kept me in bondage for years. I think I have lately had a great deliverence from it ; but it now makes me feel humble to think I was so blind as not to see the actual truth about it long ago. If I have found deliverance from a bondage of that kind, it is natural I should try to help others into freedom from such bondage.

We have completed an additional tier of shelves in the store, to be used partly for displaying fruit, and partly for depositing boots and shoes, from the Shoe-shop. A glass case, with a counter in front has also been completed, for keeping an assortment of bags, which will at the same time furnish room for some of the best boots and shoes. All these are valuable additions, and give the store an air of completeness, which it has not had heretofore. The painting is now being done, and all will soon be ready for use. The joiners are now at work on the Office room in the south part of the store building, making new desks and fitting it up for use. **B.**

Henry Blood was criticised night before last. His improvement the past winter is quite manifest, but he has many faults yet to overcome, and as he has commenced work in the Trap-shop, it is desirable that our men working there, should watch over him and help him, and criticise him when necessary. He seems to take criticism well and is desirous to overcome his faults.

WILLOW-PLACE ITEMS.

Orrin Wright commenced work in the Silk-factory

Monday morning. It is intended that he shall get a familiar acquaintance with the whole business.— Ernest also resumed work in the Machine shop at the same time.

The close of the school and the classes gives business a lively start over our way. The first team in the morning and the last one at night are again crowded to overflowing, which makes it necessary for some of the men to walk.

The women rooming in the bedrooms contiguous to the old parlor sitting-room, spend their leisure hours in "cutting up" rags for a carpet for the room. We remember the days of "Auld lang syne" when similar bees were held on the same spot, and for the same purpose.—The women also, who room on the second floor of the Middle house, are cutting rags for a carpet for the center room of that chamber.

Our elocution drill does not seem to loose any of its charms, but is still kept up with a good deal of enthusiasm both by men and women, Some one counted fifty-two women, who took part in the exercises at the last meeting of the class. Only about half of them could be accommodated on the stage in the Hall, the remaining half occupying the floor below.

The letter published in yesterday's DAILY from B. T. Munn was superscribed, "To the President of the Oneida Community, White House, Oneida Co., N. Y."

It seems that our neighbor Olmstead is having trouble in his family, one of his boys a lad of fifteen or sixteen having recently ran away.

Mrs. Langstaff is chief and overseer of beds, bedding and quilting, the latter of which is done as formerly, in the chamber over the tin shop.

EVENING READERS.—G. W. Hamilton Newspapers, E. S. Burnham Letters.

Yesterday's temperature—
17 A. M., 23. 13 M., 41. 9 P. M., 31. Mean 34½.

THE O. C. DAILY.

VOL. 3.   THURSDAY, MARCH 7, 1867.   NO. 56.

MR. OLDS'S REPORT.

" I have very satisfactorily accomplished all I tried to do. I have settled up all the most difficult matters in relation to the fruit. There has been considerable damaged fruit in consequence of bad packing, and we have had some loss in consequence; but on the whole we have come off pretty well. Those who had been dilatory in regard to remitting, came forward and settled up accounts honorably, and most of them allowed us interest. So I can say it has been successful so far.

" As to the state of the country, in regard to business I might say it was the dullest time I ever found. A great many are failing, especially among the clothing dealers, and those who bought bags and dealt particularly in ready made clothing. They bought when goods were up, and now are losing and are unable to get money enough to pay their bills. One large house in Milwaukee, Simons, Brooks and Wells, expect to lose all it has made for the last two or three years. In ordinary times I should have received a large order for bags from them, but now they said they did not dare to give one. Business will be late in that region this spring. The Trap-business promises well. The country is not so full of traps as it has been; there are not so many of the bogus traps.— Most all our customers are satisfied with our prices now, and will deal in our traps entirely.—In regard to Fruit: The only trouble will be in filling orders. One man in Chicago, gave me an order for 724 dozen. There are 950 dozen now ordered in Chicago. The prospect is that we shall have a demand for all the fruit we can put up. I am speaking only for the West. I don't know how it will be East. Take things out and out, our fruit has been better this year than it was last. There are some exceptions, but as a general thing it looks, and is better. Many who have put up their own fruit, like ours so well that they will depend upon us, instead of trying to put it up for themselves.

" People don't like the jellies first-rate. Some speak of them as very good, but at the same time you feel as though they were not quite satisfied with them. The steward of a hotel in Detroit, I learned had made some complaint of the jellies, and said he was going to criticise us some. I called on him and told him I heard he had some complaint about the jellies, and that we should be glad to hear any criticism about them, or any of the fruit. I told him I didn't think the jellies were first-rate; and finally confessed just how they were made, of apple juice flavored with different kinds of fruit. My confession and statement that I thought they were not very good, took the starch all out of him, and he was disposed to speak well of them. Some spoke of them as very fine, but a half dozen or more complained some. They were not well packed and many of the tumblers were broken. So it may be said the jellies did not give satisfaction.

" I had a good time confessing the truth. I owned up we had made some mistakes and were under criticism and judgment concerning the subject. I told them we solicited any criticism from parties who had bought of us. I spoke freely of these things to Mr. Burbank of Chicago and asked for his criticism. He is a man of good taste, and his wife has had more or less experience in preserving fruit. Her fruit is very nice. She has many good ideas on the subject. He has written out some things in the way of criticism of our folks. I had to urge him some at first, and told him not to be afraid of offending us. He does not understand our views of criticism, and was a little fearful of overdoing it. He was more disposed to praise us; but I told him that would take care of itself, and that we wanted him to give us the benefit of his judgment, that we might improve.

Mr. Hamilton's suggestion in a letter read last night, that all jobs requiring the time and attention of the carpenters and joiners, should be deferred, and their strength and energies turned toward building the new house for the children, was heartily sympathized with, we should judge. A. L. Burt said that the only carpenter-work that could not be put off, was putting in new sills to the Mansion House and building a shed back of the store. Mr. Kinsley reported that he made a beginning on the new house yesterday, by commencing to saw timber for floors.

W. P. Item.—The old omnibus, bought two or three years ago for $50.00 has been taken over to the blacksmith's shop to be rejuvenated. When it was taken apart, the springs alone were found to weigh 300 pounds. A new body is being made at the depot which will be furnished with a top. The re-born (!) vehicle is destined for the Willow-Place route.

Mr. Bradley has engaged of Mr. Rawson, 200 bushels of peas, for canning the coming season, at one dollar per bushel.

Mr. Olds returned yesterday from his long trip west, and his report which we give to-day, will be read with interest.

Mr. Thacker reports that the tax on fruit and vegetables is removed. So say yesterday's papers.

A snow-storm is in progress this morning, which promises fair for a little more sleighing.

Yesterday's temperature—
7½ A. M., 26; 12 M., 42. 9 P. M., 32; Mean 33½.

THE O. C. DAILY.

VOL. 3.   FRIDAY, MARCH 8, 1867.   NO. 67.

REMARKS BY W. B. BURBANK ON FRUIT AND VEGETABLES, 1866.

White Raspberries, all right.

Red,   "   "   "

Black,   "   require a little more sugar.

Strawberries, very nice.

Plums, Lombard, Damson, and G. G., all right.

Cherries, Red and Black,   "   "

do. White, *do not keep well*, the pit comes out and the cherry spoils, the syrup thickens, and looks like a soup. Whether the fruit is too ripe or cooked too much, I do not know.

Peaches, *very nice*, much better than 1865.

do. Pickled, "   "   "   "   "

do. in brandy should be extra nice and better brandy than last year.

Quinces, good, *a little more care* in pearing and cutting would help the appearance very much.

Pine-apple, *splendid*.

Pears, very nice.

Barberries, would preserve a few cases.

Currant-Jam, very nice.

Jellies, *indifferent, should be better*.

Tomatoes, very good—better than New Jersey.

Sweet Corn, very good, except a few cans.

Green Peas, were four or five days too old.

String Beans, good.—I think there is a better kind of beans for your purpose. Lima beans: did not have any, a good article would *sell well*.

The jars having a screw top do not work well, many of them come off—some of those I had leaked out—both the Pickled and Brandy Peach.

Chicago, Feb. 26, 1867.

We received from the O. C. Agency, March 1st, an order for seven dozen Bags amounting to $128.29.—Four dozen of these, (all leather with the exception of one) had to be made. We sent them yesterday, March 7th. Mr. Hamilton's note to Mr. Woolworth came just in time to add a little to our satisfaction in trying to be prompt in filling the order. We hope our Agency brothers will be under the necessity of sending many such orders. We will agree to fill them as soon as possible after date of order.

We planned a box in which to pack these bags, 44½ inches by 32½ and 32 inches in depth and handed our measurement to the carpenter, who after several hours work, came to inform us that the box was made, but it was impossible to get it through the doorway of the packing room, neither would it go the front door-way. No way remained but to pack it in the carpenter-shop, where there was one front door-way large enough to allow it to be passed through.—We shall know better next time, and have two boxes made instead of one.   N.

THE BEGONIA—A CURIOSITY.

Having on hand a large *Begonia* plant, of the silver-leaf variety, some three or four weeks ago we florists, thought it advisable to divide the same into several smaller ones. In doing so we had occasion to cut off some of the larger leaves. They looked so rich and pretty, that it seemed too bad to throw them away, so Mrs. S. suggested the idea of cutting them into pieces of from one and a half to two inches square, and putting them into thumb pots for propagation. She did so, and the result has proved perfectly satisfactory.

From these bits of leaves, we have now on hand, nice, fine growing plants, besides several others that are sprouting. Mrs. S. had previously read of this method of propagating plants. Of this plant, it may truly be said, " Whose seed is in itself."   S. W. N.

The criticism of our way of making jellies, occupied the most of the meeting hour last night. Mr. Thacker gave a history of the difficulties that attended his first attempts at making jelly, and the reason for adopting the mode pursued the last two seasons. It was evident to all that a spirit had crept in, and taken the lead the past summers, that was more desirous to make money and put things through, than to take a course that would satisfy our customers and prove to them that we are strictly honest, and intend to do the honorable thing. Mr. Cragin remarked that he hoped the subject would now be dropped; he thought Mr. Thacker would have true instincts in the matter, and the right course would be taken.

When at Utica a few days since, I saw Dr. Howard who had the charge of Victor for three or four months. He said that V. was improving very fast, and that they allowed him to go to church every Sunday. He also attended a bible class, the teacher of which (a very fine young man) had taken quite a liking to him.   W. G. K.

Two or three sleigh-loads of women enjoyed a short sleigh-ride yesterday afternoon—the sleighing being quite good.

Yesterday's temperature—

7½ A. M., 23.   12 M., 34.   9 P. M., 28.   Mean 31.

THE O. C. DAILY.

VOL. 3. SATURDAY, MARCH 9, 1867. NO. 58.

THE MILL WATCH.—The round of duties brings us here about once a month. How do others feel we wonder during a three hour's captivity in this still, quiet corner of our domain—not a sound other than the subdued murmur of the waste water below, and the gentle tick of the clock above. They seem to chime together in conscious unison. But the stillness! Who can better appreciate this, than one of a household of two hundred men, women and children perpetually on the go. Why, it is perfectly delicious—you seem to encounter a totally different sphere—a good time and place for reflection, they say, and so indeed it is; a good time for reviewing the past—one's experience, for instance, since the last watch, a month ago.

A capital time for study—for elocutionary exercise, (for there is no one to be disturbed, and you may roar away to your heart's content.) Bring your music too with you—horn or fiddle—no matter what. Make the most of these rare hours. But I could wish they were a little earlier in the day—that's all. What has become of the rats? They used to scamper about overhead in perpetual jubilee. But I see Miss pussy is about, perhaps a rare specimen of her kind. Some engage a companion on these occasions, "*pour passer le temps.* But we are not come to that yet, though we used to do it: but the "times are changed"—that's a fact.

So good night
For "all's right."

A SUGAR SNOW.

Floating down o'er pond and meadow,
O'er road and fence and forest drear,
Decking all with downy mantle—
The tenderest storm in all the year.

Dreamily I watch the floating
Feathery flakes of silver haze,
While memory my heart is filling
With maple-groved New-England days.

The noble trees, their life-blood ebbing
From the trickling spile to the bucket low;
The crotched stakes—the kettle swinging—
The ruddy fire, that mocked the snow.

The nectar thickens! Give the signal!
In joyous groups we gather round;
As we cool on the snow the waxen treasure,
The merry laugh and shout resound.
                                          VERMONT.

A committee was appointed by Mr. Cragin, consisting of W. H. Woolworth, George Campbell, L. T. Waters and C. A. Macknet, to devise a plan for reducing to a system, the ordering of goods from New-York

The committee met and after a discussion as to how we should get at a method, with as little machinery as possible, they proposed that a Blank Book should be kept in the Office, in which all orders made by the heads of departments, should be registered. All other persons wishing to order through the Agency, should consult either Mr. Woolworth or Mrs. Waters.

The practice of persons applying directly to our New-York agents when they are at Oneida, was criticised and not considered legitimate.

Mr. Cragin introduced in the meeting last night, as a topic of conversation, the subject of our hired help, and the boarding-houses. He raised the enquiry whether the time had not come, when, instead of barely maintaining our ground (and in some cases not even that), against the spirit we meet in our hired folks, we should not now make an aggressive movement—try to elevate and convert them. The talk will be sent to the Communes in manuscript form, so we forbear to report further.

W. P. ITEM.—Passing through the Machine shop, I noticed lying upon a lathe, a row of short steel bars of graduated lengths and sizes, reminding one of a line of Corinthian columns seen in perspective. On enquiry, I was told it was a series of screw taps varying in size from one inch down to one eight. Considerable attention is being paid now-a-days to getting up systematic sets of tools for our own use.

The sleighing we have had yesterday and the day before, has made lively times, not only with our own teams, but with those of our neighbors. Mr. A. Kinsley reports that there were more logs drawn to the saw-mill yesterday, than on any one day during the winter.

The subject of the auction has been spoken of in meeting, two or three times within a week, but it was decided last night to defer the discussion of the subject, till we have more light, or hear from Mr. Noyes.

Three acres of ground directly north of the cowbarn, and one on the other side of the road nearly opposite, are being prepared for strawberries.

E. P. Inslee left last night, for New-York. He will remain there for a time, for the purpose of studying the art of composing and arranging music.

Traps ordered the past week,	103	doz.
Hooker & Co., for California,	26	"
Other Parties,	26	"
Agency,	56	"

Yesterday's temperature—
7½ A. M., 31. 12 M., 31. 6 P. M., 33. Mean 31.

THE O. C. DAILY.

VOL. 3. MONDAY, MARCH 11, 1867. NO. 59.

BUSINESS MEETING.

Charles Cragin stated that they wanted some four or five more girls than they now had in the Silk-Factory. He thought it more profitable to hire girls from twelve to sixteen years, as they did not require as high wages as women, and for the work wanted, girls could do about as much as women. They will be paid from $1,50 to $3,00 per week and board at home. Every girl on Turkey Street had been picked up; plenty could be got at the Castle, if they could be brought to the shop every morning, and carried home every night. Mr. Budlong who carries the mail is probably the only man who would do such a job for us. He has been offered $150 a year for such service, but asks $250. In a few months we shall want ten or fifteen more girls. If we are going to make the silk business a paying thing, we shall have to take hold of it in some such way and sustain it. We find so far, that it is pretty close business, especially if we put up silk honestly. If closely managed it will yield a fair profit.

Messrs C. A. Cragin, G. W. Hamilton, Mr. Kellogg and Mr. Cragin were appointed a committee, to ascertain the most economical and best way of procedure.

Mr. Thacker said in view of taking our present cow-barn for a fruit-house next year, we shall want more barn room provided somewhere else, this year. It has been proposed, that when we move the cows from their present place, we take them to the Hitchcock farm. There are some old barns over to Willow-Place, whose frames are remarkably good; some proposed having them taken down and put up on the Hitchcock place, and others thought they might be wanted where they were, and it might be about as cheap to put up new ones. A committee consisting of the farmers, Mr. Thacker, Mr. Conant, Mr. Barron, Mr. Kellogg, J. H. Barron, Mr. Kinsley, and A. L. Burt, were appointed to settle the matter as they think best.

G. W. Hamilton thought it was time to decide what we are to do in the Trap-shop—the amount of traps we are to put up for the summer and fall trade. We want the best judgment and wisdom and it was a matter that required some study. E. H. H. had said, that he wanted to see the shop better stocked than last year. We have enlarged our market—there are not now, many traps of any kind put together. Left to the following committee, to report next Sunday, or sooner: G. W. Hamilton, Mr. Campbell, Mr. Olds, Mr. Newhouse, Joel Higgins, and Mr. Woolworth.

Mr. Worden said the question of Mr. Dunning's continuance at the Boarding-house had been before the committee more or less; they are willing to go on indefinitely; he had written out a little scheme of regulations, which he proposed for the consideration of the Board and the family. He had read the paper to Mr. Quance, who wished that something of the sort might be printed and put up at the boarding-houses, to which we could refer boarders as the expression of our wishes. The wish was expressed that whatever might be put up, might not carry the idea of restraint, or law, but something that expressed our wish for their elevation. Their habits of being out late nights and playing cards was also spoken of.

[The document to which Mr. W. refers, is not ready for publication, but we will give it to-morrow, perhaps.]

Article of agreement between the Oneida Community, L. H. Bradley agent, and ——— ———

I, ——— ——— do hereby agree, and bind myself to furnish and deliver the coming season, to the Oneida Community, L. H. Bradley agent,— ——— ——— bushels of marrow-fat peas, as follows: One half of the crop is to be sown at least one week later than the previous half, in order not to have the whole crop ready to be gathered at one time, thus giving ample time for gathering and preserving the same in good order. The peas are to be picked at the proper state of maturity for preserving; which time is to be indicated by the purchaser, and the peas to be delivered at the Community preservatory, at, or before eleven o'clock of the same day on which they are gathered, and for which the Oneida Community, L. H. Bradley agent, agree, and herein bind themselves to pay one dollar a bushel on delivery of the same. A few bushels, more or less, than the number specified, will not be considered a breach of contract, and furthermore, in case of failure to fulfill the contract from short crops, resulting from unforeseen causes, the producer will not be held responsible.

Signed

W. A. Hind's letter to Mr. Cragin was read in meeting Saturday evening, which drew out some testimony from some of the members in reference to chess-playing, which will probably lead to its unpopularity among us for some time to come.

Temperature Saturday and Sunday—
7¼ A. M., 26. 12 M., 42. 6 P. M., 39. Mean 36¼.
7¼ A. M., 46. 12 M., 40. 6 P. M., 43. Mean 43.

THE O. C. DAILY.

VOL. 3. TUESDAY, MARCH 12, 1867. NO. 60.

Oneida, March 11, 1867.

DEAR BRO. HAMILTON:—I have made the proposition of placing the wood-shed back of the Tontine, so as to occupy one half of the lower story for storing preserved fruit the present season, and thus save the time and expense of putting up a temporary building for the purpose. I have spoken to Abram and others about it, and they like the plan. The front of the shed will stand on a line with the row of apple trees, and covered by Tontine and the engine room, leaving room for an ice-house between it and the road crossing the swale, and a passage between it and the two buildings to the anticipated clothes-yard.— Thus situated, the wood can be sawed by steam-power, and thrown directly under the shed. One half of the building can at once be filled with wood, and the remaining half as soon as the fruit is packed and shipped in the fall. Will you give us your mind on the subject? We have also examined the timbers in the two barns at Willow-Place, and find them in good condition with the exception of some of the sills, and have decided to take them down and move them to the Hitchcock place, and set them up there, a plan of which, I will present when I see you. Some wish has been expressed that we might put off the building of the store shed this summer, which would reduce our jobs to two—viz. that of the children's house, and the barns. What do *you* say to that proposition? Yours with love,　　　　　　　　　　　　　H. T.

Oneida, N. Y., March 11, 1867.

The following brief report I give, as the result of my late business trip.

Collections,	$8,565.44
Bag orders,	$441.75
Trap ”	$52.73
Fruit ”	$925.45
” ” next season,	$4,000.00
Silk ”	$286.75
Cash sales for silk,	$373.62
	$13,945.74

Gone from home seven weeks, and expenses, $264.80
　　　　　　　　　　　　　　　　　　　　　　　C. O.

The following is the document referred to, in yesterday's DAILY:

"The Community Boarding-Houses indicate *business;* and whatever may interfere with that, must be considered illegitimate—they are appendages to our shops, which are for *work*, and work and worship including improvement in general, are what all are there for.

"They are instituted to furnish meals and lodging for workers, and are responsible for accommodation and promptness in the office.

"Boarders therefore should not hinder or in any way interfere with the office of these institutions, which may be done variously—viz. by thoughtlessly making unnecessary work about house—in their rooms &c., by keeping late hours—returning late at night and the like.— Also by bringing in company to tax attention and burden the housekeepers with what belongs not to them.

"Hence parties and visitations for pleasure purposes are objectionable.

"As to definite rules, we can say distinctly that, while we sympathize with innocent and youthful sports, we cannot in any case allow gambling or card playing. That late hours tend to disorder and should not be indulged in, and when warm weather comes we shall expect tobacco-smoking to disappear altogether from the apartments of our Boarding-Houses."

Col. Smith, (now one of the firm of Kingsbury Abbot and Hale of Rome), called here yesterday, and gave an order for three No. 13 R. R. Bags for carrying samples. As he wished to visit the Silk-Factory, I rode over with him in his carriage. On the way he spoke of the tendency of people to misrepresent us. Said the same was true of the Mormons. He was very well acquainted with Brigham Young, and the leading Mormons, and he found them a very peaceable and orderly people. While in military command of the district of Salt Lake, he had many familiar talks with Brigham, and had taken his daughters to dances. He thought there was much more morality among the Mormons than had been credited to them.
　　　　　　　　　　　　　　　　　　　　W. G. K.

A man jumped from the Express train yesterday, when it was whirling past the depot, struck his head on the rails and was killed instantly.

G. R. Kellogg has taken J. H. Barron's place in transacting business at the depot. J. H. B. is to assist A. L. Burt in carpentry and joiner's work.

We have this morning what we should call in Vermont a sugar snow-storm, mild and "tender."

Mr. Kelley started this morning on his regular peddling trip.

Mr. Morse from Cayuga, staid here last night.

Yesterday's temperature—
7½ A. M., 42. 12 M., 44. 6 P. M., 38. Mean 41½.

THE O. C. DAILY.

VOL. 3. WEDNESDAY, MARCH 13, 1867. NO. 61.

Not long ago I found the old Community register, in which no entry had been made since 1857.

The last, indicated a free discussion of the question of enlargement at Oneida, and the purchase of Parson's farm for the purpose of increasing the dairy, farming facilities, &c. Ten years had produced quite a change—as now we were proposing to diminish land and stock.

This old Journal seemed very instructive so far as it was kept, in its record of Births, Deaths, marriages and the like which have occurred. But ten years was a great gap and many had come and gone—some had been born, several had died, and no visible Record could be found.

Having a passion for statistics, and finding co-operative sympathy in Mr. Abbott, we joined efforts, and by dint of recollection, general inquiry &c., we have succeeded in adding a few leaves to the old Register—giving dates of all the births in the O. C. since its beginning, also all the deaths. Then we have the names of all the seceders, giving as near as we could ascertain, the time when they joined and when they left, and finally we transcribed the record made on the 20th of Feb. 1866 of all persons then, at any place, belonging to the O. C. and branches, together with the age, weight and higat of each.

The whole number born in all the Communes since the beginning of the O. C., was thirty-eight, average two and one ninth a year.

Whole number of deaths including Mrs. Martha Burt and Mrs. Jones, was sixty, average three and one third per year, allowing it to be eighteen years.

The number seceding in that time was one hundred and fifteen.—On the 20th of Feb. 1863 there were at O. C., two hundred and nine members—at Wallingford, forty-four—at Willimantic Silk-factory, three—at N. Y. Agency, including Miss Nunn, seven—in all two hundred and sixty-three.

Persons wishing to consult these records, can find the book in care of L. A. Thayer.

Counting Mrs. Bushnell, Mr. Leete and Mr. Herrick, twenty-two members have been added the past year, and one born.   M. L. W.

[We will give the remaining statistics to-morrow.]

We received, one day last week, a letter of five or six pages, finely written on foolscap, from a man by the name of Leonard, dated, Oberlin College, Ohio.—We should judge, from what we picked out of the letter, that there was some interesting matter contained in it, and that the writer was intelligent—looking toward us with considerable earnestness, but it was so long, and so blindly written, that I doubt whether any one here, read the letter clear through. Contrasting in length with the above, we give below, two letters received day before yesterday.

Cameron, N. Y., March 4, 1867.

DEAR BROTHERS AND SISTERS :—I confess Christ in me a bond of union with the Truth and with all who seek to do the will of God " on earth as it is done in Heaven." Yours in Christ,   S. E. A. DASCOMB.

Warwick, Orange Co., N. Y., March 8, 1867.

TO THE ONEIDA COMMUNITY. FRIENDS :—Will you receive into your family a boy of sixteen years, in order to teach him good morals, and some kind of a trade, to remain till twenty one years of age—then longer if he and yourselves desire it.

Very respectfully yours,   ALICE CAPES.

We received a letter yesterday from Mrs. Chesbro, requesting us to take herself and family into our employ. She says that Mr. C. is greatly changed; she believes he has had a genuine conversion, as he expresses confidence in the Community, and a belief in our doctrines. She says, that Mr. C. and their son would be willing to work for half the wages that they get now, if they could only quit dealing with the world.

We have some new shades for the lamps that hang on each side of the Hall, which are splendid and attract a good deal of admiration. We shall not attempt a description, for we cannot do them justice; but all who saw those that Jane Seymour cut more than two years ago, can form some idea of the way they are made, and of their beauty. They were cut by Portia and Beulah, and have cost them considerable labor.—All lovers of the beautiful will appreciate them we are sure.

Quite stirring bees have been held the two last days in the room below the Printing Office, for the purpose of papering grape-boxes. There were some less than a thousand to paper at the beginning, and it will take, it is thought, three more bees to complete them.

CORRECTION.—In Thursday's DAILY, March 7th, on the last page, the fourth line from the top, for the word timber, please read boards.

Yesterday's temperature—
7 A. M., 12. 13 M., 44. 6 P. M., 46. Mean 40⅓.

THE O. C. DAILY.

VOL. 3. THURSDAY, MARCH 14, 1867. NO. 62.

CONTINUATION OF STATISTICS GIVEN YESTERDAY.

Of the 209 persons young and old at O. C. on the 20th of February 1836,

63 were born in the state of New York,

60 in	Vermont,	30 in		Mass.,
18 "	Conn.,	10 "		N. J.,
6 "	England,	4 "		Maine,
4 "	Illinois,	3 "		Canada,
2 "	Ohio,	2 "		N. H.,
1 "	Maryland,	1 "		Iowa,
1 "	Wisconsin,	1 "		Missouri,
1 "	Virginia,	1 "		Scotland,
1 "	Ceylon.			

[At Wallingford,]

16 in New York, 13 in Vermont, 9 ". Connecticut. In Maine, N. H., Mass., N. J., Maryland, Michigan, one each.

[At New-York Agency,]

In New York and Mass., one each. Vermont 2, Connecticut 3.

[At Willimantic,]

In Vermont, Connecticut, and Maine, one each.

Born in the month of Jan., 17; Feb., 14; March, 22; April, 11; May, 22; June 15; July 19; August, 12; Sept., 23; Oct., 16; Nov., 13; Dec. 33.

No. under 10 years of age was 26.						
"	over 10	under	20	",	29.	
"	" 20	"	30	"	33.	
"	" 30	"	40	"	29.	
"	" 40	"	50	"	31.	
"	" 50	"	60	"	36.	
"	" 60	"	70	"	22.	
"	" 70	"	80	"	3.	
"	" 80	"	90	"	4.	

The oldest on the 20th of Feb. 1866, was eighty-six years twelve days. Heaviest, two hundred and nineteen and three fourth pounds. Lightest, eighteen three fourth pounds. Tallest, six feet two inches and a half. Shortest, two feet three inches. Average weight, one hundred and thirty two pounds. Average height, five feet two inches and about a half.

At O. C. ninety-nine were male, and one hundred and ten female; at Wallingford seventeen male and twenty-seven female; at New-York six male one female; at Willimantic one male and two female.

Average age at O. C., was thirty-seven years and twenty-nine days; at Wallingford thirty one years, seven months and fourteen days; at Willimantic twenty-eight years, eleven months and three and a third days; average age of the six in New-York, was thirty-one years two months and five days.　　M. L. W.

EVENING READING.—We were listening to the reading of " Dixon's New America" with much interest, and had traveled with him to Salt Lake City, when the book was sent for. Of coarse we promptly sent it to the call of the CIRCULAR; but another one was promised. We have been waiting as patiently as we could un ler the circumstances, but no book has yet appeared to us. So in want of something, our reader gave us last evening a reading from one of Prof. Agassiz' Lectures, which some called rather dry.　　M.

HORTICULTURAL ITEMS.—The fruit-buds on the plum and cherry-trees, appear to be dead, pears are injured considerably, and apples some.—Several apple-trees were cut down yesterday back of the Tontine, to give place for the Wood-shed.—Twenty-five loads of manure were drawn last Monday for the hot-beds.—Trimming apple-trees appears now to be the order of the day.

W. P. ITEM.—The first one of the series of weekly meetings to be held by the Willow Place people at the shop, came off yesterday at half past twelve in the Trap-packing room. The chief design of these meetings is to promote unity among ourselves, and as we attain this, its influence will doubtless be felt among the employees.

We had a long letter yesterday from A. Naramor, of Utica, Michigan, and the same again, and written in *mongrel* poetry. We give just a specimen,

" Would you have any objection
Taking one to your perfection,
If not what would your standard be
For 'mittance to Community ?"

Vernon, March 5, 1867.

Mr. M. L. WORDEN:—You are hereby notified that you were elected Path-master for the ensuing year.　　A. PHISTER, TOWN CLERK.

A letter was received from H. R. Perry yesterday, dated at Harrisburg Penn., where he was spending Sunday. He goes from there to Pittsburg.

The criticism of the Trap-Shop has occupied two evenings.

Yesterday's temperature—
7 A. M., 33. 12 M., 48. 6 P. M., 38. Mean 39½.

THE O. C. DAILY.

VOL. 3. FRIDAY, MARCH 15, 1867. NO. 63.

As there seems to be quite an appetite for statistics at the present time, a paragraph concerning women's business, and business women, may not be amiss. It may be interesting to some to learn how many of our most efficient women are occupied outside of the common household work. The counting-room has four appropriated to it, the store one, the silk-factory three, printing office four, dentistry one, bag-shop seven, bag-bees one, shoe-business one, green house one, school-teaching one, librarian and company one. Total twenty-five; besides, an average of twenty-six a day at bag-bee.—Then from June to Nov., three women are entirely appropriated to the fruit business, and four to the company business, with continuous bees through the season, of *all* the women and children that have any time to spare.

From the one hundred and eleven females that we now number, take these twenty-five, or average for the year twenty-eight or twenty-nine, and also deduct the twenty-eight who are disqualified for the labor department by infancy, age and infirmity, and of the remaining fifty-three, six are under fifteen years of age, and six are *over* sixty-five, you have left, forty-two reliable women to attend to the household work.— Cooking, washing, dairy, bringing up children, all the sewing, dress-making, hat-making and braiding; preparing bedding for the boarding-houses; and one woman to oversee them. To assist in the house-work, six men are appropriated, and four hired girls.

П. M.

Nemaha, March 7, 1867.

DEAR MR. NOYES:—This is my first attempt to write since I was sick.—I long to get back among the Community friends. If you will forgive me and take me back, I will try to prove to you my thankfulness by being as good a whole hearted Community boy as I can. I have no money. Father said he should collect all my wages until I was of age. So I have only tried to earn my board and clothes. So you see that I cannot get a dollar a head. This too I have to ask of you. And if my faithfulness to the cause can be the least return to you, how gladly I will show it. I would like to say more but I am not very strong yet.

I confess Christ in me a Community spirit and a spirit of improvement. CHARLES MILLS.

TO THE COMMUNITY.

I am thankful for the privilege of visiting you—thank you for your kindness and affection to me.

I feel a higher appreciation of the truth, and a firmer union with you. I have ever thought Mr. Noyes a man inspired of God, raised up by him, to lead his people out of the bondage of sin, into the light and life of Christ. I confess my union with Christ, with Mr. Noyes and the Community. SUSAN F. DUNN.

TRUE BEAUTY.

Oh! there's beauty all around us,
  Both in nature and in art,
But the brightest, richest, rarest,
  Is a soft and loving heart.

If our path be sad and lonely,
  Bidding tears of anguish start,
Then how sweet, how doubly precious,
  Is a pure and trustful heart.

Loveliness of form and feature,
  May a thrill of joy impart,
But it fades before the sunshine,
  Of a true and faithful heart.

Beauteous groves and smiling landscapes,
  Of earth's pleasures form a part,
But they fail to cheer and gladden,
  Like the fond confiding heart.

Outward beauty is but fleeting,
  Inward wealth can ne'er depart,
Covet then the richer treasure,
  Of a meek and lowly heart.

A letter was read . . . New-York City, making inquiries in behalf of a lady in England, who had seen Dixon's book, and wished to know more about the Community. He stated that he had read the CIRCULAR some, himself, and wished to know more about our doctrines, particularly " Male Continence," as he had not the first idea what was meant by that term.

Yesterday was colder, (with the exception of one day, the 13th of Feb.), than any day we have had, since the last day of Jan. It was real cold this morning, but the sun shines beautifully, which must modify the atmosphere before many hours.

Yesterday's temperature—
7 A. M., 16. 12 M., 22. 6 P. M., 20. Mean 19½.

THE O. C. DAILY.

VOL. 3. SATURDAY, MARCH 16, 1867. NO. 64.

WILLOW-PLACE ITEMS.

Mr. Dunning of Willow-Place has drawn an outline plan, of an addition to the Boarding-House, which he thinks necessary for the accommodation of the employees at the Shops there.—It is a plan for placing a wing next the kitchen to extend west fifty feet, and be twenty-five feet in width for a dining-room, having a basement, wash-room and sitting-room for the men.

Over the dining-room he proposes bed-rooms, as more facilities for lodging are needed.—Last fall, in our hurry there, some twenty had to be lodged out at the neighbors.—Mr. Cragin has interested himself in having some kind of assembly room or chapel, where meetings could be held with all the hands occasionally, or for evening schools and lectures. He considers that object his pet, next to the children's new house.

Some think Mr. Dunning's plan would answer the purpose as the large dining-room might be used for meetings as well. M. L. W.

SILK-DEP.—Four girls were hired at the Castle yesterday, for the Silk-department. Our painter Mr. Austin is to bring them up to the Shop every morning, and carry them back at night, for $4.00 per week.

L. F. Dunn is engaged in perfecting the measuring machine used in spooling silk. The machine at present does not work well with white Twist, and it is in regard to this difficulty Mr. D's attention is chiefly directed.

The first lot of drab Twist was received from the Dye-house yesterday.

FINISHING-DEP.—The group of quandam pan riveters are now scattered about the shop. Mr. Delatre runs a Press, O. H. M. the Drop, Mr. J. Kinsley a lathe, Mr. Kellogg a milling machine, Mr. Jones a riveting vise, &c., &c.

The O. C. Saw-mill is kept running now night and day. The great number of logs in the mill-yard—our own and our neighbors, crowding it full—and the demand for lumber necessitating this extraordinary effort.

Daniel Knowles and a hired man alternate in keeping the mill vibrating. Each work half the day and half the night.

BAG-SHOP ITEMS.

We have plenty of business on hand. Our orders come in much faster than we can fill them. We have had since March 1st thirty orders including O. C. Agency order for 40½ doz. Of these but nine have been filled, the most of them having been received (many of them through our Agents) within the last five days. With our improved arrangements, and the general enthusiasm manifested by those who work here, we expect to be able to fill our orders pretty promptly. We have at present five men and six women of our own family, and nine hired men and eight women. N.

Changes seem to be the fashion now-a-days. Just as our Bag-orders began to press in upon us, there was a sudden demand for more room. The men were crowded, the hired girls were crowded. Something must be done. It was proposed, at length, to remove the partition between the men's room and our women's, thus allowing the men the entire room to themselves, and that the hired girls should be moved into the room back of the one they had occupied, giving them too, more ample accommodations, and that our women should take their room, which, with the addition of the bed-room, it was thought, would make a pleasant place for our work.

This plan being acceded to, we had a merry bee to clean the room, without disturbing the hired girls, who kept busily at work, as though nothing had happened. With the assistance of A. and H. in taking down partitions, and the prompt and energetic action of C. E. and M. all were nicely settled the next afternoon, and ready to commence work with renewed zeal and energy. One of the hired girls said, " You Community folks get up a bee and carry things along, no matter how great, and you all seem so harmonious too." M. E.

A letter was received yesterday from a young man, a German, by the name of William Weber, of New-York City. He had heard of the Community through Mr. Bloom—had read " Salvation from Sin," which Mr. B. gave him, and is now reading the " Berean." He expresses himself as intensely interested. He says he has confessed Christ, and though he feels weak, yet he hopes to gain strength.

Little Eugene has had rather a hard time with the chicken-pox, but is getting better now. All the children that had not previously had the disease, have had it, with the exception of Virginia, who for some cause seems impervious to it. We hope the time is not distant, when we shall not be subject to the plagues of the outer world—when we shall surround ourselves with an atmosphere that Satan's spirit cannot penetrate.

Traps ordered the past week,	114½ doz.

The principal orders were—

Jacob Underhill & Co., for Oregon,	40	"
A. F. Shapleigh & Co., St. Louis,	20	"

61½ doz. of the above were large traps.

H. W. Burnham came yesterday afternoon.

Yesterday's temperature—
7 A. M., 16. 12 M., 26. 6 P. M., 23. Mean 21½.

THE O. C. DAILY.

VOL. 3.   MONDAY, MARCH 18, 1867.   NO. 65.

BUSINESS MEETING.

G. W. Hamilton reported the action of the committee on traps. They have decided on the following quantity to be made by the first of Sept: 12,000 of No. 0, 50,000 No. 1, 5,000 No. 1¼, 10,000 No. 2, 8,000 No. 3, 8,000 No. 4.—This to meet the early trade. 50,000 more to be made immediately after, for the later demand. If the demand be greater, to modify accordingly. It requires some $9,000 more of stock than we have now; some of it needs to be ordered immediately. Now is the best time to buy iron. Voted that the report be accepted and acted upon.

The kitchen department would like a couple of mop-wringers. Voted that they be obtained, if such as we want can be found in the market, and that Mr. Barnham see if he can find the article in New-York.

Mr. Thacker said it seemed necessary to have some protection to the lawn on the road-side. We did not seem to get a fence there and perhaps we did not want any. He thought of proposing for the time being, if we were not ready to do better, to put up some nicely turned posts, some 8½ feet above ground, with chain that will keep cattle off. He would like to see a couple of suitable posts put up to show where we have an entrance to our grounds. Some suggested putting up iron posts with chain. Some thought we might get up a tasteful style of iron fence. Referred to Mr. Thacker, Abram, S. W. Nash, and lawn committee.

A note from E. H. H. was read, expressing agreement with Mr. T's plan about the wood-shed, also suggesting that in the line of building we should attend to the first things, first. It was mentioned that besides building the barns, it was important that the Willow-Place boarding-house be enlarged to accommodate the help we require in making up these traps. The wood-shed will soon be wanted on its new site, and the teamsters can best attend to removing the wood now. Martin thought it would be cheaper to saw our wood by horse-power than by steam, others thought his objection to such an arrangement would be obviated by a short rail-way and truck running along by the wood-heap.

Voted that we stake out the place for the wood to-morrow, and that the teamsters commence removing it at once. For executive committee on this and the shed, Messrs. Kinsley, Kellogg, Sears, Abram, Martin and Homer were appointed.

Mr. Kinsley said there was considerable to be done by somebody at the saw-mill. We have logs enough to make 400,000 feet of boards, of our neighbors and our own,—one third more than we had last year. Customers are wanting their logs sawn, and basswood is worth $2.00 more a thousand, to be sawed in the spring, than it is to be sawed in August. Mr. K. did not wish to take the responsibility of the sawing and not have the logs sawed out. Decided that we advertise for a sawyer, and that Mr. Horace Burt and Daniel Knowles in connection with the hired sawyer, attend to running the mill night and day for the present.

Attention was called to the extravagant use of coal at the boarding-house. Mr. Worden is requested to regulate the matter.

———

It snowed and blowed yesterday, and last night it was so tedious that there was some hesitation about the folks who were expecting to start for New-York and Wallingford at midnight, being able to go, but they finally decided to make the attempt. They found plenty of drifts this side of the Hamilton bridge, but succeeded in getting through, without much trouble, thinking that the rest of the way would be better.—The snow flew so, that Homer said it was with difficulty he could see his horses, and he could not have done even that, only as one of the horses was black.—Finally at the foot of Mud-creek hill, they turned over into a snow drift, and the horses relieved of their burden went merrily on, taking with them the forward trucks, which in the tip-over had been detached from the back runners. Homer waited only long enough to see that the folks were not hurt, and then went on after the horses, which he found standing by a fence about half a mile from the place from which they started. They had turned out of the road, and come in contact with an open gate, which had arrested their course. He speedily returned to the company he had left so unceremoniously, found them all right, and came back home, no harm having been done, except an injury to one of the horses. All seemed (when the truth came to be known) to have started contrary to their better instincts. The company expect now, to start this afternoon at 5 o'clock.

———

CORRECTION.—Owing to the careless arrangement of a sentence, in our item in Saturday's DAILY, we have made it appear that our bag orders are more than is really the case. We should have said, that we have had since March 1st, orders for 40½ dozen bags, including O. C. Agency order, mentioned in the DAILY of March 8th.   N.

———

The loom has been removed from the Mill chamber, and put up in the north garret of the Mansion House. The warp for ninety yards of carpeting is colored, and warped. Mrs. Conant commences to-day (what looks to us like a big job) weaving it. The yarn (thanks to Mr. Herrick) is first-rate.

———

At a meeting held Saturday evening by the Horticultural group, including the farmers and fruit preserving company, much love was expressed toward Mr. Thacker, and a spirit of brotherly love prevailed, that made the meeting one of union with each other, which was very inspiring.

———

The Bag department was criticised on Friday and Saturday evenings. Last night Mr. Noyes's last talk on the "Soft Heart" was re-read, and much sympathy expressed for the same; also some interesting testimony of experience was given, relating to softness of heart.

———

Temperature Saturday and Sunday—
7 A. M., 10.   12 M., 31.   6 P. M., 25.   Mean 20½.
7 A. M., 28.   12 M., 46.   6 P. M., 30.   Mean 34½.

THE O. C. DAILY.

VOL. 3.   TUESDAY, MARCH 19, 1867.   NO. 66.

O. H. Miller offered himself for criticism last night, and the general testimony was, that he had made good improvement since his last criticism. He is more industrious, and works more harmoniously than heretofore—takes suggestions from others in a better spirit, and though some remains of his old tendencies occasionally show themselves, and he needs to be thoroughly in earnest to overcome his faults, yet it was thought he had formed a purpose to lay down his own indivduality, and organize into the Community spirit. Much good feeling was expressed toward him. Mr. Cragin made the following remarks on his case:

"I recollect sometime ago, I don't know how long, perhaps a year or two, when Mr. Miller was out peddling, he sent home brief letters, two or three times, that were very edifying. They indicated that he had a mind and heart interested in the truth; and I never have heard that Mr. Miller, during this time of conflict, has made war upon the Community, or quarreled with its principles. He acted very differently from other persons who have finally left us. His great difficulty has been with himself. He has been at war with himself. As others have said, his propensities to manifest his own individuality, and his desire to be free and independent, have been very strong. But I think his course has led him finally to see that this very spirit, which was so tenacious of its independence and individualism, has finally brought him into the worst possible state of slavery.

"I presume we shall sometime have Mr. Miller's experience this past winter. I think it would be interesting, if it could be brought out in a simple, truthful way. A person so thoroughly cut off from the fellowship of the Community must have a pretty hard time. I now feel like encouraging him, and letting him know, as Mr. Woolworth said, that our hearts are ready to sympathize with him, and love him, just as soon as it is manifest that he is seeking a soft heart. Probably the truth is, Mr. Miller has not been aware that he has been possessed by a terrible devil of unbelief. That is the great enemy that abuses us all, whenever we are abused. It has abused Mr. Miller shamefully. I am thankful that God is here with us, and that he can cast this devil that causes the hard heart and the spirit of unbelief out of every one of us. I am very thankful that this work is going on so quietly, and yet so strongly. I believe there is a good deal of earnestness here in the family to get entire freedom from unbelief; that is the very devil himself.

"I am satisfied there are a few yet in the family who are troubled with that principality, and that the devil has possession of them and prevents them from opening their hearts to God, and asking for the prayers of the family to deliver them from the devil. I expect that the work will go on till this great principality of unbelief is cast out of the whole Community. I do not feel so much like laboring with individuals, as I do like striking at the very centre of that spirit of hardness. The apostle James says, 'resist the devil and he will flee from you; draw nigh to God and he will draw nigh to you.' There is a double operation, and we cannot accomplish one point without the other. Resisting the devil draws us to God.

"It is the soft heart that melts the hard heart. The soft heart is in Christ; and if we are ready to confess our faults, and to see this hardness in the light of truth, as a foreign element—that the devil is a personal being who can imprison us, as officers of a government imprison criminals, and that we have need of the personal influence of Christ to deliver us from his iron grasp, we shall cry earnestly to God for help. I hope Mr. Miller will get such indignation against the spirit of unbelief and the devil, that it will make him a new man. I am not afraid of his being fanatical in regard to seeking a soft heart, for fanaticism doesn't run in that direction. He should not be ashamed of the truth, but free to expose the works of the devil upon him."

Winter seems not to be content, to let us off with what experience we have had with bad roads &c., between here and Willow-Place.—Yesterday morning found the snow piled into the road, just as it has been a number of Monday mornings during the past winter. While on the way yesterday morning, the sled runner, which had been damaged by Sunday night's adventure, gave way near Mr. Hubbard's, putting an end to all progress with the team. The girls together with one or two men, took refuge in Mr. Hubbard's house, surprising Mr. and Mrs. H. during their morning's nap. Meanwhile the teamster returned with the horses to the barn for another conveyance, which was quickly procured; as we understand the horses took fright on their way back, and made light work of getting through the drifts between them and the barn.— However, 7 o'clock found all hands ready to commence work at the shop.   C. A.

The Bag-department had a meeting yesterday for the purpose of promoting unity and organization among its members. An earnest spirit was felt, and the hope and feeling was expressed that the Bag-business would now take a new start and gain a reputation for enterprise and industry which it has lacked somewhat, in the past. It is an excellent business school for our young people. A strong desire was also expressed that our influence upon our hired help may be such, as to win and draw them to Christ and the Truth.   D. H.

The teamsters commenced moving the wood from the shed yesterday. It is estimated that there is not far from 200 cords.

Yesterday's temperature—
7 A. M., 17. 12 M., 37. 6 P. M., 23. Mean 23½

THE O. C. DAILY.

VOL. 3. WEDNESDAY, MARCH 20, 1867. NO. 67.

We had a free meeting last night and the revival spirit seemed to be in our midst—a mellowness of heart which we all sensibly felt. Mr. Woolworth said:

"I have had some thoughts in relation to the soft heart. I do not know but we make too hard work of getting a soft heart. My feeling is that it is in us, and all we want is to be able to believe and confess it.—We have not got to ascend up into heaven to get it, nor descend into the deep. 'Whatsoever things ye desire believe that ye receive them, and ye shall have them.' I hope we shall not make too hard work of getting the soft heart, but believe like little children that we have it, and confess it in simple faith.

"I realize every day that God has come near to us, and that his spirit is pressing down upon us. He is ready and anxious to give us, every one of us, repentance, faith and the soft heart. I desire very much myself, to be a good medium of the spirit that brings softness of heart.—I have felt very sensibly to-day that Mr. Noyes was with us; and I felt that it was due to him, that we should give him credit for the work that is going on here. This is the result of his spirit and his words. He is a medium of God's grace and the revival spirit."

We think that our last snow-storm was not "The tenderest storm of all the year," for it was so filled up our Willow-Place road, that a load of nineteen individuals, en route for W. P. Factory yesterday morning, was tiped over into the snow; men, women, buffalo-skins, cushions and dinner-basket all in one oblong heap. As we were picking ourselves up, J. Freeman manifested signs in his quiet, earnest way, that he would be glad of some assistance; and sure enough, his leg was caught under the seat, and he stretched out on the snow; he was helped to his feet however, without sustaining any injury. It was thought that there was a good spirit manifested by those who fell at the bottom of the pile, inasmuch as they waited so patiently to be released of their burden. The affair created a hearty laugh; there was however, a little regret expressed by some of the ladies, that G. W. H., our worthy foreman, (who, by the way, gloated o'er a tip over) had not been in the place of one unlucky fellow who found himself on the lower side of two individuals more burly than himself, besides sundry buffalo robes, cushions &c.   J. P. H.

Mr. Kellogg in speaking of the above affair, said the thing was handsomely done; that a pie was taken up from the snow neatly frosted, the basket of lunch unopened, the horses stopped in a twinkling, and nobody hurt.

We received through H. R. Perry, an order from John Unruh of Philadelphia for 3½ doz. bags. Value $225,04. We have also received through Mr. P. two orders from Harrisburgh, Penn., and one from Wheeling, Virginia. This last order is dated March 13. He says "I go to Zansville, Ohio, to-night." We will take this occasion to thank our Agents for the clear and definite way in which their orders are made out. It saves a great deal of vexatious conjecture as to what is really wanted.   N.

Mr. Kelly writes from Rochester, March 17th.

"I am having pretty good success in getting orders especially Bag-orders. I expect to take the 10 A. M. train for Bath, to-morrow, and shall get to Ithica about Tuesday night or Wednesday morning, and to New-York Thursday night. I have a good room with a stove in it, so I am by myself all day. It is a little lonesome, but I have a good time to reflect and pray.

"P. S. A new motive for our honesty. I heard some men talking about the O. C. the other day, not knowing that I belonged there. They said we were good people to deal with, were honest; but the motive of our honesty was to disarm opposition, so that we could live out our social principles."

One who reads the daily papers pretty closely, recently remarked to an admiring audience: "I see the papers these days, contain a good many of Artemus Ward's witty sayings since his death." It is gratifying to learn that the great humorist hasn't lost his cheerfulness since going to hades, and that he still keeps up communication with the press.   D. B.

The machine used for making strawberry boxes, is removed from the mill to the cellar of the New-House, and work on the boxes will be done there, for the present, by Mr. Whitney.

WATCHING.

I sat on a low cushioned chair,
  My arm did a pillow sustain,
On which lay a cherubic form,
  All restless and moaning with pain.

I lulled it with soft soothing tones,
  And moistened its feverish brow,
But I was not with it alone,
  Angels seemed hovering round.

In my spirit I seemed to hear
  Their loving and musical tones,
"We are watching beside you here,
  For the little one is our own."

Our Saviour once said, we are told,
  That a blessing to such is given,
"Their angels do always behold
  The face of our father in heaven."

               VERITE.

Yesterday's temperature—
7 A. M., 24.   12 M., 33.   6 P. M., 31.   Mean 29.

THE O. C. DAILY.

VOL. 3. THURSDAY, MARCH 21, 1867. NO. 68.

Riley, Sandusky Co., Ohio, March 14, 1867.

Mr. S. Newhouse, Sir:—I wish you would please send me your opinion on this growing mink business, did you ever try, or know of its being tried? The big men here, are all talking about raising minks; they seem to think that there is an immense amount of money to be made in the operation. I have never known of its being tried. I am now engaged capturing minks for a gentleman of Fremont, Ohio. He is going into the business extensively, he depends on getting his mink to start his menagerie with, of me, and I think if he can grow mink, I can, but I should like to hear from some person that knew of its being done, and how they manage to keep them in a healthy condition.

I have several live mink on hand now. I keep them in large boxes with a small ten by twelve enclosure within the large one, for them to nest in. I feed them the carcasses of muskrat, fish and mice, and keep a sap-trough full of water, but they don't appear to have the same rich and glossy color that they wore when first taken. I would very much like to have your opinion, and if you have ever tried the experiment, I would like to hear of it. I am going west;—to catch mink for this market. I mean to capture them alive, just as soon as the spring trapping is over. I shall be gone about two months, and then I think of coming to Oneida to see the trap-makers. I have catched some mink with the little No. 0 trap, that you sent me last summer, and it will hold them just as well as any trap and don't injure the foot so much. * * * * *

I introduced the 1½ here and the rat-trappers are all going to have that kind of trap for their next year's trapping. They will send for them just as soon as they sell their furs this Spring.—There are no mink trappers here but myself, but there are several here that have mink dogs and they do kill some few.

The Community have been sending me the Circular for some time and as I never have sent them anything in return for it I will here enclose one dollar. I suppose according to the Circular it is all in the family, so I send it to you.   S. Shannon.

———————————

It was with difficulty that we could restrain our wrath, in reading in the last week's Circular, what Dixon said about Mr. Noyes, every thing about it was so untruthful, and in reading the Circular that came yesterday, we were somewhat vexed, and not a little amused at his attempt to make us figure so conspicuously in the drama of Oneida life, when the truth in the matter is, we did not have five minutes conversa-

tion with him. On being introduced, he caught at the name, and said "are you the mother of the young man that was criticised last night, and did you sympathize with what was said of him?" Our reply that we certainly did sympathize with the criticism was all the ground he had for saying, as he does, that "sister Jocelyn, the culprit's mother did not certainly spare the rod," for we did not open our lips in the criticism the night before.

———————————

I wonder if our distant Communes, think of us all as busy as bees—full of life, just as we were when they last saw us! Wonder if they know of the energetic bag-bee, that meets an hour during the forenoon, where the girls are just as merry as of old, and the work is thrown off as by magic. Wonder too, if they think of us women, as ambitious elocutionists—who, three days in the week, meet from four until five, to vociferate "ba, be, bi, &c.," and to read according to the best of our yet quite limited knowledge. And then do they ever think of the supper hour, and imagine the Willow-place company just returning home, rushing down the archway steps, like grenadiers—and the tide of life in the kitchen—the enthusiastic table waiters, running in all directions—the buzzing and humming in the dining-room, just as ever. Can't you see it all? Of course you follow us into meeting, and can doubtless picture to yourselves the scene in the upper sitting-room, after meeting; as well as the company that flock in the lower room of the tower, to hear, and see and feel all that is to be seen, and heard and felt.   L.

———————————

An order came day before yesterday for 50 dozen No. 0 traps, which found us wholly unprepared to meet it, as we had allowed our winter stock of that kind of traps to get very low, before putting up the supply for the Spring. So we all turned out yesterday and finished up what parts of that kind of traps we had ready, making more than enough for the order.

———————————

The Circulars did not reach us till nearly noon, yesterday. In the meeting, Mr. Woolworth invited the family to express their minds about them, which they did quite freely. They were spoken of as being very interesting of late, and edifying, particularly the last, which was rich and juicy.

———————————

Mr. Woolworth said last night that some persons had expressed a wish to have their pictures taken, and such were requested to leave their names at the Office, as our financiers were willing to expend ten or twelve dollars for that purpose now.

Yesterday's temperature—
7 A. M., 17. 12 M., 33. 6 P. M., 33. Mean 27¼.

THE O. C. DAILY.

VOL. 3.   FRIDAY, MARCH 22, 1867.   NO. 69.

Mrs. Towner writes, Cleveland, March 15th :

"I have been quite a recluse during the winter—have scarcely been away from home and have received but little company. I had a very quiet time indeed, when all the children were at school and Mr. Towner away to the Law College.—I improved it in reading the New Testament and Berean what time I could spare from household duties. In reading the New Testament now, I get entirely different ideas from what I used to, when I was in the orthodox church. J. H. N. has made it plain to my understanding, and I wonder that theologians should have so distorted its meaning. I find in reading the Berean that I can comprehend the meaning of that, much better than I could one year ago. When I was at the Community you explained many points and made them plain, that before had seemed mystical.   *   *   *   *

"I regret that I have so poor an account to give of Minnie Wait, but she has really gone to California with a Mr. Brown from Long Island—perhaps you remember him. I understood that he had been on a visit to the Community within the past year. Just before we left Berlin, he and Minnie came to Mr. Lasley's and spent the evening. I was rather suspicious of her then—thought she evinced considerable interest in him—his conversation that evening I knew would have a tendency to weaken Minnie's faith in the Community, if his words had any weight with her.

"He claims that he was led by the spirit of Christ to separate from his wife and children, and go about on a mission. He said that Mr. Noyes is right in his belief, but could not live in accordance with it, and that no one else could. I asked him what he had reference to? but he said he couldn't explain in what particulars, but he inferred so from Mr. Noyes's criticism of him."

Extract of a letter from Francis Morris, of Meadville, Pa.

"Mr. Noyes, Sir:—I wish to have you continue sending the CIRCULAR to my address. Its weekly visits find a hearty welcome to my house. I think some of its teachings are in advance of the age, but in one thing I think you took a step backward, that was in discontinuing the use of Graham bread; my experience is opposite to the purport of yours, as it is given through the CIRCULAR by your Society. Some years ago I was pronounced consumptive by some two or three of the allopathic M. D.'s"

The writer goes on to relate his experience, his being given up as a hopeless case of consumption, and his having his health perfectly restored in one year by living on Graham bread.

WILLOW-PLACE.—If you take a stroll among the many departments of business at Willow-Place works, you will at length find yourself in the office of Mr. Newhouse, or "The Canadian Trapper," according to Dixon. You will always find him working at his vice, or lathe, doing some "Nice Job;" why? because he never makes other than a "Nice Job" of any thing he does. No matter what he is doing, whether filing and fitting trap-patterns, fitting up a diminutive screw-plate, adding all the elaborate and latest improvements to his foot-lathe, fixing a rickety horse-pistol or filing a fish-hook point; it is all the same to him; nothing ever leaves his hands until it is finished in the most approved manner. After watching and studying his operations awhile, you will discover that he has an inexpignable contempt for anything like a botch. So much for the old Trapper.   J. P. H.

Mr. Noyes and Charles Cragin came yesterday afternoon. Charles had been to New-York for the purpose of purchasing stock. Mr. Noyes took us entirely by surprise, this time, as not one of the family knew that he was coming. It is a treat to see him here again, though we are deprived the privilege of hearing his voice. In the evening a part of the manuscripts containing Mr. Herrick's criticisms the past year were read, and the remainder of them will be read to-night at 7 o'clock.

Dixon's book has again been received and we commenced reading it last night. We went down to Salt Lake and there left to "soak," as one of the young girls said, and we are now glad to go on with the writer, though in reference to what he says about the Mormons, the thought is continually arising, "Perhaps that isn't so exactly." This feeling detracts somewhat, from the pleasure we should otherwise have in reading the book.

We have churned the past week, forty-two pounds of butter. We have about twenty new milch cows, but the family and boarding-houses, together with several calves we are raising, require the most of the milk and cream, so we are not likely to make much butter at present. We appreciate very highly what butter we can get of our own make.

A tall man from Jersy City staid here last night.—We understand that he is an agent of Thompson & Co., Steel manufacturers, with whom our people have dealt largely.

Yesterday's temperature.—
7 A. M., 31. 12 M., 48. 6 P. M., 43. Mean 41.

THE O. C. DAILY.

VOL. 3.   SATURDAY, MARCH 23, 1867.   NO. 70.

Extracts of a letter from H. A. Warne, Fort Madison, Iowa, to Mrs. Bushnell, dated March 16th.

"Be assured that no evil thought of the Community obtains welcome entrance. If the spirit of distrust gets in, it is through some secret door of which he has discovered the spring, and when entrance has been gained, I feel unhappy until he is pushed out.—One thing is certain my interest in O. C. is still active, and increasing.

"I have been reading the book you gave me [the Berean] a third time and am near the end again. This time I have given special attention to the bible references, and even pressed my Greek testament into the service—(according to my ability.) I find my views coming more and more into harmony with the Berean, and find myself more and more separated from old friends. I believe I shall find myself generally cast out, judging from the signs of the times. These things trouble me much less, however, than the moral and spiritual strain of life long prejudices and teachings. I do sincerely desire to do God's will and to follow the truth, but the way of truth is not always clear to my mind.

"I have thought that I can see progress, and greater ability to contend with the powers of darkness, but the warfare is a stern one and I have been compelled to cry out, 'would to God it were morning.' There has been much comfort to me in the article ' Principalities and Powers.' I thank you for your belief that God will perfect his work in me.

"My correspondents I find are all for some reason becoming offended with the tone and matter of my letters, if I may judge from their silence, but they may think better of the subject after a little silent process of digestion. At any rate their defection shall not move me from my course.

"Perhaps you would like an extract from a letter to friend G. which he is very remiss in answering, although he previously acknowledged the receipt of my manuscript ' Two Classes of Believers.' He pronounced it ' excellent' and said he had lent it to a Congregational clergyman (also a preacher of present holiness) who liked it very much. I know this man well, and know him as an earnest good man.   *   *   *

"I recently received a very earnest appeal from an old and dear friend, a young but very popular minister, to go actually to work immediately in the ministry and lead my fellow men to Christ, suggesting that I may be fleeing like Jonah from duty. He urges me by all the excellences and gifts which he believes me to possess, by all there is to be done, not to delay a moment. It would be hard to satisfy men standing where he does, that my present life of unseen struggle

and spiritual activity, is the noblest and most useful activity for the present time. And yet I am persuaded it is so. I told him that I was waiting orders, not his, but God's. It would be poor service that the undisciplined recruit could do, should he rush into the field of battle without proper weapons, without instructions, without a leader, however ardent might be his spirit. Not so are battles won for God or man. That is savage warfare; I will none of it.

"As for ' the work to be done'—it were folly for my ardor to attempt outrunning God's. He loves the sons of men better than I love them, albeit I do earnestly desire to be of use in saving them.—I will seek discipline, seek knowledge, seek spiritual fitness, seek to know perfectly the will of the Captain of salvation, and await his orders when to fight. Yes, seek to fight in company with his disciplined hosts—with the Oneida Community, if God shows me that they are his peculiar people—not with some guerrilla band, even if they seek to fight for Christ."

———

The criticism of the Machine-shop was in order last night. It was thought there had been a good degree of enthusiasm in work among the hands the past winter, and a good state of feeling and harmony had existed there. Some thought there was a lack of order in the shop, and a lack of carefulness, in some cases, in thoroughly finishing work, before it was sent away.

We understand that the " Canaan Trapper" has made application for a belt of *hoop iron*; being fearful he says, that Dixon and J. P. H. may " bust him up."

D.

———

The weather is quite spring-like to-day, more so than for many weeks.

———

10 o'clock A. M.—E. H. Hamilton and M. a. Miller have just arrived.

———

Traps ordered the past week,   73¼ doz.
The principal order was—
W. M. Wyeth & Co., St. Joseph, Mo., 50 doz. No. 0.

Bag-orders for the week,   39 Dozen.

———

Yesterday's temperature—
7 A. M., 35.   12 M., 40.   6 P. M., 33.   Mean 39½.

THE O. C. DAILY.

VOL. 3. MONDAY, MARCH 25, 1867. NO. 71.

BUSINESS MEETING.

A paper was read from Mr. M. L. Worden, path-master, relating to road improvements and repairs. It is thought not expedient for the present to do more than the usual repairing on the roads. Filling up bad places, and rebuilding the dyke bridge should receive early attention.—Executive committee, Messrs. Worden, Clark and Whitney.

Thanks were voted to Joel Higgins for his faithful services as president of the Business Board. His resignation was accepted, and F. A. Marks was appointed to fill that office.

A paper was read from Mr. Worden proposing to discontinue boarding our help—paying them more wages and having them board themselves. Some discussion on the subject was elicited. Our neighbors stand ready to board, if they have the prospect of steady boarders. It was thought to be a good plan to build tenement houses, and rent them to hired people. It would deliver us from a great deal of perplexity and trouble. The boarding-house committee were authorized to consult with Mr. Noyes and Cragin on the subject, and to act promptly and in harmony with their wishes.

Mr. Clark wished to know, or to have it decided upon, what the demand for teams would be at Willow-Place this year. A double team running morning and night, and one horse for the daily chores, will probably be sufficient. It is the calculation to have a steady driver.

AN ACKNOWLEDGMENT.

Shall we receive a benefit and say nothing about it? Away with such a thought. There is the dentist department, for instance: I am sure there is a great deal done there, and much that is very valuable. Not long since, I heard of a case of tooth filling that occupied over nine hours, and upon only one tooth. The patience and perseverance of the parties were worthy of note. The case, it appears, allowed no intermission, so that they had to forego the ordinary meal at noon—nay, such was their enthusiasm, that during the whole time, they discarded all refreshment. I wish some one would give us a few items relating to that branch of our business. Perhaps some one will.

Well, I started with the intention of acknowledging a personal benefit in the line of tooth cleaning Saturday forenoon—an operation simple in itself, and generally quite disagreeable to the party operated upon—but in this case, the operator contrived to make it decidedly otherwise. Thorough, enthusiastic, and kindly considerate, there was evidently a desire by the operator that you should rise from your seat perfectly satisfied. In a word, by simply resigning yourself to the circumstances, you would *very* likely wish the operation indefinitely prolonged. M. A. D.

Mr. Hamilton reported, Saturday evening, that Mr. Noyes had expressed some dissatisfaction with the way the O. C. is mixing up with the world at the boarding-house, and in our school. He thought these things ought not to be tolerated. Accordingly a committee was appointed to look into the matter and see what could be done. They met yesterday, and in reference to board, they thought the best thing for all concerned, would be, to buy a small place near the shop, and have a little family of our own located there.

We had a call yesterday from a Mr. and Mrs. Nellis, of Bath. They came in company with a gentleman and lady from Canastota, at whose house they were visiting. Mrs. N. we understand is a friend of one of Mrs. Bushnell's intimate friends, who is somewhat interested in the Community. They expressed themselves as much pleased with their call, and took with them when they left, several Nos. of the CIRCULAR.

A note to the family was read last evening from Miss Susan Dunn, relating some of her past experience, her firm confidence in Mr. Noyes, and her wish to connect herself with the Community. Mr. Woolworth said he had talked with Mr. Noyes about her case, and he said he should not object to her uniting with us, if she could come here and be a help to us.— The subject was referred to a committee.

A letter was read last night from Mr. Noyes to W. G. Kelley, saying that he sympathized with the idea of inviting his brother Daniel to return to the Community; he thought he had acted manly in the matter. A vote was then taken by the family which was unanimous, and leave will accordingly be given him to return.

Mr. Kelley gave an interesting account last night of his call on Mrs. Otis, and his pleasant chat with Emily's brothers. He also told us of his going to Ithica and his indefatigable efforts to gain some clue to the history of the Platts, which he at last effected. His story was quite amusing.

On dit.—Important changes under consideration at W. P. regarding employe's finding board outside, and to accommodate our own men inside—a branch of the O. C. to be established at W. P. Full report when plans are perfected and approved by general assembly at evening session. REPORTER.

It is decided that Martin Kinsley shall go to New-York and take the place of Mr. Easton about the middle of April.

Temperature Saturday and Sunday—
7 A. M., 33. 12 M., 50. 6 P. M., 40. Mean 40¾.
7 A. M., 30. 12 M., 48. 6 P. M., 43. Mean 40¼.

THE O. C. DAILY.

VOL. 3.   TUESDAY, MARCH 26, 1867.   NO. 72.

BOARDING-HOUSE.

Mr. Kinsley reported that he and Mr. Kellogg called upon Mr. Atkins this morning to see if he would rent his house. He would not rent it. Then they asked if he would sell, and found that he would for $2,000, but not less. They would not give the price, so the matter dropped.

Mr. G. W. Hamilton then said, that a little after eight this morning Mr. Worden arrived at the shop "puffing and blowing," and invited the Committee on the boarding-house question to return home immediately, as Mr. Noyes had something to communicate. They accordingly returned, and met Mr. Noyes who said something to this effect.

"It was reported last night that we wanted to get a place for our family to board, and it was suggested that we hire or buy Atkins's place. Why not take immediate possession, if you can, of our own property over there, and turn your boarders off to board among the neighbors?" There was some talk about preliminaries, after this. Mr. Worden and my brother went over and broached the subject to Dunning. He took the plan easily, I understood, and said he should not stand in the way of our carrying out our plan. I supposed he was in good faith. At noon when the hands came from the boarding-house there were indications that they had learned something new. I went up and asked Mr. Dunning if he had reported our plan to the boarders, and he said he had told them they would have to find other places to board after a week from to-day, as the Community wanted the boarding-house. The hands in the shop were in more or less excitement all the afternoon. Meantime Mr. Worden and Myron had been around among some of the neighbors to see if they were willing to take boarders. Some appeared ready, and others were not. I had a talk with the hands just as they quit work, and found some of them took it rather hard. I told them we would try and find places for them to board, and there our responsibility would cease. They felt better when they understood the matter. We have about twenty hands in the machine, trap and blacksmith shops, and were expecting to get some more soon."

Mr. Cragin:—I confess I feel thankful for the move. I am glad there is so hearty a response on the part of our business men to carry out promptly Mr. Noyes's proposition. This move is calculated, I think, to secure to us a permanent victory that will make future enlargements in business a great deal easier. Mr. Noyes took the ground that our businesses are increasing, and will require a great deal of hired help and that when we had paid them a fair compensation for their services, we should have no further connection with them. He thought we should have no difficulty in securing all the help we required; and if a boarding-house is needed over there, some person would come forward sooner or later and establish one. There are many persons who can make it profitable to keep boarders. Then I like the idea of having our own family placed beside our business. The trap and silk businesses are our largest, and those upon which we shall mainly depend for our income, and it seems very desirable that we should have a permanent family there.

Then this satisfies all my desires or proclivities for preaching to outsiders. We can have our meetings and other means of improvement there, and exert an influence in a quiet way, that will gradually tell upon the people about. It may damage our business some for a while; but we can afford that, if spiritual interests demand the change, and I believe they do.

WILLOW-PLACE ITEMS.

The wire cable that has done duty on our dumb waiter for more than two years, has at length shown unmistakable evidence of wearing out. It is accordingly being replaced by a new one of similar material.

A set of twist drills has just been bought for the Machine-shop at a cost of $45.00. These drills are short steel bars of different sizes, graduated in diameter from one and one fourth inches down to one thirty-second of an inch. They derive their name from deep spiral grooves which are cut in their sides, something in the style of augers. Two patent "chucks" for holding the smaller drills, have also been procured: price $28.00.—For the benefit of the initiated, it might be added, that the machinists are also going to have complete sets of "taps," "reamers" and "mandrels."

A Miss Dunn (a cousin of Leonard and Fidelia), who has been in Ohio some two or three years, and is on her return to Vermont came here yesterday.

A man also by the name of Cleveland, from Ohio, called and wanted to join. He said he wanted a home, and he thought we were a happy harmonious people.

"Winter still lingers in the lap of Spring," giving us cold raw weather. Some one remarked that they heard the blue-bird a day or two since, but we think they must have been mistaken.

Mr. Noyes and Woolworth went to Utica yesterday to see Victor. They did not return till after meeting —consequently no report as yet.

E. S. Burnham sprained his ankle a few days ago, and at the present time is obliged to use crutches for walking.

Charles Van Velzer started this morning on his first peddling trip for the season.

Yesterday's temperature—
7 A. M., 42.   12 M., 44.   6 P. M., 33.   Mean 39⅔.

THE O. C. DAILY.

VOL. 3. WEDNESDAY, MARCH 27, 1867. NO. 73.

In the meeting last night, Mr. Woolworth gave a particular account of his and Mr. Noyes's call on Victor the day before, and the state in which they found him. He does not wish to return to the Community, and Mr. N. considers him more or less, under the same spirit of insanity that has so long had possession of him. He thinks the doctors have done all that they are capable of doing for him—and they are willing he should be returned to his friends next month.

Mr. Woolworth then read a letter Mr. Noyes had written to Mr. Mead, of Brattleboro, in which he proposed sending Victor to the Water-cure for a time, where Mr. and Mrs. Mead are boarding, and wishing them to take him under their charge, thinking that the change would be a benefit to him. The doctors say he should be kept quiet, so that his mind may have a chance to recover its healthy tone. They do not consider him capable of going into the world, as he wishes to do, and taking care of himself.

A man by the name of Bush, from Westfield, Mass., writes:

"I have been making up my mind now two years to write to you, and now I take my pencil in hand to do so.—I have read the CIRCULAR for two years, and I have had the "Berean" also to read, but I might at the same time say I had not read it, as it is a very deep book for those that are no better read in the bible than myself. I have thought a good many times I would write to you and ask you if you would be so kind as to give me employment in some of your departments of labor as a hired man, so that I can place myself before you for criticism, so as to make me a better christian. A better christian I say—I cannot call myself such, as I am a wicked man I think, but I want to be a good christian. After all I am not the worst man—I am trying to be a good man. I am what they call a *saw dust* man, that is, a vegetarian. And now my dear friends will you give this letter a fair reading and consider my case and give me employment if you can?"

WILLOW-PLACE ITEM.—Mr. Town has agreed to board the eight girls who have been living at the Boarding-house, with the distinct understanding that the Community takes no responsibility in regard to them, further than to pay them their wages in full, every Saturday night. The girls were told that Mr. T. would board them if they chose to go there—but the matter was optional with them; we would pay them $3.00 extra per week and they might board wherever they wished. This arrangement seemed to satisfy them perfectly.

Mr. Worden and Myron find that several of our neighbors are willing to take boarders—one man offering to make room for fourteen.

We have thought it would not be amiss, to speak of the practice of exaggeration in relating things, that prevails to some extent in the Community. It is very annoying, when you are desirous to come at the exact truth in a matter, so as to report it correctly, to find after it is in print, that it is not exactly true, and to have persons come to you with, "that wasn't so, nor so!"

The desire to tell a "big story," especially where we have figured largely ourselves, is a weakness of human nature, but it should not find place with us, for a moment. Let every one act conscientiously— "guard his lips," and he will soon overcome the propensity.

Last Monday, a span of horses attached to a waggon with side seats, and containing a trunk, started suddenly from the front of the New House, where they were quietly standing, and without any apparent cause of fright, ran furiously to the barn, whirled around it, emptying out seats, trunk, &c. in their rapid course. They then ran back from whence they started, making a not very graceful curve as they dashed around the house. All attempts to stop them proved futile, till running into the hedge on the north side of the lawn, their course was suddenly arrested.

NOTICE.

Whoever comes to New-York had better give the Express man who takes their trunk-checks the name *Oneida Community*, 335 *Broadway, Room 9*, as there have been several mistakes from persons giving their own names with the simple direction. 335 Broadway, which includes 93 different rooms. Thus the baggage is detained, and a liability to extra expressage incurred.

O. C. N. Y. B.

We are having new Ingrain carpets for the Reception, and lower sitting-rooms, which cost $1.45 per yard. Both carpets cost $181,25.

10 o'clock A. M.—Rumor says that all but two or three of our shop hands are going to quit, also that Mr. Town has refused to board the silk girls.—Still we all feel that the present move is an inspired one, and must go through. We have made traps before without hired help, and we can do it again.

WILLOW-PLACE.

Yesterday's temperature—
7 A. M., 26. 12 M., 32. 6 P. M., 30. Mean 29¼.

THE O. C. DAILY.

VOL. 3. THURSDAY, MARCH 28, 1867. NO. 74.

Lexington, Mass., March 23, 1867.

ONEIDA COMMUNITY, FRIENDS:—In the early Autumn of 1862 I spent a very pleasant and profitable week with you, and shall ever be grateful for the kindness and courtesy extended to me. I left you feeling that you were honest, religious and moral. That I differ with you upon religious or social matters is nothing to me. I shall ever be glad to know of your prosperity and happiness. Occasionally I see a CIRCULAR and many good items in it. Was rather surprised to see in Feb. 11, 1867 "The Bran Bread Bore." Surprised that because a few of you had been disappointed in trying to fully follow Graham, you should go to the other extreme and discard *all* that he advocated. It "wheat meal" is bad as tobacco—has "connected with it a personal *spirit*" "an evil sacrament" "in communion with the devils of dyspepsia," that you "eat *damnation* in meddling with it," as professed christians, please tell me why Jesus (the leader of christianity) ate whole wheat and allowed his disciples and followers to do the same? More than this, I think you will find if you search, that all the bible writers ate "bran bread," that *superfine* flour is a comparatively late invention.

Search for physiological facts, and you will find "fine flour" causes more constipation, and through constipation more chronic disease, than any other one kind of food, unless perhaps measly pork.

Yours for truth,   J. H. BEMIS.

MARCH 23 —"The robins are come, the robins and bluebirds too."—"Impossible? you do not mean what you say. The ground still covered with snow: robins? bluebirds?"—"Aye 'tis true sir. Those same robins awoke me with their carrol this morning.—Hearing a new strange sound, I jumped from my bed and looking from my window, on the topmost bough of yonder elm, I espied two red-breasts. They were singing their morning song. The sun's rosy light had but just commenced to faintly dapple the checkered sky—now in dialogue they chatter, and now they try in song the scope of their voices. Earnestly they contend, every feather quivers with emotion, every muscle is apparently strained to its utmost tension, but neither can fairly claim the supremacy of voice. The smaller one evidently had the clearer shrill voice on the high notes, while the larger one put in the deeper tones with great effect."

"Well, how about the bluebirds? you won't say you actually saw them, you only *thought* you heard them; I see, humbug, eh?"

"No humbug at all. Not only I, but my friend C— saw them just yonder among the cherry and plum trees. They gave no song, but were intently securing their morning meal. They were jumping from twig to bough—chirruping and piping faintly their few words, a little more loudly perhaps when occasionally they either of them secured an unusual large prize in the shape of an insect larva. They were busily engaged picking these from under the points of the old loose bark."

"Ha, ha, chickadee—dee," my friend exclaimed and significantly continued, "you think it is spring? robins, bluebirds, poh!" And he turned abruptly and left me.   ROBIN BLUEBIRD.

Just as we were taking our proof, yesterday, and were about to print the first and last pages of the DAILY, one of the girls from the business office, came out and gave us a written communication from Willow-Place, that had just been sent over. We have been in the habit of feeling that every thing that comes from Willow-Place is important, and must receive early attention. Our compositors had all left, and so barely glancing at the article in question, and without giving it a moment's thought, we hastened with all possible speed, to get some one to set it up.

The query did cross our mind why there should be so much haste to publish a mere rumor, when our folks were such matter-of-fact people, but supposing that they knew their own business best, we proceeded to do what we considered ours. Judge of our chagrin, on learning afterwards, that the item in question was written by one of the boys, and sent over without the knowledge of any of the business men in the shop.

OUR ENGINEER.

The engine-room is a very busy place. Taking care of the engine, heating water, keeping up steam for the kitchen, drying clothes, printing, making soap &c., &c., keeps a person busy enough and continually on the watch, and it needs a faithful man to do it, one that does not have a look-out for his own individual interest. Our present engineer is very faithful; on hand early and late, and willing to accommodate every body, when it does not interfere with more important duties. I have often thought him a noble example of faithfulness and industry. All honor to faithfulness.   OBSERVER.

J. P. Hutchins takes James Vaill's place in the kitchen, and James commences work to-day in the Bag-shop.

We have a cold blustering storm in progress this morning, making it rather tedious to be outdoors.

Yesterday's temperature.—
7 A. M., 30. 12 M., 36. 6 P. M., 32. Mean 31¼.

THE O. C. DAILY.

VOL. 3. FRIDAY, MARCH 29, 1867. NO. 76.

ALL RIGHT AT WILLOW-PLACE.

When a sudden and unexpected stoppage of a train of cars occurs, jerking passengers from their seats, and producing a general scare, a sort of babel confusion usually follows. But when the cry is heard from the *inspector*, "all right," and from the conductor, in a stentorian voice, "*all aboard*," followed by a move of his hand to the engineer to set his ponderous machine in motion again, quiet and confidence is as suddenly restored, as it had been disturbed, among the unharmed passengers.

So at Willow-place, a sudden change in our boarding programme for the present year, was equivalent to a stoppage of our business train for a day or so. But yesterday the employees, having recovered from the unpleasant sensations occasioned by an unexpected *switch-off* on to another track, and being reassured that all was right regarding their own interests and well being, entered as cheerfully upon their work again, as though nothing had occurred to disturb, for the moment, the harmony and good-will that has prevailed between the two forces.

The disposition on the part of employers to be governed by right, reason, peace and good-will toward their employees—in a word, to do unto them as they would be done by, under similar circumstances, cannot fail, in the long run, of securing faithfulness and respect in return. Like begets like. Generosity and brotherly kindness, on the part of overseers and foremen toward those under them, will surely yield corresponding fruit. "Whatsoever a man soweth that shall he also reap," is a maxim that all business men will do well to study.   REPORTER.

Mr. Woolworth remarked in meeting night before last as follows:

"While coming home from Utica the other evening Mr. Noyes made a remark about Victor that interested me.—Speaking of the trial that Victor's state was to him, he said it seemed the greatest affliction of his life; and yet he recognized God's hand and providence in it, and realized that it was working for good, not only to himself, but the whole Community. He did not know but all this talk and experience about the soft heart had resulted from that. He said it certainly had kept his heart very soft and humble. I know that Mr. Noyes's talks on this subject, have been a great blessing to the whole Community. It seemed to be this power that took hold of Victor. Mr. Noyes's labor to produce a soft heart in him seemed to reach him more than any thing else. He expressed his appreciation of it and desire for it."

Mr. H. R. Perry writes from Richmond, Ind., the 24th of March:

"Our bag customers are generally pleased with our goods, but I find the country is full of agents from Newark and New-York. A gentleman at Louisville Ky., said that four bag agents from the east met in his store a few days since. One told him he could "sell forty per *scent* cheaper as any *jody*," but he did not give him any order, but he did give us one. I suppose on the whole I have got a fair proportion of orders in that line.

I think we shall have a good demand for traps for the Fall trade, as merchants have generally sold out pretty close, and there are no heavy over stocks on hand. The imitation traps have hurt us some the past season, but I think we gain on them."

Messrs. Clark and Conant have finished removing the wood from the wood-shed, although they have encountered almost daily, snow or rain storms, since commencing the job. Their employees have persistently continued their labor with a good deal of zest, judging from the flow of jest and joke. By measurement I find one hundred cords—128 feet per cord—or about three hundred cords stove wood, has been taken out and one hundred cords of three feet wood has also be n removed from around the shed. This has been distributed at the boarding-houses and smaller wood-sheds, and the balance so disposed as to be most convenient for repacking in the shed when it shall be placed on its new site. The carpenters are only waiting for the cold weather to release its grip, (which as yet holds on firmly), when they will saw the shed into two parts, place timbers under the posts for the working of rollers—suitably brace and strengthen the parts, then trundle it off to its new location. The knowing ones say, "it will be only a little-before-breakfast-play-spell to remove and adjust the parts on the new foundation."   ITEMUS.

At a meeting of the Silk agents at New-York a few days since, it was decided to have the agents on their return, give a report in brief, of the amount of sales made while absent.—During my last trip of about two weeks, I took orders and delivered of Silk $977.31, of Bags $1,606.19.   W. O. K.

Yesterday's temperature—
7 A. M., 25. 12 M., 40. 6 P. M., 32. Mean 32¼.

THE O. C. DAILY.

VOL. 3. SATURDAY, MARCH 30, 1867. NO. 76.

Dansville, N. Y., March 26, 1867.

MR. JOHN NOYES, DEAR SIR:—I contemplate a trip for my health, and wish to go on some trapping or hunting expedition, or to get into some associations of that sort. Knowing that you had dealings with men of that stamp, in selling traps, and that your people had some of them been out on such a tour, I thought you could assist me. Will you be so kind as to drop me a line, and give me any information that you can, that will assist me to a communication with such parties: by so doing you will confer a great favor on your friend and well wisher.

I have been brief, thinking it better than to trouble you with more words than necessary. I have no claim on you, nor do I wish to tax you, but would like your advice. Yours for Christ and Humanity,

F. WILSON HURD.

TRAP-SHOP.—Four or five barrels of finished Traps, constitute our present stock in hand; and some Fox-traps that are ordered are yet to be finished. Parts of traps, of nearly all kinds, though in limited quantities are on hand, ready to be put together.

One obstacle to successful Trap-making which has never been thoroughly overcome, presents itself with renewed force this spring. It is in the "swaging" or as it is usually called "rolling" springs. For the last year, this work has been done entirely by our own men; as, indeed, the greater portion of it always has been. But the work is pretty severe, and our "Roller men" are gradually giving out. To flank this difficulty, it is proposed to make our No. 1 springs something as the No. 0 springs are made—i. e. punch them out of sheet steel. Five hundred pounds of steel have accordingly been ordered to experiment with.

Mr. Cragin invited the architects and a few of those who are living, or have lived with the children, to meet to discuss the proposed children's house, its internal arrangments &c. Mr Hamilton presented a plan he had hastily sketched, embodying the most important ideas that had been suggested to him by different individuals of the family, remarking before exhibiting his plan, " I see we must set a limit to the building, that we may be able to build it for about $6,000 as Mr. Noyes suggested. In this plan the main building is 46 by 44 ft., the wing 36 by 27, this is as large on the ground, as we can build for that money. In the main building first floor, I have a large sitting-room 18 by 26 ft., a large closet and spacious bed-room opening out of it. On the other side of the hall a dining and play-room 18 by 20 ft. for small children. In the wing I have provision for closets, boys boot-room, bathing-room, water closet for little ones, boys work-room, bed-rooms &c. Up stairs I have a central dressing-room, with as many bed-rooms opening into it as possible." A few alterations were suggested by those present which Mr. H. liked. There was a good brotherly spirit manifest on the part of all, which made it easy to give and take suggestions. The plan as amended was unanimously adopted. Mr. H. will now perfect it, when it will be shown to all who wish to see.

ONE WHO WAS PRESENT.

A SCENE AT THE BARN.

"A chiel's amang ye takin' notes,
An' faith, he'll prent it."

"Pull away boys—pull steady, he'll give up soon. Take him right along. Don't go round in a circle, go straight ahead. Keep him agoing, There is no danger of hurting. Whoa, wo, wo, pony. Now you act kinda good. There, that kinda suits me."

Hearing the above conversation as I was passing the yard at the barn, I was curious to know what was going on behind the board; on climbing up the high fence and looking over, there was our good natured boss-farmer with two other persons, his helpers. The three had hold of one end of a rope, while in a noose at the other, was a yearling colt's head; the men were tugging and pulling one way, colt braced on all fours mulishly resisting and pulling the other, man-power a little the stronger of the two forces.

A bow-legged crook-backed Irishman, standing at a little distance back, so as to be safe, with both hands thrust into his breeches pockets, coolly remarked as he watched the performance, "shure—and—and—and—the colt is a bigger man than all o' yese. Faith, and is'nt he a great little horse? Be jabbers, and he'll be after putting his fist in yer face, and he does that way, Och ! and he will."

This last was spoken to the man who stood nearest the colt, just as he was performing some eccentricities, such as rearing, then bounding forward, falling upon his knees, and placing his fore feet nearly on the head of one of the men. After dangling at the rope's end and gyrating to his utmost satisfaction, the colt was halter-broken.

AGRICOLA.

Mr. Aiken was criticised last night by his request. It was thought he had improved much, since his last criticism, though it is still manifest that he needs more softness of heart. His place is a difficult one, subject to many temptations, and he has in the past been liable to irritation and fault-finding. He is a good steward—provides liberally for the family, and makes it easy for the kitchen folks and others, to consult with him or make suggestions.

There are six of the little girls of Edith's age, taking lessons on the piano and harmonium, and we understand that they learn quite readily.

Yesterday's temperature—
7 A. M., 25. 12 M., 32. 6 P. M., 34. Mean 30¼.

THE O. C. DAILY.

VOL. 3. MONDAY, APRIL 1, 1867. NO. 77.

BUSINESS MEETING.

Imme-liate attention to the lawn at Willow-Place was recommended by the Business Board.—It had been proposed by Mr. Noyes that Mr. Cragin should superintend making improvements over there; accordingly he was appointed chairman of a committee, composed of Messrs. Woolworth, S. W. Nash, Ellis and Mrs. Miller.—A committee to organize the family at Willow Place was referred to Mr. Woolworth, Mr. Cragin and the general meeting.

Abram brought up the matter of remodeling several old buildings at Willow Place to make tenement houses of them. It was thought this had better be done right along, and a committee was appointed consisting of Abram, Homer, A. Kinsley and Mr. Campbell, to decide upon the plan. According to last year's statistics, every man boarding himself saves us sixty dollars per year.

The Water-pipe needs to be laid pretty soon, so that the preserving department may have an abundant supply of water in time. A new reservoir will need to be located on a lower level. Some skillful engineering is in requisition. A greater supply of water can be got by bringing it on a lower level than its present run.—G. W. Hamilton thinks that then, by means of a wind wheel, it may be raised to any desirable height so as to supply running water to the upper rooms. Committee to act in the matter, Messrs. G. W. Hamilton, Woolworth, Abbott, Sears, Whitney and Kellogg.

Mr. Noyes's reply to Mr. Hurd's letter published in Saturday's DAILY.

Oneida, March 30, 1867.

Mr. F. WILSON HURD, *Dear Sir:*—On receipt of your letter, I consulted with Mr. Newhouse, our leading woodman, and learned from him that you would probably not be able to find a *trapping* party at this season of the year, as trapping is chiefly a winter business, and usually commences in the Fall. But he said that excursions to the North Woods, or "Brown's Tract," for the purpose of hunting, fishing and recreation, generally start about the first of June; and that he could introduce you to a man who gets up a party for such an excursion every year.

By my request he has called on the man, Mr. K. C. Wilson, of Madison Co., New York, about ten miles from here, and has just informed me that Wilson with a party of four others, expects to start for the North Woods the last of May or the first of June. The other members of the party, will be a Daguerreian artist from Syracuse by the name of Thayer, a son of Gerrit Smith, and two men from the head of Oneida Lake, named Messenger and Chapman.—They expect to be gone two or three weeks. Their destination is the head of West Canada Creek about forty miles northeast of here, where they expect to find for game, plenty of deer, speckled trout, ducks, partridges, &c. They have a good boat and shanty already in the woods. If such a party as this would suit you, (and for purposes of health, it would probably be better than a trapping party) you can make your arrangements as to time, outfit, &c., with Mr. Wilson by letter; and when the time comes, if you will call on us, we shall be happy to give you any assistance in our power.

Yours truly, J. H. NOYES.

The following is a report of my late business trip:

Collections,	$203.51
Trap orders, net,	$272.00
Silk "	$59.45
Bag "	$1,383.00
Advertising Commissions,	$30.00
I was away four weeks, expenses,	$145.16
Less railroad passes and hotel bill,	$32.35
Cash expenses,	$113.81

Parties who had our fruits last season, spoke highly of them, and said they should want more of them this season. I found business generally very dull at this time, but I think the prospect is fair for a brisk campaign for us, particularly in fruit and traps.

H. R. P.

BAG-SHOP.—Every month's experience brings with it, abundant reasons for faith and perseverence in doing business as unto the Lord. We have never found that keeping religion and business separate, has worked well for either. The thorough organization which we have in the Bag-department at this time, we believe to be the result of prayer and inspiration.

Mr. Noyes' talks about a soft heart have created an atmosphere in which it is easy to pray and be receptive to God in all things. We expect in a spirit of unity with God and each other, to accomplish all that the family hope we may, and make the department a means of income not only financially, but spiritually.

Muslin Bags made last month,	80¼ doz.
Leather, " " "	36¼ "
Orders for the month,	108 "
Bag Sales,	$3,043.42

N.

SOLDIERS WANTED!

Wanted, immediately, any number of volunteers to serve the spirit of truth, during endless ages. Their fitness for the service, will depend very much upon the possession of a disposition to be improved and rejuvenated, by criticism, crucifixion, and similar refining appliances.

The object of the campaign is twofold. First, the extermination of selfishness and egotism, wherever found, as the deadly enemies of humanity. And, second, the establishment of the reign of purity, peace and love on earth,

P. S. None need apply who do not covet the art of knowing how to *die*—at least, to the *old* adam, who dwells alone in the little world called *isolation.*

By order of the we government, RECRUITER.

Mr. Hamilton left for New-York, Saturday afternoon, and Mr. Olds and H. R. Perry returned home at the same time.

Temperature Saturday and Sunday—
7 A. M., 83, 12 M., 44, 6 P. M., 38, Mean 38.
7 A. M., 40, 12 M., 54, 6 P. M., 46, Mean 47¼.

THE O. C. DAILY.

VOL. 3. TUESDAY, APRIL 2, 1867. NO. 78.

NOTES OF TRAVEL.

I left our brothers at the "Abbey," on the night of the 17th. and took passage by steam-boat for New Haven arriving there at 5 A. M. I left the boat at an early hour for our home in that city, where I found a happy group of brothers and sisters. The call was rather unexpected, which made it the more interesting. I spent several hours there, noting with interest the pleasant aspect of things, in-doors and out. It is indeed a well chosen spot for the accommodation and comfort of our brother students. May they prosper and grow in every good work. At 3 P. M. I left for Wallingford reaching there about 5 o'clock. The family there was surprised to see me. It was a pleasant meeting however, (especially to me). I was glad to see old friends "once more." I parted with them the next morning with much love and many good wishes in my heart for their prosperity. I returned to New Haven where I remained till 2 P. M., then left for New York.—After some consultation with the brothers there, I left on the 11 o'clock train for this *dear* home, arriving about 2 o'clock in the afternoon. In another article I may say something about my visit at the N. Y. B. C. O.

When a hoop encircles a barrel of sparkling wine, we say it preforms a good office, and when it gracefully rolls and skips before the stick of a rosy cheeked child, we say, what a pleasant thing. But when it presumes to encircle dainty feet, what then! Did you say naughty thing? Some of us did, a day or two since, when one or more of these aspiring hoops encircling a pair of nimble feet, came dashing through the shop. The saucy hoop stirred up dust, made war with chip and shaving, made a furious charge on an unfortunate cup of varnish, which had to prostrate itself and yield up all its costly treasures. The lady rushed on, as though mischief was honorable, leaving the knight of the brush in amazement. A LOOKER ON.

APRIL-FOOL.—Yesterday as Martin and George Kellogg were coming through the Castle, in front of a store door, and in the middle of the street, lay a nice bundle. Dr. Cherry, who was riding with them, suggested that it might be a package of raisins. Martin jumped out of the wagon and as he picked it up, a small boy opened the store door saying, "April-fool Mr. Oneida Community." Martin jumped into the waggon taking package along. After they were through the village upon examining the bundle the contents were found to be—*hay!* Dr. Cherry, it is hinted, was interested in the plot. ITEMS.

ERRATA.—Several errors occurred in yesterday's DAILY. In the report of the business meeting; for wind wheel read wind-mill. We copied the expression, word for word from the business record; and the mistake in question must be charged back on the reporter. In our ignorance of terms we did not know but a wind-mill might properly be called a wind-wheel.—Also in Mr. Noyes's letter at the commencement of the second paragraph, read Mr. H. C. Wilson, Oneida Valley, Madison Co., New York.

WILLOW-PLACE ITEMS.—The boarders at Willow-Place recently presented Mrs. Dunning with a handsome silver castor, adorned with bottles of cut glass. The value of the gift is estimated at fifteen or twenty dollars.

Our folks had their dinners brought over from home yesterday and set out in the dining-room that we usually occupy. The Dunnings are very busy packing their household goods and cleaning house, preparatory to leaving. They intend to depart about the middle of the week. The boarders are mostly settled in their new abodes, and things are moving along as quietly as usual.

The fish-pond over by the park, was drawn off yesterday, for the purpose of raising it higher. Several pickerel that were put there last Spring, were taken and put in Willow-Place pond. If they do as well as pickerel generally do, in five years the family can have a meal of fresh fish quite often.

STOCK REDUCED.—Since the new programme for farm and fruit went into operation, there has been a beginning at reduction of the stock. Six cows have been disposed of and twelve hogs, amounting to the sum of $600.00. AGRICOLA.

A stirring criticism of the evening readers, as given by Mr. Noyes in his room yesterday, was read by Mr. Woolworth last night. As the document will be sent to the other Communes, we will say no more of it.

Will persons who send us articles for publication, particularly poetical effusions, give us their names, as we sometimes wish to consult them about said articles. ED.

The committee appointed to consider Miss Susan Dunn's application for membership, decided to accept her proposal. She is accordingly considered a member of the family.

Seven hot-beds have been made containing in all, 403 square feet. Two of the beds (140 feet), have been filled with earth and are ready for planting.

Why is it dangerous to sleep on a train of cars? Answer to-morrow.

Yesterday's temperature—
7 A. M., 44 12 M., 48. 6 P. M., 42. Mean 44.

THE O. C. DAILY.

VOL. 3. WEDNE DAY, APRIL 3, 1867. NO. 79,

VISIT TO THE N. Y. B.

The object of my visit more particularly was, to consult with the brothers there, on matters of business. That branch is the center of operations in all commercial matters, the head quarters of all the agents. It is the point to study all questions pertaining to our several branches of business. I feel a clear medium there, which makes it an edifying, attractive place. I think there is a good spirit at work, guiding and controlling all affairs in a successful way. The angel of God is encamped around about them, to keep, and protect them from evil. The few days I spent there, (they seem but few, although the most of two weeks), were very profitable to me. In our consultations we arrived at some very satisfactory conclusions, especially in regard to the silk manufacturing. In starting that business we find ourselves under the necessity, in the first place, of making a good article, the very best that *can* be made. No " pretty good," or " fair" article, will answer the purpose, we *must* have the best. Perhaps there is no business in which there is more cheating, than in the manufacturing of sewing silk.—In attempting to reform and revolutionize this business, we meet difficulties at almost every step. But we are bound to conquer, and we'll succeed in establishing it on a basis above the mere competition of the world. If we carry righteousness and honesty into the business of manufacturing, we are *sure* money and all manner of success will follow.

C. O.

WILLOW-PLACE ITEMS.

SILK-DEPARTMENT.—There are now thirty-one girls employed in the Factory, of whom six have been engaged this week.

Twelve of our girls are between ten and fifteen years of age, and how to work them economically, yet not opressively, has become something of a problem. Elizabeth's time is considerably occupied with the general management of the winding and cleaning, and Harriet and Olive are engaged in the spooling room. After due consultation, the following plan has been adopted for trial. Mrs. Waltch, a winder, whose disposition and temperament seems well adapted for the the task, now has the immediate supervision of the girls. Her time is wholly occupied in looking after them—picking out the snarls they make, &c. At 10 A. M. and 4 P. M. recesses of fifteen minutes are given that they may have a run in the open air—how the plan works shall be daily reported.

A new bag-maker, named Wiegand, a German,

came yesterday from New-York. He has commenced work to-day. He does well, is young, and **promises** well, so says the bag foreman.

ANOTHER SUGAR SNOW.

Faintest foot-falls coming, going,
   Downy garments rustling by,
Strong white arms, a moment showing—
   Lift the curtains of the sky.

Sweeping down, the forest swaying,
   Wildly whirling everywhere,
Landscape hiding, stragglers blinding,
   Avalanches in the air.

"Sound the trumpet down the valley!"
   Cried an angel from the cloud;
Down the slopes the peal broke gladly,
   Leaped in echoes long and loud;

Thrilled the hillsides and the hollows,
   Shook the air and depths profound,
Pierced the ears of sleeping millions,
   Woke the nations under ground.

Soon, I saw the grass and flowers,
   Mantling all the valley warm,
Saw the blue-bird, and the robin,
   Saw the angel of the storm.

ONEIDA.

DEAR RECRUITER:—In answer to your advertisement for volunteers to serve the spirit of truth through endless ages, the undersigned offers himself as a medium of Christ to do so, and for the object of the campaign specified therein, or for any other work it may require of him. Complying with the terms of application, he covets earnestly the art of knowing how to die. Any advice given him at any time to that end will be gratefully received. WILLIAM JONES.

Mr. G. W. Noyes came yesterday afternoon, and L. F. Dunn left this morning for Wallingford via. New-York.

Mrs. Morris, with a lad of sixteen years, (her husband's son), and a little child of her own, arrived this forenoon.

ANSWER TO YESTERDAY'S QUESTION —Because they run over *sleepers.*

Yesterday's temperature—
7 A. M., 40. 12 M., 48. 6 P. M., 40. Mean 42½.

THE O. C. DAILY.

VOL. 3.   THURSDAY, APRIL 4, 1867.   NO. 80.

At early dawn, on the morning of the first of April, a rosy crimson slowly creeps up the eastern horizon, along the hilltops—up the western, climbs a dark dense cloud. Just as a rich glow has beautified the fleecy edge of the onward moving cloud, a little song sparrow comes fluttering along, and perches on a bough near my chamber window. Now he chatters and tells his story of scenes and things in the far south, whither he flew last Autumn for a more congenial clime. He says that for a summer residence, and for the purposes of rearing a family he would much prefer a climate like this. He hopes to present at our dining-room door, bye and bye, a little brood of Mr. and Misses Sparrows, to pick the crumbs that fall there. He says " I will sing all this day, on the trees that stand where the children's yard used to be, as a slight token of my thankfulness for last year's "favors." Here he commenced the following song in Dutch, which I did not fully understand. Twee, twee, twee, tee-we, teo-we, teweet, teweet, twit, twit, twit, twee, twee-ee-ee-ee-ee running all together at its close. Here raindrops lightly tapped upon my window-pane and I withdrew. The little songster however, kept his promise, and gathered around him a bevy of little birds, who entertained us several hours, with their charming music. April 2nd. Where are the birds now ? A cold, snowing, wintry day. March forgot to take old blusterer, as she left, and so we have one more reminder of the winter that is over and gone: R. B.

"Halo dar Sambo. How many toes has Mr. President Jonson ?"

"How many toes has Mr. Jonson ? De same, as many as anybody else I spose, dun no, nebber seed his toes. What's dat you mean Jerry ?"

" What a fool you'se be sambo, yah, yah, yah, don't you see, he has eighteen ?"

" Eighteen toes ! Dat's a wopper no how ; don't bleve noting bout dat."

" Ise gwine to tell you big ting; Mr. Jonson has ten natral toes and den he has eight (V) toes.

Mrs. Otis writes to Mrs. Bushnell :

" I often think of the friends at O. C. with satisfaction and increasing interest. I was very thankful for Mr. Kelley's visit, although far from being pleasant. Had it been aside from the family, I should have heard more from you all. Tell him his call was not in vain, for it strengthened my faith, and I then saw clearer than ever, the darkness and bondage of the letter, and the purity and liberty of the spirit."

Mr. Hatch has fitted up a show-case for the children in which all the nice things that have been given them from time to time, that have hitherto been kept in boxes and drawers, are now placed, so that they can all be seen at a glance. They make a fine showing, and we notice that the children take much satisfaction in looking at them, as do others of the family.

We are told that the house at Willow-Place is rapidly being transformed into a more attractive looking abode, by cleaning, whitewashing, papering, &c., &c. Some of our women go over every day, and prepare dinner for our hands there, and we are gradually getting entire possession of the place, though the Dunnings have not moved yet, but they expect to this week.

A little German boy came into the Business-office a few days ago after a paper. One of the women generously offered him some apples. Finding his little hands could not hold them all, she put the remainder into what she supposed to be his pantaloons pocket when lo ! they rolled down his leg on to the floor.

Mr. John Hutchins staid here night before last. He was on his return from the state of Maine where he has passed the winter. He states that the winter has not been as severe there as in this state, the mercury sinking at no time lower than twelve degrees below zero.

Two car-loads of coal that our people bought at Syracuse, arrived at Oneida depot last Monday, and our teamsters brought home eighteen tons yesterday, and will bring the remainder to-day.

Our evening meetings have been very interesting two or three nights past. Mr. G. W. N.'s presence with us is much appreciated, and we regret that his visit must be so brief.

Six Norway Spruces that stand west of the Tontine, and in the way of the wood-shed are being taken up and set out south of the site of the children's new house.

John Norton reports that with two hired men he is finishing seven hundred cans per diem, or a little over four thousand per week.

Said Jessie to one of her companions the other day, " How egotistical you are ! Mrs. Noyes don't like *egotisticalness.*"

The weather to-day is fine, warm and spring-like, no mistake.

Yesterday's temperature—
7 A. M., 33. 12 M., 44. 6 P. M., 44. Mean 40⅓.

THE O. C. DAILY.

VOL. 3.   FRIDAY, APRIL 5, 1867.   NO. 81,

Mrs. Bushnell was criticised last night at her request. In the course of the evening and in reference to her case, Mr. Woolworth made the following remarks:

"I have sometimes felt a little jealous of her outside relations to inquirers and believers. It seemed to me that she did not transfer her responsibilities over to the Community so completely as she might, and as it would be well for her to do. She seems to keep up a kind of outside parish of her own. The effect of this, so far as it goes, is to keep her out of the Community fellowship, and to turn her thought and attention outside.

"I do not know but it is her destiny to be a missionary. Heretofore she has been very successful in that field, in presenting the truth and converting people to it. But now I think she should make it her business to seek a soft heart, and merge her life in the Community spirit. She should never go to work as an individual again, but as a member of Christ and his body.

"I think she is well posted in respect to the doctrines of Perfectionism and Mr. Noyes's views generally; but she now needs to seek identification with Mr. Noyes and the Community spirit."

Much love was expressed for Mrs. B. and appreciation of her as a woman of faith, her past services in the cause, her love of the truth and loyalty to it.

There has been a little ripple of a somewhat unpleasant character, among the Community employees for a few days past. Michael Murphy, the man who has been hostler for the past year, on being informed that his services would not be wanted after the first of April, and that the house he occupied would be needed for the new hostler, demanded extra pay for Sunday's and other hours which he claimed to be over time. On being told that his demand would not be acceded to, he replied "I shall not leave the house but by a legal process, which you must procure and serve on me."—Accordingly, the Community served a notice on him yesterday, drawn and signed with all due formality. He was prompt in obeying the summons, as he began to remove his goods immediately after, although he might have kept us from the use of the house for thirty days. He threatened to sue for bill claimed, though he has not done so, but Mr. Kinsley thinks he will. His prospects for extorting money, are not thought to be very flattering.   ITEMUS.

G. W. Noyes with little Temple started yesterday afternoon for Wallingford, and Mr. Noyes at the same time for Utica, to visit the Asylum and see Victor.—

Mr. N. received Mr. Mead's letter in the forenoon.—He returned about 10 o'clock P. M. but we have not yet learned the result of his call.

Oneida, April 4, 1867.

Although I am not able to make as good a business showing of my late trips, I feel as though I had gained quite a victory in my spirit toward the world. I have been out nine days in all.

Amount of bags sold,		$173.55.
Silk,	"	$116.45.
Collection,		$68.45.
Cash expenses,		$20.70.

I hope to do better when business improves.
                                C. VANVELZER

We notice persons raking and clearing the lawns of rubbish that has accumulated during the winter. Mr. Nash sowed grass seed yesterday on the plot formaly occupied by the White-house, also on the old croquet ground.

The Horticultural department hired two men yesterday, paying one, one dollar and fifty cents per day boarding himself, and the other, twenty one dollars per month, with board. The latter will lodge in the chamber over the tin-shop.

It commenced raining yesterday afternoon, and the snow-banks on the hills around are lessening, and will soon disappear entirely.

A small boquet of wild flowers was brought in yesterday, containing, the Hepatica triloba and the Claytonia.

ANECDOTE.

John Dine as his practice was, went to a tavern one evening, where he spent the most of the night in gambling and carousing, with a gang of others like himself. At last they proposed to have a supper, and all that could not make a rhyme were to club together and pay the bill. They all succeeded in their attempts, except John Dine, who after paying the whole bill returned home.

While knocking at the door, his wife screamed out, "who's there?" "Nobody but John Dine," said he. "Yes," replied she, "and as drunk as the swine." "Stop wife," said he, "I must go back," which he immediately did, and told the gang, that he had made a rhyme, and then triumphantly exclaimed, "I John Dine am as drunk as a hog."

Yesterday's temperature—
7 A. M., 48. 12 M., 70. 6 P. M., 63. Mean 60½.

THE O. C. DAILY.

VOL. 3.   SATURDAY, APRIL 6, 1867.   NO. 82.

Mr. Woolworth gave a particular account last night of what Mr. Noyes had told him relative to his call at the Asylum, and his conversation with Victor. Dr. Gray was not at home. Mr. N. found Victor in a softer state than he was at his last call there, and more willing to return to the Community. Mr. Noyes has written a letter to Dr. Gray, (which was read last night), telling him of his plans concerning Victor.

He proposes to take him to New Haven, and if he consents to remain in the Community, he will give him the best chance for an education that the City affords; or if he wishes it, he can go to Europe with G. W. N., or in case he should still desire to try the world, he would give him an outfit, and let him have his choice in this respect. Victor seemed pleased and softened by his father's generous offer, and thankfully accepted it. He is heartily sick of the Asylum and as anxious to withdraw from it, as his father is to have him.

Mr. Noyes expressed himself as greatly relieved, and comparatively at rest about Victor now. We are all thankful.

WILLOW-PLACE ITEM.—Twenty or thirty ducks settled down on our pond yesterday morning, thereby noticeably stirring the hunter-blood in several of our brethren. After considerable waste of ammunition, a nondescript of the duck, bearing the not particularly euphonious title of "hell-diver" was secured. Its bill was like a hen's rather than a duck's, and its toes were webbed, each on its own hook, as one might say. We were unable with our American Cyclopedia to classify it with any of the species mentioned.

TO A CLUMP OF EVERGREENS.

Ah! beautiful trees with branches so fair,
Catching the breeze, of the pure morning air,
You fear not the cold wind though blowing so chill,
But gracefully bow, as it sweeps o'er the hill.

You whisper and sigh as you wave to and fro,
Or catch the light flakes of the fast falling snow,
The lithe little snow-bird is won by your charms,
Which you do so lovingly fold in your arms.

A lesson you teach us, so fearless and brave,
To trust in *His* arm who is mighty to save,
You patiently wait for more time and more growth,
To perfect and develop your beauty and worth.

L.

Dr. Case of Vernon, came a few days ago and engaged three dollars worth of flowers from the green

horse, to grace the golden wedding, which takes place to-day. A man was sent for the flowers yesterday. They were gathered and placed carefully in a basket, and looked beautifully.

We shall be obliged to give our readers some blank paper to-day, as we have canvassed the premises pretty thoroughly for news, but do not find much to report.

A sudden change in the weather last night, and this morning the ground is frozen quite stiff, with a slight covering of snow.

Mr. Ellis reports one hundred and eight strawberry crates made and delivered to our neighbors this week.

Traps ordered during the month of March, including Agency orders,   439 doz.
Traps ordered the past week,   25 "

Yesterday's temperature—
7 A. M., 49.   12 M., 44.   6 P. M., 38.   Mean 43½.

THE O. C. DAILY.

VOL. 3.   MONDAY, APRIL 8, 1867.   NO. 83.

BUSINESS MEETING.

J. Leonard proposed that J. Freeman take his place as reporter of the Business meetings. Approved.

Mr. Worden suggested the propriety of commencing work on the road soon. Teams can be better spared now than later. Referred to Messrs. Clark, Conant and Barron.

F. Marks read the following note from the occupants of the lower Sitting-room: "The undersigned would respectfully inform the Buisness Board that they are considerably annoyed by the pounding in the cellar below. In fact it is anything but agreeable. If it were to continue only for a short time, they would not say a word, but as they understand it is to be prolonged, they would ask that it may be removed." It was decided to remove the box business to the Tontine.

Homer Barron reported that the cost of tinning the roof of the front Portico would be $11.00 per square, including the cost of putting it on. There are about three squares, or 290 feet. It was thought we could buy the tin at wholesale prices. Moved that the roof be tinned at as small a cost as possible. Homer and Abram appointed a committee to attend to it.

In conversation with a good brother a few days since, on the subject of false love, he asked me if I didn't think it was a principality to which woman yields more readily than man, or rather are they not prone to tempt man? I was compelled to say yes, I think it is so, and although I have thought much on this subject of late, it came home to my heart with renewed power.

Is it true thought I, that woman whom God has made to be a help-meet to man, is guilty of alluring him from the noble purposes which truth has implanted in him? is it because she is vain and loves attention? Let her adorn herself with a meek and quiet spirit, which in the sight of God is of great price, and she cannot fail to secure the attention and love of all those who are in heart fellowship with Christ.   R.

The controversy between Mr. Dunning and the O. C finally culminated on Saturday last, in an arbitration held at Oneida Castle. The arbitrators mutually chosen by the parties, were Mr. Dorrance by O. C., and Esqr. Avery by Mr. D. Their award (founded principally on Mr. D's. own testimony,) was that the O. C. had broken no contract—that Dunning had no cause of complaint—consequently was entitled to no damage. After their award was declared, pay for their services was offered them, which they generously refused. We shall make them a present of some canned fruit. It was decided also to make Mr. D. a present of $25. Mr. Kinsley stated that his respect for him was greatly increased by his simple truthful statement.

Mr. Daniel Kelly came Saturday afternoon. He seems very glad to get back. The following note from him to the family was read last night:

"I can truly say that I am very thankful to God for the privilege of returning to the Community. I have come this time to stay whether I like it or not. I have come on my own responsibility, and with an understanding—have enlisted for life, and have decided live or die, to serve the Lord. I shall be thankful for any discipline that will be necessary to bring me nearer to Christ. I confess my entire obedience to Mr. Noyes, and my union with him and the Community, and am ready to do anything that they or Mr. Noyes have for me to do.   D. M. KELLY.

The reading of Dixon's book was omitted last night. In meeting at Mr. Noyes request, articles were read from the "American Journal of Science and Arts," the "World," and the "Springfield Republican," disclosing some startling facts relative to the increase of abortions, and the cause, both in this country and in Europe. Massachusetts, that State that boasts of her Puritanical blood, seems to be taking the lead in this diabolical work, outstripping even New-York City in her deeds of darkness, in producing abortions. The subject will be continued to-night.

This week promises to be a busy one to the outdoor corps. The Horticulturists have the raspberries to uncover, stake and tie up, and the grape-vines to uncover, and the straw to rake off the strawberries, besides getting the ground ready for potatoes, peas, &c., &c.

We send to-day 500 Philadelphia raspberry plants to a man in Gettysburg Pa., price $15 per hundred.

Mrs. Bushnell had a letter from Albert, Saturday, informing her that his Aunt Eunice, Mr. Bushnell's sister, who lived in the family was dead.

E. S. Nash started for Boston in the night. We understand he goes to purchase leather for bags.

Forty-five yards of carpeting have been bought for the Willow-Place house.

Mr. H. R. Perry has taken E. S. Burnham's place in the evening reading of letters and reports.

Why do people who take berths in sleeping cars have two heads?

Temperature Saturday and Sunday—
7 A. M., 32.   12 M., 38.   6 P. M., 34.   Mean 34⅓.
7 A. M., 44.   12 M., 50.   6 P. M., 44.   Mean 46.

THE O. C. DAILY.

VOL. 3.   TUESDAY, APRIL 9, 1867.   NO. 84.

OUR TENT.

Mr. Newhouse pitched a tent on the lawn yesterday, contiguous to a group of evergreens, for the purpose of having it photographed for the new edition of the "Trappers Guide." It is not a "Shelter-tent," but an "A tent," which with its little sheet-iron stove, could be made as cozy and comfortable as a parlor.

The novelty of a tent on the lawn attracted groups in the early evening, who took shelter beneath the canvass (thanks to Mr. Newhouse's hospitality) from the drippings of an April sky, and listened, while reclining, to the "patter on the roof." But after meeting the tent was all aglow with light and heat, and attracted still larger groups of hilarious boys and girls with "Father Hatch," and a few staid ones interspersed, including J. P. H. who seemed as much in his element, as a fish in its native element. John could not repress his emotion, for his imagination seemed all on fire, kindled by reminiscences of his former "wood-craft"(iness).

The tent was made vocal, notwithstanding some difficulty in getting the pitch—with "Tenting to-night on the old camp ground," "John Brown" &c., &c.

Whether John P. was able to quit the tent and come down to the ordinary conditions of life last night, the writer is not informed.   H.

The great novelty and attraction with us, at the present time, is the tent on the lawn. We had three articles on the subject handed us to-day, all of which we should be glad to publish had we room. We quote the following from J. P. H's. description of the scene: "In all we numbered twenty-four, consisting mostly of laughing girls. It was the strangest camping adventure that I ever embarked in. The muffled music had a wild and weird charm about it, only felt to its fullest extent, by those who have tasted of a wild forest-life.

"After the singers and all had retired to the house, Mr. N. and myself were left alone, to fancy ourselves, for a moment, in that dear old forest, once so congenial to our unregenerate natures."

The meeting, last night was one of intense interest. Many communications were read from the women, relating what they had seen, known and felt, of the dreadful evils attending the act of producing abortions in any way, and expressing thankfulness to God, that we as a body are delivered from all temptations of that kind, and are protected by the continence of the man, from the torments of fear in respect to undesired procreation. Women in the world are often put under a terrible pressure, to violate their conscientious scruples, and fine sensibilities, in order to escape the almost unbearable evils that stare them in the face in respect to bearing and rearing children.

Yesterday we got possession of the house at Willow-Place, and I imagine we felt like soldiers who had stormed a fortress, and had driven the enemy out and were rejoicing in our victory. We had a good time confessing Christ, and inviting the angels and the Primitive Church to come in and dwell there. The result of our confessions was electrifying, and the work of white-washing, cleaning &c., went off with new enthusiasm.

I think we may expect new inspiration and success in our business there the coming season.   C. O.

The old dining-room at the Willow-Place house has been enlarged and made more attractive, by removing a partition between it and a bed-room at the east end, making both rooms into one. More room is to be added at the west end by taking out a partition there. This room is on the north side of the house and will be contiguous to the kitchen which was enlarged last fall.   ITEMUS.

Thirty thousand strawberry plants have been engaged at $3.50 per thousand by H. G. Allen in New-York. They are to be delivered at the express office in four different lots.

This is for the convenience of setting out the plants more leisurely than we could were they all to come in one lot.   L. H. B.

---

11 o'clock A. M.—The following letter to Mr. Noyes is just received:

State Lunatic Asylum, Utica, April 6, 1857.

DEAR SIR:—Yours of the 5th is received. I should commend the New Haven and sea-voyage project.—The latter would probably be the best.

Yours very truly,   JOHN P. GRAY.

The job of moving the wood-shed was let to a man yesterday morning. The O. C. furnish him two men and he is to supply the balance of the help wanted to place the shed on its new pegs, (cedar posts), for thirty dollars.

The women's carriage was taken to the depot yesterday for repairs. It is to be newly lined, painted and varnished.

Mr. Clark was engaged with three teams yesterday in moving the new sawyer's family.

One of the tenement houses was shingled yesterday, by Mr. Thayer and others.

Answer to yesterday's conundrum. Because their feet are a head!

Yesterday's temperature—
7 A. M., 43.   12 M., 60.   6 P. M., 45.   Mean 49.

THE O. C. DAILY.

VOL. 3. WEDNESDAY, APRIL 10, 1867. NO. 85.

EVENING MEETING.

Mrs. Miller:—I was speaking of my difficulty with my eyes, when Mr. Noyes remarked that he was conscious of a good work going on in his own physical system, commencing with his stomach. He thought this began with the casting out of the bran-bread devil. A good work was then done.

He said the stomach was the center, and bore the same relation to the whole body, that God does to the Church; it is the creator and distributer of life and health. A good healthy state of the stomach will circulate a healthy tone through the whole system, as that is directly connected with all the ganglia of the nervous system. It is connected with the brain, and from the brain by means of the spinal cord it distributes life and health through all the functions of the body, the eyes among the rest. In the stomach too, he said, was formed that of which our blood was made; and from the stomach it was distributed by means of the blood all through the system to every part. So it is true, in every sense, that the stomach is the center, and that there is the place to look for the beginning of health.

He said in reference to the eyes, that miracles were formerly performed upon them by Christ, for instance, but that God did not repeat himself, and that he did not intend to repeat that same act.— God does not work in an incoherent way, doing a little here for this individual, and a little there for that one, without any connection; but he works from a great center. Our business should be to go back and get into communication with the spirit that performed those cures, such as healing the blind. Christ overcame the principality that produced blindness; and so in every other specific case, he overcame the principality; and finally overcame the devil as a whole. What is wanted is that we should become one by faith with that great spirit.

We go back to that spirit in reference to our souls. We find we must reckon ourselves saved by the faith of Christ; and why should we not do the same in reference to our bodies? The Second Coming, and all our great doctrines and discoveries, have a direct tendency to make us go back and seek the faith that makes us one with Christ and the Primitive Church.

Mr. Noyes said in all his discoveries and searchings after truth, he is in the habit of working from the center outward. He finds that is God's way, and the true way to discover truth.

The threatened writ from Michael Murphy was served yesterday on Mr. Kinsley and Martin, specifying that they refuse to pay for services rendered by said Murphy on Sundays, and extra hours during the visiting season. It is thought that he is lame, from the fact that he was paid monthly, a sum which he accepted without any demand for extra pay at the time of each settlement, and has no account of the time worked, now. After he had moved and locked up the house, he came to Mr. Clark and said, "The law allows me to keep the house thirty days, but it is too bad to keep your new hostler out of the house, and make him walk from Willow Place. As for that Martin Kinsley I would not give him the keys for a million of years."

"Well," said Mr. C. "I don't know much about the matter, and do not want any words with you about it, won't it be best to let the subject drop?"

"Mr. Clark you have always used me well," he replied, "and I have nothing against your hostler, here are the keys, and you can move your man in as soon as you choose, but I will sue Martin, that is what I will." ITEMUS.

WILLOW PLACE ITEMS.—Mr. Millbury, our night-watchman now occupies the little cottage west of the Shop, where Mr. Goakes has lived for two years past. The old house between the cottage and the Shop, is going to take a new stand this spring—a few yards south of where it now is, half a dozen little stakes indicate its future position. A wing will be added on its east side.

Our silk-dyer, Mr. Holland, takes some criticism in regard to, dyeing, thus: "Please be free to find fault with our work, as we are anxious to suit you."

Letter from F. W. Hurd to J. H. Noyes.

140 South 9th St., Brooklyn, N. Y., Apr. 6, 1867.

DEAR SIR:—Your favor of the 1st. inst. was very thankfully received. The party referred to will not answer my purpose, as I wish to be gone from four to six months and get permanent good; nevertheless I am very grateful to you for your interest in my welfare. If I can reciprocate at any time I hope you will give me the opportunity. With love to all of your blessed family and to particular friends, I am yours for Christ and humanity, F. WILSON HURD.

Messrs. Worden, Clark and Conant commence mending their ways to-day, a reform much needed, some think, as the roads are only a succession of jolts and gullies: these are being leveled up and leveled down. Five teams are at work at this, and are drawing stone chips from the quarries at Willow-Place, which are being spread on the road-way surface, which will give a hard smooth track.

News came to us yesterday, that Mrs. Burt's sister Mary Ann, was dead; cause unknown. A. L. Burt has gone there to-day, to learn the facts in the case, though the funeral is not to take place till Friday.

W. G. Kelley started this morning on his regular peddling trip.

Yesterday's temperature—
7 A. M., 47. 12 M., 50. 6 P. M., 47. Mean 48.

THE O. C. DAILY.

VOL. 3. THURSDAY, APRIL 11, 1867. NO. 86.

Mr. Hatch requested last night, the criticism, or any suggestions of improvement of the children's department. Mr. H. was spoken of as being a very good father, patient with the children, and untiring in his endeavors to benefit and improve them. The children too, were spoken of as being in a very good state generally, though some criticism was given of their manners at the table and elsewhere. Mr. Hatch thought there was a lack of responsibility on the part of the family, to check and criticise the children when they were in fault, and some thought that in a few cases among the older ones, there was a want of respect, and giving heed to reproof, when given by persons not immediately connected with the children's department. It was thought too that the children's room was kept too warm, though with their present inadequate means for ventilation, perhaps it cannot well be avoided. It was remarked by some one, that every thing indicated that we were none too soon in building the children a new house.

The wood-house in its new place, stands on cedar posts set in the ground as it did on the old site.— Night before last the posts on the east side were put in position and the building settled to its final place and leveled. The west side standing simply on slight "shores," waiting to have the cedar posts set. The posts on the west side are about ten feet long, half of them above ground. Yesterday morning we commenced to raise the building a few inches higher to admit of adjusting the posts. We proceeded with the utmost care. On lifting it with the "jack" the shore was freed so that it was likely to fall of itself. I took hold of the thing to remove it, when following some sudden curious instinct, I simply readjusted it, placing a prop against the base to hold it in position in case the jack should fail, it would catch the beam, and so prevent accident, then stepped back to watch the work go on, when quick as a flash, out went the jack and down came the timber, which was suddenly arrested by that providential shore. We said, "Thank God for that shore."
Relating the matter to Mr. Parker, the man who has the job of moving the building, he said had it not been for that shore, you would probably have had the whole concern down on your heads.   J. H. B.
[I should have said one half the shed. J. H. B.]

LOVE AND GLUTTONY.

Last spring the robin was welcome, as he came with love in his breast and music in his throat. His brisk and gallant attention to his mate was pleasant to behold. But after a fine honey-moon, his care for his belly, became all absorbing, spoiling his song and making his presence a nuisance, so that he became a subject of searching criticism, and slunk away like a naughty boy, sent supperless to bed. A week or two ago, he began to peep round the corners (as it were) to see if father and mother would forgive and receive him. His whistle was faint, his bearing timid, but as pleasant and forgiving looks were cast toward him he grew bolder; his music became more lively, and his gambols more graceful. Now a flock of redbreasts may be seen on the lawn daily, sporting, making love and collecting the tit-bits, which they seem to eat sparingly, and enjoy with modesty. May they learn by the past.   HOPEFUL.

TALK AMONG THE CHILDREN.—" Won't you help me fix my table," said a little eight year old to another a couple of years older than herself, as she placed her tiny set of China on a little bench on which her kerchief was laid for table-cloth. "Won't you help me make a party and invite the folks."

" No I won't" coolly replied the elder, " you don't think I can waste my time waiting on you ?" quoting the saying which she had heard dropped from some adult. "I am very busy with *my* things, you don't suppose I will, do you ?"

" Yes I should think she might shouldn't you ?" said the first to Lydia, another smaller girl than either of the other speakers. " She is bigger than me and"—

" Well I shant Miss, you needn't tease any more."

" I spose" said Lydia "it won't do any good to say more, she is cross and won't help you, cause she has got her *won't* up."

" I aint neither" said the older, with an air important, "I would help her but she is always so *maticular*."   L.

We had an artist here yesterday, to take a photograph of the tent on the lawn, its interior arrangements, furniture &c., &c., with Mr. Newhouse, his dog and his traps. There were three different views taken, all of which are said to be very good.

Mrs. Chesbro wrote, requesting that her husband might come and make us a visit. She says he wants our advice. We have written inviting him to come and make a visit of a day or two.

It commenced raining yesterday forenoon, and rained quite hard almost constantly, all the afternoon and evening.

The men we hire this year are mostly German, and we find them much more reliable than the Irish.

We heard yesterday of the death of George Vaill.— He died at Bellevue Hospital.

Yesterday's temperature—
7 A. M., 42.   12 M., 46.   6 P. M., 43.   Mean 45½.

THE O. C. DAILY.

VOL. 3.   FRIDAY, APRIL 12, 1867.   NO. 87.

A curious letter was read last night, addressed to F. A. Marks, from Franklin Lewis, a little dried up man who worked for us two or three years ago. He wants to join the Community. He says, " I came out to Mich. to join with my brother in raising hops ; chances are good, plenty of hop-poles cheap, but my mind is every now and then thinking I would enjoy myself better with your people. I could bring with me about $200, &c. Fred you know what I am, and I want you to intercede for me—talk with Victor, and Mr., I can't think of his name, was one of the super-intendents in the Fruit-department, and get them interested in my favor and give me an answer as soon as you can. Frederic I have been thinking of this thing ever since that woman left me." [Meaning his wife.] " Write me as soon as you can, it will save me the expense of getting *hop-roots*."

F. A. Marks replies, that, " As our Community is a religious society and admits, as members, only those who understand its principles thoroughly, and your letter shows a total ignorance of such acquaintance, it will be almost unnecessary to say that you may as well buy your *hop-roots*."

WILLOW-PLACE ITEMS.—Just now the Foundry is out of a job. The water-pipes and silk machines are all done, and it is rather early to begin on hop-stoves and Children's-House window caps, so the foundry men are having a brief respite from their usual routine.

The hum of the saw-mill may be heard on Willow Street at any time of day or night, now-a-days. The hired sawyer commences work at noon, and runs till midnight or thereabouts. Then Mr. Kinsley takes it, and keeps it going till noon again, frequently assisted by D. F. Knowles, especially during the forenoon.— Over 22,000 feet were sawed out last week. At the present speed, two weeks more will conclude the necessity of night running.

Mr. Bradley who has worked in the drying-clothes department since about the 20th of February, finished his course there, last Saturday. Mr. Horace Burt who has been Mr. B.'s assistant, continues in the business, with Mr. H. R. Perry for a helper.

Mr. Bradley takes charge of the strawberries the coming season. He reports three acres uncovered.— The Wilsons look promising ; of the other kinds he remarks " this deponent says nothing" there being six varieties. The vines were mulched so heavily last fall, that they appear as fresh and green as though they never had passed through a winter—four loads of straw having been taken off the plantation.

Mr. Dewy, a musician from the depot, was here yesterday, tuning the pianos. While at work in the Hall, he heard some one say, " *haw buck*," whose voice sounded familiar. He stepped across the stage, and out on to the balcony, to see who it was. He smiled approvingly, on seeing it was Homer Barron, as he said " Halloa ! if there isn't Barron, your depot man, driving Oxen." " How are the mighty fallen," he didn t add audibly, though possibly he thought it.

Mr. Clark reports for yesterday, one team drawing lime for making mortar to plaster the wing of the Burt-house, and repairs at Willow-Place—one team drawing iron for the shops, and fourteen Cases of traps drawn to the depot.

GREENS, GREENS.—Mr. Nash's mantle has fallen on many shoulders judging from the numerous green-parties, now-a-days. We think it will be difficult for him to pass for the *green man* at O. C. hereafter.

Four hundred dollars worth of cows and other stock have been sold this week.   ITEMUS.

Mrs. Morris and her sons are still here. The oldest one (eighteen years old, instead of sixteen as before reported) has gone to work in the Trap-Shop while he stays. He is a tinman by trade. Mrs. M.'s visit is prolonged, that she may hear from her husband, who has gone to Vineland, and ascertain what his plans are for the coming season, and whether he intends to meet her at this place. Mrs. M. has had several talks with Mr. Cragin, and seems to be getting pretty deeply interested in the Community and its principles.

Chicago, April 9, 1867.

ONEIDA COMMUNITY, Gents:—Ship by rail six No. 3, gent's leather Lunch-Bags; three No. 5, do. do. do; three No. 3, gent's cloth Lunch-Bags, and three No. 5, do. do. do.

What is the prospect for your fruits this year, and where had we best send our order, so that we may be sure it will be filled ?

And we are &c. yours, Stanton & Co.

We had orders through H. R. Perry for five leather Lunch-Bags.

Mrs. Burt arrived in the night.—E. S. Nash, also some time yesterday.

A RIDDLE.—What is it that should fit closely, in order to set loosely ?

Yesterday's temperature—
7 A. M., 38. 12 M., 40. 6 P. M., 40. Mean 39½.

THE O. C. DAILY.

VOL. 3. SATURDAY, APRIL 13, 1867. NO. 88.

A. L. Burt said night before last :—" In conversation to-day at the dinner-table at Canostota, something was said about our system of life, and I mentioned the fact that we paid considerable attention to education. There was quite a talented lady present, who seemed to apprehend that this would lead to considerable difficulty. She suggested that when we get persons well educated, they would find our sphere not large enough for them, and would be swinging off on their own hook, and deserting us. I answered that we made education entirely subservient to religion, or the true relation to God, and when that was once established there would be no difficulty, or danger, in giving all, the highest degree of education."

The Horticulturists commenced plowing and subsoiling the strawberry ground to-day. Four acres and a half are to be set to strawberries this spring. They are to be cultivated in hills, set one foot apart in the row, the rows thirty inches from one to the other. Two acres and one half are to be Wilson, seven eighths of an acre Triomphe de Gand, one eighth of an acre Agriculturist, one half acre French Seedling, and one half acre of these kinds for a plant bed. Four new kinds are bought, which are to be tested on our grounds the coming year, viz : *Juconda or Knox's seven-hundred, New Jersey Scarlet, the Philadelphia*, and *Durant's Seedling*. The last two are quite new.

The following notice has been posted in the vestibule at the new house for several days past. It has been signed by a large portion of the members of the family :

" TO WHOM IT MAY CONCERN."

" Those having charge of the strawberries, propose the following arrangement for the family beds the coming year : Each person desiring to have berries which they can feel free to pick when they choose, during the berry season, can have twenty-five or thirty hills, near the fence and road just north of the new proposed fruit-house. A stake with each persons name written thereon, will be placed at the end of their bed. The strawberry *superintendent* will set the plants, cultivate, mulch and hoe them, leaving the cutting of the runners for those who can do it.— All persons who would like a bed on the above conditions will please affix their names below, and *signify what variety they would like* to have planted. These berries are for next year's picking."

The job of moving the wood-house was finished yesterday, we know, for we saw Homer hand Mr. Parker, the man who has been doing the job, a roll of green-backs, as we were going to supper last night.

Rain and wind have prolonged the job, and made handling plank and timbers, muddy, disagreeable work. However Mr. P. appears to be a good natured, jolly kind of man, so that nothing has seemed to mar his good feeling.   ITEMUS.

WANTED TO JOIN.

Wednesday, Mr. Cromwell came up from Troy to join the Community. He was a young man and well to do in the world ; knew nothing about us however, never had seen the CIRCULAR, or read a word of our writings ; had heard that we were "a good people and Free-lovers, and that was what he believed." " No we are not Free-lovers as that term is generally understood ; and we required a thorough acquaintance before admitting to membership." " How long does it take ?" " It took me two years and I lived up this valley only about fourteen miles and used to come here quite often." " Had we a constitution and laws ?" " We had not. We printed a paper however." A copy of the CIRCULAR was given to him and then he left. His visit lasted about five minutes.   U.

WILLOW-PLACE ITEMS.— Young Mr. Morris finds employment over at W. P. I noticed him yesterday morning, "pointing dogs," snugly sandwiched between little Nell and golden-haired, celtic Tona.

Night before last about ten o'clock, our Vermont neighbor, Mr. Macoy and family arrived. He called at the house first, but not raising any one, he went to the shop, and after considerable altercation with watchman Millbury, was finally let in. He wanted the key to his newly bought house. Mr. Campbell sent him to the house again, to get Mr. Kinsley up. This was at length accomplished.

The Macoys refused to accept of a night's lodging in our house, probably fearing to crowd us. Accompanied by Mr. Kinsley they went to their own house, effected an entrance at a window—opened their goods, got out their beds, and by 12.30., got fairly stowed away for the night.

As Mr. Worden was riding home from Willow-Place yesterday, sitting in the back part of the wagon on a tub of butter, the driver, unexpectedly whipped up the horses, and the sudden jerk tumbled him out of the wagon, heels over head, and hurt his right shoulder and hip considerably, so that he is not able to use his right arm at all. He has gone down to the depot this morning to see the doctor.

Abram and C. A. Burt went to their Aunt's funeral yesterday.—Mr. Burnham arrived in the afternoon.

Yesterday's temperature—
7 A. M., 43. 12 M., 51. 6 P. M., 53. Mean 45½.

THE O. C. DAILY.

VOL. 3.   MONDAY, APRIL 15, 1867.   NO. 89.

BUSINESS MEETING.

Mr. Underwood proposed that the room left vacant by the office folks, be divided into two dressing-rooms for visitors. Refered to Messrs. Woolworth, H. Barron, C. W. Underwood, Mrs. H. C. Noyes, Chloe Seymour and L. T. Waters.

Mr. Ackley wished to have something done about the garden at Willow-Place. Such vegetables as are wanted fresh, might be raised there. A committee was appointed to attend to the matter.

Mr. Kellogg said he had been a member of the horse-committee for four or five years, and would like to resign. Mr. Woolworth moved that Mr. K.'s resignation be considered when we have bought all the horses we want. Approved.

Mr. Woolworth said he had a request to make similar to Mr. Kellogg's. Thought perhaps he had better defer it till next week. Mr. Kinsley. "I think you had better bring forward your business now." Mr. Woolworth. "Well, I have been a member of the committee on distribution of help three years or more, and would like to be discharged." Mr. Kinsley. "I move that Mr. W.'s resignation be considered when we have distributed all our help." Decided that Mr. Woolworth be relieved, and Mr. Hatch appointed to fill his place.

F. Marks reported that Mr. Rockwell wanted five or six acres of land subsoiled. Referred to Mr. Clark and Kellogg.

Messrs. Conant, Clark and Kellogg were appointed to stake out gardens for our tenants.

Mr. Noyes wrote the following, which he designs to have printed, to show to our visitors, and send to those who may request to make long visits:

"NOTICE TO VISITORS."

"We esteem it a privilege as well as a duty to entertain strangers and to open our doors hospitably to all. And in order that we may do this on the largest scale, without burdening too much our own resources, it is necessary that visitors should observe the following limitations:

"1. Visits extending to several days should not be made without previous agreement by correspondence, and should not be continued beyond the term agreed upon.

"2. Visits not thus arranged for, should be limited to the day on which they are made, and should not require a night's lodging.

"These rules, of course, can be modified in special cases, if good reasons appear. ONEIDA COMMUNITY."

Mr. Noyes has been a good deal stirred up, lately, about our visitors, not only here, but at Wallingford. The Morrises have stayed a long time, and Saturday a stranger lady, named Raymond, thrust herself in upon us without any previous notice or correspondence. She said, as she came in, "I don't know but I am intruding." Miss Chloe did'nt reply, for she thought it was true. Mrs. R. is an M. D. and is acquainted with S. P. Andrews, Mr. Sands and Newbold, and last, thought not the least, with Amasa Carr. She says Mr. C. speaks well of the Community, but thinks Mr. Noyes arbitrary. She and the Morrises will leave this afternoon.

Mr. Noyes thinks that now, as we are to have more room soon, we shall be able to take in several new members, and the question before the family is, who shall be invited? He thought we needed to make the boundary line between us and the world more distinct, and seek by prayer and fasting, inspiration to direct us in our choice. A meeting was held in the back parlor yesterday, to consider and talk over the matter, and another will be held to-night.

Our people planted potatoes, and sowed peas Saturday.—Mr. Aiken starts for New-York to-day. He expects to be gone about a week.—We have beautiful weather these days, inviting to out-door sports and rambles.—The classes for Elocution are all dissolved. Thanks to Mr. Underwood for his indefatigable labors with the women's class.—One hundred bushels of barley were bought and drawn home Saturday. The farmers intend using that amount for seed.

The Horticulturists went as far toward plowing strawberry ground Saturday, as to get into the field with plow and teams, but finding themselves short of help, and much rubbish to be removed, ground leveled where potatoes had been buried, &c., &c., the job was deferred till to-day.

Mr. Hatch has taken down this morning, the little shed, formerly called the dry-house, which stood in front of the room occupied by the children. The occupants of the Mansion House are glad enough to have it removed.

Mr. Worden's arm and side are some better. The examination of the doctor resulted in the discovery that no bones were broken—no joints dislocated; only a severe sprain, which he would soon get over if he was careful.

Mr. Burt came yesterday forenoon, and he with Mrs. B. went to New Boston in the afternoon, to do what they could toward settling Mrs. B.'s sister's estate.

A place for playing croquet, has been prepared on the lawn south of the Mansion House, and yesterday, play there was lively all the afternoon.

Answer to the Riddle in Friday's DAILY. *A trap-dog.*

Temperature Saturday and Sunday—
7 A. M., 35. 12 M., 50. 6 P. M., 47. Mean 44.
7 A. M., 43. 12 M., 65. 6 P. M., 58. Mean 55.

THE O. C. DAILY.

VOL. 3.   TUESDAY, APRIL 16, 1867.   NO. 90.

Sunday was spent by the Office hands in moving the Business Office, from the New House to the place that has lately been fitted up for it, in the south wing of the Store. There was a very helpful spirit manifested by many not immediately connected with the department, and for an hour or two, things moved pretty lively. The moving of the safe was the thing of the most importance, but it was rendered quite easy by the help of no less than twenty men, a pair of oxen and a stone-boat. Things assumed a fair degree of order at half past twelve.

Our Office is divided into two rooms—the first or outside one is fifteen feet by twenty—the second or inner Office about twelve feet square. In the outside room, is a high desk extending across it from east to west, in the centre of which is a paying counter. It is furnished with drawers and racks for books and is grained to correspond with the room. In the same room is another high desk, smaller and of a plainer pattern, for our depot agents, and those who wish to write letters occasionally.

In the inner room we have a low double-desk—a large cupboard with numerous pigeon holes, in which to pack away files of bills &c., and shelves to keep our stationary and various other things. The estimated cost of finishing the rooms, making desks and other fixtures is not far from $200. The rooms are light, airy and quiet—three things which we appreciate and highly value. We feel like dedicating it to a good spirit and desire it always to be a place where Christ and the angels will find comfort in being present with us.   A.

We ought always to be cheerful. But says one, "how can I be, when I am sober and under great pressure of doubt and temptation?" That is the very time to be cheerful, for in this, you will surely dispel the clouds of unbelief that oppress you. Christ says, "be of good cheer, I have overcome the world." A cheerful heart, bright as a May morning, sparkling with gratitude to him, will provoke to love. Its radiance will extend to others. Who does not like to see a bright, cheerful face and smiling countenance? Try it, and see if you are not successful.   z. v.

Mrs. Morris and sons left yesterday, with the expectation of remaining at the station till they could hear from Mr. Morris, and learn what he would have them do, and where go. Their place at the west is rented, and they do not have possession till fall.— They have passed the winter in Ohio with their friends, but do not wish to return to them, and would prefer to remain at the East for the summer, could they get board and employment. Mrs. Morris gave Mr. Cragin

ten dollars. Mrs. Raymond on leaving, gave Miss Chloe a five dollar bill, and wished to have the CIRCULAR sent to her.

Mrs. Susan Dunn's niece is still here, though she spends most of her time at Julia's. She expects however to leave for Bakersfield Vt. to-morrow. The following note from her was handed in, and read in meeting last night :-

                                    Oneida, April 15.

DEAR FRIENDS :—Being some acquainted with you through the CIRCULAR and many dear friends here, I desire to become stronger in the truth through inspiration, and to be taught of God to do his will as it is in Christ. I confess Christ in me a savior from all sin, and through him to have eternal life. I confess my union with Mr. Noyes and the Community.

                                    MARIAN DUNN.

WILLOW-PLACE ITEMS.—The photographic artists from Oneida, were at work over our way yesterday. One view was taken from the ridge-pole of the old barn, north of the shop, and another from a platform in the field south-west of us. We caught a glimpse of the "negative" of the north view; it really looked grand.—C. C. H. has started the Rollers again, on a lot of large springs. A set of pulleys are being fitted up for the machine, so as to make it run more slowly, in order that some new hand may learn.

A Mr. Doolittle from Clinton, writes to know if a lecture from him on the " Reminiscences of the War" will be acceptable to the Community. He states that he will charge us nothing but his expenses in coming and going. Mr. Woolworth wished to know the mind of the family in reference to it. A few expressed a wish that he might come. Mr. Noyes said "tell him that we will pay for the use of his Hall, and furnish him with an audience."

By his request Mr. Kellogg was criticised last night, which was mostly of the kind we all like best, viz. commendation. It was thought he had improved very much of late—had grown young—was a man of good judgment, and was reliable in every respect, loves improvement, plodding, &c. Much love was expressed for him. The meeting was closed by a "secular" song, "The Monks of old," sung by H. W. B.

Now that the Business Office is removed to the store building, it is proposed to have a place in the Library to deposit letters for the mail. This will save persons the trouble of going to the Office at a late hour, and after it is closed for the night.

Mr. Newhouse reports good success in trout-fishing last Sunday. He caught twenty-five of the "speckled beauties," the most of them nice and large.

The new croquet ground was spoken of last night, and persons were exhorted to continence in respect to sports and pastimes.

Two teams were engaged yesterday moving the Dunnings. They have gone to Clinton.

Yesterday's temperature—
7 A. M., 52.   12 M., 74.   6 P. M., 70.   Mean 65⅓

THE O. C. DAILY.

VOL. 3. WEDNESDAY, APRIL 17, 1867. NO. 91.

Oneida, April 17, 1867.

DEAR O. C. DAILY:—The CIRCULAR, I notice, wishes information respecting the "numbers, objects, and characteristics of the new hive," meaning the new Community family at Willow-Place, which the CIRCULAR understands is already established.

Before proceeding to enlighten the *Luminary* of *Mt. Tom*, we will just say that its understanding that a family is already established there, is a *mis*understanding, such not being the fact—yet we hope it will be true by the first of May. As the family therefore is still in embryo, we cannot say precisely what number of members will compose it, but somewhere in the neighborhood of thirty-five all told. But we can speak more accurately a month hence. The objects of this new scion of the O. C. are three-fold. 1st. To shorten the range of our home influences upon our extensive and increasing businesses at W. P. 2nd. To save time, perplexity and expense, of thirty or more efficient workers of our own, in going to and from their business. 3rd. A family there will enable us to exercise a more vigilant outlook for the Community interests in that locality, and to exercise a better influence upon our employees.

A word more about a Community family. Materials for such a family is one thing, and a very good thing too, but the family itself is quite another. A Community family implies an organization with vital functions and members; a father and mother, a family meeting every evening, family criticism as often as its members desire or require it, in order to secure the perpetual blessing of unity, brotherly love, and a spirit of improvement; and whatever else may be instructive, edifying, musical and refining to our life and character. These ordinances we call the vital organs of a Community body or family, and without them in healthy exercise, a Community with us, would be simply a *body* without a soul, an institution not very productive of peace and happiness.   c.

Howard Junction, Ill., April 8, 1867.

FRIENDS OF THE COMMUNITY, ALL HAIL!—It is most two years since I have seen any of your members, but I have kept booked up in regard to your success in the acquiring of the things of the world, and spiritual growth, through the mediumship of the CIRCULAR, which has found its way to me, though I have been wandering from town to town through the principal places in the northern and western States, for we have not yet the privilege of singing to our "*South Brothers.*" I rejoice in your, thus far, successful experiment in the *new life*, and pray you may continue to be a bright and shining light, and draw all the world unto this eternal truth.   *   *   *

The little gift I received when about to leave you, my daughter still carries, reminding us of *your good works.* I refer to the traveling-bag, and I have preached many a sermon in favor of progress, taking this Bag for my text.   *   *   *

I hope to be able to call on you on my way East. We are all tired and need the rest and quiet of home. My place is Lynn Mass. I have another one in Hutchinson Minn., and I trust we have a home in the hearts of the American people.

God hasten the day when we shall see eye to eye and all shall know the Lord.

"'Tis coming at the step of time,
    And this old world is growing brighter,
We may not see its light sublime,
    Yet high hopes make the heart throb lighter.
We may be sleeping in the ground,
    When it awakes, the world in wonder,
But we have felt it gathering round,
    And heard its voice of living thunder.

        'Tis coming, coming, coming,
        Yes, Yes, 'tis coming."

God bless you all and the rest of mankind and bring us to the light.

Yours truly,   JOHN HUTCHINSON.

Mr. George Fitch, formerly a resident of Putney Vt., and an old schoolmate of G. W. N., called here yesterday, with the intention of stopping over one train.— He enquired for Mr. Noyes, who invited him to spend the night, which he accordingly did. He resides at Grand Rapids, Mich.—has been to Putney, and is now on his return. He appeared much pleased with his visit, and expressed a good deal of interest in our prosperity. Said it surprised him to see a body of persons in such a world as this, not at work for themselves.

It commenced raining yesterday and rained all night. This morning the lawns are clothed in a mantle of green, and the buds on many of the trees are nearly ready to burst forth. The rapid change from cold weather to such summer-like days as we are now having, seems magical.

Music seems to be reviving, somewhat, among us.— Before the close of meeting last evening we had two quartette songs, a solo by Abram, and a piece of music on the piano, by A. M. Hatch, and after meeting, some chants and anthems, in which our visitor, Mr. Fitch, joined.

Digging was commenced Monday for the iron aqueduct. Two hired hands are engaged in the work, with Mr. Abbott to oversee it.

Yesterday's temperature—
7 A. M., 50.   12 M., 72.   6 P. M., 62.   Mean 64½.

THE O. C. DAILY.

VOL. 3. THURSDAY, APRIL 18, 1867. NO. 92.

Mr. and Mrs. Burt did not return from New-Boston, where they went Sunday afternoon, till yesterday. They report a settlement of Mrs. B.'s sister's estate effected, in which Mrs. B. took for her share, a note of $1000, due next Oct., besides some portion of her deceased sister's personal effects. There were many unpleasant things connected with the settlement, owing to Mr. Lee's hard state and unreasonable conduct, but both Mr. and Mrs. B. feel greatly relieved, and are thankful that every thing is closed up between them and Alonzo. Mrs. B. told her brother that she never expected to see him again. Mr. Cragin said in reference to the whole affair:

" Mr. Noyes thought it would be well to suggest to the family whether it would not be expedient or advisable for Mr. Burt to see Leonard hereafter, and if he finds him disposed to do justice to the Community, and take a manly position, let him have that thousand dollar note. The business men might think of this.

" As the case now stands, there is no obligation on the part of Mr. Burt or the Community, to make this proposition to Leonard, as he has thought best to take such a course, as to exclude generosity on the part of the Community toward him. If this course should be thought best, it is suggested that we might let Mr. Smith have control of the money for Leonard's benefit, so that it will not be wasted by him.

" I like the suggestion to give Leonard this money, because it will enable us to show to the world that we are not afraid of what the devil can do to us, and that we can turn round and be generous to our enemies.— I think, too, it is worth a thousand dollars to get Mrs. Burt free from the oppression she has been under from the Lee family."

Mr. DeLatre:—I like the proposition very well; but on the other hand I must confess I have a poor opinion of Leonard's character, and fear he might take this as a bribe from the Community. I hope he will be made to feel that it is no such thing.

Mr. Cragin:—I rather think Mr. De Latre's fear is groundless. Mr. Smith reports that the difficulty with Leonard is already settled, and there is now no possibility of his making any move to injure us. Then this money comes from God, or the death of a woman rather than from the Community. It is to be remembered that Mr. Burt labored with this sister, to induce her to make her will in favor of Leonard. This she was disposed to do, but neglected it. If she had done so, the whole $3000.00 would have gone to Leonard. As it is, I should like to have it go to him as a sincere gift from the Community.

I do not feel myself, that Leonard is a reprobate,

that God cannot save. I don't wish to put myself in that position toward him. And then his wife is a very fine woman, and liked and respected by all our folks who have formed her acquaintance. His children are the grandchildren of Mr. and Mrs. Burt, and may be said to have some claim upon them. I should like to go to Rondout, myself, as the agent of the Community, and carry this note and deliver it up to Leonard.

While we think it best to be always cheerful, at the same time there must be a sober, interior, earnest, prayerful spirit, that is on the watch to hear the voice of God, the whisper of the invisibles, who are ever ready to inspire our hearts with faith, love and heroic action. The true spirit has in it both elements, and so blended, as to produce a state of heart, that is always edifying, whose influence is good, radiating the spirit of both elements, the serious and mirthful combined.—Christ was a perfect representative of these two elements, the serious always predominating. He was ever serious, and yet we see flashes of the mirthful, beautifully manifested from time to time. We can learn of him.   z. v.

The big Lawsuit, Mich. Murphy *versus* Martin Kinsley, comes on to-day at ten o'clock A. M., at the depot. The case should have been tried a week ago, but for some cause was adjourned. Myron officially subpenaed the witnesses for the defendent, (a half dozen of the men, two women and three of our employees,) paying each twenty-five cents to secure their attendance. We will give results tomorrow.

Miss Marion Dunn did not go yesterday as she expected. The following note from her to Mr. Noyes will show how her mind is working. Mr. Woolworth remarked after the note was read, that her case would be considered to-night:

MR. NOYES, DEAR SIR:—After your kind counsel last evening, I felt stronger in the faith, to become a faithful seeker after the truth, as found in Christ, and a resurrection of him in my heart. I wish to stay here and be one of the true believers and seekers of a soft strong heart. I trust you as my father and leader, and pray God to help me conquer my old enemy, and live for the right.   MARION DUNN.

Mr. Meeker's article on " Oneida Community, Free-Love, Free-Lovers and Perfection," published in Tuesday's " Semi-Weekly Tribune," was read last night in our meeting, and gave us a good laugh.

At our 7 o'clock reading, we have commenced the book, Dixon's " Holy Land."

Yesterday's temperature—
7 A. M., 46. 12 M., 47. 6 P. M., 59. Mean 51½.

THE O. C. DAILY.

VOL. 3.   FRIDAY, APRIL 19, 1867.   NO. 93.

EVENING MEETING.

Miss Marion Dunn's application for membership was considered in the meeting. Mr. Woolworth said:

"This appears to be quite an interesting case. It is thought to be a genuine birth of a Community child, and that she really belongs to us by conversion.— When she first came here there was considerable interest in her case; but afterwards all seemed to give her up, as she visited with Julia Hyde a good deal, and had considerable sympathy with her, while she was apparently, rather indifferent toward us and the truth. But for some reason she became interested, and her heart was won by the truth.

Fidelia :—So far as I have been able to judge, I have felt that her conversion was sincere. I think there has been a great change in her spirit within a week or two.

Mr. Underwood had studied her case and learned something of her history. She had been affected by the truth, somewhat, years ago in Vermont; had a strong affection for her aunt, and had sympathized with her a good deal. Her aunt brought her up.— She afterwards went to Ohio to live with her uncle, and in a measure got away from the truth. In coming here she had been brought into closer, more vital connection with the truth than ever before. He felt that she had been led all the way along by God, and that she could not escape; that her conversion was real, and that she will remain steadfast to the truth.

Many of the Vermonters expressed a good deal of interest in the case, and thankfulness for the way it had turned out. Then Mr. Woolworth said: "Are we ready to receive her as a child of the Church? Those in favor of doing so, please say, Aye." [Unanimous vote to receive her.]

Mr. Burnham writes from Troy, April 17th:

"I am pleased with the gradual openings for trade which present themselves to me here in Troy. Smith and Brown, one of the heavy houses of the city promise to try our silk the next time they are in need. Mr. Brown made some respectful inquiries about the O. C. and I was able to bear good testimony touching our religious and social principles. I gave him the last two numbers of the CIRCULAR. Geo. Bristol & Co., another Dry Goods house who buy silk of us, are very friendly. Dodge Brothers, Shoe Manufacturers, declare that they do not hesitate to buy silk of us, because they feel assured that what the Community does, will be done right. The evidence with me is increasing every time I pass over my route, that the business public are coming to place implicit confidence in the word of the O. C. This gives me boldness, and at the same time it stimulates me to seek humility and faith, that I may *ever* represent the true Community spirit."

The Horticulturists have at present, nine hired men. We have hired some women to tie raspberry vines. I sometimes have my patience tried considerably, in teaching some of the men how to tie up vines, especially one man who cannot talk English.

Yesterday while at work, he would scatter the strings about the vineyard. I kept telling him not to do so; but 'twas of no use, he would look up, laugh, and say "string, string." Finally I took some strings from the basket and scattered them about; he looked at me; I pointed at them, then at him; then shook my head. He seemed to comprehend at last, and I had no further trouble with him.   J.

April 17, 1867.

MY DEAR SIR:—Your very kind note just came, and I will share your generous hospitality Monday next—will lecture on Tuesday evening as you may arrange, and according to the custom you mention. I will get in Troy at 9½ and take the first train via. Schenectady to Oneida, expecting to be met there by your conveyance. I send blanks for notices if you wish to use them, erasing as much as you choose.

Truly yours, WM. A. DOOLITTLE.

Mr. Noyes suggests it would be a popular thing for us to invite our neighbors, and the public if we please, to come and hear Mr. Doolittle's lecture. We can furnish some musical accompaniments and make a pleasant thing of it. Mr. D. was Chaplain in Sheridan's army. If we satisfy him, it will amount to giving a valuable, entertaining lecture to the public.

The Justice's Court of Oneida, yesterday, took the "evidence" in the suit of Mich. Murphy vs. Martin Kinsley, but adjourned the "summing up" and decision till Wednesday next. The second suit, of Murphy vs. Community cows, for trespass or cabbage stealing, was wholly adjourned till next Wednesday.— Truly, "Littergation" does "move careful."

Our people did not get home from court, yesterday, till nearly sunset. The women thought that waiting at the tavern all day, was rather dull business. They were not called into the court-room at all.

House-cleaning commenced last Monday, with two of our women and one man. We presume help will be hired to assist, before it is finished.

Yesterday's temperature—
7 A. M., 43. 12 M., 45. 6 P. M., 47. Mean 45.

THE O. C. DAILY.

VOL. 3. SATURDAY, APRIL 20, 1867. NO. 94.

WILLOW-PLACE—TRAP-SHOP.—The inspection of a lot of 14,000 Muskrat Traps commenced yesterday. A hired man is learning the art, under the special supervision of S. Newhouse, *formerly an experienced Trapper, and for twenty-five years past, well known as a maker of Traps.* The nuts used in making traps have been obtained at Southington Conn. for several years past. They are quite costly, and this spring, experiments are being made in the direction of manufacturing them ourselves. —Mrs. Story, the widowed daughter of Mrs. Macoy, commenced working in the Silk-Factory yesterday morning.

The fine weather yesterday afternoon tempted us to a ramble, and following our deepest attractions, we, together with a sister for company, wended our way over to Willow-Place. On reaching the house and not seeing any one to direct us, we entered at the front door. We were never in the house, and entirely unacquainted with its construction. We went from room to room, but found no one except a man engaged in plastering; every thing was in disorder. On penetrating to the kitchen we found our sisters, Mrs. Conant, C. A. Reid and Jane Abbott, busy as bees, cheerfully doing up the work after dinner. In the present stage of repairing the house, the kitchen does double duty, answering the purpose of a dining, as well as a cooking-room. After resting ourselves, we went out and took a look at the pond, and thought what a nice place it was for bathing and other purposes, and so pleasant to look at. On seeing the boat we were tempted to try our skill in rowing as we used to of old; but alas! it was fast locked. After calling on Mrs. Macoy, who was once a pupil of ours for two seasons, and whom we had not seen for thirty years, and stopping at the trap and silk, factories a short time, and screaming into the ears of the girls there, a few questions which in turn were answered in screams, we started for home, thankful that we could appreciate more fully, the labor that was necessary to be done on the house and grounds, in order to make the place a fitting abode for a Community family. We would mention here, that some of the chambers are finished and painted, and look very neatly, and repairs below are in rapid progress, so that the house promises when finished to be a pleasant, attractive place.

Five hundred strawberry plants were set yesterday afternoon, and six or eight men are setting plants to-day.

Forty-five hundred plants came from L. L. Whitlock yesterday afternoon; wonder when they were shipped! Can H. G. A. tell? They appear well, but look as though they had been some time on the way; possibly the Express Company in N. Y. need a friendly expostulation. Hope to have twenty thousand sent the first of next week; (though possibly more are on the way.) Will H. G. A. attend to that? We intend setting from five to six thousand per day, if we get the plants, and the weather is favorable. L. H. B.

A Welch woman named Jones, came here yesterday and wanted to stay over night, and longer if we would employ her. She has been living at Dansville and on her way here had her pocket picked, of $25, and so to get on, she had to pawn her clothing on the way. She has formerly lived at Gerrit Smith's ten years. We shall give her money enough to carry her to Utica, this afternoon.

Bags ordered to April 17th., 69 dozen.

As orders still accumulate faster than we can fill them, we have extended the time of labor to eleven, instead of ten hours a day. Our hands, on our proposing this extension, assented unanimously. By this arrangement we make three days work extra a week. N.

The following placard is being printed, to post in public places in our immediate vicinity.

"A Free Lecture at Community Hall, by Wm. A. Doolittle, (formerly Chaplain in Sheriden's army), Tuesday April 23. Subject, Reminiscences of the War. Lecture to commence at 7½ o'clock, P. M.

We notice in the "*Democratic Union*", published at Oneida, eight or ten items of Oneida Gossip, taken from the CIRCULAR.

The cellar for a new tenement house has been dug at W. P., and a commencement made for drawing sand for the children's new house.

A new fancy two horse wagon, made by order, for plying between here and the depot, was brought home yesterday; cost unknown.

Mr. Clark reports a new horse bought a day or two since costing $190.00.

Traps ordered the past week, 72 doz.

Yesterday's temperature—

7 A. M., 33. 12 M., 54. 6 P. M., 50. Mean 47½.

THE O. C. DAILY.

VOL. 3. MONDAY, APRIL 22, 1867. NO. 95.

BUSINESS MEETING.

Mr. Kellogg wanted to know if we should keep the cows belonging to our workmen in our pastures.— There are now seven or eight, and the number is constantly increasing. Refered to Messrs. Cragin, Clark, Kellogg, Kinsley and Conant.

Mr. Campbell said there was great need of a cistern at Willow-Place for the Silk department. It should be placed under the building where it would not freeze. Charles Cragin, Mr. Kinsley and J. H. Barton appointed committee to act upon it.

Mr. G. W. Hamilton said that we had bought a boat load of coal which is waiting at Albany for navigation to open ; but as only a part of it is good hard coal, he wanted to know whether more should be bought now. The only coal that we can get now is stock coal, which is not as good as fresh. Mr. Campbell thought we had better buy the best coal we can get. It would be cheaper in the end, though we should pay fifty cents per ton more for it. Voted to wait till we can get good coal before buying.

Mr. Hatch said that the small children in going to the privy, met with visitors who talked with them and asked them questions. He had been by there when he knew the children were there and strangers talking with them, but could not do any thing about it.— He suggested that a temporary necessary be built for the exclusive use of visitors. The matter was refered to Messrs. Woolworth, Kinsley, Underwood and A. L. Burt.

Mr. Hatch thought his appointment on the committee for distribution of help was more than he could well attend to. Mr. Clark thought he was a very convenient person for that office, as his business kept him generally at the house. It was finally agreed that he should try it for a few weeks, and if it proved unsatisfactory, some other appointment would be made.

J. S. Freeman was criticised Saturday night, by his request, and last night the following note to the family was read.

"I would like to take this opportunity to make public some of my recent experience. For some time past my mind has been directed to the doctrine of Salvation from Sin, with the purpose of making it practically my own. I have believed that entire Salvation was possible in this world, and that I should have it ; but I can now say, it is mine. I believe that Christ is in me, and that his victory over sin and death is mine ; his righteousness is mine. Not that I have done some great thing, I have only ceased "going about to establish my own righteousness," and have submitted myself to the righteousness of God. I am very thankful for the expression of kindness and criticism given me last evening. J. S. FREEMAN."

In meeting, last evening, Mr. Cragin brought up the subject of having the children have better accommodations for sleeping the coming summer. He thought the bakery ought to be moved away, as the room over it was made uncomfortable by the heat from the chimney and through the floor. Some suggested that the Tent-room be given up to the children and the folks that sleep there, move into the Avenue rooms. After considerable talk, Mr. Noyes proposed that all the partitions in those rooms be taken away, and it be converted into one great hall, for the use of the children. The great objection to those rooms, as they are, is a lack of the means of ventilation. A committee was appointed to meet on the spot, in the morning, and decide what shall be done.

In the confusion we had in the office Saturday forenoon, consequent upon setting up and printing the hand-bills for the lecture, some things that occurred last week, and should have been reported, were forgotten.

Martin sprained his ankle Thursday night, which prevented his going to New York Friday, as he intended, and as Louise Vanvelzer was to accompany him on her way to Wallingford, she concluded to go, Friday night, alone. In the evening before she left, she gave us some excellent music on the Harmonium. —Martin's ankle is a good deal better.

Mrs. Bushnell received a long letter from Mrs. Dascomb Friday in which she says, "I do not need to tell you that my eyes are opened to see the truth, and that I am rejoicing in the freedom and fulness of the Gospel. *The veil is rent*, that concealed the inner sanctuary, and I can no longer rest down in the letter, in *dead works*, now that the spirit of Truth opens to me the heaven of God—now that Christ is come in the flesh.

She has confessed Christ publicly, and her union with Mr. Noyes and the Community, and expresses a wish, (though not with much expectation that it will be granted) to join the Community at no very distant day.

We had the song, "The Pacific Railroad" to close the meeting last night.

It is a dark morning and rains without any intermission.

Mr. Kelley returned home, Saturday, and in the meeting last night, gave a brief sketch of the incidents of his trip, which we presume will be reported.

ERRATUM.—In Saturday's DAILY toward the bottom of the third page, for three days work extra, read eighteen days.

Temperature Saturday and Sunday—
7 A. M., 54. 19 M., 60. 6 P. M., 53. Mean 59.
7 A. M., 49. 19 M., 53. 6 P. M., 53. Mean 41½

THE O. C. DAILY.

VOL. 3.   TUESDAY, APRIL 23, 1867.   NO. 96.

REPORT OF THE COMMITTEE ON CHILDREN'S DEPT.

The Committee on improved accommodations for the children's department, respectfully submit to the consideration of the family the following changes and alterations:

"The room over the bakery would answer very well as it is, by enclosing the chimney with a wood casing, leaving a vacuum of a foot or more between it and the chimney, allowing the heat to pass into the room above. The next change proposed, was to enlarge the north room by removing entirely, the three bed rooms now connected with it, so as to make one large room for a general play room, meeting room, &c., &c. The size of it would be 15½ by 36 feet, containing four windows on the north, one on the west and two on the south; affording ample means for ventilation and good air. For additional sleeping accommodations, a door could be cut through at the foot of the chamber stairs, into the room now occupied by the two Messrs. Kinsleys, Mrs. Underwood and Lady Ellis. This room with the one occupied by Mrs. Jane Kinsley, or some other room in that vicinity, and one up stairs occupied by Mr. Ackley, would be all the rooms the children's department would require, in connection with the one leading out of the room over the bakery. The north room will overlook the small yard, that is to be, bringing the indoor and outdoor play grounds in close proximity to each other. And by a little expense of paper and paint, the north room can be made quite a presentable place for the exhibition of our little ones, of whom we need not be ashamed, and in whom, as Community children, we have a growing and an abiding interest.

"P. S. Room No. 5, now occupied by Miss Thomas, with two children, will be retained by the children's department."

———

Nr. Noyes has been collecting the statistics of the Community children, which were read last night, for the edification of the family.

Mr. N. remarked to Mr. Woolworth (which Mr. W. reported) that "These statistics, which have been read, are but a small part of what he intends to bring out. He is going on to give a statement in respect to the children generally, that were born out of the Community, and get at all the facts and statistics in relation to their previous state, and their present condition, showing the effect of their Community training and education.

"He says what we have done in the line of propagation, is but a small part of what has been done for the children of the Community, as a whole. Almost the whole of the generation, between twenty and thirty, were formerly in the children's house, and had a course of training and discipline there.

"A. J. Davis tells what condition our children are in. I suppose he has found it out by clairvoyance. I believe he claims that he looks right into things here."

Mr. Cragin:—If he does so he must have looked at the children through very weak, sore eyes.

———

Willow-Place Works, April 22, 1867.

DEAR MR. NOYES:—I want to express my gratitude to God and to you under God, for the salvation that we men are realizing from the marriage system of the world. When I think of what would have been the probable consequences if I had remained in the world, and fallen into the marriage net, it fills my heart with thankfulness and softens it. The least I can do is to offer myself to you and the church, to make whatever you can of me, which I do heartily.

Yours lovingly,   G. W. Hamilton.

———

An arrangement has been made by H. G. Allen, with the People's Line of Steamboats, whereby goods of all kinds passing between Oneida and New-York will be carried on the river for fifteen cents per hundred pounds. All persons sending goods, as freight, up or down the river, should mark them "Care of People's Line."   **E. S. B.**

Our new member, Miss Dunn, is one of our type-setters, and the two girls Charlotte Maria and Annie Kelley, after more than twelve months service, are relieved, and engage in work in other departments.— We should judge that they had made good improvement for girls of their age. Rosamond is about commencing to learn the art, under the supervision of Miss Sophronia, who belongs to our regular corps of Office hands.

———

A letter from Victor to his father, which was mailed a week ago, and was sent to Wallingford, was read in meeting last night; also Mr. Noyes's reply. Poor boy! he is tired of his confinement, and would doubtless think that his father's answer to his letter, was "Long, long, long, on the way."

———

We were told by one of the Bag-shop hands, that Jerome Petre had been hired as evening watch at the mill, so that our men can be relieved of that duty.— We are to pay him one dollar per week for his services.

———

Why is a king's servant like matrimony?

———

Yesterday's temperature—
7 A. M., 44. 12 M., 50. 6 P. M., 44. Mean 46.

THE O. C. DAILY.

VOL. 3. WEDNESDAY, APRIL 24, 1867. NO. 97.

Condemnation, discontent and fear, are three of the worst enemies we have to contend with. They stand ready to contest every step we take in our progress towards heaven and full fellowship with Christ and the Primitive Church. The devil as the representative of these three great dragons "was a murderer from the beginning," and is now waiting under condemnation for the past, and under a tremendous pressure of discontent in the present, with a "fearful looking for of judgement and fiery indignation" that shall destroy his kingdom. Under these circumstances, he seeks to insinuate himself into our spirits and make us feel as he does in this matter. But we shall overcome, for "greater is he that is in us than he that is in the world."

Testimony for Christ and the truth, will give us the victory. Let us assume that the past is forgiven, and that we are contented with the present, and that there is a glorious future before us. Condemnation, discontent and fear, belong to the devil, and not to us. z. v.

Some remarks about butter, which enters so largely into our daily fare, may not be thought amiss by the Community, from one who buys and generally provides it.

He would say that it is his intention *always* to provide a good article—but that it is sometimes difficult to obtain the same—that he buys the best he can in the limits of the neighborhood round about, and from all he gets he selects what he judges best for table use, and allows the balance to go into the kitchen for cookery.

It is his impression, that on account of the number of cooks and persons engaged in cellar and kitchen, the butter gets more or less mixed and mingled, so that offensive butter comes before people at table, from that cause, occasionally.

All should know that good butter, exposed for but a short time to the peculiar atmosphere of a cook-room, will be impaired in flavor and quality.

Hence the need of observing something like the following:— Keep the table butter distinct from the other, and as closely from the air as possible.

If necessary to use or put on table, parcels the second time, have them taken up speedily and repacked or placed in the coolest and best condition for keeping —and by all means don't mix two sorts—or butter of different firkins together.

Within the past six months, preceding the first of the present, $3,109.44 have been paid for butter alone, at the counter of the business office.

M. L. WORDEN.

Sitting by the window, yesterday afternoon, we saw Ann S. Bailey pass by, in close conversation with a gentleman, very fine looking, and remarkably white and delicate. Some one told us, that it was Mr. D. the lecturer, who had just arrived. We wondered, and were not a little tried, that a stranger should find any of our women, so familiar and easy of access.

Then came another report, which was, that it was not Mr. D. but a cousin of Ann's. This relieved our mind somewhat, but upon enquiry, no such cousin could be found. At last the secret came out. It was our friend and quondam fellow-helper in the office, E. M. Mallory, who had donned male attire, and was taken round by Ann, to see the curiosities of Oneida life.

The whole affair, as it was talked over after the lecture, caused a good deal of merriment for the girls, and was well calculated to dissipate the unpleasant thoughts that might linger in the minds of some, after passing with the lecturer over battle-fields, and listening to the groans of the wounded and dying.

The lecture last night was pretty well attended, the house being more than two thirds full. It will be needless to attempt a description of it, as we noticed D. J. Bailey taking notes. Suffice it to say, that we heard enough of the blood and carnage of a battle-field, to last us a life-time. It was quite a relief, when he ceased his tale of horror, long enough to give us a few specimens of negro praying. The exercises were opened by a piece of music on the piano, played by A. M. Hatch, and "Who'll save the left," by Abram, and at the close the song so popular with us, "The Pacific Railroad" was sung.

We heard Mr. Worden say that the last lot of potatoes he bought, cost one dollar per bushel, and one man of whom he expected to obtain some, would not sell them short of ten shillings per bushel.

A Mr. Docker, a man afflicted with the shaking palsy, staid here last night. We will speak more of him tomorrow.

Mr. and Mrs. Burt left on the night train for Wallingford. They expected to stop at Kingston and see Leonard on the way.

It is quite cold to-day, and is snowing a little, as it did also yesterday morning.

Answer to yesterday's Conundrum.—Because he is (*high menial*), hymeneal.

Yesterday's temperature—
7 A. M., 34. 12 M., 40. 6 P. M., 40. Mean 38.

THE O. C. DAILY.

VOL. 3. THURSDAY, APRIL 25, 1867. NO. 98.

VISITORS.—Mr. Joseph Decker has a family in Port Leyden, N. Y. Eight years ago, he was at work in the *Tribune* office, sleeping by day, and toiling by night, under a hot gas-light, when he was suddenly struck down and became a trembling and jerking paralytic. A German by birth and highly educated, an accomplished musician, linguist and politician, of great power of will, and strength and endurance of mind and body, all places of honor seemed open to him, until he was driven upon hidden rocks and wrecked .

A printer by profession, a chum of Speaker Colfax, when the latter edited the *South Bend* (Indiana) *Register*, afterwards, for several years, a *Bohemian*, roaming all through the Southern States, going over-land to California, and thence to Australia, working here and there as fancy dictated, acquiring the *lingua* of the Chinese, in San Francisco, where he helped to issue a paper in four different languages, he has had a large experience of mankind and many vicissitudes. Now, he thinks he does well if he succeeds in hitching himself along over a mile of space in a day, selling a patent kerosene burner. He tells touching stories of exposure and suffering on the road. He set out for Vernon, yesterday forenoon, in the storm, with much quieter nerves, and a calmer and happier countenance, however, than he had when he presented himself at our door, the night before.   U.

Our lecturer, Mr. A. Doolittle is a resident of New-York, thirty years of age; has three children, girls, the youngest, two, and the oldest, eight years of age—separated from his wife three months ago, and she has taken the three little ones, and gone back to her friends. Alledged cause of separation, uncongeniality ; real, adultery on his part.

He left this morning. The Community offered to pay his expenses in coming here, or to give him a nice traveling bag. He chose the latter, and selected a handsome "promenade" Satchel, which he said he would present to his mother.

Mr. D. expressed his appreciation of the kind hospitality of the Community, and complimented the women for their modest demeanor.

The carpenter's and joiner's departments were brought forward for criticism, last night. The criticism turned, principally, on A. L. Burt, the chief and head man of the business. He has improved a good deal, and much love was expressed for him. Still, he has defects of character which need to be corrected—old weaknesses which yet cling to him, and which, in his present position, he should be in earnest to over-come. The post he occupies is a trying one, attended with many perplexities, which calls loudly for patience, and he should take a position in his business transactions, that would ensure the sympathy and co-operation of the family.

THE RAIN CONCERT.

Millions of tiny raindrops
   Are falling all around ;
They're dancing on the housetops,
   They're hiding in the ground.

They're fairy like musicians,
   With anything for keys,
Beating tunes upon the windows,
   Keeping time upon the trees.

A light and airy treble
   They play upon the stream,
And the melody enchants us,
   Like the music of a dream.

A deeper bass is sounding,
   When they're dropping into caves ;
With a tenor from the zephyrs,
   And an alto from the waves.

Oh ! tis a stream of music,
   And Robin don't intrude
If when the rain is weary,
   He drops an interlude.

It seems as if the warbling
Of the birds in all the towers,
   Had been gathered into raindrops,
And was coming down in showers.

               .R.

We have hired a woman to assist in house cleaning. The old Tent-room, and other rooms on that floor, are undergoing a thorough purgation, to day, under the superintendence of E. F. Hutchins.

The evidence in the second suit, Murphy vs. Community, was taken yesterday. No verdict on either of the suits, has yet been given, as the law allows the justice four days to decide.

Our first report from New Haven was received, yesterday, and read in meeting last night. Thanks to the writer.

They are papering, to-day, the inner room of the old Business-Office, and the bedroom attached.

Mr. Bradley reports that one acre and a quarter has already been set to strawberry plants.

Mr. Aiken returned from New-York, yesterday afternoon.

Yesterday's temperature—
7 A. M., 39.   12 M., 44.   6 P. M., 40.   Mean 41.

THE O. C. DAILY.

VOL. 3.   FRIDAY, APRIL 26, 1867.   NO. 99.

The meeting hour was entirely taken up, last night, with newspaper reading, letters and reports, and yet we had no outside correspondence, except two letters from Mr. Bloom to Miss Nun, to the first of which, Miss N. wrote a reply, which was also read. Mr. B. wishes to come and see his boys, as he calls them, but as Miss N. told him they did not wish to see him, and there was no use in his coming, he submitted, with a better grace than we should have expected of him.

A LONG YARN.

Quite a number of our family, including Messrs. Noyes and Woolworth became personally interested in a long yarn last evening—not a Sailor's yarn but Aunt Sally's yarn, the ball of which was carelessly amusing itself on the floor during the family meeting hour. But straying too far from its base, it was suddenly caught among numerous walking beams, as they were carrying their respective owners out of the Hall, involving Aunt Sally's knitting work in other business than building up a stocking.

Indeed, a sudden *emeute* broke out, each combatant doing his best to extricate himself from the wooly antagonist. G. W. H. joined Aunt Sally's forces, and did manly service in rescuing the unfortunate ball from its perilous condition, and just in time to save its abduction to the enemy's camp. But the scene was highly amusing to lookers on, when the battle of disentanglement was at its hight, reminding one of the saying, that, "It is much easier to get into difficulty, than to get out of it." Any fool can do the former, but it takes a wise man to get out of it, unharmed.

C.

TO THE COMMUNITY.

I have felt severely judged by the late criticism of the gossipping spirit, and wish in the most effectual way to separate myself from it. Nothing too bad can be said of it. I confess Christ a savior from it. My heart is thankful for the late disclosures, though it has caused me great suffering. I have no recollection of ever hearing of some things that were charged to me, but I have said enough, and plead guilty to the charge of gossip, and trust that that spirit has now received its death blow.   JANE F. KINSLEY.

Yesterday, while talking with the little ones, about God being every where, in the thunder, rain, &c., little Harold says, "Does God make it thunder?" and "where does it come from?" After satisfying his mind about it, he says, "Where does the rain come from?" Ans. "From the clouds," "And how does it get up there?" Little Harley replies, "it comes from the Ocean and Sea;" then with a look of wonder and amazement, he exclaims, "well, how does it get up there?"   M.

We noticed, a few days since, a man at work in different rooms, putting on plastering where it had fallen off. Taking all our buildings, with the constant jarrings to which they are subjected, by so many persons coming and going, this kind of repair, has to be often repeated.

Why is a person thus employed like a woman mending pants?

A MIDNIGHT HYMN.

The authorship of the following beautiful hymn of trust is unknown. It was found treasured up in an humble cottage in England:

In the mid silence of the voiceless night,
When chased by airy dreams the slumbers flee,
Whom in the darkness doth my spirit seek,
 O God! but Thee?

And if there be a weight upon my breast—
Some vague impression of the day foregone—
Scarce knowing what it is, I fly to Thee
  And lay it down.

Or if it be the heaviness that comes
In token of anticipated ill,
My bosom takes no heed of what it is,
  Since 'tis Thy will.

For O! in spite of past and present care,
Or anything beside, how joyfully
Passes that almost solitary hour,
  My God, with Thee!

More tranquil than the stillness of the night,
More peaceful than the silence of the hour,
More blest than anything, my bosom lies
  Beneath Thy power.

For what is there on earth that I desire,
Of all that it can give or take from me?
Or whom in heaven doth my spirit seek,
 O God, but Thee?

As a part of the new goods have arrived, there is a rush of the women to the store this morning, for dresses; calico, muslin, and thin worsted, for summer wear.

Messrs. Delatre and Ellis took a handcart yesterday, and cleared the highway, from the large barn to the mill, of all the unsightly rubbish that had accumulated the past winter.

Our people have been straightening the fence north of the new burying-ground, which improves the looks very much, we are told.

We have charming weather again to-day, the air clear and the sun shining brightly.

Yesterday's temperature—

7 A. M., 39.   12 M., 50.   6 P. M., 52.   Mean 47.

THE O. C. DAILY.

VOL. 3. SATURDAY, APRIL 27, 1867. NO. 100.

WILLOW-PLACE.—A man has been hired and set to learning the art of "running the roller," the most arduous part of trap-making. It is expensive teaching a new hand; and, with an eye to economy, the present pupil was furnished with strips of wood, instead of costly steel, which he "rolled" with all formality, for the first half day. This caused some joking on the part of the hands, but it evidently "paid." He is said to do very well now in rolling springs, and promises to meet the demand.

The experiment of making No. 1. springs from sheet-steel, is progressing. A curious visitor, yesterday or the day before, would have found an interesting group at work "plating" a lot of these springs, now undergoing the necessary manipulations. G. W. Hamilton was "heating," C. C. Hatch "putting them through," and Mr. Newhouse "running the press." Presided over by such geniuses, why should the experiment not prove a success, and greatly reduce the labor and cost of the process of spring-making?

I join heartily with Mrs. Kinsley in her efforts to put down gossip. When living in the world, I have had my indignation kindled against this spirit, on witnessing the evil effects of it in neighborhoods, and surely if it is not to be tolerated in the world, it should not be with us, who are striving to put down evil in every form, and whose every day lives should be under the governing influence of him who hath said, "Do unto others as you would that others should do unto you," and "by love serve one another," not by gossip and tattle.—Confessing Christ my ability to overcome all evil, I would desire more than ever to put myself under the watchful care of the church, that in some way I may become useful in the advancement of Christ's kingdom. Yours for truth and righteousness. S. UNDERWOOD.

Since the above was written, my mind has been aroused to take a more searching look, at this spirit of gossip, and it is not enough for me to say that I very much dislike it, but I must say, that I hold it in abhorence, and confess my separation from it. I feel the spirit of Christ strong in me to assist my earnest efforts in keeping it down. While striving to shun even the appearance of evil, I ask the prayers and sympathy of the church. S. UNDERWOOD.

Yesterday a man wanted some raspberry plants and I went over to where they were, with him. He said he would take some black-caps. I uncovered them and put some in his basket; finally he said he did not want that variety, was sorry he put me to so much trouble &c., mildly remarking that "Some people were born to have trouble." He said he would take

the Philadelphia and wanted large plants; he then said he wanted some small ones, because they would grow better. He said he knew Mr. Thacker and Mr. Newhouse, and kept repeating it. I felt as though he was trying to get them cheaper, but after a while he ceased and took a few plants. I noticed two little boys he had with him which were quite disobedient, and I was shocked to hear him use profane language before them. I felt thankful that our children were brought up to fear God, and were saved from the vices of the world. s.

FOUR YEAR'S GROWTH AND PRODUCT OF THE AYRESHIRES.—A three year old heifer and a three months bull calf, were bought about four years ago this spring, and last summer, another bull calf was bought. Besides these, we now have four full blooded heifers, from three to thirty months old. The oldest heifer is giving milk. There are eleven half breeds, which will be milked this summer. We have ten half, and one three-fourth blooded, this spring calves.

Total at the present time, seven full blooded animals, twenty-one half, and one three-fourth blooded; twenty nine in all. ACCOLA.

Noticing three or four teams passing several times a day, the field where we were setting strawberry plants, loaded with slabs, cut to four feet length, we felt a little curious to know, from whence so many slabs came, and whither they were going. On investigation, we learned that they came from Willow-Place sawmill, and go to the carpenter's shop, to be converted into lath for the children's new house, and other buildings. On the green at the north end of the mill, the bag and carpenter's shop, most of these slabs having been converted into lath, lie piled up, having also been tied into bundles, containing one hundred each. U. O.

Mrs. Waters reports a great improvement in the spirit of the women in respect to getting cloth for dresses. She thought the term "rush," as used in yesterday's DAILY, would not convey a correct impression to the other Communes, as most of the women went to the store only by her invitation, and were modest and moderate.

Mrs. Miller's report, last night, of Mr. Noyes's talk on the spirit of gossip, and the need there is of placing new members under the immediate guidance of the wisest and best, will be read with a great deal of interest. Recent developments here, certainly render such a step imperative.

Last night Mr. Noyes actually "talked" in meeting, for the first time since he came on his present mission. The sound of his voice sent a thrill of delight and thankfulness through one heart, at least; and probably the feeling was common to all.

The Reception-room was cleaned yesterday, and the new carpet put down.

Hired masons are now laying the cellar wall to a new tenement house at Willow-Place.

Yesterday's temperature—
7 A. M., 47. 12 M., 66. 6 P. M., 62. Mean 58½.

THE O. C. DAILY.

VOL. 3.　MONDAY, APRIL 29, 1867.　NO. 101.

BUSINESS MEETING.

Shall we paint the dwelling house at Willow Place, this spring? It was left to the discretion of the committee on finances, as to whether it will be painted this spring or next fall.

How far shall we lend our horses to our hired men? There was some feeling that we were doing better by our hired men, in lending them teams, than by our own folks. We are often put to considerable inconvenience, by not having carriages and horses, because they were lent to hired men. It was thought we had better charge for the teams, as by that means it would curtail the demand. It was thought that, hired men wanting horses, should apply to the foremen of their department, and then have him communicate with Mr. Clark.

Mr. Hatch would like to know, if the large class of boys, at the children's house, would go to school this summer? The impression of the board was, that it would be well for the boys to go to school one half of the day, and then be at liberty to work with the men the other. Matters were left, however, to the discretion of Mr. Hatch.

Mrs. Miller reported, last night, the following:—"It will be remembered that it has been proposed that we should organize a new and special department, for the care and education of new members. Mr. Noyes has nominated Mrs. L. A. Thayer as head, or mother, of that department. He remarked, that he thought she had natural gifts or qualifications, that fitted her for being a mother, particularly for new members. She has exercised her gifts a good deal in the past, perhaps in her own strength and on her own responsibility; and now he thought of making her a Community servant, in the business. He thought her talents would be brought into exercise and be edifying to all.

"For some time past, Mrs. Thayer has withdrawn from any particular oversight of new comers, and has sought deeper interior experience. I should think such a preparation would well fit her for the present appointment.

"Her business will be to study the wants of this department and find out who are proper subjects of care—those that have joined us within a year. She should learn their cases and wants, and have a motherly watchfulness for them. She would be their adviser in respect to their reading. She is very familiar with all the Home-Talks and other writings of the Community, and has been a loyal member of the Community from the beginning. She would be able to advise new members about their reading, and about their associates or companions in business, and in other respects.

I think she has proved herself capable and worthy of this office."

[Mrs. Thayer was unanimously voted into the office of mother, to new members.]

Mr. Cragin: It may be remarked, that Mrs. Thayer will keep open with the central members of the Community, and receive advice from them in regard to her course.

Mr. Kelley called at the Asylum, Saturday, when at Utica and had a talk with Victor and Dr. Gray.—There are still manifest indications that Victor is not yet dispossessed of the spirit of insanity, and his letter to his father received last week gave us the same impression. The Dr. says now, that he will not, probably, entirely recover under six months. Mr. Noyes's letter to him was read, which touched the heart of the Community with deep sympathy for Mr. Noyes, and a prayer that if it is God's will, the bitter cup he is called to drink, may speedily be removed from his lips.

F. A. Marks offered himself for criticism. He has a good deal of responsibility and much to do with hired help, and needs the help and advice of the family. In the course of the criticism Mr. Cragin proposed that the heads of the different departments, should meet and consult together through the season as often as once a week, and relate their experience in dealing with hired help.

WILLOW-PLACE ITEM.

One bale of raw stock valued at $1175, was bought last week, and one "book" weighing four or five lbs. of a new kind of silk, known as Re-reeled Tsatlee, to experiment with. Despite the late rise in gold, raw silk is held at very reasonable prices, and the importers complain as usual that they are losing money.

We thought yesterday, as we saw the fishing rods pass our window that the fish in Oneida Creek would have a hard time; but we heard afterward that the tempting bait offered them was cautiously refused, and so the fishermen and women returned empty handed.

It is whispered round, (though not officially announced,) that the suit Mich. Murphy vs. Martin, is decided in favor of the latter.

Martin starts this afternoon for New-York. His ankle of course is nearly recovered.

Answer to the conundrum, "Why is a man patching up broken plastering, like a woman mending pants?" Because he is repairing (*breaches*) breeches.

Temperature Saturday and Sunday—
7 A. M., 46.　12 M., 41.　6 P. M. 34.　Mean 41¼.
7 A. M., 35.　12 M., 43.　6 P. M., 46.　Mean 41.

THE O. C. DAILY.

VOL. 3.　TUESDAY, APRIL 30, 1867.　NO. 102.

We hear some of our enthusiasts exulting in their success, with the much esteemed *Arbutus*. The plants are actually in blossom, although set out late last year, after a journey from Connecticut. The lucky individual whose unswerving faith in the experiment, led him to persevere in the enterprise, describes the entire gratification of his *motherly* feelings, on first beholding these pearly tokens of the travail of his soul. Henceforth, that pretty little nook of ours, ("Spring Grove"), will have one more charm.

East Palmyra, N. Y., Apr. 24, 1867.

Mr. W. H. Woolworth, Dear Sir:—Yours of the 20th was received in due time. I thank you for your kindness to me and regret the circumstances that prevent me from being one of your number, during the coming summer. At present I am suffering with chills and fever, which totally unfit me for labor.— You need not put much dependence on my help at present.

With best wishes for you and yours, I remain as ever,　　　　　　　　　　　BELL HUDSON.

Last night, when just on the edge of sleep, I was startled by a man saying in a loud voice: "*John Noyes, up comes John Miller.*" Then he took me by the hand, and led me where I saw John Miller half reclining on a bench, and partly asleep. The man said—"*He sleeps finely this forenoon.*" Then the vision disappeared, and I awoke with a rush of love for John Miller, in my heart.　　　　　　　　　　　　　　J. H. N.

WILLOW-PLACE.—By the sudden breaking of a strap, belonging to the drop in the Finishing shop, the "monkey," or hammer, unexpectedly descended, alighting upon the middle finger of George Waters, who was working the machine. The man hastily withdrew his finger, leaving the skin above the last joint, behind.

A sink-room 18 feet long and 8 feet wide, has been partitioned off, in the south-west corner of the Trap packing-room, for the use of the Silk department.

The Willow-Place garden has been prepared for planting, and yesterday, we put out several varieties of raspberries. We intend setting sixty-one grape vines, of our best kinds, so that in a few years the family there, can have all the grapes they want. Several kinds of strawberries have also been set.

A few minutes spent at Willow-Place sawmill. A log having been rolled on to the carriage, adjusted, and the dogs driven into the two ends, the saw starts with such a clatter, that I was curious to learn how many cuts it makes per minute. Taking out my watch I attempted to count, but did not succeed till I first got my hand in tune with the saw, and counted the down beats of my hand. Three times counting came out three hundred and eighty-four down strokes of the saw per minute. The log was sixteen feet long; each board sawed, gave eighteen feet board lumber. The saw cut one board in one and three fourth minutes. It cut a little over forty-eight one hundredths each downward motion. Half a minute, usually, was consumed in returning the carriage and re-adjusting the log for the saw, all of which was so quickly performed that the saw once started, does not stop till the log is finished. After deducting time spent in getting logs on to the carriage, and the sawed lumber off, this would give over three thousand feet for every ten hours.— Were there no hindrance, the saw would cut 4,800 feet in ten hours.　　　　　　　　　　　　U. O.

Our hostler is an Englishman, and before coming to this country, he worked in a brewery. He says it was his practice to drink thirteen quarts of beer, daily, and the effect was to increase his weight to 230 lbs., and that was his weight when he commenced working for us. The hired men plagued him considerably, especially when he was mowing, because he sweat so profusely. After working for us a year, his weight gradually decreased, till now he weighs only 150 lbs. He has proved himself an industrious man.

The family had a rich treat of maple sugar, last Sunday. It was not melted, as heretofore, but simply broken up and placed upon the table, ten ounces being apportioned to each individual. The sugar was brought from Vermont. As we design to melt our portion, we thought of that bank of snow in sight, on the West hillside, that still defies the warm sunshine and the rain, as we should like to "Cool on the snow the waxen treasure," &c.

The carpet has been taken up, in the Lower sitting-room, and the room cleaned; and so, as the floor was uncovered, last night, a dance of an hour after meeting was proposed, which was quite lively, Charles Van and C. A. Cragin playing the violin. They are putting down the new carpet to-day.

Most of the cherry trees on the sand hill have been taken up to make room for a pear orchard.

Silk sales since last reported,　　　$3,079.00
Bag orders "　　"　　"　　　$　272.10
　　　　　　　　　　　　　　W. G. K.

Yesterday's temperature—
7 A. M., 49.　12 M., 54.　6 P. M., 44.　Mean 49.

THE O. C. DAILY.

VOL. 3. WEDNESDAY, MAY 1, 1867. NO. 103.

EVENING MEETING.

Mrs. Miller:—I would like to offer for criticism a spirit in which I have been involved with others—that of sucking Mr. Noyes and letting him do most of the thinking and talking, and waiting on inspiration for us all. I feel that this is wearing upon him. We are making an unnecessary demand upon him; and this attitude of ours does not tend to develope inspiration in us. If we really want to help him, and work with him, we must have independent inspiration, and not make him furnish it all for us. I feel that we ought to be able to add to his comfort and edification, and not demand that he shall be talking something for us all the time. That is a spirit we should all seek to get rid of.

Mr. Reynolds:—I think we can all have a spirit of edification, so that we can speak to the edification of Mr. Noyes and of one another. I desire to have that spirit.

Mr. Woolworth:—God wants mediums, or vehicles of his spirit, and a great many of them too. He is not dependent on the great and mighty things of this world; he can use the weak things in a way to confound the wise and the mighty. I know we can offer ourselves to God and become mediums and instruments of his spirit.

Mr. Cragin:—Mr. Noyes came to my room, yesterday, and threw out a suggestion for me to think upon; and now I will throw it out here for the family to consider. It was to have a Bible-class, for an hour or so, in the middle of the day—say from half past twelve till half past one. It would be free for all to attend who chose, but there would be nothing legal about it. It would be more especially adapted to new members; and it could also be open to outsiders, and the visitors that call to see us during the summer. Heretofore we have had music for an hour, or three quarters of an hour, all through the summer; and why not now, have a Bible-class in its place, that will be edifying to ourselves and possibly to those outside?

This idea struck me pleasantly. I confess, I have a new appetite for getting hold of the spirit of the Bible, and the spirit of those who wrote it. We know that the whole system of Communism, and all the doctrines of that system, which form our platform of faith, and even the truths of our social system, comes from the Bible, and are found there in spirit. We ought to be able to clearly demonstrate to people, that we stand on Bible ground. I should be glad to have all our young people be able to prove that all our doctrines, however offensive to the world, are from the Bible; and that the fruit these doctrines produce, is good fruit.

However, I won't enlarge upon the subject to-night. I hope the family will think about it, and pray about it, and see if we are prepared to take such a step, and make such sacrifices as may be required for carrying it out. Perhaps to-morrow evening we can talk about it some.

———————

A party of three, headed by the veteran angler, B. B., visited last Monday, the trout-brooks in the valley of the Sconondoah, a few miles South-east of the Community domain, and for a few hours indulged in their favorite sport. The morning dawned propitiously; but alas for fickle April! before the first trout had hardly been bagged, a cold drizzling rain swept down upon the party, and seemed to chill the trout even, for it was, seemingly, with the greatest reluctance that they quit their covert places for the bait; and then their torpor and indifference, so unlike their usual alert, positive movements, made the bite hardly perceptible. But notwithstanding the draw-backs, the party, by perseverance and the most alluring attractions, induced forty-three trout, (how handsome they were!) of more than medium size, to quit their cold isolation, and incorporate themselves with a higher life.   H.

———————

A certain little boy, one day, lost his new hammer, and after searching every nook and corner of the room, he exclaimed in a flood of tears, "I have lost my little hammer! I cant find it *any where*—*God knows where it is, but I know he won't tell me.*"

———————

Quite a nice door-yard fence is being made in front of the rooms occupied by the children. The yard is considerably larger than the old one and the fence is on a range with the chain-fence at the north end of the Mansion House.

———————

If May does not announce her advent with blushes, she does it at least with many tears, as the clouds are pouring down torrents of the watery element upon us this morning. Vegetation smiles gratefully, for the favor, and in token of her approval, puts on her very best attire.

———————

A vote of thanks was given to H. A. Noyes, last night, for furnishing us with so much that was interesting, of the sayings and doings of her uncle, W. C. Bradley.

The trio from Wallingford, Mr. Thacker, Mrs. Allen and Charlotte Leonard, arrived safely yesterday afternoon.

ERRATUM.—In yesterday's DAILY, on the third page, fifth line from the top, for three hundred, read two hundred.

Yesterday's temperature—
7 A. M. 49, 12 M. 60, 6 P. M. 49, Mean 59½.

THE O. C. DAILY.

VOL. 3.   THURSDAY, MAY 2, 1867.   NO. 104.

EVENING MEETING.

Mr. Noyes presented his ideas in writing, last night, on the proposed Bible-class, after which the following remarks were made:

Mr. Woolworth:—It will be a new thing to start a protracted meeting and make it interesting in the summer. If the churches got up a revival, they could not carry it through the summer, but had to wait till the busy season was over. Isn't that so, Mr. Cragin?

Mr. Cragin:—Yes, sir, they had to give way to the flesh and let it have its protracted meeting. The ideas presented by Mr. Noyes, interests me very much indeed, and they are the true ones to carry out, if we undertake the work, and it looks encouraging and hopeful to me. All that have spoken about it, seem to feel a lively interest in the movement. It will demand faith on the part of the whole family. As Mr. Noyes says, we must avoid the evil he has pointed out; and by doing so, we shall secure the good, and have a series of meetings that will have the true ring to them. I am confident that the thing can be so conducted, by a company of artistic managers, as to bring into a course of meetings, the whole past history of Communism, in such a way as not to have it appear obtrusive or very prominent. We have ample means for presenting a variety, and as he says, have a very acceptable meal every day. I think, hitherto, we have allowed our light, here, to be "hid under a bushel," I was going to say; but perhaps we have not had the lamp lighted and in good operation till now. If this Community is the candle that is to give light to the world, then we ought to put it *on* a bushel where people can see and feel it, and not hide it *under* a bushel.

The world is evidently calling us to speak in meeting. No doubt they will flock here more this year than ever before. G. W. N. has written that he has commenced the pamphlet that Mr. Noyes proposed to have got up, and that he is going to put into it, the article in the *Berean* called "Two Classes of Believers." That article is really our platform. Those familiar with it will remember that it takes believers in a crude condition, or state, and carries them along into higher and higher classes still, till they are in the resurrection. It takes persons in the sinful state and carries them on an improved railroad track, upon which cars are run, bearing them forward from one station to another, till they are perfected in Christ.

The article in the *Berean* above referred to, was then read, after which the meeting closed.

It is very interesting to notice the spiritual education our children are receiving. At their meeting yesterday morning, they were asked to report what they could remember of the evening meeting the night before, and so one and another reported what they could remember, and among other things, what Mr. Hamilton said in his letter, about faith and believing. On being asked to explain what they understood by faith—one says "it is to believe in God." "Very well, but I want you to illustrate it in some simple way so that these little ones can understand it." "Well if Mr. C. should say that on a certain day he was going to Utica rain or shine, if we believed his testimony, we should have faith in him."

In speaking of fellowship, they were asked what it meant? one says "it means to get near to each other." "What, when you children get near together, is that fellowship?" "No sir," replied several promptly, "we must get near God, and to those better than we are, who will improve us."   M.

An able Divine in speaking of well authenticated miracles, said that the greatest of all, was Jonah's swallowing the whale, and its remaining in his belly three days unharmed. One of the deacons, observing the ludicrous mistake he had made, stepped up to his pulpit, and pulling him gently by his coat-tail, whispered in his ear his great mistake, telling him he thought he would like to correct it. "What mistake asked the minister?" "Why, you said that Jonah swallowed the whale, when you meant to have said, that the whale swallowed Jonah." "No matter, no matter," replied he, "that only makes the miracle the greater."

A short time since a box containing a dozen cans of fruit, was sent to Mr. Holland, of Willimantic, as a token of our appreciation of his continued kindness in giving us all the information in his power, about silk-making. Acknowledging the present, he added, "Your Lombard Plums, I have always thought, since I first tasted them, were superior to anything in market; they have less of the dried fruit flavor, than any other."   C.

Mr. Woolworth's announcement, yesterday, at the dinner table, of C. S J.'s admission to the New York Bar, was followed by the usual demonstration of light movement of the feet. We congratulate him on the successful termination of his course of study. He will be pleased to hear of Mr. Noyes's proposal for him to accompany G. W. N., to London and Paris.

The Hall was cleaned yesterday, though it rained incessantly all day. The sun shines however at intervals, this morning, but it is rather cold.

A young man of seventeen or eighteen years, a nephew of Mrs. Kelley is here on a visit.

Yesterday's temperature—
7 A. M., 58.   12 M., 56.   6 P. M., 64.   Mean 59.

THE O. C. DAILY.

VOL. 3.   FRIDAY, MAY 3, 1867.   NO. 105.

VISITORS.—We had a Chicago man here yesterday, Mr. Haines, a lawyer, and at one time Editor of the *Legal Advertiser*, a paper that we exchanged the CIRCULAR for. He wanted to see Mr. Noyes. I told him that Mr. Noyes could not talk with him, as he had difficulty with his throat; but he said if he could see him *he* would do the talking. I invited Mr. N. in, and introduced him to Mr. H., who introduced him in turn to his wife, another lady and her son who were present. He told Mr. N. he was sorry he was in such poor health, to which he replied, that he hadn't been in better health for thirty years, and that his trouble was all in his throat, which he had worn out by talking; "but," said he "I am waiting for the resurrection." Saying this he left the room.

Then Mr. H., wanted to know if he could talk with me; I told him he might, and we sat down and talked, and he bored me pretty badly before he got through; I was glad Mr. Noyes had escaped him.

I found he was very much set against the marriage system, he even went so far as to prefer Mormonism or polygamy, as an evident improvement on the marriage system of this country. He was quite a rambling talker—wanted to give me his ideas in regard to the different forms of government, and what he considered the right kind. I saw that he evidently came more to be listened to than to hear, yet he expressed a very decided interest in our movement; I believe he still takes the CIRCULAR. He thought we should by all means, become incorporated. If we only lived in the West, he thought he could help us to get an incorporation act, that would be a real benefit to us. I told him we had a lawyer who had just been admitted to the New York Bar, and that we were going to set him about the business by and by. He wanted our people to carry them to the depot, which we did, charging three dollars for our services.   U.

Since my late criticism I have been looking over my past life. I find that a spirit of egotism has been very strong. I wish to be rid of that spirit, and to do that, I offer myself to the family, to be dealt with as they may think best. My prayer is that I may have grace to show a true spirit of obedience. I hope I shall be able to prove by deeds, that it is the true desire of my heart to become a true Community man. I confess Christ a soft heart that will feel the spirit of the Lord at all times.   D. F. KNOWLES.

Auburn, May 1, 1867.

FRIEND HINDS: O. C.—Would a visit from your humble servant, next Saturday afternoon, be agreeable, and acceptable, if so, please let me know by return mail.

I am receiving the CIRCULAR quite regularly now, and am much interested in it. I have a good deal of instruction to ask of you when I may see you, and until then I remain,   Your true friend,
GEO. E. THOMPSON.

Mr. Woolworth replied, to the above letter, inviting Mr. T. to come for a short visit, but informed him that Wm. A. Hinds is at Wallingford.

We had a discussion, last night, drawn out by the reading of Mr. Hamilton's letter to Abram, in which Mr. H., raises the inquiry, whether we had not better make our calculations to light the children's new house with gas. Before deciding the question, it was thought best for Mr. Cragin and some others, to go to Durhamville Gas-works, and learn all they could about the manufacture of gas at that place.

It is a bright cool day, and outdoor business starts lively this morning. We noticed that there was a white frost, and that water standing in puddles was frozen. The leaves of the white lily are drooping, and the fragrant hyacinth meekly bows its head, thus affirming by unmistakable tokens that it has been bitten, though we trust not mortally wounded.

TRAP-SHOP.—3,000 No. 3 traps have just been put up, and 7,000 No. 0 are under way.

Preparations are being made to fit up part of one of the cellars under the Machine-Shop for a cistern. It will be lined with brick, and a double bottom laid.

Bags made in April,	70¼ doz.
" ordered "	113¼ "
Bag sales for April,	$3,536.98

Yesterday's temperature—
7 A. M., 36.   12 M., 42.   6 P. M., 39.   Mean 39.

THE O. C. DAILY.

VOL. 3.   SATURDAY, MAY 4, 1867.   NO. 106.

OUR LAWSUITS.

The decision of the Justice in the case of the Murphy Lawsuits, was received yesterday. It will be remembered there were two suits. One for damages to his cabbages, and the other a claim for pay for working overtime, nights and mornings and Sundays. The damage to the cabbages was laid at eighteen or twenty dollars, and the judgment rendered was the following:

Judgment for Plaintiff,

Damages	$5.00
Costs	$5.35
Total	$10.35

This judgement being against the Community, they have the above amount to pay.

The amount of extra pay claimed in the other suit was one hundred and ninty-three dollars, to which the Community brought in as an offset, a counter claim of thirty-six dollars and forty-four cents, for rent and one or two other items. There was also a claim of twenty-five dollars for damages to our Grapes, by his hens, which the justice ruled out, as being properly a separate cause for action.—The judgement in this suit was in favor of the Community, and was the following:

Judgment for Defendants,

Damages	$10.35
Costs	$ 6.05
Total	$16.40

It will be seen that the judgment in this suit is for just the amount the Community have to pay in the other, with the cost added, which of course Murphy pays. The Community come out, therefore, with virtually nothing to pay but lawyers fees, besides receiving a little bonus in the shape of a twenty-five cent fee to those who were summoned as witnesses. Mr. Kinsley offered to call the claims even, and settle before the trials, but Murphy refused.

The trials were before Justice Loomis.

———————

Seeing our friend B. B., the Chief Baker, wending his way toward the "*Petre Swamp*" with a tin pail of hot water and some amputating instruments in hand, I was quite curious to know what pet project he was now nursing, or upon what enemy he was about to bestow a practical *cursing*. So an hour later I was seized with a tramping fever that carried me in the same direction. Arriving at the southern extremity of the Community domain, west of the dam, my curiosity was happily gratified. Perched upon a tall, but young apple tree, the amateur fisherman, nursery-man, baker, etc., was at his favorite spring employment of fruit grafting. To my surprise I found that nature had been growing quite an apple orchard among under brush and scattered forest trees on a beautiful plateau of rich, virgin soil, which Mr. B. had discovered, and where he had been spending his leisure hours for several days, in converting those wild, unfruitful stragglers, into civilized habits of producing the choicest kind of fruit. In a few years the horticultural department will be gathering hundreds of bushels of nice fall and winter apples from that locality, which I propose to christen the "Bristol Orchard."

c.

———————

A woman by the name of Hall, came here yesterday, and wanted to join. She knew nothing about us or our principles, never having read any of our writings, but simply wanted a home. She is a widow, and on visiting her friends at Rome, and hearing of our institution, she came here hoping to find a home with us.

Her story is a sad one. She lived very happily with her husband, but four years ago he was induced to try his fortune in the West, and started with a company, to cross the plains for Idaho, and was never heard from afterwards. She supposes he must have been killed by the Indians. She had previously buried two little boys, with diphtheria, and after her husband left, she gave birth to a daughter, and that too, was taken sick and died last fall, so that she is without any near relatives, and is very lonely. She is only thirty-three years old, is good-looking, and intelligent. She asked to be hired, and our people have engaged her in the washing and ironing for one week on trial. She returned to Rome this morning, and is to come back and commence her labors next Monday.

———————

WILLOW-PLACE ITEM.—Some kind, impulsive, unknown friend, (?) fearing, doubtless, that our bees in the front yard would prove an annoyance this summer, quietly abstracted all the honey from the hives, and thereby succeeded in starving them to death. The bees had survived the winter and were doing well when this mishap overtook them. On exactly what night the job was performed, or what finally became of the honey, are questions with which we do not particularly concern ourselves.

Mr. Noyes is full of enthusiasm over his new project of a daily meeting, new thoughts and new ideas continually opening to him upon the subject. We hope the family will enter into the spirit of this new opening for missionary labor, and have a "zeal for God" which is "according to knowledge."

A Mr. Fox, of Durhamville, has a patented machine for manufacturing gas, like the one Mr. Hamilton has seen, and our talk in the DAILY, of yesterday, about "Durhamville Gas-works," is proved to be nothing but *gas*.

Traps ordered during the month of April, 191 doz.
Traps ordered since May first, 30 "
The large order, given by the Hudson Bay Co., in January, has been shipped, and to-day we have no unfilled orders on our books.

Yesterday's temperature—
7 A. M., 36, 12 M., 43, 6 P. M., 44. Mean 40½.

THE O. C. DAILY.

VOL. 3. MONDAY, MAY 6, 1867. NO. 107.

BUSINESS MEETING.

Mr. Delatre noticed trees cut upon the farm ; hopes Mr. Thacker will put a stop to such waste.

Abram said there was still considerable carpentry work to be done on the Willow-Place house—that John Leonard had worked on the house, instead of in the machine shop, as was expected of him when he went over there. Abram thought that a good work had been done there, and that he and his men might now attend to more important jobs. Left to the carpenters, Mr. Cragin and W. P., shop hands.

Mr. Clark expects a boat-load of coal this week ; a man wanted to unload it. Referred to Messrs. Clark and Kinsley.

Mr. Hatch spoke of the children's yard ; said Mr. Noyes wanted it fitted up for gymnastic exercises, and made attractive to visitors. Committee appointed to carry out Mr. Noyes's wishes in reference to the same, Messrs. Hatch, Kinsley, Kellogg, Conant and G. W. Hamilton.

Mr. Worden on repairing the road, suggested the propriety of hiring a man a few weeks, to break stone. It was shown that broken stone did not amount to much, unless it was put on a prepared foundation ; it was also thought that the new road, talked about, should be determined, so that labor be not misplaced.

Mr. Reynolds wants the new sky-lights, that were to be put on the roof of the store, made and put on soon.

Mr. Thacker said he had been called upon to find a place for our dairy, but had not succeeded very well. He had looked at the store cellar. In case we took a portion of that, we should need to put up a plastered partition, and have a separate entrance. He had thought about having the Dunn cottage removed to some place where it was shady, to use for dairy purposes, but did not know where. Mr. T., is to call in such counsel as he wishes, to assist him in deciding the matter.

FRAGMENTARY CONVERSATION AT THE TABLE, SATURDAY.—*Mr Noyes :*—This has been an eventful week, a week of great things ; there has been a constant roar of big guns. Monday, C. S. J. was admitted to the bar ; Tuesday, the *Tribune* published Meeker's article ; Wednesday, I got off my great gun on Diotrephasis ; Friday, the *New-York Herald* republished the O. C. from the *Tribune* with remarks, and right at the pivoted point the *Herald* states our position more correctly than has been done by any other paper. They say that " Fourierism failed because it made the Community support the individual." Whereas, we "are successful beyond any other association for the reason that we make the individual support the Community." The first encouraged laziness, and so Communities started under that system, sowed the seeds of dissolution at the very commencement, while our system abolished laziness at the start.

I am getting so that I can command a battle, whose armies reach from here to the Rocky Mountains, without speaking a word.

TALK AT THE TABLE SUNDAY.

H.—" Do you want we should have a dance to-night, Mr. Noyes?"

Mr. N.—" No, I am sick of dancing as we carry it on, all our hired help are doing the same thing. It is old fogyish, dirty."

H.—" Well, we wont have any till you want one."

Mr. N.—" I will tell you ; my plan is to have an oval area north of the house, on the lawn. Have it thirty-six feet wide at the center, and sixty feet between the extreme points the other way, and have an Asphaltum floor. Have roses and flowering shrubs bordering close around the oval ; outside of this, have seats for those who wish to look on, and just outside of this, a belt of shade trees, and have a musician stand elevated near the center of the floor-way on one side. Eleven setts of cotillions could be accommodated on this area. We will have all dancing done in the most artistic manner, and it shall be done not for the benefit of those who dance, but for those who look on ; have it so that if we want to entertain visitors, we can start a dance—and let them look on ."

These ideas were uttered in a loud whisper, and sympathized with by all who sat near enough to hear.

Mr. Noyes had the outlines of his plan sketched on a large sheet of paper and posted in the vestibule, yesterday afternoon. MICROPHONY.

The women who constitute the first company for Willow-Place were busy yesterday, picking up their clothes, and packing their trunks, preparatory to moving to-day. They consist of Mrs. Miller, Ackley, Whitfield, Virtue, Martha, and the silk girls, Elizabeth, Harriet and Olive. Mr. Ackley is to be the kitchen man, with George Henry as assistant. The house is nicely fitted up and the new carpet put down in the large front room, and the old reception-room carpet in another room. The two girls expect to stay two weeks only, and then have their places supplied by others.

There is a great stir this morning, of persons running to and fro, collecting and loading trunks, boxes, beds, bedding and furniture, for Willow-Place. It is some rainy, but that does not prevent the big wheel from moving forward.

Mr. Easton came about noon Saturday.

Temperature Saturday and Sunday—
7 A. M., 50. 12 M., 60. 6 P. M., 59. Mean 56½.
7 A. M., 44. 12 M., 60. 6 P. M., 63. Mean 55½.

THE O. C. DAILY.

VOL. 3.   TUESDAY, MAY 7, 1867.   NO. 108.

W. P. CORRESPONDENCE: A HAPPY OMEN.—Our Sitting-Room stove, a "Morning Light," was brought from home and set up over here, without particularly disturbing the fire within. The family, we trust, stood transportation equally well.

We had an interesting evening meeting for our first one. Among other things, a report of J. H. N's. talk over here in the afternoon, about the Bible was given. We are to have reading from the CIRCULAR, Tuesday noons, and perhaps reading every day at that hour, following home fashion.

G. W. Hamilton was appointed Newspaper Reporter, H. E. Allen Letter Reader, C. A. Burt Chorister, C. A. Cragin Reporter. The following is a list of the resident members. W. R. Inslee, J. F. Sears, G. W. Hamilton, J. C. Higgins, C. Higgins, R. Hawley, A. Hawley, C. A. Burt, M. Kinsley, E. Noyes, G. Campbell, O. Wright, D. A. Abbot, C. C. Hatch, J. Freeman, H. Blood, C. A. Cragin, J. C. Ackley, G. H. Burnham. Vibratory member, G. Cragin, together with the women mentioned in yesterday's DAILY.

A Mrs. Kilbourn, a woman with a "mission," came here yesterday. She walked up from the depot, and sat full two hours without taking off her bonnet and shawl, though she was invited to do so, when she first came in. At last she said, perhaps she had better remain over night, and in the morning we might conclude to let her remain with us. As it rained, we suffered her to stay, but told her plainly that she could not join. She made us think of Mrs. Field—had the same wild and unearthly look with her eyes. She is a widow and has lived at the West, Mt. Pleasant, Iowa, where she has two sons settled, but for ten years she has traveled and lectured most of the time. Is full of the marvelous, has spiritual insight of persons and things, heals the sick and the insane, and has foreknowledge of what is in the future. She says she is clairvoyant but is disowned by spiritualists, on account of her adherence to the Bible. Her husband was a graduate of Hamilton College, and for a good many years they lived in Tennessee and taught there, and founded an institution that bore their name. She professes to have great skill in teaching music, on an improved plan, and volunteered to impart her knowledge to us. It rains so, to-day, that we are fearful she will not be able to leave.

MR. WOOLWORTH:—I think as it was said in my last criticism, that I have been under W. A. H.'s spirit. I know that my relation to him was the commencement of my bad experience, and brought me into a hard unbelieving state. I wish now to separate myself from him entirely, or any one else who cannot help me to become a spiritually minded woman. I wish to become a true helper to Christ and the Church. I confess my hatred of unbelief, and I pray for a soft heart, a new conversion, and a spirit that seeks to know and do the will of God.   H. SIBLEY.

NUMBER OF HIRED PEOPLE EMPLOYED BY THE O. C. AT THE PRESENT TIME.

Silk-Factory, mostly women and girls,			81.
Bag-Shop,	23.	Shoe-Shop,	2.
Trap-Shop,	27.	Machinists,	2.
Horticultural Dept	10.	Farm,	7.
Tailor's Shop,	3.	Washing Dept.	3.
Tin Cans,	2.	Teaming,	3.
Carpenters including Masons,			8.
Foundry & Sawmill,			6.
Miscellaneous,			4.
Total,			131.

Mr. Leete went home Friday, sick. Mary Leete wrote yesterday, "Father is too sick to keep his promise of writing to your folks, and requested me to write and let you know how he is this morning. He was in extreme pain Saturday, and has had a good deal of fever until the latter part of last night, when it left him. His foot and wrist are better, but his hip is not as well, though he thinks the crisis is past, and he will get better now. Mother does not get much better of her fall a week ago."

Miss Nun requested criticism night before last. She has commended herself to the family, by her capability and thoroughness in business, and has shown a good deal of heroism in ignoring her bodily difficulties. She has improved a good deal since coming to the Community, though there are still defects in her character, the result of her early education, which she would do well to seek earnestly the aid of Christ to overcome.

Mr. Kelley writes from Rochester, May 5, "There is quite a stir here to-day, about O. C., on account of the *Tribune* article about us, being published in the *Rochester Democrat*, and their remarks upon it. I have sent a copy to Mr. Noyes. Got orders for twenty-four pounds of our silk, notwithstanding the excitement."

Young Penfold, Mrs Kelley's nephew, left for home yesterday. A note from him addressed to the family, was read in meeting last night, in which he expressed a deep interest in the Community, and confessed Christ in him a Savior from sin and selfishness.

Mr. Noyes went over to Willow-Place yesterday afternoon, and staid and took supper at the new Commune. He reports all right there.

BIRTH.—Yesterday, May 6, Mother O. C. was delivered of a fine youngling of about two tons weight.— At last accounts, mother and child were doing well.

Yesterday's temperature—
7 A. M., 54.   12 M., 56.   6 P. M., 55.   Mean 55.

THE O. C. DAILY.

VOL. 3. WEDNESDAY, MAY 8, 1867. NO. 109.

Elenton, N. C. May 1, 1867.

Mr. J. H. Noyes, Dear Sir:—In one month from to-day my engagement here closes, and I return to the North. I have no offer for the future and must seek employment. This I can of course find. But my heart's desire is, to become more intimately connected with the O. C.; still I will wait if it be God's will. I offer you a whole heart and willing hands, to help on the car of reformation.

Are you yet sufficiently acquainted with me to admit me on trial? I dislike returning to my relatives; for I have already suffered much abuse for the position I have taken. Still I will willingly continue to suffer if that be best.

Please inform me at your earliest convenience in regard to this matter, that I may arrange my affairs accordingly. Yours truly,
D. Edson Smith.

The article in the *Tribune*, respecting the O. C., brings us a great many letters of enquiry from persons who have heard about us for the first time. One man writes to "Elder Noyes," from Woonsocket, R. I., stating that he had read a notice of our society in the *Daily Providence Post*, relating our condition, objects and principles, and he expresses a wish to know more about us, so that if he desires, he can become a member. Another writes from Cincinnati, saying that he had just finished reading an article in the *New York Tribune*, entitled "Oneida Community, how they live &c.," and had become quite interested. He says "I learn that you publish a paper for gratuitous distribution; if such is the case, I should be very much pleased to receive a copy, as I am anxious to become acquainted with your peculiar plan of life."

Willow-Place:—The Foundry is again running on plow and machine castings.—Improvements are still the order of the day, in our new home. Two closets were formed, yesterday, by cutting doors into hitherto unused nooks, between the partitions. Bedrooms begin to assume the delicious home look, which pictures, ottomans, and above all, a woman's touch can give. It really begins to feel real "homey." We heard of one chap going over to O. C., on business, during the afternoon, who declined to stay to supper, alleging that he began to feel a little homesick!

Our eccentric visitor, Mrs. Kilbourn left this morning, notwithstanding it rained hard. She has spent much of her time while here, in writing to Mr. Noyes, Mr. Underwood, and others, giving her opinion of our position and state, in language very mystical and unintelligible. She wore her hair which was quite short, tied up in a knot on the back side of her head, with the ends hanging, which gave her a very grotesque appearance, and it was with difficulty that bursts of laughter could be repressed by the girls and some others, as she came into the dining-room to take her meals.

From Mr. Kelley, Lockport, May 5th.:

"I should think that most of the papers are copying that article from the *Tribune*. You have of course seen the *New-York Herald* of May 3, with its long editorial about it. I expect it is going to produce a great stir all over the country.

"Owen Gaffney of Rochester (a large wholesale dealer) thought we must have paid these papers pretty handsomely for advertizing us so extensively. He could hardly believe me when I told him we had not. He said it was a good deal in our pockets, and to verify what he said, he gave me his first order for silk."

John Freeman returned yesterday, from Schenectady. He has been gone two weeks, to assist his folks in moving. He says his father met him very cordially, with "How do you do Mr. Community," and for a week said nothing to indicate any unfriendliness toward us. After that, he began to show his "cloven foot," and at last could not say any thing too bad about Mr. Noyes. John was glad enough to get back home.

We received a letter yesterday from Mrs. Morris, dated Blairstown May 2. She with her son, went directly home after leaving Oneida. Mr. Morris is still in Vineland, and will call here on his return the first of June. Mrs. M. writes, "I earnestly desire that you may progress onward and upward, and when it is God's will to show me the truth, as you see and understand it, that I may confess Christ in me a savior from all sin."

Dear Mrs. J.:—In your statistics yesterday, "Silk-Factory, mostly women and girls, 31"—Should be, Silk-Factory *all* women and girls, 32.   H. E. A.

Mrs. Tobey's half-sister, Mrs. Clark, from Whitesboro, came here Monday afternoon, and left yesterday afternoon.

Yesterday's temperature.—
7 A. M., 48.   12 M., 50.   6 P. M., 46.   Mean 48.

THE O. C. DAILY.

VOL. 3. THURSDAY, MAY 9, 1867. NO. 110.

Our noon meetings commenced Tuesday, May 7th. An introductory talk was read from Mr. Noyes, which made it plain that the Community was founded on the Bible. As the CIRCULAR had just been received, the remainder of the hour was spent in reading it. Yesterday, we had a continuation of Mr. N.'s talk on the Bible, the beautiful poem of Park Benjamin, from the Spiritual Magazine, entitled "Press On"—the Home-Talk, "Union with Christ," from the same—Mr. Bolle's article in the last CIRCULAR—and the song "We're Marching along," by the children. Quite a pleasing variety.

We had a letter, some time last week, from a Jew, named Mermelstein, of New York City, expressing a wish to come and board with us ten or twelve days, for the purpose of getting acquainted with us, and our principles. He sent on his testimonials. Mr. Woolworth replied to the letter inviting him to come and make a visit.

He writes the second time: "I can well understand why an infant Community should find it difficult to afford entertainment to the many curiosity seekers, but for my part, I could not afford to spend my money for mere curiosity, but having some views which I suppose coincides with yours, I was desirous to learn more of your system, in order, that if you are correct in your views, I might cast in my lot amongst you. But I shall not burden you, especially as you take no money for entertainment."

He made some inquires in his last letter respecting our doctrines which we are told Mr. Noyes will reply to. He is a convert to the Christian religion, and has labored among his brethren, in the East.

FOREIGN CORRESPONDENCE.

W. P. May 9.—We are having quite a wet time over our way. For two or three days it has rained almost incessantly; consequently "Skinadore Creek," (as the natives call it) is out on a "bender." The flats, quarter of a mile north-west of the Shop, are under water. Some people say it is the highest nothing-but-water freshet we have had for many years, though it does not rise as high into two or three feet, as it did two years ago, when blocked with outgoing ice at various points.

In meeting the other evening, H. E. A. read a note from E. Y. J. about the funny woman that was at O. C., adding at its close, "See Daily." C. A. M. meditatively—" Let me see, we havn't ever heard anything before, about this Miss C. Daily have we?" We thought not.

"Is the storm over?" "Yes," said K., "all but finishing off, which will probably take one day more, and then, and then, if we could have warm"—"Stop; stop," said G., "there is no use in saying if we could have this or that, we should be suited and made glad &c. We must get top of all that." "What," said K., "get top of the weather?" "Certainly we should. The thing is not among the impossibilities." "Well, G., please tell me how it can be done, for I have been under the weather principality long enough. I am beginning to feel as though I had got it on my brain already." "Here it is—leave this world and get into heaven; that is, leave sin, selfishness and all manner of unbelief and rise into the world of faith, joy, love, peace and thankfulness, and your days of trouble will be over." c.

Mr. Hatch reported some conversation he had with Mr. Noyes, on the subject of singing in our daily meetings, somewhat as follows: "Mr. Noyes said there ought to be twenty persons here so full of inspiration that they could any of them start tunes whenever there was occasion, and lead right off boldly. I thought myself if we had the true revival spirit that would be so. Mr. N. said we were going to have a revival, and I felt when he said it that it was true—one that shall extend to our singing. Mr. N. said he would appoint me to select about a dozen tunes and have the family drill on them, and learn them so that we could strike into one at any time, without any preparation for books and instrument, thus making our singing spontaneous and inspiring, as it used to be in old revival times. I told him I would try and carry out his plan, and I want to call on the whole Community to take hold and assist me."

Mr. Clark has been out a day and a half, selling hop-stoves and plow-castings. He reports his sales at from five to six hundred dollars.—We went yesterday, to see the Creek run away. It is quite a long time since we have had such a freshet. Though the high water is cutting into the banks, damaging the meadows considerably, yet it was sport to see the great masses of turf plunge into the water, after the water had undermined them. Those of the Bag-Shop hands who live at Pine-Bush, had to be taken home by a team, the water being so high that they could not walk. U. O.

James Vaill was criticised, last night, by his request. It was thought that he had improved, and he was commended for his faithfulness in times past. He has lately fallen into some of his old practices, which it requires downright earnestness and sincerity on his part to overcome. If he would be saved from the temptations with which he is from time to time assailed, it is necessary for him to separate himself from his father's spirit, and seek a conversion of heart, which he very much needs.

A vote was taken, last night, on D. Edson Smith's request to become a member, which was unanimous in favor of inviting him to join.

Yesterday's temperature—
7 A. M. 44. 12 M. 46. 6 P. M. 48. Mean 46.

THE O. C. DAILY.

VOL. 3.　　FRIDAY, MAY 10, 1867.　　NO. 111.

EVENING MEETING.

Leonard Dunn's letter on the teeth was re-read last night and discussion called for. Frederick Norton gave his opinion of the state of the teeth in the Community, which was a more hopeful view of things, than Leonard had taken. He thought that in eight months or a year, they could most likely catch up, and be able after that to keep the teeth of the Community well filled and in good order. The only fear was, that in the interim some valuable teeth might be lost for want of time to fill them promptly. There was considerable talk about mallet-filling, and the question arose how far we should avail ourselves of it at the present time. It was finally, at Mr. Noyes's suggestion, decided that small cavities in the front teeth should be filled with gold, and malleted, but large ones, with amalgum, except in the case of front teeth where they could only be saved by the malleting process.— Much confidence in, and commendation of our dentists was expressed, and thankfulness that a good spirit prevailed in the shop.

Mr. Underwood:—We had a visitor here to-day from New-York, a hat manufacturer, 440 Broadway. He has made two or three calls at the Agency. He is a warm admirer of the *New-York Herald,* and has been a constant reader of it for some twelve or fourteen years. It is his daily food. He knew who was the author of the late editorial respecting the Oneida Community. It was written by Mr. Hudson of the *Herald.*

This visitor was a sample of a great many that I suppose we shall have, during the summer; people induced to come here by these articles in the papers, just for the sake of learning, in a superficial way, what kind of people we are. I didn't like his nimbus very well; he was inclined to make himself altogether too familiar.

Mr. Reynolds:—He probably has good teeth if he makes the *Herald* his daily food. [Laughter.]

Mr. Woolworth:—Perhaps he has false teeth. Mr. Noyes says that Mr. Reynolds's remark brings us back to the same subject of teeth, and he thinks if we have a hymn, it should be on the same subject. Can you give us something appropriate, Mr. Hatch *!*

Mr. Hatch suggested " Be Gone Dull Care." This was sung, and made considerable sport. Mr. Woolworth suggested that it might be easily adapted to the teeth.

Thursday, May 9th.

DEAR MRS. THAYER :—Father had a very bad spell last night, that has left him so weak that he can scarcely speak, this morning; he is very low indeed. He would like to have some of you come out and see him, and all the rest of us wish it too. Come as soon as

you can; if you can, and could some one stay all night? I did not expect he would be here this morning, at one time, but he is spared, as yet, for which we are very thankful.　　Your sister in Christ.

　　　　　　　　　　　MARY LEETE.

Noon :—Father is no better. I should have sent this in the morning, if I could have found any one going to Oneida. Cannot some of you come if it is late when you get this, for we are all alone.

　　　　　　　　　　　MARY.

Immediately after the above letter was received, Mr. Kinsley and S. B. Campbell started for Verona.

Thursday noon.—The meeting was opened as the others have been, by a communication from Mr. Noyes, then an article from the *Home Journal* entitled " The Hope of Religion," and after that, the " Home-Talk" "Setting the Lord always before our face." Mr. Cragin, Mr. Hatch and others, made some remarks, and the exercises closed with a song.

It is a long time since there has been any complaint of our bread, but on the contrary, I often hear the remark at the table, " what nice bread we have." Jane Abbott has resigned her post in the bakery department, and Mr. Bristol has now the whole charge of making and baking our wheat bread; and also takes care of the room. I heard considerable commendation expressed for him, not long since, by some of the sisters.　　　　　　　　　　　s.

People often ask, "How do you manage to keep your hired men busy when it rains?" We have had quite a number of jobs, such as making boxes, shoveling over manure, fixing barrels, &c. At the same time we have had considerable rain, and should not object to being informed of indoor jobs, in wet weather.

Mr. Abbott reports, that the rain has done considerable damage to the ditches that were dug for the aqueduct, they having caved in, in a good many places. It will probably take three days work to dig them out again.

There is considerable stir and moving these days. To-day, Mr. Worden is moving back to his old place in the Tent-room, and Mr. J. Kinsley takes the room vacated by him, one of the bed-rooms on the north side of the Lower Sitting-room.

The sun shines upon us once more; a welcome sight—the drenched earth, we are sure, will greet with gratitude his kindly rays.

Yesterday's temperature—
7 A. M., 45.　12 M., 49.　6 P. M., 48.　Mean 47½.

THE O. C. DAILY.

VOL. 3. SATURDAY, MAY 11, 1867. NO. 112.

EVENING MEETING.

The expediency of playing Base Ball was discussed. It was decided that we better drop it, for the present at least, on account of its sacramental character, which was believed to be bad. The idea was suggested of getting something in its place, that old and young, men and women, could join in. This started the question, whether young men have not a *natural* desire for bold, vigorous exercise, that the other sex and elderly men could not well join in. This view was eloquently maintained by Messrs. A. L. Burt, J. H. Barron, &c., though they were ready to abandon ball playing and seek this exercise elsewhere. Mr. Woolworth summed up the discussion as follows :

" Mr. Noyes remarks that we are in a progressive school that is different from that of the world. We take up things and suck the marrow out of them, and then leave them and go to something else. We sucked chess pretty well, at one time ; but we have left it, as it seemed to become a bad ordinance to us. Then our dancing has not been very satisfactory lately. Our hired people have gone into it, and run it pretty bad, and we have dropped it. So of music. The Lord seemed to limit us in respect to that. We had a good time with it ; but now have left it for something else. This seems to be the way the Lord leads and educates us. The question is whether we have not got all the good out of this game of ball, and should seek something else that has more marrow in it. [Voted out.]

I am thankful that the school we are in, trains us in this way. It is an indication of life and vitality, and freedom from routine, fashion and habit. The way to get new things is to let go of the old ones. If we keep sucking the old bone, we shall not get a new one.

———◦⟨◦⟩◦———

Mr. Kinsley reported that he found Mr. Leete in pretty feeble condition. He was surrounded by his family and two doctors who had been called in, so that there was little chance to do much for him. After going home he had grown much worse, his foot becoming so painful that he could not step on it, when the family became much alarmed and he yielded to their desire to call in medical aid. This gave some relief at first, by spreading the disorder to different parts. He told Mr. K. he was contending with a family affection that has no Christ in it. He was very glad to see Mr. Kinsley and Mrs. Campbell, and said he felt they brought the Community spirit with them. He wished the Community to pray for him, and asked for any advice or criticism. Mr. K. thought him better when he left, but he was so much under the influence of medicine, it was hard to tell. His battle is a hard one and it is yet doubtful how it will end. He is surrounded by the family spirit, that however much we may sympathize with him, we can do little to help him.— Mr. Woolworth has gone to Mr. Leete's to-day.

WILLOW-PLACE ITEMS. May 10 :—The old shed, west of the Shop, has been moved forward, and placed over its new cellar. J. H. B., D. Knowles and E. Van, are now at work fitting it up. A cellar is also being dug, near the Foundry, over which the building, formally used as an iron house, is to be placed, and fitted up for a tenement house.

Evening meeting.— Mr. Cragin made some remarks showing the importance of keeping in sympathy with Oneida, in the move lately begun. A general expression of interest in, and appreciation of the noon meetings, followed ; then some talk about studies. It was hoped that the young men would keep up a bright interest in their intellectual pursuits, and, with all due respect to Base Ball, etc., not let such athletic exercises abstract too much time.

A spirit of contentment and happiness pervades the family, and though there is plenty of work done, especially by the women, all testify that they enjoy themselves much.

———◦⟨◦⟩◦———

C. Van returned Thursday night, from a peddling trip of nine days. The storm kept him two or three days from doing much business, and on account of the mud, rain and high water, he was obliged to leave his team at Canandaigua. He will go out there again Monday next, and resume his peddling.

———◦⟨◦⟩◦———

Mr. Olds left quite unexpectedly night before last for Milwaukee. He had a letter from a man who is friendly to us, that a firm that owes us over $300 had failed, but that if some one came on immediately perhaps the debt could be secured. Mr. O. expects to go on his peddling route, and will be gone some weeks.

———◦⟨◦⟩◦———

THE SPIRIT'S WHISPER.

Softly, gently, Christ is speaking
In our hearts, and kindly seeking
From the outward to attract us,
Where the cares of life distract us.

Listen ! 'tis the spirit's whisper,
Soothing as an evening vesper,
" Trust me, I am with you ever,
Nought our bond of love can sever.

When the heart is torn and bleeding,
I for you am interceding,
Keenly feel your weight of sorrow,
Give you hope of rest tomorrow.

For your growth and comfort caring,
With you all your burdens sharing,
Can you fail to look within you,
To the Power that yearns to win you."

———◦⟨◦⟩◦———

Yesterday's temperature—
7 A. M., 55. 12 M., 58. 6 P. M., 57. Mean 56⅔.

THE O. C. DAILY.

VOL 3.   MONDAY, MAY 13, 1867.   NO. 113.

BUSINESS MEETING.

The Dentists would like a pipe to carry water down from the sink, and also if possible have water brought up by a pump. Referred to Messrs. Abbott, Whitney, and F. Norton.

Mr. Clark thought that the man who drives the Willow-Place team, Mr. Christian, has a very trying place to fill. There are a great many things to be done, and he has to wait a long time here and there. There has been some disposition to criticise him, both here, and at W. P., which he does not like very well. Mr. C. thought it would be well for those who have any fault to find, to come to those who have charge of him.

The drain from the Mansion-House that empties into the elm-meadow, is filling up the old frog-pond and does not run off. This matter should receive prompt attention and was referred to the standing sanitary committee. Several of this committee being away, others were chosen. The following are the committee as they now stand: Messrs. Nash, Abbott, Ellis, Underwood and Miss H. Matthews.

There ensued some talk about the proposed telegraph, between here and W. P. Homer said he had made some inquiry about the cost of it, and thought it would be cheaper to be thrown into the general line, than to take a private, independent line from here to W. P., as in the general line we should need but a small battery; independently, a large one. The company would "throw a loop" around us for five hundred dollars, and supply us with the necessary instruments. Then this five hundred dollars would be so much stock in the company, and would entitle us to the usual dividends. Moreover, as it is customary for operators to communicate with each other, without charge, the correspondence between here and W. P., would not probably cost us anything.—Mr. Hatch is requested to detail one of the boys to carry any message the office-folks may have for W. P., and the folks there may make a similar arrangement.

WILLOW-PLACE ITEMS, May 12.—The Willow-Place family gratefully acknowledge the receipt of a handsome number of books, from the O. C. Library, including works on Science, Art, Religion, Politics and Fiction. It is also whispered that we are to be presented with the Unabridged Webster, which now adorns the Library-table. M. Kinsley has been appointed Librarian.

The family have decided that the proposed driveway, in front of the house, is, on the whole, undesirable; also that it is inexpedient to establish a croquet ground over here, at present. C. C. Hatch and O. A. Nash, form a committee to beautify our grounds with flower-beds, shade-trees and the like.

O. C., Sunday afternoon. Our whole family, with the exception of Mr. and Mrs. Ackley, who are keeping house, are over here on a visit. Our Oneida home is very dear, we find, and we return to it joyfully, yet leave it again without a regret.

Saturday evening, Mr. Hatch called for about twelve volunteers, to cut up turf for turfing the children's new yard. A dozen names were quickly registered, and the job was executed in about an hour, yesterday morning, before breakfast, and the turf drawn and deposited in the yard, so that the experience, so trying to some of the mothers, of their little ones rolling and playing in the dirt, seems likely to come to an end. We reckon it did not pay.

John P. Hutchins requested criticism last night.— The principle fault found was an unwillingness to take responsibility. He was commended for his perseverance in writing for the CIRCULAR, and for the good success he had had of late in that direction. It was thought that he needed the same energy of will in his spiritual and business transactions, that he had shown in writing. He has improved, and much love was expressed for him.

One of the boys in writing from Willow-Place says, "I like my new home very much. I love our new mother too, for she is such a nice mother to us. We boys are going to have an hour a day to read the Bible and study arithmetic. We are to commence at the beginning of the Bible, and read it through, and Mrs. Miller is to meet with us. I feel thankful for such a privilege, and confess Christ a Savior from sin and selfishness."

There were two or three strangers in at our noon meeting, yesterday. All Mr. Noyes' Bible-talks were read—a poem entitled "The Acorn"—some remarks, and a general raid against the sleepy spirit. The meetings for the young people, were held as usual, at four o'clock.

It seemed real good to have the Willow-Place family with us, yesterday. It is nothing new, at Oneida, for children to stay with their parents Sundays.

The carpenters commenced work, this morning, on the Mansion House, putting under new sills &c.

Mr. Noyes started Saturday afternoon for New-York and Wallingford.

Mr. Leet was some better Saturday.

Temperature Saturday and Sunday—
7 A. M., 50.   12 M., 50.   6 P. M., 56.   Mean 54.
7 A. M., 52.   12 M., 53.   6 P. M., 54.   Mean 53¼.

THE O. C. DAILY.

VOL. 3. TUESDAY, MAY 14, 1867. NO. 114.

Mr. F. K. Phœnix, of Bloomington, Illinois, an old neighbor and friend of Mr. Meeker, came here Sunday. He is a horticulturist, and a reformer—an Eclectic, he styled himself, believing there is good and evil in all movements, parties, sects and circumstances; and that it is the duty of rational beings, to seek out and appropriate the good, and reject the evil.

He had an intense desire to understand the interior life and workings, of such organizations as the Shakers and the Oneida Community; but confessed after three or four hours of questioning, that we were too much for him, and that he should have to go away with the object of his visit unaccomplished. We expressed a willingness to help him all we could.

"Oh well," he replied, his mind tugging at the problem despairingly, "I don't know enough, I am not wise enough to get at it."

He carried in his pocket the Circular containing Mr. Meeker's sketch of the Community, and referred to it occasionally, but was unable to see everything in Mr. Meeker's way. He noticed young men associating with young women, and wondered Mr. Meeker could say, it was not allowed; and also that we never prayed. He thought we were a praying people. He wanted to know which we put first, the individual or the institution, and then he asked for some statistics of our children which were given him, whereupon he remarked—that he did not know but it might be said of us, that the persistent refusal to have children for so many years, was about as bad and unnatural as abortion. We joined issue on this point. He attended both meetings, and in the evening listened to the criticism of John Hutchins, and heard as many repetitions of, "I like John," as Mr. Meeker reports of Homer, on a similar occasion.

He left for the station after meeting, intending to take the early morning train for New-York. U.

Sunday night.

Dear Mrs. Thayer:—Father had a very bad afternoon and night, after Mr. Woolworth left us yesterday, which has left him weaker than when he came in the morning; we kept him on stimulants all night. His pulse was very low, in the early part of the night, but stronger towards morning. I talked with him, last night, and he said it would be a great help to him to have some of your folks stay with us, and if they could, I wish they would come. I looked for some of you to-day, and hoped you would come, and mother did too. I ask the sympathy and prayers of the Community, and confess my union with you in Christ.

With love, Mary L. Leete.

Monday morning:—Father rested better last night.

I shall send this by a neighbor this morning, on the first train. Mary.

S. W. Nash and Mrs. Langstaff went to Mr. Leete's, yesterday. Mrs. L. designs to stay a few days and assist in taking care of Mr. Leete.

The job the carpenters are doing, interferes considerable, with the work in the kitchen and dining-room, and makes a good deal of confusion there. Abram reports good progress, and good success yesterday, and a good helpful spirit all round. The dining-room was cleared and made ready for the workmen at eight o'clock yesterday morning, and though on entering it, at noon, for our dinner, we had to "move careful," (as the floor boards that had been taken up were laid down loosely,) yet the family expressed little inconvenience in taking dinner and supper there as usual. To make it easier for the kitchen folks to-day, it was proposed by some one, last night, that we have bread and milk for dinner. In response to that suggestion, a person in one corner of the Hall, called out "and can all that don't like bread and milk, have some beef steak?"

We have twelve peach trees all in bloom. Although the mercury stood last winter at 30 degrees below Zero, there is a fine prospect of some peaches. The trees were first tied down to stakes near the ground, and then covered with evergreens and straw to protect them. As an experiment it is a success, and raising them might be made profitable in a cold climate.

The Burt-House is at the present time occupied by two families, the Porters on the south, and Andrew Heyl on the north end of the house. A leanto has just been completed for the benefit of Mr. Heyl's family, on the back side of the part of the house they occupy, which they design to use for a kitchen in summer and for a wood-shed in winter. A shed a little distance back of the south end has also been put up for the benefit of the Porters.

The farmers are engaged in carting manure to-day. The ground is still too wet to plough.—We notice a heap of stone on the plat where the children's new house is to stand, from which we draw the inference, that a beginning is commenced, of drawing stone for its foundation.

There was some talk last night, about the practice of giving the children candies, which was thought not to be good for them, especially that that was colored. The practice will be discontinued.

Yesterday's temperature—
7 A. M., 53. 12 M., 58. 6 P. M., 59. Mean 56⅓.

THE O. C. DAILY.

VOL. 3. WEDNESDAY, MAY 15, 1867. NO. 115.

EVENING MEETING.

Mr. Woolworth :—Our principle of ascending fellow-ship seems to be on trial somewhat at the present time; at least it is pretty distinctly published and set before the world, and perhaps in the worst light. There is no doubt but that the devil intends to make it as odious as possible. But it is more and more clear to me that it is a divine and heaven-born principle. It is one of the foundation stones of Communism, and Communism never can exist without it. I am certain, too, this is where the individual's salvation, you may say, begins. It is the only sure path for old and young to walk in. It is the path to freedom, and the very shortest cut we can take to the largest liberty, if that is what we are after. I am interested that we should see the truth about this principle, and be con-verted to it, if we are not already. I don't know how many of us there are in the Community, who are not thoroughly converted to it; but I believe when it is seen in its true light, as the road to happiness and sal-vation, we shall seek to be converted to it.

Mr. Reynolds :—I believe this principle contains the great secret of the final unity Christ prayed for, that " they all may be one"

Mr. Woolworth :—Yes, as Mr. Reynolds says, it is the way to realize Christ's prayer that we may all be one. There is no other possible way in which organ-ization and unity can be realized except through central, ascending fellowship, with all hearts turned upward.—Marriage or worldly unions proceed on the opposite principle, of horizontal or descending fellow-ship. Unions starting on that basis, end in disintegra-tion and death, or in any amount of misery. Our union based on the ascending fellowship results in making us all one. This principle is under reproach now, but I am sure it will shine out bright, sooner or later. If we are faithful to it, it will lead us into full fellowship with Christ and Paul, and the whole Prim-itive Church.

We received an order from Mr. Stacy, of New Al-bany, Ind., (through Mr. H. Perry), for four and a half dozen bags, valued at two hundred and fifty-nine dol-lars and twenty-three cents, to be forwarded May 15th. We expected to send them to-day, but received a note from Mr. Stacy, saying that the water had been so high all Winter and Spring, that all trade is cut off; men are out of money, and cannot trade with him, and he has no money to pay the bill if we send the goods. He is sorry he has to send us such word. We like his honorable dealing, and feel that it is prov-idential that we received the note in time to prevent our sending the goods, which under the circumstances,

would have been rather an uncertain business transac-tion. We distributed the bags into other orders, and consider ourselves the gainers.

After consulting with Mr. Woolworth and Carrie, we have decided to call upon our Agents for more or-ders. We think we are gaining on our present ones sufficiently to justify our so doing. We hope to have them all filled by the 25th. N.

Noticing that the CIRCULAR raised the inquiry how the present health of our hostler is, compared with what it was when he drank his daily beer in such large quantities, I ventured to ask him more of his experience in the line of breweries and beer-drinking. He told me he did not drink nearly as much as some other workmen, and that there was one man who ofttimes, drank nine gallons in a day. Men who work in the breweries, have all the beer they wish to drink, gratis, and when one barrel is gone, they open another. He says he is glad that he lives where he cannot get any—that he never felt better in his life. When he drank beer, he felt obliged to keep drinking continually, for if he stopped, it seemed as though he was all on fire, and he had to drink more to satisfy his unquenchable thirst for it. He said that if some of his old neighbors should see him now, they would think he had been sick. He is evidently thankful for a home in America. Y.

On account of a change in the mail train, our letters that go out in the afternoon, have to be mailed a quar-ter to twelve; consequently it will not be strange, (judging from the past,) if the DAILY, on account of its frequently unavoidable tardiness, should be delayed till the ensuing day. We will do our best, however to get it through in season to send out the day it is printed.

We are thankful that the CIRCULARS come regular-ly now. The noon meeting, yesterday, was spent in reading the last one, which we thought rich and juicy.

Mr. Nash returned yesterday morning, from Mr. Leete's, and reports Mr. L. better and in a hopeful way.—He left him in good spirits.

Miss Clara Wait whose present home is in Lewis Co., in this State, came here yesterday. She intends to make a visit of a day or two.

An uncle of L. A. Thayer, Mr. George Warner, of Michigan, came here last evening.

Mr. Noyes arrived in the night, accompanied by Mr. Herrick.

Yesterday's temperature—
7 A. M., 63. 12 M., 61. 6 P. M., 53. Mean 59½.

THE O. C. DAILY.

VOL 3. THURSDAY, MAY 16, 1867. NO. 116.

EVENING MEETING.

Mr. Wadsworth:—We had some conversation, last evening, about the ascending fellowship. I don't know but the feeling has obtained a good deal, that the principle was adapted particularly to the young, or intended exclusively for the young folks. I understand that it is good for all classes, and indispensable for old and young, high and low. We cannot any of us do without it and prosper. I understand that Mr. Noyes is really more devoted to it than any of us; it is his daily bread and life. I cannot get along without it, but grow more and more dependent upon it, and seek it as the only true way to live, prosper and grow.—The Primitive Church that we covet fellowship with, count their years by thousands, instead of by scores, as we do; and we are anxious, very anxious for their fellowship, and seek it above everything else, and prize it above everything else. We never think of the Primitive Church as old folks. We do not consider Paul an old man. He is younger than we are in spirit.

Milwaukee, May 12, 1867.

DEAR CARRIE:—It is well I started immediately for this city to look after the note of Ledyard & Carll. I reached here last evening a little after 8 o'clock, not in time to see them, or find out any thing very definite.

I learned this morning from A. H. Gardner & Co., that they wrote to us the next day after J. M. Allcott & Co. did, reporting further about the matter. (I saw a copy of the letter this morning). As near as I can find out from parties here, they have sold every thing for money, in hand or in notes, which they have in their pockets. I expect they will pay us—at any rate I shall meet them in that spirit, with the expectation that God will help me to manage the case *wisely*, and in a way to reach their hearts, so that they will be willing to pay the *full* amount. It is *certain* they have the means to pay, and there will be no excuse, unless they *intend* to defraud us; we will wait and see.

In case they refuse to pay, we have *friends* here who will help me to their utmost extent to get our pay if possible. I find they have a bill against J. M. Allcot & Co. of about $180, which I think we can secure, and I presume more can be found, enough perhaps to cover the note.

Be assured I shall be on the alert, bright and early to-morrow morning, trusting God and the invisibles for wisdom to *do* the *very best* thing. Will report further as matters progress. Very truly yours in the service,
CHARLES OLDS.

Miss Wait left early this morning for home. A committee was called yesterday forenoon, to investigate her case, and hear what she had to say. She stated that her object in coming here, was to learn more of our foundation doctrines and get help. She says she has been trying for two years past to clear herself from the false influences she has been under at Berlin Hights, and extricate herself from the snare into which she had fallen. For this purpose she has secluded herself from all society and books, except the Bible. She thinks she has returned to Christ in a repentant spirit, and to find him near to her. She has formerly read our writings some, but for two year has known little about the Community or our publications, and she is so situated now, that she thinks it would not be right to have the CIRCULAR sent to her. She seemed soft and receptive. Mr. Cragin and others gave her some good advice, for which she seemed thankful. Her home is with a sister, and she has the care of an aged mother who is entirely helpless.

WILLOW-PLACE, May 16.—C. C. H., has unturfed several variously-shaped plats on our lawns, for flower-beds. Rosebushes and other perennials are set out about the house front. The aquarium is established at the kitchen door just outside. Rubbish is removed, holes are filled up, and gradually, nature and order begin their reign about the premises. Indefatigable Mr. Higgins flies hither and yon, piling up wood, fixing the fences, looking after the garden, feeding the pigs, etc. He is about commencing his summer campaign against dock-root.

Mrs. Dunning made us a short call, yesterday. She was apparently quite enraptured with the quondam boarding-house; declared she shouldn't have known it. Her health has been very poor since she left here; she is troubled with hemorrhage of the lungs, and was on her way to the doctor's.

Evening Meeting:—After the reports, came some earnest talk and testimony about the ascending fellowship. At the meeting's close, we had, as we frequently do, Congregational singing with violoncello accompaniment.

Mr. Stillman, Mr. Noyes's old friend, came here yesterday. After he was seated in the parlor, Mr. Noyes was invited to go in, and see if there was any one there whom he knew. No, there wasn't—no familiar face. We were told however, that Mr. S. recognized Mr. N., though perhaps he would have failed to do so, had he not expected to meet him.

Mr. Malcom, a teacher of piano music, from Philadelphia, came here last night. He gave us some specimens of his skill in the use of the instrument, after meeting.

In meeting last night a letter from Mr. Dixon to Mr. Noyes was read, also Mr. Noyes's reply. Copies of the letters will be forwarded.

Yesterday's temperature—
7 A. M., 59. 12 M., 61. 6 P. M., 48. Mean 53.

THE O. C. DAILY.

VOL 3.   FRIDAY, MAY 17, 1867.   NO. 117.

"What shall we do?" said one of our women to another, yesterday morning. "We are all as busy as bees, now. Whom shall we find to put into the company depar'ment? We had to take S., out of the Printing office, because she is going to Wallingford, and E., has taken her place, and Mrs. B., has gone to W. P., and we must get some one to fill her place, and you may say what you please, neither W. nor Y. are real strong women!" "Perhaps not, yet," said the other, "but they will be. For nine years before I came to the Community, I did not know what it was to have a well day, and now look at me. I don't know what it is to be sick these days."

We looked at her full form, and round rosy cheeks, the very picture of blooming health and youthfulness. "Hurrah!" exclaimed the listening brother, "hurrah! for Communism and Male Continence! O ir women are growing young. Several have been drafted, and some supplied, and the responsibilities are all the while increasing; but if we hire a woman to run the sewing machine, and perhaps two more to wash dishes during the visiting season, our women will continue to make sport of their work, and to grow young, and in the favor of all the people."   v.

Mr. Melville Malcom left this morning for Niagara Falls, accompanying Mr. Stillman as far as Syracuse. He is a single man of some upwards of thirty years of age. We were a little disappointed in him. He presented himself to us in quite a superficial light, notwithstanding his father, the Rev. Mr. Howard Malcom, is a reputedly religious man, and a thinker and author of some note. He has two brothers, also, who are pastors of Baptist churches. He should be a strong interior man. There may be a deeper side to his character which we failed to reach; but it seemed to us as though he had dissipated his spiritual patrimony, and lost the magnetism of a continent and growing manhood. He is near-sighted, and has a nervous affection of the eyes, which keeps them constantly in motion, rolling and glowing, in quite a disagreeable manner. His piano playing, though pretty good, was not particularly brilliant. It is to be considered, however, that he has been entirely out of practice for the past three years.—He played a piece entitled "Falling Leaves," and "Capt. Shepard's Quickstep," and one or two other pieces after meeting, last night.

When he left, this morning, he expressed his thankfulness for the privilege of making this visit, and the hope that he might sometime be permitted to join us.

Mr. Olds writes: "The *Chicago Republican*, of May 10th, copies the entire article from the *New-York Tribune*, without a word of comment.

"The failure to connect at Detroit, broke the line of connection the rest of the way, and so gave me a few hours at Chicago which time I improved calling on our customers, and I was too busy in this to hear any thing of this article in the *Republican*. Just as I was about to leave the city, one of them said to me, (with a countenance indicative of pleasure, as though he had discovered something new and interesting), 'I was reading an article in yesterday's *Republican* about your Community; I had supposed till then, you were a branch of the Shakers.' 'O no,' said I 'we are not Shakers.' 'What do you pay for such articles? I suppose that is the way you advertise. That article is worth a *thousand dollars.*' I replied, we do not pay for notices of that kind, as news-paper editors are pleased to find such matter to publish about us, and we regard them as valuable advertisements."

WILLOW-PLACE, May 17.—Seated beside a "straightening block," hammer in hand, we saw Mr. Herrick with a white apron on, yesterday afternoon, straightening irons, up stairs in the Finishing Room. He showed us his toil-browned hands, and explained a machine he had just invented whereby he could assure himself that the bars were straight, a matter which his eye, unaided, was unable to decide.

Messrs. Stillman and Malcom paid us a short visit in company with J. H. N. The last named promises to come over and attend our meetings some of these days.

Various little house-hold improvements and conveniences are added almost daily to our home, much appreciated, though scarcely reportable.

We welcome another resident—a sister has lately joined her fortunes with ours—R. M. B.—she is welcomed—and—isn't home-sick the least bit.

Veroaa, May 16, 1867.

DEAR BROTHER NASH:—I am lying about as when you left me yesterday—quite as comfortable, and my leg about the same, except that the appearances are more like dropsy. The swelling receives a deep indentation that remains some moments. I hope this is sent to carry off the former disease with out suppuration, which I rather dread. But if that should be required, I trust to be able to say, "Thy will be done."

HARLEY N. LEET.

Our people have received a boat load of coal, one hundred and two tons, from New-York, which was unloaded at the wharf, yesterday.

H. W. Burnham arrived here last night, and starts on his peddling route again to-day.

Our visitor, Mr. Warner, left in the night.

Yesterday's temperature—
7 A. M., 46.   12 M., 54.   6 P. M., 53.   Mean 51½.

THE O. C. DAILY.

VOL. 3. SATURDAY, MAY 18, 1867. NO. 118.

Mr. Bennett made us a call yesterday—a son of the first white settler in this neighborhood—the man after whom Bennett's corners, up here, was named. He said when his father moved in, there were none but Indians living here; and he lived right in the midst of them. He knew all these hills and vallies, and the turnings and windings of the creek, as well as he knew his own house. He said great quantities of blackberries grew here, about forty years ago; he remembered what sights of blackberries grew right about here where we are located.

He thought the soil naturally well adapted to growing berries and grapes. Wild grapes in large quantities used to grow here. He went over to buy some plants, and seeing so many fruits cultivated, reminded him of old times. After his father moved in here, a Dutch family came, and these two were the only white families for some time. He now lives north of the depot, where he owns one hundred and fifty acres of land. He was greatly astonished at the change that had taken place here.

DEAR MR. WOOLWORTH:—I feel very thankful for your sincerity with me, and for the spirit of brotherly love you manifested, in telling me the truth.

I am anxious to begin life anew—have a new conversion—a spirit of faith and humility, and be a help to Christ and Communism. I believe that God is good, and stands ready to help any person, and is a rewarder of those who diligently seek him. When I am tempted to discouragement, I find that by turning my attention inwardly and reading the Bible and Berean, my faith is strengthened, and I feel at such times, as though I was building a new foundation on a rock.

I never felt more earnest for salvation; I am thankful for existence and a chance to fight the devil. I confess my love for you, and my confidence in you as an inspired man. I confess Christ the controller of my passions and desires.   Your loving brother,
SIDNEY Y. JOSLYN.

Mr. Barron was criticised, night before last.— The principal faults pointed out, were undue prejudice against individuals, stiffness of character, too much gravity and not enough vivacity; an overestimate of New-England men, and too frequent mention of Vermont, and old experiences when living there. Mr. Noyes's criticism of him was, that not long since, Mr. B. gave him a false alarm by his incessant coughing. Mr. N criticised him some and his cough soon disappeared. It was thought that Mr. B., had improved in reference to the faults above specified, and he is a man that is much appreciated and loved—is a ge-

nial companion in labor, and is loyal and true hearted.

Mr. Warner, Mrs. Thayer's uncle, who has just visited us, is having considerable trouble with the "powers that be," in relation to his matrimonial connection. He is over sixty years old and has recently married his niece, a young woman about thirty, who has lived in his family the last ten years: she is his third wife. The church, (conspicuous among whom is a lawyer), are in quite a ferment about his marrying his niece, and Mr. W. is in great tribulation for fear they will separate them. We should judge from what L. A. Thayer reported, that it was a real love match. Mr. Noyes remarked that it was a striking case of the ascending fellowship.

Mr. Kelley returned yesterday. When in Cleveland he called on Mr. Towner, and spent two nights there. He liked the family very well though he felt called upon to administer a little criticism. He thought the little girl fairly ruled the house, the parents could not, or did not enforce obedience. Mr. Towner was sensible of this state of things, and was thankful for Mr. K.'s sincerity—said he would start anew, and try to govern his own house.

Mr. K. spent Sunday in Oberlin, and went to hear Prof. Finney preach.

Mr. R. N. Adams writes from Savannah, Georgia, for the purpose of gathering information respecting the Community.

He with several others, are desirous of forming a Community in Florida, on the Indian river, south of latitude twenty-six, and he wishes to know if he can unite with us and have a branch South. He wants to know the laws, rules, &c., that govern us, and asks for a copy of our paper. He says the country where they propose to locate, has a delightful climate, and produces all the tropical fruits in abundance. He says in conclusion, "Could we induce any to come from your Community, and how many?"

The trade at the store steadily increases. Since getting our new goods, the amount sold daily, averages at about fifty dollars. One man not far from here, who has a son engaged in the mercantile business at the depot, comes here, frequently, to buy goods.

Mr. Blood left Thursday night for his old home, in New-Hampshire. He has business and expects to be gone about two weeks. He has seemed a good deal softer of late, and we have good hope of a permanent cure of his past difficulties.

We get a glimpse of the sun now and then, but it is only a glimpse. It is pretty cold and backward for the season.

Mr. Conant reports that he commenced ploughing last Wednesday.

Yesterday's temperature—
7 A.M., 50. 12 M., 62. 6 P. M., 52. Mean 54⅓.

THE O. C. DAILY.

VOL. 3.   SUNDAY, MAY 19, 1867.   NO. 119.

Mr. Edwin A. Stillman resides in the town of Candice, the Southwestern corner of Ontario Co., N. Y., where he is engaged in the business of manufacturing lumber. He has a steam stave and saw-mill, and he took this trip for the purpose of making contracts, having no intention of coming to the Community, when he left home. Indeed it is only quite lately that he learned that Mr. Noyes was here. He heard of the fanatical Bible Communists years ago, but did not know that Mr. Noyes, or "John" as he calls him, was their leader. He was full of anecdotes and reminiscences of old times—thirty years ago. He said the last time he was with "John," they were traveling on foot on the horse railroad from New York to Newark. They ran horse cars then, between those cities, which stopped at all the stations. They walked on ahead of the car intending to jump aboard when it came by. In answer, however, to the driver's call to do so, when the car overtook them, "John" swung his hat and shouted, "No! We are in a hurry and can't wait!"

He described his conversion. He was studying for the ministry, and two of his brother Reverends, Adkins and Neal, hearing that he was leaning towards Perfectionism, came in to see him one day when "John" happened to be present. Adkins, however, nothing daunted, began to labor with him, and in the course of his remarks misquoted a passage from the Testament, to justify something he had previously said, whereupon "John" turned to him, and quietly told him that he lied, and then repeated the passage word for word, and showed him that his reasoning was entirely fallacious. "The battle that followed settled me," said Mr. Stillman, "and I have not swerved since."

In walking over to W. P., Thursday afternoon, Mr. Stillman started out in advance of Mr. Noyes. When Mr. Noyes overtook him he turned and greeted him with, "How do you do to-day, John?" and they walked on together after that and conversed.

"I believe I spoilt a Baptist minister when I got you, didn't I?" said Mr. Noyes. Mr. Stillman thought at first that he referred to Neal. Finally he saw the point and responded, "That is so, and I have never been sorry."

He was shown all through the works at W. P., and then into the dwelling house, and from there over to the Foundry and Saw-mill, and on our way back, we pointed out the boundaries of our land, and finished up with a thorough inspection of the Great Eastern and Horse barn. He got a pretty good idea of our material basis, but was not very much inclined to talk about our present spiritual position. He appeared, however, to have all his old love for "John."

We should have mentioned that Mr. Stillman lived for thirty years, under the impression that Mr. Noyes was in favor of the dispersion of believers; hence he had not looked for an organization.   v.

C. Van Velzer saw Mr. Carr while out on his peddling trip, and reported the interview to the meeting somewhat as follows: "Carr met me with a, 'Halloo here, how do you do? I'm glad to see you.' Then he shook hands quite violently. He asked how we were getting along, and I told him finely, better than ever before. Then he asked 'How is Noyes?' 'Mr. Noyes is doing finely,' I said, 'and we are all doing a great work.' At this he shook himself in his old style, and I said 'yes' two or three times over. He finally said Mr. Noyes would have to make his base a good deal broader before he would have much influence in the world. I got away from him as soon as I could and took another Car! [Laughter]. Before I left he said 'Well, Charlie I'm awful glad I am out of the Community.' I replied 'I am sure we are all glad you are not there.' This made him stutter a little. Though his way of speaking of our leader was very offensive to me, I thought the best way was to keep cool and get out of his way as soon as I could.

Mr. Woolworth:—What about Willow-Place?

C. Van:—He said, 'I suppose you have got a family over at Willow-Place now.' 'Yes,' I replied 'we have a very prosperous family started there.' 'Well,' said he, 'that's just what I proposed years ago.' [Laughter]. He said if we had done it when he proposed it, we should have been two or three thousand dollars better off.

Mr. Woolworth:—We seem to be warping up to his idea. Mr. Noyes says he don't know but Carr has fore-ordained all we shall do for a century to come; but he hopes we shall sometime get ahead of him. I don't wonder he thinks our platform rather narrow.

C. Van:—He said once, "Well, I like the Community folks, but there are some things I can't stand. I cannot swallow the social theory yet."! I felt a very bad spirit in him, and I could not bear him. I had about as lief meet a drunkard or a crazy man. He did seem like a crazy man, I thought; there was a wild, sickly look about him.

Mr. Kelley called to see Victor, yesterday, and thought he appeared better than when he last saw him. He carried him several Nos. of the CIRCULAR, with which he seemed much pleased; he opened a drawer and put them out of sight as quick as he could, which indicated, Mr. K., thought, a fear that the Doctor would see them.

The farmers commenced sowing barley yesterday. They hope to complete the job in less than a week.

The atmosphere was clear last night, and the full moon shone bright in the heavens. To-day is tolerably warm and sunny

We had an order yesterday, for 150 dozen traps. They were packed and shipped at noon.

Yesterday's temperature—
7 A. M., 47. 12 M., 50. 6 P. M., 48 Mean 48¼.

THE O. C. DAILY.

VOL. 3.   MONDAY, MAY 20, 1867.   NO. 120.

BUSINESS MEETING.

Only two or three persons responded promptly to the bell for business meeting, this morning. It was suggested that those present transact their business and then adjourn.

John Conant wanted to know what was to be done about setting some posts for hanging clothes. It would be necessary to have thirty-five or forty of them. Mr. Thacker thought it would be better to bolt the cross pieces on to the posts, than to fasten them as the present ones are fastened. The matter was left to John and Mr. Clark with authority to hire a man if necessary to set the posts.

Mr. Thacker said Mr. Noyes had spoken to him about the wearing away of the bank of the Creek and wanted to know if something could not be done to prevent it. He would like to have all think of it and offer plans at the next meeting if they choose.

Mr. Clark said we were having a great call for horses this season. The team-work of the farm has been delayed till now by the rainy weather, and we have coal, stone, brick, lime, sand &c. to be drawn. Some of our work will have to suffer unless we have more horses. He thought one span of heavy horses to relieve George Kellogg's team would be enough. He needs heavy horses for the depot team. Referred to the horse committee, Messrs. Kinsley, Clark and Kellogg.

Geo. Kellogg wanted to know the mind of the board about getting another hostler. The present incumbent of that position is only on trial, and is thought to be too inexperienced and careless to do the work which will be required, when we have a great number of visitor's horses to care for. We want a smart intelligent man for hostler, one who is educated to it. Referred to the hiring committee, Messrs. Barron, Kellogg and Kinsley, and also Mr. Clark and Geo. Kellogg.

It was proposed that the financial committee consider the matter of painting the fence on the opposite side of the road, and if best have it done soon.

I have for some time past felt distressed and burdened with one serious fault in my character, have had an earnest prayer, a hungering and thirsting for salvation from a very strong propensity to look on the dark side, to think evil, to be doubtful, suspicious and unbelieving. It has constantly laid me open to the devil's thought and view of things, and has made me hard, cold, hopeless and discouraged. I have from time to time had victories over it, yet it seems to be the fault which most sorely besets me. It has been so strong in me that I have almost despaired of the grace of God to overcome it. About a year ago, in

some conversation with Mr. Noyes, he said to me, that my victory would come in connection with the victory of the church; that it would not be an individual affair.

I have rejoiced in the noon meetings, and been much interested, but have not felt my heart softened and touched as I wished, until Saturday, when I felt that my heart was melted and broken and converted; that I was born again, when the Community was converted. I confess that the loving mind of Christ has taken the place of doubt, evil-thinking and unbelief. I trust to the same power that produced the change to make it permanent. I confess my union with Paul, and his boldness and freedom to be inspired and fruitful to God.   H. MATHEWS.

Mr. Herrick gave an eloquent description, last night, of the young men's meeting, the spirit of unity that prevailed, and the benefit he had received in attending it. We thought of the words of the Psalmist "Behold how good and how pleasant it is for brethren to dwell together in unity." Surely God and the Primitive church are in our midst, and Christ's prayer "That they all may be one," is fast being realized.

I want help to overcome a spirit of hardness and unbelief that I have had for a long time. I have been so tempted that life had begun to seem hateful to me. I could see nothing in this life worth living for, nor any hope for what might come after. I pray that I may not give up to temptation, but I desire God's help and the help of the family to overcome it. I confess Christ a spirit of faith; I know that without him there is no happiness, nothing worth living for.   MINERVA.

God's care over his children is sometimes so strikingly manifest, that the most unbelieving cannot help acknowledging his fatherly protection. When Mr. Kelley was out on his last trip, he was very anxious, one morning, to take the earliest train. He looked for his trunk, it was fast locked in the baggage-house. He ran to look up the baggage-master, but he was no where to be found, and so the train, to his chagrin, passed on and left him. He learned, afterward, that the same train on which he was so anxious to take passage, was by some accident, all smashed in pieces.

Mr. Woolworth inquired last night, what the family thought about closing the store, and refusing to sell goods, Sundays. After some discussion of the subject, it was thought that the better way would be to keep the store open a little later Saturday night, than has been our custom, that our workmen, and others, may have a chance after their week's work is done, to make purchases if they wish, and then keep closed doors, (as well as window blinds), Sundays. A printed card should be put upon the store door notifying our customers of our change of policy.

Yesterday's temperature—
7 A. M., 47. 12 M., 50. 6 P. M., 48 Mean 48¼.

THE O. C. DAILY.

VOL. 3.   TUESDAY, MAY 21, 1867.   NO. 121.

EVENING MEETING.

Mr. Hatch spoke of the singing. He wished there could be more inspiration and enthusiasm in it, and less tendency to drag. This drew from Mr. Noyes the following remarks:

"I think we have handled music enough, here, to make all kinds of music sacred to us. I don't think the band music we used to make here, was profane. To me it was sacred. I should not have the least objection to the introduction of piano and orchestral music and songs into our noon meetings, for the sake of variety. The style of such music might be tempered and moderated to suit the occasion. When Edward Inslee returns, I am in hopes that we shall connect, to a certain extent, the old musical entertainments, we used to have, with these meetings. I see no reason why we may not. Music is a sacred thing to me, the whole of it. I had as lief have Mozart's Requiem played by our band, in one of the noon meetings, as any Psalm-tune we have. It would be full as sacred to me. Edward Inslee is probably getting an excellent education in the science of music; and I hope when he returns we may give him an opportunity to exercise himself in connection with our meetings, and on liberal principles.

I don't think we ought to require a certain variety of words in order that we may make worship of music. Music in itself, without words, is a means of worship; and we ought to rise up into the harmonies of heaven that we get in music that is really good, without any words. Then you see we should get the use of all instrumental music, and of brass bands, orchestras and organs. I think a good lively blast on the bugle, chords a good deal better with what we are doing in our noon meetings, than a droning Psalm-tune sung through the nose. The Bible represents that the judgment is coming with the sound of the trumpet. It is not to be heralded by Psalm-singing through the nose. I hold those meetings of the old orchestra were just as sacred as these we are having now, and think both should be combined. And I guess among the other conversions here, the Community will have to be converted from a kind of Psalm singing cant.—I do not wish to have it understood, however, that I think any less of these songs that we have. I simply want to feel that our drill in the past was sacred business, and that we are going to have the use of that kind of music.

Some twenty-four or twenty-five years ago, my brother Norman said to me, (on an occasion of an outburst of persecution from a sister), "How can you get along and live with such an opposing spirit?" I told him I felt that I was sailing in a boat alone.

"O, yes," said he "some one else has expressed such a view of holiness, of launching out in a large vessel with many small boats coming in all directions toward the big ship." Since then my experience has been in a small boat, sometimes drifting onward, sometimes swamped in darkness, when a flash of light from the ship would show me the way out.

When I came here, I lost my boat and saw I must get on board the ship.—After drifting about, I almost became discouraged about ever getting aboard, and for a few days my heart has been filled with anguish. I saw myself clinging to the outside of the ship, and completely fastened—I could see no way to extricate myself. Last night, after retiring, I was so overcome with the intensity of my feelings, I thought I would say to the family cast me away, I shall only be a burden to you, when something seemed to say, "Look." Instantly I felt a change, quick as lightning—I felt an intense love for Mr. Noyes—he lifted me on board the ship. Thank God, thank God for Mr. Noyes.

SUSAN F. DUNN.

WILLOW-PLACE.—S. W. N. and C. C. H. are engaged upon our lawn, setting out bushes, flowers etc. M. H. K., is laying a plank-walk from the front door around to the back.

Quoit-pitching is quite popular with us. After supper on pleasant evenings O. C., G. W. H. and others, usually have a friendly set-to. Some of our neighbors following as is the custom, our fashions, have taken up the game: certainly better for them than beer-drinking and cigar-smoking.

As we expect Paul to visit us this summer, the question came to me, "how shall we prepare to meet him?" The churches, looking back through a long line of bishops and elders, see Paul and the Primitive church a long way off. But we find that Mr. Noyes is a link that connects us directly with them, and makes them feel very near us.

General conversation about Paul's character in our meeting—his tireless enthusiasm, and freedom from egotism, were commented on. G. C. added as he left, "I hope we shall all dream about Paul to-night."

Two men stayed here last night; one was a man who lives near Manlius, an acquaintance of Mr. Worden, and the other a German from New-York city, who had seen and read some Nos., of the CIRCULAR at the Cooper Institute. The latter sails next week for Europe, to attend the Paris Exposition.

Our people bought a span of horses, yesterday, and paid $500 for them. They also sold one of our horses, old "Rattler," for fifty dollars.

The trio from Wallingford, G. W. N, C. S. J. and Mrs. Baker arrived safely in the night. It is needless to add that we were *very* glad to see them.

Yesterday's temperature—
7 A. M., 50. 12 M., 58. 6 P. M., 58. Mean 55½.

THE O. C. DAILY.

VOL. 3. WEDNESDAY, MAY 22, 1867. NO. 122.

Mr. and Mrs. Macoy called here last Sunday afternoon. It was the first time that Mrs. M., had ever been here, and she expressed a great deal of delight and astonishment at the works of skill and art that on every hand met her gaze, saying repeatedly, that it seemed like heaven. O, how she wished that all Cambridge, that had persecuted them so much, for only coming to live in our neighborhood, could see the beauty of our surroundings, and the happiness that beamed from every countenance. If she could have her way, she would bring them all here, for once, and let them have one good look with their own eyes. We told her that the outward, that she so much admired, was only a slight semblance of the greater work that God had wrought in the hearts of the men and women of the Community. Yes, she supposed so, but how could people talk so, and be so blinded by prejudice.

Some parts of the Mansion House, have been in the utmost disorder for nearly a week past, pulling off the plastering on dilapidated walls, and putting on new; papering &c. What used to be called the "lower tent-room" is being cleaned, to-day, preparitory to papering.—Mr. Hatch, in attempting to cut a door through, on the west side of the room, encountered a formidable obstruction in the shape of a large upright beam, and so the idea of a passage to the room direct from the children's entry was given up.

The bed-room in the North-west corner of the children's front room, has been removed, and to-day the masons are plastering up the broken walls. The room is plenty large enough now, and the other two bed-rooms will remain as they are.

When meeting was nearly through last night, one of the young girls arose and made the remark, that John P. Hutchins would give us a song. John seemed to be taken all aback, but finally succeeded in singing, after a fashion, an old love-song, which ended tragically in shipwreck and death. We understand that the young lady had previously told John, that she would announce his intention to sing, if he would agree to carry it out, and he not believing that she would dare do it, consented.—The meeting was closed with the "Pacific Railroad" song, and a piece of music on the piano by A. M. Hatch.

WILLOW-PLACE :—Boating promises to become quite popular with us, this summer. Some of the young men tempted C. A. M., into a moonlight excursion on the water, the other night. We talk of raising the bridge at the upper end of the pond, so as to enable us to sail clear up to the head-gate.

Our evening gathering looked a little thin, as several of our folks were visiting "Oneida Creek," nevertheless, we had an interesting discussion concerning the ascending fellowship.

GRAMMATICAL :—Do *not* say, " It looks nicely," " It looks neatly," " She looks beautifully ;" but instead " It looks nice," " It looks neat," " She looks beautiful." You would not say, " It is nicely," " It is neatly," " She is beautifully," if you had sole reference to the appearance.

RULE.—In all such cases in which a neuter verb may be substituted for the one used, without materially affecting the sense, or in which the verb used is more nearly neuter that active in signification, the adjective should be preferred to the adverb.   *v.*

We should think that our two brothers, who are destined for a mission to the Old World, were enjoying their visit here very much. We sincerely hope they will, while at Oneida, take in large draughts of the breath of heaven, and become so saturated with resurrection life, that they can cross the " rolling deep" without experiencing the torments of sea-sickness.

I am thankful for my late criticism, or for any experience that enlarges and softens my heart. I desire a spirit that is open and receptive to good at all times. I confess an unshaken confidence in Mr. Noyes's inspiration, and the triumph of Bible Communism throughout the world. I confess Christ a Savior from evil in all its forms.   A. BARRON.

Mrs. Dascomb continues her correspondence with us, and manifests a good deal of firmness in her adherance to the truth. Mrs. Bushnell says she is placed in very trying circumstances, the relatives with whom she lives, having a good deal of bitterness toward the Community.

We had a letter from D. Edson Smith a day or two since, expressing his thankfulness for Mr. Woolworth's letter, inviting him to come on with his wife and make his home with us. He wrote that he should probably be here, about the first of next month.

DEAR MRS. J.—You served me right—I sent you a blotted, scribbled manuscript and now suffer the consequences. It should have read, " In the evening meeting, C. A. Miller remarked, ' As we expect Paul etc.' " Is it worth your trouble to correct it ?—C. A. O.

The meetings at noon continue to be very interesting. Yesterday, the most of the *Herald's* article on the O. C. was read, which afforded us a good deal of entertainment.

110 hills of watermelons have been planted over west, on the sand hill, and 100 of muskmelons near the large reservoir.

Yesterday's temperature—

7 A. M., 54. 12 M., 63. 6 P. M., 64. Mean 60.

THE O. C. DAILY.

VOL. 3.   THURSDAY, MAY 23, 1867.   NO. 123.

Mr. Olds writes :—" Chicago, May 16.—Business is rather dull in the bag line just now, in this market. I find that parties are out of stock, but they are afraid to buy, as they say they are selling nothing, to speak of for cash. They cannot collect pay for goods sold last fall and winter, and so fear to buy, as they know they must pay us in thirty days.   *   *   *

It is a matter of thanksgiving that we are getting so many orders for traps, at the present time. I believe we shall have a great demand this fall. There is no large stock on hand, and parties will be ready to order early. Some are ready to give orders now, to be filled the first of August. Every thing looks encouraging in the line of traps and preserved fruits.

I have plenty of business in the way of answering questions about the O. C., since Meeker's article appeared in the papers of this city and Milwaukee.— W. B. Burbank asked me to go to his house, yesterday, and take dinner with him, said he and his wife had some things to say about preserving fruit &c. While at the table his wife commenced by saying, " I was reading a very flattering article in one of our city papers, a few days ago, about your Community." "Yes," said I, " It was copied from the *New-York Tribune*; rather an exaggerated account." " I didn't know before," said she, " that you were doing such an extensive and flourishing business." A lady friend of theirs was present, also a brother of Mr. B. Mrs. B. seemed very much interested in the article, and went on to introduce me as a member of the O. C., to her lady friend, and proceeded to tell her what a business we were doing in preserving fruit, &c., &c. At length she became interested too, and the quality of our fruit was pretty freely discussed. The strawberry-tea question was alluded to, which produced some merriment. None of them seemed disposed to go into particulars of this story about us, but talked about it in a general way. Mr. B., and his wife both are very anxious to visit us, say they think of going East in July, and shall surely call."

WILLOW-PLACE ITEMS.—Three children, Harry C., Willie S. and Anna B., are spending a few days with us. The patter of little feet in the hall, and many shouts and laughter from parlor and kitchen, rather pleasantly disturb our customary quiet.

The birds about here, are acquiring rather expensive habits, owing, we fear, to living near us. They are in the way of lining their nests with silk ! Bits of waste which get scattered about outdoors, they appropriate for their own use. One oriole that had got her nest well begun in an elm tree near by, happened to discover a small handful of waste that Ernest had left on the fence, when she immediately deserted her first nest, and commenced another with the newly found supply. " We can show 'em," as E., says, in proof of the statement.

Verona, May 22, 1867.

DEAR MRS. THAYER:—Thinking you would like to know how my father is this week, I will write a few lines and send this afternoon. He has been quite sick with a cold on his lungs, and fever, Monday and yesterday, but is somewhat better to-day. We think he took cold by waiting on himself nights.

NOON :—Father has been up to dinner with us, and is sitting up now.   MARY.

Mr. Leete writes, " when I am weak then am I strong. My faith and trust and hope increase, and I expect soon to be my own master—the servant of Christ ever. I think something good is coming of this unusual experience."

Talk in the meeting last night about G. W. N. and C. S. J.'s contemplated European tour. G. W. N. gave a crude programme he had in his mind of their course while there, with the probable expense, subject to any alterations that the family might think proper, or that the leadings of Providence might indicate. It was remarked, that the brothers should not feel cramped or stinted financially, but should be free to follow the leadings of the spirit. Mr. Noyes thought there might be Providential openings in London that would require their presence there some time.

A full report of the talk will be given in manuscript.

The length of the iron aqueduct we are laying, including the branches, will be about 160 rods. Its object is to convey the water that now runs in wooden conductors, from the spring to the house. The wooden pipes have caused us considerable trouble by bursting and leakage. It is also our purpose, to connect other springs with those that are now brought in logs. The cast-iron pipes are constructed in pieces eight and a half feet long, and four inches in diameter on the inside, with the sides one fourth of an inch thick. One end of each piece is made larger, to receive the end of the next piece and the joint is made tight by pouring in melted lead.   J. A.

Mr. D. H. Hamilton and his wife, from Maine, came here, yesterday morning. They had previously informed us of their intention of making us a visit. Mr. Brewster also of New Jersey, arrived yesterday.

Mr. and Mrs. Brown, (Helen Underwood that was,) staid here last night, and left this morning.

Yesterday's temperature—
7 A. M., 50.   12 M., 58.   6 P. M., 52   Mean 53½.

THE O. C. DAILY.

VOL. 3.   FRIDAY, MAY 24, 1867.   NO. 124.

New York, May 21, 1867.

J. H. NOYES ESQ.—Dear Sir:—I take the liberty of addressing you upon a subject of deep interest to me, and, I believe, one which has engaged your attention for many years.

Some time since it was my privilege to attend the sick bed of a friend, who had upon one occasion left his home and sojourned with your Community for a long time; he deserted it by the advice and influence of his friends, and the matter remained a secret from almost every one. But disease came. Pain brought reflection—reflection occasioned remorse—the story he told me of the quiet, peaceful life he enjoyed while a member of "the family," and his useless regrets at having ever been induced to quit it, led me to reflect somewhat upon the subject myself, and I may safely say, that my investigations have been in every way, to the welfare of my soul. The love of Jesus, since I began to see the light, has filled my heart, and I am determined, if God almighty spares my life, to live according to the dictates of his holy word and commandment. Now I wish to be advised of the means of grace, and I, therefore, address myself to you as the person most qualified to instruct me in the way of glory. What requirements are necessary for admission to a full communion with your society.

I have just come from my home in the South to this city, and am busy settling my worldly affairs, that I may have nothing to occupy me for the rest of my life but the service of Christ and him crucified. Should your answer be favorable, I will bring into the family the sum of $6,500 dollars, invested in U. S. 7 3-10 Treasury notes. My wife and two daughters will become sisters—and together we will tread the "straight and narrow path" which leads to heaven. If you can send me any printed matter bearing upon the subject, I shall be happy to receive the same, and will compensate by return mail.   Yours in the faith,

P. RICQUE, OF GEORGIA.

WILLOW-PLACE TRAP-SHOP STATISTICS.

No., 0 Traps on hand	4,108.
" 1 " " "	12,000.
" 1½ " " "	1,519.
" 2 " " "	2,909.
" 3 " " "	686.
" 4 " " "	879.

IN THE WORKS.—FINISHING DEPARTMENT.—No. 0, stock for 10,000 ordered. No 1, 35,000 under way. No. 1½, three or four thousand just commenced. No. 2, the Fall supply just commenced. Nos. 3 & 4, getting stock together.

FORGING DEPARTMENT.—31,000 No. 1 springs finished. Nos. 2, 3 & 4, the lots are well started. Not far from 40,000 chains in the aggregate of the different sizes are to be made this summer. M. Kinsley is preparing to take hold of the job.

Six hands are employed in the Forging, and nine in the Finishing-Department, aside from our own folks.

In a letter received from Mr. Blood, dated Mason Village, May 19th, he says:

"At Worcester I called to see some old shop-mates; one of them jokingly said he thought of trying to join the Community, and the other made the remark, that if he could only have things as they were represented to be there, he would think it was a heaven upon earth; upon which I said a few words suggesting purification of his heart as the proper and absolutely necessary preparation for the heavenly state, *any where.*"

Our Spring is very backward; the trees seem struggling to put forth their leaves, and vegetation generally is laboring against adverse circumstances. We still have cold rains, and much unpleasant weather. The farmers cast a longing look toward their unsowed fields, but doubtless feel in their hearts that God is still the God of the elements.

Our noon meetings continue to be interesting. The young people, in particular, are gradually getting their liberty to speak, and use their tongues in favor of the truth. We trust that the revival spirit will finally sweep away every barrier to perfect freedom of speech, in the whole Community.

We are fitting up the company dining-room to-day, the milk having been removed to the room beneath, where it was kept last year.

The florists are to-day, moving out many of their plants from the Green-house, and setting them in the flower-garden north of it, for a summer's residence.

Our people are moving the tin cans out of the old packing-shop, to prepare it for the dwelling of one of our workmen and his family.

G. W. N. entertained us last night, with relating many interesting incidents in the life of Dr. Lyman Beecher, whose biography he has recently read.

Silk sales since April 30,	$2109.88
Bag orders,	$304.68

W. G. K.

Yesterday's temperature—
7 A. M., 54. 12 M., 65. 6 P. M., 52. Mean 57.

THE O. C. DAILY.

VOL. 3. SATURDAY, MAY 25, 1867. NO. 125.

There was a large supper-party held in the dining-room, yesterday, given in behalf of our three brothers who were to leave for Wallingford in the night. Mrs. Miller, Mrs. Ackley and H. E. Allen, were here from W. P. Sentiments were called for, but there was little response. Mr. Cragin said, however, that Mr. Noyes had remarked, that when he came here the first time, it was for the purpose of investigating social science, and the last time, to investigate the science of the Bible.

G. W. N., spoke about the *Herald's* having given the world a page of *O. C. anica*—and he said that perhaps he and C. S. J., would be prepared, on their return, to give us another chapter on Oceanica.

The trio left at midnight in fine spirits. Our prayers go with them.

We ship, to-day, to Wm. Topping & Co., fifty-five old style Lunch-Bags to be sold at auction, as "Traveler's Sample Cases."

We also ship to Stanton & Co., Chicago, nine Leather, and six Leather Cloth Lunch-bags, ordered by him in April. We have filled within a week, twenty-two orders, and have a larger stock of ready made bags on hand now, than at any time within the last six months. We have twenty orders on our books yet unfilled, which we hope to dispose of the coming week.

The Lord prospers us, and the revival spirit in our hearts, gives us inspiration to do with our might, what he gives us to do.

Will our Agents please to be particular about giving the right initials, in sending us the names of their customers, who order bags. N.

Plastering, papering, whitewashing and cleaning, all beautifully intermixed, have for several days been transpiring at the Mansion and middle house. The New House is entirely free from all this disorder, the cleaning there having been finished more than a week ago.—Every thing in the line of repairs however, approximates toward its close, when the improved aspect of things will amply repay us for all the inconvenience we have suffered, while the work of criticism has been going on.

C. S. J. gave us last night, at Mr. Woolworth's request, a brief history of his course of study, both at Yale, and Columbia College, together with his examination and admission to the bar.

The fruit-preserving corps have received a barrel of pine-apples, which they are putting up for the sake of experimenting with their new bottles.

A quartette song, a duet and a solo were sung last night at the close of meeting; also a song by the children, and a piece of music on the piano.

The sun really shines, to-day, and not a cloud is to be seen in the heavens.

We really shall be obliged to send out, to-day, for a rarity, some blank paper, as our copy runs short, and we have no letters that are interesting, or items of news to report.

Yesterday's temperature—
7 A. M., 40. 12 M., 60. 6 P. M., 62. Mean 56¾.

THE O. C. DAILY.

VOL. 3.   MONDAY, MAY 27, 1867.   NO. 126.

BUSINESS MEETING.

Mr. Jones presented the remedy which had suggested itself to his mind, for preventing the Creek from wearing its banks. The cause of its wearing, is the crookedness of the stream and the softness of its banks. He proposed that where the bank was thus washed, the stone and gravel on the opposite peninsula be thrown up against it, making a gradual slope toward the center of the stream. This would tend to straighten its channel and at the same time harden the bank.

Abram reported the planing-machine, at the carpenter-shop, very much out of repair. He would like a new one, and thought perhaps the machinists could make one. J. F. Sears, D. M. Kelly, Mr. Woolworth and Abram, committee.

Mr. Nash wished to have some one that he could call on at any time, to mow the lawn, this summer. He had applied to the distributers of help, and to the farmers without success. Messrs. Nash, Hatch, Woolworth and Kinsley, appointed committee with full authority to do the very best thing that can be done.

Mr. Inslee said the machinists have an application from Mr. Farwell, for a cleaner. He wants to know how soon and for what price we can make one for him. We are deficient in help for the wood-work, and for painting, and if Victor Hawley goes into the fruit-department as is expected, we shall be unable to fill the order, for he is our principal help on that work.

The matter was referred to Messrs. Cragin, Woolworth, Campbell, Thacker and Inslee.

The water at W. P., is very hard; disagreeable to the taste, and thought, by some, to be unhealthy. It is desirable to have a filter. We have one here which is out of order. Mr. Cragin thought perhaps we might exchange it for a larger one. Mr. Campbell, Mr. Ackley and Mrs. Miller will decide what is best to be done.

There was some talk about horses for the W. P., folks. Mr. Clark said he did not like to have young and irresponsible boys come after horses. There is need of brotherly love and kindness. Mr. Campbell was chosen to consult with the Willow-Place folks.

———

Mr. and Mrs. Hamilton our visitors, left this morning after a stay of five days. A meeting was held with them yesterday, in which they both related their past history and religious experience, quite minutely. Mr. H. was early in life religiously inclined and studied for the ministry, but his health failing he gave up study. He was at first a Congregationalist—then a Methodist—afterward a Millerite; but as the doctrine of the second Advent of Christ, according to Miller, failed, he did not know but the Bible might be in fault, and so he laid that aside, and sought truth by the study of nature and phrenology.—He has dipped into mesmerism, psychology and free love, and has taken a deep draught of spiritualism. He seems now to have given them all up, except phrenology, which at the present time is evidently his hobby, more than any thing else. His mind appears to be in a chaotic state, and though we have hope for him that he may be able to clear himself from the effects of his past course, yet we feel that he is not, at present, in any state to connect himself with the Community.

Mrs. H. told her story in a very simple and interesting way. She is naturally cautious and fearful, and has never sympathized fully in any ism that her husband has been drawn into, and has suffered intensely in consequence of his erratic course. She has evidently been the ballast that has kept the family from destruction during the storms that have swept over them. She says her mind is so much affected by the past, that she cannot see things clearly now, but seems in earnest to find the truth, and come into sympathetic relations with us. She thinks her visit here will be a great help to them, and when told that she might be called to take the lead of her husband as she had been less involved in error than he, she said if she did, it would be the first time, as she was naturally very receptive and not disposed to take a leading position. They are both more or less tinctured with universalism and believe that all men however wicked are progressing toward good, and will in ages to come be saved, and evil put out of existence.

We had some talk, last night, about the present state of our finances. We are considerably cramped just now, and as work at the machine-shop is called for, it is desirable that Victor Hawley should remain there, if possible, instead of going into the fruit-preserving business, as he was expected to. This led to some talk about D. A. Abbott's case, and his fitness to fill the place needed in the fruit business, and an eloquent appeal to Daniel from Mr. Cragin, urging him to forget the past and begin anew, begging him to become reconciled to Mr. Thacker, and take his place as a helper to him. Mr. Cragin's words brought tears to our eyes, but, we are sorry to say, produced no softening effect upon Daniel, who, we fear, may lose the present golden opportunity of reconciliation to God and an honorable place in his kingdom.

———

In the young men's meeting yesterday, a very interesting note from Mr. Hamilton to Daniel Abbott was read, which called forth an expression of love for Mr. Hamilton and thankfulness to him for his kindness and faithfulness with the young men.

———

Although it rained Saturday afternoon and yesterday, it is clear and unclouded to-day. We are thankful for fair weather.

Temperature Saturday and Sunday—
7 A. M., 63.   12 M., 68.   6 P. M., 54.   Mean 65.
7 A. M., 54.   12 M., 68.   6 P. M., 58.   Mean 56½.

THE O. C. DAILY.

VOL. 3.   TUESDAY, MAY 28, 1867.   NO. 127.

WILLOW-PLACE:—C. C. Hatch measured off half a square rod on our lawn, and counted therein five hundred and twenty full-blown dandelions, not to mention a quantity culled for greens just before. Guess Wallingford will have to give us the "belt" on raising dandelions.

Evening Meeting.—The more thoroughly to unite our various business interests, and promote brotherly love and union in our family circle, G. Cragin proposed, some days since, that we devote an occasional evening to free discussion of business matters, and have the whole family take part. Last evening it was proposed that we have a course of criticism of the different departments as an introductory step. This being sympathized with, and many volunteers offering, G. W. H.'s case was first taken. In the kind yet faithful criticism that followed, perhaps the most noticeable feature was the brotherly way in which it was given.

OUTDOOR ITEM.—One of our hired men appears to be quite mulish. We asked him to call at the office and settle; his reply was, that he should do no such thing unless he could receive pay for seven months' work, declaring that he hired out for that time, and should not leave. The fact is, he was hired with the understanding that we should keep him as long as we were satisfied with him. It is to be hoped that foremen of different departments will hire no person that has been discharged from some other department of labor, without a recommendation from the foreman under whom they have served. It might be mentioned that the hired men have been signing an agreement, drawn up by a lawyer at Oneida, that puts an end to all such disagreeable disputes.

We have heard since the above was in type, that the man referred to, has taken the money that was his due, and has left.

Coming down the road that leads through the plum-orchard, yesterday, I was met by one of the hired men on horseback, who said, "Dennis McCarthy is almost dead, he's been drinking ice-water." Hurrying to where the sufferer was lying, I found him cramped with pain, caused by recklessly drinking cold water, while very warm. Some whisky and strong pepper tea was administered to him, as soon as they could be obtained, which relieved him, so as to enable him to be taken to the boarding-house, a part of the way to which, he walked. He was doing well when last seen.

F.

The kingdom of God might be likened to a man building rustic work, who collects a multitude of poles, sticks and roots, large and small, straight and crooked, some very crooked, perhaps. He by faith sees the structure he designs to build. His eye surveys every stick and traces every crook, to see what it will make. Then his hand reaches for the foundation members of the building, which are united to form their part and support the weaker ones. Then piece to piece is added with reference to every other piece, in size as well as shape, until every member is put in its proper place, to form a harmonious and pleasing structure. As the work proceeds, it is amusing to see how reluctant each piece is to leave its temporary place (among society did you say?) The piece on top of the heap, will cling to its neighbor with great tenacity and the builder generally has to pull and tug, to get its consent to be cut, pierced or sawn asunder for the work's sake. The more curved and valuable the piece is, the more it clings to others, and much caution is needed to get it free to go through the ordeal, which all have to pass alone; but when it has received all necessary preparation and rests in its place, how it ornaments the structure. Then much has to be cast aside as unfit for the work. This might envy the good, as it stands a monument of symmetry, unity and beauty, yet formed of individual pieces, woven together like the temple of Christ.

A LEARNER.

A man from the depot, a tinman, who keeps hanging baskets made of wire, for sale, sent one of them up here, yesterday, for our florists to fill, which they immediately proceeded to do.

They first lined the basket with nice moss, then filled it with earth, six varieties of hanging vines were planted equidistant around it, gracefully falling over its sides. A nice fuchsia ornaments the center of the basket, space between that and the circumference being filled up with verbenas and other choice flowers. The man gave, as his reason for wanting the basket filled, that it would show persons the use for which it was designed, and save questioning.

We have at last succeeded in cutting a passage through, from the children's entry into their new room, alias, lower tent-room, by removing the stairway that conducted to the chamber above, the entrance to which is now effected through the upper tent-room. Another door from the entry, is to be cut through into the large room that has recently been fitted up. A partition is to be put across the entry, to divide the front entrance from the sink-room.

Some conversation, last night, about our croquet ground. It is quite desirable that it should be kept neat and in order, and the balls and mallets properly cared for. It is under the daily inspection of visitors, who on visiting the flower-garden, seem to take much pleasure in witnessing the game.

A committee was appointed to attend to the matter.

Georgiana Sears arrived safely in the night.

Yesterday's temperature—
7 A. M., 56. 12 M., 60. . 6 P. M., 62. ., Mean, 59½.

THE O. C. DAILY.

VOL. 3. WEDNESDAY, MAY 29, 1867. NO. 128.

EVENING MEETING.

Mr. Woolworth said in meeting last night, that he had been disturbed a good deal by seeing Sarah Olmstead about the premises, with her usual brassy appearance. She comes in and makes herself quite at home, and shows her friends around the house. To-day, she wanted to see Grace Mills, and seems determined to get into communication with her. Grace treated her very coldly, scarcely speaking to her, yet on leaving, she threw her a kiss, which G. did not notice. It is to be hoped that if she persists in coming, either Grace or some one else, will tell her plainly that we do not want to have any thing to do with her. It is impudence in her to thrust herself in here, when she must know that her presence is a nuisance.

Mr. Kelley called again yesterday, to see Victor. He liked him better than when he saw him last. It appears he has undertaken to defend the Community in the Asylum. Mr. K., told V., that Dr. Gray told him when he was there before, that he (Victor) was doing well, and might be able to leave the Asylum sooner than he had supposed. Victor replied that he was willing to stay as long as the Dr., thought best— Mr. K., had quite a conflict with him, when there last week, and the effect has been good. Victor was very glad to see him, and earnestly requested him to call as often as he came to Utica.

WILLOW-PLACE :—A. L. Burt's quartette club favored this quiet home with a call last evening, and agreeably surprised us with some of their finest pieces. They have our hearty thanks, and the assurance that they will ever be welcome.—We have bees after supper for putting things to rights about the grounds. We are improving the walks at present. These bees are enthusiastically attended, and are quite musical.

Things are much as usual in the Shop. Some repairs are to be made on the trap-rollers.—Among our visitors yesterday, was Miss G. Sears of Wallingford.

Our Oneida friends are often attracted to the pond where they are quite successful as anglers.

MEETING :—The criticism of Mr. G. W. Hamilton was continued in the same brotherly spirit as on the previous evening. We are anxious to perfect the spirit of unity and organization in business. G. seemed thankful for the advice and hints given him. The feeling of harmony and union with Christ was complete. Mr. Cragin made some edifying remarks at the close.—Very latest news.—It rained during the night.

On going down to supper, last night, we found our five long tables all blazing with winter-green (Gaul-theria Procumbens) berries, and every body enquiring "Where did they come from?" No one could tell. Only the steward knew that they came from the West by R. R., accompanied with the following note:

North Manlius, Onondaga Co.
O. C.—Please accept one bushel winter-green berries. With respect, ———

We thought they must have been busy fingers that gathered so many. The berries were nice and appreciated by all. We imagined we were wise enough to guess who the donors were; any how, we extend our thanks and hope they may never do a worse thing.

We discovered written on a newspaper, in the bottom of the box that contained the berries, the name, Leander Wilcox. This gives us a clew, by which we shall doubtless be able to unravel the mystery connected with the box, and also give us a chance to tender our thanks to the generous givers. The berries afforded the family a rare treat.

Miss Eliza Patten, daughter of a sister of Chauncey Dutton, called at the Community, a few days since. It will be remembered that both Chauncey E. Dutton and his sister were in communication with Mr. Noyes, in his early religious experience, and in some measure co-workers with him. Much interest is felt in Eliza on this account. She expressed a strong desire to visit us again, and become acquainted with Mr. Noyes. She was presented with a very nice satchel on leaving, with which she seemed much pleased.

Mr. Kinsley and L. A. Thayer went to Verona, yesterday. Mr. Leet has had the swelling on his leg lanced, and the sore discharges quite freely. His disease has proved itself to be erysipelas. Mr. L. thinks he shall come to Oneida, as soon as he is able to ride. He feels that his sickness is doing a good work in his own heart and spirit.

Daniel Bailey is making a visit at Willow-Place and staid there last night. Mr. Ackley was over here yesterday, and spent the night. Mrs. Bushnell has taken Mrs. Bolles's place, and Florence, Virtue's, and so the wheel keeps moving.

The lawn is being mown for the first time this season. We saw Mr. Easton out this morning, though it rained some, with his tall boots on, scythe in hand cutting down grass, farmer-like.

The weather, to-day, is like summer, no mistake, almost sultry. We welcome the change with gladsome hearts.

Yesterday's temperature—
7 A. M., 69. 12 M., 67. 6 P. M., 68. Mean 64½.

THE O. C. DAILY.

VOL. 3. THURSDAY, MAY 30, 1867. NO. 129.

We give a few extracts from Miss Clara Wait's letter, received a few days since. The letter is mostly quotations from her diary:

"May 17th.—I feel quite settled in my mind, relative to my visit to Oneida. I write to give expression to what I find in my heart. I feel very happy and am instructed and strengthened in the Lord. My heart rises towards God in the inspiration I have breathed at Oneida.

"Sat. 18.—I received a letter, to-day, from Mrs. Wm. A. Hunter, of Berlin Heights, which proves more fully how hades-haunted the socialists are there, and too, how much so I have been, up to the present time. I realize more and more the truthfulness of Mr. Cragin's criticism of me, I see how unbelief is the root of all the confounding of moral and spiritual distinctions in my mind.

"Monday 20.—Wrote to S. A. Story of my visit, its effects upon my mind and the unity I realize with Mr. Noyes and the Community, and the importance I feel of a full acceptance of the doctrine of an uncreated personal devil.

"Tuesday 21.—A day of trial of mind. The dividing line between God and those who are for him, and the devil and those who are for him, must become clearly defined in my mind." I realize a change in my spiritual and mental condition, since my visit. Spirits who came before, as advisers, now come as accusers and reproachers. They ignore personality in Christ, or the devil. Through my late experiences, I am seeing how I have been ensnared and deceived in the past.

"Friday 24.—I accept Mr. Noyes, as Christ's divinely appointed leader, and the Community as fellow-soldiers, to whom I look for drill and discipline. I desire to join you in the war against Satan and his followers, and believe I can serve the cause of Christ more effectually, under your leadership, than single-handed. I realize that my pride and self-will have been the devil's strong-hold. I desire that humility, repentance, and a soft receptive heart may be given me. I confess love for your spirit and life."

In our meeting, yesterday noon, just as the clock struck one, Mr. Herrick rose and said, " Our missionaries are at this moment, about starting out from New-York-harbor. Europe sent us the cholera. Mr. Noyes published the tract, ' Salvation from Sin' and posted up hand-bills in different places in the City, notifying the inhabitants that the sentiments therein contained, were a perfect antidote to the cholera. Now we send back to them living embodiments of Salvation from Sin, and the revival spirit."

TO G. W. N. AND C. S. J. ON THEIR DEPARTURE.

Brothers, we give the parting hand but shed no parting tear,
For though you launch on Ocean vast, you have no cause for fear,
For God doth hold within his fists, with iron grasp, the wind,
And the ever foaming Ocean, in the hollow of his hand.
The Macedonian cry is heard and angels point the way,
And fearlessly and joyfully, you listen and obey;
Perchance the word has gone before, and messengers from heaven,
To the Old World have whispered truths, that to the New, are given.
Then speed thee on thy mission, spread the news o'er land and sea,
That the Bible is our talisman, a bond of unity,
That Christ and Paul our leaders, will all nations blend in one,
God's kingdom be acknowledged, and his will on earth be done.

Elder Wheeler, from Underhill, Vermont, came here, yesterday. He has a son living in Wisconsin, and is on his way to visit him. He is a Free-will Baptist and an acquaintance of the Kinsleys, and several years ago, he became very much interested in our doctrines and saw the truth clearly. He gave up preaching for a time, and promised well. But his wife was exceedingly bitter toward us, and succeeded in hedging up his way. She died a year ago, and he soon after married a widow lady, who has several children and considerable property, and he has relapsed again, we understand, into occasionally preaching in the old way. He has long been anxious to visit the O. C., and appears very friendly.

A supper party was given, yesterday, in the dining-room, to our outdoor workmen, nineteen in number, in which Mr. Thacker and the foremen of the different departments participated. The object in getting the workmen together, was to let them know who their leaders were, and Mr. Thacker's position as general overseer. They appeared quite pleased with the supper.

A little ragged boy was seen, yesterday afternoon, on the lawn in earnest conversation with Mr. W. We drew near expecting to see tears in his large black eyes, but we found that he was trying to buy a colt that had been foaled in the morning. "For," said he, "it is just the size for me to ride on, and I have money."

DEPARTURES.—E. S. Nash, Sophronia S. Higgins, and little Maud, last night, for Wallingford.

Yesterday's temperature—
7 A. M., 64. 12 M., 76. 6 P. M., 72. Mean 70⅔.

THE O. C. DAILY.

VOL. 3.   FRIDAY, MAY 31, 1867.   NO. 130.

Extract from a note received from C. S. J. yesterday :

On board Cunard Steamship, Tripoli,
Jersey City, Wednesday noon.

" When this reaches you I shall be at sea, and far out of sight of land. Our accommodations are every way comfortable, and the officers and crew seem to be kind and accommodating. I put myself in the hands of God, and go forth to meet, I know not what. God knows, and I feel perfectly quiet and peaceful about my future."

WILLOW-PLACE :—New Haven and Wallingford are not the only kaleidoscopical (!!) families, we find: indeed, for continual shifting, W. P., perhaps, takes the lead. Hardly an evening passes but shows two or three new faces in our sitting-room, filling the places of as many absent ones. Last evening, we counted five women, accompanied by a protector, who took to the plank, after meeting, for the mile-and-a-quarter tramp.

Our lawn grows daily in attractiveness. A rustic seat adorns one spot, the gift of Mr. Ellis. After supper, bees toil diligently at our front walk. The deep emerald of the luxuriant grass, the bright hued dandelions, and the fragrant apple-blossoms add their varied beauty to the scene.

Our enthusiastic, but not thoroughly initiated horticulturist, mentioning the shrubs he had set out, included a " Flowering—Flowering," couldn't quite think what nut it was, but at length hits on one that sounds particularly familiar, " Flowering Peanut."

A TIME-PIECE FOR ALL.—Let us have a great big clock with a stroke loud enough to be heard all over the farm. Fix him up on the cupola—every one would know the hour. Watches would hardly be needed, except when you go from home—very little watch cleaning and repairing then. None would be tempted to regret having given up a watch.

We might, in the course of time, (or eternity) have a regular chime for every hour—music in the open air —a communising of time and tune, as it were,—all would hear it together. What say you ? And then we might have a watch or two always to spare, kept hung up in the office, for any one who might really need it.   EXCELSIOR.

In proportion as God's spirit works among us, in the same ratio does Satan thrust in his fiery darts of temptation, urging to the two extremes of over-action and unbelief, producing accusation and discouragement. But we are not ignorant of his devices. His attempts to " sow discord among the brethren,"—to get in little slivers of distrust, have been exposed and foiled, and hearts are knit more closely together, thus making the words of scripture true, " The wrath of man" (and devils), " shall praise him and the remainder he will restrain."

Mr. Clark reports his sales, for two days, of castings for plows and hop-stoves, at six hundred dollars.

Mr. Kellogg sold stock to the amount of four hundred and fifteen dollars, yesterday. Three hundred dollars were paid down, and the balance is to be paid when the stock is driven away. The Community receive fifty cents per week for pasturing, while the cattle remain. The stock sold was mostly cows of a second quality. Billy Smith says "they are the poorest cows the Community has got."

A heifer, full blood Ayshire, sixteen months old, introduced another little stranger to the Community yesterday, giving us eight full blooded animals at the present time. The new comer is a heifer. ACCOLA.

Mr. Guiteau came yesterday forenoon, and leaves for home to-day. He regrets that his stay here must be so short—said his business in New-York, detained him longer than he expected, and he was obliged to reach home this week. He saw his son Charles, while in the city, who has commenced the study of law, and has become so religious, that he has joined Henry Ward Beecher's church. Mr. G. spoke of C.'s condition as a marked case of diotrephiasis.

HORTICULTURAL.—Worm's nests on the apple trees are quite numerous; we commence a raid on them to-day.

We have sold between four and five hundred dollars worth of Grape-vines, this spring.

The first dinner for the season in the company dining-room, was furnished yesterday, to two gentlemen who called for it.

Notwithstanding the rain and mud, we finished yesterday, setting out five acres of strawberry plants.

Traps ordered during the month of May,   406 doz.

Yesterday's temperature—
7 A. M., 60, 12 M., 64, 6 P. M., 58.   Mean 60½.

THE O. C. DAILY.

VOL. 3.　SATURDAY, JUNE 1, 1867.　NO. 131.

The Committee to whom the use of the Willow-Place team was referred, have made the following arrangement:

It is to leave the office for W. P., promptly at seven o'clock in the morning, taking the passengers and other material that are ready to go at that hour. It will leave again for W. P., usually, on the arrival of the mail, about half past ten.

In the afternoon it is to leave the office for W. P., at one o'clock, and again, usually, at half past four. In the intermediate time, it is to be at the service of the W. P., family, and on no account be called upon to do service here, when it is wanted there. Persons having occasion to use a team, will please bear this in mind; it being the only one there is for service at that station. The business there, sometimes suffers serious inconvenience, by the team being called upon to do chores here.

Mr. Wheeler left yesterday in company with Mr. Guiteau. They expected to travel together as far as Detroit. Mr. W. as we should expect, is a very unhappy man. He saw the truth of some of our doctrines, several years ago, and for a time was very zealous. He afterward relapsed into his former state, and with the exception of the doctrine of the "Second Coming" has no belief now in common with us. He acknowledged that he took a very foolish step in marrying as he did, so soon after the death of his wife, but he wanted a home, and was overpersuaded to do it. His wife professed a great deal of love for him and does at the present time, but from some unaccountable reason, has proposed that they should separate. He says he does not know for what cause, but we doubted some, whether he was perfectly sincere in saying this; he does not expect to return to her, and is without a home. He is reaping the bitter fruit of his doings, and we could not suffer our hearts to be drawn into sympathy with him, or in any way help to turn aside the just judgments of God, though as a victim of Satan we pity him.

A Mr. Kent, from Michigan, came here yesterday. His home is near Lansing, and hearing of our Community, and that there was a lady living in Lansing, [Miss Burgess] who had been a member of the O. C., he went to see her. He did not get much acquainted with her, but she lent him the "Berean," which he has studied indefatigably the past winter, and has had the reading of the CIRCULAR some, through Miss B.'s brother. He said he felt that he *must* come and see us—he could not stay away. He has a wife, (who does not sympathize with him at all,) and three children. He made comfortable provision for them before he left, and hoped we would give him employment and let him remain here through the summer. Miss Burgess and Homer have bought a house and lot, and live together, the latter working at the saddle and harness business.

Grace Mills offered herself for criticism. The family thought she had improved a good deal, and had manifested more or less earnestness since her return; but she needs to separate herself more thoroughly than she had done, from William and her other relations, and the world, Sarah Olmstead in particular, and attach herself, by her openness and sincerity, more firmly to the Community. She needs a new conversion: she is in the habit of reading novels, and works of fiction, which was thought to be in her present state, very injurious, and had the effect to dissipate her mind, and give her a disrelish for Mr. Noyes's writings, and more important reading. It was remarked that the true revival spirit would take away her taste for light reading.

Will our Agents please to notify us (the Bag Dept.) when they allow a per cent to any of their customers, new ones more especially, as we have had several instances lately, where parties have complained that we did not give them the per cent promised by our Agents, about which we had not been notified.

When two or more parties have goods sent to them in the same box, have it understood and agreed to by said parties.

State by what route goods are to be sent, also, where freight or expressage is to be prepaid, whether it is for the whole or part of the distance.　　N.

The rain has ceased, at least for a while, and the sun once more shines upon us, which is truly delightful. As a matter of course, the outdoor work comes with a rush, ploughing and preparing the ground for barley, beans, corn, potatoes, beets, carrots, &c. I noticed a man harrowing a piece of land with oxen, who were floundering about in the mud knee deep. As far as I have noticed, I have felt a good spirit among all hands, foremen and workmen, and have not heard a word of grumbling any where.　　Y.

Mr. Conant reports that the barley was all sowed yesterday.

Yesterday's temperature—
7 A. M., 48.　12 M., 58.　6 P. M., 61.　Mean 55½.

THE O. C. DAILY.

VOL. 3.   MONDAY, JUNE 3, 1867.   NO. 132.

BUSINESS MEETING.

A communication was read from Mr. Worden, in which the enquiry was raised, who shall take charge of his responsibilities while absent at Wallingford. At Mr. Worden's suggestion, and the approval of the Board, Mr. Barron is to take charge of the interests of the Boarding-house, and the care of the highway to devolve upon Messrs. Conant, Clark and Barron.

Carrie has some trouble in regard to paying our hired hands—one man was paid two dollars at the barn, and soon after came to the office to settle, and was paid his full wages. It was decided by the Board, that our hired men should be paid only at the office, or if circumstances occurred, that made it necessary to pay them elsewhere, it should be reported at the office immediately.

Mr. Inslee presented a letter from L. F. Dunn asking for a lathe to be built for Wallingford. After some discussion, it was thought it would be a very convenient thing for Mr. Burt and others, and the machinists were requested to keep the subject in mind and get one up as soon as their other business will permit.

Mr. Clark said that those now buying hop-stoves **wanted pipe with them. He makes from two to three** cents per pound on the pipe, and when he goes out with a load, he can make from nine to ten dollars per day. He wanted to know the mind of the Board about buying pipe and about going out himself with the stoves. Messrs. Clark, Campbell and Kinsley were appointed committee to decide.

SATURDAY EVENING.—*D. A. Abbott:*—As I publicly refused to go into the fruit-business, when Mr. Cragin proposed it here the other night, I wish now, as publicly to accept of Mr. Cragin's proposition, and take that or any other position the Community may offer. [Applause.]

SUNDAY EVENING.—*D. A. Abbott:*—I take this opportunity to thank the Community for any criticism I have had in the past, and confess Christ a whole savior. I think I gained a victory this afternoon, over the spirit I have been under. [Applause.]

I was reading some in the Testament, and read the verse where Paul says: " He that soweth sparingly, shall reap also sparingly ; and he that soweth bountifully, shall reap also bountifully." I think in the past I have testified very sparingly, and consequently I have reaped but sparingly. In future I intend to testify bountifully of God's goodness to me. [Applause.]

Mr. Morris writes a long letter, giving his sentiments in full. We have only room, to-day, to give what he says on business, and perhaps shall be able to publish the remainder of his letter, or portions of it to-morrow. He writes :

" Please tell me whether your business Agency are prepared to, and feel competent to purchase general stock of merchandize for merchants. For instance a merchant in Blairstown, who trades from forty to fifty thousand dollars per year, wishes to buy in New-York, instead of Chicago. Are any of your agents judges of that kind of goods? have they had experience in that line &c.? If said merchant deposits with them by draft, and sends on his orders, which never exceed his deposit, what commission will you charge for doing the business? I have been inquired of in regard to it, and while I was ready to vouch for the integrity of the firm, I am not prepared to say about these other matters. There is quite a feeling here in favor of buying in New-York at present, and the idea of a responsible Agency takes well. Their orders and remittances would perhaps, be sent in, once or twice per month. I have agreed to write for some parties here."

Our visitor, Mr. Kent, related some of his experience in meeting, last night. He is so honest and earnest in his search for truth, and has such a straightforward and original way of telling his story, that we were touched with his simplicity, though at times the whole room was convulsed with laughter,

Our beautiful hedge that has hitherto been the glory and pride of our grounds, presents this spring, a blackened appearance. It is evidently dead, and though some faint signs of life are here and there visible, yet the probability is, that it will all have to be cut down.

A Mr. Covenhoven, of Boonville, an acquaintance of J. P. Hutchings, staid here over Sunday. He has been a reader of the CIRCULAR a good many years, and is very friendly.

D. Edson Smith came Saturday. He left his wife, at her fathers, a short distance from here, we do not know the name of the place.

An order for 480 dozen traps was received a day or two since.

A good beginning of corn planting was made Saturday.

Temperature Saturday and Sunday—
7 A. M., 64.   12 M., 82.   6 P. M., 70.   Mean 72.
7 A. M., 66.   12 M., 74.   6 P. M., 63.   Mean 67¼.

THE O. C. DAILY.

VOL. 3.　　TUESDAY, JUNE 4, 1867.　　NO. 133.

Blairstown, May 28.

DEAR BROTHERS AND SISTERS OF ONEIDA COMMUNITY :—After a good deal of wandering, I am again at home with my family in pretty good health. Mrs. Morris's health is much improved. I now return my thanks to you for your hospitality to my family whilst visiting you ; they are glad they have been to see you. Mrs. M., is quite in love with you, and were she converted to what you call religion, would be ready and anxious to offer herself as a candidate for membership with you. She talks about you every day— can't rest till she reads the CIRCULAR—has a picture of your dwelling framed and hung up in her sitting-room.

I regret that I could not get to see you, but it seems as though the fates have decreed otherwise. When I got through with my business, it seemed best for me to hasten home. Byron was interested in you, but thinks the lesson I have taught him, would have to be unlearned there, that of free and independent thinking, and he has no disposition to give that up, neither do I wish him to. It has cost me more than any thing else, to assert my own individuality, and do my own thinking, as there have been plenty of others insisting in doing my thinking for me, and urging me to have faith in Christ &c. all my life, and threatening me with damnation, if I did not believe as they did. But whilst I have ever been very accommodating, it was just as impossible for me to be an orthodox christian, as it was to have red hair, or to fly. Still I pass along, and do think that the members of the different churches love me better than they do the members of the church to which they do not belong, and I certainly think I love them better than they love one another. (I mean members of different churches).

Notwithstanding you seem to feel it your province to annihilate spiritualism every week, I still love you, for I am a Communist and you have demonstrated the practicability of Communism, and I feel that I am under great obligations to you, and hope I shall ever pray for your prosperity ; and also if your theology is right, I may be favored to see it, and that if you are hugging some delusion, such as a personal devil, resurrection of the body, final damnation of a part of the human family, Christ being God, &c., &c., that you may see it.　*　　*　　*　　*

I have yet to find the first *Bible* man or woman, that looks on you in any other light, than a band of lewd men and women, or has ever subscribed for your paper ; and yet to find the first spiritualist but what wishes you well, and looks up to you as doing good, quite a number of them taking your paper. But it is very likely that you are being of use to them, for in joining with others in persecuting them, it will probably have a tendency to purify them, for I have to acknowledge that we are not as devoted or as practical perhaps, as would be best.

Now friends think me not rude or offensive, for I feel that I ought to write, and that you would expect to hear from me, and surely whilst I respect you for your earnestness and zeal, you will not disrespect me for my frankness.　*　　*　　*　　*

I send one dollar, please send me that new book you have published, and remember that none of this letter is for the paper.

Please have the CIRCULAR sent to Blairstown, Iowa, as I can't pretend to do without it. If there is any thing for you to learn, may God and the good spirits assist you, as well as all others who are seeking to know the truth.　　　Yours with good wishes.

ISAIAH MORRIS.

WILLOW-PLACE :—A fine melodeon has been rented for the use of the W. P. family. It was obtained from a music dealer at Oneida, who charges two dollars per month and takes his pay in bags. Many who have heard it, think its tones are superior to the harmonium, especially the bass. The price of the instrument is $220.

Evening Meeting.—Criticism of H. Blood. The principal faults mentioned were freedom with the hired men, lack of politeness especially in addressing his superiors, and a habit of thrusting his opinions forward in conversation. He was thought to have improved much since coming over here to live ; seems to be anxious to seek the ascending fellowship, and as a general thing, is a faithful boy to work.

One of our hired women who worked in the laundry, spoke in a saucy way to Mrs. M. yesterday, who replied that we did not want folks that worked for us to talk in that way. She was quite angry and began to look about and pack up her things. John Conant paid her and she left without further ceremony, leaving us minus one woman in the washing.

In speaking of the hedge, yesterday, we should have mentioned that it was the privet hedge, that is winter-killed, and that the barberry and buckthorn hedges have not, as we know, sustained any injury.

We greeted the CIRCULARS very early this morning, or rather they greeted us, as on rising we found them lying at our doors, waiting for admission.

We had a thunder storm, accompanied by considerable wind, about noon, yesterday.

Rain is still abundant, with only an occasional *sprinkling* of fair weather.

Yesterday's temperature—

7 A. M., 78.　12 M., 78.　6 P. M., 68.　Mean 71⅓.

THE O. C. DAILY.

VOL. 3. WEDNESDAY, JUNE 5, 1867. NO. 134.

JUNE 4—The reading of Mr. Isaiah Morris's letter in the O. C. DAILY this morning, has stirred my spirit. I consider his advances toward us as thoroughly insincere, like those of Warren Chase. He pretends to love us and accept our Communism, while he evidently despises and hates our religion, our Christ, our Bible, every thing that has made us Communists, and gives us the success which he admires. His letter, with all its smoothness, is thoroughly disrespectful toward us, virtually accusing us of superstition and mental bondage, and actually accusing us in so many words of persecuting the spiritualists. He is evidently one of the great class of self-conceited blockheads, who have no fixed belief except in their own wisdom and independent sufficiency. The visit of his wife and son, so far as he is concerned, was an imposition. I doubt whether he is sincere in giving the reason for not coming himself. His spirit has no home here. That is probably the reason he did not come. He is simply an infidel spiritualist, and has not accepted one word of our faith-testimony in the paper or elsewhere, and is not likely to. You can see in all his sugary expressions, that he is praying and expecting that we shall find out the error of our ways and come over to his side. While he shoves aside as trash all that distinguishes us from himself and the infidels, he asks us to accept him as a friend on the bare ground of his sympathy with us in Communism. This is just the way Warren Chase courted us. I don't want such lovers. There is no possibility of making even a beginning of Communism with Morris's avowed ideas of personal independence, so that all he says about sympathizing with our Communism is a sham.

J. H. N.

The above communication from Mr. Noyes was read in the noon meeting, yesterday, and the idea was suggested to publish and send it to Mr. Morris. But Mr. Noyes objected, and thought some other person should reply to Mr. Morris's letter. He had no objections, however, to our publishing the article in question, for the benefit of the Communes. Mr. Cragin is writing to Mr. M. to-day, and will give the substance of Mr. Noyes's talk on his case.

WILLOW-PLACE ITEMS :—Our Commune is certainly growing ; forty-two persons took dinner here yesterday. We had twenty-three visitors from O. C., during the day. This class of visitors is quite popular with us ; our housekeepers notice that the female portion of it take as naturally to dish-washing and housework as fashionable callers do, to gossip and tattle.

D. J. B., is spending a few days with us. He was noticed, yesterday afternoon, in company with two or three children, fishing in the pond.

The Trap order of 4th inst., leaves us one thousand five hundred No. 0 Traps on hand. One ton of steel has been ordered, with which to test further the new method of making springs.

J. F. Sears is putting the last touches to a fine microscope. It will be of somewhat higher power than the first one he made.

MONDAY EVENING, JUNE 3, 1867.—With June began our spring, not to say summer, this year. Last Saturday was a beautiful day, and all hoped, and many believed that summer weather would soon appear with her settled habits. But up to this time many variations have been observed, of sun and shade, of cloud and wind and rain, which leads one to moralize some, and wonder at the causes of so much cold and rain as have prevailed.

All at once it seemed to be made clear that our acquisition of Russian America was the main cause. It is true that the creation of a British confederation by the sanction of Queen Victoria in consolidating the Canadas, New Brunswick, Nova Scotia &c., had modifying influences : but the great cause must have been, Secretary Seward's Isothermal current, let loose upon the cold regions of the north.

That's what the matter is—all this spring that stream of hot air has been rushing down and melting into the snow, and icy mountains of British America : sending up vast exhalations of vapor, which by the further action of political influences, Northern and Southern combined, have swung round the circle and reached us in copious showers.

SIGNED, "MY POLICY."

Omaha, May 27, 1867.

DEAR SIR :—I have for the past two years been thinking of making an application for membership in your Community; have also a friend of about my own age, who has for some time been of the same opinion. I write this in all sincerity, both for the sake of myself and friend ; we are aged respectively twenty-one and twenty-five, am myself a widower, can give good references. Please write soon as possible, and state terms of admission &c. Address R. C. Dunnington, Omaha Nebraska.

Our people actually made a beginning, day before yesterday, of putting down the iron aqueduct. We are thankful for this fine sunny day, which gives a new impetus to outdoor work.

Mrs. Aiken has a brother, and his wife and child visiting here.

Bags made in May,	98¼ dozen.
Value,	$3,880.71.
Bag sales for May,	$3,886.03.

Yesterday's temperature—
7 A. M., 78. 12 M., 74. 6 P. M., 68. Mean 66¼.

THE O. C. DAILY.

VOL. 3.   THURSDAY, JUNE 6, 1867.   NO. 135.

WILLOW-PLACE:—G. W. Hamilton spends his days at O. C. helping lay the iron piping for the new aqueduct. We wish the enterprise success.

MACHINE-SHOP:—J. S. Freeman has been doing some work, (cutting gear for a lathe) for a firm in Rome, to the amount of $43,00.

The price of our hired melodeon is $120, not $220 as previously reported. Please note the difference. It appears to be a very fine instrument. Its tone is sweet and sufficiently powerful for our requirements.

The event of yesterday, was Mr. Noyes's visit and stay over night. Our meeting was of thrilling interest, and withal very mirthful. Mr. Noyes's talk sent a thrill through every heart. The meeting will be reported in manuscript. We are very thankful for this visit of his, and feel that good will spring from it. He is up at breakfast with the rest, looking much at home.—We are mowing the lawn.

A cellar has been dug, and the old iron house, so called, near the foundry, has been moved a little distance and placed over it. The workmen are going right on to fit it up as a double tenement house.

In meeting, last night Mr. Easton was called on for a story—he wanted time to think—Mr. Herrick was then called on to tell a story while Mr. E. was thinking one up. Mr. H. wanted time to think too, and would prefer to have Mr. E tell his, first. Mr. E. finally, by the suggestion of some one who had heard him relate it, told about his first experience in witnessing "table tippings." He was quite young and got thoroughly scared, by the table spinning round the room, untouched by mortal hands.—Afterwards he told us of a scene on board a schooner off cape Hatteras. There was a man so completely stupified with sea-sickness, that it was impossible to rouse him. In the tossings of the craft, a dish of apple-sauce was thrown from the table and the contents cast directly in his face and the only movement he made, was just to turn himself over.

A committee was appointed to decide upon the price for meals, horse-keeping, &c., the coming season. A few meals are now called for almost daily.

Several letters were read, two of which were from persons wishing to join, one a man from Kansas and the others from New-York city. The question was asked by Abram, "Who answers all these letters, or what disposal is made of them?" Mr. Woolworth.— "I dispose of them in quite a summary way; those from the city I refer to the Agency, for papers or information." It is getting to be quite a business though, and takes not a little time if only short answers are given.

The meeting was closed by the club singing the Nicodemas song.

Tuesday, Lady Campbell accomplished a feat, which some of our younger women would scarcely dare attempt. She walked over to W. P. and back, much preferring that manner of locomotion to riding in a carriage. She met with some obstructions in the outset, from persons trying to discourage her from attempting to go on foot, but she persisted in trying the experiment and set out on her pedestrian route, accompanied by four of the small children. She started about 10 o'clock A. M. and returned between four and five o'clock P. M. Instead of lying down to rest, as most of the women would have done, she did several errands, making calls here and there, and testified that she was not in the least tired, and suffered no inconvenience from her long walk, but on the contrary, felt that it had done her good.

Miss Thomas sprained her ankle slightly a few days since, but is recovering from it. She writes to Mr. W. "It is a real trial to be deprived of the noon meetings, to say nothing of the evening meeting; and yet I am having an experience that I could not have been saved without. I confess my union with the family and the revival spirit. My heart is with you in the noon meetings, though I am a wounded soldier."

Mr. Noyes's stirring railroad talk was read at our noon meeting, yesterday, which, together with additional remarks on the same subject by Mr. Herrick, had a rousing effect, if we may judge from the testimony that was afterward given. Mr. Cragin's letter to Mr. Morris was also read, and the exercises closed with the appropriate song "The Pacific Railroad."

Mrs. Newhouse went to the depot twice, yesterday afternoon, for her mother whom she was expecting on the two o'clock train; but she did not find her, either time, and returned quite disappointed. Mrs. Hyde had been invited to make the O. C. a visit.

Mr. Kelly returned from his peddling route last night, after an absence of a little over a week.

Mr. Worden and Mrs. Burnham left this morning for Wallingford.

The Edmonds, Mrs. Aiken's friends, left this morning; also Mr. Kent started for his home in Michigan.

Yesterday's temperature—
7 A. M., 62.   12 M., 68.   6 P. M., 72.   Mean 67¼.

THE O. C. DAILY.

VOL. 3.   FRIDAY, JUNE 7, 1867.   NO. 136.

A TRIP WEST.

My object in making the trip, was, in the first place to ascertain what the prospects were, for the coming fruit crop, and secondly, to post myself more thoroughly in regard to Bartholomew's new method of preserving fruits in their natural state. The following is a brief report of my observations in a somewhat hasty trip as far west as Westfield, New York, via. the N. Y. C. railroad: From the Seneca river to the end of my route, I found the apple and pear bloom very abundant, and the universal answer to my inquiries was, that the present prospect of a crop of those fruits, was never better; especially in the first tier of counties along the lakes, and also from other parts, reports are flattering. The prospect of the peach, plum and cherry crop, is not very good except in Orleans and Niagara counties. In the latter it is claimed that the prospects were never better for all kinds of fruit, and the same is claimed for Orleans, but from my own observations I judge that Niagara stands at the head. There are scarcely any peaches this side of Orleans; no cherries, or plums with the exception of a partial crop in the vicinity of Rochester and north of Fairport, near the lake shore. There will be however, plenty of the common sour cherry beginning with Wayne county, as far west as I went.

In regard to the second object of my trip, I will say that I found Mr. Bartholomew a rather unpretending, modest sort of a man. A genius and a worker; and I judged, scientific in his investigations and discoveries. He generously offered to give me all the desired information, in regard to his new discovery in preserving fruits, &c.

His principal depot and place of operation at the present time, is in Buffalo, with parties who have applied for the right of that city, and who are now testing his system.

Mr. B. does not pretend that he can preserve soft fruits, such as strawberries, raspberries, &c., and keep them in a perfect state longer than a few weeks beyond their natural period of ripening, but fruits of a firm texture and tough skin, may be kept in a perfectly fresh state a year or longer. I saw oranges and lemons in cases, that were subjected to treatment more than a year ago, that looked fresh, and appeared to be perfectly sound. Also a fall apple that was taken from a case of eleven bushels, the first of June. The apples were put in the case the early part of winter, and on being opened were found unchanged. The case was again sealed up, and is to be opened again the first of July. The process of preserving fruit by this method, is simple and cheap. Mr. B., said that five minutes was all the time required, to put through the process

of treatment, a case of apples of the capacity of twenty-five bushels, and I would recommend that some further notice be taken of this new method of preserving fruits, by the O. C.   H. T.

WILLOW-PLACE:—Business moves steadily on. Some excitement was occasioned, yesterday, by Mr. Burland having notified his boarders to quit at the end of this week. He finds he is running behind. G. W. Hamilton and Myron arranged with him to try it a little longer, and plainly tell the boarders how it is, and see if they will not pay more or be content with cheaper board. They now demand fresh beef, roast or steak, once or twice a day.—The tenant-house west of the shop will soon be ready for plastering.—The new-mown hay on the lawn, sends up its pleasing perfume.—G. R. Kellogg brought the much coveted filter, last evening, and it has been located in the cellar. It cost fourteen dollars, expressage included.

Our pond is a great luxury. It is pleasant to fish in, sail on and bathe in ; and it also furnishes us a regular nightly concert. Blessed be the music of the mill-pond. These sunny days have made the water very inviting, and bathing after work hours, is becoming highly popular with the young men. The meeting was in part devoted to discussing our relations to the water. The hired men wish to have the privilege of using the pond. J. C. Higgins, Myron and Roswell were appointed a committee to talk with the shop-hands and learn what will satisfy them.

We wish to be liberal and try and gain the good will of all the people in this vicinity. But more on this subject when the committee report. Meantime our young men are exhorted to seek to make bathing an ordinance of worship; not to remain in the water too long; not to be noisy, but modest and quiet; and finally not to make the other sex discontented with a state of things that at present debars them from this luxury, which they enjoy fully as much as men do. It was hoped the women would be patient till a floating bath-house could be erected. The desire was expressed that we might soon have such a building. There was a unanimous feeling in favor of removing the spring-board.

ON THE MOVE.—Mrs. Higgins moved yesterday, into the room vacated by Mrs. Burnham, and Eliza Burt takes the room occupied the past winter by Sophronia. Mrs. Smith when she comes is to have Eliza's room.

Mrs. Hyde came yesterday forenoon. Her right wrist that was broken some time ago, she still carries in a sling, and has but little use of her hand.

It is the warmest day of the season. The mercury stood quite early this morning, at 88 deg. in the shade.

We finished setting out our tomato plants, 7,550 in number, yesterday. Last year we had only 2,100.

THE O. C. DAILY.

VOL. 3.　SATURDAY, JUNE 8, 1867.　NO. 137.

Oneida Castle, Sunday June 2.

Mr. Noyes.—*Dear Sir :*—A few days since while visiting the Community, a note was handed to me from you, accompanied by a most beautiful satchel. The note I read with the greatest interest, as it contained allusions to my mother, and also to my beloved uncle Chauncey. Being very young at the time of their deaths, I knew but little of either of them; but the memory of my mother has ever been most sacred, and her letters, of which we have a few, are very precious. Her faith I venerate.

With her beautiful character and almost faultless life, I have wished, Oh, so many times, that she might have been spared to us; but she died. I suppose it was God's will.

When now and then I meet one who knew her they indeed seem near to me. And now permit me, Dear Sir, to express to you the respect I feel for one whom doubtless my mother had the kindest regards for, as her only brother's best friend.

Accept my sincere thanks for your kind note, and also for this elegant present. It will be to me a souvenir of the friendship between yourself and my beloved mother, and I shall ever remember you, myself, with kind regards.

Hoping to have the pleasure of meeting you at no distant time, I remain 　Yours very respectfully,

ELIZA PATTEN.

A curious feature in many of the oldest church yards of England is the old fashioned doggerel epitaphs, so old that the storms of ages have well nigh obliterated the stone letters.

One from the county of Devon, dated over two hundred years ago, says :

"Here lyeth Jayne Kente,
When hyr laste was spente
She kycked up hyr heels and away she wente."

Another in an adjoining county which had been erected to the sacred memory of " Joele Hardy," says:

"Here lies father, mother, brother, sister and I,
We all died in the same year,
Only they lie buried at Loosin,
And I lie buried here."

At Winchester Cathedral, in Hampshire, is a very old tombstone (I forget the date) erected to the memory of a British soldier, who died from the effects of drinking when over heated. One of the verses runs something in this way :

"Here lies the British Grenadier,
Who died from drinking cold small beer,
Stranger take heed by this man's fall,
Drink XX (double X) or none at all."

Another in Somerset runs thus ;

(N. B. the interred is supposed to have had a wooden leg.)

"Here lies old Betsy Booden,
Her woo'd a liv'd longer,
But her cood'n,
Old age and sorree made her decay,
'Till her old hooden leg
Carr'd her away."　　　　A. E.

TALK LAST NIGHT.

After the reading of the Home-Talk, on " The revival spirit and unity," several expressed themselves as in hearty sympathy with it, and confessions of the revival spirit were abundant. The unity existing between Geo. E. and Theodore was very gratifying to all, and was thought to be an inspired work—inspired unity that has developed itself in a healthy way. They have been through a great deal of tribulation on that point and more or less chafing and friction, as they were of different tastes and temperaments. Their experience is very encouraging to all and especially to the young. Mr. Noyes thought it was a great triumph in regard to our university.

The large spruces removed last year, all promise to do well, and some are hoisting their beautiful cones in token of triumph. Those moved this spring, also look well, though many circumstances appeared against them. May they grow and flourish to help beautify these hallowed grounds.　　SPRUCE.

A lover of nuts invites all his brethren in nut craft, to help cultivate the youthful trees, so that nuts may be abundant. Baby trees also are offered to nurses, who will treat them kindly and teach them to be fruitful.　　ALMOND.

A woman writes to us from Williamstown, Mass., urging us to receive her as a member. She is a widow with one child, a lad of six years old.

She says "O, I beseech of you not to read my letter before the Community, and then turn a deaf ear to my request."

They are painting to-day, the children's door-yard fence and the floor to their large front room and entrance hall. Also the portico of the New House is under the same treatment.

Mr. Blood returned from his visit East this morning.

THE O. C. DAILY.

VOL. 3.   MONDAY, JUNE 10, 1867.   NO. 138.

BUSINESS MEETING.

Miss Nun said that the Bag Department had concluded to have bag-frames of a different pattern from those they have been making, and she wanted to know whether they should be bought, or made at W. P. If made there it will require forty or fifty dollars worth of tools. Some thought it would be cheaper to buy. Referred to a committee consisting of Messrs. G. W. Hamilton, M. H. Kinsley, G. Campbell, J. F. Sears, E. S. Burnham and Miss Nun.

The wood that was taken out of the shed is suffering for want of shelter. A committee composed of Messrs. Clark, Barron and Miller were chosen, with authority to call for bees after supper, or at other times till it was all put in the shed.

Myron Kinsley brought up the subject of a bathing-house at W. P., and also of letting the hired help go in to bathe. Mr. Woolworth thought it was very desirable to have a bathing-house there. Mr. Noyes had spoken to him about it, intimating that the hired girls of the Silk-factory might be permitted the privilege of the water, and perhaps the hired men could enjoy the same. Myron gave his estimate of the cost of a building of forty or fifty feet in length, but it was thought questionable whether we could build on such a large scale this season. Mr. Inslee, G. W. Hamilton, Mr. Woolworth, Myron, Chairman, and Mrs. Miller were appointed committee to see what can be done this season, to give the women the privilege of bathing.

Mr. Abbott wanted some one to take his place in looking after the water, and to see when it should be used, &c., and also to look after the pumps. He said water was very scarce now, notwithstanding our heavy rains. He had thought of Daniel Abbott as one that might take his place. It was thought best to let the matter lie over another week and consider it.

Mr. Woolworth proposed that Mr. Barron, Mr. Thacker, Homer Barron and Abram Burt be appointed committee to see about finding a lodging-place for our workmen, and not have them lodge on our premises. Approved.

Dear Mr. Noyes:—I have had a feeling since meeting to write you about the desires of my heart. The talk this evening about shyness hits me, and I wonder when I shall ever get over it. I do so long to be God's free woman. I think I have the same shyness toward God and the Primitive Church, as I have toward my superiors. I like to sit and listen, and catch the sparks that fly from one and another, but I feel that I do not throw my whole soul, might, mind, and strength into the work as I ought. I know I have some of the true tinder in my heart, for every time you talk, I feel the fire of God's love burning within me. I believe I shall yet be able to throw aside every weight that hinders me in this race for freedom. I wish to thank God for the victory we women have gained over special love—I know it is a victory we never should have gained, if you had not led the way. The other day Ann Bailey was reading a letter reporting your conversation about the girls, when you were at Wallingford, and every word of it found an answering place in my heart. I could not but compare my present feelings on that subject with the feelings I used to have a few years ago. I used to look upon all such things with rather a jealous eye, fearing that they might get the hearts of all the men, so that there would not be much left for us older ones. But I do not feel so now. I am thankful that they are attractive and lovable, and that they are getting where you can use them in the cause of Communism. I wish to give them their true place, and be a help and support to them in my spirit. I confess my love for them, and that your hopes are my hopes in regard to them.   Your loving sister,   C. A. REID.

. We had quite a spirited talk last night, about sprained ankles, the cause &c. In some cases it was thought to be the result of carelessness, and persons thus afflicted would get good out of it, (no thanks to the devil, however) and learn a lesson of carefulness. Considerable indignation was expressed toward the spirit that was trying to cripple us in this way.

Mr. Hatch called for a bee Saturday evening, to sand and level up the croquet ground, and yesterday forenoon at ten o'clock, it was all completed. Mr. H. expressed his thankfulness last night at the readiness with which the men took hold of the job; it was evidence to him that the revival spirit was working into our business.

D. Edson Smith went for his wife Friday, and returned with her Saturday. They both seem thankful for the privilege of entering our school, and we trust they will prove themselves studious scholars, and be a help to the cause.

Our carpenters are making some improvements in the company kitchen. They have taken away the two bedrooms connected with it, and have moved the stairs leading to the cellar, back against the wall on the north side of the house.

Mr. Cushman, and a Mr. Burke, a singer, and traveling companion of Mr. C., called here and took dinner Saturday. They gave us some good singing in the Hall, with harmonium accompaniment.

Our people are cutting down the hedge to-day. We are having beautiful weather.

THE O. C. DAILY.

VOL. 3. TUESDAY, JUNE 11, 1867. NO. 139.

We are deeply interested in the task Mr. Noyes has set the older members of the Community, viz., that of grading the railroad track he has surveyed, and clearing a passage through to the upper terminus.

To conquer the principality of unbelief that has for so many centuries held undisputed possession there, is no small affair, and as it is a work that belongs to veterans in the service, it is expected that all such will take hold of the job with determination and energy, and thoroughly equip themselves for this new fight of faith. We cannot employ hired workman (paddies) on this celestial railroad, but each one is expected to take the shovel and pickaxe, and by hard toil, overcome the thousand impediments of unbelief that with giant strength block up the way. We may be forced to dig tunnels through mountains or under the beds of rivers—to cut our way through rocks of granite hardness, but with unity of purpose and the voice of our leader cheering us on, and with the hope of victory near, we shall be able to lay bare the old track worked eighteen hundred years ago. Then the shout will go up on the whole length of the line, that " death is swallowed up in victory." Let the united thanks of all that are to come after and the feeling that we are at work for God and outraged humanity, as well as our own individual happiness, give us courage to enter our names at an early date, to serve in this great and holy enterprize.

Frequently during our meetings, people in different parts of the room are annoyed by being unable to tell what is said in other quarters. We often hear the cry "louder," and even then fail to get satisfaction. Why should we not put an end to this positively vicious state of things, and seek and expect a radical conversion in respect to our method of talking in meeting? Now, when the men have something to say they are quite apt to get very much interested in something on the floor, which brings their heads below the range where speech can be made articulate ; while the women when about to address the meeting, are fearful lest time may be lost, and so give special attention to their work. In consequence of this state of things, ludicrous scenes occur. To illustrate: Last night Mr. Reynolds said something that was inaudible on the other side of the room, and Mr. Hatch made some remark upon it, which in turn was not heard by Mr. Reynolds. It was then suggested that they both stand up and repeat their remarks, and accordingly Mr. Hatch rose and in his clearest tenor said : " We out this side have to take it for granted that what Mr. Reynolds says is true and edifying, for we cannot hear a word." Then Mr. Reynolds, standing erect and speaking in his most sonorous bass, replied : " I said

I hoped I should always have a spirit that looked at good and eschewed evil. I lost all my upper teeth a short time since, which makes it difficult for me to be heard. I expect when I get my new teeth I shall speak so as to make this hall ring." [Applause.]

Mr. Hatch :—Perhaps Mr. Reynolds is in part excusable." [Both took their seats amidst considerable laughter.] B.

OBITUARY.—Alas! the voice of lamentation and mourning is heard in our midst. Mighty men and strong arms, have laid all desolate, amidst sighing, and sorrow of heart. The much admired, and once beautiful privet hedge, is no more ; but is numbered with the things that were. Well, we bid it farewell, it has had its day. Thousands have admired its beauty, and now let it be forgotten, whilst perchance something better, and more attractive may spring up in the future, and occupy its place.

A RECONCILED MOURNER.

Who can account for the difference in taste ? While the general feeling of the Community is that of regret, at the loss of the hedge, we heard two persons yesterday, express great relief and satisfaction at its extermination. They thought it cramped and shut us in, bounded our prospects &c., and belittled our grounds.

We received a long letter from D. H. Hamilton, in which he says : " I feel since my return, a continual drawing toward the Community, as I said, I left my heart with you. Did you psychologise me, or did I find my affinity?" He seems full of his own opinions in relation to his own case—thinks we lacked true discrimination in our judgment of him.

We were quite surprised this morning, to see some of the girls whose countenances are naturally somewhat pallid, blooming with rosy cheeks. But the mystery soon came out. Miss Chloe had found, in the Reception-room, a paper of red powder, (supposed to have been left by some visitor), and the girls out of sport had been trying it on their cheeks.

We had some interesting talk last night about the encouraging prospect of our Purchasing Agency, drawn out by a letter received from H. G. Allen, together with Mr. Herrick's testimony of personal experience.

Mr. Ellis is engaged in fitting up the old Business-room, putting up a counter &c. for a ticket Office, and gentleman's dressing-room.

A young lady from the depot, a pupil of Mr. Gliddon, the music teacher, was here yesterday, and sung two or three songs, in the Hall.

THE O. C. DAILY.

VOL. 3. WEDNESDAY, JUNE 12, 1867. NO. 140.

Utica, June 7, 1867

DEAR FATHER :—As Mr. Kelley's visit gives me an easy and inexpensive mode of communicating with you, I seize the opportunity to drop you a few lines. He easily obtained permission for me to accompany him to the city to get some necessary summer clothing, and having transacted our business, we adjourned to the sitting room of Bagg's Hotel, as the most convenient place for writing, attainable under the circumstances.

I have been very much interested in your " Noon Discourses," as reported in the CIRCULAR. The last discourse but one, upon the present living magnetism of the Bible, contained important truth.

Kelley tells me you want to have me co-operate with Theodore and George E., in forwarding the University project. Well father, if you will take me out of the Asylum, I will try. I surely never felt better, both in mind or body, nor more appetite or capability for work. Can't you give me a trial? God knows I have had (and have now) no personal feeling toward you or the Community. It has been (and is) with me a question of principle; of right and wrong, and if I find hereafter that I have been in error, I will gladly humble myself at your feet. But let me beg you to give me an opportunity—give me a chance to work, and no longer rust out my life at (I speak calmly) this Hell upon Earth—the N. Y. State Lunatic Asylum.

Yours affectionately,
VICTOR NOYES.

P. S. I shall be glad to see or hear from you if you feel inclined. V.

ANSWER.

Oneida, June 10, 1867.

DEAR VICTOR :—I do not write to make you say or do anything that is contrary to your honest convictions. But I think that God's providences are speaking to you and you ought to understand them. In leaving a heaven on earth, you have got into a " hell on earth." I acted on convictions as honest as yours when I proposed to submit the question of your insanity to the scientific authorities at Utica. They decided that I was right. In April they talked as though you were nearly well. I knew you was not because you held on to the ideas you got when you was wildest. But I said nothing to them, and made preparation, as you know, to dispose of you as well as I could. Finally Dr. Gray decided that you was not fit to be discharged. I took this as an indication of God's providence and God's will concerning you. I think you ought to do the same, and not ask to be discharged till you have learned the lesson which he is teaching you by this confinement. I am very sure that the ideas you have about me, and about the Community, and about liberty, are not the result of sober reasoning, nor even of common worldly influences and teachings, but are thrust into your mind by the same spirit that used to tempt you to *swear* when you was a little boy. I shall never believe your mind is sound till you get rid of those ideas. Even if they were true in themselves, they got into your mind in company with an insane spirit, and will have to go out with it. You will have to be modest enough to acknowledge that you have been insane, (which you have hardly done yet) and wipe out all the notions that you have adopted during your insanity, and begin again as a little child. Till you do this, I do not believe you will escape confinement in some form, even if you should be discharged from the Asylum. God will hold you if Dr. Gray does not; and I believe that Dr. Gray would agree with my judgment in this matter. If you do humble yourself as a little child, you will soon be discharged, and will find a blessed revival home ready to receive you. J. H. N.

COON-HUNT NG.—Yesterday afternoon, Mr. Bristol, while walking out, discovered a large raccoon up in an ash tree, over in the Petre swamp. He came home and in company with J. N. N., and S. Y. J., returned, taking with them a gun and a clothes-basket; the basket to catch the animal alive in, if possible, it being our intention if not successful, to shoot him.

J. N. N. climbed the tree and shook it, which had the desired effect; down he came to the ground, and Mr. B. tried hard to put the basket over him, but missed it, and he started through the swamp. I sprang forward with the intention of catching him, but found myself deep in the mud. At this point I was going to fire at him, but a voice cried out, " catch him alive, catch him alive," and so I desisted, and in a twinkling he was out of sight. A long and fruitless search was the grand finale of *our*, or at least *my*, first coon-hunt. Y.

We have received recently two letters from a young man twenty years of age, by the name of Joseph Cadman, of Cambridge Vt. In the first letter he wanted we should send him some of our pictures, and the " Hand-Book," which we did; and in the second one, he acknowledges the receipt of them; says he takes the CIRCULAR and likes to read it, and asks if he can come here at any time and join. He says he has no bad habits such as using tobacco or strong drinks of any kind.

Mrs. Conant finished weaving Saturday, our long web (one hundred yards) of rag-carpeting, commenced March eighteenth. The job has been delayed on account of Mrs. C. having been called to serve, several weeks, in other departments of labor.

Mr. Herrick leaves this noon for New-York, and D. A. Abbott for Wallingford.

THE O. C. DAILY.

VOL. 3. THURSDAY, JUNE 13, 1867. NO. 141.

Vernon Centre, Tuesday, June 11, 1867.

To the Oneida Community, Oneida, N. Y.—
As Secretary of the "Vernon Agricultural Society,"
I desire to make the inquiry of you, whether you
would be willing to join with us in holding another
"Industrial Exhibition," as you did last Fall. Without your aid and co-operation we dislike to undertake, and as the officers of the society will be called
together this month, to make final decision, your
prompt response will much oblige. Should you feel
disposed to join with us, I will notify you by letter,
that you may send a delegation to confer with us at
that time, to take such measures as will insure success as we achieved last fall. Such matters are attended with some considerable expense and trouble,
(like every thing else), but they seem to pay in enjoyment, if nothing else.—We shall hope to hear
favorably from you, as soon as practicable, and much
oblige your friend and obedient servant,

Levi T. Marshall.
Secy. Vernon Agl. Soc.

After reading the above, last night, Mr. Woolworth
inquired what reply we should give to Mr. M.'s letter.
Mr. A. Kinsley thought that the Vernon Fair held
last fall, was the most satisfactory of any our people
ever attended; others thought so too. Mr. Noyes
said that as we had had one good Fair with the Vernon folks, we should be likely to have another one
equally as good. The only hesitancy was, that there
was talk that a Fair would be held at Oneida, next
Fall, in which case it would be expected that we
should assist, which we should not do, if we co-operated with Vernon. The matter was left for decision
with Mr. Thacker, Thayer, and Mrs. Vanvelzer.

On hearing Mr. Herrick's confession read, it came
to me very forcibly, that I was a Diotrephian.

Till then I could not see that I had the same disease that I saw so prominent in others. I then seemed to take a look at myself, and could "see myself as
others see me." The way that it seems to work in my
case is this; my thoughts are always running off on
some side or branch track, as it were, where I was
the chief man in the concern. I do not think that
down in my heart, I have been disloyal to Mr. Noyes,
but somehow I have always, in thought, built air
castles, great projects, where *I* was the one man looked
up to. I would be very loyal to Mr. Noyes and the
Community, but would be away off in some distant
place where I could be head, as chief missionary from
the Community. This spirit would have a very strong
hold on me whenever I had the "blues," as it is called.
It would lead me into darkness continually, and long
ago I saw the bad effects on myself, but for all that,
the spirit in me that wanted to be greatest, was so
strong that I have clung to it, as something good.

For a week or two I have felt a desire to have a
spirit that would honor Christ and help the revival
spirit, but there seemed to be some obstruction in the
way, which I have prayed to have removed, and when
it flashed into my mind that I was a Diotrephian, I
saw *that* to be one of the obstructions, and I pray for
help to overcome it. I have tried of my own will to
overcome this way of thinking, and have never succeeded in affecting a cure. The reason has been that
egotism has been afraid of being hurt, afraid of having
some one else know what I was thinking of, and I
now want to give it a thrust every time I can. I pray
for a true revival spirit.   J. D. Conant.

We had a long letter from our late diotrephian visit-
or, Mrs. Kilbourn. She is spending the summer with
a friend at Utica, "to recruit her exhausted powers,
arising," as she says, "from her arduous mental labors."

She sent us a letter she had written to her brother,
a sheet of foolscap written all over, which she says
she would like to have us print in our little Daily,
but not in the Circular. She says "By the powers
vested in me, as the anointed one of the second resurrection, I send forth the harvesting angels, who will
now begin their systematic work &c."

Mr. Vanvelzer had a narrow escape from being
dashed to pieces, yesterday, while riding in a wagon,
by the running away of his horse. Something broke,
and let the wagon forward on to the horse's heels, when
he kicked up and ran over two narrow bridges and a
narrow road, with deep ditches on each side. Mr. V.
held on to the reins till one of them broke, and this
turned the horse and wagon nearly round, which
checked his course, and enabled Mr. V. to jump out
and seize the horse by the bits.

We had a letter, yesterday, from Mrs. Loomis, the
first we have heard from her since she left the Community. She makes great professions of love and loyalty to Mr. Noyes—says she sincerely invites the criticism of the family in her isolated position, yet persists
in finding fault with the course Mr. Hamilton took
with her—thinks he had personal feelings—was not
satisfied with the way she joined, &c.

We have Mr. Moulton & Co. from Rome, here to-
day, taking pictures of different portions of our
grounds. They are now, (half past nine), taking a view
of the buildings, from the top of the horse-barn.

Mary Leete is with us. Her father is slowly regain-
ing his health and strength, and thinks he will be able
to ride as far as Oneida in a few days.

We finished planting corn, yesterday; about ten
acres of sweet corn and two of the yellow. When
think it will ripen?

ic

THE O. C. DAILY.

VOL. 3.   FRIDAY, JUNE 14, 1867.   NO. 142.

Troy, June 12, 1867.

DEAR MR. NOYES:—I had an interview, last night, with John L. Steele, the student of St. Joseph's Theological Seminary, of this city, and supplied him with the "Hand-Book," "Salvation from Sin" and Cooley's edition of the "Bible Argument." It remains to be seen what the effect will be, but at present the case is an interesting one. He is a young man of twenty-three, an American, born a catholic and bred in the church service, and destined by his parents for the priesthood. He is quite talented and has an investigating mind; thinks for himself and does not allow the church to think for him. He believes the Bible, not as St. Augustine says, because the church says it is true, but because in itself it commends itself to his reason. For saying this much in a sermon he recently preached in the Seminary, he has been called a heretic, and the Bishop of Albany has been called to labor with him. Still, I infer that he stands quite high in the Seminary and is thought considerably of by the faculty. I presented to him your experience at Andover and Yale, your rejection by the Seminary &c., in which he seemed to take special interest. I preached to him Salvation from Sin and the Second Coming. He was with me nearly two hours; says he shall read the books I gave him with great interest, will visit New-York 335 Broadway, during vacation, in about two weeks, and I recommended him to go and see Theodore at New Haven. I rather like the man, but he has a battle to fight if he joins us and he knows it. Details if wished when I reach O. C.

I learn that the Baptist church, in Albany, are much disturbed by the doctrines and practices of the O. C. We are preached against and discussed in their conference meetings with "holy horror." I was called to account, yesterday, in our behalf, by a man who had attended the Baptist meetings. The interview was a brief one and will probably be renewed. The conviction grows on me that the hold we have on the business world, will go far towards stopping the mouths of carping church members.

I have a prayer in my heart that I may appreciate your great love for the church and that I may abide in that love.   Yours for obedience.

H. W. BURNHAM.

Extract from C. Olds' letter, dated Freeport June 10.

"In answer to your enquiry about the O traps, you can tell Mr. Newhouse that there is a little quadruped about the size of a red squirrel, found in the valley of the Mississippi and the Missouri, that burrows in the ground, throwing up hillocks from twelve to fifteen inches high. They are a great pest to the farmer in his cornfields and gardens. This animal (Mr. N. will understand by this time) is called the gopher, and you may be sure they do go-for the farmers fields in earnest, and destroy with great rapidity. They are paying bounties on every one that is caught. Every farmer's boy, and I suppose every body else, is in for catching them, and here is where most of the O traps go. I presume, however, some are bought to catch the common house rat. But the great demand has been to supply the market in Iowa. They are just the trap for that business, and will, no doubt, drive out all other cheap traps. Confessing my union with Christ, Paul and all the Primitive Church, I am yours for the revival spirit.   Good night.   CHAS. OLDS."

WILLOW-PLACE, June 13.—Last evening C. A. C. said he had been Willow-Place journalist about a year, and as J. S. F. had consented to take his place, he would like to tender his resignation. It was accepted and J. S. F. elected in his place. A vote of thanks was awarded to Charles for the faithful and able manner in which he had performed that service.

What to call O. C. is a question that has long perplexed the W. P. Commune. We can't call it *home*, for our home is at W. P. on Turkey Street, east of the Trap-Shop. We do not like to call it *Oneida*, for that sounds cold and foreign; besides it does not distinguish it from the Oneida Depot. If we say *Oneida Creek*, we are met with "*Skinadore*" *Creek*, which is quite repugnant to us when applied to our beautiful home. But now we have a name. It is proposed (as we are the offspring of O. C., its son or daughter), that we call it *Mother*. "We are going over to Mother's!" How does that sound?

The machinists have sent off their pulleys to-day, which they have been making for W. C. They are intended to run the printing-press, those now in use being too small.

The sound of the croquet mallet is heard after meeting these fine moonlight evenings. A picture of the ground with persons playing the game, and others looking on, was taken yesterday. Several other groups of men, women and children were taken in the course of the day, but it was windy, and some of the efforts at picture taking, did not succeed. At nearly sunset however, most of the family were gathered *en masse* on the lawn, the wind having lulled, when, we are told, a very good picture was taken. We shall see. It was a day of considerable confusion and weariness particularly at the children's hour, as the children had to be fixed, and taken out several times. It is said that the best photograph was that of all the children grouped together, taken near the lamp-post. The disturbing influences that were felt in the atmosphere called out considerable talk last night, and some new ideas on the subject presented by Mr. Noyes, which will be reported.—The men staid here last night, and are at work again to day, on some parts of our grounds.

THE O. C. DAILY.

VOL. 3. SATURDAY, JUNE 15, 1867. NO. 143.

Warrensburg, Johnson Co., Mo.

MR. J. H. NOYES. *Dear Sir:*—I have been reading an article in one of the St. Louis papers, taken from the *New York Herald,* entitled "Communism, The Oneida and Wallingford Communities." This is the first that I have known of the existence of such a society. As there are many things in the above mentioned article, agreeing with my views, I seek to learn more of you. Being raised religiously (my father, Wm. Chamberlain, of Vermont, and my mother's father, Ard Hoyt, of Connecticut, were ministers of the Presbyterian church, and missionaries to the Cherokee Indians, under the American Board) and educated to our stern doctrines, I have never been able to advance any ideas of my own in favor of a religious reform. Our church, I have often compared to the Jewish church at the time of Christ's appearance on earth, our elders are often true types of the Pharisees, of those days. Now I have a wife and two children living, and three gone home to their brighter abode. Our love towards each other, is such that, I think if it were necessary, one would be willing to die for the other. In case we were members of your society, could we preserve our social relations and still form the proper relationship with the family at large? Or would we (man and wife, of course that relationship being destroyed in the society), have to pair off with other members of an oppsite sex, in case it was contrary to our natural feelings?

Now Sir, my object is to obtain correct information in regard to this thing, not for the benefit of the curious world at large, but for myself and family, who wish to have good will toward all men, and obey God's great commandment of "love thy neighbor as thyself." With great respect,

P. O. Box No. 138. Wm. H. CHAMBERLAIN.

At the noon meeting, yesterday, Mr. Cragin spoke of the small children, who have been in the habit of coming in with their mothers. He thought it had a tendency to distract the attention of the mothers, and hinder them from entering into the spirit of the meetings, and taking part in them.—This talk led to some criticism last night of some of the mothers. Mr. Hatch thought that of late, a sickly philoprogenitive spirit had crept in, which had affected the children, making them peevish and irritable; they suffered more, and required more discipline in consequence of it. It is for the interest of both children and mothers, that the care of the children should be left to the children's department, which certainly merits the confidence of all the mothers, and their outlook for the physical comfort and wants of their children, certainly does not forward their spiritual training and growth, but on the contrary impedes it.

The criticism was received in a good receptive spirit, and the mothers expressed their thankfulness for it, and desire to profit by it.

We had another letter last night, from a man in New-York city, making inquiries about the Community. He had seen the *Herald's* article, and wanted to know if it was designed as an advertisment—wished to know more about us—wanted to come and work, and get acquainted.—Also a letter from Mr. Brewster saying that he was visiting his *quondam* wife, (who is now divorced for the second time), and preaching the truth to her, and he felt that she had a receptive spirit toward it. He is going to take his daughter with him on his return, and will call here.

Fifty applications for membership have been received since last January. About three fourths of them came from heads of families who wished to bring their children to the Community.

Supposing these families to average four members each, (which is probably a low average), then we should have had by receiving them, an increase of one hundred and forty-eight members, that, added to the one fourth of single applicants, would swell the number to one hundred and sixty-one.

DEAR MR. WOOLWORTH:—In the past I have been troubled more or less with fellowship and sympathy with my father, but late disclosures seem to have set me free. I can now see as I never did before, the utter loathsomeness of the Hutchin's spirit. I believe it to be an *infidel, reprobate* spirit. I am thankful that I am cut off from the world and grafted on to Christ's church, and I desire my worldly friends and especially my father to feel this.—Yours for the *truth,* cut where it may. E. F. H.

Three young men from Hamilton College, came here, Thursday, and called for dinner. Some delay occurred occasioned by their not applying to the right persons. When their dinner was about ready, they were seen quietly driving away. As the ticket Office is now ready for use, no such thing is likely to occur again.

Our wood-house now, presents a sleek and finished appearance. The south end is being rapidly filled with wood, one or two bees having been held for removing it. Two bents on the north end are finished off for the benefit of the fruit-preservers.

Mrs. Bushnell has gone into the school as teacher for the present.

We had a thunder shower in the night.—Mr. H. W. Burnham came this morning.

THE O. C. DAILY.

VOL. 3.   MONDAY, JUNE 17, 1867.   NO. 144.

BUSINESS MEETING.

G. W. Hamilton said that Mr. Noyes had spoken to him several times within a few months about instructing some one to fill his place at the Trap-shop, with a view of his going to the Agency, and he wished the Board to consider the matter and appoint some one for that purpose. There was some talk about dividing the responsibilities of the Shop, and inviting L. F. Dunn home to take a general oversight. The whole matter was left to Messrs. G. W. Hamilton, W. R. Inslee, A Kinsley and Mr. Woolworth as committee. Mr. Noyes and Cragin were invited to meet with them, this afternoon at two o'clock.

Some improvements proposed in the kitchen at W. P. Referred to Mr. Cragin, Mr. Kinsley and Homer Barron.

Abram reported that the water-wheel at the 'mill was pretty much worn out; shall we put in a cast-iron wheel, as Mr. Holmes had recommended us to do? A committee was appointed to decide upon it.

We had a series of thunder showers, Saturday afternoon and evening, in which the rain literally poured. It continued to rain more or less, all night, and at intervals yesterday, so that the ground is well soaked.

E. P. Inslee and James Hatch, arrived Saturday, a little after noon.

The questions we print below, are from Mr. Noyes, and were suggested by Mr. Cragin's proposing the day before, that the family be questioned on the leading articles read in our noon meetings.

QUESTIONS: 1. About Conversion. Bring out the idea clearly that it is a *movement*—a change of place—a transfer or transportation of the heart from one spiritual region to another—a change of residence in the spiritual world—a journey from Satan to God—from the spirit of this world to the spirit of heaven. This is the general conversion, but there must be many particular conversions. So we may compare the whole to a railroad and the particular conversions to the different stations on the road. The first conversion is turning the attention obediently toward God, "The fear of the Lord is the beginning of wisdom." The last conversion is victory over death, "The last enemy that shall be overcome is death." These are the two terminal depots. Between them there will be conversions to perfect holiness, to communism, to victory over shame, jealousy, &c., &c.

2. About Revivals. They are conversions of *masses* instead of individuals—i. e., transportation of carsfull and trainsfull over the same route above described—gregarious movements—emigration of multitudes from Satan to God.—Sympathy and contagion come in to help. The greater the number to be transported, the easier it will be, because it will pay to grade and build railroads. We are preparing to transport all that will go, clear through. This is what we mean by our celestial railroad.

The following questions, by Mr. Noyes, were handed in at the noon meeting yesterday:

What is the great doctrine of the Bible? What may be called the right and left hands of God? What is true religion? What is faith? What is the "work of God?" What is salvation? Is faith a single act or a continuous work? What is conversion? In the natural state where do men dwell? Where do they dwell when they are saved? How are they carried from one state to the other? Where is the great transportation company that carries men over this route? Who is the head of it? In what sense did he go over the route? Did the Primitive Church go over it? What is the lower terminus of it? What is the upper terminus? What is the office of the Bible? What is the office of our writings? What is the object of the Daily Paper? What is the object of the university? What is the object of the Community? What is the office of our daily meetings? What is the office of criticism? What is the object of our various businesses? What is a revival? Wherein does our revival differ from the old fashioned revivals?

W. C., June 12, 1867.

MY DEAR A:—The women here had a very interesting meeting a few days ago, and I wish some one had taken notes of Mrs. Skinner's and others remarks. Mrs. Leonard opened the meeting by alluding to the subject of dress—said she thought we ought to dress as "women professing godliness" and to please the Primitive Church, but she did not think we did, when we gave so much attention to unnecessary trimmings &c.—she had felt anxious about expense in that direction—wished to co-operate with the family at Oneida in economizing. Her anxiety in the matter had kept her awake nights. She wished to lay the subject before the women and have their help. A good many new dresses had been bought, and a great deal of pains taken to get ribbon, buttons and belts to match them. It had been quite a tax on Jane at New Haven to seclect these articles, and had taken a great deal of time to say nothing of the outlay. For example, Helen Miller said she and Jane spent three hours looking for a belt ribbon, and finally got one that cost eighty-two cents. (It was for a short dress). Mrs. Skinner thought that the spirit of the world about dress, came in upon us more or less every Spring. She said if any one ought to dress, it was the old—the young looked well enough without. She held up Mother Noyes as a good example for the girls to follow in this respect, said she ought to be taken as such. They all think of her as a pattern for them in her christian character, and why should they not think that inspiration extends to this part of her life.

Mrs. S. spoke highly of Mrs. N.'s faithfulness in little things. She believed the reason why God chose her to fill the place she does in the Community, was that she was meek and faithful, and the girls need not expect to be chosen to fill any high office until they were faithful in little things.—Mrs. S. while speaking more particularly of mother Noyes's self denial and simplicity about dress, said with much spirit, "God will dress her *beautifully*." * * *

Yours affectionately.   SOPHRONIA.

THE O. C. DAILY.

VOL. 3.　　TUESDAY, JUNE 18, 1867.　　NO. 145.

Verona, June 11, 1867.

J. H. N. DEAR BROTHER:—Your letter, received last week was very cheering, like a bugle note of victory. The "curious query" which you propound, [see Mat. 9 : 2,] has often excited my curiosity—a serious curiosity. The connection between sin and sickness, and the *duty* of those who are free from sin, or who testify to freedom from sin, to maintain freedom from sickness also, is a subject that has been pressing upon my mind for many years, and as I have sometimes feared even to the neglect of the "Greater Miracle." I am not a close, deep thinker; and can not always trace back satisfactorily, from an effect to its certain cause. But the clear teaching of the New Testament on this point has satisfied me, that among the gifts that Christ has received for, and given unto men, the deliverance from sickness, and from all evil, is certainly included. The inference follows that when we come short of the possession, the cause must be in ourselves. I find it pleasant at least, if not necessary, in drawing nigh to God to do so with the feeling that in my flesh there dwelleth no good thing. My late experience has been quite interesting to me. One point among others like—I had some dread of an erysipelas swelling, somehow I had got an idea that it was a long, tedious, and somewhat precarious affair. And I prayed if possible this cup might pass; adding always, "not my will but thine be done." To this prayer the heavens were brass, and the case of Saul came often to my mind, "whom God answered not, neither by dreams, nor Urim, nor by prophet." I did not go to Endor, but after some days I saw that the Father's will was better for me than my own, for he loved me better and wiser, than I do myself. And I was led to drop the condition and say, "Father thy will be done" and a voice in my heart seemed to speak these words, "Let the flesh suffer all that God hath appointed it." Afterward whatever shrinking of the flesh I saw, I called it of the flesh, and asked no favors for it. In this state of mind there was peace, and even abundant joy. And when suppuration came and the crisis, I was probably as calm and unconcerned as any one of the group, if not more so. And four days after, perhaps it was five—the doctor said, let the wound heal up, there is no further need of probing it, and it did heal up without further trouble. The muscles of my limb however, are rather slow to render their accustomed willing service.

All this does not solve your query; and I do not propose to make any further application of it than to say, that I was not conscious of any conviction for sin, either specific or general, other than my inability to draw nigh to God in prayer. I hope to see some talk, or hear it, by you on this subject.

Yours in the service of Christ.　H. N. LEETE.

Minerva Barron's case was brought up for criticism last night. She has, for a long time, been under a hard, unbelieving spirit, and though industrious and faithful in her work, yet her efforts to free herself from this spirit, have been feeble and have failed, hitherto.

Her difficulties and the hard unbelief of the Barron children, was thought to be traceable, evidently, to their parents. Homer's experience shows what God can do in breaking this unbelief up, and giving glorious deliverance, and he should take hold and help the family, particularly his parents.

It was thought that Minerva was more honest toward the devil, in confessing him, than toward Christ, in confessing him true and faithful to his promise, in spite of the contradictions of feeling.

As it was some expected that Mr. Kelley would bring Victor home with him yesterday, a move was made to furnish him with a suitable room. Abram and F. Marks moved into the tower, and Fidelia and Marion moved over into the bedroom vacated by A. and F. They had fairly got their things all moved and arranged, when Mr. K. arrived, bringing the information that Dr. Gray did not think it best for Victor to leave the Asylum yet.

Immediately, every thing in the room, aforsaid, began to assume a retrograde motion, and, all hands assisting, were soon returned to the same spot they occupied in the morning. Marion not being used to Community ways, was at first, some tried, but soon got over it, but Fidelia said *she* did not care where she moved, if they did not move her out of the Community.

One sentiment expressed by Mr. Noyes, in the course of his remarks yesterday noon, on "The Providence of God over us," ought to be written in letters of gold and indelibly stamped on every heart. The idea was this, that, "whatever our circumstances, however much we may be tempted to chafe with evils in persons and things around us, yet we have no excuse for being fretful and cross, since in *all cases* God's Providence arranged this very thing in reference to us and for our education. Every thing should be taken respectfully as coming from God."

Mr. Bradley started, yesterday, for Albany and Troy, to see about procuring currants for making jelly, and also to find market for our strawberries, should they chance to ripen this summer.

Mr. Hawley has left the kitchen and James Vanvelzer has taken his place. Mr. H. has served long and faithfully there, and his services are much appreciated.

Thunder storms are very frequent this summer. We are now, (nine o'clock) in the midst of one.

Mr. Leete came here yesterday, to recruit his health.

THE O. C. DAILY.

VOL. 3. WEDNESDAY, JUNE 19, 1867. NO. 148.

WILLOW-PLACE ITEMS.—Yesterday afternoon, two little boys aged about eight and twelve years, children of Mr. Phillips, were crossing Mud-Creek on a log, when both fell in. The oldest managed to scramble ashore, but the other was drowned. Search was made for the body by his father and others, without success. After supper several of our men went over to the Creek, and Myron and Orrin waded the stream about an hour and a half, but found nothing. This morning Myron and Cornelius rose at three o'clock—renewed the search, and found the body about half a mile below the place where he fell in.

It was lying near the bank face downward and partly exposed above the water, which had fallen during the night some four or five feet. Myron and C. C. H. carried the body home, washed and laid it out. The parents were very grateful, and the neighbors who were present, thanked them in behalf of the whole neighborhood.

The machinists have completed another silk-cleaner for our own use. This is the fourth and last we shall need. One more spinner and another winder are to be made which will take up about all our accommodations. The number of machines will then stand thus: five winders, four cleaners, one doubler, four spinners, stretcher, soft silk winder and two spoolers.

[The following notice has been printed in large type and posted at W. P.]

The Willow-Place Pond is open to the public for bathing purposes between the hours of twelve and one at noon, and eight and nine in the evening. It is expected that people will confine themselves to the above mentioned hours, and will use their best endeavors to keep the bathing place neat and clean.—Loud shouting and boisterous noise will not be allowed.

By order of the Committee, M. H. Kinsley, R. Hawley and J. C. Higgins.

A few days since, one of the workmen in the Trap-shop, chanced to get his finger between a small belt and pulley, which were in rapid motion, and in an instant it was snapped off at the first joint.

Mr. Bradley when at Utica a few days since, went into a chair-shop owned by a German firm, to purchase some chairs. The good German had never heard of the O. C., and would not trust him without the cash down. Mr. B. left the shop and went into a trunk manufactory where he had arranged to meet Mr. Kelly. While waiting, he remarked that he had found a firm in Utica, that did not know of the existence of the O. C. "Where did you find such persons?" asked the man where Mr. B. was waiting.

"A door or two from here, the chair store." "Did you want any goods of them that they would not let you have?" "Yes, two dozen chairs." "I'll go with you and make it all right," he said very pleasantly. "I'll be very much obliged to you if you will," replied Mr. B. Entering the shop the gentleman said, "let this man have all the goods he may want, all is right; we would be glad to swap our concern any day for theirs." "All right, all right," said the old German, and the chairs were immediately brought forward. This shows how people estimate us financially.

NOTICE:—Sometime ago I saw a poor unfortunate wheelbarrow chained by the leg and locked to a post. Now I had heard of ladders running away and of their peeping into ladies windows, and even to have supported them in their descent from their father's protection, and have seen them fastened with lock and key, but to think of a wheelbarrow getting off the track! Well now I want to give warning to a high fruit stool (that for various purposes, I adopted a short time since) which is already learning to use its long legs, running away, staying out nights and forgetting to come home for duty in the morning, &c. May a hint to the wise be sufficient. ALWAYS RETURN.

Last evening E. P. Inslee related the course of study he pursued in music, while in New-York. He proposes still to continue his studies forenoons, work at W. P. afternoons, attend meeting there, and stay all night if he chooses. He took lessons one week in vocal music, and is ready to impart the knowledge he gained, to clubs, quartettes, &c., and do all in his power to improve our congregational singing.

A new martin's house has been made and put up on the east side of the Tower, just above the upper tier of windows. The old one on the west side is small, and the birds have refused to notice it. It is too late, perhaps, to expect that they will occupy the new one this year, but as it is large and well adapted to their gregarious propensities, it is to be hoped that a community of them will take possession another Spring.

Mr. Bradley came home last night, and reports good success in obtaining currants. He made arrangements for the disposal of a portion of our strawberries in Troy.

E. S. B. thinks H. J. S. must have had a "*full head on*" when he wrote his "Millenial Sermon," for the last CIRCULAR.

Eight barrels of pine-apples have arrived, and a bee for preparing them for canning, is called for this forenoon.

THE O. C. DAILY.

VOL. 3. THURSDAY, JUNE 20, 1867. NO. 147.

Among the numerous letters received yesterday, was a long and spicy one addressed to Mr. Noyes, from a lady in Rockland, Maine, Miss Lucretia E. Pilsbury. She sent the *Tribune's* article about the O. C., enclosed in her letter. She says:

"The enclosed article cut from one of our Rockland papers, I read with much interest, and was not, as the correspondent anticipated people would be, either startled or appalled; but *was* much surprised that I had not heard of your Community before. I really hope you will be kind enough to answer this letter. I wish to know how much of this article is true, and how much is false." [She goes on to ask a multitude of questions about us, which were quite amusing.] She says again, "You may think I am asking too much, but *I* do not. * * *

"One portion of the account given of you in this article I enclose, I do not fall in with; I will leave you to guess what it is, and I know too, you will guess wrong; I should think you more than common gifted if you should guess right. The vision of your delectable savannah, has haunted me ever since I read this account of you. I see you all seated in your Hall, of an evening, reading your papers and correspondence, to ready and willing listeners, and my vanity goes so far at this moment, as to imagine you reading my letter, and wondering what manner of person I am."

"Extremes meet," I thought yesterday, as I saw before the portico a swarthy low-browed Italian, patiently grinding music from an old hand-organ and a little girl, mayhap his daughter, waiting with a weary air to receive the pennies that the children delightedly put into her tin-cup, as she held it out to receive them. After listening a moment, I wended my way to the Hall, and what should I behold but the faces of our sable friends Mr. Bailey and son of Vernon, entertaining quite an audience with violin and piano. They play much better than formerly, those say that have heard them. Though of the accursed race of Ham, their faces were bright and intelligent, and their manners easy and courteous. Their winters are spent in New-York, where they earn much by playing for dances. The Italian would no doubt have scorned his African brethren, but in my heart I was thankful that the good time was coming when the whole earth should dwell in perfect unity.   B.

As James Hatch was emerging from the grove over east of the Creek and horse-barn yesterday, he heard a report of a gun near by, and at the same instant felt the raking of something across his leg on the outside of his pantaloons, which produced a stinging sensation. On looking down to see what caused it, he saw that a bullet had passed through the bottom of his coat which was buttoned closely at the time. James then saw two young men coming, one with a revolver in his hand, who proved to be Byron Olmstead. He made a great many apologies, said he was shooting at a mark, &c. J.'s escape from being wounded if not from death, was certainly a very narrow one, and is another striking proof of God's providential care over us.

VARIETY THE SPICE OF LIFE. We have had beautiful garlands of roses encircling the white arbor for a number of years past, but this year the scene will change, giving place to a lot of vigorous sprouts, which hope sees adorned with beauty next year. Also the Bignonia, or Trumpet-flower, the pride of the middle house, has, for unknown reasons, retired from the scene, a grief to many. But cheer up, a young sprout, a new creation now appears; see it attracting particle to particle and building up, which in time may rival its predecessors and show that nothing can be lost.
                                                ROSE TRUMPET.

A man by the name of Norman Safford, of Deansvile, writes to "Brother Newhouse," making application to join. As an apology for calling him brother, he states that he thinks they agree on the point of the common relations of life. He says in conclusion, "I have some money laid up, am a blacksmith by trade, earn two dollars per day, and think I could help in your Trap shop, if you think me worthy of your *honorable consideration*."

In the course of Mr. Noyes's criticism of low speaking in the Hall yesterday noon, he said that persons did not get half the benefit of their confessions, when they spoke so low that only a few who sat near could hear, he wanted them to speak with spirit and power—produce a sensation. On this Mr. Easton said, "what if Christ should confess us before the Father and the angels in the same low tone of voice? would that thought be pleasant to us?"

A full-blooded darkey, a son of South Carolina, came here yesterday, and rapped for admittance at the Tower door. On being told that the Brick house was a dwelling house instead of a Trap-shop, as he supposed, he withdrew—wandered around a while then took his departure.

Two hundred and sixteen bottles of pine-apple were put up yesterday, and only two of the bottles were broken in the whole process, and those by accident.

Victor came home quite unexpectedly last night. We are all very glad to see him.

ERRATUM.—On the second page of yesterday's DAILY, toward the top, instead of "and posted," read, "is to be posted."

THE O. C. DAILY.

VOL. 3.   FRIDAY, JUNE 21, 1867.   NO. 148.

Syracuse, June 18, 1867.

ONEIDA COMMUNITY, *Gentlemen:*—A few days ago I met your Mr. Vanvelzer Jun., who inquired about Mr. Appy. Last week I met him at one of his concerts, and he said he would be happy to make your people a visit and give a concert.

He has two sisters, who sing charmingly, and a splendid pianist, making in all one of the finest concerts I ever heard. Now if he goes to your place he would like to pay his expenses from the concert, and get some strawberries and have a good time generally.—I have no doubt you would be much pleased with his music, and be more than repaid for any trouble they would make you. Now if you desire to have them come, please write me by return mail and state the time and such other arrangements as you may wish to make, and I will convey your invitation to them with pleasure. Respectfully, H. P. STARK.

An invitation will be given to Mr. Appy, to come the last of next week, or if he chooses the fourth of July.   [Ed.]

WILLOW-PLACE.—We had a very enthusiastic bee after supper last evening, for making the proposed bathing-house and platform. There was quite a large delegation from mother's, and good progress was made toward building the fence and the house, and part of the platform was laid. The water of the pond has been kept low, several days, so that work can be done below the usual water line.

Our trade with the Indians or rather the squaws, seems to be on the increase. Mrs. Abbott has the two last months, taken of them twenty dollars in money, (besides some baskets), in exchange for broken pieces of bread, pudding etc. The year and a half that we were in the business of dealing with them, we paid into the treasury $160, besides purchasing of them $40 worth of baskets.

The letters from G. W. N., and C. S. J., were received yesterday, and read with thrilling interest. Mabel went over to meeting, last night, to hear her fathers letter read, but came home quite disturbed, because, as she said, folks laughed about her father being sick; *she* didn't laugh, but if it had been G. W. N. that was sick, she would have laughed too.

Mr. Vanvelzer makes quite a business of selling old clothes that the family have cast off, to our workmen, the Indians and poor families around us. He sold twelve dollars worth, one day last week. We hope none of the young men or boys, will take advantage of this, to throw aside their coats, pants, &c., till they are pretty well worn, or till advised to, by their mothers.

The repairs on the children's house and yard are at last all done—completed—finished. The floors are all nicely painted, and every thing looks first-rate. Mrs. Miller came over last night for the purpose of seeing the improvements there, and hearing the foreign correspondence read. She staid all night.

We hope our readers will cast the mantle of charity over the errors that from time to time, occur of late, in the DAILY, as in our eagerness to get them into the mail in season, sometimes our proof-sheet has only the merest glance.

One of our little boys, a five-year-old, on hearing some one say, that it was with difficulty that Myron lifted the dead body of the little boy that was drowned, from the water, said, " God could lift him easy, with only one hand."

I want to thank the family for the criticism I received, the other evening. I cannot express my gratitude for it. I confess my faith in God and my separation from unbelief; also my union with Mr. Noyes. I want to be a help to him.   MINERVA.

Mr. Clark has been out a part of two days, this week, and sold six hundred dollars worth of hop-stoves and pipe. He estimates the profits on the whole to be not far from one hundred and twenty-five dollars. He also sold some few plow-castings.

Traps ordered yesterday,

John Nazro & Co., Milwaukee,	854	doz.
Lyman & Macnab, Toronto,	02	"
Total	916	"

All to be shipped by Oct. 1st.

Our people commenced haying yesterday.—We saw two thirds of a box of ripe strawberries yesterday; the first we have seen, with the exception of a few Oneida seedlings, that were handed us a few days ago.

Leander Wilcox's two girls are in our employ. The oldest one works in the washing and ironing, and the other at the Silk-Factory.

Mr. Thacker last night called for a bee, to assist in cutting up pine-apples to-day. We have 2000 on hand.

We counted fifty-four men, women and children, at the bee this forenoon, eight of whom were hired men and women.

We commenced, Tuesday last, sending our milk to the Cheese-Factory.

THE O. C. DAILY.

VOL. 3. SATURDAY, JUNE 22, 1867. NO. 149.

We had a continuation, last night, of the talk we had a few days since, on faithfulness in little things. It was brought out by Abram and Mr. Hatch saying that some of their tools were taken and not returned to their proper places, which caused them considerable trouble. The question of faithfulness at length, after much exhortation from Mr. Noyes, turned on this; will we commence a reform by being faithful to God and the truth, by giving utterance to our thoughts in a distinct manner, and loud enough to be heard by those who sit in remote parts of the room ? Mr. Noyes thought if we conquered *this* spirit of unfaithfulness, it would be easy to overcome all others.

We can say for ourselves in reference to this subject, since we have realized more fully, that good spirits were present with us, and that all our acts were scrutinized by them, that when we are tempted to leave things out of place, set things down in a careless way or to not return borrowed articles promptly, or if we are behind time in our business, we have felt the lash of conscience, that would not let us rest till every thing was set right, and we could feel that we were doing by others, as we would have them do by us.

We had four applications by letter last night, for membership. One was from C. C. Rutherford, a single man of Lebanon, Indiana. He writes that he is crippled in his " rite arme," but receives $180 per year, which if he becomes a member he is willing to turn into the society. Application No. 2 is from D. K. Newhall, who writes from Saratoga Srings, but does not seem to be a resident there. No. 3 from Edwin M. Sherwood of Peoria, Illinois, and lastly, Mr. Steel, our Troy correspondent, intimates that it is probable he may want to unite with us at no very distant day. His case is a very interesting one.

A man by the name of P. G. Mitchell, of West Liberty, Ohio, writes :

" I have had a good many discussions concerning the O. C. Most persons seem to think that it is nothing more than a Community of sensualists. I am glad to say that I have disabused the minds of many persons on that point, and with the help of the CIRCULAR, I have shown (with my limited knowledge of the Community), that they aim higher than the world is willing to acknowledge. I am sorry to see that so many are prejudiced against you, but in every case where I have talked with men and explained the matter as I understand it, they have acknowledged that ' It is not such a bad thing after all.'

"Yesterday, I was talking with some gentlemen on the subject, and a young man (a runner for some wholesale house), came in and regaled us with his views of the O. C., according to the teachings of the *New-York Herald*, and drew largely upon his imagination in order to fill up. When he was through, I quietly told him what I knew, and gave him the CIRCULAR to prove it, and I soon convinced him and the company, that he knew nothing about the O. C."

Mrs. Emily Miller, a niece of Mrs. E. Hall, of St. Catharines, Canada, writes a good letter to her Aunt, in which she says:

"Your ideas of the Bible (and when I say you, I of course, mean the Community), agree so well with ours in many respects, that I read them with pleasure and satisfaction. I have believed fully since I first knew you, that Mr. Noyes is a chosen vessel, a man of God ; or in other words, deeply imbued with the spirit of God, for if not, he would ere this have fallen from his high estate ; one so much looked up to and loved, would be in great danger of becoming vain and self-righteous, and he has ever been the same; fighting manfully for the *right*, and *truth*. But few could have stood as he has, a rock in persecution, and a rock in prosperity."

We have several hired people from Taburg, Oneida Co. I heard one of them remark that he was disappointed with the Community, he found things so different from the reports—everything so orderly and quiet, no selfishness, and all striving to promote each others happiness, and finally said, that he knew it was a nice place to live, and he believed he should like it. I am thankful that our workmen feel so good toward us.   s.

A committee consisting of C. W. Underwood, Mr. Woolworth, Mr. Aiken, E. P. Inslee, H. C. Noyes, Chloe Seymour and H. M. Worden, were appointed last night, to make arrangements for the Fourth of July.

Thanks to Mr. Skinner for correcting us on pages. On examination, we find we are thirty pages ahead. We will put ourselves back in the present number, as we regulate a clock, to the true time.

Our calls for meals, from visitors, are less frequent than they were a year ago. The most we have furnished in one day is only twelve.

Mr. Noyes and Victor have gone to Utica to-day, for the purpose of settling up with Dr. Gray, and to get him to give V. an honorable discharge.

We have splendid weather these days.

THE O. C. DAILY.

VOL. 3.   MONDAY, JUNE 24, 1867.   NO. 150.

BUSINESS MEETING.

Mr. Cragin reported the action of the committee chosen a week ago, to find some one to take G. W. Hamilton's place in the Trap-shop. They think it is best to divide the responsibility, and have appointed a committee consisting of Roswell Hawley, Joel Higgins, Myron Kinsley, Alfred Hawley and Mr. Campbell, chairman. Mr. Cragin thought this committee might meet every day and organize themselves together in such a way as to do the work more efficiently than it ever had been done. The Community spirit working through the organization, would secure a very effective administration. It was thought Mr. Campbell should take more responsibility than he has. He might have some one help him in the details of packing, keeping the books, &c. It was left to this committee to select some one for this purpose.—G. W. Hamilton is desired to feel responsible for things in the shop, till they are able to get along without him. He should keep an outlook for the business there, and be free to make suggestions when they were needed.

Mr. Woolworth hoped we should be able to fill all the orders for traps. It was thought best for this committee to meet to-day for the purpose of considering how many traps will be needed, and get ready to meet orders.

The cistern at the Bag-shop is out of order. This introduced the subject of cisterns in general. G. W. H. thought some one ought to study the science of making cisterns. We have hitherto found it very difficult to make a durable and water-tight cistern. Mr. Cragin wished the talk of Mr. Noyes, Friday evening, on the subject of faithfulness, could be printed, and every one have a copy to carry in his pocket. He thought that unfaithfulness and hurry in making cisterns, was the great fault. A committee was appointed to investigate and report.

WILLOW-PLACE.—A bee at half past five, Saturday night, and another at five, yesterday morning, finished the principal part of our bathing yard and house. The bathing yard, as we may call it, is a space under water twenty feet long and eighteen feet wide. It is enclosed by the outside fences and a railing which comes near the surface of the water, which effectually protects persons from getting out of the yard into deep water. This yard has a floor consisting of two platforms. The first is twenty feet long (the length of the yard) and six feet broad, with a depth of about two feet. The second is twelve feet broad, and has a depth of three feet at the shore side, and four feet at the outer side. It is an excellent place for learners. Those who can swim may plunge off from the old platform which has not been moved. This work has been carried through in a real Community spirit, only four bees being required to do it.

As Mr. Easton is to start for New-York this afternoon, he requested the criticism and advice of the family, last night. But little fault was found with him, and a good deal of commendation and love was expressed for him. His talk has been edifying in our meetings, and he is a good example in that respect. The heartiness with which he has taken hold of business, and his willingness to change, when called for, was spoken of, as excellent traits in his character. His tendency to talk too much was considered quite a fault, though it was thought by those who were acquainted with him in New-York, that he had improved a good deal in this respect.

A "Royal Oak," on the lawn, has a double set of leaves; one of last years growth, and one of this. The last year's leaves cling to the tree, fluttering through all the vicissitudes of the winter, defying frost, wind and snow, to drive them from their parent stems. We looked to see the new offspring of this spring, crowd them off and set them adrift in the world, but they still dispute possession with the new comers, and we have the novel spectacle of a tree with green foliage interspersed with brown.—Will not this afford a text for H. J. S?   H.

We clip the following from a letter received yesterday, from Wm. M. Knight, of Kenton, Ohio:

"Enclosed you will please find $37.50 for which send me by Express, one dozen No. 1¼ Traps and the balance in No. 1 Traps, all with chains. I have used your traps for several years, and find your No. 1 is sufficiently strong to hold a large wolf, having caught seven of them in that size, and no one ever making their escape."

We had two bees yesterday, for picking strawberries, which resulted in gathering 210 quarts.—More than 1300 quarts of pine-apples have been put up.—Mr. Olds returned from his tour West, Saturday.—A Mr. Leffingwell, a nephew of Dr. Jackson, of Dansville, staid here last night.

The corps that wait on company, had busy times yesterday. Strawberry short-cakes were furnished for the first time. There were twenty dinners called for, and a good many luncheons, strawberries and cream, and ice-cream. There was a helpful spirit, the family being quick to respond to any call for assistance.

THE O. C. DAILY.

VOL. 3.   TUESDAY, JUNE 25, 1867.   NO. 151.

EVENING MEETING.

It was proposed by Mr. Woolworth to talk about *horses*, and though it might not be a very interesting subject to the family at large, it is still a Community interest, and is growing more and more so. That department seems now to be experiencing a vein of ill luck. The committee have purchased several horses this season, and have done well; but the last horse which they obtained by exchanging the one bought in Canada some time since, and a note of one hundred and twenty-five dollars, did not prove so favorable.—The horse, though fine looking, is nearly blind, and probably had been so for some time. Mr. Kinsley's instincts were not in favor of buying him, as the man seemed so anxious, or in a hurry, that he thought there was something wrong. Afterwards, the remainder of the committee concluded to proceed and close the bargain. Mr. Woolworth knew nothing of it.

What was criticised most, was lack of unity and consultation, and a spirit that makes haste. The position held by that committee is an undesirable one, and it is also an important one. It is all-important that they should be inspired, and act in harmony with one another and with the financiers. If the lesson of unity and inspiration should be learned by this affair, Mr. Woolworth thought it would be money not lost.

Mr. Clark and G. R. Kellogg were exhorted to softness of heart and brotherly love, as they are in almost constant contact with the outside world, and have special need to be in earnest on this point.

Mr. Leffingwell, our visitor, left yesterday. He is book-keeper of the Scientific Polytechnic Institute, Brooklyn, and his home is near Cayuga Lake in this State. He wrote the day before he came, informing us of his wish to make us a short visit, and his desire to bring a lady with him. For some cause he came sooner than he expected when he wrote, and did not wait for a reply to his letter; and the lady of whom he spoke was hindered from coming on account of her brother's illness. He writes:

"On my way homeward from Brooklyn, I am accompanied by a lady teacher in the Packer Collegiate Inst. of that city, who is very desirous of visiting your Community, in company with myself. She is a member of Mr. Beecher's Church, in Brooklyn, and has only recently been interested in your religious faith, by the series of "Noon Discourses," on religious topics, which have lately appeared in the columns of the CIRCULAR. I visited you about two years since, at Oneida, and have since then renewed a somewhat casual acquaintance, by visits at your N. Y., Branch. I think Mr. Underwood has met me in both places.

"Now if it would be entirely convenient for you to receive our visit (which will be of one day only,) will you meet us at Oneida Junction, Tuesday afternoon, 25th inst.   *   *   *   *   *

"I rather fear all this may seem somewhat presumptuous or presuming on a slight acquaintance, but the acquaintance on my part is much older than on yours. It was through my cousin Giles E. Jackson, of Dansville, who died in 1864, that my first knowledge of you began, and a regular subscriber for three years to the CIRCULAR, may be allowed, it seems to me, to feel something of the "stranger" feeling, wearing off."

WILLOW-PLACE.—After meeting last night several of the young women went out to the pond to try their new bathing-place. They returned exclaiming that it was "delicious! splendid!" The water was real warm, and there was no danger of getting over one's depth. Olive and Minerva swam off in the pond while the rest remained within the railing and took lessons. —They wish all their Oneida sisters to enjoy this luxury, and accordingly extend them a cordial invitation to come when they can. It has been proposed that women have the pond from nine to eleven in the forenoon, and from one to four in the afternoon.—Mr. Noyes thinks that the girls of the silk-room and also the neighboring women, may be permitted to use the yard from six to seven in the afternoon every day but Sunday. It will probably be kept locked at other times.

The silk department, yesterday, sent off 104 pounds of waste silk that have been accumulating since they first began the manufacture. It cost from $11.75 to $12.00 per pound, and is sold as waste at $1.75, to a firm in Hartford. This firm manufactures it into a second quality of silk by a process which they keep a secret.

I desire to thank God for his goodness to us, and for his care over us. I confess he is worthy to be trusted under all circumstances; I feel ashamed of myself that I do not trust him more. I desire in the future to honor God with more faith, which I think would please him. I am satisfied he will take better care of us and of our businesses, than we can ourselves, if we will let him. I confess Christ a whole Savior, and a soft heart.   ENOS KELLOGG.

The hired men are at work ditching, this forenoon, between the fruit-house and the stone reservoir. This indicates to us the glad news that laying down the *main* aqueduct, at any rate, is nearly completed.

There were 143 quarts of strawberries picked yesterday.—Haying is progressing finely, with scarcely a sprinkling of rain. The grass is very heavy.—Mr. Brewster and his daughter are here.

THE O. C. DAILY.

VOL. 3. WEDNESDAY, JUNE 26, 1867. NO. 152.

I think perhaps it would be well to publish in the DAILY, some account of my success in settling that affair in Milwaukee, of Ledyard & Carll. Perhaps it is not necessary to go into all the particulars, but simply to report how the case stands. I did not succeed in collecting the debt, as I seemed to anticipate in my first letter. I found the parties had sold out, closed up their business, and got every thing into their own hands. It was pretty evident they could pay the debt, or at least a part of it, but they proved to be bad men, dishonest and not disposed to pay. I then consulted a lawyer who rather advised me not to commence any legal action, as he thought it would be of no use, &c., said he could not guarantee success in the matter. Under these circumstances, I did not feel clear to make any moves, involving expense, and so finally concluded, by advice from O. C., to leave the note in the hands of some one who would do the best they could to collect it. I accordingly left it with A. H. Gardener & Co., (who, by the way, recommended this firm to me at first) who will act in the case as they would if it was their own, and manage it for our interest. I have written them since I left, not to settle for less than fifty cents on a dollar.   O. OLDS.

VISITORS.—Mr. Horner, from Philadelphia, made us a call Monday, with Mr. Wood from New York. Mr. Horner had read Dixon. We had considerable talk with him. He was a religious man, and as we unfolded our principles and gave him a view of our position in the resurrection, he appeared to be profoundly impressed. Indeed, both these gentlemen seemed to have a respect for the Community bordering upon reverence, which made conversation with them easy and pleasant.

Mrs. H. M. Knox from St. Paul, Minn., called here, with several of her friends and relations from Knoxboro. She expressed herself as being in love with our preserved fruits. She said they were in great demand in St. Paul. There was another party consisting of J. H. Warren from New York, a son of Mr. David Warren, and Mrs. Thomas Barbour from Patterson, New Jersey, Miss Gaffney, from Rome, Italy, and Miss Walsh, from Dublin, Ireland; all of whom were very much pleased with their visit.   U.

A BRIDGE ACCIDENT.—Two of the O. C. teams were sent to Rome, yesterday, for lumber. Good luck attended the expedition, till within two miles of home, on the return trip. On reaching the bridge over the Sconondoah Creek a short distance above the Community Saw-mill and Foundry, Charles Primo, the driver of the forward team, advised the driver of the other team to remain on the hill, till he, Primo, had crossed the bridge, as he entertained some suspicions that the old structure was not altogether safe. Indeed, the reputation of the bridge, for soundness and safety, has not been good for some time past, and only a short time since, the Vernon commissioner of highways, had been notified to inspect the same. He did so, and pronounced all right. But his judgment did not relieve our teamster from his fears, so he drove on to the decrepit frame, slowly and cautiously, and when horses, wagon and driver were fairly suspended, the treacherous timbers gave way, precipitating them all into the shallow stream, some ten feet below.

As the south side gave way first, the load of lumber was capsized as it went down. The driver, by a remarkable instinct or presence of mind, seeing himself going down, pulled upon the lines so as to save his head from striking the rocks, otherwise the fall would undoubtedly have proved fatal. The horses were much bruised as well as their driver. One of the horses had his mate killed a few years since by a similar accident on Mud-Creek. The town of Vernon seems to be very unfortunate in having poor bridges and poorer commissioners or inspectors. Somebody should lecture the town on the subject of faithfulness, and the criminality of unfaithfulness in little things.

                                                                C.

In the evening meeting, last night the fruit campaign, on which we are now entering, was spoken of, and a desire expressed by those immediately connected with it, that it might be pervaded by a spirit of brotherly love, and faithfulness to God's inspiration that would ensure success.

Mr. E. Hall and O. L. Vanvelzer went out peddling last week, and were gone four days. They report their sales as follows:

Sales by E. Hall,	Silk,	$258.00
" " "	Thread,	2.10
" " "	Bags,	56.75
Sales by O. L. Van,	Silk,	$217.50
" " "	Bags,	9.00

Mr. Noyes has been absent at W. P. the last two evenings, and Mr. Cragin has attended meeting at O. C. We understand they are to exchange in this way for a week.

570 quarts of strawberries were picked, yesterday, and a small bee this morning at five o'clock, to pick French Seedlings.

Mr. Brewster made a short stop this time, having left, with his daughter, yesterday.

THE O. C. DAILY.

VOL. 3. THURSDAY, JUNE 27, 1867. NO. 158.

W. P.—C. A. C. reports an important improvement in the silk-machinery. At the second doubling, if there is an uneven tension in the strands, one of them will be loose and the other too tight, or *vice versa*, thus injuring the strength of the silk.—Charles wrote to Mr. Holland, at Williamantic, to know if he had any way of overcoming the difficulty, and he answered that he had not, and if Charles could devise some method, he would make better silk than the manufacturers now do.

He and J. Sears have, therefore, studied long and hard on this problem, devising no less than eight different plans, but with indifferent success. Finally, it occurred to them that they might get some ideas by going to the cotton mills at Utica. They did so; told the superintendent of the mills, their difficulty, and asked him if he had ever had any such trouble with his cotton. "Yes," he replied, "and we have conquered it." He then showed them his method, which is to cover the traverse-bars with a kind of thick felt cloth, which checks the threads as they pass over it. He then gave them half a yard, (it is worth $5.00 per yard) telling them to try it. They have done so, and have found it a perfect success. Inspiration and Providence is as manifest in this circumstance, as it was at the beginning.

Caldwellville, N. Y., June 25, 1867.

My Dear Friends, Beloved in Christ:—I am conscious of an impression on my heart akin to inspiration to write to you, hoping and expecting that this missive will meet a loving response. It is no fancy subject, but one, as it now stands, fruitful of pain to me. I much desire to know from you what it is that separates you from me. Not me from you, but you from me. Calling upon memory for a cause, the only one offered is this: At the request of Mr Cragin I stated some facts as they occurred at a certain time. I need not repeat them, it is a painful theme. I heartily forgive the one who did me the wrong, and wish that memory also would cancel the record. I love him as a member of the body of Christ. I love the Community as the only body God has raised up to exhibit the true principles of heavenly life. And beyond all other men I honor and love John H. Noyes as an apostle of Jesus Christ. Why then must we be estranged? Pity it is, that those who have the same faith and love should be in the least degree separated in heart. 　*　　*　　*　　*　　*

I wait for your reply until you shall be furnished from inspiration, with matter suitable.

Your brother in Christ,

G. W. ROBINSON.

After some talk upon the subject of Mr. R.'s letter, it was proposed as a means of helping him into good relations with the Community, that he and his wife be invited to come and make us a visit as long as they may choose.

Accident.—Last evening, after meeting, as Erastus Van was running with all speed, from the house to the Tontine, he was suddenly arrested by the open ditch, left unguarded and unlighted by those laying the iron pipe. His fall was very heavy, and striking his head and face on the pipe, bruised him severely. This morning he finds himself, as well as could be expected, after the bruising. Is it not the duty of every one obstructing public passages in any way, to see that they are either lighted or barricaded at night? B.

The following is the result of my late business trip:

Fruit Orders, 1289 doz.		$6,445.60
Trap	"	3,240.93
Bag	"	399.57
Silk	"	483.55
"	Sales	146.35
Collected for Agency		189.35
"	" O. C.	842.28
Total		$11,747.03

Distance traveled by R. R. and Steamboats, 2,418 miles. C. O.

Mr. Noyes's letter to Mr. Bloom, inviting him to make the O. C. a visit, was read last night, and approved. Then there was some talk about our boys working with the hired men, Mr. Hatch thought it had a bad effect. It was decided to hire boys to assist the hired men, ride horse, &c., when necessary.

Fidelia and Marion have moved four times in a little over a week. Last night they took possession of the old Reception-room, where, it is to be hoped, they will be permitted to repose in peace for the present, though they are beginning to feel that moving is only sport.

Yesterday, Jessie asked her mother if she had read Mrs. Miller's piece in the last CIRCULAR. *Mrs. B.—* "Yes, I have read it twice." *Jessie,* (with much warmth and earnestness). "Why then don't you do as she did, let God cure your foot?"

Thirty-nine dinners were furnished, yesterday, to visitors. A large number were in at the noon meeting.

Mr. Clark sold yesterday, $400 worth of hop-stoves and pipes. Profits about $100.

We had for dinner yesterday, strawberry shortcake and green peas.

The little girls of Edith and Mabel's age alternate, and spend each a week at W. P. They consider it a great treat.

THE O. C. DAILY.

VOL. 3.   FRIDAY, JUNE 28, 1867.   NO. 154.

When Mr. Noyes and Victor went to Utica, last Saturday, they carried to the Asylum, as a present, two cases of preserved fruit; one case in bottles, for the Superintendent and his assistants, and the other in cans, for the inmates of the convalescent ward. Victor received the following response from the latter, a day or two since. We omit the two last verses:

State Lunatic Asylum, Utica N. Y.
June 25, 1867.

The Gentlemen, Residents in Hall number "One,"
Acknowledge with greatest of pleasure,
Your gift of canned fruits, which enlivened their Sunday dinner, with joy beyond measure.

On the motion of Seely, the undersigned were
By unanimous voting selected
A committee of three, the thanks to declare,
For your gift, so much unexpected.

'Tis said that of *pudding*, the proof of its goodness
Is mainly in *chewing the string*;
Our test of your present, amounted to a rideness,
For it caused from the spoons, *joyous* ring.

And when in last search, not a lingering drop
Could the busy spoon find, and the feasting was over,
We looked as content as a boy with his top,
Or as Durham in a rich field of clover.

Very suggestive, your present is surely,
And a theorem new introducing:
'Tis that *Lunies* need not to be kept too demurely,
Forbidden to shout or to sing troo-roo-roorly,
Since a Noyes may be *some* good producing.

By the Committee,   { McCay.
                         { Boyd.
                         { Malcom.

V. Noyes Esqr., Oneida N. Y.

VICTOR'S REPLY.

Oneida, *June* 27, 1867.

TO THE MEMBERS OF THE COMMITTEE:

DEAR SIRS :—Your favor of the 25th inst. was received last evening, and though wholly unexpected was none the less welcome. Permit me, gentlemen, to congratulate you on the possession of such happy poetical powers, for truly the merits of our trifling gift (which was also the gift of the Community) were sung with an originality and genius which would have won applause even at a banquet of the *literati*. In fact it did elicit both laughter and applause, when read in public assembly of the brethren here—a body of people, let me assure you, possessed of no mean taste in such matters. And here let me add—for justice really demands it—that I have received nothing but the kindest of treatment from my friends here, both previous too and since my confinement at the Asylum

and I wish to repeat now, what I often said while at Utica, that the Community had always been to me the pleasantest of homes.

Please give my respects to all the "boys," both patients and attendants, and believe Dear Sirs, the hope that youand all my numerous friends there, may early regain the blessings and rights of liberty and citizenship, is most fondly cherished by

Yours respectfully,   V. C. Noyes.

Mr. Cragin received a letter from Mr. Morris, yesterday, in reply to one Mr. C. wrote him some time ago. Mr. M. does not take his criticism at all, but on the contrary says that he was surprised and grieved, to find us as "despotic and intolerant" as any of the churches. He says he is thankful that he is getting his eyes open—has been drawn toward us heretofore, but shall be more cautious in making advances in future, and we have so misjudged *him*, thinks it not safe to trust either our inspiration or judgment in the future.

He closes his letter by saying: "Mrs. Morris joins with me in love to you. As ever yours," &c.

DEAR BROTHER NOYES AND THE O. C. FAMILY.—I have become convicted by the truths read in our hearing, that I need a new conversion, and a deeper work of grace in my heart and spirit, to enjoy a revival with the Community family. I know that the devil has had a strong hold on me through egotism, and isolation. And now I wish to take a humble, child-like position before my brethren, and invite their criticism, and the Lord being my helper, I will trust God's grace and his appointed means to deliver me from the thraldom of evil spirits. Yours for victory over the world, the flesh and the devil.   CORNELIUS HIGGINS.

There was some talk last night about bees. Mr. Bradley wished to know how much time the family could afford to spend in bees. The berries are large, and there is the prospect of a heavy crop. They are gathered much nicer, and the beds left in better order when picked by our people, but he did not want to tax the family too much, as there would now be a demand for help in putting them up. The bees have thus far been well attended.

It has been decided, for many reasons, not to attempt putting up the children's house this year and to defer laying the walls, till next spring. The children have quite satisfactory accommodations now, and room enough to make them comfortable; more so then ever before.

The Fruit-preservers commenced putting up strawberries to-day. A bee to assist in preparing bottling, is called for this forenoon.

THE O. C. DAILY.

VOL. 3.   SATURDAY, JUNE 29, 1867.   NO. 155.

Good! Grand!! Glorious!!!

Thank God, the job of laying the iron pipe, to conduct the water from the springs to the house, after much labor and persistent effort, is finally successfully accomplished. That is all we expect to do at present. (For the branches we still use the old pump logs.) At four o'clock P. M, yesterday, we completed the union which connects the iron pipes with the reservoir, and this morning it is discharging one gallon in fourteen seconds, or 195 barrels per day. The old aqueduct has, of late, discharged only about sixty barrels per day, from the same springs; the remainder must have leaked out, though not in a way to be discovered on the surface of the ground.

The length of the aqueduct now laid, is 155 rods, and its weight about 41,000 pounds; 1150 pounds of lead and about 140 of tarred rope or cord, were used n calking the joints. The tarred cord causes the water to taste of it some, but we expect it to improve soon. The family can now have all the water they want for bathing purposes. The aqueduct has cost a good deal of hard labor and expense, yet we consider it a wonderful success, and a cause of thankfulness to God. At another time I may speak of the process of laying it.   J. ABBOTT.

WILLOW-PLACE.—Two fine swarms of bees came out yesterday from their parent hives, alighting on one of the lower branches of an appple tree near by.— They were each soon provided with a habitation by Mr. Newhouse, who now reports them as having "gone to work"—probably at house-cleaning, painting, papering, &c., if we may judge by the swarm from the Oneida hive.

We met in the parlor after supper last evening, and listened to the reading of the correspondence from abroad. It was very interesting, and afforded us a rich treat. After the reading was over, the young men assisted in clearing off the tables and washing the dishes. Several of them were seen with their hands in the dish-water, others carrying the dishes away, and the work was quickly accomplished.

Ormond has somehow got an idea that it is dangerous to go in the water, and has had several times of whimpering about my going in swimming, saying that I should "*go to the bottom.*" Yesterday, after John Hutchins and I had been playing croquet, we proposed a bath, and I took Ormond along, thinking it might cure him of his fears. John went in first, and I stood by Ormond to watch the effect. As John struck out into the stream, Ormond's mouth began to pucker, and in a doleful voice he bawled after him, "John, come back! do come back! You'll go to the bottom, and *won't play croquet any more!*" Poor fellow! he has got an early peep into the darkness that bounds human life. But we cured him, so that at last he enjoyed our splashing and swimming.

J. R. N.

A gentleman and two ladies, from Auburn, or near there, called yesterday afternoon, and enquired for Mr. and Mrs. Cragin. Mr. C. after hearing their names, recollected having seen the women, and was some acquainted with them in 1837, when he lived in New-York, but has known nothing of them since. They are spiritualists, and came on purpose to visit the Community, and had never heard of Mrs. Cragin's death.

The reading of the letters from London was listened to by the family last night with all-absorbing interest. It hardly seems a reality that our brothers who were so recently with us, are in that old city, gazing upon the wonderful works of past generations, of which we have so often read and pondered.

1200 quarts of strawberries were picked yesterday and 200 picked at a bee this morning at five o'clock. The dew was very heavy, and almost cold enough for a frost. The women complained of cold fingers, and came in with their clothes dripping wet.

In the emergency for help in the preserving-rooms, to-day, it was proposed last night, that the Bag-shop hands be invited to assist. Accordingly all the hired girls are on hand, this morning, with one exception.

Strawberries are dealt out to the family very liberally this year. We had them for supper last night and the night before. 778 quarts were put up yesterday.

Mr. Bradley has resigned his office of taking charge of picking strawberries, and D. E. Smith has taken hold of the business. Mr. B. goes out to buy fruit.

Mr. Clark sold, yesterday, $375 worth of hop-stoves and pipes; profits above first cost of material and labor, $85.00.

Thirty-five meals were called for yesterday.

THE O. C. DAILY.

VOL. 4.   MONDAY, JULY 1, 1867.   NO. 1.

BUSINESS MEETING.

Mr. Barron said the hired men had been in the habit of playing ball, after supper, in the pasture. Mr. Conant had objected to it, and they had played somewhere near the boarding-house. They are quite interested in the game, and he did not know but we ought to look into it and keep it under our control. We sympathise with them in playing ball. Mr. Barron and Frederic were appointed committee on the subject.

Mr. Covell informs us that he will have a boat-load of coal here for us Monday morning,—would like us to be ready to take care of it. Left to Messrs. Kinsley, Clark, Conant and Hawley.

Mr. Kinsley said we had a large pile of wood exposed to the weather, and as the wood-shed is full, it is desirable that there should be some place provided that it might be put under cover. A leanto on the west side of the shed, was spoken of, but the matter was left to Messrs. Kinsley, Thacker, Abram and Homer.

Mr. D. Kelley said that the wagon repairing was getting to be quite an item, and we have good facilities for doing the work here, but it was difficult to give instructions for blacksmithing at W. P. He thought it would pay to have a blacksmith over here for a while.

The contemplated shop to be erected, at W. P. was spoken of as desirable. Committee on the above, Messrs. D. Kelley, G. W. Hamilton, J. Higgins and Mr. Campbell.

We have had some trouble with horses getting out of the barn in the night, and doing damage to the lawn. It was thought there was rather a loose state of things at the barn, in this respect. Our people use the horses all times of night, and do not always understand what their responsibilities are in respect to fastening them. Printed instructions should be put up, and perhaps chains, to keep the horses in their stalls. Mr. Hawley will see that things are set right in this respect.

————————

The process of laying iron pipe is as follows : In the first place a trench has to be dug about 3 feet deep, 16 inches wide at bottom and 30 at top, more or less.— As we lay the pipe, the ditch has to be enlarged against the joints, by digging it deeper and wider, to enable us to see on the under side, so that we can work all around the joint. Then a right selection of pieces, and grading to fit them, is made (as many of the pieces are sprung in casting). Next, some eight or ten yards of tarred cord is tamped into the joint—a slow process ; then clay has to be worked to the right consistence and pliency, and is packed about the joints, with an opening at top to pour in lead. The clay is held to its place, by a bank of mellow earth being pressed against it. For melting the lead we used a common coal stove, with some 12 feet of pipe to give it draft—the pipe being supported by a stake driven into the earth, and fastened to it. The stove had to be moved and set up as we advanced, every ten rods or less, as we could not well carry the lead and keep it hot enough over five rods each way. It required a very hot fire to melt the lead and make it hot enough to pour around cold iron. We used both stove-coal and charcoal, and made a fire on top as well as under the lead, and had to blow it with a hand-bellows, to bring it to a proper heat. It averaged four pounds of lead to a joint, though often a pound more was used, that had to be trimmed off with a chisel. After pouring the lead, and removing the dirt and clay from the joint, and trimming off all unnecessary lead, it had to be tamped on all sides with a heavy hammer to make it tight. In laying the pipe we averaged about twenty pieces—ten rods—per day, though we might have laid more had we not been hindered by leaky pipes.— Some persons may be surprised that we use so large pipe (4 inches in diameter) to bring so small a quantity of water. One reason is, we expect to bring more water, by adding other springs to those we now use ; but the principal reason is, the small amount of fall there is in the distance—there being not over one foot of fall from where the water is received to where it is discharged ; which causes it to move slowly, requiring a large pipe to discharge a small amount of water.

Much more might be said which I omit, fearing I may be tedious.   J. ABBOTT.

————————

Mr. Kelley returned Saturday. He called at Mr. Bushnell's, but was treated rather coldly. At Mr. K.'s suggestion, Albert got the consent of his father to come this way, when he goes to Amherst College, as he expects to some time this week. When at Dansville, Mr. K. called on Dr. Jackson, and was treated with a severe letting alone. The Dr. passed right by him without deigning him a word or even a look.

————————

Mrs. Freeman and her sister, Mrs. Shaw, with their two little girls, came here Saturday, and expect to stay several days.—Mr. and Mrs. Cornell, and Mrs. Wheeler, (the three persons spoken of in Saturday's DAILY) left for home Saturday forenoon. Mr. Cragin carried them down to the Depot.

————————

Mr. Thacker said, last night, that they wanted all the help from the family, for four days to come, that was possible for them to furnish, as the fruit-preservers hoped to put up, at the least calculation, 1000 quarts per day.

————————

116 meals were furnished to visitors, Saturday, which together with ice-cream, lemonade, horse-keeping &c., amounted to $100. Sixty-four regular meals were called for yesterday.

————————

The grass on the lawn, is being mown the second time. From our window we can see Mr. Cragin using the scythe, quite dextrously we should judge.

THE O. C. DAILY.

VOL. 4.   MONDAY, JULY 2, 1867.   NO. 2.

Carthage, N. Y., June 26, 1867.

DEAR FRIENDS :—I am still striving to do the commandments of Christ. I find much help and strength in the Bible, but more in renewing the covenant daily between me and the Lord. I realize my strength and patience increasing as I wait upon him, and deepen my consecration by obedience and submission. I am encouraged greatly of late—feel that I am gaining the victory over sin and Satan. I desire to hear from you as from home. Through increasing love to you I am coming more into love and unity with Christ. I confess faith and confidence in the ascending fellowship. My feelings of devotion to Christ, through what I have learned of you, remind me of Daniel praying with his windows open toward Jerusalem. My love for, and confidence in you, increase in proportion as they are assailed by evil spirits. Mrs. Thayer asked me when I left if I had been paid for coming. I felt paid then abundantly; now, I realize that a hundred times the cost of my visit would be no recompense for the loss I should now feel, to be placed back in my experience where I was before. I confess the Lord a sure guide out of Satan's dominions—a keeper of my thoughts and purifier of my affections.

> Yours fraternally,   CLARA WAIT.

Saturday one of our workmen was in Rome, and stepping into a store he noticed some strawberries, rather small, and not very attractive to the eye. On the boxes was printed, " Raised in the O. C. garden." On asking about them, and telling the store-keeper that he knew they did not grow at O. C., he finally said that they were raised about two miles from Rome, and remarked that they had to put the name " O. C." on the boxes in order to sell them.—I wondered if this would ultimately be the case all over the world.   s.

YESTERDAY'S ITEMS.—Among the company that visited the kitchen, was an old lady, who was wonderfully taken with our steam operations. At length she said she should like to see us wash dishes, as she had heard that we did *that* by steam. She was quite surprised when told that we washed our dishes just as other folks do.

A man here from Oriskany Falls, said he had noticed one thing that gave him much pleasure, which was, that every one he saw here seemed to be " well shod." This must have been quite creditable to Mr. Vanvelzer, we thought. The gentleman must himself have been of the same craft.

1276 quarts of berries put up. There were continuous bees from half past seven, A. M. till seven P. M. Every thing went off pleasantly.

Mr. George Bayne, of Philadelphia, formerly a member of the Brook-Farm Association, called. He remarked, in speaking of Horace Greeley, that his course latterly, proved him to be an insane man.

A report of the committee that was appointed to make arrangements for the Fourth, was read last night. It was remarked that we should have our noon meeting as usual, on that day, though perhaps it would not be held at the usual hour. Mr. Cragin has arranged with H. R. Perry, to deliver a lecture or oration, on the occasion.

A Mr. Marsh, of Wisconsin, writes to obtain explicit information relative to the regulations and laws that have governed our society, that have made it so completely a success, while so many other attempts at Communism have failed. He thinks we must have discovered some way by which the " Golden Rule" can be put in practice, in our every-day life.

Our people made and sold to Henry Wilson, for a festival, fifty quarts of ice-cream, at forty cents per quart. To-day they have agreed to make forty quarts more for Vernon, at sixty cents per quart.

Port Jackson, June 29.

Accept thanks for the specimen copy of the CIRCULAR you sent, and containing directions for Fruit-preserving. If " Outside Barbarians" can take the paper, enclosed is one dollar and my address. D. P. LUKE.

We have received a letter from Mr. Stark, of Syracuse informing us that Mr. Appy's engagements were such, that he could not visit us till some time in August.

Mrs. Louisa Waters is fairly installed in her new office, as assistant at the store in place of Mrs. Aiken who is honorably discharged.

Mr. Robinson writes that he thankfully accepts the invitation to visit the O. C., and will be here in a few days.

THE O. C. DAILY.

VOL. 4.   WEDNESDAY, JULY 3, 1867.   NO. 3.

To the Noon Meeting. —Since our noon meetings commenced, I have had a fresh baptism of the pentecostal spirit, and have had the happy experience that I was blessed with, when a young convert. The resurrection power of Christ has invigorated my spirit and body, and now I want to thank Mr. Noyes publicly for the privilege of living in this beautiful home, where I can learn to do the will of God more perfectly, and enjoy the assurance of an everlasting home with God and his saints.

It is my most earnest prayer that I may be a helper to Mr. Noyes in establishing the kingdom of God on earth. Mr. Cragin has been a benefactor to me ever since I first confessed Christ, and I am glad of an opportunity to thank God publicly for choosing such a faithful man to help me and the church of God.

D. J. Bristol.

Who does not remember how that every Wallingford journalist has very properly eulogized the beautiful river—the splendid accommodations they have for bathing, and how we, thinking of our muddy Creek, awkwardly kept silence, well knowing we had no such luxury of which to boast? Will not some one or all of our sisters there, make their very prettiest bow, and congratulate us on at last having an excellent bathing-place?

Yesterday afternoon, by the kindness of Mr. W. who procured a conveyance and officiated as driver, we (a party of fourteen women and girls) had the pleasure of going to the Willow-Place pond, where for half an hour, our enjoyment was intense. We will not attempt to describe the delight; all who have tried it, know the sensation, and those who have not we hope will soon have an opportunity. In our party were some beautiful swimmers, and the fearlessness with which they plunged into the treacherous looking depths of water, was wonderful. [Perhaps it will not be out of place to say that we hope due caution will be used by all going in there, that they will not be too daring, but use the blessing wisely.] We stopped a few moments in the house, where we were received with the hospitality which is very noticeable in our new family.

On our way home, it was moved we give a vote of thanks to our driver. Be assured it was heartily given.

E.

Willow-Place.—There was quite a large fire near the depot yesterday. About 11 A. M. the smoke was seen from the shop windows, rising in huge black columns to the very clouds. It lasted about two hours, and caused some feeling of alarm in those whose homes were in that direction. We hear to-day that the property was a total loss, there being no insurance. It was the burning of a large brush-heap, and doubtless the work of an incendiary.

Our mother supplies us very liberally with rich, red strawberries. We sometimes have them two or three times a day. We are very thankful for such an indulgent mother.

We enjoy Mr. Noyes's visits and talks very much, and are glad he feels so much at home here.

Interesting letters from G. W. N. and C. S. J. were received again yesterday, and read in meeting last night. It is wonderful how God opens the way for the introduction of truth into that Old World. It is interesting too to note the part that Mr. Dixon plays in the great drama, although entirely unconscious that God is using him in his service.

Mr. Wilson brought back, yesterday, half the ice-cream he bought of us the day before. Not being used to dealing in that article, there proved to be twice as much as he wanted. Our people paid him five dollars for it, (just half what he paid for the same) and will freeze it over to make it serviceable.

In speaking of Mr. Nash's sickness, last night, Mr. Cragin said he believed that the *devil* was having a paralytic stroke these days, and some one replied that it was to be hoped he would not be able to wag his tongue again at present, if at all.

They have six girls in the ironing, and expect two more to help to-day. The laundry corps are putting things through, as the room is wanted for other purposes to-morrow.

Mr. Whitney reports that our bottles are proving themselves first-rate; out of more than five hundred used yesterday, only three were broken.

The bag-bee's are discontinued for the present, or until the press of business in fruit-preserving is over.

H. G. Allen and F. W. Smith came a little after noon yesterday.

Mrs. Slocum, the wife of Dr. Slocum, and a lady friend of hers, staid here last night.

We furnished twenty-five meals to visitors, Monday, and seventy-seven yesterday.

Bags made in June,	58 1-6 doz.
Bag sales, " "	$2,521.10

1,884 dozen traps were ordered in the month of June.

We shall not be able to issue a Daily to-morrow.

THE O. C. DAILY.

VOL. 4.   FRIDAY, JULY 5, 1867.   NO. 4.

EVENING MEETING.

G. R. Kellogg :—I heard at the Depot that we had from two to eight thousand visitors here to-day.

Mr. Kelley :—One man called this evening and said he had been waiting all day, at the Depot, for a chance to come up, and several other parties were also waiting there. He said there was not a horse to be had within forty miles of Oneida.

Mr. Smith :—There was a peddler here to-day, selling "magnetic balsam." He was quite astonished when I told him we had a much superior article, and enquired what it was. I told him it was *faith in Christ.* He said nothing more about his medicine after that.

Mr. Woolworth :—So far as I know, our company behaved very well. They were orderly, respectful and good-natured.

Mrs. Underwood :—I was very much pleased with their deportment. I noticed that the Indians show signs of increased civilization, as many of their squaws begin to wear hoops. [Laughter.] I did not see any of them wearing waterfalls, but presume we shall see them next year.

J. P. H. : I heard an old lady say that the last song "Cousin Jedediah," was better than any theater.

Mr. W. :—Some one asked Mr. Noyes what part of the celebration he enjoyed most. He told, and says he will repeat it here if desired. [Applause.]

Mr. Noyes :—After dinner I felt the heat considerably, and was in quite a state of perspiration. I went to my room, locked the door, put down the curtains and stripped myself; took a sponge and sponged myself all over with cold water; then lay down upon the bed in that condition for about an hour, and gave myself to meditation and fellowship with the Primitive Church; and that was the best part of the celebration to me. I think there was a better feeling here this time than ever before. It seemed to me there was less labor and anxiety, and more faith and genial spirit on our part, and also on the part of those who came here. I enjoyed the day very well, though, as I said, I enjoyed my closet and meditations better.

H. M. W. :—Mr. and Mrs. Porter spoke of Mr. Perry's oration. They liked it very much indeed, and said they had similar views about Christ. They believed he was to be the sovereign of the world, and that the issue was coming soon. They thought the lecture was delivered in a fine manner.

The Fourth passed off more pleasantly than such days generally do with us. The weather was pretty warm, but a slight shower at about ten o'clock laid the dust, and modified the intensity of the heat somewhat. A party of ten came between six and seven o'clock A. M., with the intention of staying all day, and called for breakfast, which was furnished them in the east room of the middle-house. At half past two o'clock we had our lecture in the Hall, of the merits of which we cannot speak, not having been able to hear it. The Hall and gallery was crowded, and not half of our people could get in. Besides music by the Brass Band, between four and five o'clock we had singing in the Hall. A quartette of two women and two men from Hampton also sang three or four songs with Harmonium accompaniment, which were pronounced first-rate. A comic song by G. W. H., "Cousin Jedediah," which was heartily cheered, closed the performances of the day, though persons continued to call for supper, ice-cream, &c., till nearly ten o'clock.

The only annoyance we witnessed was that of the Indians, who came with all their children and babies, and took possession of the shade of the Butternut tree, together with all the seats on the lawn in front of the Mansion house. They were at times quite noisy—the children dodging round among the evergreens, breaking off twigs, &c. They were furnished with all they wanted of broken pieces of shortcake, the same as last year. They made it a regular gala-day, and staid from ten o'clock till seven.

JULY 4th, 1867.—343 meals taken.

Cash received at Office, Dinners &c.,	$413.16
" " Ice-cream, Strawberries and cream,	67.28
" " at Store,	144.32
" " " Fruit-house Strawberries,	38.00
Total,	$653.76

In a private note C. S. J., writes:

Tower of London, Saturday, June, 15.

"I have n't forgotten my promise to write you from the Tower of London, &c. We have just been shut up in the cell where Sir Walter Raleigh was confined for twelve years. It is about two thirds as large as the bedroom I occupied at Oneida when I was there last. We saw the block on which so many of those old fellows had their heads chopped off, and the axe with which it was done; the place where Anne Boleyn had the same operation performed on her, &c. I thought of you and wished you were here with us.—You would like to see Queen Victoria's crown and the Koh-i-noor—the largest diamond in the world."

Eleven visitors staid here Wednesday night.—Dr. Slocum came in the afternoon, and left yesterday afternoon, with his wife and son and the lady who came with his wife.—Mr. Robinson also came day before yesterday and is still with us.—Mary Leete and her sister and child came yesterday, and staid over night.

Mr. and Mrs. King, an uncle and aunt of H. R. Perry are here on a visit.—Twenty three loads of hay were put in the barn Wednesday.

THE O. C. DAILY.

VOL. 4.   SATURDAY, JULY 6, 1867.   NO. 5.

Mr. and Mrs. King, my uncle and aunt of Fulton, N. Y., who have been visiting here for two or three days, were very much pleased with the Community and its surroundings. They left for home yesterday. They have been reading the CIRCULAR for several years, and it was at their house I first heard of the O. C. The superabundant religious coat, by which they are surrounded, has prevented them from getting a very strong hold of our religious faith. They are however very warm and reliable friends of the O. C., and will be glad to extend their hospitalities to any of our folks who may have business in Fulton.

A day or two before coming here, Mrs. King remarked to one of their neighbors, a Mr. Folger, Deputy Sheriff of Oswego Co., that she was about to visit the Community. He said he would just as soon go to the Five Points. "Well, said she, "*you may have a good deal of knowledge of the Five Points*, but I think you had better wait until you know something about the O. C. before you condemn it."

They very well remember hearing Mr. Noyes preach 32 years ago in Cayuga Co. They did not hear of him again for 20 years, and were agreeably surprised when they first saw the CIRCULAR, and learned that **his ideas had crystalized and formed the O. C.** They say he was a very *boyish-looking preacher*, but they recollect very well that

"The preaching of this preacher stirred the pulses of the world;
Errors that were deified, into darkness then were hurled."

They say his sermons caused a terrible rattling among the dry bones, and life-long church members declared they had never heard the gospel before.   H. R. P.

WILLOW-PLACE.—Our garden has done very nicely under the care of Mr. Higgins and Mr. Miller. It occupies about one and a quarter acres of land, and contains a very good variety of fruits and vegetables. There are seventy-two grape-vines, of eight varieties, one quarter of an acre each of raspberries and strawberries, and a goodly quantity of peas, beans, sweet corn, tomatoes, etc. We have been well supplied with beet-greens, spinach and lettuce, and have had very nice green peas once or twice.

The younger girls of the Silk department, are given a recess of half an hour every afternoon, during which they recreate in the pond, under the care of one of the older girls. Their happy faces and elastic steps prove that they receive benefit and pleasure from the exercise. Their recess is from four to half past.

We had some talk, last night, about our system of reporting, and some dissatisfaction expressed about the way it had been left of late. D. J. B. upon whom this business principally devolves, has not recently been regular in his attendance at meetings, and has failed in some instances, to give notice of his intention of staying away, to others who are ready to officiate as reporters in his absence. A little understanding will doubtless set all things right.

Then followed some criticism of Mr. Kelley. In his business transactions of the Fourth, there was some manifestations of his old weaknesses—carelessness and forgetfulness.—It was thought he had not been wide awake to judge and separate himself from the spirit of his parents, where his difficulties, particularly his loose business habits, seem to root.

Mr. Noyes sent an invitation to Mr. Bloom, by letter, to make the O. C. a visit, and the following is Mr. B.'s reply:

143 *West Houston St., Ludlow Place,*
New York, July 1, 1867.

DEAR MR. NOYES:—I thank you for your expressions of peace and good will, and heartily accept any measures that will please Christ and provoke to peace, love and unity. Therefore, I shall be happy to visit Oneida at the earliest moment that my school duties will allow. I am in two schools, one of which has vacation now, while that of the other will begin about the 10th of August, when I shall be free. I should be glad to be met at the depot, and will give you timely notice of my departure for Oneida. I shall look forward in anticipation of an edifying visit.

Yours Truly,   M. L. BLOOM.

I find that quite a number of the family have got the impression (how I cannot conceive) that I was born at the South, or that most of my life has been spent there. This is an error. I was born in Vermont, and have spent most of my life in the States of New York and Iowa. Three months in Missouri, nine in Virginia, and seven in North Carolina, covers all the time spent by me at the South.   D. E. S.

A lady who called here yesterday, seemed very curious to know all about our children—asked a great many questions, and among others, if we ever whipped them. *Miss Pomeroy.*—"Certainly we do if they deserve it." *Lady.*—"Do you whip those that are not your own?" *Miss P.*—"Oh, they are all ours." *Lady.*—"Do you use a machine?" *Miss P.*—Laughing,—"The machine that every faithful mother uses in correcting her child."

As three or four of our girls were passing down the stairway from the Hall, on the Fourth, a man, a stranger, was seen to stare at them with a good deal of earnestness in his countenance; then turning round, he said to those near by, "Well, them gowns *is* pretty!"

Mr. Noyes left yesterday noon, for New-York, New Haven and Wallingford, to "swing round the circle," as he said, and return to O. C. Monday.

Mr. Worden, to our surprise, has just arrived.

THE O. C. DAILY.

VOL. 4.　　MONDAY, JULY 8, 1867.　　NO. 6.

BUSINESS MEETING.

At ten minutes past eleven this morning there were three persons present besides the Chairman and Secretary. These were considered a quorum, and they accordingly proceeded to business.

Mr. Nash reported that he had the material ready for building the front fence, and he wanted help to put it up. Messrs Thacker, Kellogg, Abram, and Mr. Nash were appointed committee.

J. P. Hutchins said that the noise of heating water in the kitchen was a great nuisance to all who worked there. It is almost intolerable, and is kept up most of the time that work is going on there. Those especially suffer from it who work at the dishes. J. P. H. said, "There is not a woman in the kitchen who would not shower blessings on the heads of those who would put a stop to it." A good strong committee was appointed to investigate the thing, and if possible provide some remedy.

While passing through the children's room just after the noon meeting, yesterday, we were greeted with, "*Stop and look into the next room—open the door carefully—make no noise.*" We obeyed wonderingly. The blinds were partially closed, which gave a slightly mystical appearance to the room, and sure enough, there in very truth was a "mystic ring." Twelve little innocents, all wrapt in the arms of Morpheus; it was as if they had all tumbled down on the floor in sport and at that moment been overtaken with slumber, so careless and graceful were their attitudes, and yet so symmetrical their circle. But this was no farce; they were truly sound asleep this time, and all unconscious of the many gazers who soon flocked in. There was not only the usually quiet Theodora and Virginia, the sedate Anna, but the hopping and skipping little Fanny, stalwart George, and even the irrepressible Ormond, all taken captives, and sleeping as peacefully on the hard floor, as if it were the softest bed. We regret that Mr. Smith could not photograph the scene, for it was a fair and rare sight indeed. AITERCUL.

A young man named Dana Ward, who is in our employ, consented to act as hostler on the Fourth. He worked pretty hard, and was furnished with all the lemonade he wanted during the day. He drank very freely, and at the same time ate freely of the lemon and peel. After meeting, Mr. Quance, the keeper of the Boarding-house, came over in great haste, to get help, saying that young Ward was in great distress. A Dr. was sent for, and he has had distressing spasms ever since, till yesterday, when he seemed some better, and hopes were entertained of his recovery. The Dr. says that his sickness was caused by the poison there was in the peel.

Botanical specimens sent to S. E. Johnson, by C. S. J., from different localities.

1st. Gorse, from Whetmore, in Staffordshire, 2nd. English Daisy, from St. James Cemetery in Liverpool, 3d. Groundsel, from near Northampton in Northamptonshire, 4th. Buttercup, from Berkhampstead in Hertfordshire, 5th. Holly, from Regent's Park, London, 6th. Fir, from Buckingham Palace.

Since Mr. Smith joined us, the question has arisen, "Can we not make photography serve us in copying Mr. Noyes's Home-Talks, and thus save much time and trouble." Last night we saw a specimen of Mr. Smith's attempts at photographing some talk we had at the noon meeting, which was very legible, and Mr. S. says, promises success in that direction.

We also saw a nice picture of his, a view taken from the south end of the garret.

The carpenters have put up a building eighteen by thirty-six feet and one and a half stories high, to be used for the present, to lodge extra help. The design is in the fall to build a cellar and move the building over it, when, with the addition of a leanto, it will make a double tenant-house. The location is east of the school-house.

Mr. Robinson left, Friday afternoon, having staid only two nights and about one day and a half. We were quite surprised that he should go so soon, but he may have had good reasons for going.

We had a bee last night after supper, for picking strawberries, which was thought to be the last one we should need, though there will still be berries to pick, for two or three days to come, but not in large quantities. Two hundred quarts were picked.

We had letters again Saturday, from our TRANS ATLANTIC brothers. They are having wonderful success in presenting the truth to the *Literati*, and men of high rank in the old World.

Our flower-gardens are now in all their glory, roses, white lillies &c. in full bloom. The air all around is filled with their delicious fragrance, and the lilly sprinkled in here and there, presents a beautiful appearance.

Mrs. Freeman and Mrs. Shaw, with their little girls, left for their homes this morning. They have been here about nine days.

4,100 quarts of strawberries have been put up this season. The Fruit-preservers are at work putting up pie-plant to-day.

THE O. C. DAILY.

VOL. 4.   TUESDAY, JULY 9, 1867.   NO. 7.

O. C., July 9, 1867.

DEAR BROTHER GEORGE E. :—Mr. Bartholomew of Westfield N. Y. will be here in eight or ten days to exhibit his new process of preserving fruits &c.— Well, I understand that you and Theodore anticipate coming to O. C. before long. Therefore my object in addressing you at this time is to inquire if you could not make it convenient to be here during the experiment. The process involves chemical principles, and would be interesting to you, as well as gratifying to myself to have you here. We shall however retain the apparatus for further experiment with the different kinds of fruits.   Yours very truly, H. T.

Mr. Jones was criticised at his request last night.— As the criticism is all to be written out for Mr. J.'s benefit it will probably be forwarded, so we will only say that it was thought Mr. J. had improved in a good many respects, since his late sickness. His cure seems to have been the result of faith in God in respect to disease. But little fault was found with him at the present time, and much was said in his praise.

After Mr. Jones' criticism, Mrs. Higgins said :

"I have had some experience within a few weeks that I would like to speak of here. It is well known that I have had to use crutches for the last three years. I got better, so that I went with one crutch. A short time since I had a slight fall, which obliged me to use them both again. This led me to see that I had not been thankful for the improvement I had already made, but was instead, constantly looking foward to the time when I should be well. I felt thankful for this hint, and thought I should always be grateful, even if I had to go on crutches all my life. In about two weeks I got better, and am now able to go more or less with only a cane.

Mr. Hatch.—I confess it has made me feel thankful to see Mrs. Higgins' improvement.

Mrs. Higgins.—I have dreamed a good many times of walking, and it was always connected with faith. I believe if I ever walk it will be through the working of the resurrection life of Christ. I attribute my present improvement to that source. The noon meetings have been a great help to me.

Mrs. Hawley testified to a new spirit working in her of love for the members of the Community, which was an evidence to her, that she had passed from death unto life.

Mr. Woolworth.—I thank God for the revival he has given us, and which is still progressing.

LETTERS READ LAST NIGHT:—James Meadowcraft, of Otranto, Iowa, writes for information of our Community system, and wants we should send him some of our papers and pamphlets that he may inform himself of our terms of admitting members. He says in closing, "Men and women of the Oneida Community, I hope and trust and pray, that the great Author of all, will enable you to perfect your attempted good work."

An elderly lady, of Concord, N. H., writes the second time, urging us to accept her as a member. She says: "Though getting a negative answer to my application for admission to your Community, I presume again to plead my case, though told that most that Communities wanted, was the property of its members. Acquaintance gained of you through reading, leads me to trust that it is not the case, &c."

Also a letter from Mary A. Bryan, of Whately, Mass., who is sick of the world and would like to find a home with us.

We hear persons express a great deal of fellow-feeling for our much esteemed brother, D. P. Nash, in his affliction, and we trust he feels the heart of Oneida throb in sympathy with his, in passing through this season of trial. His kindness, and readiness to lend a helping hand to a brother or sister, when such help was needed, are remembered by all, as is his loyalty to Christ and Mr. Noyes, and his willingness to serve the church to the extent of his ability. We cannot but feel that the power of the resurrection, that is working mightily among us, will conquer the enemy, and give *him* in turn a paralytic stroke that will greatly weaken his kingdom. We are glad to hear, through Mr. Noyes, that Mr. N. is better.

Seventy-five bushels of cherries were received last night. It will take nimble fingers to put them all up to-day.

We are refreshed this morning by the early arrival of the CIRCULARS.

Henry Allen left for New-York Sunday night.

Mr. Noyes returned as we expected in the night

THE O. C. DAILY.

VOL. 4. WEDNESDAY, JULY 10, 1867. NO. 8.

EVENING MEETING.

After relating his experience at N. Y., W. C. and New Haven, Mr. Noyes said:

I came away Monday, early. I might say as I said 4th of July, my best experience was in my closet. I made a closet of the cars, coming home. I had a book and read until I had forgotten all about the cars and company, then I went into a season of meditation and never had a better time of interior experience. I made the journey very pleasantly—no waiting or watching. The time seemed very short. My heart was at home with God and I enjoyed it very much. I recommend that way of traveling, if possible—to go into your closet, shut your door, and mind nothing about the outside-world. In fact that is a good thing to do anywhere and everywhere. You are not likely to waste much time in that position. The most profitable and refreshing of any time we spend, is that which we spend in communion with God and meditation. Meditation with Christ is the best kind of industry we can have. It is not time lost—but time gained—time redeemed and put to the very best use. It refreshes and rests us, and fits us for all other labors. It is, you may say, the breeder of all other industries; labor in the Lord; an act of the heart and mind which brings us into direct communication with God, and enables us to resist the devil and lifts us towards the resurrection. That kind of labor prepares us for all other labors—refreshes us and gives us strength, hope, courage and vigor.

Mr. Woolworth:—I desire that we may all cultivate this same habit—this state for communion with God, waiting on him and talking with him. I am sure it will sometime become natural to us. We shall not be able to live without it, for it will be the breath of life to us.

Mr. Noyes:—It will take the place with us that smoking does in the world. It will be our rest and enjoyment. The world seek relief from labor by smoking and strong drink. That is their retirement from labor—that is called refreshment all up and down the railroads. Restaurant! It is a great hoax. They don't get refreshed—on the contrary they get cast down, and are made gloomy by such restauration. But you retire into your heart and have a good time with the Lord, and you will find that it is a refreshment better than lager beer, or *German pipe.*

O. C. July 9.

DEAR BROTHER SEYMOUR.—I don't remember of your having tried the Oneida Seedling strawberry at W. C., or whether you have had any personal acquaintance with the berry. I have appreciated the fruit of this variety the present season, more than ever before, and having a good word to say in its favor, I would propose to you to set out a few square rods of this variety for the special benefit of lovers of good strawberries. My conclusion, in regard to the Oneida Seedling is, that in quality and delicacy of flavor, it is not a whit behind, if not superior to "Burrs New Pine," and were the berries as large as the Wilson, it would even rival that far famed variety in productiveness. The undersize and tenderness of the berries are faults that must always exclude it from the list of market varieties; but as a table fruit, and for the construction of the much-esteemed Community strawberry-short-cake, it stands unrivaled by any strawberry that I am acquainted with. The fruit begins to ripen a week earlier than the Wilsons, and holds out about as long—plant perfectly hardy.

Yours very truly. H. T.

FROM OUR NOTE-BOOK OF 1851.

There is unsullied, pure, a fount of love,
Proceeding from the throne of God above,
And reaching e'en to earth: the crystal flow
Is fertilizing all these vales below,
Destroying noxious plants of thrifty yield,
Long by tradition cultured in our field.
Oh may this beauteous stream unceasing run,
Till man's redeemed and heaven on earth begun.

Mrs. L. A. Thayer was at the Depot yesterday, and saw Mr. Cart at one of the stores, and had some talk with him. He seemed glad to see her, and enquired some about the Community, but did not stop to talk long. He appeared to be doing business in the village, as Mrs. T. noticed him passing from one store to another, with his carpet-bag.

WILLOW-PLACE.—Our evening meeting Monday, was occupied with criticism of C. A. Burt. He was advised to separate himself from the spirit of the Lee family and to keep up his testimony for the right.

A Lady, the matron of King's Co. Hospital, was here yesterday, with a party from Rome. In looking at our conveniences for washing, she said, that in their institution they had a wringer similar to ours, but did their washing by hand.

We were entertained again last night with letters from our London correspondents. I suppose we must think of them now as in Paris.

1,541 quarts of cherries put up yesterday. We give from four to eight dollars per bushel.

Mr. Leete is with us again and attends to business as usual.

Mr. Whatley, Mary's father, came this morning.

Fifteen barrels of pine-apples have just arrived.

THE O. C. DAILY.

VOL. 4.   THURSDAY, JULY 11, 1867,   NO. 9.

Buffalo, N. Y., July 7, 1867.

MY DEAR SIR.—In sending a copy of my "Outlines" permit me to congratulate your family Community on its great success. You have demonstrated that brethren *may* dwell together in unity. You have proved the great spiritual law, that if the kingdom of heaven be first and honestly sought, all other things follow as a necessary sequence. For myself, although I have professed Fourier, I have never held to his completeness. For twenty odd years, I have held fellowship with professing evangelical christians, and still hold. At Brook-Farm, I was a black sheep in the flock for maintaining that every Fourierite must be born again, or he would never see the kingdom of heaven. * *

Whatever difference we may have as to the interpretation of Bible doctrine, I believe your devotion to the sacred canon is the great bulwark of your freedom. Of all calamities that could happen to you, the loss of this would be the greatest. And it was very encouraging for me to read in your pamphlet that after twenty years of experience, your attachment to the sacred volume was stronger and more abiding than ever. With this lamp to your feet, and this light to your path, you may enter the sacred realm of the human heart, and seek to solve its enigmas. Whether the earthly kingdom can be made to conform to the heavenly, is to my mind simply a question of time. *

Without broaching such a thing as membership, it has occurred to me that I might be one of your eighty *hired servants*, whose happiness is obviously more enviable than anything I know of here. I desire an opportunity of living a quiet and godly life—that's all! But that is a good deal, to me. I have no family except a wife, who has exactly the same desire. We never had children. I was educated a printer, but my sight failing me, I was obliged to take to other pursuits. My wife is a superior cook, dress-maker, milliner, tailoress, or anything at all about a house. I think I could earn my way, at your place. If not, we could be discharged without ceremony. * *

Yours sincerely,   GEO. BAYNE.

A long letter was read last night, from S. Haworth, Lewis Co., Mo., written in quite an earnest spirit. In closing he says: "Please inform me whether you have any *test* by which you judge of a person's fitness to become a member, except that of personal acquaintance. If not, could you give employment to a family while such acquaintance should be made?

"Our family consists of myself, nearly thirty years of age, my wife, twenty-four, and two sweet little girls, one two years, and the other six months old."

We received a letter yesterday, from our late visitor, Mr. Kent, of Lansing Mich, which is quite characteristic. He says, "Oh how I wish I could write and tell you how I feel. If I could only see you and have another talk with you, it would do me so much good; I can talk better than I can write. I feel as though my whole soul was wrapped up in the Community cause &c."

A letter was received yesterday, from Miss Munson, who is still at Dansville, though she expects to leave soon. She expresses her regret at not seeing Mr. Kelley when he was there. She writes:

"I have been very happy since I wrote you last, and I feel that I am very near to Christ. I ask your prayers and criticism. I thought the criticism I received from some of the friends at the Community was rather hard, at the time, but now I can see it was just what I needed."

There was a company of six young people here from Rome Monday, and among them was a young lady and her brother from New-York City. The young man asked his sister if he should buy her a book, to which she gave an affirmative answer. He went into the Office and procured a Hand-Book, and coming back threw it into his sister's lap. She took it up and opening it at " Male Continence," read that article clear through; then turning to her companions, she was overheard to say, " It's too bad—an imposition, to offer such a book to the public! but don't say anything about it, Charley didn't know what was in it." She said that she and her brother would have been very sorry to go back home without coming here, when they were so near.

The strawberry season is now over; and I confess the Providence of God during all our picking.

Number of quarts picked	8,103.
Amount paid for picking	$85.12.
The least number of quarts picked in a day	143.
The greatest number picked in a day	1,273.
The highest price per quart for picking	.05.
The lowest " " " " "	.01.

D. E. S.

A gentleman from Rochester, who is here on business staid over night, also two women and a man who, came, thinking to find Dr. Lawrence here; we have not learned much about them.

The hour for meeting, last night, was mostly occupied with newspaper reports and letter reading. Mr. Noyes was not present.

These cool days we are having, bring us flocks of visitors, mostly of the better class. Fifty dinners were furnished yesterday.

John P. Hutchins leaves to-day, at noon, for Wallingford via. New-York.

THE O. C. DAILY.

VOL. 4.   FRIDAY, JULY 12, 1867,   NO. 10.

A VISIT TO WILLOW-PLACE.—A very quiet little nook indeed. The moment you enter the house, it is palpably a different atmosphere, you miss your bearings. If you want a bustle, it is close by, just step into the great factory, and the scene is entirely changed; so you may take your choice. But our Scion has a great advantage in the power of withdrawing occasionally and so completely, from the din and bustle of life. It must be a pleasant change to spend a week or two there. Cherish your privilege.

Our daughter is truly an amiable lassie, to judge by the welcome you receive. But she must look out not to get into the habit of talking in an under-tone; that sitting-room (tho' exceedingly nice) is so much smaller than our great hall. Beware of the trumpet that gives an " uncertain sound." But the change! both inward and outward—the Boarding house into a Bible Commune. That alone gives a sort of charm to the place, does it not ? another spot on earth converted into a Commune—changes like this, it is, that will transform the wilderness of this world into a garden of roses. God speed the day. These are merely our impressions. You know all about the place—amount of land—size and condition of the house—average number of inmates—thriving garden—snug little pond and bathing-place—abundant water power, and mammoth factory. One thing in particular we noticed, and that was an *open fire-place*, all alive with " lambent flame." Hold on friends, to that precious relic—it tells of merry hours around the family hearth.

We had also the pleasure yesterday, of a visit at W. P. and the exquisite enjoyment of a bath under the shelter of their new bathing-house. Everything in, and around the house seems home-like and Oneida-like. The house is certainly very convenient and commodious for such a family, and the chambers cozy and nice. We almost envied them their window blinds, so admirable for shutting out the hot sun, thus making their rooms cooler and pleasanter.

We staid to meeting, and tho' the room where they meet is not as large as the old parlor at the Mansion-House used to be, yet there was something in the arrangement of the tables, and the happy groups gathered round them busy with their needles, that reminded us of those old times and gatherings. We returned home after meeting in the carriage accompanied by Mr. Noyes and Maria Barron. On stepping into the carriage Mr. N. inquired if the springs were good—he thought their strength would be pretty well tested.

Mr. Hamilton's telegram, yesterday, announcing the fact that a house was engaged in New-York, and would be ready for occupancy next Monday, sent a thrill of delight through all hearts, and a feeling of gratitude to God, that his Providence had opened the way, and that the time had come for the introduction of a Community family, composed of men and women, into the heart of the city. Mr. Noyes said in speaking of the experience of the brethren in New-York, that " They had drove out the cholera from the city, and felt strong, now, to drive out sin, which was really as much a disease as the cholera." In speaking of the strength of the Community, he referred to the passage of scripture, " One shall chase a thousand and two put ten thousand to flight."

Mr. Francis, the former proprietor of our place, was here a day or two since. He has not been to O. C. for ten years, and he expressed his delight and astonishment, at seeing his old place in its new and improved dress.

959 quarts of cherries were put up yesterday, and over sixty bushels arrived last night. The quick ding, ding, of the bell early this morning, is the signal that help is wanted in the preserving-room, and all hands are flocking thither.

A company from New-York who took dinner here yesterday, hinted to H. Sibley who waited on the table, that our napkins would be more acceptable to the company, if we would use a different kind of soap in washing them.

It is quite amusing to witness the operations of our new hay-spreader. It reminds one of a horse kicking with all spite, though to make the figure good, a horse should have several hind feet, instead of two.

Our noon meeting yesterday, was attended by quite an attentive audience from outside. Sixty-five dinners were furnished to visitors.

Over two thirds of the haying is done. Our people got twenty-five loads into the barn yesterday.

We had showers just before night, which continued at intervals all night.

Milford Newhouse arrived yesterday.

THE O. C. DAILY.

VOL. 4.   SATURDAY, JULY 13, 1867.   NO. 11.

We give below, a part of a letter Mrs. Bushnell received yesterday, from H. A. Warne.

Fort Madison, Iowa, July 7, 1867.

" Your last letter was very *plain* but kind, and I certainly felt disposed to accept the justice of the criticisms you conveyed to me. And as I write these lines I feel a softness of heart which leads me to look to Christ for deliverance from all the old life of legality, and to desire the spirit and temper of an obedient child.

" I often think of you and am glad in the thought that you find the Community so satisfying. Perusing the CIRCULAR weekly, in a friendly, listening spirit, I learn more and more to appreciate the cheerful tone of Community life, and the earnest enthusiasm for progress in everything good.

" I sometimes compare my present enjoyment of its pages with my critical, captious feeling a year ago. What a distance my mind has traveled in that time! I scarcely know myself, and I have been told by one, that she could not have believed it possible that I should become so changed. And yet after all, my friend, I am inclined to think it more a work of separation from old things, than a joining with new. Reorganization and establishment seem but begun. Certainly one thing has been accomplished, many trammels to freedom of thought have been cut, and I dare to look things squarely in the face which I fearfully avoided only a year ago. Yes, I have lived a very long and thoughtful year since last July.

" The Noon Talks, by J. H. N., have, like everything of the man's, a peculiar attraction to me.—Then, too, your traveling brothers, the tall lawyer, and his friend G., whose initial is so familiar, are representing O. C. across the water, and writing very frank letters to the folks at home, and to all concerned. I like their letters and wish them a hearty God-speed.

" I am still in Fort Madison you see by this letter. I have my foot in a bog; there is no knowing when I shall get it out. I am busied much as when with you in Bath, (excepting the teaching). I compare my own list of botanical collections every week with that in the CIRCULAR, with interest. Who is that lady ?"

We received yesterday, a long letter of eight pages, foolscap, from a woman named Angeline Budine, of Tioga Co., Penn., about one third of which, is written in bungling rhyme. Her parents joined the Shaker's when she was a little child, and she says that she was brought up from infancy to worship mother Ann, and to believe that if she left the Shaker's she should go to hell. She says:

" Many times I had imagined that I had nearly overcome my propensities, by living a life of celibacy, but to confess the truth, instead of overcoming and subduing my passions, by living a Shaker's life, they grew stronger ; and not finding the work what I expected it to be, I withdrew, and resolved to believe in nothing, unless I could find something to satisfy my soul." [It appears she found a husband, for she continues,] " Mr. Budine and I have been like two lost sheep on a barren mountain, waiting the call of a shepherd."

WILLOW-PLACE.—C. C. H. was cutting out some stuff with the Circular saw, yesterday, when the stick was caught by it and hurled directly to a window on the opposite side of the shop, a distance of more than ten yards, breaking out three panes and the intermediate sash. The stick was four feet long by two inches square. Fortunately no one was crossing its path, or serious consequences might have ensued.

On coming down stairs this morning quite early (of course this is a very indefinite term) we were somewhat surprised to see two young women from O. C. which feeling was not at all diminished when they quietly told us they had " been in the pond." The spirit of " old-grannyism" must have received a severe thrust this time, as the morning was one of the coolest we have had for some time.

Dr. Bishop of Saquoit made us a visit yesterday.— In the course of a conversation with him and Mr. Sellew, another visitor from Penn., the Dr. remarked, that a married lady of his acquaintance, who had been here several times, and had studied our folks somewhat, had said, that in her opinion there could not be found elsewhere so large a number of people on the face of the earth, so free as we were from sensuality and licentiousness.

John Leonard has taken the place in the kitchen vacated by J. P. Hutchins, and is quite pleased to change his employment, as he has almost always worked at his trade.

Mr Jones gave us last night, a history of his life and religious experience, which occupied a half hour or more, of the meeting.

1,861 quarts of cherries were put up yesterday, and forty bushels brought up from the Depot, last night.

H. W. Burnham arrived yesterday.

THE O. C. DAILY.

VOL. 4.　　MONDAY, JULY 15, 1867.　　NO. 12.

BUSINESS MEETING.

J. Conant said that the weekly ironing was a very laborious and costly operation. Considerable money is paid out every week for the ironing, probably five times as much as for the washing. Those connected with that department are anxious that a mangle or some other apparatus should be procured that will do the work rapidly and well. Mr. Burnham proposed to enquire at Troy and Saratoga, when he goes there, to find what apparatus is employed in the collar laundries and hotels. Mr. Burnham, Mr. E. H. Hamilton and H. Allen were appointed committee to investigate and report as soon as possible.

Mr. Hatch reported that those who have charge of the furniture, found it difficult to get a supply, without buying, and furniture is now very costly. He thought a man might be hired to make what bedsteads, stands, bureaus, &c., we may need. A man might be employed half the time at this business. Messrs. Hatch, A. Burt and D. Kelley were appointed committee.

Mr. Woolworth said he had received a letter from Mr. Leander Wilcox, in which he proposes to come and work for us, and board his daughters, who are now in our employ. He is a shoemaker by trade, but is a universal genius, a good mechanic, and would perhaps prefer some other business to shoemaking. It was thought Mr. W. might take that tenant-house near the Trap-shop, which has lately been fitted up, and work in the shop. Referred to the Trap-shop committee.

A good letter from J. W. Towner was received yesterday, from which we have room only to make a few extracts.

"Some time has elapsed since I have written to any one of you, but my eyes are turned toward you continually, and my heart yearns for you with increasing warmth and tenderness. We, meaning myself and family, are enjoying a good degree of health and contentment, and are striving to enter in at the 'straight gate' of unselfishness and love to God and man. Pray for us that we may not be of those who strive and shall not be able.　＊　＊　＊

"We have thought much and have anticipated fondly the possibility of our becoming fit to come into closer union with you, to become, perhaps, members of some one of the families of the O. C.; yet now as ever, we feel willing to wait, and obediently to watch and pray for the full incoming of the kingdom into our hearts and lives, as it shall please our Lord and Saviour.　＊　＊　＊　＊　＊

"But upon one point let me acknowledge just now to feeling deep solicitude. Our oldest boy, Arthur, now sixteen, and rapidly developing into manhood is the source of the anxiety to which I refer. Generally teachable, obedient and well disposed, he is yet easily influenced by his surroundings, and I find myself unable as at present situated, to do by him, and for him, what he needs. In the first place, I am unable to give him proper and adequate employment. He inclines to mechanics, wants to learn to work in iron, to build machinery, &c. I can not get him a place to work and learn any trade of this kind, without an apprenticeship for a term of years, and this would separate him from me to such an extent that I shrink from such a course. Besides, in a city like this, spite of all precaution, he is often exposed to various pernicious and corrupting influences and associations &c. How often for his sake I have wished we were with you—that even he were."　＊　＊　＊

Miss Nun handed in a note, which was read in meeting last night, in which she exposed some of the difficulties and temptations that have troubled her of late, and invited the criticism or advice of the family. She was so sincere in her expose of the workings of evil spirits upon her, that but little was said in addition. Mr. Cragin remarked, in speaking of her case, that the spirit that sought place and distinction directly, was sure to defeat its own end. God has a place for every one of us, and is educating us to fill it. Some one remarked that the way to seek honor, was to be ambitious to serve.

Mr. Hatch, H. R. Perry and some others told of their temptations, and with the rest Mr. Perkins said *he* was tempted greatly to do all he could to serve the cause ; Mr. Woolworth replied that he hoped he would not try to resist that temptation, but persevere. The meeting closed with an old song "The Pilot," by H. W. B.

WILLOW-PLACE.—Charles Cragin returned Thursday, from a trip to New-York and Paterson, which he made for the purpose of visiting silk-manufactories and buying silk. He learned nothing of importance, however, about silk-machinery, as that of the silk-manufacturers at Paterson, was decidedly inferior to our own.—He bought a bale of silk containing one hundred and seven pounds, at $11.87½ per pound.

Mr. Bolles and his little charge came Saturday. The joy of the smallest children at seeing Maud was unbounded, and their manner of expressing it was an interesting sight.

Over 100 acres of our grass have been mown. Thirty-six loads of hay were put into the barn last Saturday, a large day's work.

W. G. Kelly and Victor start on a peddling trip together, this morning.

Mr. Noyes and H. C. Noyes left Saturday noon for New-York.

THE O. C. DAILY.

VOL. 4. TUESDAY, JULY 16, 1867. NO. 13.

Winchester, Va., July 12, 1867.

DEAR FRIEND:—I have sent you $10.00 by Express, which was the most I could command just now. I had hoped to be able to forward to you by this time the entire amount I was owing you, but as I found I could not conveniently do so I have thought best to send a part of it. I regret the more not being able to send it all, since it costs me the same [.50] to send but a part. I hope to have it in my power to forward the remainder before a great while—am extremely sorry to have kept you waiting for it thus long; but I have done the best I could do.

I am still with my relations, where I expect to remain, and am living an easy and comfortable life, much happier than when under the dominion of my tyrannical "lord and master." * * * *

My eldest son did not return to Virginia as I hoped he would when I parted with him last summer at New York, and I cannot avoid feeling anxiety on his account, for I fear with his peculiar notions he will never be able to take proper care of himself. But let him, do as he may or go where he may, I never expect to take another such a "leap in the dark" to look after him as I did when I followed him to New York. I leave him in the hands of God hoping for the best.

I hope you will write to me, as I shall be anxious to hear that you have received what I have sent you.

Yours truly, S. A. SHERRARD.

The young men's meeting Sunday, was unusually interesting. Mr. Burnham, Mr. Olds, Mr. Campbell, Mr. Hatch and other men of that class were present.

The conversation at first turned on the goodness of God, and thankfulness was expressed for conversion from a hard heart to a soft one. Nearly all testified to the goodness of God to them.—"Faith-facts" and miracles were then discussed. Some had found it difficult to believe that the cure of Mrs. Hall was a miracle, but this unbelief was removed by the late reading of "Faith-facts." The work of saving souls was considered a greater miracle than that of saving the body. This greater miracle has been strikingly manifest among the young people, during the last few months.

There was considerable freedom, especially among the young men of Ernest's class. J. F.

A letter was received, a few days since, from a man in Sacramento City, Cal., by the name of Albert A. Harris, making enquiries about the requisite qualifications for admission to our society. He had read the *Tribune's* article about the O. C., which he says was "reprinted in the papers of the distant Pacific shore."

Also a letter from O. T. Judd, of Colorado City. He with another gentleman by the name of Bassett, are desirous of establishing a Community home at the West, and he thinks the world does not present a more inviting field for Communism, than the place where they are located.

GOOD-BYE.
BY J. WILLIAM VAN NAMEE.

Good-bye—my friend—good-bye,
  God speed thee on thy way,
And while thou rid'st the deep,
  May Boreas lightly play
Upon the ocean billows;
  May skies above be fair,
  May God extend his care
To thee, my gentle friend,
  While on the deep blue sea;
And when thou'rt safe, oh, send
  A word of love to me.

The ship that bore you from
  My side, will bear me back,
  Across the ocean's track,
A line from thee, loved friend,
  And when at night, I bend
  In evening prayer,
  I'll surely bear
Thy name to Heaven, and plead
  That God will send
  In safety back to me—
  My childhood friend.

There was some complaint made last night, in meeting, about the indiscriminate shooting of birds, by some of the boys. There is no objection to destroying the robin, as we have proved him to be the big glutton of his race, and the devourer of our fruits, but the other birds should be left unmolested.

Portia had a sister call to see her yesterday, with some of her relatives who live at the Depot. Her sister expects to be married in the spring, and offers Portia a home with her. We understood that Portia gave her some good testimony and to understand that she was not in need of a home.

The chain fence extending from the road east of the Mansion-house, north to the drive-way that crosses the lawn, is finished, with the exception of painting the posts.

Our people employed hired women to gather strawberry leaves yesterday. We noticed the floor in the room where we dry clothes, covered with them.

The Fruit-preservers are at work at pine-apples to-day.

THE O. C. DAILY.

VOL. 4.   WEDNESDAY, JULY 17, 1867.   NO. 14.

WILLOW-PLACE.—Our noon-meetings, yesterday, and to-day have been occupied with reading reports of O. C. noon-meetings and evening conversations. Last evening, as was to be expected, the conversation was about the advance movement on New-York. Mr. Cragin remarked that the hearts of all the Communes were present at the evening gathering of the New-York family.

Last evening Portia gave a very interesting report of her conversation with her sister. When her sister first met her she gave way to tears, and asked Portia if she didn't want to go away. She replied that she did not. Her sister could not believe her, and afterwards when she pressed the question again, Portia told her she did not want her relatives to treat her like a little child any longer, she was old enough to have a mind of her own. She had chosen the Community, had a good home and did not wish to leave it. Portia had formerly esteemed her sister the strongest, and had leaned on her, but now told her she had Christ and the resurrection in her heart, and she was the strongest, and her sister would feel it sometime. She criticised her some for giving way to tears, telling her she ought to weep for herself, hers would be the hardest lot.

After meeting, we were all summoned into Mrs. Miller's room, where "sweet cider" was passed round. We then listened to the eighteen birth-day notes, that were written to Harriet Olds. They were really a rich feast. Some were humorous, all were good and edifying.—A cheerful looking group was the whole family, seated in a semicircle around the open fire of Mrs. Miller's old fashioned fire-place, while Harriet read her letters.

About half the family remained to await Mrs. Skinner's arrival, some reclining on the lounges, others sitting round the red blaze, telling stories, &c. Mrs. S. came about 12 o'clock, and was heartily welcomed by the family.

Perhaps the readers of the DAILY will say, " We have not heard from the children's house for some time."—We say that's so—but we intend you shall hear from us oftener. First, we can say in truth that we are all well, thankful and happy; not one complaint of sickness through the fruit season thus far, and all are ambitious to help wherever they can.—Willie, Georgie and Harry are enthusiastic to supply the family with shavings. Every morning the question is, " Can we get some shavings?" " O yes you may." So off they go harnessed to their little wagon forgetting everything about them but their present calling, even their school which they appreciate much. Now you will see them all (over twenty-five

in number) engaged in shelling peas, with a grand finale of throwing pods. Maud has just returned from a visit to Wallingford, much to the gratification of the small fry, as is manifest by their constant attendance upon her every want, and a good deal she does not want.   L.

Edwin Spaulding writes to his uncle S. W. N. as follows :

" I thank you for your plainness in pointing out the reason for my leaving O. C., and I believe that the reason which you give was the true one at least in part, but believe me, I did not see it in that light at the time. I now see that it was a lack of faith and confidence in the Community, which impelled me to act as I did.

" As to my demanding more money from the O. C. for my services : there is no act in my whole life that has caused me so much pain and regret as that, and it is with shame and sorrow that I acknowledge that I was actuated by a most selfish and bad spirit, but when I got to Lowville, my old employers told me that I might have had $2.00 per day if I had not made a fool of myself in going to O. C. and leaving them, and advised me to prosecute for my due &c. Yet this was no excuse for my doing as I did, and I am determined as soon as God gives me the means, to more than repay the amount which I extorted from the Community."

We had five letters from outsiders last night the reading of which, together with newspaper reports occupied a large part of the meeting. Before the close however, the "Canadian Trapper," who returned from New-York yesterday, was called on to report.—His talk about the new locality of the N. Y. B. and a description of the house, furniture, fixtures, &c., &c., was listened to with deep interest. Mr. N. related his meeting with Carr and his conversation with him.—Mr. Woolworth said that Carr seemed to be ubiquitous crossing our track at every point.

In addition to the botanical specimens sent by C. S. J. and published in the 6th No of the DAILY, we give the following:

1st. Elder, from Rotten Row, 2d. Yew, from Hyde Park, 3d. Blackthorn, from Kensington Palace, where Queen Victoria was born, 4th. Elm, from Marlborough House, where the Prince of Wales lives, 5th. Hawthorne, from the Tower of London, 6th. Hepatica, also from the Tower, picked on the spot where Anne Boleyn was executed, 7th. Clover, from Westminister Abbey, picked in the old Cloister where the monks used to recreate.

244 cans of peas have been put up.

THE O. C. DAILY.

VOL. 4.   THURSDAY, JULY 18, 1867.   NO. 15.

Mr. Noyes's talk, the evening he spent at New-York, was read last night. It sent a thrill of joy through every loyal heart and a feeling of gratitude to God that we have lived to see the day

"That kings and prophets waited for,
But died without the sight."

There was a very free spirit of testimony in the meeting. Mr. Woolworth remarked: "I confess my union with the Primitive church. I believe there is where our power lies—our strength and our victories. A superficial observer that sees only the external world, will see only evil, perhaps—selfishness, oppression, sin and death, suffered to reign and hold high carnival in this sphere; but to one who sees the great principality in the heavens, and that the kingdom of God was established eighteen hundred years ago, and has been living and reigning since that time, mere externals will seem very insignificant—our trials and sufferings will all be swept away when that church is recognized and let into this world by faith. I believe they are near us and near the world, and are pressing their way into this world, and that sin and selfishness will flee before them.

Mr. Underwood:—I believe there is the secret of our success as a Community, the secret of our power and unity, as manifested day by day. Visitors, with whom I talk about that church, seem to be struck with our attitude in relation to it. I press that point very often, for I feel in my heart that it is a very vital one to us. I confess unfaltering love and loyalty to Mr. Noyes and the Primitive church.

Mr. W.:—I confess that our citizenship is in heaven, with the Primitive church, our conversation is there with them. If we can dwell in that sphere, as I know we can, we shall rise above the lower magnetism, into the higher magnetism of Christ and good spirits.

Last evening a Mr. Nevoni, a young man from Palmyra, entertained us in the Hall with playing on the Piano and Violin. He has taught music for seven years as a profession, and becoming acquainted with Charles Van, was induced to call. He played "The last rose of Summer" with variations, "Humming Bird Waltz" of his own composing, and a piece giving imitations of Fife and Drum, Guitar, Band, Banjo, &c. on the Piano. He also played simultaneously, Yankee Doodle with his left, and Fishers Hornpipe with his right hand. This last was very cleverly done, and elicitated much applause from the family.

On the Violin, he performed "Yankee Doodle," with many variations, and gave an imitation of the Organ. Altogether it was quite an enjoyable affair. Mr. Nevoni staid over night with us, and left this morning.

F. W. S.

Yesterday while sitting sewing with our little four-year-old Fanny by my side, she suddenly drew a little closer to me and with bright eyes and animated countenance, (without a word having been said on the subject) said, "The king is a man, and he kills the little baby boys, but he didn't kill little baby Moses, for the good woman hid him away in the bushes where the naughty king couldn't find him."—The simple childish manner of telling her story, touched and interested me, and from the earnest manner in which she related it, I could but note the impression it had made upon her infant heart. I believe that the good seed thus sown in these tender minds will in due time spring up, and that we are not laboring in vain.

E.

It seems to me that the difference between the righteous and the wicked, is, that the righteous are thankful to God for all the good things they have, and delight to praise him for every little comfort they enjoy, while the wicked do not appreciate God's gifts, but greedily appropriate them, and then go their own way in pursuit of more, all unmindful of the giver.—I thank God that I am learning to love him. I thank him for the ten thousand good things he gives me. Most of all I thank, and praise him for his goodness, in opening my spiritual preceptions so that I can see and feel him from whom all good comes. I love him with an unspeakable love, and I thank him for every token of his love for me.

T.

100 bushels of peas are on hand this morning, all of which are to be put through the shelling, boiling, and canning process to-day. Two machines are running, the largest of which, has a wringer, or rubber roller attached to the under side of the wooden roller to carry off the moisture. Mr. Burt will be interested to know that it works first-rate.

Two ladies were here yesterday, from Gerrit Smith's; one was an elderly woman and very fleshy, and a relative of Mr. S.'s. They attended the noon-meeting awhile, then went to their lunch. When they left, it took two or three hands to assist in getting the fleshy woman into her carriage, she was so afraid of falling. She bought $60.00 worth of preserved fruit.

Mrs. Skinner came over to O. C. yesterday forenoon, and staid to dinner and the noon meeting, and returned to W. P. in the afternoon. It seemed good to see her at Oneida once again. We understand that she will be over every day to attend our meetings at noon.

About 100 quarts of raspberries were sent to Saratoga yesterday, for which we get twenty-five cents per quart. We have been selling for twenty cents.

The water is drawn off from the mill-pond, and the carpenters are making a new water-wheel and also repairing the flume.

THE O. C. DAILY.

VOL. 4.   FRIDAY, JULY 19, 1867.   NO. 16.

DEAR FATHER NOYES:—I feel like relating to you some of my late experience. Previous to the noon meetings, I felt a good deal of pressure in and around me from hadean influences. I had a consciousness that we were nearing the final conflict with the great principality of death. When these meetings were proposed, I believed they were inspired of God as a direct counter movement to concentrate the attention and life of the Community sufficiently to meet the exigencies of the case. Immediately my attention was turned from myself in prayer for the success of the cause, and the more I saw the interest you manifested and the importance you attached to them, the more I became enlisted. My faith has been steadily growing and my bodily health improving.

I am now prepared to take up the testimony which I so heartily gave when I was first healed, and to reiterate in the face of any unbelief in the Community, and all unbelief outside of it, that *I am well*; that Christ has saved me from all sin and disease. Henceforth my testimony shall be, "I live yet not I but Christ liveth in me." &c.   H. A. HALL.
P. S.—I have for some weeks been counted in with the rest of the women in the distribution of labor, and have had the unspeakable pleasure of learning from the "board," that I have given satisfaction. H. A. H.

At our noon meeting yesterday, after the reading of the article in the Berean, entitled "Our relations to the Primitive Church," a letter that Mrs. Skinner had received from Augusta was read, which gave an account of the examination and final success of our New Haven students. A round of applause followed.

The recent Home-Talk "Grace better than Law," was re-read last night, and also Augusta's letter, which many of the family had not heard. This drew out a good deal of testimony of personal experience, on the subject of the Providence of God and his care over us as a body, and as individuals, and some narrow escapes from being harmed by accidents, were mentioned. The case of our young men at New Haven, was spoken of, and their success attributed to the good Providence of God, that had attended them through their whole course of study, and given them favor both with professors and teachers.

Mr. H. Conn, of the firm of H. Conn & Co., Boston, spent two or three hours here yesterday. H. C. & Co. are tanners and leather dealers, and furnish us with most of our bag-leather. They make very nice leather, and the popularity of our leather bags is, no doubt, due in part to the superiority of the stock we get from this Boston house. Mr. C. praised our Bag-shop as being pleasant and attractive; he bought five bags. We gave him the "Hand-Book," and a photograph of the buildings and grounds; he had seen the pictures somewhere and admired them. He remarked, while looking through the fruit-department, that he saw there was much that he could learn here in respect to economy; that every body seemed to be busy. Mr. C. said as he drove away, that his wife wanted to come here, and he thought she would next time.   H.

Fidelia gave us some interesting facts last evening, relative to the way the girls at the Bag-shop take criticism. She said she had been under the necessity of criticising some of them at different times in a very sincere way, and they had invariably taken it well, and thanked her afterwards for it, and seemed ambitious to overcome the faults for which she criticised them. This seems hopeful in view of the extension of criticism among our hired help. Perhaps as we pass out from under this ordinance, our mantle of sincerity may fall upon the world around us. If judgment is first to begin at the house of God, it certainly will not stop there.

[Ed. CIR.—Please don't copy the above into your columns.]

While Victor and I were at Albion, Wednesday morning, there was quite an excitement created in the village, by the road passing over the sewer suddenly falling in, and swallowing up a span of horses driven by a negro man. There sat the driver in his carriage in utter amazement, the horses having suddenly gone down some eight or ten feet into the sewer, breaking the pole of the carriage as they disappeared. The canal had broken a leak through the culvert into the sewer the day before, and had loosened the stones covering the sewer, so that the weight of a team broke through. The hole where the horses went down, had the appearance of a large well. The horses were extricated after much labor, without serious injury. K.

WILLOW-PLACE.—Yesterday noon the CIRCULAR was read, and last evening the talk of Mr. Noyes in New-York, which called forth enthusiastic applause. At the close of the meeting, G. W. H., who arrived in the afternoon, gave us a description of the N. Y. house.—Augusta's letter to Mrs. Skinner, about the success of the students, was read this noon, and caused hearty rejoicings.

---

945 cans of peas were put up yesterday. A part of the peas that we can, are picked in the afternoon, brought here toward night, and are spread out to prevent them from heating—the remainder are picked in the morning, and brought about eleven o'clock. It is cool weather, which is quite favorable to the peas being put up in a good, fresh state.—Mrs Van is making jelly to-day, of the currants that have been sent from Wallingford.

ERRATUM.—On the last page of yesterday's DAILY, about the middle of the page, for $60.00 read $6.55.

THE O. C. DAILY.

VOL. 4. SATURDAY, JULY 20, 1867. NO. 17.

In meeting, last evening, A. L. Burt said: "In going over to Willow-Place to-day, Mr. Hubbard drove out with his team just as I was passing his place, and asked me to ride. I got in and he began talking about the CIRCULAR. He expressed a good deal of interest in G. W. N.'s letters from Europe, particularly the last one.

"I then mentioned to him about George and Theodore, that they had graduated, and he said he was glad of it. He then remarked that they had a grand chance when they were young, and were both naturally smart young men. "The fact is," said he, "your young folks, every one of them, have better advantages for getting a good education, than any rich man in the country about here can give his children, because you bring an influence to bear on them."

Mr. Cragin:—It must be only about three years since George and Theodore were taken from our business and sent to New Haven. I think our various businesses are the very best primary schools that our young people can have, as a preparation for a College course, or a liberal education. [Approved.] And then, in addition to that, all our young men and women have a purpose in life, after they have educated themselves so far as the College and schools can confer education upon them. The idea of devoting one's entire faculties and powers to the service of Christ, and the diffusion of the knowledge of God in the world, has a wonderful effect upon the character and mind. In the world, a great many young men are sent to College who have no purpose as to what business or profession they will devote themselves, until after they have obtained their education.

Mr. Woolworth:—I thought this one great cause of the success of our young men there in New Haven: they had a definite purpose in life, and they directed all the energies they had to the fulfillment of that purpose. It was not a mere individual purpose with them, but they were seeking education with a view to future usefulness in the service of Christ and God's Kingdom.

Some time in June a man by the name of Henry K. White Esq. of Whately, Franklin Co. Mass., wrote a letter to the O. C. stating that he had a friend, a lady, at his house, with her two little children, whose husband had left her, and who was desirous of becoming acquainted with us, and joining our society. He represents the woman as young, good looking, respectable and interesting, and inquires what is necessary to be done that she and her children, may become members of our society. Mr. Woolworth replied that we did not receive members on a slight acquaintance, and the first step toward forming such acquaintance

would be to study our writings, and he referred her to Wallingford for papers, pamphlets, &c. The next we hear is from the woman herself, Mrs. Mary A. Bryan, July 5th, stating that she had received the Hand-Book and CIRCULAR, had carefully perused them, and was more anxious than ever to become a member. Mr. White writes in the same letter, saying that Mr. Bryan would take one of the children from her, if he knew of his wife's intentions, and says "If you will accept Mrs. B., the sooner she leaves here the better it will be;" and for testimonials to her good character he referred us to Drs., deacons, and select men of the town of Whately, where she had always lived.—Mr. Woolworth wrote the second time that it was impossible for us to receive the lady, but gave her permission to come, and make a short visit. Judge then of our suprise on receiving last Tuesday, the following letter:

Whately, Mass. July 15.

MR. WOOLWORTH:—*Sir.*—Yours of the 8th was duly received, and in reply I would say that Mrs. Bryan will be with you, (if nothing prevents) Thursday P. M. I hope you will receive her with that sympathy she needs. She feels that your principles can do much for her and her children. Had *that* principle of self-control been understood and carried out, much of her misery might have been avoided. She would like to give herself and her children into your hands to be guided in the right way. She longs to reach the perfect state.

There is one thing she feels anxious about. She wishes you to know the fact before she reaches you, for she abhors deception. She expects soon to be a mother again, and she would go to you at this time, so that this one might particularly be the child of the Community. [!] The people of Whateley have known Mrs. Bryan all her life, and you can satisfy yourself in regard to her character, by applying to the persons mentioned in her letter or any one else in town. Her husband is a rascal, and I hope he will never find her. We commit her and hers to the care of the Community. Watch over and direct them in the right way.

Yours sincerely, H. K. WHITE.

Mr. Woolworth immediately dispatched a telegram to Mr. White, telling him that *Mrs. Bryan positively must not come here.* The dispatch seems to have been effectual in stopping proceedings, as no such woman has yet made her appearance. It seems evident that there was a concerted plan to pack her and her children off upon us—a very cool proceeding, to say the least. The telegram cost us $2.85.

Mr. Shelley came here in the afternoon, yesterday, and staid over night. He is on his way to Indiana.—Mr. Schuyler also, the sub-editor of the *World* is with us. We understand that he expects to take board and stay somewhere in the vicinity several days. He made the remark soon after he came, that "he didn't see but we were pretty much like other folks."

Our hearts were made glad yesterday, by the receipt of letters from our brothers at Paris. It seemed a long time since their last, ten days ago.

THE O. C. DAILY.

VOL. 4.   MONDAY, JULY 22, 1867.   NO. 18.

BUSINESS MEETING.

Croquet playing was spoken of as quite a disturbance when carried on at improper hours. Those who room near the grounds are disturbed both early and late. But generally it is a very pleasant, musical sound, and persons should not permit themselves to become so nervous as to be annoyed by it. Mr. Hatch thought india-rubber might be put on the ends of the mallets to deaden the sound.

Mr. Campbell said some one was needed in John Leonard's place to do the wood-work and pattern-making in the Trap-shop. It is not best to have John go back there, for he needs the change. Charles Burt would do very well if he was not wanted to pack traps. Messrs. Woolworth, G. W. Hamilton, Inslee, Campbell and J. Sears were appointed committee.

Mr. Hall, of whom we buy brick, is about to burn one kiln, and wants us to take them away as soon as they are burned. If we build, another year, the brick had better be drawn now, and put under cover. If not, they had better be sold, as we may engage brick of him another year. Mr. Hall makes about 14,000 per day. We have bought 125,000 at $6.25 per thousand. Messrs. Kinsley, Hawley and Clark are committee.

Mr. Woolworth remarked that dealers are writing to us every day, saying they shall want a good many traps. "Everything looks like a storm at W. P. before long. I suppose they have the ropes well manned there."

G. W. Hamilton:—I have noticed since coming back that the trap-men have their attention taken up a good deal with ditching, &c. I think they ought to be relieved from that business and devote themselves entirely to trap-making. Approved.

F. Marks has been chairman of the Business Board for some time, and to-day wished to be relieved from that duty. Mr. Kinsley moved that he be relieved till next Sunday. Approved.

Grace Mills has been under some trial and temptation of late, and yesterday, in the young women's meeting, which was held in the Hall, she was criticised quite sincerely, and advised to take some practical steps to clear herself from the Olmsteads. The Olmstead boys have taken a good deal of pains of late, to speak to her when they have met her, calling her "Gracey" in quite a familiar way, which has annoyed her much. When the meeting was over, and as Grace was coming down into the lower hall, who should she see directly before her, but Sarah Olmstead. She went immediately to her, and told her she wanted to see her, and Sarah replied "I want to see you Grace," and so they went out together. Sarah told Grace that she wanted to show her a letter she had just received from Ellen. Grace replied that she did not want to see the letter, but she wanted to tell her that she, (Grace) did a mean thing in leaving the Community as she did, and she came back to confess and repent of it. Grace then had freedom to tell Sarah what she thought of her, and in S.'s attempts to justify herself she told two or three downright lies, which emboldened Grace to tell her all she wanted to. She told her that she did not want her to come here—didn't want her or her brothers to speak to her. Sarah made an attempt to draw Grace into having another interview—wanted she should meet her somewhere, that she could give her back her letters; but Grace refused and told her to burn them, she should not meet her. We learned that the Olmstead boys were seen in the afternoon over on our grounds at Spring-Grove, shooting, and on their return they passed through our hall as familiarly as though they were at home, stopping at our water-tank to drink.

———◆———

Mr. Cragin introduced the subject of "reflection and prayer," last night, as worthy of our consideration and attention. He thought that neither the young or the old, could live near to God, without having seasons of withdrawing from the outward world, and listening to the voice of God in their own hearts, and praying to him. Much testimony of personal experience, and the good effects of such seasons followed.—The devil feels particularly interested to distract and divert the attention at such times, and it is right on this point that we need to "contend earnestly," for the faith that believes that God will assuredly "bring into captivity *every thought* to the obedience of Christ." Glorious deliverance!

———◆———

Yesterday, as Mr. Kellogg was standing on some high steps at the barn, reaching up and attempting to knock down a rake that was on the hay-loft above him, the steps suddenly tipped over, throwing Mr. K. with considerable force, across the lower stair. He hurt his side, which is pretty sore and lame to-day, but he thinks he shall get over it in a few days.

———◆———

We had two bees yesterday, for picking raspberries, one before breakfast and the other after supper, in which 277 quarts of berries were picked.

———◆———

97¼ dozen traps ordered for the week ending July 20th.

THE O. C. DAILY.

VOL. 4.　TUESDAY, JULY 23, 1867.　NO. 19.

Mr. Shelley, of Indiana, left here yesterday, after a visit of three days, for his home in the West. He called at O. C. a year ago last April, to spend an hour or two, but was so much interested in what he saw and heard, that his call was prolonged to three days. For a year past he has resided in Newark, N. J., manufacturing a patent whip-socket—a very nice thing. He owns one half of it, provided the patentee is not litigated out of his invention by another claimant to the same thing.—Mr. S. met a committee yesterday, of sixteen men and occupied nearly two hours in giving us a sketch of his life, religious experience, &c. He was born in 1834, and when about sixteen years of age was converted or got religion, as he called it, in a protracted meeting; but did not join the church, not seeing any particular use in that. The pentecostal spirit possessed him for a while, but in trying to live it out, practically, he found himself quite alone. Professors of religion were glad to have him work for them on that principle—it pleased them well to have little jobs of blacksmithing done for them without pay. Mr. S., however, soon got tired of working for that kind of religion that brought him no bread and butter.

But just as he discovered, to his great disappointment, that the religion of the churches was not the genuine article of the apostolic stamp, he formed the acquaintance of a Dutch shoemaker who had formerly lived in Penn., and had been a subscriber to Mr. Noyes's publications. The Dutchman reported that Mr. Skinner, of the Putney Corporation once called upon him and remained his guest over night. This German friend loaned Mr. S. papers and books, the contents of which were eagerly devoured. From that time to the present, he has been a firm believer in Mr. Noyes and the Community, as door-keepers to the Bible and the apostolic church. His faith has carried him through a great many trials safely, insanity among the rest.

He hopes ere long, to become a member of some Commune. He said to the writer on leaving, "Do you think I shall make a good soldier?"　　　c.

A Miss Williams, from Philadelphia, came here yesterday and staid over night. She has a sister living not far from Canandaigua, and she is on her way to visit her. Miss W. is thirty-six years old, and dependent on her own efforts for support. She has kept a shop in Philadelphia, and hired girls to assist her in dressmaking—but her health failed, and she wearied of so much care. The last year she has spent with her friends, but says as her health has improved, she must again seek employment. She would have liked to work for us in the Bag-shop for a time, if the work had not been too hard. She had from time to time

heard of the O. C., but had never read any of our writings, and was very glad of the opportunity to call here. She said she had always been religiously inclined, though she had never made a profession, and the necessity there was that she should work incessantly, had precluded her from giving the subject of religion any very serious thought.

The following letter was directed to "President Bible Communists."

New Orleans, July 16.

FATHER NOYES, BIBLE COMMUNISTS, ONEIDA NEW YORK.—*Sir*:—Be kind enough to inform me by what means persons obtain permission to enter your Community. Also the rules in regard to the admission of women. Be specific in regard to regulations in regard to work, how many hours each day, also how the labor is distributed among men and women. I am very much interested. Please direct Col. Andrew Daly, New Orleans Post Office.

A lot of raspberries, 475 quarts, reached us yesterday, from Palmyra in a damaged state. About thirty quarts were thrown away and the remainder made into wine. Mr. Bradley engaged the Express Co. to send them through the same day they were shipped, but they remained in Syracuse over Sunday. When they arrived at the Depot Mr. B. refused to take them off the hands of the Express Co., but they engaged to pay all the damage, if we would take them home and do the best we could with them. Mr. Thacker has offered to pay five cents per quart for what he used.

The carpenters are making some changes of machinery at the shop to facilitate the box business.—They have also put in a new water-wheel, which gives equal or greater power than the old one. It draws 96 inches of water, while the old one drew 144 inches.

We have 70 bushels of peas on hand this morning, and expect more at 11 o'clock. There is not one case of "busting up" among those that were experimented with, nearly two weeks ago.

Mr. E. H. Hamilton arrived yesterday afternoon. His coming was an agreeable suprise to the family.

---

450 quarts of raspberries were gathered from our bushes yesterday.

A house owned by Mr. Dole, of Pine-Bush, was destroyed by fire, last night.

THE O. C. DAILY.

VOL. 4. WEDNESDAY, JULY 24, 1867. NO. 20.

In meeting last night, Mr. Underwood said :

" We had a good many visitors to-day, including a party of native Greeks, consisting of Mrs. Dr. King and her three daughters. She was born in Smyrna. Her daughters are married and reside in this country. They all talk Greek fluently as well as French, and when they did not wish to have us understand their remarks, they would run into Greek and jabber like monkeys, much to their own apparent edification ; but it was not particularly interesting to me.

" We talk about the inquisitiveness of the Yankee, but I think the native Greek is more than a match for him. These people were very inquisitive, and sharp and shrewd in their observations. They seemed to lead right to the center every time they asked a question.

" One thing about them that I liked very much was, that they appeared to be fully devoted to Christ. They said if we followed Christ we could not go wrong. I rarely meet with visitors who find so many points of sympathy with us as these did. They were all religious people, and one was a member of the Congregational church.

" Dr. King was not with them. He is some twenty years older than his wife, and is now about seventy years old. He is a very fine scholar, speaks seven languages fluently, and is perfectly at home in the Arabic tongue. Mr. Reynolds has heard him preach.

" Mrs. LaSalle, one of the daughters, had a very active mind, and appeared to be well read. She saw at once that the center of our faith was the Second Coming of Christ, though she herself believed that the Second Coming was yet future. They were much pleased with our confessions of Christ, and thought that was the real substance of all true religion. They inquired into our system of criticism.

" Though the daughters left Athens when children, one only nine years old, they have a very vivid recollection of Greece. They saw our passion-flower in the green-house, and said it grew wild in Greece, and was so prolific that they could hardly kill it out of their gardens. The mother is going back to Greece this Fall, and one of the daughters accompanies her to visit her native place.

Mr. Brewster writes from Red Bank, N. J., July 20.

" After long and mature deliberation and to the best of my ability, (counting the costs and responsibilities of so sacred a union), I offer myself and all of my interests and services, to Christ and the Oneida Community and desire to become a member of your family, if I may be thought to be worthy of so sacred a relation. ' For I had rather be a *door-keeper* in the house of God, than to *dwell* in the tents of wickedness.'

" My fellowship with you rests on a union of ' faith and purpose,' which binds me to you with a strong cord ; I am moved by the same inspiration, and feel the throbbings of new friendships based on faith in Christ, and heirship to the kingdom. I seem to be dying daily to old friendships and institutions, and feel that ' whosoever shall do the will of God the same is my brother, and my sister, and my mother.' "

Mr. Hamilton related, last night, some conversation he had on the cars with Mr. Root, who seems to be a staunch friend of the O. C. He told Mr. H. he was talking with two clergyman not long since about the Community, one of whom seemed to hold our principles in abomination. Mr. R. defended us with a good deal of warmth, said we were an upright people, and our word was as good as a bond or deed, and would be taken as sufficient security wherever we were known.—When will these overseers of the morals of the people and defenders of principles, learn to take the Bible as their standard, and judge the tree by its fruits ?

MORE BOTANICAL SPECIMENS FROM C. S. J.—1st. Fir, from Greenwich Observatory, the center of the longitude of the world ; 2nd. Arancana, from Sydenham Palace ; 3d. Plain-leaf, from the Church-yard of St. Giles Cripplegate, where Milton was buried and Cromwell was married ; 4th. Horse Chestnut, from the celebrated Chestnut Avenue, in Bushy Park, near Hampton Court Palace ; 5th. Fuschia, from Kew.

There were six houses burned at Pine Bush instead of one, as reported yesterday, and also a barn. We understand that they all belonged to Mr. Dole, who is a bachelor and seems to be doling out a life of " single wretchedness," judging from his dilapidated looks, and care-worn countenance.

Mr. Bartholomew of Westfield N. Y. came yesterday ; he will stay a day or two.—10 o'clock—Theodore and George E. with H. C. Noyes, have just arrived.

THE O. C. DAILY.

VOL. 4.   THURSDAY, JULY 25, 1867.   NO. 21.

Probate Office, Ottawa Co. Mich., Grand Hann, July 16.

To whom of the O. C. these presents shall come :—Having occasion recently to visit your County, and while waiting for a certain train of cars, I called for a few moments at your Community, and was so delighted with the beauty, order and neatness, as well as the thrift that I witnessed on every hand, that I have ever since felt an earnest desire to know more of an association enjoying such apparent quietude, happiness and prosperity, a knowledge of which I had not time to obtain when calling, as above stated.

I am informed you have pamphlets and other publications that will afford all the information I desire respecting your Community as regards the *principles* that underlie and have been adopted as the foundation of your Association. I am also informed you have a paper entitled the CIRCULAR published in Connecticut. If for the public, I desire to become a subscriber and enclose herewith $1.00, which may I trouble you to forward to the office of that publication, requesting the paper sent so long as the subscription price is canceled thereby.   *   *

Very Respectfully,   A. W. TAYLOR.
Register and Judge of the Probate Court of Ottawa County for the past nine years.

West Boylston, July 22, 1857.

DEAR COMMUNITY :—Perhaps I ought to commence my letter with an apology for my assumption in writing you my first letter. You must have thought me assuming, to decide for myself from so slight evidence as a newspaper article, that you were a prosperous and happy Community of Christian perfectionists, with whom it was so very desirable to unite. And also for so far presuming upon my own worthiness, as boldly to ask a correspondence with a view to membership. But I trust you will pardon me when the case is fully set before you.   *   *   *

As to the merits of your Community, after having gleaned what knowledge I could from your "Hand-Book" and the CIRCULAR, and giving much careful thought to the subject, I find my first impressions unchanged; and have been able to form decided opinions. The inspiration of facts and circumstances previously known to me, and some knowledge of human nature, had enabled me to form a pretty correct estimate of the merits of your Community, from that newspaper article.   *   *   *

Permit me to say a word on the subject of sexual relation, as I believe it to be of the first importance ; and that right views upon it, are absolutely essential to the success of Communism. I was satisfied before reading your publications, that your course in this relationship, must be different from any of the many corrupt and corrupting systems known to prevail in the world. For there is not one, I believe, among them all, which would not be the death of any Community (save the little family) in less than twenty years. Even the sacred institution of marriage as it is commonly held, though the best form of this relation in the world, except your own, is, from its very nature, exclusive and selfish, and as generally practiced, debasing to both body and soul. And I believe a Community formed of married couples, would thereby contain antagonistic elements, which would in the nature of things prove its destruction sooner or later. I conclude your system of sexual intercourse is right, and with "continence" as a conservative principle, (it is also the only true principle of righteousness and purity) faithfully adhered to, and your hearts all bound together in true christian faith, love and unity, you must succeed. But without all these you could not have succeeded until now.   *   *

I remain yours truly for Communism and true Christian fellowship.   D. R. LAMSON.

———————

The time was when hay-making was the grand event of the season with the farmers, occupying nearly or quite two months, working early and late. But how changed now. The farmer may lie abed till the dew is off the grass, then harness up a span of horses, seat himself on a funny sort of a two-wheeled carriage, drive into the meadow of blooming grass and flowers, and enjoy a four hours drive, not on a dusty road, but in elysian fields where if he be a godly man and a lover of truth, he may enjoy himself in prayer and praise to his heart's content. Behind him as he drives around the field, he leaves the grass all cut and handsomely spread. He then returns to his house, eats his dinner with an appetite a king might envy. After dinner he may take a nap, if he chooses, and then call for his favorite span of dapple grays, and seat himself on another two-wheeled machine, still more funny than the mower, called the spreader, and off he drives for an afternoon pleasure trip, looking as though he had a dozen little animals in his rear kicking up their heels furiously. Then for a change, he attaches his team to a raking carriage, and again plunges into the cured hay, the sweet savor of which might easily cheat one into the belief that he was sailing on an ocean of perfumery.

But the practical little DAILY did not ask me for a millennial sermon, but an item of business. So here it is—Commenced haying about the 20th of June—finished July 19th—Carted into barn 230 loads of well cured hay. Mr. Conant proved himself a competent commander of the forces under him. The hired men worked with a will and enjoyed the sport mightily.—C.

———————

Mr. Tobit called here yesterday, staid over night, and leaves to-day.

Yesterday was the hottest day of the season, the mercury rising in the shade to 93 deg.

THE O. C. DAILY.

VOL. 4.   FRIDAY, JULY 26, 1867.   NO. 22.

EVENING MEETING.

After the reading of Mr Noyes's discourse about belief in the miracle wrought in the cure of Mrs. H. A. Hall, the conversation turned upon the subject, and the testimony was unanimous that the raising of Mrs. Hall was a real miracle, effected by the same agency that performed Christ's miracles. Mr. Bolles and others gave their reasons for belief in the fact. One of the best proofs is that Mr. Noyes fully believed it; and he is not a man to be easily deceived. Then there are some twenty other unimpeachable witnesses besides; the presence of Mrs. Hall as a well woman, twenty years after the time when the doctors said she was incurably diseased—the fact that Mr. Hall recognized the miracle, and that it led to his conversion, should be taken as very strong evidence. In fact, there is no chance for doubt, and all testified that they did not doubt it. At the same time several said they had not fully realized its importance heretofore, and were very thankful for the issue Mr. Noyes had made. Mr. Hamilton made the following remarks:

" The more I think of it, the more glad I am of the issue Mr. Noyes sets before us in this discourse about the case of Harriet Hall. It is the issue of unfeigned faith. This Community stands upon unfeigned faith in the will of God working through Mr. Noyes and other members of the Community. Mr. Noyes is not the man to bear false witness or to be deceived. I hope that an earnest spirit of self-examination, on this point of belief, will go all through the Community. The spirit that questions the genuineness of this miracle is a sneaking spirit of darkness that ought to have no place here or anywhere.

" I confess that I had unfeigned faith in Mr. Noyes when I joined this Community; and I believed that the power of God working through him, raised Harriet Hall. We can never be vital members of this Community unless our hearts are filled with this unfeigned faith in the power of God. God can give us this faith. I say let us value and confess what we have had and look for more."

North Elba, N. Y. July 20, 1867.

C. W. UNDERWOOD.—DEAR SIR:—Feeling a strong desire to communicate with the Community through you, I improve the earliest opportunity since my arrival home yesterday, to write a few words, although I do not expect to be able to say anything that will be edifying to you; but I long to express my overwhelming admiration for the mode of life which you appear to be living, an admiration which I involuntary experienced and which I could not resist. When I first went there it was out of mere curiosity, but I found everything so different from what I expected

and so near like my ideal of true happiness, that I confess I cannot resist the desire and earnest wish, that I too belonged to the O. C.   *   *   *

I have no doubt but the first experience of a life of Communism, in ignoring and wholly departing from the old mode and system of social life, would perhaps be attended with some trials and afflictions; but on the whole greatly preferable to the life that a great majority of mankind are now living, both in a social and material point of view. With an earnest desire for the success of your enterprize, I remain truly a friend to human progress. HIRAM A. LUSK.

[As the report from W. P. came too late for publication yesterday, we give a portion of it to-day.]

A slight change in the hours for bathing was made. They are as follows: Women, 9 to 11 A. M. and from 1 to 4 P. M. Men, 11 to 12 A. M.—4-30 to 6-30 P. M. Neighboring women, 4 to 4-30—6-30 to 7-30. Neighboring men, 12 to 1—8 to 9. It is desirable that the outside women be permitted the exclusive use of the pond from 6-30 to 7-30 as it is the only hour they can have. The pond promises well to become a popular if not a fashionable watering place. The prejudice, if there has been any, among the women of the neighborhood, is gradually wearing off, and every day introduces a number of new comers to the luxury of the bath. A company of them came at their appointed hour, this evening, and seeing a number of our men pitching quoits in the orchard, inquired of Harriet A. if it would be proper for them to go to the bathing-place. She said she thought it would be; so they went right along without minding them. Thirty-four women from O. C. including some little girls, came over to-day. It is estimated that no less than one hundred different persons received the benefit of the pond to-day, July 24.

In our meeting Mr. Underwood gave us a very interesting account of the Grecian visitors. Their pointed questions, pertinent remarks and their unbounded frankness were astonishing.

We have a Michigan rose, (single,) which runs over and covers the roof, at the north end of the Greenhouse. It is now in full bloom and makes a fine show, particularly from the west windows of the Brick house. We counted on one cluster, thirty-two buds and ten blossoms. Our hollyhocks too, of which there are an almost endless variety, from the black and variegated, to the most delicate white, now add great beauty to the flower-gardens, as do also the fragrant, charming pink, which is now in the high tide of its glory.

We had for dessert yesterday noon, ice-cream, which was very nice, and was dealt out very liberally. As the weather was quite hot and sultry, it was a very acceptable treat.

THE O. C. DAILY.

VOL. 4. SATURDAY, JULY 27, 1867. NO. 23.

O. C. July 25, 1867.

Mr. E. S. Bartholomew, the inventor of Bartholomew's improvement in preserving fruits, meats and other substances, arrived here Tuesday, the 23d, with his apparatus, according to agreement, and proceeded to make arrangements for testing the efficacy of his invention here on our premises. Accordingly, yesterday was occupied in preparing several small wooden cases, made air-tight by glueing and pasting paper over the joints. The cases were then filled with the following articles, viz., butter, eggs, fresh beef, lemons, and three varieties of raspberries. The contents of the different cases, were then put through the process separately, by attaching an india-rubber hose to the case, and connecting with the machine, by which the oxygen is exhausted, and the space filled with carbonic-acid-gas. The hose is then disengaged, and the aperture in the case closed and sealed. Thus far we are well pleased with the experiment, and have taken measures to secure a Community right, provided we are satisfied with further experiments with different fruits, at the end of thirty days. H. T.

W. P. Vegetable Garden.—Some one has said that a well kept garden is a sign of good morals.—But be that as it may, a luxuriant growth of a great variety of vegetables, free from weeds, is highly prized by those who are not in bondage to the daily use of meat. The W. P. family were particularly fortunate in having two such men assigned them as Messrs. Higgins and Ackley. Although it was very late in the Spring before it was decided to have a garden at all, the success of the enterprise has exceeded the most sanguine expectations. The W. P. family have had *peas* as often as every other day, for a long time, besides furnishing mother O. C. with twenty-seven bushels. Yesterday, full-grown new potatoes graced the dinner table. But the beauty of their garden lies in the fact that not a weed is allowed to disgrace the soil of the vegetable paradise. This interesting fact is due chiefly to Mr. Higgins, whose hatred of weeds can be measured only by his hatred of sin. The moment a weed of any description pops its head above-ground, the avenging blade of its mortal enemy, is sure to fall upon it. Indeed, one could easily imagine that the parasite intruders often die of fright at the bare sight of the grim image of their foe.—Moral. Let selfishness in any and every form be regarded as noxious weeds, in the soil of human nature, to be hated and destroyed as a curse to society and as a sign of insanity in those who tolerate it, and this world would soon become a heaven upon earth. O.

The Rev. Mr. Waugh, a Presbyterian clergyman formerly of Saquoit, came here the other day. I thought when I first saw him that he was a little queer. He acted like a man who felt that he had the disagreeable duty to preform of looking this thing through, and he was bound to do it in a thorough and systematic manner. Passing along the walk by the dining-room where the visitors were eating, he looked in, and turning to Mr. Purdy who was walking with him he jerked out "I'm going to have some dinner, come, ain't you?" Then he dodged in. Mr. Purdy had been to dinner. I was a little in advance and although I knew that he had not got his ticket, I thought I would say nothing, but see how the girls would manage him. He seated himself at the table and said emphatically, to Martha who was standing by, "Black tea!" "I will take your ticket sir, if you please," said Martha. "Ticket! Ticket! what ticket? I don't know anything about any ticket." "The ticket for your dinner," replied Martha. The visitors tittered, and one of the men told him to give the young lady a dollar, and she would get him his ticket. He gave her the money and she brought it over to the office laughing, and then returned to wait upon him.

Later in the day, I made the rounds with him, and had a talk with him, by his request, on our social and religious principles, which was long and serious. Mr. Purdy was present. He had spent nearly a year and a half with Dr. Jackson at "Our Home," and when we were talking about the general laxity that prevailed in the marriage relation, he remarked to Mr. Waugh that Dr. Jackson believed in loving his wife, but he did not believe in confining his love to her, and that he was in the habit of going into the bedrooms of his lady patients, in the morning before they were up, and kissing them all round; which seemed perfectly to horrify the good old man.

Each of these gentleman bought a "Hand-Book" before they left. Mr. Waugh will probably read his from a strong sense of duty, but with fear and trembling. U.

Mrs. Hawley's sister, Mrs. Bristol, with her daughter, and Mrs. Canfield, all of Derby, Conn., came in the night, accompanied by James Prindle.

Mr. S. has just brought in a box of raspberries of the "Hornet" variety, which are the nicest and largest raspberry we ever saw.

Mr. H. R. Perry starts to-day for the Southwest.— He goes out as an agent for the O. C., and will go as far as Little Rock, Arkansas.

The teams are all engaged at the present time, in drawing coal from Durhamville.

Letters were received again yesterday, from our European tourists, which were full of interest.

Traps ordered the past week, 743¼ doz.

THE O. C. DAILY.

VOL. 4.   MONDAY, JULY 29, 1867.   NO. 24.

BUSINESS MEETING.

It has been proposed to have a dairy house built. Mr. Thacker wished that a committee be appointed to consider the matter, and if they approve, have the house built so that it will be ready for use in the Fall. This was sympathized with, and a committee appointed consisting of Messrs. Thacker, Abram Burt, Kinsley, Worden, E. H. Hamilton and J. Hawley.

Mr. Hawley reported that we have an opportunity to hire a first-rate man for hostler. He is a brother of Mr. Quance that keeps the boarding house. Mr. Q. asks forty-three dollars per month, and house rent. This is considered a high price, but Mr. Thacker thought it was better to have an experienced, reliable man there, if we have to pay more wages. The present hostler will ask about the same, if he stays in that business. The house intended for the hostler is now occupied by two families. Hostler and house are referred to the barn committee.

The pavement of the court has become quite uneven, and it is desirable to have something done to it. Decided to have it leveled up and sand put in. Mr. Nash and Abram committee.

Mr. Woolworth said Mr. Bennet had applied for help to build a stone road for a short distance from Durhamville. They calculate that about forty rods of stone road and the rest of gravel, will make a good and cheap road. Referred to Messrs. Worden, Kinsley, Hawley and Woolworth.

There is a great deal of inexperienced help in the shop, who need a good deal of oversight. There will be considerable inspecting to be done, and any person that can help, will be welcomed in the Trap-shop. Theodore hoped all the trap-orders would be filled, for we want all the money we can get. Mr. Woolworth and Mr. Kinsley are to do what they can to get help.

Mr. Nash proposed to make a walk along the driveway like that to the store. This was approved by the Board, and Mr. Nash and Mr. Worden are to see that it is done well.

A letter from D. H. Hamilton of sixteen pages of letter paper and four pages of note added as a postscript, was duly received as a reply to one written to him by the writer some weeks since. On the whole I like the document for one reason, namely, its impudence. Disguises are all thrown off. He stands out fearlessly as the champion of the no devil theory, spiritualism and all modern improvements on the old way of getting to heaven through the crucifixion of egotism. With Hamilton it is evident enough that egotism or diotrephiasis is substituted for the cross of Christ. Well, both parties have a better understanding of each other now, than before the courtship and criticism we kindly offered him at his request.   C.

A document was read last night from John Leonard relative to bringing science, particularly chemistry into the kitchen, and have bread, biscuit, griddle cakes, short cakes &c. &c. constructed on scientific principles. George E. and Theodore were called on and made some remarks upon the subject; the use of soda, fermentation in bread-making &c. It was thought that the kitchen group should study the different combinations in cooking, and as much as possible inform themselves as to general principles. Our bread has been very nice of late, but the biscuit deserve a good deal of criticism. It was thought that the women on the whole had done pretty well, but that perhaps the time had now come, when they are to receive a thorough education in culinary science.

We had music in the Hall last night, at 7 o'clock which strongly reminded us of olden times, when we had a full orchestra. Mr. Hamilton with his bass-viol, Theodore, George E. and Frank Wayland with their violins, were a great addition to our otherwise small orchestra. The music was quite cheering. We had also, at the close of meeting, two songs by a quartette club, accompanied by music on the harmonium. The most of our employees and neighbors were present at the 7 o'clock concert.

I confess that my heart is *strong* in God. I rejoice in the Lord for the *great* salvation he has wrought out for us both for body as well as the soul. I confess myself a subject of this *full* salvation. I pray for the manifestation of a spirit of humility and a soft heart.   H. A. HALL.

We had a small shower in the night, which was very acceptable as rain was much needed. It will serve to lay the dust if nothing more.

F. W. Smith and C. Van will leave to-day for New York. Mr. Kelly also started this morning on his regular peddling trip.

Traps ordered Saturday, over 900 doz.

THE O. C. DAILY.

VOL. 4.　　TUESDAY, JULY 30, 1867.　　NO. 25.

Rockville Center, Queens Co. L. Island, N. Y., July 26.

JOHN H. NOYES AND COMMUNITY :—*My Dear Friends :*—You may recollect a letter which I wrote conjointly with Mr. Hare, to you more than a year since. This is possibly all you know of me. That letter we have ever thought of as a testimony, or record of the time when we became willing to give up all to Christ, and become thereby subordinate to God. Since then, I have received and read your paper weekly. My appreciation is necessarily the measure of myself. A knowledge of you and what you have accomplished, is to me important or otherwise, in proportion to my conception of the object in view. So I can at best, give you but my own dimensions; a matter of itself unimportant. But I would like, however, if I could, to express to you the satisfaction I derive from a communion with the spirit of your life. Although I neither see you or correspond with any of you, yet you are " my mother my sisters and my brethren." While it is the will of God that I should remain in isolation and at a distance from those who more than all others "do the will of my Father in Heaven," I can only say may " His will be done," for " He doeth all things well." If I truly believe this, and my trust is equal to my belief, there is no place left for anxieties or undue solicitude. Do I covet the benefits of criticism, or in short, of a full Communistic life ? I have prayed to be saved from the sin of idolatry; and the attainment of desirable conditions with all the good things pertaining to your Community, could not compensate for the sacrifice, if I were to substitute personalities and organization for that of which they are but the representative. So I leave it all with Him " who seeth not as man seeth," and perform from day to day my duties joyfully.

The CIRCULAR connects with *life*, and if I did not read a word of it, I should feel it, and become conscious of its character, through the subtle spirit with which it is more or less impregnated. Our little Psyche, two and a half years old, has several times asked to lay the palm of her hand upon its pages, and when interrogated as to why she wished to do so, replied, " Because it makes me feel good." I have a family interest in you as a body and as individuals. I accept all that you recognize as essential to success. Hope based upon any thing less than that to which you have attained, will inevitably fall short of the glory of the resurrection. In the certainty of consecration to God through Jesus Christ, I remain your sister,　　GRATIE HOWARD HARE.

The raspberry-bee this morning was a very enjoyable affair so far as certain individuals were concerned. After waking the sleepers at five o'clock F. Marks and I proceeded to the field. The air was still, the sky cloudless, and the bright rays of the smiling sun fell on the dewdrops, and converted them into bright gems, so far as appearances went. The sultriness of a few days past was replaced by a cool, bracing atmosphere, which with the cheerful sun tended to buoyancy of spirit.—Arriving at the berry-patch we failed to discover any signs of pickers; so we entered into profitable conversation until twenty-five minutes before six, when we concluded to return. We had but just started when the laughing countenance of Mr. D. appeared in the distance, and a little behind him C. L. They thought they must be the last ones, and so indeed they were, first and last.

It was proposed that as it was such a beautiful morning we should continue our walk to the next eminence and " View the landscape o'er." So off we started as merry as little children. The road lay along by the grapes, whose rich foliage, and abundant clusters of smooth round fruit, glistening in the rays of the sun was a sight of beauty sufficient in itself to repay all it cost. On reaching the top of the hill and feasting our eyes with the view presented, we concluded to pay a visit to " Spring-grove," miscalled the " Park," it being but a nook of the park-proper.— The suggestion met with applause, and was carried out to the edification of all concerned. After sufficiently gratifying our senses with the beauties of nature, we wended our way homeward, thankful for the *institution of bees.*　　D. E. S.

A Mr. Baker, formerly deacon of the Baptist church in Pulaski and an acquaintance of Mr. Abbott, came here yesterday, spent the night and left this morning. He was a come-out-er from the church in that place in the days of Myrick, and his radicalism drew after him a good share of the church members. Mr. Abbott says his views now harmonize more with Gerrit Smith's than with any other system of beliefs, and he is a frequent visitor at Mr. S.'s house.

Mrs Hawley's friends leave to-day, all apparently quite gratified with their visit—Mrs. Canfield particularly so. Mrs. C. expressed her delight at seeing the children so orderly and obedient, and wondered what means we used to produce a state of things with them so much superior to any thing she had ever witnessed elsewhere.

THE O. C. DAILY.

VOL. 4. WEDNESDAY, JULY 31, 1867. NO. 26.

After it was decided that I should come to Oneida and take charge of the preserving business this season, I was led to study the subject with a view of making some improvements by way of labor-saving machinery &c. By the time I had arrived here, I had blocked out in my mind one or two little machines that I saw would materially facilitate some parts of our work. Not being a regular bred mechanic, I sought aid in carrying out my enterprises, and found it in Mr. Inslee and J. F. Sears. In presenting an outline of a machine that I wanted for the purpose of cutting up string-beans, I asked Mr. Inslee if he thought it practical? After a little study he replied, "Yes, I think it is ; but we must consult J. Sears, and devise the best plan for its construction." Accordingly J. was consulted, and on being asked if he could make such a machine, replied, " Yes, I can get up just what you want." Well, the first steps to be taken was to procure a pair of rubber rollers of suitable pliability, that were deemed indispensible, and without which it was useless to proceed. Accordingly, application was made to our Agency in New-York, and the city ransacked in search of the article, but nothing suitable could be found, and no firm would undertake to make a single pair for less than fifty or seventy-five dollars. This outlay to begin with, was not deemed advisable, as the project was considered as something of an experiment. However, Mr. H. and Mr. E. H. H. continued the search for the desired rollers, and finally came across some rubber tubing, that as far as pliability was concerned, they thought might answer the purpose. Accordingly samples were sent, and it was decided that by placing one piece of tubing within another, of larger size, a fair roller could be constructed that possibly might be made to answer the purpose. Accordingly, the tubing was sent, the rollers formed, and in due time the machine was finished, and has to-day been put in operation, and we are happy to say, performs the work well, far exceeding our expectations. One other machine previously constructed, was one for the purpose of slicing and quartering Pine-apples, which saves the labor of at least three hands, and does the work much better than it could otherwise be done. But what I was most interested in, was in seeing how beautifully Community life is adapted to all our wants. For instance, one, perhaps, invents and another judges as to its practicability, and still another has the genius and qualification to execute and put the thing into operation. Surely " The eye cannot say to the hand, I have no need of thee, nor again, the head to the feet, I have no need of you, &c."   H. T.

YOUNG MEN'S MEETING, July 28.—Theodore had some thoughts about the noon-meetings which he had expressed to individuals, and he was requested to repeat them. He remarked that his father said a short time ago, that the true kind of improvement is to be doing something all the time that requires courage. There has been a great victory gained by the young women in getting freedom to speak, but that should not be the stopping place. They must look around for something to be done that requires the same courage. Let those who have only made confessions, try to bring out some new idea every time they speak.

Mr. Noyes told him that when he was a young man, he made the following resolution in reference to writing and speaking : If he had God's truth in his heart, he would find *some* way of imparting it to others, if he could only express it in a plain way, very well ; if he could communicate what he had to say in an artistic manner so as to make a sensation, so much the better.   J. F.

Mr. Elkanah Ingraham of Jackson, Mich., came here Sunday, and staid over night. He was on his way home from New-York, where he had been to attend a convention of the heirs of Timothy Ingraham, one of England's wealthy men three or four generations ago—of whom he is a lineal descendant. Property to the amount of untold millions is in question. The entire city of Leeds, having a population of 250,000 is built on leased ground belonging to this estate. A reward of $20,000, raised at a similar convention a year ago, had brought the last will to light, and there was no doubt in the mind of Mr. Ingraham, but that the heirs would soon come into the posession of this magnificent property, the estimated value of which is $500,000,000.

Mr. Ingraham had read the CIRCULAR a year and a half, and was considerably interested in us, so much so indeed that he inquired what steps he should take in order to join the O. C. He formerly resided on Quality Hill, and some upwards of thirty years ago he boarded for a while with Mr. Burt. He is a carpenter, millwright and machinist by trade, has a wife and one child at home, and is sixty-six years of age.   U.

LIGHT WANTED.—Mr. Barron said to me, a day or two since, " What shall be done with our boarding-house ?" The O. C. owns the house and the furniture—supplies the table and pays a man and his wife so much for superintending the establishment.— But their time of service soon expires and they do not wish to renew the contract. We would be glad to rent the house to some reliable person who has a gift for the boarding business, so as to be relieved entirely from the responsibility of providing for tables after the fashion of the world, and not after the fashion of Communism. The O. C. want light on the subject in order to act wisely. We appeal to our sister Communes for suggestions if they have any to offer. " In a multitude of counsellors there is safety."   c.

Mrs. Hyde leaves for Buffalo to-day, after a stay of nearly eight weeks. She returns improved in body and stronger in spirit than when she came.

THE O. C. DAILY.

VOL. 4. THURSDAY, AUGUST 1, 1867. NO. 27.

Mrs. Sarah Crosby a widow lady from Groton, N. H. writes,

" I greatly admire your fourth of July Celebration ; think your orator took up the stitch you thought you dropped five years ago. I think if this nation be a Christian nation, or even if a large portion of it were Christian, such would at once declare themselves annexed to the Kingdom of Heaven—proclaim Jesus Christ president, and lift up their standard of a universal peace-government and evince by their daily lives that they were honest souls before God. What a change would speedily come over our crazy nation, which has encountered the most horrible of all bloodly wars ever enacted as I look at it, and still another war of principle is upon the nation, which if truth and righteousness predominate, it will come out of the terrible furnace of tribulation purified and fitted to enter the Kingdom of Heaven, and proclaim Christ their King and Lawgiver.   *   *

" You seem to encourage people to relate or give a sketch of their experiences through the CIRCULAR.—To me their articles are interesting ; hope you will benefit mankind greatly thereby. As your Community are so liberal in the distribution of the paper, I suspect you are rich in perishables and well able ; really, it is an evidence of benevolence little practiced in our wicked world."

BOTANICAL SPECIMENS SENT AT TWO DIFFERENT TIMES BY C. S. J.—1st. Moss, from Salisbury Plain ; 2nd. Clover, from Motly Abbey ; 3d. Thistle, from the shores of Southampton water, near the Isle of Wight ; 4th. Elm, from the *Jarden des Tuilleries* ; 5th. Box, from the grave of Abelard and Heloise cemetery, *Pere de la Chaise ;* 6th. Chestnut, from Notre Dame ; 7th. A bit of bark from a Cedar of Lebanon ; (a rare specimen.) 8th. Sycamore, from the *Jarden des Plants*, Paris ; 9th. Cypress, from the *Bois de Bologne ;* 10th. Larch, from the *Champs Elysees ;* 11th. Cherry, from Versailles, picked near the Little Trianon ; 12th. Orange, from the Tuilleries ; 13th. A little flower from St. Cloud, (name forgotten.)

A man by the name of William Buel, of Illinois, writes to the " Superintendent of the Perfectionists."

" I believe we cannot be consistent in carrying out our existence without perfect *love*, and for a man or woman to be eternally tied down to *one*, and only one to *love*, that solitary one and none other, never was the design of Providence in the creation of man and woman. Why should a man be tied to a woman he *hates* or a woman to a man she *abhors*. I would like to visit you and spend a few days. My SOUL is full of love to all, I have no one I hate. Love is the essence of life, love is the cement of society, love is the fulfilling of the law &c."

A Miss Andrews, from Concord, N. H., a maiden lady, aged fifty-two years, came here yesterday. She has written us several letters, signifying her wish to join, and Mr. Woolworth replied to her, giving her permission to come and make a visit. She has followed teaching, a part of the time at the West and South, for years, but would like now to find a permanent home. She has taken the CIRCULAR for a few months, and professes to be very much interested in reading it. She has formerly been a member of the Congregational church, but becoming convinced that the churches were all wrong, she has, she says, been striving to find out what was religious truth, and *where* it was to be found.

All persons ordering goods, should be particular to designate to which department they belong. A sewing-machine came recently ; it was thrown off at Willow-Place, the box knocked open and after a delay, reloaded and taken to Oneida Creek. A barrel of O chains, weighing 900 pounds came, and as they were expecting chains for the lawn, it was brought here, unloaded, opened, then reloaded and carried to the Trap-shop. Thus any one can see the importance of attending to little things.   x.

We have 1,540 grape-vines in bearing, principally, the Concord, Deleware, Hartford Prolific, and Diana. The three former promise well, but the latter is inclined to rot. We do not consider the Diana a very profitable grape, and shall take most of them up the coming Fall, and put out choice varieties, Israellas, Adirondac &c.   r

We had a letter from Meroa Kneeland yesterday. She works out doing house-work and gets $2.00 per week. She says she and Emily are both homesick, want to get back to the Community, and asks if the time has not almost come for her to return.

The weather is cool and we have considerable company these days. Twenty-seven dinners were furnished Tuesday, and twenty-one yesterday.

Mr. Hamilton, Mrs. Skinner and Jessie, expect to leave to-day, Mr. H. for New-York and the two latter for W. C.

Mrs. Hatch has a brother and his wife, from Springfield here on a visit. Mrs. Leete is here also, staying a few days.

852 tumblers of currant jelly, (the pure juice of the currant), were made and put up yesterday afternoon.

We have finished canning peas, or nearly so, having put up in all 4,852 quarts.

THE O. C. DAILY.

VOL. 4.   FRIDAY, AUGUST 2, 1867.   NO. 28.

Gilead, Lewis Co., Mo., July 21.

DEAR ONEIDA COMMUNITY :—I have wanted many times to write you, since I commenced reading your paper (the CIRCULAR) not many weeks since, but as many times has my heart failed me and I have asked myself if you in your fullness of happiness, cared for "such a worm as I." But I am very lonesome, so will venture this once at any rate, and if I make too great a bore of my letter, there are plenty of ways in which you can rebuke me, and I will try to accept it with all the grace possible.

I am very much interested in your principles, and believe with my husband (S. Haworth, Mo.) that you are living the only truly christian life. The idea of Communism is no new one to me, though I never saw it so closely allied to the precepts of Christ before. Indeed it seems as though the same spirit was breathing from every page of "holy writ." I never realized it so fully until reading the CIRCULAR, so I have to thank you for much light that I have received.

We once undertook to help form a Community, but oh, the miserable failure we made, because our house was not built upon a rock, but had a sandy foundation instead. I had a vague impression then of what you have since made a substantial reality, viz., that in order to have the right kind of a society, one in which confidence and love shall rule over distrust and coldness, and spirituality and harmony over sensuality and discord, we must go to work scientifically with the great loving Father of the universe for our leader, doubting not that if we earnestly desire it, we shall be guided into all truth.

I sometimes seem to get very near you through the CIRCULAR, and many sad and turbulent feelings are soothed, through the influence which seems stealing from you to me through its columns. I can only say for the present, God bless you all. Earnestly,

SARAH E. M. HAWORTH.

We thought when the hour for sending the mail was changed from a quarter past twelve to a quarter before, that we should not always be able to get the DAILY out in season to send the same day, and we failed at first to do so in several instances; but latterly, by commencing a little earlier in the morning we have succeeded though sometimes with a good deal of effort and at the very last moment. A few evenings since, it was announced in meeting, that the mail would go out still a quarter of an hour earlier for a time, at half past eleven, for the purpose of going round by W. P. and taking whatever they had to send, from there. We have succeeded thus far since the change, in getting the DAILY into the mail, but it needs omniscience, almost, to see *all* the errors in the proof-sheet, with sometimes only a half minute to glance it over. We hope our readers will take this into consideration, and while we do not wish to screen ourselves from just criticism, and should be glad of any suggestions of improvement, yet we like to have persons know just how we are situated, that they may be able to sympathize with us, and not be too critical or severe, when every thing is not *done up* in the very best way.

Our old omnibus, that has been undergoing repairs at the Depot, was brought home a few days since, very much improved in looks, newly cushioned and made comfortable every way for carrying persons to and from W. P. and elsewhere in rainy weather. A company of fourteen girls, with Mr. Hawley for driver, went over to W. P. in the new carriage yesterday afternoon, with two span of horses attached, to pick string-beans for our dinner to-day.

When they arrived there, one span was disengaged from the carriage, and the other fastened to a ring that was drove into the barn.—One of the horses that remained attached to the wagon was the one that has made himself so famous from time to time, by running away. The barn-door blew back, hit the horses, and in a twinkling the ring was drawn out and they were off at full gallop. They were stopped by one of our teamsters just this side of Hamilton bridge, without having sustained any injury, either to horses or omnibus. Mr. Cragin thought this incident was a seasonable check to any pleasure-seeking spirit or love of display that the new vehicle was tempting us into.

WILLOW-PLACE, Aug. 1.—The noon and evening meetings here, are characterized by the same revival spirit that works at O. C. and the other Communes. They are very interesting and growing in freedom. Last evening Mr. Noyes's talk about unbelief was read, and heartily sympathised with, and also "Education of young Women." It was remarked that in the crusade against false love, there came a time when it was decided that the Community had cast it out, and then the victory began to be realized. It was a unanimous feeling that we regard the spirit of unbelief, fear and the dumb-devil, in the same light, as conquered by the Community.

Thankfulness was expressed for Mrs. Skinner's visit here. It has been very profitable to us, and was thought would tend to unite this family with the paper.

Mrs. Kelley had an aunt and her husband from New Hartford call here yesterday. Her aunt came much prejudiced, but left quite softened and pleased with what she saw.

Mr. Olds' sister and her husband came here yesterday, to make a visit.—Miss Andrews left this morning.

THE O. C. DAILY.

VOL. 4. SATURDAY, AUGUST 3, 1867. NO. 29.

We have received a letter from Nathaniel Randall of Woodstock Vt., in which he expresses a desire to learn more about us, and, with his wife wishes to make the O. C. a visit. He says, "I was one of the first to engage in the Skeneateles Community with J. A. Collins. I spent $1000 in that enterprize and then went back into the world to gamble and overreach my brothers and sisters, for a livelihood. I have succeeded in acquiring property, and am worth enough to live without any more labor, but am no better satisfied. I want to work for humanity while here.

"I am a joiner, a watch-maker and M. D.; a very handy man in any thing that is useful to fallen man."

Also a Mr. John O. Waide, of Camelton Ind. writes, making application for membership, with a request to visit us in September.

A SHORT SERMON.—"Behold I stand at the door and knock; if any man hear my voice and open the door, I will come in to him and sup with him and he with me." Rev. 3: 20.

In the above passage three conditions of the heart are requisite, in order to realize in our experience the promised blessing.

1st. Faith in God's word—a belief that he is actually seeking for admittance into our hearts.

2nd. A listening attitude and control of the attention that will hear his voice.

3d. An act of the heart that opens wide the door, and gladly welcomes Christ as our guest.

The closing clause of the verse, shows the blessed results; a feast of love, in which Christ sups with us and we with him; a reciprocal action. "My beloved is mine and I am his."

"PARODY ON THE VALE OF OVOKA."

There is not in the wide world so blest a retreat
As ours, where pure spirits in harmony meet;
Oh, the last ray of feeling, e'en life must depart,
E'er the charm of this valley shall fade from my heart.
Yet it is not that nature has shed o'er the scene
Her purest of crystals, or brightest of green,
'Tis not the soft magic of streamlet or hill,
Oh no! it is something more exquisite still.
'Tis that friends the beloved of my bosom are here,
That makes each dear scene of enchantment more dear;
And it shows how the beauties of nature improve,
When we see them reflected from looks that we love,
Sweet home of contentment! full long may I dwell
In thy charming retreat, with the friends I love well.
'Till the storms that we meet in this cold world
     shall cease,
And all hearts in one spirit, be mingled in peace.

Yesterday morning, while waiting upon the children's breakfast-table, those of Emily Easton's age, I had occasion to correct them, for calling griddle, or pancakes, *panny-cakes*, and I had them all repeat it over after me, so as to be sure they understood the difference. They went on with their breakfast, when, Emily wishing for some more of her favorite dish, says, "I thank you for some tin—some more *tin-pancakes*. It was said with an air of assurance that she had certanly got it right this time, and much to the amusement of the children and all who heard it.
                                                                E.

Willie came along this morning with a little handful of salt. As he opened his hand his countenance beaming with an air of confidence and satisfaction he exultingly said, "I am going to catch a bird!" We remembered the falsity of that saying was explained to him the other day, but the seed sown had taken root and must be proved false before he could abandon it, or distrust the words of those whom he had every reason to believe. Shall we not sometime learn that "words are seed sown."
                                                                L.

A few evenings since, it was announced in the meeting, that the Bag-shop corps had filled all their orders, though Mr. Kelley brought home more orders (we don't know how many) the same night.

In addition to the order for traps, of over 900 doz. published in Monday's DAILY, we have received for the week ending Aug. 3d, 380½ doz.

The farmers have commenced digging muck on our lot of land which was purchased last Fall, near the Cheese-factory.

We received 160 quarts of whortleberries yesterday, and are putting them up to-day.

THE O. C. DAILY.

VOL. 4.   MONDAY, AUGUST 5, 1867.   NO. 30.

BUSINESS MEETING.

Geo. E. said that a bathing place was needed here where elderly women can take a warm or cold bath at any time. He had thought one of Mr. Bristol's rooms would make a very good place for it. A connection could be made with the dish-water tank, to secure warm water, and with the other pipe for cold water. It would be large enough for two persons, and a stove could be put in for winter. It was considered very desirable to have such a place, and Messrs. Cragin, Thacker, Geo. E. Cragin, Mrs. H. C. Noyes and Maria Barron were appointed committee.

Mrs. Mallory said that the distribution of help for washing, seemed to be at loose ends. They could not tell whom to rely upon for help. It requires two men, one for two days of the week, and the other for three days. It would be a great help to that department, to have some one who understands it do the rinsing, and not have a different person every week. Messrs. Kinsley and Hatch are to have special supervision of that department.

Mr. Woolworth wished to know if that old cottage could be moved and made into a tenant house for Mrs. Goakes. Mr. Kinsley thought it could be moved but might go to pieces in the operation. Messrs. Kinsley, Hawley and Abram Burt, committee to ascertain what they can about it, and report next week.

Mr. Cragin remarked that as he came from the Post-office, this morning, around by W. P., that he thought our premises looked rather shabbily, especially before those tenant houses. A good fence should be built, but some draining is needed first. Mr. C. proposes to look into the matter further and report again.

I hope light *will* come to us on this Boarding-House question. One thing is clear—its expensiveness; but whether we shall gain by getting it farther off, or nearer to us may be considered.—It certainly would be a relief to have nothing to do with the board of outsiders; pay them simply for services rendered, including board, and let that be the end.—But there is a lack of houses and homes for workers in the neighborhood, and hence our perplexity.—Our present outlook is for tenements on, or near our domain to accommodate employees.—The question might be asked, are we making the most of such houses as we have ? I think not when we rent them to such young families—families that can furnish but one hand, and he quite liable to be kept at home part of the time to take care of wife and babies.—Older families where man, woman and children can all turn into one business or another, and if one gets sick the others can take care of him, is what we want in preference. "I can't think of any more now."   M. L. W.

Yesterday a party of six, with a team, went off on an exploring expedition, to see what the prospect is for fruit the coming Fall. The route lay up the valley through which for several miles meanders the Oneida Creek; then we turned to the right and passed over the hills on the west side of the valley, into a narrower one, down which our course was northward, for some distance, when we recrossed the hills, stopping a short time to lunch in a grove on the summit.

After dinner, we stretched ourselves upon the bosom of mother earth, with seat-cushions for pillows, and after a pleasant chat, all fell into a meditative mood. It was a grand place for reflection in that temple of God's. We arrived home safely, after seven hours pleasant ride.—Prospect for fruit not very promising; yet there will be a surplus in some orchards.   D. E. S.

A Mr. Crocker and his wife, from Lebanon Springs, came here yesterday forenoon, spent the night and will leave to-day, Mr. C. was formerly a resident of New Orleans, and in the late war lost $150,000. He still owns 400 acres of land near that city. He lives with his second wife, and she in turn, lives with her second husband. They have each a child (a boy and girl) living with the Shakers, but they are not well satisfied to have them remain there, as they are jealous of the influence the Shakers are exerting over their young minds.

The father of W. G. and D. M. Kelly came Saturday for a visit. He remarked in meeting, that for a year past he had made the Berean his study, and could now indorse its principles wholly; he had read it before, but with his mind much prejudiced; consequently had not seen its truths as he now saw them.

G. N. Miller arrived at O. C. Saturday. Mr. and Mrs. Burnham, Mrs. Hatch's brother and his wife, left for home this morning, after a stay of four or five days.

Another letter from C. S. J. was received Saturday. He gives a grand description of the Alps, and his sensations on first seeing them.

A gentleman from Watertown, the Editor of the *Watertown Reformer*, a paper published in that place, gave us a call of an hour, yesterday.

Mrs. D. E. Smith gave birth to a baby boy this morning, weighing seven pounds and thirteen ounces.

THE O. C. DAILY.

VOL. 4. TUESDAY, AUGUST 6, 1867. NO. 31.

EVENING MEETING.

A talk was read last evening, on the Diotrephian spirit, showing its manifestations in various ways, which led to a general and very interesting conversation on the subject. All seemed to think that that spirit had effected them in some way—some had gained victories over it, and all were sure of victory through Christ—through the "blood of the Lamb and the word of their testimony." This spirit was considered the greatest enemy to Christ—to humility and meekness, and thanks were expressed that the judgment is let loose upon it. Mr. Woolworth quoted this passage of scripture: " How can ye believe who receive honor one of another, and seek not the honor that cometh from God?" And said, " Is not the desire to secure the honor and approbation of our fellow men, one form of the Diotrephian disease? It is death to faith. It seems to me that one way in which this disease works, is through the spirit that seeks honor one of another."

Mr. Underwood thought this spirit one of the most subtle and powerful enemies to unity, and a friend to isolation. Mr. Noyes, in defining and exposing it, has struck a death blow not only at individual egotism, but at all forms of society that are sustained and nourished by this spirit. Purge a man from the Diotrephian spirit, and he can unite with his fellow-men, with Christ and the primitive church; but if he is not purged from this spirit, he will be like Thoreau and others, who spend their lives in building up self, having no reference to the kingdom of God.

Mrs. Miller said she had formerly been affected by this Diotrephian spirit in reference to love, but for some time past had felt that it was enough for her to be loved. Love in itself is a good thing, and she did not consider how much or how little she had, but was thankful for it, and received it as God's gift.

Theodore had found in his own experience, that when he had set his ambition on accomplishing something for himself, and would work hard on it, just before he had got to it, it would be accomplished by the Community, in season to gain the end and give that spirit a hit. He desired that his ambition should be kept in the Community channel. He wished to work hard for education, but he desired to do it for the Community, and that they might get the reward.

It is interesting to watch the spirit of receptivity our little ones have, and their readiness to believe what is told them in good faith. They seem to understand that the devil is the author of all evil, whether in the form of disease or a bad spirit. While talking with little May last night, about God making us good, she looked up very earnestly, saying, "Where is God, where does he live?" "In our hearts," was the reply, " but," said she, " when I am naughty, don't the devil live there?"

A few days ago, little Harold was sick, and while lying in the crib, he broke out very indignantly and said, " I don't want the devil to make me sick." M.

Mr. Kellogg is suffering still from what he considers the effects of his fall, though at first his cough seemed to proceed from a severe cold. The following note to the family will show the working of his spirit under trial:

" I desire to 'confess with my mouth the Lord Jesus,' and I 'believe in my heart that God hath raised him from the dead.' I also believe that the power that raised Christ from the dead is in me a Saviour from all sin, I confess I am a son of God, therefore I say to the devil, hands off, and let Christ have possession of his own. I am thankful to be placed in any circumstances that will purify my character and cleanse me from everything offensive in his sight." ENOS KELLOGG.

San Francisco, Cal. July 8, 1867.

Will the Secretary of the Oneida Community, be kind enough to forward to me such information written or printed, as may be convenient, about the Society of Communists at Lenox. I am a respectable citizen, and am long a convert to Fourier's idea of a Community of kindred spirits. I have but distant ideas of your internal economy, but it strikes me you are on the right track. I am anxious for light, am sincere, and shall hope to get a letter soon.

Very Respectfully, T. H. ROSE.

Mr. Leander Wilcox has rented a house on Turkey St., about half a mile beyond W. P. and has moved his family in there. He will work for our people in the Trap-shop.

Though the weather is fair and delightful and the evenings splendid, yet the ground is dry and parched and we need rain.

W. H. Perry has gone into the Store as an assistant in place of the women who have been discharged from that office.

| Bags made in July, | 54 11-12 doz. |
| " sold " " | $1,806.51. |

THE O. C. DAILY.

VOL. 4. WEDNESDAY, AUGUST 7, 1867. NO. 32.

Mr. and Mrs. Hathaway, Mr. Old's sister and her husband, leave to-day. The following communications from them were handed in, and read last night in meeting:

"Having received at your hands a generous hospitality, for which I desire to express my thanks, I feel that I cannot leave you without saying a word touching the impressions that I have received. In comparing you with the christian sects around you, I see that you have many advantages. I shall be quite unable to tell you how beautiful it seems to me to behold a family so large, and so interesting, worship the Father with one heart, and that heart all aglow with his love.—Fully endorsing the remarks that I have listened to, with regard to the subject of faith, I must say that it seems to me that much of your success is justly attributable to your unflinching integrity.—In illustration of this I will relate from memory an incident that I read in the CIRCULAR, several year since. One of your dealers in sewing silk, somewhere I think in one of the Western states, called upon a person, who, it seems had been one of your customers and who about that time had bought of other parties a quantity of silk, which he alleged to be cheaper and better than that from the Community. But your agent maintained that he had doubtless been imposed upon, and proposed to test the matter by weight, which test revealed the fact that it was very much in favor of the O. C.

"This carrying religion into business, or rather, making your business a preacher of your doctrines, seems very excellent to me."   P. M. HATHAWAY.

BY MRS. C. O. HATHAWAY.

"The human soul is so constituted from its origin, with such power of receptivity, that it cannot long contemplate an object of good, but that it becomes assimilated to it. So it seems to me that this Community by keeping ever before it the divine example of Christ, has come to love and follow that example ; and as he is 'the chief among ten thousand, and the one altogether lovely,' the fruits of that ever present example must be good and lovely. During my most pleasant visit of nearly a week amid the attractive scenes of this Community, I have seen neither a repellent look, or heard a harsh or impure word among its members. This proves to me the truth of the divine assertion, 'by their fruits ye shall know them.' Christ says 'If ye love me ye will keep my commandments.'—I have been impressed also with the appearance of bodily strength and vigor in the members of this Community, by which I am reminded of an allusion in Isaiah. It is said that the eagle sheds its feathers every spring, when it becomes dull and weak, but with the growth of its feathers its strength and vigor return, and its 'youth is renewed.' Thus this allusion is made very significant. 'They that wait upon the Lord shall *renew their strength*, they shall mount up with wings as eagles, they shall run and not be weary, and they shall walk and not faint.' In the one hundred and third Psalm, allusion is made to the same fact. 'Bless the Lord O my soul! and forget not all his benefits, who forgiveth all thine iniquities ; who healeth all thy diseases; who redeemeth thy life from destruction ; who crowneth thee with loving kindness and tender mercies ; who satisfieth thy mouth with good things, so that *thy youth is renewed like the eagle's.*' "

[The following is from Mrs. Canfield, our late visitor, to E. G. Hawley.]

"How much I would like to ramble on those elegant lawns of yours, and listen to that divine music that you will have to-day. Cousin, do you know I cannot conceive how any one can help being religious in such a heaven—every thing in and around you is enough to inspire one. In the busiest hours of the day, quietness even to solemnity, pervades the whole place—all is order and every thing has the precision of clock-work. Every one springs to his or her duties with a will, and each enjoys the rest between working hours as heartily. How much I enjoyed my visit I never can tell you. That cinder in my eye came near spoiling my visit ; thanks to Dr. C., I shall always remember him with gratitude. Thanks, ten thousand thanks for our kind reception and entertainment."

The notice of T. R. N.'s lecture night before last, at 7 o'clock, was by some unaccountable neglect, omitted yesterday. We hope it will not be considered stale to-day. The subject was "The relation between the animal and vegetable world, chemically considered" with explanatory diagrams on the black-board. The lecture was very edifying and instructive, and made us feel more then ever the importance of a thorough knowledge of chemistry.

Our teamsters are engaged now-a-days in drawing the brick that was engaged last spring, for building the children's new house.

T. R. N. and Mrs. L. T. Waters leave the O. C. at half past eleven A. M. to-day.

THE O. C. DAILY.

VOL. 4. THURSDAY, AUGUST 8, 1867. NO. 33.

Mr. L. I. Bigelow made quite a formal and elaborate little speech on his introduction Sunday. He faltered a little in its delivery and his voice trembled. This might have been owing to nervousness; but it struck me that he was really somewhat awed, when he found himself face to face with a Community man. He is the editor of the *Watertown Reformer*, and author of "Bench and Bar," a work which is favorably noticed in a late number of the *Home Journal*. He was on his way to Hamilton, to deliver an address before the alumni of the university, and their friends.

He was pretty well informed with regard to the O. C.; had read Dixon and the newspapers, and claimed to be free from prejudice. He is a small, nervous man, not more than thirty-five years of age, has light eyes and hair, is quick of apprehension and talented, but not profound.—He was a rapid talker; asked a great many questions; and when I told him of the Second Coming of Christ, of the Primitive church, and of our relations to that church he said, he did not see how we could be consistent and live otherwise than we did. He will write a sketch of his visit for the *Reformer*. u.

Mr. Woolworth said in meeting last night:

"We received a telegram from Henry Allen this afternoon that mystified us not a little, it was so indefinite. I showed it to several, and finally to Joseph, hoping he could throw some light upon it. It read as follows: 'Mr. Noyes wants the help at Wallingford immediately on the paper.' Joseph said he heard them say something about wanting Theodore and also George E. but more especially Theodore. Then George Kellogg remarked that when they first received the telegram at the Depot they made it out, 'Mr. Noyes wants the order help at Wallingford immediately on the paper.' They could not make sense of this, so they left the 'order' out but retained the 'the.' Finally Carrie suggested that *the order* should read *Theodore*, and that seemed to be the solution of it. But to be sure I went down to the Depot, and they called back to Albany to have them give the message again, and it came out all right: 'Mr. Noyes wants Theodore's help at Wallingford on the paper immediately.'" Theodore has gone and will probably get here to-day. A boy is employed in the Telegraph Office at Oneida and probably his wits are not as sharp as they will be when he is older.

[Extract of a letter from S. E. Johnson to S. J. Clark.]

"Yesterday, I had another package from C. S. J., which came very artistically arranged. The contents were as follows:

1st. Mint, from Zurich Switzerland; 2nd. Linden blossom, from the shore of Lake Zurich; 3d. Grape leaf, picked near the spot from which the large picture at Oneida was taken, (a different species from anything we have growing here.) 4th. Legume du Sweitz! 5th. Swiss Mulberry blossom, from the banks of the Aar at Berne; 6th. Bluebell, from the valley of Leauterbrunnen at the foot of the Jungfrau; 7th. Fern, from Interlachen; 8th. Alpine plant, picked from a Swiss chalet, half way up a mountain; 9th. Specimen of Alpine mosquito. He and I had a war of extermination and I beat. Here I have embalmed it as those old cannibals used to the skins of their enemies. 10th. Pink, from Lucerne; 11th. Swiss Arbor Vitæ, from Freybourg; 12th. Swiss Oak, from Freybourg; 13th. Swiss Honeysuckle, from the banks of Lake Geneva.—You would be delighted to see them, they are glued on so as to make a pretty border. Then he sent a miscellaneous collection of flowers, part Alpine, and two or three from the Eastern portion of France on the German border."

One of our teams attached to a load of brick, narrowly escaped being precipitated through the Castle bridge into the Creek, one day this week. There were two or three teams near together, and the driver of the one that crossed first, noticed that the bridge seemed weak, and that there was a perceptible giving away under his load. He intended as soon as he was well across, to warn the teamster behind not to cross; but before he had time to give the warning, the other team was on the bridge. This driver seemed to realize the same "weakness" as the other, only a little more so, and as he looked back, he noticed that the back end of his wagon was *going down*. This frightened him, and he made such a desperate demonstration that his horses took the fright also and sprang forward with such energy, as to rescue driver and all from their imminent peril. The bridge is a high one, and the descent if it had been made, must have proved tragical in the extreme. Verily a good Providence is over us. H.

Mrs Mary S. Arnold, of Galveston, Texas, came here yesterday, with the intention of staying three or four days. She became partially acquainted with our writings through Mr. North, and has corresponded with our people more or less for three or four years.

A man by the name of Martin Lewis, from Hudson City, N. J. came here yesterday, and spent the night. He is a friend of Mr. Franks, a reader of the CIRCULAR, and seems to be well posted in our doctrines.

Twenty-two dinners were furnished to visitors yesterday, besides luncheons, berries and cream, ice-cream, pie, lemonade, &c. &c.

Mr. Carpenter and his little son, and J. J. Skinner arrived a little after noon yesterday.

THE O. C. DAILY.

VOL. 4. FRIDAY, AUGUST 9, 1867. NO. 34.

Prescott, August 6. 1867.

My Dear Oneida Friends :—Phebe has informed me that you have accepted the renewal of my confession in the Circular, for which I heartily thank God. The very appearance of separation from your fellowship is agony to me. My heart is without a home in one sense, although I have done nothing but what I thought God would be pleased to have me do. I offer myself anew to him and to his service, willing to be to do or to suffer for him and the building up of his cause and kingdom in the world. May we not hope that he has in store great good for this people ? I believe it is so. I should love most dearly to be with you in your social gatherings and listen to the many voices that I heard when I visited you. That visit has been a very bright spot in the history of my life, for which I have always been very thankful.

Mr. Hinds has been a faithful, kind and true friend to me, and I take this opportunity to acknowledge God's kind care over me in this instance.

Mary A. Sibley.

A Disinfectant.—Is this coal tar that we are using in making side-walks, a disinfectant? If it is, that consideration would add materially to its value. One can readily become reconciled to a very disagreeable smell, provided the said smell is doing duty as a *sanitary committee* in keeping at *bay* numerous vagabond diseases which usually take advantage of the "high tide of the flesh," to float in upon society generally. Another idea in connection with coal tar, occurs to me, which may possibly be turned to good account, so here it is. Some people possess a decided fancy to perfume their persons with *musk* which is not probably, a *dis*infectant, while quite as *dis*agreeable to some, if not more so, than *coal tar*. If, therefore, the latter has the utilitarian advantage of protecting the public against common foes, then its character as a perfumer, would be readily tolerated, and a small quantity carried in the pocket would thus serve a double purpose. But seriously, the best and safest protection against disease of all kinds, the surest disinfectant and the very best perfume—the sweetest and purest—will be found in the simple compound, *belief and confession of Christ.* His spirit is the charmer of all charms, the perfume of all perfumery. c.

Willow-Place.—The letters that Mrs. H. A. Noyes wrote to Miss Maria Clark before Mrs. N.'s marriage, are being read in our noon meetings. They are very interesting and instructive, and form a most complete index of the workings of her mind when she first embraced the truths brought out by Mr. Noyes. She always regards Miss C. as her teacher, and often ex-

presses her willingness to receive advice from her.— Her characteristic faithfulness in little things appears on almost every page.—As a supplement to these letters, a criticism of Miss Clark given in 1850, and letters to her of the same date, from Mrs. Noyes and Mr. Cragin were read. The criticism was to the effect that legal obedience to her mother drew her away from following on to know the truth.

A good deal of thankfulness was expressed last night, by the family, for the good health that generally prevails, particularly among the children. It is the "high tide of the flesh," and God seems to be carrying us through this season of temptation safely.

Mr. Cragin spoke of the victory our young people have gained over the dress-spirit the past year; he thought that spirit was pretty well subdued—he had seen nothing in the family to criticise in reference to dress, this summer, or for some time past.

Strange Phenomenon—Walking-Shears.—We have heard of walking tables, but now our shears, for cutting tin, have absconded. If any one will return them, or give information where they may be found, they will confer a great favor on the

Tin-Workmen Co.

Fruit is rather scarce this season. We shall not be able to get near the quantity we want of some kinds for preserving. Raspberries have been a short crop. Plums are scarce and will come very high. Peaches will be a short crop in this state. Pears, and apples even, are a failure in this section. The grape crop, however, thus far promises to be abundant. H. T.

Mrs. N. A. Morse, of Lafayette, and a niece of hers, a Miss Cook of St. Louis Mo. came here just before dark last night. Miss C. is acquainted with Mrs. Leonard's brother, Josiah, who was desirous that she should visit the O. C. before her return West.

The weather is hot and sultry and the clouds continue to withold their precious contents. We hear there are plenteous showers all around us, but they pass us by with only an occasional sprinkling.

Our Dentists have taken in $20.00 for a set of teeth made for the wife of one of our workmen, and they are making another set for an outsider, valued at about the same.

I take this method of letting our agents know that all of the Red and Orange Raspberries put up this season, are ordered. I would refuse all orders for these fruits. E. S. B.

An asphaltum walk along the drive-way from the Tower to the north entrance to our grounds, was completed yesterday.

Charles Mills suddenly made his appearence at the O. C. this morning.

THE O. C. DAILY.

VOL. 4. SATURDAY, AUGUST 10, 1867. NO. 35.

Akron, Ohio, Aug. 7 1867.

Probably you have heard ere this that I am on the road talking *Bags* and *Traps* to old customers, and introducing them to new ones. I had a good visit at the Agency—got a little posted in silk matters and started.

I have been out long enough already, to be *homesick* if I would give place to such a temptation, but I know that God goes with me wherever I go, and wants me to be just where I am, so such temptations do not trouble me. But I feel that I am out at sea, and when in a few days I get to Morrow, Ohio, I hope to find some Daily Journals there, and if so I shall feel that I have *touched land* again.

You will recollect that I have for a number of years been very cautious about becoming *fanatical*. Unbelief has always been much pleased with my caution in that respect, but has taken advantage of it so as to keep my heart back and my intellect in the front. I have been thinking about this a good deal since the criticism given me, especially by Mr. Hatch, and I am fully determined that hereafter my heart shall have its proper influence in leading me.

Paul followed hard after Christ, and Mr. Noyes follows hard after Paul, and I feel safe in following hard after Mr. Noyes. Since I read the first volume of the *Witness* and saw what a *rock* Mr. Noyes was, when God had shown him the truth, my love for him and confidence in him have constantly increased. My ambition is to become like him a truly spiritually minded man, and so strong that he can, if he wishes, swing me around the globe and see me come back as true as the needle to the pole.

Unbelief has at times cautioned me against committing myself too strongly to Mr. Noyes, but finding its influence getting less and less over me, it finally wanted to know, a few days since, if I accepted the healing of Mrs. Hall, as a *miracle*, and I said yes, and that I fully accepted any and every thing that Mr. Noyes accepted in regard to the past, and was determined to accept every thing he may believe in future.

Unbelief then cautioned me against becoming *fanatical*, and asked what I should do if Mr. Noyes should by-and-by come to the conclusion that the moon was made of *green cheese*. It wanted to know quite triumphantly if I would accept his conclusion in that case. That puzzled me for a while, but finally God showed me the *point* and I said *yes, when Mr. Noyes* comes to *such* a conclusion I shall be quite ready to accept it. Unbelief stared at me a moment, and then retired discomfited, while I shouted in its ears *Hurrah* for Mr. Noyes, and I have not been troubled since.

Yours Truly.   H. R. PERRY.

WILLOW-PLACE.—The shop is now at full tide of business. Entering the Forge-shop, your path is obstructed by piles of springs in different stages of formation, and your ears are greeted with the clash of the presses, the rumble of the ponderous rollers, and roar of the fan.—The chain-makers seem to be doing their utmost, one gang of welders working ten and the other about fourteen hours per day. The Finishing-shop is also well manned. To-day witnessed the successful trial of a new method of making the cross-pieces. It consists in punching, cutting off and pointing them at one stroke: a process which before required three strokes, and 'till recently, four. To make a lot of 50,000 cross-pieces, required by the former method three weeks; they can be done by the new one in about one week.

The number of persons in the various departments stands thus:

		Hired		O. C.
Finishing Dept.,		25,		7.
Forge	"	"	15,	" 2.
Machine	"	"	2,	" 6.
Blacksmith	"	"	3,	" 1.
Chain	"	"	18,	" 2.
Silk	"	"	36,	" 4.
Total			63.	Total 22.

In addition to the above, we have a carpenter, and employ three hands in the Office, and also what we call irregular help.

A man who calls himself a hermit came here yesterday and took supper with the family. His real name however is B. T. Munn and he has written us once or twice not long ago. He lives in a little cabin he has built in the woods near Skeneateles, and spends his time in reading, writing and study—is a great admirer of Socrates—Jesus Christ and of nature.— He looks the picture of health, though rather awkward in his manners, owing doubtless to his seclusion from society.

Charles Mills reports, that as far as he knows, his father lives pleasantly with his new wife, but his neighbors do not like him at all. He is always in a quarrel with them, has had several lawsuits, in one of which he got beat, and appealed it. His wife is a religious woman and does not like his litigious tendencies. Charles wants to remain—thinks he is now ready to take a through ticket. He has written to Mr. Noyes, and will wait his decision.

It really rains this morning, and the prospect now is, that we shall have a showery day. We are thankful.

Mrs. Smith's father, Mr. King, came yesterday; also Mr. Bloom to make his long contemplated visit.

412½ doz. traps ordered for the week ending August 9th—to be delivered immediately.

H. W. B. arrived about midnight.

THE O. C. DAILY.

VOL. 4. MONDAY, AUGUST 12, 1867. NO. 38.

TRAP DISCOUNTS—TO AGENTS.

Our Trap-trade is growing continually, and now embraces a large list of customers from nearly all accessible parts of the North American continent.— These customers range from the single trapper to the great fur-company, from the small country retail store-keeper to the large city wholesaler. For reasons which I will not now give, we are obliged to vary our prices to these different classes; and the object of this preamble is, to introduce *a rule of discounts* to guide our agents in giving rates.

Our customers are divided into four classes. No. 1 —the *Wholesale dealer*. No. 2—the *jobber*, No. 3— the *Retailer*. No. 4—the *Trapper*. We give our largest discount, 15 per cent, to No. 1; 10 per cent, to No. 2, 5 per cent, to No. 3, and List to No. 4. To avoid confusion it is very important that these rates be as strictly followed as possible by our agents. Experience is proving that they give general satisfaction to our customers.—As it is difficult to make a rule that will apply justly in all cases, some room must be left for exceptions—as for instance, where very large retailers should receive jobber's rates, or when in order to introduce our traps, it might be expedient to offer an extra inducement for a limited time, &c. But generally these exceptions should be referred to the Home-council.—Many houses claiming to be whole-sale dealers, are properly classed as Jobbers—and agents should be wary in giving the No. 1 discount. Where the agent is not well posted as to the general trade, it is well to confer with the Home-council before doing so. It sometimes makes dealers better satisfied with the No. 1. discount to only offer them *Leah* first. They all want *Rachel*.   E. H. H.

BUSINESS MEETING.

Mr. Van Velzer desired to be relieved from the responsibility of the Shoe-shop. Mr. Woolworth and others sympathized with the change. It is a very important matter and needs a good deal of consideration, as whoever takes that place will necessarily have much to do with the family. Referred to Messrs. Van Velzer, Cragin, Campbell, Woolworth and Mrs. H. C. Noyes.

Mr. Kinsley reported that the old cottage was unfit to be moved. If any use can be made of it in its present location, it had better remain there.

Joel said that the blacksmiths could not do all the jobs that are brought to them, and keep up with the trap-tools. Mr. Kinsley proposed that those who could postpone their blacksmith work for a while, had better do so. Approved.

G. W. Hamilton reported that he had bought a mangle for $75.00.

As Mr. Aiken and Barron, both wish to be relieved from their Boarding-house responsibilities, it was voted that they continue to act till they nominate their successors.

Mrs. Arnold left this morning for Boston, where she will remain a few days, and then go to Maine, where she expects to spend a few months with her friends and relatives. The following note from her to the family, was read last night:

DEAR FRIENDS :—I have now been with you several days, and the longer I am here and the more I see of you, the more I feel the congeniality of spirit for which I have pined many long years. I have never made a public profession of religion ; I now desire to confess Christ as my Savior ; I confess my love to him to exceed by far my love for anything earthly. I think I can truly say " Thy will O God not mine be done." I have always waded through a sea of opposition, and expect to continue to do so.   M. S. A.

P. S.—I have been prompted several times since I have been here, to confess Christ in the meetings, but my large caution or Satan or perhaps the two combined, have been arguing "you had better wait ; perhaps you are not quite strong enough in the faith ; you might be sorry afterwards," &c. &c. I propose to defeat the combination of opposing forces, and confess Christ a living Savior in my heart.   M. S. A.

San Francisco, Cal., July 8, 1867.

Please foward to me a list of such publications and prices as your society has published on your peculiar doctrines and principles. I am interested to learn more of the working of that system, which I have long believed to be correct.

Am a respectable man, and write with good intentions.   Yours truly,   T. H. Rose, M. D.

J. J. Skinner gave us last night at 7 o'clock, a lecture, or description of his course of study the year past, and a programme of what his studies are to be the coming year. It made us feel that it was no *idle* thing to be a College student.

Mr. W. H. Perry has a niece, Mrs. Pert, and her son from Bergen, visiting here. She lives near neighbor to Mr. Herrick, and expressed her surprise to hear that Mr. H. was connected with the O. C.

The women in the Community have been busy enough for a few days past, in getting The Bloods ready for leaving. They expect to go to-night.

ERRATUM.—In Saturday's Daily third page instead of 63 for total of hired help, read 99. Quite a difference.

Mr. Carpenter leaves for home to-day.

THE O. C. DAILY.

VOL. 4. TUESDAY, AUGUST 13, 1867. NO. 37.

Col. Boeck of the Danish army, came here from Ilion Saturday night after meeting, and remained till Sunday evening. He was sent to America by the Danish government, for the purpose of making a contract for 30.000 Remington rifles, and he will stay at Ilion until they are all finished and inspected, and the last box shipped to Denmark, which will not be accomplished before the last of Jan. 1868.

He is fifty years of age, has been in the army thirty-seven years, and expects to remain there until he is sixty-five, when he will be allowed to retire and still to draw pay. He has a wife and five children in Copenhagen, and he has the privilege of going to see them occasionally, and remaining with them a short time. Once he staid at home fourteen months. This was his longest visit during the thiry-seven years that he has been in the army.

Parents in Denmark are obliged to send their children to school from their sixth to their sixteenth year inclusive, and they can not even take them to a foreign country until their education is completed.—Col. Boeck is a member of the Lutheran church, well educated, and a mild and affable man. U.

It is quite amusing to see how readily our children change, and how easily they make new plays. Harry K. came along yesterday flourishing a little whip, (a short stick with a string tied on), and says, "don't you want to take a ride over to Willow-Place?" "Certainly," we said, "but where is your team?" He conducted us to the settee. As we were about to take our seat, he discovered that in his absence to look up passengers, another company had taken possession of his carriage. After some debate with Harry B. who had present possession, as to the right of ownership, he walked off without seeming to be disturbed, whirling his whip, leaving his passengers to get to W. P. as best they could, and was soon seen riding horse-back on a broom-stick.

In our public meeting a few evenings since, some one confessed their thankfulness for the health of the children. We, of the department, feel that no part of the credit is due to us, but we can see distinctly that it is attributable to the Community spirit and that only. Our aim is to stand in a receptive attitude to the Community and infuse their spirit into the children. L.

Mr. Towner writes August 3, 1867:

"I am working as hard as I can to build up a business here, but I must confess to but little heart in it. I daily cry out 'who shall deliver me from the body of this death,' that is lurking everywhere in our selfish society? And the answer that comes to me is that Christ alone can give the victory. For this I pray, for this I hope. The 'Home-talk' in last CIRCULAR on 'Hard Times,' is keen as a dissectors knife. How can I, how can any one of us who live and move where this selfishness reigns, but feel condemned? I can not. Like Paul, 'I groan waiting for the adoption, to wit the redemption of my body.' But I trust the cheering promise that 'we shall be delivered from the bondage of corruption into the glorious liberty of the children of God.'

Yours Faithfully, J. W. TOWNER."

In meeting last night, a good deal was said in commendation of the Blood family. Mr. B. is a nice workman, is industrious and faithful in his business, very quiet and accommodating, and withdraws peaceably. Mrs. B. has proved herself a woman of faith, is public spirited and has been good help in the women's department of labor. The children have steadily improved, and we regret that the husband and father should be so unwise as to take his family out into the cold, selfish world again.

Mr. B. remarked to some one after meeting, that his commendation was wholly unexpected—that he took no credit to himself for faithfulness &c—that it was natural to him.

Not long since I overheard a stranger relate the following anecdote of Mr. Burt: "In the early days of Perfectionism when Mr. B. was full of enthusiasm, he was riding with a man, who by some means fell from his horse and hurt him severely. Mr. B. spoke up with considerable energy, 'thank God, thank God.' 'What' said the man, do you thank God for my fall?' 'I thank God it is no worse,' replied Mr. B." The person that related this circumstance, said he believed that was the true way, and if people would notice small events and thank God for special providences, they would be greatly blessed. He said he had a high opinion of Mr. B.—thought him a noble man. 's.

Our Brass Band has received two applications within a few days, one from Vienna and the other from Vernon, to attend their respective Fairs. The Community will decline the invitation, and think it a sufficient excuse that the Band has for some time past been out of practice.

Mrs. S. J. Clark and Charlotte Leonard are duly appointed to succeed Louisa T. Waters in her office of distributer of clothing among the women.

Last night about midnight, the O. C. went through the disagreeable operation of venesection, and quite a quantity of Blood was drawn off. The good effect upon the body remains to be seen.

THE O. C. DAILY.

VOL. 4. WEDNESDAY, AUGUST 14, 1867. NO. 38.

THE BOARDING PROBLEM AGAIN.

The greatest obstruction to the growth of our silk and bag manufacturing businesses is found to be in the boarding problem. We can obtain any number of operatives provided we could get them boarded within reasonable distances of our Mills and Shops. Shall we not be led, ultimately, to carry out the idea, vaguely entertained a few years since, of erecting a large commodious Hotel to be conducted by Community men and women, furnishing the tables precisely as we do those of our own? Establish rules and regulations of a civilizing character and then charge so much for board, or in other words sell the board thus provided, just as we would sell any other commodity, for so much per day or week to our own operatives first, and then, if there is room, to others. Have no mixing up of work and board, but say to our employees we will pay you for your services leaving you free to board yourselves wherever and however you please. Here is a Hotel where board can be had on certain conditions, &c. Let the business be conducted by itself just as we would conduct any other branch of enterprise, calculating on making a fair profit on the investment. We believe in carrying the Community spirit and enterprise into every department of legitimate business, and there is no one business probably that needs communizing more than that of public *homes*, as Hotels and boarding-houses may well be called, and notwithstanding the many criticisms brought against these public places of entertainment, they are constantly increasing and are becoming more and more a necessity.   c.

[To be continued.]

EVENING MEETING:—The remarks by Mr. Noyes about organization and co-operation among those connected with the press were read, and much appreciated by the meeting. Mr. Smith thought it no diotrephian spirit to believe that God caused the invention of the art of printing for the benefit of the Oneida Community, because he is using the Oneida Community to further his cause.

G. E. C. in:—We have two good illustrations of the power of the press in the *New York Herald* of this country and the *London Times* of England. The *Times*, especially, has more immediate control over the English nation than the Queen, the House of Lords or the House of Commons even. In fact the *Times* newspaper does not hesitate to criticise the Queen and give her advice. The *Herald*, in much the same way, is a tremendous power in this country. Then the part the paper performed in the Mills war gives a very good idea of the power of the press when well organized.

Mr. Woolworth:—I suppose Satan has tried to wield this power of the press and get it completely into his own hands. But I am sure it will be rescued in the end, and made to wholly serve the cause of truth, civilization and general enlightenment; and sooner or later it will undermine and overthrow Satan's kingdom. Thoroughly organize the press under the guidance of inspiration and it will be a tremendous engine for good.

TO THE COMMUNITY.—DEAR FRIENDS:—As I am about leaving you for a time, I feel that it is due to you and the cause of Christ that I express what I feel in my heart is the truth about you. I came here a stranger and you took me into your hearts and showed me more by example than precept, that the chief business of life was to seek the kingdom of God and his righteousness. I feel that I and my children have been made better and happier by a year's sojourn in the O. C. family. I have been strengthened and confirmed in my early religious aspirations, and have felt a new purpose to serve God and seek to do his will. I feel that I and my children have received nothing but the kindest attention from all, and on leaving I feel that we are taking leave of a family home where the love of Christ is the ruling influence. I think that in coming here I have learned more thoroughly than I could elsewhere, the true spiritual unity of Christ and believers. I go away with my heart strengthened to do whatever Christ has for me to do or suffer, and I shall joyfully return when it is his will for me to do so.—Thanking you all heartily for what you have done for me and my children, and confessing my love for and union with you all in Christ, I am your sister,

MARY L. BLOOD.

At the close of the noon meeting yesterday, music was called for, and E. P. Inslee on the cornet, C. Van violin, and Florence piano, were accompanied by four girls or young women in a schottisch dance on the stage, much to the delight of the audience, particularly the strangers who were present. It brought to mind the words of the Psalmist, "Praise God with the sound of a trumpet: praise him with the psaltery and harp: praise him with the timbrel and dance: praise him with stringed instruments and organs."

Mr. Nathaniel Randall, of Woodstock Vermont, a part of whose letter was published in the DAILY of Aug. 3d, with his wife and little son, came here yesterday. Mr. and Mrs. Vanvelzer were formerly acquainted with Mr. R. and considered him a very good man.

CORRECTION.—Toward the bottom of the third page in yesterday's DAILY, the last line of the piece relating to the Bloods, should read, " was *not* natural to him, but was due to God."

THE O. C. DAILY.

VOL. 4. THURSDAY, AUGUST 15, 1867. NO. 39.

THE BOARDING PROBLEM NO. 2.

Something has been said in favor of building a large number of tenant houses in order to accommodate small private families, which would, in the course of time, raise up scores of children to be made available at an early age in our businesses. This view of the case looks quite feasible and would, no doubt, work as well here as it does in the large Factory Villages of New England. But are we called to follow the old beaten paths of the world? I think not, but called rather to strike out into new paths demanded of us by the inspiration of heaven and seconded by a progressive civilization. Faith in science, and in Christ the soul of all science, will surely lead us to anticipate great changes in the social, as well as in the political economy of life; changes that will in a great degree, harmonize with the fundamental principles of Communism. Indeed, if we interrogate the spirit of the day of Pentecost, which has reappeared in Communism, we are enlightened at once as to the nature of the changes now impending. In all civilized nations, so called, the *watch-words* are *co-operation—combination* and *unity of interests.* Kings and Emperors would be glad to combine in order to protect their tottering thrones, but they are too selfish to do that. Their subjects, the common people, being less selfish can combine: hence their growing power.

In all our plans, the *future* must be regarded as *present.* Our greatest present want is more faith in the spirit of Communism. Let *her* be our adviser. As one who is forever patching up an old house will get no time to build a new one, so one who from the habit of unbelief hugs his old life, will never put on the new life of Christ. We believe in scientific propagation. Let us work for that. But if we build twenty tenant houses, we work for haphazard propagation for marriage and for selfish society. Let us not do evil that good may come. Our ideas on extension and growth must be organized so as to harmonize with our interior. [To be continued.]

Carthage, Jeff. Co., N. Y., Aug. 8., 1867.

DEAR MRS. THAYER:—I desire to express to you my love and unity with you, and with Christ. I am struggling along, keeping my eye on "The mark of the high calling of God in Christ Jesus." The inspiration of God is given me in proportion to my faith. Sometimes it seems as if the sun does not shine, but faith reveals bright rays and I revive in hope of more light, which comes to me in due time. I do not count my trials as great, only such as are common to those who seek full salvation from sin, I apprehend. I am striving to live Godly in Christ Jesus, and am perse

cuted in spirit by former attendants, who are artful and watch for opportunities to turn my attention and mind in old channels, and often bring doubts and questionings relative to the fellowship of Christ and his people. * * * * *

You are my teachers in Christ. But for your people I do not know that I should have ever believed in Christ. I believe Mr. Noyes has brought the Kingdom of God to this earth. The hatred and opposition of evil-unbelieving spirits to Mr. Noyes—the Community and your doctrines, which are the doctrines of Jesus Christ and of Paul, are to me a test of their truth. They teach that progression will set us all right; nay, we are all right now—the corn in the blade—the ripe, perfect seed will in due time appear.

Faith in Christ is the only means by which light has dawned upon my soul. The doctrines of spiritualism ensnared and deluded me, and I was deceived by their charming promises. But my soul never found rest in their falsehoods. When I was left quiet, and uninfluenced long enough to come into communion with my own spirit, I found myself crying for salvation from sin, I saw that I needed a Savior. The seducing charmers would say—come on—come on—there is rest, perfect rest ahead. I found that the farther I went the farther I was astray. I became conscious that I was lost. But when I sought Christ I found him a Savour from sin; a Redeemer. The Bible is a new book to me since I have received faith in Christ. What was before figurative, dark and uncertain in meaning, is now simple, easy and plain. Spiritualists do not know that they are followers of Satan. They do not believe in God, the devil or the Bible. I thought I believed in them, but I now know I did not, I was bades-haunted. Yours, CLARA WAIT.

WILLOW-PLACE.—We do not have much incident to narrate. Our time is taken up with our daily employment, our noon meetings and evening meetings, all of which we greatly enjoy. The spirit of organization is waxing stronger and stronger in every department of the shop and in the family.

The comers and goers are many, but their stay is short. Sometimes they come before supper and return to O. C. before meeting: sometimes they make us an hour's visit after meeting; and not unfrequently do they come and go before breakfast. The young men have fitted up the boat with keel, mast and sail, and with a stiff breeze and an oar for a rudder, it plows through the water at a marvelous rate.

Mr. Bradley has been out on a fruit-searching trip, and succeeded in getting thirty bushels of whortleberries paying $4.50 per bushel. He bought them about twenty miles west of Rouse's Point. Eleven bushels were sent up from New-York and reached us about 5 o'clock last night, and soon after a bee was called for to pick them over, as they needed immediate care. Seventeen bushels of those Mr. B. bought came in the night and the remainder we expect to-day.

THE O. C. DAILY.

VOL. 4.   FRIDAY, AUGUST 16, 1867.   NO. 40.

THE BOARDING PROBLEM NO. 3.

It is said that man, by nature, is a religious animal, and true to his instincts he builds meeting-houses. But christianity, the soul of civilization, civilizes the religious passion in man, leading him out of the letter of dead forms into the spirit and soul of true worship. Meeting-houses belong, not to christianity, but to Judaism. Christianity worships God in the living temple of the human soul, a temple which the Creator himself made for that very purpose. Christianity, therefore, would build *eating*-houses, rather than meeting-houses, as places of true worship. Christ, evidently, was more at home on festival occasions where eating and drinking were going on, than in the synagogues among self-righteous Pharisees. To save the body by purifying the passions and appetites, was just as much the mission of Christ as saving the soul. The two interests were combined. "Man shall not live by bread alone." His twofold nature requires two kinds of food; a mixed diet, visible and invisible. One is just as real as the other, and they should be taken together. Every meal a sacrament—the Lord's supper. Christianity will build Hotels rather than Churches, instituting daily meetings after dinner, and evening gatherings after supper. Landlords and stewards will supplant dyspeptic preachers, and like Stephen of old, will be full of inspiration and power. Communism combines the four great interests of humanity, physical, moral, intellectual and spiritual, regarding them all as public interests. So our buildings are public buildings for the common good of all. Community workshops are primary schools, the operatives are students preparing for the university. Hotels conducted by the Community spirit will be homes for students of both sexes. When Communism is rightly understood, the better class, lovers of improvement, will seek for admission to our workshops as the best place for laying an educational foundation.   c.

It may not be known, generally, that our people have for some time past, been using one of Mr. Barnes Davis's horses for his keeping, with the stipulation that the horse should not go to the depot only twice a day, and then not to be drove singly, as on some occasions he had been known to run, when used alone. Well, Mr. D. heard that we had violated the contract, and he came over in great wrath a few days ago, and talked pretty hard and swore some, though he said he waited after hearing it till he thought his anger had pretty well subsided.

Mr. Woolworth brought up the subject last night, and considerable criticism fell on Mr. Clark and G. R. Kellogg, who were the chief transgressors.—It was thought they would do well to go and see Mr. D., confess their fault and thus clear the Community as a whole, from any participation in the wrong.—General dissatisfaction was also expressed at our people taking a horse to keep in such a way. Mr. Woolworth offered to pay Mr. D. all the damage he required for the extra use of the horse, but he said it was not money he wanted he felt misused; and we felt so too.

Mr. Bloom sent in a note to the family last night from which we extract the following:

"For the kind greeting and hospitality extended to me, I thank you, one and all.—During my brief visit here, I have availed myself of this providential opportunity to get nearer to God. Hence I have spent much of my time in deep reflection, and lived mainly on the word of God, having little demand for bodily sustenance or outward action. I have earnestly desired that this visit might be fruitful to God, and that my spirit might be pleasing to the Community. Here really is my home; and at last, I believe I have reached home, home, dear, dearly loved home. And in bodily presence wherever I may be, still in spirit I will evermore be home.

"The great barrier that has in the past so constantly obstructed the attainment of my ideal, has been completely removed; for which I most heartily thank God. Time will heal all soreness and efface all unpleasant associations.—I confess my love for Mr. and Mrs. Noyes and the Community, and all the family of Christ in heaven and on earth."

While destroying worms this morning and reflecting on their ravages and ugliness, the pleasant and consoling prophecy of Joel came to mind. After telling of the great and good things which the Lord would do for the people and land, in the good time coming, he says in the 2nd. chapter 24th. verse: "And the floors shall be full of wheat and the fats shall overflow with wine and oil. And I will restore to you the years that the locust hath eaten, the cankerworm, and the caterpillar and the palmer-worm, my great army that I sent among you. And ye shall eat in plenty and be satisfied, and praise the name of the Lord your God." Then he goes on to tell of other great and glorious blessings that the faithful may attain, so that we may go on with good heart destroying evil and cultivating good.   A LISTENER.

Mr. Reynolds had some conversation the other day, with a man from Michigan about fruit. He said that peaches were very abundant in that State; he had forty acres of this delicious fruit which he had sold for $15,000, and only fifteen acres were in a good bearing condition, the remainder being young trees. He said our preserved fruits were considered the best in the country and were sought after in Michigan with the greatest avidity.

It rains gently and steadily this morning, much to our gratification.

THE O. C. DAILY.

VOL. 4. SATURDAY, AUGUST 17, 1867. NO. 41.

THREE HANDED CLOCKS.

While on a recent trip through the western part of the State, my curiositoy was excited by observing that many of the clocks in the Hotels, Stores, &c., where we stopped, had a *third* hand. At first sight this third pointer (which was similar in size, but different in appearance from the minute hand), seemed so utterly superfluous and out of place, that it reminded me of the old adage about " the cat with two tails;" but on inquiry I found the use of this third pointer was to show the difference between the mean solar, or true time, and the railroad time. This difference of time between the railroad and the sun, as you may say, becomes more and more marked as you proceed west. At Rochester it amounts to more than sixteen minutes. The *cause* of this discrepancy as I was informed is simply this: railroad time means N. Y. City time, and as Rochester, for example, is about 250 miles west from New-York, the difference between the relative time of the two cities must be considerable. Hence the employment of this third hand on the clock-face, to *point out* that difference.

v.

Our omnibus is a great convenience and luxury to us this hot weather. Besides being a protection against the rays of the sun, it is easy of entrance, and its neatly cushioned seats are very inviting to lovers of ease and comfort. It is driven over to W. P. many times, some days, loaded with persons who go to enjoy the pleasure of a bath in the pond. It is so capacious that a small room full of children can be loaded into it without inconvenience. It was driven over to W. P. two or three times last Sunday, carrying twenty adult persons each time.

What will satisfy the heart and give contentment is certainty—assurance. No one can be perfectly at rest while there remains a shadow of doubt in the mind about his present state in relation to Christ and the truth. If we are thankful for any one thing more than another, it is that the hankerings of our heart after truth have been satisfied, and Christ's words " Ye shall know the truth," been verified in our experience.

M. s. Blood writes that they all reached Mason village, N. H. safely; that very little was said on the way; that it was with difficulty she could repress her tears, when she thought of the home they were leaving—but after a night's rest, sue felt strong and courageous to meet whatever was before her. Henry writes that things look pretty small and weedy.

Total No. qts. of Raspberries picked this year,	4,942.	
No. picked by the Family,	1,129.	
" " " Hired Help,	3,813.	
" of Red ones,	1,648.	
" " Black "	3,296.	
" " White "	598.	
On one acre of second years bearing,	1,754.	
Amount paid for picking,	$140.74.	

D. E. S.

Mr. Bloom left for home yesterday. We felt that he was full of the Diotrephian spirit—full of self-complacency, and instead of being humbled and softened, by his past course, his trials seem to have exalted him in his own estimation. He thinks his experience may be the means of helping others, and he evidently feels qualified to teach.

We learned this morning, that Mr. Burbank, from Chicago, one of our fruit customers, with his wife, called here several days ago, spent the afternoon and took supper. Mr. B. has ordered this year, $4,100 net of our preserved fruit. They expressed themselves delighted with the appearance of things at the O. C.

A new coal-tar walk has been laid in front of the Store building, extending from the north end of the platform in front of the Shoe-shop, to the south end of that in front of the Office, thence across the road and connected with the walk built last year, between the New house and the highway in front.

The $10.00 that Mrs. Sherrard wrote that she sent some time ago reached us Tuesday. We have written her that we shall consider the remainder of the dept $10.00 discharged and she need give herself no further trouble about it.

Mr. and Mrs. Nash of New-York called here yesterday, and took dinner. Mr. N. is the proprietor of a large Restaurant in the City. They praised our dinner.

It still continues to rain and has with little interruption since yesterday morning. Our lawns in token of their gratitude for the favor are putting on their greenest and prettiest robes.

---

448 Doz. traps ordered for the week ending Aug. 16th—to be sent immediately.

THE O. C. DAILY.

VOL. 4. MONDAY, AUGUST 19, 1867. NO. 42.

BUSINESS MEETING.

Mr. Miller wanted to know if there was water enough to supply a trough by the road-side. It would be a great convenience to the public as well as ourselves. There is a long stretch of road here, without any watering-place. Messrs. Worden, Abbott, G. W. Hamilton and Mr. Miller are constituted a committee to investigate it.

Mr. Van Velzer reported that the committee appointed to consider the propriety of relieving him from the Shoe-shop, met, and concluded that the time had not come for so important a change. So the man who now helps him will remain, and relieve Mr. V. as much as possible.

Some complaint has been made of the clothing department—that our own men were not able to get the clothing made that they need. Several instances were related in which persons had been measured for coats, pantaloons, &c., and nothing had been done about making them. At the same time Mr. Porter has caught up with his measurements, and is making winter-clothing for the boys. Mr. Woolworth suggested that Mr. Aiken present that department for criticism this evening. This was approved.

[A very sincere and searching criticism of Mr. Aiken occupied pretty much the hour for meeting, last night. It will be reported.]

G. W. Hamilton remarked that the matter of heating dish-water, was still unsettled. He proposed that the water be heated at the Tontine and conveyed to the kitchen in pipes. A committee was appointed to meet this afternoon, viz., Messrs. Woolworth, G. W. Hamilton, Geo. E. and John Sears.

Charles Cragin said he wanted ten or twelve small girls now, and it is impossible to get them boarded near the Factory, and as Mr. Austin's engagement will soon expire, we shall need a double team to carry them back and forth. There are also twelve or thirteen boys who now walk to the Castle, but will not do so after cold weather commences. Mr. Wescott, who now owns a horse and wagon, and comes every day from the Depot, can do this work a great deal cheaper than we can, as it will make but little more work for him, and only one trip per day. He has expressed his willingness to try it, and wishes that the Community, at first, would furnish one horse and a wagon, but if the experiment proved satisfactory to both parties, he would prefer to own them. The committee, Messrs. Hamilton, Hawley, Campbell, Charles Cragin, Kinsley and Myron, meet this afternoon.

[The committee met as agreed, and report that admitting the fact that it is best to push the silk business steadily along, no better way than the one proposed of furnishing the needed help for the present, is discoverable. As to price, it was concluded to wait till to-morrow and hear what proposition Mr. W. will make, as he has agreed to be ready with his figures.]

We sat up late Saturday night, feasting our eyes on the beauty of the landscape as seen from our window, lighted as it was by the full moon, shining in clear and silvery brightness—not a cloud was to be seen. Between two and three o'clock A. M. we were roused from our slumbers by the heavy report of "heavens artillery," the bright flash of lightning, and the pouring of the rain. In the morning it was all fair again, but in the afternoon there was another thunder shower accompanied with wind, which blew furiously for a short time. It is pleasant again this morning. The weather seems to be getting out of the deep rut of dryness it has been in, during the summer, and is learning the good effects of change.

G. E. Cragin was called out of meeting Friday night, to go over to our boarding-house and see one of the girls there who had fallen down and seemed to be in a fit. It was supposed at first that what ailed her might be the effect of laudanum she had taken, and yet from her appearance, and also the small quantity administered, he thought that could hardly be the case. It finally came out that she had been frightened by one of the boarding girls who wrapped herself in a sheet and came suddenly into her room. George E. took the occasion to caution the family against venturing on any thing of the kind, as such sudden frights were sometimes attended with serious consequences.

WILLOW-PLACE.—The other evening Mr. Cragin nominated Mrs. Miller to read the Home-Talk entitled "Spiritual Justice" and then give the substance of it to the family. She did so and gave us a very complete digest of it, and said she would recommend it as a good exercise for all. Last evening Victor presented the talk on "Attention to the Truth."— This seems to be the inauguration of a series of lectures somewhat after the manner of the Theological class of last winter. Several volunteered Friday evening.

Mr. Cook from New-York, of the firm of Bertram and Cook, manufacturers of preserves, jellies,&c., was here Thursday and Friday of last week, and spent several hours each day. His wife came with him the first day. His business was to show Mr. Thacker about setting a new kettle we have been purchasing to increase the heat in preserving peas, corn, &c.

G. E. C. gave a very interesting lecture last night at 7 o'clock on "food." He dwelt particularly on the three essential ingredients that constitute a healthy diet, viz. sugar, starch and fat. We conclude the lecture will be reported.

Of the black and red varieties of cherries put up in glass we have but few that are not ordered. Our Agents will please take notice of this and take no orders for the above kinds.   E. S. B.

Mr. Olds leaves to-day for a trip to the far West.

THE O. C. DAILY.

VOL. 4. TUESDAY, AUGUST 20, 1867. NO. 43.

Hart Lot, Aug. 16, 1867.

DEAR BROTHER:—I arrived home Tuesday, fatigued and soiled. I was glad to get home, but I was sorry to leave you. My thoughts are continually of you and yours. It seems as though my life was misspent in the avocations of the world, and yet I think it necessary for me to school myself thoroughly in the principles of the Oneida Community, before I shall be prepared to enter the association—and to become a member of it is my hope and wish. All I have to regret is that I have lived so long without the sanctuary of perfect holiness. I regret that I have countenanced so long a system of selfishness and pride, wholly at variance with my heart. Please be charitable to my infirmities; for they are those of our nature and can be overcome only by the severest discipline. I have been accustomed to think on principles, though not directly at variance, yet not entirely in accordance with yours. The fault is not so much lack of love, as of information. The information I did not seek because I knew not where to look. I was willing to accept of it come from what source it might; but I thought I was alone in the world; all around me looked dark and gloomy. My relatives and friends have long since deserted me, leaving me to struggle alone against the conservatism of the world. Now my heart is rejoiced, joy and gladness reign where but a short time ago sat darkness and despair. * * * * *

I hope to look for that guidance and instruction from the fraternity which my inexperience requires. I hope the love which I feel toward you is reciprocal, without it I should be most miserable; especially after I had flattered myself with the hope; this, I think, you cannot fail to grant. The only evil with which I have to combat is selfishness; and this I have heretofore rather encouraged, than restrained. Teach me how I may overcome it. I look to you as a brother, hoping you will point out my errors, and endeavor to restrain that selfishness which is the root of all worldly war. * * B. T. MUNN.

DEAR FRIENDS:—The generous spirit that has been manifested toward me, in being willing to sacrifice so much to afford me relief from the constant confinement of the Shoe-shop, has touched my heart, and I felt like praying that I might take the course that would best please God. In all my reflections on the subject, I would be thrown into perplexities and darkness, until I turned my thoughts upon Mr. Radford as the person to relieve me. Then light began to break in and I can now see clearly my way to be absent from the Shoe-shop a part of the time, and have the business go along regularly with-

out the perplexity of introducing an entire stranger, and the additional expense of $15.00 per week; two things I confess that have been a trouble to me when thinking of the subject. Now all that remains to be done to afford me relief, is the contemplated alteration of the shop. [Taking down the partition between the two rooms.] As soon as that is done, and we get fairly settled, I can be at liberty to be absent from the shop, if need be, half the time. I have made arrangements with Mr. Radford to run the shop whenever I wish to be away. The things I think I need most, are a soft heart, fresh air and exercise.

I have to labor under bodily and spiritual infirmities, but I believe the Community spirit will enable me to do what is set before me. The deepest feeling of my heart is that there is deliverance ahead for me, and the good time is coming, coming right along.

L. VAN VELZER.

WILLOW-PLACE.—J. F. Sears and Victor have put up two force-pumps for the Trap-shop. One returns the salt water which flows down from the tempering vats, to a tank placed near the creek, thus keeping the water cool enough to harden the springs. The other one pumps water to a barrel in the finishing-room, from which it is carried in pipes to the welding furnaces to cool their tongs. Both are of course run by machinery.

Beulah takes her turn at W. P. this week.

A young man by the name of Joseph Cadman of Cambridge Vt. wrote to the O. C. sometime last Spring requesting us to send him some of our pamphlets and pictures, and expressing a wish to join. He seemed honest, though very ignorant, and after writing the second time the correspondence dropped. About two weeks since, he came on with the urgent request, that if we could not receive him as a member he might at least work in some of our shops—said he would work for nothing, &c. Mr. Macoy was acquainted with, and spoke well of him. Not being able to get board in the neighborhood of W. P. we concluded to board him and try him for a time. He takes his breakfast and supper here, his dinner at W. P. and lodges in one of the rooms of the old tool-house.

After reading Mr. Noyes's talk last night, on "Picnics," some amusing stories of personal experience in pic-nic-ing were related, which caused a good deal of merriment. Thankfulness was expressed that we had got by the pairing off season, which had formerly been the bane of such social gatherings, and a fruitful source of evil-thinking. Some testified to having had pleasant times the present season, in attending picnic parties, which they attributed to the absence of the exclusive, pairing off element.

Maj. Geo. A. Cantine, of Buffalo, a correspondent of the *Springfield Republican*, called here yesterday, and seemed much pleased. He was at the noon meeting, and was seen taking notes and also took some statistics from Mr. Underwood. So we suppose we shall be "written up" once more.

Mrs. Howard, Harriet's mother, of Belchertown, came here last night after meeting.

THE O. C. DAILY.

VOL. 4. WEDNESDAY, AUGUST 21, 1867. NO. 44.

EXTRACTS FROM LETTERS.

FROM H. A. WARNE.—"It has been gratifying to me to see how much more liberal and kindly the tone of the press is growing in its portraiture of Community life. Feeling very kindly disposed myself, I desire to have all see as I do the purity of motive actuating the Community. And certainly there is much about your social life, with its unselfish Community of goods, its spirit of brotherhood, its love of beautiful surroundings, eagerness for culture in every direction and its earnest religious spirit, to attract the attention of all who hope for the 'good time coming.'

"It is not in vain, I think, that philosophers have dreamed of Utopia and the New Atlantis, and the oppressed have believed in a better time coming when the spirit of selfishness should be broken and the poor and the landless should be seen no more. I thank God there is to be an end of the old things, and all things shall become new."

Miss Munson writes that she is having trouble at the Cure, in consequence of Dr. Jackson having heard that she was promulgating the O. C.'s doctrines. She is entrusted with the care of a girl who has fits, or she says she would leave there at once. She says in her letter:

"Last Tuesday evening, I went out to make a call. Dr. Jackson sent three men all over the Cure for me, as if life or death depended upon my being found. I returned about half past eight, he said it was too late to see me then, but I was summoned to his office at half past five in the morning. He seemed to be in a rage, and told me, he had it from good authority that I had been proselyting and spreading the Oneida views through the Cure. He said he had just got rid of one woman for promulgating Spiritualism, and now he would get rid of me. I told him I had not been proselyting, for I did not believe in it, but I never had refused to lend the CIRCULAR to any one who wished to read it. I told him the world was wide, and I had lived in it once, and presumed there was room for me now. He said when I came here, I had not a place to lay my head, nor a dress to my back. I told him I had plenty of places where I should receive less persecution than I was receiving at his hands, and I never wanted for a dress yet.

"I said I supposed he had no objections to my stopping until I could make arrangements to go. He said he had, if I could not mind my own business, and keep my tongue still; he also said if I would not promise him that I would not mention the Oneida Community while I was on his grounds, I could pack up my trunk that morning and go to the Bruister house or the Cobbler's, the latter a low Dutch family.

"He said if I was a Communist I had better go there and live with them, said he had been damned with their heresy long enough and he would not stand it any longer. He told me more than a dozen times, in the course of the conversation, that I had no sense; he said if I had had, I never would have taken the CIRCULAR, and if I had known anything, I should have kept it out of sight. He says, 'don't you know as soon as it is known that you believe in that doctrine, they think you will sleep with the first man that comes along?'

"Mrs. York one of the best physicians here, has been giving private lectures to the ladies; she advised them all, to buy your tract, on 'Male Continence.' I was asked to send for a dozen and did so. I do not know whether the Dr. knows it or not, he said nothing to me about it, so I think he does not.—I pray that my religion, may never keep me shaking in my boots, as his does."

NOTES OF SPECIMENS SENT BY C. S. J. TO S. E. J.— 1st. Nightshade, from Lausane; 2nd. Alpine violet, from the top of the Col de Trient, 5000 or 6000 feet high; 3d. Alpine Rhododendron, from the top of the Col de Balme, 7000 feet high, by the side of a snowbank. This flower only grows on the highest peaks; 4th. A flower picked half way up the Auguille, a mountain by the side of Mount Blanc, 12,500 feet high; 5th. Alpine rose, from the foot of the *Glacier de Tour;* 6th. Alpine pink, from the foot of the Glacier D Argentiere; 7th. Specimen of Mount Blanc mosquito or gnat; 8th. Alpine sorrel, from the valley of Valocine; 9th. Shamrock, from the Valley Gos Perrou; 10th. Moss, from Le Tete Noir; 11th. Fern, from the valley of Trient; 12th. Fig-leaf, from the Castle of Chillon. The tree from which this was picked, grows on the narrow wall about a foot wide, between the castle wall and the Lake—South side. 13th. Ivy, from the Castle Chillon; 14th. Fern, from Vevay Switzerland; 15th. Oak, from Vevay; 16th. Willow, from the junction of the Rhone and Arne, below Geneva; 17th. Legume, from the ruined Castle of St. Germain, valley of the Rhone; 18th. From Lyons; Mediterranean Cypress, from the cemetery of Marseilles; 19th. Oleander, from the shores of the Mediterranean; 20th. African Cypress and blossom, from Marseilles; 21st. Creeper, from Dijon.

George E. said last night that he saw Mr. Kellogg playing croquet and he thought it did him good. He felt it would do all our elderly folks good to play every day, and he hoped they would do so.

Clifton M. Nichols, Editor of the *Daily Republic,* Springfield, Ohio, called here yesterday. He too intends to write something about the O. C. for his paper.

THE O. C. DAILY.

VOL. 4. THURSDAY, AUGUST 22, 1867. NO. 45.

Mason Village, Aug. 19.

DEAR MRS. T.—I thought I would try and write a little to you this morning. We are stopping with Mr. Blood's cousin, a Mrs. Whitaker, a sister of the one that I told you about. They live in her house, and we are using her rooms. I shall commence keeping house to-morrow, in a small way, using Miss Robbin's things as she is not at home. I shall like it better as I can live more simple and the children will not be tempted to eat and drink what is not best for them.

Mr. Blood proposes to start to-morrow in search of employment. He has labored very hard to convince me of the error of my ways, but he either does not use the right kind of argument, or I am very hard to be convinced, for he has not succeeded, but, on the contrary, I am stronger in the faith than ever. I am sure if you had heard him talk to me, you would not have thought him a *silent man* by any means. I assure you I had all that I could bear, for the first three days after coming here. But I find by casting out self and turning to Christ, and taking this as a necessary discipline, I can be calm and at times joyful. One day, I believe it was Saturday, I got away down where it was dark, and a feeling of discouragement began to come over me. I began to say to myself, it is too bad that I am brought here to suffer, away from those that love me and can help me to grow better.—Well, I was getting into a dismal way when I chanced to see the file of CIRCULARS that M. J. gave me, which I had not had time to look at. I took it up and opened it, and my eyes fell on these words written with a pencil. "Courage, courage, courage, God will give us the desire of our heart, if we have faith in him. Sophia." It was just what I needed. It carried me in spirit back to those dear sisters, who were so much more than natural sisters to me, and I had a joyful time. The tears flowed freely, but they were tears of joy and peace, and I have felt stronger and less inclined to yield to temptation in that respect since. The children, all but Mary, express their desire to go back to Oneida. Their father, after having talked to me, asked them, H., I. and E. if they wanted to go back and leave him. They told him they would like to have him go too, but they would go alone, if he would let them. They are very good children and give me lots of comfort. Eddie came to me the other day and says: "Mother, I think if I confess Christ in my heart every day, perhaps he will help us to go back." And Ida says: "God knows what is best for us and he will bring it all out right." So God comforts me through my children.

In seeing how things are here, I feel a strong desire to have Henry go back to you. * * M. L. BLOOD.

O. C., AUG. 20.—We finished the wall and turfing of the Creek bank above the bridge near the boarding-house yesterday; and to-day have finished grading, and commenced walling the bend in the Creek east of the cow barn. We also tried our new kettle with the calcium bath, putting through the process twenty-one cans of peas; cooking them forty-five minutes. We found no difficulty in raising the heat to two hundred and forty with less than twenty pounds of steam. In fact before we were aware of it, the temperature went up to two hundred and fifty-five, caused by the rapid evaporation, and we were obliged to add water freely in order to keep the temperature down to the proper standard of two hundred and forty degrees Fahrenheit. H. T.

Miss S. Augusta Story writes from Benton Co., Mo. " By prayer and meditation and patient waiting, I find Christ my blessed Savior, but I did not know this until I confessed him my *whole* Savior. Doubt and unbelief was the devil's stronghold in me, but they fled away, when Christ came in power to root them out. I believe, through faith in Christ, I have won the victory and though troubles and trials are around me, I can bear them all for Christ's sake."

NOTICE TO AGENTS.—Our whortleberries have cost us more than it was calculated they would at the time we made our estimates. You will therefore understand the price for this fruit, as given in the current price-list, is for whortleberries without sugar. Those put up with sugar should be 75cts per doz., in advance of those without. We have but few with sugar, and those we have can be easily disposed of.—E.

Mr. Guiteau writes that his wife is now on a visit East, and will be gone till the middle of Sept. He does not know whether she will visit Oneida, as he said nothing to her about it, wishing to leave her free to do as she chose. He says, " my son Charles is at Chicago, and I shall look for him here the last of the present week."

G. W. Hamilton exhorts the family to be enthusiastic in helping all they can at the Trap-shop. About a dozen of the boys who work there, are offered higher wages for picking hops, and will leave next week for that purpose.—For the last five days our trap-orers have averaged 117 doz. per day.

The double tenement house at the foundry, is completed and one family have moved into it; also the small house at W. P. that has been " under treatment" is finished, and Mr. Christian is moving in.

We have engaged a woman (on trial) to take L. A. Thayer's place in running the sewing-machine. She commences to-day.

Mr. Reuben Holmes and his wife, whose present residence is in Ohio, came here yesterday and staid over night.

THE O. C. DAILY.

VOL. 4.　FRIDAY, AUGUST 23, 1867.　NO. 46.

Newburyport, Aug., 18, 1867.

DEAR FRIENDS OF ONEIDA:—Though I have not arrived at the point from which I promised to write, I do not find myself inclined to wait longer. I may as well talk to you on paper, for I find myself either speaking with you in my mind, or of you to my friends, nearly all the time. I am sure my spirit has been with you ever since I left you. I sometimes ask, what meaneth this great light that seems to illumine my whole soul—what this sunshine in my heart? I need not ask, I know. I hope you have not missed any sunshine since I left, for I seem to have brought away a great deal, but as your fountain is a never failing one, I *know* there is no want of it in that dear, dear home; it is seen on every countenance, it is felt in the very atmosphere you breathe. I only wish I was one of you, and if I do not become so it will be because you won't have me; it is as I told you I feared, you have spoiled me to live any where else.

I do not think I can go South again to live, if I do, it will be only to wilt and die; the climate is too debilitating for me now. I have borne it while younger, I cannot bear it at this age, and I do not wish to try. I will write to my husband and children to-day, **tell them about my visit to you, tell them** how I feel about it, and get their minds on the subject. Mine seems to be made up, and I have not yet found an inclination to change. I have seen many railroad tickets since leaving you, but none of them said anything of that route you were speaking of while I was with you. When you have discovered where the company is that issues them, (and it is my opinion you will find it not far from home), I propose to apply for a through ticket. I believe I am willing to pay the price, and what is unusual on other routes, I should have no objection to work my passage besides. Much love to the family.　M. S. ARNOLD.

P. S. What I desire to know particularly, is the minds of the family in regard to my fitness to be among them. Will they please talk to me, and ask me questions or find me out in any way possible to satisfy themselves in regard to me. Outside affairs can be arranged afterwards.　M. S. A.

* * *

Rockford, Ill, Aug. 19, 1867.

J. H. NOYES ESQ. DEAR SIR:—For more than a year I have been a reader of the CIRCULAR. At first curiosity prompted me to read it, then interest. Although once, in my ignorance, I heartily despised the Community, I now fully believe yours is the only true mode of life.—I realize now what a slave I have been to early education and prejudice; that selfishness has deformed my whole life and dwarfed all its enjoyments. What shackles have I unwittingly worn, and how my soul reaches out for help, for counsel, for relief.—Now, therefore, I take the liberty of writing you; hoping you will pardon me if I have taken too great a liberty.—I want your advice and sympathy, as the isolation I feel is very oppressive—I am suffocated by feelings long pent up.

I read in the CIRCULAR that those who wish to join the Community must secure confidence by deeds. What must I do to secure your confidence? *I* would join you, that I might learn the way of life.

I am a childless widow of twenty-eight years. Previous to my marriage I followed teaching, and am now engaged in that business.—Hoping to hear from you at your earliest convenience,

I am, most respectfully,　MAGGIE SATTERLEE.

* * *

The fruit department was brought forward for criticism last night, by the request of Mr. Thacker. A communication from him to the family, stating just how matters were going, and what proportion of the peas and fruit were spoiling, preceded the criticism. The whole will doubtless be reported. Some talk followed about the proposal made long ago, by Mr. Noyes, of converting the big barn into a Fruit-house. Mr. Cragin thought it was time that some action was taken on the subject.

* * *

A party of ten, from Clinton, were here yesterday, and took dinner. Among them were two of the College Professors, and a Methodist minister and his wife, Mr. and Mrs. Hard. They gave us some very good vocal music in the Hall, and one young lady played the Harmonium. Opposite to where they registered their names was written, " A very fine dinner."

* * *

WILLOW-PLACE.—Our agents need not solicit orders for No. 1¼ traps that will have to be supplied before Oct. 1st. Those we have on hand and have stock for are ordered, and we shall not be able to get malleable stock in time to get another lot much before October the first.　G. W. H.

* * *

Leo Miller, one of the big guns of Spiritualism and a popular lecturer on the subject, in this region, called here yesterday. He seemed quite interested, and sympathizes with our views fully on some points.

* * *

In the postscript of a note from C. S. J. dated " Falcon Hotel, Stratford on Avon, Aug. 10," he says, " This letter is written in the room where Shakspeare used to come and smoke his pipe and drink his beer."

* * *

Young Cadman attends the evening meetings, and confesses Christ with the family, with how much sincerity we are unable to say.

THE O. C. DAILY.

VOL. 4. SATURDAY, AUGUST 24, 1867. NO. 47.

[We make the following extract from a letter received from S. C. Burnham, Mrs. Hatch's brother, of Springfield, who visited us recently.]

" We shall ever remember our visit among you with great pleasure. It is a grand triumph to have such a control of business, giving such a variety of employment to all, and putting the Community on a self-sustaining basis. Your social system, too, so far as we can see it while on a visit, seems to work to a charm. There is surely harmony and good feeling everywhere apparent, and an entire absence of discord and strife. Every one seems to be busy and industrious, and yet no one is overworked, or employed in that which is not agreeable to their wishes or health. And your warm affection for each other seems unbounded, so that your Community home has so many attractions, that you have no occasion to seek outside of it for pleasure. I see, also, the work of self-denial among you. It is a strange sight to see so many men together and no tobacco ; so many women that are not following the fashions of the world, and trying to outstrip each other in elegant and costly dress. There seems to be an absence of selfishness, and a way of living for the good of each other which are very endearing to me. I have seen it exhibited to that extent nowhere else,

" I called on Mrs. Horace Burt, Saturday evening, and talked with her about three quarters of an hour. I told her all about our visit, explaining to her, as I was able, the religious views held by the Community, speaking to her of the various employments in which you are engaged, and the beautiful harmony and kind affection exhibited in every department, by all the members of the large family. I found her exceedingly guarded in her conversation. I talked with such emphasis, and eulogized so warmly the various workings of the Community, that, had a third person been in the room, they might have thought I was trying to bring her over to the faith of her husband. But I could get no response from her. She paid strict attention to what I had to say, and seemed very much interested, but was very careful how she replied. She made some inquiries about dress, the keeping of the Sabbath and prayer. She thinks a longer dress would be more appropriate, especially on the elderly ladies, that the Sabbath should be set apart as a day of rest and holy meditation, and that vocal prayer and the reading of Scriptures should be a prominent exercise in your religious meetings. There are others here who say, " *I join in that.*" I told her the Community would be happy to have her pay them a visit ; she would be very kindly received and enjoy it much. She thanked me for calling, and telling her about our visit, but said nothing to indicate her desire to visit the Community."

The little girls of Carrie Bolles and Marion Burnham's age have been piecing a bed-quilt under the supervision of Miss Pomeroy, and it was put on to the quilting-frames yesterday. A company was invited by the young misses to a quilting in the afternoon, and a supper party followed in which the girls acted a conspicious part, giving us a very pretty song after we were seated at the table. The whole quilting and supper were quite an enjoyable affair. We understand there is another quilt nearly completed made by the same group which is the third one in all that these busy little fingers have made, and some of them are very good quilters, and used their needles quite dextrously on the quilt yesterday.

Our morning-glories are now in all their *glory*, and make a fine show, particularly the row Mr. Ellis planted, which occupies the same place it did last year, west of the Mansion-house. It is curious to watch them as night approaches, cautiously rolling up their leaves and withdrawing from the outward world as much as possible, toward the interior for a nights repose ; and then they rise so early in the morning and adjust themselves, that no one is able to see them in their night-dress.

J. P. Hutchins will be glad to learn that the pipes for conveying hot water from the Tontine to the kitchen are being put down, so that the noise of heating dish-water that has been so annoying to the family particularly at meal time will be heard no more.

Some of the family are exceedingly annoyed and made uncomfortable, by persons keeping their rocking-chairs in motion during our noon-meetings. We know it is thoughtlessness that causes them to do so, and feel that a "hint to the wise" will suffice to correct the evil."

The Horticulturists have received a very nice and acceptable present, from W. A. Hunter of Berlin Heights, of a half dozen grape-pickers, or shears, which are very convenient for picking grapes and thinning the clusters.

Mr. Ford, Anne Eliza VanVelzer's uncle and his wife, came here yesterday, spent the night and left this morning ; also two of Mrs. Perry's nieces.

Mr. Kinsley reports that the last load of the 100,000 brick that were engaged last spring was drawn yesterday.

Mrs. Reeve from Berlin Heights, who has for a long time talked of coming to visit the O. C. arrived yesterday.

Mr Thacker leaves to-day, for Baltimore via New-York. He goes to oversee the putting up of peaches,

THE O. C. DAILY.

VOL. 4.   MONDAY, AUGUST 26, 1867.   NO. 48.

BUSINESS MEETING.

Frederic Marks said that in muddy weather the omnibus is too heavy for two horses, and it is unsafe for the driver to manage four horses on account of the narrow seat and low foot-board. Messrs. Kinsley, D. Kelly, J. Hawley and Frederick Marks, are to see what is necessary to do to it and have it done soon.

Mr. Thacker suggested, before he went away, that the milk be kept at home, for the purpose of making what butter we can. Messrs. A. Kinsley, Barron, Kellogg, Mrs. A. Burnham and Mrs. Kinsley committee.

Mr. Campbell brought up for consideration by the Board, the subject of having a horse at W. P. Messrs. Campbell, Kinsley, Hawley and Woolworth committee.

A larger press for the Trap-shop is needed for punching springs by the new method. By the old method some experienced man is required to roll and head the springs, and more time and labor is expended than by punching them. The present press is an old one and liable at any time to fail us. Besides, a heavier press would do the work with less wear and injury to the dies and punches. There seems to be no reason why we may not with such a press, punch out larger springs than the number one. The cost of it would be between $500 and $1,000. The question seemed to resolve itself into one of finance, so Messrs. Campbell and G. W. Hamilton were appointed committee to consult with the financial committee.

[The following remarks were made by Mr. Cragin in meeting last night :]

" We have abandoned all worldly institutions for the sake of being God's little children. It is not a mere sentiment, or abstract theory, but an absolute fact, that we have taken God for our father and Christ for our mother ; and for that reason we have given up marriage and every other form of selfishness, that we may all be one under the guidance of the inspiration of resurrection life. We are not setting up business for ourselves as some great persons, but are simply following Mr. Noyes in taking God for our father. What good there is in us, and whatever good we have done, should be counted the result of God's spirit working in us. We are being educated by him into fit mediums through which he can work and diffuse his spirit and power into the world. I confess the childlike spirit that trusts God as a father in regard to all that he does.

Now, for instance, we have a boarding-house that is causing us considerable perplexity. We have got to find some person to take it off our hands or devise some other course. We have a good many boarders there that we employ in our business, and they must be provided for in some way. I believe in looking to God for wisdom about the matter. I don't believe we are carrying on any business that God is not interested in ; and if I thought we had a business that he did not favor and inspire, I should wish to abandon it at once.

Two of our girls, Beulah and E. H. Mallory went into the pond at W. P. yesterday morning, for bathing, and while E. who is a good swimmer swam out into the pond, B. not knowing how to swim remained within the enclosure where the water was scarcely up to her neck. In attempting to float lying on her back, or rather in trying to extricate herself from that position her head went under the water. Elizabeth saw her struggling, but did not immediately apprehend what the matter was—thought she was sporting, &c, but soon comprehending her danger she came to her rescue. This circumstance led to some talk last night about the girls going into the water, their over anxiety to learn to swim, and criticism of the spirit of daring and risk that some of them had shown. It was thought this hint was timely, and more caution will be observed in future.

We heard a person relate an incident that happened to himself many years ago. He was a pretty good swimmer and never afraid of venturing into deep water. One day he and another man were swimming near the shore of a river, when he was suddenly taken with cramping and could not help himself in the least. He sunk to the bottom of the river and was rescued from drowning by the timely assistance of his companion. This experience he said, had made him cautious ever after, of going into the water alone, and also gave him anxiety for others.

G. E. C. gave us a lecture at 7 o'clock last night on " Digestion," or the manner in which our food and drink are disposed of, after being taken into the stomach. It was quite instructive and edifying. We also had a German dialogue spoken on the stage, after meeting, by J. J. Skinner and James Van which was quite amusing, as most of the family could not understand one word of it.

An earnest call to the family last night from Mr. Campbell and G. W. H. for all the help that could possibly be furnished in the Trap-shop the coming week, as the work there is very urgent.

M. L. Worden and Mr. Whitney started yesterday morning in pursuit of blackberries and have not yet returned.

Our barley is nearly all harvested, and threshing it commenced Saturday.

Trap-orders for the week ending Saturday Aug. 24.   1,814½ doz.

THE O. C. DAILY.

VOL. 4. TUESDAY, AUGUST 27, 1867. NO. 49.

Williamstown, Ky.

ONEIDA COMMUNITY:—Having heard frequently of your people, I have become anxious to gain some knowledge of the theoretical basis on which your Community is founded. Please forward to me a CIR-CULAR and if there are any publications which might be useful, mention the prices and how you wish re-mittance. I have for a long time been searching after truth and comparative mental composure on earth. If what little I have heard about you be true, in connection with what I perused in a work by Dixon (of England) entitled "New America," I would visit you in the Spring or next Summer with a view of uniting with you.

Hoping to hear from you soon I have the honor to be your obedient servant, WILLIAM B. BABINGTON.

Another letter from Kentucky, from J. J. Smith, of Bardstown, was received Saturday. He says, "I am desirous of learning on what conditions a person is admitted into your Society. I am generally consid-ered a useful man, am a native of England and thirty-six years of age."

Some may be interested to know of the articles transported daily by the express wagon to Willow-Place, the Foundry and the Boarding-house. The fol-lowing constitute all the articles taken over during the day (Monday) and will serve as a specimen:

Persons; bed-cord; cradle; keg of butter; ten pounds do; pail of lard; plow point; twenty-five pounds of Indian meal; two lots of eggs; a feather-bed; five pillows; two coverlids and two pillow-cases; three bushels of apples; one of potatoes; a firkin of miscellaneous articles; a firkin of sugar; box of su-gar; a basket of ice; four loaves of bread; three long bars; a barrel, box and basket of green corn; oil-can; ten miscellaneous articles; mail-bag; three letters; two straw beds; *black-mail*; a package of hard ware; eight miscellaneous articles; a box, and lastly, a load of iron to the Foundry and back with castings. z.

WILLOW-PLACE.—Mr. G. W. Hamilton went to Syracuse yesterday, to see on what terms Mr. Wescott's brother, (a machinist,) will work for us. His terms are $3.00 per day and a permanent job. He promised to come to-day or to-morrow to see the place and the work. He has worked longer at the trade than Mr. W. and we hope he will be as valuable a man. We are paying him $3.00 a day, but would rather pay him $3.50 than have him leave us.

The bathing-yard was put in repair yesterday.

Miss Harriet Mathews and Alice Nash, are with us this week.

G. W. Hamilton started for New-York in the night.

PASSING AWAY.

Some things there are, that are passing away
From the true heart that is seeking for truth;
Depths of tradition and bigotry's sway,
Fears that have tortured our manhood and youth.

Long cherished habits are passing, yea passed,
Habits that held us in bondage to pelf,
And the new habit forever will last,
Of love to our neighbor as well as ourself.

Sorrow and trial are passing away,
Anguish of heart we shall soon no more know,
These are the things that must fade and decay,
E'en death, our most potent, invincible foe.

A lighted kerosene lamp was accidentally dropped on the floor and broken last night, in the room over the store. The flame was instantly communicated to the oil, and the room for a moment seemed all ablaze. It was soon extinguished, however, by throwing a piece of canvass, which was near at hand, over the ignited contents of the lamp. No damage was done to the floor.

M. L. W. & Co. have sent us ninety quarts of blackberries, which are being converted into jam to-day. Sixty-five quarts of pears were preserved in bottles yesterday.

A daughter of the Mr. Holmes who was here last week, and her husband, from Hamilton, staid here last night. We understand they have come for the purpose of negotiating with our folks about taking our boarding-house.

A minister from Schenectady was among our call-ers yesterday; also a Mr. Prime of New-York, pub-lisher of the *Herald* of *Health*.

ERRATUM.—A mistake occurred in yesterday's DAILY. For "trap-orders" read traps ordered.

The CIRCULARS came bright and early and spark-ling with life this morning.

THE O. C. DAILY.

VOL. 4. WEDNESDAY, AUGUST 28, 1867. NO. 50.

Athenæum Office,
20 Wellington Street Strand W. C.,
Aug 13, 1867.

DEAR SIR:—Your brother, who left me a few days since will give you any news of me you will wish to hear—you and the Community.

Lord and Lady Amberly will pay you a visit at Oneida in three or four weeks with a letter of introduction from me. Would thank you to send from January last, copy of the CIRCULAR to Lady Dorothy Nevill, Dangstein, Petersfield(?) England, for which I enclose a dollar.

With my best wishes to all my old friends at Oneida, Yours very truly, W. HEPWORTH DIXON.

Mr. Woolworth remarked last night: "Those who provide refreshments for company experience some pressure and embarrassment, as there is more or less feeling in the Community that this department does not pay ; and in consequence there is more or less of a grudging spirit about providing stores for the department. It is, perhaps, an open question, whether we better go on with this department or consider it closed for the season. But at all events, let us have no half way work about it. If the Community think we have done enough and now better suspend, we will be ready to close it; but while we continue the business I hope we shall be thorough and hearty in it.

I don't quite like this talk about its paying, which takes a merely financial view of the subject. I suppose we should have thrown it up long ago if we had looked merely to the question of dollars and cents ; but it has not been conducted on that principle. In Mr. Noyes's view of the matter the financial question has been secondary. This talk about the profit of the business does not sound quite right to me. I should rather consider it in other lights, although that has some bearing of course. [Mr. Woolworth's remarks were heartily approved.]

Miss Maria Barron then testified that the department was profitable financially considered, and stated in proof of this assertion that $1700 has been received for entertainment this summer.

SPECIMENS FROM C. S. J.—1st. Acacia, from Brussels ; 2nd. Poppy, and other flowers from the battlefield of Waterloo ; 3d. Clover, from "Belgic Lion," field of Waterloo ; 4th. Beech, from the forest of Soignies—Ardennes as Byron calls it ; 5th. Quack, from the citadel of Antwerp ; 6th. English golden-rod, from Shakspeare's cliff, Dover ; 7th. Flemish Acacia and Lime, from Boruges, near the "Belfry ;" 8th. Laurel, from the Battle Abbey, Sussex ; 9th. Oak, from a Battlefield of Hastings ; 10th. Ivy, from the Castle of Hastings ; 11th. Grass, from Ashford in Kent ; 12th. Foxglove, from Canterbury in England ; 13th. Honeysuckle, from the Cathedral of Canterbury ; 14th. Harebell, from the Inner Temple, London ; 15th. Hop Clover, from Magdalene College, Oxford ; 16th Broom, from "Addison's Walk," on the banks of the Clearwell, at Oxford ; 17th. Box, from All Soul's College, Oxford ; 18th. Daisy, from Baliol College, Oxford, picked near the spot where Cranmer, Latimer and Ridley were burnt ; 19th. Ivy, picked on the wall of the old Church at Stratford, on Avon, where Shakspeare was buried, about ten feet from his grave ; 20th. Yew, from the banks of the Avon, at Stratford ; 21st. Rose-leaf, from the garden of the house where Shakspeare was born, close by the back door.

Mr. Worden and Whitney returned yesterday noon. They report that they engaged 300 quarts of blackberries at McConnelsville at one shilling per quart to be sent by R. R. They then went seven miles into the woods and obtained 215 quarts at eight cents per quart. They wrote last night to have two more crates, 120 quarts, sent in order to supply the family with some fresh ones for present use. The berries are better than last year, very nice and come in good shape. We are to have them for dinner to-day.

The kitchen group furnished the family last night with a rich treat of ice-cream and crackers, which were passed round in the Hall just before the close of meeting. We had quite a merry time—a sacrament some called it. The rattling of dishes and the liveliness of the scene in passing them round, reminded us of old parlor times, when similar events were of frequent occurrence.

We had a lively bee after supper last night, for clearing up and setting in order the grounds south of the Mansion-house, or between the house and the croquet grounds. Another bee is called for to-night to complete the job.

Young Cadman got homesick, and left for Vermont this morning. We offered to employ him in the shop if he could get board but we could not board him here any longer. We paid him $12.00 for his services.

We finished threshing barley yesterday.

H. W. Burnham came yesterday afternoon.

THE O. C. DAILY.

VOL. 4. THURSDAY, AUGUST 29, 1867. NO. 51.

Baltimore, Aug. 26.

DEAR MRS. J.:—I left New-York last evening at half past seven o'clock for this place, in company with H. G. Allen. At about twelve o'clock and when three or four miles this side of Philadelphia, the sleeping car in which we were snugly ensconced, made two or three violent jerks and then came to a sudden stop. I said to H. " The cars are off the track." At the same moment I heard some one outside cry out : "For God sake stop that train, they will run into us." On pulling on my boots and going out, I saw a train close behind us, but it had nearly stopped its headway. I then passed forward and found the second car ahead of us, off the track and partly capsized, and the next ahead of that, standing at nearly a right angle across the track, with the forward end plunged into the bank on the left hand side. The trucks and all the under gearing were swept clean from under the two conches, and lay scattered about in much confusion. Fortunately, and what seemed miraculous was, that but one man was seriously hurt. We thanked the good Providence, that things were no worse, and went back to bed, leaving the work of reconstruction to those to whom it belonged ; and spent the remainder of the night quite comfortably. The accident delayed our arrival here some three or four hours. H. T.

"Our Home," Dansville, N. Y., Aug. 26, 1867

DEAR FRIENDS:—I made you one visit last June, made very pleasant through your cordial welcome ; and yet not all I had anticipated, in that I hoped to introduce to you a lady friend of mine, who has long been wishing to see you at home. I think I wrote something of her in my note which came while I was there. She is a teacher of high rank in the " Packer Collegiate Inst.," of Brooklyn, a member H. W. Beecher's church, but very much interested recently, in your writings through the CIRCULAR ; and was very greatly disappointed in not being able to make the intended call.

I write to know if it will be convenient for us to call on our way back to Brooklyn, on the 7th prox—(Saturday), spend the Sabbath, leaving Monday morning. I am not yet entirely sure that the visit can be made even now ; but what I wish to know is, whether the time and occasion of the visit will be acceptable to you.   *   *   *

I am yours very truly, ALBERT J. LEFFINGWELL.

I would like in a public manner to confess my separation from the spirit of Mr. Hazelton and Wright. My acquaintance with them was brief, yet nevertheless, I might have taken on a spirit which deserves expulsion, and I will here say for the satisfaction of the family, that whatever heretofore may have been my tendencies toward spiritualism, I never entertained the least sympathy for infidelity, for from my early youth I have most sacredly reverenced God and Jesus Christ his son. I am well aware that in my search for truth, I took on much that was error, and though long cherished and religiously believed in, it has since been dispelled by the hearty acceptance of a more inspiring and purifying faith in the doctrine of salvation from sin as promulgated by Mr. Noyes. I desire to be subordinate to him and the Church.   S. UNDERWOOD.

Mrs. Mary E. Tillotson writes from Vineland, and wishes us to take her son, a lad of fourteen years, into our family with the object of making a Communist of him. She offers to pay us $75.00 a year for the first three years, when she thinks he can well pay his way, and when of age, if he chooses to remain, as he is an only child, she will make a will in his favor or in favor of the Community.

She says : " My boy has some knowledge and appreciation of your ways, and has to-day been scanning the picture of W. P., reading about the bear-catching and getting interested in the trap-works."

A Mr. William Pinkham from Fond Du Lac Wis, came here yesterday and spent the night. He is brother of the Pinkham spoken of in the CIRCULAR of June 10th and is on his way to New-York, and from thence he is bound for California, where he expects to establish a Community under the guidance of Washington and Franklin, he says. We believe he is under the particular direction of his brother in this move.

A Mr. Rogers and his wife from Walpole Mass. came here yesterday afternoon, and inquired if they could stay three or four days. Miss Chloe replied, that perhaps they could stay over night. They have been from home four weeks visiting at Vineland and Hammondton, N. J. Mrs. R. is a feeble woman, and they are journeying for the benefit of her health. They know little about the O. C. having seen only a few Nos. of the CIRCULAR.

THE O. C. DAILY.

VOL. 4.   FRIDAY, AUGUST 30, 1867.   NO. 52.

Baltimore, Aug. 27.

Weather fine, but rather warm. There are several steamboats and sloops in this morning with peaches. Prices too high to purchase as yet, ranging from one twenty-five, to two fifty per crate. Several other boats will be in this afternoon, when we shall expect lower rates. Melons are more plentiful here than apples are at the north. Yesterday there were fifteen or twenty vessels lying in a compact body at the wharf, all loaded with melons. The crews, which are composed of negroes were having a fine time I judged. While the masters seemed to be making sales for their cargoes, nearly every negro's face was completely buried in a huge water-melon; and the waters in the dock were literally covered with melon rinds. This is rather an old fogy City. Quite a marked contrast between this, and our northern Cities in many respects. The trucking is chiefly done by negroes and I could but notice the clumsy looking carts and truck-wagons, as compared with those at the north. The big teams from the country are mainly composed of six heavy mules, with a huge clumsy looking wagon, and a negro driver seated on one of the hindmost animals, with a short black whip in one hand, and a single line in the other, extending to the near leader horse. Thus equipped the driver, by the crack of his short whip and an occasional twitch of a single line, makes his way through the crowd of vehicles, with as much ease seemingly, as the man with a single horse and cart.

Truly yours,   H. T.

It is very clear to me that for two or three weeks, the devil has tried to hinder my testimony, by producing confusion of thought and utterance; but let obstructions be what they may, I cannot afford to concede this point to him. I know that he who owns me and cares for me, is stronger than he who is against me. I will yield myself to him to be guided and controlled by his spirit. I confess *that* faith and softness of heart which will make me a partaker of his resurrection. I earnestly desire to bear fruit unto God—to have my whole attention so fixed on him and interior truth, that the devil can find no loose thread in my life by which he can influence or distress me.

H. A. HALL.

Mrs. Reeve left for home last night at ten o'clock. Mr. Kelley went at the same time, and will accompany her as far as Buffalo. Those best acquainted with Mrs. R. liked her very well. She seems honestly seeking for truth, and desirous to wipe out by repentance and confession, the stain that may attach to her in consequence of her connection with the free-love movement at Berlin. She is a woman of a good mind, and seems to comprehend our fundamental doctrines, which she has studied carefully for the last year and a half. She appears to have no doubts about the Community or Mr. Noyes' position as an inspired leader.—Perhaps it is not generally known that she is a sister of Mr. Towner.

To THE FAMILY:—I have been here now nearly one week, and am unable to discover in myself any opposition to anything, and not only that but it is what I have asked for and through grace have come to *love* with all my heart. I would tender my sincere thanks to one and all, for the kindness I have received at your hands. Whatever may have been discovered in my character that is objectionable, by any one, I will thankfully receive a knowledge of, either in public or private as you may think proper. That I may become one with you and one with Christ, is the earnest prayer of a sincere heart.   MARTHA S. REEVE.

WILLOW-PLACE, Aug. 28.—The silk-business is constantly growing and demanding more room. C. A. C. finds that by moving the machines nearer together, he can put four more in the room he now occupies. We had quite an enthusiastic bee after work-hours yesterday, and moved the machines on one side, making room for two cleaners.—Mrs. Higgins came on a visit yesterday and remained over night.—The talks on self-limitation, and God in the interior of things, were read in our evening meeting. They were appreciated by the family.

J. S. F.

A rather comic song [Old Simon the Seller,] was sung by H. W. B. at the close of the noon meeting yesterday. When called on to sing, Mr. B. consented, saying at the same time that the song he proposed to sing was not a very pious one. Several strangers were present, some of whom were overheard to say, that " the close of the exercises were not much like the beginning, but the song was admirably executed."

OUTDOOR ITEMS.—Several hired men are building a stone-wall on the bank of the Creek east of the large barn, to keep the water from wearing the bank.

The pear trees east of the road have mostly been taken up; they were either dead or dying.—The first clusters of grapes, [Hartford Prolific], were picked to-day.

A Mr. Greaves who was a law-student with C. S. J. in New-York last winter, called here yesterday and inquired for him.

Mr. Morse from Cayuga spent the night here.

THE O. C. DAILY.

VOL. 4. SATURDAY, AUGUST 31, 1867. NO. 53.

We called in to the Shoe-shop yesterday and found it greatly improved by the changes recently made. The partition is removed that separated the two rooms and also the ceiling taken down between the shop and the bed-room Mr. Van has occupied, and shelves put up on which boots and shoes are nicely arranged. The northeast window is also closed up, and the shelves extend clear through the back side of the room. The hired men work in the west part of the front end, with a screen about ten feet long and five and a half high, which partially shuts them off from the main room, while at the same time they are able to see persons who step in for work when Mr. Van is out. Another advantage of the present arrangement is, that it is thought one stove will suffice for warming the whole room. Mr. Van is much pleased and the family generally with the alterations.

The weather is really very cool for the season and a fire does not come amiss. We sat for an hour at an open fire-place at W. P. yesterday and enjoyed it much. It brought fresh to our mind "Auld lang sine," childhood's days, a circle of brothers and sisters and the paternal roof. We trembled some last night lest Jack Frost should steal over our grounds while we slept. We thought particularly of our vineyards and the fine hanging clusters, and went to sleep with a prayer in our heart that God would protect his own property from the ravages of the destroyer. It is some warmer this morning.

[Song by Rev. J. S. Taylor, with very slight alterations by E. H. Hamilton. Taken from the DIADEM, a small collection of tunes and hymns for Sunday Schools.]

1 Dare to be right! dare to be true!
We have a work that no other can do;
Do it so bravely, so kindly, so well,
Angels will hasten the story to tell.

Cho. Then dare to be right! dare to be true!
We have a work that no other can do;
Dare to be right! dare to be true!
We have a work that no other can do.

2 Dare to be right! dare to be true!
Other men's failures can never save you,
Stand by your conscience, your honor, your faith;
Stand like a hero and battle for truth.
Cho. Then dare to be right! &c.

3 Dare to be right! dare to be true!
Love may deny us its sunshine and dew,
Let the dew fail, for then showers shall be given;
Dew is from earth, but the showers are from heav'n. Cho. Then dare to be right! &c.

4 Dare to be right! dare to be true!
God, who created us, cares for us too;
Treasures the tears that his striving ones shed,
Counts and protects every hair of our head.
Cho. Then dare to be right! &c.

5 Dare to be right! dare to be true!
Cannot Omnipotence carry us through?
City, and mansion, and throne all in sight,
Can we not dare to be true and be right?
Cho. Then dare to be right! &c.

6 Dare to be right! dare to be true!
Keep the great judgment seat always in view;
Look at your work as you'll look at it then,
Scanned by Jehovah, and angels, and men.
Cho. Then dare to be right! &c.

7 Dare to be right! dare to be true!
Prayerfully, lovingly, firmly pursue
The pathway by saints and by seraphim trod,
The railway that leads to the City of God.

Cho. Then dare to be right! dare to be true!
O. C. must carry this railroad clear through.
Then dare to be right! dare to be true!
O. C. must carry this railroad clear through.

A long letter was received from Thomas North yesterday. Mrs. Arnold who is an intimate friend of Mr. N., it seems has written to him intimating that he does not stand in the best relations with the O. C. He expresses himself quite surprised at this, and goes over in his letter his past history in connection with us and the criticism Mr. Burt gave him, the spirit of which he says he heartily accepted at the time, and is still thankful for.

The woman that came to take L. A. Thayer's place in sewing on the machine staid only four days. One cause of her leaving was her weak eyes, and another reason which made us willing she should go was that her work was far from satisfactory.

Mr. Barron and Mrs. Hatch went to Hamilton, Thursday, to see Mr. Ingols, the man who talks of renting our Boarding-house. Mr. I. will be here to-morrow and if he concludes to take the place we will report further and state the conditions.

The trade at the Store averages now about fifty dollars per day.

Mrs. Howard left in the night. The family felt quite near to her.

THE O. C. DAILY.

VOL. 4. MONDAY, SEPTEMBER 2, 1867. NO. 54.

BUSINESS MEETING.

The roof of the Bag-shop needs some repairing. The carpenters have been expecting to shingle it, and it was thought they might be reminded of it. Also the cistern of the Bag-shop has long needed repairs. This and the roof were referred to the carpenters.

Mr. Kellogg reported for the committee chosen to decide whether the milk should be kept at home for making butter, that Mrs. Kinsley kept the milk one day, weighed it and made it into butter. It was found that the average worth of the butter was equal to that of cheese. Whether we continue to make butter is left with the above committee to decide.

Mr. Barron reported the result of his conversation with Mr. Ingols. Mr. I. will be here this afternoon to close the bargain. He will pay ten per cent on the property which is valued at about $23,000. He wants a shed built for two carriages, and stable room for two cows and a horse, also a place for hogs enough to take the refuse from the kitchen and table. Mr. I. has great confidence in the Community, and it was hoped that the building committee, to whom with Mr. Barron the matter is referred, would be prompt in getting everything ready for him.

BALTIMORE, AUG. 27.—I will report that 186 crates of peaches have been purchased for us this morning, at an average price of $1.85 per crate, and that nearly two hundred busy hands are engaged in the work of packing them. The shippers are playing the mischief with the packers in this market. There being such a demand for peaches in sections where there are none raised this season, shippers have the advantage of the packers, as they can afford to pay higher prices, and thus secure the peaches, or compel them to pay the same rates. Consequently they will not be as low as was anticipated. Peaches come into this market in three grades, viz., extra, prime, and those called common, or scalawags. Of course the packers can't touch the extras, and there is a lively competition between the packers and shippers for those called prime; and the Arab's take the rest. (The name Arab is given to designate a class of packers, that put up all the miserable stuff that is found in the markets). The first class of peaches here, are truly very fine, and a lot turned out of the boxes is a sight worth looking at, and as the saying goes, "would be beneficial to sore eyes;" large, red-cheeked melting peaches, that are not only pleasing to the eye, but touch the palate in a sense most exquisite, &c. Then just think of such peaches served up in ice-cream for the the dessert, at dinner. But enough said or I fear I shall make your mouths water. I am told that there are sixty packing houses in this City, and probably the smallest firms pack double the quantity of fruit, &c. that we do.   Yours very truly,   H. T.

BALTIMORE AUG. 28.—The Baltimore and Ohio railroad passes through one of the principal streets of this city. But the locomotive is not allowed to pass except at certain hours of the night. Consequently the cars are drawn through each way by horse power. Five powerful horses are hitched to a coach and driven tandem without the aid of a line, but guided and urged forward wholly by the crack of the whip, which may be heard at almost all hours of the day and night. On the arrival of a train, a courier starts off on the track on horseback, giving notice by loudly blowing his horn, that a train is coming; presently you hear the sharp crack of the driver's whip, standing on the platform of the car, and also blowing a horn, which is the signal to clear the track. Thus one by one the cars are passed to and fro through the City. At the time the road was chartered, it was thought a fine thing to have a railroad pass through the City, but now that its population has grown to the number of three hundred thousand, and the principal streets become densely crowded, it is considered a great nuisance, and notwithstanding the precaution taken, accidents frequently happen, and more or less lives are lost annually.—I guess you would think we eat some peaches if you should step into our room at the Maltby House and see the pile lying on the carpet before us. H. G. A. has had several hearty laughs at me for getting up in the night to eat them. You would not think it strange if you should once get a taste of such delicious fruit.

Thursday morning, Aug. 29.—We have just made another purchase of peaches of 116 boxes, at $1.50 per box. We shall probably buy fifty or seventy-five more, and that will finish our job. They will all be packed to-day. I shall leave for New-York in about an hour, leaving H. G. A. to see the job completed.
          Yours truly,   H. T.

G. E. Cragin gave a third lecture last night, which was a continuation of the subject of Digestion. He showed us by diagrams on the blackboard, the position of the nerves that connect with the stomach and lungs, and gave us the scientific cause of the loss of appetite on suddenly hearing bad news or being frightened, &c.

It was reported last night that all the trap-orders on hand will be filled to-day. Work has been put through at the Trap-shop the last week or two, with more then railroad speed, and with great enthusiasm.

We had quite a spirited talk last night, and criticism of the hurried way the work in the dining-room is done, waiting on tables &c. We shall expect a speedy reform.

Mr. Bradley reports that he has secured 100 bushels of the egg plum at $4.50 per bushel, and starts this morning to look up more.

We commence packing tomatoes to-day.—Old Mrs. Olmstead was buried yesterday.

Mr. Thacker returned Saturday afternoon.

Traps ordered since Aug. 24th.   1,898½ doz.

THE O. C. DAILY.

VOL. 4. TUESDAY, SEPTEMBER 3, 1867. NO. 55.

The negro population of Baltimore must be quite large, I judge. They perform most of the hard labor, especially the loading and unloading of vessels.— They seem cheerful, and work lively, and as far as I observed, are well treated, and they in turn are polite, and will not run against you in carrying their load, though their way may be ever so much obstructed, but give timely warning to get out of the way, by calling out, " Look out sah !" and then give you time to step aside. They handle the crates of peaches with considerable skill, and with much greater care than we should expect from white laborers at the north.

I was surprised at the lack of business along this railroad between Baltimore and Philadelphia. The stations on the road are unimportant, merely places to take on, and put off a few passengers, and they are few and far between. The country most of the way looks well, and some parts are truly fine, and the broad Delaware flowing through it, adds very much to its beauty. It appears that navigators of these waters are subject to disasters, as well as mariners on the broad ocean. In passing, I saw a schooner sunk, with her masts sticking out of the water, and the sails still hanging to her booms. She may have been caught in the storm last night, or perhaps collision with another vessel, sent her to the bottom.

NEW-YORK, AUG. 29.—Arrived here at half past five this evening and can hardly realize that within the short space of seven and a half hours I have passed through portions of five of the States of the union.

H. T.

A letter from Mrs. Bronson, Derby, Conn, aunt to E. G. H. says that Mrs. Bristol and her daughter who visited the Community a few weeks since, have both been greatly benefitted by their visit. Mrs. Bristol lost a daughter two years ago, (twin sister of the one who was here,) in consequence of which she has at times been partially insane. She is now joyous and happy, and thinks her visit here will do her good for years to come. She also has a son who believes in the Community.

Mrs. Blood writes that they are to move into a house about half a mile from the Village, on a cross road not traveled much. She says Mr. B. has been looking for a place to work about a fortnight, and has at length succeeded in getting employment in a tin-shop in Milford, Mass., about eighty miles from Mason Village She says she has strong hope that Henry will be back here in a few weeks. She thinks Mr. B. has about as much as he can attend to, and don't get much comfort from his family either.

WILLOW-PLACE :—Mr. Wescott brought up his first load of little girls this morning. Fourteen little Anns, Maggies and Janes, averaging about eleven years of age. Their first day's work was done " as well as could be expected," and at night when seated in the wagon, they looked as happy as larks in the prospect of having a nice ride home. This accession increases the number of hands in the Silk-room to forty-eight.

Mrs. Lynde was sincerely criticised Saturday night. She has been in a hard, disobedient and fanatical state for some time past, and the family have had long patience with her. Last night she seemed quite softened and confessed that she had been under a hard diabolical spirit—that she had clung to her outside friends, which had separated her from the family entirely, and made her disobedient.

The contract between the O. C. and Mr. Ingols, was completed yesterday, and the papers signed last night after meeting, and It will take effect between the fifteenth and twenty-second of this month. The agreement extends to the first of April next, but if either of the parties wish to dissolve the contract before that time, they can do so by giving the other thirty day's notice. The property is valued at about $2,800 instead of $28,000 (a mistake of the compositor) as reported yesterday.

ERRATUM.—In the item on filling trap-orders in yesterday's DAILY, an omission occurred in the first sentence, which makes the meaning rather obscure. It should have read thus; " It was reported last night, that all the traps ordered, that were to be shipped by the first of Sept. &c."

Report says that D. J. B. swam across the W. P. pond and back, a few days since, a distance of over 200 yards. This is thought to be quite a feat performed without the aid of feet.

The dining-room was taken in hand yesterday, and nicely white-washed by one of the girls, or rather a young woman. So much for a beginning of reform there.

Four hundred and thirty-five cans of tomatoes were packed yesterday. We shall commence putting up corn to-day.

The farmers sold their barley 794 bushels for $1.26 per bushel which amounts to just $1,000.44.

Bags made in August,	74¼ doz.
" ordered in "	71¼ "
" sales, " "	$3,105.36.

THE O. C. DAILY.

VOL. 4.   WEDNESDAY, SEPT. 4, 1867.   NO. 56.

EVENING MEETING.

The reading of late discourses from Wallingford and New-York lasted till five minutes to nine, and was frequently interrupted by hearty applause. The ideas contained in "Self-Limitation in Business," were especially appreciated. Sympathy was expressed for what was said about Mr. North and Mr. Freeman. John Freeman was very thankful for what Mr. Noyes said about that letter. Mr. Woolworth then observed: "We have a good deal of matter before us to think about and digest. I don't know but you would call this cramming, wouldn't you George E. ?"

George E. —It might be considered in that light.

Mr. Woolworth :—How do you like what is said of the fruit-preserving business, Mr. Thacker ?

[Mr. Thacker liked it. Mr. Kellogg was especially thankful for what was said about getting into debt. Many others heartily joined with him.]

Mr. Hatch :—I like the suggestion about the "Noah's ark" very much indeed. [Warm approval, and laughter.]

C. A. Macknet :—I should like to respond to Mr. Noyes's call to the women, and desire to take hold and work with a strong heart and hand.

Mr. Woolworth :—I should like to have John Freeman consider what is due from him to his father, considered in the light of truth and righteousness, and render it, even if it should call him back there.

[Approved.]

Mr. Hatch :—I like what was said about Mrs. Noyes and Carrie. [I do, I do, I do, &c.]

WILLOW-PLACE SEPT. 3.—After meeting we occasionally have an impromptu party or concert.— Last evening candy of different kinds, cake and parched corn were placed on the tables and all were invited to help themselves. Then Beulah sang "Fine Clams," and Mr. Campbell gave us the nasal twang and drawl as sung by the original clam-sellers. "Old Dog Tray" followed and "Nelly Bly," the song "A Thousand Years," and "Johnnie Comes Marching Home again" were sung in full chorus.

The packers announce that they have packed all the traps ordered to this date.—C. C. H. and Milford have struck their tent (which has for some time been pitched on the lawn in front of the house) and repaired to the house, not on account of the cold, but because the tent was becoming mildewed.

SEPT. 4th.—G. W. Hamilton arrived last night. He reports that on account of the condition of our finances, the large press will not be built this season.

Thirty-one men worked last night from half past six to half past nine. It is expected they will do so for the rest of the week.   J. R. F.

We were a good deal interested and affected by Mr. Noys's talk on self-limitation and continence in reference to expenditure, and we had a desire that the women might take hold of this matter of finance, and show by deeds that they can save and economize, if they cannot be producers. We for one are willing while our large debts remain uncanceled, to help in the only way we are able, and that is in curtailing as much as is possible the expense of clothing, and to look around and see if we cannot manage to get along mostly, with what we now have for six months to come. We ought to realize that what articles of clothing we get at the Store is as really money paid out as though we went to the Depot to make the purchase. Will the old and the young think of this subject seriously—see where they can curtail expense, and thus help our financiers in paying our debts.

The hop-pickers are as thick as hops these days, loads of them passing daily, and many stopping at O. C. A company of them, sixteen in number, called Sunday, among whom were Emma and Mary Jones's sister and their brother's wife. In getting luncheon for her sisters, Emma found herself involved in the necessity, she thought, of furnishing lunch to the whole company gratis. She thinks she shall not get caught so again.

The bag-bees, that have been suspended during the pressure of business in fruit-preserving, commence again to-day. They will be held as formerly, in the upper Sitting-room between ten and eleven o'clock A. M.

J. J. Skinner and H. M. Hutchins leave us to-day noon, the former to resume his collegiate course at Yale, and the latter for New-York.

We were greatly rejoiced and thankful, yesterday noon, to hear of the safe arrival on Monday, of our trans-Atlantic brothers.

Machine twist manufactured at the Silk Factory,		
W. P. in August,	201¼ lbs.	$3,689.50.
Sent to O. C. Agency,	243½ "	$3,882.37½.
Miscellaneous Sales	30 "	$ 460.13.

Traps ordered yesterday,	637 doz.

THE O. C. DAILY.

VOL. 4.   THURSDAY, SEPT. 5, 1867.   NO. 57.

Berlin Heights, O. Sept. 1, 1867.

DEAR MRS. J.:—I wish to send the outgoing of my heart O. C. ward. I cannot be too thankful, for the good that Mrs. R. brings from you all. I feel much benefited by what she has learned: shall endeavor to appropriate it to the best advantage. I know that Christ will succeed with me, for he assures me of it every day. My heart says, almost unceasingly, that Christ is there and I am safe. I *do* love Christ, for he has befriended me; he has come to me, and saved me, where devils are as thick as grasshoppers in Kansas; and I believe, if he so desired he could continue to save me here in spite of all the diotrephians, and other devils that abide in this place. Yet I very much doubt if he desires us to stay in this continual warfare for any great length of time. I must give Mr. Noyes's writings credit for being the medium, at least in a great degree, through which Christ has been enabled to come to my heart. To-day I read the cure of Mrs. Harriet A. Hall in the book of confessions that Mrs. R. brought, and so far from having a doubt, as to the truthfulness of it, I could not restrain the tears that came as my heart recognized the great goodness and devotion to God's will of Mr. Noyes and Mrs. Cragin. How many things I find in the volume of CIRCULARS of 1851, that start the tears, and fill my heart all full, and make me know, *yes* make me *know* that your God is my God, and my God your God.

I am very thankful for all the suggestions that were made to Mrs. R. and I feel assured that we shall profit by them. I have never found it so easy to stand up for any unpopular thing, as for the truths that come from Mr. Noyes and the O. C. The help of Christ makes many things easy that once were difficult. * * * * * *

With this you have my most sincere blessings,

G. W. REEVE.

Mrs. Reeve writes that she arrived home safely, and feels much strengthened by her visit, and by her confession made while here, that Christ was in her heart and had saved her from all sin.

Mr. Noyes's talk read last night, on the boarding-house question, will give the O. C. a chance to turn a short corner once more. A man is dispatched to Hamilton to day, to notify Mr. Ingols that we wish to have the contract made with him a few days ago, dissolved. He will doubtless think we are a strange and fickle people, but perhaps Mr. Barron who is the man deputized to notify Mr. I. of our change of policy, will explain the matter to his satisfaction. The business men, particularly the boarding-house committee, feel greatly relieved at the contemplated change and all the family, so far as we know, enter into the plan heartily.

WILLOW-PLACE:—About a quarter past seven, last evening, those who chose gathered in the parlor to hear read, from the *Semi-Weekly Tribune*, some extracts from Queen Victoria's memoirs of Prince Albert.

In meeting after the talk on finance was read, there was some discussion about our Trap-business. Mr. G. W. Hamilton said that Mr. Noyes was anxious we should make the most of this business, as it looked as though the Lord was going to help us out of debt through it. There seemed to be an instinct that we should be sure and have traps to fill all orders.—Lillie and Marion B. are here.

A woman calling herself Mrs. Bigelow, came here on foot yesterday. She seemed very strange and odd; said she was a Spiritualist and a lecturer. In the course of her talk with Mr. Underwood, she confessed that she was the wife of the crazy-headed Pinkham, the woman referred to in the present Vol. of the CIRCULAR, May 13th, under the heading "A pair of Diotrephians." She seems to hate Pinkham with perfect hatred, and bears the name of her first husband. She leaves this forenoon.

Improvements in the dining-room continue to progress; new white curtains have taken the place of the old yellow ones, and one of the tables is taken entirely away, and chairs substituted for stools, around the east table. We design as soon as it can be brought about, to have all the stools removed and chairs take their place.

Seventeen thousand two hundred and twenty-nine traps have been packed and shipped during the past three days, Monday, Tuesday and Wednesday, Sept. 2nd., 3d. and 4th. The following table shows the number of each size shipped in that time:

No. 0 Traps,	2,580.
" 1 "	13,236.
" 1½ "	636.
" 2 "	459.
" 3 "	234.
" 4 "	84.
Total.	17,229.

Traps ordered yesterday,   263¼ doz.

THE O. C. DAILY.

VOL. 4.   FRIDAY, SEPT. 6, 1867.   NO. 58.

Mr. Barron returned last evening reporting that Mr. and Mrs. Ingols were somewhat taken aback by our proposition to give up the contract we had made with them. They had, during the three days the contract was in force, rented their tenement, sold their wood, gathered wild berries for drying, and had been very busy generally in getting ready for their new calling. Previous to the engagement Mr. Ingols had contracted for the building of a market wagon, which Mr. B. agreed to take off his hand, when completed. This was satisfactory to Mr. Ingols who, on the whole, behaved gentlemanly under the disappointment, losing none of his high regards for O. C.

The more we reflect upon the matter the greater is our conviction that we have done the best thing for Mr. Ingols in nullifying the bargain before he became more deeply involved in the enterprise. Perhaps our anxiety to get the boarding business entirely off our hands, was so great, that we were not sufficiently quiet to hear what those wiser than ourselves had to say about it. Well, this new branch of industry before us is coming right along. We do not see far ahead yet. The first battle, however, in this warfare, will be with *dirt.*—Communism and dirt will never agree to live in the same house so long as it has the means to procure soap and sand, water and lime and other deoderizing and purifying compounds.   o.

LOVE.

Love lingers not where sorrow dwells,
She cannot bide the downcast face,
Where laughter rings like golden bells
Is her abiding place.

Love follows those, though seeming vain,
Who gild life's path with faith and hope;
She smiles on those who smile again—
Not on the misanthrope.

Love ne'er can be disconsolate,
For love is happiness untold;
Oh then, whate'er may be thy fate,
Be cheerful, bright and bold.

Then fairer than a morn of Spring
Beneath the sun's unclouded glance,
Shall be thy life, for love shall fling
O'er all, her radiance.   F.

[Clara Wait came here yesterday.—This morning she handed us the following communication.]

"Whoso offends one of the least who believe in me, offends me." I have offended Christ by speaking evil of his followers at O. C. when I was in sympathy with lying spirits and a hades-haunted Spiritualist—deceiving and being deceived. I spoke evil of things I understood not, and should have utterly perished in my delusion, had not the Lord called me to turn about and leave my evil way and repent and seek to undo all the evil of my life—forsake sin and Satan, and turn to Christ, whom I knew not, and in whom I did not believe, until I found that evil spirits, the doctrines of Spiritualists, and my own unredeemed carnal nature, had well nigh destroyed moral distinctions, so that I could call evil good and good evil, and see no difference. I learned of Christ and came to believe him a Savior from sin and Satan through Oneida, whom I now fully believe to be followers and disciples of Christ—the only true representatives and embodiment of the Kingdom of God on earth. I now seek unity and fellowship with them as the children and church of Christ."

WILLOW-PLACE.—There was some conversation last evening about reporting, and it was generally felt that the other Communes ought to hear more of what is done in our meetings. It was thought unnecessary yet to have a written report made as is done at N. Y. and W. C. but it was decided that O. A. N. take the post of journalist and expect to fill one page of the Daily every day with a condensed report of our meetings.

We had an earnest talk again last night about work at the Trap-shop. G. W. H. said that what they needed most was some one of our own folks there who was capable of overseeing the work of green hands and boys. The family will look round and see what can be done.

A man and his wife who came here yesterday from Verona Springs, made themselves quite disagreeable by their impudent questioning, their coarse remarks and their peering round into private rooms. Miss Chloe and Mr. U. criticised them some which seemed to have a good effect.

Nearly eleven hundred cans of tomatoes were packed yesterday; also twenty-two dozen of crab-apple jelly was made. Twenty-five crates of nice plums received yesterday and will be packed to-day.

The W. P. Band, the music of which consists of drums and fifes, gave us a serenade last night just at dusk, and also by request performed two or three tunes on the stage after meeting.

Two ladies from Washington, a mother and her daughter, came here yesterday. They thought we kept a hotel and they came to stay a few days and recreate. They spent the night and will leave to-day.

Twenty-five meals were furnished to visitors yesterday.

Traps ordered yesterday,   28 doz.

THE O. C. DAILY.

VOL. 4.   SATURDAY, SEPT. 7, 1867.   NO. 59.

DEAR DAILY :—I have the impression that some of our members have failed to get a clear understanding of the boarding-house problem as presented by Mr. Noyes in a late talk on the subject. As I understand him, his idea is that we start another branch Commune at our boarding-house building over the Creek, whose business· will be to provide accommodations for a limited number of guests or boarders, for certain prices ; and as soon as the way opens, invite those who have and who are almost daily applying for the privilege of working for the O. C. We are doing almost the same thing now in providing meals for daily visitors. We cook for them, we entertain them, invite them into our noon meetings, &c., &c., only, we do not *lodge* them. It is virtually pushing Communism to the front again on a different line. Christ is to subdue all principalities and powers, that is to say, bring them into his service or dash them in pieces. Hotels are a principality. Christ is bound to take charge of them. Under him we propose to march to this new front and make a beginning on a small scale. We make the move primarily for the sake of Communism, not for the convenience of our hired help. Perhaps very few of our present operatives will avail themselves of this new home. It is something like building a school-house in a battle-field. It is to me an order from head quarters to march on the enemy. I shall obey, let come life or death, unless the order is countermanded.   C.

Mrs. Howard writes to Harriet, Belchertown, Sept. 1. " My own spirit is full of thankfulness and love, and I feel like a new woman ; in the strength of Christ I purpose a steady and unceasing confession of Christ before my own family and before the world, when they come and eat at the same table with me.

Things here look small and of little consequence, and I feel homesick or soul-sick, to think of living here, (if it can be called living,) as we have. I desire to work for God and his people, and whatever I do to glorify him and have his will done in me as it is done in heaven ; I thank you Harriet and all that dear family for their kindness and love to me. I feel unworthy of it, but Christ is worthy and I confess him in me a living witness for the truth, therefore " Inasmuch as ye did it unto one of the least of these, ye did it unto me."

The bag business has grown so large that the old door of the mill was found to be too small for its accommodation, so that the old one has now been discharged and a pair of good sized new ones more than fill the place. Then the many busy feet going and returning, have nearly worn out the plank walk; this is also repaired, and hopes are entertained that the mill will become more attractive, and that the bag and other businesses will still continue to grow.

AN OBSERVER.

A man by the name of Buss from Oswego Co. came here last night. All he knew of us was what he had read in the *World*. He seemed oblivious of our outward surroundings, and occupied himself wholly while here in the investigation of our principles. He has rather a rough exterior but Mr. U. thinks him intelligent and a rather interesting man.

1058 cans, and 664 bottles of plums were packed yesterday ; all of first quality. Also 125 jars of crab-apple pickles were preserved. We have on hand to begin our day's work with, 18 crates of peaches, 13 of plums, and a lot of string beans. We expect more plums to-day.

Mr. Noyes's talk about the noon meetings met with a hearty approval. It is to be hoped that the revival spirit will continue to inspire our business with resurrection life and enthusiasm, so that we shall lose nothing by giving up our noon gatherings.

Mr. Samuel Holmes from Cambridge center Vt. a cousin of the Burnhams came here last night. He had business in Oneida Co. and called to see his relatives. He was here twelve years ago, and thinks things have changed some since then.

J. H. Barron is appointed to succeed Mr. Aiken as steward, and Mrs. Allen will be associated with him as stewardess.—Mrs. Bushnell is selected as overseer of the dining-room and dish-washing.

James Van is released from the kitchen and goes to the Trap-shop, and the women in that department do for the present, with only the help of one man.

We had hard thunder showers yesterday afternoon, accompanied with high wind, and to-day is as fine a day as a pure air and bright sun can make it.

Six or seven little girls with Miss Pomeroy to oversee their work, go over to the Trap-shop to-day, also four boys.

The roof of the New House is being painted over.

Traps ordered Sept. 6th.,   196¼ doz.

THE O. C. DAILY.

VCL. 4.   MONDAY, SEPT. 9, 1867.   NO. 60.

BUSINESS MEETINQ.

S. Y. J. said there were several hundred hop-poles in our swamp that might be cut and sold. They will bring $17.00 per hundred. Messrs. Thacker, Kinsley and Conant were appointed to consider the subject.

Mr. Clark wished to be relieved from all responsibility about horses. He nominated Frederick Marks to take his place on the horse committee. Approved.

Mr. Underwood said he had to answer a great many questions every day as to what that building is across the way. There is nothing to show that it is a store. He wished that a sign with "O. C. Store," painted on it in large letters, could be put up where it could be seen from the house. There are probably a great many visitors who would like to make purchases if they knew we had a store. Mr. Aiken was appointed to look after the sign.

The Lawn Cammittee hoped that shooting among the trees of the lawn would be discontinued, as it defaces and injures the trees. Frederick Marks said the robins were destroying the grapes very rapidly, and would continue to do so if they were not shot. Some one inquired if there was no way to scare them away from the grape-vines. "Nothing but shot will scare them," said Sidney, "and they are not always afraid of that; sometimes they will stop to eat after they are shot." The subject was left to the discretion of Mr. Thacker and F. Marks.

W. P. SATURDAY SEPT. 7.—The coming of the children this morning to help in the trap-shop, was quite inspiring, they were so enthusiastic and hearty.—They were accompanied by Mr. Hatch, M. D. P., and H. M. Worden their teacher, who worked with them. They did good service, assorting between fifty and sixty hundred weight of iron in a few hours, a piece of work which would have occupied as many hired boys all day, and who would have been paid ten cents each an hour. A vote of thanks for the children's help was proposed in meeting this evening and unanimously passed.

Three teams started this morning at one o'clock for Utica, to procure leather scraps for use in the "toms," that returned at seven this evening with very large loads, which they got gratis; each of which would have cost seven dollars in Rome, besides the trouble of drawing them. There are four loads more to be had at the same place on the same terms.

The enthusiasm in the trap business runs high, and many are the volunteers for service in that department. We see *how* many there are at dinner and noon-meetings. To-day our family at dinner numbered sixty-four, just double the number of resident members. There is a short trap-meeting almost every evening.

Last night a letter from Mr. North was read, in which he states that he is in debt $5000. He says:

"Since I wrote Mr. N. and O. C., I have accepted a power of Attorney to sell territory for a patent right called "Improved bored well," for the counties of Cayuga, Onondaga, Madison and Oneida. I have done this with the purpose of moving, say to Oneida Station, or some other post near O. C., and operate in this business from there as head quarters, in case O. C. could not furnish me exclusive business, and even then, perhaps it might be so arranged that the one would not conflict with the other, &c."

It was thought the only thing we can do for Mr. N. will be to furnish him with work in our shops, if we can make room for his family in one of our tenement buildings. It was thought by Mr. Cragin and others that the very best thing for him, was to come down from his ministerial dignity and go to work like any common mortal and earn his living.

He seems now to be connected with an unlucky principality, and perhaps by having him near us we can learn the cause of his bad luck and help him out of it.

Among our visitors Saturday, was Dr. Dwight, of Columbia College. New-York, C. S. J.'s tutor, and his wife. He has a summer residence in Clinton where his family are stopping, and he came from there here. He inquired for C. S. J. and also wanted to see Mrs. Bushnell; said a friend of his wished him to see her. On Mrs. B. inquiring who it was, he said it was Esq. Rumsey, of Bath, whom Mrs. B. knows to be her enemy and bitter toward O. C., and a great friend of Mr. Bushnell. The Dr. is one of the delegates to the N. Y. State Convention now in session at Albany.

The noon-meeting yesterday was taken up with discussing the boarding-house question, which resulted in appointing three or four members to select a strong committee, which was reported in the evening meeting to consist of twenty-four men and women, who are to meet this morning at half past eight o'clock. All the family feel desirous that Mr. Noyes's ideas on this subject should be fully carried out.

We have put up in all 2,400 cans and bottles of plums which are perhaps all we shall be able to get this season. We commence packing corn again to-day.

Miss Susan Dunn started this morning for Northern Vt. She goes to settle up her temporal affairs, and will make her stay as brief as possible.

Traps ordered Saturday and Sunday, 621 1-12 doz. including thirteen Bear-traps.

THE O. C. DAILY.

VOL. 4.   TUESDAY, SEPT. 10, 1867.   NO. 61.

O. C., Sept. 9, 1867.

DEAR FATHER:—It is my wish and the wish of the Community to return to you the fifty dollars which I contributed toward the Printing-Office fund while I was under age. I felt at the time that I was the Lord's, and all that I had belonged to him, and when the CIRCULAR was in want of funds, believing that it was devoted to the interest of Christ, I sent what I thought I could spare to Wallingford, much as *you* would contribute for the support and instruction of the freedmen. I now feel that I ought not to have acted without your consent, and that in some sense you have a claim on the money; that it is your due.

We are in somewhat straitened circumstances, financially, but instead of letting it harden our hearts and make us shut up our sympathies for those in like condition, we desire to have it soften our hearts. We want to do what is right and merciful, and treat those who are in such circumstances just as we would like to have the Lord treat us. We feel like sending you not only the fifty dollars but a barrel of flour also. The Community have none other feeling toward you than that of peace and good-will. They will be glad to deal generously with you if you will cease your opposition, but their purpose is to deal righteously with you in any event. Yours for a continuous soft heart,   JOHN S. FREEMAN.

WILLOW-PLACE, SEPT. 9.—Four or five of the young men worked almost all day yesterday in the shop, getting a press ready for making springs by the new method. A brief description of the process by which the *small* springs, at least, are made, may not be out of place here.—Instead of cutting the steel into short pieces and forming the springs by heating and rolling, it is cut into pieces eight or nine feet long and annealed. After this, it is put into a large tom where it is kept tumbling until it is bright and quite free from scales. The springs are punched out while the steel is cold. They are then ready for the second press, which forms the bows, without requiring the steel to be heated. They are finished in the usual way. Making springs by this method, saves eight heats on every spring, and also is a great saving in time and labor. Only half the amount of coal heretofore used, will be required to manufacture them in this way. More steel is used in making a spring by this process, but this expense is more than covered by the saving in other respects.

A slight accident happened a day or two since. One of the pulleys which runs the toms in which the steel is scoured, was placed rather too near another pulley, and the consequence was that the belts which were running on each, got mixed up. One belt broke and getting wound into the machinery, threw the tom six or seven feet from its place—quite a feat considering that the weight moved was at least one tun. No serious damage was done, unless the thorough frightening of several boys at work in the room, might be called so.—Ellen Hutchins and Frank Hillerman are members of our family for the present.

Ex-Mayor Grove, of Utica, the present editor of the *Utica Observer*, was here with his family yesterday. They were accompanied by Mr. A. Hubbell, another Ex-Mayor, and his wife, also Mr. and Mrs. P. C. Costello, of Camden. Mr. C. was a member of the State Assembly at the same time that Mr. Hubbell served in the Senate, two or three years ago. There were also a lady from Boston, Mrs. Greaves, and Mr. Henry A. Vintor, of a piano manufacturing firm in Broome St. N. Y. Mr. V. played a few pieces in fine style on our piano in the Hall. His mother was here with him.—There were twenty-four meals furnished in all; a rare thing for Monday.

NOTICE TO AGENTS:—You will please take no orders for the following fruits: Yellow Spanish Cherries in cans, Lawton Blackberries and Pine-apples in cans. We have a good many more orders for the first above mentioned, than we can possibly supply; have not succeeded in getting *any* of the second mentioned to put up, and have so few of the third, that they will all be sold without any exertion on the part of agents.
                                                    E. S. B.

Only 200 cans of corn were packed yesterday, as it was found to be rather too small. We then fell back on tomatoes, and put up 970 cans. We have commenced packing fruit in cases for shipping, and hope soon to realize some returns for our outlays in this department.

Harriet Howard's sister Louisa came here last night. She walked up from the Depot and round by W. P. and got here about half past ten o'clock. We understand she came to work for us.—Mr. Easton also arrived in the night and was warmly welcomed.

101 bushels of tomatoes were picked in our fields yesterday and 96½ of them taken to the Fruit-house for preserving.—Little Eugene was welcomed to the children's department yesterday, and seemed to enjoy highly his first day's experience there.

Some criticism of Charles Mills, last night. He does not commend himself to the family as being a sincere and earnest Christ-seeker but on the contrary is frivolous and worldly, and mixes up with the hired folks.

77½ dos., and two bear traps ordered yesterday.

THE O. C. DAILY.

VOL. 4. WEDNESDAY, SEPT. 11, 1867. NO. 62.

W. P. SEPT. 10.—Some extra exertion being necessary to finish a lot of springs, volunteers were called
for who thought they could add four or five hours to
their usual day's work, without drawing too largely on
their reserved force. A caller at the forge-shop at
any hour before one o'clock A. M. would find there
a busy group of young men. The foreman of the
department, a book keeper, an M. D. fresh from Yale,
one or two men from the silk-factory, a machinist and,
perhaps the foreman of the bag-shop, with some regular trap-makers form a very efficient force. Some
of the hired men work at traps evenings, until half
past nine o'clock.—Miss Maria Barron is to spend
her forenoons in the office here, assisting Mr. Campbell with the books, while C. C. H. helps in the shop.

Mr. Easton took his place in the trap-works in
good season this A. M. We are glad to welcome
him.—Our meeting last evening was chiefly occupied
with talk about allowing strangers to go through the
silk-rooms. It was thought there was a way in
which permission could be refused, which would
make persons feel almost as well as though their
desire had been granted. All such requests should be
met with good nature, and politeness should be cultivated.—The reading of the life of Dr. Beecher for
half an hour between seven and eight in the evening
proves very interesting and is attended by all who
can leave the Trap-factory.

[Mrs. Mathews, Harriet M's mother, writes to her
from Chicago.]

" I get the paper every week and it is a very great
comfort to me, as well as a deal of company and instruction. The poetry, ' Fulfill your Mission,' was
eminently so, not only to me but to other of the inmates, [of the Home for old ladies.] I felt that I
could be." A true disciple sitting at the Saviour's feet,"
and what Queen could be in a more exalted station.

" I was glad enough to see Mr. Olds, felt something
as Paul did when his friends met him at Appii-forum.
I also thought how I wish I had such a son, one who
could speak the language of Canaan. But I am glad
I have one daughter that can. I am very thankful
that the Community has saved you for me." [Intense
worldliness, affliction and early deaths were the lot
of her other daughters and sons.]

" I was happy in the receipt of your nice little package; somehow you always hit upon the very things
I am in most need of; some of my troubles were much
relieved thereby. My health has been very poor of
late, and I sometimes think I have not long to stay.
But I have many comforts, and I feel a quiet, thankful spirit, and a thankful mood is a comfortable one."

Mr. Perry writes from Peoria, Illinois, that the imitation traps do injure our trade some in that section.
Though all admit that our traps are the best, yet many
say they can make a larger profit on the others. He
writes :

" I am still outward bound but hope to get on the
home stretch, by-and-by. The Lord owns a great
amount of very fine country out this way, but a very
crazy set of people have got possession of it. I shall
be glad to return home, for I had rather be a door-
keeper or hang out clothes in the house of the Lord,
than to be a traveler among the tents of wickedness.

" I have had a good deal of profitable experience
since I have been out and find myself growing more
and more in love with organization in Christ."

REBUS.

Take the name of the God that o'er music presides,
And Æneas's wife to great Priam allied,
And the fair vestal maid whom Leander adored,
Whose fate in the Hellespont many deplored,
The time of the year that with youth doth agree,
And one of the graces, the first of the three,
And lastly the muse of profane history.
The initials of each, together when joined,
Will spell a hard name which in Scripture you'll
        find;
Likewise of a matron or elderly dame
Who dwells at O. C.: will you please guess her
        name ?

The Foundry has made and disposed of seventy-one
hop stoves this season ; also purchased 7,800 pounds
of ready made stove pipe, which has been sold with
the stoves.

Sales of stoves,	$2,541.88.
Cost of stoves at Foundry,	$1,906.41.
Profits,	$ 635.47.
Sales of pipe,	$1,150.00.
Cost of pipe	$ 900.00.
Profits.	$ 250.00.

H. T. CLARK.

Correction.—On the third page of yesterday's DAILY
for the name Vintor read Vinton : also on the third
page of Saturday's do. for Buss read Russ. We blunder on names more then any thing else, particularly
where they are unfamiliar ones.

The weather is as fine as a clear sky and bright sun
can make it. The nights are pretty cool, but we hope
the frost will delay its annual call for some time to
come.

We have eight new tables in the dining-room four
on the east and four on the west side of the room.
Most of them are oval-shaped and will seat eight
persons each.

The work of packing tomatoes has been prosecuted
with energy the last two days, 1,800 cans having been
put up.

Traps ordered yesterday.   232½ doz.

THE O. C. DAILY.

VOL. 4. THURSDAY, SEPT. 12, 1867. NO. 63.

EVENING MEETING.

Mr. Noyes's recent discourses about Paul are highly appreciated here at Oneida. Last evening Mr. Woolworth remarked upon the subject as follows:

"I think Mr. Noyes's whole course in respect to Paul has been very admirable. Go back thirty years or more and you will find him standing up and defending Paul against Boyle and T. R. Gates, and the whole crew that assaulted and denounced him as being jesuitical, carnal and double-minded. Mr. Noyes defended him then, and has stuck to it through thick and thin ever since. Paul is his hero now, and justly. I believe this is the true kind of hero-worship."

G. E. Cragin:—I think the secret of Mr. Noyes's success both spiritually and temporally is, that he has adhered to Paul, and Paul has worked through him.

Mr. Underwood:—Evidently this devotion to Paul has brought Mr. Noyes into connection with the Primitive church, and hence with the spirit of organization which has been the real foundation of this Community. Paul was a great organizer; and is yet, no doubt.

Mr. Woolworth:—I confess my union with Mr. Noyes in his devotion to Paul. Mr. Noyes compares Paul's career to running backward. Paul said, "I run not as uncertainly." There is the secret of his career: there is no uncertainty in it, for he steadily kept his eye on Christ. He was making bold outs all the time, but was sure to get back safely.

Mr. Woolworth remarked just before the close of meeting last night, that G. R. Kellogg had reported that the Fire company from the Depot would be here about 9 o'clock and inquired of George if he knew what they expected of us. G. did not know. This broke up the meeting, as there was immediately a low buzz of conversation. Mr. Woolworth said "talk loud and laugh loud if you wish," at the same time setting the example himself. Soon the Hall was pretty much cleared of occupants, and music was heard in the distance, and the dancing of torch-lights seen approaching. The company consisted of about sixty, including the Brass Band. They made a fine show in their uniform marching round the circle in front of the New House several times. After a while they were invited into the Hall and played several pieces of music, and our people in turn favored them with songs and music on the piano, and cornet.

It was quite a puzzle for a time to decide in what way we should furnish entertainment, as we had no cake suitable for such an occasion. A happy thought at length occurred to Mr. Woolworth. Three or four months ago on the occasion of his birth-day he had received a present of a large fruit-cake, which he proposed should be cut up and served round, which together with crackers, cookies, raisins, wine and apples passed round in the Hall was sufficient and answered a good purpose. It was about eleven o'clock when they retired from the Hall, lighted their torches and commenced their march homeward. On the whole we enjoyed the affair, and we think they did. They were all very civil and respectful.—Mr. Woolworth addressed a few words to them thanking them for the pleasure their call had afforded us, which was responded to by one of their number, (Dr. Cherry), who said if we ever found our beautiful home invaded by the devouring element, we should find in them willing hearts and ready hands to serve us.

W. P. SEPT. 11.—A trap meeting was called last evening, in which the night work was discussed. How to make it most profitable temporally and spiritually is the question. There seems to be a purpose not to let the spirit of dissipation, which is so commonly the accompaniment of night work, have a place among us. Letting the spirit of organization into the business, was thought to be one of the best measures we could take to insure success. It was proposed that G. W. Hamilton be a committee to see what work was most needed, and all who were willing to work should let him know it. He is then to organize a company according to his best judgment. This plan was followed in the work last night, and all say that it went off the best it ever has. A spirit of unity and strength prevailed in the meeting.

Mother Noyes's hard-times bedquilt covered our center-table this noon, and was surrounded by a group admiring its beauty and looking it over, trying to recognize pieces like dresses they had seen worn by mother Noyes and others. It is a monument of the patience and skill of its maker.

NOTICE TO AGENTS.—Do not take any orders for Gage plums in cans. We have orders on our books for 20 doz. more than we shall be able to supply. Also our stock of Gage plums in glass is nearly exhausted, so nearly in fact, that Agents had better consider them as erased from the list. E.

Mrs. Bailey has sewed since the first of Aplrl, 103 straw hats, bleached 100, pressed 195, altered or repaired 46, and colored 19. The above statement shows that the *heads* of the Community are pretty well cared for.

A Mr. Luther Meacham, an elderly, white-haired man from Binghampton staid here last night.

One thousand and thirty-six cans of corn were packed yesterday.

Traps ordered yesterday, 219 doz.

THE O. C. DAILY.

VOL. 4.   FRIDAY, SEPT. 13, 1867.   NO. 64.

Milwaukee, Wis., Sept. 8, 1867.

DEAR BROTHER:—Perhaps the following notice will interest the O. C., as it appeared in the *Milwaukee Sentinel* of Thursday's issue, Sept. 5.

"THE TRAPPERS GUIDE:—We have received from the agent, Mr. Charles Olds, who is now stopping at the Newhall House, the above work by S. Newhouse and other trappers and sportsmen. It is a complete manual for capturing all kinds of fur-bearing animals and curing their skins; with observations on the fur trade, hints on life in the woods, and narratives of trapping and hunting excursions. It will prove an invaluable aid to sportsmen generally and will have a large sale. It is on hand and for sale by the Wisconsin News Co."

Since the appearing of this notice, there have been several inquiries for the book. The proprietors of the News Company are anxious to get the ten copies ordered, as they are having calls and no books. I sold them two copies last evening, which they seemed pleased to get. They propose to make an effort to sell a large number, selling them on the cars, and pushing the sales by distributing the circulars all through the country. They spoke of ordering 100 copies, if we would make a greater discount. The prospect is, it will have a large sale in the West.

I am going to St. Paul, and shall probably find sale there. I shall present the Guide to the editor of some city paper there, who will give it a notice. I expect the *Chicago Republican* will give it a notice, as I left a book at the office before I left that city. The prospects and indications for business are encouraging.

    *   *   *   CHARLES OLDS.

To-morrow morning, Sept. 14th, we purpose to take possession of the boarding-house. But what shall we christen this young Communistic child of ours? Shall we call it the boarding-house family? That does not sound well. Shall we call it Hotel family? That sound does not seem to reach the right spot. I should like "*Creek house*" much better, standing as it does, on a bluff overlooking the little stream below. We will leave the subject open, however, till all the Communes send in their preferences as to a name. As it is Father Noyes's child, perhaps he may have a fancy to give it a name.

The cabinet officers for this young Commonwealth are M. L. W., Secretary of the Commissary department, L. H. B., Secretary of Culinary department, L. A. T., S. A. B. and H. N. O. Executive committee of the interior. L. A. T. Secretary or Chairman. c.

It seems that thieving on a small scale is no uncommon occurrence among the families of our workmen. S. Y. J. caught a youngster last night in the attempt to carry off pound sweets from one of our apple trees in the Weed-lot. S. had been for some time suspicious of his depredations, and seeing him pass the house just at dusk, he secreted himself behind a tree in the orchard where he could see him, if he came into the lot, and watch his approach. Presently he appeared and commenced a vigorous clubbing of the tree. S. stepped out from his hiding-place and seized the lad by the collar and shook him. He was terribly frightened, and blubbered out a promise that he never would steal from us again—if he did, he would pay fifty dollars and take a good thrashing into the bargain.

Over west near the vineyard lies a pile of tin cans, or "swelled heads" as they are called, awaiting burial. A few days since our people discovered four of these cans lying by the fence south of the Weed-lot, with a hole punched in the end of one, and ears of green corn and apples scattered round on the ground. It looked as though the purloiner supposing he had got a nice treasure in the cans, waited only to get behind a fence or in some sly place, to taste the bottled sweets. The stench that followed the opening of one, probably frightened him, and he dropped all and ran for dear life. There was a board knocked off from the fence, done most likely by his haste in climbing over.

Fruit orders are plenty these days. On Tuesday of this week we received eleven orders amounting in the aggregate to about $1,200. We have orders for 3,900 cans of peaches, 7,836 of corn and 9,636 of tomatoes. According to present appearances, we shall not get enough corn to put up a great deal more than is mentioned above, but we hope to get from 12,000 to 15,000 cans of tomatoes. The expense of putting these up, is very slight in comparison with that of putting up fruits, and we are confident that a very large business can be done with a small amount of capital, if we limit ourselves to such things as grow in our immediate neighborhood.   E.

We had a call again yesterday from a band of musicians, who rode round in front of the New House "discoursing sweet music," and scattering their programmes profusely in all directions. They had their horses richly caparisoned in crimson and were connected with a company from New-York who are entertaining the inhabitants of the Depot for two or three nights with their theatrical performances.— They gave Mr. U. four admission tickets.

Five hundred and eighty-three cans of corn were packed yesterday and five hundred and twenty-eight of tomatoes.

We have a new and nice spread for the piano, which improves its looks wonderfully.

Traps ordered yesterday,   290 doz.

THE O. C. DAILY.

VOL. 4.   SATURDAY, SEPT. 14, 1867.   NO. 65.

[Mr. and Mrs. Randall, our late visitors from Wood-stock Vt. have sent us the following rhapsody:]

" Our short visit at your beautiful home, with its elysian surroundings and attractions, seemed more to us like Paradise of old than earthly temples reared by human minds and hands. And all these masterly material comforts, beauty and loveliness, made manifest by a few earnest, conscientious souls, in less than a score of years. It don't seem possible. This tells what co-operative minds and hands can do for the comfort, beauty, security and happiness of men and women in this life of rough and tumble, where might is right in the eye of church and state, where politician and priest, lawyer and doctor exercise their strength and ingenuity in overreaching the common people for selfish ends.

"A question arises in our minds, have your souls outstripped the brotherhood, mentally, socially, morally and spiritually, in the same ratio that you have materially ? If so, what evidence of higher wisdom and purer life do we want ? I hope it is so. Many of your thoughts, rites and practices seem a great way above the legal ways and isolated life of the rich and poor.—Your generous hospitality and christian graces were so apparent for our care and comfort, that I could not feel at ease without due acknowledment to you and the whole fraternity.   Yours sincerely,
NATHANIEL RANDALL."

Charles Mills left this morning for the West. He remained with us long enough to prove himself an out and out scamp and the Community sent him off. He proved himself in many ways to be devoid of conscience or regard for truth and positively hypocritical and dishonest. His affinities and associations were principally with outsiders, not excepting the Olmsteads, where he went secretly for one or more evening calls. When questioned about going there, he plumply denied it, though he had previously admitted to Grace that he had been there. One of his plots that came to light at the Trap-shop was to persuade the hired men and boys, particularly the latter, to strike for higher wages ; and even boasted to Grace that that was one way in which he could increase our financial embarrassments. He came to us with high professions of spirituality and unity with the Community. His first public testimony was, that " although he had been absent from us in body, *he had been present with us in spirit*," &c. He was told that such testimony was more damaging to his cause than most any thing else he could say—that if he would begin to confess his faults, and do works of repentance that we should begin to have some fellowship with him.—He evidently had some intention of going to W. C., as he told Grace that he should see his mother within three days. Mr. Kinsley went with him to the Depot with the purpose to buy his ticket to Ill. and see him started Westward. This test of Grace's loyalty has been good, and her character shines the brighter for it and has increased our confidence in her.   W. H. W.

There was some talk last night about our butter-nuts. Mr. Hatch said we had a good many and our neighbor's boys were carrying them off pretty fast, and unless they were gathered soon, there would be none left to gather. Mr. Woolworth proposed that we set apart a certain share for our employees and have them confine themselves exclusively to what was apportioned them. This was approved and a committee appointed to see that it was done. Afterwards followed some talk about affairs at the Trap-shop, suggested by word sent over by G. W. H., to the effect that he wanted O. C. should remit none of her zeal in furnishing help at the shop—that the battle was not yet won, as we had 37,000 traps to be made and shipped by the first of Oct., and large orders were coming in daily.

W. P., SEPT. 13.—We had a call a few days since, from a trapper fresh from the North woods. He represents the woods as swarming with bear and otter, and said he caught a bear the day before coming here, and is going back to try one of our bear-traps, which he thinks will be just the thing. He has engaged to capture and deliver at Rome, a living bear.

Last evening much good-will was expressed for Mr. Cragin, who has so faithfully attended our meetings this summer. He has done much to help this infant family to gain strength, and to keep free from worldly influences. We hope and expect he will have good success in his new enterprise. He is with us for the last time to-night.

NOTICE TO AGENTS: Owing to the high price of Pears it has been decided to advance the price of that fruit $1.00 per doz. making the present price $6.50 in cans and $8.00 in glass.—It is quite desirable in all cases, that Agents sending orders for any of our productions should send shipping directions with the orders. By doing so they would save those at home who have charge of the shipping, a great deal of perplexity, besides suiting customers.   E.

The kitchen folks are delighted with the cessation of the noise of heating water by steam in the back room. Besides conveying hot water in this underground way for kitchen purposes, there is a pipe and faucet at the west sink in the back room and also in the little entry between the children's room and the hall of the Mansion-house.

S. B. C. takes charge of letters and reports in place of L. A. T.

Traps ordered yesterday,   256½ doz.

THE O. C. DAILY.

VOL. 4.   MONDAY, SEPT. 16, 1867.   NO. 66.

BUSINESS MEETING.

Attention was called to the floor of the piazza in front of the Mansion House which is in a very dilapidated condition, and dangerous to walk over. Decided to refer the matter to the buidilng department, and have it put in a safe condition immediately. Mr. Cragin here remarked that he thought the foremen of the different departments should try to be present at the business meeting every Sunday, so that they can be consulted on subjects pertaining to their departments.

As there is but little to be done by the men who have been hired till the first of Nov., to work on the farm, Mr. Conant wanted to know what was thought about buying tile for laying one hundred and fifty rods of tile drain; the cost would be about $50.00. It was thought the men could go on with the digging, and when the tile is needed, if thought best, it will be bought.

Mr. Cragin suggested that some man like Mr. Kinsley have the general oversight of the hired men, and discharge those who are not needed and who are hired by the day, and to shift those who are engaged till Nov., to places where their help is most needed.

Mr. Kellogg said Mr. Thurston had complained to him several times, about some cows he bought of us last spring. He seemed to think they were not what they were represented to be. Mr. Worden mentioned another case of dissatisfaction. It was decided to have Mr. K. write to Martin Kinsley who sold the cows and find out what he has to say about them, and what he thinks had better be done, and have the letter read in our next meeting.

Mr. Woolworth thought there might be a committee appointed to look into this Midland Railroad project, and see what interest we have in it, so as to be able to answer any inquiries in regard to it. Left with Mr. Cragin to choose a committee.

OUR NEW COMMUNE.—The little band elected to bring into existence another Commune accomplished the object Saturday Sept. 14. Our first meeting was held Saturday evening. Two being a quorum for starting a Community family we had that and one more. But an interesting meeting does not depend upon numbers, provided there be a unitary, faith spirit to ri*act the presence of him who said " where two or three are gathered together in my name there am I in the midst of them." And truly we felt that time and space were abolished on that occasion so that we realized the presence of good spirits from all the Communes, both visible and invisible, wonderfully strengthening our hearts for the new work given us to do. But more anon.   C.

The Community had a grand butternut crack and roast-corn picnic yesterday P. M. at three o'clock, over on the island. The day was as fine as a day could well be, and every thing conspired to make the affair an enjoyable one. Most of the family were present including W. P. Commune. As we approached the spot (which nature has made a lovely one, and man with little labor might make still more so), we perceived active preparations being made for a roast and a crack. Four fires were blazing, and long sharp pointed sticks for holding the ears of corn while roasting, were furnished to all who wished to try their hand at this primitive mode of cookery, and stones and hammers for cracking. Heaps of corn and piles of butternuts were in readiness and the hammer and the roaster were soon in vigorous use. The kitchen group also furnished the company with plenty of the nicest kind of bread and butter, to which ample justice was done. Then followed sports—leap-frog, fox and geese, blind man's buff, &c.

In the evening meeting Mr. Woolworth proposed a vote of thanks to the getters up of the party, which was heartily given. He said he felt it was a success; a vote of thanks was also extended to those who worked all day at the Trap-shop, [three men and two women in the forenoon, and four men in the afternoon.] Near the close of the meeting, cake, crackers and wine were passed round in the Hall. The song "Speak a kind word when you can," by Abram, and three comic ones by H. W. B. and G. W. H. closed the evening exercises.

Mrs. Blood writes Sept 4th, " I think Mr. B. wishes to make me as comfortable as possible, and then he wants me to give up the Community—think no more about it—teach my children right contrary to your teaching, and be a happy and respectable woman. Do you think I can do all that? If I do not I am told I shall have all my children taken away from me, and he does not know but he shall get a divorce; thinks he can get one without any trouble. I do not fear either, for I do not think he would dare make the attempt.

" He told me the night before he went away that if he had the means to take care of them he would take every one of the children with him, and I should not go. The devil shall not have the pleasure of seeing me sit and mope and be miserable over it; I will do with my might what my hands find to do, and trust God for my future."

One of our best cows fell, in the night, into a ditch that was being dug for a drain to the cellar of one of our tenement buildings, and was found nearly dead, and died soon after.

A brother of Mrs. Hatch, Mr. Burnham, and his wife, from Bridgeport, Conn. are here on a visit.

Ira S. Hitchcock died Friday and was buried yesterday.

Twenty-one dinners were provided for visitors yesterday.

Traps ordered Saturday and Sunday, 500½ doz.

THE O. C. DAILY.

VOL. 4.   TUESDAY, SEPT. 17, 1867.   NO. 67.

[Felix Snelling writes the following to J. H. Noyes from Philadelphia, Sept 1st :]

" Many times have I desired to express some kind thoughts to the Community but for the positive injunction that my letters were not acceptable. I have often occasion to talk about the O. C. and always take pleasure in correcting wrong impressions and misrepresentations which are afloat, and I am truly glad of your continued success in setting the world an example of the only true way of living. As for myself I am still struggling with adversity but hope for better times to come.

" We are in good health. Felix is nine years old and has remarkable talent for music. God bless you all. Mrs. S. unites with me in the kindest regards and feelings toward you and the Community.

Yours Truly,   FELIX SHELLING.

WILLOW-PLACE.—It is found to be a great help to the business in the shops, to keep the spiritual atmosphere clear; and to insure this, the subject is often presented in our meetings. It is a vital point with us to keep our connections good with each other. It is a good time to study organization when we have so much business on hand. We find that the arbitrary way of governing the hands, which is in use in other establishments, does not suit us, yet we must see that we make the most of the time of those we hire. The foremen should not work too much themselves, but be around among the workmen fresh and lively, generating enthusiasm.

G. W. Hamilton reports the traps shipped since July 31st, to be 74.620. Orders on hand to be filled by Oct. 1st, 43,298 traps. There is no danger of getting out of work immediately.

Some may be interested to know how much the wages of the workmen in the different departments of the factory amount to per week.

Trap-shop,	$394.34.
Silk-factory,	$143.50.
Machine-shop,	$36.00.
Blacksmiths,	$42.90.
Foundry,	$36.00.
Total,	$652.74.
Cash paid,	$618.87.

An extract of a letter from Mrs. Bristol, our late visitor from Derby, Conn., says, " Nathan, (her husband) desires me to thank you all at Oneida for your kindness to us while at your place. I also thank you and all for the kindness we received. I would have expressed my gratitude before we left if I could have had an opportunity. Cornelia made herself so very conspicuous that I appeared better in the shade.—

Martha (her daughter) said that it was very good of the folks to keep the horses waiting so long at the depot for us, (they waited over one train). Then again we occupied three rooms and you must have had considerable washing for us." [One of the rooms mentioned here was occupied by James P.] E. G. H.

ANSWER TO THE REBUS IN LAST WEDNESDAY'S DAILY.

Take the name of Apollo, who o'er music presides,
And Æneas's wife, Crusia, to Priam allied,
And Hero, fair maid, whom Leander adored,
Whose fate in the Hellespont many deplored,
And Spring, that in freshness, with youth doth agree,
And Aglai, of the graces, the first of the three,
Then lastly, blind Homer, sage muse of hist'ry.
The initials of each, when together they're joined,
Will spell the name Achsah, which in Scripture you'll find;
Besides, at O. C. dwells an elderly dame,
Who, (if we mistake not) has just such a name.
W. C., Sept. 14.   A.

[In a letter from Mrs. Wealthy Knowles, dated Champion, Sept. 1st, she says:]

" Atwood still seems discontented away from the Community. I think it would be better for him as well as for me, to seek spiritual fellowship and union with you, than to spend our time mourning over our circumstances; if we are with you in spirit, it will work out into outward things in time. It is a fine day and my mind has wandered away to your beautiful home many times. How pleasant it must be there. It is about three years since I was there, but it does not seem so long. Well, my heart is with you. I think I understand the feelings of our friends across the ocean, 'That distance is nothing; time is nothing; circumstances are nothing; but unity is every thing.'"

In compliance with a vote taken by the business board Sunday, M. L. W. with three teams and six or seven men commenced repairs on the road yesterday, between the Store and the Hamilton bridge. Mr. W. hopes to continue the good work begun, during the week, or until the entire road clear through to W. P. is thoroughly repaired.

H. W. B. gave us last night, some incidents of his late trip, which were quite interesting, but which we have not room to recapitulate here.

One thousand and thirty-six cans of corn were packed yesterday, and one hundred and thirty-six of peaches.

150 lbs. of grapes, [Hartford Prolific,] were picked yesterday which will be sent to Boston.

Traps ordered yesterday,   78¼ doz.

THE O. C. DAILY.

VOL. 4. WEDNESDAY, SEPT. 18, 1867. NO. 68.

Champion, Sept. 14th.

BROTHER WOOLWORTH:—I suppose you would like to hear how I get along peddling. Well, the first day the change was so great, every thing so new and I so green in the business, that it threw me into a strange sort of confusion which I fear failed to give the Romans a very high appreciation of me as a peddler. However the next day I gathered myself a little, and got the hang of my load, so that I could find what I wanted, and as Mr. Mr. M. would say the first few days had tolerable luck; picked up about $175.00. The next two days I followed on the track of another silk-peddler and sold only $3.95.

I am staying over Sunday at Mr. Atwood Knowles', and if ever I saw a homesick man, he is one. Nothing goes to suit him, and he has made up his mind to sell out and get back to the Community if he can. Poor man! I am sorely tempted to feel sorry for him. They both appear soft toward us, and express their regrets at the course they have taken.

It has been beautiful weather thus far, and I have enjoyed the trip. When I left home, I left the shoe-shop behind, and I presume it has been managed as well as if I had taken it with me, and certainly my load has been much lighter. I think peddling agrees with me, for I have had a good appetite, have slept well nights, have felt first-rate ever since I started, and have not been tempted to feel cross, but on the other hand have been happy and thankful.

Yours in the service, L. VAN VELZER.

W. P., SEPT. 17.—G. E. Cragin has taken Charles Burt's place as Alfred's assistant in overseeing the hands in the finishing-room. Night work goes on in the Trap-shop with unabated vigor, and those who do not work, must learn to sleep with the music of clattering machinery constantly in their ears.

J. P. Hutchins and Charles Marks arrived this afternoon from W. C., and met with a hearty welcome.

Ellen H. has been indulging her taste for white-washing at the expense of our kitchen, and that hith-ertoo rather dingy looking apartment now presents a very cheerful appearance. The wall over head is of a snowy whiteness, and the side walls are brushed over with a mixture which gives them a delicate pink shade, and which does not "rub off" as whitewash usually does. We can recommend her as an artist in this business.

This evening just as Mr. Westcott was starting with his load of nineteen girls, one of his horses got its foot over the neap, and falling down broke it and the reach. The girls left the wagon rather precipitately, and were obliged to wait for Mr. W. to go over to O. C. for another conveyance. When he re-turned with the omnibus the little girls seemed quite delighted.

The carpenters have commenced work on the west roof of the Mill building. They are to shingle it, take out the dormer-windows and put sky-lights instead. It is a pretty heavy job, and will take 50,000 shingles to do both sides. Abram's best workmen are missing, the Trap-shop attractions having drawn them off. Yesterday was a real warm day, the mercury standing at two o'clock in the shade at 85 deg. and scarcely a breath of air stirring. It was so uncomfortable, working on the roof, that D. M. Kelly was obliged to quit, and Abram said he felt at times as though he should melt. We are thankful however for this warm weather, as it is just what we need to ripen our grapes, tomatoes and corn.

A lady's meeting was held in the Hall yesterday P. M. at three o'clock, for the purpose of ascertaining the minds of the women in reference to the *kind* of flannel they would choose to have purchased for their wrappers, drawers &c; whether a mixture of cotton would not be better and more economical on the whole. It was decided to get flannel with a small mixture of cotton. As usual a large basket of unmarked clothes was brought forward, which drew out an earnest exhortation and criticism from H. C. N., which we hope may produce good results.

Mr. Noyes's talk on "Retrospection" was read last night. We believe with him that the last year has been a remarkable one, full of big events to us, and our cause. Mr. Woolworth said he hoped the family would look round and gather up all the interesting facts that have transpired among us the past year, and report them.

CONUNDRUMS.—Why is a decayed tooth like a trap-order? Because both have to be filled.—When is a clock like a naughty child? When it strikes.—Why is a pig like a tree? Because it roots.—Why is a fish, handy to weigh? Because it carries its *scales* with it.—Why is a dentist like a mathematician? Because he extracts the root. H. C. W.

Two hundred boxes of grapes, (mostly pound boxes) were packed and shipped yesterday. Our grapes were never nicer than this year.

One thousand two hundred and eighty cans of tomatoes were packed yesterday.

Mrs. Hatch's friends, the Burnhams, left for home yesterday morning.

Traps ordered yesterday, 182 doz.

THE O. C. DAILY.

VOL. 4.   THURSDAY, SEPT. 19, 1867.   NO. 69.

Berlin, Thursday evening, Sept. 12, 1867.

DEAR FRIENDS:—I cannot feel to retire for the night, until I give some vent to the thankful feeling for the letter we have just received from you. We were not looking for a letter; some one has said "blessed are they who expect nothing, for they shall not be disappointed."

How much I feel the truth of what you say of ——. That weakened state of spirit; it would rise up, but it is paralyzed. I know this same thing has been a great trouble of mine, and hence the necessity of leaving this place. We have just been reading the cure of Mrs. Hall again this evening, and the O. C. inspiration against unbelief seemed pouring right into my heart till I was indignant with this villainous devil, as I never had been before. I want to thank God for the O. C., for setting up his kingdom on earth, for I believe from the depths of my heart that the O. C. is his kingdom. How blessed that message this evening from the O. C. to my heart, that told how terrible is unbelief, and gave me new life. The devil keeps suggesting that it would at least be more modest, not to make claim just yet that I am saved, but I am determined not to hear it, and much less to heed it, for I am assured from a much more reliable source that I am saved.—Mr. and Mrs. Lesley think Mrs. R. borders on fanaticism in her enthusiasm for Christ and the O. C. Also think that Mr. Noyes and the Community fail to sufficiently recognize similar cures and manifestations among spiritualists. They thought Mr. Noyes and the O. C. should be more modest in claiming that it was God in the case of Mrs. Hall, and not in some cures among spiritualists. Yet Mr. L. says he looks not for salvation in spiritualism, but thinks it belongs with the hadean world, &c. &c.,

I have $100.00 that I am making no use of now. If the O. C. can use it to advantage, I should be glad to have them do so. If desired, I will send it in whatever manner you may suggest.—Hoping for entire unity with Christ, Mr. Noyes and the Oneida family,

I remain as ever,   GAYLORD W. REEVE.

EVENING MEETING. *Mr. U.:*—Four Spiritualists were here to-day. The first call was by Mr. Benton and wife, from Troy. He represented himself as a cousin of Mr. Reynolds; but Mr. R. thinks the relationship more distant. He acknowledged himself to be a Spiritualist, but went into ecstasies over what he saw here, and said he certainly must join us.

The next call was by Mr. Chauncey Barnes, the man who made himself so conspicuous in the recent Spiritualist's Convention at Cleveland, He came to have a talk with "brother Noyes," and had a great deal that he wanted to say, but as Mr. Noyes was not here he finally concluded to leave. I walked with him as far as the corner by Mr. Hubbard's. We stopped there and stood by the roadside and talked. Presently Mrs. Bigelow passed by, the wife of the diotrephian Pinkham, making the fourth Spiritualist. She was on the opposite side of the road, and when I asked Barnes if he knew her, he said he did not; but on my telling him who she was he did know her, and motioned her to come over. She obeyed the wave of his wand, and I left them talking there by the roadside.

Victor:—I confess my sympathy with father's judgment of the Boston school of literature. I have been conscious, when reading it, of a subtle infidelity and unbelief in God and his power and wisdom. I desire to separate myself from it entirely.

W. P., SEPT. 18.—The water in the pond is so low to-day that it is deemed advisable not to keep the machinery running every night; therefore work that requires the wheel to run will be carried on every other night, only. There seems to be a general feeling of trust about the water, feeling that the Lord will look out for the best interests of his business.

There was a meeting of the hired men to-day called at one o'clock in which they were exhorted to be prompt at their work when the bell rings, and make good time; fill out all the moments. They were told to go to work in the morning where they left off the night before unless otherwise ordered. The meeting continued only ten or fifteen minutes, but it is thought to have made a good impression on the men. Several expressed themselves afterward, as well pleased with it. There were eight hired men and boys present. The first bell is to be rung at five minutes before the time to go to work instead of fifteen, as has been the custom. Just after meeting this evening we were called out on the piazza by singing from a quartette of young men (some of our shop hands), who had stationed themselves just outside our gate. They sung two or three songs very well and were cheered.

The women propose to assume the duties of the evening watchman as long as the men are obliged to work nights.

The mercury stood yesterday, for three or four hours in the middle of the day, at 89 deg. and though we had a refreshing shower at five o'clock, yet the night was excessively warm, and the morning is equally so.

NOTICE TO AGENTS.—Do not take any more orders for pine-apples in cans, peaches in bottles, or sweet corn. We shall hardly get corn enough to fill what orders we have already.   E

455 cans of corn were packed yesterday, including 40 cans for one of our neighbors. Also a lot of pickled pears and pears not pickled.

Traps ordered yesterday,   144 doz.

THE O. C. DAILY.

VOL. 4.   FRIDAY, SEPT. 20, 1867.   NO. 70.

How to Govern.

Those who govern *best* are those who *seem* to govern *least*. This assertion may appear somewhat paradoxical at first sight, but let us take an interior view of the proposition before rendering an adverse verdict. The best example of superintendents or managers of men, the world ever saw, were *Christ* and *Paul*. From their teachings we learn that the true, scientific method of inducing men to do as you want them to, is to understand the art of putting your own will and disposition into them. Here the supposition arises, what if your disposition leads *you* to *shirk* all you can yourself, while you require the uttermost faithfulness on the part of those under you? Now it will not be difficult to discover that the more you govern others in such a spirit the more you would diffuse among them a spirit of *eye-service* and unfaithfulness. Or, in other words, the more government of that kind, the less obedience you would reap. While, on the other hand, a foreman who can say, sincerely, "It is my disposition to govern others by example—that I will require no greater obedience, no more faithfulness of those under me, than I render to those above me," is one who will govern most perfectly without seeming to govern at all. Indeed, such foremen would govern men by the new covenant principle, by the diffusion of a good disposition into them, a disposition to do the right from choice—from attraction. A true foreman or a father, therefore, whose office it is to govern others, is one who possesses the most *humility*, the most *faithfulness* and the most *obedience* to the light and truth within and above him; one, in short, whose meat, drink and every pleasure, is found in the spirit of perpetual service for the good of all. And will it not be one function of Communism to educate men to govern others by the *infusion* of a true, righteous *disposition* that will make it easy and natural for men to govern themselves, instead of being governed by the action of coercion and legislative law.   c.

W. P. Sept. 19.—Notice was given at the supper table, that help was needed in the chain-shop for an hour, and that women would not be refused employment if they chose to volunteer. They *did* choose and soon there was a merry group surrounding the fitting table, reminding one of old times at W. C.

A little talk was had in meeting about promptness in getting to work at the ringing of the bell. We exhort our help to be on hand, and it is important that we set them a good example. The moral effect of having all begin work at once, would be worth a good deal. If people wish a little leisure, let them take it at some other time; begin promptly if you quit fifteen minutes afterward.

The subject of the Midland R. R. is exciting the attention of the Oneida people; so much so that the inhabitants have resolved themselves into a committee of the whole to raise the necessary subscriptions—viz., $150,000.

Last evening a delegation of about a dozen called on us to ascertain what assistance can be afforded by the O. C., urging by earnest argument that we should be largely benefited and intimating their expectation of liberal encouragement in the way of taking stock.

We claimed time for consultation and promised to give a definite answer within a week.   m. l. w.

Miss Clara Wait left for home yesterday. She has been here two weeks, and has improved in health and strength of spirit, and leaves feeling that her visit has been a great help to her every way. She has made herself quite useful in various ways, has engaged in work with the women, and seemed much like one of the family. She is sensible that her connection with spiritualism and free love requires great earnestness on her part to free herself from their paralizing effects. Her case seems hopeful.

Several errors were left uncorrected in our little sheet, yesterday, owing to the drive and push we had at the last moment, to get it out in season for the mail. There was an error in the W. P. report, but as we followed the copy strictly, we do not plead guilty to that. The number of the hired men present at the meeting spoken of, was eighty instead of eight.

A Clergyman by the name of S. S. Hughson, of Newark, N. J., with his niece, Mrs. Tucker, came here yesterday. Mr. H. was acquainted with Mr. Inslee who came over from W. P. to entertain him.—Also Mrs. Perry's brother, with his wife and daughter came last night.

One of our men at the Trap-shop, asked a little dirty looking boy what made his face so dirty? "Oh!" said he, "I worked in the tom yesterday."

There were thirty-seven dinners ordered yesterday. Among our visitors was a party of fourteen from Verona Springs.

Mr. Aiken left for New-York yesterday noon, accompanied by Arthur Bloom, who is en route for W. C.

Traps ordered yesterday,   184¼ doz.

THE O. C. DAILY.

VOL. 4.   SATURDAY, SEPT. 21, 1867.   NO. 71.

"Reflector" Office, Schenectady, Sept. 18, 1867.

Mr. UNDERWOOD, DEAR SIR :—My paper goes to press this P. M. I have delayed sending the other papers promised until I could post them together.

My own report in the *Reflector* you will observe is quite as extended as brief space will allow, and simply gives a superficial statement, as announced to you at time of our interview.

I trust under the circumstances it will prove satisfactory to your society, and I would be pleased to have a line in reply from you in regard to its reception.—" Kringle" of the " Dorpian" is a young man twenty-two years of age. He has informed me since my return that he would have preferred to have accompanied me before writing anything of the Community in the way of burlesque humor ; and would have taken that step had he known sooner of my projected trip.—Should you stop off at this depot at any time on your way to Albany I hope you will drop in at the *Reflector* office. And with sincere personal wishes I remain Respectfully and truly,

W. VAN SANTVOORD.

Mansfield, Tioga Co. Pa., Sept. 1867.

BROTHER CRAGIN :—Your reply came duly to hand and contents noted. I thank you for the faithful and frank manner in which you deal with my case. It is in accordance with my spirit and convictions. Your suggestion that I would probably find the main difficulties of my case in the " family and ministerial enclosures," I think contains a good deal of truth.—At dinner one day, I read your letter to Mrs. North, closing with the remark, " Every word of that letter is true—Mrs. N. what do you think of it ?" She answered " I have no longer any opposition to you, but am ready to go with you wherever you go."

The well arrangement did not cost me any thing. My leading inspiration is to go to work for O. C. and hold every other enterprise subject to it. If the one cannot be made to harmonize with the other, then the wells must bore themselves. My feeling is, any work I can do or *learn* to do for O. C., I am ready to do.

So soon as I finish my present engagements, I shall make tracks for O. C., Providence permitting. Yes, " Yours for unbounded confidence in Mr. Noyes."

THOMAS NORTH.

FITTING AMUSEMENTS AT W. P.—Last night about quarter to seven a large load of Oneidians arrived and immediately commenced operations in the Chain-room and vicinity. Fitting, trying, mending and sorting were all going on, under the management of M. H. Kinsley. Mr. Kinsley Sr. started the bee, bringing the folks over in the omnibus with a four horse team.

Twelve of the party were women. Just before nine they were invited to the house to wash ; after which ceremony, ice-cream and cake were passed around. A song or two followed, when the party started homeward. Myron reports thirty-six hands at work, twenty-four from O. C. ; work executed as follows :

10,000 " fits" made ; 1,500 chains tried ; a large quantity malleable iron sorted, and a lot of swivels " turned ;" as much work as twelve boys would do in a day.

Miss Munson writes that Dr. Jackson has not recovered from the fall he had, about the first of Sept., which was noticed in the papers. She says :

" He seems to be afflicted in many ways just now ; his character as a minister runs very low, and the ministers in the Cure have all left, and the talk is that a stop will be put to his preaching. I do not know how it will end, but I am sure there is one who will see justice done." Miss. Munson is expected to visit he O. C. next week.

We should like to know from our friend G. E. C. (if not too busy at the Trap-shop), whether it be good economy in point of health, for the kitchen folks to be inhaling for hours that peculiarly rank emanation which infallibly attends the concoction of those (alas !) popular things called *nut-cakes*.

We doubt whether it would not have defied the vocabulary even of a *Shakspeare* to convey an idea of its rare pungency. SANITARY.

Mr. Pinkham who called here a week or two since seems to have experienced a sudden conversion to our faith, and instead of going to Cal. to aid in establishing a Community as he intended to do when here, he, writes making an earnest request to join us.

Yesterday at three o'clock the mercury stood at 92 deg. There was a shower between four and five and the weather is cooler this morning.

The result of the last two days packing at the preserving house are as follows : 1,521 cans of corn and 412 bottles of peaches, pickles &c.

The company from W. C. did not arrive till six o'clock this morning. Mr. Nash bore the journey very well.

Mrs. Dascomb came here yesterday, to make her long contemplated visit.

Traps ordered yesterday,   234½ doz.

THE O. C. DAILY.

VOL. 4. MONDAY, SEPT. 23, 1867. NO. 72.

BUSINESS MEETING.

G. R. Kellogg wanted to know if orders for castings could be promptly filled at the foundry. There has been some trouble in getting castings that are wanted by different parties, and it was hoped that we should not get a reputation for slackness and forgetfulness, as was reported in some cases. It would be better not to take orders, than to take them and not fill them promptly. It was thought that persons should be particular to write down all orders, and not leave them to the memory of Mr. Campbell or any one else. Mr. Campbell has too much other work to do to attend to the castings properly, and see that they are sent away as soon as made. Messrs. Campbell, G. W. H. and Inslee were appointed to systematize the foundry business.

"B. H. C."—Just nine days old this twenty-second day of September is this Community child, and there is one thing quite remarkable about us, some think, viz., that we can *talk* while so very young. But we can. Indeed we did a good deal of talking the very hour we were born, so great is the development of that gift in us—a gift so handy to have, as Meeker would say, especially in a child like *we*, so full of wants. But a grave question arises, "How much will our kind, large-hearted mother and brothers and sisters wish to hear our prattle? Will our talk edify them?" Perhaps they would say, "Tell us all the *good* news you can and let the bad news go unreported, as that belongs to a certain *old egotist* whose name we care not to mention." But he is no relation of ours, and, moreover, he can do his own reporting, which, however, he don't like to do, for he knows that all honest folks regard him as the prince of liars. We have to confess however, to one feeling which came knocking at our door, that we were missionaries in a field very remote from civilization. Well, perhaps we are a missionary, and if so, we can say that the *natives* treat us kindly. They appear to like our kind of preaching, which goes directly to the right spot they say, when they are hungry, which we judge is quite all the time.　　　　　　　　　c.

Mr. Noyes's talks on "Finance", and "Antidote for trouble in the flesh," were re-read last night, followed by interesting conversation on the subject, expressive of sympathy with Mr. N.'s ideas, and a desire that continence in reference to expenditure and getting into debt may govern us in the future. G. E. C. was then called on to give some report how matters stood at the Trap-shop. He stated that there were now on hand orders for 25,000 traps, 15,000 of which were to be made and shipped by the first of Oct. He then gave a particular account of the manner of making springs by the new method.

J. H. Barron:—I have had a new appreciation of the "Canadian Trapper" since the new improvements in spring-making. [Applause].

G. E. Cragin:—I ought to have remarked, that the improvement originated with Mr. Newhouse, and that he has been the father of it all the way through.

In Mrs. Blood's letter received Friday last, she sends us the following extract from a letter she received from Mr. B.: "I feel that something must be done soon, some sort of a decision. As I said, I want to be patient, but I am also disposed to meet the issue fairly and squarely, not to shirk it, but to walk right up to the breach at once if need be, and while I pray "O Father, if it be thy will, let this cup pass from me," will say, "nevertheless, not my will but thine be done." I have little strength enough to do that which it is needful for me to do, at the best; yet when I see you so ready to be led away into by and forbidden paths, so ready to put aside your solemn obligations and follow cunningly devised fables, it takes away *some* of that energy that I need for my every-day labor. That God may forgive you and turn you back to the truth, as he has me, is the prayer of

　　Your loving husband,　　D. E. BLOOD.

We had a grand tomatoe bee yesterday, which lasted from eight o'clock, A. M. till half past three P. M., (with only an interval of about an hour and a half for dinner and noon meeting), in which 1,835 cans of tomatoes were put up. We were pleased to see the activity and enthusiasm that prevailed, particularly among the young women and girls.

The work of the last two days in packing amounts to 3,450 cans of tomatoes, and 117 bottles of peaches. Whole number of tomatoes packed thus far, 8,300.

NUT-CAKES.—Having had no practical experience in frying nut-cakes, I am unable to give an opinion as to its being unhealthy or the reverse. Hot steam is enervating and relaxing, and the fumes of boiling oil may have the same effect. However if not too long continued, I do not think the exposure to the fumes of hot oil will result in any serious disturbance. The heat is worse than the odor. Don't quit nut-cakes quite yet.　　　　　　　G. E. C.

There were picked and prepared for market yesterday, 184 one-and-a-half pound boxes of grapes and nineteen four-pound boxes. Our table was furnished bountifully with this delicious fruit last night, the first we have had this season.

Mr. Van Velzer returned from his peddling trip last Friday. He reports that he enjoyed it much and had fair luck.

Mrs. Smith with her babe went Saturday to visit her father and mother.

Traps ordered Saturday,　　　　　211½ doz.

THE O. C. DAILY.

VOL. 4. TUESDAY, SEPT. 24, 1867. NO. 73.

Mr. Woolworth brought up the subject, last night, of horizontal fellowships, and their bad effect upon James Hatch and Manly Aiken, who have been very intimate for some time past; he was a good deal tried with both of them, particularly the latter—said he should not have brought the subject up in this public way if he had not labored with Manly considerably in private to no purpose. The shop hands do not respect him as foreman, and our own folks who work there are very much tried with him. It was thought that Mr. Bolles, who labors in that department, should be associated with Manly as foreman, as Mr. B. would be a great help to him in checking the spirit of frivolity and worldliness he meets in the workmen.

W. P., SEPT. 23.—A little incident occurred to-day which shows that our influence on the hired help in the shop is tending to make them take the right course when away from us. A young man seventeen years old came to Myron to know if he could get a place to board at Mr. B.'s. He had boarded at home, but said his mother (a widow) did not wish to have him there longer. Myron, suspecting something was wrong, went up into the silk-room and talked with his older sister about it. She said he was disrespectful to her and his mother, and behaved so badly this morning that his mother boxed his ears, which made him very angry, and he declared he would leave home; she wished he would if he could not behave better. Myron and Geo. E. talked with the young man about his course, advising him to ask his mother's forgiveness and mend his ways. He acknowledged that he had done wrong, but could not think of making a confession. M. saw his mother, who begged him to use his influence to make her son do what was right, saying he had more influence over him than any one else. He talked with the young man as he would with a brother, until he broke down and cried like a child. He said he would go and ask his mother's forgiveness if M. would go with him, which he did, and the thing was settled to the satisfaction of all parties. [Please don't copy the above into the CIRCULAR.]

An unearthly din was heard just as meeting was out this evening which we found to be created by thirty or forty men and boys engaged in the very refined amusement of "horning" a newly married couple. The persons honored in this way, were Mr. Town, one of our nearest neighbors, and Mrs. Story, daughter of Mrs. Macoy, who by the way is said to have another husband still living.

During the past week I have been engaged with several men and teams at road repairs. About one hundred dollars were expended in labor, and those parts most liable to become rutted in the wet season before us, received attention.

Gravel from the Creek was applied to the central part with the view to prevent water standing on the track, and thus rendering it soft and muddy by travel, and the heavy traffic our road is subject to. But at best we seem to be doomed to mud and bad roads at intervals in this vicinity; until, at least, a sound material is applied, and much more system is adopted in constructing them. Broken stone of good quality may answer, but iron tracks for wheels to move on, perhaps will yet be necessary to secure the desired results. M. L. W.

Mr. Pinkham came here again yesterday, and took dinner with the family. He said when he was here before, he was a sinner, but he had experienced a great change and thought he was now saved from sin. He would like to join but seeing that his fitness for such a step, was questioned, he concluded to go back to Wisconsin and go to work at his trade, that of a carpenter. He seems anxious to learn more. He says he has read since he was here, "Salvation from Sin", and the "Hand-book" which have greatly enlightened him.

The people of Oneida Depot have sent word to the directors of the Midland Railroad Company that they have raised the $150,000 required of them. The actual subscription is only $138,000; but a half dozen of the influential citizens have assumed the responsibility of the remainder. They requested Mr. Hubbard to try and learn what the Community would do. Mr. Hubbard told them that he thought the Community would be liberal if the road came near by, but if it run at a distance they would give nothing.

Mr. Perry's brother and his wife, Mr. and Mrs. Goodell, and their little girl, leave to-day for their home in Courtland Co. Mr. G. was very much pleased with the Community and thinks his sister is well off and her children nicely cared for.

The shingling of the west side of the Mill is completed and the carpenters will wait awhile before attempting to do the other side. Box-making is in great demand these days, both for fruit and traps.

Mrs. Abbott has taken of the squaws the past year, (for broken pieces of bread, cold puddings, &c.), $100.00 in cash, and $45.00 worth of baskets.

☞ All persons are requested to be prudent in the use of water till the preserving season is ended. J. A.

It is pretty cold this morning and there was a slight frost last night.

1,086 cans of corn and 88 of pears were packed yesterday.

Traps ordered yesterday, 166 doz.

THE O. C. DAILY.

VOL. 4. WEDNESDAY, SEPT. 25, 1867. NO. 74.

ODDS, ENDS AND PINS.

When the O. C. had a house in Brooklyn, Mr. Noyes at one time had an inspiration for picking up *pins*, as he chanced to discover them in walking the streets of the city. It was to him a good ordinance, an act in which he could worship God just as truly as in preaching a sermon. He enjoyed it too, mightily, and his enthusiasm was contagious, for all in the family tried their luck at *pin-hunting*. But none were so successful as the original inventor of that source of pleasure. I dare not say how many thousand pins were accumulated in that way, but the family were fully supplied with the article. Moreover, in picking up pins, Mr. Noyes picked up many a bright thought that he *pinned* to his memory, and subsequently worked over into edifying fireside talks. I have been reminded of that interesting experience by reading a short article in the last CIRCULAR on the economy and order in the character of Christ. We talk well and truthfully when we insist upon converting all our schemes of money-making into ordinances of the worship of God. Now why not do the same thing in studying economy —*saving* money? To save money or to make money from the pressure of worldly fear, and similar motives, is a bad ordinance we say, because it is a confession that we are orphans, or that our father is a poor vagabond, leaving his children to shirk for themselves. But to save money in the various ways that true economy would suggest, from motives of love, of doing good to others, and, above all, for the sake of pleasing him who said " gather up the fragments that remain, that nothing be lost," can be made an ordinance of worship as truly as that of making money, and would have no belittling effect upon the character when done joyfully and enthusiastically.—In our next, we will pin on a few practical suggestions. c.

Mr. Underwood was passing near one of our westerly vineyards last evening before supper, where he saw three children—two girls and a boy—come out and run. He thought best to investigate, and so pursued them through the corn-field to the fence, where he overtook the smallest girl. He took her to her mother ; also three bunches of grapes which he picked up in passing through the corn. The mother and child were both very sorry and wept. The little girl asked forgiveness, and he readily forgave her, as he considered the older girl chiefly to blame. He learned that the mother and child were visitors in this vicinity and that the other children were Mr. Petrie's.— The oldest girl Alice Petrie told the other one that she was picking the grapes for her mother. Mr Underwood then called on Mrs. Petrie, and inquired for her daughter Alice. Alice was called in,

and he stated the case and showed the grapes. Mrs. P. seemed very indignant, and said he might do what he pleased with the girl, but that she should give her a good whipping at any rate. Alice seemed sorry to have been caught, but not at all repentant for the wrong. Mr. U. said he thought Mrs. P. had no such keen sense of the immorality of the act as the other woman had manifested, though she was evidently sorry it had happened. He had intended to give the grapes to Alice if she seemed repentant and soft-hearted, but he saw so few signs of anything of the kind that he brought them away with him. He thought Mrs. P. would probably give Alice a good whipping, and that would end the matter.

Mrs. Dascomb left yesterday. The clandestine manner of her coming here did not please us, and she was advised not to protract her visit. She remained one day longer than was anticipated, waiting for her satchel which was miscarried to Hamilton by the stage-driver. Mrs. Dascomb's family (the Averills), hold high position in the aristocratic world, and have a basis of wealth and talent ; and they are very jealous and sensitive respecting Mrs. D.'s course, and threaten her with the Lunatic Asylum if she comes to the O. C. Her older brother, Gen. Averill, has promised her a home for herself and boy on condition that she will submit to his military will and discipline. She revolts at this, and thinks she may gain an independent livelihood by teaching, in which she has had experience. Her younger brother professes to be in the confidence of the men who are taking steps, or meditating steps for the suppression of the O. C. by legislative enactment. He told Mrs. D. that the preliminary steps would be taken by the Constitutional Convention.—Mrs. D. seems to be firmly attached to Community principles, and says she has a clear and satisfactory understanding of Mr. Noyes's position in this dispensation of the incoming kingdom.

Mrs. D. read copies of some of her letters to Gen. Averill in which she gives him some wholesome criticism, and lays bare some of his social deviations. Her brothers respect her religion, but think she is wild about the Community.

Esq. Rumsey, the first Lawyer of Bath, and a member of the Constitutional Convention is an intimate acquaintance of the Averills, and hence their knowledge, probably, of the threatened proceedings against the O. C. w. H. W.

A call last night for help in the preserving room to-day, where we should judge they are having lively times. We have one hundred and twenty-five or one hundred and fifty bushels of tomatoes on hand, which must all be put up to-day. As meeting closed Mr. Woolworth said " Don't forget the tomato bee."

2½6 cans of corn were packed yesterday and 90 of pears ; also 89½doz. tumblers currant jelly manufactured.

Traps ordered yesterday, 183½doz.

THE O. C. DAILY.

VOL. 4. THURSDAY, SEPT. 26, 1867. NO. 76.

H. G. Allen reports that he left New York about three weeks ago, visited Boston, Portland and Bangor; thence round through Canada, and finally down through to Oneida, where he is very happy to call.—He learned in Portland that only about half the usual amount of corn was being canned this season.—The trap-business in the regions he visited is in better shape than formerly. Many parties in Canada have ordered early, and expect to want more when business gets well under way. The popularity of our traps increases. He sold seventy-five copies of the " Trapper's Guide," and could have sold more if he had had them with him. One book-seller told him he had calls for fifty copies last winter, but could not obtain any in New York; which leads Henry to conclude that Canada will prove a good market for the book, and that in connection with the trap-trade we shall yet make money out of it.

The crops in Canada are excellent. The elections have retarded the fall trade some. Henry says there seems to be a growing conviction in Canada that they shall yet become a part of the United States. Good-will toward our government and people is increasing.

There seems to be a good deal of humbug about the Canada gold-mining. Those who assay the ore are often in league with the speculators in mines.

W. P., SEPT. 24.—Our little family is subject to more or less change from time to time. This week has brought more than usual of these changes. Mr. Burt and D. A. Abbott have taken up their abode with us for the present. George Henry goes to O. C., and Lorenzo takes his place here in the kitchen. Virtue and Charlotte Maria are here in the place of Frank and Alice.

Our meeting this evening has been occupied by giving advice and criticism to George Henry and Orrin. George Henry was commended for many good traits, and criticised for being independent and allowing himself to get a dislike to work he has to do, and for being lazy about learning to speak and behave correctly. Orrin appears to be in a very unsatisfactory state. His difficulty seems to be that he likes to be independent, has thrown off his allegiance to his father but has not taken any one else in his place. It was thought he would never be free from his father's influence until he submits himself to some one else.

We heard the following anecdote related of a Spiritualist. A woman lost her husband by death, and on reflection she found regrets and a bad conscience for the treatment she had given him while living, and wished to call him back to make confession. So she got a circle and medium, and her husband came, to whom she made ample apology, and a reconciliation seemed affected, when the widow asked him if he would not like to return and live again with her? " Well," he replied, " I guess I had rather stay where I am." " But where are you ?" said the affectionate wife. " Oh, in hell of course !" was his reply.

The carpenters are engaged at the present time in making improvements at our new Commune. They are converting the wood-shed into a room for the hired men to wash in—are going to finish it off, lath and plaster it and build a chimney. They are also putting up another shed joining on to the old one, and expect to take down the partition running through the kitchen making it one large room.

Is not the persevering industrious spirit of Paul very manifest when shipwrecked on the coast of Melita. Instead of rubbing his white hands, as a modern Bishop would have done, he appears to have been the first to gather sticks and recruit the fire. This was rewarded by the opportunity he had of performing the only miracle of the kind on record.   C. E.

Mr. Hawley has a niece by the name of Brooks, with her husband and little boy here on a visit. Miss Munson from Dansville also came yesterday. She thinks it doubtful whether Dr. Jackson ever recovers from his fall.

The company from W. O. arrived safely yesterday afternoon, and received a hearty welcome. H. G. Allen came in the forenoon.

The kitchen company had a bee at five o'clock this morning for opening clams. We expect to test their good qualities at dinner.

2,280 cans of tomatoes were packed yesterday.—There were 916 cans of corn put up the day before, instead of 216 as reported.

We have just heard that Rosamond, our youngest helper in the office, is drafted for W. O. We shall miss her.

2,125 pounds of grapes have been picked, 1,650 pounds of which were Hartford Prolific.

230 1-6 doz. traps ordered yesterday, including one large bear-trap, No. 6.

THE O. C. DAILY.

VOL. 4.   FRIDAY, SEPT. 27, 1867.   NO. 76.

WASTE NOT, ABUSE NOT.

One of the great advantages of Communism is, that the interest of one is the interest of all. There is scarcely anything required to be done or desirable to have done, but that every member of the Community can, in some way, participate in its accomplishment. For instance, the O. C. has given itself the job of paying off its debt just as soon as it is possible to do so by steady industry and frugality. Now, as it amounts to about the same thing whether a penny is *saved* or *earned*, all who can *save* money are rendering service in extinguishing the debt of the O. C. as truly as those who earn it by hard labor. If I have my boots mended so that they answer all the purposes of a new pair (except in looks), several dollars are thus saved to the O. C. treasury. The same would be true of garments of every description. Let every one ask himself the question, "Can't I have my pants or coat mended and made comfortable six months or a year longer, and so save ten or more dollars toward liquidating our debt?" Let those who have more dresses, or stuff for them than they need at present, distribute to those who do need them, and so save the expense of buying new ones. Perhaps the color or style does not suit you, then rally your patriotism, and sacrifice your taste to the cause.

Indeed, one can hardly realize, in so large a family as ours, how much might be saved by taking care of property of all kinds, particularly so, in small things. The spirit, probably, that needs cultivating most, in many of the younger members, if not in some of the older ones, is one that will take care of things that would otherwise be destroyed. A word may be said too about the treatment of books. Evidently our books do not have the care in being handled and used as they deserve. When books are ill used it indicates, to say the least, that they have been in the possession of persons who lack refinement and consideration. Good books are costly and valuable. We pay money for them freely because we love knowledge. We love to associate with the great minds of past ages through their writings. Books personify their authors; treat them with due respect. We call a steam engine a wonderful invention bordering on the miraculous. A printed book through which an invisible man speaks, is scarcely less so. Indeed, there is a sense in which all things are clothed with sacredness, because created by infinite wisdom or by man who was created in the image of that wisdom; hence all things should be treated with respect.   C.

A long letter was received from Mr. Blood yesterday, written in a very pious strain, for the purpose, he says, of finally settling up with us. He says he once wrote us some letters commending and endorsing our system, but that, on account of our deviation from, or going beyond the Bible in our social principles, he has changed his mind and returns to the Bible standard. He says "I confess with shame, that I neglected and 'went out of' the gospel of Christ in seeking in *any* way unto any system that sanctioned and practised sexual intercourse upon any other principle than 'every man having his own wife and every woman her own husband,' and I confess my return to the *letter* and *spirit* of the gospel and it is my inflexible determination, to make it in the future, by the blessing of God, a 'lamp to my feet and a light to my path.'"—He warns us that unless we do return to the Bible, we shall in the course of time crumble away and be known no more on earth as an organization.

Rockford, Ill., Sept. 22, 1867.

MR. W. H. WOOLWORTH, DEAR SIR:—I arrived here a week or ten days ago, and had not five cents left. My object in writing is to know about that money you was going to send. Will you send it to Thomas Mills, Rockford, Ill., because I shall not be here for five or six months. I have hired out as brakeman on a passenger train, from Detroit to Chicago.   Respectfully,   C. MILLS.

[The money referred to by Charles, is what he claims of his mother's estate, and which Mr. W. told him before he left he would look into, learn the facts in the case, and see that justice was done.]

Mr. Woolworth remarked last night that there was a good deal of work done nowadays, and inquired if any one felt oppressed by it. W. G. Kelley thought we escaped in a good degree the pressure of disease that was felt outside, through our enthusiasm in business. Indeed, some of our members have been seriously attacked, but in every instance we believe, are on the gain, and some entirely recovered.

2035 cans of tomatoes were packed yesterday.—Twenty-four barrels of quinces were bought at Fairport, at five dollars and fifty cents per barrel.

A committee was appointed last night to select articles for the fair which is to be held at Oneida next week.

The currant bushes sent to us from W. C. arrived yesterday.

141½ doz. traps ordered yesterday.

THE O. C. DAILY.

VOL. 4. SATURDAY, SEPT. 28, 1867. NO. 77.

Morrow, Ohio, Sept. 23, 1867.

DEAR MR. WOOLWORTH:—I enclose some orders as you will see. I called on our trap customers in Cincinnati on Saturday last. They had received their traps and were well pleased, and said they were selling well. Howell, Gano & Co. will send another order in a few days. The Cincinnati men who have heretofore thought the imitation traps would answer for their trade find them slow sale, and say when they can work off their stock they shall buy of us altogether.

All bag dealers like our bags, but say they are too good—too expensive for selling. Even our best customers sell ten times as many from Peddie and other manufacturers. I go to day to Circleville and on toward Pittsburg. I expect to get home in about ten days. I wish to confess my union with Mr. Noyes and the Community. Yours, H. R. PERRY.

In the *La Science Sociale*, a semi-monthly paper published at Paris, of the date of Sept. 1st, mention is made of the O. C. It states that two young men, members of the Community, had been at Paris, and had given curious information about their Association, which had called the attention of the *publicistes européens*—those who had been and still are interested in Communism. The paper states that "The O. C. was founded in 1847 by John Humphrey Noyes, *petit-fils* of an English puritan." Two columns of this paper are filled with a description of the Community, taken we should judge, from the newspaper articles circulating in this country.

W. P., SEPT. 26.—It is quite the fashion to call a bee after supper, when there is a piece of work that needs to be done immediately. A bee was announced this evening for work in the silk-room on a new spinner, and for making iron headed bobbins. It proved to be a very pleasant enthusiastic affair, and a good deal of work was done. One more such bee will finish the business. There was some music mixed with the work. The double drag was played on blocks of iron with hammers, and manly voices rang out in song above the clatter of hammers.

Mr. Kelley overheard some conversation about the Community while riding on the cars yesterday.—Blind Henry and the miller of Oneida took the lead in the conversation, though all in the cars seemed greatly interested. As the *facts* stated were before unknown to the O. C., it may be well to record them for the benefit of interested friends. The miller said the Community were doing an *immense* business, and kept *ten* teams on the road; for the sustenance of which, he, said miller, sold said Community $500

worth of feed per month. Another man observed that you could not go to the Community without meeting at least one, and perhaps two or three Community teams on the way. Blind Henry said: "The Community people are talked about a great deal, but I think they behave about as well as the rest of us, and I don't know but a little better." The same man further remarked that he had read the CIRCULAR, and found it *thoroughly orthodox.*

After reading what Mr. Noyes said about Mr. Blood last night, there was a general burst of indignation and criticism of him and his course while here, and a recantation of the commendation given him the night before he left. His letter which was received a day or two since gives us a pretty good clue to the workings of his mind while he was here. We sincerely pity his family.

Mr. Shelley came yesterday. He has settled up his affairs at the West and has come East with the intention of going to Newark and closing up his whip-socket business there, so soon as he shall have manufactured enough of that article for the fall trade: he will then offer himself to the O. C. for membership. He seems to be a man of the true stamp and mettle, though rather uncultivated.

Our cows are reveling in clover fields this fall, and as a consequence we have the nicest kind of butter. The dairy folks report that they churn some over 150 pounds per week. We have done getting meals for visitors, and to-day they are moving the milk into the company dining-room.

We hear at the present time the music of the loom in the garret at the mansion-house and that of the sewing-machine in the old reception-room. Mrs. Conant is weaving a web of twenty-two yards of rag-carpet for the sitting room at the new Commune.

There is a good deal of moving and changing rooms nowadays. We heard one of the girls say yesterday in reply to an objection her companion made to moving so often, "Why, you don't want to be a cabbage do you?"

We had a call yesterday from a Mrs. Spencer who has resided twelve years at the Sandwich Islands.—She is an acquaintance of H. R. Perry and was much disappointed in not seeing him.

Sympathy was expressed by Mr. Kinsley and others with Mr. Noyes views in reference to our taking stock in the Midland Railroad.

There are now at the children's house twenty-nine children, under twelve years of age, eighteen of whom are under seven.

Traps ordered yesterday, 178¼ doz.

THE O. C. DAILY.

VOL. 4.   MONDAY, SEPT. 30, 1867.   NO. 78.

BUSINESS MEETING.

The letter from Martin Kinsley to Mr. Kellogg in relation to Mr. Thurston was presented. He said that he did not misrepresent the cows to Mr. T., but on the contrary he (Mr. T.) had seen them milked and seemed satisfied with them. He thought he could not reasonably demand damages, and that the reason of his dissatisfaction was the low price of cheese this season. The subject is left in the hands of Messrs. Woolworth, Kellogg, Conant and J. H. Barron.

Abram wished to know what was to be done about painting the W. P. house. It was postponed last Spring with the expectation of doing it this Fall. If it is to be done at all this season it will have to be done next month. There will be no economy in putting it off. It can be done better and cheaper now than in the Spring. The Board therefore voted that the house be painted this Fall. Committee on colors, Mrs. Miller, J. H. Barron and Abram Burt.

F. Marks wanted to know how we should supply apples to the Wallingford, New Haven, New York, W. P. and B. H. Communes. They have no apples in Connecticut this season. Mr. Woolworth thought it might be well to use limitation in regard to apples, as in other things, and not be quite so free as we have been accustomed to be. Much would be saved by having some person look after the apples and see that they do not rot. Mr. Thacker said after we get thro' our other preserving we had better can a part of the apples for future use.

W. P., SEPT. 28.—A company of fourteen women and girls, and eight or ten men, came over from O. C. this evening and spent two hours in the chain-room. They "turned" one bbl. of swivels, "tried" a large number of chains, and "fitted" enough to keep two presses at work all night welding. Myron has eleven boys from the depot, who are going to work at chains all night.—Twenty-one thousand traps have been finished, packed and shipped, within the last six days—an average of thirty-five hundred per day.

One might imagine from the number and variety of spiders to be found in our house that it had been selected by them as a general rendezvous. Some of the girls not liking their company, have for the past week been waging a war of extermination with them. The number of spiders killed is one hundred and forty.—In our meeting this evening the talk about Mr. Blood was read, and heartily endorsed by all the family.

Last night just before ten o'clock we heard the music of voices and the ringing laugh in the old reception-room, and, in quest of items, we ventured to look in to see what merry-making was going on at that late hour; and sure enough there was a company of six, with a basket of butternuts, grapes, bread and butter, cheese and cake, seated in a circle (some on the floor) enjoying a sumptuous repast, not the least of which was, if not "a feast of reason," at least "a flow of soul."—The company with four more, had started just before night for a picnic, but being overtaken by cold and rain, they retreated, and not wishing to be entirely thwarted in their plans, had chosen this unique way of disposing of the contents of their baskets.

Friday afternoon, after receiving Mr. Noyes's opinion on the Midland Railroad, Mr. Woolworth requested Mr. Worden to go down to the Depot, and inform the Oneida delegation that called on us some eight or ten days ago, of our decision.—They had expected a favorable report and were quite disappointed and expressed their regrets at our conclusion in reference to this project. Mr. Worden told them that we were friendly to the enterprise, and should the road be so laid as to come near and give us a depot, the O. C. would do its best to aid it, although all our means were employed and needed at the present time in our business.

Our beautiful summer-like weather received a sudden check yesterday. In the forenoon it was uncomfortably warm, so that muslin dresses seemed desirable; but in the afternoon and evening we were obliged to wrap ourselves in flannel in order not to be uncomfortable. It was some rainy and windy during the night, consequently no frost. This morning at 7 o'clock the mercury stood at 38 deg.

We had some talk last night about the family spirit, as it was thought that some of our members were suffering bodily as well as in spirit in consequence of the influence emanating from that principality, Harriet Howard and Mary Jones in particular.—Louisa Howard has been in the family some time, but she is worldly, and does not commend herself to us as in earnest for salvation.

The business of corn packing has closed for this season. Eight thousand cans have been packed, thus exceeding our programme three thousand. We shall probably reach our mark of fifteen thousand cans of tomatoes by the middle of the week.

A new song entitled "The American Ensign" was sung by a Quartette club yesterday at the opening of the noon meeting, and again last night. The music was charming.

Mrs. Brown, Mrs. Underwood's daughter Helen, staid here over Sunday. Mr. North also came Saturday, and Mr. Aiken.

552 boxes of grapes (820 pounds) were packed Saturday and Sunday.

Traps ordered Saturday and Sunday, 3144 doz.

THE O. C. DAILY.

VOL. 4. TUESDAY, OCTOBER 1, 1867. NO. 79.

Berlin Heights, O., Sept. 25, 1867.

DEAR ——— : I do not wish to surfeit you with letters. This morning I sent to the Express Agent, at Berlin Station $200.00 directed to Mr. W. H. Woolworth, Oneida Community Oneida N. York.— Ordered it sent by M. U. Express. This letter will be mailed one day later. Mr. John W. B. Randolph sends one hundred.—Mr. Randolph has been a reader, and an advocate of the doctrines of Mr. Noyes and the O. C. for nine years past. He sent for the "Berean" and "Bible Communism" in 1858. We feel that he is with us in spirit and in deed.

I think it was in the year 1858 while Mr. Randolph and myself were living under the same roof, that I remarked to a friend of mine, (a young man,) that I wished to do something to make the mice that found their way into our buttery, superstitious. My friend, not in sympathy with Mr. Randolph, said he thought to let them (the mice) read the Berean would have the desired effect.

I awoke quite early this morning, and thought with my head that it would be a good time to write you, as the mental sky would be clearer in the morning.— In fact I think it has been so many times, and I have had a kind of theory that each day was a miniature life-time, and as a consequence have thought of the evening as the most unfavorable time for inspiration. But the inspiration I have now seems to be quite the reverse of that. After working in company with Christ all day, and having been made to *feel* so good, I come home at night wanting to tell. * * How very near I feel to you this evening as I write, and how much the devil tried to thwart my purpose in writing. I want to confess Christ a power in me to overcome all such devils.

I should like to make the mark on this paper that would just express the feelings of my heart. But I will trust for the present that you can guess near enough. G. W. Reeve.

Mr. North leaves us to-day for his home in Pa. On Sunday morning last he disclosed to the writer the fact that another string to his bow had been added since penning his last letter to us. A friend of his in the West, on learning through Mr. Guiteau that he had sold out his mercantile business, made proposals to him to accept an agency in a Life Insurance Co. Upon the receipt of the proposition, Mr. North replied to it, asking for more definite terms. Having received them he left soon after for the O. C. Looking at the matter from a purely worldly stand-point, the offer was a decidedly liberal one. As a *solicitor* of premiums on life insurance, Mr. N. no doubt has more than ordinary ability.

After listening to all that he had to say on the subject, I replied that the O. C. had never assumed any responsibility whatever respecting his course, or of his affairs, either temporal or spiritual; for he had never been in circumstances that would justify us in doing so. Moreover he had not hitherto, solicited the exercise of any such function on the part of the O. C., unless, indeed, his first letter to Mr. Noyes, a few weeks since was such an application. But even that appeal for advice was virtually countermanded in a subsequent letter to the O. C.

As to his accepting the tempting offer, we could not take the responsibility of advising him. He could remain, however, an outside friend as he had been, rendering such aid to the cause in the way of writing for the CIRCULAR as he had inspiration and ability to do. It was quite evident that, aside from obstructions to a closer union of his family, he himself is in no condition to enter the service of the O. C. as a hired laborer. On the whole, therefore, it was quite a relief to learn that he had the prospect of a business that would in a year or two, if successful, enable him to liquidate his obligations to the world. But "strait is the gate, and narrow is the way, that leadeth unto" Communism, "and few there be that find it." c.

A copy of Mr. Woolworth's reply to Mr. Blood's letter was read in the meeting last night. Mr. W. had **freedom to tell him some plain, cutting truths, which,** although it may not benefit him, is nevertheless a help to us in clearing the atmosphere of any remains of his diabolical spirit. Those who have copies of Mr. W.'s letter to Mr. Blood, sent out yesterday, should read *interlarded* instead of *interluded*, as written.

Traps packed for shipment during the week ending Saturday Sept. 28, 1867:

No. 0 Traps,	1,140.	No. 0 with chains,	960.
" 1 "	3,090.	" 1 " "	13,790.
" 1¼ "	192.	" 1¼ " "	576.
" 2 "	108.	" 2 " "	1,278.
" 3 "	108.	" 3 " "	147.
" 4 "	84.	" 4 " "	120.
Total,	4,728.	Total,	16,871.
		Whole number,	21,599.

At 9 o'clock last night the murcury stood at 38 deg. and at a quarter to six this morning at 28 deg. There was a white frost spread over the fields, and the grapes are considerably damaged. The day is bright and promises to be warmer than its predecessor.

We forgot to mention yesterday, that we had a dance Sunday night after supper, the first we have had since Feb. 20th. It went off nicely.

Ten hundred and forty-six cans of tomatoes were packed yesterday.

Mr. Shelley left in the night for Newark, N. J.

Traps ordered yesterday, 421 doz.

THE O. C. DAILY.

VOL. 4. WEDNESDAY, OCTOBER 2, 1867. NO. 80.

Cleveland, Sept. 27 1867.

Mrs. J. ——: I embrace this opportunity to express my thanks to the Community. But for Mr. Noyes's exposition of the new Testament, I know not that I should ever have accepted Chirst as a Savior. It is over a year since I accepted your faith. I have read the CIRCULAR three years or more, but the first years of reading it, made but little, if any impression upon me, as I was so infected with *hadean* spiritualism, that I was impervious to any thing else. Long years I wandered in the wilderness of so called spiritualism; but I rejoice that I have at last found rest in Jesus Christ. My mind so long steeped in gloom, is now buoyant with hope. It seems as if new life was infused into my being—that I have indeed passed from death unto life. I desire above all things to be free from all sin—to be in perfect subjection to Christ—to be obedient to the heavenly calling. Yours in the faith, HENRIETTA SWEET.

[Miss Sweet is a sister of Mrs. Towner and has formerly lived at Berlin Heights.]

(Extract of a letter from James Meadowcraft, of Minnesota:)

"The article entitled 'Victory over Sensuality,' in the CIRCULAR for Sept. 9th, I am rather at a loss to understand. The ideas I have gathered from reading the pamphlet 'Salvation from Sin, the end of Christian Faith,' are, that an individual who has really accepted Jesus Christ as a whole Saviour, is thenceforth and forever preserved from sin—that Jesus Christ dwelleth in him, saving him even from a tendency to sin; in fact that our Saviour has done and will continue to do all the fighting; that his gospel invites not to battle, not to a warfare with principalities and powers of darkness, but to a feast—a feast of love. In the article I have alluded to, we are summoned to do battle with the old man, the flesh and the devil, a whole principality of evil which must be conquered before we can obtain peace. Dear friends, this to me is an unexpected difficulty. I have been fighting the devil all my life; he would, right or wrong, make an infidel of me. I thought when I read 'Salvation from Sin,' that I had at last, in the providence and mercy of God, found something to save me; that in accepting of Christ as a Saviour, the victory over sensuality and all other evils and principalities of evil, was won, and won forever."

Our mangle is said to be a great help to the laundry department, but its good qualities have not been so fully tested as they will be when it is connected with the steam power, which we hope to have accomplished soon. Turning it by hand is rather hard work.

Mrs. Mallory thinks, judging from the short experience she had in using it, that it saves the labor of two hands; smoothing all the table-cloths, towels, pillow-cases, handkerchiefs and all plain under garments that have no buttons on them.

Mr. Noyes's late talks, "The Inner Man," "How to be Fruitful," and "The Paper: How to Edit it," were read last night, and listened to with all-absorbing interest. Mr. Woolworth said: "I think Mr. Noyes is stripping this subject of the resurrection and the inner man of a great deal of mystery and unreality that has heretofore surrounded it, and is treating it in a very practical, tangible manner. He makes the subject plain and intelligible to our understanding and comprehension."

The following is a summary of my late trip West:

Trap orders, net,		$4,641.
Bag " "		1,666.
Fruit " "		1,037.
Silk " "		177.
Total,		$7,521.

I was away from home two months. Expenses, $331.32. H. R. P.

Two gentlemen called yesterday, one from New York and the other from Utica. Both were acquainted with some of our members. We have bought goods of the New York gentleman. They were quite jovial over their dinner, and praised it a good deal.—The Newyorker is an iron merchant, and the Utican cashier of a bank.

Another letter was received from Mr. Blood yesterday, which was a sort of re-hash of his last one. Mr. Cragin received one also, which he said he should burn, and give it no further notice. We wish Mr. B. could be made to know how slightly his missiles affect us.

About a thousand pounds of grapes were packed yesterday and eight hundred and seventy pounds the day before. The bag business crowds just now, and it is rather difficult to get what women's help we need to pack grapes.

Flora Whiting has taken Rosamond's place in distributing the DAILIES, and also the CIRCULARS.—Charlotte Maria is with us again for two or three weeks in place of Phebe, who has gone to Willow-Place.

There is a change in the hour of the mail, so that it is not made up at O. C. till a quarter to one o'clock P. M. This is a great relief to those who have the most to do in getting out the DAILY.

Dinners are called for by visitors more or less almost every day, which are furnished them in the family dining-room.

Traps ordered yesterday, 121½ doz.

THE O. C. DAILY.

VOL. 4. THURSDAY, OCTOBER 3, 1867. NO. 81.

W. P., Oct. 1.—Our men set it for their mark to send off thirty thousand dollars worth of traps during the month of Sept. Last evening it was reported that the sales for the month amounted to $30,198.44.

A young man belonging to this family having volunteered to do the milking for a time, went bravely at his work this morning; but the cow seemed to be unwilling. After some discipline, and a good deal of chasing, she was at length cornered and submitted to be milked. Just as the work was nearly done, a man passing by remarked, " There is a smart fellow, *milking on the wrong side of the cow!*"

The paper received to-day, was spoken of by many this evening in terms of high commendation. The first article in particular was liked.

Oct. 2.—It being necessary to finish a lot of No. 1½ traps immediately, a grand bee was called. A goodly company from O. C. were on hand, and at seven o'clock the work began and continued until nine.— Our meeting was omitted; the family came together after supper and listened to the reading of journals and reports.

Among the curiosities brought home by H. R. Perry is a cone, ten and a half inches in length, and four in diameter, taken from one of those mammoth trees in California. It is gummy, and similar in appearance to the cones that grow on our pines: also an ivory ball, manufactured in China, some less than two inches in diameter, cut from a solid block of ivory and curiously carved, with four little balls inside, one within the other, all cut and carved similar to the outside one. But what attracted our attention the most, and excited our admiration as a work of art, was a Lincoln badge, woven in Coventry, England. It is a perfect likeness of that unfortunate man, with the stars and stripes and other ornamental figures beneath, and the words, " The ever lamented President Lincoln," and above it, the American eagle with extended wings standing between two urns, and the United States motto waving over its head; and still above this, Lincoln's memorable words, " I have said nothing but what I am willing to live by, and if it be the pleasure of the Almighty God, to die by'; " also the date of his assassination. The badge is made of the finest silk, about a foot in length and two inches in width, and considering that it is all woven, it certainly is the finest specimen of delicacy of design, and skill in the art of weaving that we ever saw.

The cone and badge will be placed in the show-case where all can see them if they wish.

The O. C. had a slight ripple on the surface of its life yesterday, caused by the sudden appearance of Lord and Lady Amberly. They staid about ten minutes. Mrs. Sedgewick, the wife of Mills' lawyer, of Syracuse, came with them. H. C. Noyes was introduced to them, and went over with them to see the children. They kept up such a fire of questioning on our social practices, that H. C. N. said she felt when they left, as though she had been bombarded.

Another sensation was felt in the afternoon by a call from the notorious Grove Loomis. He was accompanied by a lady, and they walked round the premises, the barn in particular, Tontine, Store, &c.

After Grove Loomis's call was mentioned last night, the question was asked if the family thought that our property at the barn, Tontine, Bag-shop, Shoe-shop and Store, was considered as secure as it could be made, and those having charge of these departments were exhorted to look into the matter.— While we feel that " unless the Lord keep the city, the watchmen labor in vain" yet this trust in God will not justify us in leaving property carelessly exposed.

Hearing one of the ironing girls making some remarks about something that happened at the Boarding-house, I took occasion to inquire how they liked the new administration. One of the girls answered that she never saw so great a change in a house in her life. " Like it?" said she, " we cannot tell how much we like it. I do not know but we are crazy some of the time, we are so happy." " What is it," I inquired, " the change outwardly or spiritually?" " Both," was the answer. E. F. H.

[We give the following letter just as it is written with the orthography, capitals, &c.:]

Office of R. W. Ulery,
Real Estate Agent and Notary Public,
Blairstown, Benton Co., Iowa, Sept. 26, 1867.

O. C.
Walengford }

Gents :—Pleas find Enclosed Fifty Cents for whitch you will Pleas Send one Doz. Coppies of Mail Contingence or Self Controle in Secual intercoarse Send soon to R. W. ULERY.

1,073 cans of tomatoes have been packed within the last two days making a total of 15,670. We shall probably not reach much over 16,000, as the frost has cut off the remainder of the crop.

Sales for the month of Sept.

Traps,	$29,014.28.
Bags,	$3,951.50.
Preserved Fruit,	$1,071.16,

Traps ordered yesterday,	337½ doz.

THE O. C. DAILY.

VOL. 4.   FRIDAY, OCTOBER 4, 1867.   NO. 82.

GOD GIVES US ALL THINGS TO ENJOY—NOTHING TO POSSESS.

Paul says that God gives us richly all things to enjoy. Here is an open secret, we might say, that civilization has hardly yet discovered. The question, how to appropriate the wealth of enjoyment so freely offered to us, is one of great significance. There are multitudes who abound in what the world calls wealth, but who are actually poorer than paupers in every thing like true enjoyment of it. And the question may be asked seriously, is not the idea an insane one, that the possession of property, persons or things, necessarily insures enjoyment of them? One who does not intrinsically possess himself, is in no condition whatever to possess other persons' things. God only possesses that power, and therefore has wisely connected all true enjoyment with himself. If the O. C., therefore, was conceived in the spirit of that principle, that God is the *bona fide* owner of all things—persons included—its perpetuity and growth will not be questioned by believers in God and the Bible. And by recognizing a truth so radical as the foregoing, in practical, every-day life, the Community has verified the apostolic statement, that God gives us richly all **things to** *enjoy.* **It is in this way, and in no other, that** the O. C. is made happy—happy in knowing *how* to enjoy all things as belonging to God, by knowing *how* to serve him for the love of that service. And when we cease to find enjoyment in any given course, the presumption is, that God's inspiration in it has run out; for without inspiration there can be no genuine enjoyment in any thing; but with it, all things are fruitful sources of joy and satisfaction.

A few years since the O. C. had an inspiration to borrow money for the purpose of building up the Trap-works at W. P. and we took pleasure in so doing. But we find that we no longer have inspiration to do business upon borrowed capital, while on the other hand we realize a full flow of inspiration and pleasure in working to cancel our indebtedness, and to secure a sufficient surplus to supply all of our legitimate businesses with the requisite capital without borrowing. Communism has had to assert its freedom from legality in finance, as well as in religion and morality. To trust our temporal affairs to the guidance of the wisdom of heaven, instead of the wisdom of this world, has been about as hard a battle to fight, as that of trusting the salvation of our souls to grace and truth rather than to law and duty-doing. But we are sure to conquer in the former as we have done in the latter.   c.

W. P., OCT. 3.—Another enthusiastic bee this evening for finishing traps.—We gathered in the sitting-room immediately after supper, and listened to the reading of part of the correspondence, and again at nine o'clock to finish it. It was thought we could fully agree with what was said in the talk about the uses of the paper, and the same subject will be discussed in our evening gathering. Some advice and criticism was given some of the young men who seemed to have got off the track. It is vastly more important for us to see that we have a good spirit than it is to make traps; that is our first business, and these young persons can help more by having thorough union with Christ and the family, than by making traps for a year. The meeting continued with great earnestness until nearly half past ten. Most of the young men expressed their determination to take sides with the truth against the faults criticised.

Lousia Howard was in our meeting last night, and seems to have experienced quite a change. She confessed that she came here full of unbelief and prejudice and disposed to think evil. Mr. Woolworth told her plainly what he thought of her case, and she is now thankful for his sincerity, though at the time, she thought him unnecessarily severe. It is to be hoped that this is a new era in her life, and that she and Harriet may be the means of saving their parents and brother.

There was a good deal of testimony given last night in commendation of the CIRCULAR and the various ways in which it is doing good not only among ourselves but in the world outside of us, in circulating the truth. Many of the members testified to having had in the past, their attention arrested, and fastened on the truth by reading the CIRCULAR; others that Mr. Noyes's writings seemed to be the key that unlocked the treasures of the Bible and made its truths easy of comprehension.

Mrs. Guiteau made us a call of two or three hours yesterday and took dinner—she was accompanied by a friend of hers, a lady from Syracuse. She has been absent from home about eight weeks visiting her friends who live in this vicinity.

Our meeting last night seemed quite thin, between twenty-five and thirty of the family having gone over to help at the Trap-works.

There was an urgent call for help at the Trap-shop to-day, as many of our hired men will be absent attending the Fair.

There was a frost again last night, about as severe as the first. The thermometer stood a little before sunrise, at 27 deg.

Among other things sent to the Fair to-day, are twenty-one varieties of grapes.

A Mr. Reid from Ovoca a place near Bath, staid here over night. He came wanting to join.

Traps ordered Oct. 3, 784¼ doz., including two bear-traps.

THE O. C. DAILY.

VOL. 4. SATURDAY, OCTOBER 5, 1867. NO. 83.

Miss S. Augusta Story writes from Fort Lyon, Mo.: "I feel since I confessed Christ my whole Savior that God has pardoned my past sins, and that he has granted me repentance unto life. I ask your advice, what I had better do. I want to place myself in your hands as my teachers and leaders. I am but a babe in Christ, and I ask to be taught of you, to be guided and directed. It seems to me that I am ready to stand purification by fire; that I can lay *all* on the altar, self, friends, a good name, all things, and come free and willing, without reserve, to you. I have taught school for a living most of the time since I was eighteen, excepting the year of my married life. My husband obtained a divorce and is married again. I was married when I was about twenty. I am now thirty-two. I place myself in your hands by God's leading I believe, and I ask your advice what to do."

W. P., Oct. 4.—The Fair drew away thirty-five of our hired hands from the Trap-shop to-day, but O. C. sent a generous supply of men and women to help fill their places. Another company came this evening and worked until nine o'clock. Mr. Woolworth was among the number.

Roswell reports that the finishing department is not waiting for springs! And that the forge department can turn out 2,500 finished springs per day.

It was the testimony of many of the family this evening that work had gone off remarkably well to-day, and they had enjoyed themselves in it. The talk last evening cleared the atmosphere perceptibly.

Mrs. Blood and Henry both write in great perplexity of mind, in consequence of the course Mr. B. takes in reference to the latter, he insisting that Henry shall look at the Community through his (Mr. B.'s) eyes. He wants to take him to Milford and put him into a machine shop, and Henry wants to come back to the Community and his mother is very anxious about him.

Mrs. B. says in her letter, "I sometimes say after reading Mr. B.'s letters 'Oh dear! what shall I do? was ever a woman placed in such circumstances?' But after a time I get quiet, and think of what Mr. Cragin and other good friends tried to impress on my mind, that 'God arranges all our circumstances, and will take the best possible care that they serve his purpose and our best good.'"

When Hannah, the colored woman, brought her baby here it excited the wonder of our little ones. "Could it laugh?" "Had it got teeth like us?" Is it black?" Has it got feet?" and all kinds of questions concerning it. Finally Ormond inquired quite soberly, "*Could God get in its heart too?*"

The other morning I said to Ormond, "I am going to turn over a new leaf about you now, and you are not going to expect any more from me than the other children do." He went out under my window and took up a limb of a lilac bush, and asked if that was the new leaf. I told him it was not. The next day he came along and said, "*Mamma, have you got the new leaf in your pocket?*"

The other morning Harry Burnham, having slept with his mother, awoke very early. She persuaded him to lie still, promising to get up soon. Presently she said "*Well, now I will get up*," but did not for a minute or two. Harry turned to her quite reprovingly and said, "*Why don't you get up? God sees you and hears you. You said you would get up.*" His mother said she felt all the forenoon as if she had been criticised.

These items will show how children remember and reflect on what is said to them.　　H. M. W.

Mr. Nash, it is thought, is steadily, though slowly, improving. At times he can move one of his fingers on his palsied hand. Mr. Smith, who has the care of him, left him for a short time yesterday, and on his return he found Mr. N. stretched on the floor, laughing heartily at his ludicrous position. In his attempts to turn himself, he had fallen flat on his back, but was not hurt in the least.

Two of our hired men who had charge of our cattle that were taken to the Fair, yesterday, got drunk, and some of our folks who were there finding that the cattle were left without care, drove them home.—One of the men was taken home on a load of coal, dead drunk. It is to be hoped that they will be immediately discharged from our employ, though it seems to have been their first offence.

Our people had good luck yesterday, in selling grapes at the Fair, having taken in about $20.00 and getting an order for $50.00 worth besides. They were expecting to sell a good many more to-day, but it rains this morning, and people if they are wise, will stay at home.

Beulah runs the sewing machine now, and likes the business. The machine is settled at last in its old place, the north garret of the Mansion-house.

Our meeting was thin again last night, as more of the family were missing than the night before; Mr. Woolworth with the rest.

A Mr. Burbank staid here last night.

Traps ordered yesterday,　　339 doz.

THE O. C. DAILY.

VOL. 4.   MONDAY, OCTOBER 7, 1867.   NO. 84.

BUSINESS MEETING.

The subject of a new ice-house at W. P. was brought before the Board for consideration. The present one is not suitable to keep ice through warm weather. It is about empty now. It was referred to Messrs. Kinsley, Ackley, G. W. Hamilton and A. Burt, who are to consider whether we had better build a new house or make the present one answer till we are better able to build.

Mr. Kinsley wished to know how we should accommodate our new hostler with a house. It is desirable to have him live as near to his business as possible. Several places were suggested, but the matter was finally referred to Messrs. Kinsley, J. Burt and A. Burt.

Mr. Kinsley said he had been on the committee for tenants and tenant-houses for a long time, attending to their wants and listening to their complaints, and he would like to be relieved from that office. It was not a very attractive one. Mr. Woolworth suggested that Mr. Kinsley keep that place till he makes it attractive. Generally sympathized with.

Abram Burt wished there could be a horse for jobbing. He could not always anticipate his wants, and could not always get Mr. Miller's team to draw lumber, &c., to places where he needed it. Some thought the horse Mr. Miller drives might do more than it does. Mr. Hawley, F. Marks and A. Burt were appointed committee to consider how he can be accommodated.

The committee on butternuts report that they think there are not far from seventy-five or one hundred bushels on the ground, and the question how they shall be gathered remains unsolved. It is hoped the nuts will not be wasted.

There are two or three jobs to be done at W. P. that require teams and digging. The teams required will be at liberty in about a week. Left to G. W. H., Mr. Burt, G. Campbell and J. Higgins.

Mr. Cragin received a letter yesterday from Mr. Newbould, in behalf of Mr. and Mrs. Hare, lately of Modern Times, who, he says, would be glad to work in some of our work-shops, for such wages as we may think fit to give. He says of them, " Mr. Hare is a very faithful and intelligent worker, when under direction, but his shrinking and sensitive nature debars him from combatting with the world. He cannot ask for employment, nor negotiate with strangers, and suffers consequent poverty. The same sensitiveness prevents his seeking fellowship with you. I do so for him, feeling sure that in himself and family you will find gratifying adjuncts. His scientific and philosophic thought has revolved him through doubt, back into an enlightened acceptation of the Community theology.—Mrs. Hare is of a very gentle, amiable temperament, with keen perceptive faculties and considerable mental cultivation. Both are healthy, able workers, and earnest, religious people."

A very good letter from Mrs. Hare was published in the Daily of July 30th.

W. P., Oct. 5.—Two men have been perseveringly painting all day on our house, in spite of the rain.—By the way this rain is very much appreciated by our people, for we are short of water; though not as short as in days of yore at our old grist-mill, when Mr. H., the miller, was seen franticly rushing at some cows that were drinking from the almost drained pond.

A new welding press is in successful operation in the chain-room, which will greatly facilitate business in that department.

Twenty-one thousand and sixty-three traps shipped during the last six days, (about the same as last week notwithstanding the Fair) and between twenty-four and twenty-five thousand have been ordered in the same time.

Our people suspended work at W. P. yesterday, out of respect to the feelings of our neighbors (Mr. Adkins in particular,) who were disturbed by the clatter of our machinery Sundays. Mr. Cragin and others thought we should lose nothing by this rest from business, for our pond at W. P. is low and needs filling up, and perhaps the spiritual pond there may need replenishing; and taking time for reflection and joining the family at O. C., may serve that important end.

There was considerable talk last night about the stirring up of the Depot folks about us and the newspaper articles, in consequence of our refusal to take stock in the Midland Railroad. Mr. Burt and others gave their opinions on the subject of the " Depot building us up" as they assume is the case, and thought that when the truth was known, the shoe would be on the other foot.

Bags made in Sept.	86¾ doz.
" ordered " "	123 "

We sometimes receive orders from our Agents, that are a week old before we get them. Would it not be better for all orders to be forwarded as soon as received, instead of waiting perhaps a week or more, merely because the Agent will then be here himself.

We had two bees in the afternoon yesterday, one for picking the remainder of the tomatoes, and the other to gather in the grapes. The work was accomplished in a little more than two hours.

Mr. Van Velzer starts this morning on a peddling trip of a week.

$34.00 worth of grapes in all, were sold at the fair.

Traps ordered Saturday and Sunday, 489½ doz.

THE O. C. DAILY.

VOL. 4.   TUESDAY, OCTOBER 8, 1867.   NO. 85.

Messrs. Burt and Newhouse visited Oneida yesterday, and had some conversation with some of the influential men there, on the subject of the Midland Railroad, and our views respecting the enterprise. The following statements were made in meeting last evening: All worthy people in the village are not disposed to sympathize with the manner in which the Oneida papers have treated the question of our refusal to subscribe to their fund; though at the same time they are disappointed and rather sore at our supposed refusal. Mr. Burt fully explained our views. They accepted them in part, especially that we had helped them in the past more than they had helped us. They looked upon the article in the *Democratic Union* much as we do, and said it would have no influence in the place. Still, they claimed this road would benefit us if it did not come close and give us a depot, as it would reduce freight rates by competition, and double the value of our real estate. Mr. Burt conceded the first point, but to the second he replied that we were not, like the farmers around us, intending to sell out, and that the only effect of increase of value in real estate would be to double our taxes, a favor which we could cheerfully dispense with. To this they said little or nothing. Mr. Stevens admits that the route we wish the road to take is the straight one from the end of the Lake up through the valley; that he first advocated it on that ground; and that in order to bring the road where the Oneida people want it, a bend of over two miles will have to be made; thus turning their plea for a straight road, bending to accommodate no one, against them into a stronghold for us.

Oneida's subscription is conditional, as follows: If the road comes within the borders of their corporation they will do so much: if not they will do nothing. Thus they boldly justify in themselves what they condemn in us. They made no secrect of the fact that they would never consent to Mr. Burt's plan, of running the road east of Oneida and giving them a depot near the mouth of Scouondoa Creek; though they admitted its advantages. Mr. Stevens thinks he could bring the road so as to give us a depot near the site of the old red schoolhouse. Mr. Littlejohn will soon be at Oneida and Mr. Stevens intends to try and bring him up here that he may compare notes with us, and examine the merits of the two routes.

DEAR DAILY:—By the force of circumstances, I again find myself in my old place—tempering springs in the Trap-shop. It so happens that much of my labor has, thus far, been in the night. Perhaps if I were an owl I should not mind it; but trying to sleep daytimes never amounted to very much with me.

However, in the still hours of the night, when machinery has ceased to roar, and the busy laborers and foremen have ceased their toil, I have ample time to reflect on my ways. I think how soon was I snatched from my quiet hill-side home, in the old state of Connecticut, to mingle in this ferment of business. I was there just long enough to learn that old Connecticut is fair; and to fall in love with her rocks and mosses—her old pastures and babbling brooks—her sweet ferns and wild roses. I repeat the old strain, "I lost my love when enjoying her most."

But what shall I say now? I have discovered that Oneida too is a fair maid—at least her maids are fair. She offers her hand to me. Shall I refuse it because I have a sweet-heart elsewhere? Woe is me if I do. You may, if you please, tell my fair Connecticut that I am going to have other sweet-hearts besides her, so that when she sends me away again I shan't so much care.   Yours truly,   J. P. H.

Mrs. Reeve writes from Berlin Sept. 28th.

"Surely God is just like a Father and he is a 'rewarder of all those who diligently seek him.' How much more abundantly is the prayer of my heart answered than I ever dared to hope for; little did I think that what I wanted was faith in Christ which is the basis of christian Communism. The Father 'knoweth the things we have need of before we ask him.' At times I feel like singing, running, dancing, working, playing, crying, (for joy) all in the same minute, but as I can't very well I just keep right on steadily at work.

There is one thing for which I feel especially to thank God, it is this, that I have no cause for hesitating about opening my heart to you; not that there is nothing to be corrected, but you will be true; just as ready to reprove as to commend; it is what I love.— I want no dark corners, I want the light everywhere. You will tell us if our letters come too often, and are too long; we know you have a work of your own to do, and it is our desire to be helpers in that great work. God bless you all."

Having occasion to send to Mr. Rawsons this morning for a chicken, Mr. Woolworth sent them a half bushel of grapes, and acting on Mr. Noyes's late suggestions, "to overcome evil with good," and also his own inspiration, he sent the Olmstead folks the same amount.

A general bee for gathering butternuts yesterday afternoon, resulted in collecting only ten bushels.— Our neighbors have taken their share first, which leaves ours rather spare.

The supper hour is changed from six o'clock to half past five, and to-night at 7 o'clock we commence reading, in the Hall, the life of Dr. Beecher.

THE O. C. DAILY.

VOL. 4. WEDNESDAY, OCTOBER 9, 1867. NO. 86.

THE CONVERSION OF TRADES.

Trades and businesses need to be converted to God as truly as any other class of sinners. The business world is one of the strong-holds of satan, the source of floods of unbelief that drown all convictions and thoughts about God, truth and righteousness. It is, moreover, the strong-hold of selfishness, claiming great respectability under the title of usage and custom. But venerable and hoary-headed as selfishness is, under the cloak of trade and commerce, it is being impeached, so to speak, by a congress that has been in session for 1800 years—a congress that believes, with a united voice that the resurrection power of Christ is abundantly able to carry on every kind of legitimate business in this world in the spirit of perfect truthfulness and integrity.

Indeed, as believers in a celestial railroad, as well as terrestrial ones, we opine that the former is now not only under contract, but actually in process of construction, and its route surveyed, which will run through the very heart of commercial-dom. All trades, therefore, not devoted to its construction and patronage, will not be likely to prosper in the long run, as heaven has, virtually, declared that all business on the road will be done on communistic principles. Hence the only alternative, ultimately, for every business will be, conversion to the common cause of God and humanity, or destruction and outer darkness.— And this is no fiction but sober truth. Precursors of Communism are everywhere seen in the wake of civilization, in such forms as free trade, free schools, combined industries and fraternal associations of almost endless variety of character. Such are the signs of the times, visible to all who, with Paul, recognize the fact that "God hath made of one blood all nations of men &c." Conversions, therefore, of trades to God, is the same thing as conversions to Communism, and the latter is already in the field, laboring with as much zeal for a change of purpose in doing business, as ever characterized the labors of Lyman Beecher for the conversion of souls. [Continued.]

CORRECTION.—The omission of the little word *or* occurred in Mr. Cragin's article of Friday, about the middle of the first page, which essentially altered the meaning of the sentence. It should have read thus: " One who does not intrinsically possess himself is in no condition whatever to possess other persons *or* things."

Dangstein, Petersfield, Sept. 23, 1867.

Lady Dorothy Nevill, having received the CIRCULAR and having seen therein " Business Announcements," would feel greatly obliged if she could have price-lists sent her of the famous Rat-trap made by the Community, also the prices of Traveling-bags, Preserved Fruits, Jellies and Sewing-Silks, etc. She is most grateful for the CIRCULAR, which is most interesting, and which she hopes may be continued to her.

Lady Dorothy Nevill would like to know when she sends an order, how and to whom she is to remit the money for the said order. I. HONDAY.

W. H. WOOLWORTH'S REPLY.

O. C., Oct. 9, 1867.

LADY DOROTHY NEVILL:—Your welcome letter of the 23d ult. came to hand yesterday. We take pleasure in complying with your request as far as possible, and send you with this, printed price-lists of our principal productions, with the exception of Sewing-silk, of which we have no *printed* list. We manufacture at present, of silk, machine-twist only—black and white—which we wholesale at $14.00 per lb.

You will observe that the assortment of Preserved fruit is very much reduced, the demand for many kinds having already exhausted the supply. If you should choose to order any of the Community productions, you will please remit by draft on some Banking-house in New York city, payable to the Oneida Community.

Your words, appreciative of the CIRCULAR, are cheering to us. We shall continue to send it to you with pleasure. Very respectfully yours,
Oneida Community,
by W. H. WOOLWORTH.

DEAR DAILY :—I wish to make use of your columns to publish the letter alluded to in one of the Journals read last evening. It read thus: " I wish to express my appreciation of the CIRCULAR and the great good it has done and is still doing. For one thing it has given me an opportunity to preach the doctrine of Communism in its pages, and I expect still more to do so. It gives others the same privilege, and I hope many more will improve the opportunity."

H. BURT.

They moved yesterday, the building, (that was put up hastily last summer, for a lodging place for our workmen,) over the cellar that has been dug for it and will finish it off immediately for some of our tenants.

Mr. Woolworth remarked last evening that he had a good deal of faith in the power of good-nature to overcome evil. He thought Paul was a good specimen of this spirit; he exhorts " Rejoice evermore," &c.

Hurrah for progress ! We are happy to inform our readers that the mangle is at length connected with the steam-power—that it works finely, and that the laundry corps are jubilant over its success.

The teamsters are at work on the last boat-load of coal, and hope to finish drawing it this week.

Traps ordered Monday and Tuesday, 217½ doz.

THE O. C. DAILY.

VOL. 4. THURSDAY, OCTOBER 10, 1867. NO. 87.

CONVERSION OF TRADES. NO 2.

The revival spirit that is working so bravely in all branches of our businesses, is a leaven that will continue to work, we trust, by the force of its own integral laws, till the entire business world, with all its trades and professions, is as truly and thoroughly consecrated to the service of God as it has been to the service of mammon. One's business is so often a part of one's life, that the conversion of the one without the other, would not be a conversion of the whole man at all, but simply a fraction of a man. Hence, one's business needs the benefit of crucifixion and resurrection—a surrendering to God—as truly as the soul and affections. In communism, all businesses, without distinction, are consecrated to the service of heaven from their birth, but require much spiritual labor and many conversions in the beginning, to keep them from falling from grace. By thus making them ordinances of the worship of God, every trap, every bag, every bottle of fruit, and every spool of silk, manufactured under the influence of the Pentecostal, revival spirit, will carry abroad *honesty* and *faithfulness* in every fibre of their composition. They are silent but potent preachers of that gospel which says " Seek first the kingdom of God and its righteousness, and all these things shall be added." The trapper will trap with communism; the traveler, with his bag, will travel with communism; the tailor will stitch communism into his garments; and the consumer of preserved fruits will eat communism, and find it sweet to his mouth and stomach too, as it will digest well.

And all this is as it should be. The present age is a commercial and business one, and a gospel is no gospel that cannot grapple with it and convert it to God

[Concluded in our next.]

Mr. Reeve writes in reply to the question " what disposal shall the O. C. make of the $200 he and Mr. Randolph sent, and whether they wanted our notes for the same ;" " Please say to Mr. Woolworth first, for Mr. Randolph; He wishes to have the O. C. pay him, without interest, fifty dollars of the one hundred, at some future time if he shall feel that he needs it.— He will give ample time in his notice if he shall want it. Then he wishes a copy of the " Trappers Guide," ¼ doz. copies " Hand Book," ¼ doz. do. " Salvation from Sin," and ¼ doz. traps, five of No. 0. and one of No. 1½. with chains.—The remainder of the $100 to go to the support of the cause of Christ as the O. C. shall see fit.—For my part, please send the same as to Mr. R. (with the exception of " Salvation from Sin") with the addition of one doz. copies of " Male Continence." They may all be sent in a little package by express, I suppose. The remainder we give to the O. C. In so doing I feel that we are only sending it home.

P. S. I forgot to say that Mr. R. and myself would each of us like a medium sized satchel, sent with the other things mentioned."

Mr. E. H. Hamilton's sudden appearance yesterday, was a joyful surprise, and his talk last night full of edification. Considerable conversation was had about the newspaper articles concerning the O. C., recently published at the Depot, and it was the general feeling that they were not worth minding, as they evidently do not express the feelings of the majority and the better part of the inhabitants of Oneida.

What a glorious thought, that we can become united to the great family of heaven, whilst here on earth—daily treading mansions of the blessed, working for God and praising him in all we do, instead of thinking, as the world does, that we must wait until after death before we can realize any of these good things. E. F. H.

Mrs. Bointon, from Hartford, Conn., a cousin of Mr Reynolds, with her husband, called here Tuesday on their way to Montreal. They staid three or four hours and took dinner. Mr. B. came with his mind a good deal prejudiced, but left with his feelings much modified. They both seemed pleased with their call.

It is a sentiment of Demosthenes, that " He who receives a benefit should remember it forever, if he would approve his honesty ; but that he who confers the benefit should instantly forget it, unless he would betray a sordid and illiberal spirit."

Mrs. Freeman writes to John that Mr. F. did not tell her of the receipt of the fifty dollars he received from O. C., nor where the barrel of flour came from, and she did not know of the facts till John wrote informing her.

A large company went over again last night to W. Place to assist at the trap-works, consequently the seven o'clock reading was omitted.

Two men staid here over night, one, Wm. H. Culver, from West Troy, and the other, Robert Hannah, from Oriskany.

Our grapes, or a portion of them, are rapidly being converted into wine and vinegar.

Traps ordered yesterday,   30¼ doz.

THE O. C. DAILY.

VOL. 4.   FRIDAY, OCTOBER 11, 1867.   NO. 88.

CONVERSION OF TRADES. NO 3.

Thirty years ago Charles G. Finney might possibly have converted New York city could he have got the two giant trades, dry goods and groceries, on to the anxious seat to be prayed for, as he did other sinners. But those principalities were too much for him. It is true they built him a tabernacle to preach in, but with a tacit understanding that they should have seats among the ruling elders. It proved a fatal compromise. The tabernacle was a failure. Finney preached, but made no converts. Indeed, the commercial spirit was so strong and artful that it got the preacher on to the anxious seat; but not liking it he fled to the woods at Oberlin. Ah! those merchant princes were "bully" devils, with which Finney had not power to cope. The tabernacle was built expressly to catch the well-to-do class of upper-tendom. Communism has begun the work where Finney failed and left it, but on scientific principles. And it is a curious fact that the O. C. tabernacle—if we may call it such—is located directly opposite the ground on Broadway where the *Finney tabernacle* stood. Worth st. was formerly Anthony st., and the old tabernacle was on the east side of Broadway, on the corner of Anthony. Splendid dry goods stores now occupy the same site, as much as to say, "We dry goods conquered Finney and his revival, and drove them out of town." But don't boast; a greater than Finney is in your midst, although you know it not.

To save human souls, God clothed his only begotten son with human nature, and set him to work to conquer it. The business world must be conquered in the same way. And, to accomplish this noble work, God has brought Communism into the field, clothed with the spirit of business, energy and enterprise, ready for any and all kinds of service, whereby every trade and profession, needful to God or man, may be converted to honesty, truth and righteousness, and made acceptable servants of heaven on earth.   c.

Miss Munson left this morning after a stay of over two weeks. She goes to Worcester where she has a brother living, and from there to Boston to see her children. She thinks she may get work in some cotton factory. She would have been glad to have staid at O. C. but we did not feel that she was yet prepared to join. She is so much under the influence of the Graham principality—so much of a body-tender, that we shrink from very close contact with her. Still, she thinks she is ready to cast off all her old habits, or those that conflict with the truth, and we think there is a degree of honesty and integrity in her character, that will bring her into closer relations with us at some future time. She is quite skillful with the needle, and worked industriously for us while she was here. On leaving we made her a present of a small ladies satchel with which she seemed much pleased. The following note from her to the family was read in meeting last night :

DEAR COMMUNITY FRIENDS :—I leave you in the morning and I must say, that I feel sad in doing so, but I should feel very different from what I now do, if I had not faith to believe, that he who careth for the shorn lamb will care for me. I confess Christ, and a soft heart. I have asked him to make me as a little child, that I may learn of him and all above me. I ask for criticism and hope it will be freely given.— As this is the last time I shall meet you at present, I will bid you all good bye, thanking you for your kindness to me, and the beautiful present given.

SUSAN B. MUNSON.

W. P., Oct. 8.—Grapes have been quite freely distributed in our shops to-day, and the hands seem to appreciate them. The shop-men and boys were requested to assemble in the forge-shop at noon. They didn't know the reason of the call but supposed there was to be a meeting, so the grapes that were presented were a surprise.—Business in the silk department is pretty lively these days. A third spooler has been started and is to be fitted up as soon as may be.— Other silk-machinery is being made as fast as the calls for machine work from the Trap-shop will admit. Orders from the Agency are frequent and urgent.

Work in the shops evenings is to cease promptly at half past eight, that we may not lose our meetings. Work had better suffer than to have our meetings neglected, and it *will* suffer if our meetings are not kept bright.

OCT. 10.—Mary Leet spent the afternoon here. She has assumed the short dress, and before returning to O. C. she had her hair cut short, which very much improved her appearance, and made her seem quite like our folks.—Mr. Hamilton passed the evening with us, and gave us some report of things at W. C. and New York. He also made some interesting remarks on justification, humility, and a soft heart, which led to a free talk on these subjects. Such conversations seem to draw on us the spirit of heaven, and make all feel earnest.

As hard colds are quite prevalent among us, there was some talk last evening on the subject, and a criticism of the spirit that lets in such nuisances as colds and coughs upon us.

A Mr. Fisher from Danbury, Conn., staid here last night. He is a Sandemanian [see Cyclopædia] and came, he said, out of curiosity.

We had a thunder shower between seven and eight o'clock last evening, with very vivid flashes of lightning.

Traps ordered yesterday,   90½ doz.

THE O. C. DAILY.

VOL. 4, SATURDAY, OCTOBER 12, 1867. NO. 89.

Black Creek, Wilson Co., N. C., Oct. 5, 1867.

O. C., DEAR FRIENDS :—I read the CIRCULAR and like its teachings. I would like to join the Community, provided you thought me worthy. Could I get employed by you at some kind of work, with a view of joining after sufficient acquaintance? I am a farmer, and a poor man, but I think you are no respecter of persons on account of property. I was in the rebel army at the age of sixteen years, and believed in the right of our cause; but now I am glad the emancipation of slavery has taken place, although I never wish to see a negro put on social equality with a white man. I am twenty years of age, and sound constitution, and am willing to work for the interests of the Community; but I am still in my sins. Mr. Noyes, with God's help, cured Mr. Burt and Mrs. Hall, and I would like for him to try his hand on me, although I fear I am too far gone for much hope. Oh, that I could enjoy the peace you all do. Hoping to hear from you soon, I am, Respectfully yours, H. D. LUCAS.

Mr. Guiteau writes Oct. 4th. "My son Charles has made us a visit lately, was here about two weeks. I am not pleased with the state of his mind, but after hearing what he had to say, I came to the conclusion that it was of no use for me to undertake to influence his course; he labors under a species of insanity that nothing but the long suffering of God can overcome and I am not sure that that will reach his case. I know of no other way but to leave him where he is. While he was here Mr. Carr called and spent two or three hours. I thought Charles seemed to have quite a relish for his talk. During the conversation I took occasion to say to them both that I thought it would be well for them to be cautious about what they said in reference to Mr. Noyes and the Community. My own judgement is that neither of them have known Christ or comprehended Communism, notwithstanding they have so long been connected with the Community."

We have a namesake living a mile and a half from Mr. Leete's in Verona, an old gentleman 97 years old, and a daughter who is considered partially insane.—One night last week a man rapped at his door, and on being asked what he wanted, he thrust in his cane, pushed the door open and went in. He told the old gentleman he wanted his money. Mr. J. replied that he had none for him; upon which the stranger drew from his cane a dagger or some deadly weapon, and threatened him unless he produced his money. In the meantime, the daughter had the presence of mind to take an old tin-horn, and stepping outdoor blew it with violence, which the robber hearing, fled precipitately without much ceremony.

A back-woodsy looking man, a stranger, called a day or two since at the Office, and after inquiring for the *head-man*, asked in a low, confidential tone, if we adopted children.

"*Head-Man.*"—No, we don't often adopt children unless we can have the parents or guardians come with them.

Stranger.—I have a little girl, eight months old, that I want to dispose of if I can find a good place.

H. M.—You want to give the child away do you?

S.—Yes.

H. M.—Are the parents living?

S.—Yes.

H. M.—Do they live near here?

S.—No, at quite a distance.

H. M.—(turning away) We don't like to take children in that way—the Community is not an Asylum.

S.—(following after) Then there is no use trying farther?

H. M.—No, it will be of no use.

[*Exit stranger.*]

Two hundred and eighty-five gallons of wine have been made from grapes rendered unfit for market by the frost. Also one hundred and sixty gallons of the juice of poorer quality will be turned into vinegar.

Packing pears and quinces and making jellies is the business that is being prosecuted at the preserving-house at the present time. Also load after load of these goods are daily being shipped to their places of destination.

It is requested that persons will be a little more careful about leaving the *Dailies* around where strangers will read them. A pile of old ones was carried into the Library yesterday, by some one, and left lying loosely on the desk, and Miss Chloe found the stranger who staid here the night before, looking them over and reading them at his leisure. The proper place to deposit them is at the printing-office.

Mr. Littlejohn and Mr. Stephens called here yesterday, to see our people on the Midland R. R. project. Mr. Hamilton gave a particular account last night of the interview with them which will be reported in manuscript.

On Thursday a letter was received from Baldwinsville informing us that Mr. Robinson was very sick and not expected to live and requesting some of our people to come immediately. Mr. Hatch and Emma Jones went the same afternoon.

☞We received a letter yesterday, from Paris, dictated by Mademoiselle Bocugue, making many inquiries relative to our Society and upon what conditions a person can join.

Traps ordered yesterday, 267 doz.

THE O. C. DAILY.

VOL. 4. MONDAY, OCTOBER 14, 1867. NO. 90.

BUSINESS MEETING.

Mr. Miller said that he could not carry all the persons that go to W. P. with one horse, and wanted to know if the Board would sympathize with his having another one. The Trap-shop committee together with Mr. Cragin are to consider the need of another horse, mornings and nights.

Mr. Perry wanted to know if something could not be done to procure through rates in the shipment of traps and other things. Parties out West can get goods cheaper from New-York than they can from here, and sometimes insist on having their traps sent from there. It was proposed that some one go to Albany and see what can be done. Messrs. Hamilton, Burnham and Perry were appointed to consider the matter of sending some one.

The tenant-houses near the Trap-shop are destitute of any place to shelter their wood or for the men to wash. Mr. Milbury has ten boarders and Mr. Christian twelve and all are obliged to wash out doors. Proposed that sheds be built large enough to shelter the wood, coal &c. and afford to the men a place to wash. Left to the Building-Committee with power and recommendation to act.

Mr. Hatch said it had been the practice to have the boys in the children's department furnish coal, kindlings &c., to those rooms occupied by persons unable to get them themselves. But the boys he had last winter had gone to other places, and as the family had failed to furnish him with more, he would like to have the men take charge of those chores without being appointed to it. Mr. Hamilton thought it was a privilege to do chores, and thought Mr. Hatch might give notice that he had some privileges to dispose of, and that he would accommodate persons with them as far as they will go.

Berlin Heights, Ohio, Oct. 0, 1867.

Mr. Woolworth, Dear Sir:—I send to-day by express, $300 to you for the use of the O. C., without interest. I do not want your note; you may keep a book account of it. I will give you timely notice when I want it. As I am selling-out here, I may have a few hundred more to spare you if acceptable.—I am in hopes the time has come for me to retreat from this terrible battle-field—this hades-haunted hill—this diotrephian head-quarter, in this world; for

> " My ear is pained, my soul is sick, with every
> day's report"
> Of silly women and vile men, with which this
> place is filled.

I believe that God has sent me here to be buffeted of the devil for my own good. I am a rough-hewn stick, that will take considerable counter-hewing, planing

and sand-papering, to make fit for the kingdom.—I am glad that my lot has been cast here, for here the power of the spirit, through the writings of J. H. Noyes, has brought me to feel and confess Christ in me, a whole Savior from sin ; which has brought me much peace and rest, although closely surrounded by those possessed of " seducing spirits and doctrines of devils." Although this is a hard place, there are some good honest souls here, that are almost persuaded to believe.

I have always thought my speech and letters contemptible, and for a contemptible letter to be sent from this place, I would think the time had not come, so I have written the O. C. but seldom. I thought it would be hard for you to believe that anything good could come out of Berlin.

Since G. W. Reeve and wife have confessed Christ, I feel greatly encouraged and strengthened, and would say that for the last nine years I have been looking toward O. C., hoping at some time I would be made fit to live in that family, or some of its branches.

With much love, hope and faith, I am yours as ever,
J. W. B. Randolph.

Notice to Agents.—I have to give notice hereby, that nearly our entire stock of fruits is exhausted. We have on hand only Peaches in cans, and a few doz. bottles of Strawberries and Pine-Apples. The Strawberries and Pine-Apples in bottles will have to be used to make up for our lack of these fruits in cans ; so that orders for fruit should be limited to Peaches in cans Of vegetables, there still remain unsold about 150 doz. Tomatoes and 160 doz. String-Beans.　E.

Mr. Noyes's talk on the policy of the O. C. in reference to the Midland R. R. was re-read last night as many of the family had not heard it. Mr. Hamilton related some conversation he had with Mr. Hubbard, which goes to show that Mr. H.'s sympathies are with us in this war, rather than with Oneida, and that in consequence of his, Mr. H.'s refusal, to comply with their wishes he is set down in the same category with the O. C.

Mr. Hatch returned Saturday from Baldwinsville. He left Mr. Robinson some better, but the doctors think there is little hope of his recovery. He is surrounded with a world of unbelief, death and the family spirit, and under such circumstances Mr. H. thinks his restoration to health is doubtful. Emma stays two or three days longer.

A tall man by the name of Gage, from Vineland, staid here over Sunday. He is a spiritualist and with his wife visited here several years ago. H. W. B. also spent Sunday with us.

26,000 traps were made packed and sent off last week—the largest week's work ever done in the shop.

252½ doz. traps ordered Saturday and Sunday, including three bear-traps.

THE O. C. DAILY.

VOL. 4. TUESDAY, OCTOBER 15, 1867. NO. 91.

EVENING MEETING.

Mr. Woolworth.—I have thought about Paul considerably lately, and have had some experience that has made me realize that it is a practical thing to have fellowship with him, and come into such vital sympathy with him that I can have the same spirit and the same wisdom, heroism and power that he had. Paul had tremendous heroism, courage and boldness. He faced death without fear or flinching. I have felt something of the lion-hearted spirit that Paul had working in my heart lately—the spirit that fears nothing that man can do to us. Man can only kill the body. "The fear of man bringeth a snare." Paul did not come into that snare, he was above it. I realize that God's inspiration and providence match; and if we can only be receptive, and have our hearts open and sensitive to God's voice, we shall be led aright.

Mr. Hamilton.—I am glad to hear what Mr. Woolworth says about Paul and his own experience. All such experience is public property, and is valuable to each of us. I confess my union with Paul, and his public spirit and devotion in building up and edifying the church.

Mr. Woolworth.—I am thankful for Mr. Hamilton's visit here. I think it was timely and inspired. I am thankful to have him here just at this crisis we have been in lately.

Mr. Hamilton.—I am thankful to come here. Outward things are pleasant to me; but my interior experience has been the pleasantest part of my visit. My heart has been filled with a good deal of comfort and joy.

Mr. Horace and Wm. Perry both find their wardrobes materially reduced by some means not altogether mysterious. The former mourns the loss of a valuable overcoat, and the latter the loss of at least three good vests. A combination of circumstances make it pretty evident where these things have gone. In the first place, they were hanging in the closet of the room where Charles Mills roomed, (H. R. Perry's room, he being absent at the time,) and in the second place, Charles was away late on the night before he left—at Olmstead's it was conjectured; and thirdly, he declined to go down with George Kellogg to the Depot, protesting that he was going on foot, and only consented to ride after being told that he would get no money unless he should ride down with George and take the cars; and fourthly, we have the testimony of our neighbor Rawson, that Charles was back at Olmstead's the day after he left the Community. Those who helped pack his things are sure these articles were not among them; but that they were smuggled off to Olmstead's hardly admits of a doubt. **R.**

Mr. Reeve, in speaking of repairs on his engine, boiler, &c., says, "I suppose it always costs largely to undo and do over; yes, it costs the old man, but the new one realizes a great gain." Mrs. R. writes, "I confess to having such a strong desire to be with you in person, that I was unable for the time to say 'the Lord's will not mine be done.' But a victory is gained and I feel anew God's love, and not only a desire to know and *do* his will, but a trusting confidence that all will be well, and that whatever way God directs will be best."

W. P., Oct. 14.—Another large bee was called and well attended, in the chain and finishing departments, last evening. According to present appearances we shall be able to catch up with the orders this week. The present working capacity in the shop is estimated at three thousand traps per day.

The meeting hour was occupied with testimony of the goodness of God, relating experience, and exhortations to unity. All should see to it that no slivers are allowed to get in and create discord.

Mr. Hamilton cautioned the family last night, about saying too much to neighbor Hubbard about our enemies at Oneida, as everything said to him would doubtless be reported to them, which would have a tendency to increase the feud already existing.

From our window where we usually sit afternoons, we have a fine prospect of the intermingling of evergreens with the bright colors of autumnal leaves.—We wish Mr. Whiting was here or some other artist, to sketch the picture.

Mr. Abbott has been laid up for some time past, in consequence of pleurisy, and also rheumatism in one of his legs, which makes it difficult for him to walk.

Mr. E. H. Hamilton leaves to-day for New-York, Marion Dunn and little Coset'e accompanying him on their way to W. C.

The amount of goods sold at the Store yesterday, to outsiders, was $112, the largest sale ever made in one day.

Traps ordered yesterday,   98 doz.

THE O. C. DAILY.

VOL. 4. WEDNESDAY, OCT. 16, 1867. NO. 92.

Carthage, Oct. 13 1867.

DEAR MR. CRAGIN:—I wish to thank you for your faithfulness in showing me my connection with evil principalities, and to tell you that I thank God for so faithful a man as you are to the truth and for the opportunity I have had to become acquainted with you. Through the discrimination I was able to exercise in the light of your criticism and others at Oneida, I was able to judge all my connections with spirits. I have rejected all communications and refused to pay any attention to visions since my return. I am determined to keep my attention fixed upon Christ and to trust wholly in him and the power of his resurrection. I find peace and rest to my spirit in Christ, and through faith I am steadily gaining in health and strength. I believe the devil held power over me by distracting my attention from Christ through hadean spirits. I confess love for you as my instructor in Christ. Yours, CLARA WAIT.

Miss Wait says in a letter to Mrs. J.

"I thank God every day for the Oneida Community, and feel that I am 'growing in the knowledge of God and in fellowship with you.' I am greatly benefited by reading the Noon Discourses. I pray in faith and receive what I need daily. I confess my love for Christ and the Primitive Church and Paul, and unity with and loyalty to Mr. Noyes and the Community."

When we get afflicted about some small affair that is trying to engross the whole of our large hearts, perhaps some friend will say, "Never mind; turn your heart to God, he will satisfy it." This is well said, but it would be more satisfactory if we had some idea of *how* the Lord would satisfy our hearts. Well, he has various ways; some of which are so simple, that when our trouble is gone we can hardly realize that we have had any. All we need to do is, to tell the Lord that we have got a job too big for us—a burden on our hearts; and that we are going to cast it on him whether or no; and if he has another job ready for us well and good; it not, we shall wait until he has. He likes such faith and trust as this, and will be quite apt to say, "Yes, I have business enough for you—just all you can do," and before you are aware of it, a stream of life and love will rush upon you from all quarters; not only from heavenly sources, but from all of your fellow-mortals, and you will find yourself so overwhelmed with the goodness of God that you will have to pray to him with all your might, to help you mow it away. J. P. H.

W. P., OCT. 15.—The large number of traps ordered to-day gives us an assurance that we shall not get out of work immediately. In meeting this evening,

G. W. H. remarked that the thirty-seven molders employed at the malleable iron works, where we get iron, have been put on to our work. God makes men work for and accommodate us. Geo. E. wished to recognize the providence of God in enabling them to get some machinery, that had broken down, in running order much sooner than was expected. Mr. Campbell and others wished that the caution about speaking too freely to Mr. Hubbard about our views of the railroad and the Oneida people, might be extended to talk in the shop and with our neighbors on the same subject.

H. W. Thayer and his mother started in the night for Massachusetts. They go to visit their relatives. They expect to go to W. C. before their return. Louisa Howard accompanied them. She does not yet seem ready to join us heartily, and it was unpleasant for her and for us, to have her work in our shop and board with the other hands. She thinks she shall go home, and, by cutting the links that connect her with the world, prepare herself at some future time to join the O. C. Whether she will do that, remains for the future to disclose.

We heard yesterday, that one of Olmstead's boys had reported that Charles Mills, the day he left, went as far as Canastota station, and then returned; that he had taken a bundle of clothes from us, and buried or hid them somewhere, and came back after them. This confirms our suspicions of him, and also Mr. Rawson's statement.

Miss Susan Dunn returned yesterday. She met Marion at Oneida depot, and had a chance to converse with her a few minutes before the train left.— Miss D. has settled up all her affairs in Vermont quite satisfactorily, we believe, and is glad to get home.

Mr. Hamilton talked some before he left about our bees; he said he hoped we would make them religious bees, and not suffer them to run into frivolity and pleasure-seeking.

We are having beautiful days and splendid nights, the full moon shining with unwonted brightness.

We finished harvesting our beets yesterday, 1,000 bushels.

We have sold our mill-stones for $150.

Traps ordered yesterday; 707 1-6 doz.

THE O. C. DAILY.

VOL. 4. THURSDAY, OCT. 17, 1867. NO. 93.

EVENING MEETING.

An unfortunate affair happened at Willow-Place on Tuesday, which is making some disturbance.— The following is a brief account of Mr. Burt's report of the case, as presented in last evening's meeting:

Sometime since two boys were dismissed from the shop for disobedience. Myron afterwards saw their mother, and she pled with him to take them back, saying they were poor, her husband sick, and that the wages of the boys mainly supported the family. She asked Myron to take them and govern them as he would a child of his own, and if they needed it punish them. Myron consented out of benevolence, and the boys returned to the shop, but soon were in mischief again. Myron whipped one of them, and called upon the mother and reported it. She approved his course. The other boy recently started some machinery contrary to orders and got his finger pinched in the gearing. Tuesday he started the dumbwaiter, though he had been told not to touch it, and seeing some one coming he ran off and left it to go up at its leisure. At this Myron and George E. took him in hand, and presented the alternative of leaving the shop or taking a whipping. The boy preferred to be whipped, and Myron took him up in the garret and switched him on the bare skin with a little stick that George E. said could do him no injury.

Yesterday morning neither of the boys came to the Shop. Myron then went to the Castle where they live, and saw their mother, when it appeared the boy had complained of his punishment and created quite an excitement. His father had taken him to Durhamville. Myron followed and was there served with a warrant by the sheriff.

Last evening Mr. Burt, Mr. Kinsley, Geo. E. and Myron waited upon the boy's mother. The father was absent, though he had agreed to meet them. He demanded $50 for damages. They thought it would not be wise to pay anything, as it might confirm the rumor that the boy had been abused; and so no conclusion was arrived at. They found the story had been well circulated and terribly exaggerated. Frank Hyde told them he had heard the boy was whipped nearly to death. The mother of the boy admitted that she told M. to punish her boys, and that he was not injured, though it appeared the end of the stick had drawn blood in several places. Then the fact that he walked with his father to Durhamville, showed that he was in usual health.

After hearing this report the meeting unanimously took the following attitude: The Community entirely disapprove of the course taken with this boy, and wish to have it so understood, and the facts fully known. Messrs. Burt and Kinsley are to try and settle the difficulty at once by leaving it to arbitrators.— The boy deserved all the punishment he received, but our folks were not the ones to administer it. We especially deprecate the measure just at the present time. It is evident that the devil is wide-awake to do us mischief. Hints were given about laying hands on the boys in the shop. It was thought we should dismiss any boy we could not control without resorting to punishment.

The following is as near a correct statement of the amount of grapes harvested as it is possible to produce:

Total number, 16,139 lbs.

Deleware,	4,490 lbs.
Hartford Prolific,	2,297 "
Concord,	2,829 "
Miscellaneous varieties,	523 "
Total of good grapes,	10,139 lbs.
Damaged by frost,	6,000 lbs.

It might be mentioned that those that were damaged by frost were made into wine and vinegar. 280 gallons of wine were made, and several barrels of vinegar. s. y. j.

Mr. Conant reports that our people finished digging potatoes yesterday, having put about 800 bushels into the cellar. It is thought that we have used not far from 200 bushels in the family the last two months, making in all raised this year 1000 bushels. They are very nice.

The corn is being put into the barn, and husking it commences to-day. We do not intend to buy husks for beds this year as we did last, and now is a good chance for those who want husks, to help themselves.

Emma Jones has not returned yet. She has written once that Mr. Robinson was failing. Mr. Hatch goes there again to-day to see how the case stands, and why Emma stays so long.

One of the black men in our employ is to assume the responsibility of hostler and is to-day moving into the white house, so-called.

T' ans ordered yesterday, 185 doz.

THE O. C. DAILY.

VOL. 4.   FRIDAY, OCT. 18, 1867.   NO. 94.

HOW FAMILIES ARE MADE.

I am not going into a long, philosophical disquisition on the origin of families, or how they were created before the flood. Suffice it to say, however, that Billy and Anna meet at a dance, at a boarding-house, in the factory, or elsewhere, fall in love, court a while, then marry—sometimes from necessity to save appearances. There you have a modern family. Their fitness for each other, and for the office of parental responsibilities, had never entered their minds. Pleasure-seeking was the incentive to the contract—propagation a contingency. The training of their children to obedience and the fear and love of God, does by no means follow as a necessary sequence from the marriage vow. Probably in six cases out of ten these parents have no government at all over their children, allowing them to grow up in the spirit of animal willfulness and disobedience, to be a *curse* instead of a *blessing* to society. Now where is the sacredness of such contracts between the sexes? Had Billy and Anna, in coming together, the remotest thought of consecrating themselves or their affections to God or to society, or to any being higher and better than themselves? Nothing of the kind. The sacredness of any act lies in the fact that the object upon which it is bestowed has been set apart, consecrated to a superior being or cause, to which one owes allegiance and gratitude for favors received. Of course there are some noble exceptions to this general, irresponsible method of creating families. Were it not so, the redemption of the world would be extremely problematical. And these exceptions, where marriages are made subservient to the public good, are resultants from influences coming down upon marriage, counteracting its natural selfish, exclusive tendencies, from Christ's gospel, the spirit and principles of which ignore all institutions necessitated by the spirit of selfishness and self-seeking.

[We omit the remaining paragraph for want of room, and will insert it tomorrow.]

EVENING MEETING.

Mr. Newhouse.—Dr. Whetmore was at the shop to-day with a friend who is a Democrat and supports the *Democratic Union.* This man said he was perfectly disgusted with the course this paper was taking with us, and should have no sympathy with it if it continued. He thought it a very unjust attack, and that they did not assign the true reason, which was simply to get money out of us. He thought these articles were doing us more good than hurt.

Mr. Woolworth.—Well, I am thankful for the chastening the Lord is giving us. I think we may take it all as from the Lord. We are having a good deal of prosperity, and I don't know as we should sail along safely without some ballast of this kind. I think the Lord is showing his love for us in it.

[Homer Barron had been made blue by these attacks, but had gained the victory over such temptations.]

Mr. Woolworth.—The Lord seemed to brace me up before the attack came. I think I received a baptism of Paul's spirit. I was never more sensible of rising above all fear of death or persecution. This was a mystery to me at the time, but I have since interpreted it as a baptism of Paul's spirit.

J. H. Barron.—Mr. Davis said that Baker, the editor of the *Democratic Union*, told him that he could take our publications and go before the Grand Jury and get the Community indicted for keeping a bad house. Davis replied that he could take a file of the *Democratic Union* and get *him* indicted for treason.

W. P., Oct. 16.—The painting of our house is completed and we feel pleased with its appearance.

Eleven thousand eight hundred and seventy springs were bent and tempered between seven o'clock Tuesday morning and one o'clock at night; the links were put on the next day and they were ready to go into the water. Two thousand of these springs were cut from the steel and made throughout. This is the largest days work ever done in the forge-shop.

Mr. Cragin was at our meeting and remarked that the lesson for us to learn from the late affairs at the shop, was humility. He felt no personal criticism toward Myron or G. W. H. They should not be cast down and disabled by allowing their attention to turn upon themselves. All were exhorted to close up the ranks and cement our union more closely than ever.

Mr. Noyes's article that was written with a view to being published, and which he left to the discretion of the O. C. is in the hands of the Editor of the *Oneida Dispatch* and will appear in that paper to-day. There seemed to be a clear instinct in the minds of the leading business men here that the time had come to publish it, and on their showing it to Mr. Jenkins he thought it was just the thing. Mr. J. went and consulted the Editor of the paper who offered to publish it without cost to us, or if he charged anything it would be only three dollars.

The father of the boy that was whipped refused to settle on any terms short of our paying him $50.00, and so the case will be tried, according to law to-morrow.

The Bag-shop bands had a lively bee at the shop last night after supper, which lasted till nearly meeting time. There were forty present and considerable work was accomplished.

Emma Jones returned yesterday. Mr. Robinson is better, and since dismissing his doctors, entertains the hope that he shall recover.

Traps ordered yesterday,   78 dos.

THE O. C. DAILY.

VOL. 4. SATURDAY, OCT. 19, 1867. NO. 95.

HOW FAMILIES ARE MADE.
[*Concluded.*]

But, says one, is not marriage a natural institution, and therefore inevitable, in the very nature of things? Marriage is just as natural as slavery, and no more so; but a union of the sexes is not only natural, but desirable and beautiful, harmonizing with the eternal fitness of human susceptibilities and attractions.— But is a union of the sexes safe without the law of marriage? No, nor with it either, while men and women are under the power of sin and selfishness.— The law, marriage law included, was made for the lawless and disobedient, not for the obedient and righteous who are free from sin and consequently free from unrighteousness, possessing the disposition to do right from choice.   o.

We had a stirring meeting last night, in which both our neighboring Communes were present. Mr. Noyes's talk, and W. C.'s testimony on Ann Eliza's case was read, which was sympathized with and heartily endorsed by all. Her case stands out in bold relief, and shows of what mischief an unsubdued will like hers is capable. Mr. N.'s talk on the principle of the ascending fellowship made that subject easy of apprehension, and many expressed themselves as seeing in the light of his argument, the truth on that subject with greater clearness than ever before. The meeting held until nearly ten o'clock.

We were surprised night before last at the arrival of Mr. Atwood Knowles and his wife. Mrs. K. received rather a cool reception. Mr. K.'s object in coming was to look up a place near the O. C. as he has sold out where he is, and wished to locate near us. He talks of buying the place on Turkey-street next beyond Mr. Macoy's on the same side of the road, and went to look at it yesterday, and got the refusal of it for a few weeks. Mrs. K. appears much softened. She had a talk with Mr. Woolworth, in which she confessed her faults in the past, and seemed repentant. The following note from her to the family was read in meeting last night:

To THE COMMUNITY:—I am glad of an opportunity to acknowledge my faults. I am sorry that I let such a hard spirit take possession of me when I was here last. At times I would try to extricate myself, but as often fell back, and my temptations became stronger every time. I confess I have no fellowship with such a spirit. I desire a soft heart, one that Christ can easily mould. I accept the criticism of the Community and hope they will be free to criticise me in future. I see now that I was deceived, as has been said, and put light for darkness and darkness for light. I confess my union with Christ and the Community.

                           D. W. KNOWLES.

What corn we had (less than two acres) was picked in the field a few days since, and the ears deposited in the big barn, and Thursday morning the husking commenced and was completed yesterday. Women and children and some men, with pumpkins, stools, boxes and cornstalks for seats, enjoyed the pleasant pastime of husking it, for the weather was warm and summer-like. The only regret was that there was not more of it, as a good many more husks than were obtained are needed in the family. We hope another year the quantity of corn planted will be doubled, at least.

Four of our men have gone down to the Castle this morning to meet the legal authorities, when we opine, somebody will be obliged to take another whipping; it may be the father of the boy this time, and it may be the O. C.

Notwithstanding the rumors afloat about us, this fine weather brings us a good many visitors—nice-looking people too—and some dinners are called for almost daily.

Two vagrants, a man and a woman, were found stretched upon the straw in our barn-yard yesterday morning. They came to the house for some breakfast.

Mr. Noyes's article alluded to yesterday, came out in due form in the *Dispatch*, without note or comment by the Editor.

A small bee for paring and putting up pears is in progress this morning. Our fruit-preserving is gradually closing up.

The weather has been very warm for three or four days past; the mercury stood at noon, yesterday, at 74 deg.

The new sign over the Store door, "O. C. Store," looks well, and puts on a finish that was much needed.

Twenty barrels of apples have been bought for W. C. and were shipped by canal yesterday.

Traps ordered yesterday,   235½ doz.

THE O. C. DAILY.

VOL. 4.   MONDAY, OCT. 20, 1867.   NO. 96.

BUSINESS MEETING.

Mr. Kinsley said there was a tendency to over-load the omnibus. The inside is filled and often the top heavily loaded. It will carry all that can get in, and two persons may ride with the driver, but the top should not be loaded. That is made as light as possible, merely for shelter.

Mr. Conant wanted to know if that road between the corner and the red school-house is to be straightened, as he might do something toward making the fences this Fall. Mr. Burt proposed that we let it be for the present, till we see how the Midland Railroad is coming out. We may want to make a straight road to our depot if we have one, and in that case we should not want to lay out much on this road.

Mr. Smith wanted to know the mind of the Board about having a coal-sifter for the house similar to the one they have at the Trap-shop. That is in the form of a cylinder, about six feet in length and two in diameter, set on an incline and turned by a crank. The cinders are thrown into a hopper at the upper end and the crank is turned, and the whole mass commences its downward career. The ashes fall out by the way and the cinders drop down from the lower end of the cylinder into a box. The advantages of this arrangement are ease, dispatch, and freedom from dust. The cost will be between twenty and twenty-five dollars. It was reported that Mr. Whitney had some ideas on coal-sifting. Messrs. Clark, Smith and Whitney were appointed committee to see what can be done.

Homer wished to consult with the Board about making beef of our oldest Ayrshire. He has been advertized for sale some time, but there does not seem to be much prospect of selling him. He will make excellent beef and we shall probably realize as much by killing him as he has cost us. Being put to vote, the sentence of death was pronounced on him.

W. P., Oct. 17.—A new spinner has been started this week and another winder and spooler are nearly ready to run. The silk business is pretty lively these days.

The exaggerations and variations of the late affair which come to us, have tended somewhat to cast a shadow over some in the family, which makes things go hard. We had a good free talk about it this evening, and concluded that it is not our business to give attention to this devil's scare, but go on with the work of making traps, which God has set us about; be good natured and courageous, and show people that we are doing all the good we can. Paul is a good example of one who was not turned from his business of preaching Christ, by trials and persecutions. We should go on cheerfully in the place where

God has put us and expect he will take care of and inspire us in it.—After meeting George E. and Edward gave us some music on the violin and melodeon.

Myron's law-suit, which was to have come off Saturday, was adjourned till next Wednesday on account of the sickness of the boy's mother, who was M.'s principal witness. But as it seemed desirable on many accounts that the affair should be settled soon, it was decided in the noon-meeting yesterday, that Mr. Burt and G. E. Cragin should go down and see the boy's father, and try to induce him to act a reasonable part, and settle without farther controversy. They went accordingly, and though they did not succeed in softening Mr. Lambert's feelings toward the O. C., yet they got his consent to settle it with his lawyer, Mr. Shoecraft, if they could. Mr. Burt and Geo E. went down toward night to see Mr. S., but found him in meeting and only had a chance to say a few words to him. He thought there would be no difficulty in settling it, and some of our folks have gone down this morning to see what can be done, as Mr. S. agreed to meet them at eight o'clock at his office.

Our noon meeting yesterday, was occupied in talking over W. P. affairs and criticism of the spirit that sinks down, and is childish and egotistical when reproved. This spirit has been sensibly felt in the Trap-shop of ate and has affected the business there a good deal.—Mr. Woolworth said last night, that we want to help the Trap-shop all we can; they need help now, as much as they have in the past, as large orders continue to come in; and we are helping them by laboring to remove the difficulties that stand in the way of unity.

As there are so many flying exaggerated reports about that unfortunate affair at the Trap-shop, it was thought best to call together this morning all the workmen there, and also at our boarding-house, and give a truthful account of the whole matter, that the blame might rest where it belongs, and not on the Community as a whole.

Mrs. Hatch has retired from the children's department, and Miss Chloe Seymour takes her place as mother at the children's house.

CORRECTION.—There were thirty barrels of apples sent to W. C. instead of twenty, as reported in Saturday's Daily.

The mercury stood yesterday, at one o'clock, at 84 degrees in the shade. We have splendid, unclouded weather.

The last load of our coal (400 tons) was drawn Saturday.

Mr. Thacker left in the night for W. C.

947 doz. traps ordered Saturday and Sunday.

THE O. C. DAILY.

VOL. 4.   TUESDAY, OCT. 22, 1867.   NO. 97.

EVENING MEETING.

Mr. Burt reported that he and George E. called on Mr. Shoecraft, and plainly told him our views and wishes respecting a settlement of the whipping case, and showed him a statement written by Myron which produced a very favorable impression on him. Mr. S. thought it would be the best thing to settle it. Accordingly Mr. Burt rode back to the Castle and brought Mr. Lambert down. After some talk with his lawyer, Mr. L. agreed to settle for $100. Mr. Burt was not at liberty to give so much. He finally offered to pay Mr. L. $50 and Mr. Shoecraft's fee of $35. Mr. L. accepted, and a receipt in full was made out and signed ; so that no action can now be brought for the whipping of the other boy, as there had been some threat of doing.—After the settlement Mr. S. frankly expressed his views. He owned that the reports in circulation and his examination of the boy, at first worked upon his feelings a good deal ; and he was free to say he thought we had escaped easier than we should if it had been left to the law, as he had already made out the papers for carrying it to the county court, where he thought it would have cost us two or three hundred dollars. He said the boy's pantaloons were stiff with clotted blood, and that he counted seventeen places where blood had been drawn ; that this was witnessed by a crowd at Durhamville and produced a good deal of excitement. Still, our account convinced him there was no design to be cruel, and that it was intended for the good of the boy, who had not received any real injury. Had he known the whole story at first he would not have had anything to do with it ; and he would now do all he could to correct false reports ; would go to Durhamville himself and correct impressions there.

Mr. Lambert rode up home with our folks in sight of all the lawyers round the Castle hotel. It is expected his boys will return to the shop. Mr. L. thinks we will have no further trouble with them.

Mr. Kinsley said he examined the boy and would be willing to take his oath that there were not over seven spots where blood had been drawn, and that the clotted blood was all mere falsehood. George E. admitted to Mr. Burt that the whipping had been more severe than he had represented to the family. Mr. K. thought the whipping entirely out of place and too severe any way, and was sure Myron would not wish to have it excused ; and still he did not wish to have the family credit Mr. S.'s story. He was sure George E. would consider it greatly exaggerated. Mr. Woolworth thought the truth was somewhere between our first impressions and Mr. S.'s representation. He was glad the case was disposed of, as it had created bad vibrations and unpleasant sensations. He moved it be dropped and considered settled. This proposition was received with applause.

W. P., Oct. 22.—Last evening just as meeting closed, G. W. Hamilton who was sitting by the window, exclaimed " what is that?" and made a sudden exit through the window, saying as he went, " nothing dangerous." All of course rushed to see what it was, and saw a bright blaze rising from the ground near the shop at the north end. The men seized pails of water and started on a bee line for the shop, over fences and ditches, and it being pretty dark some collisions occurred, and one man got the benefit of a ducking. The fire was nothing dangerous, as it happened, though it might have been so in the night. It was supposed to have been occasioned by some one throwing a lighted match from the window on a heap of scraps, sawdust, etc., which had been emptied from the tombs. Too much care cannot be taken about danger from lights and matches.

To the Family.—For some time past I have been going through a very severe criticism and judgment of the flesh. I recognize it as an act of discipline from a kind and loving father, and I very much desire to learn the lesson intended by it. I confess my union with Christ—with the resurrection energy of his spirit let whatever may happen to the outward man. I confess a soft and obedient heart, and my union with Mr. Noyes and the family.   John Abbott.

John Leonard gave us last night, a third article on " Chemistry in the Kitchen." The subject discussed this time was the manner of making coffee. John was commended for studying improvements in the kitchen and for improvement in coffee-making.

A long and a strong bee is called for this morning, and a *pair* of paring machines are in brisk motion, which *pare pears* and quinces very rapidly. We had nineteen barrels of quinces on hand to dissect this morning.

Between seven and eight hundred bushels of apples have been purchased for family use. Mr. Perkins furnishes our table with the nicest kind of cider of his own manufacturing.

We sent this morning to a man in New-Jersey 8,000 Philadelphia raspberry plants, for which we receive $500.

58¼ doz. traps ordered yesterday, including two No. 5 bear-traps.

THE O. C. DAILY.

VOL. 4. WEDNESDAY, OCT. 23, 1867. NO. 98.

EVENING MEETING.

Mr. Woolworth.—I had some interesting conversation with Mr. George Hamilton to-day. I think he is getting a very great blessing out of this late experience, and that it is going to result in a new birth to him. He is getting so that he clearly sees the spirit that has been upon him, and is judging it very sincerely. He is rising up into thankfulness and victory, and the truth is making him free. He confesses that he has had the diotrephian spirit in a subtle form, and yet it has been very strong upon him in the way of jealousy. He traces it back to the time Mr. Reid was connected with the trap-business. We all know Mr. Reid had a great deal of inventive genius and ability in getting up tools and contrivances for saving labor in trap-making. George's jealousy worked toward Mr. Reid in a very subtle, and yet devilish, cruel way. This has run all through his experience.—I think this is a common enemy, and such a victory is a common blessing that we can all rejoice in. I told George that I considered all the trial and tribulation, and all the money it has cost us, as mere dust in the balance.

Mr. Kinsley.—I think the change in George is very manifest. In a business meeting we had over to Willow-Place to-day, and again in meeting him over here this afternoon, I was struck with the softness manifest in his speech and look.

Mr. Woolworth—I believe it is true that the Lord is taking measures to have our revival go on. This late experience has been directly calculated to remove obstructions—pride and hardness of heart. I confess the experience has increased my faith in God, and my belief that his kingdom is coming in this world. There is power in his kingdom to save men from egotism and the old life. That power has come into this world; Mr. Noyes is the representative of it; this Community embodies that power. To me this experience of G. Hamilton's is one of the greater miracles.

Reading, Pa., Oct. 12, 1867.

EDITOR OF THE CIRCULAR, DEAR FRIEND:—Enclosed please find 50 cts., for which you will please send me one doz. of " Male Continence," for distribution among my free-thinking friends. I read and pass around the CIRCULAR. I see that your institution is an improvement on the old theology, but believe you could do more good by not adhering quite so much to Christ and him crucified, and adopt some of the principles of the " Harmonial Philosophy." If modern Spiritualism is not a reality, then I doubt very much the Spiritualism of old.

If you think proper you may print the lines I have sent you, with your criticism upon the same.

Please let me know the price of your sewing-silk in large quantities. If there is a chance to make a percentage on it, I may order a lot to wholesale out in small quantities through the country.

Yours with great respect,

PETER ZIEBER.

On Monday last our youngest children enjoyed what to them was a rich treat. The day being exquisitely fair and warm, we took them out to walk.—First we stopped on the lawn and let them sport awhile among the autumnal leaves. They were full of fun and would roll and tumble and cover each other with leaves. After awhile we concluded to give our boarding-house Commune a call, so after calling them all together and organizing the company, numbering sixteen, Mary B. started on, taking Eugene in his little carriage while I brought up the rear. Not a word of discord was heard on the way and all seemed very happy. We met a cordial welcome and were taken into the parlor where the children played awhile; but soon Georgy asked permission to run in the yard and then all followed suit, down to little Minnie; and such a screaming, running and jumping, hopping and skipping, (each trying to outdo the other,) I seldom if ever witnessed. Their lungs had full scope for they had liberty to make all the noise they pleased, a favor seldom granted. After staying about an hour, we returned home thanking God for Community discipline and education, that enables so many little ones to play together in such perfect harmony.

M.

A Mr. Bush from Westfield Mass. came here Saturday, and left this morning. He is a subscriber, and has long been a reader of the CIRCULAR. He is a whip-maker by trade, and came with the hope of getting employment in some of our shops. At first we thought of hiring him to work in the Bag-shop, but on reflection we thought it not good policy, as he has a family, and his wife is opposed to our principles.—He gave Mr. Hatch two and a half doz. very neat little whips, of his own make. Whether he thought Mr. H. would need to use them himself, or whether he designed them for playthings for the children, we can't say.

Mr. Kelley writes from Elmira Oct. 18:

" I came through last night from Jamestown to this place. Gen. Sheridan was on the same train. I had a very good opportunity to see him and hear him talk. I also shook hands with him on one occasion when there were but few around, and he was offering his hand. He is a plump little man—head as round as an apple—no corners left. He has a pleasing smile, and speaks more with his eye than with his tongue. His general build, I should say, is Nepoleonic.

Mr. Perkins reports that he has made 480 gallons (16 barrels) of cider from our apples, and 250 gallons (8 barrels) of vinegar.

ERRATUM.—In yesterday's *Daily*, on the second page a little above the middle, for *lawyers* read *loungers*.

Traps ordered yesterday, 575¼ doz.

THE O. C. DAILY.

VOL. 4.   THURSDAY, OCT. 24, 1867.   NO. 99.

Berlin Heights, Ohio, Oct. 18, 1867.

DEAR FRIENDS:—It is evening and Mrs. R. and I
have just been visiting Mr. and Mrs. Lesley. We find a
blessing to come home; yes we come *home*: come
home to O. C. We couldn't touch Oneida while we
were there. It seems much to us as though they were
too anxious to hitch on to the world. I seem to feel
you reaching out after us more than usual this evening.—Only a night or two since Mrs. R. was introduced to a Mr. Lawrence, as a brother Oneidian, by
Mrs. Dr. Karshner. He seemed to be quite in sympathy with O. C. but in the course of his remarks he
said he thought that Mr. Noyes, would have to change
somewhat and not make so much distinction between
the O. C. and the so-called infidels. Mrs. R. told him
she thought he would find the change in others, not
in Mr. Noyes. Then I thought of reading his writings of 1851, and still farther back, and those written
at various periods; and these words came to me: " He
is without variableness or shadow of turning." The
same spirit pervades every thing that we find that
comes or has ever come from Mr. N. We find the
same life, and the same food in all.—God be praised
for Mr. Noyes.   *   *   *   *

It is Sunday evening, and Mr. Randolph, Mrs. R.
and I, had an evening meeting from seven till eight
o'clock. We read from " Confessions and Reports."
Best of all, at eight o'clock Mrs. Wm. A. Hunter
came in, and acknowledged Christ in her a savior from
impatience and irritability; and told us that she had a
few days ago felt like confessing Christ in her a hope
of glory, and had so confessed him. I must confess
that the tears came readily to my eyes as she made me
feel that there was no sham in the confession. She
confessed again her love for, and faith in Mr. Noyes·
I *do* think she and Mr. H. are on hopeful ground. It
is such a blessing, and gives me so much joy to have
any one in this place speak well of Mr. Noyes.

Of late, for a few days past, I have been over-anxious
to get away from here. But Christ assures me that
the way will be made plain and easy when the time
comes. It is my desire, if I am found worthy, to unite
with the O. C. so soon as the way is open to leave this
place; and if not worthy to unite, to live near.

With much love,   G. W. REEVE.

Mrs. Reeve writes, " I can say as Mr. Reeve does
God be praised for Mr Noyes, and to-day especially, I
have come to be thankful for my deliverance. What
am I that Christ should show me such favor. Though
at times I am buffeted and nearly ready to sink yet I
know Christ is near and will watch over me, and will
not let the powers of darkness wrest me from him.—
Mrs. Dr. K. has just been in a few minutes, and
seems quite indignant at Mr. and Mrs. Lawrence for
settling themselves on to her, and has something to
say about folks leading purposeless lives, and going
uninvited from place to place, and waiting to be turned
out before they go. This is why I feel so thankful
because my faith in Christ and O. C. is *such a protection.*

There was some talk again last night about the
whipping affair. It was thought that Myron was too
sensitive to look steadily at the truth, and his father
was warped in his judgment by the family spirit, and
between them both, M. was losing the softening effect
that God designed by this chastisement. Mr. Burt
and Geo. E. both confessed that they had to struggle
against a spirit that would make them look at the case
in a more favorable light than the truth would justify.
It is a high attainment to have that clear-sighted, godly sincerity, that impartially judges our own acts and
motives, and estimates them truthfully.

There is no established name for our new Commune
—once the Boarding-house. The " Creek-house" has
been proposed, also the " Midland-Railroad-house,"
and the " Midland." Some object to " Creek-house"
as not euphonious, and " boarding" does not sound
like home. Is there any objection to " Midland," and
as it is between the two other Communes is it not appropriate, the word coming from *medius*—the middle.
Packages marked M. D. will go there.   *   *

The old furnace has been taken away from the Mansion-house, and a smaller one put in its place. The
hot air from the new one is not admitted into the old
Reception-room, which is warmed by a stove.

George Bayne, of Philadelphia, formerly a conspicuous member of Brook-Farm Association, came here
yesterday and is still with us. He is much interested
in our movement and would like to join.

A brother-in-law of Leonard Burt's wife, Mr. Hayes,
staid here night before last.

Traps ordered yesterday,   194 doz.

THE O. C. DAILY.

VOL. 4.　　FRIDAY, OCT. 25, 1867.　　NO. 100.

OUR SILK-BUSINESS.

It is now about twenty months since it was proposed to send Charles Cragin and two female associates into the outside world to learn the business of manufacturing silk twist; and, if successful, return with the spoils as a basis of another Community enterprise.—The growth and extensiveness of this business, in so short a time, has been a remarkable one indeed and speaks for itself. But the point to which I wish to call the attention of the Community is this. Charles Cragin, as is evident to every one who has taken any notice of him, or the business under him, needs very much to have associated with him, a competent young man possessing talent and enthusiasm for that post. The business has grown to such dimensions already that C. can do justice, neither to the Community, to the business, nor to himself. If the O. C. is wise therefore, it will take some action immediately to investigate the matter, and see if the powers over us are not ready to re-enforce that department with the desired strength.　　　　　　　　　　　　　　C.

W. C., Oct. 22.

Dear ———— :—Having arrived safely at W. C., I thought I would report myself. Nothing of note occurred on the way, with the exception that our iron horse gave out when in the vicinity of West Springfield. He met with some accident to his vital parts I judged, as I saw the white breath gushing forth from his brassy chest furiously. We were not long detained however. It being down grade, we switched the old fellow off the track, and let the train pass on without a motor, running some three or four miles to the bridge, where we met another engine that drew us into the depot. Quite a number of the passengers, some of them women, supposing we should be detained some time, left the cars and undertook to foot it to Springfield. They were not a little chagrined when they saw the train passing them before they had walked a third of the way, and under such headway that rendered any attempt to get aboard hopeless. I thought how much the world generally would be benefitted by a little study of the lesson of patience.—All are well at W. C. I believe. I have the pleasure of meeting Mr. Solon Robinson here.

　　　　　　　　Yours truly,　　H. T.

" Midland" is a better name than " Creek-house" for our boarding place. Still, we should prefer something a little more descriptive, poetical, and, if you please, historical, than either. " Willow-Place," the name with which we christened our offshoot last Spring, fulfills these conditions perfectly, and we all like it, notwithstanding it is suggestive of neither silk-spinning nor trap-making. For similar reasons " Brook-Farm" would suit us exactly for our new Commune. This name has been a synonym of failure; we should make it one of success and righteousness, and thereby rescue it from the oblivion into which it is passing. There are various considerations in its favor, which, however, will, no doubt, occur to the minds of others, and therefore they need not be presented here.

　　　　　　　　　　　　* * *

W. P., Oct. 24.—A new plan is being tried to secure faithfulness and good behavior in the little boys who work in the Trap-shop. A week ago word was given out that prizes would be awarded to those boys who should do the best in work and general deportment in the shop, for the ensuing week. The distribution of prizes took place to-day at noon in the inspecting-room, in the presence of a large majority of the hands employed. The prizes consisted of a pair of boots, a cap, a tippet and one or two pocket-knives and pocket-books. George E. made some appropriate remarks to the boys, then called the names of six who came forward as they were called, with very large smiles on their faces, and received their rewards with evident satisfaction. G. then told the boys that there would be another meeting a week from to-day when we would have something else for them. This plan promises to work well.

We rode over to Vernon yesterday afternoon, and on our return, about sunset, we met, midway between Mr. Hubbard's and W. P., one of our young women trundling a very small wheelbarrow, such an one as our little three-year-old boys use in their play. The ludicrousness of the thing attracted our attention at once, and we were anxious to learn the cause of so strange a procedure. The facts, when known, were these: Mr. Campbell came over here from W. P. with an old gig, a miserable rickety thing, and when ready to return he invited a certain lady to ride home with him. As there was some hesitancy on the part of said lady to comply, a friend of hers who was present, said, jokingly, " If you'll go I will come after you with a wheelbarrow." She was taken at her word, and Miss ——— jumped into the gig, telling her ladyfriend that she should hold her strictly to her promise, which our heroine felt bound to fulfill to the letter, and which certainly required some moral courage, as every one who met her gazed and wondered.

There was a very enthusiastic bee at the Bag-shop last night, where were present forty men and women, twelve of whom came from W. P., which was a pleasant interchange of good offices. The rooms were brilliant with lights, and the shop outside had almost the appearance of an illumination.—Mr. H. went over after the W. P. company with the omnibus, and carried them back in season for meeting.

20 1-12 doz. traps ordered yesterday including one bear trap.

THE O. C. DAILY.

VOL. 4.   SATURDAY, OCT. 26, 1867.   NO. 101.

Hamilton, Oct. 23, 1867.

MR. NOYES:—When I saw the first article in the *Democratic Union*, I thought it unfair as well as unjust, being the production of ill-will and disappointment because the Oneida Community do not assist to build a Rail-road that is to be of vast importance to the village of Oneida.—I saw the intent of the writer, "After You," was to create prejudice in the mind of the public toward the Community. I accordingly wrote a reply to it and sent it to Mr. Baker, Editor of the *Union.* Up to this time I see it is not published and probably will not be. Verily the Oneida paper is down upon you like a "thousand of brick."

This reply is at your disposal. I would reply to this Schenectady man but the *Union* probably would treat it the same as the other.

Very respectfully yours,

CARLTON RICE.

P. S. I this moment learn, i. e. am so told, that the author, "After You,"is the Editor of the *Union* himself.

———————

The Bag business is passing through some changes in the method of conducting it. In two particulars especially is it found desirable to improve arrangements. Working with direct reference to orders was found quite inconvenient, as it required constant and perplexing attention to carry through the various parts of the many kinds of bags in the small lots, and also consumed the time of the hands in their constant change of work. The plan of operation which is now being worked into, is to start the bags in gross lots, of from two to sixteen dozen, according to the prospective demand, which is quite definitely gathered by reference to past sales. This change of policy is nearly completed already, and reduces the labor of superintending very materially.

The other change inaugurated, which is more important, and more difficult to effect, is to have the work done by the piece instead of by the day. The old vicious hireling system of the world, which is only one remove from slavery, requires, in order to get the most work for the least money by the day, a kind of driving, quite distasteful to Community people; and in the absence of this, the selfishness of hirelings takes advantage of our lenity to make a great leak in the profits of our manufactures, which are already reduced to the very minimum. We are learning by special tests, as fast as we can get at it, what it is really worth to do each part, and as soon as practicable intend to have it done by the piece. One man who works by the piece earns a third more pay than when he worked by the week, and the work per piece does not cost us so much, all because he has the more healthful motive to accomplish work, rather than the depressing spirit which watches the clock and seeks dilatory expedients to kill time. Doubtless every man who works for money will do much more when he knows that he will get every cent that he earns, and that every blow struck is so much cash in his pocket. The production is considerably increased already by these changes, and three additional hands have been put on.—

There are some thirty hired men and women and six of our own folks stately employed, with volunteers occasionally, and generous bees of the family. Considerable work is put out to neighboring families.

As soon as our orders and shelves are filled, so that every order for regular varieties can be shipped on the next train after the order is received, we intend to start trunk-making in a small way, to save our customers the always irritating charge of packing-boxes which are worthless to them, and which are considerable trouble for us to get up.   L. B.

———————

Yesterday morning, Mr. Smith on entering Mr. Nash's room, was met with the exclamation, "I had as lief have a dead man as —— to sleep in the room with me, I could not wake him anyhow. I called as loud as I could, rattled my cane, then flung it toward the bed, threw my pillow and slippers, but all would not rouse the fellow." The room showed the effects of his night's struggle, for every thing within Mr. N.'s reach was turned topsy-turvy. The truth was he had occupied the room alone; the person who was to have stayed with him had forgotten to come. Mr. N. was quite as well as usual yesterday, and Mr. Smith thought, and Mr. N. felt that the experience was good for him, but we hope such a thing will not occur again. —It was too bad.

———————

"Brook Farm," appears objectionable as a name for the Community beyond the creek, for it is neither euphonious nor indicative of the character or occupation of the family, and comes to us with infidel associations and the prestige of failure. The family there will have nothing to do with farming. As has been hinted it wants a name that is pleasing or poetical.— Now what would meet the demand better than some liquid Indian name ? Please think of it, and don't be hasty in choosing a hackneyed name.   * * * *

———————

A lady remarked after meeting last night, that it seemed as though God was lifting the curtain to show us what was transpiring behind the scene.

———————

Mrs Allen has been engaged for two or three days in making "Black-Jack," with very good success. A barrel and a half has been made.

We have just heard that Mr. Robinson died night before last.

Sales at the Store, to outsiders, for two days past, $140.

We furnished ten meals to visitors yesterday.

Traps ordered yesterday,   121 doz.

THE O. C. DAILY.

VOL. 4.   MONDAY, OCT. 28, 1867.   NO. 102,

BUSINESS MEETING.

The mind of the Board was asked in regard to buying logs, when Mr. Burt suggested the expediency of packing our traps in barrels instead of boxes; that is the 25 dozen boxes. One of these boxes costs us about seventy-five cents, while a new barrel costs only forty cents. This would have some influence on the number of logs we had better buy. It might also reduce our transportation rates, as barrels are easier to handle than boxes. It was decided to have the trap-committee institute some experiments in regard to packing traps in barrels, and confer with the committee, Messrs. Clark and Kinsley on buying logs.

A committee was appointed last year to consider the propriety of buying a force-pump for the trap-shop for use in case of fire, but no action was taken by it. G. W. Hamilton thought there was too much risk in the shop to let the matter go along much further without some decisive action. The cost of such an one as we should need with the appurtenances would be from $500 to $600. It is proposed to have a cast-iron pipe run up through the building to which hose may be attached in any story. The matter was deferred last year on account of the outlay required, so that it now becomes one of finance. Mr. Woolworth remarked that as we do not take insurance policies we might afford to pay out a few hundred dollars to insure ourselves. Referred to the original committee, Messrs. E. H. and G. W. Hamilton to consult with the Agency folks.

The subject of a dry-house for the silk-department was brought up for consideration by the Board. As things are now, the silk has to be dried in the office or in the sink-room, and as these rooms are in use during the day, this work has to be done in the night, requiring a vigorous fire to be kept up all night. It is thought unsafe to have such a fire in any part of the building and that we had better build a brick room for the purpose outside of the shop. A house 14 by 16 would be large enough and would probably cost about $200. The work of drying the silk is the most wearing and disagreeable that Charles has to do, and such a house will be a great help to that department. An executive committee was appointed, viz: Messrs. Burt, Kinsley, G. W. Hamilton, C. A. Cragin and Miss Harriet Allen. It is desirable to have the work done without delay.

Hold up friends! hold up! enough said; we are content with our name, *Boarding House.* It is a very plain, prosaic one, to be sure, but then, so is our business a plain one, nothing poetical about that. Our house too, standing here quite naked and alone, is also a very plain affair; and, morever, we communists who run this machine, would be regarded, probably, by strangers, as belonging to the same category of plain commodities. Neither is there any thing in the situation or surroundings, suggestive of poetical beauty; hence deserving, for its own sake, a corresponding appellation. Under such circumstances it would be decidedly incongruous to attach a musical or romantic name to a business or place that does not suggest the remotest idea of any natural connection between them. But when *Brook-Farm* was proposed, as an appropriate name for our premises, we thought, verily, the sun had gone down on this subject, and persons were groping about by *star-light*, and that it was high time to close the books for subscriptions to this *name-stock* enterprise.   [Continued.]

Some three or four of our men went to the lake fishing, yesterday, and about the same number went hunting, which led to considerable talk last night about the expediency, just at this time, of giving our neighbors cause to think evil of us by indulging in these amusements, Sundays, particularly hunting. A good spirit prevailed, and all seemed desirous to act in union with Mr Noyes, and avoid every thing that might give offence to our neighbors.

A Mr. Carey, an Uncle of P. A. Sibley, writes to her from West Brookfield, Oct. 2nd: " Your social ideas I believe are based on good morality and sound common sense, but little known to the outside world. You and the Community have my best wishes for their continued success in all that pertains to elevate men, women and children to the high standard of virtue, love and peace."

A Mr. Chester Hare from Syracuse, staid here over Sunday. He was and old acquaintance of Mr. Van Velzer, and of E. H. Hamilton, and was disappointed in not seeing either, as Mr. V. is away peddling.

Our people have just completed a new omnibus similar in construction to our other one. It was built for the purpose of carrying the silk-factory girls to and from their boarding-places.

Three of the avenue rooms have been vacated, and the partitions between them are being taken away, for the purpose of making one large room for the children to play in the coming winter.

Mr. Olds returned Friday and W. G. Kelley Saturday.—D. A. Abbott started Saturday night for W. C. via. New-York.

The grape-vines are all trimmed, laid down and covered with earth.

Traps ordered Saturday and Sunday,   858 dz.

THE O. C. DAILY.

VOL. 4.   TUESDAY, OCT. 29, 1867.   NO. 103.

THE NAME QUESTION CONCLUDED.

Now as boarding is, at present, our business, we find a growing friendliness to the name. Indeed, in looking over the world we see that it is little else than one great boarding-house. Every body boards in one way or another. Strictly speaking. nobody lives at home or keeps house permanently. A wife does cooking, washing &c. &c., for her husband. In that case, a man boards with his wife; and then, he is not always suited with his board. In Washington City, it is said that one half the inhabitants board with the other half; but which half secures the best end of the bargain or the most happiness is not stated. Christ understood the exact situation of things.— He had no home, not even a boarding-house.— "The foxes have holes, the birds of the air have nests" said he, "but the son of man hath not where to lay his head." He had as much love for home, "sweet home," as any one, and was bound to secure it, not only for himself, but for all who were worthy of it. We judge this to be so by his saying, "in my father's house are many mansions—I go to prepare a place for you." Here a true home was promised them, and they are now in the enjoyment of it. The enemy and destroyer of all peaceful, permanent homes, is the old serpent, death. Let us all go in as Christ did, for a victory over the enemy that shuts us out of our own true home in the bosom of God. Until then, we are soldiers, having no abiding place, but are thankful for tents, boarding-houses, shanties, or whatever will serve our present needs. Don't let us forget that we are *soldiers in battles, daily*, not on furlough, sporting bright uniforms to tickle our vanity by attracting attention.   C.

I give below the summary of my late trip:

Trap orders,	$13,850.84
Fruit "	$3,129.31
Bag "	$1,240.96
Silk "	$246.10
Orders for Trappers Guides	$206.25
Collections	$10,868.58
Total	$30,554.04
Expenses	$328.67

The criticism of James Vaill occupied the most of the meeting hour last night. He has been tempted into some of his old habits of late, and is full of frivolity and nonsense. He needs sincere repentence and conversion to God. He has given evidence by confessing his faults from time to time, that he has the love of the truth in his heart, but he inherits bad blood

and needs earnestness and entire openness, and the help of the family to overcome his temptations and make him spiritually minded. Mr. Woolworth said he hoped all would pray for him.

Mr. Kelley learned when at Oberlin, that one young lady had been discharged from the Oberlin school for her belief in, and sympathy with the doctrines held by us, and her refusal to tell the names of other of her associates who were interested in the O. C.

We had a very pleasant and lively bee, of about an hour and a half, at the Tontine after supper last night, for paring and cutting apples. About sixty of the family were present and nineteen bushels of apples were pared and cored.

We fail to-day, the first time for many weeks, to get sufficient copy to fill our DAILY, and shall be obliged to send out one blank page.

Our splendid weather which has continued for many weeks, seems to be drawing to a close. It is quite warm and rainy this morning.

Traps ordered yesterday,   55½ doz.

THE O. C. DAILY.

VOL. 4. WEDNESDAY, OCT. 30, 1867. NO. 104.

Charles Olmstead handed our folks the following letter, which was directed to his address, with these words written on the back of it:

"Please give thos note to charles Mills in the Com buy his request."

Tecomseh, Jhonson Co., Oct. 15, 1867.

Dear Son Charles Mills your letter is to hand asking if I want a box of fruit trees, you had better not meddle with any sich buisnees so soon going to Oneida, I would like Trees, but I would not pay the express charges on them, you had now better Settle down quietly and submit your self to the Community althoug I have no more faith in them now then when I left them I would liked to had you got you a good wife and Settled down Steady and carred on my farm for years, I could have given you a good chance, I kneed some one all the time, I am now sick and have been for most three month, with Tiford Fevor I want one favour of you, *Its this*—find out how the Community makes three Kinds of Bread—Brown—, *Graham Bread*, and *white Bread*, write to me gust how its done. I would like to know who paid Grace expences to the *Com.* please to write all the perticulars about the Bread Soon, I shall git the Baby and Mother and my self likeness tooken and send it to Oneida So they can see the great appostate once more Frances sends her best wishes from your father **William Mills.**

charles Omstead I shall write your folks soon a good buisness letter about matter. **William Mills.**

DEAR MR. WOOLWORTH:—I feel this morning like writing a few words to you. It has been a great trial to me to be unable to take part in the business campaign this Fall and the summer past, but I believe that God is a kind and loving father, and does not afflict willingly. I have been led to look over my past life and judge it, for it looks very hateful to me. I have felt like judging my parents too, for my father had a hard unbelieving spirit for a good many years before he died, and my mother has been sick ever since I can remember. When she was about my age, she had a paralytic stroke on the right side of her body, which caused her much suffering and from which she has never fully recovered. For several years I have been troubled some as she was in my right side, but for three weeks past it has given me a good deal of trouble and suffering, not only in my leg but my arm also, which seems to me to be the cause of my foot's tardy progress. I believe there is a wicked principality connected with it, and I feel the need of help to overcome it. I ask God every day what I can do to help forward the work of salvation in myself and others and obtain resurrection life, which

I so much need. Any criticism or advice will be thankfully received. Confessing a soft heart, and my union with you and the family, I am yours in hope of the resurrection, **L. E. AIKEN.**

W. P., Oct. 29.—Business in the shops goes on smoothly this week, but we are unable as yet to give the exact number of traps made during the present month. Some reading from the *Circular* this evening. The present number is particularly refreshing; though all the late issues have been filled with power and edification.—Mr. Ackley and Mrs. Campbell were elected several evenings since, to prepare a pantomime, and this evening they were called on to present it. One end of the room was cleared for their use, and a box was brought in by Myron and placed on the floor.—Two persons apparently beggars entered. The woman seated herself on the box while the man begged in silence for something to eat, which M. appeared to give them and one would have thought they were half-starved to see them eat. Soon some old clothes were asked for, when M. pointing to the clock set the man to sawing wood and seized the opportunity when they were both off the box, to put a slanting roof on it which drew shouts of laughter, and exclamations of "Mr. Burt's well-curb," from the spectators. The man sawed vigorously for a time, looking often to see if his time was not up. Finally, M. appeared to satisfy their demand for old clothes and dismissed them to the barn. Our W. C., beggars were easily recognized and heartily laughed at.—G. E. C. and H. M. W. are to give us the next pantomime.

We had just corrected the proof of the inside pages of the DAILY yesterday, and started the press, when lo! to our great consternation, one of the pages was precipitated on to the floor beneath, and the type scattered in all directions. What was to be done? Quick as thought we dispatched a hand to recall our compositors, who with the assistance of our publisher, succeeded in getting the paper out in season for the mail. In its reconstruction however, the initials (c. o.), of the person who gave us the table of statistics, was overlooked and omitted.

We had two bees last night, one company going over to the Trap-shop, and another assembling in the Tontine for paring apples. Nearly the same number attended at the latter place, and about the same amount of work was done, as the night before; and we learned that a good deal of work was accomplished at W. P.

New-York, Oct. 29, 1867.

DEAR O. C. DAILY:—If you want a distinctive name for that *boarding*-house, why not call it "*The Crayin House.*" You are *welcome* to the suggestion. Yours truly, and always happy to see your sprightly face, **E. H. H.**

Traps ordered yesterday, 129 doz.

THE O. C. DAILY.

VOL. 4.　THURSDAY, OCT. 31, 1867.　NO. 105.

EVENING MEETING.

Mr. Newhouse:—One of the reporters of the *New York Herald* came to the Willow-Place works this afternoon, accompanied by a lawyer by the name of Dodge, who formerly resided at Oneida Castle, and Dr. Whetmore and Pat Ferrol. They looked around considerably and appeared to be very much pleased with what they saw. They were surprised to see so much business being done there. The reporter had called for the purpose of seeing what he could and " writing us up," as he expressed it. His time was limited as he wished to return in season for the evening train.—They requested me to come over here with them, and I did so. I looked around for Mr. Underwood, but could not find him; so I showed them through the hall, library and reception room, and then went out to the fruit-house. They appeared very much interested, and very sorry that they had so little time, as they wanted to have some talk. The reporter thought he should call again sometime. They did not stop here over fifteen or twenty minutes.

Mr. Dodge had been absent thirteen years and did not know that we had put up any new buildings. He was much surprised at the improvements we had made. The reporter said our place beat the Central Park. Pat Ferrol told this man that he must write up the *Democratic Union.* They were all down on the way this paper is treating us. Pat said they had no friends at the Depot and he didn't know how they managed to keep the subject in the papers at all.— These men were all Democrats but Dodge.

Had our name-seekers accompanied the writer to the top of the tower, one bright day not long ago, and from there rested their eyes sympathetically, on the *Boarding-house* and its surroundings,—the old barns, the apple-trees, the growing cabbages, and the corn and beans apparently within a stone's throw of the house, the cows and young cattle contentedly grazing in the clover meadow round-about, within easy call of a boy standing in the doorway, and the creek marking and washing the boundaries, and purling on its way just under the windows of the " Old Farm-house," perhaps they would have agreed with him, that nature had stamped this picture with the title *Creek-Farm.* Indeed, on that mellow Indian Summer day, the *Boarding-house* appeared to be *wreathed with beauty, and farming associations*; and so it appears to the writer now, and also the business conducted therein.

From *Creek-Farm,* to *Brook-Farm,* was only a step, the past history and relations of this last, not being then regarded as of much account, in the light of that spirit, which is making all things *new.* He is happy to say however, that he is perfectly satisfied, for the present, with *Boarding-house,* and thinks, that after all there may be no better name for our new Commune, unless, indeed, we accept the suggestion of E. H. H. and call it, *The Cragin House,* which has also been somewhat canvassed here, during the past week. He is glad to express his appreciation of the remarks on this subject in Tuesday's DAILY.

* * *

Two men called into the printing-office yesterday, by permission, who said they were printers by trade, and wanted to look around. We told them there was not much to be seen—that we were a small affair &c., but they seemed curious and examined both presses and the type in the drawers, and wanted to know about the paper we printed. We showed them a DAILY which one of them seemed anxious to take with him, and after looking them over, we selected one, which we gave him, with which he seemed much pleased. The other man said he did not blame us for not wanting our family matters circulated outside; he should not care to have his home affairs known to the world around him.

J. M. Beckett of Boston has written us another of his queer letters. The DAILY copied from them last year. The one just received contains a fruit order, and the envelope was superscribed, " Oneida Community *Phroot rh'ume,* Oneida N. Y." The letter begins thus:

" Com-mu-ni-tye ! Please send me by the cheapest and best route, of course." [Then follows the order,] " Will remit on receipt of Invoice *and sarse.*

Most corpulently Yours,　　J. M. BECKETT."

Forming good resolutions and putting ourselves into God's hands for the correction of our faults, requires great moral courage, and abandonment of egotism. Exposure of the workings of our old life, of satan's strong-holds in us, must come first or last, if we are to be saved.

We had still another paring bee last night attended by some less than sixty of the family. We make our sweet apples into cider-apple-sauce which we put into bottles for family use, and instead of drying our sour ones, they too are preserved in bottles, as last year.

Our rain-storm is over, and the sun shines this morning bright and warm. The month of Oct. has been remarkably fine, as was its predecessor, Sept.; scarcely one unpleasant day.

H. M. Worden has left the school, and gone over to W. P., for a few weeks. Portia has taken her place, and will remain teacher for the present.

Traps ordered yesterday,　　　　10 5-6 doz.

THE O. C. DAILY.

VOL. 4.   FRIDAY, NOV. 1, 1867.   NO. 106.

EVENING MEETING.

Mr. Bolles reported that four of the German workmen, Young, Woolfe, Hoffman and Fritz, had given notice of an intention to leave our service, assigning as a reason that they did not like the board. These men have given such entire satisfaction that it had been determined to raise their wages. They were notified of this, but it didn't move them. They complained of the way the Yankee boarders treated them. German immigrants are very sensitive to ridicule, and some of our boarders are pretty rough, not scrupling to call these men "Dutchmen," "sauer-kraut," etc. This is thought to be the chief cause of their disaffection. They were finally told that we would set a separate table for them and let them choose their bill of fare. At this they agreed to think of it and give us their decision to-morrow.

If these men quit it breaks the business right in two. Mr. Woolworth suggested that the aim should be to educate men who live right around us to do this work, so that we shall not be dependent on foreigners and liable to be left just at the critical moment. Mr. Bolles felt that this was another attack of the devil on our business enterprise but thought that good would come of it.

There was some talk about the boarding-house. It seems hardly expedient to attempt to curtail the meat diet or to be too economical there. Mr. Bolles thought the pies rather thin and the sugar a little too brown. On the other hand Mr. Worden said the boarders, with the exception of the Germans, were entirely satisfied with the quality of the food, and better pleased with the boarding arrangements than ever before.

Mr. Woolworth.—I confess I have a desire in my heart to profit by the circumstances we are in. It is a time of considerable trial and perturbation, and the devil seems to be very active. God is also very active. I think this is a good school for us, in which to educate our hearts, and discipline us to give our attention to God in the midst of excitement and clatter. Paul and the Primitive Church went through a great deal of experience far worse, and much more trying. Our trials and afflictions are not worthy to be compared with theirs; and yet they serve to bring us into sympathy with them and make us appreciate the trials they went through. [Heartily appproved.]

COMMUNISM A BUILDER.

Here and there individuals are found who possess a wonderful talent for remodeling and creating new, useful, and beautiful things out of little or nothing, as it were; such, for instance, as making new garments out of old ones, causing ugly things to look comely; finding materials and tools to work with where others would find none. In fine, possessing the faculty to improve every thing upon which they can lay their hands, and by so doing, turn every thing to some good account. Now Communism possesses just that sort of disposition and genius. It came into the world to save men, not to destroy them; to do good not evil: to build up, not to pull down; to make bad men good by reconstructing them, leaving out the selfish element of slavery to sin, and putting in the Christ element of love; to make good men better; to enlighten the ignorant; to humble the proud; to criticise the self-willed and conceited; to comfort the afflicted by turning their attention to the better life within; to liberate the oppressed; to do justice to all; to think evil of none, and to instruct every one to seek not his own, but the good of others. In a word, Communism is the *incarnation* of vital christianity, the practical embodiment of the gospel of Christ, which exhibited, in a remarkable manner, its natural disposition on the very day of its birth, by causing men who drank in its spirit, to speak the word of God with great power and boldness; to lose their covetousness and hardness of spirit in the twinkling of an eye; "to eat their meat with gladness and singleness of heart;" to find themselves unselfish and generous, saying, one to another, that these things which we possess are not our own, but belong to God and to his children; so we will hold them in common for the good of all.   [To be continued.]

W. P. Oct. 31.—The number of traps made in the last two months is 160,000; 90,000 of which were made the present month. The number of pounds of silk made during the month of Oct. is 444½; valued at $6,116.45. Silk sold and sent to O. C. A. amounts to $6,098.75.

Mr. Noyes's letter to Mr. Woolworth recommending the raising of wages without solicitation from employees, was received with approbation. This course has been pursued to some extent in the Trap-shop. Considerable talk followed, on our policy toward the help. Making presents seems to be better in some cases than raising wages. Some of the boys and girls in our shop cannot afford to go to school, but would like an evening school. Can we not help them to one in some way; if we could, it would have a good effect on them and on the world around us. We want a spirit of liberality toward our workmen and not the spirit of the world which grinds them down and seeks to get all it can from them for the least money. Next week we shall commence carrying the boys who live at the Castle and Depot, to and from the shop, as we do the girls.

Mr. Vanvelzer returned from his peddling trip yesterday, having been absent ten or eleven days.

V. C. N. and E. S. B. Left in the night for W. C.
Traps ordered yesterday,   142 doz.

THE O. C. DAILY.

VOL. 4. SATURDAY, NOV. 2, 1867. NO. 107.

COMMUNISM A BUILDER.

[Concluded.]

And all these remarkable changes in the habits, feelings and disposition of men were the natural, logical results of the working, transforming influences of the spirit of life that raised Christ from the dead.— Here, it might be said, was the first application of God's wonderful invention of reconstructing individuals or the manufacturing of good men. And, truly, it is an invention as marvelous as it is simple and effectual. But the process, says one, of making good, sound, honest men! tell us, if you can, how it can be done? for honest men and true, are the want of the age. The cry, yes the agonizing cry of every trade, every business, every profession, from the pulpit, the bar, the dispensary and the political forum, is heard, give us honest men; men, who are true to the public good, true to the majesty of simple truth, regardless of consequences to individualism or self-interest. Now just such men were manufactured in the Primitive Church. Paul is one of them and is a sample of the men wanted everywhere. How suddenly he was *reconstructed* after Christ met him on the plains of Damascus.

The son of God in his work of regenerating or re-molding men, reverses the process sometimes seen when a carpenter builds a new house over an old one, by building a new house *inside* of an old one. The reason for such a peculiar procedure is simply this—if Christ should begin to build on the outside of a character first, the devil would give him trouble and bother him very much by attempting to pull down his work, or by diverting attention to outward things etc.; but by beginning at the center of the *interior* life the builder can work on unmolested, and for the simple reason that the devil has no interior—no life within a life, hence can only look outward and in a straight line, possessing as he does no more knowledge of the work Christ is about in the inner, refined sphere of humanity, or where souls live by faith, than a beast of the field does of agricultural chemistry. Here Christ lays his foundation so deep in the purely spiritual part of human existence that no amount of evil on the surface of life can for a moment disturb it. And upon this foundation, communism is a builder.   c.

———

W. P. Nov. 1.—When Myron was at Oneida a few days since he saw the carcass of a bear which was killed at Oneida lake, near the place where our people used to camp when spending a night there. A young man who was out setting traps started the creature which gave him quite a fright as he had no gun with him. He went home for his gun, and some men went back with him and killed the bear.

A new machine for riveting has been procured for use in the Trap-shop which promises to be a great saving of time and money; doing the work of several men.

There was another distribution of prizes to-day among the small boys in the shop. This seems to have a good effect on them. Our neighbors recognize the fact that our shops are a blessing to the young men and boys in the neighborhood. One man remarked that working in our shop had been the making of the Hubbard boys and Fred. Davis. They were good for nothing before.

———

The grand *finale* of our apple-bees came off last night, in which ninety-two persons participated.—There were twenty-seven from W. P., and the only fault found was that the sport ended too soon, a quarter past seven. 103 bushels in all, have been pared and cored, 44 of sweet and 59 of sour.

———

The difficulty among the German hands at the Bag-shop was satisfactorily arranged yesterday, and three of them are to remain. The fourth, Mr. Woolfe, will leave, as he is not liked very well, and is thought to have been the mover of the disaffection among the rest.

A THOUGHT.

I.

Winter nears us, Autumn's flying,
Vegetation weeps, seems dying,
But however stern appearing,
Nature's rest is sweet and cheering.

II.

So when God sends tribulation,
For our good, our education,
Let us not repine or wonder,
Though he speaks in tones of thunder.

III.

Heavy chastenings now so grievous,
Oft from serious faults relieve us,
And the stripes so wisely given,
Prove a precious boon from heaven.

IV.

Patience when temptations buffet,
Is the grace that most we covet,
But our hearts with strong endeavor,
Seek the rest that lasts forever.

———

Traps ordered yesterday,   215¼ doz.

THE O. C. DAILY.

VOL. 4. MONDAY, NOV. 4, 1867. NO. 108.

BUSINESS MEETING.

It was proposed that measures be taken to recover damages for the injury done to one of our wagons some time ago in falling through the wheel-barrow factory-bridge. The Board of Auditors of Vernon meet soon, (14th inst.) so that we can have a committee to estimate the damages, and present them to that Board for payment. Messrs. Clark, Hawley, Kinsley and D. Kelly were appointed committee, Mr. Kinsley Chairman.

The subject of removing the bell to the roof of the middle house was brought up for discussion. During cold weather when the doors and windows are pretty much closed, the bell cannot be heard in the upper sitting-room, and persons often remain there after the bell has rung for meeting. Its location on the middle house will also be more convenient to the Tontine and other places. Messrs. Clark, Hatch, A. Burt and J. H. Barron are committee to look into the matter. The propriety of getting a larger bell was suggested. The committee will take this into consideration.

It is desirable to have some bathing conveniences for the use of Mr. Daniel Nash. It is considerable work for one man to carry water to his room for that purpose two or three times a week, and it was thought the plan offered last August of having a bath-room in the mansion house might be carried out and thus accommodate others as well as Mr. N. The subject was postponed at that time on account of our financial pressure, and it was recommended that the committee appointed then, reconsider the matter with Mr. Nash's case in view. That committee consisted of Messrs. Cragin, Thacker, Geo. E. Cragin, Mrs. H. C. Noyes and Maria Barron.

[The subject of the location of the place for bathing, was discussed in meeting last night and after considerable talk, it was decided to fit up the bathing place in the children's sink-room for the accommodation of Mr. Nash, (as it would be in his present state, almost impossible to take him down stairs,) and to build another room on the lower floor as was proposed for the accommodation of elderly persons as soon as it can be done conveniently.]

Charles Cragin reported that he did not consider himself over-worked in the silk business, but he liked the idea of having another man learn the business so as to take charge of it should he want to be spared from it for any reason. It is quite a costly business to teach any one, as a great deal of botch-work is made and it injures the character of the silk. He would like to have a good selection made of some one to be instructed so that he will understand the business as well as he does himself. Mr. Burt thought we should select some one who should qualify himself to take charge of the business at W. C. Charles A. Cragin, Messrs. Woolworth, Burt, Campbell, H. Barron, H. E. Allen and Elizabeth Hutchins were appointed a committee to make a suitable selection.

Mr. Kinsley said he was placed last week on the committee for buying logs, and if the responsibility ended in purchasing them he would have no objection to the appointment; but it involves attending to the teams and seeing that the logs are drawn to the mill, and keeps him out of the winter classes. He had that post last winter, and thought he would like to be relieved this winter in order to have time for study. Mr. Woolworth proposed that as Mr. Kinsley has charge of the distribution of help, he could divide his responsibilities in a way that will admit of his attending the classes.

Mrs. Dascomb writing from Cameron, Oct. 27, says, " In joy or suffering, my heart ever turns toward the Community as the spot where the true light is now shining more brightly than among any other people upon the earth. I felt very near you before my visit, and on my way to you I felt like one who after a weary absence, and toilsome journey approaches home, with all its endearments ; and how disappointed and heart-broken I was, the first two days of my visit, to find that I was not so near you as when away. I can only compare my experience at that time and during some dark hour's since, to that of one suspended between the heavens and the earth as nearly as I can imagine that to be. I am very sorry I caused you so much trouble, etc."

Mr. Wm. A. Hunter of Berlin, who, it will be remembered, worked for us a few weeks several years ago, and afterwards proposed to join, and held some correspondence with Mr. Cragin relative to the matter, writes that he now sees he was not prepared to join at that time—that since Mrs. Reeve's visit here, he and his wife have had their interest newly awakened, and he desires, (to use his own expression) to " hitch on" just where he left off—thinks he is at least fifteen years behind the Community.

We judge from letters received from Berlin, from time to time, that there is an earnest spirit at work there, and that some are sincerely judging and separating themselves from their past lives.

We have had considerable high wind for two days and some rain, though the weather is quite warm. The wind blew quite a gale last night when the W. P. family left for home which made it rather unpleasant for them.

Traps ordered Saturday and Sunday. 219 doz.

THE O. C. DAILY.

VOL. 4.   TUESDAY, NOV. 5, 1867.   NO. 109.

Los Angeles, California, Oct. 6, 1867.

MR. WOOLWORTH:—I received a kind of Circular or Community letter from you, recently. Feeling somewhat interested in the success of Community experiments, I wish to know of your people. Please write me your style of living. How many hours per day do you work? What hour do all rise, and what hours do they eat?—and tell me what dress your men adopt? Do your folks shave or wear whiskers? or is it optional; also the dress of the other sex.

For years I have been a believer in your Community ideas—I know not what your religious notions are; my own are modified from what they were. I was a Baptist, but am somewhat more liberal than formerly, and think any tree that bringeth forth *good fruit* is a good tree.

I am a bachelor forty-five years old. For many years have been a teacher, though formerly I was a Doctor. I have charge of the Los Angeles grammar school.—I shall be glad to hear from you; I have long had serious thought of giving my personal attention to your experiment, and investigate its claims to the confidence of honest men, who think society as at present organized a lamentable failure.

I have sent money to Wallingford for your paper to be sent me here, I believe also I have ordered some books from you.—Give me light, I am a seeker for truth, light and better hopes.   Yours truly,

T. H. ROSE.

W. P., Nov 4.—Our three teams which left the ticket-office this morning conveying women, boys and girls to our shops, created quite a sensation. One of our hired men carries eighteen boys back and forth every night and morning now. The man and team stay over night at one of the hotels at the Depot.

Mr. Burt on retiring Thursday night, could not find his night-shirt, so was forced to go without it.—The next morning he told his trouble to Hattie Mallory, who made his bed the day before, rather feeling that there had been some carelessness on the part of the person having the care of his room. She went with him and they searched the room, but no night-shirt could be found. It was very mysterious. Saturday evening while preparing for a bath, what was Mr. Burt's astonishment to find between his shirt and under-shirt, his *lost night-shirt!* He must have been in a brown study when he dressed, Thursday morning.

Mrs. Bristol and Annie Kelley take the places of S. B. C. and H. M. Worden in our family. Jane L. Abbott will remain with us for the present in the place of Portia.

The judgment on special love and the marriage spirit has been searching me of late, and stirring me up to sincerity and earnestness—and the principality in favor of selfishness and slavery has also been very busy in stirring up, exciting and aggravating the old, selfish life, and hence an exceedingly sharp conflict between the two, which made me realize the truth of what Mr. Noyes says in the article, "Principalities and Powers," "that every believer is little more than a battle-field on which invisible hosts contend." The result of this battle has been on the one hand to greatly humble me, and show me the utter worthlessness, hatefulness, meanness and unfaithfulness of my old life—and on the other hand to establish my heart in the truth that God has a purpose concerning me,—to save me from all this, and I *know* what he proposes to do, he can and will accomplish. The talk on spiritual slavery opened a great door of hope to me.—I feel like taking a new departure, in faith and devotion to the truth—like girding myself anew as a good soldier in this warfare with the marriage principality—The earnest prayer of my heart is for patience, and the repentance which will separate me from the works of the flesh and the hard heart.   H. MATHEWS.

Mr. Woolworth inquired last night if any one would volunteer to give us a pantomime—said he did not know but it was time for us to follow suite with the other Communes—thought perhaps we had been so much absorbed in the moral war that was going, that the spirit of the thing had not reached us yet. He would like to have some one give us a pantomine of this war, and asked if it was considered ended? Some thought it was. Mr. Delatre and J. P. H. were finally selected to try their skill in this mute way of communicating thought.

M. D. Pomeroy had a fall night before last, which sprained one of her shoulders. She suffered a good deal with it yesterday, but feels better this morning, and we hope it may not prove as serious as we at first feared.

A cousin of Harriet Sibley, a Mrs. Green with her husband, from Milford Mass., came here yesterday and staid over night. They are recently married and are making their wedding tour.—Mrs. Bushnell's son came also last night.

The company from W. C., arrived safely in the night.

Traps ordered yesterday,   153 doz.

THE O. C. DAILY.

VOL. 4.   WEDNESDAY, NOV. 6, 1867.   NO. 110.

Syracuse, Oct. 31, 1867.

ONEIDA COMMUNITY:—*Dear brethren and sisters
in the Lord:*—I wish to propose myself as a member
of your society. I am forty-five years old, weigh
185¼ lbs., enjoy good health, by occupation carpet
weaver, can turn my hand to almost any thing, and
desire to live with congenial spirits who love the Lord
and are in his kingdom here below. My wife says
she will give her written consent that she is willing to
have me join you, which was all the question against
me when I called to see you, so if you vote for me to
come, send me your paper directed to Charles E. Post,
Salina, Onondaga Co., N. Y. A well wisher to the
cause of union,   O. E. POST.

W. P., Nov. 5.—The work of grading around the
factory has been vigorously prosecuted for several
days, and is not yet finished. The earth removed is
carted to the flat between the willows on the northwest side of our house and the barns below, to make
a road to be used in drawing stone and all other
teaming, instead of having it all go through our lane.
This will be appreciated by our family, especially in
the summer.—Mrs. Thayer spent a good part of the
day with us; we were glad to see her.—James Hatch
is a member of our family for the present.

Nov. 6.—A flock of wild geese passed our house
this morning, flying so low and making such a noise
as to awake some members of the family. There are
also a flock of ducks on the pond and Mr. Newhouse
is out with his rifle.

It may be remembered that last spring the team
Charlie Primo drives, fell through the bridge near the
wheelbarrow factory, in the town of Vernon. A committee has been appointed to estimate the damage
and present the claim to the Town Authorities. Meantime, however, quite a strong feeling in favor of relinquishing the claim, or giving it to Charles Primo,
was found to exist. Mr. Woolworth had conversed
with Mrs. Miller on the subject and found her anxious
to have the matter dropped. Charles Primo will present his claim for personal damages. Mr. Woolworth
said his instinct prompted him to favor giving our
claim to Primo and letting him make the most of it.
The meeting unanimously favored this idea. Charlie
has proved himself to be a faithful servant and a
staunch friend of the Community.

The thanks of the Community are due to the HON.
DEMAS HUBBARD JR., member of Congress from the
Nineteenth Congressional District of this state, for valuable Public Documents. Mr. Hubbard, a Republican
associate, and warm personal friend of Judge Holmes
of Morrisville, is a resident of Smyrna, Chenango Co.
On his way home from the Central R. R. a few weeks
ago, he and Mrs. Hubbard and some of their friends,
made us a call of an hour or two, and took dinner; and
in looking over our library afterwards, Mr. Hubbard
volunteered a donation of such Reports of the Heads
of Departments at Washington, as he thought would
be useful and desirable.   U.

Mr. Nash is steadily gaining in power to control
his body. Yesterday he succeeded in getting from
his chair on to the bed, without assistance. He worked
his chair to the foot of the bed, grasped the bedpost
with his well hand, drew himself on to his well foot,
wheeled round and sat down. He then worked himself toward the head of the bed, threw himself on his
back, put his well leg up, and then with a rolling
jerking motion succeeded in getting the lame one on.
This he did several times.   D. E. S.

We had two pantomimes last night on the stage;
the first by W. G. Kelley, designed to represent Mr.
Burt's affair of the night-shirt, and the other by J. P.
Hutchins and Mr. Smith, intended as a representation of the forgetful watcher, or Mr. Nash's night's experience when left alone. They were both quite
amusing and their subjects easily recognized by all.

The ground this morning is white with a thin mantle of snow, and the evergreens have put on a delicate
fairy-like covering. The little boys and girls are out
with their sleds in great glee, but as the sun shines
brightly their sport must soon be over, and these pre-
monitions of winter melt away.

Albert Bushnell left this morning. He sung two
very good songs last night, accompanying them with
music on the harmonium, and playing very acceptably
some good pieces besides.

Said A. to B. I can place four figure ones, so that
when added, they shall make precisely 12. Will
some one tell how it is done?

Traps ordered yesterday,   87 doz.

THE O. C. DAILY.

VOL. 4. THURSDAY, NOV. 7, 1867. NO. 111.

Chicago, Nov. 4, 1867.

MR. CHARLES OLDS, DEAR SIR:—Yours of the 29th Oct. was duly received, have not had a minute's leisure to answer. I have been very busy repacking fruit and delivering it to customers; shall finish the job this week and make collection, so that I can send you a draft next week; at the same time may send you notes as we talked about. I have received all the fruit that you shipped, not enough of some kinds, and plenty of others. I was obliged to cut order for B. O. raspberry. I have found but one or two broken bottles; there is about the usual quantity of fermented fruit in which the corks are loose. The jellies came in good condition; not one broken tumbler as far as opened. The quality is *very much* better than last season—in fact it is *very nice*. The peas and lima-beans we have eaten and find *good*, as are all the fruits we have tasted. The case of pickled tomatoes came to hand with the other fruits. We have eaten of them and find them *excellent;* in fact, nice, nicer, nicest. We had no idea that tomatoes could be made into so good pickles. Please accept our thanks for the very nice present. Very truly yours,

W. B. BURBANK.

To MR. E. S. BURNHAM, DEAR SIR:—Yours of Oct. 28th came to hand last week, but for want of time has not been answered. I think Mr. Old's advice about shipping my last order was sound, as it was too small a lot to ship alone. I am short of the raspberry, damson plums, pickled peaches, blackberry, raspberry jam and Lawton blackberries. The fruit, came in good condition, only one bottle broken. The jam very nice, as are the jellies—not one broken tumbler. Very truly yours, W. B. BURBANK.

W. P., Nov. 6.—Charles A. Cragin, has been looking about to-day to see if we can get the evening school, for the boys and girls in the shop. The last plan proposed is to secure the use of the school-house on the street, and hire the teacher of the day-school, Mr. Fish, to teach in the evening. Charles first called on Henry Wilson, who is one of the trustees. He thought our evening school would be a good thing, but was not enthusiastic; did not know about having it in the school-house; it might be damaged—thought we might make a room in our old paint-shop near the Foundry—would consult the other trustees about it and let us know. C. then went to the school-house to see if we could secure the services of the teacher. Mr. F. was very polite. He said he would teach three evenings in the week, if paid for it, but could not tell how much he should want until he had tried it. C. met Mr. Williams, another of the trustees, and was introduced. On mentioning the school project to him

that gentleman remarked that he might as well tell him as any one that people in the village thought we were exerting a bad moral influence on the young people in the neighborhood. C. told him that that need have nothing to do with the question of the school, as we did not expect to send our children or have anything to do with it except to foot the bill.—Mr. W. thought the town would not do more than give us the use of the room, if they did anything.—We must pay for fuel and lights. He would consult with the other trustees, another of whom came in just then and C. lingered to see if something would not be said to him about it. Nothing was said, however, and C. came home feeling rather disgusted at the lack of public spirit displayed.

The children had a nice ride one of the last of the fine days we have been having. There were two companies of them, the largest children going in the forenoon and the little ones in the afternoon. The omnibus was brought into requisition, which by the way is a great comfort and convenience. We took the first party into the pine woods, near Pine-Bush where some public-spirited person has put up a large swing, and they had a fine time swinging, running in the woods and covering themselves with leaves. The little ones went in the afternoon and enjoyed the ride, which to them is a ride with a wonderful sight of pleasure attached. Every thing we pass comes under their notice, and draws out expressions of admiration and pleasure. L.

Mr. Woolworth remarked last night, "I have had a new desire lately that we might be true followers of Mr. Noyes,—receptive to his spirit of faithfulness to the truth and Christ. He is looking and praying for greater manifestations of God's power and wisdom, and resurrection life. I offer myself as a medium of that spirit."

Mrs. S. B. Campbell has been nominated to the office Mrs. L. A. Thayer held, of adviser and counselor of new members. This is subject to the approval, or otherwise, of the family. It was thought that was a good office. Mr. Noyes created it and wished to have it perpetuated. [Mrs. C. was elected to the office by a unanimous vote.]

A small party was got up yesterday, in the old parlor-room for Mrs. Ellis. It was her eighty-fifth birth-day, and she was highly pleased with the treat.

The New-Jersey man has ordered 1,800 more raspberry plants for which he pays $140.

J. P. Hutchins and H. M. Worden start to-day noon for W. C.

It is a pretty cold morning, the mercury standing at twenty-four deg.

Mr. Thayer and his mother arrived home yesterday.

Traps ordered yesterday, 101 doz.

THE O. C. DAILY.

VOL. 4.   FRIDAY, NOV. 8, 1867.   NO. 112.

EVENING MEETING.

The talk headed "Is A. C. Smith the Man," was read and indorsed. Mr. Woolworth said, "I believe Mr. Noyes has got at the root of the matter now. As he says, he has dug all around Mr. Smith heretofore and tried to justify and save him. I should like to know how many felt any sympathy for him while he was here on his visit. So far as I know the Community did not have much to do with him. He spent most of his time with Mr. Pitt. I went to Mr. Smith's house and staid over night after he had left the Community. I was out peddling at the time. It was the worst hole I ever got into. I was glad to get away again, and wondered what I went there for. He was full of bitterness toward Mr. Noyes and the Community. At the same time he was scheming for his children, to get them married and settled, and was almighty pious, praying, exhorting and rolling up his eyes in the most solemn manner." Mrs. Hawley, Mr. Nash, Mrs. S. B. Campbell, Mr. Kelley, etc., joined in confessing separation from Mr. Smith. They thought his spirit dark and selfish, and were very glad he was brought to the judgment.

[We are glad we have a man among us who can detect hypocrisy and open it to the light, however deeply it may be covered with the cloak of religious sanctity. The bible doctrine, "by their fruits ye shall know them," should be brought into requisition in judging Mr. Smith.]

Mr. Woolworth.—I felt a good deal of interest in Mr. Noyes's talk about German literature, and his judgment of it. I would like to know what Mr. Perry thinks about it.

Mr. H. R. Perry.—I felt that Mr. Noyes had given a very correct judgment of German literature, so far as I know anything about it. I think his estimate of Goethe a very truthful one. I have very little sympathy, or none at all, with the generality of German ideas. I like to read German, sometimes, as I should Chinese if I knew anything about it, or any other language.

Mr. Woolworth.—Have you ever studied the effect of it upon yourself and your experience?

Mr. Perry.—I have somewhat, and think its effect was bad for a time, till I was enabled to understand Mr. Noyes and the Community, and that overcame it.

Mr. Woolworth.—Did it produce skepticism?

Mr. Perry.—Yes sir, its tendency was that way.

[Mr. Woolworth then asked D. J. Bailey what he thought about it. He replied that he sympathized with what Mr. Perry said. Formerly he was dazzled by the writings of Goethe; but about a year ago he went through a judgment that opened his eyes to their true character and put him in a position to fully indorse Mr. Noyes's judgment of German literature. He liked to study German for the mental improvement it gave, and with a view of making it useful hereafter, but had no sympathy with peculiar German ideas.]

W. P. Nov. 7.—Mrs. King, a woman who worked at Willimantic when our girls did, called here to see them on her way home from the West. She spent most of the day in looking around here and at O. C., and seemed pleased with all she saw. Her sister has written asking for a place in our shop. She has been invited to come if she thinks she shall be suited with arrangments for board, wages, etc. Mrs. King left at eight P. M., C. A. Cragin taking her to Oneida with the horse and carriage.

In our meeting some talk was had on the state of feeling in the village about us, as reported yesterday. It was thought best for Mr. Burt and C. A. Cragin to investigate the matter a little—see Mr. Williams and find out what he meant by the remark he made to C. A. C. Some thought our working Sundays had caused bad feelings in our neighbors: others that they were jealous because we were a little larger and more prosperous than they. Messrs. Williams and Wilson had been used to being looked up to as the most important members of society here, and did not like to be overshadowed by us. It is our policy to secure good feeling in them if possible.

Some of the visitors who have been here this Fall, have remarked that they never saw better hogs than those we have. It is truly wonderful, the amount of kitchen refuse they will stow away. Two of them were killed yesterday, and one of them weighed 470 lbs., the other, 630 lbs. and was eight feet three inches long. As a scavenger among beasts the hog has no equal.

SOLUTION OF THE QUESTION IN WEDNESDAY'S DAILY.—The figure 11 with 1 divided by 1 (written fractionally), added, equals 12.   J. B.

[We fail in fractional type and communicate our ideas without them the best way we can.]

CIDER-MAKING No. 2.—Eight barrels of cider and six of vinegar. Forty one bushels of the apples were bought. This finishes our cider-making for this year.

Mr. Smith has quite a passion for work in the printing-office, and spends his leisure moments in type-setting. He has had a little experience heretofore.

Traps ordered yesterday,   247¼ doz.

THE O. C. DAILY.

VOL. 4.   SATURDAY, NOV. 9, 1867.   NO. 113.

WILLOW PLACE, Nov. 8.—Mr. Noyes's judgment of Mr. Smith was very heartily endorsed by our family. Many stories were told of Mr. S.'s doings in Newark. Mr. Burt said that one of the first things Mr. S. said when he came here to live was, that if we did not look out he should get ahead of us all. Charles Cragin remarked that he always did want to lay a good many of his troubles to Mr. S. and he did not know but he could now. He feels very thankful to Mr. Noyes for his labors in behalf of the Cragin family, and feels encouraged to think he shall overcome his difficulties.

Charles C. reported the results of the talk Mr. Burt and he had with Messrs Williams and Wilson. They went first to Mr. Williams. Mr. B. introduced the matter by asking an explanation of the remark he made about our influence on the young people around us. He was quite ready to give one. He said we employed quite a number of rather wild young men from Utica, also a great many girls and boys from the village, and they got acquainted and *would* be together evenings, even if we kept them separate in the shops : this did not elevate the morals of the young. Another grievance, was our running our machinery on Sunday. It did not speak well for the neighborhood to tolerate such a thing. He mentioned Dixon's book, making the complaint that some papers have, that the whole country was in danger of being classed with us and the Mormons. His mind was clouded by misrepresentations of the whipping affair. His private grievance, was trouble in getting his logs sawed at our mill. He thought the business at the mill had been very poorly conducted this season. The school subject was introduced and he was of opinion that on the whole we ought to have the use of the room and would use his influence to have us have it.

Mr. Wilson received them very cordially. He had nothing to complain of but the Sunday work: had thought of coming to us about it. He had evidently been thinking of the school question, and was very decided in his mind that the school-room ought to be used, and that the district might furnish the fuel. He will see the other trustees and let us know soon. Mr. Fish will teach for one dollar an evening, three evenings each week.

PREMIUMS AWARDED TO THE O. C. AT THE LATE FAIR HELD AT ONEIDA.
[From the Democratic Union.]

Best Ayrshire bull, $10.00 ; best two-year-old bull, $2.00 ; best two-year-old heifer, $2.00 ; best grade two-year-old heifer, $2.00 ; second best working-cattle, Allen's best Farm Book ; sweet corn, six turnip-beets, parsnips, yellow onions, three heads cabbage, three cauliflower, three stalks celery, five golden Japan squash, best three pumpkins, best three watermelons, 25 cts. premium each. Best and largest variety of vegetables, presented in best condition, diploma and Thomas's Farm Implements. The committee feel under great obligation to the Oneida Community for their very fine display of vegetables. Best sample of roll butter, $1.00 ; best specimen of manufactured silk, 50 cts. ; best steel traps, diploma ; best table boquet, 50 cts ; best hand boquet, Culture of House and Ornamental Plants ; best show of pansies, 50 cts.

For twenty varieties of grapes shown by O. C., Fruit Trees of America. Of canned and bottled fruits the committee exclaim " no use of talking—Oneida Community can't be beat—they have too many witnesses—we give them what they deserve, the first premium ; diploma and one dollar."

A Miss Holley, an Anti-slavery lecturer, called here yesterday to solicit our subscription to the *National Anti-slavery Standard*. She pressed the thing quite immodestly, said with our principles of freedom she didn't see how we could live without that paper &c. She was told that we were striking at the root of all slavery, selfishness, and believed in living without sin. She believed in that too, and thought herself, the existence of O. C. was a miracle. She seemed to be a woman of talent and culture.

W. G. Kelly made some exposure in the meeting last night, of a spirit of forgetfulness and lack of order and organization in his habits, that produces confusion and disqualifies him to do business correctly. Mr. Woolworth thought Mr. K. had set a good example of sincerity in confessing his faults and called on C. Vanvelzer to open himself to the light. C. told some of his temptations, as did also his father and all three expressed themselves desirous to walk in the light, in connection with their experience when peddling.

I wish to acknowledge my sympathy with Mr. Noyes's article on trap-setting; and confess my desire to entirely rid myself of the spirit which would appropriate the love of others, which alone belongs to God. I know that I have in times past been subject to that spirit; and in Mrs. S.'s case have been the object of idolatrous love. I confess my entire separation from a trap-setting spirit.   D. E. S.

There was a woman staid here last night, who was in pursuit of a home. She said she would like to stay here as long as she lived, if she died in any decent season.

Traps ordered yesterday,   115 doz.

THE O. C. DAILY.

VOL. 4.   MONDAY, NOV. 11, 1867.   NO. 114.

BUSINESS MEETING.

Mr. Thacker said he had talked with Mr. Noyes and Mr. Hamilton about building a force-pit for forcing plants for the garden, and they thought it might be carried out. Mr. N. thought he should be in favor of spending a small amount in that direction. At present, our hot-beds have assumed such dimensions that they take the greater part of the manure for heating them, which we need on the land. The building would need to be about 11 by 60 feet, and would cost about $300, to be heated by coal or wood. We have material enough on hand to reduce the extra expense to about $200. As there is some brick and stone work to do, it will have to be built right away, before cold weather commences. It was voted that Mr. Thacker have the privilege of building the forcing-pit.

There has been a good deal said about having a place for skating, and such a place would be quite a luxury to the Community. Mr. Burt and others went this morning to examine a spot that had been spoken of, and found that with little trouble they could flood over an acre of land and drain it at pleasure. It would require an embankment about four rods long and six feet in hight, and also a gate in the dike, to let in the water. Messrs. Burt, Hamilton, Woolworth, Campbell and Myron H. Kinsley were appointed committee to investigate the subject and report next week.

Homer being called upon said he had no business to present, but would like to say a word in reference to the skating project. Sometime ago we made what might be called a solemn vow that we would get out of debt and have money enough on the first of January to stock our businesses, and he thought we should not allow such a leak as that would be. It would require some outlay, and he thought we should forego luxuries at such a time as this. This was sympathized with and Mr. Woolworth moved that Homer be added to the committee. Approved.

Abram Burt thought there ought to be a pair of scales at the mill. They often want to weigh articles such as nails, paint, &c. but have no way of doing it without coming up to the store. The bag-department have need of one very often. It was thought a pair of scales that would weigh from 300 to 500 pounds would be adapted to their use. Abram was given leave to get a pair.

WESTON THE PEDESTRIAN.—Yesterday forenoon we were much surprised, and not a little grieved, to learn that several of our young men, and some older ones, visited the Depot Saturday evening, to witness the arrival of the great Weston ; but most of them returned without the sight, not having had a particularly edifying time of it. Well, at the noon meeting, a report of which will be sent to the other Communes, the action of the young men in thus representing the whole Community at the show, without the knowledge or consent of the administration, was kindly but sincerely criticised. That principality of gambling and pleasure-seeking represented by Mr. Weston, was handled by some of the speakers without much mercy. The result was, truth and sincerity triumphed in the meeting. Late in the forenoon we were informed that the walking gentleman had purposed at the beginning of his big job to call at the O. C. And true enough, a request had been sent to us by the aforesaid gentleman, for permission to call upon us at two P. M. Of course permission was given ; and in about an hour after we had given the small lion of the day a pretty thorough criticism, Mr. Edward Payson Weston, staff and attendants arrived, followed by quite a crowd of assorted outsiders. Messrs. Burt and Woolworth were appointed a committee of reception. The curiosity to see the owner of such a wonderful pair of walking beams was very great indeed. As Mr. W. was escorted into the Hall the multitude followed. Edward Inslee and others entertained them with music for awhile, which all seemed to enjoy wonderfully.

On the whole it was quite an episode in our daily life and not a little dramatic withal. Mr. C. who was the most severe the hour before in the work of criticising the whole fraternity to which Weston belongs, was seated beside the pedestrian, holding free conversation with him during the musical performance.

Weston is a citizen of Boston, gentlemanly in manners, very slim in person, delicate in appearance, and has no surplus flesh. Expressing as he did a wish to go on the stage for the purpose of being introduced to those who might crave the honor, and offering to shake hands with all who wished it, indicated a streak of vanity in his composition. On ascending the stage he bowed gracefully to the audience and remarked, that he did not feel like making a speech until he had accomplished the work he proposed to achieve, and if he failed in that, he should not care to talk much. On the whole the affair passed off very pleasantly. In the forenoon Mr. W. attended the Baptist church at the Depot, the pastor of which, we are informed, is the enviable author of the articles on the O. C. in the *Democratic Union*. So it may be published to the world that the two institutions which were favored with the presence of the distinguished pedestrian, are the Baptist church and the Oneida Community.

SERVANT.

Our two or three days of cold weather passed away, and we are having a warm Indian summer. Visitors continue to give us calls more or less daily.

H. W. Burnham passed Sunday with us.

Traps ordered Saturday and Sunday, 251 doz.

THE O. C. DAILY.

VOL. 4.   TUESDAY, NOV. 12, 1867.   NO. 115.

Michigan, Nov. 1867.

COMMUNITY FRIENDS:—I purpose writing you a few lines by way of remembrance. It is nearly five months since I visited you. In the mean time I have had the pleasure of hearing from you once a week, while you have not heard from me only once. Now the thought arises, how are you going to form an acquaintance with me, which seems to be the only desideratum at present. It seems to me, that to acquire the object sought, there should be reciprocal action between us. Now take it for granted that this is the right construction of the case, the question arises, how are you going to know me only through the medium of correspondence, and then how will you know whether I am sincere? " By their fruits ye shall know them." Now my prayer and desire is to convince you that I *am sincere*, and I have no other way but by simply telling you of it, and you have no other voucher but my word. Now what shall I do? I feel that I ought to devote my time and talents to the cause. My *proclivious propensity* is manual labor—how I would like to work in that capacity. * * You may rely on me henceforth, as one who is ready to do his duty. God has began a great work on earth and I would like to help him. I will stand and .../ picket duty until I am released, be it by death or by a general order. More anon.   AUSTIN KENT.

W. P., Nov. 11.—The evening school commences to-night. Mr. Fish consents to try teaching four evenings instead of three.—Lorenzo invited criticism this evening, which was kindly but thoroughly administered. He was very well liked for some time after coming here, but of late he has not given very good satisfaction. He was criticised for a lack of simplicity and respect; for being forgetful. His alimentiveness was thought to be quite out of order; he eats inordinately. He was advised to ask Mr. Ackley's pardon for talking disrespectfully to, and about him, and set it for his purpose to satisfy Mr. A.—Mr. Noyes's talk about the way people judge him was read, and many expressed their sympathy with the truth as there presented, and their gratitude for all that he has done for us. We thank God for Mr. Noyes.

Last Saturday evening, H. W. B. reported his call on the Troy and Schenectady Editors, who had published Mr. Freeman's articles, and was cordially received by them. The Editor of the *Troy Whig* said he would gladly publish John Freeman's articles, or a portion of them, as he would like to give expression to both sides. He was aware that Mr. Freeman was very bitter against the Community. The Schenectady Editor was too busily engaged writing to talk much, but would give the subject his attention, and would perhaps publish a part of John's articles. The Troy Editor wished to exchange with the CIRCULAR. H. W. B. intends to call on the Editor of the *Albany Evening Journal* on his return.

Last evening Mr. Woolworth reported that Gen. Wilson of the U. S. A. made us a call during the day. He is commissioned to buy preserved fruits and vegetables for the army on the Plains. Having made large purchases in Baltimore he was on his way to Portland to procure preserved corn and lobsters, and called here to learn what we were doing in this line and what we expected to do next year. Gen. Wilson has been in the army fourteen years, and is supposed to have taken active part in suppressing the rebellion. He spoke of the peace with the Indians of the Plains as a "humbug," and said he was positive they would renew their attack whenever circumstances favored. They were willing to suspend hostilities now because winter was coming on; but nothing short of their extermination would give lasting security. Meantime the Indian agents are circulating flattering reports of peace, in the hope of securing supplies that they can sell and speculate with. Isn't this a hopeful commentary on the integrity of governmental officials?

A PIG! A PIG!—Quite an excitement was created among the girls last night, by Mr. Hawley telling them that he was going down to the Depot in the night after some one who was expected on the cars—that he had received a letter (a telegram the girls stated,) but as Mr. H. willfully refused to inform them who it was, their curiosity was excited to the highest pitch. Many were the offers to sit up and get refreshments for the new comer, which Mr. H. told them was not necessary. This morning the whispers went round " who is it? who has come? and no little mortification was felt, and displeasure at Mr. Hawley, when it was known that the new comer was only a *pig*.

WESTON ONCE MORE.—The very latest news we have heard about the pedestrian, Weston, is that his mother lives in the Oneida Community, and his call upon us Sunday was simply to see his mamma. The report will surprise no one however when it is understood that it came from a prolific little village about four miles north of us somewhat given of late to the production of *fulmen brutum*. [It was a mistake that Mr. W. *offered* to go on the stage, as he went on by request.]

Traps ordered yesterday,   6 doz.

THE O. C. DAILY.

VOL. 4. WEDNESDAY, NOV. 13, 1867. NO. 116.

Boston, Nov. 11, 1867.

ONE IDEA COMMUNITY:—Enclosed is a check for one hundred and six dollars. Your invoice says $106.09 but 2 errors sent the 9 cts. to pot. I have to buy these fruits for my neighbors, who believe what I tell 'em when I say your folks are neat as wax. Heaven forgive me for the awful responsibility I assume in so saying. We can buy tomatoes here for $2.75 called better than yours, but me see the Irish gals going to and fro, and our stomachs revolt at the *idee*. For my commissions and trouble in your behalf, send me the CIRCULAR one year. At the end of the year I'll remind you of the fact unless Miles Grant's *eend* comes to pitch us all into KAIOSS.

Yours in the usual smudge of materialism,

Jm. BECKETT.

Hadley, Nov. 10, 1867.

MR. S. NEWHOUSE, SIR :—I have just been reading your book the *Trapper's Guide*, and have been very much pleased and entertained with it. I would like to ask you a few questions if it would not trouble you too much to answer them. I am a farmer's boy, 21 years old, strong and healthy. I have often thought I would like to go on a trapping expedition, but never knew much about the business until I read your book. I have trapped some for muskrats, using your traps which are the best I ever used. I have known them to hold by one claw.—I would like to go on a trapping expedition with an experienced trapper ; could you direct me to a suitable person with whom I could make some arrangements ? I suppose it is too late to go this fall, but I thought there would be no harm in writing and see what I could do. W. C. DICKINSON.

W. P., Nov. 12.—Several days ago complaint was made to us by the parents of a young man who works in the shop, that he, their son, was suspected of having taken money from his brother and sister. Myron went down to see his parents about it, they having desired him to use his influence to make the young man confess it, and while talking with them, the son came in. He stoutly denied the charge for a time, but at last confessed all with many tears.—Yesterday Myron was called aside by four men who work in the Trap-shop, and board at Mr. Christian's, who complained that money to the amount of twenty-eight dollars had been taken from their rooms, and from the rooms of some of the silk-girls who boarded there. They suspected a sister of Mrs. Christian, who has worked there. Myron consulted Messrs. Woolworth and Cragin, and by their advice reported the complaint to Mr. C. He immediately set about finding the thief. The person suspected was found to have spent more money at our store than she could have earned. She stoutly denied all charges, but left home soon after being questioned. She is keeping company with the young man mentioned above, and accounted for the money she had spent, by saying he gave it to her : this he denied. Mr. C. having got all the facts he could, hunted up the girl, and made her confess to all but thirteen dollars, which she still denies having taken. This girl was discharged from the silk-shop for dishonesty. They wish to keep the matter as still as possible, so request our people not to mention it outside our own circle.

DEAR MR. WOOLWORTH :—My late experience has given me a new appreciation of the work of salvation. I see it is one thing to be saved from sin, but quite another to be saved from our old life, which is outward and superficial, liable at any time to be thown off the track. This experience has cost me from time to time much suffering, mortification and condemnation, and has driven me to God with renewed earnestness to be saved from it. After all, I find myself up to this time in an unconverted state, and feel the need of help and strength to rescue me from such a diabolical influence. I see very clearly that I have inherited this superficial part of my character from my father, who although strict in the observance of the ordinances of religion, was a very superficial insincere man ; thought more of pleasing man than God ; while my mother was a very conscientious God-fearing woman, and secured the love and respect of her children. I felt this morning like bringing out my experience into the light ; I want the truth and nothing else. I have allowed myself to drift along in this way long enough ; my heart is stirred up in earnest, to find out the cause and cure. Yours for a true spirit of repentance,

M. D. POMEROY.

A Miss Williams whose home is in Hartford, Conn., and who has been passing some time in the western part of this state, came here yesterday. She called here last summer on her way West and wanted we should give her employment ; and now on her return she is anxious to work for us, that she may inform herself, she says, of our faith, and become acquainted with us with a view of joining. She seems to be a woman of considerable refinement and cultivation.

Tryphena and child and H. C. Woolworth arrived safely in the night.

Traps ordered yesterday, 151¼ doz.

THE O. C. DAILY.

VOL. 4.   THURSDAY, NOV. 14, 1867.   NO. 117.

Albany, Nov. 12, 1867.

ONEIDA COMMUNITY, GENTLEMEN :—Your favor of the 8th. inst. with $3.00 to pay for a bbl. of facing sent last March (and for which you say the amount was sent by mail in May and never received by us), is received. We return four shillings, keeping only cost of facing. Had you only sent twelve shillings we should not have found fault. We appreciate your magnanimity, and more so as we last week got muddled up with outside barbarians and have had to make a change of base. We went in for about $3,000 which places us in a tight place, and dollars look big to us just now. I have read much on community systems : they have had my sympathies and best wishes over twenty years. Whenever you come this way, if convenient, call and make my house your home.

Please accept our thanks.   L. A. Orcutt & Co.

The Register, in which for about five and a half years persons visiting us have recorded their names, is filled to its utmost capacity. Visitors from Cal., Col., Texas, Minn., Wis., and nearly every one of the United States, have left their autographs, besides others residing in England, Scotland, Ireland, France, Italy and Greece of the old world. Among the most noted are W. Hepworth Dixon, William Heywood, Dr. Speigle friend of Humbolt, Judge Mason of Hamilton, Miss Susan B. Anthony, B. G. Noble Lieut. Gov. Wis., Dr. Dwight of Columbia College, Mr. Foucou who came from France to inspect the mines of this country, carrying with him on his return, photographs of the Community which he presented to the French Socialists, Henry Edgar, also a Frenchman and philosopher of the Positive School, one of the number chosen by Compte to present his system when the world is prepared, at present a resident of Long Island, with Prof. Appy formerly of the Italian Opera, N. Y., Juvenelia Tinker, Miss Hewlet, John W. Hutchinson, Miss Kate Foster of Utica, and other musical characters; Newspaper Reporters, Professors and Students from different colleges, Authors, Speakers, and last of all the pedestrian Edward Payson Weston.—Recorded, are the names of nearly 16,000 persons, probably about one third of those who have visited here during that period, including in the unrecorded names, Lord and Lady Amberly and Ex. Gov. Seymour.

Mrs Reeve writes that snow fell at Berlin, Oct. 30th over seven inches on a level, and that many fruit trees were broken down they were so loaded. She says, " Notwithstanding all the clouds, the cold, and the storm without, there is a bright spot within ; the sun of righteousness shines and a fire is kindled on the altar that cannot be quenched. How our hearts go out in thankfulness to God, that he has given us a taste of his life, so that we are no longer dependent on our outward circumstances or surroundings for happiness.

The reading of Mr. Wright's letter called forth a burst of indignation from the family. We can scarcely find language to express our abhorrence of such a cool, deliberate, and satanic spirit as was manifest in that letter. His hypocritical course while with us was scarcely equaled, even by Mills. We sincerely hope that every remaining vestige of his spirit will be forever wiped out from our midst.

Miss Nun had a fall down stairs last night, over to the Boarding-house, which has bruised her considerably. It was dark and as she went in she took an open door, which was the wrong one, and fell to the bottom of the cellar stairs. She is rather sore but no bones broken.

Mr. Whitney who is appointed to take care of the fires in the furnaces the coming winter, employs his spare moments in riveting jaws and posts for the Trap-shop. He is quite a help in this way, and does the work in his own room in the old tool-house.

We had another communication from J. Leonard, last night on reform in the kitchen, with some suggestions of improvment there in various quarters, which we thought good. It speaks well for John that his mind is active in this direction.

The farmers are fortifying the banks of the Creek on the Hamilton meadow, by throwing in stone and brush to prevent the water from wearing it.

Last night was very clear and the moon shone brightly—if the "stars of heaven fell," as was expected, we failed to see them.

The weather is growing colder and there are indications of snow. We are pretty well prepared for winter.

Mulching strawberry vines is going on these days. There are between four and five acres to be covered.

Our people have engaged Miss Williams to work in the Bag-shop, and she is to board at Mr. Porters.

We were credibly informed this morning, that the Trap-shop hands were up with their orders.

We had a bee this morning for opening clams. We shall test their qualities at dinner.

Our apples (200 barrels) are all safely housed.

Traps ordered yesterday,   5 doz.

THE O. C. DAILY.

VOL. 4.   FRIDAY, NOV. 15, 1867.   NO. 118.

Dangstein, Petersfield, Oct. 31, 1867.

Lady Dorothy Nevill is greatly obliged for the letter, etc. from the Community. She would like to order some of their articles, but as she cannot *resell* them, she only wants some exclusively for herself. Not knowing what the rules are in this respect, and not knowing any Banker in New-York, she could not pay beforehand and she is afraid the Community require cash payment. If they would trust her, she would faithfully pay the *amount the moment* the articles arrive. Messrs. Trubner, with whom she has dealings, says he would pay anything for her to the Community, or she would pay through her Bankers, Messrs. Drummond of Charing Cross. She is well known to Wm. H. Dixon. If the Community would allow her to pay when the articles arrive, she would like to have one dozen rat-traps without chains, one Lunch-bag 11½ inches, with all necessaries ; and a box of a dozen bottles, or quarts of any vegetables or jams or jellies, they could spare her. She would like to have them, if possible, of different sorts, as she merely wants them out of curiosity. She would like them sent by the cheapest route, directed to her, 29 Upper Grosvenor Street, Hyde Park, London, that being her town residence. She would like the CIRCULAR to be sent as usual here. Should the Community not be able to agree to her terms, or not be able to send her such small quantities, she will not put them to the trouble and expense of answering her. She will conclude from their silence they can do nothing in the matter.

[Our people will forward the articles required to Lady Nevill as soon as they can be collected and packed.]

W. P., Nov. 12.—Last evening a small Teuton was discharged from the shop, for disobedience and disrespect. This morning he came back bright and early on foot, accompanied by his mother, who could scarcely speak a word of English, but who was very earnest in her pleadings to have him taken back. The boy had to act as interpreter. She said his father had given him a good whipping, and she thought he would do better, but if he does not " you do *so* ! *so* !" at the same time enacting a vigorous pantomime of a whipping. Myron signified to her that we should not do *that* ! The boy will be tried once more.—Milford and Earnest devote two hours each day to practice in drawing and engraving, with G. N. M. for tutor.

The talk on spiritualism was read this evening and drew out interesting remarks on the subject. We had quite a free meeting, and much appreciation was expressed of the home spirit. Now when there is so much venom displayed in the Oneida papers, and which is chiefly aimed at Mr. Noyes, we need to draw together and strengthen him.

PRACTICAL PROBLEMS. NO. 1.

We have some trouble with our jaws. Trap-jaws, we mean. They break. We shall send the broken ones back to the foundry. Possibly some of the bad ones have got into our traps which have been sent away. And should they break, and the game escape, what would the trapper say ? We dare not imagine. Is it unfaithfulness at the malleable iron works ? Unspoken thoughts are as busy as bees about having our own malleable iron works by next spring. Can it be done ? Does our debt say no ? Well, we must pray about it. Our Trap-works will be incomplete without that addition. But where or how shall we board and lodge the men and boys required to run the works? Must we depend on Oneida and run a line of coaches to carry operatives back and forth, subject to many contingencies ? No, that is too expensive—It is unnatural. Our silk-works too, are straitened in the same way. So, here we are again, confronting the Boarding-house problem, but hopefully this time. There is light ahead.

When we entered the printing-office a few mornings since, we beheld our press all taken to pieces and lying in scattered fragments on the floor. It was undergoing the necessary process of cleaning. How could it ever be put together again ? But it was in the hands of a skillful machinist, who after scraping and rubbing the pieces and removing all the dirt that had been accumulating for years, quietly readjusted its parts, and presented it to the office hands greatly improved. Is not this the way, thought we, that God deals with the human machine ? He takes it all to pieces and for a time it seems totally worthless : but every part is carefully preserved, which after being rubbed and scoured thoroughly, by criticism and judgment, the work of reconstruction commences. Every piece is carefully gathered up by the great Machinist, and put in its true place, and a new structure created out of the old one, fitted to be cogged on to the great machinery in the Heavens.

The stone work of the forcing-pit is completed, and the masons have commenced laying the brick. The building is twelve feet four inches wide, by sixty-eight feet long, including the fire pit. The walls will be three feet high above ground. The building is situated south of the horse-barn.

C. A. Macknet leaves for New-York to-day.

Traps ordered yesterday,   149 doz.

THE O. C. DAILY.

VOL. 4. SATURDAY, NOV. 16, 1867. NO. 119.

A PEEP BEHIND THE CURTAIN.—A young lady from Pratts Hollow, came here yesterday for the purpose of joining. Her mother and a white-haired old man accompanied her. These two ladies had managed, through the agency of one of the merchants of Munnsville, to engage this old gentleman, a resident of that village, whom they had never before seen, to meet them at the house of a relative in that vicinity, and to bring them in his carriage from there to the Community. The young lady asked for Mr. Noyes when she came in, and on learning that he was not here, she inquired for the head of the family, with whom, she said, she desired a private interview. Mr. Woolworth was duly presented and the ladies were invited into his room, where they told their story, from which it appeared, that the daughter was the wife of a man of more than twice her years, a violent, reckless, drinking fellow, well known to the writer, who abused her badly and persistently, and had even threatened to hang her. She had borne with his tyranny and neglect to the last degree of endurance, and had finally concluded to leave him and seek an asylum in the Community.

She had called here several times, and she thought she might be contented and happy with our people. Mr. Woolworth inquired if she had any children? She replied that she had none. He then asked her if she expected any, whereupon she turned with a half smile to her mother, who helped her out by saying, that she didn't expect any, and she didn't want any, and she didn't mean to have any.—She was quite a good looking woman, only twenty years of age, and very much the superior, one would think, of the person she wedded. "How came you to marry such a man," inquired Mr. Woolworth. No reply. "Did you love him?" "No, she didn't think she ever did." The mother said, had she been at home at the time, the marriage would never have taken place. The whole party took dinner with us, and then there was some consultation, after which we gave them our decision.

The young lady is not a religious woman, and she knows nothing of our faith, or of the Community, further than she has gained by hearsay, and accordingly, she was told that the most we could do for her at present would be to employ her, and we did not think best even to do that, unless she could get a written release from her husband, or his permission to enter our service. There were enemies on all sides of us, lying in wait and watching for opportunities to make mischief, and we found it necessary to be circumspect and prudent. They were very much disappointed with the result, and inclined to be a little ungracious before they left. They didn't think there would be any trouble, and evidently had no fears that the Community was about to be broken up. U.

Amherst, N. H., Nov. 12, 1867.

J. H. NOYES ESQ., DEAR SIR:—For two years past I have been a constant and interested reader of the CIRCULAR which has been sent to me, gratuitously, by the generous Community. The doctrine therein promulgated is producing a deep impression upon my mind, and is gradually changing my religious views from Orthodoxy to Perfectionism. My mother is a member of the Baptists. A few years since I came near joining the same, but did not. Since then my mind religiously, has been unsettled. Will give you a little of my history, then you can understand my case better. Am twenty-three years old—unmarried—tall and slender, six feet—weight 145—temperament nervous sanguine—have tendency to lung disease.

[He goes on to say that his father died of consumption when he was nine years old, leaving his mother and three children almost penniless. He worked on the farm till he was eighteen ; afterwards in a printing-office, then engaged in peddling, and acted as traveling agent for his health. He says in conclusion :]

Mr. Noyes, cannot the Community furnish me a situation to travel with their silk, and pay me a fair salary sufficient to support myself and family ? As I am now situated, my mother and sister to look after, I don't think it would be right for me to join the Community even were I prepared to do so, which I know I am not. The future looks dark and gloomy to me, but I trust that God will bring me out of these melancholy feelings and cause me to rejoice ; perhaps I am too selfish. I do hope that soon I may be settled in that religious belief which will make me happy here and hereafter.—My object in securing a traveling situation with you, is to prepare myself to be *fit* to be one of your band at some future day—can furnish testimonials as to character—use neither tobacco or intoxicating liquor.—I trust you will *find* the time to reply and give me such counsel as you think I need ; whether you desire my services or not, but if possible I should be happy to be where I could feel the spirit of the Community, and feel that I was doing God's will. Respectfully yours, HENRY C. DODGE.

The Community sent yesterday, a present to Miss Clara Wait, consisting of an Alpaca dress-pattern with belt-ribbon and trimmings, and a ladies leather satchel. The O. C. have thought of making her this present ever since she was here, but have for some cause postponed it till now. Mr. Van Velzer met her when he was out on his last peddling trip, at a store, two miles from her home, and at her urgent request called on her the next day, Sunday, and staid over night. He was pleased with her state and her sincerity, thought she had grown strong spiritually and physically since she was here. We liked her letter received a few days since very much.

G. N. Miller leaves for W. C. to day and C. A. Burt for New-York.

THE O. C. DAILY.

VOL. 4.   MONDAY, NOV. 18, 1867.   NO. 120.

BUSINESS MEETING.

Several of our hired men in the Bag-shop have asked the privilege of making a skating-park on the flat where we have talked of having one. They were willing to do the work, and if they could have a team to do some necessary plowing, they would bear what further expense it might require. Messrs. Thacker and Newhouse were chosen to ascertain if there are any objections to granting their request.

Mr. Horace Burt said he had been disturbed lately by the disorderly conduct of our hired men in that part of the shop in which he works. They talk a great deal about things that do not concern their business, and in doing so have to raise their voices to the highest pitch, and neglect their work. At times they break out with the most hideous noises, howling and mewing, and often throw things back and forth across the shop. Yesterday, they threw several times at him, hitting him once. He desired to have the support of the Community and Trap-shop committee in preserving order there. Mr. Burt's remarks were sympathized with. We are behind other establishments in that respect. They make strict rules that there shall be no unnecessary talk while at their work. The subject was finally referred to the Trap-shop committee.

Four or five of the silk-girls will board at our Boarding-house this winter, and will want to be carried to and from their work morning and night. The committee to whom the matter was referred met and concluded that Mr. Wescott's man will drive up and get the girls in the morning, and at night Mr. Miller will leave W. P. at a quarter of five, with those who wish to quit at that time, and return in time to bring the girls at six.

There are several brothers (colored men) working for us who would like to have some accommodations nearer their work than they now have. They propose fitting up the old paint-shop near the sawmill. They are found to be good reliable workmen, minding their own business, and respectful to others. As we find it difficult to procure good help, it is very desirable that they should be accommodated. Messrs. Kinsley, Campbell, F. Marks and J. H. Barron committee to investigate the matter.

PRACTICAL PROBLEMS. NO. 2.

Communism is a *doer*. It seizes questions in a practical way, and by so doing discovers the possibilities and impossibilities of many things. For instance, Communism has demonstrated that an unselfish individual or society can do things which it would be impossible for a selfish individual or a selfish society to do. The boarding-house question, or the question of securing help contiguous to our shops and factories, is one pregnant with difficulties if viewed from a worldly stand-point. But Communism has taken off its coat, so to speak, and grappled with it; and after a trial of two months it feels entirely confident of ultimate success in making Community boarding-houses attractive houses to all well disposed persons, without being demoralized by the business. In order to secure that end, however, those who undertake the management of such establishments must represent fully the Community spirit.

Serving tables is a business of unparalleled magnitude, and the mischief of it is, that the devil is *steward* of this great kitchen of the world, while Jesus Christ, who actually owns the human race, and who should have the entire management of its dietetics, is only allowed occasionally to serve tables on church communion seasons, where a few crumbs of bread and a little weak wine is served out to the guests. Now I protest against such treatment of Christ. Go to one of these monthly celebrations of the sacrament and witness the ceremony—see their long disfigured faces, calling up unpleasant memories of their past sins, and cherishing no hope or expectation of doing any better in the future. Is there any resemblance between so sad a looking company, and the multitude on the day of Pentecost, where all souls were full to overflowing with joy, eating their meat with gladness and singleness of heart? The world can be civilized **in its alimentiveness only by casting the devil out of** the pantry and kitchen, and by inviting Christ in, as head steward. The truth is, there is life and death in the ordinance of eating and drinking. There is great significancy too, in the exhortation of the apostles when deacons were to be chosen, whose office was to serve tables, that they should be men of honest report, full of wisdom and the Holy Ghost, men who were not afraid to say with Paul, " ye cannot be partakers of the Lord's table and of the table of devils." These are the men we want now to take charge of Boarding-houses, Hotels and eating saloons. The martyr Stephen must be invited back to render assistance in this labor of serving tables. He is alive yet, and 1800 years have only increased his ability to do heaven's work in this world.

The criticism of C. S. J., L. F. D. and others was read in meeting last night and heartily endorsed by the family. We sympathize with Mr. Noyes in his efforts to drive the slave holding spirit from our midst.

At seven o'clock this morning the mercury stood at twelve deg. above zero. The ground is slightly covered with snow.

A committee has been appointed to organize classes in study for the winter.

Traps ordered Saturday and Sunday,   254¼ doz.

THE O. C. DAILY.

VOL. 4. TUESDAY, NOV. 19, 1867. NO. 121.

W. P., Nov. 18.—Our pond is fairly frozen over, but the ice is not yet strong enough for skating. We have to thank our Mother O. C. for a sewing-machine. It is not a new one to be sure, but it is new to us, which with children, often answers just as well. It is certainly a very useful addition to our home comfort.

A meeting of our employees was called to-day, and some criticism of their rowdyism out of the shop as well as in was given. Mr. Adkins and Mr. Wescott indorsed the criticism.—In a meeting of our business men this morning Alfred received some criticism. This evening he said he thanked the committee for their sincerity to him. He felt at first like persisting in his assertion that he was not competent to be foreman in the shop, but he soon came to himself and felt that though he might not of himself be fitted for the place, he knew that with the help of Christ and the family, he could do well in it. He desired the help of his superiors and wished to be receptive to their spirit and advice.

———————

C. B. H.—Since Miss Nun had the misfortune the other evening to enter the wrong door, only to find herself among cabbages and potatoes at the bottom of the cellar, instead of among the members of our family, we thought it advisable to publish a card, giving specific directions for finding the Community sitting-room, reception-room, parlor and Mrs. Thayer's bed-room, all of which, constitute one room fourteen feet square. Directions—Enter the north front door of the two story white house (we have a brown house with a north front door), and, if the object of your visit is to see the men boarders, turn to your right, which will land you in their sitting-room (now under repair), but if you wish to see the Community family by finding your way to their sitting-room, turn to the left. Should you, however, desire to repeat Miss Nun's exploit of leaping into the cellar, go *straight ahead*, and if you are under full speed, you may possibly land at the bottom without touching a single step of the stairs, as she did. We beg to say, however, that we do not advise trying the experiment as the invisibles might fail to be *present* to take charge of *you* as they, or some other unseen power, did of our *worthy* sister, whose call, if not her fall, was one of business rather than of pleasure. Perhaps that accounts for the miracle in her escape from more serious injury.

———————

What we seem to need, is some business that we can carry on in connection with our trap-business, to which we can shift our help when our trap-trade slackens up. A year ago we had sixty hired hands to work for us on traps, and before the winter was over we had to discharge all but about eighteen or twenty men. Last fall we once had ninety hands, and we have over sixty now, and nearly all of them are good, steady, faithful hands, and they are anxious to work for us, and probably would work for less wages, if they could have work all winter. In selecting this help we have probably tried two or three hundred hands, first and last, and instructed them more or less in the business, at a great loss, and then they proved to be such help as we did not want. Now unless we have some business besides the trap-business, we shall probably have to discharge the most of our help, and then when the trap-trade starts up again go through this sifting process again.—The malleable iron business has been mentioned; the objection to that is, unless we have a large capital that we want to tie up in our business, we shall have thirty or forty more hands to discharge when the trap-trade slackens.

The bag-frame business helped us to keep our help employed last year, some, but the objection to that is, we do not have enough of any one kind to make it pay.—Let us all watch and pray and see if the Lord has not something more for us to do. J. C. H.

———————

A young man of the name of Baerman, a graduate of the Van Rensselaer Institute, Troy, and one of the engineers of the Midland Railroad, called here Saturday, and spent several hours. He thinks the road will be completed between Oneida and Oswego within a year. It will cross the Central, at a point a quarter of a mile west of the Oneida Station. As there is a great scarcity of good building stone, near the route surveyed, the gift of our quarry, in his estimation, was really a magnificent donation. He is acquainted with the leading projectors and managers of the enterprise, and he said that he should use what little influence he could bring to bear, in favor of locating the road as near to our domain as practicable. He expressed himself as being well pleased with his visit. U.

———————

Amsterdam, Oct. 22, 1867.

THE DIRECTORS OF THE ONEIDA COMMUNITY,—GENTLEMEN :—The present is serving to pray you to send us the price-current of your conserved meats.

Soliciting the favor of an early answer, we remain Gentlemen, yours truly, C. HUIZER & Co.

———————

Mr. Nash rode over to W. P. yesterday and staid half an hour. He wants to go to work and thinks he might do something about the traps in his room with his right hand. He asked the other day if he could not have a trundle-bed put under his bed and have two children sleep there, that he might take care of them.

———————

ERRATUM.—On the third page of yesterday's Daily, sixth line from the top, for attractive *houses*, read attractive *homes*.

THE O. C. DAILY.

VOL. 4. WEDNESDAY, NOV. 20, 1867. NO. 122.

THE INVISIBLE O. C.

In looking at the O. C. from a worldly stand-point as in looking at trees, men can see only half of her—the external and least essential half. The Community has an interior domain with facilities for the cultivation of crops much more extensive and valuable than her physical possessions, as seen by an unbelieving world with the natural eye. And one of the most valuable commodities of her invisible industry is, *unfeigned faith*, the cultivation of which, is the business of all, old and young, men and women, the robust and healthy, as well as the feeble and unhealthy. No one can be exempted, or have the disposition to be, from this interior work. Moreover, the winter is the harvest season for all the staple crops of the *unseen* Commune, such as faith, love, meekness, gentleness, goodness, patience, and whatever grace can comfort, strengthen, and beautify the inner man. But faith—that living faith of Christ, the gift of God to us, that works in our souls by love, purifying our hearts, and overcoming the world in us, is the great life-crop, or spiritual wheat-crop, with which our inner man is renewed day by day. Indeed, this practical faith in God, in Jesus Christ, in the Primitive Church and in the Bible, is as truly an actual substance, a necessity of life, and as essential to the continued existence of the visible O. C., as physical food is to the animal man. Without faith in God, man is not a man in the sight of heaven, or at best only half a man and that the poorest and of little worth to God. To build up the O. C. financially, to increase her trade and industries, and to make her a power in the business world—such a power as will please heaven—we have only to look after the interests of the interior O. C. and see that good health, unity and industry is going on there, and the outward Community, the only one the world can see, will take care of itself, or we should say, will be taken care of by Him to whom all power was given both in heaven and on earth. o.

We make a few extracts from a letter received from Mrs. Blood of Nov. 17th. She writes as follows:

"I have had some *very cloudy weather* since I heard from you last. Indeed there has been many days when there did not seem to be one ray of sunshine. But I thank God the clouds are drifting, and light and peace have once more come to cheer and strengthen me. I sometimes wonder if you realize how much help I get from O. C. I wish I could help you as much as I am helped by you. I thank God daily that he led me to the Community. I am trying to teach my girls to work, so they will be able to help more when they come back; for you see we have not given up the idea but what we shall come back; that is one of the bright things we look forward to. I have not seen Mr. Blood but once since Aug'st. He came here about four weeks ago and staid three days. He was very pleasant but we did not have any special conversation until the night before he went away. I had gone up stairs to bed with Mary when he sent Ida up to ask me if I would not come down and talk with him. He wanted me to promise him not to say any thing about the Community; that if any one asked me about it not to testify in favor of it. *I did not promise* I could not. I think it was very hard for him (feeling as he does about the O. C.), to come home and have all his children even *Mary* tell him they wanted to go back, and she told him she should go if she had to wait till she was of age. I think he wished he had left us there. He went away the next day the saddest looking man I ever saw.—We have a family in the house with us; the woman is a few months over seventeen and is living with her third husband and the other two are living. She was married to the first one when she was but eleven years old; it was her mother's work and was to get money."

Rain has been withheld from this section for many weeks, except in limited quantities, just enough to wet the surface of the earth, and the consequence is that there is a great dearth of water in the land. The streams are very low, springs are failing, and wells that were never known to be dry, refuse to yield their accustomed supplies. The inhabitants of Pine Bush resort to the Creek for water, and one of our neighbors who lives half a mile away, comes to our barn to water his horses. Our neighbor Parsons too has to come down from his *high estate* to the valley for water, we are told. The O. C. has as yet suffered no lack; thanks to a good providence that gave us a new iron aqueduct last summer, without which we should doubtless be in the same straits as our neighbors. As winter seems now to be setting in it is feared this dearth will be protracted.   H.

Mr. C. Roby, an agent of the great steel manufacturing firm of Hussey, Wells & Co., Pittsburg, Penn. called here yesterday. He was accompanied by a Mr. Taylor of Portland Me.—Mr. Roby was well acquainted with Adin Ballou and he also knew the history from the beginning of the Hopedale experiment. This association failed on account of a lack of unity and agreement among its members. It was a joint-stock concern, and it resulted, as a matter of course, that the I spirit prevailed. Since the death of his only son, a very promising young man, Mr. Ballou had changed very much. He had apparently lost all heart and enthusiasm for the cause of Socialism, and seemed to be settling into a slow decline.   U.

We are having a driving snow-storm from the south-east. There is a nice foundation for sleighing, as the roads have not been cut up in consequence of heavy rains.

Traps ordered yesterday,   845 doz.

THE O. C. DAILY.

VOL. 4.   THURSDAY, NOV. 21, 1867.   NO. 123.

Mr. Underwood reported in meeting last night that a man by the name of Smith visited us Monday, and staid over night. He came from New York expressly to see us, but remained at the Depot from Saturday night till Monday. He had considerable talk with leading men at Oneida ; and Mr. Underwood took pains to draw him out, in order to learn how the good citizens of that place represent the Community to strangers. Mr. Smith talked with Lawyer Snow, Mr. Messenger and Mr. Allen, the keeper of the National Hotel, where he stopped. Snow said we were very fine people, and recommended him to us. Messenger said there was some envy of our prosperity on the part of some in the village, but that we were very fine people, and, if he called on us, would treat him with the greatest kindness and courtesy. Mr. Allen took him to his private parlor, and among other things, in a long talk about the Community, observed, that if he was a young man without ties or outside obligations he would not ask for a better home than the Community ; and in that case he should join if he could get in.—Mr. Smith is a native of Ireland and has been in this country eight years. He was steward in the Government Hospital for the Insane, at Washington, for a year or two ; and on resigning was appointed supervisor of the Maryland Insane Hospital. He had warm testimonials from both institutions. He became much interested in us; read considerable from the Berean, etc., while here; and finally wanted to give us what property he had which consisted wholly of cash. Mr. Underwood told him we could hardly take such a donation ; but recommended him to call on Mr. Hamilton at the Agency and thus renew and improve his acquaintance with us.

Mr. Underwood thought this gentleman very sincere and candid. Being heir presumptive of the large estate of a rich uncle in the north of Ireland—which becoming known in the cities where he had resided since coming to this country, he had been subjected to the maneuvering of managing mothers on behalf of unmarried daughters. This had completely disgusted him with the marriage institution of the world, and he said he should never marry.

To THE O. C. DAILY.—I have a new appreciation of the value of the confession of Christ, as a means of grace and salvation. Nineteen years ago with fear and trembling, I confessed Christ in me a savior from sin. I now have to acknowledge with unspeakable thankfulness that through much weakness, foolishness, and temptation on my part, he has been faithful to his promise, " Whoso confesseth me before men, him will I also confess before my father in heaven." With gratitude for past mercies, I renew my confession of him as an everlasting savior of soul and body, not doubting his promise that he would do us as "exceeding abundantly above all that we can ask or think" and gladly surrender to him heart and life and all that is dear, to be used in his service anywhere and in any capacity, trusting his grace to make me faithful and obedient. With the same gratitude I have to acknowledge my everlasting indebtedness to Mr. Noyes for the knowledge of the truth that brought me to my first confession, and for the strength and support of his spirit in maintaining it. Without it, I do not see how it could have been done. That I may have grace to make a proper return of loyalty and service is my earnest prayer.   GEO. CAMPBELL.

W. P., Nov. 20.—G. W. Hamilton reported some talk he had with Mr. Clark of the malleable iron works. Mr. C. seemed interested in watching the moral war, and quite anxious that the O. C. should not suffer in the encounter. He takes the ground that society around us has nothing to do with our social relations : have no more business with them than with the private affairs of any family. If we are, as some of our influential neighbors testify, perfectly upright in our dealings, orderly, good neighbors etc., that should secure us peace.—Mr. Campbell reports that old Mr. Wilson is quite interested in the CIRCULAR. Mr. C. gave him a copy last week. Tuesday he came to the office for another, and after reading in the office for half or three quarters of an hour, asked permission to carry the paper home. He liked Carlton Rice's letter, said it was just the thing, just what ought to have been said. He spoke of the comparison of us with the Mormons by the Oneida paper, and said we were no more like the Mormons than heaven was like earth.

A DREAM.

I thought 'twas the judgment; how solemn it seemed,
As weary I lay on my pillow, and dreamed
That the record all kept through my life was disclosed,
And all my dark deeds to the light were exposed.
I wept as I pondered with bitterness deep,
That as I had sowed, I the harvest must reap
Of repentance, that follows the deeds of the flesh,
Which now to my memory were called up afresh.
And is there no hope? and a voice soft and clear
Said, " Why do you ask it ? you've nothing to fear,
These dark works are Satan's, confess and forsake,
And I from your spirit the burden will take.
Be sincere with yourself; look the truth in the face ;
'Tis only your old life that suffers disgrace,
And that at the best is fit only for hell;
Be bold, and the truth with fidelity tell."
I woke, and the vision was lost to my sight,
And around me were drawn the dark curtains of night,
And I felt that the judgment in mercy is given,
Our guilt to wipe out, and thus fit us for heaven.

40 1-6 doz. traps ordered yesterday, including two bear-traps.

THE O. C. DAILY.

VOL. 4.   FRIDAY, NOV. 22, 1867.   NO. 124.

West Dryden, Tompkins Co., N. Y., Nov. 16, 1867.

ONEIDA COMMUNITY, DEAR FRIENDS :—You seem dear to me although I have never seen any of you. I have been a constant reader of the CIRCULAR for over a year; this may account for it. Through the CIRCULAR, I learn that you employ quite a large number of persons in your Trap-works and elsewhere.

The writer of this is a young man of twenty-one, who would like to get into some other business than farming, especially during the winter. He has always lived on a farm with his parents, who have two younger children, so that his services are no longer needed. Have you a place open for such an applicant or would you be willing to employ such an one if you were sure about his good character? If so, please answer this and oblige, Yours truly, F. SNYDER.

The following prayer of Mrs. Mary E. Cragin was found in the cover of an old book in the library. It was transcribed by Mrs. Sarah Seymour in 1851 :—

"O Lord! thou hast sent the spirit of thy son into my heart, and I can with my spirit call thee Father. This is thy gift to me, and I thank thee that I can approach thee, not only as a king and judge, but as a father. I am thy daughter, thy child, and I thank thee for the measure of faith which thou hast given me. I thank thee for Mr. Noyes to go before and point us to thee, and I have a request to make which is this; that thou wouldst please to give me faith suitable to thy generosity. I wish to do thy riches and generosity justice—I do desire that I may so appreciate thy promises as to come boldly and ask thee to use all my talents for thine own purpose, and give me grace to have permanent inspiration as Mr. Noyes does. I pray for faith unfeigned in thy generosity, and when I see weaknesses in my spirit, may it be but inducement to faith. I feel that thou art drawing me with cords of love to abandon myself to thee without reserve. Every item of happiness shall play back into thy hands and promote union between me and thee. I will believe thee and trust thee and love thee for thou art worthy. The God of Abraham of Isaac and of Jacob who led Israel through the Red Sea, and who raised Christ from the dead, is *my* God, and I will trust him with my whole heart. I desire that you may be honored and believed on, as a present, Almighty and companionable God as thou wast then. Wilt thou make me an engine of thy praise and glory for thy namesake. M. E. C."

The new wax thread sewing-machine at the Bag-factory, is now run by water power, and by extending the shaft four feet, the old machine can be worked in the same way. Running these heavy machines by foot power has been quite laborious work, but by the present arrangement about half the labor is saved and more is accomplished. Considerable of the work formely done by hand, is now done upon the machines, and still further improvement in this direction is in prospect. Much credit is due to Edward Inslee for an ingenious device of brake and pulley attached to the treadle, by which the machine is instantly stopped or started by a slight movement of the foot.

L. B.

We have received a letter of ten pages from a widow lady by the name of Pease, at present residing at New-Lebanon Centre, N. Y. She has two children, a boy and a girl, and is urgent to join our society though she evidently thinks us a Community of spiritualists. She sends her picture and says, " If you desire to have some of your mediums tell you all about me, you will have my picture to assist them." She closes by subscribing herself a " true inquirer after the true *road* to the true, pure and *holy* religion."

There have been within a few days past some improvements made around the dish-washing establishment in the kitchen—a new floor laid which was much needed, and a water-pipe to conduct the hot water directly into the rinsing-box. We have also a lot of new dishes which add much to the comfort of our dining-room.

Traps ordered yesterday,   66¼ doz.

THE O. C. DAILY.

VOL. 4.   SATURDAY, NOV. 23, 1867.   NO. 125.

Berlin Heights, O., Nov. 17, 1867.

DEAR——:—I feel that I am ready to say with considerable vehemence that I want to migrate from this port of the habitable sphere. I begin to feel as though I were a stranger in a strange land : my *home* has left, and I am intent on following it as soon as possible. Christ has spoiled me for this locality. I want to tell you how I value your suggestions, to flee from this place, or rather if I could, what Christ makes me feel about it. (Excuse the *I's*, for this is a great place for *I*, and it is difficult to keep *I* in place). Almost every day makes me feel that I am somebody else, not *one* of them in any sense whatever. I can't help contrasting what Christ does for me nowadays, with what I did for myself in former days ; or what I attempted to do. My inclinations take the better road without so much care and anxiety as one necessarily encounters when they have the responsibility of saving themselves. I am made alive to, or conscious of the power of Christ in me. The more and better our relations with Christ, the more desire we have to disconnect ourselves from most of our neighbors in this place. We have incurred Mr. and Mrs. Lesley's displeasure, as well as that of others. We are informing our neighbors here, that it is our intention to sell out and move away as quick as possible. We hope to be able to leave by spring if not before. Mr Randolph left us last Wednesday, and it seems a month almost. He was the only one here, that was fully with us.   *   *   *   Last evening we were shown a letter from Clara Wait to H. K. Reed, a diotrephian of this place, in answer to something he had written her. I think he will not attempt to communicate with her any more. What she said was quite brief and to the point, and Mrs. Reeve and I sympathized with it much, though I think Mr. Reed did not.—Hoping to live and work with you, at some future time,   I remain as ever,   G. W. REEVE.

Vinton, Benton Co., Iowa.

I am going to write a little to you about myself, for I have no one I can talk with confidentially about what I want to know. I joined the Methodist church about two years ago, and I have tried hard to live right, and have partly succeeded in overcoming some of my besetting sins, but I can't be what I desire. I long to live without sin. Do you think it is possible here on earth, to live so that the petty cares and vexations of life do not irritate and make me cross and impatient ? The sum of the whole is I can't find Christ, and I don't know how to find him ; in spite of all the telling the way is dark, and for some reason God won't make it light for me. I have read a great many novels and romances, in my life, and when I made up my mind to try and lead a new life, I quit reading such books, but I could not give up day-dreaming, and I have imagined about as many romances as I have read ; and these foolish idle thoughts keep my mind away from God, and I sometimes think that this is the barrier between God and my soul. If I was sure, I would try and give them up ; but indeed I believe I could as easy pluck out my right eye or cut off my right hand. It is the very light and joy of my life, half of which has passed in dreams, until I can scarcely tell the real from the unreal. Now what do you think of my case ? Is there any " balm in Gilead" for me ?

MRS. WM. K. GREY.

W. P., Nov. 22.—A week ago Mr. Williams one of the forge-shop men who has been in our employ, in attempting to drive a piece of hardened steel out of an anvil where one of the boys had placed it, struck off a piece of the steel which flew into his left eye, entering the iris and cutting a gash one fourth of an inch long. He did not notice it much that day, but it has proved a serious matter. It is the opinion of G. E. C. and also of Dr. Carpenter who has attended him, that he has lost his eye. He has gone to Utica to consult an oculist. It is supposed that the steel is still in his eye.

We have had a searching criticism for two evenings past, of Mr. Joslyn and the Joslyn family, which it is hoped may end in their dissolution as a family, and if there is any thing left that is good in them, that it may be absorbed into the Community family. We sympathize heartily with the judgment of the licentious, pleasure-seeking spirit, both in Charles and his father, and appreciate Mr. Noyes's labors in his efforts to expel such a diabolical element from the Community. We confess our separation from that and from the family spirit and our reliance on Christ to give us that repentance that is thorough and sincere.

It may interest Mr. Noyes to know that Miss Eliza Patten (the same whose letter to Mr. N. was published in the Daily of June 8th), was married last Thursday to a man by the name of Alexander Stuart. Mr. S.'s father lives in this vicinity, but the young man owns property in Missouri, whither he intends to take his bride.

The weather is mild again and the snow has disappeared except a little on the hills.

Traps ordered yesterday,   125 doz.

THE O. C. DAILY.

VOL. 4.   MONDAY, NOV. 25, 1867.   NO. 126.

BUSINESS MEETING.

Mr. Clark having some difficulty in getting men to chop the wood in our wood-lot on the hill, is authorized to pay more per cord in order to have it cut in the early part of the season.

The Board decided to pay Mr. Hubbard something to take down his fences between his house and W. P. for the winter, to prevent the drifting of the snow. It costs us more to break roads than it would to take down the fences and nail the boards on in the spring. To be attended to by Messrs. Worden, Thacker and Clark. A fence should be built around the school-house near the boarding-house, and convenient gates be made for access to it. Referred to the building committee and foreman of the farming department.

We are now obliged to supply the boarding-house with water by drawing it there with a team, from the large reservoir. It was proposed to lay pipes from a spring 150 rods distant, which would insure a good supply of water, but it may be cheaper to dig a well east of the house. Messrs. Worden, Cragin, Sears and Bradley were appointed committee to consider the propriety of digging a well.

The committee chosen last week to confer with Mr. Rawson in reference to the skating-park for the hired men of the bag-shop, find that it is not practicable to make one at the place spoken of, but recommend a spot between the mill and the bridge. Four or five rods of pipe will enable them to flood it at pleasure. Left to the same committee with power to act.

PRACTICAL PROBLEMS. NO. 3.

Society at large holds the O. C. responsible for the moral conduct of her employes. That is right, and we accept it so far as this, that we will not employ persons whom we know to be vicious and immoral, and who purposely lead others astray. It is our aim in hiring help, to secure such only as will commend themselves to us and to our neighbors, by their good behavior, both in our shops and in their respective boarding-houses.

Situated as our works are at W. P., on a street where families had previously located themselves, they could not feel otherwise than slightly solicitous about the social influences that would be brought to bear upon their families by the hundred or more of young men and women, many of them strangers from abroad, whom we are employing in our factories. And some of these families have children too, which would naturally be thrown into the society of these operatives, particularly so if the families to which the children belonged took boarders. These employes may conduct themselves orderly while engaged in work on our premises, conforming strictly to the rules and regulations of the shops. But still, some of them may be persons wholly destitute of moral integrity, and consequently dangerous members of society. Now how shall these things be averted? How can we get sufficiently acquainted with our employes to discover the real *animus* of their characters?

Often, it is found that the most dangerous men in society—those who are preeminently wicked at heart, real emissaries of Satan, are outwardly highly polished and attractive in their manners, appearing to a superficial observer, as angels of light. To exclude such characters from our work-shops and farms would require an acquaintance with them that could not be formed during the period of work. Out of twenty-four hours only ten of them are employed on our premises; the remainder of their time is spent at their boarding-homes or elsewhere. The only possible way therefore for the Community to offer anything like a guarantee for the good behavior and moral integrity of her employes would be to establish boarding-houses of her own, superintended by Community men and women—true deacons of the church.

At this time when there is an unprecedented failure in the springs and wells all over the state, it may be interesting to know precisely how the springs hold out which supply our aqueduct. The water was started in the iron aqueduct soon after the ground had been thoroughly drenched with rain; it then discharged by exact measurement, (July 7th) 18 quarts per minute. One month later, it discharged one quart less; since then, there has been a uniform decrease in the water of one quart every twenty-three days, so that the discharge Nov, 20th, was thirteen quarts per minute, that being five quarts less than when the springs were at their maximum hight. This proves them to be very durable, the decrease being less than one third, after about five months in which there has not been rain sufficient to affect deep springs.   J. A.

O. C. Nov. 25, 1867.

CARLTON RICE, DEAR SIR:—We send you to-day in care of the Stage-driver, a small case of preserved fruits, as a slight testimonial of our appreciation of your friendship and kindly offices in behalf of the Community.—The "moral war" is apparently ended, and rather ingloriously for the attacking party. The Oneida people as a whole never seemed more anxious than now, to manifest their good feeling toward the O. C.   Truly yours, W. H. W.
                                   For the Community.

We never had such a sense as now of the utter selfishness of the family spirit and the cover it gives to all iniquity. The judgment that has been going, has opened our eyes wide, and we loathe it with that loathing that, it is hoped, will purge out the last vestige of that spirit from our being.

Traps ordered Saturday and Sunday,   114 doz.

THE O. C. DAILY.

VOL. 4.   TUESDAY, NOV. 26, 1867.   NO. 127.

Mr. Bacon, one of the Depot landlords came here Sunday afternoon, with a friend of his, a Mr. Nichols from St. Lawrence County, and staid perhaps two hours. He is the man with whom Mills and his children boarded during the Mills' war. Mr. Nichols had heard some bad stories about us, and being in this vicinity he called here for the purpose of learning what kind of people we were, and the secret of our union and prosperity. He was somewhat of a skeptic, believed in a God that was prisoned in a network of laws of his own making. I was thankful for the opportunity of broadly stating some of our leading principles before these men; our relations to Christ and the Primitive Church, the place that we assigned to the Marriage institution as being well adapted to a slavish, egotistical life, but perfectly incompatible with an unselfish form of society; and also in regard to our faith in the Providence of God. Mr. Nichols demurred as a matter of course to some of the conclusions reached, particularly with respect to the providential care of God in arranging and matching our circumstances to our various needs and conditions; but Mr. Bacon took sides with me in every issue that we made on this subject, and I could feel that he had a deep respect for our faith and religious standing.   U.

The classes are all organized and some of them commenced their course of study yesterday, and others are waiting for books. The following is the programme, for study: One class in Chemistry, one Nat. Philosophy, one in Phonography, one in Composition, one Geography, one in Mental Arithmetic, two in French, two classes in Thompson's Arithmetic, and three classes in Algebra, one in Robinson's and two in Davie's.—In addition to these we are to have, as last winter, a school for the young men of Ernest's age, at the Dunn Cottage, H. R. Perry, teacher, and another for the young girls taught by Tryphena Seymour.

The *Daily Union* notices the Trapper's Guide as follows:—" The above is one of the most interesting books that has lately fallen into our hands. It is a manual of instructions, for capturing all kinds of fur-bearing animals, and curing their skins; with observations on the fur-trade, hints on life in the woods, and narratives of trapping and hunting excursions. It is a valuable and interesting book for gamesters, excursionists and boys; full of illustrations of life in the woods, wild animals, traps, &c."

The old Reception-room that has stood the test for years without alteration, has at length yielded to the carpenter's instruments. The partition is removed, the alcove taken away, and a small clothes-press is to be put up on the south side near the door. The room now contains two beds and a trundle-bed, and five occupants.—Poor old room, what remembrances dost thou call up! But the car of progress calls for change, and we gladly yield to its demands.

W. P., Nov. 25.—Our family seems to be undergoing a change preparatory to getting settled for the winter. The three youngest members, Ernest, Orrin and Milford have been transfered to O. C. to attend school. Mr. H. Burt has applied for membership and been admitted. Our classes are organized and will commence study as soon as books, slates, blackboards, etc., are procured.

It seems as though everybody and thing were on the move, nothing stationary. Many hands are called into requisition, in carrying beds, bureaus, &c., &c., from one house or room to another. Sixteen persons moved yesterday and to-day, among whom was Mrs. Baker who has removed to the upper sitting-room, so that it will be convenient for her to attend meetings.

We had a letter from J. W. Towner a day or two since, in which he commences to give us the history of his life, in order, as he says, to our fuller acquaintance with him, and to let in the light upon his past course. He says " You can do what you please with this document, even to publishing it in the CIRCULAR if it is thought best."

Mr Kelly says there is a tailor living in Bath, N. Y., who claims to have made Lord Amberly's first pants. This tailor was employed by Lord Russell and other English Lords, to one of whom he gave offense by dunning him—this he assigns as the cause of his coming to this Country.

The Camellias of which there are several varieties, are now in full bloom. One kind is of the purest white, and of exquisite delicacy and beauty. The Augusta rose-bush is thickly budded and will soon add much to the attractiveness of the Green-house.

Charlotte Leonard has taken Minerva Barron's place as assistant in keeping the books at the Bag-shop, and Minerva, Beulah's, in running the sewing-machine. Beulah and E. F. Hutchins have gone to W. P. to remain permanently, or for the winter.

Traps ordered yesterday,   5¼ doz.

THE O. C. DAILY.

VOL. 4.   WEDNESDAY, NOV. 27, 1867.   NO. 128.

Carthage, Jeff. Co., N. Y., Nov. 24, 1867.

DEAR MRS. J———:—Your two letters were duly received, also the Express package. Thanks to the Community for the valuable gifts. They are *acceptable*, the more so as tokens of interest and love from you. They are to me evidences of the favor and approbation of God. My heart is stirred up to renewed consecration to Christ and to you. Your letters were timely helps to me—many times I have thanked God for them, coming as they did when I was assailed by malicious spirits. They left when your letter was handed to me and have not attempted to disturb me since. They have met with no favor, or listening ear, from me since I was at O. C. last. I thank God anew for the O. C. and confess anew my unity with you and with all my superiors in Christ and the kingdom of heaven. I am glad of the documents relative to Mr. Wright, although it is not likely that he will write to me again. You say the CIRCULARS were superscribed Clara Wait, Carthage. Mr. Vrooman says there is another Carthage P. O. in the western part of the State to which mail matter is sometimes carried which is intened for this place, if Jefferson Co. is not put on, which is probably where the CIRCULARS have gone. I have inquired for them at the Office twice and Mr. Vrooman has inquired nearly every week for them too, so I think the above explanation is the true one. Mr. V. was at the Office yesterday, and told them the CIRCULARS had been sent there for two months or so. They said no such papers had been received there.   Yours truly,   CLARA WAIT.

W. P., Nov. 26.—We heard from Mr. Williams through one of the shop hands a few days since. The oculist whom he consulted, told him that his left eye was destroyed, and there was great danger of his losing his right eye. It was only by paying fifty dollars down, that the man could be induced to undertake to save it. It is a pretty hard case, and some of our people feel that we ought to do something for Mr. W.—One of the chain-shop boys complained Monday morning, that his money was stolen on Saturday, by one of the other boys. In trying to ferret out and settle this matter, it was found that the same boy who stole the money, also stole a cap from one of the stores at Oneida. He confessed everything, and gave the cap to Myron, who went down to see his parents about it to-day, and left the cap with them for the boy to return to its owner, and apologize, as he has promised to do. While talking with them, Mrs. Toher came in, and was earnest in her expression of gratitude to the O. C. for the blessing they had been to her and other poor people in the place. She said she was married . and lived with her husband five years, and became mother to five children. Then her husband died and she had supported her children by her own labor alone until this fall, when three of them, found work in our shops. She said it was a shame, the way the papers at Oneida had treated us, and if a vote of all the people were taken, they would be stopped. All the poor people would vote for it. One of the merchants who came. down on us at first, spoke about the school we had started, commending it.

W. P.—DEAR O. C. DAILY:—Will you please tell J. P. H. that this is the second time I have found my love when desiring her most. Perhaps this will offset the two times he has "lost his love when enjoying her most."—I have had quite a desire to live at W. P. ever since the family was first organized, but circumstances which I was content to believe God arranged, prevented me, until some two months since when I was permitted a three week's stay, which only deepened this desire. Now imagine my delight on being invited to spend the winter here.—There are three studies I intend to pursue this winter. First to learn to love the Lord with all my heart, second, Grammar, third, Writing.
                                            E. F. H.

The struggle between Autumn and Winter is still going on, now this, and then that prevailing. At the present time the ground is unfrozen. We have dark cloudy weather and the atmosphere is quite warm. We hope for rain, and there are many indications from time to time, that the clouds are about to bestow their precious contents upon the earth, but as yet our hopes in this respect have proved futile.

We often hear persons say when they have had something which was enjoyed with peculiar appetite and relish, "*it went right to the spot.*" This expression, though more forcible than elegant, involuntarily arose in the mind of one at least, after reading the CIRCULAR yesterday. Many thanks to the purveyors of the "round table."   H.

The men constituting the Bag-shop corps, went out yesterday afternoon, and threw up an embankment about four feet high for the skating-park. All is now ready for laying the pipes that are necessary to flood it.

CORRECTION.—In inserting the notice of the Trapper's Guide in yesterday's Daily, we should have said that the *Daily Union* from which it was taken, is published in Block Island, Illinois.

Much sympathy was expressed last night with what Mr. Noyes said in his talk about Mr. Shelling's musical career in the Community, and a desire manifested to do him justice.

Traps ordered yesterday,   26 doz.

THE O. C. DAILY.

VOL. 4.   THURSDAY, NOV. 28, 1867.   NO. 129.

HIS NAME IS LOVE.

While meditating alone in my room one evening, on various subjects none of which appeared to hold my attention with much firmness, something seemed to say to me in a tone of parental affection, "do you know God?" "Know God," I repeated, with a slight tremor in my voice, "I hope I do." But that answer was unsatisfactory to my inner self. I soliloquized thus, should I say I *hope* I know my mother who had brought me into the world, nursed me, clothed and educated me, and did all she could for my happiness and well being? No, indeed, I should not; simple honesty, if nothing more, would require me to say, "Know her? to be sure I do, better than I know myself. She has been all in all to me, and to say I *hope* I know her, would be evidence of my insanity". But the same voice continued, "To know God is eternal life, and that eternal life is *parental love* with which no earthly mother's love, for tenderness, watchfulness and gentleness, can compare. And this love," said the voice, "is God, the Creator of all things. Now do you say you *hope* you know God?" This was too much for cold unbelief—my heart melted and tears flowed. "Oh, my father, my father!" I exclaimed in broken accents, "your goodness has overtaken me at last and conquered my hard impenitent heart. I did not know that my father's name was *Love* till now. I did not know that it was my *father* for whom my soul pined and hungered, during the many years it was seeking rest and finding none in earthly lovers."

I imagined that there was a special somebody that needed my love, and that I needed that somebody's love; so I wandered about to find my lover, my special mate, and how many times have I fancied that I had been at last, successful in my search for the one love made expressly for me, a poor forlorn egotist, but only to reap disappointment. Cheated continually, my soul was unsatisfied, saying to me in a tone of gentle rebuke, "It was not love that you found when you grasped the creature for whom you was ready to lay down your life. It was simply a temple like your own, more beautiful perhaps, but a temple cannot love any more than a house can love. It was not made to love, but to *serve* love, to be filled with love, filled with him who is love. There is but one love in the universe, and that is uncreated. All true lovers, so called, are servants of the one universal, common love and nothing more." Had I known my father earlier I should not have been a heathen so long, worshipping temples instead of life and love. God is love and Jesus Christ the only begotten son of love. I can now say I know God.   *Novus Homo.*

In a letter to Mr. Cragin, Mr. Reeve writes:

"We had been looking to the mails rather anxiously, but not impatiently, for something from O. C.: and we have received more than we dared to hope for. Yesterday we received a note from Mr. Woolworth, with the correspondence concerning A. D. Wright. How well we appreciate the care the O. C. have for us, I will not attempt to say with my pen. If our hearts were inked over, and we had some of that thin paper that answer so well for transferring, we might send an impression: and perhaps we have already sent one by telegraph. How I thank God for your letters, the spirit you send in various ways. We shall endeavor to make the best use of all the good things you send us. They are sacred to us as things coming from our own family."

Mrs. Reeve says in addition, "I like what Mr. C. says about studying; I had intended to do what I could in that direction. I feel that if the devil brought us here, that God, will lead us away, when we prove ourselves faithful to him and to Christ. It seems to me that however truthful we have been as the world goes, we have now to learn to be truthful and truth-loving as a little child learns to walk. It is our desire to be sincere—how my soul has hungered after sincerity, honesty and truthfulness (as held by the little band at O. C.), and been thrust back to feed on the husks and crumbs of the world, until it was nearly famished, and was hard to realize that sincerity could exist under the sun. My heart is so full, words seem empty, and fail to express what I would be glad to."

Mr. W. H. Perry was criticised last night by his request. He wrote out a history of his past life, and course in the Community, which opened the way for the family to be very sincere. Such a spirit of prolonged disobedience as his confessions disclosed, few if any have been guilty of in the Community.

The forcing-pit has received its roofing of glass, and the building is nearly completed with the exception of hanging the doors, and laying down the flue-pipes, which will not be a long job. Providence has blessed us with favorable weather for doing the work, for which we are thankful.

The Advance comes to us now and promises to give us some wholesome reading.

Traps ordered yesterday,   19 doz.

THE O. C. DAILY.

VOL. 4.   FRIDAY, NOV. 29, 1867.   NO. 130.

W. P., Nov, 28.—All the family were requested last evening, to be prompt to breakfast this morning, and much curiosity was excited by so special a request, which was gratified only on seeing ourselves at the table, where we found oysters, smoking hot prepared for us. They were sent by Joseph, to Myron, on a wager which he lost two years ago or more.

After listening to the reading of the report by Mr. Noyes, "A Proposition," this evening, Mrs. Ackley remarked : "I wish to join Mr. Noyes in dedicating Alice and her gift for singing, to God." This was responded to by all.—Hearty sympathy was expressed by the family with Mr. Noyes's nomination of Geo. E. Cragin, and a desire to help in the work of establishing and organizing the second generation. Love for, and confidence in Theodore and George were testified to by many.—Myron has been in some trial and darkness for some weeks. This evening he related some of his experience and confessed his separation from his old life and the spirit of discouragement that has possessed him of late. He wished to begin anew to give himself to God and his cause. He invited advice or criticism from the family. He was advised to seek the ascending fellowship and appreciate it more than he has in the past. He has a tendency to allow himself to criticise some of his superiors and take exceptions to their criticism. He should seek a soft heart and let the work God intended for him be done in him.

We had two visitors from the West, Wednesday, Mr. William Buel of Oconee, Shelby Co., Ill., a distant relative of Gen. Buel, and Mr. Louis Kelley, of Marion, Grant Co., Ind. The last named came from Indiana on purpose to see the Community, and to learn the conditions of membership; reached here at about eleven o'clock A. M. in company with Mr. Buel, with whom he fell in on his way up from the Depot, staid to dinner, talked and looked around, and upon learning that we expected persons who joined us to bring their families with them, or to get their freedom from family ties and obligations, through union with Christ and the Providence of God, set out on his way home at three P. M. of the same day, perfectly satisfied and contented.

Mr. Buel remained over night. He wanted to join, badly, or to be put in the way of joining, and it didn't seem as though he could possibly wait. His life thus far, he claimed, had been a hard one. When I showed him into the Hall, he looked up at the frescoed ceiling, and around upon the walls, and the cozy comfortable seats, and exclaimed, "Happy family ! Happy family !" and then raising his face and eyes and clasping his hands, "Gracious God ! how I wish I was a member of it !" He had a "sorry" cast of countenance, no doubt had cultivated an unthankful spirit, and quarreled with his circumstances, and was evidently in search of better conditions. He brightened up very much while here, and when shaking hands on leaving, said fervently, "God bless you and this Institution ! Heaven rain upon you, and upon all here !" Perhaps we never had a more continent visitor than Mr. Kelley, nor one apparently more unreconciled to his lot, and at the same time so favorably situated, so far as this world's goods are concerned, than Mr Buel.   U.

Miss S. Augusta Story who has been expected here for sometime past, came yesterday. She arrived in the morning and waited at Oneida till nearly night, not knowing our people, or what hour they went down. She seems very glad to get here, but is very tired, having started from her home in Missouri, Monday morning and traveled nights without much interruption. It is expected that Miss S. will help at our Boarding-house where she will become more acquainted with us, and we shall in turn ascertain whether she is prepared to join us as she proposed to do, some months ago.

A letter was received yesterday from a lawyer in N. Y., whom C. J. Guiteau has employed to collect wages which he claims his due, for services rendered us while he was here. He claims the moderate sum of $9,000 being $1,500 per year for the six years he was with us; also interest on the $900 dollars he put in. Such audacity is without a parallel in the history of the Community, throwing even Mills' course and claims upon us quite into the shade.

Thanksgiving day passed without the usual accompaniments of roast turkey etc., as has been our wont in past years. There was nothing in particular to distinguish it from other days, except the shutting up of the Bag-shop, and dispersion of the hired hands. The day was warm, dark and slightly rainy.

The call from Wallingford for Mrs. Conant, who is mother of the washing, has caused a good deal of stirring up all round to supply her place. Emma who has been in the Office only three weeks, leaves, and H. C. Woolworh takes her place.

Last night Mr. Delatre made an expose of some of the dark passages in his past life, which is another evidence that the truth is searching us and the work of judgment still going on.

We understand that the boarders at our Boarding-house last night, had a nice time in making molasses candy. They behaved well and enjoyed the sport.

Traps ordered yesterday,   84 doz.

THE O. C. DAILY.

VOL. 4. SATURDAY, NOV. 30, 1867. NO. 131.

I wish to thank the family for their faithfulness to me in criticism, which I indorse heartily as from the Lord, believing that it will have the effect to clear me from the thralldom in which I have been enshrouded. I find it already easier to resist the course I have been pursuing so long, and believe that I shall be able to come off victorious through Christ.

I am bent on revenge on the enemy, and swear in my heart the devil shall pay for it. But words are cheap things, and you desire *deeds*, which I trust in God I shall be able to give, confessing Christ my ability to do so.—I fully indorse Mr. Noyes's views in regard to fasting, and believe that there is salvation in it for me, which I desire to avail myself of.

W. H. PERRY.

Hamilton, Nov. 28, 1867.

MR. WOOLWORTH, DEAR SIR:—I this day (Thanksgiving day), received a case of preserved fruits and jellies, from my friends, the Oneida Community, and I received it with thanksgiving. The specimens are very nice, and fully sustain their reputation, and I can't tell when I ever received a present I more highly prized than I do this, coming as it did so unexpectedly. Be so good as to express my gratitude to the Community for this kind expression.

I see the fire into the O. C. from Oneida has grown feeble, though weak in the beginning, especially its poetry. Doctor Franklin used to say, "The surest way to kill an enemy was to let him alone." Perhaps it has been so in this case. Very respectfully to you and the Oneida Community, I am your friend,

CARLTON RICE.

De Ruyter, Nov. 26, 1867.

To THE EDITOR OF ONEIDA COMMUNITY, GENTS:—Please send me your paper as I wish to know something of your social Community and take this as the first step. I hope to be able from this one advancement to satisfy myself more fully as to the good which I may derive from the information I shall be happy to receive. Confidentially, Yours Respectfully,

MANSEL E. BURDICK.

Two of our elderly men whose eyes are rather dim, when walking the other day on the bank of the pond at W. P. espied something in the water near the opposite bank. One says to the other "What are those?" pointing to the objects seen. "Why stumps of trees to be sure," said the other. "No they are not stumps for they keep moving; I think they are turkies, quite a flock of them too." A young man coming along just then, set them right by informing them that the objects at which they were gazing, were only the reflection in the water of the heads of several cattle grazing near by. This incident was related by one of the parties concerned, who is a good joker, to amused listeners, and he did not spoil the story by sparing himself.

Why is your mother's mother a nice woman?
Because she is a *Grand*mother.
Why is your mouth like a trap?
Because it has *jaws.*
Why is a spider like a top?
Because it *spins.*
Why is an ear of corn like an army?
Because it has *kernels.*
When is a man like a chimney?
When he *smokes.*
Why are your teeth like trees?
Because they have *roots.* H. C. W.

Rain fell in small quantities yesterday afternoon, for two or three hours, but the weather during the night changed, the wind blew very strong, and this morning the ground is frozen stiff.

The men's sitting-room at the Boarding-house is newly papered and painted, which improves its appearance very much.

Chemistry in the kitchen No. 5th., by John Leonard, was read last night. Some parts were very amusing to say the least, and some one remarked that they thought J. had struck a good vein.

Our copy runs short to-day, and so of course, we shall be obliged to make our *Daily* short, which we regret.

Mr. Underwood, Mrs. Stephens, C. A. Macknet and little Cosette arrived safely yesterday noon.

Traps ordered yesterday, 3 doz.

THE O. C. DAILY.

VOL. 4.   MONDAY, DEC. 2, 1867.   NO. 132.

BUSINESS MEETING.

Mr. Reynolds desired to have some improvements made in his room at the store. A half day's work by a joiner will enable him to work to greater advantage. Mr. Reynolds and Mr. D. Kelly will carry the work through. It may be well to state here that Mr. Kelly takes the place, as foreman of the carpenter's shop, in Abram Burt's absence.

As it is near the time for taking our annual inventory, Mr. Woolworth thought the foreman of the different departments had better buy as little stock as possible. We should thus save a great deal of handling over. It is a poor plan to buy stock merely to keep the hands at work. If we have nothing for them to do in which we are sure of success and profit, we had better let them go. Mr. Kinsley and Carrie were appointed committee to consider what help can be spared and thus reduce our expenses in that direction to their minimum. In view of our determination to get out of debt we had better curtail our expenses generally as much as we can.

A man has been hired to drive the W. P. team, and the committee thinking that some one or two persons should be responsible for his direction, have appointed Mr. Aiken and Anna Hatch, to whom persons will go when they wish anything done by that team out of its usual line of duties.

Mr. Abbott is slowly improving. We make the following extracts from a long note from him to the family, read last evening:

"I have had some experience during my late sickness, interesting to myself, and perhaps it may be to the family, if I can clearly present it. For some time I had been oppressed by a dark, unbelieving, discouraged spirit. I saw so much evil, both within and without the Community, that it seemed absurd to expect any great immediate amelioration of the condition of mankind; or, for the aged to think of escaping the common lot of mortals, in respect to putting off the earthly body; mere testimony of the resurrection was unsatisfactory, while unattended by that power that raised Christ from the dead. Bodily infirmities and old age seemed pressing upon me with irresistible force, until it appeared to me, to be the course of true wisdom, to become reconciled to what seemed inevitable; and I became so far reconciled to die, that I could look death in the face without a shudder.—In this state of mind, I was led into a retrospect of my past life. I could see in it no cause for self-complacency; but much for sorrow and repentance; it seemed almost a blank. Still there were a few instances, in which I was conscious of yielding to the leadings of Christ, according to the best of my ability.—One effect of my sickness has been to reduce and criticise an inordinate alimentiveness that has oppressed me, and to bring it into more subjection to interior, spiritual life.—Another important effect of my late experience, has been a thorough investigation and judgment of my social character, not only since my connection with the Community, but during my previous married life.—Another lesson has been to trust Christ as a savior of the body. I seemed to be shut up to the necessity of trusting Christ alone for deliverence from the bodily afflictions which I suffered. I am conscious that my recovery so far as it is affected, is wholly due to resurrection life working in me.

"I believe the most important lesson I have learned by my late experience, has been full trust and confidence in God as a financier.—I have felt to judge and clear myself from the worldly, unbelieving, idolatrous love of money, to which I had been deeply in bondage while living in the world, and which has had more or less influence over me since living in the Community.

"The first real desire I had to get well was that I might see, and if possible co-operate with the church in the development of Christ's financial principles in the world. I am thankful that Carr's financial influence is being purged out of the Community, and that Mr. Noyes is having a chance to lead. It is certain that all financial prosperity depends on the inspiration and favor of God, and not on human prudence and foresight.—In conclusion, I wish to thank God for all his dealings with me, both for his judgments and his mercies. I wish specially to thank him for the improvement there is, both in my body and spirit. I confess a spirit that is soft, humble and receptive to the ascending fellowship.   JOHN ABBOTT.

Mr. Woolworth said last night, that he had reflected a good deal within a few days on the text "All things work for good" &c., and thought that God was proving it true in our case. In the *Moral War*, in our judgments, criticisms and tribulations, the good results are already very apparent.

It commenced snowing Saturday afternoon, and grew cold and was very blustering all the evening and during the night. It continued to blow and snow more or less all day yesterday and up to this morning, yet there is not snow enough on a level to make sleighing.

Mary Jones has gone to W. P. to remain for the winter; so it is expected there will be no more changes this winter of women or girls, as has been the practice heretofore.

We had a dance last night after supper, which many seemed to enjoy much, particularly the children.

Fidelia has changed places with Minerva Barron and leaves the Bag-shop for the present.

Traps ordered Saturday and Sunday,   281¼ doz.

THE O. C. DAILY.

VOL. 4. WEDNESDAY, DEC. 4, 1867. NO. 133.

W. P., Dec. 2.—Our classes are fairly started, numbering six,—Composition, University and Elementary Algebra, Geometry, Grammar and Spelling. As we have no school-rooms we receive our course of Geometry and Grammar at the tables where our dinner is served up to us. Our Algebra and spelling classes seem thoroughly wide awake though they are held in the same room where some of the members are accustomed to spend many hours in sleep. All seem enthusiastic and inclined to improve their time and make the most of their opportunities. We ask and expect the blessing of God on our efforts to improve our minds and expect he will help us to keep a healthy ambition free from competition.

Beulah will take, for the present, the responsibility of reporter for the O. C. *Daily* from Willow-Place. May success crown her efforts.

If the readers of the *Daily* should have missed its appearance yesterday, we give as the *principal* reason, that on coming to the Office we found we had *nothing* to report, not one solitary item. We hope this may not occur again.

We find it pretty difficult at this season, some of the time at least, to get interesting matter, incidents and items for the *Daily*, and we wish the family would take it into consideration and lend us a helping hand. We remember we had the same difficulty last winter. There are plenty of facts occurring almost daily in our large family, in the different departments, which if reported, would be read with interest, and occasionally a stray one reaches us; but we are far from gathering up *all* that would edify or amuse the readers of our little sheet. Ought there not to be a person selected from the kitchen group, for instance, the children's department, the schools and classes, the Store and business Office, who should have a lookout for our wants in this respect, and report from time to time, such items of interest as come under their observation?

The class of young girls commence their studies for the winter with a good degree of enthusiasm. A good spirit prevails.

A slight collision occurred yesterday, between the teacher and one of them, the scholar answering back hastily. This morning she asked forgiveness saying she thought she did wrong, and was sorry, and confessed Christ a soft heart. The rest of the class seemed touched, and all joined in the confession of Christ in their studies.—This little incident seemed to let in the revival spirit. T.

One day last week, a well was begun on the Hitchcock place, intended to meet the wants of the Boarding-house, as water has failed there, and been drawn from the O. C. kitchen for some months past. The digging proceeded for two days, and on the third, water appeared, and stoning and digging were carried on together, until rain set in, and the work was broken off. It has been cold and stormy ever since. So the well has remained in *statu quo* up to the present time, with the exception of filling up with water to the depth of two and a half feet of the nine which had been reached. MORE ANON.

Nov. 30, 1867.

I have heard of the Community and think if it is as I have heard, I should like to join you if you would accept me. I am a widow, my husband died in the army and I don't like to get married again. I have one child a nice little boy five years old. I am twenty-nine years old and if you will please write me your rules of taking any one, and if you will take me and my boy, I think I will come. Please write soon and let me know. Yours respectfully,

ARDELL TOLTS.

The crisp morning air, and the creaking sound of the snow beneath our feet, remind us, if nothing else, that it is cold weather, and that winter, that has for many weeks threatened us, is fairly ushered in. The sound, too, of sleigh-bells is heard in the distance, though the sleighing, judging from the depth of snow we see around here, can't be very good.

Mrs. Mallory has gone into the washing again, after being out between two and three months. She will feel quite at home in the business, as she was mother in that department previous to her sickness nearly two years.

Our people had quite too many porkers, namely twenty-one, and yesterday they butchered twelve of the number. Five of them dressed are judged to weigh at least twenty-five hundred, and the twelve forty hundred.

The meeting hour last night, was taken up mostly with reading reports. At the close we had music from Abram and others.

Abram leaves to-day noon for New-York, and takes with him Harley, who is destined for Wallingford. Alas for our music. !

Traps ordered Monday and Tuesday, 42¼ doz.

THE O. C. DAILY.

VOL. 4.   THURSDAY, DEC. 5, 1867.   NO. 134.

Post Office, Mount Marius, N. Y., Dec. 3, 1867.

JOHN H. NOYES, DEAR SIR:—In your CIRCULAR of Nov. 28th., I read, " A woman called in pursuit of a home; she said she would like to stay here as long as she lived, if she died in any decent season." I feel an interest in that paragraph. A woman called on me who was seeking a home and I directed her to the O. C. She said she had been nurse in the army during the war, in New Orleans and elsewhere. You would favor me by telling me whether you accepted her or not. I think from her energy she would be of great service to you and I judge from all I hear and read of you, that you would make her future more peaceful and hopeful. At least I trust she is with you, for it grieved me to think she must wander without a home when she seemed so capable of earning her way well. Tell her to write to me if she is with you, and oblige me by stating yourself as to the fact.

Respectfully, REBENN MOSES SANFORD.

ASSISTANT P. M.

P. S. Your European correspondence has been very interesting to me, the best I have read from that country.

W. P., Dec. 4.—Mr. Williams who was mentioned some days since as having his eye seriously injured came into the shop to-day. He seemed bright and cheerful and expects to return to his work again in a few days. One eye is totally lost, the other has recovered. Besides the loss of his time and traveling expenses, he has paid the doctor some fifty-eight dollars.

A couple of boys in our employ, having imbibed a good deal of cider, and made themselves merry thereby, went into the school-house and damaged some books belonging to some of the scholars. This morning the father of one of the children whose books were injured, called to settle with the boys. Our folks advised them to settle; but not until the man had gone and Myron suggested to them that the Sheriff might appear next, did they seem inclined to do so; then they scampered off as fast as possible to pay the amount, a dollar for each book. Perhaps it will be a good lesson to them.

The skating on the pond is said to be *splendid*, by those of our folks who have tried it. A number of our hired hands were seen there yesterday noon, evidently enjoying it very much.

A man living in Cincinnati, Ohio, by the name of Thomas Willis Jones, made application some weeks ago to join, and was invited to make the O. C. a visit. He writes that in consequence of an accident that happened to one of his feet, in which a great toe was injured, he shall not be able to travel at present. He says in addition to the above :

" I take advantage of this opportunity to offer a few reasons for desiring to join the Community. I desire occupation, honest society, religion without cant and to be free from Politicians, Lawyers, Doctors, Soldiers and ungodly people. All this I believe is to be found in your Community, the Constitutions and doctrines of which, I have read with great attention. I have also read Mr. Noyes's " Salvation from sin" with, I hope, great advantage, certainly with great satisfaction. So far all is well, but I think it right to tell you that I am advanced in years, of strong constitution, sound " mind and limb," *all but the toe*, willing to be useful in any capacity, but I am not a mechanic, my means are limited," &c.

The skating-pond made for the benefit of the hired help and others, has been completed by raising a bank from the bridge to the point of high land at the foot of the tail-race of the mill. The pond is flooded by tapping the flume, and conducting the water through the lower story of the mill by means of logs, through a four inch bore. The pond was partially filled with water yesterday, but it is feared the volume of water will prove too small, in case an attempt should be made to flow the pond in a cold day, by the water congealing as it flows in, thus forming bad ice.

Thankfulness was expressed last night for the general good health of the family, particularly the children. There is considerable sickness outside, yet we feel little of the pressure upon us.

Traps ordered yesterday,   101 doz.

THE O. C. DAILY.

VOL. 4.   FRIDAY, DEC. 6, 1867.   NO. 135.

EVENING MEETING.

After Mr. Underwood had finished reading the two talks on a "New Era in Love," and the love of money in the Joslyn family, Mr. Woolworth put the following question:

"Do you indorse that, Mr. Joslyn?

Mr. Joslyn.—Yes, Sir, I do, with all my heart.

Mr. Woolworth.—Do you Mr. Perry?

Mr. Perry.—I do.

Mr. Woolworth.—Well, do the whole Community indorse it? [Loud applause.]

Mr. Joslyn.—I hope Mr. Noyes will never have any more trouble with me on this subject. I have never been conscious of thinking evil of what he has done for Victor. I have always felt perfectly at ease respecting what he has done about him, and I should if he had spent twenty-five dollars a week upon him. Since those affairs Mr. Noyes refers to, I have never felt like resisting him. I have never felt any quarrel respecting any of Mr. Noyes's actions in building up the Community. I have felt no quarrel about what he has done for individuals in the Community. I sympathize with all Mr. Noyes has done, all that he is doing, and all that he will do. [Applause and laughter.] I have full confidence in him as a man of God, and I always have had.

Mr. Perry.—I have been satisfied for sometime, that my trouble about finances was altogether too worldly. I want a spirit of true foresight and sympathy with Mr. Noyes.

Mr. Woolworth.—I am satisfied that Mr. Joslyn has had confidence in Mr. Noyes as a man of God, as he says; but at the same time this root of evil has been in him. I hope this is going to dig it out.

Mr. Joslyn.—I don't wish to have it understood, from anything I said, that I resist the criticism, for I accept it all.

Mr. Woolworth.—I very much like Mr. Noyes's idea, that we may get out of debt so as to do liberal things and generous acts to the whole universe. [Approved, Mr. Joslyn cheerfully and heartily joining with the rest.]

Mr. Underwood.—That is a glorious ambition for us.

George E.—I confess hearty sympathy with the talk about a New Era in Love. [Generally indorsed.]

WILLOW-PLACE, Dec. 5.—Dropping in for a short time last evening upon this little family, we could but notice the contrast of the present with a few weeks ago. Then on every hand we would hear, "So many traps ordered to-day; a bee to-night; telegraphed to Wallingford for more help; coming to-morrow," and like expressions. The sound of the drop would greet us first in the morning and last at night, and business seemed in the very air, and stirred every fibre of our being. But now a change; books, books, and classes, classes, everywhere. The enthusiasm is for study. The large number of the family a while ago, has dwindled down to twenty-seven, and with them is the same earnestness in this direction as hitherto for business.

Resources for amusement seem to remain, and last evening a thriving club composed of the kitchen corps of women, kindly volunteered to interest the family. When it was first announced, we were on the alert for pantomime, but the melodeon was brought in, around which they grouped themselves, and then sang with a great deal of energy,

"Mary had a little lamb, its fleece was white as snow,
  Shouting the battle cry of freedom,
And everywhere that Mary went, the lamb was sure to go,
  Shouting the battle cry of freedom.
CHORUS.—The union forever," &c.

From the cheers that followed, the song seemed to be appreciated and they no doubt were fully rewarded for their effort.   AN EX-MEMBER.

The twelve hogs have been weighed and disposed of. The largest one weighed 637 pounds, and the smallest, 147 pounds. The aggregate, including untried fat, was 4,685 pounds. Five of the twelve averaged 544 pounds each. Part of the lot was sold yesterday at Utica by Mr. Kinsley, for $377.82, cash, being 4,198 pounds, at nine cents per pound. The balance was sold at home. Since May last, eleven others have been butchered; weight, 3,675 pounds; the value of all, together with pigs sold, gives a hog revenue of $820.15 the past season, produced mainly from the refuse of the kitchen and dairy.

George Larkins, one of our hired men, died yesterday morning at his residence near W. P. Foundry. He leaves a widow and two quite small children in poor circumstances; also two children in England, which he had by his first wife, and whom he designed to send for as soon as he was able.

It is a very blustering day, though not very cold.

Traps ordered yesterday,   125 doz.

THE O. C. DAILY.

VOL. 4. SATURDAY, DEC. 7, 1867. NO. 136.

Humbolt, Kansas, Nov. 24, 1867.

DEAR FRIENDS, BROTHERS AND SISTERS:—I desire you to send me two of your choice traveling leather bags, one smaller than the one you gave me when I was with you, the other the *Lunch-Bag*, the size of those I saw. I inclose a draft, $20. I do not know the price of your best bags, but please send the articles and the balance shall be adjusted in the future. * * * I failed to come to see you last Spring as I thought, and I may never visit you again, but I esteem you a city on the hill—a beacon light—an oasis. I never can forget the great pleasure I had in the two days I spent with you. I speak of you often in my rounds and commend your virtues. I feel I am with you in sympathy and charity, and shall pray you may exist and prosper, until the whole earth shall be filled with the knowledge of Jesus. We differ in minor things, but so few, I could almost say I indorse and recommend you to the rest of mankind. God bless the Oneida brotherhood and sisterhood; may you prosper in the spirit and grow in grace. Farewell.

Yours truly, JOHN W. HUTCHINSON.

N. B. I wish you could establish a family here on the Neosho valley, the finest in Kansas. The land is very rich, plenty of good timber, good water and good people in this part of the State. Land may be bought for $2.00 per acre, worth with you, $500. All kinds of fruit may be grown here. Apples five years from the seed, peaches three. There are plenty of coal-beds, and black walnut for timber. J. W. H.

Clinton, Penn., Nov. 31, 1867.

J. H. NOYES, DEAR FRIEND:—I have been reading the CIRCULAR more or less during the last two or three months, and feel very much interested in the truths there set forth, especially so in the Home-Talks by yourself. I have come to feel that you have *the truth*, and the truth being what I do above all things else desire, I feel like getting better acquainted with you. I think the O. C. is living the truth, and I think likewise that I belong with you; I wish therefore to come and see, and if I find that you have the truth, and together we find that I am fit to be one of you, then I will gladly join. I wish to know if you can give me employment on my arrival with you? I am a man twenty-five years of age, have had a little experience at a great many kinds of work, but my main business has been farming. My father is quite wealthy but I have not the least idea that he will give me any money (though a kind old man), to go to the O. C. with, he can't see it yet, poor man! I leave quite a good home and kind friends, but I do feel that *the truth* is worth more than houses, or lands, or friends, or aught else; that the love of God is all that is worth seeking for, and I am willing to be an outcast if it must be so. * * * B. V. EATON.

W. P., Dec. 6.—The talks, "The Love of Money" and "A New Era in Love," were read this evening, and heartily sympathized with by all. Then G. W. H. gave an account of his trip to Utica and Watertown, in search of a good machine blacksmith to take the place of Mr. Pritchard, who has been discharged for drunkenness. He has worked for us some time, and is an excellent workman, but has been in the habit of going off on a spree, and though agreeing to come back the next day, would be gone three or four days. About a year ago G. W. H. told him if he knew of his doing so again we should discharge him. Last Saturday he went off, taking with him Mr. Ellis, the best workman in the Trap-shop. Monday they came back, and saying they did not feel able to work, they went to the cider-mill. Myron went to their boarding house and found them beastly drunk. Mr. Pritchard said he was not *half* over his spree and that Mr. Ellis should not come back to the shop again. Myron told him to come the next morning or we should discharge him; he did so and seemed sorry for what he had done. Mr. P. took his things and left. Mr. Glidden, one of our machinists, said his respect for us was increased by the course we had taken in the affair.

It has been a statute of the State of Maine, that a citizen of that state who should erect by the road-side a watering-trough, and keep the same supplied with running water, should have an annual allowance in his taxes of three dollars. Well, this is so good an idea, that I wish the same, or something similar, could be enacted by our State, or established by the several towns. Three dollars a year, might be an inducement to, and perhaps a compensation for the work, while the good realized to the public, would be immeasurable.—The inference is, that the State of Maine which has taken the lead in temperance, sought also to provide a cheap and sufficient substitute, and I am sure it would be highly beneficial.

A PATHMASTER.

The class in Chemistry is now well under way, and the study promises to be very interesting. It has somewhat taxed the ingenuity of our teacher, to obtain material for properly illustrating the subject under consideration. Thursday night's express-bag from N. Y., brought a retort, glass bottles and vessels of different sorts, which to *our* eyes look quite imposing. D. E. S.

THE O. C. DAILY.

VOL. 4.   MONDAY, DEC. 9, 1867.   NO. 137.

BUSINESS MEETING.

We have been in the habit of sending our canal freight to Mr. Bennett at Durhamville, who ships it when he gets an opportunity. It is thought however, that freight lies in his storehouse before it is sent much longer than is necessary, and J. H. Barron proposed that we take it hereafter to Clark & Harvey's, only a few rods further. They are reported to be more thorough business men, and as there are two in the firm, one or the other will generally be on hand to catch opportunities to ship goods. This proposition was indorsed by the Board, and Mr. Hawley will instruct the teamster accordingly. As Mr Bennett's storehouse is somewhat nearer than that of the other firm we will continue to *receive* goods through him, so that he will not probably have occasion to feel slighted.

Black Creek, Wilson Co. N. C., Nov. 30, 1867.

Mr. W. H. Woolworth, DEAR FRIEND:—What can I do to repent of my sins and be saved? My heart is so hard, it seems impossible. I try to do better and cannot; I have no religious friends to talk with, not one. Oh that I could be with some of the O. C., that they might advise me what to do. It seems as if I cannot appreciate God's kindness; in fact I sometimes think I am an infidel, and at others, that I am insane. I have been tempted to commit suicide. I used to believe in Universalism, and I fear I am not cured of it yet. I received the Tract which you sent me, but I can't repent, I wish I could. I fear there is no hope for one who has done as bad as me; if I could think there was any hope, I think I could do better. What shall I do? please tell me, and oblige your obedient servant,

H. D. LUCAS.

Mr. North writes to Mr. Bolles from Freeport, Ill., Dec. 4th.—"I would suggest that, to Mr. Guiteau and myself, a somewhat detailed account of the outside pressure, the church at Oneida, has been laboring and suffering under for several months past, would be of special interest just now. I think we can say that we desire the fellowship of your sufferings, and count it honor to suffer with you for Christ's sake. If you feel free to communicate to me as per the foregoing request, it will not gratify an idle curiosity, but operate for our edification, and to give tone to the fellowship of suffering. Mr. Guiteau wishes to say that he sympathizes with the sentiments of this letter, and with O. C. in the special suffering experience they are now having, and hopes for the working out of salvation as the result."

Julia Hyde writes, "I am better in some respects, do not suffer quite as much all the time, around my heart, but I am weak. I am quite patient and happy most of the time, although there are times when everything looks dark and dreary. But I will stick to my confession of Christ as my only hope, as the Savior of my soul. I thank God for his mercies to me, which are many, and I wish to offer myself anew, body and soul, to Jesus Christ. I am astonished sometimes, at the evidence I have, of God's care over me. Why was I, more than others, made to listen to his voice."

Mr. D. P. Nash received a benefit last night in the shape of a criticism from a committee. He was commended for his former usefulness in the Community, and for the improvement he has made in certain directions during the past six weeks. A general desire was manifested to hold up his hands and strengthen his faith. It was thought that God had called him to a new field of labor, and that he could aid Mr. Noyes and benefit himself more, by setting his face firmly toward the work of becoming patient; of holding still in the position in which God has allowed him to be placed, and thus gain the spirit of fortitude and meekness only attainable by bearing the cross. Mr. Nash seemed very thankful for the criticism.   D. E. S.

Through the kindness of the family several of the new members are to have the benefit of a few lessons in dancing. Special thanks are due to Mrs. S. B. C. for engineering the matter, to Mr. Clark for volunteering to teach; and to Charles Van for offering to play. The school meets in the ironing-room Sundays at four P. M., and Wednesday evenings from six to seven.   D. E. S.

Yesterday forenoon the weather was very boisterous and stormy, but in the afternoon the wind subsided and the snow fell very fast, and is now of sufficient depth, we should judge, to make good sleighing. At seven o'clock this morning, the mercury stood at four deg. below zero.

Night before last the weather being very boisterous, one of our men asked, why it was like a person using a pocket-handkerchief?

Because it blows, it snows. [its nose.]

A Mr. More from Hygeania staid here over Sunday; also H. W. Burnham.

A report of Mr. Inslee's criticism given last night, will be published to-morrow.

Traps ordered Saturday and Sunday,   39 doz.

THE O. C. DAILY.

VOL. 4.　　TUESDAY, DEC. 10, 1867.　　NO. 138.

SUNDAY EVENING MEETING.

Mr. Inslee had asked for help, and the meeting was devoted to a thorough investigation of his state, and its causes. The younger business men at Willow-Place, are anxious to introduce some new business that will give steady employment to the hands, and take full advantage of our water power. Mr. Cragin, and others thought God would give us business enough, as soon as there were the proper spiritual conditions ; viz., a thorough organization among such men as Mr. Inslee, Mr. Newhouse and George Hamilton. Mr. Inslee's faults were set before him in a kind, but sincere manner. He dislikes responsibility, and has put the foremanship of the Machine-shop, mainly on to John Sears, so that young men working there, hardly know who is foreman. It was generally testified that he had never been head of his family ; that his wife, with all her legality, ruled him ; that he was subject to fits of condemnation for having left her as he did ; that he had never had control of his children, and consequently had not brought them to Christ ; that he had never thoroughly judged his connection with Charles Weld and A. C. Smith ; that he had a great deal of respect for worldly religion ; never had studied Christ's character only in a one-sided way, regarding him as the Lamb of God, perfectly yielding and docile to his Father, but quite overlooking his character as the Lion of the Tribe of Judah. It was thought there was some of the lion in Mr. Inslee, if he could only be aroused ; but the spirit he is under makes him torpid, spiritually lazy and inclined to say, Good Lord, good devil, or that all is good. There seems to be a subtile spirit of Universalism over him. When he first commenced on the silk-machinery, he acted like an entirely new man, and seemed full of Mr. Noyes's inspiration. It was hoped he would now take hold and clear himself of this vascillating state, and be a strong man in the cause, and not have to be pushed on by others. He must take hold and strike for himself, and be willing to strike a pretty hard blow too, if he would be free. He once knocked a man down ; and it was hoped he would now come up to the scratch, and do the same thing for this principality that has so long abused him, and hindered the work of truth and righteousness.

Hamilton, Dec. 8, 1867.

Mr. Woolworth, Dear Sir :—Hon. Henry M. Rice Ex-U. S. Senator from Minnesota, a younger brother of mine, is expected to be at my house next Christmas day. He is agent for the Minnesota, and other north-western tribes of Indians. If you will send a few sizes of your traps such as are used by those living in that country, I will give them to him to take home with him. It might be the means of a call for more of them. Also if you will send me a few ounces of the varieties of your sewing-silk, I will do the same with it. The Indians (the friendly), use much silk in the manufacture of their fancy articles, stringing beads &c. And for myself, if you will be so good as to send me one of your traveling bags, such an one as Mr. Noyes showed me when he was at my house, I will send to you the price on receiving it. Some two years since Mr. E. H. Hamilton of your folks sent me an invitation to attend with my family a concert to be given by the Community. I was not able to attend then. Are you to have one or more the present winter ? and could I consider Mr. Hamilton's invitation a standing one ? If so, I should take great pleasure to visit your family, with my wife and five daughters. I observe that "After You" has given up the chase ; been better not to have undertaken it. He has gained nothing, nor harmed the Community.

With great respect I am yours truly,

CARLTON RICE.

W. P., Dec. 9.—John Freeman has gone from the Machine-shop into the Silk-factory as assistant, and also with a view to learning the details of the business, and rendering himself competent to become foreman.—Mr. Williams has returned to his work. Our folks have paid him his wages for the time he was away.—As Victor Hawley was engaged to-day in repairing the walter belt, the string with which he was sewing it together, gave way and as he was drawing toward him at the time, the belt awl struck him just below the left eye, going in half way to the bone. A narrow escape and should be a warning to those having occasion to use awls, to draw away from, instead of toward them.

Mr. Sears was criticised last night at his request. Much was said of him that was commendatory of his course in the Community, his faithfulness in business &c., yet as a spiritual man he had failed to commend himself. An influence seemed to overshadow him, the same as Mr. Inslee, that shut out his true character from view. He was exhorted to search into the past, and see if he could not discover the cause of his difficulties, and strike a blow that would bring him deliverance.

A new member was added to the family yesterday, a little girl baby. It was welcomed as all such gifts are, and together with its mother is doing well. The baby weighs seven pounds and six ounces.

Traps ordered yesterday,　　　　46¼ doz.

THE O. C. DAILY.

VOL. 4. WEDNESDAY, DEC. 11, 1867. NO. 139.

A Mr. Solomon Haworth of Lewis Co. Mo., writes us a long letter, making inquiries about the prospect of his hiring a tenant house of us next March, and getting work in some of our shops, so that he can support his family, while they should become personally acquainted with us, and we with them. He says in conclusion:

" The truth is, I feel that I desire to enter into your school with my whole heart, believing as I do that you are earnest workers in the cause of truth and righteousness in the earth; and I would much prefer laboring for you than for men of the world who do not consecrate their all to God. "

A letter received yesterday from Mr. Haworth's wife, is so good, that we give it entire.

Lake Side, Wayne Co., N. Y. Dec. 4, 1867.

DEAR O. C. :—I wonder if you have forgotten me ? Be assured I have not forgotten you; you have been in my thoughts more than anything else for more than seven months, and you have grown very, very dear to me. I have wanted to tell you so before but hardly dared to, but I can withhold the confession no longer, nor do I believe it would be right for me to. **I was much interested in your principles before I com**menced reading your paper with my husband last summer in Missouri. I learned many new things from the CIRCULAR, but I have not commenced yet to learn all that I feel that you are able to teach. In your principles I find an antidote for all the evils that now inflict society, and I dare hope for the time when Communism shall cover the land as the waters cover the sea.

I am now visiting my relatives in this part of the country. I came from Missouri the latter part of Oct. with my two babies alone. My husband is teaching school in Missouri this winter. I believe I shall never leave this State again without going to see you, and I might as well say it I suppose, I believe I should never, never want to leave you. I have asked myself the question often lately, can I ever, ever endure to go off alone and humdrum along through life as almost everybody else does? Sometimes my heart sinks at the thought that perhaps I may have to do so. Then I pray for my children's sake and for my own, that I may not have to do a thing that seems so dark and dreadful to me. My faith grows stronger and stronger that I shall yet enter Christ's kingdom here upon this earth, and that I and my babes shall by that means be saved from the sins that glitter and glare in the broad way that the world seems pursuing with such headlong speed.

I have not seen the CIRCULAR except the old numbers that I brought with me, since I left Missouri. I shall feel more at home when I can again resume the reading of it on my return to Marengo, where my mother resides and where my husband directed it to be sent. With much faith and love I am sincerely your friend, SARAH E. M. HAWORTH.

W. P., Dec 9.—Just as meeting was out to-night we were suddenly startled by a noise as if all the Trap-shop machinery, drop, toms and all had suddenly started in our cellar. What *is* it? thought we. On going down there we saw C. C. H., his brother and Mr. Ackley, with the tenor and bass drums and a tin pan. What is this *for* said we? Then we learned that notwithstanding the many patent mouse-traps " Newhouse's superior steel" among the rest, that it was found necessary to resort to this unearthly din, in hopes to drive the rats and mice away. Possibly it may have the effect to drum up more recruits.

We heard a person express himself yesterday, as being thankful for bare salvation; said he had no aspiration for place or distinction, yet he had a desire that God would make the most of him for his own service.

Mr. Easton entertained us last night, with a history of his connection with the Young Men's Christian Association in New York, and its languishing condition at the time of his joining.

Traps ordered yesterday, **26 doz.**

THE O. C. DAILY.

VOL. 4.   THURSDAY, DEC. 12, 1867.   NO. 140.

B. H. C.—Our family, all told, numbers thirty-one souls, six of whom are Communists, one a probationist, one a hired helper and twenty-three are boarders. Of the latter, sixteen are women and girls, and the remaining seven are men. Two evenings since, Mr. Bradley opened a school from seven to eight for the sterner sex. In the course of the week, Mrs. Thayer will do the same for the young women, or as many of them as choose to attend.

The opening of a free school for the benefit of our employes, is highly appreciated by most of them, and in due time, I opine, when Communism is better understood, the opening of a free church, or free religious meetings in our boarding-houses, will be still more appreciated by all who have honest, religious proclivities. Indeed, wherever there is a Community family, if it consists of only two, there will be found a school, a church and a theatre, or the spirit of them, if not the form; and a home is not a home without them. Communism virtually implies the confession and presence of an indwelling Christ, as an all-sufficient savior from sin, ignorance and selfishness, with free criticism added. As it is, in isolated families in the world, the members of them must go to somebody's church to buy their religion, just as they go to a store to buy their groceries, to some academy to buy their education, and to some theatre to buy their amusements. All very expensive methods of supplying one's legitimate needs, to say nothing of the liabilities of being terribly cheated and imposed upon. But Communism is not a trafficker in human affections, nor in any of God's generous gifts to man, but an authorized distributer of them, according to actual, meritorious deeds. If men do not study Communism, therefore, as God's way of keeping house and raising up a family, so much the worse for them. But selfish men say they can't see it; no more can the devil.   c.

Mr. and Mrs. Smith received an invitation from Mrs. S.'s father to come home to Christmas, and attend the wedding of one of Mrs. S.'s sisters, and the following is her reply:

DEAR FATHER:—We received your kind invitation to visit you on the 24 inst., to-day. But I fear it is but a trap of the devil to draw my attention from spiritual matters. For some time past I have been examining the great question, "what must I do to be saved." To be one with Christ requires the spirit that recognizes no relations outside of Christ's people. He said he would not own his own mother unless she did his Father's will. I confess Christ in me a Saviour from all sin. I have much to do to rid myself of my old life, and cannot at this time think it best to put myself under influences which tend to divert my attention. I still love you all, but I love Christ more, and pray that you may yet be one with me. I shall be glad to hear from you all at any time. I have been in a sinful unbelieving state long enough, and am going to try and become one of Christ's children. If I should come there now, I think it would be a detriment to me; therefore I think it best not to come.

Your loving daughter,   FRANCES.

Mr. Thayer on his late tour to Mass., was presented with two large, beautiful pictures, by his brother-in-law, Mr. Spooner, who is an artist. One is a large photograph of the late President Lincoln. This picture is a valuable acqusition and now graces the vestibule of our Hall. The other represents the Soldier's Fair held in Springfield, Mass., Dec. 22, 1864, and hangs in the upper sitting-room. Pictures of persons who attended the fair are said to be taken separately and afterwards arranged; a difficult piece of workmanship we should think. Among the most conspicuous personages are Gov. Andrews and his staff. This picture excels in detail and minuteness anything of the kind we have seen, and highly commends the taste and skill of the artist.

Many thanks are due to Mr. Reynolds who volunteered to frame these pictures, which is nicely done, the frames being of black walnut with a gilt edge.

R. G. H.

Mr. Hamilton's letter to Mr. Woolworth, in reference to hiring a store in New-York, was read last night, after which, Mr. W. called for some expression on the subject from the family. It seemed to be the unanimous feeling that the brethren in N. Y. should be left free to follow their own instincts in the matter; that they in their position, were best qualified to judge of their wants, &c.

The Dunn Cottage was found to be too uncomfortably cold, particularly for the feet, and the young men's school was moved yesterday, and is now held in the attic of the Tontine, in the room occupied by O. H. Miller.

After Mrs. Smith's letter was read last night, Mr. Woolworth remarked that he was thankful that natural claims were being subordinated to God's claims in this world.

At half past seven o'clock this morning the mercury stood at five deg. below zero.

Mr. Easton left in the night for New-York.

Traps ordered yesterday,   200 doz.

THE O. C. DAILY.

VOL. 4.   FRIDAY, DEC. 13, 1867.   NO. 141.

A Mrs. Pease, from Lebanon Center, Mass., came here yesterday, the same lady whose letter is mentioned in the *Daily* of Nov. 22d. Her father is a Methodist minister and lives in Canaan of the same State. Mrs. P. has been stopping for six weeks past with a Mr. Crocker a leader of Spiritualism and a free-lover. Mr. C. is living with his affinity, having discarded his wife and child, and left them without the means of support. Mrs. Pease it seems has been for some time unsettled in her mind and anxiously seeking for truth, and she went to Mr. Crocker's for the purpose of investigating the mysteries of Spiritualism and to cast in her lot with them if she was convinced they were the true people. Mr. C. found her a dull scholar, told her she was not sufficiently developed to fathom its mysteries, but urged her to join immediately—to sign their documents, in proof of her sincerity. Mr. C. is gathering his forces for a Community, and is going South to establish one as soon as everything is arranged to his mind. He once called at O. C. with his wife, and Mrs. P. tried to draw out some information about the Community from him, and wanted to come here and see for herself, but he objected; but as she was irresistibly drawn in this direction, and on Mr. C. leaving home for New-York she started for Oneida.

She thinks by coming here the snare that was being thrown around her is effectually broken. She said she was convinced that we have the truth for which she has so long been seeking, and she should not rest till she had examined our system thoroughly. She started for home this morning, having taken with her the Hand-Book and Salvation from Sin, and will send for the CIRCULAR as soon as she gets employment or finds a home.—The following letter is from Mrs. C. No. 1, who was at New Lebanon at the time of Mrs. P's leaving.

New Lebanon Center, Dec. 9, 1867.

MR. NOYES.—As I have visited your "Divine" Community and realized a force of equity and truth flowing therefrom, I take the liberty to open a correspondence with you, trusting it will find access to you, and I also may receive a response to it. I have a friend by the name of Mrs. Rachel E. Pease, residing in this family, who is truly desirous of investigating the way to true happiness, and she seems to turn her mind and feelings in this direction. Can you see it proper in your judgment, to confer with us upon this special matter? If so, I can assure you it would afford much consolation to me and my friend.

My address is No. 103, Elm St., Newark, N. J.

Very truly yours, MARY E. CROCKER.

P. S. Mrs. R. E. Pease has concluded to go herself,

therefore, that you will welcome her to you kindly, and receive her as one among you, is my sincere prayer.   Yours again, M. A. C.

Lyons, Dec. 9, 1867.

MR. L. VAN VELZER:—I am happy to hear that I have been able to respond to one of your many kindnesses to me by assisting that young man. I do not consider it worth mentioning so small an amount as seventy-five cents, but inasmuch as you have taken notice of it sufficient to forward the small amount, which I might never have thought of again, I certainly can't help but acknowledge the receipt of the same. [When Victor was at Syracuse just before he left for W. C., he met Mr. Cady, who kindly gave him the money referred to.] I heard the boy say he was going home but was out of means, and the respect I have for your Institution as well as the kind treatment I have received from some of its members and more especially from yourself (for I shall ever bear witness to your many kindnesses to me in former years), prompted me to ever be mindful of you and yours; hence my relieving that young man, if you might call it relief. I asked him if he wanted any more money, he said No. I thought if a man had all the money he wanted he was all right. Ever bearing your hospitality in remembrance, I remain yours &c.,   E. H. CADY.

P. S. If at any time I could afford you or your people aid I would most cheerfully. ....

One of our young women being anxious to disprove the assertion of one of the men, " that more women occupied beds alone than the men," has taken pains to collect the following facts :

No. of double beds,	45.
No. of single "	87.
No. of Gentleman's double beds,	9.
No. of Ladie's " "	27.
No. of Gentleman's single "	48.
No. of Ladie's " "	39.
Whole No. of beds including trundle-beds,	140.

Our large uncut wood-pile is fast melting away before the sharp teeth of the circular saw, driven by steam-power, which we think is a great improvement on horse-power for such work. On inquiring of Mike, who is one of the sawyers, how he liked the power, he answered, " O! he ish a steady hoss," meaning that the power did not fag.   H. T.

At seven o'clock this morning the thermometer stood at fourteen deg. below zero.

THE O. C. DAILY.

VOL. 4.   SATURDAY, DEC. 14, 1867.   NO. 142.

A DIALOGUE.

A.—Counterfeiting is bad business, very bad, and I am very sorry B. to see that you are engaged in it.

B.—What do you mean, A.?

A.—I mean just what I say, that you and C. are coining spurious money, and passing it for genuine, among the ignorant. Don't you understand?

B.—Well, I suppose you mean that I am involved in false love.

A.—Yes, I do. False love, is counterfeit love, and to coin it and pass it off for true, genuine love, is worse than stealing. Heaven alone issues the genuine greenbacks and they are very different bills from those that you are issuing I can assure you. The paper on which your bills are printed is very coarse and the engraving is poorly executed indeed. Besides, they do not read like the genuine. On the genuine you will find in the center, in letters of gold, the words "Ascending fellowship." In your counterfeit you have substituted "Horizontal fellowship," for ascending. Moreover you are continually tormented with the spirit of fear; fear that somebody will examine your counterfeit currency in the light. And what is still worse, you are laboring hard, most of your time, in trying to persuade yourself that it is no worse for *you* to pass spurious love than it is for D. You say that D. is passing it freely among the *noritiates*, and you don't see why you have not just as good a right as he to do the same. You have just the same right as D. which is no right at all. Falsehoods have no rights whatever, and what is false love, but falsehoods? Love is the food of the soul, so when you eat false love, you are cheating your own soul—starving it on sugar-plums—giving it the dyspepsia. Now B. you had better abandon at once, this way of life, and begin to do business like an honest man. Turn states evidence and expose all your associates in counterfeiting the true love of God. Heaven's police is after these gangs of counterfeiters, and they cannot long elude the light of day.   DETECTIVE.

We had quite an interesting meeting last night, in which the spirit of brotherly love prevailed. Mr. Kinsley and others expressed their sympathy with Mr. Noyes's appointment of George E., as successor of Mr. Woolworth in the oversight of the family, and their desire and willingness to sustain the second generation in responsible positions.

Mrs. Maria Kinsley said she wished to separate herself from her father's spirit; she had done it in private, and tried to help herself in that way, but she now wished to do it more publicly. Her father was an irreligious man, and had a cough similar to hers, and she might have inherited his infirmities, but that was no reason why she should not hope to overcome them. Many expressed their sympathy for Mrs. K. and a hope that she might get a victory over the spirit that oppressed her.

A No. of the *Optimist*, a paper published at Berlin Heights, and which we should call *blue* literature, was sent us yesterday by J. W. Towner. It contains a reply to one of Mr. Towner's articles published in the CIRCULAR, and is an attempt to prove that Mr. T. was a downright hypocrite when he was a member of the Berlin fraternity. Mr. Towner writes that if that is the case, he thinks the O. C. ought to know it. The paper also contains some of the mystical sayings of a Miss Brown, a seeress, or medium we should judge, respecting the state of the Oneida Community, but as the paper is not to be found this morning, we will not attempt to speak of it further.

A letter received from Mr. Reeve a few days since, states that he is selling out and disposing of his property in Berlin, and thinks he shall be ready to move away by the first of March. He don't mention that he has any place in view, but he is anxious to quit Berlin at any cost. I suppose he would be right glad to cast in his lot with us.

Mr. Nash says he has sat up all night, or nearly so, for two nights past, to keep a fire in the Green-house, to protect the plants from freezing. A fire has also been kept up nights in the fruit-house.

Yesterday at four o'clock P. M. the mercury stood at six deg. below zero; at a quarter to ten, at twelve, and this morning at seven o'clock it had sunk to twenty deg. below zero.

Traps ordered Thursday and Friday,   55 doz.

THE O. C. DAILY.

VOL. 4.   MONDAY, DEC. 16, 1867.   NO. 143.

BUSINESS MEETING.

It was proposed to have a light door with a window in it at the foot of the stairs in the arch-way. As it is now, nothing can be set in there without freezing, so that we are to a great extent deprived of the use of it. A light door that can be easily closed will keep the whole building warmer. Messrs. J. H. Barron, Kelly and Whitney were appointed committee to determine the shape, double or single, and see that it is put in.

As the ice is getting to be thick enough for cutting, it was proposed that we take hold of the job and do it up about next Tuesday. Messrs. Kinsley, Burt and F. Marks committee to make the necessary preparations.

There has been some difficulty in keeping the reception-room warm enough to be comfortable to visitors. They should have some place to go to, and if we cannot warm it with the furnace we must put up a stove there. Messrs. G. E. Cragin, Clark and Woolworth, committee to attend to it.

Messrs. Inslee, John Sears and G. W. Hamilton were appointed to ascertain the cost of making iron rollers for the mangle to take the place of the wooden ones they now have. The repair of the revolving wringer is referred to the machinists and wash-room folks.

G. E. Cragin said he had been looking over the books and found that our payments for hired labor between the present time and the first of last January amount to $36,000, and before the end of the year they will probably reach $40,000. We are not so nearly out of debt now as we were a year ago. The time of the men has not been kept as carefully and accurately as it should have been, and the books must determine how much we invest in the different departments. Mr. Kinsley and Carrie have been appointed to cut down the help, but Carrie has too much to do just now to attend to it. We should have a committee large enough to look into every department, and see how little hired help we can get along with. Accordingly Messrs. G. E. Cragin, Campbell, Miss Nun and Mrs. Van Velzer were added to that committee. George E. wished every one to study the matter and see how much we can reduce our expenses this winter. We want to keep constantly before us the fact that we have vowed to get out of debt, and keep out.

ADVANTAGES OF CONCENTRATION.

An army that has weakened its center by throwing out widely extended outposts, might be said to be in bad position, and liable, before it could concentrate its forces, to be attacked and overthrown by the superior force of an enemy. Oneida, as a center, might be said to be placed in similar circumstances, financially. The disadvantages under which she labors, in the support of her outposts, is perhaps weakening her financial power and making her liable to disaster and ruin. But put a stop to the unavoidable expenses of men and means, in the support of distant colonies, by concentration and the employment of the forces in productive labor, and the scale would soon be turned, and the result would be accumulation and power. God undoubtedly, had an important object in view, in establishing these outposts, and when his ends are accomplished, he will perhaps order a retreat, and conduct the forces back in safety. CONCENTRATIONIST.

Friday evening after the talk of Mr. Noyes on Mr. Worden's case was read, a general criticism of him followed. Last night Mr. W. handed in a note, which after being read, Mr. Burt, Mr. Abbott and some others followed up the criticism given the night before. Mr. W. was exhorted to take hold of the job given him by Mr. Noyes, and judge the Manlius principality and not shrink because he had been connected with it. The following is the note referred to:

I wish to separate myself in any way I can, from the evils and errors of my past experience, whether as a New-York Perfectionist, or as a Communist, and presuming that several may be present to-night who were not when the criticism came up, I wish them to be free in the expression of their thoughts at this time.   M. L. WORDEN.

Mr. C. W. Underwood had a sincere, searching criticism Saturday evening which was continued last night. He has been in a very unsatisfactory state all through the Summer and Fall, and his treatment of Harriet Sibley has been very ungentlemanly and cruel from first to last. His influence also on the young girls and women generally, has been very far from satisfactory.

The skating-pond about which the Bag-shop hands were so enthusiastic, is likely to prove an entire failure. After filling it with water a fine sheet of ice was formed over it, but before long it was found that its "bottom had fallen out," or the water had leaked through and rendered it useless.

The original Ayrshire heifer has been quite prolific, and through her a number of fine bloods have been added to our stock. On the third instant, she brought her fifth heifer calf in annual succession, which is true to the breed, and looks well.

G. W. and T. R. Noyes have just arrived.

THE O. C. DAILY.

VOL. 4. TUESDAY, DEC. 17, 1867. NO. 144.

EVENING MEETING.

George E.—I went down to Oneida this morning, to see if the editor of the *Democratic Union* would publish a small document, or squib, written by Mr. George W. Noyes. No name was signed; but it purported to be from one of the inhabitants of this neighborhood, and went on to say that Mr. Freeman's charge that we did not give anything to the poor, was true; that though we paid all our lawful taxes, we did not contribute anything to the support of the poor-house, penitentiary, &c. I thought I would see Dr. Carpenter first, and learn what he thought of it. He looked at it and said he did not know whether the editor would publish it or not, but he would take it right over and ask him, and make it a special request. He took it out and I waited till he returned. The editor glanced at it, and said he would look it over carefully afterward and decide. He thought he would publish it, but said if he did he should put in a note, saying it was the very last he would publish on either side; that he was heartily sick of the whole thing; that he had been dreading a long letter from Carlton Rice—who was a regular buster at writing when he got going—in reply to the article against him in his paper, but that it had not yet come.

Then he said the *New York World* had come out strong in favor of the O. C., and it was of no use for him to keep on the other side, and he was going to give it up. Dr. Carpenter said that one of the editors of the *World* was a personal friend of his, and was at Oneida recently, when he brought him up here, but did not introduce him, as he wished to remain unknown. He seemed to think quite a favorable impression was produced on the editor, though his call was brief. He probably questioned Dr. Carpenter a good deal. I got the impression from the Dr. that Mr. Baker, the editor of the *Democratic Union*, had flatted out on the question of the moral war, and was sick of the whole thing and going to retreat.

Mr. Woolworth.—This back-down of the *Democratic Union* seems to be the signal for us to advance. [Applause.]

Lisbon, Ill., Dec. 10, 1867.

J. H. NOYES, DEAR SIR:—I have read the Hand Book of the Community, and the CIRCULAR for the past two years, and think I understand the object and aim of the Community, so I write to you for advice about joining. I am a young man eighteen years of age, by profession a farmer and mechanic. I have never joined any church because I never found any whose creed I could subscribe to, till I came across the creed of the Community, which I think I fully understand and believe. My parents belong to the Congregational church, but would have no objection to my joining the Community. I think that Communism shows the only true way for people to be happy in this world. I have counted the cost and I wish to join the Community or serve it in some way or other; but I wish advice of you as to what I had better do in my situation; I think you know what would be best in my case. Do you think there will be any new Communities formed very soon?

Yours truly, G. B. CLARK.

We have received a letter from Mrs. E. Chynoweth dated Madison, Dec. 11th, written in a good spirit and in a style of simplicity which always characterizes her communications. She says:

"I often ask myself if I should be willing to leave my family to live in the Community and when I think not, I fall into condemnation and think I never shall be what I ought to be. I have many attractions in the world, a kind husband, good children and a pleasant home; but I try to keep in mind that my relation to them is not permanent. I accept them and am thankful for them as the gifts of God, and pray that they may not draw my heart away from him. Outside of my family I have few friends because I am so much at home. I think I am somewhat of a *slave* to my family; I don't speak to complain, for I follow my inclinations. I sometimes think if I was not so necessary to them they might not be so willing that I should enjoy my own way of thinking. Mother made me a visit of a few weeks last Fall and I can remember it with thankfulness for I do not think I was once irritable to her. I tell you all these little things because they come into my mind and I want some one to tell *little things* to. My children all attend school yet, except Fred; he is in the news depot connected with the P. O.; he does not care as much for books as the others do. The three oldest will graduate next June."

The W. P. family were all over again to the meeting last night. The thought of the drawing together of our scattered family, and the concentration of our forces at Oneida, though in the future, makes all eyes glisten and all hearts beat quicker. The visit also, of our Wallingford brethren, brings strength and comfort, and their assistance at this time will be much appreciated. Surely "our cup runneth over."

To-day we commence getting ice. The young men's school is suspended during the time, and all hands that can be spared from the shops, are called into the service. The weather is moderate, and the sleighing is passable.

The women had a bee yesterday forenoon, in the upper sitting-room at the Brick-house, to make mittens for the men to use in handling ice. They made twenty-three pairs.

THE O. C. DAILY.

VOL. 4. WEDNESDAY, DEC. 18, 1867. NO. 145.

EVENING MEETING.

After the reading of the talks from Wallingford, the following remarks were made:

T. R. Noyes.—I want to be perfectly free to move in the direction of spiritual vision. I don't want anything to stand in the way of it.

G. W. Noyes.—It seems to me this is the lesson we are invited to at the present time. I don't know as I can add anything by way of elucidating it, but I feel my heart drawn in this direction, and I think this is the door of happiness and salvation for us. I don't see it in any other direction, and I don't want to see it in any other direction. I know that I shall have all due outward happiness in following upon that search.

Mr. Woolworth.—I believe this microscopic vision will open a new world of beauty, happiness and refinement. It is a kind of vision that discloses God to us.

W. P., Dec. 17.—It should have been reported that we commenced the eight hour system in the Trap and Machine-shops Saturday. About eight o'clock that morning it was discovered that the water was low in the pond, so low indeed, that at ten the works were stopped all around. At one place in the dyke there was found to be only fourteen inches of water below the ice. To-day however, the busy hum of machinery gives notice that there is plenty of water again. Knowing ones say there is certainly going to be a thaw ere many days.—The annual campaign for getting ice commenced yesterday.—As we have not been favored with the fine snow-storms our Wallingford sister speaks of, several teams were engaged yesterday in drawing snow on to the road in various places between us and O. C. for the easier passage of the ice teams to-day. As we were riding home last night some one suggested that we were going for the purpose of breaking the road, a laughable idea, considering the very slight amount of snow to be seen.

Dec. 18.—Some of the worthy members of our family, created quite a sensation on coming to breakfast this morning, by declaring that there had been an earthquake; that about ten minutes after three o'clock they were awakened by a jarring of their beds, and a stand which stood unevenly in the room of one of them, was heard to rattle very decidedly. Does Oneida know anything of it we wonder?

The *Daily Press*, a paper published at St. Paul, gives the following notice:

"*The Trapper's Guide*, by S. Newhouse, and other trappers and sportsmen. A Book for the Trapper, the Hunter, and the Farmer; thirty-two full page illustrations and numerous wood-cuts. Published by the Oneida Community, Oneida, N. Y.

Apropos to the trapping season comes the above useful and charming volume,—just the desideratum for all hunters, lovers of wood-craft, excursionists and boys. It tells how to trap all fur-bearing animals and cure their skins, how to live in the woods—to build boats and fish in the winter—how to destroy the pests of the farm and how to hunt deer, buffalo and other game, and tells where the best traps are made.—It also gives narratives of the exploits and experiences of trappers and sportsmen; all told in the most charming manner.

The book is an exquisite volume, clearly printed on good paper, and very finely illustrated with representations of animals of all kinds, &c.

It is just the thing so much desired. For further information, see advertisement in another column."

From the *Daily Pioneer* published at St. Paul:

"THE TRAPPER'S GUIDE.—This book contains much valuable information for trappers. It tells how to trap all kinds of fur-bearing animals; how to cure their skins; how to live in the woods; how to build boats, and fish in winter; how to destroy the pests of the farm and poultry yards; how to hunt deer, buffalo and other game. It tells where the best traps are made, and abounds in narrations of the exploits and experience of trappers and sportsmen, old and young. It is just the book for lovers of wood-craft. Price, bound in cloth, $1. For sale by Combs & Whitney."

Some of our classes have been suspended till after Christmas. Taking the inventory, preparing for concert and getting ice, pretty much breaks us all up. Well, we had started off on a straight line for the winter, and these interruptions may serve to make us more flexible and shape our course more in a curvilinear line, which is said to be the line of beauty. We want to be where God can use us, at a moment's warning, for such purposes as he may choose.

G. W. N. entertained us last night, by giving a description of the English railroad cars, in what respects they differ from the American. He spoke likewise of the habits of the people, thought in neatness, they compared favorably with the French and German population, and also with the American; more particularly in the use of tobacco.

Some of the family were aroused from their slumbers and considerably frightened last night at about three o'clock, by what appeared to be an earthquake. The house was sensibly shaken, stoves rattled and there were two very distinct shocks.

J. J. Skinner and T. C. Miller arrived safely in the night.—We have just heard (11 o'clock), that H. W. B., Frank and Alice had also arrived.

THE O. C. DAILY.

VOL. 4.   THURSDAY, DEC. 19, 1867.   NO. 146.

EVENING MEETING.

G. W. Noyes.—I feel that this is an interesting concentration of our people just at present. It amounts to a sort of convention, and reminds me of what Mr. Burnham said in conversation with me a little while ago, that it seems to be somewhat like the concentration we had at Wallingford last year, which was very pleasant and profitable. I think it is a good time for us to cultivate a good spirit, as has been suggested in this report read to-night. It seems to me that we are invited to look to God for a good result from this concentration, and expect that he will make it an occasion of blessing us with a good spirit, and of giving the good spirit the start in the Community.

Mr. Burnham.—The thought in my mind arose from a little conversation we had with Mr. Hamilton just before leaving. He expressed the hope that we would come here as the mediums of a good spirit. I felt his words sink into my heart and was thankful for them. There was but very little said any way; yet I felt that he was the medium of a good spirit to me, and I wished to communicate that spirit, as far as I could, to others. Since coming here, that Christmas-week at Wallingford has been in my mind. That was a very edifying week indeed: a good spirit seemed to overshadow it which drew the men together and united them. I had an idea in regard to the concerts we have had in the past, that though they served a valuable purpose there was always more or less of a distracting influence connected with them; but it seems to me that we have attained to an experience at the present time where we need not be distracted. We can give all the attention to the subject that is required, and yet be single-eyed and come out without any harm. At any rate I felt a prayer in my heart that we might do that. [Approved.]

George E.—I wish to recognize Mr. George Noyes and Theodore as mediums of Mr. Noyes's spirit and be receptive to them. [Indorsed by others.]

Mr. Woolworth.—I have been interested in the new developments at Wallingford in relation to music and art, and I hope that spirit will take possession of this movement. I hope we shall forget the things that are behind and enter upon a new dispensation in music and art. [Approved.]

George E.—I like that very much indeed. I think this concert will be the beginning of a new era here at Oneida, not only in art but in love.

T. R. Noyes.—I think the Community is called to begin a new life, forgetting the old things and pressing on to the new.

G. W. Noyes.—It seems to me that this union will be one of resurrection to the whole of us, if we make it serve unity.

———————

W. P. Dec., 18.—Getting ice continues to be the order of the day. Mr. Burt reports to-night, that yesterday and to-day, 80 cords have been got out and drawn away, including that taken by our neighbors. This is a much larger quantity than has ever been drawn before. Our neighbors pay us twelve shillings per cord, we getting out the ice and helping them load it. The amount thus received, Mr. B. thinks will pay all expenses. With the aid of the ice-plough, two men are enabled to cut fast enough for twenty teams. This is a decided improvement on the old way. The work will be finished to-morrow.

Our evening meeting, after reading the heart-stirring talks, was occupied with earnest confessions and conversation. The heart of the family responds to the truths Mr. Noyes is so constantly giving us, and we all desire to keep in step.

———————

THINGS NOT GENERALLY UNDERSTOOD.—It is quite common to see tin pans and tin fruit cans, and tin ware generally, turned bottom-side up on the stove or some other surface, to dry. A little forethought would show that just the opposite course should be taken. After a vessel has been properly drained, place it right side up, with the bottom resting on a warm surface, and it will be found to have dried in a very short time. On the contrary, when placed with the bottom side up, the vapor arising from the moisture within, cannot escape, and the ware is liable to become rusted before the inner surface becomes dry. Dairy men and dairy women, would find their milk-pails and milk-pans smelling much sweeter and purer if they would practice placing them right side up in the sun.   T.

———————

It was proposed in meeting last night that classes in study should not be broken up any more than was necessary; that it would be better for the family not to give up study entirely, as it was thought at one time we should have to do. There will necessarily be a good deal of excitement, but there will be those among us who will not need to give the subject of the concert much attention, and who can go on quietly with their studies as they have done.

———————

Upon Mr. Nash going to bed for two nights past I have been unable to find his night-cap. Mrs. M. has also made fruitless search for it. This morning, having occasion to change his shirt, the missing cap was found part way down his back. It had worked off his head some night, down between his shoulders and shirt and there remained concealed.   D. E. S.

———————

Mrs. Perry's sister, and her daughter with her husband and their two children, staid here last night.

THE O. C. DAILY.

VOL. 4.　　FRIDAY, DEC. 20, 1867.　　NO. 147.

A Mr. Andrew Findlay, of Chicago, writes to the O. C. giving a history of his life and asking advice as to his future course. He states that he visited us eighteen years ago and though he had previously heard that we were a licentious people, yet our appearance at that time, dispelled every such idea from his mind. Since then he has lost his wife, who he says was sorely troubled by the devil, and last year married again. He says he got hauled through the filthy slime of Spiritualism, then Swedenborgianism, and got slightly covered with its frothy scum. He lost $4,000 by a land swindle which he says was a stupid action on his part, and a high handed swindle on the other side. He says " The swindle being settled, I wish to commence business in some shape that would be most profitable, keeping in view a union with you as soon as you thought best. Could your agents call on us the first time one visits the West? Please consider me as waiting for orders, ready to use my means and time for whatever is thought to be of most use for the advancement of Christ's cause."

We extract the following from a letter received yesterday from Horace B. French :

" Has it ever occurred to you that as my mother carried some money and other property and put it into the Community as her all, for the cause of Christ and her support, and that she being suddenly taken away without scarcely any expense, that I her only child and heir ought to have at least a small part of that property? We all know that mother set her life by me, and next to her salvation all the thoughts and aims of her life were, ' What can I do for my children?' Now with the kindest feeling to all I ask has justice been done me? Is it right that I should be denied some small boon, the proceeds of that mother's property? I admit the property was small, yet the right is just as sacred to me as though large. You have had it and the use of it for years; while I as is well known to you all have ever been a friend to the O. C., yet from that day to this have ever felt wronged, and wondered why (though I presume it did not enter your minds at the time), you did not say, ' Here Horace, your mother is dead ; we are rich, you are poor ; take this your mother's money and God bless you.' Some may call this begging, but if you are candid and in favor of fair dealing you will not see it in that light, for asking a thing morally and lawfully your own, cannot be begging."

We hope the above will not draw on the sympathies of any in the family. The Kinsleys can place the matter of French's claims in a very different light.

A part of our swamp meadow is unproductive.

The soil being made up chiefly of vegetable matter, the surface becomes dry and loose, and the grass, what little takes root, fails and ultimately dies out. Such soils are almost wholly lacking in silica, an important element in the structure of the different grasses, and stalks of plants and grain. In order to supply this want, Mr. Conant is occupying his spare time in hauling on sand and loam from a neighboring knoll and spreading it on the surface, which we think will improve the soil and increase its productiveness.　　　　　　　　　　H. T.

Gill Hall, Allegany Co., Dec. 10, 1867.

MR. J. H. NOYES, DEAR SIR:—I am an earnest seeker for the truth as it is in Christ Jesus—am willing to make any sacrifice, that I may know what a *true life* is, an be enabled to *live it.* Therefore I desire to visit you. Will it be agreeable for me to spend two or three months with you as a boarder, or if my friends refuse to give me money, could you furnish me with some light work by which I might pay for my board? You will oblige me by answering soon.

Yours in love of the truth, ELIA M. WALLACE.

Night before last, the family finished reading, in in the Hall, the life of Dr. Lyman Beecher, and we can't but feel that he was a great and good man in his day. He failed however, to see the light of the gospel that was just breaking in upon the world, and the dawn of the millennial glory that he longed for, and hoped was not far distant.

One of our members had the curiosity yesterday, to look over the contents of a box of sweepings, and found the following articles : two hundred pins, eight needles, two shawl pins, a band-box full of rags, one pair of shoe strings, one spool of silk, and various buttons and other notions.

G. D. Allen and W. G. Kelley arrived yesterday afternoon. Mr. K. reports that he left the CIRCULAR containing the first No. of the article entitled *Black Mail*, in the hands of a person at Elmira, to be delivered to Thomas K. Beecher of that place.

Last night at half past nine o'clock the thermometer stood at one deg. below zero, but this morning it has risen to twelve deg. above. It is quite blustering and stormy, the wind driving from the south-east.

We have one camellia at the green-house which is exquisitely beautiful. I would recommend to all lovers of flowers, to call and see it.　　　S. W. N.

The W. P. family were all over last night (with the exception of Mr. Higgins), and expect to be here every night till after Christmas.

We are having orders for the *Trapper's Guide* for holiday presents.

THE O. C. DAILY.

VOL. 4.   SATURDAY, DEC. 21, 1867.   NO. 148.

Hamilton, Dec. 19, 1867.

MR. WOOLWORTH:—I have received both your letter and the articles. I will remit to you for the bag soon. I thank you for the invitation to the concert but regret it is so soon. For a number of reasons it will be difficult to come before New-Years; two of my daughters are not at home and will not be at that time of the concert, and if I were to come I would like all of them to come with me. Most any time after the first week in January with a few days notice I could come, and should be much pleased to do so.

The communication "Morality" I have seen, and have a very lengthy reply to it about ready. I fear Baker will not publish it. I intended to be severe on "Morality" as I believe he is the one that has been "After You," and now after me. Also if it is published and Rev. Freeman sees it, it will stop his pen. Also if published it I think will stop these City sectarian papers shedding their lustre at the expense of the Community.—In my note to the *Union* I shall tell him he is largely responsible for this "Moral war" in lending his press to keep it up. He evidently does it to make his paper interesting. With respect to you and your family I am yours,   CARLTON RICE.

E. P. Inslee was criticised last night at his request. His faults as pointed out, were self-conceit, a professional spirit in music and clinging to old ideas and lifeless forms, the brass band &c., instead of organizing under the new dispensation in music that is now coming in. He was thought to have been in a good spirit last Summer for a time, and his efficiency was commended; but for some time past he has been hard and uncongenial, which it was thought was caused by the influence of false love that he has been under. In the course of the evening the following remarks were made:

T. R. Noyes.—In my experience in college, in contact with George E., I learned the lesson that I must use my professional skill as something gained for the whole Community, and have an ambition to bring everybody up to my level, and not feel that I was going to stand head and shoulders above the rest. If I gain anything, it is so that the Community can have the benefit, and I desire to have all advance as fast as they can. I should be happy to-day if everybody knew as much about science as I do, and I want to work for that end. I know that is the only true way to be happy in it; because if I consider my knowledge as property that I have gained for a mere professional end, it cuts me off from common sympathies and brotherly love.   [Approved.]

G. W. Noyes.—The more of that spirit any of us

can attain the better. I cherish in myself a very deep anticipation that God is going to embellish this Community, and make it a school and an ornament to humanity, in the way of art. I believe it will shine, and its light will be diffused abroad in the world as a high temple of the fine arts for the glorification of God and the exaltation of humanity. And to that end I am satisfied that the spirit Theodore manifests must get full possession of the Community. We shall prosper in art and science so soon as we cast out this egotism that is ready to take hold of our attainments to exalt ourselves. I presume all God waits for in this Community, before giving it a tremendous impulse forward, is that we should be ready to diffuse to the world as Community property whatever he gives us, and not hold it as our own. We must diffuse it and level up continually. I think with that spirit the Lord is willing to give us gifts of all sorts: we can each of us have gifts from the Lord God himself in the line of art, if we will only pour what he gives us into the lap of the Community.

The work which was commenced a short time since, that of repairing some of the appurtenances of the dish-washing department, is completed. The repairs not yet reported, are as follows:

Convenient shelves put up on the north side of the sink where our tin ware is washed, or on the spot formerly occupied by the steam tub; a new table on the south side, boarded up on the west and east sides, while on the south side are inserted doors; in this cupboard are placed those unsightly swill-tubs, which have so long been a nuisance to refined eyes. The old benches on which the dish-racks are set before rinsing, have been replaced by more substantial ones, made with banks, so that it will be impossible to knock baskets of dishes off them. Thanks for improvements.   D. E. S.

A young widow lady from Skeneateles came here day before yesterday, for the purpose she said, of joining. All she knew of us, was the knowledge she had gained from the perusal of a few Nos. of the CIRCULAR, and from a partial acquaintance with Mr. Munn, who had visited the O. C. and was very much enamored with it. She insisted that her object in wishing to join, was on account of our religious principles. She left yesterday morning.

Traps ordered since Friday, Dec. 13th,   122 doz.

THE O. C. DAILY.

VOL. 4.   MONDAY, DEC. 23, 1867.   NO. 149.

Black Creek, Wilson Co., N. C., Dec. 15, 1867.

Mr. W. H. Woolworth, Dear Friend:—Yours of the 9th inst. is at hand, and was read with much interest. I now resolve to reform and be a better man. You are very kind to advise me what to do; you asked me if I could not visit you? No, I am unable to pay my expenses from here to Oneida; I wish I could, but I am a poor man. I want to talk with you, and the rest of the O. C. The people laugh at me for taking the Circular, but I do not care for it. I love the O. C. and its friends, and wish you success if I never see you. I believe you are right, and believe that Christ can save me if I believe on him, and I believe that Christ was the Son of God, and if he saves me it will not be because I deserve it, but because he is good and merciful. Oh, that God would soften my hard heart; I believe he will, and that he is at work on me. I am cured of drinking whiskey and chewing tobacco. I will not be ashamed to confess Christ in me a Savior from sin.

Please excuse a badly composed and badly written letter, and write to me as soon as possible. I am your sincere friend,   H. D. Lucas.

If Oneida has failed hitherto to manifest her enthusiasm at the prospect of a personal reunion with her sister Communes, they will be guilty of that neglect no longer. Saturday evening after hearing all the circumstances related by G. W. N. and Theodore, that led Mr. Noyes to make the proposal, there was a general outburst of feeling, stamping of feet, and clapping of hands, and when a vote was called for there was not one dissenting voice. What a power we shall be when all our strong men and woman are concentrated in one harmonious family!

DAILY PROVIDENCES.

I.

The drops that fill the ocean,
    Are gathered from the rill;
And thence, by brook and river
    Their destiny fulfil.
The power that guides the river,
    Must every rill control;
Or, left to other guidance,
    The river would not roll.

II.

The gorgeous, grand Cathedral
    Is laid up stone by stone;
And each for its position
    Is fitted one by one.
Had these been left in quarry,
    Or scattered wide and free,
What use would be the Builder?
    Where would the temple be?

III.

So, too, the mighty army,
    With bannered pomp and power,
That wrecks the works of ages
    In one destructive hour;
Doing by combination
    What no one singly can:
Yet these from untaught masses
    Were gathered man, by man.

IV.

If in this world's collisions
    Conflicting powers allure,
With little things ungoverned
    Will great events be sure?
No, he who builds, or battles
    Must do it by a plan;
And He who governs nations
    Must supervise the man.

A son of Erin, on getting into a boat that was lying against the shore, soon found himself adrift, and fast being wafted by the wind and tide out into deep water. The wind and waves becoming more and more boisterous as the boat receded, and Pat not knowing how to manage the craft, and seeing no way to extricate himself from his perilous condition, became terribly frightened, and besought the Lord for help, in prayer. He began by saying that he was not in the habit of troubling him for favors of any kind, and if he would only condescend to help him this time, in his very great distress, and place him once more on dry land, he would never ask him for any more favors.   T.

The following is the closing paragraph of a letter received from Vineland N. J., Saturday:

"Should you come into this neighborhood, or any of your family, I should be much pleased to have you stop with me.—Your hive is pretty full and you will need to swarm in due time, and I think this part of New Jersey offers many inducements to a society like yours. We have large tracts of cheap and good fruit lands, in a mild and healthy climate, near the best markets, with connecting railroads.

Fraternally yours,   John Gage.

Very little business was transacted at the meeting of the Business Board yesterday, and what little there was, not of sufficient interest to report.

We have had two or three days of thawy weather, but it is colder to-day and very blustering, the wind driving furiously from the north-west.

We had no noon meeting yesterday, the Hall being occupied with the rehearsals.

G. W. N. gave us another talk last night, on England which was very entertaining.

THE O. C. DAILY.

VOL. 4. TUESDAY, DEC. 24, 1867. NO. 150.

CHRIST AND PAUL COMMUNISTS.

That Christ and Paul were Communists in every fibre of their nature no one will question who studies them faithfully and impartially. Not a particle of the pride and egotism of individual sovereignty about them. They lived, moved and had their being in the *we* spirit. Christ lived for his father, and the father lived in Christ. So Paul lived for Christ and Christ lived in Paul. The less was an abode for the greater. " God was in Christ reconciling the world unto himself," and Christ was in Paul and in the other apostles, doing the same thing. One faith, one life, one love, flowing from the center outward through vitalized mediums or channels. And as the life of God is a unit, it would follow, as a natural sequence that all who partake of it, would become a part of that unit, hence the interest of each, would be the interest of all, and the interest of all, would be the public interest ; and the public interest is Communism. Now as like begets like, the converts of Christ and Paul would be converts to Communism. And we venture to say that no one can read the gospels or the epistles of Paul with his eye on Communistic principles without believing that to be a disciple or follower of Christ, is to be a Communist. Indeed, the New Testament, as a whole, is nothing more or less than a record—a brief history of the birth and developments of heavenly Communism on earth, and Christ and Paul were the most prominent exponents of its spirit and principles.   c.

We received yesterday, a letter from our late visitor, Mrs. Pease, urging us to receive her and her little girl on trial immediately, as she dreads to meet the displeasure of her father, should he know of her proposed connection with us. She says :

" I feel to say I can, and am willing to pass through *all* your criticisms. I hope to be truly humble, and with your help overcome this hard, selfish heart, that *I* too, may be one of your number in purity and humility, and live (shall I say it), a sinless life. I can but try, with such Christians as I believe you to be, to help me. How strange my business terminated after I found peace to my soul ! I prayed that if now I was in the right way, my temporal affairs might prosper, and truly they did ; and as everything seemed to go wrong on my deciding to become a spiritual believer, if I could, so everything seemed to take the opposite course as far as they have gone now."

Last night a deep feeling of thankfulness seemed to touch all hearts, and many expressed themselves grateful to God and to Mr. Noyes as his instrument, in saving them from false love. Considering how deeply the O. C. has been involved in this false element in the past, and how much labor it has cost Mr. Noyes and others to eradicate it, our present freedom from its pernicious influence, may be set down as a great manifestation of God's power, and his care over us.

Mr. Underwood complained last night that he had lost his *awl*, that it had been taken from the library. G. W. N. said he thought it was quite a pathetic case and implied a good deal, if Mr. U. had really lost his *all* ; to which Mr. U. replied that it was nevertheless true.

The Hall is decorated with evergreens preparatory to Christmas night, and the family are invited to attend the rehearsal to night at six o'clock. We do not know whether to expect Mr. Rice and family to-morrow, as we have received no reply to Mr. Woolworth's last letter.

The Bag-shop is shut up for two weeks, and the hired hands scattered for the holidays.

D. P. Nash gets over to meeting about once a week, usually Sunday evenings.

We have just heard of the arrival of E. H. Hamilton.

We shall print no Daily to-morrow.

THE O. C. DAILY.

VOL. 4.   THURSDAY, DEC. 26, 1867.   NO. 151.

It is credibly reported that the N. Y. C. R. R. Co. seriously contemplate the building of a section of a new R. Road from Wampsville to Utica, thus cutting off the great angle made in going to Rome and materially shortening the distance between the two points. A meeting of the directors has been lately held in Utica to consider the project. Vernon capitalists are sanguine that this road will be built soon, and that it will give them a Depot. The prospective Midland road undoubtedly operates as an incentive to the directors of the Central road to make every possible improvement.

The O. C. will very likely get the desire of her heart yet in respect to R. Road facilities without asking favor of the Depot. Look out for "porridge!"

H.

The following is the programme of last night's entertainment:

PART I.

1. OVERTURE. "Tancredi."
2. CHORUS. "By the Rivers of Babylon."
3. LITTLE FOLKS.
4. SOLO, Cornet. "Una voce poco fa."
5. BACKWOODS COURT SCENE.
6. SONG. "The Pacific Railroad."
   Words by T. L. Pitt, Music by L. P. Inslee.
7. SONG. "Cousin Jedediah."
8. SCENE FROM "EGMONT." Farewell scene between Prince Ferdinand and his friend Count Egmont, who is under sentence of death.

PART II.

1. CHORUS AND TABLEAU. From "Il Trovatore."
2. A DRUM PIECE.
3. SOLO, Violin. De Beriot's "6th Air."
4. SONG. "The Charming Young Widow."
5. HERR VON SPLUGEN and his Wonderful Box.
6. SONG.
7. FARCE. "Don't Meddle."
8. SONG AND TABLEAU. "Pilgrim Stranger."

We might say much of the concert had we time. The Hall was crowded, and the gallery filled to overflowing, so that few of our own people attempted to get in. All strangers however, got seats, and judging from their outward demonstrations, enjoyed the treat much. Every thing went off satisfactorily on our own part as far as we know. As Herr Von Splugen was leaving the stage, after having exhibited to the audience his wonderful box, its magical properties &c., the box commenced following its master, and a fall leaf to the box was raised up on one side, on which was written in plain characters, "After You," with the picture of an *animal* beneath it. This caused vociferous and prolonged cheering. The evening was dark, some rainy and windy, and not very pleasant for persons who lived at a distance. The exercises closed about half past ten o'clock.

The scene in the upper sitting-room the first of the evening was an interesting sight. The children were all there with their mothers or guardians, and such lively times! such flittings to and fro and such a chattering! The little ones were dressed in white and looked like little fairies. Their appearance on the stage was one of the best exhibitions of the evening, and drew out considerable applause from the audience.

A letter was received yesterday from Carlton Rice, expressing his regrets that he was not able to attend the concert. He sent us his article written for publication in the *Democratic Union*, giving us liberty to suppress it altogether, or to alter any passage about us, that was not strictly true. We shall offer it to the *Union* for publication, though it is very doubtful whether they accept it.

Received this week an order from Treadwell & Co., of Boston, for 78 doz. traps, mostly large ones, including three doz. bear-traps for the Cal. market. They gave us the privilege of doubling the order, on condition that they should have six months time for payment.

We had a noon meeting yesterday, at half past one o'clock, to read the correspondence and reports that were left unread the night before.

Our dinner yesterday, consisted of chickens and baked ducks, with their accompaniments.

The weather is warm and spring-like and the sun cheeringly smiles upon us.

G. D. Allen and F. W. Smith left for New-York in the night.

We have plenty to do to-day in regulating and cleaning.

THE O. C. DAILY.

VOL. 4.   **FRIDAY, DEC. 27, 1867.**   **NO. 152.**

EVENING MEETING.

After the reports from Wallingford were read the conversation turned upon our relation to Mr. Noyes. It was considered a fact that the devil had a special spite against him; and it was hoped we should search ourselves carefully and see that there was no element among us that did not recognize Mr. Noyes in his true position. Theodore said that two years ago he got as much in love with his father as a spiritual man, as he ever did with a woman, and that it "shattered special love all to pieces," and was the foundation of all the spiritual progress he had made since. This view was heartily concurred in by others; and the wish was unanimous that we might come into vital union with Mr. Noyes, and open the judgment upon everything that hinders it. Mr. Hamilton was conscious that his unity with Mr. Noyes had made him what he is, and he was glad to confess it. Mr. G. W. Noyes and many others made similar confessions. Mr. Hamilton had been forming a purpose there in New-York to avail himself of every good opportunity to bear witness concerning Mr. Noyes and show the world just what kind of a man he is. This purpose was commended, and many said they were ready to confess Mr. Noyes before the world. Then as to the question of despotism: It was thought we should meet that boldly, and let the world know that this is *an absolute despotism toward evil.* Then on the other hand Mr. G. W. Noyes testified that Mr. Noyes's influence tended to make him free. He was a freer man now than he ever could have been but for that influence, and he was growing freer every day, and coming out into a life of perfect romance, beauty, love, hope and courage. He did not feel such an influence to be a despotism. Many joined in this, and bore similar testimony. Some one observed if this was a despotism it was a glorious one. Mr. G. W. Noyes said Christ was just as much of a despot as this: "He made the devils howl when he came among them, and drove them out into the swine."

Mr. Hamilton said the world cried despot to Mr. Noyes, but those of us who are honest and true call him father and liberator. Mr. Woolworth remarked that this love and unity must be genuine and thorough, and free from all man-worship and idolatry, which Mr. Noyes hates when directed toward himself, or any one else.

It is now some more than eighteen years since I first began to study Mr. Noyes's writings. At first I read them out of mere curiosity, without much faith in him or his writings. I soon became convinced that his principles were true, and that he was inspired to introduce the kingdom of heaven on earth. This conviction brought on a fierce struggle between my sense of duty, and my worldly attachments and ambitions which lasted for months. Finally the truth triumphed and I was enabled to make a full surrender of myself to Christ and to Mr. Noyes. I can say now after eighteen years of experience in the Community and personal acquaintance with Mr. Noyes, that I have not been tempted to doubt his inspiration, nor to be sorry that I connected myself with him. On the contrary my faith in and love for him increases every day. I wish to dedicate myself anew to the cause that he is laboring for, and I pray that I may be filled with the same spirit that actuates him.

J. C. HIGGINS.

Mr. Hamilton spoke last night of Mr. Bolles' case. He has not been in a good state for some time, and a committee was called the day before, who sincerely criticised him. Mr. H. said he thought Mr. B. represented the Methodist principality, and it was that power we were dealing with, and not with Mr. B. as an individual; said he hoped he would take this view of his case, and clear himself from the false religious element he had been under all his life.

Mrs. Dascomb writes to Mrs. Bushnell from Fulton, where her son has gone to attend school. He was taken sick with diphtheria, and she is quite anxious about him. She has not heard one word from the O. C. since she was here, though letters have been sent her. She has been to Bath, and thinks as a general thing that public opinion is not as bitter against Mrs. B. and the Community as it has been; says she had some talk with Mr. B., and his rancor is still unabated.

We hear from various quarters outside, commendations of the concert, and much satisfaction expressed with its general character. Pussy, on the magic box, called forth much discussion, some affirming, neighbor Hubbard among the rest, that the picture was designed to represent a cat to be sure, but with *pole* prefixed, and that it was the most fit representation imaginable.

It is a very dark, rainy, windy morning. There are few days lately, that we do not have pretty high winds from some quarter or points of compass. Now it blows cold, and now warm. We hope the elements will at length settle into a calm, and have no more bluster for the season, but we are thankful for rain.

DEPARTURES.—Mr. E. H. Hamilton and Alice Ackley in the night for New-York, and T. R. Noyes and T. C. Miller for Wallingford.

THE O. C. DAILY.

VOL. 4. SATURDAY, DEC. 28, 1867. NO. 153.

Fairfax, Vermont, Dec. 23, 1867.

MR. PRESIDENT, DEAR SIR:—I feel it a duty to write to you now, and tell you what has been going on in my mind for the past week, although I am a stranger to you, and to the members of the Community. Often have I heard of the Oneida Community, but never, till last week, have I been able to ascertain what views they held, or what things they practiced. All I could know of them was, that they were a low set of people, whose practices and beliefs were all different from the world. Last week I was able to peruse a small pamphlet published in Brooklyn, N. Y., in 1857, entitled *Bible Communism.* I am glad that such a work ever came in my hands, for it has chased from my mind all the prejudices common among Christians toward your Community. To-day, Sunday, I am a different man from what I was a week ago. I must acknowledge that your views are in accordance with the Bible and especially with the New Testament. I have done as you wished of every reader of your work. I have taken my Testament and looked at every passage of Scripture you quoted, and found the same as in your work. I cannot help saying, that you are right, and that having the Bible as a guide, it is impossible for you to err. * *

I am a Protestant, and have been in connection with several Baptist churches. I am a French Canadian, born and brought up in the Roman Catholic belief until five years ago, when I was able to read the Bible, and since, I have abandoned my former ideas. To what shall I attribute my falling in with your book? Is it not a decree of a Providence all divine? I cannot see it in any other light. You have been, or your book has been the cause which made me come to a full sense of my depravity, and has made me to understand that there was something else I should know. Hoping a speedy answer, I remain,

Yours truly, LUDGER C. VINCENT.

DEAR MR. WOOLWORTH:—I thank you and the whole family for your faithfulness in criticising me; I accept it all as from the Lord. I have been enabled to see my old life as I never saw it before, and the terrible thralldom I have been under. That *self-complacent, self-justifying, cruel, sensual, devilish marriage principality;* that's what it is. That was the spirit that corrupted my fellowship with Mrs. M., the year after I joined the Community, and I am convinced that it has clung to me since. I confess Christ my ability to renounce it now and forever.—I agree with you that I made a fool of myself in that affair with Louisa Wightman. I see nothing in my past life, either in the Community or out of it to be complacent about. I have abused the confidence of my best friends—I hate and loathe my own life. There is nothing in it worth saving, and it is my prayer that it may *go to hell,* where it belongs. I submit my case to the Community, confessing that Godly sorrow which works repentance unto life. Truly yours,

C. W. UNDERWOOD.

TO THE FAMILY:—I wish to improve this opportunity in confessing my love for Mr. Noyes, and loyalty to him and the cause of Christ. I am satisfied that I have been under the influence of devilish and wicked spirits, the selfish marriage spirit, and family ownership and idolatrous love. These influences have cast a cloud over me most of the time since I have been here, and have made me gloomy and dissatisfied. I am satisfied that I have never wholly given my family up to God and the Community heretofore, and now I wish to render to God what belongs to him, and accept all things as gifts from him. I confess Christ in me the ability to do this, and a Savior from my old life, which is becoming very hateful to me. I desire to join Mr. Noyes's Young Men's Christian Association, and offer myself wholly to the Community and to God, without reserve. I desire to become a perfect medium of Mr. Noyes's spirit, and be obedient to his will. I invite the aid and prayers of the family to sustain me in these resolutions. Confessing my union with Mr. Woolworth, Mr. Cragin, G. W. Noyes and the family, I am your brother in Christ, C. E. CARPENTER.

Mr. Robert Stuart, who with his wife, was among the wounded at the late terrible railroad catastrophe, is a cousin of Alex. Stuart, the husband of Eliza Patten. He was married to Miss Eliza Merrill, about a week before the marriage of Eliza Patten, and with his wife went West. They were on their return from their wedding tour, when the accident above referred to, happened to them. Mr. Merrill, the father of Mrs. Stuart, has, until recently, lived neighbor to Mr. Patten, but now resides at Oneida Lake. The unfortunate couple were in the last car that took the frightful leap, and Mr. S. is so badly injured that little hope is entertained of his recovery. Mrs. S. though severely bruised, it is thought may survive.

The spirit of good-will to all, which blossomed out in the Christmas work-boxes at W. C. was operating in the same way at the Boarding-house. A nice work-box, with accompaniments was presented to the hired girl, who was so delighted with it that she could not sleep, Christmas night.

114 doz. traps ordered during the week ending Friday Dec. 27, including three doz. bear-traps.

THE O. C. DAILY.

VOL. 4. MONDAY, DEC. 30, 1867. NO. 154.

BUSINESS MEETING.

Some discussion ensued as to how many hands we had better retain in the Trap-shop. Sometime ago we decided to make a quantity of traps ahead this season so that we should not be hurried in the Fall, and be obliged to hire so much inexperienced help. The question is, how far shall we follow that decision in our present circumstances. The general feeling was to keep the smallest number of hands that would do our work, but the amount of work to be done is not yet decided upon. Myron and G. W. Hamilton have collected statistics which enable them to ascertain the amount of work a certain number of hands will do. It was recommended that they send them to E. H. Hamilton and Theodore, and get their minds about it.

In a line with this Mr. Burnham reported that the committee for cutting down the hired help at the Bag-shop, had reduced it about one half. As there will be few bags sold during the next two months, and it is quite expensive to warm that large building it was recommended to suspend work entirely for a while. The matter was referred back to the same committee.

[The committee met in the afternoon and decided to continue the work but condense, and all work in the large south room.]

W. P., Dec. 30.—Nothing very startling happens nowadays in our family. After having spent Christmas and the evenings of Christmas week at mother Oneida's, we are quietly settled again in our accustomed ways. Our classes commenced again with new interest, and also our home-like evening gatherings.

The skating for a few days past has been decidedly the finest of the season, and has evidently been enjoyed by our own folks and a number of outsiders. This morning, however, the glory seems to have departed, for on looking out nothing but one wide sheet of snow is to be seen. Who knows but we are going to have sleighing again by way of variety?

Thanks to J. N. Norton's kindly care, the omnibus, which has served us so well has been provided with lanterns outside and a bright little lamp inside, which promises to make our evening rides much pleasanter.

I wish to begin anew in seeking to possess and exhibit the positive principles of Christ, peace, fellowship and unity. In looking back to my past, or first religious experience, I find I never got hold of anything at all satisfactory, only as I yielded myself trustingly to God, and took in the positive spirit of humility and love. I desire now to resist evil insinuations and temptations, by drawing nigh to God in the meekness and simplicity of my first love. My hope of overcoming is by cherishing this love, and by strength-ening the things which remain in the direction of devotion and fellowship with Christ. I shall rely on this spirit to aid me to discover, confess and judge that in the past which has abused me and the truth, and from which I pray for deliverance. M. L. W.

The severe cold weather during this month did little or no injury to the fruit-buds,—even the more tender varieties of cherries and plums have received scarcely any damage. We seldom have the mercury sink to twenty degrees below zero, without doing more or less injury to fruit-buds. We have known the buds of the Heart cherries to be killed at eighteen below zero. We account for this difference, from the fact that the fine and dry weather of last autumn was favorable to the maturing and ripening off of the wood and buds of fruit trees. It is also noticeable that the fruit-buds are unusually small, which undoubtedly is a favorable condition in order to withstand the severity of the climate. Peach buds of course, will be found killed, if unprotected, where the mercury has sunk as low as fourteen degrees below zero. T.

TO THE FAMILY.—I confess Christ a humble and broken heart which is receptive to the truth in the spirit. I confess Christ my strength and wisdom to judge the principalities under which I have been educated, and a spirit of thorough sincerity in all things. I confess true reverence for my superiors, and a subordinate spirit. I thank God for victory over false love, and pray that the love of God and the ascending fellowship may possess my affections entirely. I confess my hatred of egotism and independence, and desire the help and prayers of the family. L. BOLLES JR.

E. H. Mallory's case was brought up for criticism last night. It was thought she had been under the influence of her father's spirit for some time past, which had made her disobedient, independent and disrespectful to her superiors, particularly to her mother whom she has treated cruelly. This poisonous influence had through her, spread itself over the young people, or those of them with whom she has been intimate. Her father's character was pretty thoroughly judged, and Elizabeth was exhorted to hate, and separate herself from his spirit, if she would save her own soul.

I confess I have been pretty deeply involved in false love, and it has caused me misery and suffering. I hate it, and am ready to publicly renounce it forever. I pray that the love of God may fill my heart, so that false love can find no place to creep in. I confess my loyalty to the ascending fellowship, and a true spirit of humility. HARRIET N. OLDS.

The snow fell about two inches last night, and there is some prospect of more.

THE O. C. DAILY.

VOL. 4.   TUESDAY, DEC. 31, 1867.   NO. 155.

"There is no place like home" has been said and sung by nearly all the civilized world, yet they cling to and defend a system which sooner or later tears the majority of homes to pieces; and never will a perfect home be realized by any one till they take Christ's home for a pattern. The kingdom of heaven is represented as being a home, and it is the privilege of every one to enter at once into Christ's family in spirit if not in body. The great distinguishing feature of a heavenly home is that true love fills every heart; while in worldly society false love, which is the very core of selfishness and idolatry, gains a foot-hold in almost every heart, breaking up families that its idol may be the better monopolized. God hates such idolatry, and will sooner or later destroy it by death. But let a person become united to Christ, and his heart filled with the love that he had when he prayed that all his followers might be one, even as he and his Father were one, and your heart has found a home that will be eternal. I confess Christ in me a savior from false or idolatrous love. I love all men and all women in the degree that they show the fruits of Christ's spirit dwelling in them.   D. E. S.

I think it is true, as was said in a late Home-Talk that all our victories over evil come through unity with Mr. Noyes. In my case the truth demands that I should bear witness to the fact that he has been my savior. He found me swamped in infidelity and unbelief, sinking in darkness and insanity, and his despotism towards evil saved me. But I have great reason to know that there is a positive, malignant, lying spirit, full of enmity to him, which is exceedingly subtile and indefatigable in its whispers and suggestions, misrepresenting his spirit and actions, which would take advantage of every superficial act or mistake, to make things *appear* wrong, and stir up an unbelieving conscience against him I have had great temptations and conflicts from this spirit, and great discouragement about ever getting a perfect victory over it, and I am glad of this opportunity to expose it and offer it to the judgment—to declare my everlasting separation from it, and to join with my whole heart in the war against it. In searching into its real character as I have from time to time in the past, I see clearly that this same spirit if it could have its way, would lead right on to evil thinking and doubt about the Bible and Christ and God, and leave one ship-wrecked as to faith and hope and eternal life. I pray for deep and true repentance and indignation against this spirit. H. MATHEWS.

At a recent call Tryphena Seymour made at Mr. Hubbard's, the conversation turned upon the articles on Black Mail in the CIRCULAR, C. J. Guiteau's character, &c. Mrs. H. said that Guiteau called there two or three times before he left the O. C. the last time, and was there when Tryphena called to bid her parents good bye before leaving for Wallingford, but staid outdoor until she had left. He told them he was going to leave, and wanted Douglas Hubbard should carry him to the station, but as he refused, they thought he must have gone on foot. Mrs. H. remarked that she wished folks who were intending to leave the Community, would not come to her house—she thought more of *our* friendship, than that of any seceders.

A subscription of twenty dollars has been made up by the hands at the Trap-shop for Mrs. Larkins, the widow of one of our employes who died a few weeks ago. They wanted the Community to head the list, but Mr. Campbell, after consulting with others, did not like to do that, but thought we might give her the rent of the house where she lives, and perhaps a barrel of flour. The Business Board were in favor of doing something for Mrs. L., and appointed Messrs. Burt, Campbell and Myron committee to determine what we had better do for her.

DEAR MR. CRAGIN:—I wish to separate myself from the hard, disobedient spirit that has been over me. I indorse the criticism of Mr. Underwood, and can say that I have not any sympathy for him. I confess my hatred of false love, and pray that the love of Christ may fill my heart, so that I shall never seek for any other. I thank you for your criticism of me, and for any more you have at any time.
                                    MARTHA J. HAWLEY.

Miss Munson writing from Boston, says: "I called on Dr. Child and Lawyer Giles last week, and they both wished to be remembered to the Community. Dr. Child who has traveled a good deal, says you have no idea how many friends you have about the country. I also called on Mr. Ballou, who takes the CIRCULAR. He says he is coming to spend a week with you when that 'Hotel' is in running order."

We have pretty cold weather again. At seven o'clock this morning the mercury was down to zero.

END OF VOL. IV.

THE O. C. DAILY.

VOL. 5.   WEDNESDAY, JAN. 1, 1867.   NO. 1.

To THE FAMILY.—I wish to testify to the truth by acknowledging that Mr. Noyes has been a liberator and saviour to me. It was through his teachings that I found Christ to be " the chief among ten thousand and the one altogether lovely," and God the fountain of all goodness. It was through him I was saved from the marriage principality and false love, for which I can never be too thankful. I have never doubted that he was chosen and inspired by God to preach the true gospel to the world, yet I have been tempted at times by a spirit that would think evil of him (and much more of myself), because I could get no nearer to him ; but for some years I have thought there was no cause for either, but that I was not civilized and soft-hearted enough to get near him, and was thankful for the privilege of being taught by him, and loving him at a distance, trusting God for the future. All the victories I have ever gaind in the past have been by taking hold on his faith, and confessing Christ my helper. Hear let me relate some experience which I have had many times within the last few months. At times when I was more tired than usual and my foot very painful, as soon as I shut my eyes I would seem to be in some frightful place—repulsive objects would stare me in the face in an impertinent way, which at first would almost make me shudder, but soon I would arouse myself to an earnest confession of Christ and the presence of good spirits, which would dispel evil ones, and leave me in peace, thanking God there was power in the name of Christ. I am thankful for any experience or suffering which tends to soften my heart and make me receptive to the truth, Mr. Noyes, and the ascending fellowship, and help me to " wash my robes and make them white in the blood of the lamb," let it cost ever so much rubbing and wringing. Salvation is worth it a thousand times.

                               L. E. AIKEN.

There was something said in meeting last night about the stiffness of the way we sit in the Hall, those who are expected to do the principal part of the talking, sitting in one corner. It was something like going into a pulpit and preaching. It was thought it would add much to the home feeling, for all to feel more responsibility in edifying the meeting. George E. said that Theodore when he was here, thought the seats were badly arranged, all facing one way ; he thought there might be a change for the better. George E. is to see what changes and improvements can be made.

Mrs. Dascomb who has been stopping for a while with her son at Fulton N. Y., had a call while there from Theodore Otis. She had a very plain talk with him about the Community. He did not make much opposition to what she said, and finally acknowledged that he thought things were pointing in that direction. Mr. O. is traveling with an agency for some new school books.

The new year comes in with storms and wind from the south-east, though it is not very cold. We hope to begin it with new purposes, and sincere and deep strivings to know more of God, and to overcome all obstructions that stand in the way of perfect fellowship with him. The past year has been full of mercies to us, and the coming one is bright with anticipations of love and unity.

E. H. Mallory's note to the family read in meeting last night, was quite satisfactory. It was thought she had made a good beginning, in separating herself from the spirit of her father, and in judging it. It is hoped she will persevere in the right direction till the love of God shall supplant every false affection, and her heart is fully satisfied.

DEPARTURES.—G. W. Noyes and J. J. Skinner for Wallingford, and Minerva Barron for New-York.

Many thanks are due to Mr. N. and Joseph for their timely assistance in the Concert.

The Office folks are at work on the details of the Inventory. Joseph's _____ _____ have been invaluable in this work.

We wish all the readers of the *Daily* a happy New-Year.

THE O. C. DAILY.

VOL. 5.   THURSDAY, JAN. 2, 1868.   NO. 2.

OUR FATHER CARETH FOR US.

A father says to his children, "you assist me in my business, look after my interest just as though you owned all my property, and do things in exact accordance with my instructions; then in return, I will look after every want of yours. I understand perfectly, all your necessities; food, clothing, education, recreation, health, and indeed, can anticipate them all, so that you need not have the slightest care for your personal welfare or of your future happiness. But in order to secure the proffered boon, you must have entire confidence in my promises and be thoroughly obedient to my will." Now our heavenly Father says as much or more, than all that, to every one of us. For proof of his care of, and generosity toward his children, see how perfectly all temporal, as well as spiritual interests for all worlds, and for all time, are wrapped up in the promise, "seek first the kingdom of God and his righteousness and all these things (such as a godless world is seeking after), shall be added unto you." But it may be asked, "why seek *first* the kingdom of God?" We answer, "because it is the source of true life and perfect health."

Intelligent parents regard the physical training of their children, so as to secure strong, healthy constitutions, as of the first importance in laying a foundation for their future education and happiness. And strange indeed, would it be, if our heavenly parents, from whom all wisdom and knowledge emanate, should not be equally sagacious and wise in securing in their resurrection children, a foundation of healthy life that would prove invulnerable to all the powers of sin, disease and death. Morover, "the kingdom of God is not meat and drink, but righteousness, peace and joy in the holy spirit." And, as thus defined, we see that it is a kingdom that must necessarily enter within the man, as a righteous disposition, a holy will, and a pure spirit, elements of unity and power, and constituting a life as infinite as it is beautiful and heavenly. Perfect health and immortal, youthful vigor, therefore, are sure to result from "seeking first the kingdom of God and his righteousness." What more could our heavenly parents do, or their children ask?   c.

W. P., Dec. 31.—The last day of the old year! We shall remember it long after its footsteps have departed. We had G. W. N. and W. H. W. with us to dinner, at which we sat in true English style, an hour and twenty minutes, while G. W. N. entertained us with lively sketches of his journeyings in the Old World. Afterward, Mrs. Miller proposed that we have a dance in the evening, and that these gentlemen return to us bringing with them a party from O. C.

So we had our supper at half past four, and in a little while after, the dining-room was cleared of chairs, tables and the stove even, which was seen standing outdoor, producing perhaps, as much effect on the atmosphere as a kettle of hot water on the icy waters of the Quinnipiac. About six we heard the omnibus coming, and soon were welcoming a merry group of twelve, six of them women and girls. Sly whispers were noticed after awhile among our guests, such as, "Too late for supper"—"No, No, don't say anything, hush!" &c. After a little questioning, we discovered that by some funny mistake, the women were told that they were invited to supper. Stopping on their way at the Boarding-house for Mrs. Bradley and some of their number who were there to tea, they found out their mistake; that it was not supper but a dance they were coming to. Amidst much laughter we led them down cellar, which became for the time the dining-room. This little incident let in the home feeling completely. The music and dancing commenced at half past six, and for an hour Cotillions, Waltzes and a Spanish dance followed each other in quick succession, the gentlemen insisting that the ladies invite their own partners half the time. In ten minutes from the time the last note of the music was heard, the dining-room (which, by the way all said made a good dancing hall,) was in order, the tables ready for breakfast, and the last adieus were said, some of them to our friends who leave us tonight for New-York and W. C. We send after them our greeting, "Happy New-Year," to all. At eight we gathered in the sitting-room and listened to the excellent reports from W. C. The reading of "Once More," and the Home-Talk from the CIRCULAR called forth hearty cheers and much earnest testimony for Mr. Noyes and the truth. The meeting was one of the best since we gathered here as a family, and we all purpose to begin the New Year in earnestness and improvement seeking.

Is it not a pleasant thing to be saluted with "Happy New-Year?" Early this morning while musing, feeling, after, and wishing to be a comfort to God, the thought that it was New-Year's morning came pleasantly to mind, with the assurance that this was the happiest beginning of the year ever past by me, because I was losing more of the old life, and getting nearer to the fountain of all happiness. Then the home feeling so much and so long desired, came clearer and sweeter than ever before, filling my heart with peace and love, giving new courage and fresh ardor for the work of the Lord.   c. e.

Two sleigh-loads of persons who live eight miles distant came here last night, to attend the concert. They probably had not heard that the concert was at Christmas instead of New-Years.

THE O. C. DAILY.

VOL. 5.   FRIDAY, JAN. 3, 1868.   NO. 3.

Miss Clara Wait writes Dec. 29.:—" My mind and feelings go out towards you and the family in love very much of late, and I desire to send an expression of it. I am aware that words may be mere empty sounds, yet I do not on that account the less appreciate them, when they are expressive of what is felt and known. I feel encouraged daily, by my growing unity with Christ. I often find my old life coming up for judgment, and as I reject and shake off the worldly, pleasure-seeking spirit, I find myself separated from what has before been pleasing and enticing in society. My heart and thoughts are being changed very fast, it seems to me. The CIRCULAR comes to us regularly now. How different are the feelings and spirit with which I receive and read it, from what were mine when I last received it in Ohio. The marriage spirit was ever the greatest barrier to my mind's receiving the truth. As my heart becomes open and soft to Christ and his people, it becomes closed and hard toward the devil and all who serve him. I pray to be taught how I may best serve Christ, and henceforth and continually labor effectually for God and Communism. I have reason to think that some of my old theories have made such deep impressions upon my habits of thinking and feeling, that they are not wholly eradicated yet. The Talk in the last CIRCULAR, ' Binding the strong man,' rouses my whole soul. What shall I do, how shall I learn what is really required to overcome the devil in me?"

W. P., Jan. 1.—A very quiet day with us, a sort of Sunday. The Shops being closed, some of our brothers busied themselves with writing or studies; others wended their way to O. C., while one of them of helpful mind, employed himself in mopping and various household ways. Our evening meeting which was held half an hour earlier than usual, was very earnest and edifying. G. W. H. who leaves us to-night on a western tour, was asked to express any thoughts he might have in relation to our business. He related some very interesting experience he had had for the past few months and then said, he thought there had been some tendency toward independence and individualism in one or two instances, and earnestly exhorted the young men who are in responsible positions to seek thorough organization and spiritual unity with those above them. He seemed to be inspired in what he said. A spirit of sincerity pervaded the meeting, and a good many of the young men gave testimony which showed that God is working in the hearts of all. We felt that our hearts were softened and that our purpose for the coming year, should be to rally round the center and become vitally united to the ascending fellowship.

Jan. 2.—In a meeting to-day of the women, it was ⟨illegible⟩ that we ⟨illegible⟩ the ⟨illegible⟩ that are behind and look toward ⟨illegible⟩ to prepare a home in our hearts for those who are coming. This evening we go to O. C. to hear the reading of the Inventory. If our Wallingford friends choose, they can imagine nearly thirty of us packed into a four horse sleigh, on our way thither.

The children had a little exhibition New-Year's day, and a small company were gathered in the school-room to hear them speak their pieces. They looked bright and happy and full of the importance of the occasion. All acquitted themselves creditably and the little ones " brought down the house" every time they spoke. Mabel related the trials of a grasshopper, ending with, " A grasshopper's feelings are not understood." She seemed fully to enter into the spirit of the song, and a general burst of laughter from the company followed. Lillie with a long dress on, acted the part of a pettish wife with Clarence Bloom, her affectionate, good natured husband. Georgie Easton, Anna Bolles and Harry Campbell stood up in line to repeat each a passage of scripture. They looked brimful of mirth intermixed with some embarrassment. Georgie was to commence ; his eyes twinkled, he stammered a little, and finally came out with " Ask and"———then recollecting and brightening up—" Ask and she will give it to you." After the exercises, Miss Portia read the credit marks, and gave two prizes, a pretty book to Carrie Bolles who had the most, and another book a little smaller to Leonora, who was only two marks behind Carrie. Then candies and raisins were passed around Miss Portia saying, " As it is New-Years I thought I would get all the children something." The exercises closed with their singing two very pretty songs.   S.

Mrs. D. who has recently visited Dr. Jackson's Water Cure, said they did not talk about much else, but the O. C. while she was there. All the assistant Physicians seemed very much interested to learn all they could about the Community. Dr. Jackson is assisted into the chapel, mornings, and prays sitting in his chair.

The *Democratic Union* of yesterday, publishes Mr. Carlton Rice's article on the Oneida Community. The editor told G. R. Kellogg that printing it, or something else, broke down his press. We do not wonder, as it is rather a heavy article, compared with some of the " light" pieces that have appeared in that paper lately.

The Inventory was read in meeting last night, and made a better showing than we had reason to expect. It will be sent on to the other Communes in manuscript.

THE O. C. DAILY.

VOL. 5.   SATURDAY, JAN. 4, 1868.   NO. 4.

DEAR MR. WOOLWORTH:—I thank God and the Community for the spiritual victories that I have gained, or that Christ has gained for me. I feel dead to my old life of selfishness, and I feel entirely reconciled to God, to Mr. Noyes, to the Community spirit and the ascending fellowship. I confess brotherly love for all that confess Christ, and do his will. I wish to be obedient to all my superiors, and be made the most of in the cause of Communism. I also confess an eternal separation from all persons and spirits that do not confess Christ, and do the will of God.

Yours in brotherly love, C. E. CARPENTER.

Jan. 1.—Having a new desire to testify for Christ and his cause, I can think of no better way on this opening year than to confess that this has been the happiest New-Year's day I ever spent. The quiet trust in God as a kind loving Father, who has given such rest and peace of heart, is so manifest it almost overwhelms me, it is so much more than I could ever ask or think of. Then I have a new appreciation of my superiors which I desire to cultivate, and by faith and earnest prayer to learn how to fan the flame and open the door of my heart to good spirits, and be a helper in the great work of concentration. I am thankful for a settled faith in Mr. Noyes as an inspired man of God, and believe that no weapon formed against him shall prosper. E. WHITFIELD.

We had a pretty sincere talk last night about Georgiana Sears' case, and Mr. and Mrs. Sears' relation to each other and to their children. The fact that considerable intimacy has been kept up between Georgia and Grace Mills and her mother, (a kind of family spirit,) was thought to be pretty clear proof that Georgia had not separated herself thoroughly from William Mills and the diabolical spirit he had toward the Community. Mr. Hatch's family was spoken of too, as being in a disorganized state, and their children were still suffering in consequence of this unnatural state of things between their parents.

The weather for two or three days has been quite warm, and though some snow has fallen, yet on account of its slight depth and the thawy weather, sleighs cut through to the ground and run hard. It is some colder this morning and the snow that fell during the night will improve the sleighing somewhat.

Our small dog (a shepherd's dog), was stolen from the barn last Sunday night. It seems that thieves are lurking around us, as Mr. Hubbard had sixteen turkeys stolen not long since, the thief taking them at two different times.

Mr. Cragin said last night that he thought the Community might with profit take a spiritual inventory, and have every thing squared up by the twentieth of February.

It is a fine time for snow-balling, and we notice that the children and others engage in the pastime with a good deal of zest.

Seven and a half doz. traps ordered the last week.

THE O. C. DAILY.

VOL. 5.   MONDAY, JAN. 6, 1868.   NO. 5.

Willow-Place, Jan. 4, 1868.

DEAR DAILY:—Since the commencement of the New-Year I have had a good many thoughts about labor—the ideas which Mr. Noyes has suggested—the plan of breaking up W. C. and N. Y. A., and concentrating at O. C. for the purpose of paying up our debts—of discharging to a great extent our hired help and doing our work with our own hands. These thoughts kindled in my heart all my energy, ambition, zeal and enthusiasm. I desire to do what I can to help in this cause and stir up in others the ambition and enthusiasm I feel myself. In thinking of the subject I concluded I would write out some of my thoughts and have them printed in the *Daily*, if approved. I have thought for one thing, since we have cut down the time of work in the Trap-shop to eight hours per day, that we men might work the eight hours and then have three hours for study before eight o'clock, allowing two hours for supper; or if we choose to take the time in the morning, we can get six hours (which is ample time for study), and not take out half the eight hours and leave others to work alone, which disarranges the business and cools off the ardor and enthusiasm. Union is strength—time is money. All the time we can work in the Trap-shop this winter, is so much money toward paying our debts; what we do ourselves we don't have to hire done. Holding these thoughts before my mind while about my work for two or three days past, has awakened in me as much enthusiasm and earnestness to "do with my might what my hands find to do," as I had during the most extreme pressure of orders last Fall. I hope others will hold the subject before their minds and act accordingly. I don't say "go boys," but "come boys." More anon.   H. B.

At the supper table last night, it was announced that there would be a gathering in the Hall, of the family, at half past six o'clock, in which there would be some games, or plays, and perhaps dancing. Accordingly, the most of the family were assembled at the time appointed, and for an hour or more we had lively times. The chairs were arranged in circles, and each circle had a play distinct from its neighbor. Next, the chairs were re-arranged, and a large circle formed in the middle of the Hall, and the popular play, "Spat them out" was entered into with considerable enthusiasm. Dancing followed, at the close of which the family were requested to be seated, when crackers and cheese, apples, dates and nuts were passed around. The exercises closed with two songs, one by H. W. B. and the other by C. M. Leonard.

Two or three years ago a lady, Mrs. H. B. Ostrum, of Titusville Pa., one of the first families of Pa., purchased one can of O. C. goods, fruits or vegetables, (the only can the merchant had may be the only one in the place), took it home, tried it, was well pleased with it; it being so much superior to any thing of the kind she ever found before, she sent by a friend to get Price-list of the O. C. fruits. She ordered, that year. Her friends and neighbors seeing and testing the fruits, were induced to order, so that now we have eight customers in that town, the total amount of whose bills, is $337.75. Meadville, a town three or four miles distant, sends five orders from five different individuals, amounting to $185.37. How many of these persons heard of our fruits through the one can, we don't know. Yesterday, we received application for Price-list from Titusville, closing with, " So far as the goods are concerned we are satisfied they are excellent."   KETCHUP.

For several days past, Mr. D. P. Nash has amused himself a few hours each day, in reading in a Vol. of the History of England. One night I remarked that my philosophy was missing. Mr. Nash said he found philosophy treated of some, in the History of England. The next night I found my book on the bed where he had been reading, and I asked him if he was studying philosophy. He said " No that was the History of England, but he found a good deal of philosophy in it." He said he had been laboring hard for nearly two days to get through the philosophical part, but had not yet succeeded. I advised him to look for the History of England in another book.

                           D. E. S.

O. C. JAN. 6, 1868.—There are at the present time at O. C., two hundred and ten members, including W. P. and B. N. Communes. At W. C. there are fifty-two, including N. H. French, and V. C. Noyes. At N. Y. Agency there are sixteen, making in all the Communes at the present time, two-hundred and seventy-eight members.

It is one year to-day since a death has occurred in any of the Communes. There have been but three deaths, for over three years, Mrs. P. Noyes, Jane Seymour and Mrs S. Hamilton. During the same time there have been five births, Ransom Reid, Maud, Eugene Kinsley, Eugene Deming Smith, and our new member, little Bertha.   J. A. & M. L. W.
                           Statisticians.

At an early hour this morning, the mercury stood at five deg. below zero.

THE O. C. DAILY.

VOL. 5.　　TUESDAY, JAN. 7, 1868.　　NO. 6.

On the supposition that we make up our minds to pack the coming season the following amount of the two kinds of vegetables, viz. 25,000 cans of tomatoes, 40,000 cans of corn, raising the crops and doing all the work ourselves, the results would be found to be very nearly as follows, reckoning the goods at list prices:

25,000 cans of tomatoes at $3.75 per doz.—$5,729.16.
40,000 cans of sweet corn at $3.75 per doz.--$12,500.00.

Total,	$18,229.16.
Cost of cans,	$4,550.00.
Cost of cases,	$506.20.
Interest on 45 acres of land,	$450.00.
Total,	$5,506.20.
Deduct,	$5,506.20.
Balance,	12,722.96.

Add to the balance $800 for 200 tons of green fodder at $4.00 per ton,　　$800.00.

We have for labor and profits,　　$13,522.96.

Then if we should decide to do the usual amount of business in packing other fruits, the profits might perhaps, be increased to within the neighborhood of $20,000.　　M. T.

W. P., Jan. 6.—The Trap-shop hands commenced work again to-day; those in the Machine and Blacksmiths shops commenced the day after New-Years. To-morrow we commence on piece work in the chain and finishing department. Thirty-six hired men and boys are at present employed in the works.

Our evening meeting was occupied with general testimony of God's goodness. For an evening or two when Mr. C. would say at the usual time, "Meeting's closed," no one would seem to take any notice of it, but on the contrary there would be a sudden appetite around for more conversation and testimony; last night it was a little amusing. The home feeling is evidently gaining ground. After meeting John Sears brought in his new microscope with one hundred and twenty objects he has been collecting. We looked at them with a great deal of interest; some of them seemed very wonderful.

How pleasant to be able to bring system out of chaos, and order out of confusion. The carpenter's shop had gone a long time without being put to rights, but we have now nearly put all things in order, and arranged lumber, tools, implements, nails, screws, &c. &c., according to their classes, as nearly as the case will permit. We have had a good time, when nearly choked with dust and blinded by cobwebs, in looking to the end, which has stimulated and given us pleasure

in what would otherwise have been very repulsive. Though we feel greatly honored in being permitted to help Mr. N. and the cause in any way, nevertheless we think that all who come to the shop to do small jobs, should act conscientiously—do as they would be done by—leave all things in order, that the shop may be kept attractive, and much labor and vexation saved. One thing more. Will persons be careful about cutting into valuable lumber, when pieces will do just as well, and avoid the waste of nails, screws, brads, &c.
　　A HELPER.

To THE FAMILY.—I wish to express my thanks to God and the Community, for salvation from my old life. I confess Christ in me a whole Savior. I also confess my loyalty and obedience to Mr. Noyes, to the Community and to the ascending fellowship. I feel that it is a great thing to be saved. God is doing a great work in me, and my earnest desire and prayer to God is, that I may be ever faithful to the cause of Christ. I confess Christ a soft heart, and a spirit of obedience.　　MARY A. CARPENTER.

I confess my *hatred* of, and separation from a spirit of special, idolatrous love, which has been over me like a cloud all my life. I have been tempted to feel that it was Almighty, that I never could be saved from it, but I believe that Christ's power is not limited.

I should be glad of any criticism the family may have for me. To know the truth and be obedient to it, is the earnest prayer of my heart, I care not where it cuts and separates.　　G. J. SEARS.

H. W. Burnham left Oneida yesterday morning. He has made himself very useful while here, and his services are much appreciated.

The weather is still pretty cold. At half past seven o'clock this morning the mercury stood at zero.

THE O. C. DAILY.

VOL. 5.   WEDNESDAY, JAN. 8, 1868.   NO. 7.

Monday evening Mr. Woolworth made the following remarks: "'The truth shall make you free.' These words have been in my mind lately with peculiar interest; and I have inquired how it makes us free, or what the process is. It seems to me that the process by which the truth makes us free is not arbitrary, but scientific. We conceive of it as a living being, a spirit that affects our life if we open our hearts to it. The truth is possessed of discrimination and power to dissect our life, and separate the good from the evil—the false from the true; and it has power to emancipate us from the devil's slavery, marriage and false love. It also frees us from the devil himself, the great slaveholder of all.

"That is the way, as I conceive of it, that the truth makes us free. It is represented as a 'two-edged sword,' capable of dividing asunder, soul and spirit, joints and marrow. It has the power of dissecting, and it does its work with perfect certainty and accuracy; it strikes the joint between good and evil every time.

"We say that the truth is our best friend, and I believe in my heart that it is. It hurts to have the knife put into the flesh, as it must be where the good and the evil, the false and the true have been mixed up, but the truth will make us free just as fast as we give it scope.

"One of the devil's devices is to try and produce alienation between us and God, by making us feel that God is our enemy if he criticises us. The same spirit makes us feel that our friends are our enemies when they criticise us and tell us the truth; and this produces alienation and evil thinking, and a disposition to shrink away into the dark, out of the light and the reach of the knife of criticism. So far as that spirit works it hinders the truth and defeats its work. It is very miserable policy to obey that spirit. I think some of the young folks here are tempted in that way: when criticism comes upon them or their friends they are inclined to think evil of it, and so let in a spirit of alienation, when they ought to draw closer to their friends and the truth."

DEAR MR. CRAGIN:—I am thankful for criticism and judgment, anything that will soften my heart and make me a medium of the spirit of Christ. I heartily sympathize with the judgment of special idolatrous love in the family. It separated me from God before I came to the Community, and has separated me from Mr. Noyes and the ascending fellowship. I confess my hatred and eternal separation from it, and desire in the meekness and humility of Christ to begin anew, and be filled with the faith and love of God. I desire true unity and organization with Mr. Hatch, and acknowledge him as my spiritual head, and pray God I may have a true spirit of love and subordination to my superiors. I pray for a spirit of repentance and brokenness of heart. I am thankful for good desires and purposes to serve God with my whole heart.   H. W. HATCH.

Our former can-maker, Mr. Quance, is expecting an answer soon, whether or not we intend to give him a job this season, of making cans. Also the farmers who have heretofore raised peas for us, are anxious to know as soon as possible, if we want them to raise for us this season, and if so, how many? &c.

How shall these inquiries be answered? Perhaps some one will take the responsibility of calling a convention for the purpose of deciding what amount of business we will do in this line, and also in other departments, the coming season.   T.

Lord, we seek the truth to know,
Though that knowledge strikes a blow
At old habits, fondly cherished,
And with care and labor nourished;
Spare not; let the judgment sever
Our old life from us forever;
That the new, unchoked may flourish
Yielding fruits that never perish.

After reading the reports and Home-Talks last night, we had some edifying talk upon self-control, the use of the tongue etc. Mr. Cragin thought persons might take some practical steps in controlling their tongues that would be of great benefit to them,

CORRECTION.—In Monday's *Daily*, on the first page, the seventh line from the bottom, for the words, *two hours* read *half an hour.*

THE O. C. DAILY.

VOL. 5.   THURSDAY, JAN. 9, 1868.   NO. 8.

Mr. Carlton Rice was at the meeting and related some anecdotes of Gerrit Smith's father. Mr. Woolworth then called on him for the story about his wife and Gerrit Smith. Mr. Rice complied as follows: "I am afraid that would be almost personal. I will remark in the first place that this happened before my marriage. I was not married till I was thirty years old, and then married a lady who was called an old maid, so that we were considered an old bachelor and old maid couple. Gerrit Smith was a great advocate of Temperance and Abolition, and my wife was a very excellent singer. She then had a very strong voice and she still sings. So Mr. Smith would get her to go to his meetings and sing for him. He with his good language and she with her good voice made the meetings interesting. On one occasion however Mr. Smith was pretty well pelted with eggs, and my wife happening to be near got a portion of them. There was not much said about it at the time, but Mr. Smith told her he would remember it. Five or six years ago next spring, he presented her the piece of property where I now reside, consisting of a house and six or seven acres of land, in consideration of the eggs that were thrown at her. She would not thank me for telling this here however."

Mr. Rice being further questioned said his family consisted of eight members. He has five daughters and one son. The son is in his eleventh year and is the youngest, and the oldest daughter is twenty-two. He had contrived to give them all a good common education, and two of them were now teaching. The girls read the CIRCULAR when at home. The oldest daughter was in poor health, but the others were all healthy and had never been doctored.

He supposed all his daughters had inherited rather uncommon voices from their mother, and when they were at home they all sung together. He has not been to Church since his quarrel and lawsuit with it, but the Church authorities told him if he would come and bring his wife and daughters, they should be well accommodated and nothing should be said about rents. He said when old Mills was at his house three years ago, one of his daughters remarked, "I know that's a hateful man by his looks." Mr. Rice made all these statements in a very matter-of-fact way, and said he did not want them to be made public.

HIGHLY FLAVORED CHEESE.

It is a notorious fact, that the cheese factories, especially the one we patronize, have made a great deal of very high-flavored, or what I should call bad-flavored cheese the past season, the cause of which, is a problem among the knowing ones, not yet satisfactorily solved. For the purpose of aiding in a solution of the matter, I would suggest, that perhaps if the farmers would take measures in some way, to ventilate and cool the milk, thus divesting it of its animal heat as soon as possible, after it is drawn from the cow, it would be a great improvement, and possibly remedy the evil altogether. The practice now is, I believe, of turning the milk as fast as drawn, through the strainer directly into the can, and thus in a confined and heated state, it is driven for miles to the factory, allowing no chance for the effluvium arising from the animal heat in the milk to pass off, which in very warm weather is liable in a short time to become tainted, thus imparting a peculiar flavor to the milk that no after process will entirely eradicate. It should be understood that decomposition once commenced though it may be retarded, the process never ceases—though ever so slowly, it will go on to completion.

Once on a visit to a condensed milk-factory I was forcibly struck with the peculiar and offensive effluvium that was drawn off by the pumps from the milk, in the process of condensing. I am not certain but it will be found in the end, that the elements contained in animal heat in the milk, is the most prolific, insipient cause of all the bad butter made.   H. T.

In a letter from Mr. Reeve of Jan. 5th he writes:
"We are inclined to think that we have been thinking more of our *own wants*, than we have of your time or opportunity to give information: hence we desire to take back any request for information concerning our living with or near you, and trust that we shall get it unasked, if it is well for us to have it. After reading Mr. Noyes's article to applicants in the last CIRCULAR, I felt sorry that we should have added one to the number, that made such an article necessary. I want to expose a complaining spirit that hangs about me, and is trying in various ways to make me feel that that article is unjust, but I may as well condemn *all* of Mr. N.'s writings as that. I intend to be honest with you and tell you *all*, whether we ever work with you in the family or not: and I know that Christ will assist me in ridding myself of such a lying spirit, as would try to make me say and feel that what I clearly perceive to be just and good, is *unjust* and evil. This evil spirit has been tormenting me while I have been writing this letter, but as I open my heart to Christ and you, it vanishes."

The family at W. P. were all here last night by invitation. There was nothing out of our ordinary course expected, except the presence of Mr. Carlton Rice, who came in the afternoon, and by the way is a plain man. The children sang two very pretty songs, and A. M. Hatch entertained us with music on the piano.

THE O. C. DAILY.

VOL. 5.   **FRIDAY, JAN. 10, 1868.**   **NO. 9.**

EVENING MEETING.

The Talk about "Man-Worship" was read, after which expressions of sympathy with it were general, and a desire that we might be saved from the spirit of man-worship—from petting ourselves or any one else.

George E. thought all might take Mr. Noyes's advice to the young women, and by so doing we shall doubtless please and help Mr. Noyes.

Mr. Woolworth.—I have felt sensible to-day of a victorious spirit—victorious over evil principalities and powers—that good is asserting itself and proving itself stronger than evil. It is due, I think, to the spirit of concentration. Though there has been no outward move, yet I think the *spirit* of concentration is moving, visibly and invisibly. Wallingford is not only coming nearer to us in spirit, but the Primitive Church is approaching us.

George E.—I have been conscious that we are assuming the spherical condition more and more, not in outward circumstances, but in spirit. Mr. Noyes's theory and talk upon this subject is very interesting indeed. The spherical condition of the body is one which is able to resist external evils of every kind. Disease generally attacks a man in the extremities, and there is where he is weakest. The more we turn within, and the stronger we become, the better able we shall be to resist attacks of the enemy.

It seems to me as though the more we concentrate here in the Community, the more we grow, though our concentration is invisible at present.

Mr. Woolworth.—I suppose these attacks from without were designed to bring us together.

George E.—Our enemies thought they were going to scatter us, but instead of that they are helping us out of the sprawling state into concentration.

Mr. Woolworth.—There has been a terrible temptation to sprawl—a rush of applicants—a cry from the West and the South, the North and the East, for us to take in new members and start new Communes: but the Lord has headed that off pretty effectually. I believe there is a gathering going on now spiritually. Our spiritual forces are concentrating and we are feeling increased power and strength in consequence of it.

Mr. Woolworth expressed his thankfulness for the evidence we have that good is stronger than evil in the conversion of E. H. Mallory and G. J. Sears, and Mr. Cragin said he hoped the family would not pet these individuals, as has been the tendency in some instances in the past, which would hinder instead of helping the work of continuous earnestness which they need to feel.

DEAR MR. WOOLWORTH:—I am thankful for the spirit of truth which has shown me that I have been in bondage to the spirit of false love that has been criticised of late. I refer to my fellowship with Mr. Leonard. I am conscious that he was instrumental in bringing me into the fellowship of the Church, for which I am exceedingly thankful. I love the truth and want nothing else. Well to go back, I came from Putney in the fall of 1857, as they were going to sell out. The idea of being separated from Mr. L. threw me into great suffering, so that for a time I was nearly or quite deranged. Then when he left for Wallingford some four or five years since, I had a similar turn; I kept my feelings mostly to myself, not for a moment doubting that my fellowship was all pure and heavenly; but the meetings of late have shown me that I was involved in the same spirit that has been criticised. One day last week the thought came to me that I had better give away Mr. L.'s picture that I knew I had idolized. This with some other little relics I cheerfully disposed of, and what I am so thankful for is, that the Lord made it so easy for me to do it.   E. ELLIS.

Charles Primo's wife is sick and has been for a week past, and as they are quite poor and in our employ, and find it difficult to get suitable help, it has seemed no more than an act of common humanity that we should help them some. Two or three of our women have interested themselves in their case, and have been there from time to time and assisted them some. On finding that their babe was destitute of suitable clothing for winter, these "sisters of charity" took it home yesterday, and with the assistance of several of the women fitted and made it some clothes. After the talk last night on petting, Mr. Cragin said he hoped our women would not *pet* the Primos—they are having trouble in the flesh, just what we might expect—we can relieve them somewhat, but he said he didn't know as the Lord would thank us for it.

Our people commenced drawing logs to the saw-mill last Monday, with seven teams. The logs were on what is called Tilden hill in the town of Vernon, though not far from Verona Springs. The sleighing is excellent, and the weather was mild and pleasant till yesterday, when it was stormy and very blustering, and on that account and the drifts, they were unable to work except in the forenoon. This morning the wind has subsided and the sun shines, the mercury standing at five degrees above zero.

A notice is put up in the vestibule that we have a 300 dollar order for bags, and a bee is called at half past nine o'clock A. M. to assist in making them. We shall continue to have bag-bees for a time.

THE O. C. DAILY.

VOL. 5.   SATURDAY, JAN. 11, 1868.   NO. 10.

B. H. C.—We have only sixteen boarders at present, twelve women and four men. Seven of the former are employed in the Silk-factory. They are taken over in the morning and brought home at night by the W. P. team. They take their dinners with them. The washing department employs three more, and the tailoring business has the services of the two remaining. Of the men, two are teaming under Mr. Conant, one is in the Shoe-shop, and one is in the Bag department. Most of them appear to have caught the intellectual contagion prevailing in the Community, being quite attentive to their studies during a portion of the evening, and it is with much pleasure that we can commend them for being very respectful to our family and to each other. Indeed the Boarding-house is an orderly, quiet Community home, a good place for study, meditation and prayer. The truth is, that when people outside of our society come sufficiently near to us to feel the nimbus of our daily life, the more they respect us. A life that is honestly and earnestly devoted to the spirit and principles of the gospel that Christ and Paul embodied in their lives, cannot otherwise than commend itself to the honest and true on the one hand, and on the other, be a rebuke to the selfish and dishonest.

If Communists therefore have the disposition and ability to make an attractive *home* for the homeless, and to make themselves *friends* to the friendless, it is due to their receptivity to the spirit of him who said, "As we have opportunity let us do good unto all men, especially unto them who are of the household of faith."   c.

Mr. Woolworth remarked last night, that Mr. Carlton Rice reported something of his affairs while here. He owns a farm near the village of Madison that is under a mortgage for some $1,890, and unless the sum is paid this month, the mortgage will foreclose, and the farm will be sold. He said he expected to be able to raise the money, as Gerrit Smith had given him some encouragement to expect that he would help him. But if he failed to get the means, he said he should be glad to have us step in and bid in the farm, and take the title of it until he could redeem it. This $1,900 is all the incumbrance there is, and he represented the farm I believe, as worth about $6,000. We did not pledge ourselves, but told him we would help him if we could; we should be glad to assist him if consistent &c. If not redeemed the farm will be sold the 30th of this month.

The inquiry raised by Mr. Hamilton in a letter to Mr. Woolworth which was read in our meeting last night, was put to John Conant who is at the head of

the laundry department, and received an answer in the affirmative. It was this, " Can the O. C. give up the room for drying clothes in the Tontine, as soon as next March, for a composing room for the CIRCULAR?" It seemed to be the prevailing feeling that some other place for drying clothes could be found that would answer for a time, or till some other way should be devised for drying them.

Hurrah for concentration! Hurrah for the removal of the Printing-Office to O. C.! The drying of clothes can be accommodated in most *any* quarter. Hurrah! *Hurrah!!* we are ready for you. The washing department says, " Come on." With united voice we cry, " Come one, come all, come great, come small." Glory! Glory! Hurrah!! Wont it be superb? Splendid? Glorious? Hurrah! Hurrah! Hurrah!!!   YOUNG FOLKS.

The bag-bees were spoken of last night, and the importance of having all the stock we have on hand worked up. A good beginning was made yesterday, and a hope was expressed that the work might not flag.

36 doz. traps ordered for the week ending Jan. 10th.

THE O. C. DAILY.

VOL. 5.   MONDAY, JAN. 13, 1868.   NO. 11.

Cleveland, Ohio, Jan. 6, 1868.

DEAR BROTHER WOOLWORTH:—Now that the spirit of "Black-mail" seems to be making its assaults upon O. C., I think it fit to report an instance of what may justly be considered as coming from the opposite spirit. I have in my hands for safe keeping a will made by John W. B. Randolph some six weeks ago bequeathing all his property to J. H. Noyes, E. H. Hamilton and W. H. Woolworth in trust for the sole use and benefit of the O. C., amounting to some $1,500 including what you now have in your hands. The will was drawn by me at his request. I have no doubt it is a free-will offering to God and his church.

G. W. H. is with us, giving us joy and edification by his presence. I confess Christ a spirit of thankfulness for what we have, and of hope that we may be prepared to receive more of the love of God.

Yours for the truth, J. W. TOWNER.

YOUNG MEN'S MEETING.—Nearly every young man present. George E. remarked that the object of calling the meeting was to promote unity among the young men. H. G. Allen said that unity had been promoted among the brethren at N. Y. by talking about concentration. It was thought that the path to freedom lies in our receptivity to our superiors. False love is distracting and leads to dissipation of all the faculties, while brotherly love satisfies all desires, and is a great promoter of fellowship between the sexes. Special love is like a depraved appetite that relies on stimulants for action. It eats like a canker, and destroys both soul and body. All seemed determined to rid themselves of every vestige of false love with its train of evils, and substitute in its stead true brotherly love, which purifies the whole being making its possessor attractive and lovable. It was thought there was danger of fostering false love and trap-setting, by a wrong use of the eyes. These windows of the soul may be made to keep alive the fires of unholy passion when all outward actions are strictly correct. It was thought that *greediness* was the essence of false love—a hoggish, devilish spirit. Amativeness and alimentiveness are closely allied, and greediness in alimentiveness must be overcome, before conquering amativeness. We must gain self-control over the lesser passions before we can expect continence in the use of the greater.

Mr. Cragin said in the meeting last night, "In listening to the remarks of the young men this afternoon in their meeting, I found my heart stirred up to thankfulness for the evidence there is, that our young men as a body, are putting on Christ in a more vital way than ever before. I think they all see the evils that have been connected with false love in the past, and that that dispensation is gone, and they are being called to this national spirit which leads to identification with Christ. I think it is true of the young women too, that they are coming into a state where they are having more attraction for this national spirit, and devotion to the good of the cause, than they ever had for special lovers. I believe they feel compensated, and that they have more real enjoyment now in one week's time, than they formerly did in months, or perhaps years, when drifted about hither and yon, under the influence of the affections. I guess a good many of us old folks can sympathize with them. We have not anything to boast of over them in that respect—at least I have not."

Mr. Woolworth.—No: we have all been children.

Some weeks since Mr. Easton wished me to inquire at Rochester, about his brother, whom he had heard was superintending putting in Water-works for the City. The first man I inquired of, happened to be the right one, as he had just sold Mr. Easton a house and lot, for $10,000. This man said that two of the Easton brothers were there; one had recently come over from England. They were both engaged on the Water-works. I saw this same man again last week, and he said that Mr. E. called at his store after I was there, and he told him that a young man had inquired about him, and said that he had a brother in the O. C. At this Mr. E. was very angry and wanted to know what right any one had to meddle with his concerns. He went on talking for a time and said some pretty hard things about his brother. The man made some apology, saying it was only incidental that his name was mentioned. He soon cooled down and then said confidentially, "If that young man calls again you inquire of him about my brother. I would really like to know how he is getting along, and his wife too, whether she is contented." He thought she was a very fine woman but could not believe she would stay there long. But said he, "If Abel and his wife *are* contented there, I think it is the very best place for them."

W. G. K.

The only business that was brought before the Board yesterday, was repairing the planing machine. There was some talk about economy in the use of coal, sifting and burning cinders &c. It was thought that the spirit of Christ's words should rule in this thing as in all other, "Gather up the fragments that remain that nothing be lost."

A little robin was seen hopping around near the Tontine, Saturday. Yesterday it was in the hemlock hedge, where it may take up its abode for the winter.

H. G. Allen came Saturday afternoon.

THE O. C. DAILY.

VOL. 5. TUESDAY, JAN. 14, 1868. NO. 12.

W. P. Jan. 13.—Messrs Campbell and Newhouse, and Myron took a sleigh-ride to Hampton to-day, for the purpose of ascertaining the best terms for which they could furnish us with castings. They agreed to furnish them for twelve and a half cents, hardly liking to do so, but willing to for the sake of keeping their hands at work during the winter. This is a cent and a half less than we have been able to get there before.—The ice-machinery has been in use to-day cutting ice for some men in Vernon. They are to draw the ice themselves.—We have a new member in our family. Mrs. Aiken has come to sojourn with us for the present, and notwithstanding her lameness she seems bright and cheerful.—Alfred reports two hands discharged from his department (Finishing), to-day.—After reading Mr. Noyes's letter to Mr. Guiteau this evening, there was an expression of hearty sympathy and approval, and it was the general feeling that Mr. G. could hardly fail to be convinced by Mr. N.'s arguments.

Jack Frost, our great and skillful artist, who so beautifully paints our windows almost every night, has condescended to go down under the mill and chisel out marvelous figures and devices, that far exceed the most delicate French lace in tasteful arrangement, and casts into the shade all human attempts at carving and polishing. This exquisite tapestry covers unsightly objects, and gives a charm which compensates for winter. But did you know that Jack was a musician as well as artist? For some time we heard what seemed to us a perfect Eolian harp, but we did not know from whence the sounds issued. The other day on bringing my ear close to the top of the lever that hoists the gate below, I heard a large humble-bee in my ear. Not being afraid of the sting, I laid my ear on the top of the lever, and the loud buzzing continued to come through the pores of the wood, which must proceed from Mr. Frost's work-shop, as no such music was heard before he commenced operations. May he have a good time and an appreciative audience. YOUNG STUDENT.

I desire to offer myself anew to Christ and the Community, and to confess my entire separation from all family ties and spirits. I feel the need of judging my father's spirit more thoroughly than I ever have. He was once almost persuaded to be a Christian—a Community man—and in turning back he has sinned against great light. He at times has some compunctions of conscience, but has plunged into business and the world, to drown all such convictions. Now that he is disabled, and is looking toward the grave, in spirit I think he clings to me with a tight grasp.

He was always very self-righteous, self-sufficient, narrow-minded, and full of doubt, fear and unbelief. I now want to confess my entire and eternal separation from *his* spirit, and the *Newark* spirit, and ask God and the Community to accept me as their child. CARRIE.

THE OPEN DOOR.

I.

The open door, the open door;
    For him who cares to enter.
With hope and fear, to chill or cheer,
    Whoever comes must *venture*.

II.

For all without, is fear and doubt,
    A status none can covet:
But saved from sin, there's peace within;
    And truth, for those who love it.

III.

The open door, the open door;
    Be careful ye who close it;
For many there with earnest prayer
    And bleeding hearts, oppose it.

IV.

Around this goal, the earnest soul,
    The true in heart, will center,
Then guard with care, lest any dare
    For selfish ends, to enter. H. N. L.

Mrs. Aiken has taken up her abode for the present at W. P. Her ankle has been so lame for some months that she has scarcely been able to stand on her foot at all. By rooming on the same floor with the dining-room, parlor &c., she will now be able to take her meals with the family, attend the evening meetings, and help herself more generally than she has been able to do while occupying a room up stairs. She seemed thankful for the privilege of this change and we are thankful on her account.

Our meeting last night was quite interesting yet scarcely reportable. Mr. Noyes's letter to Mr. Bolles was read, and some advice to Mr. B. followed in reference to the weakness and temptation under which he has been laboring. The conquest the men of the Community gained over the tobacco principality years ago, is his, if he will but avail himself of it; but he needs "himself to strike the blow," and an earnest one too, if he would enter into their victories.

H. G. Allen left for the West yesterday afternoon.

THE O. C. DAILY.

VOL. 5.   WEDNESDAY, JAN. 15, 1868.   NO. 13.

A GOOD HOME AND STEADY WORK.

A good home and steady employment is the want of thousands everywhere, a want, one would think, that could not easily be supplied. There are many however, who seem to be looking to the O. C. for these blessings, as though manufacturing homes and furnishing employment for those who need them, were our main business. Well, we confess we are doing something in that line of things, and hope to do a great deal more as we augment our capital stock. And the process of making them is a simple one. But before revealing the secret as to *how* they are made, we will ask the question, " What constitutes a good home? Is it to have a comfortable house to shelter you, and plenty of food, clothing and fuel ?" That may do very well for the animal man, but the faith man, the Christ man, must have something more. Here then is the secret of securing a good home and plenty of work, namely—give up your body to the care of your soul, and give up your soul to the care of God. Have no sham about it, let it be an honest transfer, and, in return, God will give you thankfulness and a *soft* heart. Now a soft heart is a home that is a home, and will ever continue to be a blessed one too—**with it you have all the work you can do.** It will be God's work, that of believing on his son. But says one, " Will believing on God bring me bread and butter—supply me with all the grub I want ?" Ah! have you forgotten that you gave your *body* away to your soul, and your soul to God ? Looking out for bread, then, is not *your* business but your heavenly father's, and he has said that " Man shall not live by bread alone," &c.

Now as "There is no place like home," so there is no home like a soft, penitent, loving heart. And there is no food so nutritious and healthy, as the spirit of thankfulness. You are in no danger of eating too much of it. Eat three hearty meals a day, and take lunch every hour, and you will feel all the better for it. The great mistake however, about finding a quiet, comfortable home is, that one looks for it in the wrong direction—outward. That is not the way to find a home or any other good thing. But a true home is the gift of God, as we have said, and the home of a soft heart is one that you can carry with you wherever you go. Now the heart is a wonderful thing. It has the power of contraction or expansion according to the character of the spirit that possesses it. Under the devil's influence, it hardens and contracts, but under God's influence, it *softens and expands*, so much so, that all of God's numerous family can find room there. But more in our next.

W. P., Jan. 14.—Hearing that the children attending the evening school were noisy and troublesome, Mr. Burt and C. A. C. went over there this evening. The teacher, Mr. Fish, said the children behaved very well in school, but out of it they were pretty wild. Mr. Burt talked to them some, and at first some of the younger ones were disposed to giggle, but became sober as he went on in his earnest way, to tell them that we had started this school for them at our own expense, and had considerable difficulty with the neighbors about it as they had no faith that the children would do well. Now, said he, part of your education is to learn to behave like gentlemen and ladies—we want you to improve and be an honor to us &c. They looked quite serious over it and he hopes his talk will do them good. He said they read very well for such untaught creatures. C. said that while there, he heard a great screaming down the street, and presently a row in the entry, when suddenly the door burst open and three little boys rushed in. On their way home Mr. Burt remarked to C. that he hoped we should get the whole neighborhood under our control so that we could bring them under the screws of criticism.—In yesterday's *Daily* instead of a " cent and a half cheaper," read " one cent," it was a misapprehension of the journalist.

Not long since I overheard the following colloquy between an Irishman and a colored man, neither of whom know how to read or write: The Irishman remarked that it was somewhat hard to sit all the long evening and not look into a book, and to be unable to read the paper, and know so little about the world—he said time hung very heavily indeed. But, said he, " the English language looks as it always has and always will, a mixed up mess." I could see he seemed to regret that he knew so little.

It was somewhat different with the colored man. He said the way it was with him, was, " Go day, come day, God send Sunday," and he would sit and while away time and make the most of what little he did know, and not worry about the future. I tried to reason with them a trifle, and attempted to show them the vast importance of knowledge, at least enough to read and write, but in vain, and I beat a hasty retreat, thankful for what little knowledge I possess, and the appetite I have for gaining more.   x

George Hamilton writes from Springfield, Ohio, that Western men complain pretty loudly of hard times—the hardest times they say since 1857, and consequently that collections are difficult, losses by failure, frequent. George reports very good luck in collecting our dues in the West, and we hope by vigilance and faithfulness to gather our harvest with but little loss.

THE O. C. DAILY.

VOL. 5.   THURSDAY, JAN. 16, 1868.   NO. 14.

Urbana Depot, Jan. 9, 1868.

DEAR MRS. MILLER:—I providentially had an opportunity to see or have an interview with Gov. Hayes of Ohio. When I came out I didn't expect to stop at Columbus, but finding I would have to lie over four or five hours here or at Columbus I chose Columbus. After calling on the business men I could have any prospect of getting orders from, I called in at the State-House to see the legislature in session. While there I saw an old acquaintance, who was reporter for one of the daily papers in Columbus. I stated my wish to see the Governor elect if he was in the City. He learned that the Gov. was in the City and where he lived—where I would be likely to find him, as he has not been inaugurated. Consequently, in your behalf, I plucked up courage to call upon him. After getting my name and where I came from, he was very cordial—made many inquiries about your family—seemed more interested in George than any other individual of the family—thought he was pretty smart &c. He wished to know if G. was fleshy. I told him G. had been traveling in Europe the past summer, whereupon he wished to know if the Community sent anything to the "Exposition." He spoke of visiting Wallingford some eight years since. Expressed himself as having no prejudices on account of our peculiar religious beliefs, and as well pleased at having a call from one of our people. He sent his respects to your family. I had but a short opportunity to see him, as there were others that called for him shortly after my going in. I felt that there was a Providence in getting the interview up for me.

I am having a good time in attending to the Lord's business. He manifests his goodness to me continually. What I want to learn is, to rely on him and his followers, the Primitive Church, for inspiration.

Much love to all Willow-Place. Yours lovingly,
G. W. HAMILTON.

The following is an extract of a letter from Mrs. Tryphena E. Freeman, to John S. Freeman :

Schenectady, Jan. 12. 1868.

Dear John:—I received your letter in due time, with thankfulness to you all for the ten dollars you sent. Oh the love of God! If all would trust God, none would want. The barrel of flour you sent will last, I think, till the last of April or the first of May. Your father says he will do all that lies in his power to break up the Community as long as he lives, and that is all he lives for. When you first went away your father had all my relatives on his side. Some of them said they would not do anything for me, nor come to see me. But they have given that all up.

They feel indignant toward him. Your Mother in Christ,
T. E. F.

Night before last the report of the criticism of the personal habits of the W. C. was read and Mr. Noyes's remarks on the same subject, which caused quite a sensation in our circle. A wish was expressed that we too, might let in the light upon old habits, judge them, and separate ourselves from everything that was annoying to good taste. The habits of disease and old age were spoken of, as particularly disgusting, and one elderly member said he didn't want persons should treat him as though he was an old man, and needed care and petting on that account. He thought the best way to overcome old age, (which was nothing but a habit) was to ignore it. Last night, persons were made free to say what they wished to, about the habits of the family, or of individuals, and there was considerable freedom and a good deal of mirth over some habits that were criticised.

Some time since, mention was made in the *Daily* of a lady visitor who " wished to remain here as long as she lived, provided she died in any decent season." The same person came again yesterday, her object seeming to be, to find a home. She was employed as nurse in the army, and brought a large file of recommendations which she wished Mrs. Bolles to read. Mrs. B. told her we did not doubt her honesty or faithfulness, but we could not accept her as a member, and referred her to Mr. Noyes's article in a late CIRCULAR. She thought if she could see Mr. N. it might be different, but on being assured by Mrs. B. that she had given her the mind of the Community, she decided to leave, this morning.

We would introduce to the readers of the *Daily*, Miss Ann S. Bailey, as its future Editress. In retiring from our office we desire to thank the family for their patience in bearing with our many mistakes, and hope the same leniency will be extended to our successor, who we doubt not will have the support of the family in her new position, which she enters upon with much trembling. We feel however, that she will do well in the business.
E. Y. J.

Mr. Hawley took all the children with their attendants and teacher out to ride, yesterday afternoon. The sleighing was excellent, the day fine and they all enjoyed it much. There were thirty-one, and they all went in one long sleigh, drawn by two span of horses.

THE O. C. DAILY.

VOL. 5.   FRIDAY, JAN. 17, 1868.   NO. 15.

W. P., Jan. 16.—Our great water-wheel became so loaded with ice that it was considered unsafe, so a company of the men went at it to-day, relieved it of its burden and put up a stove in the wheel room.

A lot of beaver traps which were to have been finished last September, but were laid aside on account of the hurry of other work, are now being finished.

The punching of jaws and pan-posts instead of drilling them as heretofore, proves to be a success. C. C. H. has been at work on the rollers for a day or two and is preparing to roll the great bear-trap springs to-morrow.

We haven't any little folks at our house, but once in a while we make a draft on Oneida's "happy family." Marion and Mabel are over to-night.

We wonder what W. C. would say if they knew that the O. C. talked of selling out! We wonder if they think we can go on making traps when our noble Factory lies in ruins!! And isn't our Bag business drawing its last breath? They don't know that the Democratic party have offered us eight hundred thousand dollars (!!) cash down, for our place, to turn into a Soldier's Home!! W. C. better look out! The tables may turn. While they are advertising, O. C. *may* appear to them in a more tangible form than they do to us, by merely shutting their eyes and letting the imagination work!!! "AFTER YOU."

Mr. Woolworth and Carrie went to Vernon yesterday and paid $4,000—one-half of the mortgage on the Hitchcock farm. It was not due till April first, but having the money on hand we offered it to them, and they accepted it, allowing us $36.20 for prepayment. This mortgage was given to Josiah Case, President of Bank of Vernon, March 10, 1865. The remaining $4,000 will be due October first, 1868. The amount of mortgages now stands, $19,650.

Mr. Olds reports that the large trap order from Treadwell and Co., Boston, was packed and sent off yesterday.

111 doz. amounting to $1,123.41 net. Three doz. of these were bear traps. There were fourteen cases sent to T. P. Rose, N. Y., and shipped from there to California via. Cape Horn.

Three gentlemen called at the Office the other day, one of whom made quite urgent inquiries as to where Mr. Noyes was, and when he would be back here. Mr. W. asked him if he was acquainted with Mr. N. or his publications.

"No" he replied, "but my friend here, knowing that you were in the manufacturing business, has a new kind of *buckle* which he wished to show to Mr. N., and have some talk about."

Surely, we thought, Mr. Noyes would be bored to death if he turned his attention to everything and everybody that called for him.

The Talk on "God's Love" was read in our meeting last evening, and by the expressions which followed, it evidently made a deep impression on the hearts of all. That God does hear and answer prayer and that "he is a rewarder of them who diligently seek him," is becoming a living fact to us.

Otis! Mr. Conant thinks you and perhaps some others will be interested to hear that they have drawn the first muck from the swamp near the cheese-factory. The amount drawn is forty-three loads.—Mr. Conant also reports that the teamsters are improving the excellent sleighing by drawing wood from Stockbridge hill. We have about 150 cords there, which they hope to get home while the sleighing lasts.

One of the school boys was lately overheard talking in his sleep something in this wise :

"Nine, is a common noun ; multiplied by"—

After some moments silence he again exclaimed, "Mr. Perry, it's time for spelling class." Then no doubt fancying his turn had come, he spells clearly and with considerable assurance, " B-e be, q-u-i-t-h queath, bequeath." Poor fellow!!

This morning every one's curiosity seems to be not a little aroused by the unexpected appearance of T. R. N. We hear the eager question, "What *has* he come for?" His precise mission we have not learned, but are glad to see him here on whatever business.

Mr. Aiken and Homer have gone to Utica this morning, on business.

THE O. C. DAILY.

VOL. 5.   SATURDAY, JAN. 18, 1868.   NO. 16.

EVENING MEETING.

Theodore read the report of Mr. Noyes's remarks about Carlton Rice and Spiritualism, and a letter from Mr. Woolworth to Mr. Rice giving Mr. Noyes's views. Much sympathy was confessed with Mr. N.'s ideas, and a determination expressed to keep free from all sympathy with Spiritualism, and any curiosity respecting its diabolical phenomena. We used to have Wright and Hazelton to keep us stirred up against this spirit, but since their departure we may have grown careless respecting the danger. Our weakness in this case of Mr. Rice was thought to lie in the direction of false benevolence, which leads us to magnify his services, and makes us unduly anxious to help him. Mr. Rice was sincerely judged for his relations to Gerrit Smith and this hadean mummery. He has not confessed the truth before the world and therefore can not be said to have done much for it after all. Gerrit Smith is really our enemy, because of his infidelity. There was a determination to be thoroughly separated from his spirit and from all his sympathizers.

A committee was appointed to consider the question of financial aid to Mr. Rice. This point was considered a delicate one. It was hoped he would not need aid. The committee will endeavor to look at every aspect of the case in the true spirit.

One of our trap-shop hands, George Walters, met an old school-mate at the depot the other day, who gave quite an interesting account of himself. George tells his story as follows:

"Three years ago he went to California and betook himself to trapping. The first season he had tolerable luck, though he had but few traps, and did not understand the art very well, (owing doubtless to his not having a copy of the 'Trapper's Guide.') But last Fall he went again, taking with him quite a number of Newhouse's superior Nos. 0 and 1. About fifty miles north-east from San Francisco, he found a trapping ground where mink were plenty and Comanches were not. In fact, not a hostile Indian within 150 miles. Here he set himself at work, and in three months had captured $700.00 worth of fur, and 'used up' his traps.

"They got broken, I suppose?"

"No, not exactly. A few were stolen, and then when he got done trapping he threw away what traps he had left. He used up about twelve dozen, in the two seasons. That's always the way trappers do out there—when the season's over, throw away the old traps, good ones and all—the price of a trap is nothing—when they start again, buy new ones."

(Communistic interlocutor with an eye to market.)

"Why that's a real handy way I should think!"

"Yes: black bears, panthers and wolves gave him the most trouble of anything, as they were pretty thick, and as he had nothing but a gun, he couldn't thin them out much. A few beaver and bear traps would have set him all right."

George's friend states farther than this, that the Newhouse trap came into the San Francisco market about three years ago. Before that, poor English traps and clumsy wooden contrivances were in use. Now, of course nothing but N. S. will answer. A No. 6 Grizzly bear-trap, is one of the "sights" in San Francisco. People didn't think a trap could be made so large before. The business of trapping has received a great impetus within a year or two in California, owing to the introduction of a perfect trap, and the advancement of the Pacific R. R. Sections of country, heretofore unsafe on account of the scalping knife, are now open to the public. The trap trade is bound to grow immensely in that region, especially when the railroad is opened clear through.

The young man (who is responsible for the above views), starts back to California again next month.—c.

W. P., Jan. 17.—Messrs. Campbell and Clark went to Clayville to-day, to see about getting a man to make patterns for pipe skeins and boxes for wagon axles, hoping to introduce them in the Foundry. They found him at work for another man, so not at liberty to do anything for us at present. They got however, some new ideas in regard to nicety and finish, which will be of much value should we continue the business. J. F. S. is engaged in draughting and making patterns for the corn-machine.—Mother Oneida sends us this afternoon an invitation to come over to meeting. So we have supper earlier, afterward brotherly hands help us clear it away. At half past six we gather in the parlor to hear the journals and Talks. As we finish some one says, "There! the bells!" in an instant there is general donning of shawls, bonnets, overcoats &c. We laughingly stow ourselves away under the buffaloes, and are off. So easily and quietly we make the change, like the flitting of birds in Autumn. No Cabbages we.

Our steward says: "The second half ton of cheese made for us at the factory this year, was of so positive a character that it was likely to remain on our hands indefinitely, there were so few in the family that liked it. It was sold in Utica yesterday for 10½ cts. per pound, with this reservation—if Martin gets a better price offered for it in New-York, sample having been sent him, we can send it there. To take the place of this, cheese was bought some weeks since of a factory on the East hill, for 14 cts. which is excellent."

THE O. C. DAILY.

VOL. 5.   MONDAY, JAN. 20, 1868.   NO. 20.

EVENING MEETING.

Mr. Cragin spoke of the Carpenters and gave them some good general advice, applicable in part to all new members.

Mr. Woolworth spoke of the late Talk on Northern and Southern Vermont as one that had interested him a good deal. Others heartily joined in this, especially Northern Vermont members. The meeting was then devoted to brotherly exhortation.

Manly Aiken was spoken of as lacking earnestness in seeking salvation ; and it was hoped he would give less attention to dress and hair-cutting. Mr. Aiken was exhorted to try and become a spiritual helper to Manly.

Homer Barron was commended for giving good testimony in meeting, but exhorted not to fall from the pitch of earnestness, as he is liable to do when out of meeting. He should watch his influence, and cultivate openness with the men.

Martha Hawley was mentioned as one in need of conversion from a hard heart. She has never really given her heart to God. There are hopeful symptoms in her case now. Mr. Hawley and her brothers were exhorted not to make a pet of Martha, but rather to seek to help her to conversion.

And finally the young folks generally were exhorted to be watchful respecting their influence upon one another. If they cannot help those who have taken a new stand for Christ, they should at least let them alone. Theodore was mentioned as one whose example in love could be safely followed. Many of the young folks confessed their union with him.

———————

In our noon meeting yesterday, Theodore, who, in company with George E. had just returned from a call on Mr. Carlton Rice, gave a report. Their object was to report to him the state of our finances, and that we could not help him without embarrassing ourselves. Mr. Rice seemed to have great confidence in our integrity and thought the business could be so arranged that we could help him and still not injure ourselves. The matter was referred to Mr. Noyes in perfect confidence. Following this was an earnest desire expressed to be saved from false benevolence, and to know how to treat our outside friends. Mr. Burt had been going through some judgment on this point—said that false benevolence was a weakness that he had always been liable to, and he wanted it judged without mercy. Our true outside friends are really benefitting themselves more than they are us, and we need not therefore feel under obligations to them.

———————

Among the changes made in the work this week are the following : Miss Ellen Nash goes into the children's house in the place of Florence ; Miss Eliza Burt takes Ellen's former post, that of assistant to Fidelia as mother in the kitchen, and Phebe goes to the Bag-shop in the place of Eliza. We ask wherefore Mr. Olds should sit and pare apples so quietly this morning, and are told he has taken the place of John Leonard for the present and John goes to W. P. Shall we suffer for lack of " Chemistry in the Kitchen"?

Mrs. Bradley who has been with us the past two weeks returns to her post at the Boarding-House with new zeal, feeling benefited and refreshed by her stay here. B. T. T. also goes to the B. H. and Mrs. Mallory and M. Hall come home.

———————

Sidney states that we have a larger amount of apples on hand than usual for this time of year. They disappear rather slowly, consequently they have to be sorted considerably. We grind up the defective ones and make them into vinegar for future use.

———————

As our first move towards closing up the Bag business, our agents have been instructed to dispose of our manufactured stock, by giving their customers better rates of discount, as an inducement for them to buy more, and earlier in the season than is usual. We have received since Jan. 6, orders to the amount of $1,287.00, with the assurance from some of the agents that we shall be able to sell all the bags we have made or can make, at good prices, without any difficulty.

As frames are the most unsalable stock we have on hand, we propose to make up our stock of leather, enameled muslin &c., with reference to these, which we can do and still supply our customers with any styles of bags they may order.

Our present number of hired hands is eight, four men and four women. These, with six men and three women of our family, half a day, together with the bag bees, constitute our present force. W. H. Perry is our present inspector of bags, therefore, no bags to be had hereafter, that cannot be opened when it is necessary.   N.

———————

One of the Northern Vermonters hands us the following : " The Talk on 'Two Opposing Parties' was evidently a nail in a sure place. It works like leaven in the hearts of all the Northern Vermonters, men and women. And not only so, but the other party already feel a turning of heart toward the branch criticised, and we all see in prospect a glorious union, and even went so far last evening as to reckon ourselves one."

———————

There was no business before the Board yesterday, necessarily, no report.

———————

Little Harry Kelly on being told that it was time for him to go to bed, whimpered out, " I don't go to bed now, I go at half past one."

THE O. C. DAILY.

VOL. 5.   TUESDAY, JAN. 21, 1868.   NO. 18.

EVENING MEETING.

Homer Barron thanked the family for what was said to him last evening and hoped others would feel free if they had anything in mind. " I acknowledge the justice of the criticism," he said, " and desire to be stable and spiritually minded."

Mr. Kinsley :—I am very much interested in the Talk in regard to Northern Vermont. I have a great desire for an enlargement of heart, and for a soft heart that is open to the spirit of the Putney family. I desire to remove all obstructions to full union with their spirit.

Mr. Barron :—I join Mr. Kinsley in that expression. In thinking of the Northern Vermont members, it has seemed to me that we have been *loyal* to Mr. Noyes, in a measure, from the beginning ; and at the same time I think there has been a pretty strong principality upon us that has been quite independent, and that we need to get rid of. I feel that I need to be delivered myself. [Other Northern Vermonters joined in these expressions.]

H. G. A. writes from Chicago, Jan. 16, 8 A. M. " Have just reached here after the through ride of **284 miles from Detroit, since six o'clock last evening.**" He says of Standart Brothers, Toledo, " I have been afraid they were expanding too much, and think now that they were managing things to good advantage.

" The best houses there, all complain about their collections being slow, very slow. We may sell some traps there in the Spring. Expect to get some bag-orders there on my return. Obtained orders there for seven or eight lbs. of our Machine Twist, mostly as samples, and think we shall get a good trade there in time. I feel more than ever as though I was on the Lord's business, and only wish to do what he has for me to do."

Some days ago, Milford, chancing to be over on the old picnic ground, saw a half eaten crow, and feeling certain that the work was that of an owl or fox, he was not long in procuring one of " Newhouse's Superior," which he cunningly and with true hunter shrewdness covered with feathers. This done, he returned home to await the result.

Saturday Mr. Bristol, Homer and Sidney were down in the Petrie woods hunting, when Mr. Bristol descrying what he supposed a partridge, took aim and fired. On gaining the spot where his game had fallen, he found not a partridge, but an enormous owl, measuring from tip to tip four feet and ten inches, with a No. 1 trap and chain attached to its foot. They were some surprised at this but on reaching home, Milford

was able to explain the matter. After exhibiting the prize to quite a number of the family, including the children, whose eyes for wonderment became nearly as large as those of the owl, they beheaded it ; or as little Emily Easton expressed it, " Say, you children, Mr. Sidney Joslyn cut off that *howl's ed*"

Our little fish-pond under the bank west of the house, boasts a score or more of handsome trout, weighing from one fourth to one half pound each. These speckled beauties owe their presence in these parts to Mr. Bristol's agency, and he quite naturally exercises a fatherly care over them and indulges them from time to time with a meal of fresh meat, which they eat with great avidity. To see them swarm around the hole cut through the ice, and take the pieces of meat from the hand of those who feed them is fun which an admiring group occasionally enjoy. The entertainment is heightened when a roguish hand that holds the tempting piece of meat gives a sudden jerk, as the unsuspecting trout closes his teeth upon it, landing him high and dry on the ice. How much the trout enjoy this last operation is uncertain.

G. W. H. writes from Indianapolis Jan. 15 :
" People feel somewhat better here than they do at Cincinnati, though they complain here of hard times. I do not find letters to day from home. Shall go on to Lafayette to-morrow. If I was perfectly sure that the parties in Peoria and Quincy would pay I would not go there it is so expensive, but the fact is they don't know where who is good now-a-days. The wholesale men seem to fare the hardest, they have so many outstanding accounts. I still hope for good luck, and am thankful for what we have had."

THE DARTMOUTH, a Monthly published by the students of Dartmouth college, has the following notice in its *Memoranda Alumnorum*: " Hepworth Dixon's recent book 'The New America,' contains an extended biographical history of John Humphrey Noyes, class of '30, the founder and head of the prosperous Community styled ' Perfectionists,' at Oneida Creek, N. Y."

Yesterday, Messrs Hawley and Clark spent the day in going to Clinton, Deansville and Knoxboro, for the purpose of delivering sleigh shoes and other castings, and bringing home from Knoxboro old iron for use at the Foundry.

Mr. C. B. Underwood returned yesterday from a few days visit to his daughters, Mrs. Bridge and Mrs. Brown.

It snows quite fast this morning ; some of the men say at the rate of a depth of ¼ of an inch in an hour.

THE O. C. DAILY.

VOL. 5.   WEDNESDAY, JAN. 22, 1868.   NO. 19.

EVENING MEETING.

The report of Mr. Noyes's remarks on the subject of faithfulness was read and appreciated. It drew out the following responses :

Mr. Cragin :—I believe faithfulness is the gift of God to us, and where it is recognized as such I don't think it will lead to man-worship.

Mr. Woolworth :—I am thankful that there is a foundation of faithfulness laid in this world.

George E. :—I like this idea very much of drawing toward Mr. and Mrs. Noyes, and cultivating the same spirit of faithfulness toward them that they have to God. I want to remove every other attraction in myself but the one that will draw me in that direction, and make me faithful to the truth. In studying the faithfulness that Mrs. Noyes has always shown toward Mr. Noyes, I think it will be found that one thing that constitutes her strength is, that she is instantly receptive to everything that comes from him : she does not seem to have a shadow of hesitancy, but is ready to receive whatever he proposes and trust God for the result. I think she is a model that we can all follow.

Mr. Cragin :—She had perfect faith in his inspiration at the beginning, and never has yielded to doubt for a moment since.

[A good many confessed the same spirit of faithfulness Mrs. Noyes has, and their union with her.]

W. P., Jan. 20.—Joel has been to Syracuse to-day to see about getting some springs' trip hammered for the No. 6 bear-trap. They hope to accommodate us in about three weeks. The steel will be sent them to-morrow.

Our tenant houses near us are to be left vacant, as Mr. Milbury (our former watchman) with his family, also Mr. Christian and wife, leave next week for the west. We are pleased to have them go. If Oneida has any difficulty in finding room for the coming troop from W. C., we may be able to provide some of them with *christian* lodgings.

Jan. 21.—This forenoon the waiter at the shop went suddenly from the fourth story to the bottom, having on it at the time several boxes of traps, a man and boy. As it started, the man saved himself by clinging to the floor, the boy jumping off at the next story. The waiter went on with a terrific noise, raising a great dust and striking the bottom with such violence as to cause the bursting open of some of the boxes. The cause of all this, was the loosening of the set screws that fasten the driving wheel.

This afternoon one of the small boys employed in the shop, in fun threw a handful of iron filings into the face of another boy, filling his eyes full. The poor fellow . . . . . . the Office, where two or three of our men spent an hour or so in washing out the filings from his eyes, after which he returned to his work with a cleaner face.

One of the Forge shop presses has lately been remodeled on a new plan invented by the machinists at a cost of seventy dollars. Preparations are being made for altering the large press for punching springs in the same way. It is a great improvement on the old style.

The Silk Dept. report that they have a ready market for all the silk they can make.

———————

" What is being done in your department, Mr. Kelly ?"

" Well, quite a variety of things. We have one hired man, Mr. Petrie, steadily employed in making furniture, tables, stands, bureaus, &c., &c. Another, Mr. Crain, has been getting out stuff for a partition at the trap-shop. Mr. Ellis makes boxes for packing traps and bags. He has just finished seventy for the trap-shop. You may tell Abram that we have given the planing-machine a thorough overhauling, and now it runs finely."

———————

A day or two ago we heard two ladies remarking about the weather like this :

C.—(Looking out of the window), I declare, it really seems as though it snowed all the time, and I believe it does, every day.

D.—(Born in Conn. Turning around with a great deal of sham surprise depicted on her countenance), How *can* you say so ? We have had since winter set in, five days in which the sun rose and set without a cloud, just as it does in Connecticut. *Five entire days !* What a rarity !

———————

" There were several parties of visitors here Monday. Neighbors from Smithfield with friends from a distance ; two students of Madison University on their return from North Bay, where one of them preached Sunday ; a couple from Lakeport with friends from Ill. ; a Mr. Steele from Wyoming County, an acquaintance of Mrs. Bushnell, with his daughter and several lady friends, brought over from Peterboro where they had been visiting ; and some others." So says Mr. Underwood.

———————

G. W. H. writes from Lafayette : " The prospect is, we shall have a heavy demand for traps from this State next season." And from Peoria, Ill. " I turn my face homeward this evening. I expect to be in Chicago to-morrow morning and hope to see H. G. A. I have just taken an order for ten lbs. of Silk."

———————

Won't this day of perfect loveliness and beauty atone for weeks of cloud, wind and snow ? This one whole-hearted smile makes us forget a score of frowns.

THE O. C. DAILY.

VOL. 5. THURSDAY, JAN. 23, 1868. NO. 20.

EVENING MEETING.

Mr. Aiken was criticised by request. He was commended for improvement in spirit, and manner of treating members of the family. He appears very ambitious to have the Store make a good showing, and realize Mr. Noyes's expectation. He was exhorted to be still more anxious about his spiritual balance. He takes great pains to please outside customers, but his manners to our people going there for things are still objectionable in some respects. People feel that he considers the Store his own property, and that he does not care to have them come for things, or if they do, he gives them in a way to make folks feel that they are receiving a charity. He still shows some partiality and respect of persons. Mr. Woolworth said he liked Mr. Aiken's anxiety to please his worldly customers; but he thought he should take more pains to please the Community and make the Store attractive, especially to the committee who has charge of the wants of the family. So far as he knew there was a chaste spirit on the part of the family about going to the Store for goods. Mr. Aiken's position is a trying one: his office may be to exercise a wholesome restraint in some instances. He should try and make it easy for folks to consult with him about clothing etc. His faults were thought to near . . . . mindedness. He forgets that our interests are all one. It was hoped he would study the Talk on Northern Vermont.

Mr. Leete generally goes home Tuesday morning and returns Wednesday night, spending the remainder of his time in attendance at the Store. As he was about to get into the sleigh Tuesday morning, he laughingly said, " When I get ready to go home, I'm reminded of the man who went to sea. On leaving his wife, he wrote, ' Mr. —— going to sea, his wife requests the prayers of the congregation,' for the minister to read in church. He, not minding the punctuation, made it read, ' Mr. —— going to see his wife, requests the prayers of the congregation.' This last way of reading it applies to me. I'm going to see my wife, and feel like requesting the prayers of the church."

Here is a conversation from the school-room:

Teacher.—Edith ! what is the capital of Paraguay ?

Edith.—(Snapping her fingers, and her eyes fairly dancing for merriment) I know ; Consumption!

Teacher.—What does consumption mean ?

Edith.—When folks have got the rickets.

Teacher.—(Addressing the school) Is that right ?

Marion.—No ma'am. It's a *great big cough.*

I am thankful that I have been accounted worthy to be one of its members. I am also thankful for good health and for a good appetite for work. I never enjoyed my work as I have for a few months past, or realized so much that I was working for God and his cause. I wish to give myself soul and body, unreservedly to Christ, to serve him forever, with all my soul, mind and strength. I cannot thank God enough for his care over me all my life. As well for my sufferings and discipline, as for my joys and prosperity. But above all do I thank God for deliverance from special and idolatrous love.

OLIVE CONANT.

One passing through the upper sitting-room last evening might have seen on the center table a beautifully frosted, pyramidal cake, ornamented with variously colored confectionery, and lying near it a note addressed to Mr. John Leonard, which read like this :

DEAR BROTHER :—Please accept this present as an expression, to some extent, of the sincere regard which we feel for you as a brother and co-laborer. We desire especially to thank you for the enthusiastic manner in which you have prosecuted the study of science in the kitchen. Your efforts in this respect, we think, have given an impetus in the right direction. We hope that in whatever circumstances you may be placed, you will lose none of your interest in the Kitchen Department. Confessing a lively interest in your welfare, We remain your friends.

[Here followed the names of all those engaged in the kitchen, and some others.]

As a result of the discussion on manners, one of our young women was heard to say in a very arch way, to an unsuspecting individual, " Here ! Gentlemen of the O. C. are not allowed to sit in their hats with the house on."

There was a bee yesterday afternoon for getting the Carpenters ready to leave. Are we not justified in hoping this is the last bee of the kind we shall be called on to hold ?

Messrs. Newhouse and Hawley have gone to Hampton, where the former will remain a day or two for the purpose of working on the patterns of the castings we have made there.

Temple has lately been learning about the Poles, and conceiving the idea that there must be some such arrangement about himself, cries out to his mother; " O mama ! my north leg aches."

Mr. Kelly gone to Utica on business.

THE O. C. DAILY.

VOL. 5.   FRIDAY, JAN. 24, 1868.   NO. 21.

EVENING MEETING.

Mr. Carpenter expressed thanks to the family for their kindness to himself and family during their late preparations to leave. He desired the most friendly and kind feelings towards us. Finally, he was thankful for our kindness to them all through their stay here. He had been very much benefited by his acquaintance with us. He knew he was not qualified to remain here. If God wants him here, he will find a way to fit him for a place with us. Mrs. Carpenter joined Mr. C. in thanking the Community for their kindness, and confessed Christ a soft heart and a spirit of brotherly love.

Messrs. Woolworth, Cragin and others were glad to part with friendly feelings on both sides, and though Mr. C. may be disqualified for soldiers duty at present, we shall be glad to consider him a sympathizer outside.

Sympathy with the Talk "How to be Samsonized" was expressed, and a belief that it is not only possible, but an easy thing for God to give us an increase of power and vitality, so that as children of God we shall have power in ourselves to do all things.

Mr. Woolworth.—I don't want to have any spirit in me that will limit God in respect to our bodies or souls. He owns us body, soul and spirit. I desire that he may make the most of us.

Mr. Whitney.—I desire that God may have my whole body and soul and passions. I have liked Mr. Noyes's Talks lately very much. In thinking of his remarks about fasting, I have felt like judging my past life in regard to my alimentiveness. That has been my weak point. I wish to expose the devil and clear myself from this spirit.

Then followed remarks on true love, which is a great source of strength to us. There is power in it. God has not given us a spirit of fear but of power and love and a sound mind. We have had a great deal of criticism of false love; now we want to see it displaced and the ground fully occupied by true love. And not only false love, but false benevolence should be removed. That has been as great a curse to us as false love. It leads us into fellowships that destroy our life without bringing back anything to God.

While on the cars, overhearing some men conversing about the proposed short-cut from Utica to Wampsville, I was a little curious to listen.

One of them who seemed to be well posted was very confident that it would be carried out this season.

He said that Case, of Vernon, recently attended a meeting of the Board of Directors of the Central Road at Albany, in which Vanderbilt expressed himself strongly in favor of straightening this part of the road, and selling the section from Rome to Utica, to the Rome and Watertown road. By this change they find they can save 300 miles travel every twenty-four hours.

Vanderbilt says no local interest shall influence him in the least against what is for the general interest of the road.   w. g. k.

———

Mr. Kinsley and George E. have gone to Morrisville to see Judge Holmes about Mr. Rice's farm. He is thoroughly posted about the farm, the execution of the sale being in his hands, and if the information obtained from him proves satisfactory, they will go on to Hamilton and try to make such arrangements with Mr. Rice as will enable us, in case we buy his farm, to regain the money invested in the course of two or three months.

———

Yesterday Mr. Clark went to Canastota for the purpose of delivering castings, and making a few collections.

———

Mr. Conant says the teamsters are still engaged in drawing wood and logs. Yesterday morning, however, on reaching the foot of the hill, they found the snow so badly drifted that the roads were quite impassable, and after getting a little wood that had been left there, they came home by the village of Stockbridge.

Uncle Heman says we have now for family use, about twenty-five gallons of milk; enough to keep us comfortable; enough for tea, coffee and cocoa, and occasionally a bread-and-milk supper.

———

The Carpenters took a quiet leave of us last night at 12 o'clock. They proved rather indigestible—something of a "dough-ball"—and we feel lighter to have them gone. We gave them $50.00, deducting the same from amount of inventory of their goods left at W. C., and they gave us a receipt in full of all demands whatever.

———

We are a little in the dark as to the perpetrator of the following:

"The O. C. has been forcibly reminded by recent experience that Carpenters are not always joiners."

———

Last evening one of the women was heard to say in an earnest and decided manner, "Why Mrs. Clark, that yarn isn't good for *anything.* Only think! I knit *Hemily* a pair of stockings, and she 'adn't worn 'em a week, before there was 'oles in the toes and 'oles in the 'eels.

———

It was proposed last evening to have the supper hour changed from five to five and a half o'clock.

THE O. C. DAILY.

VOL. 5.   SATURDAY, JAN. 25, 1868.   NO. 22.

EVENING MEETING.

Mr. Kinsley reported that he and George E. called on Judge Holmes, of Morrisville, and examined the papers relative to Carlton Rice's farm. The place has been mortgaged twenty-four years, and has been in court since 1864. It was consequently so involved that they determined at once to have nothing to do with it. The court has decided that Mr. Rice's title is good, though he attempted to disprove it, in order to invalidate the mortgage. In consequence of this plea of his Mr. Kinsley thought no one would take a new mortgage.

They then called on Mr. Rice and told him their decision; and at his request consented to go to Utica and see Thompson, the mortgagee, with a view of inducing him to postpone the sale for thirty days. Thompson and Rice are open foes, but Mr. Rice thought Thompson might listen to them. If he could have little more time he hoped to still raise the money. He could easily raise it by mortgaging the place Mr. Smith gave his wife, but Mr. Smith would object to it, and he does not like to displease him.

It was distinctly understood by Mr. Rice, that, after this appeal to Thompson had been made, we would have nothing further to do with the business. Our delegates thought the most charitable view to take of him was, that he was so involved that he did not know the real merits of the case. He did not tell us the whole truth when here a while since, and probably did not know it himself. He has lost his energy and is intellectually, morally and physically lazy and in bondage to Gerrit Smith. Thankfulness was expressed that we were to have nothing further to do with him.

———————

W. P., Jan. 23.—On the sixty-seventh page of the present volume of the *Scientific American* is a question stated thus: "How many revolutions on its own axis will a wheel make in rolling once round a fixed wheel of the same diameter?"

As the subject excited considerable interest among the men and some of the women, it was proposed that it be discussed at length in the evening meeting. Accordingly, one enthusiast with the aid of the blackboard and a minute machine proceeded to prove that it made but *one* when the same side of the axis was directed toward the center of the wheel. Then taking the other side of the argument, he proved that it made *two* when the axis was carried round with reference to the points of the compass.

Highly amusing discussions followed, in which no less than four machines were brought forward by as many different persons, to prove these two principles. The umpires, Mrs. C. A. M. and H. E. A. have as yet been unable to decide which is right.

Jan. 24.—Mr. Inslee reports that the waiter is again in safe and working order.

The last of the No. 6 bear-traps have been sent off.

Mr. Hawley kindly came over this afternoon with a four horse sleigh and gave us a family sleigh-ride, a nice long one. We all enjoyed it exceedingly, and offer Mr. H. our heartiest thanks.

On arriving home we found G. W. H. awaiting the warm welcome we were ready to give him. He reported himself in the evening meeting as having had a profitable time spiritually. Said he realized God's care as never before.—All expressed themselves as very thankful for the talk, "How to be Samsonized."

———————

B. H. C.—A dance is going on here this evening. It happened on this wise: Two of our best trap-shop hands leave us to-morrow, induced to do so by higher wages at gun making. But wishing for a social gathering of their acquaintances, mostly among our late and present employes, these two young men applied for a room in our trap-shop for a dance. We did not like to say *no*, and yet we could not say *yes*. So we compromised the matter by offering them our dining-hall at the boarding-house. With this offer, they were more than satisfied, highly pleased. Our boarders too, especially those whose dresses conceal the *character* of the *steps* in the performance of the dance, consider it a pleasurable episode in their monotonous mode of daily life. Well, so far they appear to enjoy the occasion much, and their behavior toward all, is commendable. Indeed, to commend themselves to our little family, seems to be their chief pleasure. The company consists of about twenty-four couple.

Mr. Whitney has been experimenting the past week to ascertain the comparative expense of using Lehigh and Scranton coal, and gives the following figures:

Lehigh used in 7 days 1,575 lbs. Exps. 71 cts. per day
Scranton "   "   "   1,645 "   "   ·59 "   "   "

Balance in favor of Scranton coal,   12 "   "   "

Mr. Ackley has also been using the Scranton coal in the kitchen-range at W. P. and considers it preferable to Lehigh.

———————

Mr. Newhouse says: "Mr. Root thought it would be a good thing for Mr. Noyes to call on Vanderbilt and have a talk with him about this scheme of straightening the Central. He said he himself had met Mr. Noyes several times, and he liked him very much, and thought him a very interesting man; and he believed if he would call on Vanderbilt it would have a good effect."

———————

Traps ordered during the week, 25 doz. Received also last night the following order from Hudson's Bay Co.:

75 doz.	No. 1.	49 doz.	No. 2.
34 "	" 3.	44½ "	" 4.
1 "	" 5,	(Bear-traps).	

Assuming that these are to have chains, the amount of the order will be, $1,902.43

The traps are to be sent in two installments; the greater part at once, and the remainder in March.

THE O. C. DAILY.

VOL. 5.   MONDAY, JAN. 27, 1868.   NO. 23.

BUSINESS MEETING.

As there are several wagons that need repairing before wheeling comes, and the blacksmiths can attend to it now better than later, it was suggested that, if D. F. Knowles could be spared from W. P., he should oversee the details of the business under the supervision of Mr. Kelly.

Messrs. J. Conant, J. H. Barron, Kinsley, Burt and G. W. H. were appointed as a committee of consultation, in reference to converting the room over the engine into a place for drying clothes, in accordance with the plan adopted by the hotels in N. Y. as reported by E. H. H. There will be no change made in the room until the return of A. L. Burt.

Mr. Ellis, in connection with the other carpenters, will fulfill all obligations we may have incurred to make rustic seats for parties who have applied for them.

Persons should not carry jobs to either the blacksmiths or carpenters unless they are really necessary; and try to be economical in both time and material. When furniture is wanted the committee should be consulted.

Every precaution should be taken to have the waiter at W. P. made perfectly safe. G. W. H. will examine the safety improvements in use in other places and report.

Mr. Kinsley went to Utica Saturday, to see about getting the sale of Mr. Rice's farm adjourned. Mr. Thompson met him pleasantly, and agreed to leave the question of the adjournment to Judge Holmes, whom he would see in a few days. Mr. Kinsley agreed to pay the cost of such adjournment—which would be merely nominal—if the mortgage was not redeemed, and the sale eventually took place. Mr. Thompson thought Mr. Rice had meant to deal honestly about the estate, but he was rather slack, and his affairs had been embarrassed. Mr. Kinsley wrote to Mr. Rice, reporting the result of his interview with Thompson; and here it is supposed our connection with the matter ends.

We quite frequently have notes read in the meeting from different members of the family which show that the good work is going on and the spirit of truth at work in searching our hearts, preparing the way for concentration, and a real *home* in which all hearts are one. Though these notes are edifying, they are rather too long to admit of printing all of them.

Among those read lately was one from D. M. K., expressing faith and confidence in Mr. Noyes and a determination to be faithful.

Another from Manly, exposing past temptations and taking a new stand for Christ and the truth.

Miss Ellen Nash confessed her hatred of false love and judged a spirit that had secretly longed for it.

She took a bold stand on the side of the Lord, and expressed her desire for the community fellowship.

One from Mr. Conant expressing his opposition to the disruption spirit, and confessing faithfulness and loyalty to Mr. Noyes.

Quite a lengthy one from Mr. Aiken to Mr. Cragin, in reference to the present disorganized state of his family. He frankly acknowledges he has never stood as the head of his family, but has always looked to Mrs. A. as his leader until two or three years ago, since which time he has neither allowed her the position formerly granted, nor yet had strength to take the place himself.

He now wishes to become organized into the Community, and be so joined on to Christ and Mr. Noyes, as to enable him to assume the true attitude in his family, and qualify him for any place the Community may think best to put him in.

The Talk on "Spiritual Astronomy" was listened to with interest. The year 1816 was mentioned as one of great scarcity occasioned by an extremely cold season. Snow fell to a considerable depth in the month of June. The suffering occasioned thereby was greatest in 1817.

We had a free stirring meeting, which lasted until nearly 10 o'clock. A report will be sent in manuscript.

When Mr. Kinsley and George E. were at Morrisville Judge Holmes presented them with seven neatly bound volumes, five of which were the "Patent Office Report" for '64 and '65, and the other two, "Report of the Department of Agriculture" for the same years.

We were pleased by a short conversation as reported to us by one of the parties. It ran like this:

Mr. X.—Well, Mrs. Z., what's the news?

Mrs. Z.—(A little coldly), I haven't heard any news.

Mr. X.—(Nothing daunted), But, how goes the battle?

Mrs. Z.—(Indifferently), Battle? I don't know what you mean.

Mr. X.—Why the battle with the devil.

Mrs. Z.—(Animatedly), I dont know *anything* about him. I don't have ANYTHING to do with him; but I should think some of the rest of you had considerable dealing with him by your testimony!

Daniel Abbott walked up from Oneida early yesterday morning; he slips into our circle very quietly, and his coming is a reminder of the many more that are to come. "*We can't hardly wait.*"

Born at O. C. on the 25th, a son to Horace R. and Amanda E. Perry. He is a fine little fellow, weighing 8¼ pounds. Last report says mother and son both doing well.

All seemed to enjoy a quiet dance last evening. It was more generally participated in than is sometimes the case, including children, elderly persons and beginners. Not the least noticable of those on the floor was Mrs. H. A. H. Sad commentary on the wisdom of the good people of Putney!

THE O. C. DAILY.

VOL. 5.   TUESDAY, JAN. 28, 1868.   NO. 24.

W. P., Jan. 27.—Our family numbers at present twenty-nine, twelve of whom are women. Georgiana has come to live with us; we notice her this afternoon busily engaged in her new occupation, that of spooling silk.

The author of "Chemistry in the Kitchen" is employing himself these days in making patterns for a machine for bending dogs.

We whirl away again to-night for Mother Oneida, and isn't it nice to live so near? But surely never was there such a load, only think! thirty-three of us, with those we take in from the B. H. C. The old sleigh creaks and groans as if in protest against being weighed down so heavily. On the way it is mentioned as a good providence that the roads are not drifted. It is very unusual for us to have so little snow and yet such excellent sleighing.

Last evening Mr. Woolworth reported that he and several of our men met Mr. Henry Wilson and Mr. Case of Vernon, in our trap-shop office and had some talk with them about the new railroad project, with a view of learning what they would like to have us do. They are a good deal stirred up, and are preparing to make a strenuous effort to have the Central straightened. The route was surveyed some years ago, and the money raised to build the road; and the Central road was pledged as before. They propose to get the record of the old survey, and all the facts, and then send a delegation to Com. Vanderbilt. They wished to have us send a delegate and help defray the expense, our share of which they thought would be from fifteen to twenty-five dollars. Mr. Woolworth told them that our man, Mr. Hamilton, was already in New-York, and if he felt like acting in the capacity of a delegate we should like to have him do so. He also told them we should be willing to share the expense of the delegation. These men are acting quietly and rather not have their movements known and talked about till they come to something. They wish to avoid any excitement. In conclusion Mr. Woolworth said, "I feel the importance of walking wisely and seeking inspiration in the midst of these conflicting interests."

It will be remembered that what was the old parlor is now six bedrooms; well, be it known that three of these rooms at the present time are occupied respectively by Mrs. Smith and her baby, Harriet Sibley and her baby, Mrs. Perry and her baby. Mrs. Ellis rooms there too, and the other day some one said to her:

"You live in babydom, don't you?"

"Baby *dumb?* My goodness, not much baby dumb about this; baby *alive* I should think!"

An anonymous contributor hands us the following

"Did you ever see a Temple cut a summerset? If not, perhaps you would like to know how it is done.

"A keg of nuts was standing on the lower stair of the Tontine. A temple passing by and seeing them, at once proceeded to elevate itself to the summit of the keg. Amid the breathless attention of an astonished crowd it slowly but surely gained the pinnacle, and stood there the cynosure of an awe-struck multitude. One moment of tottering triumph, and down came the temple, keg, nuts and all, scattering the crowd in confusion and 'wild dismay.' One instant the admiration of all—the next—a mass of crumbling ruins.

'Huge foundation stones,
all mingling fell.'

"P. S. The Temple is safe."

Last evening a gentleman called and wished to see "some of the elders—Mr. Olds or some one." The girls, highly amused, ran to tell Mr. O. of his new title; and he found the gentleman to be one Harvey Rice, a cousin of his. He has been for quite a number of years, an engineer, and is at the present time traveling on railroad business. Frequently passing us he said he thought he would stop just to see whether Mr. Olds was "dead or alive."

Mr. Olds invited him to stay over night with us. He appears a little surprised and pleased at the state of things. He too, has heard stories, and is amazed at the truth.

We asked Mr. Clark yesterday morning what he was preparing to do, and he replied:

"Well, Mr. Hall and I thought we would ride out; so he has set up in the dry goods and I in the hardware business, and we're going out to see what we can do."

"Do you really mean so?"

"O certainly, certainly; we are going to take a double team, and Mr. Hall will put in his silk, thread &c., and I'll take castings and try our luck in Hampton, Clinton, Waterville and Madison."

The Oneida "Protection fire Co. No. 2." has its first "Annual Benefit" at Devereux Hall, Jan. 29, 1868. One of the members gave us two tickets, and we bought four more at $1.00 each. The assurance the Co. has made repeatedly before that we might rely upon them for assistance, should our buildings take fire, was renewed. We shall not use the tickets, but may present them to some of our employees.

At the head of the broad stairs in the main hall can be seen a wood engraving of Prof. George Bush, which has been torn from an old copy of "Life Illustrated," and pinned up there.

Mr. Olds leaves the kitchen and goes to W. P. to attend to the packing and shipping of traps. Sidney will fill his place in the kitchen.

At seven o'clock this morning, the mercury stood at three degrees above zero. Some early risers aver that it stood at the zero point before breakfast.

THE O. C. DAILY.

VOL. 5.   WEDNESDAY, JAN. 29, 1868.   NO. 25.

Sundry visitors here yesterday. One of the number A. B. Maynard, of South Bay, for the past thirty years a speculator; at present, "A retired Capitalist," he termed himself. Our neighbor Mr. Stiles, called in the afternoon, with some of his friends, one of whom asked for the privilege of buying our "deacon skins," the coming season. In a conversation with these folks about the "Midland," Mr. Maynard said, that he didn't believe they could get the road through, this time. They couldn't do it against the capital and influence of such men as Vanderbilt, Corning and hundreds of others. They would lay down three tracks on the Central, first. "I will tell you," said he, "just how it will work. The 'Midland' will bond the farmers along the route and make them pay a percentage from time to time, until they get discouraged and refuse, and then they will be sued, and one difficulty will lead to another, and finally Vanderbilt will buy up the whole thing. Somebody will get rich out of it, but the road wont be built. If it want for the Central, it could be built easy enough; but that is laid, and legislated, you see, and they are not going to have another road built, which will bleed the life out of the Central. Not if they can help it, and they can."   C. W. U.

Yesterday Mr. Olds accompanied Mr. Rice to the Silk-factory. He was highly interested in all he saw; noticing so many girls at work he said, "I suppose these girls are all of your own family?"

"No, none of them."

"But they have on short dresses?"

"Yes a great many of our hired women prefer this dress."

"Where are the superintendents?"

"We have one man and two women of our people for this purpose. The young man is'nt in now, but there are the women at work at the books by that table." (Pointing out Elizabeth and Harriet.)

"I don't understand how it is that you can educate such young girls to superintend a business like this, and to keep books too."

"Why, how old do you take those women to be?"

"Well, about fifteen I should say."

"Miss Allen, that one, who is the younger, is at least twenty-five and I guess rather more than that."

It took Mr. Rice some little time to assure himself that they were not girls. He said our women *all* looked short and very girlish. He was greatly pleased with the trap-shop and laughingly said he guessed he should have to go into the trap business.

H. G. A. writes from Chicago, Jan. 24: "Have had an interesting talk to-day with a Mr. Brownley of St. Paul, who is engaged in the fur business. He has spent two seasons near Alaska, in British Columbia, and says that Alaska and vicinity are full of fine furs.

He thinks it only needs the yankees and our traps, to develop the fur business in this locality. They now use wooden traps, and don't understand managing the business in that systematic way we do in the U. S.

"He says that country is perfectly *lousy* with furs, as he expresses it, and that some day we shall have a big demand for traps from there.

"The same he says is true of the Hudson Bay Territory to a great extent, and the H. B. Co. do not do half of the business there they might.

"When that Territory passes out of the hands of the H. B. Co. as it will ere long, I expect we shall have the greatest demand for traps that we have ever had.

"The settling up for *blown* bottles of fruit is one of the "*little odd jobs*" I find to do. Am happy to report that our corn, peas and tomatoes stand at the head of the list here this year—jellies and fruits the same. Folks are loud in their praise of our corn and peas.

"I shall be *very glad* to face homeward, and shall expect to leave here by Monday next, reaching O. C. by Saturday or Sunday morning."

The last CIRCULAR states that there have been five births in the O. C. during the year '67. This startles us a little, for we know that we at Oneida are responsible for only *two* of them. What is the natural inference? Clearly this: W. C. *must* be the responsible party, and all unbeknown to Mother Oneida too; knowing that this would probably be discovered in the coming movement of concentration, they chose the boldest course and published it.

Well, we forgive them, and will bear it in mind when we make room for the company from W. C.

Mr. Newhouse wants us to say to Mr. Noyes, that Vanderbilt in straightening roads, is cutting off the eating houses, the one at St. Johnsville, and quite likely this one at Oneida, thereby creating a demand for Lunch Bags. Mr. Newhouse wants this considered before closing up the bag business.

There was a note read in our meeting last evening, from Mr. and Mrs. Perry, thanking God for his providential care over them, and offering their boy to Christ and the Community. If there was no objection on the part of the family, they would be pleased to call their little one, Walter Burt Perry. This name was liked and adopted.

Our newspaper report last evening was made from the CIRCULAR. It is refreshing to think there is one paper in the world that is not made up of railroad accidents, murders, robberies and politics. It is proposed that the report, on Tuesday evenings, be from this paper, at least for the present.

Messrs. Kinsley and Clark have gone to Vernon to see about buying logs.

THE O. C. DAILY.

VOL. 5.   THURSDAY, JAN. 30, 1868.   NO. 26.

EVENING MEETING.

Mr. Woolworth said he had heard considerable commendation of Mr. Whitney lately, and he would propose that we give him a public benefit. Mr. Whitney had learned to suffer need, and he thought he had reached the spot now where he could bear prosperity. He had come out from under the 7th of Romans and appeared to be living in the 8th of Rom. experience. Then in praising Mr. W. we were not exhalting an individual but magnifying the grace of God.

George E. said when Mr. W. began teaching he had to contend with unbelief, bashfulness and the forwardness of some members. He agreed to try when the committee appointed him, and had tried and succeeded completely, in spite of every obstacle. He has a splendid class now, and all the pupils think him a first rate teacher. The pupils and all joined in this commendation.

Mr. Cragin, and others, wished Mr. W. would write out his whole experience in the Community, including the tobacco conflict and the four secessions he has made. It was thought he had never really succeeded in separating from us, and especially the last time. He was commended for never having given us any trouble in leaving or while away. Mr. Hatch said he was now calling for more work.

All testified that he was cheerful and never grumbled. His experience is looked upon by all as an instance of the power of the grace of God to change character. His talk in meeting is very edifying.

Mr. W. attributed his good experience in part to being free from false love. Others joined in this and suggested that his former bad experience was in a great measure due to certain fellowships.

John Leonard was also commended as one who had made great improvement in gaining victories over old temptations. He seems to be having new experience of a very profitable character. He had a good deal of "Chemistry in the Kitchen" and it seems to have worked into his experience and heart.

The following is Mr. Thomson's decision in regard to adjourning the sale of Carlton Rice's farm :

Utica Jan. 27, 1868.

ALBERT KINSLEY ESQ.—*Dear Sir :*—I have further considered the request to adjourn sale, and have concluded to adjourn the same to the 26th day of February, 1868, to accommodate you. If you please, give the matter prompt attention, and advise me of your final determination as soon as practicable, and oblige,

Yours truly, L. M. THOMSON.

Our final determination is, that we are " Done, completely done." From the moment we decided to clear ourselves from this affair, God's providence and inspiration has attended every move, and we have not only fulfilled all our obligations, (real and fancied) to Mr. Rice, but he is now indebted to us for the adjournment of the sale of his farm.

A. KINSLEY, } *Committee.*
G. E. CRAGIN, }

Mr. Campbell tells us that the number of men now employed at W. P. is thirty-six. Distributed in the different departments as follows :

Machine-shop,	3.
Blacksmith-shop,	3.
Spring department,	3.
Chain " "	7.
Finishing " "	13.
Men of all work,	2.
Foundry,	2.
Saw-mill,	1.
Men who alternate, watching half the time and working half the time,	2.
Total,	36.

He says about half the hands employed in the Trap-shop proper, are boys. It is expected that one of the machinists will be discharged, as soon as the silk machines are completed he is at work upon.

When we go from our little office across the hall and thrust our head into the drying room, filled with long ropes covered with steaming clothes, the room heated to the point of suffocation, and see the colored man walking back and forth, hanging up wet clothes and taking down dry ones, only stopping to feed the two greedy stoves, we think what a change must soon be wrought here. Thinking of the practical part of the change, the removal of posts, bars and benches, substituting type cases, which must needs be transported, we involuntarily reflect what a labor saving operation it would be if Tirzah could only manage another earthquake as adroitly as she did that one mentioned in the CIRCULAR, thereby shaking everything into its proper place in a few moments. What think you Tirzah ?

Yesterday, Erastus Cook, an old acquaintance of Mr. Worden and distant relative of his wife, took dinner with us. C. A. C. had written to him about a patent mouse-trap, of which he has the sale, and he came here to see about selling some of them. The men say it is quite a superior trap, being always set, always baited, and has been known to catch a dozen mice at one time.

Three men had been engaged to come and thresh some clover for us, and accordingly made their appearance yesterday afternoon, and this morning, one standing at the front door may hear through the keen, frosty air the whir and hum that indicate machinery in motion.

THE O. C. DAILY.

VOL. 5.   FRIDAY, JAN. 31, 1868.   NO. 27.

EVENING MEETING.

Mr. Hamilton gave an interesting report of his call on Commodore Vanderbilt, which is probably well known to the other Communes. Mr. Woolworth also reported a call on the Cases of Vernon. They were full of interest in Mr. Hamilton's account of his interview with Mr. Vanderbilt, and to know that he was in any way considering the new project and was already weighing the facts connected with it. The Cases are gathering up facts and statistics so far as possible, with a view of sending a delegation to N. Y. Mr. Hamilton told them we did not wish to be conspicuous at all in this affair, and that we declined acting in connection with the proposed delegation. He thought we could work quite as effectually, by keeping behind the scene ourselves, and acting independently. They assented to this and were willing to have it so.

Mr. Woolworth thought the prestige of this affair, the interview with Mr. Vanderbilt, &c., was a fine thing—and that it is due to the Lord and to his providence. Mr. Hamilton said the devil is evidently trying to pull us down and throw us under by these late attacks upon us; but it is also evident that the Lord means to have us ride triumphantly over these attacks, instead of being swamped by them.

Mr. H. said it was going to be a great time of political and social excitement. Mr. Dixon's new book will soon be in the field and we do not know what that will stir up. He felt ready to trust God and accept of just such a destiny as is before us. He accepted the principles advanced in the Home-Talk just read on "The Offence of the Cross," and was willing to stake his all in the stock Mr. Noyes had put out. That will not depreciate. Others expressed their hearty sympathy with this testimony.

W. P., Jan. 30.—G. W. H. says that while away he was often asked the question how long he had been in the Community? When he answered eighteen years, the questioners appeared much astonished, but seemed to have more respect for us from having seen a person who had lived here so long.

The new riveting machine, which when we first obtained it, we were tempted to throw aside as worthless, was tried yesterday and found to work very satisfactory in the riveting of pans and jaws.

We have commenced a round of criticism; it is proposed to take the members of the family in alphabetical order, one or more each evening. A good deal of sincerity is manifested, combined with love and tenderness. There seems to be a longing in the hearts of all for the judgment.—E. H. H. is with us at supper.

Our Store serves as an excuse for quite a number of our neighbors to call and see us. Neighbors, with whom, in the past we have had more or less trouble. Mr. Olmstead calls occasionally for goods, or work at the shoe-shop, and has the reputation there of being "good pay." His sons too, now and then, give us a short call, making a few purchases, or detailing some local news. H. B. Petrie has also been seen to call two or three times of late for articles from the store. This shows that the O. C. Store is considered by our neighbors as "handy to have."   B.

Miss Mathews does the work on the sewing-machine at the present time. The other day we asked her how many yards she supposed she stitched in a week. She smilingly made answer she did not know; she did all that was brought her to do, and would try and estimate it if we wished her to. During the six working days of last week she stitched on shirts, night-dresses, drawers, skirts, dresses, aprons, towels, sheets and pillow-cases, collars &c., &c., as nearly as she could estimate it, 436 yards.

Allowing twenty stitches to the inch, we find she took 313,920 stitches. How much time would have been consumed by her in taking the same number by hand with her needle and thread?

Blessings on the inventor of the sewing-machine.

These occasional meetings between Mr. Hamilton and the family are not in the least unpleasant (!) but on the contrary are seasons of happiness and improvement to all: and we are not sad at the thought that these meetings will ere long terminate in one "protracted meeting."

Some one has suggested that a good way to rid a man of his egotism, would be to so dissolve him in sulphuric acid, as to pour him through a goose quill ! !

THE O. C. DAILY.

VOL. 5.   SATURDAY, FEB. 1, 1868.   NO. 28.

EVENING MEETING.

Mrs. Maria Kinsley invited criticism. Though she has made considerable improvement she still has faults that need correcting. It was suggested that her difficulties originated in willfulness, and she was exhorted to seek a soft heart and the spirit that provokes to love.

An unedifying state of things has existed in the lower sitting-room for some time past, and a pretty free expression was had on the subject. It appeared, that the spirits of evil-thinking, gossiping, injudicious wholesale criticism and legality, have had place there. Those affected were exhorted to examine themselves, and seek the spirit of Christ that provokes to brotherly-love and charity.

There seemed to be considerable moving going on yesterday, for when there is one change to be made, it generally involves about a dozen more. It is done something in this way: Mr. Hatch and Eliza, by planning and consulting, get a place provided for each one that they wish to move; and when all have consented to take the place assigned to them, some one begins; this looks like a quiet announcement, but could you see the bedsteads, bureaus, wash-stands, work-stands, rocking-chairs and whatnots, that have to go, you would think it quite a commotion) another takes his place, another the place of the second, and so on until all are quietly situated in their new abodes.

These frequent upheavals and overturnings are not unpleasant affairs however; the parties concerned manage to get considerable amusement out of it, and it forms part of the spice of Community life.

The teacher hands us the following:

1st Scholar.—(Looking up from her Grammar with a very perplexed and troubled expression on her face), Is it correct to say a onion?

Teacher.—No, you should say an onion; a becomes an before a vowel.

1st Scholar.—(Reading from the Grammar) Before words beginning with u long, a is used instead of an; as a onion, a university.

Teacher.—(Looking a little astonished.) Onion is not a correct example of that rule; it has the sound of u short and not u long.

2nd Scholar.—(Whose curiosity has led her to look at the book.) Why M——, It don't say a onion, it says a union!

At this point the perplexity of the scholars turned to merriment, and the teacher's distrust of the erroneous example, speedily terminated.

Mr. Abbott reports that, by recent measurement, he finds the amount of water received per minute continues to decrease at the rate of one quart in twenty-three days. We are now receiving ten quarts per minute, and should the amount continue to decrease, as it probably will until it begins to thaw in the Spring, we shall have to be economical to make it last.

Daniel Abbott says he has got every thing in readiness to commence can-making, but is waiting for tin. We have formerly purchased tin of Phelps, Dodge & Co., but don't think we shall suffer because they are so conscientious.

Mr. Conant says there is nothing to report from his department, unless it is that they have finished threshing. The teamsters continue to draw wood.

Mr. Hamilton is gone again. Surely, this is in accordance with the idea, " Meet, and pass on."

Traps sold during the month,				$1,776.86.
Bags	"	"	"	"	$1,389.53.
Silk	"	"	"	"	$1,229.25.
Castings "	"	"	"	$149.93.
Fruit	"	"	"	"	$116.44.
Total sales	"	"	"	$4,662.01.
Silk sent to N. Y. Agency,				$3,993.42.

What is the use of trying to comment on the weather? We can't keep pace with it; what we should write this morning, might be laughably amiss at noon, therefore we are discouraged about attempting anything on the subject. We have all kinds, so each one can fancy it the style that suits him best; only be careful and use the sunshine rather sparingly.

Virginia says to one of the girls, whose hair isn't very long, " You aint dot *much* air, has you?" Then, looking at her intently, " What a drate, bid forehead you've dot, hasn't you? O ! I know, it's tause your *eyes* are so *low down* !"

Mr. D. M. Kelly says there is so little going on at the shop that he did not think it necessary to keep both of his men, so discharged Mr. Petrie.

Mr. Crane is engaged in putting up more boxes for clothes, in the ironing-room. (Preparing for the coming delegation from W. C.)

For the wise ones, here is a query:
Why does the tongue never get weary?

d. w. n.

THE O. C. DAILY.

VOL. 5.   MONDAY, FEB. 3, 1868.   NO. 29.

Saturday evening, the state of feeling in the lower sitting-room was further considered. Mrs. Bolles and Mrs. Easton were criticised in quite a frank manner for the spirit they have shown. It was said that Mrs. Bolles was suffering from the spirit of Methodism, and Mrs. Easton greatly afflicted with the family spirit. In view of existing facts it would become both to be modest in criticising more experienced members.

Mr. Woolworth said criticism should be given in love and not in a personal spirit. Criticism administered in a personal spirit does no good, but is a great injury to the one who gives it.

After the Talk on Spiritualism was read it was decided by acclamation that we would not entertain Spiritualists, when known to be such, nor have anything to do with them. Mr. Cragin suggested that we include Methodism, as really a part of the hadean principality, and extend it no sympathy. Let it be understood that, HENCEFORTH ONEIDA GIVES NO PLACE TO SPIRITUALISM, OR METHODISM IN ANY FORM.

H. G. Allen reached home yesterday morning. We are glad to see him. He says we would be surprised to see how many friends Mr. Olds has on his route; says almost the first question the customers ask is, "Why, Mr. Olds hasn't quit us, has he?" Henry says these men have quite a variety of names for Mr. Olds—"Mr. Young, Mr. Youthful, The old man, Old whitey" and the like, but every body likes him and don't want him to leave his route.

In our noon-meeting yesterday the article from the *Atlantic* "Does it Pay to Smoke" was read, and if we were to take all the nods we saw as those of approval, then the piece was pretty generally intertaining as well as somewhat amusing. (We are a little apprehensive that these nods were not made in assent.)

Sunday is a great day with us for meetings. Yesterday there were twelve regular meetings, and three committees for criticism. The morning club from nine to ten o'clock; Business meeting from 11 to 12 A. M.; noon meeting from 1 to 2 P. M. At 2 o'clock George E. had a short meeting with Ernest's class of boys; at 2½ o'clock a club of women held their meeting; at three, the young men had a session in the back parlor, but gave place to the young women at four. Six o'clock brings together a class of women of the age of Fidelia and Libbie Hutchins, and seven o'clock is the time appointed for the girls meeting, and the usual meeting of the new members. At some hour in the afternoon there was a meeting of the "New York Perfectionists," Mr. Burt, Mr. Worden and others. Of course the evening meeting was joined in by all. The Talk on "Spiritualism" was re-read, and very generally indorsed. It was hoped we should be thoroughly awake on this subject.

After meeting Saturday night, at the suggestion of Mr. Woolworth, quite a large company of young men and women went down to the lower sitting-room, where they were joined by the room-mates, and had a good time singing. We feel sure that the late criticism of the inmates of the sitting-room will be the beginning of a new spirit there, and there will no longer be that marked division between the old and young that has existed heretofore. We already feel the barriers to love and unity melting away, and know they will be entirely removed.

The following note was read in the meeting last evening: I wish to thank the family for the criticism I received last evening. I feel it was true, and I now desire to separate myself *forever* from the cruel hateful spirit of gossip and evil-thinking which leads to unbelief. I also desire to be separated from the marriage, selfish spirit which is at the bottom of it all.

I wish to offer myself, soul and body, unreservedly to Christ and his church to be made a new creature. I confess my hatred of my old life and desire to be entirely separated from it. The desire of my heart is, that the love of God may be stronger in me than any other love, and feel that I can forsake all—husband and children—for the love of Christ. I wish to confess my union with Mr. Noyes and my love for the ascending fellowship. I pray for a true spirit of humility and repentance and a soft loving heart.

LOUISA EASTON.

It is a bright, clear morning, and very cold. Mr. Thacker comes up to report that the mercury fell to nineteen degrees below zero.

While the company was singing Saturday night, Mrs. Abbie Burnham was heard to say in her unapproachable style, "They voted in meeting to give up Methodism, but I suppose they must have one good suck at it, first."

We judge from the following item in the *Syracuse Daily Standard*, that the people of Springfield have adopted W. C.'s method of dealing with *tramps*:

"Professional tramps, who lodge at the station house in Springfield Mass., are required, much to their disgust, to pay for their lodging by sawing wood for two hours the next morning."

At the close of the meeting last night, the kitchen folks entertained the family with pop-corn candy, molasses candy, crackers and wine. It seemed to be a very quiet kind of enjoyment and promotive of the home feeling.

THE O. C. DAILY.

VOL. 5.   TUESDAY, FEB. 4, 1868.   NO. 30.

EVENING MEETING.

H. G. Allen reported something of his late western business trip. He had good luck in collecting; but in some cases he had to take short notes bearing interest. The parties were considered reliable, and he considers the accounts good.

He found about twelve hundred dozen traps in Chicago, so there is not much prospect of a great trade the coming spring. Customers are good-natured. Wise ones say fur is rising, and traps will be in demand in the fall. Few furs were caught last season, from the fact that the dry weather injured their market value. The mink were nearly red. Fur-bearing animals need plenty of wet weather in order to have marketable skins.

Henry was surprised to find our preserved fruits so popular, especially the corn and pease. Some said the pease were better than any they could get in summer. The jellies were not so popular in some quarters, owing to their poor quality the year before, though all who had tried them this year liked them. Mr. Olds confessed that they were made chiefly of apple the year before, and this has won for him the additional cognomen of " Applesauce."

On his return Henry rode in one of the new sleeping cars. In Canada the driving-wheel of the engine was broken. When the train was stopped they found they were near a very high bridge and their escape from a terrible accident was a narrow one. He recognized it as an instance of God's care over him and was thankful for it.

A man accompanies each of these sleeping cars to look after things. One morning Henry left his overcoat in the car as he went to breakfast, on the strength of this man's assertion that everything in the car would be safe. On returning he found his coat had been removed. He took measures to find it, but all to no purpose. The agent for these cars who lives in Rochester, considered the company responsible for the loss of the coat and recommended Henry to write to them about it.

Any one on the road between O. C. and W. P. yesterday afternoon about 5 o'clock, would have met our large double sleigh filled with a laughing crowd of boys and girls (?) on their way to W. P. As they speed along, we notice in the back part of the sleigh, an object whose towering proportions suggest a double base. Ah I now' we know " what's up." Let's follow and see. On they go, and in a few minutes come whirling up to the back door of our W. P. C. The instant the sleigh stops, the load pours over the sides and into the house, floods through the narrow passage ways and bursts in upon an astonished gram-

mar class, that are gravely discussing, " Webster was a statesman." With hasty apologies, the merry crowd rushes on, scattering to the different rooms, while the undaunted but momentarily paralyzed teacher of " Kerl" continues, " The following sentence" etc. A few minutes of noise and bustle, and the current of life flows on with its usual W. P. placidity. Supper is announced and discussed. Soon the dining-room is cleared, stove, tables and all, and,

" The O. C. Band then tuk its stand
  So swately in the parlor there;
  And soft bassoons (?) played heavenly chunes
  And violins did fiddle there."—also the double base.——The " Romanoff," " Concert Hall," " Spanish," a waltz, a schottische. " That is all." A general *glow* of talking and laughing. " The team is at the door." A hasty donning of hats, muffs and overcoats and off they go amid " the jingling and the tinkling of the bells, bells, bells."   ONE OF THEM.

W. P., Feb. 3.—This morning the mercury stood at sixteen degrees below zero. At nine the men had to stop work for half an hour and chop away the ice from the great water-wheel.

Twenty cords of stone have been sold from one quarry. Two teams from the Depot are engaged in drawing it away.

Inquiring of Joel what is going on in his department, he answers, that one of the blacksmiths is engaged in ironing a little carriage for the children's department, and that he and the other blacksmith are busy making bear-traps, one hundred No. 5 and forty No. 6.

As John Freeman is to leave in the morning for Schenectady to see his father, he asked the advice and criticism of the family. He was commended for his faithfulness, and for his earnestness in seeking the truth. He was exhorted to seek the inspiration and wisdom of God while away, and to meet his father in a soft heart. He took money with him and will do what seems best after ascertaining the exact state of affairs. He don't feel like trusting his father with money, but may pay his rent for him.

Mr. John Allen, of Oneida, was here Sunday and while in conversation with Mr. Newhouse, told him that Messrs. Hitchcock and Wells attended our concert and gave him a glowing account of " *Herr Von Splugen's* Wonderful Box." It pleased him so much he could not resist the temptation to go over and see W. about it, and this is his report of their talk:

A.—Well, you had a fine time the other night didn't you?

W.—Where? What do you mean ?

A.—Why, at the Community.

W.—I havn't been there.

A.—Yes, yes, at the concert you know.

W.—I tell you I wasn't there.

A.—But, Hitchcock and Wells say they saw you.

W.—It's a d——d lie; I didn't go near there.

A.—They said you were there *in a box!*

Here, W.'s wrath boiled over; Allen said he raved like a chained tiger. Probably this was the immediate cause of his second attack on us.

THE O. C. DAILY.

VOL. 5. WEDNESDAY, FEB. 5, 1868. NO. 31.

EVENING MEETING.

Night before last Mr. D. M. Kelly was criticised by his request, and the same subject was continued last evening. Mr. Kelly was commended for his industrious habits, and for his desire to become a spiritual man. He was exhorted to put on Christ, so that he could take his position as head of his family and do his duty respecting his children. He is a little too easy about things, and rather inclined to be spiritually lazy. It was thought he should give more attention to Mr. Noyes's writings, and if he has no time take it from his business hours.

Mr. Kelly's relations to his outside friends were thought to be a hindrance to his improvement. He was advised to look to this. In the light of the Talk read last evening it was discovered that Mr. Kelly had a tendency to promiscuous intercourse with unclean spirits.

Mr. Kelly was thankful for the criticism, and confessed his purpose to have no fellowship with any spirit that did not confess Christ.

Mr. Woolworth then said he would like to take occasion to give Mr. Olds a word of exhortation. He felt that Mr. Olds had been incontinent in his communication with our Western customers, and Henry Allen's report confirmed that impression. Mr. Olds is a sick man both physically and spiritually. He needs to learn continence in the use of his tongue. It would seem that he drops down to his customers, and does not put the Community between him and the world. Our men can, and should go out into the world and maintain their position as representatives of the Community spirit. It does not speak well for Mr. Olds that his customers are free to call him "pet names." He has evidently been to free with them; he has had a spirit that tends to promiscuous intercourse.

Mr. Olds was thankful for these hints, and hoped all would feel free to express any impressions they had. Mr. Woolworth wished Mr. Olds would study his own case, and ask God for the truth concerning his whole experience.

What shall we say by way of expressing our appreciation of the late "Home Talks?" To say they are rich, excellent and all that, is tame. Every one of them is just in time—just to the point, and more important to our growth and progress than the food we eat.

We will not mention them in detail, but we cannot refrain from expressing our heart-felt gratitude for "The True Jordan." The very idea of crossing that river at no very distant period stimulates us to bear all necessary trials and criticism with a fortitude we have not before experienced.

G. W. H. is about to take W. G. K.'s business agency, or at least a part of it. George will continue to interest himself in the trap department, and buy stock for it.

Malleable Iron manufacturers in Troy offer us trap-irons on favorable terms, guaranteeing the quality of their iron. The trap department proposes to give them an order for a sufficient amount of iron to make 25,000 traps as a trial lot.

Mr. Hubbard reminds us that Tryphena's contribution for the support of the old folks is due, and asks us to increase the amount for the coming year. As usual he is insatiable. It has been proposed that we tell him, that as the times are now, we might fairly ask for a reduction of this stipend.

A business committee consisting of H. G. A., G. W. H., W. H. W. and others met Monday at W. P. and decided to give the Cincinnati firm of Heron, Rogers & Paddock the extension they ask of their creditors; viz., six, twelve, eighteen and twenty-four months. They propose to pay their debts in four installments, at times specified above, with interest. The committee thought we should probably come out quite as well with this arrangement as we should if they were compelled to go into bankruptcy. Their indebtedness to us is $754.58.

Quite a number of the family were tried that so erroneous a statement as that about our mangle should have gone from here. It is true, there has been considerable talk about using iron rollers heated by steam, but as yet it is only talk, and we regret that such an announcement has gone forth. Several of our folks went to the ironing-room to see it and were quite overwhelmed at the difference between the mangle as reported, and the mangle as it is.

Calling on Portia's school we find she has seventeen scholars, five of whom are too young to study much, but she teaches them from a chart of "Familiar objects represented by words and pictures." This helps them to gain correct ideas of the form and color of objects.

While asking the older ones some questions on "Pelton's Outline Map of Europe," Temple scrambled up into a chair and seizing a long rod used as a pointer, he placed the tip of it on England and says, "I know what that is, my father went there." Then running the stick across the Channel into France, "And there too." The circumstance of his father's having been there had brought these places home to him and stamped them on his childish imagination most vividly.

The older ones study Reading, Writing, Spelling Geography and Arithmetic; and Marion says "We speak pieces sometimes, too."

It is a very bright and happy looking school and so quiet and orderly that it's a real pleasure to work as near it as we do, here in our little office.

Mr. Clark has started with the intention of making a circuit round Oneida lake. He will deliver castings and make whatever collections there are to be made,

THE O. C. DAILY.

VOL. 5.　　THURSDAY, FEB. 6, 1868.　　NO. 32.

EVENING MEETING.

A communication from Mrs. Conant was read, going into some historical criticism and asking the help of the family. Her case was taken up; and at the suggestion of Mr. Cragin the Bailey and Conant families were included. Mrs. Conant is at times possessed with a dumb devil that makes her treat persons ill in the way of not answering. She says she does not hear. She was a pet in her father's family which would account for much of her bad experience. In her turn she is given to petting Virtue.

There is a wrong relation between Mrs. Bailey and Mrs. Conant. Mrs. Bailey was thought to lack subordination. Her influence on Lillie is not good. The question arose whether both Mrs. Bailey and Mrs. Conant were not suffering for their past intercourse with evil spirits. They were advised to go into a thorough historical investigation of their past lives. It is possible that they are still under the influence of Mr. Bailey's spirit to some extent. The character of that is well known.

Mr. Cragin said the Bailey family in the West was perfectly chaotic. There was no real organization in it, or respect one for another. What Mrs. Conant and Mrs. Bailey need now is to prove their obedience and humility. It was suggested that perhaps Mrs. Conant had never been prepared till now for the truth, and the Community generally had not been in so good a position to tell the truth in love.

The 29th of last November, we shipped by canal, 5769 lbs of scrap steel to Prentice, Atha & Co., of Newark, N. J., Steel Works. A short time after, a sudden stop was put to navigation, by the freezing of the canal, and the steel had to be transported the rest of the way by railroad. A few days ago a letter was received from the above Co., with a check inclosed for the amount charged them, $228.13, and saying that the scrap steel had been received, but with it came freight and cartage bills to the amount of $54.72!!

This they lamented, but said of course we did not know that the canal would freeze up, and they supposed that they must stand the ill luck, but an order or two would tend to counterbalance.

The Trap Dept. did not wish to order any more steel of them at present, so it was proposed we send them $25.00, to help defray the expenses. We wrote them a kind letter, inclosing the check for $25.00. Last night we received an acknowledgment, thanking us for our kind favor, and remarking, "Business is not always so justly conducted. How pleasant t'would be if it were."　　OFFICE.

Who knew a legacy had been left to the O. C. !

Five years ago Philo Gilbert of Moravia, Cayuga Co., N. Y., by last will and testament bequeathed the O. C. one or two hundred dollars. So a man told us yesterday. We didn't know whether we had received it or not. We thought not. We said, "there was some surprise and considerable talk about it at the time, in that neighborhood. Mr. Gilbert was a Presbyterian, and the Presbyterians hoped he would endow their church, *and he didn't*. He was a queer man. He thought folks should live together like brothers and sisters, and once made a trial of the Skeneateles Community. The wonder subsided after a while. The bulk of his property went to his widow who is still living. They had no children. Terry Everson of that town administered the estate." Mr. A. H. Dunbar, our informant, staid to dinner. He is an agent for Ivison, Phinney, Blakeman & Co.

W. P., Feb. 5.—G. W. H. and Myron went to Oriskany yesterday, to see A. B. Buel about malleable iron. Upon arriving there, they found he had not yet come down from Utica, where he resides. So they took the car they had just left, not troubling themselves to get any tickets.

It happened that the conductor did not come through that car again, so when they got off at Utica G. W. H. went into the office to pay their fare, but found him engaged in conversation with Major Priest. He waited until he saw it was time for the train to leave, then went in and spoke to him about it. The conductor looked at him a while in some amazement, and then said, "Well! you are one gentleman in a thousand." Said G. "You will find it like all the men of the O. C." "I know it, I know it" said the conductor.

James Hatch is to spend his forenoons at O. C. in assisting Daniel Abbott at can-making. He has heretofore worked in the chain department.

As the matter now stands it looks as though I intended to deceive about the mangle. Such was not the case however. I wrote the article several weeks before I expected it to be published. I inquired about the mangle, and was told that iron rollers, heated by steam were expected to be put in, in a few weeks. Supposing from the information then received, that what I wrote would be a fact by the time it was published. I felt innocent of deceiving. I accept the criticism, and hope to profit by the lesson.　　D. E. S.

Mr. Abbott thinks "that robin" deserves a little notice; because, we suppose, he lacks the wit to go South as a sensible robin should, and has such a vast store of amiability, that he seems imperturbably good-natured; with the mercury nineteen degrees below zero he looks so contented that you fancy he wouldn't care to be a whit warmer if he could.

THE O. C. DAILY.

VOL. 5.   FRIDAY, FEB. 7, 1868.   NO. 33.

EVENING MEETING.

Mr. Clark had been invited to offer himself and family for criticism last evening. Mr. Woolworth said it was known to some that Florence had been under criticism of late, for a hard, independent, reckless spirit, and in studying her case they were naturally led to look at the family—to her relations with her father and mother. She is in very close connection with her father, though he says he knows nothing of her heart experience, but is all out of fellowship with her mother. Mr. Clark is no help to her, nor to the Community, in the way of bringing her to Christ. Florence has times of yielding obedience to good desires, but soon falls away into recklessness and terrible hardness. Through a very sincere, private criticism this evening, she remained as hard as adamant.

Mr. Clark has been an industrious, faithful man, and profitable to the Community in a pecuniary way, but very lazy and unprofitable spiritually. It would be better that he should stop work and business entirely, better that our Foundry should be closed than that we should make so great a spiritual sacrifice.

The relation between Mr. and Mrs. Clark was mentioned as unsatisfactory. If they could be reconciled, and come into good relations with each other, Florence would no doubt love and respect her mother. There has always been a lack in Mr. Clark as a father and husband. He has not governed his children, and as he has not taken Christ for his head, Mrs. Clark could not look up to him as her head. Thus the matter stands at the present time. The responsibility of parents to children was dwelt upon with earnestness. Finally, Mr. Clark was advised to give up his business to Mr. Kinsley, and devote himself exclusively to becoming a spiritual, earnest man—to the cultivation of a soft heart—thus beginning a new existence. Mr. Clark expressed a belief that he could do so, and it is hoped and confidently expected that a new day has dawned upon Mr. Clark and his family.

We frequently hear funny things from the different Grammar classes. From one this is reported. Parsing lesson in progress; one anxious student, anticipating her turn, inquires of her neighbor in a loud whisper, "Say, what's *love?* It's a conjunction, isn't it." Her companion made answer roguishly "I rather guess it is, sometimes." Another scholar thinking of conjunctions and trying to parse a pronoun, emphatically pronounced *it* to be *a personal conjunction!*

The hands in the Bag Dept. now work nine hours a day. All work faithfully and industriously and, notwithstanding we are few in numbers, we are progressing, slowly perhaps, but surely, to the closing of this business. How much we shall gain in material property is uncertain, but we expect to show some spiritual gains which shall more than counterbalance any loss we may sustain.

Neat, Kearney & Co., of Boston, gave us an order for six leather Lunch Bags, amounting to $40.00. We filled the order immediately.

Can our Agents give us any idea what will be the demand for bags, and when their customers will send in their orders for the Spring trade?   N.

A sporting party, mostly amateurs, bagged a fine large rabbit yesterday in our cedar swamp. The "Canadian Trapper" assisted in the capture as also his son, who performed the important office of starting the game. Then the dog, a deep voiced hound, was put on the track and the chase begun, which lasted for a half hour, with more or less excitement, when the game was brought round within easy range of one gun, which delivered the fatal shot. Poor rabbit! he was immediately taken in out of the cold and cared for, and the party had the satisfaction of thinking a humane act had been performed.

Our Chemistry class now numbers sixteen, and the interest in this study seems to be steadily increasing. We have some difficulty in reconciling the statements of our text-book (Wells') and those of our teacher, who is an advocate of the "New System" and who takes every opportunity to show the superiority of the new over the old. The study of Chemistry, theoretical and practical, with other natural sciences will undoubtly form an important part of our future educational development, so we feel encouraged to struggle on in spite of the at present confusing talk about "displacing hydrogen," "bascicity," "equivalent," "equivalence," "monads," "dyads," and "tetrads."   ATOM.

Mr. Clark reports that while gone he procured orders for the following:

2,543 lbs. plow castings at 6 cts.		$152.58.
820 " stove " " 5 "		$41.00.
3,363 "		$193.58.

One of our compositors has a grandmother who occasionally tells her funny stories, and this is one of them:

"A certain rich farmer had four highly accomplished daughters whom he had severally given in marriage. The first to a Mr. Poor, the second to a Mr. Little, the third to Mr. Brown, and the fourth and last to a man by the name of Hog. At the wedding of the youngest he exclaimed:—'With all my care and expense in educating my daughters, they have all turned out to be nothing more than *Poor, Little, Brown, Hog.*'"

THE O. C. DAILY.

VOL. 5. SATURDAY, FEB. 8, 1868. NO. 34.

EVENING MEETING.

Mrs. Clark had invited criticism, and her case was taken up. Not much was said. She was commended for meekness and humility, and exhorted to put on Christ in a way to command the respect of Florence, and all with whom she comes in contact. Mr. Clark was invited to write out a history of his life.

Mr. Cragin then mentioned Mr. Barron, and said he found him pleasant when he met him anywhere, but had been disappointed in not hearing from him in meeting.

Mr. Barron responded that he was thankful for the criticism and advice he had received, and thought it was doing him good. He had thought of writing something, but found himself under too much pressure. He said the isolation criticised had often not been from alienation of feeling toward persons, but was caused by the impression, that was settling down over him, that he was getting to be an old man; that he had passed the meridian of life and was getting to be unattractive. A spirit of discouragement had settled down on him like midnight; yet he had never lost confidence in God's power to accomplish the work he has undertaken in him.

What Mr. Barron needs is to come out of himself and testify. The Community has called on him to do that, and now let him prove his obedience. Homer said when he was a boy his father would request him to do a thing, and if he did not start promptly his father would say, " Don't let me have to speak to you twice." That ended it. He thought his father better take his own precept to himself and not make the Community speak twice. This was highly commended.

————————

Sometimes you ask a person where a certain thing is, and are told to " follow your *nose*."

Well, if you want to know where most of the family concentrate after meeting, " follow your nose" and it will almost invariably lead you to our upper sitting-room, where the men gather about the stove and the women group around the register.

Last evening there seemed to be unusual buoyancy and effervescence of spirit among the women and girls, who felt a great desire to give vent to it in some way. So games were proposed, and a circle formed, where " Hunt the thimble" was played with a good deal of enthusiasm. Either the one that hunted it was unusually sharp and discerning, or her companions lacked the unpretending secrecy necessary, for the thimble was found pretty often.

Then the circle broke up and formed a larger one on the floor, where " What to do with it" was played.

This was quite amusing. One was asked what was given her and she said, " a gorilla, and she told me to wrap it in silk-tissue paper and send it to my husband." Another had a hedge-hog given her which she was told to dust carefully and place upon her whatnot. And to end with, the last one was presented with the mangle, which she was told to cook up in good style and give to Mr. Bolles and Miss Nun for supper. Rather indigestible, we thought!

————————

Mr. Conant says since good sleighing commenced, they have drawn 230 cords of wood and 800 logs. He thinks we have had a remarkably favorable winter for this kind of work.

————————

Mr. Hawley says he and his men spent the day yesterday, in cutting hay and breaking roads. This morning he is going to Hoboken for feed, as the mill at Oneida is out of repair.

————————

Mr. Bristol remarks, " This is a fine morning—Ah! a lovely morning—this is like Connecticut."

S. W. N. reports that the mercury is thirteen degrees below zero.

————————

Among the letters received in yesterday's mail was one from Dover, Pa., with the following superscription: " Mr. Samuel Steelhouse, Idaho Community, N. Y."

————————

Traps ordered during the week,	43 doz.

STATISTICS FOR THE YEAR 1867.

175 tons of Hay	valued at		$2,800.00
1,000 bush. „ Barley	„	„	1,260.00
1,000 „ „ Potatoes	„	„	750.00
1,000 „ „ Beets	„	„	375.00
27 „ „ Clover-seed	„	„	324.00
Live Stock : 113 Head			7,215.00
Estimated value of teaming			5,800.00

Value of produce from Horticultural Dept. 6,587.54 This includes, among others, the following items: 794 bush. Tomatoes; 183 bush. Stringbeans; 152 bush. Raspberries; 253 bush. Strawberries; 820 bush. Potatoes: 40 bush, Pears; 110 bbls. Apples; 16,139 lbs. Grapes; 250 gals. Wine; 480 gals. Cider.

Work at Shoe Shop for O. C.	$2,140.71
„ „ „ „ „ W. C.	67.50
„ „ „ „ „ N. Y. B.,	41.50
„ „ „ „ „ Employees	271.23
Cash Receipts at Shoe Shop	1,640.32
Cash sales of O. C. Store	11,277.96
Silk M'n'f'd, 2,950½ lbs. valued at	40,052.49
Bags „ 10,423 „ „	84,361.80
Tailoring—this merely includes value of stock and work for men's clothing—	2,793.87

Principal articles purchased for family use,

Flour	$2,056.70
Sugar	2,130.92
Butter	4,450.09
Eggs	449.00
Beef	654.53
Fish	154.15
Apples	711.94
Potatoes	828.12

(To be continued.)

THE O. C. DAILY.

VOL. 5.   MONDAY, FEB. 10, 1868.   NO. 35.

BUSINESS MEETING.

G. W. Hamilton said the Fire Co. at the Depot were urgent that we should buy their old engine, for which they ask $150.00 and he agreed to present it to the family. Left to G. W. H. and D. M. Kelly.

Mr. Woolworth said at the present rate we are using coal, it is estimated that we shall require about one hundred tons more to last through the season. It was thought there were some fires that might be dispensed with; and in cases where but one occupies a room a portion of the time, wood could be used to advantage. Messrs. Kinsley, Hamilton, Clark, Thacker and Nash, Mrs. A. S. Burnham and M. F. Barron, were appointed a committee, to take immediate measures to curtail expense in this direction.

Mr. Kinsley thought it desirable to have a new saw put in at the Saw-mill, for the purpose of working up waste pieces into box stuff Estimated cost, $35.00. Messrs. Kinsley, Kelly, Inslee, Woolworth and Hamilton were appointed as a committee with power to act.

Mr. Thacker thought it would be necessary to have a new boiler for use in the Fruit Dept. the coming summer. G. W. Hamilton will look into the matter and see what can be done.

W. P., Feb. 6.—Cornelius reports that one of the boys in the shop, stooping for something and rising suddenly, struck his head violently against the horn of an anvil, cutting quite a severe gash in his forehead.

The race-way below the shop became so filled in with snow and ice, that the water was overflowing our neighbor's hop-yard, so this morning four of our men, with as many hired men, went down there and worked until noon; getting the race-way nearly clear. The snow blew about so furiously that some of the time they could not see each other when a rod or two apart. One of the colored men fell in, but the boys pulled him out in a hurry. *They* thought it indescribably funny to see him with his head just appearing above the water; whether *he* thought so is a question, as the mercury was three degrees below zero.

After dinner Alfred came in with a little fellow—a grandchild of our neighbor Adkins—who had caught his finger in the planing-machine and smashed it quite badly. It was bound up and he was taken home to his mother.

The first drifts of the season between here and O. C.

The criticisms go on with increasing interest. C. A. Cragin was the subject this evening.

I do not see as O. C. has lost any of her faculty to improvise entertainments. At the close of the Sunday evening meeting it was announced that the children had something to present to the family. Curiosity was of course, wide awake, and the uninitiated indulged in all sorts of speculations as to what was coming. Soon the familiar tones of the dinner bell rang out, and alimentiveness suggested something good to eat. But no! Up went the curtain, and there stood on the stage a double quartette of boys and girls dressed in costume. It was not a masquerade exactly, for their faces were uncovered, but otherwise the transformation was complete. Lorenzo Bolles (a kind of Brobdignag among the rest) was dressed in long skirts and lace cap, and well represented as some one said, a great coarse Irish girl. Edith was a handsome Highlander. Marion dressed in a "swallow tail" stuffed, looked like a veritable Tom Thumb; while Mabel her partner, dressed in enormous hoops, with a slight help of the imagination, passed for Tom Thumb's wife. A gallant sailor was represented; and so on.

Soon, with "Father Hatch" playing the violin (a thing in itself refreshing), a cotillion was formed, and the fun commenced. It was both unique and comical and every body was entertained. At the close they sang a song, the words of which were in an unknown tongue.

The charm about these "little ones" in such exhibitions is their simplicity—an element which always did and always will go straight to the heart. Says George E. to the writer: "This beats any thing you can find in New York." I admitted it and replied that it was worth coming from N. Y. to see. B.

It was so stormy yesterday, and the snow so badly drifted that Mr. Hawley thought best not to go out with the teams; therefore, we did not have the usual addition to our family, that of the W. P. folks. We noticed their absence in the meetings, but hear they have been wishing for a blockade, and we are glad to congratulate them on having their fond hopes thus fully realized.

STATISTICS CONTINUED.

Amount of Freight received by Railroad,

East,	lbs.	470,837
West,	"	154,977
Charges,		$1,636,23
Freight shipped,		
East,	lbs.	132,808
West,	"	340,366
Charges	East,	$376,33
"	West,	$1,575,05
Freight received pr. Amer. Ex.	lbs.	40,204
Charges,		$441,72
Freight shipped pr. Amer. Ex.	"	53,723
Paid M. U. Ex. on Fr't. rec'd.		$678,22
Amount estimated at	lbs.	65,899
Fr't. shipped "	"	50'000
173,929 lbs Castings from Foundry		$10,125,37
Traveling expenses of agents		$2,622,39

(This does not include O. L. Aiken's expenses.)

Tin cans made		47,000

Lumber made at O. C. Saw-mill for O. C., Basswood 162,681 feet; Hemlock 34,213 feet;

Profits		$918,05

Custom work, 207,400 feet, all kinds; profits 407,25

NUMBER OF PERSONS ATTENDING CLASSES.

Algebra 21; Arithmetic 26; Geometry 4; Grammar 44; Philosophy 14; Chemistry 16; Composition 19; French 11; Phonography 5; Spelling 4; Geography 17; Girls school 7; Boy's school 7; Primary school 17.

AN ITEM FOR VANDERBILT

Allowing ten tons to a car, the amount of freight received and shipped by the O. C. for the year 1867 would require a train of 65 cars.

THE O. C. DAILY.

VOL. 5.   TUESDAY, FEB. 11, 1868.   NO. 36.

John Freeman returned from Schenectady Saturday. He reports that his father met him in a hard spirit, but that quarreling was avoided.

The old man had received some money in advance for the board of the child that is living with them, and had used the money to pay his house rent. John paid his grocer's bill amounting to between thirty and forty dollars. John asked the grocer to receipt to the Community, but he demurred, assigning as a reason that he feared that the old man would not like it, but he would receipt to John. John asked his father if he would accept the receipt, and he answered that he would take what benefited him more than it injured anybody else. Mrs. Freeman said she had a plenty of friends who would be glad to give her a home whenever she needed. Mr. F. had a quantity of papers in envelopes, containing articles against the O. C. ready to send to whatever point he thought they would *do good*, and aid the great work he has undertaken of breaking up the Community.

The declaration in the *Daily* of Feb. 3d respecting Spiritualism and Methodism was too unqualified to express the Community sentiment fairly; the thought was simply to exclude *Methodism* from the O. C., and not Methodists.

Mr. Smith asked one of the young men to stay with Mr. Nash Saturday night, but he got the impression he was to stay there Sunday night, so went peacefully to bed and D. P. N. was left alone.

In the night he wanted the fire fixed; finding himself alone and feeling a little too independent to call on Mr. Hall, who was in the next room, he got up, put on his stockings and drawers, went across the room to the stove, fixed the fire and then made a safe journey back to bed.

This is quite a discovery—to find he is capable of helping himself so much, but we don't think he will be left alone intentionally and hope not accidentally again.

George Kellogg says he makes regularly, two trips per day to Oneida, and sometimes three and four.

At the present time he goes at 7¼ A. M. and 1 P. M., carrying the mail, passengers, bags, traps, fruit and anything else there is to go—always has somebody or something to carry each way.

The distance from our Office to the Depot is about four miles, making the distance traveled each day sixteen miles. At this rate in one year—365 days, less the 52 Sundays—he travels 5,008 miles. But we have made no account of his extra trips. Allowing fifty extra ones, eight miles each, and we find he passes over the entire distance of 5,408 miles. In the eight days including Christmas and New Years he made twenty journeys to and from Oneida.

NEW HAVEN PROPERTY.

We paid for the property :

Cash,	$1,483.49
Mortgages,	1,400.00
Paid for repairs,	635.28
Total,	$3,518.77

The sale of the same :

Two mortgages paid,	900.00
Rent of house till April 12th,	20.00
Taxes for year ending in July,	35.00
Incidentals, stamps, &c,	5.00
Cash paid by Mr. Scott,	2,640.00
Total,	$3,600.00
Amount paid for property,	$3,518.77
Balance in our favor by the sale,	$81.23

W. P., Feb. 10—Going home Sunday is something which we all look forward to during the week with a great deal of pleasure, so it was with much regret that we found ourselves yesterday morning really "snow-bound." But we made the best of it. Our noon-meeting was very free, there was a general raid against the spirit of fear and unbelief, and earnest testimony on the side of faith and the simple child-like spirit.

We had a lively dance after supper. In the evening meeting the same freedom was manifested as at noon, especially among the young men. We all felt that our hearts were strengthened and drawn together. After meeting we enjoyed a very sociable time over some butternuts and wine. Altogether it was a happy day, though we do not care to have it repeated. It is the first time in all our ten months sojourn here, that we have not been able to turn our faces, as well as our hearts, homeward.

Twenty-one men were engaged this morning, until ten o'clock, clearing out the race-way; the work is at last finished.—G. W. H. left this morning, taking Mr. Kelly's route. He is to be absent two weeks.

Two members are added to our family; Mary Baker and Edward Inslee. Mary goes into the Silk-factory.

STATISTICS (CONCLUDED.)

Greatest number of employees at any one time.

Trap Shop	84
Silk Department	51
Bag "	27
Horticulture	23
Farm	11
Fruit	9
Laundry	6
Foundry	4
Building	4
Tailoring	4
Machine-Shop	3
Blacksmith "	3
Saw-Mill	1
Total	230

Taxes (including School, Town, County and Revenue),	$12,321.22

Preserved Fruits and Vegetables.

Fruit,	10,664 Bottles	$8,204.90
"	15,356 Cans	7,852.82
Jellies, 666 doz. tumblers		2,664.00
Vegetables, 31,796 Cans		9,205.75

THE O. C. DAILY.

VOL. 5.   WEDNESDAY, FEB. 12, 1868.   NO. 37.

W. P., Feb. 11.—Mr. Higgins was criticised last evening. He was commended for the interest he took in the family last summer, taking care of the garden, &c. Then he was bright, improving and growing young; but lately he has been troubled with his old writing habits and manifested some fanatical tendencies. In this state he is unedifying to the family. He was advised to turn away from his writing, take up some study and seek to cultivate unity. This morning he expressed himself as very thankful for his criticism; said it had taken a great load off from him. He certainly seemed a great deal brighter.

Business is lively in the Silk department. They have now all the machinery they intend getting, with the exception of one cleaner. Some strict regulations have lately been made for the little girls in the shop. Hereafter they are not to leave their places in work hours without permission.

C. A. C. and John Freeman have changed lodgings, John going to the shop to sleep and Charles taking a room at the house.

Mrs. Robinson is with us this afternoon.

An itinerant lecturer and songster called here Monday. He lectures on the "Pursuit of Happiness," and sings national songs with his audience.

We first ascertained that he was not a Spiritualist, and then made the usual rounds with him, gave him his dinner, and let him go. His name was William A. Gorden.

One of the students of "Old Harvard" called on us yesterday. A bright and very suave young man, well up in Botany too, as well as in other things, we learned when showing him the flowers. Talked some about our system of education. This led to an introduction, in the Reception-room. While the two congratulated, we queried standing near, whether Yale wasn't more scientific and less literary than Harvard. Our visitor bought a "Salvation from Sin" and a "Hand Book." Name, J. L. Seward. Home, Keene, N. H. Charles Foster, of Messenger's Law Office, a college friend, brought him here by way of W. P.   c. w. u.

Yesterday, Mr. Guilford, Editor of *The Oneida Dispatch*, called at the W. P. factory, and asked Myron if we were not going to publish some statistics in the CIRCULAR this year. Myron told him he thought we should. He said he should like to print some of them, but if he waited till they came out in the CIRCULAR *The Democratic Union* would get them first, as they print Wednesday, and he doesn't until Friday.

Mrs. O. A. M. thought it might be promotive of good to accommodate this man, and a consultation with Mr. Woolworth and George E., resulted in having George go down there this morning, and give Mr. Guilford such statistics as he thinks best.

A few days since, the children's school received an invitation to attend the exercises of the girls' school. Hitherto in such entertainments, the children have been the performers; and it was quite a treat for them to be *for once* spectators. Mrs. Seymour's scholars being all girls, in the dialogue between Mrs. Credulous and the fortune teller, Charlotte Maria appeared as an astrologer. She talked in quite a professional style about consulting the stars &c., occasionally lifting her glasses and eyeing sharply her victim Flora, who acted the widow. This little old lady, apparently in deep sorrow, very gracefully performed her part. Frank rehearsed "A Solemn Trifle," (from the CIRCULAR), reciting in an *extremely sarcastic* manner, the passages descriptive of the world. Her utterance was so natural, that you really felt she was giving you *her* opinion. The girls all did well, and the exercises though short, were quite pleasing.   p.

We have lately received a letter from Charles H. Keith, Campello, Mass., a young man who has read the *Trapper's Guide* and likes it very much. He writes for the prices of our traps, and says :

"I have felt considerable curiosity to know about the O. C. If you have no objections I wish you would tell me about it. What kind of a society is it ? What are its objects ? Are all the members hunters and trappers ? If they are, I should like to join it."

Mr. Newhouse says he should tell him, that most of our leading men *were* either hunters, trappers or fishermen.

One of Mr. Parson's sons came Saturday evening, and wished to draw "Life of Fremont" from our library. Mr. Underwood allowed him to do so, telling him we wished to have good care taken of the book.

Mr. Hawley and one of the hired men, each with a double team, started for Utica yesterday morning, at about four o'clock, the mercury standing ten degrees below zero. Their business was to bring home leather scraps for use in the trap-shop.

Yesterday, Mr. Conant, with his men and their teams, drew twenty-nine loads of muck from the cheese-factory swamp. He says he intends drawing thirty-six loads to-day.

Mrs. Julia Hyde spent a few hours here yesterday. She is improving in health, but not very stong yet.

Mrs. Joslyn has gone to Utica on business, and will spend a day or two with her sister.

THE O. C. DAILY.

VOL. 5.   THURSDAY, FEB. 13, 1868.   NO. 38.

EVENING MEETING.

A lengthy communication from Mr. Olds was read, in which he related his experience in the West and invited the criticism of the family. His communication was first criticised, for being too long and seeking to make out as good a showing as possible for himself by special pleading. Mr. Cragin considered it quite a mixture of confessing and preaching.

Mr. Woolworth was glad Mr. Olds had made his confessions, and thought this intimate relation that existed between Mr. Olds and his customers explained his present weakness and sickness of soul and body. It will require earnestness on his part to clear himself, and there should be no shrinking from the truth for fear of injustice. It was suggested that he might have to go back and judge his family for lack of faith, Universalism &c.

Mr. Woolworth said that Harriet Olds was much surprised at the shortness of H. G. Allen's late trip West. She thought it remarkable, judging from her father's experience. It was suggested that Mr. Olds had failed in this respect; that he had spun out his business as he did his communication just read. He may have spent a week or two during each trip in needless and unprofitable talk with his customers. Then when he comes home he is used up and disinclined to take hold of business as other agents do.

Mr. Woolworth said Mr. Olds had been to the front and done good service, but had been wounded; and he needs now to be cured and set free from his difficulties. He may require considerable probing or surgery before he can fully recover.

Mr. Bristol's sister, Margaret, writes to him of their brother Sherlock (the gentleman that called here a few years ago), who has again gone to California, and says: "They arrived in due time, after a most prosperous voyage; as S. says, 'scarcely a ripple on the water.'

"San Juan is a village of about twelve hundred inhabitants, boasting two hotels and several stores. The religion is chiefly Catholic. Here S. and family stopped awhile with a family who seemed to be so wealthy, I've a mind to speak of it.

"The usual number at their table is twenty-five, strangers and guests always 'on hand.' They own 200,000 acres of land, 80,000 sheep, 300 horses, 3,000 cattle, five quartz mines (gold and silver) in operation, one quicksilver mine, and a line of stages from San Josa to San Angelos, running two coaches each way daily for 300 miles.

"Job would have been a very poor man in comparison, wouldn't he?

"S. is having a good time with his gun. He tells of killing thirteen wild geese at one shot and bringing home fifteen; also seeing thousands of quails in one flock &c.

"But he is the most enthusiastic about the Fruit. He went into a pear orchard 75 years old, where the fruit had been gathered, and after eating all he wished, brought home some weighing a pound each. Apples, all our Eastern varieties, grow finely and are sweeter. As for grapes they are marvelous; he called at a store for two pounds and they gave him a bunch which weighed something over, and so delicious are they, he says, one does not know how to stop eating them. Whole loads of all kinds of plums, the smallest, the size of a hen's egg. Figs, great nice figs, olives, nectarines, apricots, &c., &c. He speaks of beets weighing twenty-four pounds."

These stories would seem rather large, but Mr. Bristol assures us that his brother is just as honest as he is.

W. P., Feb. 12.—A letter was received about ten days ago from our old machine blacksmith, Mr. Pritchard, saying that he had reformed and was anxious to work for us again. Mr. Woolworth was consulted in regard to the matter, and there was some discussion of it in our business meeting Saturday night. G. W. H. has since made inquiries at Utica, which satisfied him that Mr. P. has been doing well since leaving our employ. It was decided to discharge our present blacksmith and again try Mr. Pritchard.

The water-wheel at the Foundry has frozen up several times this winter, in consequence of not being put under water. Mr. Inslee, John Sears and Victor worked three hours this morning cutting away the ice from and around it.

Two iron columns were cast to-day for the new composing-room, which are to take the place of wooden ones. A third will be finished to-morrow.

Among the noticeable things in the children's house just now, is Master Ormond, who is reveling in the delight of his *first pants*. They are certainly becoming to him and he deports himself not ungracefully.

Little Eugene is at present making himself very interesting by his attempts at walking.

Call at the green-house and you will see the Augusta rose-bush, blossoming most magnificently, it's slender vine almost burdened with superb beauties that fill the air to density with their entrancing perfume. We counted twenty-three buds in one cluster and nineteen in another. The camelias too, are beautiful.

Passing through the lower sitting-room, we noticed quite a group of persons near the register, and began rallying them about having *circles*: this charge they stoutly denied—they didn't deal in those things—but said they had been making an estimate of their years. The united age of the room-mates is 764 years, the average making each person to be 54¾ years old.

THE O. C. DAILY.

VOL. 5.   FRIDAY, FEB. 14, 1868.   NO. 39.

EVENING MEETING.

George Kellogg invited criticism. He was thought by all those most associated with him to have improved a great deal within the last few months. He has learned an important lesson in the control of his tongue. His course during the moral war was particularly commended. He was not frightened nor led into unnecessary talk with outsiders. On the one hand he was bold and fearless, on the other manly and respectful. His general course as Agent was commended. He lacks yet in softness of heart and true humility. If we can do anything to help equip him with a chronic soft heart, we shall do him the greatest favor, and he will be a grand representative of the Community.

There was some talk on the tobacco question, and a desire expressed that all might be faithful and prompt in carrying out Mr. Noyes's wishes in the way of writing out experiences. A beginning has been made. Our freedom from that tobacco principality is a great victory—a great deliverance.

O. C. has no new bread-knife, but we can boast a potato washer. This is a somewhat ingenious contrivance, gotten up by Mr. John Leonard with the help of some others. It is similar to the machines used in starch-factories for the same purpose, and consists of a wooden, slatted cylinder, about three feet in length and sixteen inches in diameter, revolving by a crank, in a water-box, three feet long by two and a half wide.

The water-box supports the cylinder at a convenient height to put in the potatoes, and allows a basket to be placed beneath it.

By removing three slats of the cylinder, that have been arranged for the purpose, you can pour in your potatoes—any quantity not exceeding two bushels—replace the slats, give a few turns of the crank, draw off the water, open a small trap-door in the bottom of the water-box, again remove the slats from the cylinder, turn it round so that the opening is brought directly over that in the water-box, and there are your potatoes in the basket, very nicely washed in much less time, and a great deal easier than by the old method.

Turnips, beets, parsnips and clams (if you have them) can be washed in this way equally as well.

In the morning we frequently hold meetings with the children, in which all their little complaints and tribulations are brought up, discussed, and satisfactorily settled.

Sometimes Father Hatch reads to them from the Bible, which they seem interested in; at the close of the reading they often start the confession of Christ.

When Virginia's turn came this morning her first attempt to speak was not loud enough; she was told to speak louder, and repeated it, but no louder than before. She made a third trial and sobbed out, " I tonfess Christ a dood spirit, dat will pease God."

This confession, with the many others, so simple and earnest, touched our hearts and strengthened them. What a blessed thing it is that these little ones are taught so young to fear the Lord and trust in him. As truly as we believe God *is*, do we believe these little petitions, so confidingly offered, are heard and attended to by him.   E. & H.

It appears that Mr. Kellogg has been having some trouble with a sick cow. Mrs. Langstaff reports a conversation she heard between Mr. K. and Mr. Worden on the subject:

K.—To-day, I've had more rejoicing over the one sick cow, than I have over the forty-and-five well ones. She is convalescent—up, walking about her room. You ought to see her room and the bed Billy has made for her.

W.—I suppose it is equal to any feather bed, is'nt it?

K.—I guess she thinks so. Billy says, he thinks it was the beets he fed her that made her sick. He thinks he shall know better next time, and not do the like again. We had a pretty anxious time until she commenced walking; she couldn't stand on her feet for several days.

Mrs. Howard writes to Harriet: " I have thought much of the condition of outsiders, as they are called in the paper, and while thinking of Mr. Noyes's article to applicants, it seemed to me there was a way to come much nearer being an insider, than outsiders have generally gained. My thought is this: let outsiders take hold and work for and with the Community; and, whilst they praise and think so much of the CIRCULAR, let them rouse themselves and see if they cannot *support* it. I think this would show their appreciation and love for the truth it contains, more than whining, making excuses of being sick or poor, &c., &c. Poor souls! why, it would be the most effectual way to get rich, and rid them of the spirit of selfishness.

" I have felt like writing a short communication to G. (he wrote on this subject, you know) to know if he would not ask outsiders, *to try and support the* CIRCULAR *one year*, and see if it would not result in good to them; but I do not know as it is my place to do so, and so I wait."

A fine morning. Mercury, eight degrees above zero. The busy folk hurrying to their work, smile and congratulate the passers, " Nice morning this !" " Aye, truly! such exhileration in the air."

Small boys go whizzing past you on their hand-sleds, while the older ones must e'en convert their shoe-soles into runners, and slide on them.

THE O. C. DAILY.

VOL. 5.   SATURDAY, FEB. 15, 1868.   NO. 40.

W. P., Feb. 13—The other day as our sawyer, Mr. Dings, was crossing the pond he saw a wild duck on the ice. He caught it and carried it into the shop; where the boys tried to feed it, but it snapped at them fiercely. Victor finally put it into the raceway, where it swims about in apparent content. He feeds it and thinks that in time it will become domesticated—(if he clips its wings.)

Mr. Campbell went with Mr. Kinsley to Clinton to-day for the purpose of getting iron for the Foundry. They brought home with them a ton of pig-iron, the cost of which amounted to forty dollars.

A gentleman from O. C., who shall be nameless, came over here yesterday afternoon bringing two young ladies with him. They remained to supper. As they were starting for home some of us heard a great laughter outside the door, and on going out there we found the three tipped into a huge snow drift. It wasn't very soft, so the girl who chanced to be at the bottom did'nt seem to think it as funny as it might have been. But this morning the gentleman came over saying the girls were all right, and that he had come with the firm resolve to shovel away that snow bank, to spare any one else a like adventure.

After the reading of the journals and reports, last evening, Mr. Woolworth said he liked the suggestion in the N. Y. Journal, to have all of our rooms provided with suitable furniture that shall belong to the room and not to persons, thus avoiding so much transportation of property. He thought the furniture and houses were worn and injured more by this, than in any other way. There has been an improvement in this respect, but it should be avoided altogether.

Mr. Cragin said he noticed the ice was already being used from the ice-house, and as we are to have an addition to our family thus requiring more than the usual supply, he proposed to have ice drawn from the pond for present use, and not draw on the summer store.

A communication from Mr. Abbott, was read exhorting to economy in the use of water, and proposing for consideration, the idea of conducting the water from one or two more springs, in addition to those now used. " It is something to think of" as Mr. Franks would say.

John Freeman fished up while at home, some old newspapers published at Albany in 1843. One of these papers contains a long article of four columns, from the pen of Mr. Freeman, which is a bitter attack on the trustees and superintendent of the common schools of Albany. Mr. F. had been teaching there. Another paper published a few days subsequent to the one containing Mr. F.'s attack, has an editorial making a humble apology for publishing the article, saying that he (the Editor) was imposed upon by Mr. F. and his friends, and made to believe that the statements were just and true, when, as he had become convinced, they were a tissue of falsehoods.

When at home John read to his mother the article in the Berean entitled " Regeneration." After the reading, his father took up the subject and declared his disbelief in the doctrine of the article. He said that folks who lived before Christ were just as well off in respect to regeneration, as those living after—that the former were regenerated by looking *forward* to Christ, and the latter by looking *back* to him.

MY TRIP AND IT'S SEQUEL.

Tuesday morning was bright, but very cold, yet as I had previously made my arrangements, I started for Utica to transact a little business, which only a woman could well do, and in which I was personally interested. I had fair success in accomplishing my business and a good time with my sisters, particularly Mrs. Wright, who seemed open and receptive to the truth, and anxious to follow it, though it should cut her off from all her friends.

I returned home the next afternoon, happy and thankful that the truth was working in the heart of at least one member of my father's family. It was nearly dark when I reached home, and after returning borrowed articles of clothing, I put my hand into my dress-pocket and took my porte-monnaie (which contained about ten dollars,) thinking I would return that also, but it was late and I concluded to wait till morning. After going in to meeting I put my hand into my pocket and missed my porte-monnaie. Where was it? I must have dropped it on the way. I was not long in retracing my steps—searched diligently for the lost treasure—ransacked drawers and desks where I should have been the most likely to have placed it had I taken it from my pocket, but it was nowhere to be found. What could it mean? Was I crazed? Had I not had it in my hand? S. says " Oh, mother! you have had your pocket picked, no mistake." But I did not believe that, though he was continually repeating it. I passed an almost sleepless night, and came to the conclusion that I had either dropped the money at the tavern where I stopped, after leaving the cars, or when on the cars had put my hand outside my pocket instead of into it, and that the idea that I felt it or took it from my pocket after my return, was a delusion.

Early in the morning I started for Oneida, went to the tavern where I had stopped and enlisted the landlady to assist in the search—had G. R. K. inquire of the conductor if he had found the missing article—but all in vain. I made a great fuss I confess, considering there was only ten dollars at stake, but I thought I should not feel justified in doing less. Last night after meeting, I went to the cupboard or desk to get my portfolio and on returning it, judge of my surprise to see my lost treasure lying on the shelf in plain sight. I could scarcely believe my senses, but it was even so. Comments are unnecessary. I took it immediately to Mr. W. though it was ten o'clock. I would not trust myself again with it lest it should be hidden from my sight. There were many to rejoice with me over its recovery, (for I did not lack for sympathy in my trouble), though there were some hints that I might be suffering from *dementia*.   E. Y. J.

THE O. C. DAILY.

VOL. 5. MONDAY, FEB. 17, 1868. NO. 41.

EVENING MEETING.

Mr. Cragin offered the Boarding-house for criticism. All concurred in the opinion that the experiment of introducing a Community family there had proved a perfect success. But little was said by way of criticism of the organization.

A little too much effort is made to entertain our own people when invited there to dinner. The steward thought the organization was better now than formerly. Still he had the impression that Mrs. Thayer and Mrs. Bradley might meet on some convenient half-way ground, in respect to cooking, in a way to benefit both. He had thought there was some tendency in Mrs. Bradley to be extravagant.

Mr. Woolworth thought the presence of Mrs. Story there was the point that principally needed investigation. She seems to be a good woman and is liked to a certain extent; but she has been deeply involved in Spiritualism and is not now free, though she is struggling hard to break its meshes. Mr. Woolworth felt that she was a good woman at heart, and had tried to be reconciled to her residence there, and frequent attendance of our meetings; but there was a secret feeling all the while that she had better return to her friends.

Mrs. Thayer said Mrs. Story had volunteered to withdraw or do anything the Community should think best. We are bound by no promises to her. This does not seem to be the time to attempt to digest a Spiritualist. The mind of the family was ascertained by a vote and Mr. Cragin and Mrs. Thayer were appointed to pay Mrs. Story liberally for her services, and invite her to retire for the reasons mentioned. It was hoped nothing would be said or done to hurt her feelings unnecessarily, or offend one of God's little ones.

The W. P. family had a *falling out* yesterday; not with mother O. C. exactly, though it came under her observation, excited her fears and awakened her most motherly solicitude for the beloved offspring. It happened on this wise:—The superincumbent mass, making in the aggregate twenty-eight souls and an avoirdupois of about 4000 lbs., was packed into one sleigh behind four spirited steeds for the usual Sunday turn-out and reunion with O. C.

All went merry as a marriage-bell, and as the fates would have it, the unlucky (or lucky) spot was not reached till a grand spectacle could be made before numerous spectators, and an immense sensation created. At the critical point the road was narrow and drifted. The snow yielded to the concentrated bulk, first one way, giving the mass a lurch to the larboard side; there was an involuntary shifting of the ballast; when down went the runners on the starboard side, and before the balance could be recovered, the center of gravity had fallen without the base, and—reader, you can imagine what followed better than it can be described. Such a confused, motley, topsy-turvey mass, with assorted sizes and very little attention paid to the arrangement of " heads and points" was not only indescribable, but irresistible.

The twenty-eight had no sooner emerged from their snow-bath, and struggled from under buffalo-robes, cushions, and other more substantial weights, than a chorus of shouts and laughter rang out, which was taken up by the lookers on; laughter and hand-clapping echoed and re-echoed, and the hilarity did not subside entirely for a half hour, during which time the scratched and bruised were cared for, and their wounds pronounced insignificant.

P. S. The "Canadian trapper" facetiously, remarked to the Jehu of this occasion that he should have had his *lanterns* on, and thus avoided the catastrophe. w. h. w.

In the noon-meeting yesterday George E. related his experience respecting the measles. When Theodore and he visited Carlton Rice, they found two of the children down with the measles. They had been in the room some time before George knew what ailed them, and when he learned he thought it best not to run. He and Theodore talked it over afterward, and Theodore thought it possible that George would take the disease and communicate it to the children at home. George however felt a strong assurance that he should not take it; he could not feel that it was necessary. They returned home, and all went well.

George then visited Mr. Rice in company with Mr. Kinsley, and found three children sick with measles. They were in the same room with them two hours, and took supper there. The air was close and rather unpleasant.

After being home a day or two George began to feel queer. In fact the symptoms of measles were well defined. Still he felt that it was not necessary that he should have them. After consultation it was decided that he better remain in his room and not expose the children unnecessarily. He remained still Saturday, and did not attend the meeting in the evening. He really felt sick. Sunday he was better; and in the evening he came to the Hall and played for a dance. A row of the little children sat on the stage in front of him, well exposed. None caught any disease. He felt nothing further of the attack. The impression prevails that he never had the measles, though no one is positive. He ascribes his escape from this attack, be it of what nature it may, to faith. His experience has served to strengthen his faith in the doctrine that disease may be resisted and overcome.

He believes from this experience, that the resurrection spirit is growing strong in the Community and that it is not necessary that our children should have such diseases as measles, hooping-cough, chicken-pox etc. The power of Christ is sufficient protection against such diseases.

These views were heartily indorsed, and thankfulness was expressed for the excellent health of the Community. Several had obtained victories in answer to prayer.

THE O. C. DAILY.

VOL. 5.　　TUESDAY, FEB. 18, 1868.　　NO. 42.

An unusual number of visitors the past three days. A West-Hartford Conn. farmer walked up from the village to see us Friday evening, arriving just as the "tintinnabulation of the bell" had evoked the usual muster and commotion.

He wanted "to connect" with the evening train, and so staid only an hour, took supper, and then walked "back again." He was on his way home from Topeka, Kan., and from "seeing to the fences and things," on a farm of his, of several hundred acres in Ia.—had land enough for a Community at West-Hartford—went down to W. C. three years ago to learn what good, if any, we derived from the use of fish guano; saw Mr. Noyes there, and became interested in us, because we were practical and progressive.

He was not a Spiritualist, but instead a Baptist in good standing, and apparently as honest an old farmer as was he "of Tippecanoe." His name was Joseph Davenport.

A sleigh-riding party, four couples from Vienna Saturday evening reaching here at six o'clock. They came to see the Community, and expected to be entertained, and had ridden so far, and were so hungry withal, that we took compassion upon them, and fed them, and their horses, notwithstanding the lateness of the hour. Two of the party were a married pair from Ill. All were remarkably well-behaved and respectful. They set out on their return-ride of three hours, a few minutes before meeting closed.　　U.

The Internal Revenue tax collector, R. H. Avery of Canastota, called here Saturday, and took dinner.

His first business was to inquire what the prospects were of having the N. Y. C. R. R. straightened. It appears he is interested in the project, and said he was going from here to Vernon to see the Cases about it. Canastota, for the past five or six years, has been quite ambitious, apparently in some rivalry with the Depot, and this may account for their willingness to have the Central taken away from Oneida.

Mr. Avery's second object in calling, was to borrow some ancient costumes for Mrs. A. who is to take part in an entertainment they are getting up, in which a New England kitchen and tea-party will be represented. In this we accommodated him as best we could.

We have long desired to make our tax returns at Oneida, and so get rid of the odious visits of lisping assessor Williams; or, as his fellow officials sometimes say, "Tommy." While in conversation, Mr. Avery volunteered to bring the proper U. S. Agent up here on his next round; when, he says, the transfer can be made, if we have a map ready showing our exact position.　　B.

Mrs. Baker is improving some; she wears a common shoe now, but does not walk, so of course she has to be waited on. A few days since she had her dinner brought to her as usual, and on preparing her coffee and attempting to drink it, she discovered that there was an astonishingly strange taste about it. She said she was at a loss to fancy what could have befallen it, it was so overwhelmingly nauseous. Suddenly the thought occurred to her to investigate the sugar, and fortunately, for those white and glistening crystals possessed no saccharine qualities, they were pure *salt*.

Mr. Clark informs us that the stove to our large, portable oven has been unsatisfactory for some time past. In the first place, it was too small and in the second place, it filled up with coals which had to be shoveled out. This proved an expense of fuel. We have introduced a new stove—one of our own make—with grates and an ash-pit, that works satisfactorily. Mr. Bristol says he can now bake bread in one half or three fourths of the time it took with the other stove and he thinks with much less fuel.

Mr. Olds has again taken his place in the kitchen.— Mr. W. G. Kelly has taken Mr. Smith's place in waiting on Mr. Nash, and Mr. Smith will work at the trap-shop for the present.—Mrs. Story's departure creates a vacancy which Phebe goes to fill for a season.

We noticed Mrs. Higgins washing dishes this morning, and that reminds us how smart and bright she is. She takes care of several bedrooms, attends the bag-bee, does all the shoe binding and an immense amount of sewing for different members of the family.

The old piano—poor, wretched, crazy thing—has lately been moved from the Tontine to the South-Garret, because it had a benumbing effect on the minds of the school boys. Mrs. Hatch suggests that this piano is to O. C., what the *hen* is to the different Express Offices of the U. S.

Mrs. Conant says they have dried the clothes in the dry-room for the last time. They will begin work there now, to convert it into an acceptable composing room. This is rather electrifying—it seems so near that it makes one's heart beat faster—a few short weeks and you will all be here. *Come quickly.*

We have just made a short tour through the different houses to see if peradventure we might haply light on some news, but alack! t'is the scarcest thing at O. C. The only thing we saw was Mr. Woolworth vigorously brandishing a broom over a large drift near his door; he paused from his arduous engagement, looked up and said, "This is a *gal*-orious morning!" and then fell at his work again most lustily.

THE O. C. DAILY.

VOL. 5. THURSDAY, FEB. 20, 1868. NO. 43.

W. P., Feb. 18.—Messrs. Case and Hills called at the Office, yesterday afternoon. Mr. C. had with him a letter from Mr. Hamilton, stating that he had seen Mr. Clark, who said that the committee were in favor of having the Central straightened, but if they were going to have to fight for the right of way, they did not want to have anything to do with it.

We have already signified our willingness to give the right of way across our land and Mr. Case wishes us to influence our neighbors, as far as possible, to do the same. He inquired how much freight we shipped during the year, and was answered, that last year the freight shipped and received amounted to six-hundred and fifty tons. Mr. Wilson was present and remarked that we had better petition for a passenger depot—said that Oneida and Vernon would probably quarrel as to which should get it, and in the meantime we could put in our claim. The other gentlemen assented to this; said they should like it much better than going to Oneida or Vernon as they have done.

Two of the Wightman girls commenced work in the Silk-factory to-day.

Another molder has been hired to work in the Foundry.

Feb. 19.—A few days ago, Mr. Newhouse and Myron went to Vernon to see a man who had a boat for sale. They offered him three and a half doz. No. 1 traps for it, but he said he had sold it to his brother. Yesterday, he called at the shop and said that his brother could not pay him until spring, and as he wanted pay now, we might have the boat, at the terms offered. Mr. Newhouse went over this morning and brought it home. It is larger than the old one and is to be nicely painted and put in order for Summer use. But it's name, what shall it be? We leave the subject open, hoping for suggestions.

A class was formed last night for the study of Philosophy. Pupils, Jane Abbott, Georgia and Mary Baker. Teacher, J. F. Sears.

Wallingford boasts a patent bread-slicer, O. C. a potato-washer, and we—well, we have a patent egg-beater and cake-mixer. It's merits have not been very thoroughly tested yet, but it promises to "be handy to have."

We notice Mr. Higgins these days busy with Arithmetic and Geography. From his countenance we judge he finds in them all the charm and more, than he has found heretofore in writing.

You may remember how your mother, on washing day, used to go to the trouble and expense of boiling her clothes—all the white clothes must be boiled—it would not do to omit boiling. "Wy-ee! they would be streaked and yellow if not *boiled*."

We launderers of the O. C. have broken from this thralldom of ancestral custom, and learned a better way. At first we ventured not to boil the sheets and pillow-cases; they looked very well. Next the women's clothes were tried; looked very well indeed. The old habit was so strong that we thought shirts must be boiled still; the shirts looked yellow, and in contrast with the other clothes, *quite* yellow. Despite our pains-taking, they did not improve, so at last we stopped boiling them, and now folks say they are brightening up every week.

The large amount of fruit used by us is the occasion of a great many stains on table and pocket linen; new boots and shoes stain white hose; we often want to use new cotton in the winter, etc. etc. All this bleaching to be done at a season when there is neither grass nor dew to do it for us, led us to look about for some method of accomplishing it. This winter we have substituted chloride of lime. It costs us eight cts. per lb., and we use it at the rate of two oz. for five yds. of cloth. By its aid we are able to do the work of our department quite satisfactorily to ourselves and our many patrons.   B.

Mr. Kelly and his corps wrought quite a change in the dry-room yesterday—pitched all the benches, posts, bars and braces out the front windows—took out the two stoves—fixed the base-boards—put up the iron columns—swept and cleared the floor, and now the room is ready for paint and white-wash. Everybody is interested in this work, and all go at it with smiling faces, willing hands and happy hearts.

We noticed two gentlemen at dinner yesterday, and asked Mr. Underwood who they were; he replied, "Oh! *Nobodies.* One was from Bath, but he didn't know our folks that came from there."

Mr. Leete says there isn't any news to be had at the store. Most of his customers, the squaws, say it is "hard times" with them, because they are no longer allowed to sell bead-work on the cars.

If we were called on to say why it is so quiet out here, we should tell you we suspected it was owing to the fact, that the boys of Mr. Perry's school are improving this lovely, spring-like morning by taking a hunting excursion. They have not strayed so far from home however, that we cannot hear the occasional report of their guns.

Mr. Leete returned as usual, yesterday, but accompanied by Mary. Since she wears a short dress and short hair she seems quite like one of us.

Mrs. Deborah Hale has been spending two days with us, and left this morning.

THE O. C. DAILY.

VOL. 5.   FRIDAY, FEB. 21, 1868.   NO. 44.

DEAR DAILY.—Mrs Deborah Hale of Genoa, Five Corners, gave some account of her experience in private conversation, which may interest some of your readers. She has been a believer in Mr. Noyes and in the truth he advocates from the first I believe.

Several years ago she parted from her husband without a penny for her support, and has since lived alone. Her son who died in the army willed his bounty and pension money to his mother, which very much enraged Mr. Hale; and when an additional bounty of one hundred dollars was offered, Mr. Hale entered a claim for it, but on being told that it must go to Mrs. Hale, the receiver of the previous payments, unless he could give good reasons why she was not worthy, he convicted her on the ground of her connection with a body of Perfectionists, who believed and practiced very bad things. This crushed her to the earth for a time, when she rallied and felt stronger than ever to face the great men of this world, defining her relations to the Community and the doctrines they hold, so far as she understood them. Their respect for her increased from this time.

Mr. Lyon, Chief Justice, and the first man of Genoa, drew up a paper, testifying to the good character of Mrs. Hale, and the dishonest, untruthful character of Mr. Hale, which was forwarded to Washington. Mr. Hale's Attorney told Mrs. Hale that he tried his best to dissuade Mr. H. from pressing his claim, but he was very bitter and determined that he would go on. "Then" said the Attorney, "I must be well paid." And, as he was well paid, he must now do his best to aid what he knew was an unjust demand. Mr. Hale cannot now pass through the streets of Genoa without being hooted at, so that he is seldom seen there.

What interested me was that all this trying experience had led Mrs. Hale to a more earnest and intelligent knowledge of God. She felt that the truth was more precious to her than a good name, and had she a million dollars at stake she would not sacrifice one iota of what she believed to be truth to retain it. She expressed a high appreciation of the CIRCULAR, and considers it a letter from the O. C. to her.   S. B. C.

———————

In the meeting last evening, a letter was read from E. H. H. to Mr. Woolworth, concerning hired help—suggesting that we retain some of our best hands, for the present at least. This was sympathized with, and it was thought we should feel free to reconsider the decision of the business meeting on this point.

Mr. Woolworth then said, "I hear that some of our folks have been having rather *emotional* experience this afternoon owing to the clams we had for dinner. How is this, where is the trouble? Shall we have to condemn the clams? Perhaps some one has some experience they would like to relate." Here followed a general buzz, and considerable merriment. That the clams were excellent, was the general opinion, but they are more apt to make folks sick than round ones, and particularly if persons are unused to eating them. Mr. Hatch thought a meal of oysters would be a good antiemetic, and serve to settle the clams satisfactorily all round.

The Talk "Remarks on the Second Coming" was re-read and very generally endorsed. Many said they had found it true that Christ responded to every act of theirs to please him. No matter how small the action if only performed in faith. We can all seek to please God in our every-day life, and in the smallest things that go to make up our experience.

———————

Several of our elderly brothers and sisters have of late testified to feeling young and strong. Uncle Elias Hall, who takes care of the calves at the barn near the Boarding-house, says he never endured the cold as well as he has this winter. Mr. Conant thinks that both Mr. Hall and Mr. Kellogg are renewing their youth. Mrs. M. Hall says she has never in her life been as well as she is this season. B. T. Thayer and others joined Mrs. Hall in testifying to excellent health. Aunt Sarah Nash is "as smart as a cricket" and is growing young and sparkling.

Mr. Knox, of the firm Keefer, Knox, Arms and Co., in company with Theodore Hand took supper here last evening. Mr. Knox brought samples of woolen goods for which he wished to take orders. Mr. Aiken did not want anything at present, and therefore gave him no orders. Mr. Leete says he has bought of this man for twelve or fourteen years, and has always found him reliable and honest.

———————

Mr. Kinsley and Homer have gone to North Bay. Mr. K. to take Mr. Clark's place in delivering, and getting orders for castings from our customers in that region, and Homer will try and find good butter for our table.

———————

Messrs. Hawley and Hall have gone to Clinton, the former to sell castings, and the latter, silk.

———————

It has been quite warm for two or three days—a south wind blowing—which has caused the snow to disappear very rapidly. It is cooler again this morning.

———————

Mr. Conant reports that they have finished drawing muck. Whole amount drawn, 340 loads.

THE O. C. DAILY.

VOL. 5. SATURDAY, FEB. 22, 1868. NO. 45.

Mrs. Langstaff sends a special dispatch to state, that from the beginning, the business of quilting has been carried on in a most unsatisfactory way.

From our remotest grandmothers downward to us, all women that have quilted have been content to rest the frame on which the quilt was stretched on the backs of chairs. This was a most uncertain support; hit the chair but slightly, it would fall backward, down would go the frame at one corner. tilting up at the other, likely as any way hitting some unsuspecting person on the head; while amidst a tumult of small screams and terrified shrieks from the women, away went the spools of thread, scissors, papers of pins, chalk, twine and everything else on the quilt in a shower of confusion, to hide themselves under beds, bureaus, stands, or any other un-get-at-able place.

Things were gathered up and put in their places, order restored and quiet reigned again, until another chair was overturned and a like scene enacted.

Well, thanks to a man's ingenuity and kindness, the quilters of O. C. need be no longer subjected to such dire disasters. Mr. Ellis has quite recently made for them four " beautiful white horses" with nicks in their backs for the frame to fit into and hold it firmly. These are vastly appreciated by Mrs. L. who has labored long under the chair dispensation.

The parties mentioned as being gone on business, have returned and report a prosperous and pleasant time, with the exception that the westward party (Mr. Kinsley and Homer) in crossing. the Lake to reach Cleveland, found several cracks and fissures in the ice and had the rather uncommon experience of getting their team and sleigh into the water.

When within about fifty rods of the north shore, they were suddenly immersed to the depth of about two and a half feet. They were obliged to take off the team, get boards to walk on while carrying the load forward to firm ice, and then by the aid of long chains the sleigh was drawn forward and re-loaded.

The most serious part of it was the wetting of one pair of feet (on a very cold day) and Mr. Vanderburgh's plow-points. B.

The O. C. Store is embellished with one of the " Oneida business directories." The following description of them is taken from the *Dispatch:*

" The frames, which are composed of black-walnut and gilt molding, are three feet and six inches square, and are divided into seventeen spaces. The central space at the top contains a clock, the oblong lower one contains three dials under the magical words, ' Breakfast' ' Dinner' and ' Supper,' set so as to indicate the hour at which the guests of the respective Hotels at which the ' Directories' are displayed, indulge in the amusing pastime of eating their meals."

On the Directory may be seen handsomely printed cards of the principal business firms of Oneida.

It was some question with the people of Oneida in which place to put this advertisement, in our store or at the Castle; but concluding this would be the most conspicuous place, they asked G. R. K. to bring it up.

The remarks in the W. C. journal, about a daily paper, were received with cheers. Mr. Woolworth said " We shall have rather lively times here then, shan't we ?" George E. thought the *Democratic Union* would stand a rather poor chance. " Yes" says Mr. W. " It will be something like having a new revolver against an old musket."

After meeting last night some of our folks seemed to be seized with a desire to sing, and sing they did. " Tappan," " Portuguese Hymn," " Devizes," " When I can read my title clear" and " Sherburne" were all sung most zealously and with " untiring effects." At length one young woman exclaimed, " Say, Father Hatch, don't you think " America" would be a good thing to go to bed on ?" All agreed it would, and accordingly the company arose and " America" was sung with great gusto ; then the merry group dispersed.

Mother Burnham seems to be missed on such occasions ; we heard it quite often said, ' If Mother Burnham was only here !' We expect she soon will be, and we are as patient as good children in the meantime.

The steward says, " Our stock of butter is nearly exhausted ; so is the supply in the country about here, making it almost impossible to procure more. The price is high, and advancing. In view of these things can we not, for the next forty days, be con-contented with a little thinner ' spread' ?"

The Bag Dept. has lately had a re-enforcement. Mr. James Van Velzer has left the kitchen to assist in this work, and George E. intends spending his forenoons there for the present. We suspect they know it is about to breathe its last, and want to make sure of having the doctor on the spot, when the time arrives.

Oh ! there comes Mr. Leete along the walk with a paint-pail. He, with Mrs. Conant as an assistant, is going to do the painting in the composing-room.

THE O. C. DAILY.

VOL. 5.   MONDAY, FEB. 24, 1868.   NO. 46.

BUSINESS MEETING.

Several of the hired men had been notified that we should not want them another year, but in re-considering the matter, in accordance with Mr. Hamilton's letter on this subject, it was decided to keep the teamsters if a satisfactory bargain can be made with them. It was thought the effect of this move on the hired men had been good. Messrs. Thacker, Conant, Woolworth, Marks and Hawley were appointed a committee for hiring help on the farm and regulating wages.

Mr. Thacker proposed, for a preserving-house, to move one or two old barns from W. P. ; for a dairy-house, the basement of the Tontine now used for fruit preserving ; for storing vinegar, cider, &c., the present fruit-house ; and for storing fruit, the north room of the Tontine over the proposed dairy-room. This last place had been spoken of for a school-room, therefore a committee was appointed to consider this part of the proposition. Committee, Mr. Hatch, Mr. Thacker, George E. and Portia.

Messrs. Kelly, Burt, Kinsley and Knowles were appointed a committee to see what can be done about the planing-machine at the mill, as the water-wheel with which it is connected is out of order.

It was proposed that John Leonard make W. P. his abiding place, and devote his time to pattern-making.

Last evening we had an entertainment in the Hall, and we were lamenting our inability to do justice to the subject, when we chanced to see the following note which we immediately intercepted and appropriated :

O. C. Feb. 23, 1868.

DEAR H. :—If you thought the entertainment two weeks ago worth a journey from New-York here, I do not know what you would say were you here to-night. We have just had a repetition of that same with a great addition, mostly for the benefit of the W. P. family, as they were not here when the children danced before. I cannot give you a full account now, but will let you have some idea of it through my eyes.

The family met in the Hall at a quarter before seven, expecting, they knew not what. At the first rising of the curtain, C. Cragin appeared with a manuscript book in hand and pantomimed C. J. Guiteau to perfection, delivering his noted lecture, in the middle of which he took off his coat and walked back to the stand in a most pompous manner.

Next Charles and Milford, representing the same personage and William Vaill, rooming together, with the chalk mark on the floor—Milford sitting as near the boundary line as possible playing the flageolet, while Charles was walking back and forth in his part of the room, reading in the most earnest manner, and as he could not make William cease his noise, he rubbed out the chalk mark in disgust.

Then Mr. Wright, (George E.) appeared to us in company with four " boys" (Fred. and Charles Marks, Dan. Abbott and Ernest) hoeing strawberries. After moping along awhile, stopping now and then to wipe the water from his eyes with the corner of his great silk handkerchief, he succeeded in getting ahead of the boys, when he stopped, and leaning on his hoe handle, narrated to them the story of his lady love appearing to him &c. ; and the last pantomime gave us the very thing itself——Geo. E. in the character of Mr. Wright, serving as Mill-watch. After seeing that all was safe he sat down to study Astronomy by the light of his lantern. He soon fell asleep, and was awakened by his angel bride (Ellen Nash) gliding about the room. At first, he started back, but on discovering the star in her forehead, and learning that it meant himself, he invited her to his arms, and as she sat on his knee, happy in his embrace, the curtain dropped. Better justice could not have been done to those celebrated men, and the family were not slow in manifesting their pleasure.

But do not imagine this was all. The curtain was again raised, and there stood Father Hatch with his company, consisting not only of the boys and girls that entertained you so much, but eight of the smaller ones, with their Aunt (Emma) whom they were visiting, and Harriet Olds, acting the part of a professional dancing-master and dressed to correspond. They formed two sets of cotillions, and danced the Romanoff through without making a mistake. The little ones danced by themselves ; George Easton, represented a little Turk, with Rose for partner, Temple, a soldier, grave as a deacon, with sparkling little Fanny, Willie, an old gentleman, wearing swallow-tailed coat, a standing collar, and spectacles ; with the once timid Dora, and Harold, to all intents and purposes, a live " Dancing Jack," and dressed like one, with sober Anna. The little girls all dressed in white. The older ones danced as before, and did well ; but the little ones and the dancing-master were too much for us—especially Harold, whose peculiar jump, diddle, or whatever it might be called, made the scene an overwhelming one. They seemed so unconscious withal, so intent on their business, and kept excellent time.   Yours truly,   s. b. c.

My oldest daughter, usually called Nelly, proposes, with the consent and approbation of her friends, to discard this name, having out-grown it, and assume her original name Helen ; substituting Emma for her middle name thereby giving Helen Emma Woolworth. " For short" she may be called Helen E.   w. h. w.

It grew very cold toward night Saturday, and yesterday morning the mercury stood at fifteen degrees below zero. This morning the air bites your ears and nose and is filled with little shivering snow-flakes struggling downward.

THE O. C. DAILY.

VOL. 5.   TUESDAY, FEB. 25, 1868.   NO. 47.

EVENING MEETING.

Mr. D. P. Nash invited criticism. He was spoken of as a man of faith, and one who loves God. Yet at present there seems to be a spirit over him that should be looked into and judged. He makes trouble for his attendants, especially for his night watchers. He has manifested but little interest in spiritual things of late, but has been given to novel-reading. This he has dropped, however, and seems to be taking a new turn of earnestness.

Mr. Nash was exhorted to give up his own will and trust to the judgement of others. It was thought there was an under-current of grumbling in his spirit. Mr. Kelly felt there was an unwholesome atmosphere in his room. He questioned whether there was not something in Mr. Nash's past life that needed cleansing. He felt there was something impure in his spirit respecting social matters. Others had similar thoughts.

Every time Mr. Nash has been criticised he has improved. Christ has power over the palsy, and if Mr. Nash gives himself wholly to his spirit there is no reason why he cannot recover.

Mr Campbell writes to us from W. P.:

"Assessor Williams called on us Friday afternoon to settle a question about our silk tax that has been somewhat in abeyance for the last three months. The occasion, was a letter just published from the Revenue Commissioner, explaining in detail a decision he made in regard to it last fall, and about which the assessor had been waiting for information. That decision allowed the deduction of the cost of the raw stock in making up the silk tax returns, and reduced the tax on silk about one half.

" Mr Assessor came here full of the idea that he had discovered a rat hole, or something of that kin, in the letter of explanation that would prevent us from getting the benefit of that deduction. Raw silk was defined to be silk that ' had been reeled from the cocoon' and the astute official bethought himself that the raw stock we used was not in that state, as he was confident he had seen it being put through that process. *Ergo*, we could not be entitled to the benefit of that decision.

" The absurdity of such an idea is apparent at a glance to any one at all familiar with the subject, though perhaps it was natural enough for the assessor to be caught with it, with his imperfect knowledge of the business and official predisposition to look out for any ' smart chances' to increase the tax returns.

" C. A. C. however, succeeded in convincing him by actual demonstration that we did not ' reel silk from the cocoon,' so he patronizingly gave up the point, and concluded he should have to allow us the deduction, contenting himself with giving some directions about amending the returns."

W. P., Feb. 24.—Joel reports some decided improvements in his department. Some complaints coming to us from trappers about the liability of our malleable iron posts for bear-traps to break, it was decided to make them of wrought iron, and over two hundred were forged last year. The best blacksmith, with a boy to help him, was able to forge only three in an hour, making the work only cost us fifteen cents a piece. Lately a pair of dies have been made by which they can be forged in the drop, now a man and boy can make one hundred and thirty in five hours, doing them much better and easier than by the old way. Joel says the new method is not perfected yet, but he expects ere long to more than double on the present speed.

Victory ! The potato-washer has been perfected ! The skill of an inventive genius has triumphed over all obstacles that appeared to the unbelieving against it.

Instead of picking the potatoes out by hand from the cold water, we now lift the washer from the box by a handle and dump them into a basket, so quick ! that one hardly believes it—and so clean too, it is truly astonishing. We can wash as many in ten minutes, as we could by hand in an hour, and it's nothing but sport. The inventor, and others concerned, certainly deserve great credit for their indomitable perseverance and energy in adding such an important machine to the number of useful inventions. We can do but injustice with words, but people wishing to see the machine work, or test its qualities themselves, can do so by calling in the back kitchen any morning at seven and a half o'clock.   KITCHEN.

Yesterday, some one made quite a sensation by posting this notice at the head of the broad stairs :
" Come and hear ' Spiritual Wives' at 6–45."

Classes that have usually met at this hour made different arrangements, the dish-washing and dining-room work were dispatched with great celerity, and at the appointed time there was a full house (as full as our present family ever makes it), eager and expectant to hear what you have already heard, therefore no necessity for comment.

In the afternoon yesterday, a little bird, perched on a twig near the window, kept triumphantly reiterating, " The snow 'll be knee deep, the snow 'll be knee deep." Perchance his prophesy may be true, for it snowed all day yesterday, it snowed all night we should judge, and it's snowing still.

THE O. C. DAILY.

VOL. 5.   WEDNESDAY, FEB. 26, 1868.   NO. 48.

After listening to the account of Mr. Shelly, in the New-York journal, Mr. Woolworth said :

" We advised Mr. Shelly, when he was here last, as he was going to Newark to close up his business, to put himself in communication with Mr. Hamilton and the Agency brethren, and cultivate their fellowship and invite their criticism. The idea was, that if he could join Mr. Hamilton and the Agency he could probably join the Community. It seems he neglected our advice altogether. I never understood that he made a regular application to join the Community, though he talked about it a good deal in a vague way. He seemed very much preoccupied with his business, the whip-socket hobby."

Mrs. Langstaff reports that she has been in the quilting business just one year. Most of the time she has had an assistant and the hired girls engaged in the laundry have generally worked there a portion of the day every Saturday.

During the year they have pieced and quilted thirty quilts, made ten comfortables, twelve new cotton ticks for husk-beds, and five pair of pillows. They have also quilted six quilts that were pieced by different members of the family. The material used for making these, has been about an equal proportion of new and old calico.

We have sold to our employees, four second rate quilts, five pair of pillows, and four feather-beds.

Mr. Conant's teamsters have been drawing stone for two days. We asked him what they were drawing it for and he said, " We never want a pile of brick without a lot of stone. We thought likely as any way our folks would be wanting to build something, and we rather draw the stone when it's good going, than wait till the mud comes."

Mr. D. M. Kelly says, they had been at work about an hour, Monday morning when suddenly all the machinery stopped. They went below and found that the new iron-bucketed water-wheel put in last fall, had become covered with ice, and in consequence, when they started, it tore off one bucket and flattened all the rest. They at once went about repairing the wheel. This they did by replacing iron buckets with wooden ones ; they had good luck, and got everything ready to begin work again this morning.

The greatest objection we see to the Commodore's scheme, of not allowing the squaws to sell bead-work on the cars, is, *Our Squaw Cupboard*. It is filled with squaw goodies, (brown-bread crusts, pudding, clam-pancakes, codfish &c.) which, until Vanderbilt's veto, we found no difficulty in disposing of for cash.

What shall be done to open trade in this direction ? The squaws must eat, but they find hard work to get money. If E. H. H. would only suggest to the Commodore the vital importance of this traffic, and the important revenue derived from it, would he not re-consider.   KITCHEN.

What a ludicrous " hash of things" we sometimes make by misunderstanding the remarks of others.

A. said, " Blessed is freedom," and her companion fancied she said something was as " *placid as farina*." M. remarked to A. " It's a beautiful morning," but A.'s ears converted it into, " *it's dreadfully annoying*." C. says, " He wants to warm his back, I guess ;" B. understands her, " *he wants a spanking, I guess*."

A party of engineers engaged in suveying a route for the Midland Railroad are now working south from Oneida up the valley of the creek toward Hamilton. There is some prospect that the road will pass near the western boundary of the O. C. domain ; yesterday the party were to be seen taking their levels around the hill passing this side of neighbor Johnson's and within half a mile of our office.

Mr. Perry just stepped in to say that he and his boys have been *promoted ;* the colored man is sick, and they are all going to hang out clothes. A pleasant recreation from their books.

THE O. C. DAILY.

VOL. 5.   THURSDAY, FEB. 27, 1868.   NO. 49.

W. P., Feb. 25.—Our meeting hour is changed for the present to seven o'clock, in order that we may read "Spiritual Wives," which is sent to us from Oneida as soon as they finish reading.

Last evening a sincere criticism was given to Edward Inslee.

Near the close of the reading hour, G. W. Hamilton made his appearance among us.

The culvert through which the water escapes into the race-way was frozen up Saturday night, and when the gate was hoisted Sunday, the water filled in to the depth of five feet—two feet above the floor of the tom-room. Some of the men have been engaged to-day in clearing out the race-way again.

The Cases, of Vernon, are at work like beavers for the straightening of the Central. They are now at work for the "right of way" i. e. they have drawn up a paper for the signatures of the land holders on the proposed route, pledging the land for $50.00 per acre. They have already obtained a good many names, and anticipate no difficulty in securing the right for the above price which one of them remarked was a mere bagatelle. Some will undoubtedly give their land. The Cases were here this week and exhibited a profile drawing of the section through which the survey was made by Jenning. This survey was made across our flat between the Trap-factory and the Creek, running just north of the W. P. pond.

The "Marriage Fund Association" of Boston have sent us two circulars, addressed to J. H. Noyes. The avowed object of this association as set forth in the circular, is to provide "some remedy that shall reach the wide spread and rapidly growing evil of abortion, and the growing tendency of our young men towards celibacy." The society claims to have a fund of $10,000 "and intend to devote their time, talent and money to promote these reforms, and now solicit subscriptions from all who are interested in this work."

Has it come to this that marriage requires such extraordinary efforts to perpetuate it?

We had no money to subscribe, but such as we had we gave, and sent two copies of M. C. to their relief.

You should look from our window just for one moment. You could not see very far to be sure, (for we are having not the "Tenderest snow in all the year," but a most frantic, blinding storm) however, you might discern Mr. Hawley's hale and hearty figure engaged in driving a span of horses that are attached to a sled on which are several barrels, from the back of the brick house round to the concrete building near the Tontine; in his wake, Mr. Bristol, Mr. Thayer, Frederic and two hired men, each armed with a tin pail. We were a little curious to know what was being done, and found on inquiry, they were transporting the vinegar from the new-house cellar to the fruit-house.

The external life of the Community is so unvaried just now that not much appears suitable for our little *Daily*; still we are conscious of a steady growth in our inner life. Not a day passes without unmistakable evidence that a good spirit is working wonders in individual character. Where once was coldness, hardness and discouragement, is now seen and felt the warm, genial influence of a soft, loving heart; and with it is a deep toned earnestness that insures continuous progress.

NEW YORK LEDGER ITEM.

A dark figure prostrate on the snow—a low moan—two stalwart men lift the form and bear it to a couch—an errand-boy dispatched to the reading-room—a few hurried words with the M. D.—he leaves the apartment—a dull dread, a dim foreboding of shadowy ills, a chill of horror—terrible suspense! * * *

The Dr. returns looking placid; "'twas nothing——slipped down the stair-way, bruised his knee slightly, but nothing serious;" so we breathe again and laugh to see how frightened we had made ourselves.   SYLVANUS.

Hacker's "Pleasure Boat," a little paper published in N. J., came to us a few days since with a friendly article of considerable length on "The Oneida Community." It also contained "The Twin Relics," "No Chance for Competition," "Appeal to all Lawyers, Justices, Judges, and Courts of Law," copied from the CIRCULAR.

Mr. Kelly very smilingly remarked to us last evening, "If you had said those buckets 'doubled up' instead of 'flattened,' you would have been nearer right."

We asked him to pardon our ignorance, and promised a correction to-day. So please consider that those buckets were not flattened but doubled up.

We heard a lady say, "If it is to remain a profound secret much longer, as to who the persons are that are coming here from W. C., they must not be surprised when they come if the sleeping arrangements are just a *little mixed*."

Uncle Heman had a mishap last evening. He lost his foothold and slipped down the steps near the dairy-room, bruising his leg. Mrs. Kinsley says it pained him considerably during the night and is swollen some. George E. thinks it will be nothing serious.

THE O. C. DAILY.

VOL. 5.   FRIDAY, FEB. 28, 1868.   NO. 60.

CARLTON RICE ONCE MORE.

The following letter speaks for itself:

Utica, Feb. 27, 1868.

ALBERT KINSLEY ESQ.   DEAR SIR :—Enclosed please find bill of sheriff ($5,50) for extra expense by adjournment, which as per agreement you promised to pay. It was much to my injury the sale was adjourned as Mr. Rice took advantage of the time by causing to be cut and carried off the premises all the wood he possibly could.

Rice is a bad egg !   Yours truly,

L. M. Thomson.

We shall notify Mr. Thomson that we knew nothing about this last dodge of Mr. Rice's, but supposed we were dealing with an honest man, which, it seems is not the case. He gave us to understand distinctly that if the sale of the farm could be adjourned one month he would do all he could to redeem it. We now find that he has used the time so obtained to clear the land of wood, and then allowed it to be sold without an effort to redeem either the land or his promises. After all what more could we expect of a spiritualist. *On commence par etre dupe ; on finit par etre fripon.*   COMMITTEE.

W. P., Feb. 27.—The other evening, during the reading of that part of " Spiritual Wives" which narrates the vision of the Rev. (!) Erasmus Stone, Mr. Burt suddenly burst forth with, " Well ! Mr. Dixon does have the greatest faculty for coloring things !" Some one said, " Did you furnish the original ?" " Yes" " Is it rendered word for word ? " " *Word for word !*" echoed he in astonishment, " Dixon has *twenty* words where I had *one.*"

We have been so fortunate all this winter as to have a good supply of rain-water. As we are dependent upon our cisterns for drinking-water we have appreciated this very much. Now, however, the cisterns are empty, and Mr. Ackley may be seen, armed with a washtub and great tin dipper, making war on the snow-banks which abound in our door-yard.

The Finishing Dept. having finished three thousand No. 3. traps are at present engaged in putting together 17,000 No 1's. A. says the No. 3's are the very last of the traps begun in the summer.

Mr. Higgins is anxious to raise lima beans in our garden next summer. He is sure it can be done, and he wishes to know if some one at Wallingford will send him some for seed.

Alas for that duck ! Scorning our attempts at civilization, it took to itself wings—or rather used those it had—and flew away.

This morning while we were quietly at work in the kitchen, the steam-pipe that is used for heating water became disconnected, and being under a pressure of forty-five lbs. at the time, it created quite a consternation, the steam driving about ten feet and making a *terrific* noise. It was a good time to observe who had the most presence of mind. Some were seen making their way for the arched-way with a considerable degree of enthusiasm. Two of the women however, did not seem to mind much about it, or else were too much frightened to know what to do—probably the latter—for they kept quietly at work and appeared undisturbed. We were all thankful that nobody was injured.   KITCHEN.

Feb. 27., Upper sitting-room, 9-30, P. M.—What is the cause of all this chatter ? Why are there so many folks here, and what causes so much enthusiasm ? Look up, as the others are all doing, and you will see suspended from the corridor twelve different patterns of paper hangings. They are all pretty—this would look nicely in a bed-room—that is just the thing for the sitting-room—but that's not the question. Which one is the most appropriate for the new composing-room ? Ah ! now you know what the discussion is. We trust the concentrated taste of this large group of interested friends will result in a pleasing selection to those for whom it is being made.

There seems to be a slight perturbation in Father Hatch's flock just at present. They are having a run of something, they do not know exactly what, but it seems to be an aggravated form of a cold. Eight of the children have already had it, and a number more show signs of coming down. You should see how jolly they are over it; notwithstanding they bark like so many little dogs, and are so hoarse they can hardly speak aloud, they are smiling and bright, and all seem to have a courageous, cheerful spirit.

Mr. Hatch says, yesterday morning in their meeting he told them he should like to hear from the sick ones, but there was not *one* that would acknowledge they were sick.

Mr. Woolworth thinks a portion of the family might indulge in a little earlier rising without any detriment to them. It has been customary for the waiters to remain in attendance until 8½ o'clock, but it was thought they should not be required to serve after 8 o'clock. Persons coming after this time should wait on themselves.

Carrie and Annie have lately taken the table-waiting in the morning; possibly their business habits and ideas of punctuality co-operated to bring about this exhortation.

Mrs. L. A. Thayer's uncle and his wife are here. They came yesterday, and intend leaving to-day.

THE O. C. DAILY.

VOL. 5. SATURDAY, FEB. 29, 1868. NO. 51.

New York, Feb. 27, 1868.

SIR:—I have been requested to procure a circular issued by your society and send it to the Greek Minister at Washington. If you have such a circular please to forward a copy to me at No. 4 Wall St., Room No. 3, and anything of interest connected therewith, and oblige, Your obedient servant,

GEO. G. MITCHELL.

To the Chief of the
Society of Perfectionists, Oneida Creek, N. Y.

We sent our CIRCULAR that Mr. Noyes prepared last summer to send to correspondents, to the writer of the above and refered him to the Agency for further information if desired.

Another consternation in the kitchen this afternoon. It had been decided to have some hulled-corn, so E. F. H. of W. P. was sent for to take charge of the business, in order we suppose, to have the work done scientifically. Mr. S. was applied to for lye (a necessary article in this line of business); it was brought and deposited in the steam boiler and a full head of steam turned on. While waiting for the lye to boil, each busy here and there, we were all suddenly surprised and filled with terror to see the lye boiling over at a rapid rate. At this juncture, V. H. came to the rescue, but before we could stop it, nearly half had escaped onto the floor. Seeing our hopes so quickly dashed, E. F. H. was heard to exclaim in a most lugubrious tone " *I am dead!*" This remark produced no little merriment among the group. A fresh supply of lye was obtained and we were soon able to proceed with our work.

The mothers thought it a good time to mop the floor, and so this job was done up a day in advance. The floor now presents a beautiful *yellowish-white* appearance. Good luck attended us the remainder of the afternoon. KITCHEN.

A few days since, we received a very lackadaisical letter addressed to Mr. Noyes, from which the following is an extract:

" I suppose politics are flung to the dogs with your people, at any rate I should hope so. I am so sadly disgusted with the way things are conducted at Washington, that I am as ever, silent. I never voted in my life, and I am glad of it. I am a man loved wherever I go, and politics would be like religion with me, were I to enter the arena. My family consists of a handsome, lovely wife, a sweet little daughter three to four years of age, gentle and interesting. I named her Evangeline, we call her little Eva, and sometimes little Evanga. My wife is about my own age, twenty-six, and romantic as myself. She is influenced by me-

and has the same belief. I have mesmerized her and . . . . I could never make it convenient to see you yet, but this coming week I shall probably give you a call. I am now at Albany disposing of my little paintings of Lake George scenery. So you can look for me about Saturday night.

" Yours in great haste and in the greatest affection,
J. H. KEITH. ARTIST."

This " *Lord Veriwpht*" arrived last evening. He looks just as his letter sounds, and Mr. Underwood says he talks in the same strain. Our folks tried hard to make him out a spiritualist, that they might have a good excuse for asking him to leave, but they did not succeed.

Mrs. Bristol, with whom the cloudy weather of O. C. has become quite a hobby, wishes to have it announced that since December first, we have had sixteen days of sunshine; nine of these have been in the present month. Having carefully kept a record, she feels sure she has given the entire number, and blandly remarks, " We have had an *unusually* pleasant winter; in fact, quite a *remarkable* one!"

Mr. Kinsley, Mrs. Abbie Burnham and Mrs. Conant are engaged in papering the composing-room. The paint has the slightest tinge of pink, and the groundwork of the paper is of the same hue. H. C. N. thinks the visions of those working in this room will be rose-colored.

Called at the Office last evening for an item. Carrie said it was a poor place for news—they do not have any. We noticed that the ledger account with Phelps, Dodge & Co. had been balanced, and a new account opened with another firm. Carrie very archly remarked she "did not like their principles and could not deal with them any longer!"

What would they say to her view of the case?

Will you invite items of history, biography and statistics, and make room for a few, daily? If so, here is the first:

John Guttenberg, born near Mentz, Germany, A. D. 1400. Printing discovered and practiced by him in 1440. He died Feb. 24th. 1468. M. L. W.

Mr. Hatch says we may report that Master Eugene has graduated; he is no longer hampered with a creeping-skirt, for he has discarded that mode of getting about and assumed the perpendicular.

THE O. C. DAILY.

VOL. 5.   MONDAY, MARCH 2, 1868.   NO. 52.

BUSINESS MEETING.

Messrs. Conant, Thacker and Kinsley constitute a committee to decide whether any more stone shall be drawn this winter.

It was unanimously decided to close the boys' school, and the classes which meet in the day time.

Mr. George Hamilton is to go to Titusville to see about procuring a second-hand boiler for use in the preserving department. There are probably a good many in the market there, and no difficulty is anticipated in selecting a good one. The cost of a second-hand boiler will be from $450 to $600, while a new one would cost us $1,000.

Several propositions were offered respecting the mode to be pursued in raising corn the coming season. Shall we raise it all ourselves and do all the work, or engage our neighbors to raise a portion, while we decide the time for picking, and either pick it ourselves, or oversee the work? Messrs. Kinsley, Conant, Thacker, Thayer, J. H. Barron and Frederick Marks were appointed committee for deciding on some course.

Decided to leave one of the old barns at W. P. for a kind of store-house, and if Mr. Thacker's building needs more stuff, to have it bought. Also suggested that those who have the buying of timber attend to it soon, that it may be drawn while we have snow.

———————

Something has been said from time to time of things in the kitchen—of an increase of machinery, &c.; which lessens the labor there very much. These are of great value; but there have also been improvements of a higher and more important character—an increase of unity, fellowship, and a feeling that it is a high and noble calling to "*serve tables*" in the church of God—a spirit of faith that we shall be helped to inspiration in preparing food as well as in other things.

Those of this department with the steward and stewardess, have a meeting once a week around the large work-table, when each member has an opportunity to make any suggestions as to food, manner of cooking, economy, the spiritual atmosphere, &c., &c. Such seasons are always edifying and enable us to go about our work again with lighter and merrier hearts.

KITCHEN.

———————

The "Midland" will dart out of the woods into the open, and enter the gully between Mr. Johnson's two sugar-loaf hills, cross the field by the old log house, separating the two springs, and then curving gracefully over the level will make for the West-hills. So said one of the surveyors, yesterday, a young man of the name of Clark from Rochester, who called here for a few minutes to look around.

The Philosophy class have been considering the beautiful working of the telegraph machine, and the question arose whether we could not have something practical for the illustration of its principles.

It was mentioned that a telegraph line might be made available in a paying sense between O. C. and W. P. to operate in conveying messages that often require a personal journey. Then all students of the science could be allowed chances of improvement by actual examinations. Shall the poles be got ready and the line established the coming Spring?

The expense need be but trifling, as we could furnish poles and do the work ourselves. Very likely our machinists could construct all the apparatus, and the wire and cost of material would not probably exceed $50 or $100.

Shall we have it?   ECONOMIST.

———————

Mr. Kelly tells us:—"Mr. D. P. Nash seems to be steadily making progress. Saturday he began for the first time moving his left arm back and forth on his lap. He also got up from his chair without any assistance and walked across the room. He has been a regular attendant at the 7 o'clock reading and evening meeting for the last week."

———————

Quite a portion of the family visited the composing-room at different times during the day yesterday. All are interested in it and desirous to have it look neat and attractive. At one time we saw there a group of laughing girls (ranging from twenty-one to thirty years of age) making for themselves no little amusement by trying that "froggy" game mentioned in the W. C. Journal.

———————

Sunday morning was very cold; S. W. N. states that the mercury was fifteen degrees below zero. It was a clear, bright day, but this morning, nothing can be seen save through a misty veil of snow-flakes.

The prediction of some one that we should have "six weeks of sleighing in March" was not ill-founded, judging from the beginning this month has made.

———————

The girls' school stops now, and their help in the house-work will be sensibly felt. The boys are to be variously distributed in the different departments of Community industry. One enters a round of duties in the kitchen, two will go to the Bag-shop, and others to the Trap-factory.

———————

Mr. Clark and Miss Eliza Burt are engaged in cleaning and preparing rooms for the W. C. delegation. They have begun on the one intended for Mrs. Skinner which produces not a few joyous heart-leaps.

———————

Mr. Keith, alias Lord Verisopht, left Saturday noon. We do most humbly wish Dickens could see him, and in his inimitable style render him immortal.

THE O. C. DAILY.

VOL. 5. TUESDAY, MARCH 3, 1868. NO. 53.

Mr. Woolworth said in the meeting last night:

" It may interest some to know that several of us have been over to Willow-Place, to assist at the celebration of Mrs. Miller's birth-day. I believe she tried to keep the day a secret. This party was quite a surprise to her. She was presented with a handsome pyramid-cake and a fruit-knife. She appreciated the knife, as she had lost the one she had.

" Nothing of very special interest took place. We had considerable entertainment with this new game of " froggy" as they call it. It was with some reluctance that the young folks entered into it, but when they got started they had considerable fun. The young women tried it, and then some of the men went through the performance, and rather carried off the palm, I thought. Finally we had a mixed game of both men and women, which was a decided improvement on anything we had had. We had some good laughs over it.

" Then G. W. Hamilton wound up with his frog song which was very amusing.

" I think there is a good home feeling over there at Willow-Place—free and genial. All seemed to be happy, so far as I could discover. It is a very pleasant place to visit."

(When they went, it snowed. When they came home, it was still snowing.)

We need only to mention the name Wm. Augustus Doolittle, to remind the Community of the lecturer who inflicted on us " Reminiscences of the War" a few months since. Well, it seems from a circular just received that W. A. Doolittle became discontented with his name for some reason (we think it was very appropriate, especially the surname) and has had it changed to Augustus St. Clair, with Rev. prefixed.

Furthermore, Wm. A. Doolittle that was, solicits an invitation to lecture to us again on—what ? Why, " Reminiscences of the War." Can we endure it ? Can we in consideration of his new name, Rev. Augustus St. Clair, consent to be bored again with his reminiscences ? " We pause for a reply."

(If it continues to snow we may be spared this infliction, without the trouble of answering his letter.)

Mr. Hawley reports he has all the business he can attend to in bringing folks from, and carrying them to their work. The Silk-factory girls have to be carried to and from the Boarding-house ; the Bag-shop hands cannot get to their work on foot, and the women that work in the washing must be brought in the morning and carried home at night.

Last night he had the extraordinary luck to overturn his sleigh, containing fourteen hired girls, just before the front door of the Boarding-house. This was royal fun for the lookers-on, and nothing serious for the dumped ones.

This morning they have been breaking the road between here and W. P., and at ten o'clock Mr. Hawley, Mr. Kinsley and a load of hired men are going to Vernon to attend a town meeting. Mr. H. says they expect to *shovel* their way through the snow.

D. M. Kelly thinks those engaged at the shop yesterday had a very narrow and providential escape.

They were planing some boards for a Mr. Thomas that lives near the Foundry. One of the knives of the planer had become worn and thin, and the boards were frosty ; suddenly there was a terrific noise, and half of one knife was hurled to the farther side of the room with intense velocity. Mr. K. said he thought by the noise that the whole cylinder had gone, but he soon discovered the facts in the case. He thinks this will teach them not to use the knives after they are worn so much as this one was. But a moment before the knife broke, Mr. Thomas stepped from in front of the planer ; Mr. K. says it would have been certain death to any one standing there, and he realized God's care over them in this accident.

(There is a little too much snow at the shop to have the boards work very satisfactorily.)

A copy of F. W. Smith's letter to Charles Guiteau was read in our meeting last evening. It was received with peals of laughter and loud applause. W. H. W. thought the charge for use of our Hall was light enough, and said speaking of the letter, " I should think it would be rather difficult to ' *rebut*' that."

(It snowed during meeting.)

" Ever deeper, deeper, deeper
Fell the snow o'er all the landscape,
Fell the covering snow, and drifted
Through the forest, round the village."
That is the way it does here.

At the breakfast table Mr. Perkins said he had got to hang out clothes ; says he, " We don't hang *up* clothes any more, we hang 'em *down*. Some of the way the snow is within a foot and a half of the line !"

COMMENT ON THE WEATHER.

Blow ! *blow !*
Snow ! *snow !*
Bluster, *fluster*, DRIFT !

If our friends do not hear from us again for a few days, they must attribute it to the snow—consider us " snow-bound."

It is a little stunning to hear the New Haven journalist talk about Spring. Possibly we may, by-and-by, but *it snows* now !

THE O. C. DAILY.

VOL. 5. WEDNESDAY, MARCH 4, 1868. NO. 54.

EVENING MEETING.

Mr. Cragin hoped we should have a spirit that would appreciate and profitably digest all the late talks from Wallingford.

H. C. N.—I hope we shall come into full sympathy with W. C. in respect to the Paper, and that it will be a central object of interest with us. We can make it easy for them to come on here, by doing what we can to create a good atmosphere for them to think and write in. I believe we can also help by writing.

Mr. Woolworth.—It is bringing a new interest, and a very important one among us. We should begin to make some calculation for it, in our minds and hearts at least. We can make a good atmosphere, as has been suggested, and I hope we shall do a good deal more than that, by getting the spirit of truth and love working up into our brains, as Mr. Noyes expresses it. I don't know what we cannot do when that spirit works in us in the true way. It is destined to work as great a revolution for human nature as steam power has effected in the world in the last forty or fifty years. This is a beautiful thought to me, and I feel its force and life. Here is something the world has not done, and can not do without Christ. In the world love is a force that destroys: it works ruin and destruction. But I know that in God's kingdom love will be made to work life and health and miracles.

Mr. Cragin.—It is a very interesting thought, that love worketh no ill to its neighbor.

B. H. C.—The Daily calls upon us for items just as though articles could be manufactured at will, or picked up like pebbles, on any ground.

Our Boarding-house life, outwardly, is quite a monotonous one. The boarders make short work of the ordinance of eating, then disappear till the ringing of the next bell. But Sunday is an exceptional day. Some leave us on Saturday to visit their friends and return Monday. Those who remain, however, (mostly girls), do not usually lack for company of the other sex from abroad. On our return last Sunday evening, from mother O. C., we stumbled upon cozy couples in various quarters. In the mens sitting-room there were not less than three couplets each occupying a corner, having willed our steady Mr. Snow into the wash-room somewhat against his sense of propriety and of equal rights. On hearing the facts we felt a little disturbed by it and thought some of calling a meeting of the feminine boarders and kindly suggest to them that if they must be sparked on Sundays that they learn to do it up in a Christian-like manner, i. e., discreetly and in order, or in such ways as the world to which they belong, approves, so as not to bring scandal upon our B. H. home.   c.

A flock of white snow-birds have been seen in the pear-orchard for several days past. Yesterday, Mr. Reynolds shot one. It was six inches long, spread of wings, twelve inches. The head and hind neck was of a yellowish-red, mottled with black; the other parts nearly white. According to Audubon, its name is the Snow-Bunting. It is sometimes called Hudson's Bay Bunting, white Snow-bird &c. It breeds in the most northerly parts of the continent, and on the islands of the Arctic Ocean. As the polar night approaches, it migrates to the south, always keeping, it is said, within the snow-line.   R.

Mr. Hawley reports fearful encounters with snow-drifts this morning. He again had the luck to eject the three Misses Wightman from his sleigh with considerable emphasis. The bobs became disconnected; the forward one pitching down and the back part of the sleigh being elevated correspondingly, the young women were in a twinkling, tenderly laid in "a soft, a downy bed."

These turnovers are getting to be of common occurrence, we hear of them nearly every day.

"The old White and black Charlie" with those that accompany them to the other place to work, had a great time breaking their way this morning. Upsetting times innumerable, they at length made the perilous journey and reached W. P., only to discover that the race-way was so filled with snow and ice that it would be out of the question to run to-day.

The shop is closed, and the hired hands dismissed, so says Myron who is over here.

Uncle John says jokingly, " G. C. wouldn't have guessed my riddle if he hadn't been plowing with my heifer; it was my custom to take tea, not three times a day, but only twice. However, there are two truths to one lie, and as the Indian remarked, that was pretty well for a poor, old Indian !" " Better, perhaps, than Dixon does," some one else remarked.

Mr. Conant says they had drawn last Saturday night, 160 loads of stone. It will require one day more to complete the work, but it is difficult to tell, from the present appearance of things, when this day's work will be done.

"Spiritual Wives" is listened to with increasing interest. We have passed the "Burnt Districts" and are now enjoying his story of Mr. and Mrs. Cragin.

The floor of the composing-room has been oiled. There was considerable discussion which was best to do, paint or oil it. Some preferred one and some the other, but the stronger current seemed to be in favor of oiling.—The carpenters bid us report, that the new type-stands are finished.

THE O. C. DAILY.

VOL. 5.   FRIDAY, MARCH 6, 1868.   NO. 56.

Last evening Mr. Woolworth re-read the Talk entitled the " Word of God," and then said, " The word of God should sanctify all our efforts and control our lives. It will sanctify our food for one thing and make it digest well. It will sanctify our fellowships to give the word of God free course, and it will sanctify all our contacts with matter and external things. The spirit of God is the great digester. It is the gastric juice of heaven, and we want it in our stomachs and in all our fellowships."

Much appreciation and thankfulness for the Talk was expressed.

W. P., March 3.—Work in the shop commenced this week under the ten-hour system; the hands like this much better, as they get more money. One of them remarked that he liked the eight-hour system but he didn't like the pay.

There is quite a reinforcement from O. C. Milford, Orrin, Charles Van and James Vaill in the inspecting-room, and H. R. Perry packing traps.

Three or four of our men were engaged most of the forenoon in cleaning out the race-way. One of them worked diligently, utterly unconscious of the cold, until his neighbor informed him that his ear was frozen, when he concluded to leave for the house.

G. W. H. left this morning on his usual two weeks trip.

March 4.—Soon after breakfast Mr. Westcott arrives from the Depot with the silk girls. They unload at the shop and just as he drives inside our gate over goes the sleigh fairly on its side. He says this is the third tip-over since starting. Luckily, the girls got out and walked each time. They were not very warmly clad and some of them cried bitterly with the cold. C. A. C. distributed a pan of apples amongst them and they went home again nothing daunted by their previous adventures.

The express man does not appear, but at ten o'clock in comes Sidney and Myron, bringing us the reports and the names of those who are coming from W. C. We read them eagerly. Only a little while and they will all be here.

In the afternoon we have a family game of " froggy" which is highly amusing. Mr. Burt and Mr. Higgins enter into it with a great deal of zest. Mr. H. thinks it is an excellent game to take the starch out of the old folks. Then we try " Old mother Grimes" which proves even funnier than the other.

A splended sun-set; the storm is over; Spring has come; and we expect ere long to hear the birds sing.

Charles Olmstead accosted one of our men in the street yesterday, and inquired if we had received a letter from a Mrs. Williams of Utica lately. He was told that we had not. He then inquired if one of our men had not been to Utica to see Mrs. Williams and Mrs. Butterfield, who are heirs to the Olmstead estate, for the purpose of purchasing their right and title in said estate. He had been told, he said, that one of our men, answering to the description of W. H. W., had been there, and offered them $100 per acre for their interest in the property. Charles was told that there was no truth in it. " Well," he said, " I didn't hardly believe it, but father was induced to believe it, and felt pretty cross about it. He thought the Community might come to him if they wanted to buy the farm."

Moving! In attempting this subject we feel some as the man in Putney did when he lost all of his ashes through the back part of his cart; he was so notorious for his use of profane language, that every one paused to hear what he would say on this occasion: his only remark was, " Gentlemen, I've nothing to say; I can't do justice to the subject." There is a great deal of sweeping, mopping, setting up of bedsteads, moving bureaus, shaking carpets, etc; and under the generalship of Mr. Hatch this seems to go off pleasantly and well. We hear they have been successful in furnishing suitable places for the nineteen that are expected.

It has proved that Uncle Heman was injured more than was at first supposed. His knee-pan was fractured and displaced. He is confined to his bed, only sitting up to have his bed made. Mrs. Kinsley says he seemed some better yesterday, but his leg is sore and painful yet. He told Mr. Abbott if he had got to be confined to his bed long, he should wish he was as poor as the man in Vermont, who, as the story went, carried a string in his pocket with a corn-cob attached to it, which on windy days he threw out as an anchor.

Yesterday was perfect in its loveliness. The sun was warm and bright and it *didn't snow.* To-day however, there is a good " spanking breeze" coming from the south. Those wise in such things say it bodes a thaw.

Prof. Frobisher has sent us two copies of the *Cooper Union Journal* " published by the literary class," and several tickets to " The People's Readings." We shall have no use for the tickets, and can send them to our friends in New-York if they desire to attend the " readings."

The teamsters are drawing coal from Oneida. There has been a car load there for several days, but they could not draw it on account of the drifts.

Mr. John Sears has been putting a line-shaft, which will connect with the one below stairs, through our office into the school-room, where it will drive the printing-press.

THE O. C. DAILY.

VOL. 5.　　SATURDAY, MARCH 7, 1868.　　NO. 57.

W. P., MARCH 5.—At seven o'clock this morning a company of men, numbering twenty-eight, each with shovel or ax in hand started for the race-way. They worked until nearly nine, getting it so well cleared that all but three left. The gate was hoisted, the bell rung to call the silk girls in the neighborhood, and again the busy hum of machinery was heard. Mr. Westcott brought his load of girls from the Depot at half past ten. One man has been employed most of the day in cleaning out loose masses of snow and anchor-ice from the race-way.

Several callers from O. C.: among them Mr. Bradley, who comes to improve the fine day by taking Mrs. Miller to ride, and two little folks, Theodora and Emily Easton, who tell us they have come to stay all night.

Orrin is a member of our family for the present.

Mrs. Aiken received a sincere criticism this evening. The family felt like making a strong push against the spirit of disease which would be glad to force itself in among us. Disease has taken root and strengthened itself in Mrs. Aiken's old life and she was advised to abandon it; not try to save it, but to yield herself entirely to the family. In so doing she will find relief from her present troubles.

Thursday evening Mr. Woolworth said he would say one word about butter, just to let the folks know we hadn't any. Homer said the three families had used of late about 300 lbs. per week, but we now have only 100 lbs. on hand, and the present prospect for getting more is a little dubious. All seemed to think if there was no butter we could easily do without it; and the announcement that we might possibly be obliged to get along with very little for a month or two, was received with cheers. How different this, from the butter discussions of former times.

It is now about two weeks since George E. began to be troubled with a pain in his side. For a week he attended to his business and was about the house, but for a few days past he has kept his bed most of the time. He don't give his malady any name. S. B. C. waits on him.

The thaw, predicted by the weather-prophets, has arrived. It rained quite smartly last evening and considerable during the night. We heard some of the men debating the liabilities of a somewhat serious freshet that seems to be impending. Mr. Hawley says the snow is so soft that it is impossible to do anything with the teams. Frederic says a company started out this morning to shovel the roads, so that a passage can be had between here and Oneida.

The children's play-room has comprised three bedrooms heretofore, but it has been thought best to repartition off one room for the use of Mr. Jones. He has lately roomed in the back part of the tin-shop, and has felt rather lonely; it is not so good for him to be isolated, and he appears much pleased with the idea of his new abode. This will be a better place for him than for others as he will not be disturbed by the noise.

As George E. is just now unfitted for his post, it was thought best to send for Dr. Carpenter to come and see Uncle Heman. Although his knee is not so sore and painful now, yet some fear it may knit together in a way to become stiff. G. R. K. will call on Dr. C. this forenoon.

We have nothing more to report and we take it for granted that our friends had rather have blank paper than a dissertation to fill up.

You can imagine what thrilling incidents might have been recorded had we gone on and filled the space. Each one can fill it out to suit himself.

Traps ordered since last reported, 29½ dozen.

THE O. C. DAILY.

VOL. 5.   MONDAY, MARCH 9, 1868.   NO. 58.

BUSINESS MEETING.

A new water-wheel is needed at the carpenter's shop for doing extra work—sawing slabs, &c. Messrs. D. M. Kelly, A. L. Burt, D. F. Knowles, G. W. Hamilton and J. Burt appointed committee to look after the wants of this department.

Mr. Thacker inquired if the well commenced last season at the B. H. C., should be finished. Objections were made to the water; it is said to be very hard. There is a spring of good water at the foot of Parson's hill that might be conducted thither in pipes, the cost of which has been estimated at from $60 to $100. Referred to the old committee and Mr. Thacker.

John Morris sent a young man here yesterday to demand pay for a sleigh-pole, which he claims was broken by turning out for our loaded teams between here and W. P. It was thought that we were not at all to blame for the accident, as our teamsters gave him fair warning to wait until they had got through the drifts, but he refused, saying he had only an empty sleigh. This is not the first time that Mr. Morris has tried to extort money from the Community. Decided to refuse his claim.

Heman Kinsley sent in a note requesting that railing be put to the steps north of the company dining-room. Homer Barron is to see that it is done. He also suggested that railing to several of the stairways at the Trap-shop might be the means of saving some knee-muscle. Myron and Mr. Burt appointed committee to see that the stairways at the Trap-shop be made safe for our elderly men who work there.

Sidney reported that the roof of the middle house leaks badly. The shingles are so rotten, that in a dry time there is considerable danger of their catching fire. Laid over until Mr. Hamilton comes. Sidney to keep it in mind and bring it before the Board again.

Messrs. Hawley, Conant and Kinsley were appointed committee to see that ice is drawn to supply the place of what has been used this winter.

The pipe conveying steam to the kitchen has failed to perform its function. The cause is supposed to be, water leaking through the outer or cement pipe and causing the steam to condense. Messrs. Abbott, Clark and Sears, were appointed committee to see that tile is laid below the pipe to draw off the water that settles about it.

Dr. Carpenter called Saturday afternoon as was expected, to see Mr. Kinsley. He thought that the patella was fractured, but that all had been done that was necessary; thought he could not have done more had he been called earlier. Said it might trouble him some by being stiff and it might not. The Dr. seemed to think he was doing well and that makes folks who were tempted to think there had not been enough done for him, feel contented.

After dinner yesterday, Mr. Hawley with a small company of armed men started out to stamp a road through to W. P. The drifts have been cut through, but the thaw has made the snow so slumpy that teams could not pass with safety. As the travel to and from Oneida is necessarily by the way of W. P., this work was done preparatory to bringing up our W. C. friends to night.

Yesterday was a beautiful spring-like day, and the sunshine made fearful ravages on the snow-drifts. To see patches of earth again and to walk on planks free from snow and ice, is a matter of no small enjoyment. This new-born warmth of Spring tingling in the veins, makes a merrier sparkle in the eyes, a more rippling music in the laugh, and brighter smiles for all.

George E. says we may report him as better this morning. He now calls his difficulty inflammation of the liver; says folks may call it bilious fever if they want to. S. B. C. says he seems bright and cheerful.

We just called in to inquire after the children. Found them holding their meeting and all present, though one or two are a little disabled yet. Mr. Hatch says they are all better and he considers the worst of it over.

Miss Susan Dunn, who has been suffering from the same thing that has afflicted the children, is reported better this morning.

The W. P. family did not join us yesterday. The roads are so bad between here and there it was thought unsafe to try to bring them over. We missed them and trust next Sunday will prove propitious for their coming.

Mr. Thayer says they start a fire in the new forcing pit to-day for the first time. They will keep it running now right along.

We of the *Daily* can't but feel, putting it mildly, some curiosity to know when we are to be dismissed. Is this our last effort? Who will answer?

THE O. C. DAILY.

VOL. 5.　TUESDAY, MARCH 10, 1868.　NO. 59.

EVENING MEETING.

Mr. Woolworth said he rejoiced in this purification from false literature, as he believed it was the harbinger of a better experience. It was thought there was a close connection between this false literature and false love, and that both produce the same effect. "Narcotic" seems to be the very term to apply to it. People resort to this kind of reading to drown bad feelings, as they would to whiskey or tobacco.

Many confessed their separation from this kind of literature and the effects of it. The general testimony was that the appetite for such reading was dying out, and a purer taste arising. Much thankfulness was expressed for the deliverance from such a feverish, foolish bondage.

Mr. Woolworth inquired if any one could report the general health of the Community and the condition of the disabled ones. All seem to be improving, and the general tone of the family is one of faith, health and courage.

Clark Roberts, of Putney, called and took dinner with us yesterday. He seemed very friendly, and had a free, gossiping talk with Lady Campbell and H. A. Hall about Putney folks and affairs. He called by request of Henry Campbell, son of Dr. John Campbell. Henry is living with Mr. Roberts and was interested to hear how the Campbell friends in the Community were prospering. Henry is without property—the Dr. having willed his property to his wife—and is dissipated, i. e. has his sprees from time to time. Henry had a sweet-heart, a Putney lass, that he had wooed and won and expected to make his bride in due time, but while he was away in the army fighting the battles of his country, his younger brother Hugh became enamored of his affianced bride, and he in turn wooed and won her heart and made her his bride. This unfaithfulness Henry took to heart, and it is more than intimated that he took to his cup as a surcease of sorrow.

Israel Keyes is reported as still a "spared monument."

Durrant Lord is pursuing the downward course of his old vicious habits. The Willard boys own the "Campbell farm," and are represented as thrifty men, carrying on farming in connection with blacksmithing.

Mr. Hatch attends to lighting the entry-ways of the old house, and often allows the children to carry the lanterns to their places because they delight in it so much. Last evening he lit one lantern and placed it on the bureau. While he went into the next room for something, little Ransom marched up to the bureau and placing his head a little on one side he exclaimed,

"Well, Mr. Lantern, I shall ask papa Hatch if I can't take you and carry you and hang you up."

Mr. Worden returned yesterday from an excursion as far west as Syracuse, where he made every reasonable effort to obtain butter. It was so scarce in that direction that he was able to bring home but one jar suitable for our table, for which he paid fifty cts. per. pound. The retail price of butter at Oneida and Syracuse is at present sixty cts. per. pound.

Mr. Worden also called on his sister who is in a very low state of health.

On the upper sitting-room center-table is to be seen a box of silk with a slip of paper near it reading thus: "The O. C. silk Factory's first attempt at colors." There are three colors, red, green and blue. This silk was an object of great admiration last evening eliciting profuse comment on its beauty and the success of the manufacturers.

The carpenters say that the planing-machine is again ready for use. The machinists made new knives for it at a cost of about thirty dollars. Mr. Kelly says this department has all it can attend to, but there is so great a variety in their work it is hardly reportable.

The first delegation from W. O. arrived in the night. They are delighted to get here, and we are more than delighted to see them. They report a pleasant but uneventful journey.

Theodore, George, Mrs. Skinner, Mary, Consuelo and Ida have been out to see the new composing-room. They pronounce it a fine room and appear much pleased with it. Miss Mary appeared especially delighted to find that the type-stands and tables could be arranged in the same way here, that they have been at W. C.

This is a dark rainy morning.—The teamsters are drawing ice from the pond to replace what has been used from the ice-house.—Mr. John Sears is over here again at work on the shafting.—Mrs. Miller spent most of the day with us yesterday and staid here last night. It is just as pleasant to have her visit us as though she lived hundreds of miles from here.

The sick folks are all said to be better this morning. Theodore says he made George laugh quite heartily by telling him about Mr. Leonard.

Yesterday we called at the Office and found Carrie busy making out the tax report, and she, Maria and Annie were rejoicing in the thought that possibly the manufacturer's tax will be removed. Carrie thinks in that case we shall fare nicely as we have no other tax to pay.

THE O. C. DAILY.

VOL. 5. WEDNESDAY, MARCH 11, 1868. NO. 60.

EVENING MEETING.

The comers from Wallingford were welcomed, and expressed themselves as thankful to be here. T. R. N. said, " I want to take hold and start new life."

Mr. Woolworth.—I like that idea, of starting new life. I confess a spirit of receptivity to new life. This Talk just read about "Dissolution and Reorganization" is very interesting to me, and seems to be full of meaning. I feel a response in my heart to that call to begin anew. [Generally approved.] I believe that is a characteristic of the gospel, that these two processes, dissolution and reconstruction, go on together.

Considerable interest was then manifested in the idea of starting a public reading of the New Testament. Several said they had read the Testament this winter with peculiar satisfaction, and hearing of the course of reading they had been having at Wallingford had increased their interest in it. Mr. Woolworth asked if Mrs. Skinner could not give us some more definite account of the readings they have had than we have received. She did so ; and it was finally resolved to start a class for the benefit of all at seven o'clock, to continue till half past seven.

W. P., MARCH 9.—E. F. H. has a decided peachant for skating, but unfortunately has not been able for some time to follow her taste in that direction, as the pond has been covered over with snow. At last the snow has disappeared and early this morning E. accompanied by Victor went to the ice with their skates, looking quite enthusiastic. When they returned they said they had had a fine time and were going again the next morning.

During the forenoon Mr. Thayer came over from O. C. and proposed to go fishing, telling Mr. Ackley that if he would allow him to cut a hole in the ice he would give him half the fish caught. This afternoon he came again and actually cut a hole in the ice and fished for some time. We have not heard that there was any spoil divided.

MARCH 10.—Our skaters found it raining this morning and concluded to postpone their skating until fairer weather.

Mr. Inslee went to Utica to-day to get a circular saw straightened. Edward is at work on the machine for bending trap dogs. Victor says he has been engaged for a day or two in putting the machine shop to rights. So much for the machinists.

We finished this evening our round of criticism. Mrs. Whitfield was the last.—Hearty sympathy was expressed with the Talk " Come to the Light."

We are tempted to express our gratitude for the weather, which is so often the occasion of grumbling.

This winter has been considered a nearly perfect one ; good sleighing and plenty of it, steady cold, with few extreme changes. Our present thaw is a model of quietness and gentleness. We had very little rain in the fall ; in consequence the ground is quite dry and drinks all the water. The heavy accumulation of snow is gradually settling away without one of those fearful floods that cause grown folks anxiety and so delight boys. B.

The committee appointed to act about the steampipe had the ditch opened yesterday and found as was expected that the cement pipe had absorbed water and cracked in several places. To remedy this, it is proposed to cover the pipe on three sides with a close plank box, and lay tile along the planks to draw off the water. This it is hoped will prove an effectual cure.

Mrs. Skinner says whenever she comes here that ditch is open, something always being done to the pipe. Just so surely as it is opened some one will walk into it ; yesterday evening one of the young women had this somewhat unusual experience.

The carpenters were busy yesterday in making another bedroom in the large chamber over the Store. It will be a very pleasant place and Miss Fidelia says it is intended for some of the N. Y. A. men.

To-day Mr. Kelly says they are " fixing up" in the composing-room, putting up a sink, and drop tables on the type-stands for folding papers.

Mr. Newhouse took the one o'clock train yesterday morning for Troy. He goes to see that our No. 3 malleable castings are properly made, and to attend to all those nice details for which our " Canadian Trapper" is so remarkable. There is no such phrase in his vocabulary as " Oh ! that's good enough."

Daniel Abbott says can-making is so monotonous that there positively isn't anything about it to report. Three of them, Daniel, James and one hired man, have made over 13,000 cans. James, a beginner at this business, can now make 350 per day ; the hired man says, old hands consider 300 a good day's work.

The second company from W. C. " came duly to hand" at 12.30 last night. They tell us we are to have another party to night from N. Y. It seems a little odd to see so many faces that have been from home so long, but it's none the less pleasurable. They have warm homes in our hearts and we trust they will feel at home.

Mr. and Mrs. Clark and S. B. C. have gone to Verona. S. B. C. had promised to visit Miss Mary Leete, and she goes to fulfill her engagement.

This party has made one or two previous attempts to go but have been prevented by snow storms.

H. C. N. and A. S. B. will care for George E. in Mrs. Campbell's absence. He is better this morning.

THE O. C. DAILY.

VOL. 6.   FRIDAY, MARCH 13,   1868. NO. 61.

EVENING MEETING.

Mr. Woolworth.—I have been preaching covetousness a little to-day. It seems to me that when rightly directed it is a good thing. Paul somewhere exhorts earnestly to covetousness respecting our best gifts. I believe God wants to make every one of us rich with good gifts and heavenly things. I think it is legitimate to covet the treasures of heaven and the best gifts that God can bestow ; covet them as much as the miser does his gold: not that we should hoard up what we obtain, as the miser does, and appropriate it to ourselves, but that we may distribute, and do good and bless others. I want to be rich, that I may have a great deal to give away, distribute and do good with. I feel covetous for such things. [Indorsed by others.]

Unity was confessed with the new members from W. C. It was thought they brought a good spirit with them. Theodore said their entrance into this family was quite a delicate operation, and all should be wide awake to see that the devil does not take advantage of it. If all are wide awake he is confident good will result from the condensation.

Theodore hoped the paper would be conducted in a way to please his father, and honor the truth. He prayed for wisdom in his connection with it. Others joined him and confessed an interest in the paper.

Our W. C. friends drop in quietly, and while they have been waiting for their "ship to come in" they have made themselves useful in the housework. At noon yesterday we saw M. L. P. washing dishes, and T. C. M. standing in a chair carving an enormous cheese. This morning they are sewing for H. C. N. and S. B. C. Mary Van assisted at washing pitchers and Ida about the knives. Some of them attend bag-bee. Miss Consuelo spent some time yesterday forenoon in making pillow-cases on the sewing-machine, and this morning she has been washing dishes. It is difficult to realize H. M. W. has been away, it seems so natural to see her flitting about the house. Mrs. Skinner takes care of one or two bedrooms. Miss Cornelia and Ella are both doing excellently well in getting acclimated.

Abram says Mr. Kelly gave him a job at the shop, and Charles is waiting for the press to come as he is going to help in setting it up.

W. P., MARCH 12.—C. A. C. ordered a lot of bobbins a while ago from Mr. Williams of Utica. Part of them arrived day before yesterday and were found to be spoiled. So yesterday he went to Utica to see about them, arriving there "just in time" Mr. Williams said, as the rest of them (over a thousand) were turned, ready to go into the tom, where they would have been spoiled like the others. The difficulty was found to be in letting them be in the tom too long.

Myron went to Syracuse to-day. His first item of business was, to order a car load of coal ; next, to see about some iron that was sent us. One hundred pounds were ordered but owing to some mistake in the figures half a ton was sent. Myron said they were willing to take it back. His third object was to hurry on if possible the great bear-trap springs which are being trip-hammered for us. They will be along Monday.

At no time since the Silk business started has there been so many applications for work in that department as now. Women and girls come daily ; four or five came yesterday. The same is true in the Trap-shop.

Last evening we finished "Spiritual Wives," and it was proposed we begin reading the Testament. This was liked by all, and we had the first reading this evening from half past seven until eight.

The Talk "The Death of Unbelief," sent a thrill through us all. Many expressed themselves as having a new appreciation of Mr. Noyes' labors. We can help him by praying that the prison doors may be opened.

Yesterday was a day of changes. Some who had been with the children through the winter, thought best to come away. Mrs. Van, who has assisted in the washing, desired to prepare for the coming fruit campaign. Mrs. Burnham, who as all know has long been a faithful distributer of work, desired a change ; so in consideration of the obvious good reasons the following changes were made. Emma leaves the children's house, and takes Mrs. Van's place in the washing, and Miss Alice Ackley goes to the children's house. Harriet Olds leaves the children's house and takes Mrs. Burnham's place in distributing work, and Mrs. B. goes to the children's house. Minerva goes to the Bag-shop to assist in closing up the business.

It is decided to use the northwest corner room on the first floor of the Tontine for a school-room. It has been used heretofore for storing cans, and Mr. Thacker, Mr. Alfred Barron and others were busy yesterday in removing them to the building in the rear of the Tontine.

Alfred will work with Mr. Thacker for the present.

We heard last evening that the car had come and notwithstanding it thundered and rained considerable during the night, and the roads are pretty wet and muddy some of the way, the men thought best to go with sleds to bring up the things. Accordingly, one drawn by four horses, another by three, and four double teams started in good season this morning for Oneida. Mr. Edwin Nash and E. S. B. have gone to see about unloading the goods and assist in getting them home.

The back parlor was too noisy a place for George E. and he has been moved up stairs into the south room in the vestibule. It is more quiet there and he is doing well. We asked him this morning how he was and he replied with considerable vim in his voice, "Tell them I'm doing gloriously." Mrs. Campbell and others think if he is kept quiet it will be but a short time before he can be about the house.

THE O. C. DAILY.

VOL. 5. SATURDAY, MARCH 14, 1868. NO. 62.

W. P., MARCH 13.—"Come! see the procession!" called some one just about dinner time. We ran to the door and there was a procession sure enough. Six teams well laden with the cargo of our ship from W. C. As they filed slowly up the hill, we watched with anxious eyes the four horse team which led the way. The road was terrible, the load top-heavy and we were saying, "If that team goes through safely, the rest surely will," when over it went and out went the contents into the snow. Some of the men went to the rescue, and very soon the line proceeded on its homeward way. We are glad to learn that nothing was injured and that they all reached home without any more adventures.

Mr. Campbell and Myron were suddenly called to the upper dam this afternoon. The water had risen two feet within an hour; the ice was blocking up and there was a prospect that something was going to happen. They went up there with ropes and pike-poles, and found a great cake of ice three or four feet thick projecting some fifteen feet over the dam. The danger was that if this went off it would raise the bridge. They worked at it breaking it away sufficiently to remove all present danger. To night Myron says every thing is doing well.

George Miller has gone into the inspecting room; he is to reside in our family. We number at present 88.

Mr. Whitney's Arithmetic class closed Wednesday evening. Several expressed themselves as having enjoyed the class and highly appreciating the opportunity they had had to increase their knowledge of this science. A hearty vote of thanks was tendered Mr. W. accompanied with cheers. He has proved a most excellent teacher. At this point butternuts were called for, and

> Soon the hammers began to ring,
> Amid the mirthful prattle ;
> And shells flew thick : on every side
> Sped *kernels*. Was it battle?

After a merry time we went to the reading, feeling it good to cultivate friendship.   A MEMBER.

Theodore, W. H. W., H. C. N. and one or two others put their heads together and plotted not how they might best weed out the onions, but by what means every cabbage at O. C could be up-rooted. After due deliberation they unanimously decided to make a different arrangement of seats in the Hall. They were successful in making an entirely new disposition of tables, benches and chairs, grouping them round the room and leaving an open space near the center.

We think this style is more conducive to the home feeling, and expect we shall all like it when we get a little wonted.

An interesting letter was received a few days since from Mrs. Blood. She is living with and caring for Mr. B.'s step mother. She says she feels it a special providence that she does not have to live with him. The letter is written in a good, courageous spirit; near the close she says, "I cannot say half I would like to, but this much I will say; my faith is strong in Mr. Noyes and the Community. If I had been a disbeliever when I left you, I have seen enough to convert me since I came here."

We heard Theodore asking Tirzah if they were not going to have some "medicated" before long. To the uninitiated this had a sound somewhat mysterious. It was something about which all those coming from W. C. seemed to have the most perfect understanding, and we were not permitted to remain long in ignorance. After meeting they had their "medicated," (known by common minds as sweetened water) and played "froggy" and "old mother Grimes," at the request of some here who had never seen these games. Some were even prevailed upon "to weave" for our amusement.

We very much admire the freedom and simplicity of the Wallingfordians and hope it will be contagious.

Jesse Dillon, of Boynton, Ill., had a small bill of traps of us ; he writes about the cost of getting them and says, "however I gess its as cheep as I could get traps here any way I am very well Pleased with them the little girles had a fine Play with those little traps and got thare fingers Pinched till they holerd good for help."

Mrs. Langstaff and Eliza are busy in unpacking and disposing of the bedding and bureaus that came from W. C. At most any time during the day Eliza may be seen carrying rocking-chairs, stand-spreads, bedquilts, or something wherewith to furnish and make comfortable somebody's bedroom.

Several of the W. C. folks have taken an Oneida cold. Mrs. Skinner, Theodore, Consuelo and Tirzah are afflicted in this way. Mrs. Skinner kept her room yesterday, but we trust she will soon recover.

Two hired men were engaged yesterday in laying the plank and tile about the steam pipe, and this morning they are filling the dirt back into the ditch. May it remain there for at least six weeks to come!

Ransom witnessing the men's operations from the window exclaimed, "That's a dirty job."

Thursday, Homer spent the day roaming about the country in search of butter. His search was not altogether fruitless for he purchased something over 100 lbs., paying forty-five cts. per pound.

The girls at the Office say there has not been such a dearth of business since they have been in the book-keeping as at present. Carrie did not unlock the safe yesterday—not any money paid out, nor any taken in.

Mrs. Jones is here on a visit; she came yesterday and Emma says she expects to leave to-day.

THE O. C. DAILY.

VOL. 5.   MONDAY, MARCH 16,   1868. NO. 63.

The Nation this week has a column and a half of review of "Spiritual Wives." The tone is contemptuous as was expected. It sums up the book as follows :

" A pretty full account, of the pictorial-historical kind, of the Königsberg Ebelians ; a newspaper correspondent's account of Prince's Agapemone ; a rather poor newspaper correspondent's account of certain half-crazed and certain hypocritical persons who figured in one or two old revivals in this country ; some desultory insufficient talk about several other people and several sects who have put in practice the theory of free love ; and some talk about a number of irrelevant matters of various kinds."

The writer is evidently a Boston literary man for he ends with the following squirm :

" Mr. Dixon has already been complained of because, in his chapters on the Agapemone, he has drawn once more into public notice persons connected with families which are, of course, injured by his exposure of the now half-forgotten crimes and follies of some of their members. We complain of him as guilty of another similar breach of good manners in dragging into his very miscellaneous assemblage of imbecile and immoral visionaries the men of Brook Farm. The objects of those men in trying their experiment, their minds and their characters, were so utterly different from the objects and minds and characters of most of the men and women into whose company he, Mr. Dixon, has seen fit to bring them, that to lead or to help his ill-formed readers to class them together is a piece of gross injustice. * * * *

" It is hardly worth while to say much about a book of this kind. On the whole, looked at from whatever point of view, ' Spiritual Wives' will do Mr. Dixon's reputation nothing but harm."

B. H. C., MARCH 15.—While at supper last evening the cry was suddenly heard, ice, ice, ice, and sure enough the whole army of ice with its companies, brigades, regiments, battalions and divisions, was now in motion for a march down the creek. A large body of these icy cohorts had chosen a sort of cove just above the B. H. as a camping ground for the past twelve hours, but now orders had been given from the Commander in Chief, for the entire army to march for the Lake. At first there was a great amount of confusion in getting into line, one squad plunging into another in mobocracy fashion ; but at last the vanguard moved off like racing cavalry which gave room for the rest to follow in due order. The sight for half an hour was very exciting.

This morning the creek is clear of ice, but the dead cakes, like dead soldiers on a sanguinary battle field, line the banks in motley disarray. The ice was very thick but it never did less damage to the banks.   o,

For a week Mr. Thayer has been heating up the new propagating house preparatory to sowing tomato and other garden seeds. This valuable addition to the horticultural department is a low brick-building with its floor somewhat lower than the surrounding ground ; is 60 feet long including the wooden anteroom which covers the main entrance as well as the two furnace doors ; is 12 feet wide, having two tables of earth extending the whole length with a passage way between them. Heat is distributed by means of a 10¼ inch earthern pipe leading along the floor from each furnace to the chimney at the opposite extremity of the house. Cash outlay $150. Labor $150. Total cost $300.   A. B.

Among the changes made this week, Miss Beulah returns from W. P. where she has spent the winter. No one will take her place to remain permanently, but the girls will go in turn, continuing their stay two weeks or thereabouts. M. L. B. and H. V. M. are the first to take their turn. George Miller will take Beulah's place as news reporter from W. P. ; he insists that he has had *greatness thrust upon him*. Permit us to hope he will be able to endure it.

Miss Harriet Allen said to us yesterday, "I hope you will glorify this day in to morrow's *Daily*." Now, nothing would suit us better than to please Miss Allen, but we don't know how exactly. Shall we say the day was intoxicatingly splendid ? or deliriously beautiful ? or, quietly enjoyable ? It was such a day as **prompts young men to lie on the grass in the sunshine,** and young women to stroll in couples on the lawn. Invalids are tempted out to breathe the pure, fresh air, and ailing children are drawn out in their little carriages. Birds sing happily, and—(Miss Allen, won't *you* please to finish this?)

H. W. B. arrived Saturday night as was expected. Last evening the N. Y. A. club kindly sang a few pieces for our entertainment. Those who are considered judges of such things, think these musicians have made great improvement. We were all pleased with their music and thankful for the training they have had.

Mr. Hawley says he should like to have Otis understand that the teamsters here are doing something if the roads are in a terrible state. Saturday they drew from Oneida twelve tons of coal and four tons of steel.

Mr. Kinsley says, " Tell the folks we bought five cows, Saturday."

Yesterday our family numbered fifty more than it did the Sunday before. This addition is most noticable in the dining-room and the Hall. Our house is fuller and the current of life seems stronger.

This morning Milford and Charles Burt are in the old school-room cleaning the press preparatory to setting it up. The girls are in the composing-room distributing what they brought with them of the last paper.

Mr. Newhouse and Mr. Abbott are quite anxious to have it reported that the blue birds have been heard for a number of days ; robins too, were seen as early as Friday of last week.

Mrs. H. C. Noyes says, " We think the ' onions' lately transplanted are growing finely and we like the variety."

THE O. C. DAILY.

VOL. 5.   TUESDAY, MARCH 17,   1868. NO. 64.

BUSINESS MEETING.

The question was raised whether it would not be a good plan to buy a few more cows and make butter for our own use instead of buying it. If we are going to lay out money for one or the other, we should save in the end by buying cows. We want to take that course which will give us the most money next August. A strong committee was chosen to consider this question; Messrs. Woolworth, Thacker, T. R. Noyes, Kinsley, J. H. Barron, Mrs. H. C. Noyes and Mrs. Harriet Kinsley. They will also consider the appointment of some one to Mr. Kellogg's place who wishes to be relieved.

Persons who go abroad to make purchases should hand in a bill promptly at the Office. There are suspicions that outsiders have bought things in our name, which circumstance will be looked into.

G. W. Hamilton reports that he went to Titusville and bought a boiler and engine for the Fruit department, of ten horse power. He expects it will be here this week.

Messrs. G. W. Hamilton, Joel Higgins, Burt, Woolworth, Thacker, Kinsley, Hatch and Theodore, were appointed committee to consider the appropriation of help to the Trap-shop. They will also select some one to work with Mr. Thayer in the Garden. There is no one to take his place, should he be called away, hired men having received the education which should have been given to some of our own folks.

The appointment of Mr. Burnham to the Bag-shop to help close the business was unanimously endorsed.

While at work on the lawn near the north gate Mr. Nash saw two men in the road in front of the large barn apparently engaged in a back-hold wrestle; he soon discovered they were fighting and called to Mr. Woolworth and Alfred Barron who went with him to the scene of action. On inquiring into the affair they found things situated about like this: the immediate attacking party was one Coloway in our employ and the party attacked Byron Olmstead. Mr. Coloway stated that he had been obliged to take his boy out of school because he was so teased and tormented by this young Olmstead; also, Byron had not unfrequently indulged in stoning Mr. Coloway's outbuildings; taking it altogether Coloway had come to a spot where he could endure it no longer and therefore had lain in wait for Byron to pass the barn in returning from school and made a rush at him with a pitchfork.

Mr. Coloway will be discharged at once.

What a gift is presence of mind! Last night as G. R. K. was discharging his load of flour at the south door of the bakery, he stood at the back end of the wagon with a barrel poised, when suddenly the endboard on which his foot rested gave way, and—he found himself on the ground. He knew the barrel would follow and remembered that falling bodies descend at the rate of 16 feet the first second; getting up was not to be thought of—the barrel was already falling—a quick roll to one side—and plump came the 212 lbs. at the safe distance of three inches from his twenty-four ribs, which, had it not been for his rather brief calculation, would in all probability have suffered incalculably.   J.

Mr. Thacker spent most of the day yesterday in locating ditches on the Hitchcock farm. He laid out 147 rods, and two hired men commenced ditching. This work is preparatory to raising sweet corn on that place.—Two hired men are sawing wood by horse power.—S. W. Nash was busy yesterday in strewing ashes on the lawn.—Frederic is making preparation to begin the work of trimming apple trees.

There is a poster at the head of the main entry-way stairs inviting all who can to come and split wood near the building back of the Tontine.

When Mr. Clark left the Foundry there seemed to be no one to take his place; Mr. Kinsley with his other cares took it until some one else could be provided. After consultation Abram has been selected and invited to take this responsibility. This is something new for him, but he takes it willingly and we judge he is glad of the change.

W. P. March 16.—T. R. Noyes is one of the "greasy mechanics." He works in the Factory forenoons inspecting traps.

A lot of 5,000 No. 0 traps are receiving finishing touches.

The W. P. family proper, now numbers thirty-five members.

Miss Portia reports they have had their first school in the new room and are pleased with their accommodations; it is a larger room, is lighter, and has also, in the minds of the children, another superior quality, it is new.

George E. is dressed to-day for the first time; he walked from his bedroom in the vestibule, through the sitting-room into Mrs. Skinner's room in the Tower.

We hear that Mrs. S. K. Dunn has arrived. She spent the night at W. P. and came over this morning.

Traps ordered since last reported 55¼ doz.

THE O. C. DAILY.

VOL. 5. WEDNESDAY, MARCH 18, 1868. NO. 65.

W. P., MARCH 16, EVENING.—G. W. H. having heard Dickens read in Buffalo, gave us some descript- of his appearance—manner, dress &c., and then read some of the selections which he heard. Before doing so he remarked that it would be impossible for him to imitate Dickens, but he would read as well as he could. So we had the Court Scene from Pickwick Papers if not by the great Charles, in the character- istic style of the great George. We question whether Dickens could do Sam Weller much better.

Tommy O'Brien, one of the shop boys, had his thumb "nipped" by the "drop" this afternoon. He was not seriously injured but was wholesomely fright- ened. He was meddling.

MARCH 17.—The proposal to buy a press for W. C. was read at the dinner table to-day all the business men being present. It was responded to by cheers.

Some seven years ago when Cornelia was "baby girl" for S. B. C. she commenced reading the Bible to her. Mrs. Campbell soon went to Newark which in- terrupted them; but on her return they again took it up and read until Mrs. C. went to Wallingford. Not long after this the paper was removed to W. C. and Cornelia went with it; so here again they read to- gether and had reached the forty-second chapter of Jeremiah when S. B. C. was called to return to Oneida. This last has been a somewhat protracted break, but the next day but one after Cornelia's arrival here, they appointed a time and have gone on with their reading, beginning where they left off.

We wonder if they will now remain together a sufficient length of time to complete it.

B. H. C.—The B. H. has been run six months by a Community family. The four members of the family entered upon their new calling with some trepidation as to their ability and fitness to make the experiment a successful one. The boarders too, at the commence- ment, were not, by any means, such as we should have selected for an experimental expedition to the frontier. At first we experienced a little heart-sinking, occasioned by the roughness of our new situation. When under such temptations we remembered him who placed us here as one who had been guilty of no mistakes in his matured plans, so we took in fresh courage to press on and came out of our momentary temptation to run up a signal of distress.

We purposed at the beginning to make a loving, unitary home for ourselves, and if successful, depend on our family contagion for securing a quiet, parental, home-feeling for the comfort of our boarders. We purposed also, to treat all with due respect and show partiality to none. How well we have succeeded in the execution of our purposes and aspirations, it does not belong to us to say.   c.

Some days since Mr. Newhouse had some conversa- tion with Henry Wilson about the railroad business. Mr. Wilson said he thought our folks too unselfish; we stood and looked on and let Vernon get a depot when we needed one more than they did; wanted to know why we didn't put in our claim for a depot.

Mr. Newhouse told him, with a very grave face that we believed Providence was overseeing this railroad building and that we should be cared for. Told him if we *ought* to have a depot, and there was not much doubt about it in his mind, we certainly *should;* all we needed to do was to wait on God about it.

Mr. Wilson assented to this, said he supposed that was the best way, but looked a little puzzled at having it laid before him in this light by our "Canadian Trapper."

Yesterday, Mr. Daniel Nash exchanged his crutch for a cane, and last night commenced going without a watchman. He expressed himself this morning as having got along just as well as though some one had slept in the room with him.

He is frequently seen through the day walking about the grounds with no accompaniment but his staff.

These fine spring-like days have tempted folks out after greens. Three or four different parties were to be seen coming in yesterday abundantly laden with their verdant burdens. We noticed six baskets well filled with "scurvy grass" standing in the arched-way, and thought of Helen Hutchins.

"Mr. Conant, what have you been doing that is reportable?"

"Not much, some of us have been looking about the farm to see what needs to be done in the way of fences and one thing and another, that's pretty much all."

"Is there anything to report from you Mr. Hawley?"

"No, nothing. It's too muddy now for news."

We are a little mortified to be obliged to correct a mistake made yesterday, but none the less delighted to state that our folks do not saw wood by horse power but by steam. That seems more merciful, doesn't it? They are busy about it again to-day.

Mr. Edwin Nash says the press is up; there is con- siderable work in details yet but the main part of the job is satisfactorily accomplished.

We were favored last evening with one of Oneida's richest sunsets; a most gorgeous panorama spread for all beholders without any miserable twenty-five cent admission fee. One young lady lately from the foot of Mount Tom was heard to say, "Oh! isn't that glorious? I haven't seen the sun set before for years."

THE O. C. DAILY.

VOL. 5. THURSDAY, MARCH 19, 1868. NO. 66.

EVENING MEETING.

The Talks from Wallingford were listened to with great interest. The ideas respecting prayer came to the hearts of all as just what they were in need of at the present time. Mr. Woolworth said he was satisfied that Mr. Noyes had brought out the true law in regard to prayer and going to God. He was conscious this law had been working in his experience and in that of the whole Community. Prayer is becoming more vital and necessary to us. At the same time it is divorced from all sense of duty-doing, and instead of being irksome becomes very attractive.

The question of the breakfast hour was re-considered. Mr. Conant was much pleased with the arrangement to have it at six but could get along if it was delayed till the old hour—half-past six. It has a good effect on the hired men to hear the bell rung early. They inquired the reason of the change, and Mr. Conant told them that the snow had gone and spring was coming with its new life and energy, and consequently we were live men now, and he hoped they would be also. The business men would be satisfied if the bell could be rung at a quarter to six, though for his part, Mr. Conant said, he *did* like to have his breakfast in the *morning*. Decided to continue to have breakfast at six.

Mr. Woolworth wished milk might be placed on the side table where those who preferred it to hot drinks could help themselves. Mr. Olds said one table would be set without cups and saucers and supplied with milk and water. Those who prefer can sit at that table, and if they require another table for their accommodation it will be furnished in like manner.

Theodore made a request that the exchanges in the printing-office should not be taken away at present till they can learn how many come to us. Also he would invite contributors to the CIRCULAR to write only on one side of their paper, as it is inconvenient for the compositors to have copy written on both sides.

As it has been decided to put up a few pease the coming season, one of our men went out yesterday to see about getting them raised for us. Last summer we paid one dollar per bushel. This year we think they can be raised for less.

Mr. Rawson says if others can raise them for seven shillings, he can. "For" says he "the Indians live just up on the back road. I am close by, you know, and can r-r-raise them as cheap as anybody."

J. Rivenburgh thinks he can raise them for seven shillings, for, "we want you to make a good thing of it—want to encourage you in your business."

Thomas Cornelius says of the seven-shilling clause, "I gues-s is fair."

The pease are to be paid for the first of November next, when we get returns from our fruit. B.

W. P., MARCH 17. EVENING.—The talk about Amusements drew out expressions of sympathy from old and young. S. Newhouse falls in heartily with the views about sporting. He says that a flock of ducks settled down on the creek yesterday, a thing which has not happened before in three years. The ducks were not molested.

MARCH 18. The forgers are rolling bear-trap springs. They expect to make forty of the great Bear-Tamers.

Our garden is being plowed and Mr. Higgins is sewing pease.

The following communication from the family at W. P. was read in our meeting last evening:

BROTHER THACKER:—We the undersigned wishing to *save* all we can, as well as *make*, offer to raise six, eight, or ten, acres of sweet corn for the preserving department.

We will take this for our gunning, fishing, and sports in general, taking care of it at a time out of regular work hours.

[This is signed by most of the men living at W. P.]

We are encouraged in regard to closing up the Bag business. Yesterday, G. W. Hamilton took a memorandum of a lot of unfashionable, steel-mounted satchels—about forty-five in all—and to-day he sold them. True they were sold at a discount, probably some below cost, but we are satisfied with the sale. They were sold to a firm in Utica for $150, on thirty days. We trust this is but a prelude of our future luck in this line of things. G. W. H. expects to take the train for Syracuse and Rochester to-night where he will try his hand at a large lot of gilt-mounted satchels. H. W. B.

Yesterday, Fidelia went into the children's house to get Temple as she wished to have him try on his summer clothes. Anna Bolles seeing him going with his mother cried out, "My sakes! I wish my mother would come and get me to go and try on *my* summer clothes."

We have been trying to get some one to say a neat and appropriate thing about this most splendid of mornings. Theodore says it is "crystalline." Mary says "heavenly" is the right word to express it, but Harriet thinks it is quite inexpressible.

Mr. Kellogg reports that a full-blood Ayrshire heifer has recently been added to this superior family.

THE O. C. DAILY.

VOL. 5   FRIDAY, MARCH 20, 1868.   NO. 67.

W. P., March 18, Evening.—Messrs. Burt and Campbell went to Vernon this afternoon to see the Cases who are so active about straightening the New York Central. The business of Messrs. B. and C. was to tell the Cases that we did not wish to take part in the project they have for buying the right of way for the R. R. Mr. Hamilton's letter giving our reasons for wishing to be inconspicuous in the matter was read to them. The Cases acknowledged the wisdom of our policy, and seemed to have great confidence in Mr. Hamilton's management.

J. Farwell, Jr., & Co., of Boston, who ordered Silk machinery of us last year have ordered another spinner and cleaner. These machines are nearly completed and will net us $700.00. This sum will nearly pay for the new presses for W. C.

Messrs. Kinsley, Clark, and Hawley went before the Board of Town Auditors at Vernon, yesterday, for the purpose of having it decided how much was coming from the town to Charles Primo, as amendment for his tumble through the bridge several months since. The claims as laid before the town meeting were, from us, for damage done to wagon, horses and harness, $150 ; from Mr. Primo, for injury received by the fall, something over $200.

The meeting was informed at this time that it was our intention to give Mr. Primo whatever we should receive, hoping our example would induce them to do the liberal thing by him. They are not Community men however, and this information had exactly the opposite effect. They concluded if we were going to give him what we realized from our claim that would be about the fair thing, and by dint of getting a lawyer on to the ground, who did a good deal of skillful wriggling, they made out the papers entering the two claims as one, and unanimously decided that one hundred dollars would be a just equivalent for all damages received by the claimants.

Our men told them we should prefer to have the papers made out separately. They had purposely made them together, knowing if they did not it would leave Mr. Primo free to sue for the balance of his claim. At this point the lawyer went to work and caused it to appear that they were not legally bound to do any thing about it, but they wished to do a generous act and would therefore *donate* $100. Our folks felt they did not care for a donation and declined to sign the papers. Charles signed the papers, accepting the proposed sum as full remuneration of his claim. He will not receive the money till the first of next January as the Board has no money placed at its disposal but must wait for the returns of the town-tax.

We have lately invested ten dollars in a farm right

to make and use "Todd's improved, patent fence."

The fence is made by stretching four wires horizontally from post to post, two at the top and two at the bottom, and then weaving in slats or pickets by alternate crossings of the wires. It is claimed that this fence has advantages over most other kinds in cheapness and rapidity of construction, durability, and ease with which it may be removed and re-constructed when it may be desirable on road-sides, to prevent the drifting of snow.

It may be made ornamental and used for door-yard fencing.

The question is often asked, " When do you expect to finish the bag business?" We cannot give a definite answer to this inquiry, but will endeavor to report progress occasionally. We have made, during the past year, 157 different kinds and sizes of bags. Fifty-two of these we have now discontinued making, forty-one of the different varieties being entirely sold out.

Our women, numbering five, now occupy the northwest room, formerly appropriated to their use. We find ourselves much more pleasantly situated for the change.   N.

The creek had so worn away the earth foundation to the north abutment of the Hamilton bridge, that yesterday afternoon a considerable portion of it crumbled into the water. The Commissioner of Highways was soon informed of the state of the bridge. It is to be hoped the repairing will be attended to with equal promptness, it renders the bridge impassable for teams. It is however, safe for foot passengers as yet, and we hope it will not obstruct the communication between here and W. P.

Yesterday afternoon, while busily engaged in the can-shop, James Hatch saw a young deer near the window. He went out and without difficulty captured it and took it in. It was very tame and seemingly enjoyed being fondled and caressed. All conjectured it must be some pet that had strayed from home. After supper as James was bringing his prize to the house for people to see it, one of the Olmstead boys met him and wanted to know if " that wasn't Mr. Parsons' deer." James told him he did not know. In the evening James called on Mr. Parsons and found the fawn belonged to him. It was kept in the barn over night and will be returned this morning.

Last evening as Mrs. Burnham finished undressing Maud she took her up and said, " This is my baby. I'll put my baby to bed." Maud made answer quickly, " Pa Hatch say mus'n't play baby." Then fearing she had not made it sufficiently impressive, " Pa Hatch spoke me *mus'n't play baby.*"

Mr. Worden says of the weather: " Quite a contrast between the weather of to-day and that of last Sunday, when two young men were tempted by the summer-like sunshine to take a swim in Oneida Creek." It has been dark and cloudy all the morning, and is now snowing quite rapidly.

THE O. C. DAILY.

VOL. 5. SATURDAY, MARCH 21, 1868. NO. 68.

EVENING MEETING.

Mr. Woolworth remarked that they had a pleasant time burying Florilla this morning. Every one appeared cheerful and light-hearted; and the whole thing seemed to him more like a picnic than a burial. He believed it was more pleasing to God than long, doleful faces, and the shedding of a good many tears; and also more in keeping with real faith and the spirit of the resurrection.

F. A. Marks invited criticism. He was believed to be improving. Mr. Thacker thought he lacked in attention to details, and was rather deficient in mechanical skill. It was hoped he would not seek to do too much work with his own hands, but rather devote himself to planning and directing. Some thought his men lost time last summer in hunting for him. A more perfect organization of business would avoid this evil.

George E.—I have had considerable experience for the last two or three weeks that has been very interesting to me, and rather new. I was never sick before; that is, I was never really prostrated. I found the great lesson I was learning was to be thankful for suffering. When I was reduced clear down to the lowest, it seemed to me I got nearer to God than ever before; and I could say from the bottom of my heart that I thanked God for suffering, or anything that produced faith and turned my heart in that direction. This experience has made me feel very much in earnest to know God for myself and seek him every day. Until my late experience I never realized the meaning of Paul's saying: "When I am weak then am I strong." I realized what it was to be strong in the spirit when the flesh was weak. I hope I shall have any kind of experience that is necessary to keep me humble and soft.

Yesterday, Mr. Thacker, Abram and others laid out the ground and set the stakes for the new preserving-house that is to be. The following item about it was handed to us:

If you would like to know where to think of the preserving business this year, you may conceive of it as in a building 30 feet wide, 84 feet in length, 1½ stories high, standing near, and parallel to, the old corn-house hill, where we as children were wont to slide on hand-sleds. The east half will rest on a wall enclosing a cellar, and the west half will be open as a place to husk corn, &c. The east half of the first floor is to be used for preparing fruit; the west half for storage of fruit and a packing-room. The chamber will be occupied for a can-shop and store-room for cans. The engine-room will be on the south side even with the east end. The bath-room immediately west of it. B.

The water wheel at the saw-mill has for some months needed repairing. Some of the buckets were broken which caused a great waste of water. Yesterday, Mr. Kinsley and Daniel Knowles made a successful attack on this job. They removed all the old buckets replacing them by new ones. Mr. Kinsley says it was a pretty cold operation as most of the work had to be done standing in the water, but they have the pleasure of knowing that they are now utilizing all the power.

George E. has quite recovered. He dismissed Mrs. Hatch (who has lately waited on him) last evening, and begins this morning to go to the dining-room with the rest of us. Little Cosette who has been quite sick is looking bright and smart again. Mrs. Lynde, Mr. Perkins and several others who have been numbered on the sick list, are improving. Most of the folks that have been afflicted with colds are getting over them, and the prevailing tone is one of health.

The carpenters have commenced work on the dry-room that is to be over the engine-room, and made on an improved plan. Yesterday, they tore down the bedroom and moved the great water-tank into the south-east corner of the room. Mr. Kelly says they expect to go right along with it now, and finish it as soon as they can. Will put up the partition to-day.

A little more moving yesterday! George E. goes from the vestibule into the second left-hand room in the lower sitting-room. Mrs. Easton and Annie Kelly who have roomed there heretofore, go into the east chamber of the middle house, in the place of Miss Frank Hillerman and Mary Whatley. Miss Frank has gone in the reception-room at the old house and Mary will move into what was once called the "snuggery." Mr. Bristol and John Conant moved from the Tontine to the south garret of the old house.

Mr. Ira Kirkland, road commissioner, came with his men yesterday and worked at repairing the bridge. Mr. Worden thinks they were quite expeditious and will in all probability complete the work to-day.

It is snowing again this morning, and the children seem to be enjoying it highly. We saw ten of them harnessed up and drawing one sled.

Mr. Thayer has finished seed-sowing in the forcing-house.

THE O. C. DAILY.

VOL. 5.   MONDAY, MARCH 23, 1868.   NO. 69.

EVENING MEETING.

After the Talks from Wallingford had been read, Mr. Woolworth said he hoped we should fulfill Mr. Noyes's expectations, and learn to be watchful, sober and chaste in the use of our tongues. He thought the Community still suffered more or less from the gossiping spirit. Barrenness is the state of reaction from gossip. When people come to meeting with nothing edifying to say it is probable they have squandered their best thoughts in idle talk.

The testimony in favor of watchfulness, sobriety and prayer, was general and hearty. Many expressed a desire to learn to speak to edification, and to refrain from idle conversation.

Mr. Nash's treatment was mentioned by Mr. Kelly, and the mind of the Community asked respecting it. All were much pleased with Mr. Kelly's treatment, and were glad to see Mr. Nash taking so much exercise. It was thought Mr. Nash's case a good one for showing that faith could cure even chronic diseases and bodily lesions. Mr. Nash walked to the bridge and to the barn to-day. All who spoke thought his improvement in the last three or four weeks very rapid and encouraging.

Mr. Cragin and Theodore expressed themselves as much interested in the financial question.

Mr. Woolworth remarked that they had fixed on the first of May as the time for closing the bag-business. If it can be finished before, it will be. This announcement was received with applause.

BUSINESS MEETING.

A building is wanted near the Trap-shop for storing such machinery as is lying about the shop unused. It was thought the old paint-shop would be a good building for this purpose. M. H. Kinsley, John Sears, Mr. Campbell, D. M. Kelly, A. Kinsley and G. W. Hamilton were appointed to see that a place is provided.

Messrs. J. Burt, Joel Higgins, G. E. Cragin, H. W. Burnham and A. Kinsley were appointed as a standing committee to look after and dispose of all dead property. Mr. Burnham requested that this committee assist him in disposing of the bag property.

An inmate of No. 10, who has been known to make profuse protestations against seeing her name in the DAILY, hands us the following item:

Still another change! Mrs. Maria Kinsley has moved into the room previously occupied by Mr. Cragin—the first room after entering the hall of the mansion house—and Mr. Cragin has taken possession of Mrs. Kinsley's former domicile, No. 17, lower sitting-room.

The occupants of the lower sitting-room are now comprised of an equal number of Southern Vermonters, Northern Vermonters and New-Yorkers—four of each—two men and two women of each. Besides these we have one native of Connecticut and one of O. C. A good combination, one person remarked.

We expect good results from such a mingling of different temperaments and experiences.

What makes it all the more interesting is, that the present arrangement is purely providential!

Mr. Thacker left this morning for Springfield, where he goes to see about engaging the corks we shall need the coming season. We had considerable difficulty with the corks last year, and our not being able to find exactly what we wanted was the occasion of more or less "blown" fruit. After we had purchased a supply for the season in New-York, an agent for a manufacturing establishment in Springfield called and offered us corks ten per cent cheaper than we had been getting them, and would make them any size we liked. It is to this house Mr. Thacker has gone. He said he expected to see both W. C. and N. Y. A. before reaching home.

This morning some of the men undertook to move the old ash-house, that has stood near the soap-house, across the swale, because where it stood it would be in the way of the proposed preserving-house. They hitched two span of horses to the building and drew it down the hill to the bridge. As they attempted to cross it one span of horses shied round suddenly, which had the effect to land old "Major" on his back in the ditch, and he pulled the horse he was harnessed with in after him. By cutting the harness some, the upper horse was released and drawn back on to the bridge. Major was not so easily gotten out, he lay there on his back perfectly helpless, and it was only by the combined strength of the other horses that he was placed on his feet again. Mr. Conant says "The horse wasn't injured, only got his back wet a little, that's all."

Mr. Edwin Nash says he got along with the printing yesterday quite as well as he expected to. He thinks the press worked very well after they once got it fairly adjusted and in running order. The printing was finished about 10½ o'clock P. M.

The office corps are engaged this morning in folding and mailing the papers.

Yesterday was a bright, sunny day, but it was rather cold and windy. This morning it is warmer, the wind does not blow much, and to sit in the lemon-tinted sunshine is a delight.

THE O. C. DAILY.

VOL. 5.   TUESDAY, MARCH 24, 1868.   NO. 70.

EVENING MEETING.

The Talk entitled "The Grace of God" was read and heartily endorsed.

Mr. Woolworth:—Mr. Noyes is constantly taking advanced positions. He takes ground in this Talk that I think we need to possess; and I believe God is calling us to it.

Theodore:—I am much interested in the parable of the sower. I think it would be well for us to study that passage. We are daily receiving the seed of the word of God, and if we are not making pretty rapid improvement it is because some of those conditions which kill the seed still exist. In thinking of the various causes it appeared to me that the temptation here at Oneida is to let the cares of the world hinder the work of the word of God in our hearts. I suppose all these amusements might be included in the cares of this world, or anything that we allow to turn us away from God and occupy our minds.

Mr. Woolworth:—I thought our desires might be compared to many open mouths, all the time seeking some kind of aliment; something to gratify and fill them, or make them happy. Mr. Noyes says he has a thousand desires. This demand creates a supply of some kind. The world, the flesh and the devil are all the time catering for our desires, and seeking to give them some kind of gratification. God is also busy. He has set his table, and now says "Ask and you shall receive." "Blessed are they that hunger and thirst after righteousness, for they shall be filled." He offers something that is enduring and eternal. I pray that our desires may turn to God and seek his table and his grace, and be filled.

W. P., March 23.—The following notice was posted in the silk-factory last Saturday afternoon:

"The Depot team will stop running for one week as the cleaning is up with the winding, and there is a large amount of cleaned silk on hand.

The team will start again on Monday morning, March 30.   O. C. SILK DEPARTMENT."

In consequence of this the silk folks are employing sixteen hands less than usual this week. The girls temporarily dismissed, are very glad of a vacation.

Two Photographers from Oneida were here this forenoon taking pictures of our hop stoves. The pictures are to be engraved for a poster which the Foundry folks are getting up.

The paint-shop that is to be converted into a store-house for machinery has been used heretofore for storing lumber. Yesterday, the teamsters were busy in drawing this lumber from that building, which is near the Foundry, and placing it in the old hen-barn. They did not get all of it drawn and will continue the work to-day.

Charles Burt and Erastus are at work in the dry-room.—Frederic, Sidney, and Alfred Barron, are trimming apple trees in the Weed orchard.—Abram and Theodore are putting up the window curtains in the composing-room.—The hum of the washing-machines can be heard, and that tells what is being done in the basement.—House cleaning is receiving a due proportion of attention.—Since the press has been set up in the next room, the only power we have to run the press on which we print the *Daily* is that generated from the oxydation of buckwheat pancakes.—It is a fine, sunny morning and the snow is nearly gone.

Last evening we were favored with an extract from Pickwick "in the characteristic style of the great George," as our W. P. correspondent hath it. The family appeared entertained.

Little Horace Perry has had quite a hard cough and Miss Chloe thought thoroughwort might do him good, so steeped up some and gave him. He bravely attempted to drink it but soon looked up at her and said, "Don't, To'e." Miss Chloe says she has not given him any since.

Traps ordered during the week,   30 doz.

THE O. C. DAILY.

VOL. 5. WEDNESDAY, MARCH 25, 1868. NO. 71.

EVENING MEETING.

Mr. Underwood re-read the Talk in which Theodore was spoken of as one qualified to take the lead in finances and develop a true policy for the Community. The nomination was received with expressions of satisfaction. It was thought Theodore was well qualified to fill such an office.

Theodore was appointed chairman of the committee for the disposal of dead property; and this committee was authorized to dispose of any property that it may be thought expedient to part with. This committee may also elect more members if those now serving think it desirable.

By request of Mr. Woolworth Theodore unfolded some of the workings of his mind on the financial question. So far as he has matured any plan, it is to look the books over and learn how the different businesses "have run" for the past four or five years; see how much capital each has required, and put the whole thing in black and white. As it is now, nobody can tell the exact amount of capital invested in the trap-works during the busiest season. The same is true of the other businesses. We should know just what each business requires. Then the central management could say to each department of industry, "Here, you can have the use of so much capital this year and make what use of it you think expedient." This arrangement would save the accumulation of dead property; educate the foreman of departments in wise financiering; and save overgrown plans in one department that would swallow the capital of the whole Community. Such is a brief sketch of a few of Theodore's ideas.

Last evening's mail brought a telegram from Mr. Noyes saying some one would be at Oneida on the 11-30 train. G. R. K. and Theodore went down to meet either Mr. J. H. or G. W. Noyes; which one it would be no one was entirely certain. It proved to be Father Noyes and be assured we are very thankful to see him. We have had a fast of over eight months. We were especially thankful to hear him say, "It seems good to get back here." He has been out to the office and thinks it very fine—if anything better than the one at W. C.

The following letter just received:

Dangstein, Petersfield, Monday, March 9.

Lady Dorothy Nevill has received the box from the Community, and although two bottles were broken, she is much satisfied with the contents. The fruits and jellies were quite excellent, but English palates did not approve of the Indian corn. If the O. C. would be obliging enough to send Lady Dorothy any more fruits and jellies she would be most grateful to them. She does not want any traps, pease, green corn, or Lunch-bag; but merely, fruits, jellies, and tomatoes. She would much like if the Community would put in a box of silk as they did last time. She still continues to be much pleased with the CIRCULAR. Lady Dorothy will pay immediately through Messrs. Trubner.

Do our people realize what an enormous affair our washing is? We now have five hired girls, two of our women and one man as a regular force in this department. Besides these there is an extra man and woman for washing days and two men to hang out clothes. This last week they had 5,054 pieces to wash and iron.

To BEULAH.—A BIRTH-DAY NOTE.

No more a prattling child you play,
And quickly change from smiles to tears:
The June of life succeeds the May,
As swiftly roll the freighted years.

Full many an idle fancy gleams
Before the plastic mind is wrought;
But soon dissolve the girlish dreams,
As wakes the woman's nobler thought.

Yes, twenty-one fleet years have sped,
Since dimly dawned your natal morn,
Strewing their roses on your head,
Perchance with here and there a thorn.

And must it fade, this fresh bright youth,
And pure ingenuousness depart?
Oh! no: believe me—'tis the truth—
Perennial youth may fill the heart,

When waywardness of human pride
To lowly Christian faith give place.
Then follow those who best may guide,
Not seek alone to win the race.

But humbly keep the narrow way,
Nor heed the tempest, nor the night;
For even now has dawned the day:
The land of *Beulah* lies in sight.

The selfless aim for others' good
To life a sweeter charm will lend,
And glorious years of maidenhood,
Replete with beauty, never end.

O. C., *Feb.* 18, 1868.

Mr. Conant says part of his men were engaged yesterday in drawing manure on to that part of the Hitchcock farm that is to be a raspberry field. Mr. C. also made a beginning on the cellar of the new preserving house.

Mr. Hawley was engaged yesterday with a four horse team drawing freight from Oneida. This freight was in part, steel and iron for the trap-shop, and the remainder, tin for the can makers.

THE O. C. DAILY.

VOL. 5. THURSDAY, MARCH 26, 1868. NO. 72.

The Talks brought by Mr. Noyes and those that came in the mail yesterday, were the occasion of a seven o'clock gathering to hear them read. These Talks are food for our souls and we desire to drink in their spirit and not "live by bread alone."

After the reading Mr. Noyes very interestingly explained to us the discovery recently made by Joseph. The business men were highly interested in it and all wondered that so simple and yet so useful a method had not been discovered earlier. Mr. Noyes said he did not believe we should make much money by it if we obtained a patent. It would be his way to have Joseph go on and get up his rule—perfect his discovery—and then make a present of it to the public through the paper. The proposal was received with cheers.

This explanation engaged our attention until 8-20, when Mr. Woolworth said there would be an intermission of ten minutes. At the expiration of this time we again assembled for meeting. After the reading of news and the journals from W. C. and N. Y. A., Mr. Burnham gave a sketch of a providential occurrence on the cars when Mr. Noyes was coming here whereby he was thrown in contact with a young Catholic priest and preached the Second Coming to him. Mr. Noyes gave some particulars of his conversation with this young man. It was very entertaining and a report will be sent.

The meeting lasted until half past nine, and then the W. P. family, who will come to our meetings while J. H. N. is here, started for home.

So passed our evening.

A party of Midland surveyors were at work yesterday afternoon on the hill-side east of Mr. Olmstead's. It seems that Johnson's sand hill is impracticable for railroad purposes, in their view, and that they will have to pass around it, and across our land, by the old red school-house to the bank of the creek. From there they have driven their stakes on a line crossing the dam and Mr. Olmstead's door-yard, to the elevation on the opposite side, and so on south. They are not now making the final survey; but are trying to find the best route, and expect to be able in a day or two, to report results to the Board of Directors in waiting at Oneida. So some of our folks say who went over to see them.   U.

W. P., March 25.—One of the Foremen of the Trap-shop whose name is not Hawley, or Higgins, or Hamilton, being down cellar the other day thought he would take a cookie from a well known basket which sat on one of the shelves. Now it so happened that certain rats had been holding a carnival in the basket and the kitchen folks had placed therein one of Newhouse's infallible traps. The result may be imagined. The fingers of the unlucky foreman striking the trap it closed on them as remorselessly as it would have on any other depredator. The kitchen folks were as much pleased as if they had caught a rat.

Miss Beulah says she was instructed to bring us the following:

Mr. De Latre was seen at work yesterday cleaning up the lawn in front of the Old House. This is the first attack on the rubbish that has accumulated during the winter. It is hoped that he or some one else will carry on the war in other quarters. The horticulturists think they might do something to improve the surroundings of the Tontine. Winter shut us up, and dirt accumulated. Now that spring has come to let us out again, would it not be well for every one to enlarge his borders and set his yard in order? Let us have a lively campaign against *all sorts of dirt and debt*.

The dentist's office has been undergoing an operation which has very materially improved its appearance. The ceiling has been whitewashed and the walls brushed over with a pink tinted solution of lime and glue. Now what could be more enchanting than to go into an office where everything is of a roseate hue, recline in the easiest of velvet-cushioned arm-chairs, and, *have a tooth pulled*.

The children's house folks furnished us the items found below:

Father Hatch has been telling the children the story of Christ's birth and childhood. This morning in their meeting he questioned them about it to see how much they remembered and understood. Asking them what the wicked king did when he could not find Christ, Willie answered very promptly, "I know! he killed all the little *babies* that were six years old."

Cosette walked up to Rose and Marion and said, "Say! *I* can sing better than Miss Alice Ackley."

In Beulah's birth-day note printed yesterday, we were unfortunate enough to have two mistakes. In the fifth verse, second line, read *gives* for give. The first word of the last verse should be *there*, not the.

While the journals from the other Communes tell of storms and snow, we are having days of wondrous beauty. This is the fifth day of unclouded glory.

THE O. C. DAILY.

VOL. 5.   FRIDAY, MARCH 28, 1868.   NO. 73.

EVENING MEETING.

After Mr. Noyes's late Talk, "The Happier Way," had been read Mr. Woolworth remarked : "I believe this is sound doctrine, and practical too. The spirit of God that has planted this Community leads right to that, if rightly carried out. I am sure of this from my own experience. It will lead every one of us toward that platform, and to Paul, if we are faithful to it. There should be no distraction in serving the Lord. I believe it is true that our happiness lies right here, in serving God with a single-eyed spirit, without distraction. This is not a mere matter of duty : our happiness and highest pleasure and satisfaction consist in it. I confess my union with Mr. Noyes on this platform of freedom from all distraction.

"I thought the Talk read last evening contained some very valuable advice and important suggestions; particularly about quitting, altogether, this talk concerning schemes and projects that we have not any capital to spend upon. I believe we have wasted, or squandered a good deal of time and life in talking over these impracticable projects. I think we ought to quit it. I believe it is true, as Mr. Noyes says, that it is the habit of the spendthrift. We shall not get rich till we get out of all these habits."

Mr. Woolworth's remarks were generally endorsed, and nearly all expressed a desire to serve the Lord without distraction—serve him with a pure heart.

W. P., March 26.—A few evenings ago the family discussed the expediency of buying some hens. The most serious objection to keeping them, was thought by one of the machinists to be that they would disturb the slumbers of the family and awaken persons at unseasonable hours by *crowing*. Another member thought that an economical way to keep hens, would be to keep them one night, and have them served up on the table next day. All objections were however overruled and to-day Myron bought twenty-six hens.

J. H. N. walked through the Trap and Silk shops this afternoon.

There was a ladies' meeting at 3 P. M. yesterday, held in the upper sitting-room. The object of the meeting was to discuss the subject of economy in clothing, time, and labor. All feel ambitious to co-operate with the men in getting rid of such hired help as we can, and feel good heart and courage to do the house cleaning, washing, and fruit-preserving, ourselves. With a resurrection spirit we can do double the work and feel it less. We desire a godly ambition for making money. It was thought to have a good effect—a wholesome restraint—for folks to keep an account of their expenses. Several have done so this year and said they had found it good for them.

After the meeting was closed, a large bundle of clothes that had been outgrown by the older children were distributed to the mothers for the smaller ones.

DEAR DAILY.—The appeal made through your sheet yesterday ... subject of *rubbish*, reminds me to say ... could help us wonderfully if our friends would only take a *negative* attitude in the matter, and avoid *scattering* the rubbish. You have no idea what a help it would be.

I have an amendment to offer to that appeal of yesterday. I should deprecate any *extension* of borders, until folks can take care of what they already have.

                                        LAWN.

Mr. Bradley has had an evening Arithmetic class this winter with a few of the men boarding at the B. H. C. He says they have been very enthusiastic and eager to learn. A few days since he closed the class. As a token of their appreciation of his kindness to them they presented him with a paper sack containing thirty oranges and twenty-four lemons.

Another splendid morning and the children are reveling in the sunshine. Mr. Hatch says they are all well now, every one. After they are dressed in the morning, they are not unfrequently permitted to make a circuit round the brick house. This they enjoy immensely, and it gives them blooming cheeks and sparkling eyes, and a better relish for their breakfast.

Thank God for so many good and happy children.

Mr. Conant says the spring work is getting along nicely. He has daily applications for work from men and boys. Some of them are so earnest in their entreaties for work that it is difficult to turn them away. He thinks we ought to have the job of hiring men to build a railroad. We should not have to advertise.

Mr. Nash continues to make progress. Yesterday he went to the wood-shed and split wood for some length of time. Of course he could wield the ax with only one hand, but he succeeded in demolishing quite a log.

We have just heard that Mr. Noyes intends to leave for W. C. to-night, taking Mrs. Skinner with him. We are thankful to have had them with us even for so short a time.

Yesterday, Mr. Noyes and Theodore were looking over the ground to see where we could concentrate and substitute our own folks for hired help. By discontinuing the DAILY it will throw four women into the work, and so dismiss three hired hands. This proposal met with hearty approval and it was decided to put it into execution at once. There will be a journal in manuscript sent to the different families, and we are much pleased to announce Mrs. S. B. Campbell as the journalist.

As we close to-day, we would like to express our gratitude for our friends' forbearance with our mistakes, the sympathy they have extended to us, and the kindness and willingness shown in furnishing items. Thanks to you all.